Lecture Notes in Computer Science 2756

Edited by G. Goos, J. Hartmanis, and J. van Leeuwen

Springer
Berlin
Heidelberg
New York
Hong Kong
London
Milan
Paris
Tokyo

Nicolai Petkov Michel A. Westenberg (Eds.)

Computer Analysis of Images and Patterns

10th International Conference, CAIP 2003
Groningen, The Netherlands, August 25-27, 2003
Proceedings

Springer

Volume Editors

Nicolai Petkov
Michel A. Westenberg
University of Groningen
Institute of Mathematics and Computing Science
Blauwborgje 3, 9747 AC Groningen, The Netherlands
E-mail: petkov@cs.rug.nl, michel@cs.rug.nl

Cataloging-in-Publication Data applied for

A catalog record for this book is available from the Library of Congress.

Bibliographic information published by Die Deutsche Bibliothek
Die Deutsche Bibliothek lists this publication in the Deutsche Nationalbibliografie; detailed bibliographic data is available in the Internet at <http://dnb.ddb.de>.

CR Subject Classification (1998): I.4, I.5, I.3.3, I.3.7, J.2, I.7

ISSN 0302-9743
ISBN 3-540-40730-8 Springer-Verlag Berlin Heidelberg New York

Springer-Verlag Berlin Heidelberg New York
a member of BertelsmannSpringer Science+Business Media GmbH

http://www.springer.de

Printed in Germany

Typesetting: Camera-ready by author, data conversion by Olgun Computergrafik
Printed on acid-free paper SPIN: 10952979 06/3142 5 4 3 2 1 0

Preface

This volume presents the proceedings of the 10th International Conference on Computer Analysis of Images and Patterns (CAIP 2003). This conference series started about 18 years ago in Berlin. Initially, the conference served as a forum for meetings between scientists from Western- and Eastern-bloc countries. Nowadays, the conference attracts participants from all over the world. The conference gives equal weight to posters and oral presentations, and the selected presentation mode is based on the most appropriate communication medium. The programme follows a single-track format, rather than parallel sessions. Non-overlapping oral and poster sessions ensure that all attendees have the opportunity to interact personally with presenters.

As for the numbers, we received a total of 160 submissions. All papers were reviewed by two to three members of the Programme Committee. The final selection was carried out by the Conference Chairs. Out of the 160 papers, 42 were selected for oral presentation and 52 as posters. At this point, we wish to thank the Programme Committee and additional referees for their timely and high-quality reviews. The paper submission and review procedure was carried out electronically. We thank Marcin Morgós from Scalar–IT Solutions for providing us with the Web-based participant registration system. We also thank the invited speakers Nicholas Ayache, John Daugman, and Dariu Gavrila, for kindly accepting our invitation.

CAIP 2003 was organized by the Institute of Mathematics and Computing Science, University of Groningen, and took place in the University Hospital. We hope that the conference proved to be a stimulating experience, and that you had an enjoyable stay in the nice city of Groningen.

August 2003

Nicolai Petkov
Michel A. Westenberg

Organization

CAIP 2003
10th International Conference on Computer Analysis of Images and Patterns
Groningen, The Netherlands, August 25–27, 2003

Chair

Nicolai Petkov	University of Groningen, The Netherlands

Co-chair

Michel A. Westenberg	University of Groningen, The Netherlands

Steering Committee

Reinhard Klette	The University of Auckland, New Zealand
Nicolai Petkov	University of Groningen, The Netherlands
Władysław Skarbek	Warsaw University of Technology, Poland
Franc Solina	University of Ljubljana, Slovenia
Gerald Sommer	Christian-Albrechts-University of Kiel, Germany

Local Organizing Committee

Cosmin Grigorescu
Simona Grigorescu
Nicolai Petkov
Michel A. Westenberg
Michael Wilkinson
Alle Meije Wink — University of Groningen, The Netherlands

Program Committee

Ronen Basri	Weizmann Institute of Science, Israel
Gunilla Borgefors	University of Uppsala, Sweden
Horst Bunke	University of Bern, Switzerland
Dmitry Chetverikov	Hungarian Academy of Sciences, Hungary
Luigi Cordella	University of Naples "Federico II," Italy
Kostas Daniilidis	University of Pennsylvania, Philadelphia, USA
Alberto Del Bimbo	University of Florence, Italy
Rachid Deriche	INRIA Sophia Antipolis, France
Vito Di Gesu'	University of Palermo, Italy

Robert Duin	Delft University of Technology, NL
John Eakins	University of Northumbria, UK
Jan-Olof Eklundh	Royal Institute of Technology, Sweden
Luc Florack	Eindhoven University of Technology, NL
Siegfried Fuchs	Dresden University of Technology, Germany
André Gagalowicz	INRIA Rocquencourt, France
Georgy Gimel'farb	University of Auckland, New Zealand
Bart ter Haar Romeny	Eindhoven University of Technology, NL
Václav Hlaváč	Czech Technical University, Czech Republic
John Illingworth	University of Surrey, UK
Atsushi Imiya	Chiba University, Japan
Jean-Michel Jolion	INSA Lyon, France
Reinhard Klette	University of Auckland, New Zealand
Ryszard Kozera	University of Western Australia, Australia
Walter Kropatsch	Vienna University of Technology, Austria
Aleš Leonardis	University of Ljubljana, Slovenia
Stefano Levialdi	Rome University "La Sapienza," Italy
Martin Levine	McGill University, Canada
B.S. Manjunath	University of California, Santa Barbara, USA
Peter Meer	Rutgers University, Piscataway, USA
Heinrich Niemann	University of Erlangen-Nürnberg, Germany
Lyle Noakes	University of Western Australia, Australia
Constantinos Pattichis	University of Cyprus, Cyprus
Petra Perner	ICVACS, Germany
Nicolai Petkov	University of Groningen, The Netherlands
Maria Petrou	University of Surrey, UK
Jos Roerdink	University of Groningen, The Netherlands
Gerhard Sagerer	University of Bielefeld, Germany
Alberto Sanfeliu	Technical University of Catalonia, Spain
Gabriella Sanniti di Baja	CNR, Naples, Italy
Bernt Schiele	ETH Zürich, Switzerland
Christos Schizas	University of Cyprus, Cyprus
Cordelia Schmid	INRIA Rhône-Alpes, France
Nicu Sebe	Leiden University, The Netherlands
Jean Serra	CMM-École des Mines, France
Nils Siebel	University of Kiel, Germany
Władysław Skarbek	Warsaw University of Technology, Poland
Arnold Smeulders	University of Amsterdam, The Netherlands
Pierre Soille	EC Joint Research Centre, Italy
Franc Solina	University of Ljubljana, Slovenia
Gerald Sommer	University of Kiel, Germany
Minsoo Suk	Sung Kyun Kwan University, Republic of Korea
Tieniu Tan	Chinese Academy of Sciences, China
Max Viergever	University Medical Center Utrecht, NL
Juan Villanueva	Computer Vision Center, Barcelona, Spain
Lucas van Vliet	Delft University of Technology, NL

Albert Vossepoel	Delft University of Technology, NL
Harry Wechsler	George Mason University, Fairfax, USA
Joachim Weickert	Saarland University, Germany
Michel Westenberg	University of Groningen, The Netherlands
Michael Wilkinson	University of Groningen, The Netherlands
Konrad Wojciechowski	Silesian Technical University, Poland
Ian Young	Delft University of Technology, NL

Additional Referees

A. Akselrod
J. Andrade-Cetto
J. Aranda
M. Artac
A. Bagdanov
R. Baldrich
M. Bjorkman
E. Borenstein
S. Bres
T. Brox
A. Bruhn
J. Cech
C. De Stefano
R. Duits
J. Edwards
F. Faas
J. Goldberger
L. Gorelick
A. Grau
M. Jogan
P. Juszczak
F. Kanters
J. Krivic
P. Krsek
H. Kruppa
B. Leibe
J. Lou
C. Luengo Hendriks
F. Moreno Noguer
C. Neocleous
X. Otazu
P. Paclik
J. Palecek
D. Paulus
P. Peer
E. Pekalska
T. Pham
J. Ren
B. Rieger
B. Rosenhahn
C. Sansone
D. Simakov
D. Skocaj
M. Skurichina
R. Sluzek
M. Spengler
V. Stepan
T. Tan
F. Tortorella
M. van Ginkel
M. Vanrell
J. Varona
J. Verges Llahi
J. Vitria
J. Vogel
L. Wang
Y. Wang
Y. Wexler
T. Weyrich
L. Zelnik-Manor
V. Zyka

Sponsoring Organizations

Institute of Mathematics and Computing Science, University of Groningen, NL
International Association for Pattern Recognition (IAPR)
Scalar–IT Solutions, Poland

Table of Contents

Analysis and Understanding

Video

Segmentation

Shape

Classification

Face Recognition

Interpolation and Spatial Transformations

Filtering

On Design and Applications of Cylindrical Panoramas

Reinhard Klette[1], Georgy Gimel'farb[1], Shou Kang Wei[2], Fay Huang[3],
Karsten Scheibe[4], Martin Scheele[4], Anko Börner[4], and Ralf Reulke[5]

[1] CITR, The University of Auckland, Auckland, New Zealand
{r.klette,g.gimelfarb}@auckland.ac.nz
[2] Dept. of Information and Computer Science, Keio University, Yokohama, Japan
shoukang@ozawa.ics.keio.ac.jp
[3] Institute of Information Science, Academia Sinica, Nankang, Taipei, Taiwan
fayhuang@iis.sinica.edu.tw
[4] Institute of Space Sensor Technology and Planetary Exploration, DLR, Berlin, Germany
{Karsten.Scheibe,Martin.Scheele,Anko.Boerner}@dlr.de
[5] Institute for Photogrammetry, Stuttgart University, Stuttgart, Germany
Ralf.Reulke@ifp.uni-stuttgart.de

Abstract. The paper briefly overviews the design and applications of cylindrical panoramic cameras characterized by a rotating linear sensor capturing one image column at time. The camera provides very high image resolutions paid by motion distortions in dynamic scenes. The images are used for stereo reconstruction and visualization of static scenes when extremely high image resolution is of benefit.

1 Introduction

Panoramic cameras are of increasing importance for various applications in computer vision, computer graphics, robotics, and remote sensing.

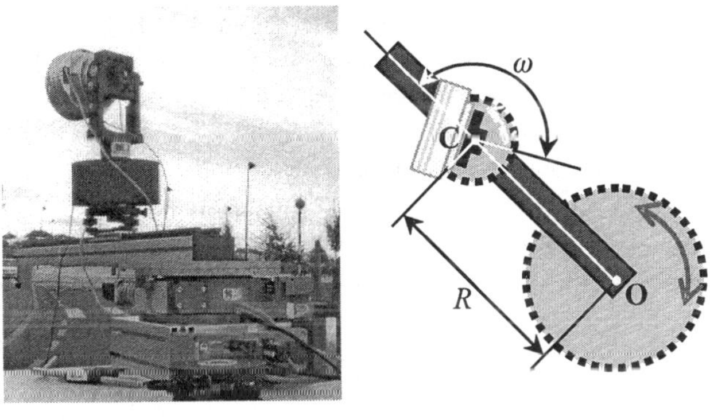

Fig. 1. Camera setup for panoramic image acquisition.

Figure 1 shows a setup of the panorama acquisition with a single-line color camera "Eyescan" built at DLR [8]. The camera is geometrically characterized by a single optical (projection) center, denoted as **C**, and a 1D linear photon-sensing CCD device.

N. Petkov and M.A. Westenberg (Eds.): CAIP 2003, LNCS 2756, pp. 1–8, 2003.

To acquire a cylindrical panoramic image, a slit camera rotates with respect to a fixed 3D axis (e.g. the rotation axis of a turntable) and captures slit images consecutively at equidistant angles. Each slit image contributes to a single column of the resulting panoramic image. The camera may rotate part of, or full 360°, producing line images with 10,200 pixels each. For the focal distance 60 mm, a full 360° image has 55,000 columns, resulting in a single panoramic image of size 3.3 Gbytes. The radiometric dynamic range is 14 bits, and the signal to noise ratio is in the range of 8 bits. The acquisition time depends on the illumination conditions and is about 4 minutes. The off-axis distance R, the principal angle ω and the camera focal length f remain constant during a panoramic image acquisition process.

This paper overviews basic results in design and calibration of such cameras and their application for acquisition and processing stereo panoramas.

2 Camera Calibration

Conventional calibration methods for camera architectures reflecting the pinhole camera model cannot be applied to panoramic cameras due to non-linearity of these latter. The non-linearity follows from the existence of multiple (nonlinear) optical centers and a cylindrical image manifold. The novel calibration methods developed for the panoramic line cameras involve specific image and scene measurements and non-linear constrained optimization techniques.

First, production-site facilities are used for extensive geometric and radiometric calibration of CCD-line cameras of super-high resolution. The main result of the geometric calibration procedure are accurate pixel coordinates in the focal plane in relation to the optical axis (interior orientation). An additional result is a space-dependent point-spread function, which is related to image resolution and image quality. Ideal parameters (e.g. the focal length f) for characterization of the systems can be derived from this measurements. Radiometric calibration is related to the signal-to-noise-ratio, signal dynamics and linearity as well as true-color retrieval. Additional measurements concern the homogeneity of the signal, e.g. photo-response non-uniformity and dark-signal non-uniformity. For the camera in Fig. 1, all these measurements are done at a special calibration facility at DLR Berlin.

Besides these production-site calibrations, values of the two dominant parameters R and ω have to be dynamically specified according to different scene ranges of interest. As shown in [4, 12], these parameters can be accurately estimated using a non-linear least square optimization. The calibration assumes that (*i*) there are at least three straight line segments in the captured real scene (e.g. a special object with straight edges), which are all parallel to the rotation axis and (*ii*) the length of these line segments and the distances between any two parallel lines are measurable.

Let us consider a pair of parallel line segments of lengths H_i and H_j in 3D space shown in Fig. 2,A. The distance between these two parallel lines is denoted as D_{ij}. The length of the projections of the line segments on image columns can be determined from the input image, denoted as h_i and h_j in pixels respectively.

Figure 2,B shows the top view of the geometry. The camera optical centers that view these two parallel lines are denoted as $\mathbf{C}_i$ and $\mathbf{C}_j$ respectively. The distances S_i and S_j

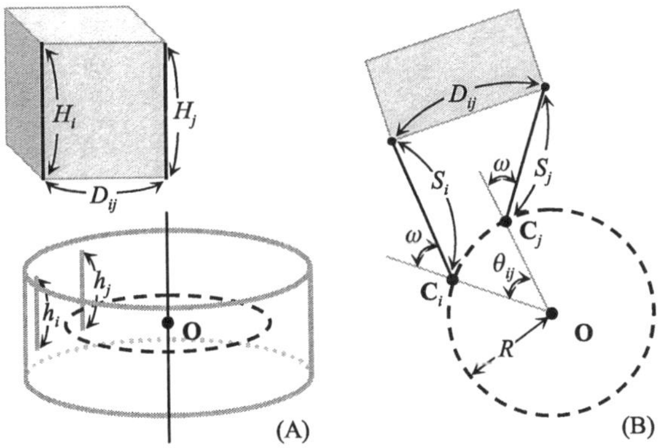

Fig. 2. Camera calibration utilizing the parallel line segments in the 3D scene.

are defined to be the shortest distances between the associated camera optical centers and the parallel lines respectively. These distances can be calculated by the following relations $S_i = fH_i/h_i$ and $S_j = fH_j/h_j$ where f is the pre calibrated effective focal length of the (line-) camera. The angular distance θ_{ij} (that is, the angle $\angle \mathbf{C}_i \mathbf{O} \mathbf{C}_j$) can be calculated as follows: $\theta_{ij} = 2\pi d_{ij}/W$ where d_{ij} is the distance between two projections of the parallel lines on image, measured in pixels, and W is the width of a panorama in pixels.

As a result, the following linear equation is obtained:

$$\begin{aligned}(1-\cos\theta_{ij})R^2 + (S_i+S_j)(1-\cos\theta_{ij})R\cos\omega - (S_i-S_j)\sin\theta_{ij}R\sin\omega \\ + \frac{S_i^2+S_j^2-D_{ij}^2}{2} - S_iS_j\cos\theta_{ij} = 0\end{aligned} \quad (1)$$

Since the values of S_i, S_j, D_{ij}, and θ_{ij} are known, the equation can be rewritten as $K_1R^2 + K_2R\cos\omega + K_3R\sin\omega + K_4 = 0$ where the coefficients $K_j; j = 1, \ldots, 4$, are calculated from the measurements from real scenes and the image. Assuming that n such equations are given, the desired parameters can be obtained by the non-linear least square error minimization:

$$\min_{R,\omega} \sum_{i=1}^{n} \left(K_{1,i}R^2 + K_{2i}R\cos\omega + K_{3i}R\sin\omega + K_{4i}\right)^2 \quad (2)$$

3 3D Stereo Reconstruction

One of important applications of symmetric panoramic images is 3D depth or shape recovery. The study of epipolar geometry of such images is essential not only for these applications, but also for panoramic visualization or simulation of walk-through, i.e. the virtual paths created between multiple panoramas. The epipolar curve equation serves as a fundamental tool for many important computer vision tasks, such as pose estimation and stereo analysis. The general epipolar curve equation for a pair of arbitrary poly-centric panoramas is presented in [4, 12]. An intuitive and practical way to reduce the

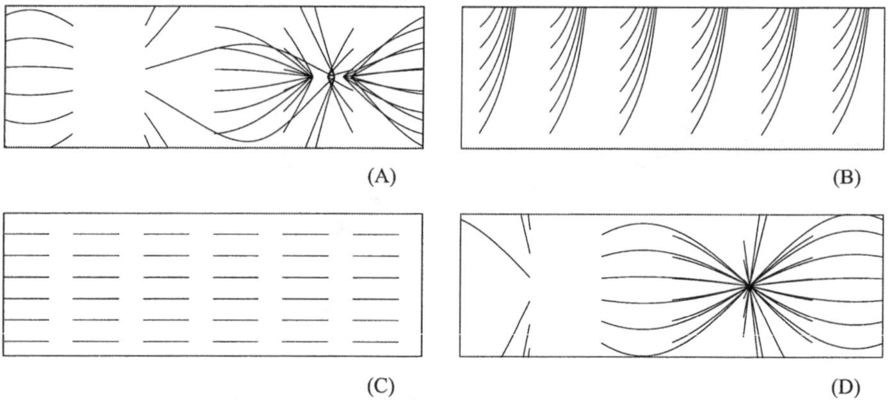

Fig. 3. Epipolar curves of four special cases: leveled (A), concentric (B), symmetric (C), and single-center (D) panoramas.

dimensionality of the general epipolar curve equation is to make all the associated axes of the panoramas leveled to the sea level. It can be achieved by mounting the camera on a leveled tripod. A polycentric panoramic pair whose associated axes are orthogonal to the sea level is called a *leveled panoramic pair*. Note that the heights of images in a leveled panoramic pair can be different. Under the assumption that a panoramic pair is perfectly leveled, the general epipolar curve equation can be considerably simplified.

Two panoramas whose axes coincide are called a *co-axis panoramic pair*. This constraint reduces two rotational and two translational parameters, and yet has its practical merit. The epipolar curves of a co-axis pair coincide with image columns under some camera setting assumptions. Also note that the implementation of such a configuration is reasonably straightforward. A normal tripod allows such a setting. Therefore, this geometrical constraint has been commonly applied in some panoramic camera architectures such as the catadioptric approach [11, 3, 6, 7].

Figure 3 illustrates the distinctiveness of epipolar curve patterns in four different geometric configurations: leveled; concentric; symmetric; and single-center panoramas.

Due to the known epipolar curves, the panoramic pair can easily be converted into the standard horizontal epipolar stereo pair having one-to-one correspondence between the pixel rows in the both images. Assuming a continuous visible surface, binocular stereo reconstruction of the panoramic scene can be obtained by one or another conventional stereo technique, e.g., by symmetric dynamic programming stereo (SDPS) [2].

Figure 4 shows the left and right stereo images of a close-range urban 3D scene and results of 3D stereo reconstruction with the SDPS (namely, the range image with the grey-coded depths and the cyclopean image fusing the stereo images in accord with visibility of the reconstructed 3D points).

Some reconstruction errors, e.g. on the sky or near the rightmost columns of the building are typical for these panoramic line cameras. Because of relatively long time for capturing a single image, the left and right images of the stereo pair differ considerably in all the "dynamically changing" areas such as cloud patterns or positions of moving people.

Fig. 4. Stereo pair of panoramic images brought to the standard epipolar geometry by rectifying the epipolar curves (upper row) and the range and cyclopean images of the reconstructed 3D scene.

4 Multi-sensor Approach

Combination of geometric 3D laser scanner data and high resolution panoramic color image data opens up new possibilities in architectural documentation and digitalization, in particular for preserving historic buildings and monuments. Distance measurements of a laser scanner provide high-resolution digital surface models. Due to extremely high resolution, panoramic images are suitable for "texture mapping" in rendering of such high-resolution surface models. As an example, results of the "Neuschwanstein project" are presented below. The project is directed on a complete 3D photometric documentation of this Bavarian castle.

Figure 5 illustrates one panoramic scan, which can be used for high quality texture mapping and the laser scanner reflection image from the same scene. Data acquisition is based on a panoramic colour camera and a laser scanner for capturing 3D information [8]. The data sets (range data and panoramic images) are co-registered to reference each other and transformed into theodolite measurements using photogrammetric bundle adjustment. Measured or calculated orientation data can be used to merge 3D scanner pixels and 2D color pixels in a virtual information space in order to generate different views, ortho images or 3D models.

The combination of laser scanner data with digital scanner panoramas is very useful in close range photogrammetry. The range and image data are transformed into a theodolitic (spherical) coordinate system with two angles, longitude σ and latitude τ, and one distance value ρ for each pixel. Both systems have data along the rotation axis in fixed angle increments, depending from the cylindrical recording system. The vertical angle (latitude) results from the relationship $\tau = \arctan(i \cdot d/f)$ combining the number i of vertical pixels of the linear size d and the focal length f of the camera. The distance to the object is unknown. The strategy to capture the distance data with the 3D laser scanner is similar to that of close range photogrammetry. A conventional gray scale image in addition to the 3D data enables immediate control of the recorded data.

The laser scanner data are already in a theodolitic coordinate system. The first step is to convert the scanner data into a format where the distance and the intensity data are

Fig. 5. Panoramic scan (a) and intensity image of a laser scan (b) of the castle Neuschwanstein.

stored in a 3D grid with equidistant angle increments. This reduces the size of the data by about a third. Calibration information is crucial for this reduction step.

The advantage of laser scanner data is the possibility to view the data after a scan immediately in 3D space (with rotation, translation or scaling). Laser scanner and camera work digitally, and the accuracy of the whole 3D digitalization and modeling approach critically depends on calibration of the systems: calibration of the rotation table of the panorama camera, and of the off-axis distance between rotation axis and projection center of the optics [4]. The viewing angle ω was kept at zero degree.

A single scan is in general not sufficient to acquire all object points due to visibility limitations. Several panorama scans from different view points require 3D modelling such that texture mapping can be based on object matching. This is done automatically by identifying control points and other characteristic points or patterns, followed by bundle adjustment. The results are seven parameters of an affine transform (including three translation, three rotation, and one scaling parameter) of the exterior orientation of every scan. The same method is used to orient the panoramic image data to the laser scan data. In addition it is possible to improve the parameters of the scanner interior orientation. If an oriented virtual 3D model consisting of any number of scans is given, any desired layout maps, elevations, scene views, or 3D object visualizations can be created. The next step is to map panoramic image data ("texture") on the laser scan based CAD model. The difficulty arises from the amount of data: one scan has more than 270 million pixels, and often there are more than just one panoramic image for one scene. Normal ray tracing algorithms require extensive computations.

Alternatively, the 3D surface models can be produced by automatic generation of optimum triangular meshes [1]. Parameters can be set to provide the required degree of detail. The size of the meshes depends on the structure of the surface. Planar surface patches generate 'rough' meshes, and fine structures have detailed meshes.

Figure 6,A illustrates the panoramic image mapping for a detail of Neuschwanstein with the approximately planar surface. First, an ortho plane was defined, and the oriented

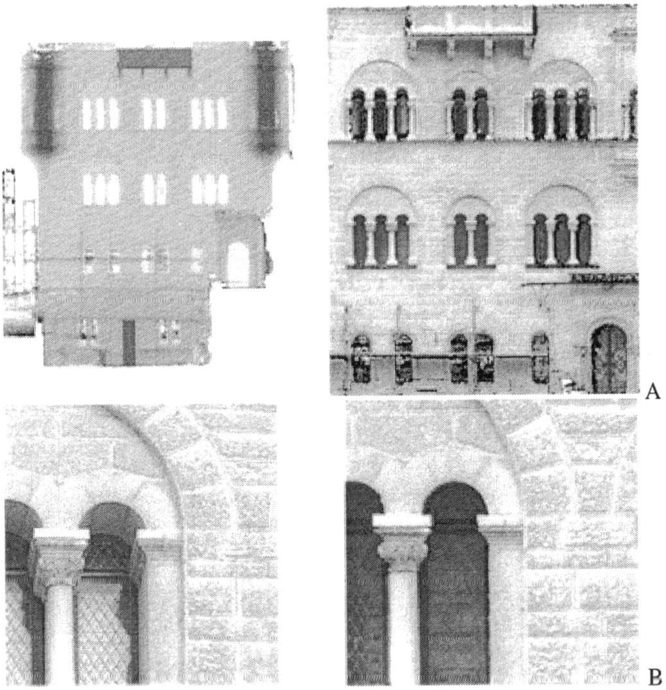

Fig. 6. A: grey coded(left) and with mapped texture (right) surface; B: original panoramic image (left) and processed ortho image (right).

panorama data are projected onto this plane. Ortho images are generated by merging 3D object surfaces and photographic information. High resolution photos need to be taken into account in addition to the laser scans. Figure 6 shows a detail of the original panorama data and the result after texture mapping onto the laser surface data.

In some cases the acquisition of 3D data from a stereo analysis module was replaced by a combination of laser data and color panoramic images. However, computation time saved by using laser data instead of stereo processing, is then needed for rendering and raytracing. It also required the development of a fast algorithm, which handles more than 1500 million points and takes advantage of the reported research on rotations and epipolar geometry of panoramic images. The problem of mesh calculation for visualizing very large clouds of 3D points has yet no acceptable solution.

5 Conclusion

We reviewed recent developments in fundamental research and application of a particular type of cylindrical panoramic cameras, in particular, acquisition and processing of panoramic stereo images. Major "milestones" have been set, but future research and design has to address more specific (and more difficult) questions, e.g., the impact of inaccurate rotations on epipolar geometry or the unification of several 3D distance maps produced by several stereo pairs of symmetric panoramic images.

Stereo panoramic images can accompany the acquisition of 3D laser scan data in order to improve the quality of the surface model derived from the laser scanner. Problems resulting from reflections on edges and corners might be solved in this way.

References

1. GIMEL'FARB, G., MARCHENKO, V., AND RYBAK, V. An algorithm for automatic identification of identical sections on stereo pairs of photographs. *Cybernetics 8*, 2, 311–322, 1972.
2. GIMEL'FARB, G. Probabilistic regularisation and symmetry in binocular dynamic programming stereo. *Pattern Recognition Letters 23*, 4, 431–442, 2002.
3. GLUCKMAN, J., NAYAR, S., AND THOREK, K. Real-time panoramic stereo. In *Proc. DARPA'98*, 299–303, 1998.
4. HUANG, F., WEI, S. K., AND KLETTE, R. Geometrical fundamentals of polycentric panoramas. In *Proc. 8th Int. Conf. Computer Vision, Vancouver, Canada, July 2001*, 560–565.
5. KLETTE, R., GIMEL'FARB, G., AND REULKE, R. Wide-angle image acquisition, analysis and visualization. In *Proc. 14th Int. Conf. on Vision Interface, Ottawa, Canada, May 2001*, 114–125, 2001.
6. NENE, S., AND NAYAR, S. Stereo with mirrors. In *Proc. 5th Int. Conf. Computer Vision, Bombay, India, Jan. 1998*, 1087–1094.
7. PETTY, R., ROBINSON, M., AND EVANS, J. 3d measurement using rotating line-scan sensors. *Measurement Science and Technology 9*, 3, 339–346, 1998.
8. SCHEIBE, K., KORSITZKY, H., AND REULKE, R. 2001. Eyescan - a high resolution digital panoramic camera. In *Proc. Robot Vision 2001*, 77–83.
9. SEITZ, S. The space of all stereo images. In *Proc. Int. Conf. Computer Vision, Vancouvedr, Canada, July 2001*, 26–33, 2001.
10. SHUM, H., KALAI, A., AND SEITZ, S. Omnivergent stereo. In *Proc. ICCV'99*, 22–29, 1999.
11. SOUTHWELL, D., REYDA, J., FIALA, M., AND BASU, A. Panoramic stereo. In *Proc. Int. Conf. Pattern Recognition, Vienna, Austria, Aug. 1996*, A:378–382, 1996.
12. WEI, S.-K., HUANG, F., AND KLETTE, R. Determination of geometrical parameters for stereoscopic panorama cameras. *Machine Graphics & Vision*, 10 (3), 399–427, 2001.
13. YAMANOUE, H., OKUI, M., AND YUYAMA, I. A study on the relationship between shooting conditions and cardboard effect of stereoscopic images. *IEEE Trans. on Circuits and Systems for Video Technology 10*, 3, 411–416, 2000.

Finding the Symmetry Axis of a Perspectively Projected Plane Curve

Giovanni Marola

University of Pisa, Pisa, Italy

Abstract. In this paper we describe an algebraic technique for the identification of the symmetry axes of a perspectively projected symmetrical plane curve. The procedure requires a limited amount of calculations and allows a highly accurate recognition of the searched symmetry axes even when the considered curve is partially occluded or not perfectly segmented.

1 Introduction

In this paper we describe an algebraic technique for the identification of the symmetry axes of a perspectively projected symmetrical plane curve. In our approach we suppose that the curve is modeled as implicit bivariate polynomial functions of degree higher than three. These polynomials are characterized by a great modeling power and are able to represent complex shapes including curves composed of disconnected elements, boundaries which intersect themselves and figures with holes [1]. In addition, the algorithm used for fitting the coefficients to the geometrical data is robust with respect to noise and performs well even when data are missing from a consistent portion of the curve [3].

Starting from a polynomial representation of the projected curve, we derive a differential form which is invariant to the perspective projection and defines an algebraic correspondence between the projected symmetry axis $\mathbf{s}$ and the vanishing point $\mathbf{p}_\infty$ of the straight lines perpendicular to $\mathbf{s}$. This gives rise to a system of algebraic equations whose solution allows us to identify the position of both $\mathbf{s}$ and $\mathbf{p}_\infty$. The procedure requires a limited amount of computation burden and has been proven to be reliable both for synthetic and real images. In addition, the location of $\mathbf{s}$ and $\mathbf{p}_\infty$ enables a partial estimate of the position of the viewing device.

2 Symmetrical Plane Curves Modelled by a Bivariate Polynomial

Consider a plane curve C_0 and assume it is modeled by a polynomial function of degree $n \geq 4$ in the homogeneous variables X, Y and W:

N. Petkov and M.A. Westenberg (Eds.): CAIP 2003, LNCS 2756, pp. 9–16, 2003.

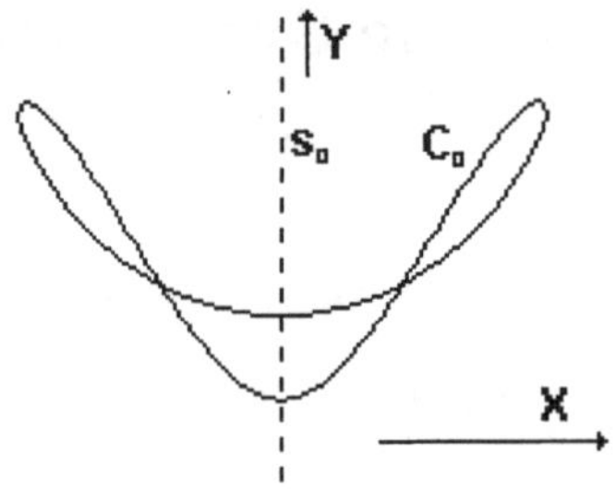

Fig. 1. Example of a plane curve symmetrical about the vertical axis.

$$Q(X,Y,W) = a_{0,0}W^n + (a_{1,0}X + a_{0,1}Y)W^{n-1} \\ +(a_{2,0}X^2 + a_{1,1}XY + a_{0,2}Y^2)W^{n-2} + ... \tag{1}$$

In particular, if C_0 is mirror symmetrical about the vertical axis, as it is shown in Fig. 1, we have $a_{i,j} = 0$ for i odd.

Let us introduce the following composite differential form:

$$\mathbf{q}_b \frac{\partial Q(\mathbf{q}_a)}{\partial \mathbf{q}_a} = X_b \frac{\partial Q(\mathbf{q}_a)}{\partial X_a} + Y_b \frac{\partial Q(\mathbf{q}_a)}{\partial Y_a} + W_b \frac{\partial Q(\mathbf{q}_a)}{\partial W_a} \tag{2}$$

where $\mathbf{q}_a = [X_a, Y_a, W_a]$ and $\mathbf{q}_b = [X_b, Y_b, W_b]$ are two arbitrary points belonging to the plane of C_0. If we chose $\mathbf{q}_a = [1,0,0]$ and $\mathbf{q}_b = [X,Y,W]$, the former being the vanishing point $\mathbf{q}_\infty$ of the horizontal axis , it is easy to see that Eq. 2 reduces to:

$$[X,Y,W] \frac{\partial Q(\mathbf{q}_\infty)}{\partial \mathbf{q}_\infty} = nXa_{n,0} \tag{3}$$

which therefore models the symmetry axis ($X = 0$) of the considered curve. Conversely, chosing $\mathbf{q}_a = [X,Y,W]$ and $\mathbf{q}_b = [1,0,0]$ yields:

$$\mathbf{q}_\infty \frac{\partial Q([X,Y,W])}{\partial [X,Y,W]} = X \sum_{i=2}^{n} W^{n-i} \sum_{j=1}^{i/2} 2j a_{2j,i-2j} X^{2j-2} Y^{i-2j} \tag{4}$$

which again models the symmetry axis ($X = 0$) of the considered curve, together with a residual symmetric curve of degree $n-2$. From Eq. 3 and 4 we can conclude that the differential form in Eq. 2 defines a double algebraic correspondence between the *symmetry axis* $\mathbf{s}_0$ of C_0 and the set of its *transverse* axes or more precisely their vanishing point $\mathbf{q}_\infty = [1,0,0]$, as shown in Fig. 2.

Assume now we project perspectively the C_0 plane curve into a displaced and rotated plane as it happens for example when we acquire an image by means of a photo camera or a TV set. Also in this case, in order to be able to represent points at infinity, we use the homogeneous coordinates x, y and w. More precisely if $\mathbf{q} = [X,Y,W]$ is a point belonging to the plane where the original curve C_0 is lying and $\mathbf{p} = [x,y,w]$ represents its perspective projection into the rotated and displaced (viewing) plane, we have, in matrix form:

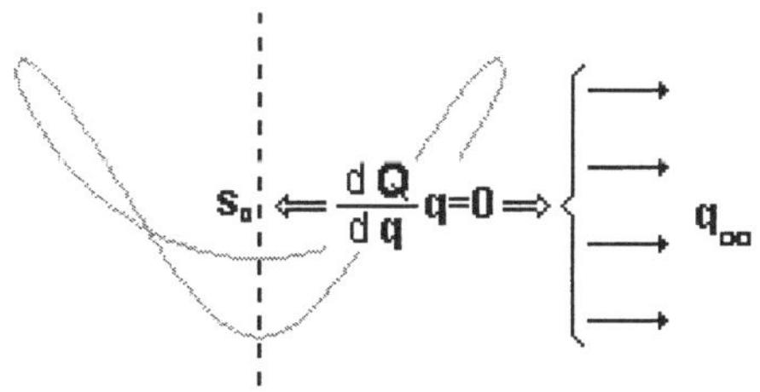

Fig. 2. Correspondence between the symmetry axis and the vanishing point of the transverse axes.

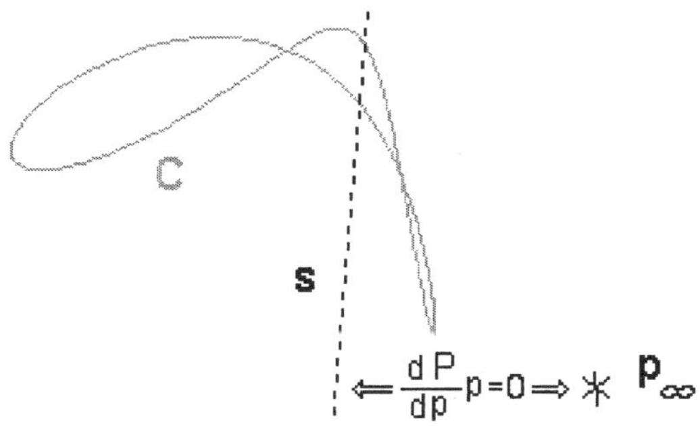

Fig. 3. Correspondence between the projected symmetry axis and the projected vanishing point of the transverse axes.

$$\mathbf{p} = \mathbf{q}\mathbf{A} \tag{5}$$

where

$$\mathbf{A} = \begin{bmatrix} r_{1,1} & r_{2,1} & r_{3,1}/f \\ r_{1,2} & r_{2,2} & r_{3,2}/f \\ X_0 r_{1,1} & X_0 r_{2,1} & 1 + (X_0 r_{3,1} + Z_0)/f \end{bmatrix} \tag{6}$$

being $r_{i,j}$ the entries of a rotation matrix in the 3-D space, $[X_0, 0, Z_0]$ a displacement of C_0 and f the focal length of the viewing device (note that a possible displacement Y_0 of C_0 along the vertical axis does not change the position of its symmetry axis so we have neglected it for simplicity). In addition it is worthwile to note that the coordinates of the projected vanishing $\mathbf{p}_\infty$ point of the X-axis coincide with the first row vector $[r_{1,1}, r_{2,1}, r_{3,1}/f]$ of the $\mathbf{A}$ matrix. By substituting Eq.5 into the right hand side of Eq.1 we obtain:

$$Q(\mathbf{q}) = \left[\sum_{i=0}^{n} W(\mathbf{p})^{n-i} \sum_{j=0}^{i/2} a_{2j,i-2j} X(\mathbf{p})^{2j} Y(\mathbf{p})^{i-2j} \right] \tag{7}$$

This polynomial function of degree n in the homogeneous unknowns x, y and w models the curve C shown in Fig. 3. We denote it by $P(x, y, w)$ and assume it has been obtained in the form:

$$P(x,y,w) = b_{0,0}w^n + (b_{1,0}x + b_{0,1}y)w^{n-1} + (b_{2,0}x^2 + b_{1,1}xy + b_{0,2}y^2)w^{n-2} + \dots \quad (8)$$

by means of the techniques described in [1]-[3].

Consider now again the differential form defined in Eq. 2. By substituting $\mathbf{q}_b = \mathbf{p}_b\mathbf{A}^{-1}$ we resort to:

$$\mathbf{q}_b \frac{\partial Q(\mathbf{q}_a)}{\partial \mathbf{q}_a} = \mathbf{p}_b \mathbf{A}^{-1} \frac{\partial Q(\mathbf{p}_a\mathbf{A}^{-1})}{\partial(\mathbf{p}_a\mathbf{A}^{-1})} \quad (9)$$

On the other hand it is well known that the following identity holds:

$$\frac{\partial Q(\mathbf{p}_a\mathbf{A}^{-1})}{\partial(\mathbf{p}_a\mathbf{A}^{-1})} = \mathbf{A} \frac{\partial Q(\mathbf{p}_a\mathbf{A}^{-1})}{\partial \mathbf{p}_a} \quad (10)$$

so that by assuming $Q(\mathbf{p}_a\mathbf{A}^{-1}) = P(\mathbf{p}_a)$, we obtain:

$$\mathbf{q}_b \frac{\partial Q(\mathbf{q}_a)}{\partial \mathbf{q}_a} = \mathbf{p}_b \frac{\partial P(\mathbf{p}_a)}{\partial \mathbf{p}_a} \quad (11)$$

This states the invariance of the differential form defined in Eq. 2 with respect to the perspective projection. Using this property together with Eqs. 3 and 4, we can conclude that if $\mathbf{p}_\infty = [x_\infty, y_\infty, w_\infty]$ is the perspective projection of $\mathbf{q}_\infty$, the following equation:

$$\mathbf{p}_s \frac{\partial P(\mathbf{p}_\infty)}{\partial \mathbf{p}_\infty} = 0 \quad (12)$$

$$\mathbf{p}_\infty \frac{\partial P(\mathbf{p}_s)}{\partial \mathbf{p}_s} = 0 \quad (13)$$

are satisfied by the points $\mathbf{p}_s = [x, y, w]$ belonging to the projected symmetry axis. In other words also in this case the considered differential form defines a double correspondence between the projected symmetry axis $\mathbf{s}$ and the projected vanishing point $\mathbf{p}_\infty$ of the transverse axes, as it is shown in Fig. 3.

Let us now denote with $\alpha x - \beta y + \gamma w = 0$ the equation of the above symmetry axis. If we solve it, for example with respect to y, and then substitute it into Eqs. 12 and 13, we obtain two polynomial equations in the homogeneous variables x and w that must vanish identically. This leads to the following system of $(n+2)$ equations of degree $(n-1)$ in the 6 *homogeneous* unknowns $[\alpha, \beta, \gamma]$ and $[x_\infty, y_\infty, w_\infty]$:

$$
\begin{cases}
\alpha\sum_{i=1}^{n}\sum_{j=0}^{i-1}(i-j)b_{i-j,j}x_{\infty}^{i-j-1}y_{\infty}^{j}w_{\infty}^{n-i}- \\
\qquad -\gamma\sum_{i=0}^{n-1}\sum_{j=0}^{i}(n-i)b_{i-j,j}x_{\infty}^{i-j}y_{\infty}^{j}w_{\infty}^{n-i-1}=0 \\
\beta\sum_{i=1}^{n}\sum_{j=1}^{i}jb_{i-j,j}x_{\infty}^{i-j}y_{\infty}^{j-1}w_{\infty}^{n-i}+ \\
\qquad +\gamma\sum_{i=0}^{n-1}\sum_{j=0}^{i}(n-i)b_{i-j,j}x_{\infty}^{i-j}y_{\infty}^{j}w_{\infty}^{n-i-1}=0 \\
\sum_{j=0}^{i}\sum_{k=0}^{n-i-1}\alpha^{n-1-j-k}\beta^{j}\gamma^{k}\binom{j+k}{k}[(j+k+1)b_{j+k+1,i-j}x_{\infty}+ \\
\qquad +(i-j+1)b_{j+k,i-j+1}y_{\infty}+ \\
\qquad +(n-i-k)b_{j+k,i-j}w_{\infty}]=0 \qquad i=0,...,n-1
\end{cases}
\tag{14}
$$

which, once solved numerically, allows the identification of both the projected symmetry axis and of the position of the vanishing point of its transverse axes.

3 Numerical Solution

It is well known that the task of finding the zeroes of a system of nonlinear algebraic equations is in general a very hard problem to deal with. In addition, the difficulty is exacerbated by the fact that the number of possible roots may be very high. Fortunately, the case of system (14) has some characteristics which render its solution quite simple. First of all, being the number of equations always greater than that of the variables, the system has in general only one set of real solutions or more precisely one solution for every symmetry axis of the original curve. Secondly, the first two equations are linear in the unknowns $[\alpha/\gamma]$ and $[\beta/\gamma]$ so that these latter can be eliminated easily. As a consequence we have only two unknowns to deal with i.e. for example the two ratios $[y_{\infty}/x_{\infty}]$ and $[w_{\infty}/x_{\infty}]$, this leading to a noticeable reduction of the dimensionality of the problem.

A procedure which has proven to be very effective in finding the above roots is based on an adaptation of a globally convergent method developed in [4]. It combines the idea of minimizing the *sum of squares* of all the individual functions $[f_1,...,f_n]$ to be zeroed, with the traditional Newton method. Even if this algorithm can in principle fail by coming to rest on a local minimum, in our case it worked successfully in all of the examples we carried out provided we start from a sufficiently large set of initial values. Note that the technique reported in [4] works only for equal numbers of equations and unknowns, whereas in our case we have n equations in only two unknowns. However this difficulty has been overcome in the present case by substituting the expression of the Newton step $\delta\mathbf{x}=-\mathbf{J}^{-1}[f_1,...,f_n]^T$ used in [4], with the equivalent one $\delta\mathbf{x}=-\left[\mathbf{J}^T\mathbf{J}\right]^{-1}\mathbf{J}^T[f_1,...,f_n]^T$ valid in general for non square jacobian matrices $\mathbf{J}=\{df_i/dx_j\}$.

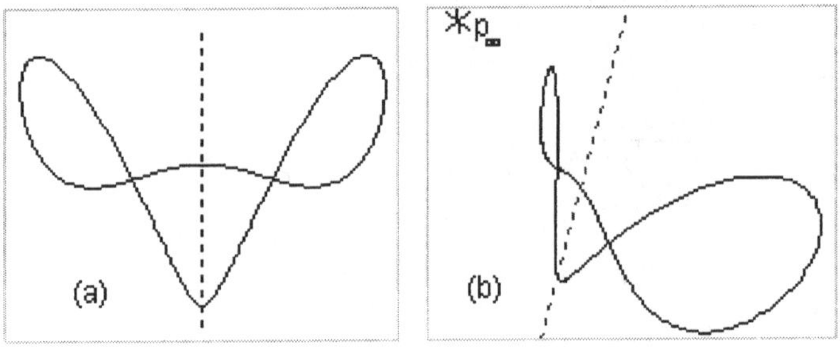

Fig. 4. Original curve (a) and projected curve (b).

Table 1. Results obtained for different initial guesses $[y_\infty]_o$ in the case of Fig. 4b.

$[y_\infty]_o$	y_∞	w_∞	Sum of squares	Comment
-100	-0.844	-0.310	0.133E-07	symmetry axis
-25	-0.844	-0.310	0.133E-07	symmetry axis
25	4.008	-0.594	0.749E-02	local minimum
100	4.008	-0.594	0.749E-02	local minimum

4 Examples of Applications

As a first example of application let us consider the synthetic curve in Fig.4a which can be modelled exactly by means of a bivariate polynomial of degree $n = 4$. It has been projected perspectively by using Eq. 5 thus obtaining Fig. 4b. Its modelling polynomial $P(x, y, w)$ has been found by using the technique reported in [3].

In order to show how the numerical procedure for the identification of its symmetry axis works in practice we have summarized in Table 1 the obtained numerical results for a set of 4 initial values of the unknown y_∞, having assumed $x_\infty = 1$ (remember $[x_\infty, y_\infty, w_\infty] = \mathbf{p}_\infty$ is the projected vanishing point of the transverse axes).

Also note that we have chosen a zero value for the initial guess $[w_\infty]_o$ of w_∞. This is due to the fact that in most practical cases we have to deal with weakly perspective or even horthographic projections so that the actual value of w_∞ does not differ substantially from zero.As we can see the technique converges toward the exact values even if the initial guess $[y_\infty]_o$does differ considerably from the actual value of y_∞. Of course only solutions with a conveniently small value of the *sum of squares* (of the functions to be zeroed) correspond to the searched roots. A relatively large value of the *sum of squares* shows that the method has failed by landing on a local minimum and the corresponding values of y_∞ and w_∞ are not solutions to the system. Consider now Fig.5a and 5b, where a synthetic curve of degree $n = 4$ with three symmetry axes is shown.

In this case, we have to use a larger set of starting points $[y_\infty]_o$, otherwise the numerical procedure would not be able to detect the position of all of the sym-

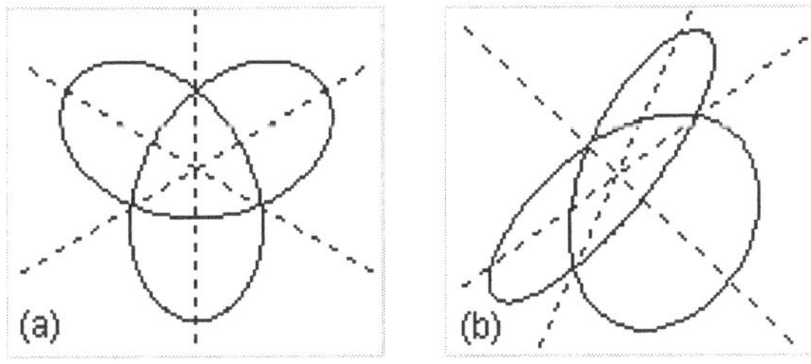

Fig. 5. Curve having three symmetry axes (a) and its perspective projection (b).

Table 2. Results obtained for different initial guesses $[y_\infty]_o$ in the case of Fig. 5b.

$[y_\infty]_o$	y_∞	w_∞	Sum of squares	Comment
−5	-5.671	-1.373	0.317E-07	first symmetry axis
−1	0.191	-0.180	0.422E-07	second symmetry axis
1	1.237	0.033	0.163E-08	third symmetry axis
5	6.286	0.133	0.324E+04	local minimum

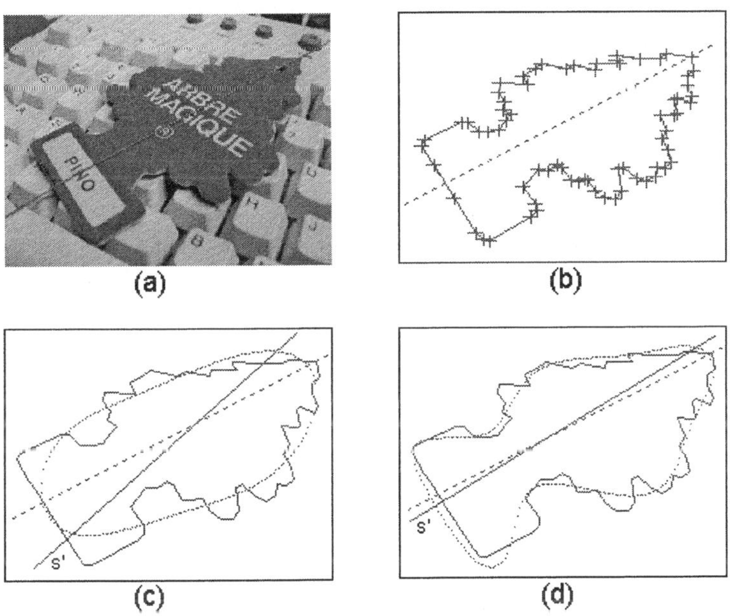

Fig. 6. Real image acquired by means of a digital camera.

metry axes. As we can see in Table 2, also in this case the numerical procedure has been able to find all of the three symmetry axes.

Consider now the case of a real image as it is shown in Fig. 6a. We have identified manually a set of 69 points belonging to the arbre boundary, thus obtaining Fig. 6b. Using the above set of points a polynomial of degree $m = 4$ and $m = 6$ has been obtained. The corresponding curves and the computed symmetry axis are shown in Fig. 6c and 6d respectively. With a polynomial of degree $m = 4$ both shape description and axis identification (continous line s') have a poor correspondence with the reality, whereas when $m = 6$ the obtained result is quite satisfactory.

5 Conclusions

We have presented a simple numerical procedure for the identification of the symmetry axes of a perspectively projected symmetrical plane curve modelled by bivariate polynomial functions. The future work will consist of testing the robustness to the noise and the ability to operate even when data is missing from a consistent portion of the curve.

References

1. D. Keren, D. Cooper, and J. Subrahmonia, "Describing Complicated Objects by Implicit Polynomials", *IEEE Trans. on Pattern Analysis and Machine Intelligence*, Vol. 16, No. 1, January 1994.
2. G. Taubin, F. Cukierman, S. Sullivan, J. Ponce, and D. Kriegman, "Parametrized Families of Polynomials for Bounded Algebraic Curve and Surface Fitting", *IEEE Trans. on Pattern Analysis and Machine Intelligence*, Vol. 16, No. 3, March 1994.
3. T. Tasdizen, J.P. Tarel and D.B. Cooper, "Algebraic Curves That Work Better", IEEE Conference on Computer Vision and Pattern Recognition (CVPR'99), 23-25 June 1999, Fort Collins, Colorado.
4. W.H. Press, S.A. Teukolsky, W.T. Vetterling and B. P. Flannery, "Numerical Recipes", Cambridge University Press, 1992

Representing Orientation in n-Dimensional Spaces

B. Rieger and L.J. van Vliet

Pattern Recognition Group
Delft University of Technology
Lorentzweg 1, 2628 CJ, Delft, The Netherlands
{bernd,lucas}@ph.tn.tudelft.nl

Abstract. In this paper we present new insights in methods to solve the orientation representation problem in arbitrary dimensions. The gradient structure tensor is one of the most used descriptors of local structure in multi-dimensional images. We will relate its properties to the double angle method in 2D and the Knutsson mapping in three or higher dimensions. We present a general scheme to reduce the dimensionality of the mappings needed to solve the orientation representation problem and derive some properties of these reduced mappings.

1 Introduction

Orientation plays a key role in the description of local structure in images. The local structure depends on patterns of intensity change. The first order intensity variation is the gradient. A collection of local gradients is needed to compute a dominant orientation and an accompanying variance that can be used to describe lines, surfaces and edges as well as texture. A characterization of "simple" neighborhoods is the dominant orientation [6, 7, 5, 2]. We define these simple neighborhoods as areas that are shift invariant in at least one direction and not shift invariant in at least one other direction, for example a line.

Orientation is direction up to point inversion, leaving room for ambiguity in representation. Representing structures in images without direction information by vectors (direction information) leads to troublesome descriptions, in the sense that it is discontinuous. Representing a line in 2D by its angle and a plane in 3D by its normal vector is therefore not a suitable representation. A consistent definition of direction is only possible in a global framework, which can be induced by choosing an origin. However, most image operations work in a local neighborhood. If we want to obtain the characterizing dominant orientation, one must average the local orientations, e.g. gradient vectors (at opposite sites of a single line or plane) pointing in opposite directions, but enforce each other. We need a continuous representation of orientation to average the orientations inside a local window.

Furthermore, a discontinuous representation is very often not suitable for further processing. Most image operators give an incorrect response to apparent

N. Petkov and M.A. Westenberg (Eds.): CAIP 2003, LNCS 2756, pp. 17–24, 2003.

discontinuities. Therefore the approach should be as follows: obtain the gradient vectors, map them to a continuous representation, carry out the averaging (or apply another filter). The interpretation of the results of the filtering operation on the new representation is then - in general - not straightforward.

A well-known tool to analyze local structure is the gradient structure tensor [6, 8, 7, 14, 2, 11, 16]. It is defined as

$$G := \nabla I \nabla I^t, \quad \overline{G} := \overline{\nabla I \nabla I^t}, \tag{1}$$

where I is a grey-value image and the overlining stands for averaging the elements over a local neighborhood. The gradient structure tensor borrows its descriptive power from the analogy to a well-known quantity in physics, the inertia tensor [13]. Maybe not so widespread known, the structure tensor is also similar to the covariance matrix $C = \langle X^2 \rangle - \langle X \rangle^2$. In statistical pattern recognition the covariance matrix is used to describe a set of points (here generated by the endpoints of the gradient vectors). The relation is given by

$$C = \overline{G} - \overline{\nabla I_i}\,\overline{\nabla I_j} \quad 1 \leq i, j \leq n\,. \tag{2}$$

The covariance matrix and the structure tensor are identical if the average (expectation) per element is zero, $\langle X \rangle = 0$, i.e. on lines and planes.

The gradient structure tensor overcomes the problem to average orientation by mapping the local gradient ∇I via a quadratic form (dyadic product) to a continuous representation which allows filtering; averaging with a weight function. The outcome cannot be interpreted directly but first an eigenvalue analysis of $\overline{G}$ has to be done, where the ratios of the eigenvalues characterize local structure [6, 15, 1], i.e. the local dimensionality. Due to the nonlinearity of the structure tensor, arbitrary linear filters may produce unexpected results.

The gradient structure tensor clearly treats gradients (x) pointing in opposite direction ($-x$) equally with respect to direction *and* magnitude

$$G : \mathbb{R}^n \ni x \to xx^t \in \mathbb{R}^{n \times n}\,. \tag{3}$$

These two properties are necessary conditions for sensible averaging of the tensor elements. In other words, rotation of the image yields a (equally) rotated result of the tensor space.

In other circumstances it may be desirable to preserve absolute differences in orientation in the mapping resolving the orientation problem. Limiting the number of elements of a mapping is important as high dimensional images have high memory requirements. We will look for the minimal set of elements to describe local orientation satisfying the following conditions.

2 Requirements of a Mapping

Knutsson proposed the following three properties for a continuous distance preserving representation of orientation: *Uniqueness, Uniform Stretch* and *Polar Separability* [10, 9]. Let be $x \in \mathbb{R}^n$:

- Uniqueness: Antipodal vectors should be mapped onto one point, this removes the phase jump, e.g. opposite gradient vectors are treated equally. $M(x) = M(-x)$
- Polar Separability: The norm of the mapped vector should be rotation invariant; information carried by the magnitude of the original vector does normally not depend on the angle. $\|M(x)\| = f(\|x\|)$, where f is an arbitrary function $f : \mathbb{R}^+ \to \mathbb{R}^+$.
- Uniform Stretch: The mapping should carry implicitly information about the distances in the original space that is rotation invariant and scales linearly with the angle between two hyper planes. $\|\delta M(x)\| = c\|\delta x\|$ for $\|x\| = const.$

3 The Mapping

A mapping that fulfills the above requirements is the quadratic form $M : \mathbb{R}^n \to \mathbb{R}^{n\times n}$

$$M(x) = \frac{xx^t}{\|x\|} . \tag{4}$$

It was introduced by Knutsson in this form in 1989 [10]. From the construction it is clear that M is symmetric and has only $\frac{n(n+1)}{2}$ independent components. The mapping is slightly different from the structure tensor G. The latter does not meet all the above requirements. The uniqueness requirement is met by G, also the polar separability as $\|G(x)\| = \|x\|^2$, but the uniform stretch property is not met as $\|\delta G(x)\| = c\|x\|\,\|\delta x\|$. The structure tensor is therefore no distance preserving mapping.

The mappings M and G are non-linear mappings, thus the outcome of filtering operations applied to the elements of M or G is subject to interpretation. For G the smoothing and an eigenvalue analysis of $\overline{G}$ is now standard. General statements are possible about the properties laid down in the requirements, the norm of a variational vector $\|\delta M(x)\|$ and the norm of a mapped vector $\|M(x)\|$. The uniform stretch property can be utilized to compute different properties than local structure by applying other filters than blurring filters[12].

For the norm in the uniformity and the polar separability Knutsson chose the Fröbenius norm

$$\|M\|^2 := \sum_{ij} m_{ij}^2 = \mathrm{tr}\,(M^t M) = \sum_n \lambda_n^2 , \tag{5}$$

where λ_n are the eigenvalues of M. In this special case, M being a quadratic form, the Fröbenius norm is equal to the often used spectral norm $\|M\|_{spec} := \sqrt{\text{largest eigenvalue of}(M^t M)}$ as M has only one nonzero eigenvalue.

At this point we notice that we can further reduce the number of independent components of M and G. The polar separability requirement guarantees for both mappings a rotation invariant norm and

$$\|M\|^2 = \lambda_{max}^2 = \lambda_1^2 = \mathrm{tr}\,(M)^2 = const . \tag{6}$$

So there is another restriction imposed on the diagonal elements of M. Therefore from the n diagonal elements only $n-1$ linear combinations are necessary and the mappings M and G have $\frac{n(n+1)}{2}-1$ independent components. This can be important as the less dimensions to process the less memory is needed.

3.1 The Mapping in 2D ($n = 2$)

For the 2D case the mapping M reads $x \in \mathbb{R}^2$:

$$M(x) = \frac{1}{\|x\|}(x_1^2, x_1x_2, x_2x_1, x_2^2)\,, \tag{7}$$

or in polar coordinates $x_1 = r\cos\varphi, x_2 = r\sin\varphi$

$$M(x) = r(\cos^2\varphi, \sin\varphi\cos\varphi, \cos\varphi\sin\varphi, \sin^2\varphi)\,. \tag{8}$$

From the above consideration we know that there are only $\frac{n(n+1)}{2}-1=2$ independent components. Linear combinations of the diagonal elements yield only one component carrying information

$$\cos^2\varphi + \sin^2\varphi = 1 \tag{9}$$

$$\cos^2\varphi - \sin^2\varphi = \cos 2\varphi\,. \tag{10}$$

To scale all elements evenly we take the off-diagonal element m_{12} twice, $2\sin\varphi\cos\varphi = \sin 2\varphi$. Combining eq.(7) with the restriction on the trace we get a *reduced set*

$$M_{r2D}(x) = \frac{1}{\|x\|}(x_1^2 - x_2^2, 2x_1x_2) = r(\cos 2\varphi, \sin 2\varphi)\,. \tag{11}$$

The Knutsson mapping M, reduced to M_{r2D} in 2D is equivalent to the well known *double angle method*: $r(\cos\varphi, \sin\varphi) \to r(\cos 2\varphi, \sin 2\varphi)$ [6, 4, 5]. Note that the double angle method cannot be generalized to higher dimensions in a straightforward manner. Already in 1978 Granlund proposed an orientation operator for 2D images

$$O := (\overline{G}_{22} - \overline{G}_{11}, 2\overline{G}_{21})^t\,, \tag{12}$$

only using these linear combinations of the components of the structure tensor to describe the orientation $\tan 2\varphi = 2\overline{G}_{21}/(\overline{G}_{22} - \overline{G}_{11})$ [4]. The functions $r(\cos 2\varphi, \sin 2\varphi)$ are the circular harmonics [3]. They form a basis of the polynomials of second degree in 2D, so the reduced set M_{r2D} (11) is indeed minimal.

3.2 The Mapping in 3D ($n = 3$)

Again we want to reduce the dimensionality of the general mapping M. For the 3D case we transfer the successful recipe from 2D; taking twice the off-diagonal elements and cyclic combinations of the diagonal elements

$$\frac{1}{\|x\|}(\underbrace{x_1^2 - x_2^2, 2x_1x_2}_{\text{again 2D}}, 2x_1x_3, 2x_2x_3, x_2^2 - x_3^2, x_3^2 - x_1^2)\,. \tag{13}$$

We have 6 components, from the above considerations we know that there are only $\frac{n(n+1)}{2} - 1 = 5$ independent components. A combination of the diagonal elements m_1, m_5, m_6 is suitable to reduce the set by one by utilizing the restriction on the trace. We choose

$$M_{r3D}(x) = \frac{1}{\|x\|}(x_1^2 - x_2^2, 2x_1x_2, 2x_1x_3, 2x_2x_3, \frac{1}{\sqrt{3}}(2x_3^2 - x_1^2 - x_2^2)) . \tag{14}$$

Knutsson 1985: In 1985 Knutsson introduced a mapping fulfilling the above requirements suitable for 3D [9]. This function $M_K : \mathbb{R}^3 \to \mathbb{R}^5$ is written in spherical polar coordinates $r \in \mathbb{R}, \phi \in [-\pi, \pi]$ and $\theta \in [0, \pi]$

$$\begin{aligned} M_K(r, \theta, \phi) \to r(s, t, u, v, w), \\ s = \sin^2\theta \, \cos 2\phi, \\ t = \sin^2\theta \, \sin 2\phi, \\ u = \sin 2\theta \, \cos\phi, \\ v = \sin 2\theta \, \sin\phi, \\ w = \sqrt{3}(\cos^2\theta - \frac{1}{3}) . \end{aligned} \tag{15}$$

Knutsson gave no derivation for his mapping M_K and said it was heuristically derived. We can derive M_K in a systematical way from the general mapping M (4).

The function M_K is in fact not different from M. M_K is the reduced set M_{r3D}(14) in spherical polar coordinates: $x_1 = r\cos\phi\sin\theta$, $x_2 = r\sin\phi\sin\theta$, $x_3 = r\cos\theta$. The extension from 2D to 3D is now no longer heuristic, as we presented its derivation. Extension to higher dimensions has become straightforward.

Another Way to M_K: The extension to 3D (15) of the 2D solution to the orientation problem, the double angle method, can also be derived by analogy transfer. The double angle method maps the tangent to $r(\cos 2\varphi, \sin 2\varphi)$. These are the circular harmonics. Now let's have a look at the spherical harmonics [3]

$$Y_l^m(\theta, \phi) = \begin{cases} P_l^m(\cos\theta)\cos(m\phi) & \text{for } m = 0, 1, 2, \ldots, l \\ P_l^{|m|}(\cos\theta)\sin(|m|\phi) & \text{for } m = -1, \ldots, -l \end{cases} , \tag{16}$$

where P_l^m are the associated Legendre polynomials. The spherical harmonics of second degree Y_2^m are (up to a scaling factor) identical to the components of the mapping M_K

$$\begin{aligned} s &= 1/3 \; Y_2^2, \\ t &= 8 \; Y_2^{-2}, \\ u &= 2/3 \; Y_2^1, \\ v &= 4 \; Y_2^{-1}, \\ w &= 2/\sqrt{3} \, Y_2^0 . \end{aligned}$$

The spherical harmonics form a basis of the polynomials of second degree in 3D, so the set of components of M_{r3D} (14) is indeed minimal.

4 Properties of the Mappings

In table 1 we summarize some properties of the mappings presented in this paper.

Table 1. Some properties of the different mappings.

	Dimension	Stretch constant	Polar Separability	Angle
G	n	–	$\|x\|^2$	–
M	n	$c = \sqrt{2}$	$\|x\|$	$\cos\alpha = \cos^2\psi$
M_{r2D}	2	$c = 2$	$\|x\|$	$\cos\alpha = \cos 2\psi$
M_K	3	$c = 2$	$\frac{2}{\sqrt{3}}\|x\|$	$\cos\alpha = \frac{3}{4}(\cos 2\psi + \frac{1}{3})$

The angle ψ of two vectors x, y in the original space can be related to the angle α that the mapped vectors $M(x), M(y)$ will form in the mapped space. Knutsson has done this only for M_K [9, 10]. For the general mapping M (4) the deduction is

$$\cos\psi = \frac{x \cdot y}{\|x\|\,\|y\|} \tag{17}$$

$$\cos\alpha = \frac{M(x)\cdot M(y)}{\|M(x)\|\,\|M(y)\|} = \frac{\sum_{ij} x_i x_j y_i y_j}{\|x\|^2\,\|y\|^2} = \frac{(x\cdot y)^2}{\|x\|^2\,\|y\|^2} \tag{18}$$

$$\Rightarrow \quad \cos\alpha = \cos^2\psi\,. \tag{19}$$

In figure 1 we plot the angle transfer functions for M, M_K, M_{r2D} between the angle of two vectors in one space and the angle of the corresponding vectors in the mapped space. We observe the following properties:

$$M : n\text{D} \to n^2\text{D} \quad \psi \in [0, 180°] \to \alpha \in [0, 90°] \tag{20}$$

$$M_K : 3\text{D} \to 5\text{D} \quad \psi \in [0, 180°] \to \alpha \in [0, 120°] \tag{21}$$

$$M_{r2D} : 2\text{D} \to 2\text{D} \quad \psi \in [0, 180°] \to \alpha \in [0, 180°] \tag{22}$$

Knutsson pointed out that the sum of two non-zero mapped vectors (by M or M_K) is always greater than zero because the maximal angle they can make is smaller than 180°. He interpreted this as a consequence of the fact that there is no fully symmetric representation[1] of two 3D lines [9], but there is one of three 3D lines, i.e. three perpendicular lines. If we map three perpendicular lines

$$\begin{aligned}
&\text{z-axis:} \quad M_K(r, 0, \phi) = r(0, 0, 0, 0, 2/\sqrt{3})\\
&\text{y-axis:} \quad M_K(r, \pi/2, \pi/2) = r(1, 0, 0, 0, -1/\sqrt{3})\\
&\text{x-axis:} \quad M_K(r, \pi/2, 0) = r(-1, 0, 0, 0, -1/\sqrt{3})
\end{aligned}$$

then the sum of these three mapped vectors is zero. Here we see the possibility to generate from two mapped vectors (by M_K) in 5D, a third vector that is perpendicular to the other two *and* that is in the image of M_K. To find a vector

[1] Fully symmetric in the sense that reflections map the lines onto each other.

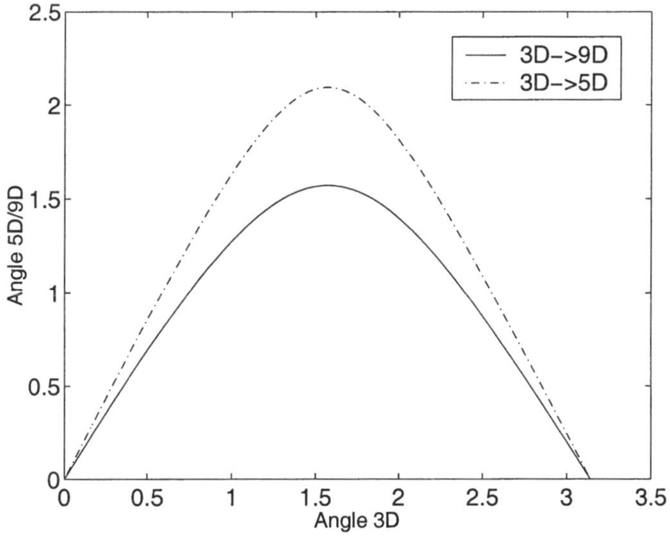

Fig. 1. Transfer function of the angle.

in 5D that is perpendicular to two other is not difficult, we want to find the one which lies in the subspace of the image of M_K. In 3D the outer product is used to obtain a perpendicular vector from two other, in 5D the sum of those three must be zero

$$\begin{aligned} \text{3D} \quad z &= x \times y && (23) \\ \text{5D} \quad M_K(z) &= -[M_K(x) + M_K(y)] \,. && (24) \end{aligned}$$

5 Conclusions

We have shown in which manner specific solutions (2D [4, 7] and 3D [9, 10]) for a continuous orientation representation are connected through a general framework for arbitrary dimensions. In a general manner we can reduce the dimensionality of the Knutsson mapping (4) and of the gradient structure tensor to a minimal set necessary to describe orientation in multi-dimensional images. The relation with the circular and spherical harmonics has become clear, as a minimal set of necessary components in 2D and 3D. Furthermore the difference between the structure tensor and the Knutsson mapping are discussed, the first being not distance preserving which is important when applying other than averaging filters. The uniqueness and polar separability are properties of both mappings.

Acknowledgments

This work was partially supported by the Netherlands Organization for Scientific Research, grant nr. 612-012-003.

References

1. P. Bakker, P.W. Verbeek, and L.J. van Vliet. Edge preserving orientation adaptive filtering. In *CVPR'99 (Colorado, U.S.A)*, volume 2, pages 535–540, June 1999.
2. J. Bigün, G.H. Granlund, and J. Wiklund. Multidimensional orientation estimation with applications to texture analysis and optical flow. *IEEE Transaction on Pattern Analysis and Machine Intelligence*, 13(8):775–790, 1991.
3. I.N. Bronstein, K.A.Semendjajew, G. Musiol, and H. Mühlig. *Taschenbuch der Mathematik.* Verlag Harri Deutsch, Thun, Frankfurt (Main), 4th edition, 1999.
4. G.H. Granlund. In search of a general picture processing operator. *Computer Graphics and Image Processing*, 8:155–173, 1978.
5. G.H. Granlund and H. Knutsson. *Signal processing for computer vision.* Kluwer Academic Publishers, Boston/Dordrecht/London, 1995.
6. B. Jähne. *Digital Image Processing.* Springer, 4th edition, 1997.
7. M. Kass and A. Witkin. Analyzing oriented patterns. *Computer Vision, Graphics and Image Processing*, 37:362–385, 1987.
8. H. Knutsson. *Filtering and Reconstruction in Image Processing.* PhD thesis, Linköping University, Linköping, Sweden, 1982.
9. H. Knutsson. Producing a continuous and distance preserving 5-d vector representation of 3-d orientation. In *IEEE Computer Society Workshop on Computer Architecture for Pattern Analysis and Image Database Management*, pages 175–182. Miami Beach, Florida, November 18-20 1985.
10. H. Knutsson. Representing local structure using tensors. In *The 6th Scandinavian Conference in Image Analysis*, pages 244–251, Oulu, Finland, June 19-22 1989.
11. K. Nordberg, H. Knutsson, and G. Granlund. On the invariance of the orientation and the tensor field representation. Technical report, Linköping University, Linköping, Sweden, 1993. LiTH-ISY-R-1530.
12. B. Rieger and L.J. van Vliet. Curvature of n-dimensional space curves in grey-value images. *IEEE Transactions on Image Processing*, 11(7):738–745, 2002.
13. F. Scheck. *Mechanics: From Newton's Law to Deterministic Chaos.* Springer, Berlin, 1999.
14. M. van Ginkel, J. van de Weijer, L.J. van Vliet, and P.W. Verbeek. Curvature estimation from orientation fields. SCIA'99, Proc. 11th Scandinavian Conference on Image Analysis, pages 545–551. Pattern Recognition Society of Denmark, Lyngby, 1999.
15. J. van de Weijer, L.J. van Vliet, P.W. Verbeek, and M. van Ginkel. Curvature estimation in oriented patterns using curvilinear models applied to gradient vector fields. *IEEE Transactions on Pattern Analysis and Machine Intelligence*, 23(9):1035 -1042, 2001.
16. C.F. Westin. *A Tensor Framework for Multidimensional Signal Processing.* PhD thesis, Linköping University, Linköping, Sweden, 1994.

Docking of Polygons Using Boundary Descriptor

A. Imiya[1,2] and S. Kudo[3]

[1] National Institute of Informatics, Japan
[2] Institute of Media and Information Technology, Chiba University, Japan
[3] Department of Information and Image Sciences, Chiba University, Japan

Abstract. We show that the polygon docking problem can be divided into two subproblems, partial matching of periodic strings and line segment intersection detection. And we show that the docking problem of a pair of polygons is solved in $O(n^2)$ times, where n is the number of edges of polygons. Using this result, we show that construction of an object from a collection of polygons whose elements have no numerical error on the expression of the lengths of edges and the angles between two connecting edges can be solved in $O(k^3n^2)$ times for k polygons where the maximum number of edges of polygonal-elements is n.

1 Introduction

In this paper, we deal with the docking problem [1] of closed planar polygonal curves. For the construction of a simple polygonal curve from two simple polygonal curves, we are required to find parts of polygonal curves which touch each other without any gaps. We convert the process for the selection of a pair of parts of polygons to a partial matching of strings.

Docking is a fundamental operation used to construct an object from pieces of objects. The problem is studied in the contexts of computer-aided assembly, computer vision, pattern recognition, pharmacy design, and genomic analysis [2–6]. For the detection of a part of the object boundary for docking operations, it is necessary to select a pairs of a convex part of an object and a concave part of the another object. These two parts of polygonal curves contact to yield a new simple polygonal curve. Recently, the partial matching of polygonal curves is used for shape retrieval and shape classification [7]. The matching of closed polygonal curves, which are boundary curves of polygonal shapes, is fundamentally converted to string matching problem, whose elements are lengths of edges and angles between two connecting edges.

The boundary curve matching for jigsaw puzzle has been studied by some authors [8–10], in the context of pattern recognition. Freeman and Garder [9] applied the chain code for the boundary expression and developed an algorithm based on string matching of sequences of chain codes, whereas Radack and Badler [8] expressed the boundary curve of a planar figure by the polar coordinate system and derived a translation invariant expression for shape matching of polygonal curves. Furthermore, Wolfson, *et al.* [10] developed an algorithm for the partial matching of sampled boundary curves. They showed that the docking of

N. Petkov and M.A. Westenberg (Eds.): CAIP 2003, LNCS 2756, pp. 25–32, 2003.

elements in jigsaw puzzle can be converted to shortest pass problem. Arkin *et al.* [3] showed that the tangent description of the boundary-curve of polygon, whose lengths are normalized to unity, is suitable for the discrimination of polygonal shapes. They employed string discrimination based on string matching for the discrimination of polygonal curves.

We combine the tangent-curve expression of polygonal curve and partial string matching for docking problem. Furthermore, we do not restrict our figures to elements of a jigsaw puzzle set. Therefore, our method solves the docking problem for any planar shapes.

2 Docking of Simple Polygons

We consider simple polygonal curves on the two-dimensional Euclidean plane $\mathbf{R}^2$. Setting $\{\boldsymbol{p}_i\}_{i=1}^m$ to be vertices of a simple polygon $\mathbf{P}$ on $\mathbf{R}^2$, we define string $P = \langle \boldsymbol{p}_1, \boldsymbol{p}_2, \cdots, \boldsymbol{p}_m \rangle$, for $\boldsymbol{p}_{m+i} = \boldsymbol{p}_i$, which follows the vertices of a polygon in the counterclockwise direction. Setting $\boldsymbol{p}_{i+1,i} = \boldsymbol{p}_{i+1} - \boldsymbol{p}_i$ and $d_i = |\boldsymbol{p}_{i+1,i}|$ we denote a triangle whose vertices are $\boldsymbol{p}_i$, $\boldsymbol{p}_j$, and $\boldsymbol{p}_k$ as $\boldsymbol{p}[ijk]$. The angle between two edges $\boldsymbol{p}_{i+1,i}$ and $\boldsymbol{p}_{i,i-1}$ is given as $\theta_i = \cos^{-1} \frac{\boldsymbol{p}_{i+1,i}^\top \boldsymbol{p}_{i,i-1}}{d_i d_{i-1}}$. Here, θ_i such that $0 \leq \theta < 2\pi$, is measured from vector $\boldsymbol{p}_{i-1,i}$ to $\boldsymbol{p}_{i+1,i}$ in the counterclockwise direction.

If triangles $\boldsymbol{p}[i-1, i, i+1]$ and $\boldsymbol{q}[j+1, j, j-1]$ defined from string $P = \langle \boldsymbol{p}_1, \boldsymbol{p}_2, \cdots, \boldsymbol{p}_m \rangle$ and $P = \langle \boldsymbol{q}_1, \boldsymbol{q}_2, \cdots, \boldsymbol{q}_n \rangle$, respectively, are connected by rotation and translation, and the contrails of $\boldsymbol{p}[i-1, i, i+1]$ and $\boldsymbol{q}[j+1, j, j-1]$ lie inside the polygon and outside the polygon, respectively, or lie outside the polygon and inside the polygon, respectively, we call this pair a docking pair. The first step for solving the docking problem is achieved by detecting a pair of chains of docking pairs of triangles such that

$$\boldsymbol{p}[\alpha(1), \alpha(2), \alpha(3)], \boldsymbol{p}[\alpha(2), \alpha(3), \alpha(4)] \cdots \boldsymbol{p}[\alpha(n-2), \alpha(n-1), \alpha(n)] \quad (1)$$
$$\boldsymbol{q}[\beta(1), \beta(2), \beta(3)], \boldsymbol{q}[\beta(2), \beta(3), \beta(4)], \cdots \boldsymbol{q}[\beta(n-2), \beta(n-1), \beta(n)]. \quad (2)$$

Using a rotation and translation invariant, we detect these chains from a pair of polygons. From P, we define a string $p = \langle \theta_1, d_1, \theta_2, d_3, \cdots, \theta_m, d_m \rangle$ which is a rotation and translation invariant expression of a polygonal curve P. Setting S to be the total length of the edges of a polygonal curve, we express the point on this polygonal curve as $\boldsymbol{p}(s)$ for $0 \leq s \leq S$. Since $S = \sum_{i=1}^m d_i$, we have the relations

$$\dot{\boldsymbol{p}}(s) = \sum_{k=1}^{i} \theta_k, \text{ for, } \sum_{k=1}^{i} d_k \leq s < \sum_{k=1}^{i+1} d_k, \ \ddot{\boldsymbol{p}}(s) = \sum_{i=1}^{m} \theta_i \delta(s - \sum_{k=1}^{i} d_k). \quad (3)$$

Therefore, string p of polygonal curve P is derived by the second derivative of polygonal curve $\boldsymbol{p}(s)$. Arkin *et al.* [3] called function $\dot{\boldsymbol{p}}(s)$ the turn function of polygon. They showed that the similarity of polygonal shapes is computed $O((n \log n)^2)$ times using the turn functions of unit length polygonal curves.

Latecki and Lakämper [7] introduced the curve evolution based on the turn functions of polygonal shapes. Our descriptor of polygonal curves is the derivation of the turn function. In Figure 1, we show the change of the tangent direction along a polygonal curve and the derivation of the turn function.

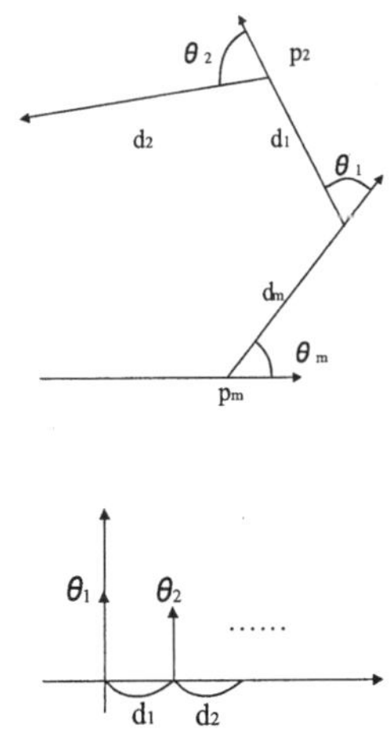

Fig. 1. The change of the tangent direction along a polygonal curve and the derivation of the turn function.

Setting $-p = \langle \theta_n, d_{n-1}, \theta_{n-1}, d_{n-2}, \cdots, \theta_1 \rangle$, we solve the docking problem using $-p$ and p. For a pair of strings,

$$p = \langle \theta_1, d_1, \theta_2, d_2, \cdots, \theta_m, d_m \rangle,\ q = \langle \phi_1, e_1, \phi_2, e_2, \cdots, \phi_n, e_n \rangle, \tag{4}$$

if relation $d_i = e_j$ is satisfied, parts of two edge-list pairs are completely matched, and, for $k \geq 1$, if

$$\begin{aligned} & d_i = e_j \\ \theta_{i+1} + \phi_{j-1} = 2\pi \ \ & d_{i+1} = e_{j-1} \\ \theta_{i+2} + \phi_{j-2} = 2\pi \ \ & d_{i+2} = e_{j-2} \\ \vdots\ \ & \vdots \\ \theta_{i+k-1} + \phi_{j-k+1} = 2\pi \ \ & d_{i+k-1} = e_{j-k+1} \\ & d_{i+k} = e_{j-k} \end{aligned} \tag{5}$$

are satisfied, triangles $\boldsymbol{p}[i+\alpha, i+\alpha+1, i+\alpha+2]$ and $\boldsymbol{q}[j-\alpha, j-\alpha-1, j-\alpha-2]$ match completely as shown in Figure 2. If there exist some partial strings which satisfy eq. (5), we adopt the partial string which maximizes the length of edges $L = \sum_{n=i}^{i+k} d_n$. Therefore, parts of polygonal curves $\Delta P = \langle \boldsymbol{p}_i, \boldsymbol{p}_{i+1}, \cdots, \boldsymbol{p}_{i+k} \rangle$ and $\Delta Q = \langle \boldsymbol{q}_j, \boldsymbol{q}_{j-1}, \cdots, \boldsymbol{q}_{j-k} \rangle$ are candidates of partial edge-list pair which are shared for the docking of two polygonal curves. We call ΔP and ΔQ the share curve pair for docking. The detection of the share curve pair is achieved by the partial matching of two periodic strings. Therefore, the time complexity of the detection of the share curve pair is $O(n^2)$, if $m \cong n$.

The string $pq = \langle \theta_1, d_1, \theta_2, d_2, \cdots, \theta_{i-1}, d_{i-1}, \theta_i + \phi_{j+k}, e_{i+k-1}, \phi_{i+k-1}, \cdots, e_{j-1}, \theta_{i+k} + \phi_j, d_{i+k}, \cdots, \theta_m, d_m \rangle$ defines a polygonal curve derived by docking a pair of polygons and eliminates the share-curve pairs as shown in Figure 2 (c). In Figure 3, we show the configuration of vertex angles of new vertices in the polygon yielded by the docking process. If a polygon whose invariant expression is pq is simple, we can completely solve the docking problem.

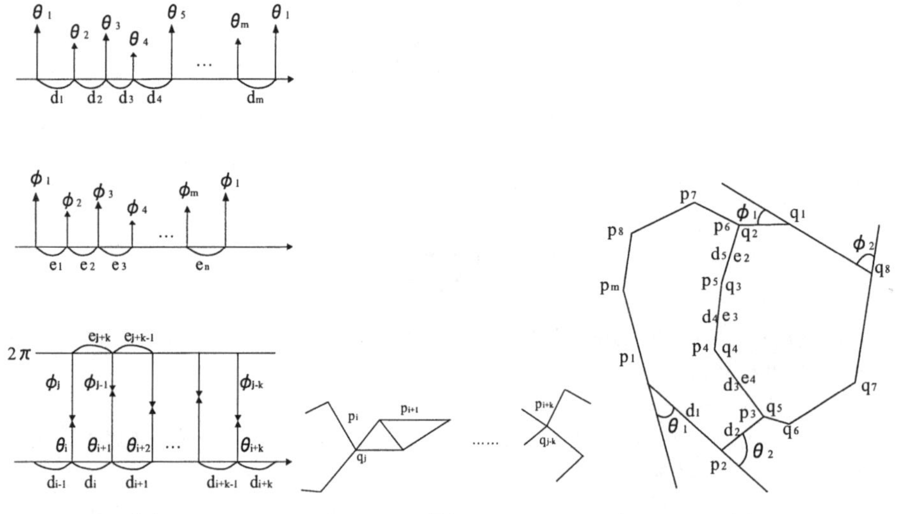

Fig. 2. Docking of polygons: (a)Partial matching of strings. (b) Partial matching of triangle chains, and (c) The turn function along a new polygon.

If we do not consider the first and the last equations of eq. (5), the relations become

$$\theta_{i+1} + \phi_{j-1} = 2\pi \;\; d_{i+1} = e_{j-1},$$
$$\theta_{i+2} + \phi_{j-2} = 2\pi \;\; d_{i+2} = e_{j-2},$$
$$\theta_{i+k-1} + \phi_{j-k+1} = 2\pi \;\; d_{i+k-1} = e_{j-k+1}.$$

In this case, pairs of vertices $\boldsymbol{p}_i$ and $\boldsymbol{q}_j$, and $\boldsymbol{p}_{i+k}$ and $\boldsymbol{q}_{j-k}$ do not touch. At each end of the shared curve, a vertex touches an edge as shown in Figure 4. Therefore, as the concatenated polygon, we have the string

$$pq = \langle \theta_1, d_1, \theta_2, d_2, \cdots, \theta_{i-1}, d_{i-1}, \psi_1, a_1, \phi_{j+k}, e_{i+k-1}, \phi_{i+k-1}, \cdots, e_{j-1}, \psi_2, a_2, \cdots, \theta_m, d_m \rangle, \qquad (6)$$

where

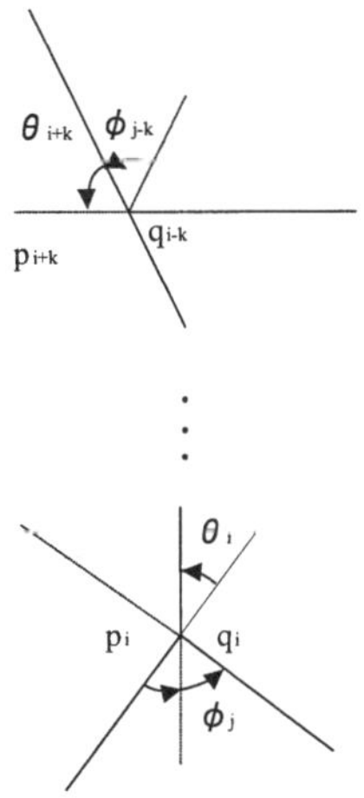

Fig. 3. The configuration of vertices and angles of new vertices.

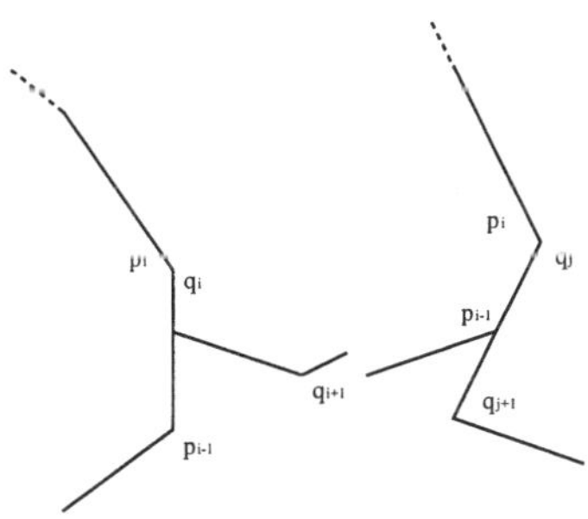

Fig. 4. Configurations of end points of curves for the docking of a pair of polygons.

$$a_1 = |d_i - e_i|,\ \psi_1 \in \{\phi_i,\ 2\pi - \theta_i\},\ a_2 = |d_{i+k} - e_{i-k}|,\ \psi_2 \in \{\phi_{i-k},\ 2\pi - \theta_{i+k}\}. \quad (7)$$

Now, we can determine the positions of vertices of a new polygon. Using positions of vertices on a plane, we can examine whether a polygon is simple or not [11, 12]. The time complexity of this process is $O(N \log N)$ for $N = m + n - 2k$. If $m \cong n > 2k$, then $N \cong n$. Therefore, the time complexity of this process is $O(n \log n)$. Furthermore, the first process is computed $O(n^2)$ times. These considerations lead to the conclusion that the docking of two polygons is computed $O(n^3)$ times, where n is the maximum of the number of edges of polygons.

3 Construction of Shape from Pieces

In Figure 5, we show an example of docking of a pair of polygons. Polygons (a) and (b) are transformed to polygon (c) by the docking algorithm based on partial string matching.

(a) (b) (c)

Fig. 5. Docking of a pair of polygons computed by our program based on the algorithm proposed in this paper.

We implemented the following algorithm for the construction of an object from a collection of polygons, where $\boldsymbol{P}$ denotes a collection of polygons.

Algorithm: *Polygon Docking*

1. If the number of polygons in $\boldsymbol{P}$ is 0, then stop.
2. For all combinations of a pair of polygons $\mathbf{P}_i$ and $\mathbf{P}_j$ from $\boldsymbol{P}$, detect the longest share curves.
3. If $\mathbf{P}_i$ and $\mathbf{P}_j$ can touch, then concatenate them.
4. Set the result of step 3 as $\mathbf{P}_i$, delete $\mathbf{P}_j$ from $\boldsymbol{P}$.
5. Go to step 1.

As shown in the previous section, step 2 can be separated into two steps and the time complexity of step 2 for each pair is $O(n^2)$. For each iteration, the algorithm tests the possibility for docking to $O((k-p)^2)$ combinations in p-th iteration. This property derives the following theorem.

Theorem 1. *Docking of k-piece polygons requires $O(k^3n^2)$ times.*

The shapes of pieces of a jigsaw puzzle are almost same. Furthermore, since practically, $k \gg n$, the total time complexity of the construction of a jigsaw puzzle is $O(k^3)$. This rough estimation of time complexity of jigsaw puzzles agrees with the grade of jigsaw puzzles, although the element shapes of jigsaw puzzles are different.

Figure 6 shows the elements for the docking of polygons. In Figure 7, we show an example of polygon construction from a collection of polygons. In these figures, (a) and (b) derive (c). (c)=(d) and (e) derive (f). (f)=(g) and (h) derive (i) as the final shape. In this example, the positions of vertices of polygons are input data. Once the share curves are detected from a pair of polygons, for the concatenation of one polygon to an other, the program computes the rotation and translation for a polygon to construct a new polygon from a pair of polygons.

4 Conclusions

We have shown that the polygon docking problem can be divided to two subproblems, partial matching of periodic strings and line segment intersection de-

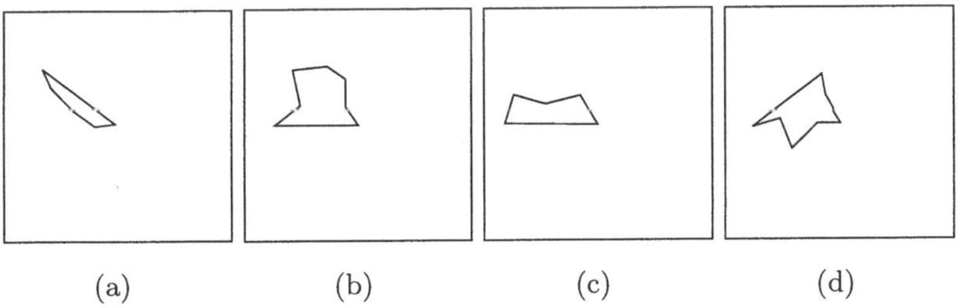

Fig. 6. The elements for docking of polygons.

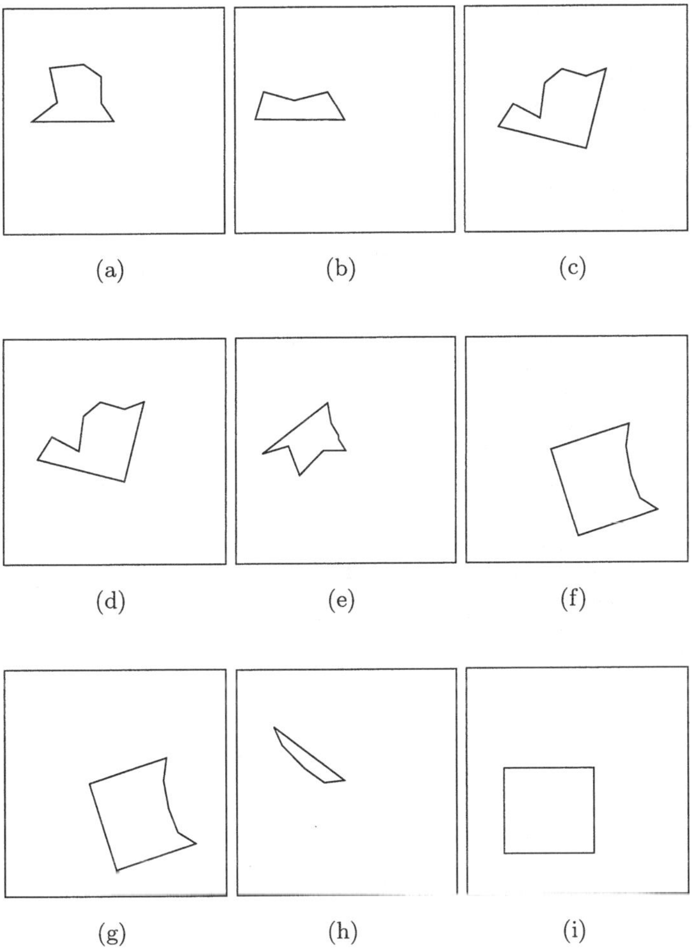

Fig. 7. Docking of polygons computed by our program based on the algorithm proposed in this paper. (a) and (b) derive (c). (c)=(d) and (e) derive (f). (f)=(g) and (h) derive (i).

tection. And we have also shown that the docking problem of a pair of polygons is solved in $O(n^2)$ times, where n is the number of edges of polygons. Using this result, we developed an algorithm for the construction of an object from a collection of polygons whose elements have no numerical error in the expression of the lengths of edges and the angles between two connecting edges.

References

1. Sandak, B., Nussinov, R., and Wolfson, H.J., Docking of conformatinally flexible proteins, LNCS, **1075**, 271-287, 1996.
2. Apostolico, A. and Galil, Z. eds., *Pattern Matching Algorithms,* Oxford University Press; New York, 1997.
3. Arkin, M., Chew, L.P., Huttenlocher, D.P., Kedem, K., and Michell, S.B., An efficiently computable metric for comparing polygonal shapes, IEEE, Tr. PAMI, **13**, 209-216, 1991.
4. Leung, M.K. and Yang, Y.-H., Dynamic two-strip algorithm in curve fitting, Pattern Recognition, **23**, 69-79, 1990.
5. Waterman, M.S., *Introduction to Computational Biology, Maps, Sequences and Genomes,* Champman & Hall;London, 1995.
6. Fu, K.S., *Syntactic Methods in Pattern Recognition,* Academic Press; New York, 1974.
7. Latecki, J.L. and Lakämper, R., Convexity rule for shape decompositions based on discrete contour evolution, CVIU, **73**, 441-454, 1999.
8. Radack, G. and Badler, N., Jigsaw puzzle matching using a boundary-centered polar encoding, CGIP. **19**, 1-17, 1982.
9. Freeman, H. and Garder, L., A pictorial jigsaw puzzle: The computer solution of a problem in pattern recognition, IEEE, Trans. Electronic Computers, **13**, 118-127, 1964.
10. Wolfson, H., Schonberg, E., Kalvib, A., and Lamdan, Y., Solving jigsaw puzzle by computer, Annals of Operations Research, **12**, 51-64, 1988.
11. de Berg, M., van Kreveld, M., Overmars, M., and Schwarzkoph, O., *Computational Geometry: Algorithms ad Applications, Chap.2.* Springer; Berlin, 1997.
12. Preparata, F.P. and Shamos, M.I., *Computational Geometry: An Introduction,* Springer; New York, 1985.

Area and Moment Computation for Objects with a Closed Spline Boundary

Stanislav Sheynin and Alexander Tuzikov*

National Center of Informational Resources and Technologies
National Academy of Sciences of Belarus
Akademicheskaja 25, 220072 Minsk, Belarus
{sheynin,tuzikov}@mpen.bas-net.by

Abstract. We propose an approach for computation of area and geometric moments for a 2D object with a spline curve boundary. The explicit formulae are obtained for area and low order moment calculation. The formulae use the advantage that the sequence of spline control points is cyclic. It allows us to reduce substantially the number of summands in them.

Keywords: Area, moment, parametric curve, spline, explicit formulae.

1 Introduction

Various applications need to compute features of plane or volumetric objects. The features often used include colour, shape and texture. Moment based features and moment invariants are among the most popular global shape features [1, 2]. Moments of zero order define the object area and volume, respectively. The object centroid is computed using first order moments and the orientation (we mean axes of inertia) – from second order moments.

A geometric moment m_{pq} of order $p+q$ for a plane object P is defined as follows:

$$m_{pq}(P) = \iint_P x^p y^q \, dx dy. \tag{1}$$

The explicit formulae for moment computation based on boundary representation are known for a simple class of objects only. The formulae for 2D polygonal objects were derived in [3]. Suppose that P is a polygon with n vertices $(x_0, y_0), \ldots, (x_{n-1}, y_{n-1}), (x_n, y_n) = (x_0, y_0)$ numbered in a counter-clockwise order. Then it is true:

$$m_{pq}(P) = \sum_{i=0}^{n-1} (x_i y_{i+1} - x_{i+1} y_i) \sum_{k=0}^{p} \sum_{l=0}^{q} \frac{p!q!(k+l)!(p+q-k-l)!}{k!l!(p-k)!(q-l)!(p+q+2)!} x_i^k x_{i+1}^{p-k} y_i^l y_{i+1}^{q-l}.$$

For $p = q = 0$ one gets the area of a polygon P:

* This work was done in framework of the ISTC B-517 project and INTAS 00-397 grant.

N. Petkov and M.A. Westenberg (Eds.): CAIP 2003, LNCS 2756, pp. 33–40, 2003.

$$m_{00}(P) = \frac{1}{2}\sum_{i=0}^{n-1}(x_i y_{i+1} - x_{i+1} y_i).$$

These formulae were extended in [4] for 3D *polyhedral* objects and higher dimensional polytopes.

Recently new results were obtained for 2D and 3D objects with a boundary defined by *parametric curves* and *surfaces* [5–9]. This became possible, because some parametric representations of a curve or a surface allow to compute moments directly. The complexity of computation in this case depends on the order of the curve/surface applied and the moment order to be computed. The formulae for area computation of objects bounded by Bézier and B-spline curves were proposed in [9]. They are based on computation of the signed area of a sector between the curve and the coordinate origin. A similar approach was presented in [5] for computation of areas and volumes. Computation of volume and moments for cubic patches was discussed and evaluated in [6]. The results presented in [5, 6] were further extended in [8].

The aim of this paper is to derive the formulae for area and low order moments of plane objects with a uniform spline curve boundary. Since the object contour is closed it is possible to use the advantage of cyclic sequence of control points. It allows us to reduce the complexity of computations and to propose efficient algorithms that might be applied in various applications.

2 Approach Proposed

We consider plane objects bounded by a closed uniform spline curve. A spline curve is defined by a sequence of n control points $\mathbf{p}_i = (x_i, y_i),\ 1 \le i \le n$. In our case it is supposed that this sequence is cyclic, i.e. $(x_{i+n}, y_{i+n}) = (x_i, y_i)$.

A spline curve consists of segments. A spline segment of order s is constructed by $s+1$ sequential control points. The number of segments in a closed curve constructed by n points equals n and an m-th segment has the following parametric representation:

$$(x(t), y(t)) = \left(1\, t \cdots\ t^{s-1}\, t^s\right) H X_m, \quad t \in [0, 1], \tag{2}$$

where

$$X_m = \begin{pmatrix} x_m & y_m \\ \vdots & \vdots \\ x_{m+s} & y_{m+s} \end{pmatrix}.$$

Here H is a fixed matrix of size $(s+1) \times (s+1)$ which defines a uniform spline of order s. This matrix defines the influence of different control points on the shape of the spline curve. Fig. 1 presents examples of cubic B-spline and interpolating curves. We discuss these examples of splines in Sect. 3.

Note that there exists another way to define splines which allows to deal with non-uniform splines as well [10, 11].

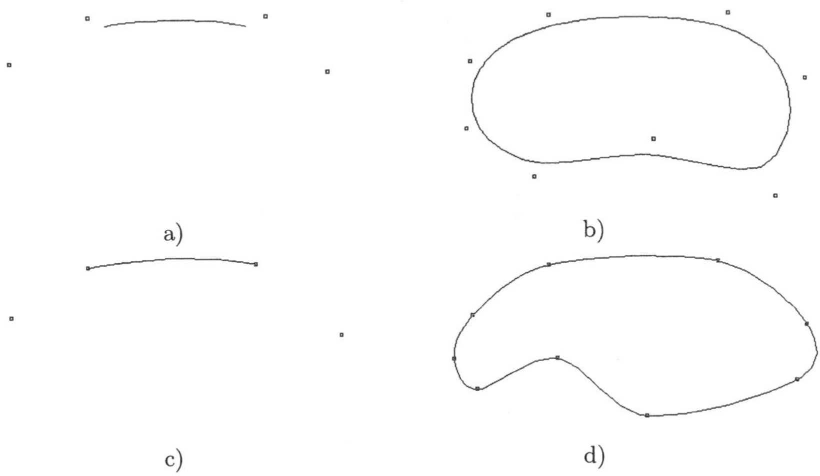

Fig. 1. Cubic B-spline: a) segment; b) closed curve. Interpolating cubic spline: c) segment; d) closed curve.

Later on we denote by h_{ij}, $0 \le i, j \le s$, a corresponding element of matrix H, i.e. rows and columns are numbered from 0 to s (we assume the same for other matrices as well).

It is assumed that splines possess the following *symmetry* property: the spline curve has the same shape for the reversed order of control points. Note that uniform B-splines [11] and interpolating splines [12] possess this property.

To compute the area bounded by a closed spline curve one has to sum the oriented subgraph areas of all spline segments. The same is true for computing arbitrary order moments for the region bounded by this curve.

One can show that the following formula holds for oriented moment computation of a subgraph U under a parametrized curve $x = x(t),\ y = y(t),\ t_0 \le t \le t_1$:

$$m_{pq}(U) = \frac{1}{q+1} \int_{t_0}^{t_1} x(t)^p y(t)^{q+1} x'(t) dt. \tag{3}$$

If the function $x(t)$ is not monotone, then the curve is not a graph of a single-valued function. However, the formula (3) is also true in this case, and it defines an oriented moment of the subgraph. Some examples of subgraphs are presented in Fig. 2. The subgraphs are shown in gray and the signs + and − on the second subgraph components denote the sign of the corresponding subgraph component area (moment) while computing the oriented area (moment) of the whole subgraph. Particularly for the closed curve (when $x(t_0) = x(t_1),\ y(t_0) = y(t_1)$), formula (3) defines the moments of a region bounded by this curve. Note that the transposition of the coordinate axes x and y in this case does not influence the region bounded but reverses the boundary orientation. Therefore, the transposition of x and y and the corresponding moment orders in formula (3) results in changing the sign only.

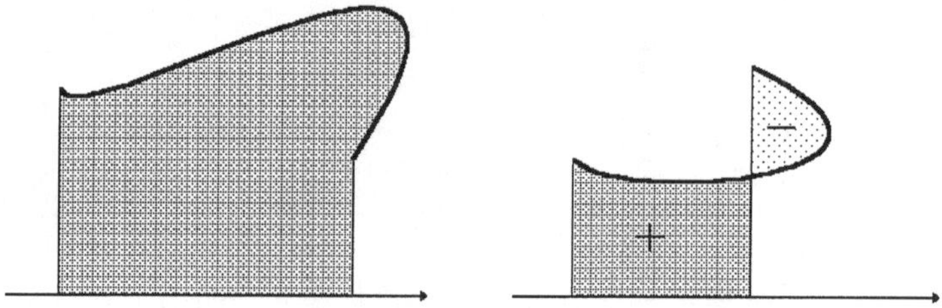

Fig. 2. Subgraphs of curves which are not graphs of single-valued functions.

In our case $x(t)$ and $y(t)$ are polynomials for every spline segment. Substituting these polynomials into (3) one gets the expression for moment computation of the segment subgraph. This expression is a form of order $p+1$ respective x-coordinates and of order $q+1$ respective y-coordinates of control points defining the segment. Therefore, one can show that the formula for moment m_{pq} contains at most $\binom{s+p+1}{p+1}\binom{s+q+1}{q+1}$ summands, where $\binom{n}{m} = \frac{n!}{m!(n-m)!}$.

For the area (moment m_{00}) the following proposition holds.

Proposition 1. *The subgraph area of m-th spline segment of order s defined by control points* $\mathbf{p}_i = (x_i, y_i)$, $m \le i \le m+s$, *according to (2) equals*

$$\mathbf{x}_m A \mathbf{y}_m^t. \tag{4}$$

Here $\mathbf{x}_m = (x_m, x_{m+1}, \ldots, x_{m+s})$, $\mathbf{y}_m = (y_m, y_{m+1}, \ldots, y_{m+s})$, *and A is a matrix of size* $(s+1) \times (s+1)$. *The elements* a_{ij} *of matrix A are calculated as follows:*

$$a_{ij} = \sum_{k=1}^{s} \sum_{l=0}^{s} \frac{k}{k+l} h_{ki} h_{lj}. \tag{5}$$

If the spline possesses the symmetry property, then matrix A is centrally-antisymmetric, i.e. $a_{ij} = -a_{s-i,s-j}$.

Formula (4) has $(s+1)^2$ summands. To compute the area of the region bounded by the whole closed spline curve one needs to add the results for all segments, i.e.

$$m_{00} = \sum_{m=1}^{n} \mathbf{x}_m A \mathbf{y}_m^t = \sum_{m=1}^{n} \sum_{i=0}^{s} \sum_{j=0}^{s} a_{ij} x_{m+i} y_{m+j}. \tag{6}$$

However, in this cyclic sum the matrix A is redundant. Since the sequence of control points is cyclic, it is possible to prove the following result.

Theorem 1. *The area* m_{00} *of a region bounded by a closed spline curve of order s with n control points* $\mathbf{p}_i = (x_i, y_i)$, $1 \le i \le n$, *is computed as follows:*

$$m_{00} = \sum_{(i,j)\in\Gamma_{00}} a'_{ij} \sum_{m=1}^{n} x_{m+i} y_{m+j}. \tag{7}$$

Here $a'_{ij} = \sum_{k=0}^{s} a_{k+i,k+j}$ *for* $a_{k+i,k+j}$ *having sense (i.e.* $0 \le k+i,\ k+j \le s$*) and* Γ_{00} *is a set of indices* $\Gamma_{00} = \{(i,j)|\ 0 \le i,j \le s,\ ij = 0\}$ *representing the first row and column of matrix* A*.*

It follows from the central-antisymmetry of A that $a'_{i0} = -a'_{0i}$, $a'_{00} = 0$. One can conclude now that for computing the area of a closed spline curve it is sufficient to find the sum of $2sn$ elements. Note, that the direct computation according to formula (6) has $(s+1)^2 n$ summands. Note also that the area computation of an object with a polygonal boundary with n vertices needs $2n$ summands.

First order moments are computed similarly. Let us consider moment m_{10}. The following expression holds for the moment m_{10} of a region bounded by a closed spline of order s with n control points:

$$m_{10} = \sum_{m=1}^{n} \sum_{i=0}^{s} \sum_{j=0}^{s} \sum_{k=0}^{s} b_{ijk} x_{m+i} x_{m+j} y_{m+k}, \tag{8}$$

where

$$b_{ijk} = \sum_{p=0}^{s} \sum_{q=1}^{s} \sum_{r=0}^{s} \frac{q}{p+q+r} h_{pi} h_{qj} h_{rk}. \tag{9}$$

Note that $b_{ijk} = b_{kji}$.

Since the coefficients b_{ijk} and b_{jik} correspond to the same element, it is important to know only their sum $b_{ijk} + b_{jik}$. So we can introduce the symmetrized coefficients $\bar{b}_{ijk} = (b_{ijk} + b_{jik})/2$. The antisymmetry property $\bar{b}_{ijk} = -\bar{b}_{s-i,s-j,s-k}$ also holds for them.

The formula (8) can be simplified similarly to the formula for the area.

Theorem 2. *Moments* m_{10} *and* m_{01} *of a region bounded by a closed spline curve of order* s *with* n *control points* $\mathbf{p}_i = (x_i, y_i)$, $1 \le i \le n$, *are computed as follows:*

$$m_{10} = \sum_{(i,j,k)\in\Gamma_{10}} b'_{ijk} \sum_{m=1}^{n} x_{m+i} x_{m+j} y_{m+k}, \tag{10}$$

$$m_{01} = - \sum_{(i,j,k)\in\Gamma_{10}} b'_{ijk} \sum_{m=1}^{n} x_{m+k} y_{m+i} y_{m+j}. \tag{11}$$

Here $\Gamma_{10} = \{(i,j,k)|\ 0 < i,j,k < s,\ ijk = 0,\ j < i\}$, *and*

$$b'_{ijk} = \begin{cases} \sum_{m=0}^{s} \bar{b}_{m+i,m+j,m+k} & \textit{if } j = i, \\ 2\sum_{m=0}^{s} \bar{b}_{m+i,m+j,m+k} & \textit{if } j \ne i. \end{cases}$$

Note that coefficients $b'_{ijk} = 0$ for $i = 2k$ due to antisymmetry property.

Therefore, one can check that the number of summands in (10) and (11) is at most $\left[\frac{(s+1)(3s+1)}{2}\right] n$ in comparison to $(s+1)^3 n$ ones using a direct computation by (8). Here $[s]$ denotes the integer part of s.

Formula (11) follows from (10), since to compute moment m_{01} we can transpose the coordinate axes and use the formula for moment m_{10} (changing the sign due to changing the orientation).

The approach can be similarly applied for computation of second order moments m_{20}, m_{11} and m_{02}. Due to space limitation we do not present here the corresponding formulae.

3 Examples

Let us consider B-spline and interpolating spline curves. Note that B-splines approximate control points and interpolating splines pass through control points.

3.1 Cubic B-Spline Curves

Matrix H of a cubic B-spline and matrix A for area computation obtained by formula (5) are given as follows:

$$H = \frac{1}{6}\begin{pmatrix} 1 & 4 & 1 & 0 \\ -3 & 0 & 3 & 0 \\ 3 & -6 & 3 & 0 \\ -1 & 3 & -3 & 1 \end{pmatrix}; \qquad A = \frac{1}{720}\begin{pmatrix} -10 & -71 & -38 & -1 \\ -9 & -150 & -183 & -18 \\ 18 & 183 & 150 & 9 \\ 1 & 38 & 71 & 10 \end{pmatrix}$$

Formula (7) for area computation for the curve with n control points is the following:

$$m_{00} = \frac{1}{720}\sum_{m=1}^{n}\Big(-245(x_m y_{m+1} - x_{m+1} y_m) - 56(x_m y_{m+2} - x_{m+2} y_m) - x_m y_{m+3} + x_{m+3} y_m\Big).$$

Moments m_{10} and m_{01} computed by formulae (10) and (11) are the following:

$$m_{10} = \frac{1}{60480}\sum_{i=1}^{n}\Big(5947 x_i x_{i+1} y_i + 5947 x_{i+1}^2 y_i + 648 x_i x_{i+2} y_i + 2710 x_{i+1} x_{i+2} y_i + 648 x_{i+2}^2 y_i + \frac{5}{3} x_i x_{i+3} y_i + 36 x_{i+1} x_{i+3} y_i + 43 x_{i+2} x_{i+3} y_i + \frac{5}{3} x_{i+3}^2 y_i - 5947 x_i^2 y_{i+1} - 5947 x_i x_{i+1} y_{i+1} + 7 x_i x_{i+3} y_{i+1} - 648 x_i^2 y_{i+2} - 2710 x_i x_{i+1} y_{i+2} - 648 x_i x_{i+2} y_{i+2} - 7 x_i x_{i+3} y_{i+2} - \frac{5}{3} x_i^2 y_{i+3} - 43 x_i x_{i+1} y_{i+3} - 36 x_i x_{i+2} y_{i+3} - \frac{5}{3} x_i x_{i+3} y_{i+3}\Big),$$

$$m_{01} = \frac{1}{60480} \sum_{i=1}^{n} \Big(-5947x_iy_iy_{i+1} - 5947x_iy_{i+1}^2 - 648x_iy_iy_{i+2} - 2710x_iy_{i+1}y_{i+2}$$
$$- 648x_iy_{i+2}^2 - \frac{5}{3}x_iy_iy_{i+3} - 36x_iy_{i+1}y_{i+3} - 43x_iy_{i+2}y_{i+3} - \frac{5}{3}x_iy_{i+3}^2 + 5947x_{i+1}y_i^2$$
$$+ 5947x_{i+1}y_iy_{i+1} - 7x_{i+1}y_iy_{i+3} + 648x_{i+2}y_i^2 + 2710x_{i+2}y_iy_{i+1} + 648x_{i+2}y_i$$
$$y_{i+2} + 7x_{i+2}y_iy_{i+3} + \frac{5}{3}x_{i+3}y_i^2 + 43x_{i+3}y_iy_{i+1} + 36x_{i+3}y_iy_{i+2} + \frac{5}{3}x_{i+3}y_iy_{i+3} \Big).$$

Example of cubic B-spline curve is given in Fig. 1 a), b).

3.2 Interpolating Spline Curves

Matrices H and A for the interpolating cubic spline passing through the control points are defined as follows:

$$H = \frac{1}{2} \begin{pmatrix} 0 & 2 & 0 & 0 \\ -1 & 0 & 1 & 0 \\ 2 & -5 & 4 & -1 \\ -1 & 3 & -3 & 1 \end{pmatrix}; \qquad A = \frac{1}{240} \begin{pmatrix} 0 & -11 & 12 & -1 \\ 11 & -120 & -143 & 12 \\ -12 & 143 & 120 & -11 \\ 1 & -12 & 11 & 0 \end{pmatrix}$$

Formula (7) for area computation for the boundary curve with n control points is the following:

$$m_{00} = \frac{1}{240} \sum_{i=1}^{n} \Big(-165(x_iy_{i+1} - x_{i+1}y_i) + 24(x_iy_{i+2} - x_{i+2}y_i) - x_iy_{i+3} + x_{i+3}y_i \Big).$$

Moments m_{10} and m_{01} computed by formulae (10) and (11) look like as follows:

$$m_{10} = \frac{1}{6720} \sum_{i=1}^{n} \Big(1643x_ix_{i+1}y_i + 1643x_{i+1}^2y_i - 136x_ix_{i+2}y_i - 302x_{i+1}x_{i+2}y_i$$
$$- 136x_{i+2}^2y_i - x_ix_{i+3}y_i + 8x_{i+1}x_{i+3}y_i + 23x_{i+2}x_{i+3}y_i - x_{i+3}^2y_i - 1643x_i^2y_{i+1}$$
$$- 1643x_ix_{i+1}y_{i+1} + 15x_ix_{i+3}y_{i+1} + 136x_i^2y_{i+2} + 302x_ix_{i+1}y_{i+2} + 136x_ix_{i+2}y_{i+2}$$
$$- 15x_ix_{i+3}y_{i+2} + x_i^2y_{i+3} - 23x_ix_{i+1}y_{i+3} - 8x_ix_{i+2}y_{i+3} + x_ix_{i+3}y_{i+3} \Big),$$

$$m_{01} = \frac{1}{6720} \sum_{i=1}^{n} \Big(-1643x_iy_iy_{i+1} - 1643x_iy_{i+1}^2 + 136x_iy_iy_{i+2} + 302x_iy_{i+1}y_{i+2}$$
$$+ 136x_iy_{i+2}^2 + x_iy_iy_{i+3} - 8x_iy_{i+1}y_{i+3} - 23x_iy_{i+2}y_{i+3} + x_iy_{i+3}^2 + 1643x_{i+1}y_i^2$$
$$+ 1643x_{i+1}y_iy_{i+1} - 15x_{i+1}y_iy_{i+3} - 136x_{i+2}y_i^2 - 302x_{i+2}y_iy_{i+1} - 136x_{i+2}y_iy_{i+2}$$
$$+ 15x_{i+2}y_iy_{i+3} - x_{i+3}y_i^2 + 23x_{i+3}y_iy_{i+1} + 8x_{i+3}y_iy_{i+2} - x_{i+3}y_iy_{i+3} \Big).$$

Example of interpolating cubic spline curve is given in Fig. 1 c), d).

4 Conclusion

We presented an approach for deriving explicit formulae for computation of area and low order geometric moments for plane objects with a spline boundary. The approach uses the property that the boundary curve is closed. It allowed us to reduce essentially the complexity of formulae obtained. This complexity depends on the order of moments considered, spline degree used and the number of spline control points. Therefore, the approach is useful for low order moments computation only.

The final formulae can be efficiently applied in various applications, when it is necessary to perform measurements of plane objects with a smooth boundary.

References

1. Mukundan, R., Ramakrishnan, K.: Moment Functions in Image Analysis: Theory and Applications. World Scientific (1998)
2. Reiss, T.H.: Recognizing Planar Objects Using Invariant Image Features. Volume 676 of Lecture Notes in Computer Science. Springer-Verlag (1993)
3. Singer, M.: A general approach to moment calculation for polygons and line segments. Pattern Recognition **26** (1993) 1019–1028
4. Sheynin, S., Tuzikov, A.: Explicit formulae for polyhedra moments. Pattern Recognition Letters **22** (2001) 1103–1109
5. Elder, G.: Linearizing the area and volume constraints. Technical Report CIS 2000-04, Computer Science Department, Technion (2000)
6. Gonzalez-Ochoa, C., McCamnon, S., Peters, J.: Computing moments of objects enclosed by piecewise polynomial surfaces. ACM Transactions on Graphics **17** (1998) 143–157
7. Jacob, M., Blu, T., Unser, M.: An exact method for computing the area moment of wavelet and spline curves. IEEE Transactions on Pattern Analysis and Machine Intelligence **23** (2001) 633–642
8. Soldea, O., Elber, G., Rivlin, E.: Exact and efficient computation of moments of free-form surface and trivariate based geometry. Computer-Aided Design **34** (2002) 529–539
9. Ueda, K.: Signed area of sectors between spline curves and the origin. In: 1999 IEEE International Conference on Information Visualization, London, UK (1999) 309–314
10. Hearn, D., Baker, M.: Computer Graphics. Prentice-Hall International (1986)
11. Watt, A.: 3D Computer Graphics. Addison-Wesley (1993)
12. Catmull, E., Rom, R.: A class of local interpolating splines. In Barnhill, R., Risenfeld, R., eds.: Computer Aided Geometric Design. Academic Press, San Francisco (1974) 317–326

Construction of Complete and Independent Systems of Rotation Moment Invariants

Jan Flusser and Tomáš Suk

Institute of Information Theory and Automation
Academy of Sciences of the Czech Republic
Pod vodárenskou věží 4, 182 08 Prague 8, Czech Republic
{flusser,suk}@utia.cas.cz
http://www.utia.cas.cz

Abstract. The problem of independence and completeness of rotation moment invariants is addressed in this paper. General method for constructing invariants of arbitrary orders by means of complex moments is described. It is shown that for any set of invariants there exists relatively small basis by means of which all other invariants can be generated. The method how to construct such a basis is presented. Moreover, it is proved that all moments involved can be recovered from this basis. The basis of the 3rd order moment invariants is constructed explicitly and its relationship to Hu's invariants is studied. Based on this study, Hu's invariants are shown to be dependent and incomplete.

1 Introduction

Moment invariants have become a classical tool for object recognition during last thirty years. They were firstly introduced to the pattern recognition community by Hu [1], who employed results of the theory of algebraic invariants and derived his seven famous invariants to translation, rotation, and scaling of 2-D objects. Since that time, numerous papers have been devoted to various improvements and generalizations of the Hu's invariants but only few attempts to derive invariants from moments of orders higher than three have been done. Li [2] and Wong [3] presented the systems of invariants up to the orders nine and five, respectively. Unfortunately, no one of them paid attention to mutual dependence/independence of the invariants. The invariant sets presented in their papers are algebraically dependent. Most recently, Flusser [4] has proposed a method how to derive independent sets of invariants of any orders. However, in [4] the completeness was proven only within a certain class of invariants and the problem of recovering moments from the invariants was not investigated.

In this paper, we present a general method how to derive rotation moment invariants of any order. Furthermore, we show that there exists a relatively small set – basis – of the invariants which is independent and complete and we give an explicit algorithm for its construction. Knowing the invariants from the basis we can recover all moments involved and, consequently, we can express any existing moment invariant of any kind in terms of the basis elements. As

N. Petkov and M.A. Westenberg (Eds.): CAIP 2003, LNCS 2756, pp. 41–48, 2003.

a consequence, we show that most of the previously published sets of rotation moment invariants including Hu's system are dependent and/or incomplete. This is a surprising result giving a new look at Hu's invariants and possibly yielding a new interpretation of some previous experimental results.

2 General Scheme for Deriving Invariants

There are various approaches to the theoretical derivation of moment-based rotation invariants. Hu [1] employed the theory of algebraic invariants, Li [2] used the Fourier-Mellin transform, Teague [5] proposed to use Zernike moments, and Wong [3] used complex monomials which also originate from the theory of algebraic invariants. In this paper, we present a new scheme, which is based on *complex moments.* The idea to use the complex moments for deriving invariants was already described by Mostafa and Psaltis [6] but they concentrated themselves to the evaluation of the invariants rather than to constructing higher-order systems. In comparison with the previous approaches, this one is more transparent and allows to study mutual dependence/independence of the invariants in a readable way. It should be noted that all the above approaches differ from each other formally by mathematical tools and notation used but the general idea behind them is common and the results are similar or even equivalent.

Complex moment c_{pq} of order $(p+q)$ of an integrable image function $f(x,y)$ is defined as

$$c_{pq} = \int_{-\infty}^{\infty}\int_{-\infty}^{\infty}(x+iy)^p(x-iy)^q f(x,y)dxdy \tag{1}$$

where i denotes imaginary unit. Each complex moment can be expressed in terms of geometric moments m_{pq} as

$$c_{pq} = \sum_{k=0}^{p}\sum_{j=0}^{q}\binom{p}{k}\binom{q}{j}(-1)^{q-j}\cdot i^{p+q-k-j}\cdot m_{k+j,p+q-k-j}, \tag{2}$$

where geometric moments are defined as

$$m_{pq} = \int_{-\infty}^{\infty}\int_{-\infty}^{\infty} x^p y^q f(x,y)dxdy. \tag{3}$$

To express geometric moments in terms of complex moments, we can substitute new variables for $(x+iy)$ and $(x-iy)$ into (1) and (3) and, consequently, derive an inverse form of eq. (2):

$$m_{pq} = \frac{1}{2^{p+q}i^q}\sum_{k=0}^{p}\sum_{j=0}^{q}\binom{p}{k}\binom{q}{j}(-1)^{q-j}\cdot c_{k+j,p+q-k-j}. \tag{4}$$

In polar coordinates, (1) becomes the form

$$c_{pq} = \int_0^{\infty}\int_0^{2\pi} r^{p+q+1}e^{i(p-q)\theta}f(r,\theta)drd\theta. \tag{5}$$

It follows from the definition that $c_{pq} = c^*_{qp}$ (the asterisk denotes complex conjugate). Furthermore, it follows immediately from (5) that the moment magnitude $|c_{pq}|$ is invariant to rotation of the image while the phase is shifted by $(p-q)\alpha$, where α is the angle of rotation. More precisely, it holds for the moment of the rotated image

$$c'_{pq} = e^{-i(p-q)\alpha} \cdot c_{pq}. \tag{6}$$

Any approach to the construction of rotation invariants is based on a proper kind of phase cancellation. The simplest method proposed by many authors is to use the moment magnitudes themselves as the invariants. However, they do not generate a complete set of invariants. In the following Theorem, phase cancellation is achieved by multiplication of appropriate moment powers.

Theorem 1. Let $n \geq 1$ and let k_i, p_i, and q_i $(i = 1, \cdots, n)$ be non-negative integers such that

$$\sum_{i=1}^{n} k_i(p_i - q_i) = 0.$$

Then any product

$$I = \prod_{i=1}^{n} c^{k_i}_{p_i q_i} \tag{7}$$

is invariant to rotation.

3 Construction of the Basis

Theorem 1 allows us to construct an infinite number of the invariants for any order of moments, but only few of them are mutually independent. By the term *basis* we intuitively understand the smallest set by means of which all other invariants can be expressed. More precisely, the basis must be *independent*, which means that none of its elements can be expressed as a function of the other elements, and also *complete*, which means that any rotation invariant can be expressed just by means of the basis elements.

The knowledge of the basis is a crucial point in all pattern recognition problems because it provides the same discriminative power as the set of all invariants at minimum computational costs. For instance, the set

$$\{c_{20}c_{02}, c^2_{21}c_{02}, c^2_{12}c_{20}, c_{21}c_{12}, c^3_{21}c_{02}c_{12}\}$$

is a dependent set whose basis is $\{c^2_{12}c_{20}, c_{21}c_{12},\}$.

Now we can formulate the fundamental theorem of this paper that tells us how to construct an invariant basis for a given set of moments.

Theorem 2. Let us consider complex moments up to the order $r \geq 2$. Let a set of rotation invariants $\mathcal{B}$ be constructed as follows:

$$(\forall p, q | p \geq q \wedge p + q \leq r)(\Phi(p,q) \equiv c_{pq}c^{p-q}_{q_0 p_0} \in \mathcal{B}),$$

where p_0 and q_0 are arbitrary indices such that $p_0 + q_0 \le r$, $p_0 - q_0 = 1$ and $c_{p_0 q_0} \ne 0$ for all images involved. Then $\mathcal{B}$ is a basis of a set of all rotation invariants created from the moments up to the order r.

Theorem 2 is very strong because it claims $\mathcal{B}$ is a basis of *all possible* rotation invariants, not only of those constructed according to (7). This is a significant difference from a similar theorem published in our recent paper [4].

Proof. The independence of $\mathcal{B}$ follows immediately from the mutual independence of the complex moments themselves (see [4] for details). To prove its completeness, it is sufficient to resolve so-called *inverse problem*, which means to recover all complex moments (and, consequently, all geometric moments) up to the order r when knowing the elements of $\mathcal{B}$. Thus, the nonlinear system of equations

$$\Phi(p,q) = c_{pq} c_{q_0 p_0}^{p-q} \tag{8}$$

must be resolved for each c_{pq} involved.

Since $\mathcal{B}$ is a set of rotation invariants, it does not reflect the orientation of the object. Thus, there is one degree of freedom when recovering the object moments which corresponds to the choice of the object orientation. Without loss of generality, we can choose such orientation in which $c_{p_0 q_0}$ is real and positive. As can be seen from eq. (6), if $c_{p_0 q_0}$ is nonzero then such an orientation always exists. Thus, $c_{p_0 q_0}$ can be calculated as

$$c_{p_0 q_0} = \sqrt{\Phi(p_0, q_0)}.$$

Consequently, using the relationship $c_{q_0 p_0} = c_{p_0 q_0}$, we get the solutions

$$c_{pq} = \frac{\Phi(p,q)}{c_{q_0 p_0}^{p-q}}$$

and

$$c_{pp} = \Phi(p,p)$$

for any p and q. Recovering the geometric moments is straightforward from eq. (4). □

As an example, we present the basis of the invariants composed from the moments of 2nd and 3rd orders, that is constructed according to Theorem 2 by choosing $p_0 = 2$ and $q_0 = 1$.

$$\begin{aligned}
\Phi(1,1) &= c_{11}, \\
\Phi(2,1) &= c_{21} c_{12}, \\
\Phi(2,0) &= c_{20} c_{12}^2, \\
\Phi(3,0) &= c_{30} c_{12}^3.
\end{aligned} \tag{9}$$

4 Relationship to Hu's Invariants

In this Section, we highlight the relationship between Hu's invariants [1] and the proposed invariants (9). We show Hu's invariants are incomplete and mutually dependent.

Let us recall the Hu's rotation invariants first:

$$\begin{aligned}
\phi_1 &= m_{20} + m_{02}, \\
\phi_2 &= (m_{20} - m_{02})^2 + 4m_{11}^2, \\
\phi_3 &= (m_{30} - 3m_{12})^2 + (3m_{21} - m_{03})^2, \\
\phi_4 &= (m_{30} + m_{12})^2 + (m_{21} + m_{03})^2, \\
\phi_5 &= (m_{30} - 3m_{12})(m_{30} + m_{12})((m_{30} + m_{12})^2 - 3(m_{21} + m_{03})^2) \\
&\quad +(3m_{21} - m_{03})(m_{21} + m_{03})(3(m_{30} + m_{12})^2 - (m_{21} + m_{03})^2), \\
\phi_6 &= (m_{20} - m_{02})((m_{30} + m_{12})^2 - (m_{21} + m_{03})^2) \\
&\quad +4m_{11}(m_{30} + m_{12})(m_{21} + m_{03}), \\
\phi_7 &= (3m_{21} - m_{03})(m_{30} + m_{12})((m_{30} + m_{12})^2 - 3(m_{21} + m_{03})^2) \\
&\quad -(m_{30} - 3m_{12})(m_{21} + m_{03})(3(m_{30} + m_{12})^2 - (m_{21} + m_{03})^2).
\end{aligned} \tag{10}$$

It can be seen clearly that the Hu's invariants are nothing else than particular representatives of the general form (7):

$$\begin{aligned}
\phi_1 &= c_{11}, \\
\phi_2 &= c_{20}c_{02}, \\
\phi_3 &= c_{30}c_{03}, \\
\phi_4 &= c_{21}c_{12}, \\
\phi_5 &= \mathrm{Re}(c_{30}c_{12}^3), \\
\phi_6 &= \mathrm{Re}(c_{20}c_{12}^2), \\
\phi_7 &= \mathrm{Im}(c_{30}c_{12}^3).
\end{aligned} \tag{11}$$

Using (11) we can demonstrate the dependency of the Hu's invariants. It holds

$$\phi_3 = \frac{\phi_5^2 + \phi_7^2}{\phi_4^3},$$

which means that ϕ_3 is useless and can be excluded from the Hu's system without any loss of discrimination power.

Moreover, the Hu's system is incomplete. Let us try to recover complex and geometric moments when knowing $\phi_1, \cdots, \phi_7$ under the same normalization constraint as in the previous case, i.e. c_{21} is real and positive. Complex moments c_{11}, c_{21}, c_{12}, c_{30}, and c_{03} can be recovered in a straightforward way but c_{20} cannot be fully determined. Its real part is given unambiguously but the sign of its imaginary part (i.e. the sign of m_{11}) cannot be recovered. The incompleteness of the Hu's invariants implicates their lower discrimination power comparing to

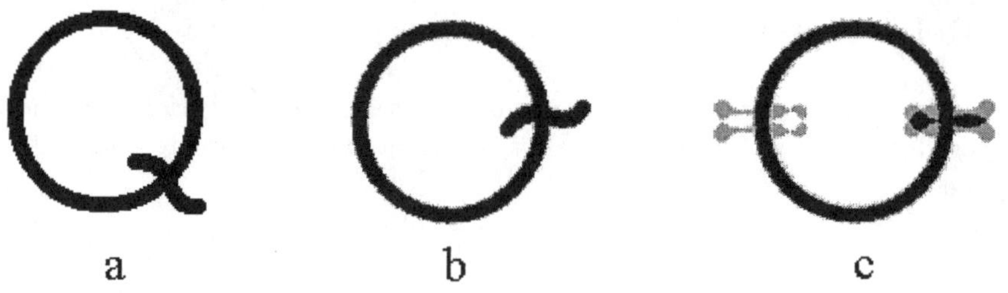

Fig. 1. The stylized letter Q: original (a), rotated to the normalized position (b), another object created according to (12)(c). For the values of the respective invariants see Table 1.

Table 1. The values of the Hu's invariants and the new invariants (9) of the objects from Fig. 1b and Fig. 1c, respectively. The only invariant discriminating them is emphasized.

Hu	Fig. 1b	Fig. 1c	New	Fig. 1b	Fig. 1c
ϕ_1	0.0032	0.0032	$\Phi(1,1)$	0.0032	0.0032
ϕ_2	$0.2128 \cdot 10^{-6}$	$0.2128 \cdot 10^{-6}$	$\Phi(2,1)$	$0.7613 \cdot 10^{-9}$	$0.7613 \cdot 10^{-9}$
ϕ_3	$0.9717 \cdot 10^{-9}$	$0.9717 \cdot 10^{-9}$	$\mathrm{Re}(\Phi(2,0))$	$0.3499 \cdot 10^{-12}$	$0.3499 \cdot 10^{-12}$
ϕ_4	$0.7613 \cdot 10^{-9}$	$0.7613 \cdot 10^{-9}$	$\mathbf{Im(\Phi(2,0))}$	$\mathbf{-0.2993 \cdot 10^{-13}}$	$\mathbf{0.2954 \cdot 10^{-13}}$
ϕ_5	$0.6609 \cdot 10^{-8}$	$0.6609 \cdot 10^{-8}$	$\mathrm{Re}(\Phi(3,0))$	$0.6451 \cdot 10^{-18}$	$0.6451 \cdot 10^{-18}$
ϕ_6	$0.3499 \cdot 10^{-12}$	$0.3499 \cdot 10^{-12}$	$\mathrm{Im}(\Phi(3,0))$	$-0.1123 \cdot 10^{-18}$	$-0.1123 \cdot 10^{-18}$
ϕ_7	$-0.1123 \cdot 10^{-18}$	$-0.1123 \cdot 10^{-18}$			

the proposed invariants of the same order. Let us consider two objects $a(x,y)$ and $b(x,y)$ in the normalized positions having the same geometric moments up to the third order except m_{11}, for which $m_{11}^{(a)} = -m_{11}^{(b)}$. In case of artificial data, such object $b(x,y)$ can be generated for any given $a(x,y)$ as

$$b(x,y) = \frac{1}{2}(a(x,y) + a(-x,y) + a(x,-y) - a(-x,-y)), \tag{12}$$

see Fig. 1 for an example. It is easy to prove that under (12) the moment constraints are always fulfilled. While the new invariants (9) distinguish these two objects by the imaginary part of the $\Phi(2,0)$, the Hu's invariants are not able to do so (see Table 1), even if the objects are easy to discriminate visually.

This property can be demonstrated also on real data. In Fig. 2 (left), one can see the photograph of a pan. A picture of a virtual "two-handle pan" (Fig. 2 right) was created from the original image according to (12). Although these two objects are apparently different, all their Hu's invariants are exactly the same. On the other hand, the new invariant $\Phi(2,0)$ distinguishes these two objects clearly thanks to the opposite signs of its imaginary part. The same is true for the picture of a beater (see Fig. 3).

It should be noted that also other previously published systems of rotation invariants are dependent. Li [2] published a set of invariants from moments up to the 9th order. Unfortunately, his system includes the Hu's system as its subset

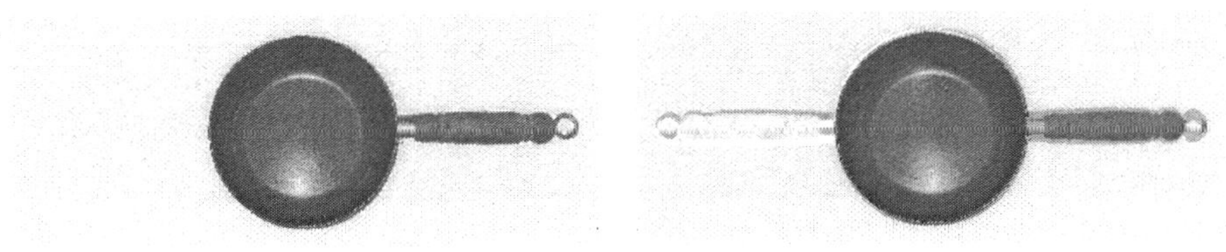

Fig. 2. Original image of a pan (left) and a virtual "two-handle pan" (right). These objects are distinguishable by the new invariants but not distinguishable by the Hu's invariants.

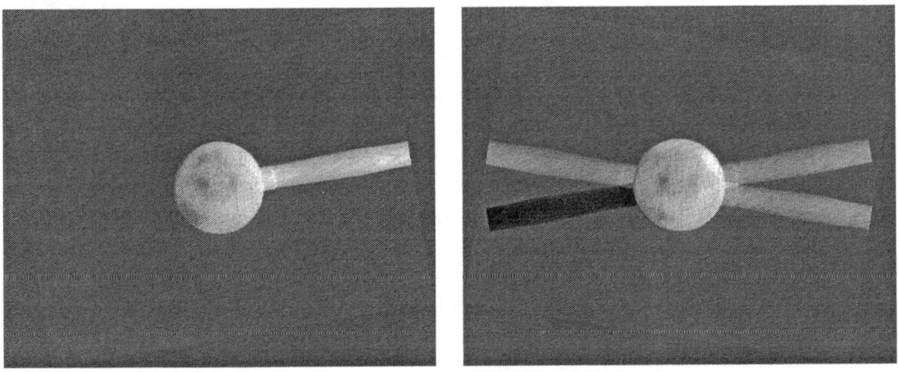

Fig. 3. Original image of a beater (left) and a virtual "four-handle beater" (right). These objects are distinguishable by the new invariants but not distinguishable by the Hu's invariants.

and therefore it also cannot be a basis. Wong [3] presented a set of 16 invariants from moments up to the 3rd order and a set of "more than 49" invariants from moments up to the 4th order. It follows immediately from Theorem 2 that a basis of the 3rd-order invariants has only 6 elements and a basis of the 4th-order invariants has 11 elements (these numbers relate to real-valued invariants). Thus, most of Wong's invariants are dependent and of no importance to practical pattern recognition problems.

5 Conclusion

In this paper, the problem of independence and completeness of the rotation moment invariants was discussed. Although the moment invariants have attracted significant attention of pattern recognition community within last thirty years, they have not been studied from this point of view yet.

The general method how to derive rotation invariants of any order was described first. Then the theorem presenting the smallest complete set (basis) of the invariants was formulated and proven. This is the major theoretical result of the paper. Finally, the relationship to the previous work was studied. It was shown that the proposed invariants outperform the widely-used Hu's moment invariants both in discrimination power and dimensionality requirements.

Acknowledgment

This work has been supported by the grant No. 201/03/0675 of the Grant Agency of the Czech Republic.

References

1. M. K. Hu, "Visual pattern recognition by moment invariants," *IRE Trans. Information Theory*, vol. 8, pp. 179–187, 1962.
2. Y. Li, "Reforming the theory of invariant moments for pattern recognition," *Pattern Recognition*, vol. 25, pp. 723–730, 1992.
3. W. H. Wong, W. C. Siu, and K. M. Lam, "Generation of moment invariants and their uses for character recognition," *Pattern Recognition Letters*, vol. 16, pp. 115–123, 1995.
4. J. Flusser, "On the independence of rotation moment invariants," *Pattern Recognition*, vol. 33, pp. 1405-1410, 2000.
5. M. R. Teague, "Image analysis via the general theory of moments," *J. Optical Soc. of America*, vol. 70, pp. 920–930, 1980.
6. Y. S. Abu-Mostafa and D. Psaltis, "Recognitive aspects of moment invariants," *IEEE Trans. Pattern Analysis and Machine Intelligence*, vol. 6, pp. 698–706, 1984.

A Structural Framework for Assembly Modeling and Recognition

Christian Bauckhage, Franz Kummert, and Gerhard Sagerer

Technical Faculty, Bielefeld University
P.O. Box 100131, D-33501 Bielefeld, Germany
{cbauckha,franz,sagerer}@techfak.uni-bielefeld.de

Abstract. Although structural approaches to pattern recognition are not as popular anymore as they were some 30 years ago, they still provide reasonable solutions for certain recognition problems. This paper demonstrates that recognizing mechanical assemblies is among these problems. We will present and evaluate a framework for visual assembly recognition that combines different structural techniques. Context free grammars are used to detect assemblies in an image. The resulting syntactic structures are translated into relational models which enable the recognition of individual assemblies.

1 Context, Motivation, and Overview

In the 1970s, structural methods were very popular among the pattern recognition community (cf. e.g. [4, 11]). Nowadays focus has rather shifted to implicit or statistical techniques, but if recognition has to deal with highly structured objects, structural approaches are still attractive. Mechanical assemblies of a number of rigidly connected parts in a certain geometrical configuration are a practical example of such highly structured objects. In assembly recognition, however, abstract structural models still play a secondary role. Known contributions to assembly recognition from sensory input apply template-based techniques [7] or they rely on detailed geometric reasoning. The latter either require sensors of high precision like laser range finders [10] or only cope with assemblies made from simply shaped objects or marked parts [9, 13].

The work reported here results from a research project on human machine interaction which is developing a robot that is verbally instructed to assemble wooden toy objects (s. Fig. 1). Since the machine shall simulate human sensing, a computer vision solution for assembly recognition is required. Moreover, since the instructor is free to decide what to construct, our setting necessitates comprehensive knowledge of how assembled objects might appear in image data. But assemblies are made of multi-functional parts which can be assembled into numerous configurations. Therefore, it is impossible to model all feasible assemblies in advance and consequently we are in need of generic and flexible representations.

The following sections will point out that syntactic models of classes of assemblies enable flexible assembly detection. However, syntax might be ambiguous. Thus, the fourth and fifth section will briefly discuss that unique graph-based models can be derived from syntactic structures and how subsequent graph matching accomplishes the recognition of individual assemblies. Finally, a conclusion will end this contribution.

N. Petkov and M.A. Westenberg (Eds.): CAIP 2003, LNCS 2756, pp. 49–56, 2003.

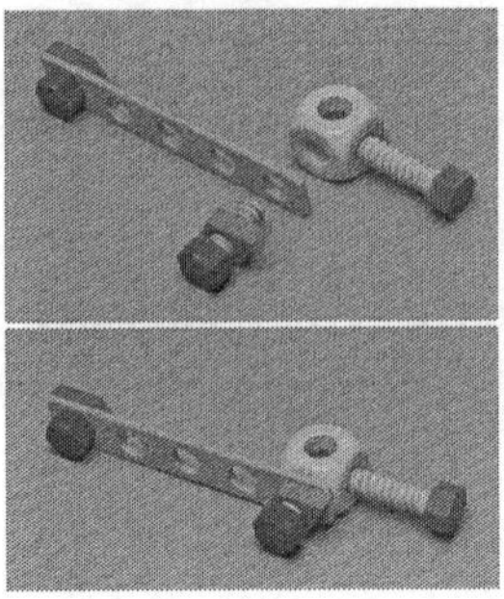

(a)

ASM → B-PRT N-PRT |
B-PRT M-PRT N-PRT
B-PRT → ASM | BOLT
N-PRT → ASM | CUBE | RHOMBNUT
M-PRT → ASM | BAR | ... |
ASM M-PRT | BAR M-PRT | ...

(b)

Fig. 1. 1(a), Construction principle of bolted assemblies. 1(b) Context free grammar for the component structure of bolted assemblies (ASM ≡ Assembly, B-PRT ≡ Bolt-Part, ...).

2 Syntactic Approach to Assembly Detection

Concerned with assembly sequence planning, Homem de Mello and Sanderson [6] proposed to represent all feasible decompositions of an assembly in an AND/OR graph. And since a comparative study by Wolter [14] yielded that this is the most efficient way to store sequence data, AND/OR graphs have become a standard technique in assembly (sequence) modeling. However, already 30 years ago Hall [5] noted that there is a one to one correspondence between AND/OR graphs and context free grammars (CFGs).

As *any* assembly can be structured according to an AND/OR graph, there has to be a corresponding CFG for *every* mechanical assembly. A syntactic model of a whole class of assemblies could therefore be obtained from unifying the CFGs of all members of that class. Although this would provide comprehensive knowledge for visual recognition it unfortunately would not cope with the aforementioned requirement for genericity. By means of our scenario, however, we will exemplify that considerations concerning the mechanical function of assembly components lead to recursive and thus compact but comprehensive models of classes of assemblies without the need for enumerating all members.

The assemblies of our scenario are bolted assemblies where a *bolt* and a *nut* may fix a series of *miscellaneous objects*. As Fig. 1(a) indicates, each of these *functional parts* might be an elementary object or an assembly. This observation directly leads to a context free grammar $G = (N, T, P, S)$ with variables $N =$ {ASM, B-PRT, M-PRT, N-PRT}, terminals $T = \{BOLT, CUBE, BAR, \ldots\}$, a start symbol $S =$ ASM, and productions P as depicted in Fig. 1(b). The terminals thus represent elementary objects whereas assemblies and their functional parts appear as variables. The first production indicates that bolted assemblies consist at least of a bolt- and a nut-part but might also have a miscellaneous-part. The other productions specify how these functional parts may look like; the bolt-part, for instance, might be an assembly or a bolt.

Note that G also generates words that do not comply with feasible assemblies. (Bolts, for instance, have a finite length but the productions do not restrict the number of objects attachable to them.) Hence, parsing images according to G must regard that only a subset of $L(G)$ constitutes feasible assemblies. To cope with this problem grammars can be

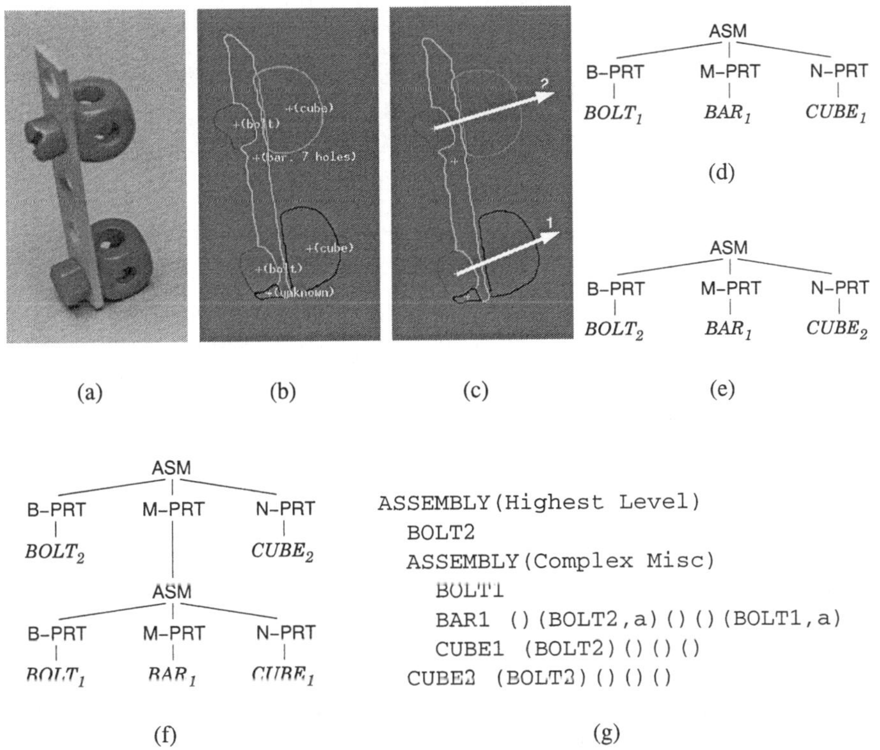

Fig. 2. Scheme of assembly detection from image parsing.

implemented using the semantic network language ERNEST [12]. Such implementations are advantageous because context sensitive restrictions can easily be modeled so that parsing will only accept feasible assemblies.

Figure 2 exemplifies the process of visual assembly detection. The entities that are examined are 2D clusters of recognized elementary objects like shown in Fig. 2(b)[1]. As explained in [1], ideas adopted from discourse parsing provide a suitable strategy to analyze such clusters. In our example, parsing started with the lower bolt and then considered the object adjacent to it. This defined a line along which further objects to be analyzed were searched for; in Fig. 2(c), this direction is indicated by arrow 1. The objects found along this line resulted in the syntactic structure depicted in Fig. 2(d). Then, parsing restarted at the upper bolt and analyzing the objects along arrow 2 led to the structure in Fig. 2(e). Since this structure shares an object (BAR_1) with the earlier found tree, the first found structure was integrated into the recent one; the resulting tree structure in Fig. 2(f) describes the whole assembly.

3 Evaluating Syntactic Assembly Detection

Figure 3 displays prototypical results accomplished with our method. Assembly structures found in the images are enclosed in black polygons. These examples illustrate that

[1] See [8] for details on elementary object recognition.

Difficulties: 0.32, 0.41, 0.53 and 0.72

Fig. 3. Prototypical detection results after syntactic image parsing.

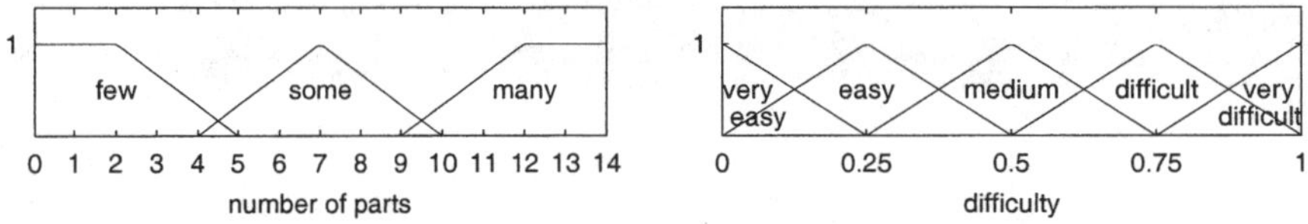

Fig. 4. Examples of linguistic variables and their fuzzy partitions.

the semantic network implementation can cope with context sensitive conditions: in the upper left, for instance, only two of the four cubes were associated with the bolt because its thread does not allow more.

The examples also indicate that there are scenes of varying complexity. Hence, it is no surprise to observe the performance in assembly detection being dependent on the *difficulty of the task* which is influenced by several factors. For instance, syntactic assembly detection from vision might be mislead, if an object cluster contains many objects so that many alternatives for parsing must be considered. As the dependency on the input makes it difficult to provide meaningful test sets[2], we decided to evaluate our algorithms with respect to the difficulty. This was assessed using a fuzzy function depending on the four parameters *number of visible parts* in an object cluster, *number of visible bolts*, *mean degree of adjacency* within a cluster, and *mean degree of perspective occlusion* of elementary objects. Suitable partitions for these variables (s. e.g. Fig. 4) as well as fuzzy rules that characterize their interdependencies were estimated from an independent training set of 70 images. Figure 5 summarizes the results obtained from this evaluation scheme. To produce this figure 164 images of assemblies were attributed to 8 levels of difficulty.

In a first series of experiments, the results from elementary object recognition were corrected manually so that the input to our parser was always correct; a second series was done without corrections. An experiment was counted a success if a correct structure was produced. As we would have guessed, easy data was always processed correctly whereas correctness diminishes with increasing difficulty.But even in difficult cases it is quite accurate.

4 Graph Based Approach to Assembly Recognition

Parsing according to simple CFGs reliably *detects* assembly structures in an image. However, the resulting hierarchical structures are seldom unique since complex assem-

[2] A test set should neither contain too many simple cases nor too many difficult ones.

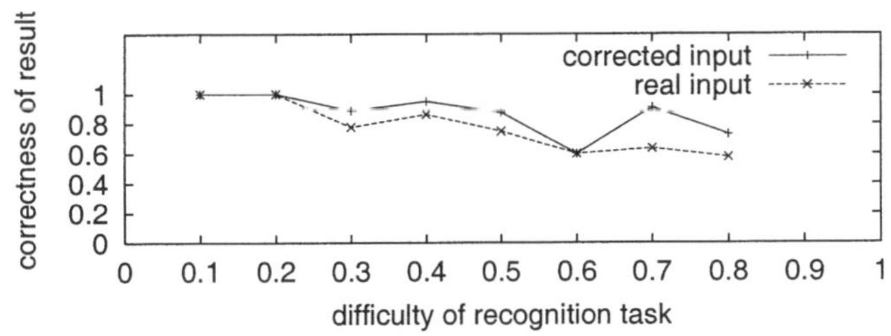

Fig. 5. Evaluation result for syntactic assembly detection.

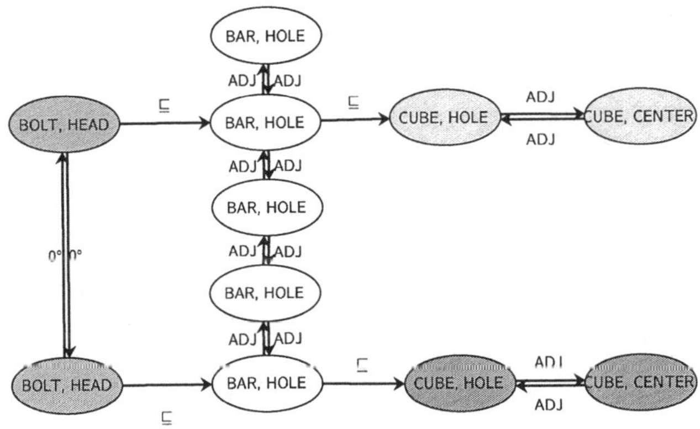

Fig. 6. Graph describing relations among the mating features of the assembly in Fig. 2(a).

blies will have numerous syntactic structures [14]. Moreover, assemblies that are made of the same parts but exhibit different part attachments may have the same description. Assembly *recognition* therefore should rest upon a more unique representation.

From analyzing the geometrical appearance of an object cluster details concerning the relations among the object's mating features can be determined. This provides topologically unique information of part attachments which can be added to syntactic descriptions leading to so called *high-level* sequence plans [2]. Figure 2(g) shows a plan that was derived for the exemplary assembly. Its global structure corresponds to the tree in Fig. 2(f), its local structure reflects mating feature relations: the cubes and the bar appear with lists of slots representing holes where some of them are labeled with the bolt that is inserted into them.

Topologically different assemblies, i.e. assemblies with different part attachments, thus have distinct high-level sequence plans. But a complex assembly may still have several sequence plans. However, augmented syntactic descriptions can be transformed into graph based models. Figure 6 shows the *mating feature graph* derived from the plan in Fig. 2(g). Each vertex is labeled with a feature type and with the type of object it belongs to. Furthermore, vertices are colored according to the object they are part of. Subparts connected via edges labeled 'ADJ' belong to the same object. Chains of edges labeled '$\sqsubseteq$' indicate sequences of subparts attached to a certain bolt. Finally, for each

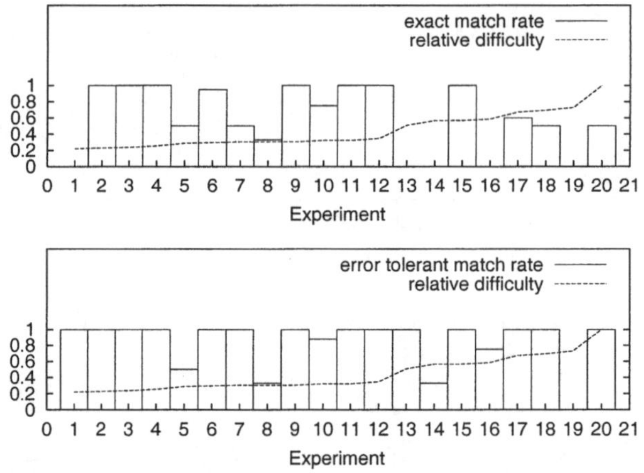

Fig. 7. Evaluation result for graph based assembly recognition.

pair of bolts connected to the same object, the corresponding vertices are related via edges labeled with the angle the bolts enclose.

As each sequence plan of a given assembly encodes the same feature relations, all plans of an assembly can be condensed into the same graph. Given graph-based assembly models like this, graph matching can recognize topologically equivalent assemblies. In our implementation we apply the Graph matching toolkit of the University of Berne (GUB) developed by Messmer and Bunke [3]: after deriving an assembly graph from an image it will be matched against a database of previously derived ones. If no corresponding model can be found our system has learned about a new assembly and will insert it into the set of prototypes.

5 Evaluating Graph Based Assembly Recognition

Based on the edit-operations *vertex deletion*, *edge deletion*, and *insertion* and *label substitution* the GUB determines error tolerant matches. We set the costs of the first three operations to 1, 1, 10, respectively, since practical experience revealed that this yields matches of well acceptable quality. The expensiveness of edge insertion is due to the fact that the GUB tends to insert edges to minimize graph distances. However, this introduces feature relations that do not exist in reality and thus will result in useless matches. The costs of label substitutions are given by the difference of label values.

Figure 7 summarizes two series of experiments conducted to evaluate assembly recognition from mating feature graph matching. Both series are based on the same test set of 111 images of different views – some of them cluttered – of 20 assemblies. In each experiment i, our system thus was faced with n_i different views of an assembly. For the first image considered in an experiment the mating feature graph of the depicted assembly was generated and stored in a database. For the remaining images the resulting graphs were matched against that database. If no match was possible, the recently found graph was stored as well. For n_i views of an assembly, an optimal performance thus corresponds to $n_i - 1$ matches while in the worst case where no match was to be found the database will will contain n_i graphs. Consequently, Fig. 7 characterizes the performance in assembly recognition using the ratio $\frac{m_i}{n_i-1}$ where m_i denotes the number of matches found in experiment i.

The upper part of Fig. 7 shows the results obtained from experiments on exact matching. In the first experiment, an assembly was examined whose mating feature graph consists of 9 vertices and 17 edges while in the 20th experiment the number of vertices and edges sums up to 118. The relative difficulty plotted in the figure was computed with respect to this number. For the first experiment it thus is $\frac{9+17}{118} = 0.22$ while for the last one it equals 1.0 [3]. In eight experiments the rate of successful recognition attempts exceeds 0.95, in seven cases it reaches up to 0.75, but in five experiments no exact match was found. Note that the latter does not depend on the relative difficulty; complete failures also happened in rather easy experiments.

The lower part of Fig. 7 shows the results for error-correcting graph matching. Here, a match was counted as a success if the edit distance between input- and model-graph did not exceed 15% of the sum of the number of vertices and edges of the model. Now there are 14 sets of views with a match rate higher than 0.95 and four experiments result in rates between 0.33 and 0.88. However, for the data considered in experiment 19, the costs of the computed isomorphisms always exceeded the acceptable threshold. An examination of the corresponding images revealed that they were perfect examples for severe perspective occlusion. Due to the rather complex geometry of the considered assembly even reasonable changes of the viewpoint led to considerable occlusion of components which caused seriously different graphs to be extracted from the images.

6 Conclusion

This paper summarized research efforts in assembly modeling, detection, and recognition. Faced with a dynamic and unpredictable assembly scenario we proposed a framework of structural methods to treat each of these aspects.

Understanding mechanical assemblies to be composed of functional parts led to context free grammars with recursive productions which model whole classes of assemblies. Implementing such models as semantic networks and adopting techniques from discourse parsing enables assembly detection from image data. Augmenting syntactic descriptions with information of mating relations yields high-level sequence plans. These plans can be translated into unambiguous graph-based models of assemblies which were used for recognition purposes. Since syntactic methods crucially depend on the complexity of the input, we applied a performance evaluation with respect to the task difficulty. As difficulty is rather vague it was measured using a fuzzy approach. The results underline that simple grammatical methods provide a flexible and reliable means for visual assembly detection.

Based on error-correcting graph matching it is possible to recognize that two reasonable complex images of assemblies show the same parts in the same mating relations.

[3] Note that graph matching is NP complete. Messmer and Bunke tackle the resulting time complexity by means of sophisticated data structures and memory organization. Practical experience shows that this allows to match complex graphs of rather high connectivity in reasonable time (i.e. matching graphs of up to 120 vertices and edges takes less than 3s on a Digital Personal Workstation (SPint95/fp95 = 13.9/18.1)).

Thus, it is possible to identify that they are topologically identical. Encouraged by our experimental result we can thus conclude that the described combination of structural methods, i.e. the integration of grammar- and graph-based techniques, indeed provides a suitable framework for vision for flexible assembly.

References

1. C. Bauckhage, S. Kronenberg, F. Kummert, and G. Sagerer. Grammars and Discourse Theory to Describe and Recognize Mechanical Assemblies. In *Proc. S+SSPR'00*, pages 173–182, 2000.
2. C. Bauckhage, F. Kummert, and G. Sagerer. Learning Assembly Sequence Plans Using Functional Models. In *Proc. IEEE ISATP'99*, pages 1–7, 1999.
3. H. Bunke and B.T. Messmer. Recent Advances in Graph Matching. *International Journal of Pattern Recognition and Artificial Intelligence*, 11(1):169–203, 1997.
4. K.S. Fu. *Syntactic Methods in Pattern Recognition.* Academic Press, New York, 1974.
5. P.A.V. Hall. Equivalence Between AND/OR Graphs and Context-Free Grammars. *Communications of the ACM*, 16(7):444–445, 1973.
6. L.S. Homem de Mello and A.C. Sanderson. AND/OR Graph Representation of Assembly Plans. *IEEE Trans. on Robotics and Automation*, 6(2):188–199, 1990.
7. K.W. Khawaja, A.A. Maciejewski, D. Tretter, and C. Bouman. A Multiscale Assembly Inspection Algorithm. *IEEE Robotics & Automation Magazine*, 3(2):15–22, 1996.
8. F. Kummert, G.A. Fink, G. Sagerer, and E. Braun. Hybrid Object Recognition in Image Sequences. In *Proc. ICPR'98*, volume II, pages 1165–1170, 1998.
9. J.E. Lloyd, J.S. Beis, D.K. Pai, and D.G. Lowe. Programming Contact Tasks Using a Reality-Based Virtual Environment Integrated with Vision. *IEEE Trans. on Robotics and Automation*, 15(3):423–434, 1999.
10. J. Miura and K. Ikeuchi. Task Oriented Generation of Visual Sensing Strategies in Assembly Tasks. *IEEE Trans. on Pattern Analysis and Machine Intelligence*, 20(2):126–138, 1998.
11. T. Pavlidis. *Structural Pattern Recognition.* Springer, Berlin, 1977.
12. G. Sagerer and H. Niemann. *Semantic Networks for Understanding Scenes.* Plenum Publishing, New York, 1997.
13. C.-P. Tung and A.C. Kak. Integrating Sensing, Task Planning and Execution for Robotic Assembly. *IEEE Trans. on Robotics and Automation*, 12:187–201, 1996.
14. J.D. Wolter. A Combinatorial Analysis of Enumerative Data Structures for Assembly Planning. *Journal of Design and Manufacturing*, 2(2):93–104, 1992.

Simple Points in 2D and 3D Binary Images

Gisela Klette

CITR, University of Auckland
Tamaki Campus, Building 731, Auckland, New Zealand

Abstract. The notion of a simple point is of fundamental importance for deformations of digital images. A point (pixel or voxel) is simple if the change of its value does not change the topology of the image. This article unifies characterizations of simple points. It shows equivalences of characterizations based on different models that are useful for the design of deformation algorithms (thinning and magnification). The paper also specifies an algorithm for identifying simple voxels.

Keywords: simple points, topology, simple deformations, thinning, shape simplification

1 Introduction and Basic Notions

Simple points are used in topology preserving digital deformations in order to characterize a single element p of a digital image I which can change the value $I(p)$ without destroying the topology of the image, in the sense that there is a bijective map between the components before and after the deformation process.

A picture element is a pair $(p, I(p))$ consisting of a location p and a value $I(p)$. A simple picture element is either a simple pixel (2D-images) or a simple voxel (3D-images). The images are defined on an orthogonal grid in 2D or 3D, either using the grid cell model where a pixel p is a closed square in 2D (2-cell) and a voxel p is a closed cube (3-cell), whose edges are of length 1 and parallel to the coordinate axes, and centers have integer coordinates; or using the grid point model where vertices of grid squares are pixel locations, and vertices of grid cubes are voxel locations with integer coordinates.

We use common adjacency concepts: 4-,8-(2D), 6-,18-,26-(3D) for the point model and 0-,1-(2D), 0-,1-,2-(3D)for the grid cell model [7, 6]. Any of these adjacency relations A_α, $\alpha \in \{0, 1, 2, 4, 6, 8, 18, 26\}$, are irreflexive and symmetric. The *α-neighborhood* $N_\alpha(p)$ of a pixel location p includes p and its α-adjacent pixel locations.

Based on neighborhood relations we define connectedness as usual [11]. An *α-component* of a subset S of C is a maximal α-connected subset of S. It is common to use different types of connectedness for $p \in \langle I \rangle$ and $p \in \langle \overline{I} \rangle$. For brevity, we call them 1's and 0's. In this paper we use α-connectivity for the 1's and α'-connectivity for the 0's where $(\alpha, \alpha') = (8, 4), (4, 8)$ for 2D-images and $(\alpha, \alpha') = (26, 6), (6, 26)$ for the 3D case. For the grid cell model, a component is the union of closed squares (2D) or of closed cubes (3D).

N. Petkov and M.A. Westenberg (Eds.): CAIP 2003, LNCS 2756, pp. 57–64, 2003.

Let $A_8(p)$ be the 8-adjacency set of p and the elements x_i of this adjacency set are numbered in the following way:

$$\begin{matrix} x_4 & x_3 & x_2 \\ x_5 & p & x_1 \\ x_6 & x_7 & x_8 \end{matrix}$$

For calculating the number of components in $A_8(p)$ Hilditch [4] defined the crossing number as follows:

Definition 1. *The number of times of crossing over from a 0 to a 1 when the points in $A_8(p)$ are traversed in order, cutting the corner between 8-adjacent 4-neighbors of 1's, is called* H-crossing number $X_H(p)$*:*

$$X_H(p) = \sum_{i=1}^{4} c_i$$

where

$$c_i = \begin{cases} 1 \text{ if } x_{2i-1} = 0 \text{ and } (x_{2i} = 1 \text{ or } x_{2i+1} = 1) \\ 0 \text{ otherwise }. \end{cases}$$

The crossing number is equivalent to the number of 8-components of 1s in $A_8(p)$ if at least one 4-neighbor is a 0.

Yokoi et al [13] introduced the notion of connectivity number in $A_8(p)$ as follows.

Definition 2. *The number of distinct 4-adjacent 4-components of 1's (0's) is called connectivity number $X_B(p)$ $(\overline{X_B}(p))$ with:*

$$X_B(p) = \sum_{i=1}^{4} a_i$$

where $a_i = x_{2i-1} - x_{2i-1} * x_{2i} * x_{2i+1}$, $x_9 = x_1$ *and* $\overline{X_B}(p) = \sum_{i=1}^{4} b_i$ *where* $b_i = \overline{x}_{2i-1} - \overline{x}_{2i-1} * \overline{x}_{2i} * \overline{x}_{2i+1}$, *and* $\overline{x}_i = 1 - x_i$ *in* $A_8(p)$.

Note that $\overline{X}_B(p)$ is equivalent to $X_H(p)$.

The *frontier* of a pixel is the union of its 4 edges and the frontier of a voxel is the union of its six faces. A face of a voxel includes its 4 edges and each edge includes its 2 vertices. Let p be an n-cell, $0 \leq n \leq 3$. The frontier of a picture element p is a union of i-cells with $0 \leq i < n$. For example, if p is a voxel (3-cell) then the frontier consists of eight 0-cells, twelve 1-cells and six 2-cells.

For the grid cell model, Kong [6] defined the I-attachment set of a point p.

Definition 3. *The set of all points of an α-cell, $\alpha \in \{0, 1, 2\}$ on the frontier of p that also lie on an α-cell of the frontier of at least one other point q with $I(p) = I(q), p \neq q$ is the I-attachment set of p in I.*

Note that the cardinality of the I-attachment set of a 0-cell is one. Examples for 2D and 3D I-attachment sets are in Figure 1.

To represent the I-attachment set of a voxel we use Schlegel diagrams as Kong proposed in [6].

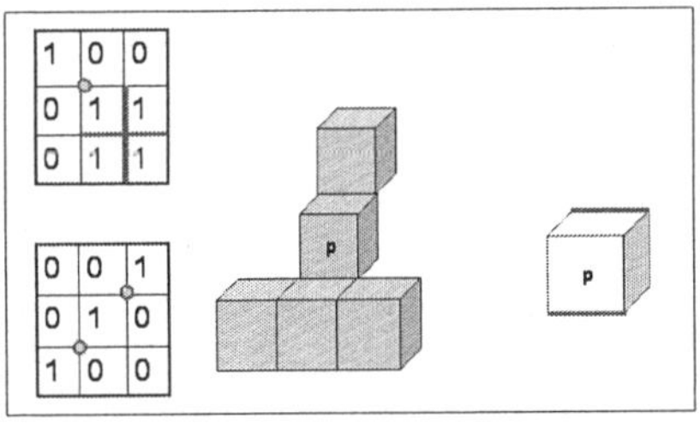

Fig. 1. I-attachment sets.

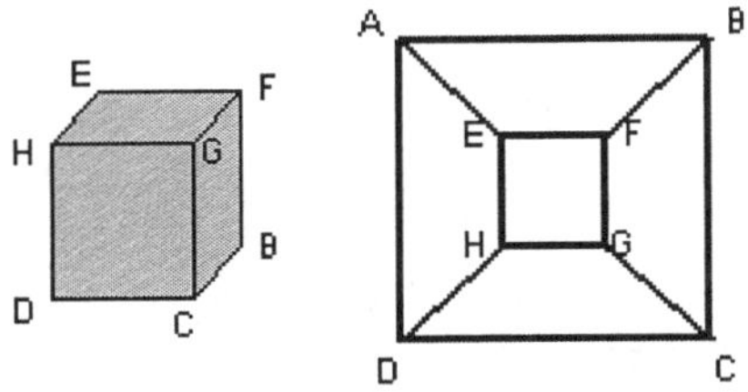

Fig. 2. Schlegel diagram: the face (2-cell) with vertices A,B,C,D is invisible on the left.

2 Characterizations of a Simple Pixel

Definition 4. *[11] A 1 of an image I is called α-simple if it is α-adjacent to exactly one α-component of 1's in $A_8(p)$ and it is α'-adjacent to exactly one α'-component of 0's in $A_8(p)$.*

Let $(p, I(p))$ be a border pixel of an image I. Then $(p, I(p))$ is α-simple in I iff p is α-adjacent to exactly one α-component of $I(p)$ in $A_8(p)$.

Note that a 4-simple pixel p can be 4-adjacent to exactly one 4-component of 1's in $A_8(p)$ and 8-adjacent to distinct 4-components of 1's in $A_8(p)$. In the example below p is a 4-simple 1 or an 8-simple 0.

$$\begin{matrix} 1 & 1 & 1 \\ 0 & p & 0 \\ 1 & 0 & 1 \end{matrix}$$

We consider both changing 1 to 0 and vice versa. Changing an α-simple point p of an α-component U results into a non-empty α-component $U \setminus \{p\}$ and a non-empty α'-component $V \cup \{p\}$, and the adjacency relations to all other components remain the same. The region adjacency trees of the original image and the resulting image are isomorphic. We extend Definition 4: A pixel $(p, I(p))$ is called α-simple if it is α-adjacent to exactly one α-component in $A_8(p)$ and it is α' adjacent to exactly one distinct α'-component in $A_8(p)$. The result of changing the value of a single α-simple pixel p is an α'-simple pixel.

A change in the value of a simple pixel delivers a topologically equivalent image [11]. Two images differ by *simple deformation* if one can be obtained from the other one by repeatedly changing simple pixels from 1 to 0 or vice versa. The set of pixels that changes the value during a simple deformation is called *simple set.* Thinning or shrinking procedures are one-way simple deformations that transfer 1's to 0's. Magnification algorithms change 0's to 1's.

Characterization 1. *A* 1 *of an image I is 8-simple in I iff* $X_H(p) = 1$.

This characterization is equivalent to Hall's characterization [2] where a 1 is 8-simple iff there is exactly one distinct 8-component of 1's in $A_8(p)$ and p is a border 1.

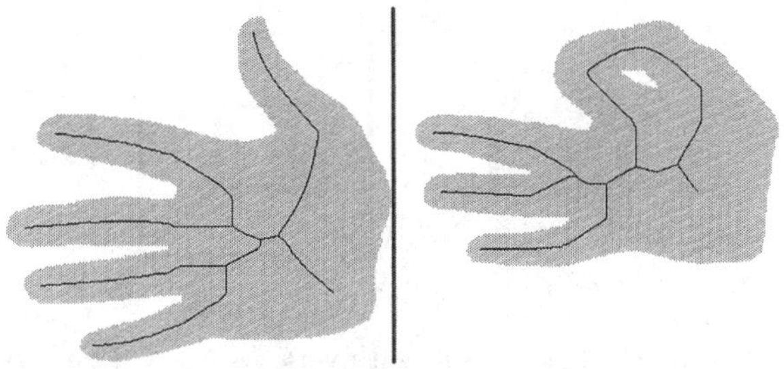

Fig. 3. Examples: Results of thinning algorithm using characterization 1.

As an illustration, for the hand gesture images in Figure 3 we used morphological closing as a preprocessing step and applied a modified sequential thinning algorithm [4] that uses characterization 1 for the test whether a pixel is simple or not.

Theorem 1. *[5] A* 1(0) *of an image I is 4-simple iff* $X_B(p) = 1$ ($\overline{X}_B(p) = 1$). *A* 1(0) *of an image I is 8-simple iff* $\overline{X}_B(p) = 1$ ($X_B(p) = 1$).

It follows that a pixel $(p, 1)$ is 4-simple in I iff $(p, 0)$ is 8-simple in I and a pixel $(p, 1)$ is 8-simple in I iff $(p, 0)$ is 4-simple in I. It follows as well that $(p, 0)$ is 8-simple in I iff $(p, 1)$ is 8-simple in $\overline{I}$ where $\overline{I}$ is the negative image of I (all 1's in I are 0's in $\overline{I}$ and vice versa). For simple deformations the use of binary images is verified by applying the characteristic function after segmentation of grey value input images. The magnified image in Figure 4 is the result of applying the same sequential thinning algorithm on $\overline{I}$.

Characterization 2. *[6] A* 1 *at p of an image I is 8-simple in I iff the I-attachment set of p is non-empty and connected, and it is not the entire frontier of p.*

We have only four ways (and symmetric cases) in which the I-attachment set is non-empty and connected and not the entire frontier. In all cases $X_H(p) = 1$ and $\overline{X}_B(p) = 1$. Even this characterization for 8-simple 1s based on the concept of attachment sets is equivalent to above characterizations based on the grid point model.

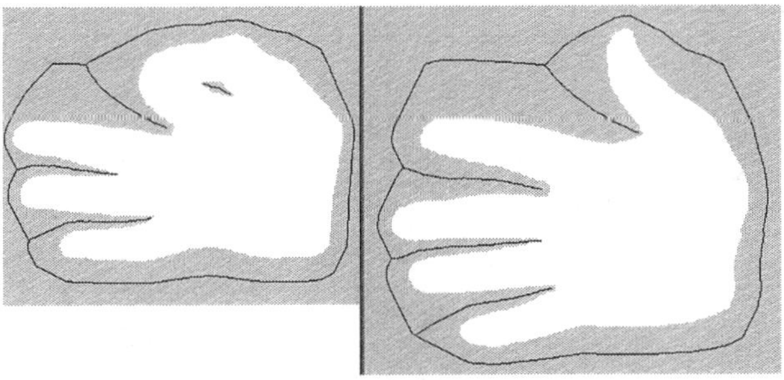

Fig. 4. Results of thinning applied on $\overline{I}$.

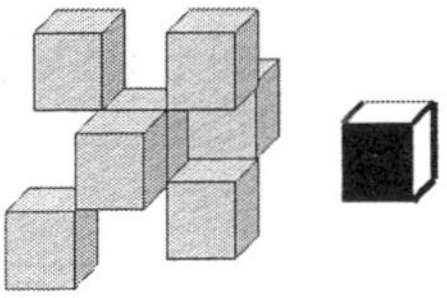

Fig. 5. The I-attachment set is not empty, connected and not the entire frontier, but p is not simple.

3 Characterizations of Simple Voxels

Characterization 3. *[1] A voxel $(p, I(p))$ of an image I is 26-simple iff it is 26-adjacent to exactly one 26-component of voxels in $A_{26}(p)$ and it is 6-adjacent to exactly one distinct 6-component of voxels in $A_{18}(p)$.*

A voxel $(p, I(p))$ of an image I is 6-simple iff it is 6-adjacent to exactly one 6-component of voxels in $A_{18}(p)$ and it is 26-adjacent to exactly one distinct 26-component of voxels in $A_{26}(p)$.

In [7] the number of 26-components of voxels in $A_{26}(p)$ and the number of distinct 6-components of voxels in $A_{18}(p)$ are called *topological numbers* relative to $\langle I \rangle$ and p. The calculation of the topological numbers of p for 3D images is complex.

Characterization 4. *[8, 9] A 1 at p of a 3D image I is simple in I iff*

- *p is adjacent to another 1 and*
- *p is 6-adjacent to a 0 and*
- *the set of 1's adjacent to p is connected and*
- *every two 6-adjacent 0's are 6-connected by voxels that are 18-adjacent to p.*

Characterization 2 for simple pixels using the concept of the I-attachment set of p for 2D images is not sufficient for the example in Fig.5. The I-attachment set of p in the frontier of p is connected and it is not the entire frontier of p and p is not simple.

Characterization 5. *[6] A 1 at p of a 2D or 3D image I is simple in I iff the I-attachment set of p, and the complement of that set in the frontier of p, are non-empty and connected.*

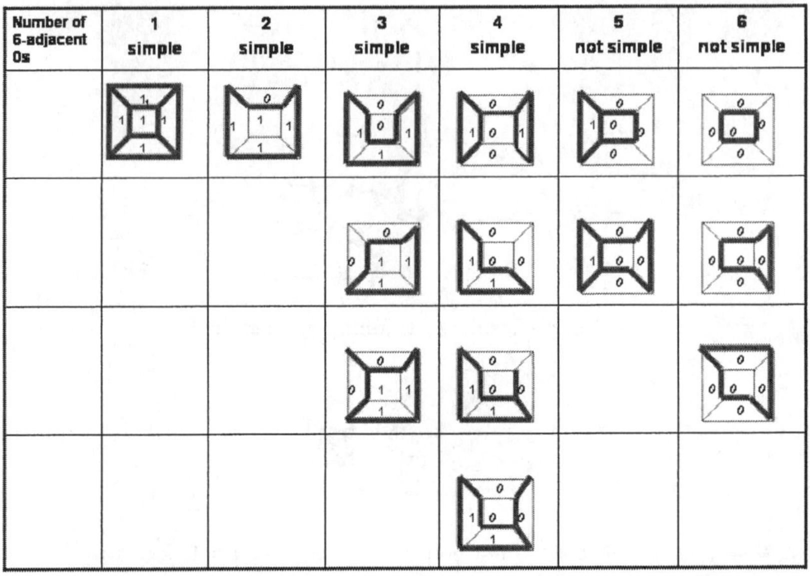

Fig. 6. Faces belonging to S are marked with 1s and edges in S are bold.

This characterization using the grid cell model and the previous characterization based on the grid point model are equivalent for 26-simple 1's.

Theorem 2. *The I-attachment set of p, and the complement of that set in the frontier of p, are non-empty and connected iff*

1. *p is adjacent to another* 1 *and*
2. *p is 6-adjacent to a* 0 *and*
3. *the* 1*'s adjacent to p are connected and*
4. *every two 6-adjacent* 0*'s are 6-connected by voxels that share at least an edge with p.*

Let N_6 be the number of 6-adjacent 0's, N'_{26} the number of 26-adjacent 1's, S the I-attachment set of p and $\overline{S}$ the complement of that set in the frontier of p.

The number of necessary computations for testing single voxels to be simple depends on N_6. If $I(p) = 1$, we store the values of all neighbors and the relative location of these neighbors in three arrays (0,1,2-cells). We use the following propositions:

1. If $N_6 = 1$ then p is 26-simple.
2. If $N_6 = 2$ and the 18-neighbor that shares an edge with both of them is a 0 then p is 26-simple.
3. If $N_6 = 3$ and two disjoint 18-neighbors sharing one edge with two disjoint 6-adjacent 0's each, and both of these 18-neighbors are 0's then p is 26-simple.

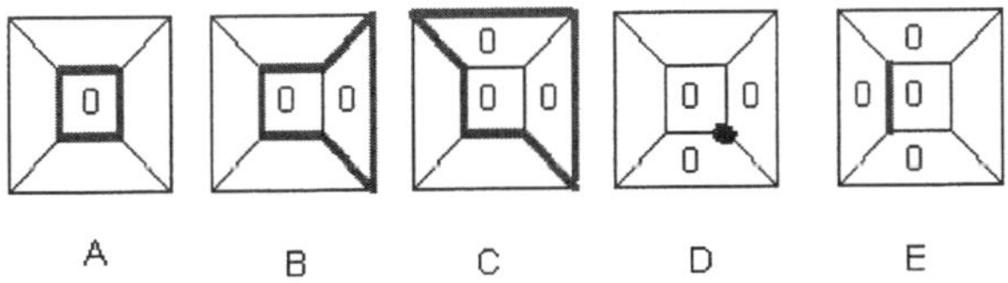

Fig. 7. Configurations A,B,C,D,E for non-simple points in 3D.

4. If $N_6 = 3$ and three disjoint 18-neighbors sharing one edge with two disjoint 6-adjacent 0's each, and at most one of these 18-neighbors is a 1 then p is 26-simple.
5. If $N_6 = 4$ and four disjoint 18-neighbors sharing one edge with two disjoint 6-adjacent 0's each, and exactly one of these 18-neighbors is a 1 then p is 26-simple.
6. If $N_6 = 4$ and five disjoint 18-neighbors sharing one edge with two disjoint 6-adjacent 0's each, and at most two of these 18-neighbors are 1's and one of these 18-neighbors shares one vertex with a 6-adjacent 1 and no 6-adjacent 0 shares four edges with 18-adjacent 1s then p is 26-simple.
7. For $N_6 = 5$ and $N_6 = 6$ we determine all non-simple voxels if $N'_{26} > 1$. p is not simple in following configurations.

The *Euler characteristic* $E(p)$ of the I-attachment set of a voxel is equal to the number of 0-cells minus number of 1-cells plus number of 2-cells [3].

Characterization 6. *A voxel p is simple iff the I-attachment set of p, and the complement of that set in the frontier of p are connected and* $E(p) = 1$.

4 Conclusions

In this paper we informed about equivalent characterizations and properties of simple points and voxels. The number of computations for testing single voxels can be reduced if the sequence of operations is based on N_0.

References

1. G. Bertrand and G. Maladain: A new characterization of three-dimensional simple points. in: *Pattern Recognition Letters*, **15**, (1994), 169–175.
2. R. W. Hall: Parallel connectivity-preserving thinning algorithms. in: *Topological algorithms for Digital Image Processing* (T. Y. Kong, A. Rosenfeld, eds.), North-Holland, (1996), 145–179.
3. C. J. Gau and T. Y. Kong: 4D Minimal Non-simple Sets. in: *Discrete Geometry for Computer Imagery*, LNCS 2301, Proc. 10th International Conference, Bordeaux, (2002), 81–91.
4. C. J. Hilditch: Linear skeletons from square cupboards. in: *Machine Intelligence 4* (B. Meltzer, D. Mitchie, eds.), Edinburgh University Press, (1969), 403–420.

5. G. Klette: Characterizations of simple pixels in binary images. in Proceedings: *Image and Vision Computing New Zealand 2002*, Auckland, (2002), 227–232.
6. T. Y. Kong: On topology preservation in 2-D and 3-D thinning. in: *International Journal for Pattern recognition and artificial intelligence*, **9**, No.5 (1995) 813–844.
7. C. Lohou and G. Bertrand: A New 3D 6-Subiteration Thinning Algorithm Based on P-Simple Points. in: *Discrete Geometry for Computer Imagery*, LNCS 2301, Proc. 10th International Conference, Bordeaux, (2002), 102–113.
8. G. Maladain, G. Bertrand: Fast characterization of 3D simple points. in: *Proc. 11th IAPR Int. Conf. on Pattern Recognition*, vol. III, The Hague, The Netherlands, (1992), 232–235.
9. P. K. Saha, B. Chanda, and D. D. Majumder: Principles and algorithms for 2D and 3D shrinking, *Tech. Rep. TR/KBCS/2/91*, NCKBCS Library, Indian Statistical Institute, Calcutta, India, (1991).
10. A. Rosenfeld: Connectivity in digital pictures. *Comm. ACM*, **17** (1970) 146–160.
11. A. Rosenfeld, T. Y. Kong, A. Nakamura: Topology- preserving deformations of two-valued digital pictures. *Graphical Models and Image Processing*, **60**,(1998) 24-34.
12. J. Serra: Image Analysis and Mathematical Morphology, vol.2, Academic Press, New York (1982).
13. S. Yokoi, J. I. Toriwaki, T. Fukumura: An analysis of topological properties of digitized binary pictures using local features. in: *Computer Graphics and Image Processing*, **4**, (1975), 63-73.

Viewpoint Selection – Planning Optimal Sequences of Views for Object Recognition

Frank Deinzer*, Joachim Denzler, and Heinrich Niemann

Chair for Pattern Recognition, Department of Computer Science
University of Erlangen-Nürnberg, Martensstr. 3, 91058 Erlangen
{deinzer,denzler}@informatik.uni-erlangen.de
http://www.mustererkennung.de

Abstract. In the past decades most object recognition systems were based on passive approaches. But in the last few years a lot of research was done in the field of active object recognition. In this context there are several unique problems to be solved, like the fusion of several views and the selection of the best next viewpoint.

In this paper we present an approach to solve the problem of choosing optimal views (viewpoint selection) and the fusion of these for an optimal 3D object recognition (viewpoint fusion). We formally define the selection of additional views as an optimization problem and we show how to use reinforcement learning for viewpoint training and selection in continuous state spaces without user interaction. We also present an approach for the fusion of multiple views based on recursive density propagation.

The experimental results show that our viewpoint selection is able to select a minimal number of views and perform an optimal object recognition with respect to the classification.

1 Introduction

The results of 3D object classification and localization depend strongly on the images which have been taken of the object. Based on ambiguities between objects in the data set some views might result in better recognition rates, others in worse. For difficult data sets usually more than one view is necessary to decide reliably on a certain object class. Viewpoint selection tackles exactly the problem of finding a sequence of optimal views to increase classification and localization results by avoiding ambiguous views or by sequentially ruling out possible object hypotheses. The optimality is not only defined with respect to the recognition rate but also with respect to the number of views necessary to get reliable results. The number of views should be as small as possible to delimit viewpoint selection from randomly taking a large number of images.

In this paper we present an approach for viewpoint selection based on reinforcement learning. The approach shows some major benefits: First, the optimal

* This work was partially funded by DFG under grant SFB 603/TP B2. Only the authors are responsible for the content.

N. Petkov and M.A. Westenberg (Eds.): CAIP 2003, LNCS 2756, pp. 65–73, 2003.

sequence of views is learned automatically in a training step, where no user interaction is necessary. Second, the approach performs a fusion of the generated views, where the fusion method does not depend on a special classifier. This makes it applicable for a very wide range of applications. Third, the possible viewpoints are continuous, so that a discretization of the viewpoint space is avoided, as has been done before, for example in the work of [2].

Viewpoint selection has been investigated in the past in several applications. Examples are 3D reconstruction [11] or optimal segmentation of image data [10]. In object recognition some active approaches have already been discussed as well. [12] plans the next view for a movable camera based on probabilistic reasoning. The active part is the selection of a certain area of the image for feature selection. The selected part is also called receptive field [13]. Compared to our approach, no camera movement is performed, neither during training nor during testing. Thus, the modeling of viewpoints in continuous 3D space is also avoided. The work of [9] uses Bayesian networks to decide on the next view to be taken. But the approach is limited to special recognition algorithms and to certain types of objects, for which the Bayesian network has been manually constructed. In other words, the approach is not classifier independent and cannot be applied without user interaction. [5] showed that the optimal action is the one that maximizes the mutual information between the observation and the state to be estimated.

In section 2.1 we will show how the fusion of multiple views can be done. We will present our approach for viewpoint selection in section 2.2. The experimental results in section 3 show that the presented approach is able to learn an optimal strategy for viewpoint selection that generates only the minimal number of images. The paper concludes with a summary and an outlook to future work in section 4.

2 Planning of View Sequences

The goal of this work is to provide a solution to the problem of optimal viewpoint selection for 3D object recognition without making a priori assumptions about the objects and the classifier. The problem is to determine the next view of an object given a series of previous decisions and observations. The problem can also be seen as the determination of a function which maps a history of observations to a new viewpoint. This function should be estimated automatically during a training step and should improve over time. The estimation must be done by defining a criterion, which measures how useful it is to choose a certain view given a history of observations. Additionally, the function should take uncertainty into account in the recognition process as well as in the viewpoint selection. The latter one is important, since new views are usually taken by e.g. moving a robot arm or a mobile platform. So the final position of the robot arm or the platform will always be error-prone. Last not least, the function should be classifier independent and be able to handle continuous viewpoints.

The realization of the described problem can be separated into two major parts. First, as a sequence of views will be necessary to compute classification results, we have to be able to perform a fusion of several views. A way to solve this problem using particle filters is given in section 2.1. Second, the main task, the planning of view sequences, must be properly formulated. An approach based on reinforcement learning [14] is presented in section 2.2

2.1 Fusion of Multiple Views by Density Propagation

In active object recognition a series of observed images $\boldsymbol{f}_t, \boldsymbol{f}_{t-1}, \ldots, \boldsymbol{f}_0$ of an object are given together with the camera movements $\boldsymbol{a}_{t-1}, \ldots, \boldsymbol{a}_0$ between these images. Based on these observations of images and movements one wants to draw conclusions for a non-observable state $\boldsymbol{q}_t$ of the object. This state $\boldsymbol{q}_t$ must contain both the *discrete* class and the *continuous* pose of the object. This fact is important for the following discussion.

In the context of a Bayesian approach, the knowledge on the object's state is given in form of the a posteriori density $p(\boldsymbol{q}_t|\boldsymbol{f}_t, \boldsymbol{a}_{t-1}, \boldsymbol{f}_{t-1}, \ldots, \boldsymbol{a}_0, \boldsymbol{f}_0)$ and can be calculated from

$$p(\boldsymbol{q}_t|\boldsymbol{f}_t, \boldsymbol{a}_{t-1}, \ldots, \boldsymbol{a}_0, \boldsymbol{f}_0) = \frac{1}{k_t} p(\boldsymbol{q}_t|\boldsymbol{a}_{t-1}, \boldsymbol{f}_{t-1}, \ldots, \boldsymbol{a}_0, \boldsymbol{f}_0) p(\boldsymbol{f}_t|\boldsymbol{q}_t) \tag{1}$$

where $k_t = p(\boldsymbol{f}_t, \boldsymbol{a}_{t-1}, \ldots, \boldsymbol{a}_0, \boldsymbol{f}_0)$ denotes a normalizing constant that is ignored in the following considerations. Under the Markov assumption for the state transition, (1) can be recursively rewritten as

$$p(\boldsymbol{q}_t|\boldsymbol{a}_{t-1}, \boldsymbol{f}_{t-1}, \ldots) = \int_{\boldsymbol{q}_{t-1}} p(\boldsymbol{q}_t|\boldsymbol{q}_{t-1}, \boldsymbol{a}_{t-1}) \cdot p(\boldsymbol{q}_{t-1}|\boldsymbol{a}_{t-1}, \boldsymbol{f}_{t-1}, \ldots) d\boldsymbol{q}_{t-1} \,. \tag{2}$$

Obviously this probability depends only on the camera movement $\boldsymbol{a}_{t-1}$. Its inaccuracy is modeled with a normally distributed noise component.

The classic approach for solving this recursive density propagation is the Kalman Filter [8]. But in computer vision the necessary assumptions for the Kalman Filter ($p(\boldsymbol{f}_t|\boldsymbol{q}_t)$ being normally distributed) are often not valid. In real world applications this density $p(\boldsymbol{f}_t|\boldsymbol{q}_t)$ usually is not normally distributed due to object ambiguities, sensor noise, occlusion, etc. This is a problem since it leads to a distribution which is not analytically computable. An approach for the complicated handling of such multimodal densities are the so called particle filters [7]. The basic idea is to approximate the a posteriori density by a set of weighted particles. In our approach we use the Condensation Algorithm [7]. It uses a sample set $C_t = \{\boldsymbol{c}_1^t, \ldots, \boldsymbol{c}_K^t\}$ to approximate the multimodal probability distribution in (1). Please note that we do not only have a continuous state space for $\boldsymbol{q}_t$ but a *mixed discrete/continuous state space* for object class and pose, as mentioned at the beginning of this section.

Now we will show how to use the Condensation Algorithm in a practical realization of sensor data fusion of multiple views. As noted above we need to include the class and pose of the object into our state $\boldsymbol{q}_t$ to classify and localize objects. This leads to the definitions of the state $\boldsymbol{q}_t = \left(\Omega_\kappa\ {}^1\varphi^t \ldots {}^J\varphi^t\right)^T$. The samples $\boldsymbol{c}$ and camera movements $\boldsymbol{a}$ are defined as

$$\boldsymbol{c}_i^t = \left(\Omega_{\kappa_i}\ {}^1\varphi_i^t \ldots {}^J\varphi_i^t\right)^T \quad \text{and} \quad \boldsymbol{a}_t = \left(\Delta^1\varphi^t \ldots \Delta^J\varphi^t\right)^T \tag{3}$$

with the class numbers Ω_κ and Ω_{κ_i}. ${}^j\varphi^t$ denotes the pose of the j-th degree of freedom for the camera position and $\Delta^j\varphi^t$ the relative changes of the viewing position of the camera.

In the practical realization of the Condensation Algorithm, one starts with an initial sample set $C^0 = \{\boldsymbol{c}_1^0, \dots, \boldsymbol{c}_K^0\}$ with samples distributed uniformly over the state space. For the generation of a new sample set C^t, samples $\boldsymbol{c}_i^t$ are

1. drawn from C^{t-1} with probability $\frac{p(\boldsymbol{f}_{t-1}|\boldsymbol{c}_i^{t-1})}{\sum_{j=1}^K p(\boldsymbol{f}_{t-1}|\boldsymbol{c}_j^{t-1})}$
2. propagated with the necessarily predetermined sample transition model $\boldsymbol{c}_i^t = \boldsymbol{c}_i^{t-1} + \left(0\; r_1 \dots r_J\right)^T$ with $r_j \sim \mathcal{N}(\Delta^j\varphi^t, \sigma_j)$ and the variance parameters of the Gaussian transition noise σ_j. They model the inaccuracy of the camera movement under the assumption that the errors of the camera movements are independent between the degrees of freedom. These variance parameters have to be defined in advance.
3. evaluated in the image by $p(\boldsymbol{f}_t|\boldsymbol{c}_i^t)$. This evaluation is performed by the classifier. The only requirement for the classifier that shall be used together with our fusion approach is its ability to evaluate this density.

In the context of our viewpoint selections the densities represented by sample sets have to be evaluated. This can be done, for example, by a Parzen estimation over the sample set [15]. For a more detailed explanation on the theoretical background of the approximation of (1) by a sample set we refer to [7].

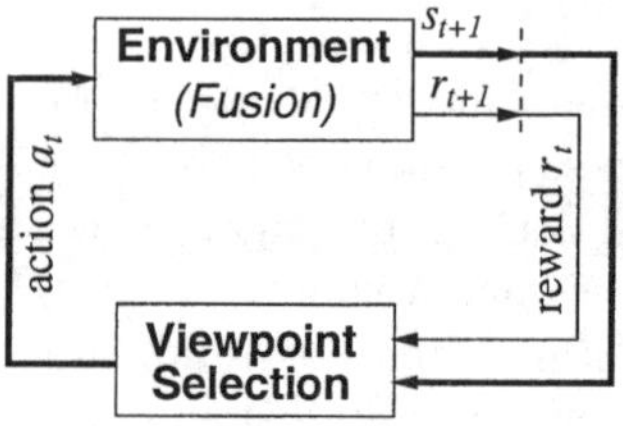

Fig. 1. Reinforcement learning.

At this point we want to note that it is important to include the class Ω_κ in the object state $\boldsymbol{q}_t$ and the samples $\boldsymbol{c}_i^t$. An alternative would be to omit this by setting up several sample sets – one for each object class – and perform the Condensation Algorithm separately on each set. But this would not result in an integrated classification/localization, but in separated localizations on each set under the assumption of observing the corresponding object class. No fusion of the object class over the sequence of images would be done in that case.

2.2 Reinforcement Learning Applied to Viewpoint Selection

A straight forward and intuitive way to formalizing the problem is given by looking at Fig. 1. A closed loop between sensing s_t and acting $\boldsymbol{a}_t$ can be seen. The chosen *action* $\boldsymbol{a}_t$ corresponds to the executed camera movement, the sensed *state*

$$s_t = p(\boldsymbol{q}_t|\boldsymbol{f}_t, \boldsymbol{a}_{t-1}, \boldsymbol{f}_{t-1}, \dots, \boldsymbol{a}_0, \boldsymbol{f}_0) \tag{4}$$

is the density as given in (1). Additionally, the classifier returns a so called *reward* r_t, which measures the quality of the chosen viewpoint. For a viewpoint that increases the information observed so far the reward should have a large value. A well-know measure for expressing the informational content that fits our requirements is the entropy

$$r_{t+1} = -H(s_t) = -H\left(p(\boldsymbol{q}_t|\boldsymbol{f}_t, \boldsymbol{a}_{t-1}, \boldsymbol{f}_{t-1}, \ldots, \boldsymbol{a}_0, \boldsymbol{f}_0)\right) \tag{5}$$

It is worth noting that the reward might also include costs for the camera movement, so that large movements of the camera are punished. In this paper we neglect costs for camera movement for the time being.

At time t during the decision process, i.e. the selection of a sequence of viewpoints, the goal will be to maximize the accumulated and weighted future rewards, called the *return*

$$R_t = \sum_{n=0}^{\infty} \gamma^n r_{t+n+1} = -\sum_{n=0}^{\infty} \gamma^n H(s_{t+n+1}) \quad \text{with } \gamma \in [0;1] \,. \tag{6}$$

The weight γ defines how much influence a future reward will have on the overall return R_t at time $t+n+1$. Of course, the future rewards cannot be observed at time step t. Thus, the following function, called the *action–value function* $Q(s, \boldsymbol{a})$

$$Q(s, \boldsymbol{a}) = E\left\{R_t | s_t = s, \boldsymbol{a}_t = \boldsymbol{a}\right\} \tag{7}$$

is defined, which describes the expected return when starting at time step t in state s with action $\boldsymbol{a}$. In other words, the function $Q(s, \boldsymbol{a})$ models the expected quality of the chosen camera movement $\boldsymbol{a}$ for the future, if the sensor fusion has returned s before.

Viewpoint selection can now be defined as a two step approach: First, estimate the function $Q(s, \boldsymbol{a})$ during training. Second, if at any time the sensor fusion returns s as classification result, select that camera movement which maximizes the expected accumulated and weighted rewards. This function is called the *policy*

$$\pi(s) = \operatorname{argmax}_{\boldsymbol{a}} Q(s, \boldsymbol{a}) \,. \tag{8}$$

The key issue of course is the estimation of the function $Q(s, \boldsymbol{a})$, which is the basis for the decision process in (8). One of the demands defined in section 1 is that the selection of the most promising view should be learned without user interaction. Reinforcement learning provides many different algorithms to estimate the action value function based on a trial and error method [14]. Trial and error means that the system itself is responsible for trying certain actions in a certain state. The result of such a trial is then used to update $Q(\cdot, \cdot)$ and to improve its policy π.

In reinforcement learning a series of *episodes* are performed: Each episode k consists of a sequence of state/action pairs $(s_t, \boldsymbol{a}_t), t \in \{0, 1, \ldots, T\}$, where the performed action $\boldsymbol{a}_t$ in state s_t results in a new state s_{t+1}. A final state s_T is called the terminal state, where a predefined goal is reached and the episode ends. In our case, the terminal state is the state where classification and localization is possible with high confidence. During the episode new returns $R_t^{(k)}$ are collected for those state/action pairs $(s_t^k, \boldsymbol{a}_t^k)$ which have been visited at time t during the episode k. At the end of the episode the action-value function is updated.

In our case so called Monte Carlo learning is applied and the function $Q(\cdot,\cdot)$ is estimated by the mean of all collected returns $R_t^{(i)}$ for the state/action pair $(s, \boldsymbol{a})$ for all episodes.

As a result for the next episode one gets a new decision rule π_{k+1}, which is now computed by maximizing the updated action value function. This procedure is repeated until π_{k+1} converges to the optimal policy. The reader is referred to a detailed introduction to reinforcement learning [14] for a description of other ways for estimating the function $Q(\cdot,\cdot)$. Convergence proofs for several algorithms can be found in [1].

Most of the algorithms in reinforcement learning treat the states and actions as discrete variables. Of course, in viewpoint selection parts of the state space (the pose of the object) and the action space (the camera movements) are continuous. A way to extend the algorithms to continuous reinforcement learning is to approximate the action-value function

$$\widehat{Q}(s, \boldsymbol{a}) = \frac{\sum_{(s',\boldsymbol{a}')} K\left(d\left(\theta(s,\boldsymbol{a}), \theta(s',\boldsymbol{a}')\right)\right) \cdot Q(s',\boldsymbol{a}')}{\sum_{(s',\boldsymbol{a}')} K\left(d\left(\theta(s,\boldsymbol{a}), \theta(s',\boldsymbol{a}')\right)\right)}, \tag{9}$$

which can be evaluated for any continuous state/action pair $(s, \boldsymbol{a})$. Basically, this is a weighted sum of the action-values Q(s',$\boldsymbol{a}$') of all previously collected state/action pairs $(s', \boldsymbol{a}')$. The other components within (9) are:

- The *transformation function* $\theta(s, \boldsymbol{a})$ transforms a state s with a known action $\boldsymbol{a}$ with the intention of bringing a state to a "reference point" (required for the distance function in the next item). In the context of the current definition of the states from (4) it can be seen as a density transformation

$$\begin{aligned}\theta(s_t, \boldsymbol{a}_t) &= \theta\left(p(\boldsymbol{q}_t|\boldsymbol{f}_t, \boldsymbol{a}_{t-1}, \boldsymbol{f}_{t-1}, \ldots, \boldsymbol{a}_0, \boldsymbol{f}_0), \boldsymbol{a}_t\right) \\ &= \det\left(\boldsymbol{J}_{\zeta_{\boldsymbol{a}_t}^{-1}}(\boldsymbol{q}_t)\right) p\left(\zeta_{\boldsymbol{a}_t}^{-1}(\boldsymbol{q}_t)|\boldsymbol{f}_t, \boldsymbol{a}_{t-1}, \boldsymbol{f}_{t-1}, \ldots, \boldsymbol{a}_0, \boldsymbol{f}_0\right)\right) \end{aligned} \tag{10}$$

$$\zeta_{\boldsymbol{a}}^{-1}(\boldsymbol{q}) = \begin{pmatrix} q_1 + a_1 \\ \vdots \\ q_m + a_m \end{pmatrix}, \quad \boldsymbol{J}_{\zeta_{\boldsymbol{a}}^{-1}}(\boldsymbol{q}) = \begin{pmatrix} \frac{\partial(\zeta_{\boldsymbol{a}}^{-1})_1}{\partial q_1} & \cdots & \frac{\partial(\zeta_{\boldsymbol{a}}^{-1})_m}{\partial q_1} \\ \vdots & \ddots & \vdots \\ \frac{\partial(\zeta_{\boldsymbol{a}}^{-1})_1}{\partial q_m} & \cdots & \frac{\partial(\zeta_{\boldsymbol{a}}^{-1})_m}{\partial q_m} \end{pmatrix} = \begin{pmatrix} 1 & & 0 \\ & \ddots & \\ 0 & & 1 \end{pmatrix}.$$

  This density transformationwhich simply performs a shift of the density.
- A distance function $d(\cdot,\cdot)$ to calculate the distance between two states. Generally speaking, similar states must result in low distances. The lower the distance, the more transferable the information from a learned action-value to the current situation is. As the transformation function (10) results in a density, the *Kullback-Leibler Distance*

$$\begin{aligned} d_{KL}(s_n, s_m) &= d_{KL}\left(p(\boldsymbol{q}|\boldsymbol{f}_n, \boldsymbol{a}_{n-1}, \boldsymbol{f}_{n-1}, \ldots), p(\boldsymbol{q}|\boldsymbol{f}_m, \boldsymbol{a}_{m-1}, \boldsymbol{f}_{m-1}, \ldots)\right) \\ &= \int p(\boldsymbol{q}|\boldsymbol{f}_n, \boldsymbol{a}_{n-1}, \boldsymbol{f}_{n-1}, \ldots) \log \frac{p(\boldsymbol{q}|\boldsymbol{f}_n, \boldsymbol{a}_{n-1}, \boldsymbol{f}_{n-1}, \ldots)}{p(\boldsymbol{q}|\boldsymbol{f}_m, \boldsymbol{a}_{m-1}, \boldsymbol{f}_{m-1}, \ldots)} d\boldsymbol{q}, \end{aligned}$$

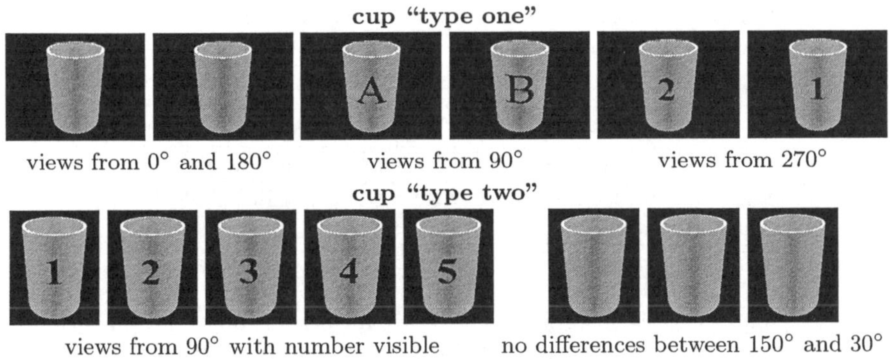

Fig. 2. Examples for objects that require viewpoint selection and fusion of images for proper recognition.

which can easily be extended to a symmetric distance measure, the so called *extended Kullback-Leibler Distance*

$$d_{EKL}(s_n, s'_m) = d_{KL}(s_n, s'_m) + d_{KL}(s'_m, s_n,)\,, \tag{11}$$

can be used. Please note that in general there is no analytic solution for (11) but as we represent our densities as particle sets anyway (see section 2.1) there are well-known ways to approximate (11) by Monte Carlo techniques.

– A kernel function $K(\cdot)$ that weights the calculated distances. A suitable kernel function is the Gaussian $K(x) = \exp(-x^2/D^2)$, where D denotes the width of the kernel.

Viewpoint selection, i.e. the computation of the policy π, can now be written, according to (8), as the optimization problem

$$\pi(s) = \underset{\boldsymbol{a}}{\operatorname{argmax}}\, \widehat{Q}(s, \boldsymbol{a})\,. \tag{12}$$

3 Experimental Evaluation

Our primary goal in the experiments was to show that our approach is able to learn and perform an *optimal* sequence of views. We have shown in several publications [3, 4] that the fusion of a sequence of *randomly* chosen views works very well in real world environments and improves classification and localization result significantly. For that reason we decided to use the rather simple — from the object recognition's point of view — synthetic images of the two types of cups shown in Fig. 2 for the evaluation of our viewpoint selection approach. In this setup the camera is restricted to move around the object on a circle, so that (3) reduces to $\boldsymbol{c}_i^t = (\Omega_{\kappa_i}\ {}^1\varphi_i^t)^T$ and $\boldsymbol{a}_t \in [0°, 360°]$. The classifier used to evaluate $p(\boldsymbol{f}_t|\boldsymbol{c}_i^t)$ for the fusion of images (see section 2.1) is based on the continuous statistical eigenspace approach presented in [6].

The four cups of "type one" in Fig. 2 show a number **1** or **2** on one, and a letter **A** or **B** on the other side. A differentiation between the 4 possible

Table 1. Results of viewpoint selection. Calculation time given is for planning one step, computed on a Pentium IV 2.4GHz.

	cup "type one"			**"cup type two"**		
	$\gamma = 0$	$\gamma = 0.5$	$\gamma = 1.0$	$\gamma = 0$	$\gamma = 0.5$	$\gamma = 1.0$
classification rate	100% (as expected)					
average sequence length	2.36	2.28	2.31	2.13	1.96	2.13
calculation time	$\approx$ 13.1s			$\approx$ 12.3s		

objects is only possible if number and letter have been observed and properly fused. In a training step a total of about 600 action-values $Q(\cdot, \cdot)$ were collected during 200 episodes; each for different settings of the return parameter γ (6). The evaluation was performed with 500 sequences with randomly chosen classes and starting views. There exists a theoretical minimum for the necessary sequence length of $\approx$ 2.3 views: Number and letter are visible within about 120° each, requiring 2 views for that case and 3 views for the remaining viewing area. The recognition rates at the end of the sequences were as expected 100% for these rather simple objects. But it is very interesting, and this is the main point, that the average length of the planned sequences shown in Table 1 is very close to the calculated minimum of necessary views. This indicates very strongly that the learned strategy for recognition is optimal. Due to the nature of the objects, the learned strategy is the same for all values of γ.

The cups of "type two" in Fig. 2 show a number (**1 2 3 4 5**) on the front side. If this number is not visible the objects can not be distinguished or localized. The cups can be classified correctly and stable within an area of nearly 120°. Localization of the cups is possible within an area of about 144°. In the training a total of about 430 action-values Q were collected during the 200 performed episodes that generated about 600 different views. The optimal strategy must bring up the number with a minimum number of views. We first expected our viewpoint selection to learn a strategy that moves the camera by 120° if the cup can not be classified, as this would result in an average minimum sequence length of 2.0. But the learned strategy — which is the same for each trained value of γ — moves the camera by 180° if no classification or localization is possible. The reason for this strategy is that it allows for a better fusion and thus for an unambiguous recognition. Surprisingly, even this learned strategy has a theoretical minimum for the necessary sequence length of only $\approx$ 2.03 steps. As the results in Table 1 show, the average sequence length required by our viewpoint selection is just about the minimal number of required views.

4 Conclusion and Future Work

In this paper we have presented a general framework for viewpoint selection and the fusion of the generated sequence of views. The approach works in continuous state and action spaces and is independent of the chosen statistical classifier. Furthermore the system can be be trained automatically without user interaction. We claim that these properties have not yet been provided by any other approach. The experimental results on two objects that require different strategies for recognition have shown that an optimal planning strategy was learned.

In our future work we will evaluate how much the planning of optimal view sequences improves object recognition rates on real world objects compared to the random strategy we used in [3, 4]. Another important point for real world applications are *costs* of movement that could not be discussed in this paper. Finally, for higher dimensional state spaces, other reinforcement learning methods might be necessary to reduce training complexity.

References

1. D.P. Bertsekas and J.N. Tstsiklis. *Neuro-Dynamic Programming.* Athena Scientific, 1996.
2. H. Borotschnig, L. Paletta, M. Prantl, and A. Pinz. A Comparison of Probabilistic, Possibilistic and Evidence Theoretic Fusion Schemes for Active Object Recognition. *Computing*, 62:293–319, 1999.
3. F. Deinzer, J. Denzler, and H. Niemann. On Fusion of Multiple Views for Active Object Recognition. In *DAGM 2001*, pages 239–245, Berlin, 2001. Springer.
4. F. Deinzer, J. Denzler, and H. Niemann. Improving Object Recognition By Fusion Of Multiple Views. In *3rd Indian Conference on Computer Vision Graphics and Image Processing*, pages 161 166, Ahmedabad, Indian, 2002. Allied Publishers Pvt. Ltd.
5. J. Denzler and C.M. Brown. Information theoretic sensor data selection for active object recognition and state estimation. *PAMI*, 24(2), 2002.
6. Ch. Grässl, F. Deinzer, and H. Niemann. Continuous Parametrization of Normal Distributions for Improving the Discrete Statistical Eigenspace Approach for Object Recognition. In *PRIP 2003*, May 2003. submitted.
7. M. Isard and B. Andrew. CONDENSATION – Conditional Density Propagation for Visual Tracking. *IJCV 98*, 29(1):5–28, 1998.
8. R.E. Kalman. A New Approach to Linear Filtering and Prediction Problems. *Journal of Basic Engineering*, pages 35–44, 1960.
9. B. Krebs, M. Burkhardt, and B. Korn. Handling Uncertainty in 3D Object Recognition using Bayesian Networks. In *ECCV 98*, pages 782–795, Berlin, 1998.
10. C.B. Madsen and H.I. Christensen. A Viewpoint Planning Strategy for Determining True Angles on Polyhedral Objects by Camera Alignment. *PAMI*, 19(2), 1997.
11. P. Lehel and E.E. Hemayed and A.A. Farag. Sensor Planning for a Trinocular Active Vision System. In *CVPR*, pages II:306–312, 1999.
12. S. D. Roy, S. Chaudhury, and S. Banerjee. Recognizing Large 3-D Objects through Next View Planning using an Uncalibrated Camera. In *ICCV 2001*, pages II: 276 – 281, Vancouver, Canada, 2001. IEEE Computer Press.
13. B. Schiele and J.L. Crowley. Transinformation for Active Object Recognition. In *ICCV 98*, pages 249–254, Bombay, India, 1998.
14. R.S. Sutton and A.G. Barto. *Reinforcement Learning.* A Bradford Book, Cambridge, London, 1998.
15. P. Viola and W.M. Wells III. Alignment by Maximization of Mutual Information. *International Journal of Computer Vision*, 24(2):137–154, 1997.

Epipolar Plane Images as a Tool to Seek Correspondences in a Dense Sequence*

Martin Matoušek and Václav Hlaváč

Czech Technical University, Faculty of Electrical Engineering
Department of Cybernetics, Center for Machine Perception
121 35 Prague 2, Karlovo náměstí 13, Czech Republic
phone +420 224 357 637, fax +420 224 357 385
{xmatousm,hlavac}@cmp.felk.cvut.cz

Abstract. We present a method seeking correspondences in a dense rectified image sequence, considered as a set of Epipolar Plane Images (EPI). The main idea is to employ dense sequence to get more information which could guide the correspondence algorithm. The method is intensity based, no features are detected. Our spatio-temporal volume analysis approach aims at accuracy and density of the correspondences. Two cost functions are used, quantifying the belief that given correspondence candidate is correct. The first one is based on projections of one scene point to the spatio-temporal data, while the second one uses two-dimensional neighborhood (in image plane) around such projections. The assumed opaque Lambertian surface without occlusions allows us to use a simple correspondence seeking algorithm based on minimization of a global criterion using dynamic programming.

1 Introduction

One of the fundamental problems in computer vision is correspondence seeking. Established correspondences (coordinates of pixels that are projections of a single point in the 3D scene) are precondition for reconstruction of 3D shape from intensity images.

The state-of-the-art approaches for correspondence seeking can be classified according to data processed as follows. The first class works with a set of two or more unorganized images. Computational binocular stereo is commonly used here. The well-known methods for occlussion-free scenes are based on dynamic programming [3]. For scenes with occlusions, pairing algorithms not imposing the monotonicity constraint are used [9]. Larger set of images can make search for correspondences easier. The verification of a correspondence candidate by comparing intensity values in multiple unorganized images is used in [8].

The methods belonging to the second class work on organized set of images, usually forming a sequence. Detecting and tracking features in sequence [10]

* This research was supported by the Czech Ministry of Education under the project MSM 212300013 and by the Grant Agency of the Czech Republic under the project GACR 102/03/0440 and by the European Union under the project IST-2001-32184.

N. Petkov and M.A. Westenberg (Eds.): CAIP 2003, LNCS 2756, pp. 74–81, 2003.

is one possibility. Another possibility is to combine wide-baseline stereo and a sequence. The moving wide-baseline stereo rig provides two dense sequences [4] in which features are tracked. Short sections of tracked trajectories are obtained and simplify finding correspondences.

Images of the dense sequence (a sequence with small interframe displacements) stacked to a spatio-temporal block are the the input of the third class of methods. Signal processing techniques (filtering) can be used to detect occlusions [2, 7]. Another example is computation of differential characteristics in local neighborhood of the current pixel to estimate optical flow. Epipolar plane image analysis [1] also belongs to this class of approaches.

Each of the mentioned approaches has different advantages and drawbacks. Wide-baseline stereo has sufficient spatial accuracy, but often cannot resolve an ambiguity due to e.g. repeating-pattern. Local methods (tracking, optical flow) usually find acceptable correspondences between adjacent frames, but error accumulation occurs for longer sequences. Tracking may allow to detect features with high accuracy, but still only sparse set of correspondences is obtained.

Our approach to spatio-temporal block analysis utilizes large data set and is supposed to provide more scene information than stereo. Ambiguity known in stereo is reduced. We use global information present in the whole spatio--temporal block (or in a single EPI) without error accumulation (as in local methods) and no features have to be detected. This allows to compute a dense set of correspondences with sub-pixel accuracy, and large distance between end frames of the sequence leads to sufficient spatial accuracy. Unlike feature-based EPI analysis methods [1], our approach is purely signal based. The difference of another intensity based correspondence verification methods (e.g. [8]) is in employing the highly organized structure of the EPI, which significantly reduces the search space.

2 Problem Formulation

We are given a dense sequence of images in which each two images are rectified. We assume no occlusions in the captured sequence and rigid opaque Lambertian scene with enough texture. This allows to use uniqueness and monotonicity constraint, and to assume that a point on the surface is projected to each image with the same intensity. Our task is to establish a set of correspondences between end images of the sequence, focusing on density and accuracy of the correspondences.

3 Spatio-Temporal Volumes, Epipolar Plane Images

Let us consider dense image sequence, i.e., the sequence with small inter-frame pixel displacements. Such a sequence can be viewed as a 3D *spatio-temporal* volume $f(x, y, t)$; x, y denote the image coordinates and t is an image index. Particular scene point is projected as a curve $\mathcal{C}_X$ in (x, y, t) space. This curve is parametrized by t. Note that such a curve need not be defined for all t in case of occlusions.

Let the sequence $f(x, y, t)$ be captured by the pinhole cameras with projection centers lying on a line (the baseline), such that all adjacent centers have the same distance. Moreover, all cameras have the same intrinsic calibration parameters, all optical axes are perpendicular to the baseline and parallel to each other. Thus, the whole sequence is epipolarly rectified, it means that each pair of images is rectified. In this casem, each curve $\mathcal{C}_X$ is formed by (parts of) a line with constant y coordinate (Figure 1a).

The baseline generates a bundle of epipolar planes. Epipolar lines, belonging to a single epipolar plane, are aligned with image rows. They are stacked along the parameter t to form *epipolar plane image* (EPI, Figure 1b).

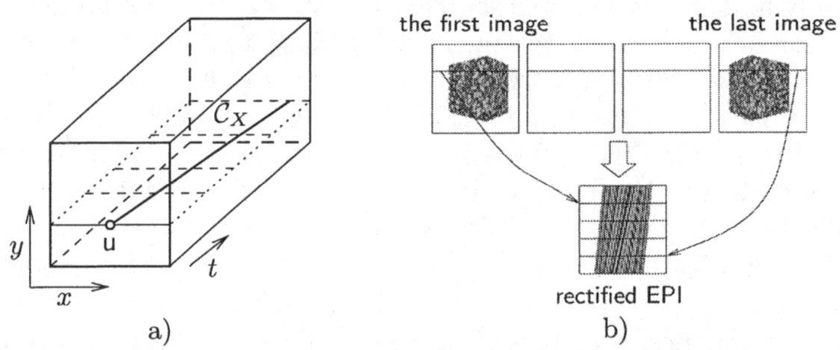

Fig. 1. (a) Rectified spatio temporal volume and (b) EPI formation scheme.

A sequence obtained under the above assumptions has the following useful properties:

- Search space is reduced to 1D only. Independence of epipolar lines allows to treat each EPI separately.
- A single scene point maps to a *straight line* in the EPI, which has in case of Lambertian reflectance a constant intensity profile.

The assumption of constant intensity of the line in the EPI corresponding to a particulare point is not entirely true in real world due to e.g. noise. Moreover, it is very difficult in practice to capture a sequence rectified accurately enough. In [5] we analyzed several phenomena violating the assumptions of the method.

4 Seeking Correspondence

A correspondence between a point in the first and in the last image is denoted by a pair (i, j) of column coordinates in the selected row. The (i, j) coordinates also determine end points of a line in the EPI (Figure 2a); such a line is a realization of a single point in the scene. Given a correspondence candidate, the cost $c(i, j)$ quantifies confidence that (i, j) is realization of some observed scene point. We used two following cost functions.

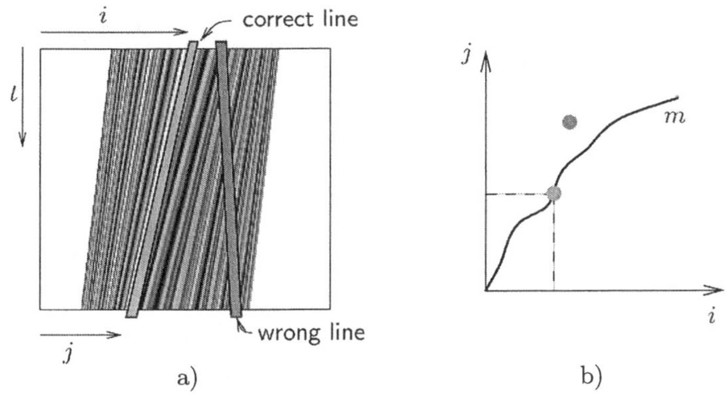

Fig. 2. (a) Selected EPI with two lines shown and (b) search space in which correspondences are sought.

The first cost function is defined considering only one scene point. The cost is calculated according to intensities along the line (i, j) in the EPI. *Variance* of the intensities was chosen as this cost, similarly as in [8]. The second cost function uses a small 2D neighbourhood around the point in each image of the sequence. We assume, that such a small neighbourhood is an observation of a local surface texture model, and we measure the consistency of all observations with this model. The sum of normalized correlations between each observation and the model serves as the consistency measure. The neighbourhood in the first image in the sequence was chosen as the model, however, other choices (e.g., mean of all observations) are possible.

The domain of the cost $c(i, j)$ is $\mathbb{R}^2$ in both cases because positions with sub-pixel accuracy can be obtained by interpolating neighbouring coordinates. Here we take advantage of the fact that there are many images at hand in the sequence. The defined cost function $c(i, j)$ allows to examine all possible correspondence pairs. We are looking for the whole set of correspondences considered as a *mapping* m between i and j (Figure 2b). The global criterion $\mathcal{J}(m)$ sums up $c(i, j)$ along m. The mapping m is a strictly increasing function because of ordering and uniqueness constraints. The estimate m^* of the optimal mapping is computed by minimizing $\mathcal{J}(m)$ by dynamic programming. During dynamic programming, discrete raster is subsampled to achieve sub-pixel accuracy.

5 Experimental Results

We conducted experiments having two aims. The first aim was to test the idea on synthetic data, which perfectly fits the assumptions of the algorithm. The second aim was to uncover the limits of practical usage on the real scenes.

5.1 Synthetic Data

Only the first cost function was tested on synthetic data, which were provided by the ray-tracer. The scene was an edge of a cube with random granite-like

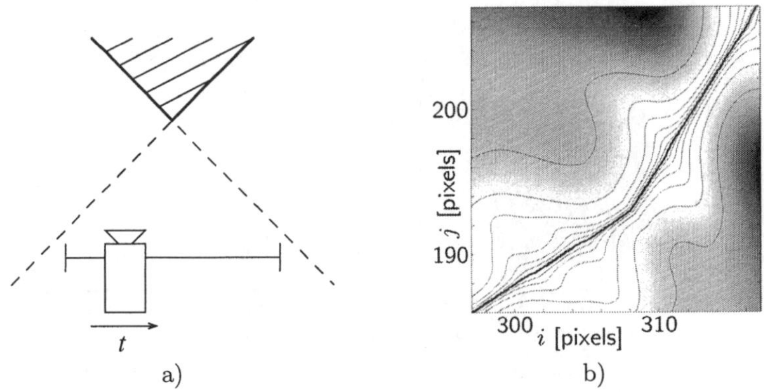

Fig. 3. (a) The setup for the synthetic experiment. (b) Result of the dynamic programming on synthetic data, the path corresponding to surface near the corner is zoomed in. The underlying image shows the values of the cost function; white means lowest value, contours (with logarithmic scale) mark equal values.

texture. The maximum and mean error was 0.13 and 0.04 pixel, respectively. The results on synthetic images are shown in Figure 3 and presented in more detail in [6].

5.2 Real Data

The studied real scene consisted of a reverse side of a single 15×15 cm bathroom tile, sprayed by a random texture. The unglazed ceramic surface is expected to have almost Lambertian reflectance properties. Images were captured by a stationary CCD camera (1K×1K resolution, 9mm chip size, 25 mm lens) placed at the distance 90 cm from the scene. The homogeneously illuminated scene was moved along the straight line by 15 cm in 1.5 mm steps; a hundred of images was taken (Figure 4). Note that we are moving the scene instead of the camera because mechanical inaccuracy during movement has smaller influence in that case. To fulfill the assumption that the surface is observed with the same intensity from an arbitrary direction, we illuminated the scene by the light source placed sufficiently far from the scene.

The movement of the tile is approximately, but not exactly, parallel to image x axis, so the sequence is rectified before the correspondence seeking. To enable the computation of rectifying homography, the tile is equipped with easy-to--locate calibration marks (chess-board). However, we need not know the full camera calibration for the rectification. Equidistant movement steps together with constant relative orientation of the movement direction and optical axis are ensured. Then the rectifying homography consists only of two elementary transformations, rotation around the optical axis and pan. These transformations remain constant for each image and thay can be computed from a set of known correspondences.

The back side of our bathroom tile is covered by regular stripe-like hollows which are approximately 0.2 mm deep—the surface is bounded by two parallel

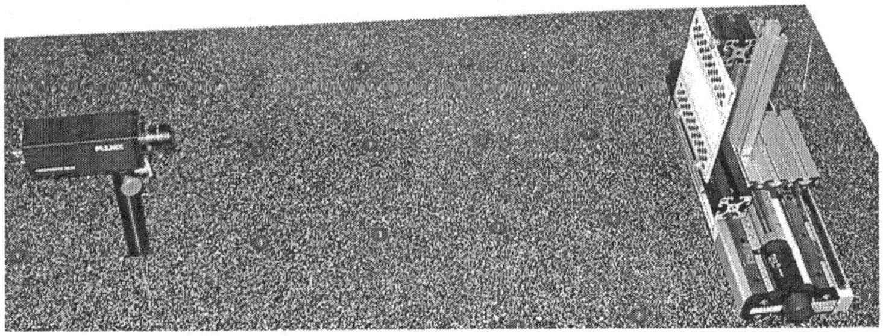

Fig. 4. Experimental setup. The camera and the moving table mounted on granite slab.

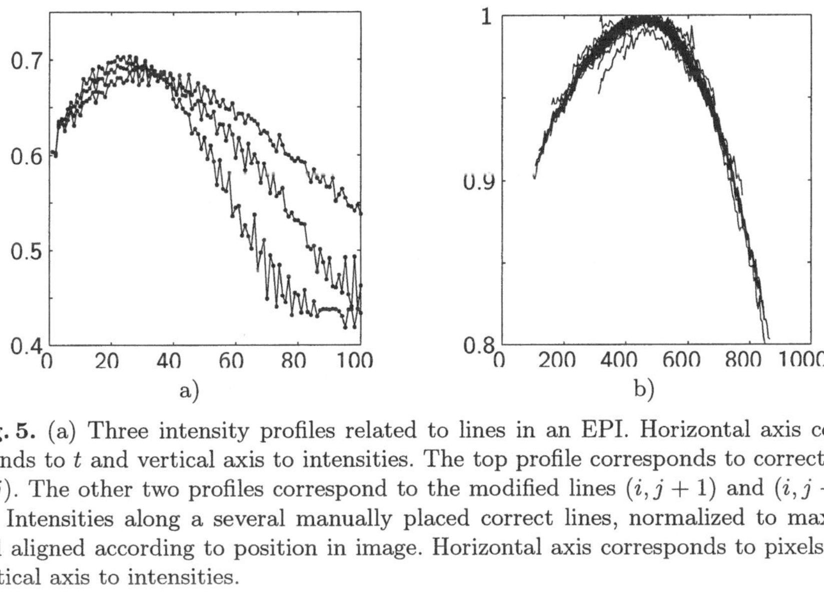

Fig. 5. (a) Three intensity profiles related to lines in an EPI. Horizontal axis corresponds to t and vertical axis to intensities. The top profile corresponds to correct line (i, j). The other two profiles correspond to the modified lines $(i, j+1)$ and $(i, j-1)$. (b) Intensities along a several manually placed correct lines, normalized to maxima and aligned according to position in image. Horizontal axis corresponds to pixels and vertical axis to intensities.

'planes' with known distance. The approximate value of disparity between border images in the sequence was 427, which leads to expected difference of a disparity around 0.1 pixel between the two 'planes'.

First, we use the variance-based cost function. Real data suffer from many phenomena, missing in ideal case, some of which are described in [5]. Figure 5 shows several intensity profiles along correct line in an EPI. It is apparent that the photometric field darkening strongly influences the profile. We measured the camera response to the constant irradiance in a few image locations (regular 10×10 grid). The third-order two-dimensional polynomial was fitted to the measured intensities and used for the correction of the field darkening.

The presence of noise and violation of Lambertian surface assumption motivated us to use the cost function based on correlation window (Figure 6).

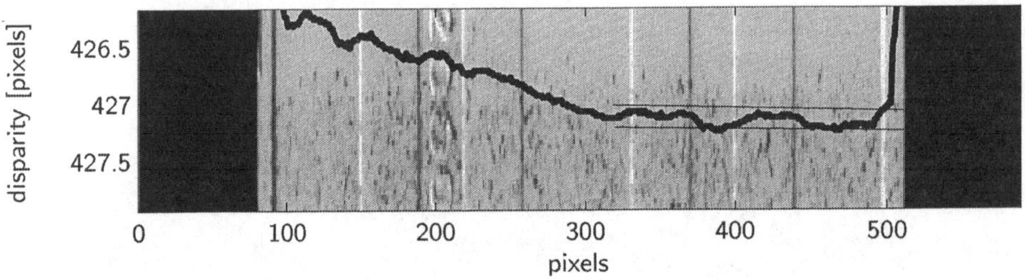

Fig. 6. Computed disparity values for a selected y-coordinate, overlaid on the first image of the sequence. Expected disparity for the two planes is shown as the two parallel lines. Let us note that the tile is non-planar in reality.

6 Conclusion

We presented the idea of how to use the set of epipolar plane images for correspondence seeking. The structure of EPI allows all image data from the sequence to be employed directly in computation. The main contribution lies in using purely intensity based method on the set of EPIs. The idea works well when the data processed are in accordance with the strict assumptions of Lambertian surface and accurately rectified sequence (synthetic case).

However, it has proven to be difficult to fulfill assumptions of the method in the real case, considering the accuracy level we aim to work at. The useful information extracted from the rectified spatio-temporal volume is disturbed by imperfection of the real measurements. As shown in [5], the inaccurate positioning of the camera has a strong influence. However, even in the real case, the results demonstrate the feasibility of the idea. The application of the stereo using the pairing algorithm [9] suffers from ambiguous matches.

Our outlook is to extend the concept on general (not-rectified) sequence. The structure of a general spatio-temporal volume, relating the image data of the dense sequence, should simplify the correspondence search in such cases. Also occurrence of occlusions can be handled more easily in this framework.

References

1. Robert C. Bolles, Harlyn H. Baker, and David H. Marimont. Epipolar plane image analysis: An approach to determining structure from motion. In *Internation Journal of Computer Vision*, number 1 in 1, pages 7–55, 1987.
2. George T. Chou. A model of figure-ground segregation from kinetic occlusion. In Eric Grimson, editor, *ICCV'95: Proc. 5th IEEE Intl. Conf. on Computer Vision*, pages 1050–1057, Cambridge, Massachusetts, June 1995. IEEE Computer Society Press.
3. Ingemar J. Cox, Sunita L. Higorani, Satish B. Rao, and Bruce M. Maggs. A maximum likelihood stereo algorithm. *Computer Vision and Image Understanding*, 63(3):542–567, May 1996.

4. Pui-Kuen Ho and Ronald Chung. Stereo-motion with stereo and motion in complement. *IEEE Trans. on Pattern Analysis and Machine Intelligence*, 22(2):215–220, February 2000.
5. Martin Matoušek and Václav Hlaváč. Correspondences from epipolar plane images, experimental evaluation. In Boštjan Likar, editor, *Proc. Computer Vision Winter Workshop*, pages 11–18, Bad Aussee, Austria, February 2002. PRIP.
6. Martin Matoušek, Tomáš. Werner, and Václav Hlaváč. Accurate correspondences from epipolar plane images. In Boštjan Likar, editor, *Proc. Computer Vision Winter Workshop*, pages 181–189, Bled, Slovenia, February 2001. Slovenian Pattern Recorgnition Society.
7. Sourabh A. Niyogi. Detecting kinetic occlusion. In Eric Grimson, editor, *ICCV'95: Proc. 5th IEEE Intl. Conf. on Computer Vision*, pages 1044–1049, Cambridge, Massachusetts, June 1995. IEEE Computer Society Press.
8. Sébastien Roy and Ingemar J. Cox. A maximum-flow formulation of the N-camera stereo correspondence problem. In Sharat Chandran and Uday Desai, editors, *ICCV'98: Proc. 6th IEEE Intl. Conf. on Computer Vision*, pages 492–499, Bombai, India, January 1998. IEEE, Narosa Publishing House.
9. Radim Šára. Finding the largest unambiguous component of stereo matching. In Anders Heyden, Gunnar Sparr, Mads Nielsen, and Peter Johansen, editors, *ECCV'02: Proc. 7th European Conf. on Computer Vision*, volume 3, pages 900–914, Copenhagen, Denmark, May 2002. Springer-Verlag.
10. Tomáš Werner, Tomáš Pajdla, and Václav Hlaváč. Correspondence by tracking edges in a dense sequence for image-based scene representation. In Tomáš Pajdla, editor, *Proceedings of the Czech Pattern Recognition Workshop '97*, pages 64–68, Prague, Czech Republic, February 1997. Czech Pattern Recognition Society.

Computing Neck-Shaft Angle of Femur for X-Ray Fracture Detection

Tai Peng Tian[1], Ying Chen[1], Wee Kheng Leow[1], Wynne Hsu[1], Tet Sen Howe[2], and Meng Ai Png[3]

[1] Dept. of Computer Science, National University of Singapore
3 Science Drive 2, Singapore 117543
{tiantaip,leowwk,whsu}@comp.nus.edu.sg
[2] Dept. of Orthopaedics, Singapore General Hospital
Outram Road, Singapore 169608
tshowe@yahoo.com
[3] Dept. of Diagnostic Radiology, Singapore General Hospital
Outram Road, Singapore 169608

Abstract. Worldwide, 30% – 40% of women and 13% of men suffer from osteoporotic fractures of the bone, particularly the older people. Doctors in the hospitals need to manually inspect a large number of x-ray images to identify the fracture cases. Automated detection of fractures in x-ray images can help to lower the workload of doctors by screening out the easy cases, leaving a small number of difficult cases and the second confirmation to the doctors to examine more closely. To our best knowledge, such a system does not exist as yet. This paper describes a method of measuring the neck-shaft angle of the femur, which is one of the main diagnostic rules that doctors use to determine whether a fracture is present at the femur. Experimental tests performed on test images confirm that the method is accurate in measuring neck-shaft angle and detecting certain types of femur fractures.

1 Introduction

Many people suffer from fractures of the bone, particularly the elderly folks. According to the findings of the International Osteoporosis Foundation [1], the lifetime risk for osteoporotic fractures in women is 30% – 40% worldwide, and 13% in men. The number of hip fractures could rise from 1.7 million worldwide in 1990 to 6.3 million by 2050. Most dramatic increase is expected to occur in Asia during the next decades. According to World Health Organization, osteoporosis is second only to cardiovascular disease as a leading health care problem [1].

In practice, doctors and radiologists in the hospitals rely mainly on x-ray images to determine whether a fracture has occured and the precise nature of the fracture. Manual inspection of x-rays for fractures is a tedious and time consuming process. Typically, the number of images containing fractures constitute a small percentage of the total number of images that the radiologists have to scan through. For example, in our test images, only 11% of the femurs are fractured. After looking through many images containing healthy femurs, a tired

N. Petkov and M.A. Westenberg (Eds.): CAIP 2003, LNCS 2756, pp. 82–89, 2003.

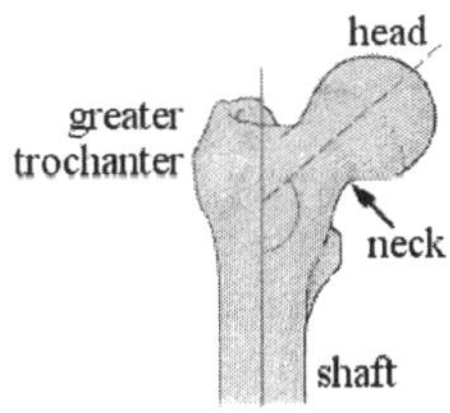

Fig. 1. Neck-shaft angle is the angle made by the shaft axis (solid line) and the neck axis (dashed line) of the femur.

radiologist has been found to miss a fractured femur among the many healthy ones. As some fractures are easier to identify than others, an automated fracture detection system can assist the doctors by performing the first examination to screen out the easy cases, leaving a small number of difficult cases and the second confirmation to the doctors. Automated screening of both healthy and fractured cases can thus relieve some of the labor intensive work of the doctors and help to improve the accuracy of their diagnosis. Therefore, this computer vision application is extremely useful for clinicians and is now feasible because all clinical radiology is going digital. Digital x-ray images are now routinely captured using digital x-ray machines.

Among the various fracture incidents, common hip fractures of the femur account for the largest proportion of fracture cases. One of the main diagnostic rules that doctors use to detect femur fracture is by assessing the distortion of the so-called *neck-shaft angle*, that is, the angle between the shaft and the neck axes (Fig. 1). The neck-shaft angle of a healthy adult femur is about 120 to 130 degrees. A large discrepancy from the healthy neck-shaft angle would indicate a possibility of fracture. Thus, this article focuses on the automated measurement of neck-shaft angle of the femur in an x-ray image and uses the measured angle to determine whether a fracture has occurred.

At first glance, it may seem that automated measurement of neck-shaft angle is a trivial task for a computer. However, it turns out to be far from trivial, especially for fractured femurs. The femoral neck usually appears as a very short segment in an x-ray image. Correct localization of the neck is a very difficult task. For certain types of fractured femurs, the necks are crashed and do not even appear on the x-ray images (Fig. 2(c, d)). To overcome this problem, we define the neck axis to be the axis of symmetry of the 2D contour of the femoral head and neck, and applies an optimization algorithm to determine the best fitting symmetry axis (Section 3).

2 Related Work

So far, we have not come across any published work on the computer automated detection of fractures in x-ray images. The closest related methods used non-visual methods to detect fractures. For example, Ryder et al. analyzed acoustic pulses as they travel along the bone to determine whether a fracture has occurred [2]. Kaufman et al. applied a neural network model to analyze mechanical vibration [3] whereas Singh and Chauhan measured electrical conductivity [4].

Most of the research efforts related to orthopaedics have instead been focused on the detection of osteoporosis (e.g., [5–7]). These methods of detecting osteoporosis usually assume that an area of interest is provided by the operator. So, there is no need to automatically detect the contour of the bones under examination. The image analysis required for the detection of osteoporosis is, therefore, simpler than that for fracture detection.

There are substantial amount of work on the analysis of tubular structures such as blood vessels and lung bronchi. In the analysis of these small structures, it is reasonable to assume certain relationship between image intensity and the position on the structure. For example, the cores method [8] and the ridge detection method [9] have been applied to 2D images to find intensity ridges which correspond to the medial lines of vessels. However, the femur is a large structure with complicated internal structure, which shows up as complex texture patterns in an x-ray image. So, standard method of analyzing tubular structures cannot work on the x-ray images of femurs.

3 Fracture Detection Method

Our method of detecting fractures in the femur consists of three stages: (1) extraction of femur contour, (2) measurement of neck-shaft angle, and (3) classification of femur based on measured neck-shaft angle. The extraction of femur contour in stage 1 is performed using a combination of algorithms, namely Canny edge detection and Hough transform for detecting significant straight line and curve features, and active contour mode (i.e., elastic snake) [10] with Gradident Vector Flow (GVF) method [11] to snap on to the continuous femur contour based on the line and curve features detected. Due to space limitation, this paper will focus on stage 2 (Section 3.1) of the process. Stage 3 will be discussed together with the experimental results (Section 4).

3.1 Measurement of Neck-Shaft Angle

To measure the neck-shaft angle, we have to recover the shaft axis and the neck axis. However, standard algorithms, such as the medial axis transform, are too sensitive to the noise along the contour, and they fail completely to extract the neck axis especially for fractured femur where the neck is crushed and distorted. Instead, a more robust algorithm that exploits the shape of the femur is used.

Computing the Shaft Axis. Note that the contour lines along the femoral shaft are almost parallel. If lines normal to the shaft contours are drawn from one side of the shaft to the opposite side, then the mid-points of the normal lines would be aligned with the shaft axis. We call these normal lines *level lines* as each line denotes a level along the shaft. (Note that our "level lines" are different from the well-known "level set" algorithm.) It turns out that level lines can also be found eminating from the femoral head, passing through the approximate center

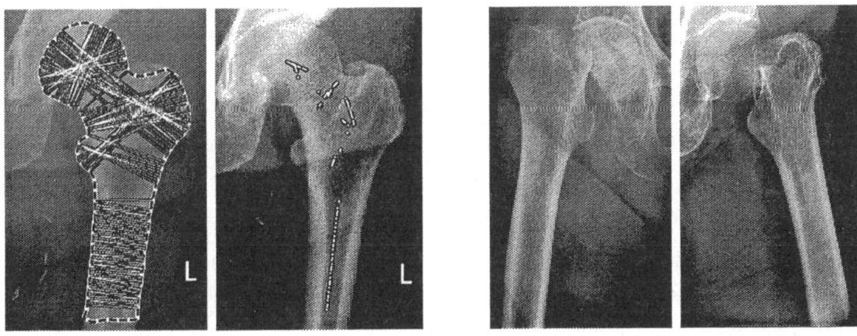

Fig. 2. (a) Level lines found in the femur contour. (b) Mid-points of the level lines at the shaft are oriented along the shaft axis. (c, d) The neck contours are compressed or absent in these fractured femurs.

of the head, and ending at the lower part of the greater trochanter. Whereas the level lines at the shaft are perpendicular to the shaft axis, those at the neck are parallel to the neck axis.

Instead of computing all possible level lines, we compute only those that intersect the snake points. First, the unit normal vector $\mathbf{n}_i$ of snake point $\mathbf{p}_i$ is computed by applying Principal Component Analysis (PCA) on a neighborhood of snake points centered at point $\mathbf{p}_i$. The first eigenvector of PCA would be tangential and the second eigenvector normal to the contour at point $\mathbf{p}_i$. Then, a line $l(\mathbf{p}_i, \mathbf{p}_j)$ joining points $\mathbf{p}_i$ an $\mathbf{p}_j$ is a level line if it is parallel to the normals $\mathbf{n}_i$ and $\mathbf{n}_j$, i.e.,

$$|\mathbf{n}_i \cdot \mathbf{n}_j| \approx \frac{|(\mathbf{p}_i - \mathbf{p}_j) \cdot \mathbf{n}_i|}{|\mathbf{p}_i - \mathbf{p}_j|} \approx \frac{|(\mathbf{p}_i - \mathbf{p}_j) \cdot \mathbf{n}_j|}{|\mathbf{p}_i - \mathbf{p}_j|} \approx 1 \ . \tag{1}$$

In the current implementation, two orientations $\mathbf{v}_1$ and $\mathbf{v}_2$ are considered similar i.e., $|\mathbf{v}_1 \cdot \mathbf{v}_2| \approx 1$ if $|\mathbf{v}_1 \cdot \mathbf{v}_2| \geq 0.98$.

Figure 2(a) shows an example of the level lines found in the femur contour. The level lines at the shaft can be easily isolated from the other level lines because they are short and are located at the lower half of the image. Given the shaft level lines, the mid-points of the level lines are computed (Fig. 2b) and a straight line is fitted through the mid-points to obtain the shaft axis.

Computing the Neck Axis. Figure 2(a) shows that there are several bundles of level lines within the femoral head and neck region. An adaptive clustering algorithm similar to that in [12] is applied to cluster the level lines into bundles according to two criteria: (1) the lengths of the lines, and (2) the mid-points of the lines. Level lines with similar lengths and whose mid-points are close to each other are clustered into a bundle. The algorithm is adaptive and it can compute the appropriate number of bundles required. After clustering, the bundle with the largest number of long level lines is chosen and the mean direction of the level lines is computed to approximate the orientation of the neck axis.

The above algorithm works well for healthy femur. However, for fractured femur whose neck is crushed, the contours of the neck may not even exist (Fig. 2(c, d)), complicating the problem of determining the neck axis. To obtain a more accurate estimation of the neck axis, an optimization algorithm is applied to compute the axis of symmetry of the femoral head and neck given the initial estimate obtained using the algorithm described above. Before computing the axis of symmetry, the femur contour is first smoothed with a 1-D Gaussian filter to remove noise along the contour. The σ value of the Gaussian should be large enough to produce smooth contour at the head and neck regions but not too large that the shape of the contour is severely distorted. In the current implementation, a σ value of 5 is used.

The general idea of computing axis of symmetry is to find a line through the femoral head and neck such that the contour of the head and neck coincides with its reflection about the line. Given a snake point $\mathbf{p}_k$ along the head contour, the mid-point $\mathbf{m}_i$ along the line joining snake points $\mathbf{p}_{k-i}$ and $\mathbf{p}_{k+i}$ is computed. That is, we obtain a midpoint for each pair of snake points on the opposite sides of $\mathbf{p}_k$. Then, a line l_k is fitted through the midpoints $\mathbf{m}_i$ to obtain a candidate axis of symmetry. If the contour is perfectly symmetrical, and the correct axis of symmetry is obtained, then each contour point $\mathbf{p}_{k-i}$ is exactly the mirror reflection of $\mathbf{p}_{k+i}$. So the fitting error E_k for l_k is

$$E_k = \frac{1}{n} \sum_{i=-n/2}^{n/2} \left| \mathbf{p}_{k+i} - \mathbf{p}'_{k-i} \right| \tag{2}$$

where $\mathbf{p}'_{k-i}$ is the reflection of $\mathbf{p}_{k-i}$ about l_k. E_k indicates how well is l_k an axis of symmetry. The best axis of symmetry is a line l_t that minimizes E_k. This procedure can be completed in $O(n^2)$ time where n is the number of snake points along the head and neck contour.

In the current implementation, the extent of the neck-head contour is empirically determined to be 40 snake points each to the left and right of a given snake point on the femoral head. The start position of the optimization algorithm is the snake point that is closest to the approximate neck axis computed in the previous stage using the level-line method. 20 snake-point positions to the left and right of the start position are considered in finding the best-fitting position and orientation of the neck axis.

4 Experimental Results

63 images each with a left and a right femur were used as the training images. The neck-shaft angles of these 126 femurs were computed and the decision threshold that minimized the number of detection error was determined (Fig. 3). This threshold was determined to be 116°, i.e., femurs with neck-shaft angles smaller than 116° were classified as fractured. This threshold value was used for classifying the other 160 test images containing a total of 320 femurs.

Table 1 summarizes the classification performance on the training and testing data. 94.4% of the training images and 92.5% of the testing images are correctly classified.

Figures 4 and 5 illustrate sample femurs that are correctly classified.

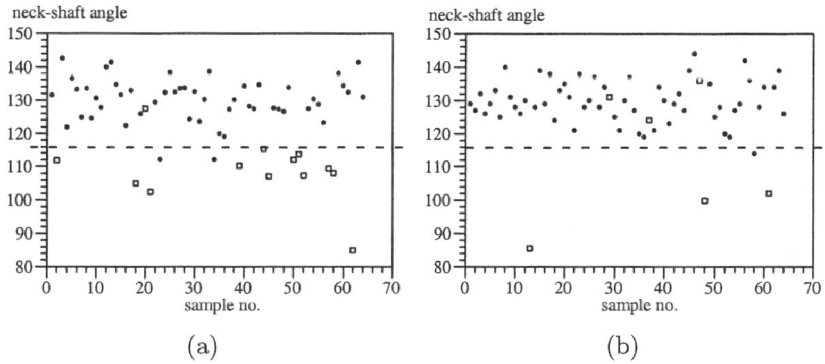

Fig. 3. Measured neck-shaft angles of training images. (a) Left femurs. (b) Right femurs. Dots: healthy femurs, squares: fractured femurs, dashed line: decision threshold.

Table 1. Summary of training and testing results.

	training			testing		
classified	left femur	right femur	both	left femur	right femur	both
correctly as fractured	12	3	15	8	7	15
correctly as healthy	48	56	104	134	147	281
sub-total	60 (95.2%)	59 (93.7%)	119 (94.4%)	142 (88.8%)	154 (96.3%)	296 (92.5%)
incorrectly as fractured	2	1	3	5	1	6
incorrectly as healthy	1	3	4	13	5	18
sub-total	3 (4.8%)	4 (6.3%)	7 (5.6%)	18 (11.3%)	6 (3.8%)	24 (7.5%)
Total	63	63	126	160	160	320

Visual inspection of the wrongly classified femurs indicate two main sources of error in the training and testing data. First, some fractured femurs are missed by the algorithm because there is no significant change of neck-shaft angle. These fractured femurs can be divided into two main categories:

1. Some fractures at the femoral necks cause the femoral heads to be displaced along the neck axes. As a result, there are no significant changes of neck-shaft angles though the shapes of the femoral head and neck regions are changed.
2. Some fractures are very slight cracks of the bones, and others are complete breakage of the femoral necks without significant displacements of the femoral heads. In these cases, there are no significant changes of both the neck-shaft angles and the shapes of the femoral head and neck regions.

These fractures can only be detected using other criteria and methods.

The second source of error is due to the misclassification of healthy femurs as fractured. These cases can be categorized into two types:

1. The femoral shafts are either very short or completely missing in the x-ray images. As a result, it is impossible to compute the shaft axes correctly.
2. The x-ray images are taken at unusual pose causing the shapes of the femurs to be distorted.

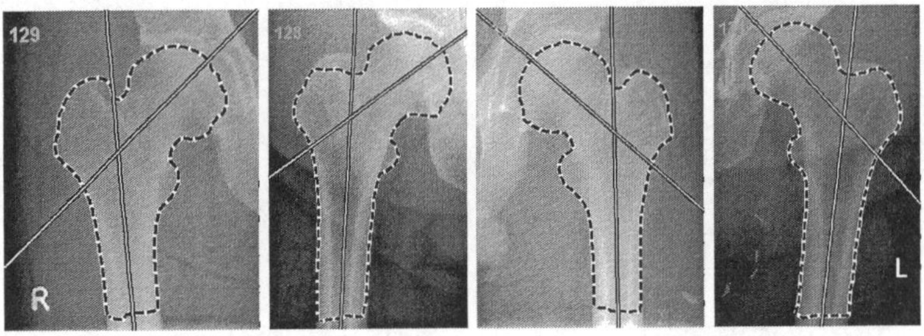

Fig. 4. Femurs correctly classified as healthy.

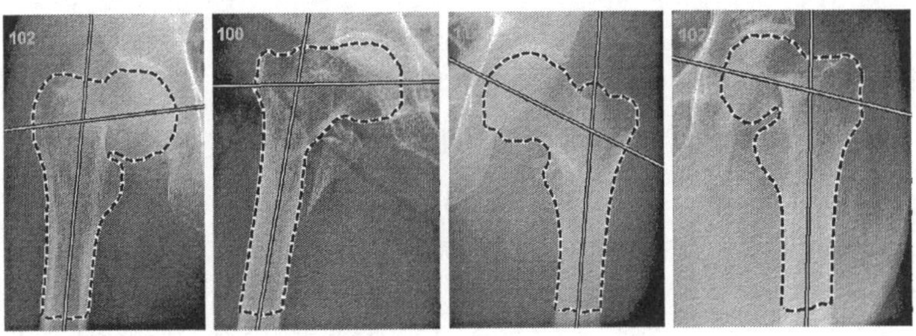

Fig. 5. Femurs correctly classified as fractured.

Table 2. Summary of misclassifications.

wrongly classified as healthy		
type	training	testing
change in shape	2	6
no change in shape	2	12

wrongly classified as fractured		
type	training	testing
no shaft	0	3
unusual pose	2	1
program failure	1	2

The first problem can be solved using methods that do not need the shaft to make correct classifications, and the second can be solved only with 3D models.

The above two sources of complications account for the majority of the misclassifications (Table 2). Only one femur among the training images and two among the testing images are wrongly classified due to the failure of the algorithm in computing the correct neck-shaft angle. That is, the algorithm fails to compute the correct neck-shaft angle for only 0.7% of the samples.

5 Conclusion

A method of computing neck-shaft angle for detecting femur fracture is presented in this paper. Given the contour of a femur, level lines that are perpendicular to the contour are computed. The mid-points of the level lines at the shaft are aligned with the shaft axis. The largest bundle of long level lines at the head gives an approximation of the neck axis. Given this approximation, an optimzation algorithm is applied to find the best-fitting axis of mirror reflection of the head-neck contour. This axis of mirror reflection is the best-fitting neck axis. The neck shaft angle can now be computed from the neck and shaft axes. Test results show that the algorithm correctly computed the neck-shaft angles for 99.3% of the training and testing images. Application of the computed neck-shaft angle for fracture detection achieved an accuracy of 94.4% for training images and 92.5% for testing images. We are investigating other fracture detection methods to complement the current method and to improve the detection accuracy.

Acknowledgment

This research is supported by NMRC/0482/2000.

References

1. IOF: The facts about osteoporosis and its impact. International Osteoporosis Foundation, http://www.osteofound.org/ press_centre/fact_sheet.html (2002)
2. Ryder, D.M., King, S.L., Olliff, C.J., Davies, E.: A possible method of monitoring bone fracture and bone characteristics using a non-invasive acoustic technique. In: Proc. Int. Conf. on Acoustic Sensing and Imaging. (1993) 159–163
3. Kaufman, J.J., Chiabrera, A., Hatem, M., Hakim, N.Z., Figueiredo, M., Nasser, P., Lattuga, S., Pilla, A.A., Siffert, R.S.: A neural network approach for bone fracture healing assessment. IEEE Engineering in Medicine and Biology **9** (1990) 23–30
4. Singh, V.R., Chauhan, S.K.: Early detection of fracture healing of a long bone for better mass health care. In: Proc. Annual Int. Conf. of IEEE Engineering in Medicine and Biology Society. (1998) 2911–2912
5. Laugier, P., Padilla, F., Camus, E., Chaffai, S., Chappard, C., Peyrin, F., Talmant, M., Berger, G.: Quantitative ultrasound for bone status assessment. In: Proc. IEEE Ultrasonics Symposium. (2000) 1341–1350
6. Matani, A., Okamoto, T., Chihara, K.: Evaluation of a trabecular structure using a multiresolution analysis. In: Proc. Annual Int. Conf. of IEEE Engineering in Medicine and Biology Society. (1998) 632–633
7. Tascini, G., Zingaretti, P.: Automatic quantitative analysis of lumbar bone radiographs. In: Proc. IEEE Nuclear Science Symposium and Medical Imaging Conference. (1993) 1722–1726
8. Furst, J.D., Pizer, S.M.: Marching optimal-parameter ridges: An algorithm to extract shape loci in 3D images. In: Proc. Int. Conf. on Medical Image Computing and Computer-Assisted Intervention (LNCS 1496). (1998) 780–787
9. Guo, D., Richardson, P.: Automatic vessel extraction from angiogram images. In: IEEE Conf. on Computers in Cardiology. (1998) 441–444
10. Kass, M., Witkin, A., Terzopoulos, D.: Snakes: Active contour models. Int. Journal of Computer Vision **1** (1987) 321–331
11. Xu, C., Prince, J.L.: Gradient vector flow: A new external force for snakes. In: Proc. IEEE Conf. on Computer Vision and Pattern Recognition. (1997)
12. Leow, W.K., Li, R.: Adaptive binning and dissimilarity measure for image retrieval and classification. In: Proc. IEEE CVPR. (2001)

Illuminance Flow

Sylvia C. Pont and Jan J. Koenderink

Universiteit Utrecht, Department of Physics & Astronomy
Princetonplein 5, 3584 CC Utrecht, The Netherlands
s.c.pont@phys.uu.nl

Abstract. In an image of a scene illuminated by a single source, such as a landscape in sun light, the light field is approximately the same at all locations in the scene. This is apparent from the common direction of cast shadows, the common polarity of illuminated and shaded parts of convex objects, and so forth. Here we concentrate upon the statistics of texture due to 3D surface corrugations. We show that patches of roughly uniform texture reveal the local direction of the illumination. In this way we are able to map the global structure of the "illuminance flow" through simple image processing techniques. We propose a theoretical treatment of texture due to illuminaton of rough surfaces and we present experiments on real textures and scenes. The illuminance flow is a robust indicator of the light field and thus reveals global structure in a scene. It is an important entity for many subsequent inferences from the image such as shape from shading.

1 Introduction

In many scenes the light field [4] is approximately the same at all locations in the scene. This is the case, for instance, for an open landscape under illumination by the sun. In the latter case all objects are being illuminated by a collimated uniform beam of a single direction. This is important because it induces a similar structure in the illumination of entirely disparate objects all over the scene. In this respect the light field can be compared to optical flow [5]. In the case of optical flow the flow of all stationary objects is due to a common motion, namely the motion of the observer. In the case of the light field the light field is the same at all object locations because it is due to a single source. Thus objects at various locations in a scene can be compared in the certainty that at least some important parameters (motion in the case of optical flow, the source in the case of the light field) are common to both.

The light field can be of various nature. E.g., the light field due to an overcast sky is quite different from that due to the sun. The former is roughly a hemispherical diffuse, the latter a collimated beam. In a collimated beam the shading [6] is due to shadow (occlusion of the source) and the attitude effect due to Lambert's cosine law. In a diffuse beam the shading is due to a complicated combination of vignetting, that is partial occlusion of the (extended) source by the object itself, and the attitude effect. In either case image texture is generated through the shading of rough surfaces [2]. This image texture is "polarized" according to the local direction of illumination. For instance a small protrusion will have a light

N. Petkov and M.A. Westenberg (Eds.): CAIP 2003, LNCS 2756, pp. 90–97, 2003.

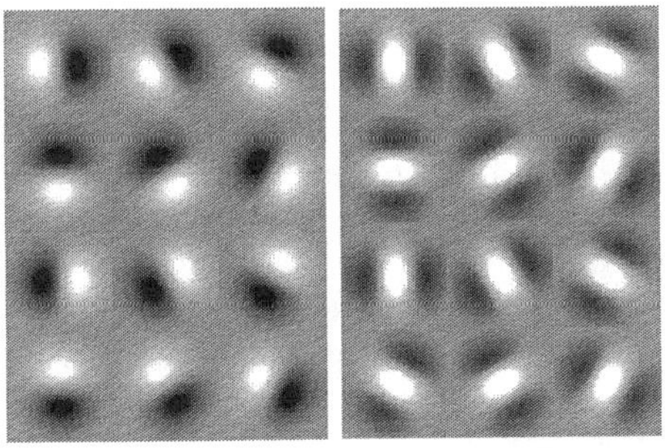

Fig. 1. At the left a set of "edge detectors", at the right a set of "line detectors". These operators suffice to compute the illuminance flow via the squared gradient or Hessian.

side facing the source, and a dark side facing away from the source, thus giving rise to a "dipole" illumination pattern in the image. The same observation holds for a small depression, except for the fact that the dipole orientation is reversed. For a rough surface one has a statistical mixture of protrusions and depressions, so the dipole patterns cancel on the average. The second order statistics of the illuminance is due to the autocorrelation of the dipoles and since the autocorrelation is insensitive to the orientation of the dipoles, it doesn't average out. The second order statistics of illuminated rough surfaces shows a pronounced orientation that is determined by the local illumination direction, which can be estimated computationally and visually for globally flat samples [8]. For globally curved samples the estimated local illumination direction will vary over the surface due to the variation of the fiducial surface normal with respect to the global illumination direction. We propose to refer to this field of orientations as the "illuminance flow".

The illuminance flow is written all over the image of a scene. It can be computed via the local second order image statistics. Indeed, either the square of the gradient or the Hessian of the image intensity reveals the illuminance flow. In a computation one has two essential parameters, namely the scale at which the differentiation is performed ("edge detectors" in the case of the gradient, "line detectors" in the case of the Hessian, see figure 1) and the scale of the averaging of the squared activity of the differential operators. The local computation yields two essential parameters, namely the orientation of the illumination (the azimuth modulo 180°) and a confidence measure. The confidence is zero if the texture is isotropic (no illumination direction indicated) and one if the illumination direction is fully determinate. We can prove (see below) that for an illuminated Gaussian random surface the confidence can be as high as 0.5.

2 Theory: Image Texture for Obliquely Illuminated Gaussian Random Surfaces

The "Gaussian random surface" is determined by the probability density function of the height in a Monge patch[11] description (i.e., the deviation $h(\mathbf{r})$ from a reference plane $\mathbf{r}(x, y)$) and by the autocorrelation function (or, equivalently, the powerspectrum) of the heights. The height $h(\mathbf{r})$ is assumed to be a stationary random function. The probability density function of the heights is assumed to be normal (hence the name). We consider only the case of isotropic surfaces here, thus the autocorrelation function is assumed to be rotationally symmetric. We assume shallow relief, that is to say, $\|\nabla h\|^2 << 1$ throughout, and thus we may omit any but the lowest order terms in the derivation. Since we eventually average over the ensemble the lowest order of interest is two (order zero is the average illuminance and and thus irrelevant, whereas first order terms will average out).

For such surfaces all spatial partial derivatives of the height are likewise normally distributed. The average product of any pair of derivatives is given by

$$\langle\frac{\partial^{p+q}h}{\partial x^p \partial y^q}\rangle\langle\frac{\partial^{r+s}h}{\partial x^r \partial y^s}\rangle = \frac{\partial^{p+r+q+s}h}{\partial x^{p+r} \partial y^{q+s}}\rho(\mathbf{0}) = (-1)^{\frac{1}{2}(p+r+q+s)} m_{p+r,q+s},$$

where the autocorrelation function $\rho(\mathbf{r})$ and the power spectrum $E(\mathbf{k})$ are a Fourier transform pair. The moments $m_{u,v}$'s are defined by

$$m_{u,v} = \int \mathrm{d}\mathbf{k}\, k_x^u k_y^v E(\mathbf{k})$$

i.e., the $m_{u,v}$'s are the moments of the power spectrum of the height. From the symmetry of the autocorrelation function we see immediately that $m_{r,s}$ is zero for $r+s$ odd. Thus odd and even partial derivatives are mutually uncorrelated.

For the isotropic case the m's can be written in terms of the "circular moments" of the powerspectrum

$$m_{u,v} = M_{u+v} \int_0^{2\pi} \cos^u \vartheta \sin^v \vartheta \, \mathrm{d}\vartheta, \qquad \text{where} \qquad M_p = \int_0^{\infty} 2\pi k \mathrm{d}k \,(k^p E(k)).$$

These circular moments depend on the particular shape of the autocorrelation function, but we will see that this dependency cancels out in the case of immediate interest here. The statistical properties of Gausian random surfaces are well understood. The theory is due to Longuet-Higgins[9], see also[1].

For our purposes we will need the means of products of partial derivatives of the height up to the third order. Notice that the illumination of a local surface element depends on the first order derivatives of the height. We need to study the gradient of the illuminance (involving the second order derivatives of the height) and the Hessian (matrix of second order derivatives) of the illumination, which involves the third order derivatives of the height. We conveniently apply the established fact that the covariance matrix of the second order derivatives (h_{xx}, h_{xy} and h_{yy}) is

$$\begin{pmatrix} \langle h_{xx}^2\rangle & \langle h_{xx}h_{yy}\rangle & \langle h_{xx}h_{yy}\rangle \\ \langle h_{yy}h_{xx}\rangle & \langle h_{yy}^2\rangle & \langle h_{yy}h_{xy}\rangle \\ \langle h_{xy}h_{xx}\rangle & \langle h_{xy}h_{yy}\rangle & \langle h_{xy}^2\rangle \end{pmatrix} = \frac{M_4}{8}\begin{pmatrix} 3 & 1 & 0 \\ 1 & 3 & 0 \\ 0 & 0 & 1 \end{pmatrix}$$

whereas that of the third order derivatives (h_{xxx}, h_{xxy}, h_{xyy} and h_{yyy}) is

$$\begin{pmatrix} \langle h_{xxx}^2 \rangle & \langle h_{xxx}h_{xxy} \rangle & \langle h_{xxx}h_{xyy} \rangle & \langle h_{xxx}h_{yyy} \rangle \\ \langle h_{xxy}h_{xxx} \rangle & \langle h_{xxy}^2 \rangle & \langle h_{xxy}h_{xyy} \rangle & \langle h_{xxy}h_{yyy} \rangle \\ \langle h_{xyy}h_{xxx} \rangle & \langle h_{xyy}h_{xxy} \rangle & \langle h_{xyy}^2 \rangle & \langle h_{xyy}h_{yyy} \rangle \\ \langle h_{yyy}h_{xxx} \rangle & \langle h_{yyy}h_{xxy} \rangle & \langle h_{yyy}h_{xyy} \rangle & \langle h_{yyy}^2 \rangle \end{pmatrix} = \frac{M_6}{16} \begin{pmatrix} 5\,0\,1\,0 \\ 0\,1\,0\,1 \\ 1\,0\,1\,0 \\ 0\,1\,0\,5 \end{pmatrix}$$

Of course any pair consisting of a second and a third order derivative is uncorrelated. This is essentially all the statistics we will need in order to analyze the statistics of the illuminance distribution for stationary, isotropic, random Gaussian surfaces, illuminated obliquely with a collimated beam of radiation.

When the illumination direction is given by $\{\vartheta, \varphi\}$ (ϑ the elevation of the source, φ its azimuth), then the illuminance of the surface around a point $\mathbf{r}$ is simply

$$I(\mathbf{r}) = I_0 \frac{\{-h_x, -h_y, 1\}}{\sqrt{1 + h_x^2 + h_y^2}} \cdot \{\cos\vartheta\cos\varphi, \cos\vartheta\sin\varphi, \sin\vartheta\}$$

By direct differentiation we find the gradient and the Hessian of the illumination. The average values of both quantities are zero: In order to arrive at relevant measures we need the second order statistics. Thus we need to find the average values of the tensor product $\mathbf{G_2} = \nabla I \otimes \nabla I$ (known as the "structure tensor"; ∇I denotes the gradient vector) and of $\mathbf{H_2} = \nabla^2 I \nabla^2 I^T$ (where $\nabla^2 I$ denotes the Hessian matrix of $I(\mathbf{r})$). This involves the averages of products of pairs of derivatives (because of the shallow relief assumption we may neglect terms with powers higher than two), these values can immediately be obtained from the covariance matrix given above. The result is proportional with the circular moments M_4 (for the case of the gradient) and M_6 (for the case of the Hessian). Notice that, though we only go to second order derivations of the illuminance, this implies derivatives up to the third order in the heights. We end up with (perhaps miraculously) identical results for the case of the gradient and the Hessian: In either case the angular dependence is given by the symmetric matrix

$$\mathbf{S} = \begin{pmatrix} 2 + \cos 2\varphi & \sin 2\varphi \\ \sin 2\varphi & 2 - \cos 2\varphi \end{pmatrix}$$

Since $\mathbf{S}$ does not depend upon the circular moments, the result is independent of the particular shape of autocorrelation function of the heights, only the Gaussian amplitude distribution is required. The eigenvectors of $\mathbf{S}$ are $\{\cos\varphi, \sin\varphi\}$ with eigenvalue 3 and $\{\cos(\varphi + \pi/2), \sin(\varphi + \pi/2)\}$ with eigenvalue 1. The so called "coherence" of the structure tensor $\mathbf{S}$, that is to say $c = (\lambda_1^2 - \lambda_2^2)/(\lambda_1^2 + \lambda_2^2)$, has the value 0.8, indicating a strong orientational bias. The eigenvector for the largest eigenvalue is thus very well defined. From the expression we see that it points in (or away from) the direction of illumination.

3 Examples

As a baseline experiment we used an example "plaster" from the Curet data base [3]. This is a globally flat sample with random, 3D surface structure. The sample was locally matte white, but due to the oblique illumination the image is

Fig. 2. The "plaster" item from the Curet database. The sample is viewed $-11.25°$ from the normal direction, the illumination direction is from the left, altitude of the source $56.25°$.

highly textured (see figure 2). It is clearly visible that this texture is not isotropic (although the 3D surface structure is!), but polarized due to the illumination direction, which is easily seen to be from the left (or the right [8]) in this figure. The image (figure 2) was rotated in Adobe Photoshop© over 30°, 60° and 90°. We ran our algorithm on these images as a test (see figure 3). We ran both the $\mathbf{G_2}$ (upper row of figures) and the $\mathbf{H_2}$ (lower row) version of the algorithm, using a ROI of four times the width of the differential operators. Thus each estimate is based upon roughly 16 independent samples. In these figures the axes ratio of the ellipses denotes the confidence, the orientation of the major axis the orientation of the illuminance. In this case the confidence level is close to the one predicted for Gaussian random surfaces. As is evident from figure 3 this is amply sufficient to estimate the local illuminance orientation.

In another experiment we used a photograph of a 3D object with a rough surface. We painted an orange matte white and photographed it in a hemispherical diffuse beam (see figure 4) and a uniform collimated beam (see figure 5). In these figures one sees both the effect of global shading as well as a texturing due to photometrical effects on the meso scale (remember that the orange was painted a uniform white: All texture is due to shading). The hemispherical diffuse beam hits the object from the top. In this case the whole object is differentially shaded (due to vignetting of the source by the global object and the attitude effect). The texture contrast is least near the top and highest near the dark pole [10]. In figure 4 we show results for both the $\mathbf{G_2}$ (top row) and the $\mathbf{H_2}$ (bottom row) algorithm, for three different ROI sizes. The ROI diameters are 1, 4 and 16 times the diameter of the differential operators. Notice that the smallest ROI leads to very noisy results (although the illuminance flow is noticeable in the Hessian results), but results in a robust measurement in the case of a ROI diameter as small as 4, whereas the ROI diameter of 16 is clearly larger than necessary. In the latter case boundary artefacts are clearly visible. The flow lines are apparently vertical straight lines in this case.

In the case of the collimated illumination (see figure 5; this figure has the same general organization as figure 4). The collimated beam made an angle of

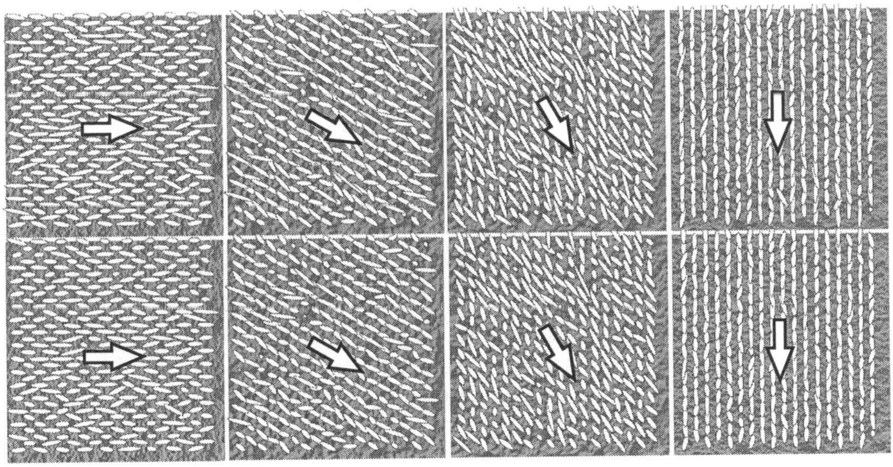

Fig. 3. From left to right the plaster example from figure 2 rotated by 0°, 30°, 60° and 90°. The images were 512 × 512 pixels. The derivative operators were Gaussian derivatives with a width of two pixels. The second order statistics was computed over a ROI of 4 pixels. In the top row we show the results for the $\mathbf{G_2}$, in the bottom row the results for the $\mathbf{H_2}$ algorithm. The arrow indicates the actual direction of illumination.

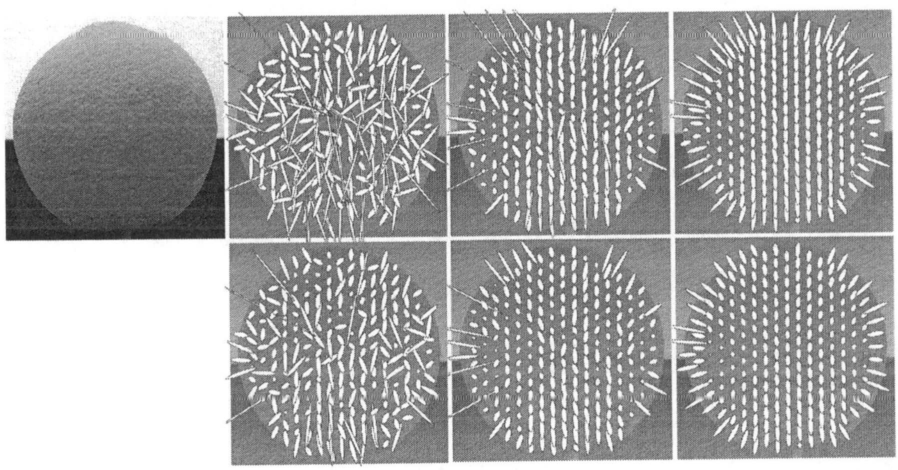

Fig. 4. Results for an orange, painted matte white and illuminated by a hemispherical diffuse beam from the top. The original image at top left measures 512 × 512 pixels. Results are shown for the $\mathbf{G_2}$ (top row) and $\mathbf{H_2}$ (bottom row) algorithm. The ROI size was varied from a diameter of 2 pixels (left), 8 pixels (center) and 32 pixels (right column).

30° with the viewing direction. The point at which the beam hits the object from the normal direction is clearly visible (the brightest point of the image). Notice that the flow lines apparently radiate out from this point (very evident in the case of the ROI diameter 4) and that the confidence, while zero near the singular

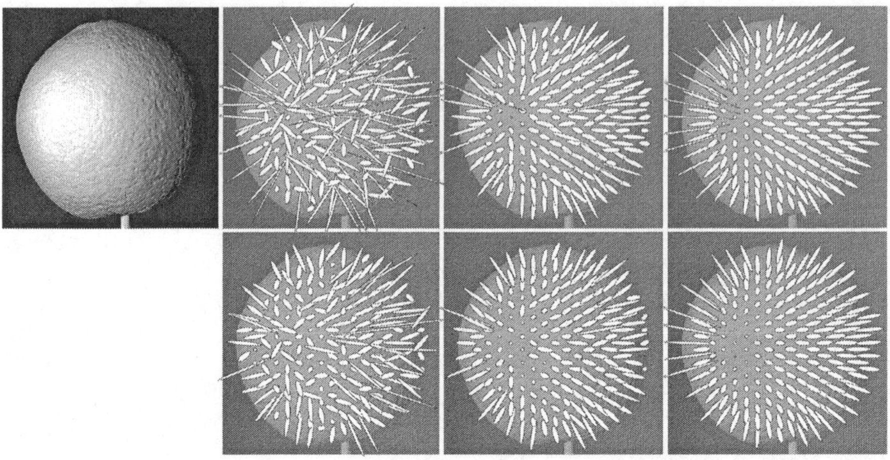

Fig. 5. Results for an orange, painted matte white (same object as in figure 4) and illuminated by a uniform, collimated beam. The direction of illumination subtended an angle of 30° with the viewing direction. This figure has the same general organization as figure 4.

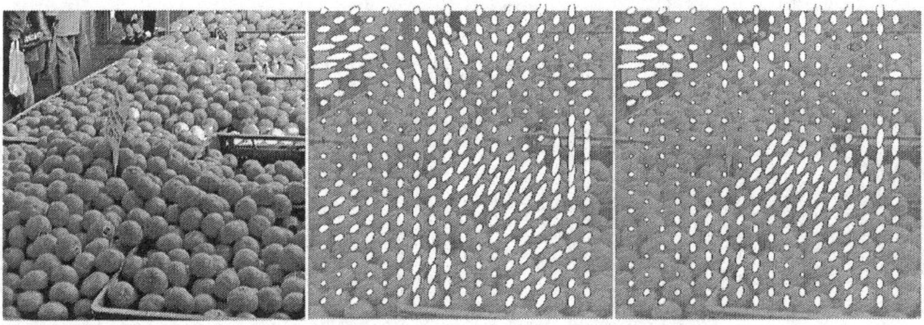

Fig. 6. Results for a scene at a market. The original image at top left measures 512×512 pixels. Results are shown for the $\mathbf{G_2}$ (middle figure) and $\mathbf{H_2}$ (right figure) algorithm. The ROI size was 32 pixels, the derivative operators were Gaussian derivatives with a width of 8 pixels.

point, increases steadily as the local normal deviates more from the direction of the beam.

In figure 6 we show the results for a natural, complicated scene: a fruit stall at a market. The figure shows the original image, the illuminance flow field derived by means of the $\mathbf{G_2}$ and by means of the $\mathbf{H_2}$ algorithm, from left to right. In this scene various parts of space are in different light field regimes. With minor adjustment of the parameters, we obtain robust results even for complicated images like this.

4 Conclusions

We have shown that the "illuminance flow" in the image of a scene can be computed robustly. The information is contained in the second order image statistics of either the square of the gradient or the Hessian. A computation involves two essential parameters, namely the scale of the operators ("edge detectors" for the gradient, "line detectors" for the Hessian) and the size of the ROI. The computations yield the local illuminance orientation along the local surface (azimuth direction modulo 180°) and a confidence. We find that for many rough surfaces the confidence is close to that predicted for a Gaussian random surface, even though most natural 3D textures are far from Gaussian.

References

1. Berry, M. V., Hannay, J. H. (1977). Umbilic points on Gaussian random surfaces, J.Phys.A: Math.Gen. 10, 1809-1821.
2. Chantler, M., Schmidt, M., Petrou, M. and G. McGunnigle (2002). The effect of illuminant rotation on texture filters: lissajous's ellipses, in: A. Heyden et al (Eds), ECCV2002, NLNCS2352, pp. 289–303, Heidelberg, Springer.
3. *Columbia–Utrecht Reflectance and Texture Database.* `http://www.cs.columbia.edu/CAVE/curet`
4. Gershun, A.: (1939). The Light Field, transl. by P. Moon and G. Timoshenko, J.Math.Phys. 18(51).
5. Gibson, J. J. (1950). The perception of the visual world, Houghton Mifflin, Boston.
6. Horn, B. K. P., Brooks, M. J. (1989). Shape from Shading. The M.I.T. Press, Cambridge, Massachusetts.
7. Koenderink, J. J., van Doorn, A. J. (1992). Generic neighborhood operators, IEEE Transactions on Pattern Analysis and Machine Intelligence 14, 597-605.
8. Koenderink, J. J., van Doorn, A. J., Kappers, A. M. L., te Pas, S. F., Pont, S. C. (2003). Illumination direction from texture shading, accepted by JOSA A.
9. Longuet-Higgins, M. S. (1956). The statistical analysis of a random moving surface, Phil.Trans.R.Soc. A 249, 321-64.
10. Pont, S.C. Koenderink, J. J. (2002). Bidirectional texture contrast function, in: A. Heyden et al (Eds), ECCV2002, LNCS 2353, pp. 808-822, Heidelberg, Springer.
11. Spivak, M. D. (1970-1975). A comprehensive introduction to differential geometry, Publish or Perish, Boston, Massachusetts, 5 Vols.

Rough Surface Correction and Re-illumination Using the Modified Beckmann Model

Hossein Ragheb* and Edwin R. Hancock

Department of Computer Science, University of York, York YO1 5DD, UK
{hossein,erh}@cs.york.ac.uk

Abstract. In this paper we illustrate the use of the Beckmann model for surface analysis problem in computer vision. The Beckmann model is a physical model that describes the reflectance of light from rough surfaces. The parameter of the model is the surface slope, or ratio of the surface roughness to the correlation length. We show how this parameter may be estimated using pairs of surface images, subject to different illumination directions. With the parameter to hand, the Beckmann model may be used to perform photometric correction, and hence shape-from-shading may be applied to the rough surfaces. This model may also be used to re-illuminate the recovered surface. We present experiments to illustrate the utility of the method for each of these tasks.

1 Introduction

Reflectance modelling is a task of pivotal importance in the analysis of image data by computer. For instance, in computer graphics it is necessary for generating realistic images of synthetic scenes. In computer vision, on the other hand, reflectance models form the basis of shape analysis techniques such as shape-from-shading and photometric stereo, and may also be used to estimate the physical properties of materials from passively sensed image data [4].

Roughness is a measure of the statistical variation in the topographic relief of a surface [2]. The most important, most frequently used, and perhaps the least well understood statistical surface parameter is the root-mean-square (RMS) roughness, σ. Unfortunately, the specification of a height distribution and the RMS roughness is insufficient to discriminate between surfaces with different length scales. Such surfaces may, however, be distinguished on the basis of their correlation function. The RMS slope which is the ratio of the RMS roughness to the correlation length is even more dependent on the measuring instrument than is the RMS roughness [2, 3].

In this paper we focus on using physics-based reflectance models which apply to rough surfaces. The effect of variable surface roughness is to alter the relative contributions of specular and diffuse reflectance to the total reflectance. The Torrance-Sparrow model [8] is among the most popular models which aims to incorporate the effect of roughness into the specular reflectance. The calculation

* Sponsored by the university of Bu-Ali Sina, Hamedan, Iran.

N. Petkov and M.A. Westenberg (Eds.): CAIP 2003, LNCS 2756, pp. 98–106, 2003.

of reflectance is based on geometrical optics, and is hence applicable when the surface irregularities are much larger than the wavelength of incident radiation. Nayar et al. [5] showed that under these conditions the Torrance-Sparrow model approximates the physical optics model developed by Beckmann [1]. One of the shortcomings of these aforementioned models is that they ignore the effect of roughness on the diffuse reflectance component. However, this effect has been incorporated into the model developed by Oren-Nayar [10]. The major drawback of both the Torrance-Sparrow model and the Oren-Nayar model is that they rely on the assumption of surface isotropy. Based on this observation, Ginneken et al. [4] have recently developed a model that can be used to predict reflectance from isotropic rough surfaces that have both specular and diffuse components.

In this paper we turn to the physics-based model described by Beckmann as an alternative to the methods mentioned above. The starting point for this model of scattering from rough surfaces is the Helmholtz-Kirchhoff diffraction integral [6]. Unfortunately, this model is limited to the case of scattering close to the specular direction. However, Vernold and Harvey [9] have recently modified the Beckmann model to overcome this limitation and have extended the model to large angles of both incidence and scatter. In this paper, we show how this improved model can be used to analyse rough surfaces.

2 A Realistic Reflectance Model

Beckmann has used the Kirchhoff scatter theory to develop reflectance models that can be applied to surfaces with different scales of roughness, i.e. slightly-rough, moderately-rough and very-rough surfaces. These models also give different scattering behaviour when the form of the surface correlation function is varied. For very-rough surfaces, Beckmann has explored the effects of a Gaussian or and exponential correlation function for very-rough surfaces. However, since it gives a better fit to measured surface data for very-rough surfaces, here we confine our attention to the exponential correlation function [2, 6]. Under this restriction, the diffuse reflectance function which results from Beckmann's model is

$$I(\theta_i, \theta_r, \phi_r) = 2\pi F^2 / A v_z^2 m^2 [1 + v_{xy}^2 / (v_z^2 m^2)]^{3/2} \tag{1}$$

The model depends on both the incidence and the reflectance angles. In Eq. (1), θ_i and $\phi_i = \pi$ are the zenith and azimuth angles of the illuminant and θ_r and ϕ_r are the zenith and azimuth angles of the viewer (on local tangent planes). Also, $v_x = k(\sin\theta_i - \sin\theta_r \cos\phi_r)$, $v_y = -k(\sin\theta_r \sin\phi_r)$, $v_z = -k(\cos\theta_i + \cos\theta_r)$, $v_{xy}^2 = v_x^2 + v_y^2$ and $k = 2\pi/\lambda$, where λ is the wavelength. The physical properties of the surface are captured by the surface slope $m = \sigma/T$ which is given in terms of the surface roughness σ and the correlation length T. This equation may also be used to model the total reflectance since the specular contribution is negligible for very-rough surfaces. The geometrical factor $F(\theta_i, \theta_r, \phi_r)$ is given in [1]. However, in this paper we use an alternative geometrical function suggested by Vernold-Harvey [9] which is described in the next section. The parameter A is the area of a plane sheet on which the scattering coefficient is defined [1].

2.1 Modified Beckmann-Kirchhoff Model

The Beckmann model fails for large incidence angles and large scattering angles. To overcome this problem, Vernold and Harvey [9] have recently developed a modification of the Beckmann model that gives reasonable agreement with experimental scattering data at both large angles of incidence and at large scatter angles. The main point considered by Vernold-Harvey in modifying the Beckmann model is as follows. Beckmann [1] has claimed that for rough reflective surfaces, it is the local surface normal direction that is of primary importance in determining the geometrical factor F. Beckmann has indicated that the local surface normal at each point on a rough surface varies as the surface is traversed, and does not coincide with the mean surface normal. Although Vernold and Harvey [9] agree with the observation that the local and mean surface normals do not coincide, they do not agree that a new obliqueness factor must be derived using the local surface normal. Instead, they claim that it is appropriate and sufficiently accurate to use the mean surface normal when modelling rough surfaces. In the Vernold-Harvey modification [9], the geometrical factor (F^2) used in the Beckmann model is replaced by the cosine of the incidence angle which comes from Lambert's cosine reflectance law. They have applied their modification to that variant of the Beckmann model which assumes a Gaussian correlation function for the surface. Here, we apply their modification to the Beckmann model for very-rough surfaces with an exponential correlation function. In this paper, we refer to this variant of the Beckmann-Kirchhoff model as the B-K model Eq. (1). Hence, by replacing the term F^2 with $\cos(\theta_i)$ in Eq. (1), the modified B-K model is

$$I(\theta_i, \theta_r, \phi_r) = 2\pi \cos(\theta_i)/Av_z^2 m^2[1 + v_{xy}^2/(v_z^2 m^2)]^{3/2} \qquad (2)$$

3 Using the Model in Computer Vision

In this section we investigate three important tasks for the modified B-K model in computer vision. The first of these is to show how the slope parameter can be estimated using a pair of images acquired under different illumination directions. The second task involves performing photometric correction to recover the Lambertian reflectance component. This allows the surface normals to be recovered using shape-from-shading. The third task is that of re-illuminating the surface using the field of recovered surface normals.

3.1 Surface Slope Estimation

For very-rough surfaces, we can use the B-K model to estimate the surface slope $m = \sigma/T$. Caron et al. [3] have recently computed the angle of RMS slope $\theta_0 = \pi/2 - \tan^{-1}(\sqrt{2}m)$. They have shown that for incidence angles smaller than θ_0, the reflectance predictions delivered by the Kirchhoff theory are reliable. Once an estimate of m is to hand, we can fit the B-K reflectance model to the data. Such a model is potentially useful since it allows photometric correction to be performed and the Lambertian reflectance to be recovered (Section 3.2).

Our technique for estimating the surface slope $m = \sigma/T$ is as follows. First, we collect images with two different angles of illumination. Using the two images we make measurements of the reflectance I_1, I_2 at a corresponding point on the surface. This is straightforward in practice since we keep the surface fixed and move the light-source direction. Let the two different angles of incidence be $\theta_i = \theta_1$ and $\theta_i = \theta_2$. In both images the planar surface is perpendicular to the viewing direction, i.e. $\theta_r = 0$. To deal with problems of local texture arising from the surface roughness, we average the intensities over local neighborhoods. Although the use of two different wavelengths is possible, here we use only one wavelength λ. Under these illumination conditions and from Section 2 we can write $v_{xy}(\theta_i) = (2\pi/\lambda)\sin(\theta_i)$ and $v_z(\theta_i) = (2\pi/\lambda)[1 + \cos(\theta_i)]$. We use the average quantities to compute the ratio I_1/I_2. From Eq. (2) we can write

$$\frac{I_1}{I_2} = \frac{\cos(\theta_1)v_z^2(\theta_2)}{\cos(\theta_2)v_z^2(\theta_1)} \left\{ \frac{1 + v_{xy}^2(\theta_2)/[v_z^2(\theta_2)m^2]}{1 + v_{xy}^2(\theta_1)/[v_z^2(\theta_1)m^2]} \right\}^{3/2} \tag{3}$$

Hence, the estimate of the surface slope $m = \sigma/T$ is

$$m = \left\{ \frac{1}{K-1} \left[\frac{v_{xy}^2(\theta_2)}{v_z^2(\theta_2)} - K \frac{v_{xy}^2(\theta_1)}{v_z^2(\theta_1)} \right] \right\}^{1/2} \tag{4}$$

where $K = \{[\cos(\theta_2)v_z^2(\theta_1)I_1]/[\cos(\theta_1)v_z^2(\theta_2)I_2]\}^{2/3}$. By substituting one of the two pairs (I_1, θ_1) or (I_2, θ_2) together with λ and m into Eq. (2), an estimate of the parameter A can also be obtained. The estimates of A and m can be used in Eq. (2) to compute absolute values of the scattered intensity.

3.2 Photometric Correction for Shape-from-Shading

With estimates of the surface slope parameter m, we may use the reflectance model of Eq. (2) to perform photometric correction and hence recover the Lambertian reflectance component $\cos(\theta_i)$ from the raw diffuse reflectance. With corrected Lambertian reflectance to hand, we can apply conventional shape-from-shading techniques to recover shape (surface normals) information.

Model as a Function of Incidence Angle. For some problems in computer vision, such as shape-from shading, it is the incidence angle behavior of the reflectance models that is of primary interest. Hence, here we derive a formula for the specific case when the angle between the light-source and the viewing directions is small (i.e. $\theta_i = \theta_r$ and $\phi_r = \pi$). When the light-source and viewing directions are identical, the maximum fraction of the surface is illuminated and visible. Under these conditions, by replacing the quantities $v_{xy} = v_x = 2k\sin(\theta_i)$ and $v_z = -2k\cos(\theta_i)$ in Eq. (2), the modified B-K model for this case is

$$I(\theta_i) \approx \lambda^2/8\pi A m^2 \cos(\theta_i)[1 + (\tan^2(\theta_i)/m^2)]^{3/2} \tag{5}$$

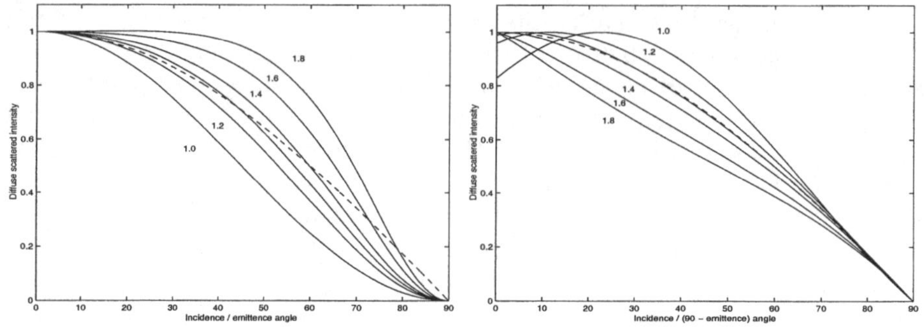

Fig. 1. Diffuse intensity by the modified B-K model vs incidence angle (degrees) for $m = 1.0, 1.2, .., 1.8$ compared to Lambertian model (dashed): for $\theta_i = \theta_r$ and $\phi_r = \pi$ (left), and, for $\theta_i = \pi/2 - \theta_r$ and $\phi_r = 0$ on surfaces with parabolic shapes (right).

In Fig. 1, we show the behaviour of the modified B-K model. The different curves in each panel show the diffuse intensity I as a function of the incidence angle θ_i for different values of surface slope m. The dashed curve in each panel is the prediction of Lambert's cosine law. The plots are for a wavelength of $700nm$. The left-hand panel is for the case where $\theta_i = \theta_r$ and $\phi_r = \pi$, while there is no restriction for the surface shape (Eq. 5). From the different curves it is clear that the larger the surface slope, the higher the diffuse intensity. In particular, for $m = 1.6$ and $m = 1.8$, the brightening effects are very intense compared to the Lambertian reflectance curve. In the right-hand panel, the light-source direction is perpendicular to the viewing direction while the surface is assumed to be parabolic (i.e. one of zero Gaussian curvature) with the minimum (zero) curvature direction along the y axis. Hence $\theta_i = \pi/2 - \theta_r$ and $\phi_r = 0$. The equation for this specific case can be derived from Eq. (2). Here, by contrast with the left-hand panel, as the surface slope decreases from $m = 1.8$ to $m = 1.0$, then so the diffuse intensity increases. Also, the maximum intensity moves away from $\theta_i = 0$ and occurs when the incidence angle is close to $\theta_i = 25°$. This behaviour also means that the reflectance function for this case is not invertible.

Lookup Table Solution. We can not recover the Lambertian reflectance component $\cos(\theta_i)$ directly from the modified B-K model since the analytic solution of the resulting equation is intractable. Hence, we adopt a lookup table approach as a practical alternative. To do this we tabulate $\cos(\theta_i)$ as a function of the computed diffuse intensity I from Eq. (5). Since the Lambertian reflectance I_L is proportional to $\cos(\theta_i)$, this allows us to approximate I_L using the measured intensity I. In practice, the larger the number of incidence angles tabulated $(0 \leq \theta_i \leq \frac{\pi}{2})$, the more precise the correction process. Once an approximate value of the surface slope is estimated $(m = m_0)$ using the technique outlined in Section 3.1, the lookup table is computed using Eq. (5).

Under conditions in which the object is illuminated in the viewing direction, the modified B-K model is amenable to our lookup table approach since, like

Lambert's law, the brightness decreases monotonically with increasing incidence angle (Fig. 1.a). As a result the reflectance function appearing in Eq. (5) is injective and invertible. In other words, each measured brightness value is related to a single value of incidence angle and hence to a single Lambertian reflectance value. Note also, that for other illumination geometries where the reflectance is directly dependent on both the incidence and reflectance angles, the lookup table approach is not usable. We have used a similar approach in [7] for Lambertian correction using the reflectance models by Wolff, Nayar and Oren [10].

3.3 Re-illumination

Once the corrected Lambertian intensity is to hand, then the surface normal directions or the surface height may be recovered by applying shape-from-shading to the corrected image. Here we use the method of Worthington and Hancock [11]. This is a geometric technique which constrains the surface normals to fall on a cone whose axis points in the light-source direction and whose apex angle is the inverse cosine of the corrected Lambertian reflectance. Once the accurate surface normals are in hand, re-illuminating object surfaces is a straightforward task. Since at each point on the surface, the local surface normal and the viewing direction are known (and fixed), we can use the modified B-K model (Eq. 2) to compute the diffuse reflectance for any light-source direction.

4 Experiments

The images used in our experiments have been captured using an Olympus 10E camera. Each surface has been imaged under controlled lighting conditions in a darkroom. The objects have been illuminated using a single collimated tungsten light-source whose wavelength is approximately $700nm$. The light-source direction is recorded at the time the images are captured. The objects used in our experiments are a terra-cotta bear and a cylindrical sandpaper.

Estimating Surface Slope. Our first experiment is to estimate surface slope m for rough surfaces composed of terra-cotta and sandpaper. As mentioned in Section 3.1, first we need to measure two mean-intensity values I_1 and I_2 for two different angles of incidence θ_1 and θ_2. One way to do this is to use a small approximately planar patch on each object surface. However, if such planar patches can not be found, one may use a planar surface of the same material and roughness. For $\theta_1 = 30°$, $\theta_2 = 45°$ and $\lambda = 700nm$, we measure the mean-intensity ratio for the sandpaper $I_1/I_2 = 1.1004$ and for the terra-cotta $I_1/I_2 = 1.1147$. Hence, using Eq. (4) the surface slope is estimated $m = 1.41$ for the sandpaper and $m = 1.29$ for the terra-cotta.

Photometric Correction. The estimate of surface slope m allows us to fit the modified B-K model to the reflectance data for each object. The next experiment is to use the raw images of the terra-cotta bear and the cylindrical

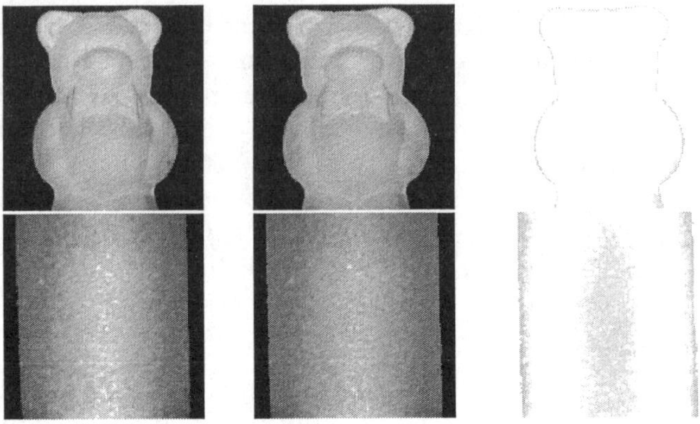

Fig. 2. Photometric correction on images of two objects with rough surfaces: raw images (left), corrected Lambertian images (centre) and difference images (right).

sandpaper together with the fitted models and perform photometric correction. Both raw images are captured under almost identical light-source and viewing directions. For each surface, we construct a lookup table, as described in Section 3.2, using the model of Eq. (5) and the value of surface slope m estimated for each surface. We present the results in Fig. 2. Here, the left-hand panels show diffuse raw images (I), the centre panels show the recovered Lambertian images (I_L) and the right-hand panels show the difference images ($|I - I_L|$). Here, the darker the point in a difference image, the larger the difference. We use the absolute function to show both positive and negative differences. It can be seen in Fig. 1.a that for $m = 1.3$ (terra-cotta bear) if $\theta_i < 45°$ then $I_L < I$, whereas for $m = 1.4$ (sandpaper), if $\theta_i < 60°$ then $I_L < I$. Although the correction process has an effect at almost every location on each surface, the differences are most marked where the inclination of the object surface is steepest. Note, also, that the photometric correction increases the contrast of the surface detail.

Re-illumination. Each corrected Lambertian image obtained in the last experiment can be used as an input image to shape-from-shading. Here we use the method of Worthington and Hancock [11]. The needle maps of the surface normals obtained using this method are shown in Fig. 3. Here the left-hand panels show the surface normals extracted from raw images whereas the centre panels show those extracted from Lambertian images. The fields of difference between these surface normals are shown in the right-hand panels. Here, the complex surface structure of the terra-cotta bear, is clearly visible. For the sandpaper, the symmetrical shape of the cylinder is nicely preserved. We now turn our attention to the effects of photometric correction process on the surface normal directions. The changes in surface normal directions occur both in the zenith angles and in the azimuth angles. The zenith angles change slightly and there is no scatter, i.e. the data points trace out a curve. Because when $\theta_i = \theta_r$, at each point on the surface, the zenith angle is equal to the arc-cosine of the brightness. Most of the

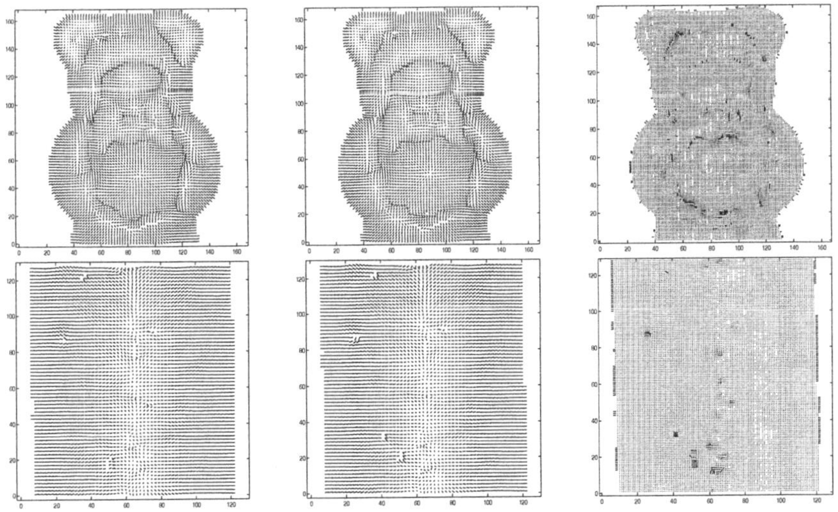

Fig. 3. Needle maps of the surface normals obtained by applying shape-from-shading to the raw images (left) and to the corrected Lambertian images (centre) shown in Fig. 2; The field of difference between these two needle maps (right).

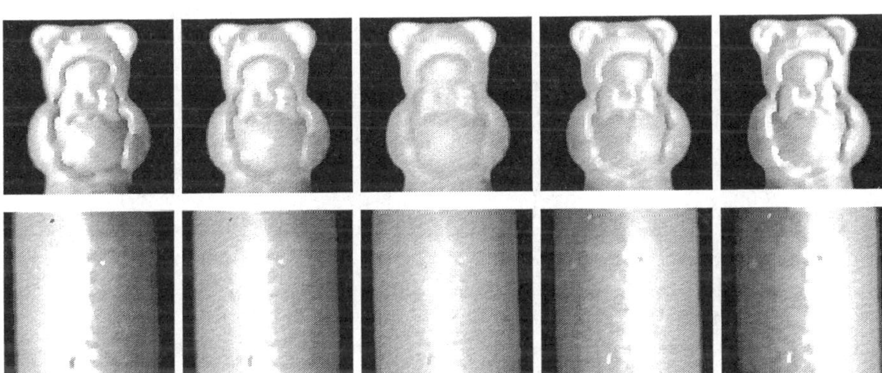

Fig. 4. Images computed using the modified B-K model by re-illuminating surface normals (Fig. 3) from 5 directions: $(18°, -90°)$, $(9°, -90°)$, $(0, 0)$, $(9°, 90°)$ and $(18°, 90°)$.

azimuth angles, however, vary significantly and do exhibit scatter. The reason for this is that the surface normals are free to rotate about the cones subject to smoothness constraints. Note that shape-from-shading results in small differences in azimuth angle near object limbs since the boundary condition constrains surface normal to be perpendicular to the occluding boundary.

Using the surface normals extracted from the recovered Lambertian images (Fig. 3, centre), we experiment with re-illuminating surface objects from five different directions. At each point on the surface, we compute the diffuse reflectance using the modified B-K model (Eq. 2). In Fig. 4, we show re-illuminations of the surface normals extracted from the two objects under study when the light-source direction is re-positioned. Here we move the direction of lighting from -18 degrees to +18 degrees to the image plane normal, in the horizontal direction. The images reflect the underlying shape of the object in a consistent manner.

5 Conclusions

In this paper, we have shown how the modified B-K model for very-rough surfaces can be used for surface slope estimation, photometric correction and re-illumination. The surface slope is estimated using a pair of images acquired under different illumination directions. Lambertian images are recovered from raw images using lookup tables for the objects illuminated nearly in the viewing direction. Once the Lambertian image is recovered, then the surface normals may be recovered using a Lambertian shape-from-shading method. Finally, we show that photometric correction improves the accuracy of surface normals, and that by re-illuminating these surface normals we obtain realistic images.

References

1. P. Beckmann and A. Spizzochino, *The Scattering of Electromagnetic Waves from Rough Surfaces,* Pergamon, New York, 1963.
2. J.M. Bennett and L. Mattsson, *Introduction to Surface Roughness and Scattering,* Optical Society of America, Washington, D.C., pp. 38-56, 1989.
3. J. Caron, J. Lafait and C. Andraud, "Scalar Kirchhoff's Model for Light Scattering from Dielectric Random Rough Surfaces", *Optics Communications*, vol. 207, pp. 17-28, 2002.
4. B.V. Ginneken, M. Stavridi and J.J. Koenderink, "Diffuse and Specular Reflectance from Rough Surfaces", *Applied Optics*, vol. 37, no. 1, pp. 130-139, 1998.
5. S.K. Nayar, K. Ikeuchi and T. Kanade, "Surface Reflection: Physical and Geometrical Perspectives", *TPAMI*, vol. 13, no. 7, pp. 611-634, 1991.
6. J.A. Ogilvy, *Theory of Wave Scattering from Random Rough Surfaces,* Adam Hilger, Bristol, 1991.
7. H. Ragheb and E.R. Hancock, "Lambertian Correction for Rough and Shiny Surfaces", *Int'l Con. on Image Processing*, vol. 2, pp. 553-556, 2002.
8. K.E. Torrance and E.M. Sparrow, "Theory for Off-Specular Reflection from Roughened Surfaces", *J. Opt. Soc. Am. A*, vol. 57, pp. 1105-1114, 1967.
9. C.L. Vernold and J.E. Harvey, "A Modified Beckmann-Kirchoff Scattering Theory for Non-paraxial Angles", *Scattering and Surface Roughness, Proc. SPIE*, vol. 3426, pp. 51-56, 1998.
10. L.B. Wolff, S.K. Nayar and M. Oren, "Improved Diffuse Reflection Models for Computer Vision", *Int'l J. Computer Vision*, vol. 30, no. 1, pp. 55-71, 1998.
11. P.L. Worthington and E.R. Hancock, "New Constraints on Data-closeness and Needle-map consistency for SFS", *TPAMI*, vol. 21, no. 11, pp. 1250-1267, 1999.

Towards a Real Time Panoramic Depth Sensor

Peter Peer and Franc Solina

University of Ljubljana
Faculty of Computer and Information Science
Tržaška 25, SI-1000 Ljubljana, Slovenia
{peter.peer,franc.solina}@fri.uni-lj.si

Abstract. Recently we have presented a system for panoramic depth imaging with a single standard camera. One of the problems of such a system is the fact that we cannot generate a stereo pair of images in real time. This paper presents a possible solution to this problem. Based on a new sensor setup simulations were performed to establish the quality of new results in comparison to results obtained with the old sensor setup. The goal of the paper is to reveal whether the new setup can be used for real time capturing of panoramic depth images and consequently for autonomous navigation of a mobile robot in a room.

1 Introduction

Real time panoramic depth imaging is an issue that is not well covered in the literature. There have been attempts or discussions [5] about it, but nothing has been done in practice so far, at least not by using mosaicing concept, i.e. the multiperspective panoramas.

In [6] we have presented a system for capturing panoramic depth images with a single standard camera. A stereo pair of images is captured while the camera rotates around the center of the system in a horizontal plane. The motion parallax effect which enables the reconstruction can be captured because of the offset of the cameras' optical center from the systems' rotational center. The camera is moving around the rotational center in angular steps corresponding to one vertical pixel-column of the captured standard image. A symmetrical pair of panoramic stereo images are generated so that one column on the right side of the captured image contributes to the left eye panoramic image and the symmetrical column on the left side of the captured image contributes to the right eye panoramic image. This system however cannot generate panoramic stereo pair in real time. To illustrate this fact, we can write down the following example from practice: if the system builds a panoramic stereo pair from standard images with resolution of 160×120 pixels, using a camera with the horizontal view angle $\alpha = 34°$, it needs around 15 minutes to complete the task.

Generally mosaic-based procedures for building panoramic images [1–3, 5–9] can be marked as non-central (we are not dealing with only one center of projection), they do not execute in real time and they give high resolution results. Thus the procedures are not appropriate for capturing dynamic scenes. The

N. Petkov and M.A. Westenberg (Eds.): CAIP 2003, LNCS 2756, pp. 107–115, 2003.

main advantage of this procedures over other panoramic imaging systems (like catadioptric systems [10]) is the ability to generate high resolution results. But high resolution results are essential for effective depth recovery based on the stereo effect.

In the next section, the geometry of the system presented in [6] is revealed. In Sect. 3 we indicate how the time needed for the generation of a symmetric panoramic stereo pair can be dramatically reduced and in Sect. 4 we go even further and explain how we can achieve real time execution. Sect. 5 presents the depth reconstruction equation for the new setup. The epipolar constraint is discussed in Sect. 6. The evaluation of results is given in Sect. 7. We end the paper with conclusions in Sect. 8.

2 Geometry of the System

Let us begin this section with a description of the old sensor geometry [6].

The geometry of the system for creating multiperspective panoramic images is shown in Fig. 1. Panoramic images are then used as an input to create panoramic depth images. Point C denotes the system's rotational center around which the camera is rotated. The offset of the camera's optical center from the rotational center C is denoted as r describing the radius of the circular path of the camera. The camera is looking outward from the rotational center. The optical center of the camera is marked with O. The column of pixels that is sewn in the panoramic image contains the projection of point P on the scene. The distance from point P to point C is the depth l and the distance from point P to point O is denoted with d. θ is the angle between the line defined by point C and point O and the line defined by point C and point P. In the panoramic image the horizontal axis presents the path of the camera. The axis is spanned by μ and defined by point C, a starting point O_0 where we start capturing the panoramic image and the current point O. With φ we denote the angle between the line defined by point O and the middle column of pixels of the image captured by the physical camera looking outward from the rotational center (this column contains the projection of the point Q), and the line defined by point O and the column of pixels that will be mosaiced in panoramic image (this column contains the projection of the point P). Angle φ can be thought of as a reduction of the camera's horizontal view angle α.

The first idea about how to capture a stereo pair quicker is to generate panoramic images from wider vertical stripes instead of just one column.

3 Building Panoramic Images from Wider Stripes

This task is by all means much faster, but at the same time we have to make a compromise between the speed of the capturing task and the quality of the stereo pair. First of all, the wider the stripes are, the more obvious are the stitches between the stripes in the panoramic image. But the real problem arises from the fact that we are not correcting the radial distortion of the cameras' lens. As will be shown in experimental results (Sect. 7), we were satisfied with

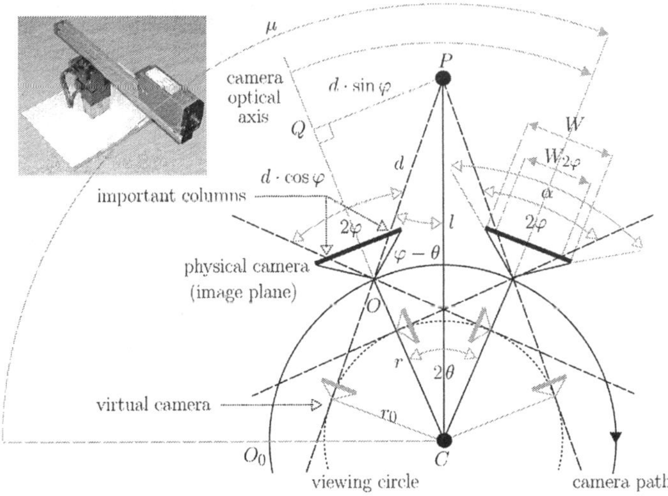

Fig. 1. Geometry of our system (old sensor setup) for constructing multiperspective panoramic images. Note that a ground-plan is presented; the viewing circle extends in 3D to the viewing cylinder. The optical axis of the camera is kept horizontal. In the small photograph the hardware part of the system is shown

the result when we used the stripe which was 14 columns wide and we think that it represents a good compromise. This statement is naturally highly related to the camera that we are using. The horizontal view angle of the camera is 34°, which means that 14 columns represents the angle of approximately 3°. In this case the building process takes around a minute.

3.1 Property of Using Stripes

If we observe the panoramic image built from stripes closely, we can notice that the image is not perfect. In this case we are not referring to stitches nor radial distortion. These problems are present, but are not too disturbing. Another problem can be noticed on close objects on the scene, which have a nice texture on them (like text). In such a case we can see that some points on the scene are not captured (Fig. 2). Of course this is partly because of the fact that we are dealing with the images, which are discrete (for an instance: we cannot take a half of a pixel), but if we take a look at the geometry of the system, we can see that this is not the only reason. If we consider two successive steps of the system, we can see that the stripes that contribute to the panoramic image do not cover all the scene.

We can write one more conclusion in regard to this property. Namely, the wider is the stripe, more scene points are not captured in the panoramic image (Fig. 2). And this holds regardless of the position of the stripe in the captured image. Naturally, by using columns we achieve best possible result (Fig. 2), though still not perfect, since the described property still holds, but is not so obvious.

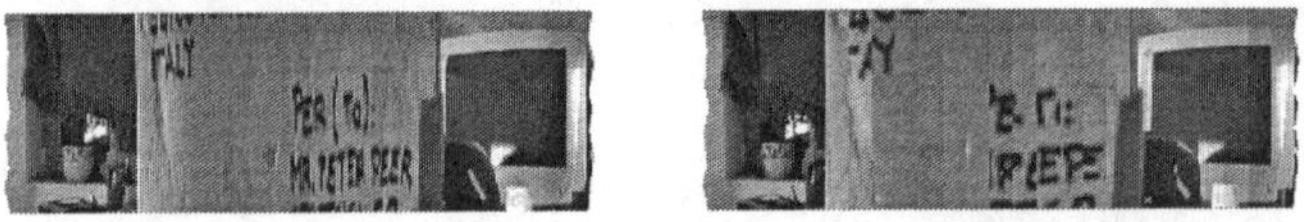

Fig. 2. The wider is the stripe, more distant are the scene points from the center of rotation that are not captured in the panoramic image: the left panoramic image was built from columns, while the right panoramic image was built from stripes (stripe was 14 columns wide). Note how very distant scene points are well captured in both examples and how some nearby scene points (text on the box) are not captured in the second example

4 Achieving Real Time

The idea for a real time panoramic sensor is actually very simple. In our old system [6] the panoramic image is build by means of moving the standard camera for a very small angle along a predefined circular path. If we could have a camera on each position on the circular path, we could build the panoramic image in real time. But unfortunately in practice we cannot put so many cameras so close together (with respect to a reasonable size of radius r). If we build a panoramic image from captured images with resolution of 160×120 pixels, then we have to put the cameras with the horizontal view angle $\alpha = 34°$ approximately 0.2° apart from each other and we need 360/0.2=1800 cameras.

In the case when we use stripes, the presented numbers get more reasonable. A 14 column stripes suggest that the cameras would be approximately 3° apart from each other and we would need 120 cameras to cover the whole circular path. If we use a camera with a wider horizontal view angle (e.g. $\alpha = 90°$), we need less cameras (e.g. 45). The new sensor does not need any moving parts, which means that we are not dealing with mechanical vibrations nor are we limited with the radius of the circle on which the cameras are fixed. The last statement about the radius enables us to make the sensor out of standard cameras that are available on the market.

5 Reconstruction

By following the sinus law for triangles, we can simply write the equation for the depth l as (Fig. 1):

$$l = \frac{r \cdot \sin\varphi}{\sin(\varphi - \theta)} \ . \tag{1}$$

This equation holds if we do the reconstruction based on the symmetric pair of stereo panoramic images built from one pixel column of the captured image.

But when we use the stripes, we have to adopt the equations according to the new building process. In this case we take symmetric stripes instead of symmetric columns from the captured image. While the column was defined by the angle φ, the stripe is defined by two such angles: $\varphi_{\min}$ and $\varphi_{\max}$. On the

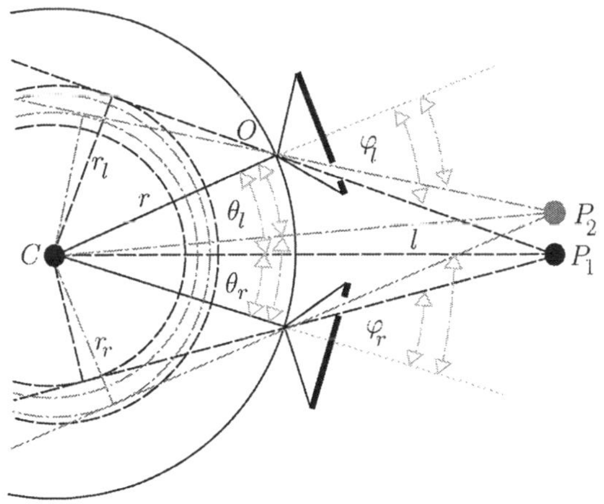

Fig. 3. Angles θ_l and θ_r are related to angles φ_l and φ_r as presented in Eq. 4. Here the relationship is illustrated for two scene points

left eye panoramic image we can assign the angle φ_l to each pixel within the stripe: $\varphi_{\min} \leq \varphi_l \leq \varphi_{\max}$. After finding the corresponding point on the right eye panoramic image, we can evaluate the angle φ_r in the same manner, according to the position of the corresponding pixel within the stripe: $\varphi_{\min} \leq \varphi_r \leq \varphi_{\max}$. Now let us assume that we can still calculate the angle θ as in [6] (see the next section to clear the issue of why we can assume this):

$$2\theta = dx \cdot \theta_0 \ , \tag{2}$$

where dx is the absolute value of the difference between x coordinates of the corresponding points in the left eye panoramic image and in the right eye panoramic image, while θ_0 is the angle corresponding to one pixel column of the captured image and consequently the angle for which we have to move the robotic arm if we build the panoramic images from only one column of the captured image. Using analogy for this equation and having in mind that we are building the panoramic images from stripes, we can write the following equation (Figs. 1 and 3):

$$2\theta = \theta_l + \theta_r \ . \tag{3}$$

When we use one column instead of stripes then $\theta_l = \theta_r$ (Fig. 1), but this is not necessary true if we use stripes. In general these two values are different, but the property following from the equation

$$\frac{\theta_l}{\theta_r} = \frac{\varphi_l}{\varphi_r} \tag{4}$$

shows that the ratio of these two values is related to the angles φ (Fig. 3). The bigger φ_l gets, the bigger gets the corresponding θ_l. Now we can simply express θ_r and θ_l from Eqs. (2), (3) and (4) as:

$$\theta_r = \frac{dx \cdot \theta_0}{(1+\frac{\varphi_l}{\varphi_r})} \ , \qquad \theta_l = dx \cdot \theta_0 - \theta_r \ .$$

We know that bigger φ brings bigger accuracy of the reconstruction process [6]. And since we would like to achieve the best accuracy possible, we take bigger φ from the two possible values (φ_l and φ_r) and associated θ and calculate the depth estimation using Eq. (1).

6 Epipolar Constraint

In the previous section we assumed that we can calculate the angle θ using Eq. (2). This equation holds if we do the reconstruction based on a symmetric pair of stereo panoramic images, which are made from one pixel column of the captured image. In this case we know that the epipolar lines are corresponding rows of the panoramic image [6, 9].

The stripe is composed of columns, each of them with a different angle φ. This basically means that we are dealing in fact with non-symmetric cases, for which the epipolar lines are different from corresponding rows. But if we look at the situation from another view point, we can establish the following: We are using symmetric stripes to build a stereo pair of panoramic images. If we lower the resolution of the captured image, we transform the stripe into a column. The symmetric stripes would become symmetric columns and we could again use the rows of the panoramic image as epipolar lines. The same conclusion can be drawn from the property of the viewing circle, which gets thicker if we use a stripe instead of a column.

7 Experimental Results

Fig. 4 shows some results of our new system. On the bottom image an example of the left eye stereo panoramic image is given. Symmetric stereo panoramic pair was build from stripes determined by $2\varphi_{\text{max}} = 29.75°$ and $2\varphi_{\text{min}} = 24.225°$. The stripe was 14 columns wide. The whole process was simulated (by rotating one standard camera) using radius $r = 30$ cm and the camera with the horizontal view angle $\alpha = 34°$.

For this image a sparse range image was calculated, which is presented in the middle image in Fig. 4. The sparse depth image was build by first detecting vertical edges in panoramic images. This information is normally essential for robot navigation. Edges were derived by filtering the panoramic images with the Sobel filter for searching the vertical edges [4, 5]. We searched only for the correspondences of these feature points on the input panoramic images. All results were generated by using normalized correlation technique [4] with a correlation window of size $(2n + 1) \times (2n + 1)$, $n = 4$. We searched for corresponding points only on the panoramic image row which was determined by the epipolar geometry. We also used back-correlation procedure [4] and the information about the confidence in estimated depth [4], which we get from the normalized correlation estimations. In this way we increase the confidence in estimated depths. Black

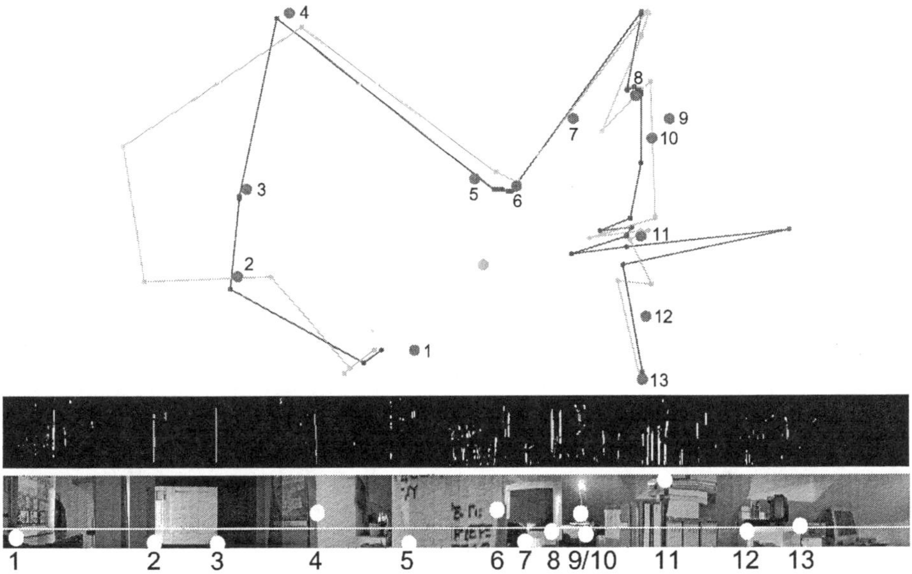

Fig. 4. The top image is a ground-plan showing the results of the reconstruction process based on the 85th row of the depth image (the middle image) from stereo pair built from stripes (*the lighter outline*) and only one column (*the darker outline*) of the captured images. The bottom image shows the reconstructed row and the features on the scene for which we measured the actual depth by hand. For orientation, the distance to the dot marked 1 is 63.2 cm

color marks the points on the scene with no depth estimation associated. Otherwise, the nearer the point on the scene is to the rotational center of the system, the lighter the point appears in the depth image.

Since it is hard to evaluate the quality of generated depth images, we present a reconstruction of the room from the generated depth image on the top image in Fig. 4. Now we are able to evaluate the quality of the generated depth image and consequently the quality of the system.

The result of the (3D) reconstruction process is a ground-plan of the scene. The following properties can be observed in Fig. 4: Big dark dots denote features on the scene for which we measured the actual depth by hand. A big light dot near the center of the reconstruction shows the center of our system. Small dots are reconstructed 3D points on the scene. Lines between small dots denote links between two successively reconstructed 3D points. The darker small points and lines were gained from panoramic images built from only one column of each captured image ($2\varphi = 29.9625°$). The lighter small points and lines were gained from panoramic images built from stripes. The result shows the reconstruction based on the 85th horizontal row of the depth image. Small dots are reconstructed on the basis of estimated depth values, which are stored in the same row of the depth image. Note that the features in the scene marked with big dark dots are not necessarily visible in the same row.

Based on this reconstruction we can see that the darker outline has one problem on the right side, while the lighter outline has one on the left side. Besides that the reconstruction is pretty consistent. Generally speaking the darker outline is better then the lighter outline. This was expected, since the nature of the panorama building process says that the quality of the depth estimations is better when φ is bigger [6]. At the same time, the quality of the lighter outline is much better than the outline which would result from the panoramic image build from one column of each captured image at a suitable lower resolution. As already mentioned, this lower resolution turns stripes into columns. But lower resolution also brings considerable decrease in the number of possible depth estimates [6]: in this presented case from around 140 possible estimates to only around 10 estimates.

At the end let us present one quantitative measure, which gives the average error of the estimated depth (l) in comparison to the actual distance (d) over 19 scene points: $AVG_{columns} = ((\sum_{i=1}^{19} |l_i - d_i|/d_i)/19) \cdot 100\% = 4.3\%$, $AVG_{stripes} = 16.1\%$. In the last result ($AVG_{stripes}$) three points were really critical, while without them the result would be much better: 5.4%.

8 Conclusions

The presented theory and initial results suggest that the new sensor could be used for real time capturing of panoramic depth images and consequently for autonomous navigation of a mobile robot in a room. Assumptions made have proved to be correct and revealed some other interesting properties of the system.

Since we can trust in estimates that are not far away from the center of rotation and the size of the angle φ prescribes the number of possible depth estimates [6], stripes suggest to dynamically modify the level of trust, since the angle φ within the stripe varies, while the procedure based on one column has a fixed angle φ. (See the two most left big dark dots and their reconstructions in Fig. 4.) We are also interested in how the system would perform in practice if we use a wide-angle camera [1] and if we correct the distortions in the captured images. This will be the subject of our future work.

References

1. Bakstein, H., Pajdla, T.: Panoramic Mosaicing with a 180° Field of View Lens. Proc. IEEE Workshop on Omnidirectional Vision. Copenhagen, Denmark (2002) 60–67
2. Benosman, R., Kang, S. B. (eds.): Panoramic Vision: Sensors, Theory and Applications. Springer-Verlag, New York, USA (2001)
3. Chen, S.: Quicktime VR — an image-based approach to virtual environment navigation. Proc. ACM SIGGRAPH. Los Angeles, USA (1995) 29–38
4. Faugeras, O.: Three-Dimensional Computer Vision: A Geometric Viewpoint. MIT Press, Cambridge, Massachusetts, London, England (1993)
5. Ishiguro, H., Yamamoto, M., Tsuji, S.: Omni-directional stereo. IEEE Trans. PAMI **14(2)** (1992) 257–262

6. Peer, P., Solina, F.: Panoramic Depth Imaging: Single Standard Camera Approach. Int. J. Comp. Vis. **47(1/2/3)** (2002) 149–160
7. Peleg, S., Rousso, B., Rav-Acha, A., Zomet, A.: Mosaicing on adaptive manifolds. IEEE Trans. PAMI **22(10)** (2000) 1144–1154
8. Peleg, S., Ben-Ezra, M., Pritch, Y.: Omnistereo: Panoramic Stereo Imaging. IEEE Trans. PAMI **23(3)** (2001) 279–290
9. Shum, H.Y., Szeliski, R.: Stereo reconstruction from multiperspective panoramas. Proc. IEEE ICCV, Vol. I. Kerkyra, Greece (1999) 14–21
10. Svoboda, T., Pajdla, T.: Epipolar Geometry for Central Catadioptric Cameras. Int. J. Comp. Vis. **49(1)** (2002) 23–37

Depth Recovery from Noisy Gradient Vector Fields Using Regularization

Tiangong Wei and Reinhard Klette

CITR, University of Auckland, Tamaki Campus
Building 731, Auckland, New Zealand
{tiangong,r.klette}@citr.auckland.ac.nz

Abstract. This paper presents a regularization based method for surface reconstruction from noisy gradient vector fields. The algorithm takes as its input a discrete gradient vector field, obtained by applying a Shape from Shading or Photometric Stereo method. To derive this algorithm, we combine the integrability constraint and the surface curvature and area constraints into a single functional, which is then minimized. Therefore, value changes in the height or depth map will be more regular. To solve the minimization problem, we employ the Fourier transform theory rather than variational approach to avoid using the initial and boundary conditions. The Fourier transform of the unknown surface is expressed as a function of the given gradient's Fourier transforms. The relative depth values can be obtained by an inverse Fourier Transform and by choosing associated weighting parameters. The method is evaluated on gradient data delivered by a shape-from-shading algorithm. Experimental results using both synthetic and real images show that the new algorithm is more robust against noise than existing methods.

Keywords: regularization, Fourier transform, gradient vector fields, shape recovery, depth from gradients

1 Introduction

Recovering depth is a central problem in three-dimensional perception. Most depth recovery techniques, e.g., shape from shading (SFS), photometric stereo method (PSM), normally provide gradient values (i.e., the discrete gradient vector field) for a discrete set of visible points on object surfaces. In order to achieve the relative height or depth values of the surface, these discrete gradients have to be integrated. In practice, however, the gradient vector fields are normally contaminated by noise because each captured image is influenced by the presence of camera noise and further measurement errors.

Assume that the surface function $Z(x, y)$ of a scene object is formed by an orthographic (parallel) projection of the surface into the xy-image plane, and defined in the image plane over a compact region Ω. The gradient values of this surface at discrete points $(x, y) \in \Omega$

$$p(x,y) = \frac{\partial Z(x,y)}{\partial x} = Z_x \qquad \text{and} \qquad q(x,y) = \frac{\partial Z(x,y)}{\partial y} = Z_y$$

N. Petkov and M.A. Westenberg (Eds.): CAIP 2003, LNCS 2756, pp. 116–123, 2003.

are only available as input data and contaminated by noise. The surface gradients can be represented in the form of an imperfect *needle diagram*, which consists of drawings of vectors (p, q) by a "little arrow".

Essentially there are two main classes of integration techniques for finding $Z(x, y)$ from $p(x, y)$ and $q(x, y)$: *local integration techniques* and *global integration techniques* (for a review, see Klette and Schlüns [6]). Local integration methods such as two-point method [1] and eight-point method [3] are conceptually simple. The surface depth can be recovered by considering the surface normal vectors at the two or eight adjacent points of a given point, computing the average tangent through the given point, and interpolating the surface depth and surface normals. Wu and Li [11] proposed a method based on the following curve integrals:

$$Z(x, y) = Z(x_0, y_0) + \int_{\gamma} p(x, y)dx + q(x, y)dy, \qquad (1)$$

where γ is an arbitrarily specified integration path from (x_0, y_0) to $(x, y) \in \Omega$. The common characteristic of the local methods is that starting with initial height values, the local methods propagate height values according to a local approximation rule (e.g., based on the 4-neighborhood) using the given gradient data. Such a calculation of relative height values can be repeated by using different scan algorithms. Finally, resulting height values can be determined by averaging operations. However, initial height values have to be provided. The locality of the computations propagates errors, i.e., this approach strongly depends on data accuracy. Therefore, local integration techniques perform badly when the data are noisy.

The equations linking the surface depth and gradients are $Z_x = p$ and $Z_y = q$, so global integration techniques (Horn and Brooks [4], Frankot and Chellappa [2], Horn [5], Wei and Klette [9, 10]) are based on minimizing the following functional (cost function):

$$W = \iint_{\Omega} [|Z_x - p|^2 + |Z_y - q|^2]dxdy. \qquad (2)$$

Comparing with the local methods, the *Frankot-Chellappa algorithm*, based on the results of the paper [2] and presented in Klette et al. [7], leads to better results for the task of calculating height from gradient. At each iteration of the algorithm, the non-integrable surface is converted into the integrable surface by orthogonal projection in the frequency domain. Nevertheless, the errors of the algorithm are high for the imperfect estimate of the surface gradient or noisy gradient vector fields. Also, the algorithm is very sensitive to abrupt changes in orientation, i.e., there are large errors at the object boundary. Noakes, Kozera and Klette [8] proposed a Lawn-Mowing algorithm for enforcing the integrability condition of a given non-integrable vector field, but there are no experimental results reported in [8] for real images.

In this paper, we describe a new integration method for depth recovery from noisy gradient vector fields. To derive this algorithm, we combine the integrability constraint (2) and the surface curvature and area constraints into a single functional, which is then minimized. Therefore, value changes in the depth map will be more regular. To solve the minimization problem, we employ the Fourier transform theory rather than variational approach to avoid using the initial and boundary conditions. The Fourier transform of the unknown surface is expressed as a function of the given gradient's Fourier transforms. The relative depth values can be obtained by an inverse Fourier Transform and by choosing associated weighting parameters. Experimental results using both synthetic and real images show that our algorithm successfully recovers the depth information. The robustness of the algorithm is illustrated by using qualitative and quantitative analysis.

The organization of the rest of the paper is as follows. In Section 2 we describe our new algorithm for depth from gradients. The experimental results using synthetic and real images are presented in Section 3. The conclusions are given in Sections 4.

2 Depth from Gradients

In this section, we use the Fourier transform theory to derive our new algorithm for solving depth from gradients problems. Instead of using the cost function (2), the following functional is minimized, in order to improve the accuracy and robustness, and to strengthen the relation between the estimated surface and the original image:

$$W = \iint_{\Omega} \left[|Z_x - p|^2 + |Z_y - q|^2 \right] dxdy + \lambda \iint_{\Omega} \left(|Z_x|^2 + |Z_y|^2 \right) dxdy$$
$$+\mu \iint_{\Omega} \left(|Z_{xx}|^2 + 2\,|Z_{xy}|^2 + |Z_{yy}|^2 \right) dxdy, \qquad (3)$$

where the subscripts indicate partial derivatives. In the above cost function, the second term of the right-hand is a small deflection approximation of the surface area, and the third term is a small deflection approximation of the surface curvature (i.e., it is a measure of quadratic variation in the surface slopes). The non-negative regularization parameters λ and μ establish a trade-off between the constraints, i.e., it is used to adjust the weighting between them. The above new cost function reflects the relations among the surface depth $Z(x, y)$, surface gradients $p(x, y)$ and $q(x, y)$ more effectively, and make the best use of the information provided by the surface gradients.

The following objective is to solve the unknown $Z(x, y)$ subject to an optimization process which minimizes the cost function W. To find the minimum of the functional W, one of the methods used in computer vision is to discretize it directly in spatial domain. The other type of methods use calculus of variations to produce the Euler-Lagrange equations. Then a discrete version of the Euler-Lagrange equations can be solved by using numerical methods. The main disadvantage of these two type of methods is that initial values or boundary conditions have to be supplied. Instead of using a discrete method and variational calculus, we use the Fourier transform theory. Suppose that the Fourier transform of the surface function $Z(x, y)$ is

$$Z_F(u,v) = \iint_\Omega Z(x,y)e^{-j(ux+vy)}dxdy, \tag{4}$$

and the inverse Fourier transform is

$$Z(x,y) = \frac{1}{2\pi}\iint_\Omega Z_F(u,v)e^{j(ux+vy)}dudv, \tag{5}$$

where j is the imaginary unit. According to the differentiation properties of the Fourier transform, we can derive the following relations

$$\begin{aligned} &Z_x(x,y) \leftrightarrow juZ_F(u,v), &&Z_y(x,y) \leftrightarrow jvZ_F(u,v),\\ &Z_{xx}(x,y) \leftrightarrow -u^2Z_F(u,v), &&Z_{yy}(x,y) \leftrightarrow -v^2Z_F(u,v),\\ &Z_{xy}(x,y) \leftrightarrow -uvZ_F(u,v). \end{aligned}$$

Let $P(u,v)$ and $Q(u,v)$ be the Fourier transforms of $p(x,y)$ and $q(x,y)$, respectively. Taking the Fourier transform in (3) and using the above differentiation properties and the following Parseval's formula

$$\iint_\Omega |Z(x,y)|^2\,dxdy = \frac{1}{2\pi}\iint_\Omega |Z_F(u,v)|^2\,dudv,$$

we obtain

$$\begin{aligned} &\frac{1}{2\pi}\iint_\Omega \left[|juZ_F(u,v) - P(u,v)|^2 + |jvZ_F(u,v) - Q(u,v)|^2\right] dudv\\ &+\frac{\lambda}{2\pi}\iint_\Omega \left[|juZ_F(u,v)|^2 + |jvZ_F(u,v)|^2\right] dudv\\ &+\frac{\mu}{2\pi}\iint_\Omega \Big[\left|-u^2Z_F(u,v)\right|^2 + 2\left|-uvZ_F(u,v)\right|^2\\ &+\left|-v^2Z_F(u,v)\right|^2\Big]\,dudv \to minimum. \end{aligned}$$

The left side of the above expression can be expanded as

$$\begin{aligned} &\frac{1}{2\pi}\iint_\Omega \big[u^2Z_FZ_F^* - juZ_FP^* + juZ_F^*P + PP^*\\ &+v^2Z_FZ_F^* - jvZ_FQ^* + jvZ_F^*Q + QQ^*\big]\,dudv\\ &+\frac{\lambda}{2\pi}\iint_\Omega \left(u^2+v^2\right)Z_FZ_F^*dudv + \frac{\mu}{2\pi}\iint_\Omega \left(u^4+2u^2v^2+v^4\right)Z_FZ_F^*dudv, \end{aligned}$$

where $*$ denotes the conjugate. Differentiating the above expression with respect to Z_F and Z_F^*, we can deduce the following minimal conditions for the cost function (3):

$$C_{uv}Z_F + juP + jvQ = 0;$$

and

$$C_{uv}Z_F^* - juP^* - jvQ^* = 0,$$

where $C_{uv} = (1+\lambda)(u^2+v^2)+\mu(u^2+v^2)^2$. Adding the above two equations together, then subtracting the first one from the second one, this results in the following equations

$$C_{uv}(Z_F + Z_F^*) + ju(P - P^*) + jv(Q - Q^*) = 0,$$

and

$$C_{uv}(Z_F - Z_F^*) + ju(P + P^*) + jv(Q + Q^*) = 0.$$

Solving the above equations except for $(u,v) \neq (0,0)$, we have

$$Z_F(u,v) = \frac{-juP(u,v) - jvQ(u,v)}{(1+\lambda)(u^2+v^2)+\mu(u^2+v^2)^2}, \tag{6}$$

where $(u,v) \neq (0,0)$. Therefore, the Fourier transform of the surface is expressed as a function of the Fourier transforms of given gradients $p(x,y)$ and $q(x,y)$. The main result is summarized in the following theorem.

Theorem 1. *The cost function (3) is minimized by taking the Fourier transform of surface $Z(x,y)$ as in the formula (6).*

The Frankot-Chellappa algorithm [2] as formulated in [7], is a special case when parameter $\lambda = 0$ and $\mu = 0$ in (3). Therefore, let $\lambda = 0$ and $\mu = 0$ in (6), we obtain that the objective functional (2) is minimized by taking the Fourier transform of the surface $Z(x,y)$ as

$$Z_F(u,v) = \frac{-1}{u^2+v^2}\left[juP(u,v) + jvQ(u,v)\right], \tag{7}$$

where $(u,v) \neq (0,0)$. The formula (7) can also be derived using the above process directly. If so, the process deriving (7) is much simpler than the one used by Frankot and Chellappa [2]. On the other hand, our new algorithm is capable of dealing with additional constraints.

Our proposed method for the task of calculating depth from gradients, use the transformation as specified in Theorem 1 after having the Fourier transforms of the given gradient field. Then an inverse Fourier transform leads to the desired depth map, which allows us to reconstruct object surfaces in 3D space within a subsequent computation step of a general back projection approach.

3 Experimental Results

To illustrate the usefulness of our method described earlier, several computer simulations on both synthetic and real images are given in this section. The discrete gradients were generated by means of some shape-from-shading algorithms. The Gaussian noise (with a mean set zero and a standard deviation set to 0.1) was subsequently added to the gradient vector fields obtained from the corresponding surfaces.

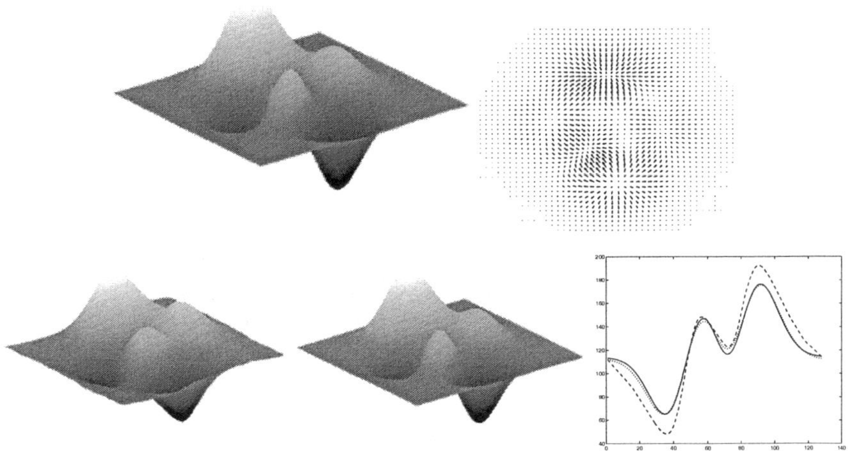

Fig. 1. Results of a synthetic image. (a) Original surface. (b) Gradient vector field.(c) Reconstructed surface with $\lambda = 0, \mu = 0$. (d) Reconstructed surface with $\lambda = 0.1, \mu = 10$. (e) $z - y$ plane sliced at x=64, where solid line stands for real surface, dashed line for $\lambda = 0, \mu = 0$, and dotted line for $\lambda = 0.1, \mu = 1$.

The following figures show the reconstructed surfaces when the parameters λ and μ are given by some specific values. Figure 1 shows the reconstructed surfaces for a synthetic image with $\lambda = 0, \mu = 0$ and $\lambda = 0.1, \mu = 1$, and the $z - y$ plane sliced at $x = 64$, where the solid line represents the real surface, dashed line represents the reconstructed surface with $\lambda = 0, \mu = 0$, and dotted line for $\lambda = 0.1, \mu = 1$. Figure 2 illustrates the reconstructed surfaces for a torus object with $\lambda = 0, \mu = 0$ and $\lambda = 0.1, \mu = 2$. Figure 3 shows the reconstructed surfaces for a vase object with $\lambda = 0, \mu = 0$ and $\lambda = 0.1, \mu = 10$.

Our evaluation is also done by providing quantitative measures on how well the reconstructed surface matches the original by looking at the Mean Square Error (MSE), Mean Normal Error (MNE) and Mean Cosine Error (MCE):

$$MCE = \left| \left(\frac{1}{N \times N} \sum_{i=1}^{N} \sum_{j=1}^{N} \cos^{-1}(\boldsymbol{n}_{i,j} \cdot \boldsymbol{n}^*_{i,j}) \right) - 1 \right|,$$

where $\boldsymbol{n}_{i,j}$ and $\boldsymbol{n}^*_{i,j}$ represent the original surface normal vector and the reconstructed one, respectively. The errors for the three images are shown in Table 1.

From the reconstructed surfaces, we can see that the depth recovery is improved by choosing corresponding regularization parameters. The mean square errors are also much smaller. Therefore, the experimental results show the proposed algorithm is a robust method for depth recovery from noisy gradients.

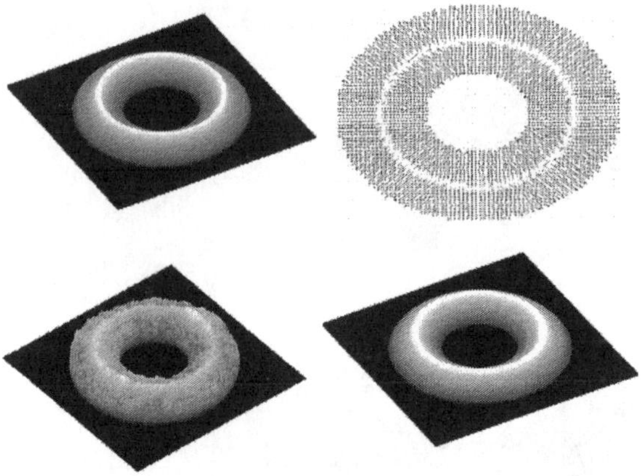

Fig. 2. Results of a torus object. (a) Original surface. (b) Gradient vector field. (c) Reconstructed surface $\lambda = 0, \mu = 0$. (d) Reconstructed surface $\lambda = 0.1, \mu = 15$.

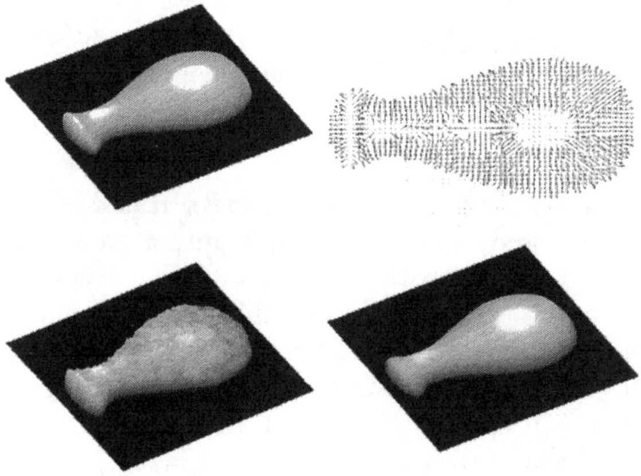

Fig. 3. Results of a vase object. (a) Original surface. (b) Gradient vector field. (c) Reconstructed surface $\lambda = 0, \mu = 0$. (d) Reconstructed surface $\lambda = 0.1, \mu = 10$.

Table 1. Mean Square Error for the reconstructed surfaces.

Surfaces	Parameters	MSE	MCE	MNE
Peaks	$\lambda = 0, \mu = 0$	14.516	0.564	1.445
Peaks	$\lambda = 0.1, \mu = 1$	7.5789	0.165	0.947
Torus	$\lambda = 0, \mu = 0$		1.374	1.184
Torus	$\lambda = 0.1, \mu = 2$		0.449	0.866
Vase	$\lambda = 0, \mu = 0$		1.155	1.629
Vase	$\lambda = 0.1, \mu = 10$		0.227	0.833

4 Conclusions

We designed a new algorithm for depth from gradient vector fields. The new cost function reflects the relations among surface depth and surface gradients more effectively than Frankot-Chellappa algorithm. The new algorithm is capable of dealing with additional constraints. The choice of regularization parameters heavily affects the surface reconstruction from noisy gradients. The relation between the parameters and noise should be the future research topic. The appropriateness of the approach has been illustrated through experiments using synthetic and real images.

References

1. N. E. Coleman, Jr. and R. Jain: Obtaining 3-dimensional shape of textured and specular surfaces using four-source photometry. *CGIP*, **18** (1982) 439–451.
2. R. T. Frankot and R. Chellappa: A method for enforcing integrability in shape from shading algorithms. *IEEE Transactions on pattern Analysis and Machine Intelligence*, **10** (1988) 439–451.
3. G. Healey and R. Jain: Depth recovery from surface normals. *ICPR'84*, Montreal, Canada, Jul. 30 – Aug. 2 **2** (1984) 894–896.
4. B. K. P. Horn and M. J. Brooks: The variational approach to shape from shading. *Computer Vision, Graphics, and Image Processing*, **33** (1986) 174–208.
5. B. K. P. Horn: Height and gradient from shading. *International Journal of Computer Vision*, **5** (1990) 37–75.
6. R. Klette and K. Schlüns: Height data from gradient fields. *SPIE Proc on Machine Vision Applications, Architectures, and Systems Integration*, Boston, Massachusetts, USA. **2908** (1996) 204–215.
7. R. Klette, K. Schlüns and A. Koschan: *Computer Vision - Three-dimensional Data from Images*. Springer, Singapore, 1998.
8. L. Noakes, R. Kozera and R. Klette: The Lawn-Mowing algorithm for noisy gradient vector fields. *SPIE Proc., Vision Geometry VIII*, Denver, Colorado, USA. **3811** (1999) 305–316.
9. T. Wei and R. Klette: A wavelet-based algorithm for height from gradients. *International Robot Vision Workshop (RobVis 2001)*, Auckland, New Zealand. In:*Lecture Notes in Computer Science*, **1998** (2001) 84–90.
10. T. Wei and R. Klette: A New Algorithm for Gradient Field Integration. *Image and Vision Computing New Zealand (IVCNZ'01)*, Dunedin, New Zealand. 109–114, 2001
11. Z. Wu and L. Li: A line-integration based method for depth recovery from surface normals, *Computer Vision, Graphics, and Image Processing*, **43** (1988) 53–66.

Bunch Sampling for Fast Texture Synthesis

Dongxiao Zhou and Georgy Gimel'farb

CITR, Department of Computer Science, Tamaki Campus
The University of Auckland, Auckland, New Zealand
dzho002@ec.auckland.ac.nz, g.gimelfarb@auckland.ac.nz

Abstract. A fast technique for synthesising large-size spatially homogeneous textures is described. It randomly samples specific continuous or disjoint signal bunches from a given small-size training image. The bunches are replicated and randomly placed into the goal texture with due account of their interdependence. Both the geometric form of and placement rules for the bunches are estimated from the training image using a generic Gibbs random field model of the texture. Experiments with natural textures show the bunch sampling avoids drawbacks of more conventional block sampling techniques.

1 Introduction

Due to diversity and complexity of natural textures, today's texture analysis and synthesis focuses on spatially homogeneous textures with translation invariant signal statistics. Most significant achievements relate to texture modelling with Markov/Gibbs random fields founded in [2, 5, 8]. The model is specified by a joint Gibbs probability distribution (GPD) of signals. After identification (parameter estimation), the model offers a Markov Chain Monte Carlo (MCMC) generation of images distributed in accord to the GPD. But the MCMC is too computationally complex for generating large-size textures being of main practical interest.

Faster texture synthesis is achieved with non-parametric sampling that implicitly involves a Markov texture model. In such sampling, the training image acts as a source of random signal samples corresponding to the marginal GPDs. The training samples are replicated to form a synthetic texture in a pixel-wise or patch-wise mode. The pixel-by-pixel synthesis [4] extends a given seed by randomly choosing each next pixel among the training or already generated pixels with neighbourhoods similar to the neighbourhood in the goal texture. However, this texture extrapolation is unstable due to accumulation of errors. Also it is computationally complex, and there are no formal criteria for selecting a proper neighbourhood for a particular texture. Much more stable and faster patch or block sampling [3, 9] replicates and permutes rectangular blocks of the training signals to form a goal texture. Major drawbacks are the verbatim replicas of the same block and false linear borders between the permuted adjacent blocks. In some cases the borders are suppressed with special post-processing [3]. However, there are no theoretically justified schemes for selecting the post-processing parameters or choosing the blocks of a proper size.

N. Petkov and M.A. Westenberg (Eds.): CAIP 2003, LNCS 2756, pp. 124–131, 2003.

This paper describes a new approach to the texture synthesis, called *bunch sampling* in [7], that bridges the gap between the fast non-parametric sampling and the Markov/Gibbs model based synthesis. In order to maintain visual and quantitative similarity between the training and synthesised texture, specific signal bunches are randomly sampled from the training image and placed into a goal texture with due account of their spatial interdependence reflected in relative positions. The shape of and the placement rules for the bunches are derived from the characteristic structure of pairwise pixel interactions for a generic Gibbs random field (GGRF) model of translation invariant textures [6].

2 Estimation of Bunch Characteristics

The bunch sampling considers a given training image as a collection of interdependent texels of different types but of the same geometric form specific for the texture at hand. According to the underlying GGRF model, there exists a regular guiding grid of independent (interchangeable) subsets of the texels. But the adjacent texels in each subset are strongly interdependent. The texture synthesis should preserve relative positions of the interdependent types of the texels but allow for random permutation of the independent texels of the same type. The placement rules specify the training and goal guiding grids and the relative positions of the texels of different types with respect to the grid.

Estimation of the Bunch Shape. Let $\mathbf{g} = \{g(x,y) : (x,y) \in \mathbf{R};\ g(x,y) \in \mathbf{Q}\}$ denote a greyscale digital image with a finite set $\mathbf{Q}$ of signals (grey levels) supported by a 2D finite lattice $\mathbf{R} = \{(x,y) : 0 \leqslant x \leqslant M-1; 0 \leqslant y \leqslant N-1\}$. Each translation invariant pairwise pixel interaction in the GGRF model of a spatially homogeneous texture is characterised by the inter-pixel shift (ξ,η) and the partial interaction energy $E_{\xi,\eta}(\mathbf{g})$. The interacting pixels form a translation invariant family $\mathbf{C}_{\xi,\eta} = \{(x,y),(x+\xi,y+\eta) : (x,y) \in \mathbf{R}; (x+\xi,y+\eta) \in \mathbf{R}\}$ of cliques in the neighbourhood graph [2, 8].

The first approximation of the partial energy is proportional to the variance of the relative grey level co-occurrence histogram (GLCH) collected for the training image $\mathbf{g}^\circ$ over the clique family $\mathbf{C}_{\xi,\eta}$ [6]:

$$E_{\xi,\eta}(\mathbf{g}^\circ) \propto \sum_{(q,s)\in\mathbf{Q}^2} \left(F_{\xi,\eta}(q,s \mid \mathbf{g}^\circ) - \frac{1}{|\mathbf{Q}|^2} \right) \cdot F_{\xi,\eta}(q,s \mid \mathbf{g}^\circ) \tag{1}$$

Here, $F_{\xi,\eta}(q,s \mid \mathbf{g}^\circ)$ is the relative frequency of the grey level co-occurrence $(g^\circ(x,y) = q; g^\circ(x+\xi,y+\eta) = s)$ in the training image.

We assume the geometric shape of a bunch (texel) relates to a characteristic structure of pairwise interactions. For simplicity, in our experiments below the structure is found by selecting a given number of the top-rank clique families, ordered by the relative partial energies of Eq. (1), among the distinct families in a large search window $\mathbf{W} = \{(\xi,\eta) : \mid \xi \mid \leq \xi_{\max}; \mid \eta \mid \leq \eta_{\max}\}$.

Figure 1 shows several training textures of the size 128×128, cut out or taken from [1, 10], and their scaled-up interaction structures in the search window $\mathbf{W}$ of

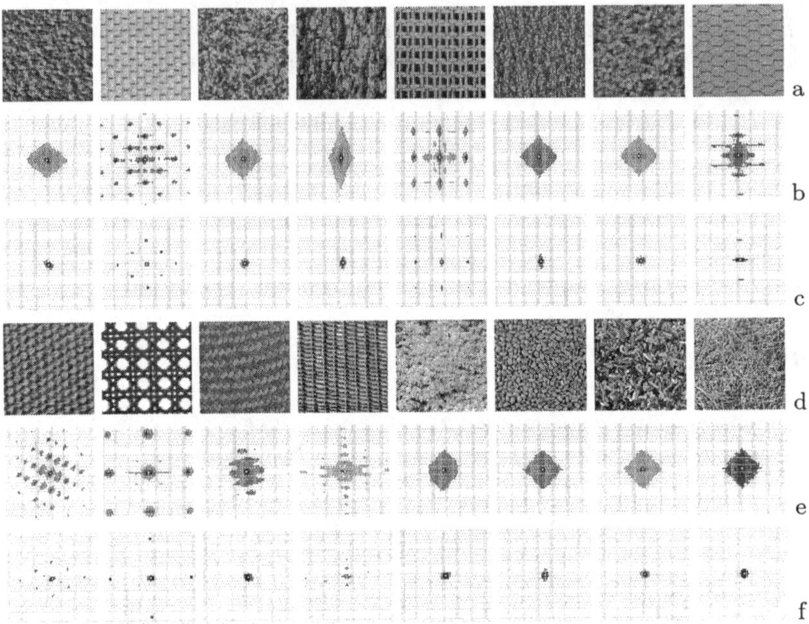

Fig. 1. Training textures 128 × 128 D4, D6, D9, D12, D20, D24, D29, D34 (a), D77, D101, Fabrics0, Fabrics13, Flowers5, Food0, Food7, and Grass1 (d) and their grey-coded characteristic interaction structures with 200 (b, e) and 15 (c, f) clique families, respectively (the blacker the point, the larger the energy).

the size 65 × 65. The energies of all the clique families $\mathbf{C_W} = \{\mathbf{C}_{\xi,\eta} : (\xi, \eta) \in \mathbf{W}\}$ form a model-based interaction map (MBIM): $\mathbf{E_W} = \{E_{\xi,\eta}(\mathbf{g}) : (\xi, \eta) \in \mathbf{W}\}$. The interaction structure shows the most characteristic neighbours of each pixel selected from the MBIM (e.g., by thresholding the energies). A geometric pattern of the characteristic neighbours, specific for each texture, determines the shape of the signal bunches. The remaining problem to be solved is how to select a range of the bunch sizes allowing to synthesise textures that are visually and quantitatively similar to each particular training image.

Deriving the Placement Rule. The GGRF texture model yields translation invariant marginal probability distributions of the signal bunches of the estimated shape. The placement rules for the texture synthesis specify the relative positions of the interdependent bunches. Assuming the spatial repetitiveness of the bunches of the same type, the texture is tesselated with a specific guiding grid that separates conditionally independent positions of the bunches from the conditionally interdependent ones. Relative position of the bunch with respect to the grid should be preserved in order to keep similarity between the training and goal textures. Below we restrict our consideration to the simple rectangular tessellation controlled by orientation and size of the estimated bunch. Generally the tesselation may be oblique-angled and involve non-rectangular cells.

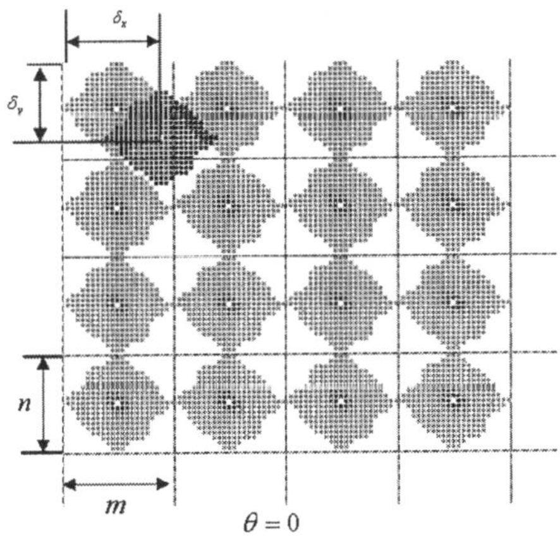

Fig. 2. Tessellation of the training texture D4 according to its interaction structure. The relative shift of a black bunch with respect to the grid is denoted $\{\delta_x, \delta_y\}$.

Let $\mathbf{A} \subset \mathbf{W}$ denote the characteristic interaction structure of the texture. Let θ denote the orientation angle between the x-axes of the lattice $\mathbf{R}$ and the placement grid. Let m and n denote the maximum span of $\mathbf{A}$ along the x- and y-axis of the grid, respectively. Figure 2 exemplifies the tessellation in the case of $\theta = 0$. For simplicity, in our experiments below the x-axis of the grid is oriented along the main principal axis of the MBIM:

$$\theta = \frac{1}{2}\tan^{-1}\left(\frac{2 \cdot \mu_{11}}{\mu_{20} - \mu_{02}}\right)$$

where the second-order central moments $\mu_{\ldots}$ of the MBIM account for the exponential dependence between the partial energies and Gibbs probabilities:

$$\mu_{pq} = \sum_{(\xi,\eta)\in\mathbf{W}} (\xi - \bar{\xi})^p (\eta - \bar{\eta})^q \exp\left(E_{\xi,\eta}(\mathbf{g})\right); \quad \bar{\alpha} = \frac{\sum\limits_{(\xi,\eta)\in\mathbf{W}} \alpha \exp\left(E_{\xi,\eta}(\mathbf{g})\right)}{\sum\limits_{(\xi,\eta)\in\mathbf{W}} \exp\left(E_{\xi,\eta}(\mathbf{g})\right)}$$

(α stands for ξ or η). In the simplest case the spans m and n of the grid cell are obtained by projecting the bunch shape onto the grid axes. Therefore the simple placement rule used in the experiments below is as follows: if $\{x_{\mathrm{tr}}^{(\theta)}, y_{\mathrm{tr}}^{(\theta)}\}$ is the position of the bunch in the training image, then its possible positions $\{x_{\mathrm{syn}}^{(\theta)}, y_{\mathrm{syn}}^{(\theta)}\}$ in the goal synthetic texture satisfy the conditions:

$$x_{\mathrm{syn}}^{(\theta)} \bmod m = x_{\mathrm{tr}}^{(\theta)} \bmod m; \quad y_{\mathrm{syn}}^{(\theta)} \bmod n = y_{\mathrm{tr}}^{(\theta)} \bmod n \tag{2}$$

The superscript (θ) indicates the coordinate axes of the placement grid which are rotated by the angle θ with respect to the initial image lattice axes.

We consider the bunches with the same shift relative to the closest cell in the guiding grid as the texels of the same type. These latter have the same marginal statistics of pixel interactions and thus are indistinguishable and interexchangeable both statistically and visually. When several output positions comply with Eq. (2), one of them is randomly selected to place the bunch. The random selection avoids the verbatim replication of large patches of the training image, so that the synthetic texture differs more from the training one.

3 Experimental Results and Conclusions

Figures 3–5 show examples of synthetic textures obtained with the bunch sampling from the training images in Fig. 1.

Fig. 3. Synthetic textures 512 × 512 D4 (a), Food0 (b), Grass1 (c) with $\mid \mathbf{A} \mid = 200$, and D101 (d) with $\mid \mathbf{A} \mid = 10$.

Visually, the synthetic and training textures are very similar. To test the effectiveness of the bunch sampling, we also compared them quantitatively. Because the characteristic GLCHs are sufficent statistics of the GGRF model, the model-based dissimilarity between the training, $\mathbf{g}^{\circ}$, and synthetic, $\mathbf{g}_{\mathrm{syn}}$, textures can be measured by the total chi-square distance between the relative GLCHs for the learned clique families $\mathbf{A}$.

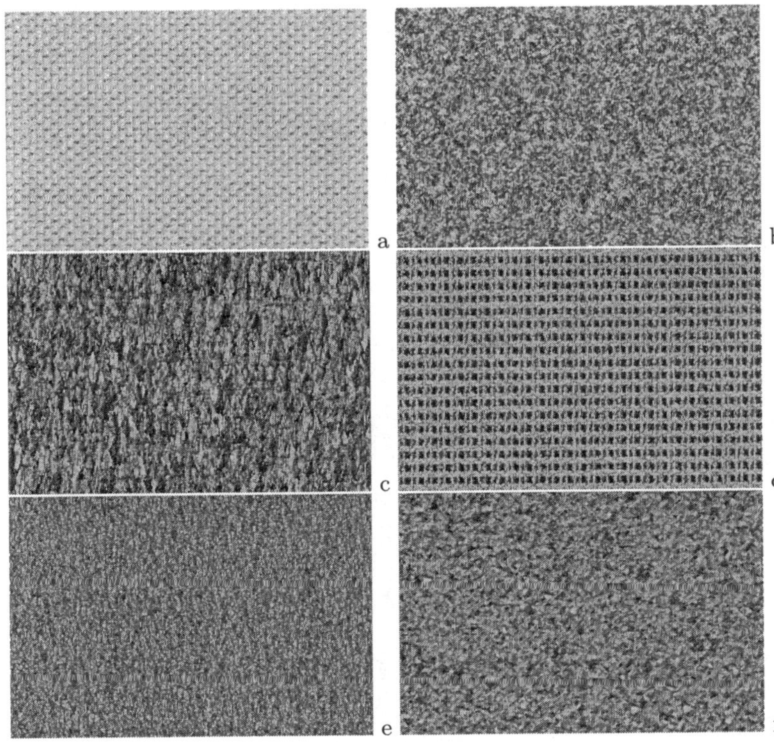

Fig. 4. Synthetic textures 512 × 334 D6 (a), D9 (b), D12 (c), D20 (d), D34 (e), and D77 (f) with $| \mathbf{A} |= 15$, 200, 200, 10, 200, and 200, respectively.

Due to the totally different nature of stochastic textures like D4 and regular mosaics like D101, these texture types set forth the different requirements regarding the shape of and the placement rules for the bunches. The stochastic textures are formed by a random arrangement of a very large number of different types of texels. The placement rule in this case is less restrictive, and the visual quality of synthetic images depends mostly on whether the size of the bunch is sufficient to represent most typical types of texels. For a regular mosaic, the bunch is usually disjoint and may be of much smaller size than it is needed for the stochastic textures (e.g., the size $| \mathbf{A} |= 10$ is already sufficient to adequately replicate the mosaic D101). However, the periodicity of the texels is the major feature of a regular mosaic, so that the placement rules play the prominent role in replicating such textures and must be estimated very accurately. Even small orientation and size errors may deteriorate the synthetic textures [7].

Figures 6 and 7 present the dissimilarities of the synthetic and training stochastic texture D4 and regular mosaic D101 for different sizes and orientations of the bunches. The dissimilarities for the texture D4 are very stable in a relative narrow range comparing to those of the mosaic D101. The synthesis of D101 is very sensitive to both the size and orientation of the learned interac-

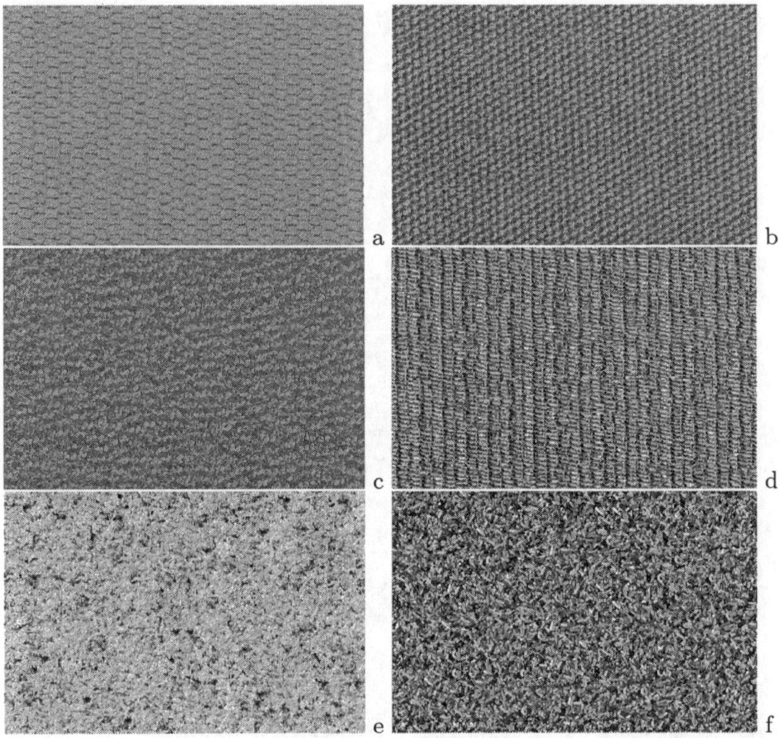

Fig. 5. Synthetic textures 512 × 334 D34 (a), D77 (b), Fabrics0 (c), Fabrics13 (d), Flowers5 (e), and Food7 (f) with $|\mathbf{A}|$= 31, 12, 200, 200, 200, 200, respectively.

tion structure. Generally, the bunch sampling behaves better with the stochastic textures than the regular ones. The quantitative comparisons in Figs. 6 and 7 can be used also for learning the proper bunch sizes and guiding grids. One may expect more realistic texture synthesis if the placement grid and the bunch size are estimated by minimising the dissimilarity between the GLCHs for the training and synthetic textures.

These and other experimental results show that the bunch sampling is able to effectively replicate a broad range of homogeneous textures even with the above oversimplified placement rules. The bunch sampling is as fast at the synthesis stage as the more conventional block sampling, but effectively overcomes the main drawbacks of this latter: the false linear borders and the heuristic choice of the block. The bunch sampling takes advantage of the explicit texture model in order to extract characteristic features of the training image. Also, the clear separation between the analysis and synthesis stages provides opportunities to further refinement of this technique. In particular, a more elaborated learning scheme accounting for spatial distributions of local energy maxima in the MBIMs might extend this approach to a larger variety of image textures.

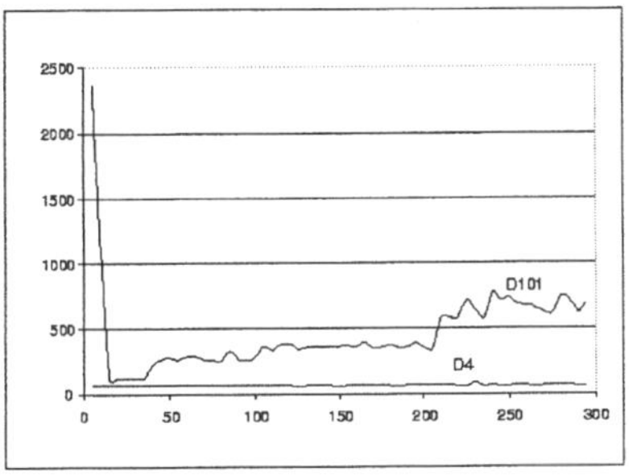

Fig. 6. Chi-square distances between the synthetic and training textures D101 and D4 as functions of the bunch size | **A** |.

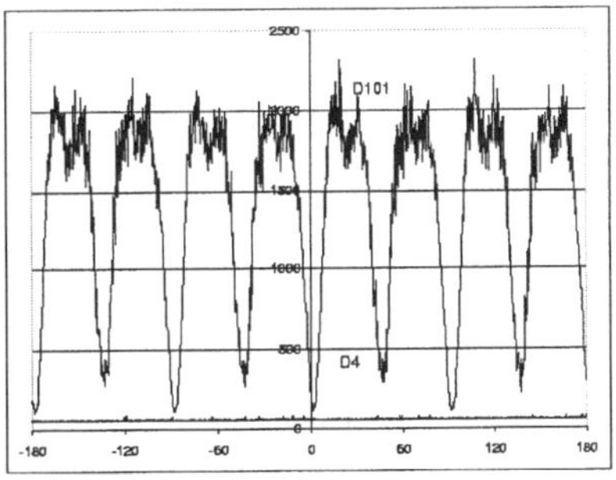

Fig. 7. Chi-square distances between the synthetic and training textures D101 and D4 as functions of the orientation angle of the guiding grid.

Acknowledgements

This work was supported by the Royal Society of New Zealand Marsden Fund under Grant UOA122 (9143/3600771) and by the University of Auckland Research Committee under Grant 9393/3600529.

References

1. P. Brodatz. *Textures: A Photographic Album for Artists and Designers.* Dover, New York, 1966.
2. G. R. Cross and A. K. Jain. Markov random field texture models. *IEEE Transactions on Pattern Analysis and Machine Intelligence*, 5:25–39, 1983.
3. A. A. Efros and W. T. Freeman. Image quilting for texture synthesis and transfer. In *Proc. ACM Conf. Computer Graphics SIGGRAPH 2001*, pages 341–346. ACM Press, 2001.
4. A. A. Efros and T. K. Leung. Texture synthesis by non-parametric sampling. In *Proc. IEEE Int. Conf. Computer Vision*, Corfu, Greece, Sept. 1999, vol. 2, pp. 1033–1038, 1999.
5. S. Geman and D. Geman. Stochastic relaxation, Gibbs distributions, and the Bayesian restoration of images. *IEEE Transactions on Pattern Analysis and Machine Intelligence*, 6:721–741, 1984.
6. G. L. Gimel'farb. *Image Textures and Gibbs Random Fields.* Kluwer Academic Publishers, Dordrecht, 1999.
7. G. Gimel'farb and D. Zhou. Fast synthesis of large-size textures using bunch sampling. In *Proc. Image and Vision Computing New Zealand 2002*, Auckland, New Zealand, 26-28 Nov. 2002, pp. 215–220, 2002.
8. M. Hassner and J. Sklansky. The use of Markov random fields as models of textures. *Computer Graphics and Image Processing*, 12:357–370, 1980.
9. L. Liang, C. Liu, and H. Y. Shum. Real-time texture synthesis by patch-based sampling. *Technical Report MSR-TR-2001-40, Micorsoft Research*, 2001.
10. R. Picard, C. Graszyk, S. Mann, et al. *VisTex database.* MIT Media Lab, Cambridge, Mass., 1995.

Automatic Detection of Specular Reflectance in Colour Images Using the MS Diagram

Fernando Torres[1], Jesús Angulo[2], and Francisco Ortiz[1]

[1] Automatics, Robotics and Computer Vision Group
Dept. Physics, Systems Engineering and Signal Theory. University of Alicante
P.O. Box 99, 03080 Alicante, Spain
{ftorres,fortiz}@disc.ua.es
http://www.disc.ua.es/gava

[2] Center of Mathematical Morphology, Ecole des Mines de Paris. 35, rue Saint-Honoré
77305 Fontainebleau CEDEX, France
jesus.angulo@cmm.ensmp.fr
http://cmm.ensmp.fr/~angulo

Abstract. In this paper we present a new method for the identification of specular reflectance in colour images. We have developed a bi-dimensional histogram which allows the exploitation of the relations between the signals of intensity and saturation of a colour image. Once the diagram has been constructed, it is possible to verify that the pixels of the specular reflectance are located in a well-defined region. The brightness is automatically identified by means of the extraction of pixels present in this region of the diagram, independently of their hue values. The effectiveness of the method in a variety of real chromatic images has been proven.

1 Introduction

In industrial visual inspection systems, the images are acquired in work environments where illumination plays an important role. Sometimes, a bad adjustment of illumination can introduce the presence of brightness and specular reflectance in the objects captured by the vision system [1]. The presence of such brightness alters the pattern recognition process because the previous stage of detection of edges in the objects fails: the brightness and specular reflectances are considered as different objects in the environment in which they are located and therefore it is not possible to perfectly detect the objects in the scene [2].

To be able to attenuate the effect of the specular reflectance in the captured scene, it is necessary to identify the brightness beforehand. Criminisi *et al* [3], and Lin *et al* in [4] use stereo images to separate specular and diffuse reflectances. In [5], Ragheb and Hancock use iterated conditional modes. Nevertheless, it is possible to use information about saturation and hue as well as intensity for the recognition of brightness in colour images. To do so, Bajcsy *et al* in [6] use a colour reflection model based on a dichromatic model for dielectric materials. In this paper we propose to exploit the existing relations between the intensity and saturation signals of a chromatic image that are obtained from a transformation of the RGB colour space.

N. Petkov and M.A. Westenberg (Eds.): CAIP 2003, LNCS 2756, pp. 132–139, 2003.

2 Colour Space Used

In the bibliography, many referenced colour spaces appear [7,8,9]. In general, they are three-dimensional spaces that can be classified in standardised systems (CIE-RGB, CIE-XYZ, CIE-Lab), physical systems (RGB and CMY), and intuitive systems, where the objective is to represent the colour information in an intuitive way (HSV, HLS, HSI, YSH, etc). The intuitive systems are widely used in image processing as they represent the information in a similar way to the human brain. In fact, they represent a single system, which Levkowitz and Herman define as GLHS [10]. The other spaces are particular cases in which a certain intensity function has been assigned to them. In this study, the intensity function employed M, is defined in [10] as the LHS-triangle model:

$$M = \frac{1}{3}(r + g + b) \tag{1}$$

By this way, the intensity signal corresponds to the projection of the colour vector **c** in the space RGB on the achromatic axis, $\mathbf{c}_a$. The saturation used in this study is the one proposed by Serra in [11], and which corresponds to the projection of the colour vector **c** on to chromatic plane $\mathbf{c}_p$, where:

$$\vec{c} = \vec{c}_p + \vec{c}_a \tag{2}$$

The value of s is given by the expression,

$$\begin{cases} S = \frac{1}{2}(2r - g - b) = \frac{3}{2}(r - m) & \text{if } (b + r) \geq 2g \\ S = \frac{1}{2}(r + g - 2b) = \frac{3}{2}(m - b) & \text{if } (b + r) < 2g \end{cases} \tag{3}$$

2.1 MS Diagram

In this study, we propose to exploit the existing relations between M and S that permit the detection of brightness on a digital image, independently of the hue of the object in which the brightness exits. We use a bi-dimensional histogram where the number of pixels that have the values M and S are represented. This way, a relationship between the signals M and S, defined above, is obtained, independently of the hue of the object involved. In Fig. 1, a colour image and its corresponding MS diagram are shown.

3 Detection of Specular Reflectance in the MS Diagram

If an object has brightness, the brightest point will have a high intensity value and low saturation, giving rise to a sensation of an intense white point without any hue. However, in the bright area the saturation generally increases as the intensity is reduced, gradually acquiring the sensation of colour as it loses intensity [12].

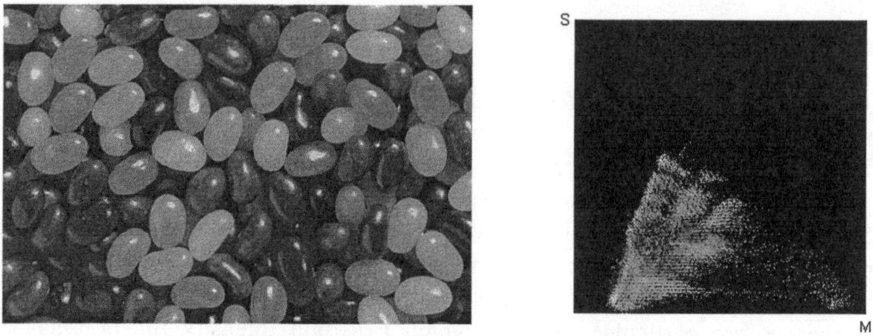

(a) colourbeans.bmp (b) MS-colourbeans.bmp

Fig. 1. Colour digital image and its MS diagram

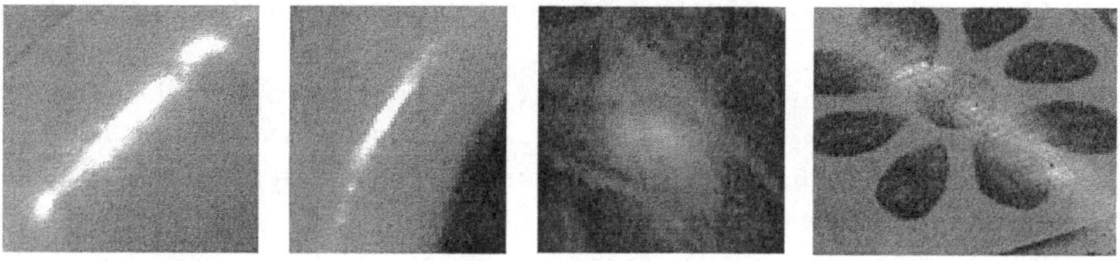

(a) life-saver.bmp (b) umbrella.bmp (c) hanger.bmp (d) table-cloth.bmp

Fig. 2. Bright areas in colour objects

In Figure 2, can be seen different bright areas from colour images where this phenomenon appears.

In Figure 3, the MS diagrams for each image in Fig. 2 are shown. In these diagrams there is no generic rule for the detection of brightness. However, the absence of such a rule is due to the fact that the dynamic range of the luminance signal is different for each image. This can be observed on the histograms of the intensity of M (Figure 4).

3.1 Enhanced Contrast and Detection of Bright zones

Before obtaining the MS diagram, it is necessary to carry out a previous step which guarantees that all the images have the same upper limit of dynamic range (255) of the luminance signal. As can be seen in Figure 2, all of the images have brightness. As is shown below, the algorithm proposed in this paper is based on the identification of brightness by means of the selection of a region of pixels in the MS diagram (Fig. 8). In Figure 3 it can be seen that not all of the bright areas in original images are in the selected zone. Therefore, it is necessary to guarantee that the bright pixels of any image are found in this zone. This process is performed through an equalisation of the histogram of the intensity signal. For the image in Figure 2.c, the process is schematised in Figure 5. Once this step of enhancement of the contrast has been achieved, the MS diagrams are computed (Figures 6 and 7).

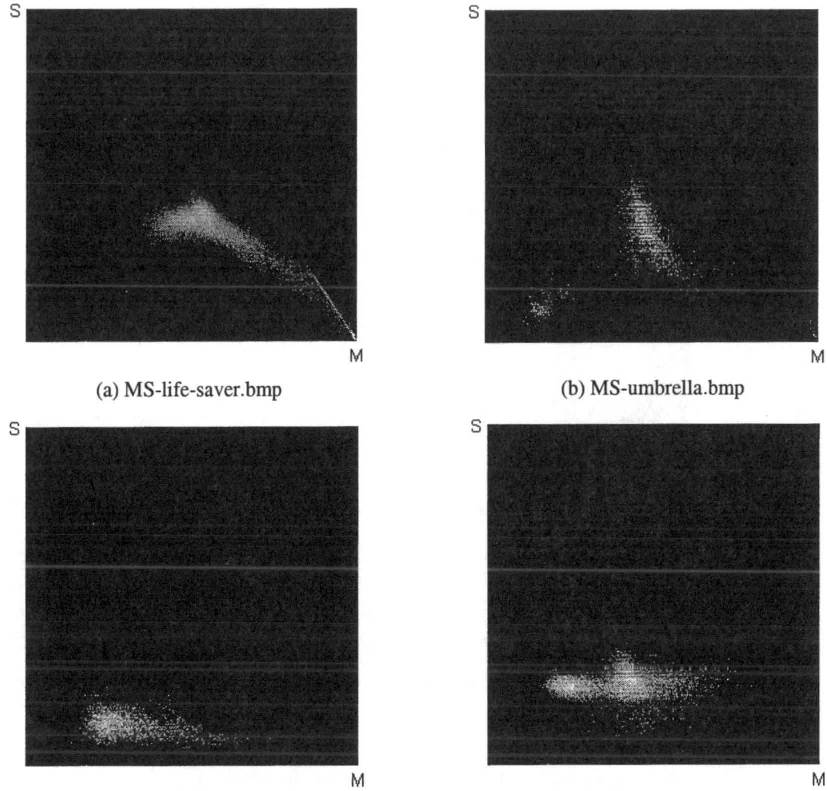

(a) MS-life-saver.bmp (b) MS-umbrella.bmp

(c) MS-hanger.bmp (d) MS-table-cloth.bmp

Fig. 3. MS Diagrams of the images in Fig. 2

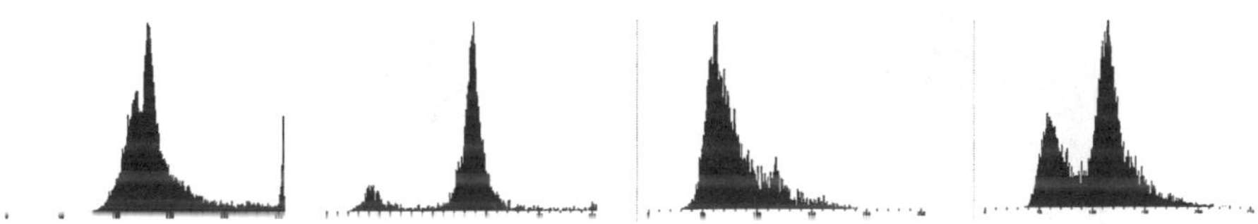

(a) Hist. of Fig. 2.a (b) Hist. of Fig. 2.b (c) Hist. of Fig. 2.c (d) Hist. of Fig. 2.d

Fig. 4. Histograms of the images in Fig. 2

From the analysis of the normalised MS diagrams (Fig. 6 and 7) and after different test in a representative selection of images, we have observed that the pixels values for M and S of the zones of brightness correspond to those ones belonging to the region mask given in Fig. 8. This set of points of the bi-variate histogram which follows a particular relationship appears in all the images where the objects have brightness. Therefore, the bright areas can be segmented by obtaining all of the pixels of the image. The values of the equalised M and S signals of the bright pixels are within the area indicated in Fig. 8. The choice of the maximum value for S of this zone has been fixed empirically after a detailed study with our database of images.

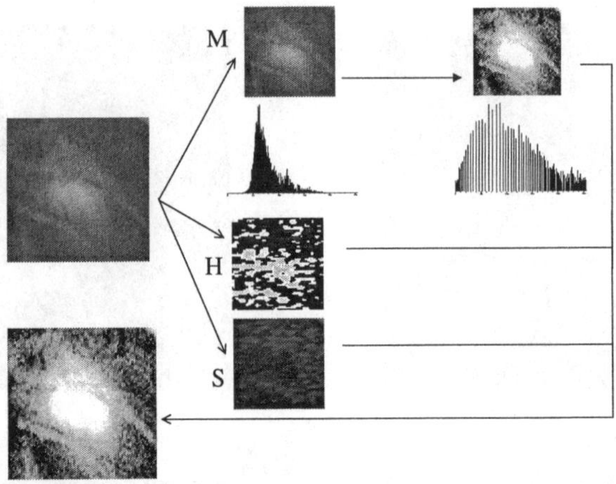

Fig. 5. Procedure for enhancement of the contrast of bright zones

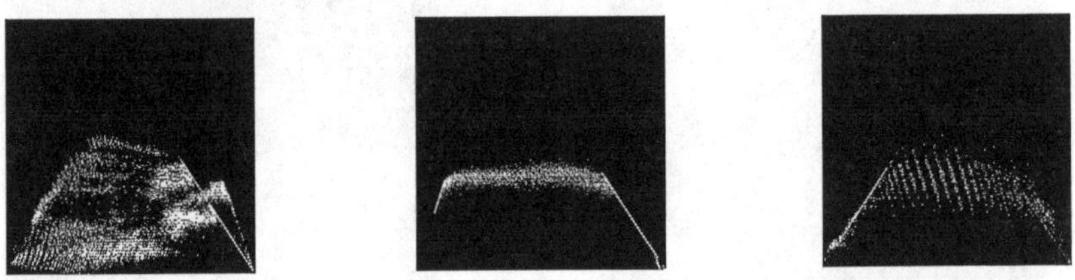

(a) MS-colourbeans-contr.bmp (b) MS-life-saver-contr.bmp (c) MS-umbrella-contr.bmp

Fig. 6. Normalised MS diagrams of the images in Fig. 2

(a) MS-hanger-contr.bmp (b) MS- table-cloth-contr.bmp

Fig. 7. Normalised MS diagrams of the images in Fig. 2 (cont)

Fig. 8. Binary mask of the bright pixels in the MS diagram

4 Results

In this section, we present the results obtained for the images analysed. The results obtained for the detection of bright areas in Fig. 1 are shown in Fig 9. In Figs. 10, 11 and 12, the results of the detection of specular reflectance on the images in Figures 2.a, 2.b, 2.c, and 2.d, respectively, are shown. From the results, the robustness of the method for the detection of specular reflectance presented in this paper, can be observed. In the results an almost complete absence of false positives is observed. This can be appreciated in Figure 11.a in which there is a white zone which is not identified as brightness.

(a) colourbeans.bmp

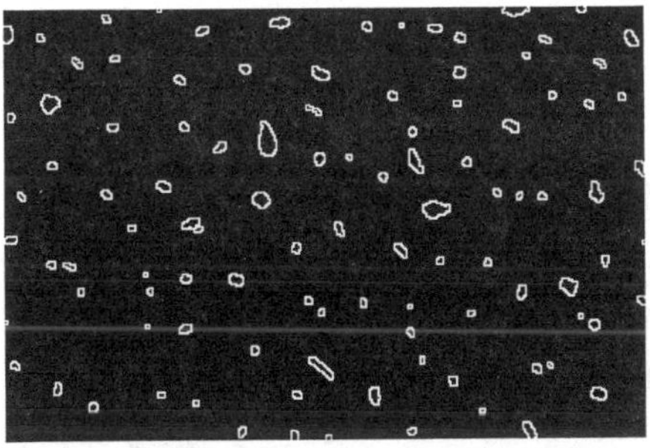
(b) brightness-colourbeans.bmp

Fig. 9. Detection of the specular reflectance of the image in Fig. 1

(a) life-saver-B.bmp

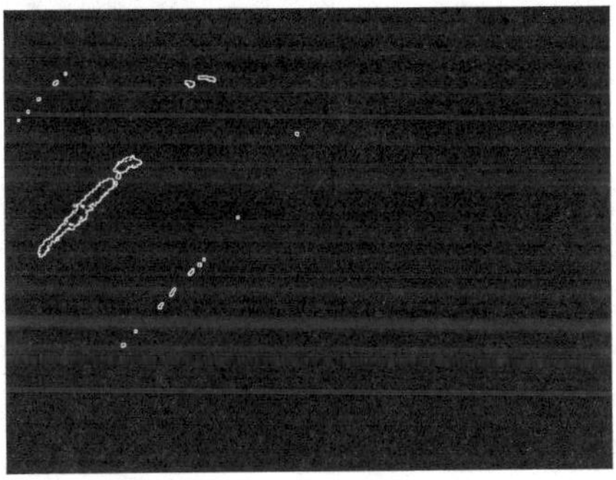
(b) brightness-life-saver-B.bmp

Fig. 10. Detection of the specular reflectance of the image (a) in Fig. 2

5 Conclusions

In this paper a robust detector of specular reflectance in colour images, based on the exploitation of the properties of the MS diagram, has been presented. Using the present approach, it is possible to automatically detect bright areas, independently of the

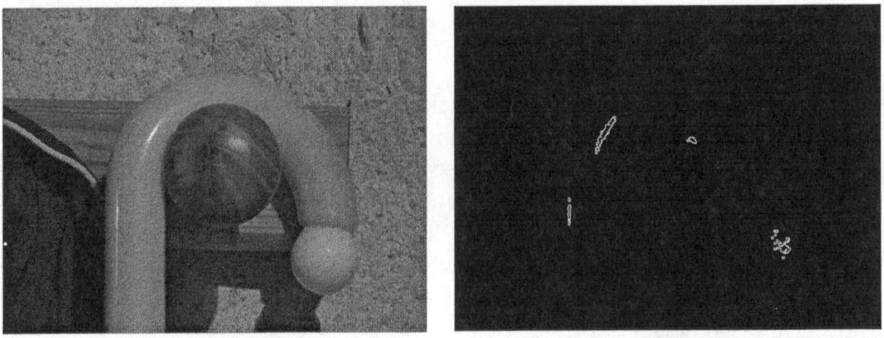

(a) umbrella-hunger-B.bmp (b) brightness-umbrella-hunger-B.bmp

Fig. 11. Detection of the specular reflectance of the images (b) and (c) in Fig. 2

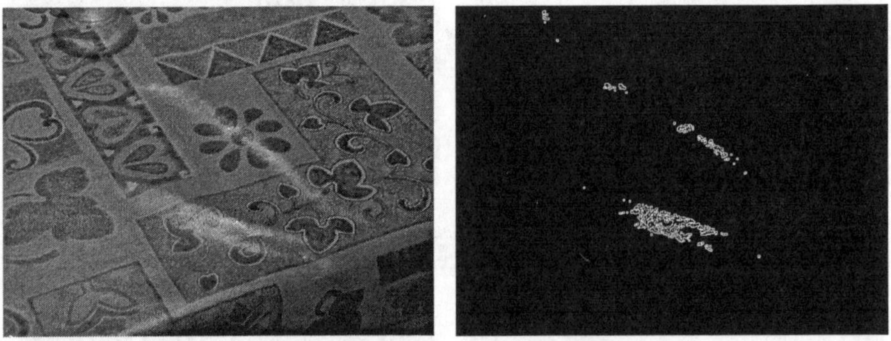

(a) table-cloth-B.bmp (b) brightness-table-cloth-B.bmp

Fig. 12. Detection of the specular reflectance of the image (d) in Fig. 2

chromatic value (hue values) in which they take place. The results obtained by means of this algorithm facilitate the later stages of improvement on the quality of colour images, such as the automatic elimination of bright areas. These pre-processing operations are interesting for applications where it is necessary to obtain a correct segmentation of the objects: manipulation, in multimedia systems, etc.

6 Original Colour Images

All the colour images in this paper are referenced as "name.bmp" and are available in `http://www.disclab.ua.es/aurova/caip2003/images`.

References

1. Gonzalez, R., Woods, R.: Digital Image Processing. Addison-Wesley (1993)
2. Ortiz, F.: Procesamiento Morfológico de Imágenes en Color. Aplicación a la Reconstrucción Geodésica. PhD. Thesis. University of Alicante (2002)

3. Criminisi, A., Bing Kang, S., Swaminathan, R. *et al*: Extracting Layers and Analyzing their Specular Properties Using Epipolar-Plane-Imaging Analysis. Tech. Report MSR-TR-2002-19. Columbia University (2002)
4. Lin, S., Li, Y., Bing Kang, S., *et al*: Diffuse-Specular Separation and Depth Recovery from Image Sequences. In: Heyden, A., Sparr, G., Nielsen, M., Johansen, P. (Eds.): Computer Vision – ECCV. Lecture Notes in Computer Science, Vol. 2352. Springer-Verlag (2002)
5. Raghed, H., Hancock, E.: Separating Lambertian and Specular Reflectance Components using Iterated Conditional Modes. Proc. of The British Machine Vision Conference (BMVC), University of Manchester (2001)
6. Bajcsy, R., *et al*: Detection of diffuse and specular interface reflections and inter-reflections by color image segmentation. IJCV 17 (2), (1996) 241-272.
7. Sangwine, S., Horne, R.: The Colour Image Processing Handbook. Chapman and Hall, Cambridge (1998)
8. Plataniotis, K., Venetsanopoulos, A.: Color Image Processing and Applications. Springer-Verlag, (2000)
9. Fairchild, M.: Color Appearance Models. Addison-Wesley (1998)
10. Levkowitz, H., Herman, G.T.: GLHS: A generalized lightness, hue and saturation color model. CVGIP, 55 (4), (1993) 271-285
11. Serra, J.: Espaces couleur et traitement d'images. Tech. Report N-34/02/MM. Centre de Morphologie Mathématique. École des Mines de Paris (2002)
12. Risson, V.: Application de la Morphologie Mathématique à l'Analyse des Conditions d'Éclaraigc des Images Couleur. PhD. Thesis. CMM. ENSMP (2001)

Skeletonization of Character Based on Wavelet Transform

Xinge You[1,2], Yuan Y. Tang[1], Weipeng Zhang[1], and Lu Sun[1]

[1] Department of Computer Science, Hong Kong Baptist University, Hong Kong
{xyou,yytang}@comp.hkbu.edu.hk
[2] Faculty of Mathematics and Computer Science, Hubei University, Wuhan, China

Abstract. We propose a novel scheme for computing skeleton of characters using wavelet transform. The development of the method depends on a new wavelet function which is designed specifically for computing the medial axis and corner points of character strokes. Based on some certain desirable properties yielded by this particular wavelet function, wavelet skeleton is defined and computed. By using multiscale corner detection with new wavelet function, a set of modifying techniques are developed to remove the artifacts of primary skeletons. Experimental results show that the proposed algorithm overcomes some undesirable effects and limitations of previous methods.

1 Introduction

The skeletons are especially suitable for describing characters since they have natural axes [5]. Representation a character by a set of thin curves rather than by a raster of pixels can reduce the storage space and processing time of character image. This representation is also particularly effective in finding relevant features for character recognition [4].

Generally, the skeleton of a planar character is referred to as the locus of the symmetric points or symmetric axes of the local symmetries of character stroke [1]. Different local symmetry analysis may result in different symmetric points, hence different skeletons are produced and a great deal of skeletonization techniques are explored. In these respects, the *Symmetric Axis Transform* (SAT) introduced by Blum [1], *Smoothed Local Symmetry* (SLS) by Brady [2] and *Process-Inferring Symmetry Analysis* (PISA) by Leyton [7] are employed. Recently skeletonization also makes great progress by using regularity-singularity analyses and constrained Delaunary triangulation technique [10]. Many non-symmetrical skeleton definitions, such as principal curves skeleton, which is [4] independent of the above symmetrical analysis are extensively developed recently.

Though more than 300 skeletonization algorithms have been proposed [5], the improvements are still needed. The existing algorithms often suffer from one or more of the following drawbacks [3, 5, 10]: 1) It may take a long time to skeletonize a high-resolution image; 2) Skeletons may not be centred inside the underlying shapes; 3) Skeletonization algorithms are sensitive to noise and shape

N. Petkov and M.A. Westenberg (Eds.): CAIP 2003, LNCS 2756, pp. 140–148, 2003.

variations, such as rotation and scaling, etc; 4) Skeletons may contain artifacts such as noisy spurs and spurious short branch between split junction points.

In this paper, a new wavelet function which is designed specifically in our work [9] for computing the medial axis and corner point of character objects is investigated. With desirable properties yielded by its wavelet transform, a maximum modulus symmetry analysis is developed and a novel algorithm for computing primary skeleton of character is proposed. A set of modified technique based on multiscale corner detection [6] with new wavelet function is developed to remove the artifacts of primary skeleton. The proposed approach not only remains the desired properties provided by the existing methods, but also improves the corresponding technique. Especially, (1) It is generally easy to determine the symmetric points from symmetric curves proposed, and a skeleton may be centred exactly inside the underlying character. (2) A proposed algorithm is robust against noise and insensitive to affine transform, such as translation, rotation and scaling, etc. (3) It is suitable for a wide variety of character images with varying grey level distributions.

2 Wavelet Transform of Images and Wavelet Function

Let $f \in L^2(R^2)$ be an image. Its continuous wavelet transform (CWT) with respect to the fixed wavelet ψ and scale $s > 0$, $W_s f(x,y)$ is defined by $W_s f(x,y) := (f * \psi_s)(x,y) = \iint_{R^2} f(u,v)\frac{1}{s^2}\psi(\frac{x-u}{s}, \frac{y-v}{s})dudv$, where $*$ denotes the convolution operator in $L^2(R^2)$ and $\psi_s(u,v)$ the dilation of $\psi(u,v)$ denoted by the scale factor s as follows: $\psi_s(u,v) := \frac{1}{s^2}\psi(\frac{u}{s}, \frac{v}{s})$. For a general theory of the scale wavelet transform, it can be found in [8]. Here two wavelets are derived from the partial derivative of $\theta(x,y)$: $\psi^1(x,y) := \frac{\partial}{\partial x}\theta(x,y)$ and $\psi^2(x,y) := \frac{\partial}{\partial y}\theta(x,y)$. Let us denote $\theta_s(x,y) := \frac{1}{s^2}\theta(\frac{x}{s}, \frac{y}{s})$. Their scale wavelet transforms can be written as $W_1^i f(x,y) = (f * \psi_s^1)(x,y) = s\frac{\partial}{\partial x}(f * \theta_s)(x,y), W_s^2 f(x,y) = (f * \psi_s^2)(x,y) = s\frac{\partial}{\partial y}(f * \theta_s)(x,y)$. Its corresponding modulus and gradient of wavelet transform are defined respectively as follows: $|\nabla W_s f(x,y)| := \sqrt{|W_s^1 f(x,y)|^2 + |W_s^2 f(x,y)|^2}$, $Af(s,x,y) := \text{argtan}\left(\frac{W^2 f(s,x,y)}{W^1 f(s,x,y)}\right)$.

To detect the edge or contour of strokes of character and further extract their skeletons, the following odd function, which is designed specifically for computing the medial axis of ribbon-like objects (such as character strokes) in our latest work [9], is considered as wavelet function.

$$\psi(x) := \begin{cases} \psi_1(x) + \psi_2(x) + \psi_3(x) & x \in (0, \frac{1}{4}) \\ \psi_2(x) + \psi_3(x) & x \in [\frac{1}{4}, \frac{3}{4}) \\ \psi_3(x) & x \in [\frac{3}{4}, 1) \\ 0 & x \in [1, \infty) \end{cases} \tag{1}$$

where

$$\begin{cases} \psi_1(x) = -\frac{2}{\pi}(-8x \ln \frac{1+\sqrt{1-16x^2}}{4x} + \frac{1}{2x}\sqrt{1-16x^2}) \\ \psi_2(x) = -\frac{2}{\pi}(8x \ln \frac{3+\sqrt{9-16x^2}}{4x} - \frac{3}{2x}\sqrt{9-16x^2}) \\ \psi_3(x) = -\frac{2}{\pi}(-4x \ln \frac{1+\sqrt{1-x^2}}{x} + \frac{4}{x}\sqrt{1-x^2}) \end{cases}$$

Apparently, the function $\phi(x) := \int_0^x \psi(u)du$ is an even function with compactly supported on [-1, 1], and $\phi'(x) = \psi(x)$ holds as well. Accordingly, for two dimension case, it is easy to see that the smoothness function $\theta(x, y)$, which is defined by $\theta(x, y) := \phi(\sqrt{x^2 + y^2})$, is the reasonable choice. Correspondingly, the 2-D wavelet functions are given by $\begin{cases} \psi^1(x, y) := \frac{\partial}{\partial x}\theta(x, y) = \phi'(\sqrt{x^2 + y^2})\frac{x}{\sqrt{x^2+y^2}} \\ \psi^2(x, y) := \frac{\partial}{\partial y}\theta(x, y) = \phi'(\sqrt{x^2 + y^2})\frac{y}{\sqrt{x^2+y^2}} \end{cases}$

Some significant characteristics of its corresponding wavelet transform with respect to image containing characters are presented below, namely:

Theorem 1. *Let l_d be a straight segment of character stroke with width d and central line l. If the scale of wavelet transform $s \geq d$, then the local maxima moduli of the wavelet transform corresponding to the above wavelet function generates two new periphery lines around the original stroke segment with the following properties: The two new lines are exactly symmetric with respect to the central line of the segment; the distance between the new lines equals to the scale s, in other words, the location of maximum moduli of wavelet transform depends completely on the scale s and the location of the central line of the stroke segment. In particular, if and only if the scale s equals to the width of the stroke segment, the locations of points of maxima moduli lie exactly in the boundaries of the stroke segment.*

An graphical example of WT moduli for two dimension case is illustrated in Figure 1. In the case of one dimension case, the above properties can be derived analogously. Let $C(t) = (X(t), Y(t))$ represent a regular planar curve where t is the arc length. The orientation is defined as : $\alpha(t) = tan^{-1}((dY/dt)/(dX/dt))$. Its corresponding modulus maximum of 1D wavelet transform $W\alpha(s, i)$ at different scales s indicate the possible appearance of singularity. They are especially applicable for detecting singular point of planar curve, such as corner point of shape, where the orientation of planar curve has sharp transitions.

3 Maxima Moduli Symmetry and Wavelet Skeleton

Maxima moduli symmetry and its corresponding wavelet skeleton can be readily defined as follows:

Definition 1. *If wavelet transform which the scale s is bigger than or equals to the width of strokes of character is performed, then the points of corresponding maxima moduli will generate the two new lines locating in the periphery of a stroke. Moreover, they are local symmetrical with respect to the central line of a stroke. This symmetry be called maxima moduli symmetry of wavelet transform (MMSWT).*

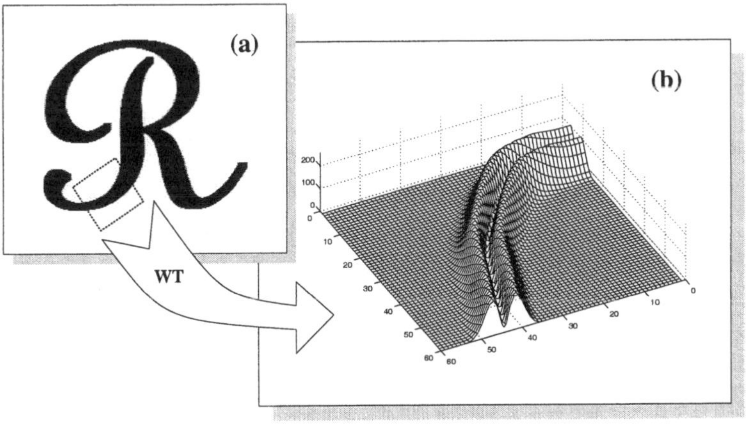

(a)

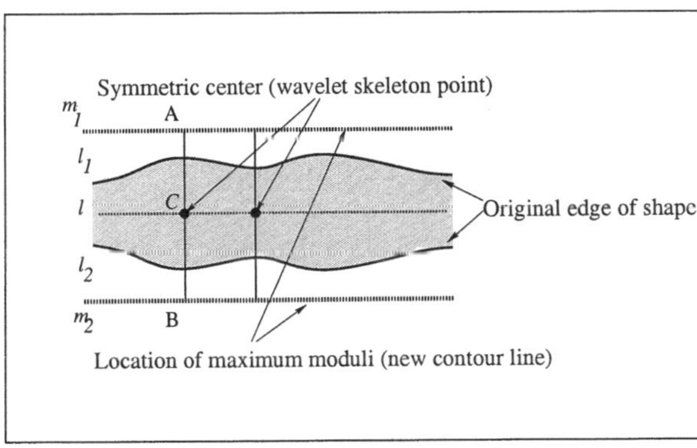

Maximum Moduli Symmetry of Wavelet Transform

(b)

Fig. 1. (a) An example of the distribution of the local modulus maxima of WT for a stroke segment. (b) The illustration of $MMSWF$ Analyses

Definition 2. *The wavelet skeleton of a character is defined as the connective curve of all midpoints with respect to all symmetrical pairs of WT maximal moduli.*

A graphical descriptions of $MMSWT$ is shown in Fig. 1(b). Obviously, it is differently from three typical symmetry analyses, i.e. Blum's SAT, Brady's SLS and Leyton's PISA. Some comparisons between $MMSWT$ and three typical symmetry analyses have made in our previously work [9]. A symmetric axis from $MMSWT$ can be mathematically centred inside the underlying character stroke. It also implicates that total computational expenditure of this algorithm is mainly determined by computing WT phase. Extra computational cost like those algorithms based on previous symmetrical analyses searching tangent circles of contours may be saved.

In practice, for every local moduli maximum point, we determine the other one as its symmetric counterpart along its gradient direction such that the distance between this symmetrical pair equals to scale s. Further, the midpoint between them will be considered as desired skeleton point. In the discrete domain, we slightly modify gradient expression by adding a small positive constant ε to prevent the expression from becoming unstable and have $tg\alpha_s = \frac{\frac{\partial(f*\theta_s)(x,y)}{\partial y}}{\frac{\partial(f*\theta_s)(x,y)}{\partial x}+\varepsilon}$. When α_s falls into a sector, it will be quantified to a certain vector, which is represented by a center line of that sector. Thus, only 4 codes are needed to be used to code these different directions. The above gradient code corresponding to every point is called it's Gradient Code of Wavelet Transform ($GCWT$).

The basic algorithm for extracting the primary wavelet skeleton is summarized as follows: 1.Select the suitable scale of the wavelet transform according to the width of strokes to perform wavelet transform; 2. Compute modulus of the wavelet transform and its $GCWT$; 3. Remove noise (it is necessary for extraction of objects in a noisy environment); 4. Compute all the local modulus maximum and determine its best symmetric counterpart according to its $GCWT$; 5. For every maximum modulus symmetric pair, search its midpoint as skeleton point.

4 Modification of Primary Skeleton

The primary skeletons obtained from the above approach do not resemble somewhat human perceptions of the underlying shapes owe to two types of losing points below, as shown in Fig. 3(c). 1. Some desired points lost from the locus of primary skeletons; 2. Almost all desired skeleton points in the intersection and loop of strokes have not been extracted accurately.

This is because that symmetric counterparts of some contour points (or maximum modulus points) of stroke do not exist and their corresponding symmetrical centers which act as skeleton points can not be detected exactly, especially in all junctions of stroke.

The first type losing point can be resumed readily by comparing the $GCWT$ of its neighbor points along the norm direction of its gradient. Namely, if some lost point which locates in the locus of primary skeleton has the same $GCWT$ as its neighbour points along the norm direction of its gradient, it can be resumed as a skeleton point. This modifying step is also called skeleton smoothing process.

We classify different kinds of contour lines into two types below: If a contour point exists maximum modulus symmetry point of WT or its correspond skeleton point can be obtained from smoothing process, it is called stable contour point. The contour line which is composed of stable contour points is named stable. If contour point which exist neither maximum modulus symmetry point nor correspond skeleton point obtained from smoothing process, then it is called unstable. The corresponding contour line produced by them is called unstable.

Almost all junctions of character strokes resulted in the second losing in the primary skeleton loci may be generalized into five typical patterns in [9]. We are mainly interested in retrieving the second losing skeleton points.

Recalling the corner detection mentioned previously, the orientation function of the contour curve $\alpha(i)$ can be evaluated. Due to desirable properties of WT with new wavelet function, WT is computed for $\alpha(i)$ and modulus maxima of $W\alpha(s,i)$ of WT will be regarded as a corner candidate. For our purpose of modifying artifacts of primary skeleton, only those candidates without symmetrical counterparts are considered as final corner points. We call these corner points as characteristic points.

In addition, we defined another two types of characteristic points below:

Definition 3. *If a point locates in the locus of smoothed primary skeleton and has only unilateral neighbour point along the skeleton locus, then it is called terminal point.*

Definition 4. *If a point locates at the intersection between a stable contour section and unstable one of stroke, then it is called intermittent point.*

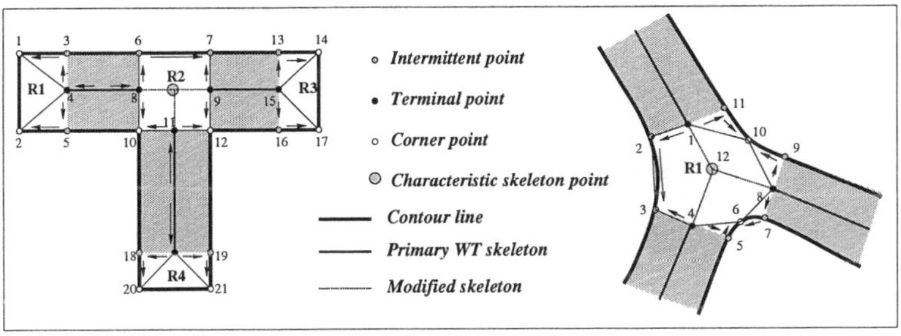

Fig. 2. Illustration of forming polygon

All computation of terminal points are involved in primary wavelet skeletons computing step, as illustrated in Fig. 2.

In practice, all these characteristic points can be used to form a polygon in the intersection according to the following steps: For every terminal point in the primary skeleton, one of two intermittent points are first searched along its gradient direction. Since every intermittent point is associated with an unstable contour line, we start tracking process from this intermittent point and go straight along the unstable contour segment until meet next intermittent point or corner point. Meanwhile, all characteristic points in the tracking path from the starting terminal point to the final corner or intermittent points are recorded as a integrated group. If another tracking group shares some corner or intermittent point with this one. then all characteristic points contained in these two groups are integrated into one new enlarging group. Iterating the above tracking and integrating process until all these characteristic points can be connected to the close polygon along the unstable contours. Some examples are illustrated in Fig. 2.

In practice, the characteristic skeleton point is taken simply as the center of gravity of the polygon. The another alternative scheme for computing characteristic skeleton is based on minimum distance-square error. Namely, the characteristic skeleton point of an intersection region can be determined by minimizing the distances from itself to all terminal points locating in the intersection region.

Fig. 3. (a) The original image; (b) The location of maximum moduli of the wavelet transform; (c) The primary skeletons extracted by the proposed algorithm; (d) The final skeletons obtained by applying the modification technique

Finally, the characteristic skeleton is linked with all terminal points in the underlying polygon region and produces new loci, which will be considered retrieved skeleton lines. The above modification algorithm is summarized directly as four steps below: 1). Detecting characteristic points; 2). Forming Polygon; 3). Determinating characteristic skeleton point; 4). Linking retrieved skeleton lines.

5 Experiments

Finally, we focus on the verification of the effectiveness of the skeletonization from the proposed algorithm by experiments. Some examples are illustrated in Fig. 3. The original image consisting of some English and Chinese words, where each character strokes with a variety of widths. We compute the primary wavelet skeletons in Fig. 3(c) and perform modifying processes on it to obtain the final skeleton in Fig. 3(d).

The image of English words "lucky" with varying grey level distribution and noises is illustrated in Fig. 4(a). The result of final skeletons extracted by using our technique is shown in Fig. 4(d). By comparing the result of the non-threshold processing shown in Fig. 4(b) with that of the threshold one shown in Fig. 4(c), we can conclude that the threshold processing of wavelet transform modulus

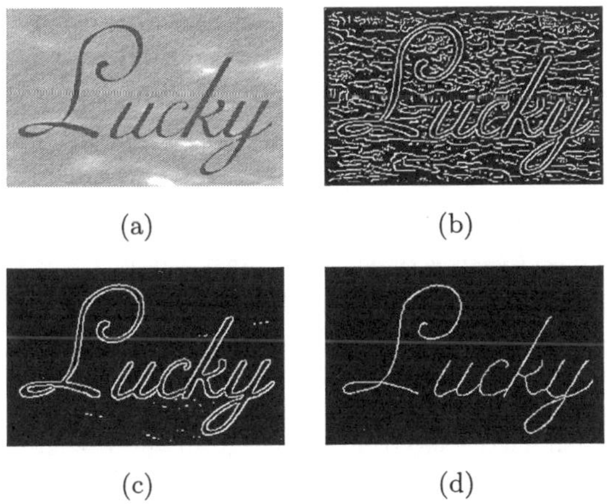

Fig. 4. (a) The original image; (b) The raw output of maximum modulus obtained from the raw wavelet transform modulus; (c) The maximum modulus detected from wavelet transform modulus with threshold process; (d) The final skeletons extracted by applying the modification algorithm

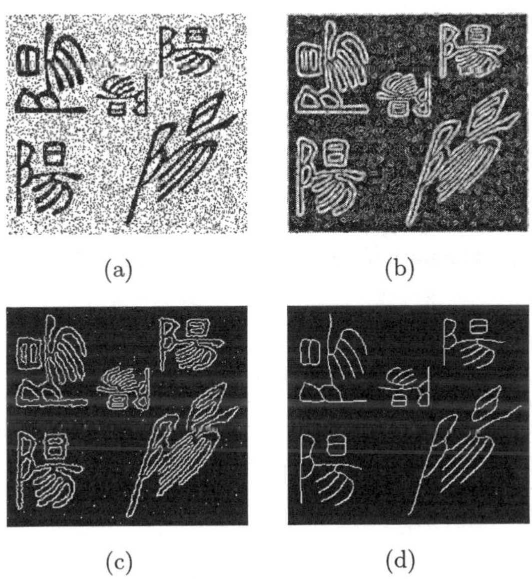

Fig. 5. (a) The original image is harmed by adding "salt and pepper" noises; (b) The raw output of moduli of the wavelet transform corresponding to $s = 4$; (c) The maximum modulus obtained from wavelet transform modulus with threshold processing; (d) The final skeletons extracted by applying the modification algorithm

is robust against the noises and the distracting background. Finally, the image with five affine transformed patterns of the same Chinese character is shown in Fig. 5(a). To evaluate affect which the proposed approach is robust against both the noise and the affine transform, "salt and pepper" noises are added. The desirable effect also verify the fact that the method proposed is insensitive to noises and affine transformation, such as translation, rotation, scaling, etc.

6 Conclusions

Some desirable characteristics of wavelet transform with our constructed wavelet function are presented. With development of wavelet transform characteristics investigation, wavelet skeleton is defined and an efficient algorithm for extracting primary skeleton of character with various gray levels and width is presented. Effectiveness, robustness and accuracy have been evaluated on different images and it also demonstrates that it may be useful in wide images containing all sorts of characters.

Acknowledgment

This work was supported by Research Grant 2002A00009 from Depart of Education in Hubei Province.

References

1. H. Blum. "A transformation for extracting new desxriptors of shape", W. Wathen-Dunn, Eds., Models for the Perception of Speech and Visual Form, pp. 362-380. The MIT Press, Massachusetts, 1967.
2. M. Brady. "Criteria for Representation of Shape", J. Beck and B. Hope and A. Rosenfeld, Eds., Human and Machine Vision, pp. 39-84. Academic Press, New York, 1983.
3. H. S. Chang and H. Yan. "Analysis of Stroke Structures of Handwritten Chinese Characters". *IEEE Trans. Systems, Man, Cybernetics (B)*, vol. 29:pp. 47–61, 1999.
4. B. Kégl and A. Krzyżak. "Piecewise Linear Skeletonization Using Principal Curves". *IEEE Trans. Pattern Anal. Mach. Intell.*, vol. 4(1):pp. 59–74, 2002.
5. L. Lam, S. W. Lee, and C. Y. Suen. "Thinning Methodologies - a Comprehensive Survey". *IEEE Trans. Pattern Anal. Mach. Intell.*, vol. 14:pp. 869–885, 1992.
6. Jiann-Shu Lee, Yung-Nien Sun, and Chin-Hsing Chen. "Multiscale Corner Detection by Using Transform". *IEEE Trans. Image Processing*, vol. 4(1):pp. 100–104, 1995.
7. M. Leyton. Symmetry, Causality, Mind. The MIT Press, Massachusetts, 1988.
8. S. Mallat. *Wavelet Tour of Signal Processing.* Academic Press, San Diego, USA, 1998.
9. Xinge You, Y. Y. Tang, and L. Sun. "Skeletonization of Ribbon-like Shapes with New Wavelet Function". In *The First International Conference on Machine Learning and Cybernetics*, Beijing, China, November 4-5 2002.
10. J. J. Zou and Hong Yan. "Skeletonization of Ribbon-Like shapes Based on Regularity and Singularity Analyses". *IEEE Trans. Systems. Man. Cybernetics (B)*, vol. 31(3):pp. 401–407, 2001.

A New Sharpness Measure Based on Gaussian Lines and Edges

Judith Dijk, Michael van Ginkel, Rutger J. van Asselt, Lucas J. van Vliet, and Piet W. Verbeek

Pattern Recognition Group, Delft University of Technology
Lorentzweg 1, 2628 CJ Delft, The Netherlands
{judith,michael,lucas,piet}@ph.tn.tudelft.nl

Abstract. We measure the sharpness of natural (complex) images using Gaussian models. We first locate lines and edges in the image. We apply Gaussian derivatives at different scales to the lines and edges. This yields a response function, to which we can fit the response function of model lines and edges. We can thus estimate the width and amplitude of the line or edge. As measure of the sharpness we propose the 5th percentile of the sigmas or the fraction of line/edge pixels with a sigma smaller than 1.

1 Introduction

The purpose of the research presented in this paper is to model the perceptual sharpness of natural (complex) images. Sharpness is an important perceptual attribute determining the perceptual quality of an image. This is, for example, important to judge image enhancement techniques. The standard RMS measure reflects the perceptual quality very poorly [2][10].

In the past, we have already done some experiments regarding the *relative* sharpness of natural images [3]. This relative sharpness is defined with respect to an original image, whereas the sharpness measure proposed in this paper is a property of the image itself. In the previous study we have seen that images can be seen as a collection of areas that are more or less uniform, separated by lines and edges. We assume that perceptual sharpness is correlated to the sharpness of these lines and edges.

To determine the sharpness we need to determine the location and orientation of the lines and edges so that we can perform measurements on their profile. To establish their sharpness we need a model for the profile. We use a Gaussian profile for the line and an integrated Gaussian (error function) for the edge.

We compute Gaussian derivatives at several scales to obtain a response function or signature. At a singularity point, the response function can be predicted given the width and the amplitude of the line or edge. Conversely, we can estimate the width and amplitude of the line or edge from the measured response function.

The measured sigmas of all points have to be combined to form one or a few measures of sharpness. An obvious measure is the smallest sigma in the image.

N. Petkov and M.A. Westenberg (Eds.): CAIP 2003, LNCS 2756, pp. 149–156, 2003.

Because measuring the smallest sigma is sensitive to noise and other artifacts, we use the 5th percentile instead of the minimum sigma. Another measure that can be used is the fraction of pixels for which the sigma is smaller than one. This gives some insight in the number of sharp lines and edges in the image.

Kayargadde [6] proposed a similar measure for the perceptual sharpness of images. He used a polynomial transform (Hermite transform), to detect and estimate edge parameters, such as position, orientation, amplitude, mean value and sigma. Our methods differs from his on three points. The first is that we detect lines and edges and determine the width of both of them. The second difference is that we perform a numerical estimation of the amplitude, whereas Kayargadde derived an analytical relationship. And the last difference is that we estimate the orientation of the structures in the localization phase, where Kayargadde determines the orientation in the estimation phase.

2 Line and Edge Detection

Before we can determine the sharpness of individual lines and edges, transients or singularity points for short, we must extract them from the image. For each transient we must also establish whether it is a line or an edge and its orientation ϕ, as defined in figure 1. Since we must deal with both lines and edges, it is logical to use a filterbank based on quadrature filters[1]. A quadrature filter is a linear, complex-valued filter. The real and imaginary part act as a line and edge filter respectively. The magnitude of the response is phase-invariant, i.e. insensitive to whether the transient is a line or an edge. This is important when we discuss the suppression of spurious responses below.

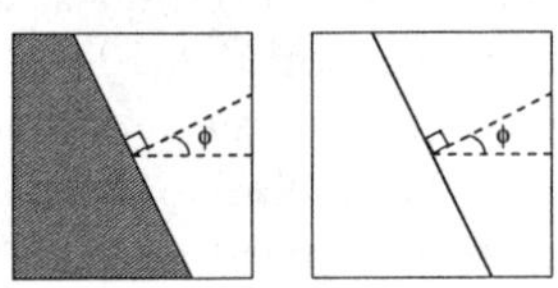

Fig. 1. The definition of orientation ϕ for an edge (left) and a line (right)

The quadrature filter is sensitive to edges and lines under a limited range of orientations. To obtain the response under an arbitrary angle we use a steerable [4] quadrature filter: the response can be computed from the filter response under a finite set of angles.The details of the quadrature filter we use can be found in [5]. The filter's characteristic frequency f_c, the range of frequencies it is sensitive to b_f and the orientation selectivity s_a can be tuned independently. Our supposition is that the overall sharpness relates to the sharpest line or edge in the image. This supposition only holds for natural images. We have tuned the filter in such a way that it will detect small-scale lines and edges $(f_c, b_f) = (0.16, 0.16)$.

[1] Knutsson and coworkers [7] were early advocates of the use of quadrature filters in image analysis.

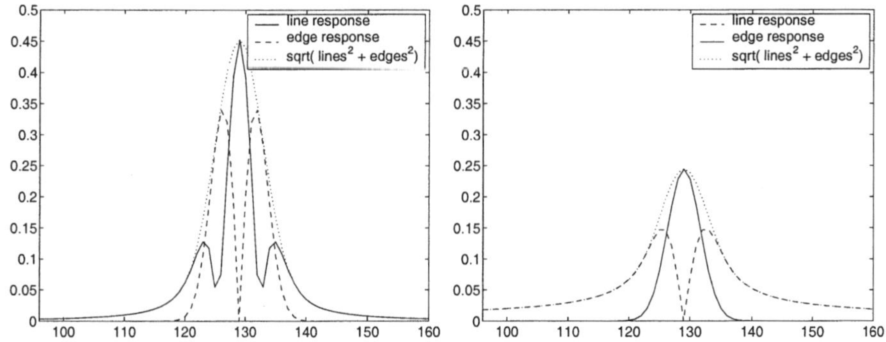

(a) (b)

Fig. 2. a) The filters responses to a line (a) and an edge (b)

The orientation selectivity $s_a = 0.185$ [5] (17 filters) was chosen as a trade-off between orientation selectivity, signal-to-noise ratio and localization of the filter response.

Our last task is to determine whether a detected transient is an edge or a line, and the suppression of spurious responses. To see why these occur, imagine a line. The line detector responds as it should, but the edge detector will also respond. It responds to the flanks of the line, although less strongly than the line detector. This is illustrated in figure 2. We resolve this problem by suppressing (inhibiting) the secondary responses. The final line response l_{line} is given by

$$l_{\text{line}}(x,y) = \begin{cases} 0 & \text{if } q(x,y) < \max_{N(x,y)} q(x,y) \\ 0 & \text{if } q_l(x,y) < q_e(x,y) \\ q_l(x,y) & \text{elsewhere} \end{cases}, \tag{1}$$

with q the quadrature filter result, q_l and q_e the quadrature line and edge component filter results respectively ($q = \sqrt{q_l^2 + q_e^2}$), and $N(x,y)$ a neighbourhood around (x,y). The size of the neighbourhood must be roughly equal to the width of the response lobes. By swapping the roles of q_l and q_e the same technique can be used to obtain the final edge response. Points for which the quadrature filter is larger in a different orientation are discarded.

3 Line and Edge Characterization

In this section we explain how we can determine the amplitude and sigma of Gaussian lines in images. We assume that the noise level is low: there is no point in measuring a subtle feature like sharpness if the image is heavily distorted. The method we use is a variation of Mallat's approach [9], using Gaussian derivatives rather than wavelets [13]. The idea is to compute the response of the Gaussian derivator operator applied across the transient, while varying the scale of the Gaussian. The response depends on both the scale of the Gaussian and that of the transient. Since we know the first, we may estimate the latter.

It is convenient to adapt a local coordinate system (v, w) at each point (x_0, y_0) that is aligned with the orientation ϕ at that point:

$$\begin{pmatrix} v \\ w \end{pmatrix} = \begin{pmatrix} \cos\phi & \sin\phi \\ -\sin\phi & \cos\phi \end{pmatrix} \begin{pmatrix} x - x_0 \\ y - y_0 \end{pmatrix}. \tag{2}$$

The singularity function of an infinitely long line and edge respectively are given by

$$\begin{aligned} h_{\text{line}} &= A\,\delta(v) = A\,\delta\big((x - x_0)\cos(\phi) + (y - y_0)\sin(\phi)\big) \\ h_{\text{edge}} &= A\,u(v) = A\,u\big((x - x_0)\cos(\phi) + (y - y_0)\sin(\phi)\big) \end{aligned} \tag{3}$$

where A is the amplitude of the transient, ϕ the angle of the transient with respect to the x-axis, $\delta(x)$ the Dirac delta function and $u(x)$ the Heaviside step function. Real transients have a finite width. We model this by convolving these functions with a Gaussian with $\sigma_{l/e}$. The width $\sigma_{1/e}$ reflects the sharpness of the transient.

To find an estimate for the width $\sigma_{l/e}$ and amplitude A of the lines and edges we construct a response function in the following way: we convolve the input image with directional Gaussian derivatives along ϕ increasing the scale exponentially: $\sigma = b^i$ $(b > 1)$ with i the free scale parameter. The Gaussian regularisation has, in general, the effect that the response decreases as a function of scale, as noted by Lindeberg [8]. We follow [8] in using normalized, or scale-independent, Gaussian derivatives. This results in more pronounced response curves. The normalization consists of multiplying the response with σ.

The response curve at (x_0, y_0) is

$$r(\sigma) = \sigma \frac{\partial g_\sigma(v, w)}{\partial v} * \big(h(v, w) * g_{s_{l/e}}(v, w)\big) \tag{4}$$

Using the commutativity of the convolution operator we obtain

$$r(\sigma) = \sigma \frac{\partial}{\partial v}\big(h(v, w) * g_s(v, w)\big) \quad \text{with} \quad s = \sqrt{\sigma_{l/e}^2 + \sigma^2}. \tag{5}$$

In what follows we consider the modulus of the response $M(\sigma) = |r(\sigma)|$. The expression for M for a line and edge respectively is given by the following two equations:

$$\begin{aligned} M_{\text{line}}(\sigma) &= |A\sigma \frac{\partial}{\partial v} g_s(v)| = \frac{|A|\sigma}{\sqrt{2\pi} s^3} |v| \exp(-\frac{v^2}{2s^2}) \\ M_{\text{edge}}(\sigma) &= \frac{|A|\sigma}{\sqrt{2\pi} s} \exp(-\frac{v^2}{2s^2}) \end{aligned} \tag{6}$$

The modulus maxima per scale are given by

$$\max M_{\text{line}}(\sigma) = \frac{|A|\sigma}{\sqrt{2\pi e} s^2} \text{ at } v = s \quad \text{and} \quad \max M_{\text{edge}}(\sigma) = \frac{|A|\sigma}{\sqrt{2\pi} s} \text{ at } v = 0. \tag{7}$$

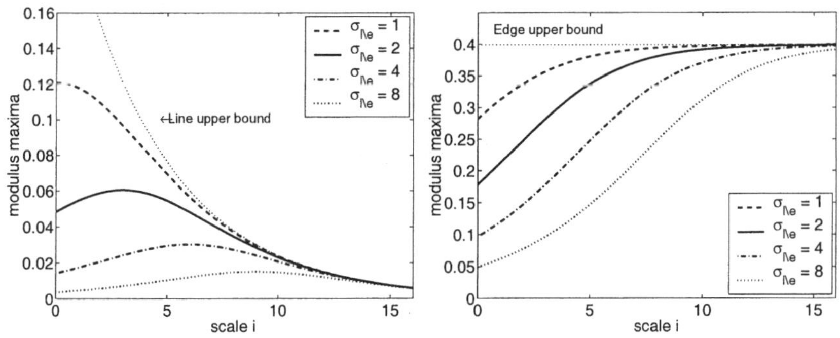

Fig. 3. The modulus maxima of the response at different scales. A = 1, b is $2^{1/3}$

The modulus maxima for lines and edges with different sigmas are given in figure 3. These responses are the theoretical responses of lines and edges. We find the sigmas of the lines and edges in the image by fitting the measured responses to the theoretical responses.

The selection of the modulus maximum for an edge is straightforward: the position of the maximum is the same as the position of the point itself. For the lines this is different, the maxima are shifted over s. To find these maxima we search for a maximum in a appropriately sized neighbourhood.

The minimalization can be done by some numerical minimization method. We use a minimalization based on the Levenberg-Marquardt method. We start with the third maximum ($\sigma = b^3$) and use 8 scales. b is chosen $2^{1/3}$, i.e. three samples per octave.

4 Sharpness Measures

The final step is to obtain one or a few sharpness measures using the sigmas. We define and evaluate two sharpness measures. The first measure we looked into is the fraction of points with a sigma smaller than 1. This is a very intuitive measure, just the number of points with a small sigma. The second measure is the sharpest line or edge in the image. Ideally, we would want to use the smallest sigma. However, measuring the smallest sigma is sensitive to noise and other artifacts. Therefore, we use the 5th percentile of the sigma as an estimate for the smallest sigma. The choice for the percentile level is not critical: the effect of changing the percentile is roughly that of a multiplicative constant.

5 Tests of the Sharpness Measures

We tested the three proposed sharpness measures using four test images. These images are given in figure 4 (a)-(d). The images were manipulated in two ways, The first manipulation is a Gaussian blurring with $\sigma^2/2 = \{0.5, 1.0, 1.5 ... 3.0\}$. In

(a) `trui` (b) `erika` (c) `cameron` (d) `lenna` (e) `bicycle` (f) `portrait`

Fig. 4. The test images

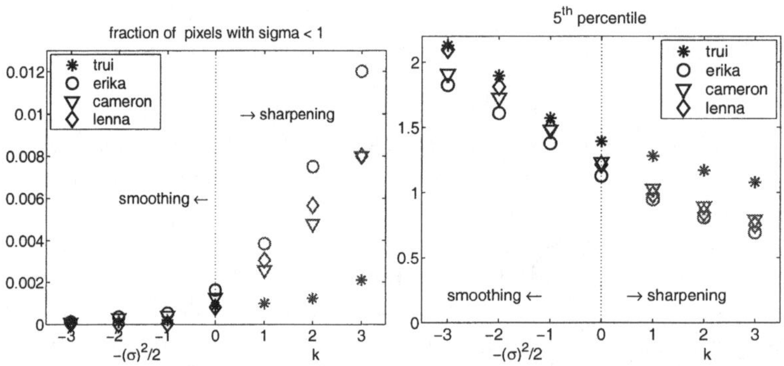

Fig. 5. Different sharpness measures. In (a) the values are inversely correlated with the sharpness of the image, in (b) the values are correlated with the sharpness of the image. The method of unsharp masking allows estimated sigmas smaller than 0.9 without problems of aliasing

the second manipulation we subtract from an image I, k times the Laplacian-of-Gaussian filtered version [14] (unsharp masking) with $\sigma = 1.0$. The k's used are $\{0.5, 1.0, 1.5...3.0\}$. In the results we plot these two manipulations in one plot by putting the original in the middle (denoted by the dashed line), with the blurring to the left and the sharpening to the right. The spacing to the left is $-\sigma^2/2$, the spacing to the right is k.

The results for the two sharpness measures are given in figure 5. We expect the fraction of pixels with a sigma smaller than one to decrease for a larger blurring, and the smallest sigma to increase for a larger blurring. It can be seen that this is indeed the case. This means that both measures can be used as a measure for the difference in sharpness between images.

We performed a small pairwise-comparison experiment to determine the sharpness of the original images with respect to each other. Six subjects compared all pairs, six subjects only the pairs without `lenna`. It was found that `cameron` is the sharpest image, closely followed by `lenna`. The most unsharp image is `trui`.

If the measures are absolute sharpness measures, this order should also be found with the sharpness measures. For the 5th percentile, `trui` is indeed the

Table 1. The Spearman rank-order coefficients per subject. The number of images in the range is 8, for which the critical value is 0.74. All values are significant. Note that subject 4 did not participate in the `bicycle` experiment

Image	sharpness measure	Subject 1	2	3	4
`portrait`	5th percentile	0.93	0.83	0.93	0.86
`portrait`	fraction of points	0.88	0.88	0.79	0.95
`bicycle`	5th percentile	0.95	0.88	0.83	
`bicycle`	fraction of points	0.95	0.88	0.83	

most unsharp image. The ordering of the other three images is not the same as as was found with the pairwise comparison experiment, but these values are not significantly different in the first place. We conclude that the 5th percentile is a promising measure. For the fraction of pixels with a sigma smaller than 1 trui is not the most unsharp image. We conclude that we can only use this measure as a relative sharpness measure.

6 Results of Perceptual Experiments

In earlier experiments [3] we asked subjects to order images that were sharpened with unsharp masking, and subsequently smoothed with anisotropic diffusion [11][1]. The images that are used in the experiment are standard ISO images (CD-ROM 12640:1997). These images are given in figure 4 (e) and (f). The correlation between the perceived sharpness on the one hand and the proposed sharpness measures on the other, is measured with the Spearman rank-order correlation coefficient r_s [12]. The null hypothesis that is tested is that there is no association between the two rankings. Each subject ordered a range of images for which the sharpness was different. The rank-order coefficients for the different subjects and ranges are given in table 1. It can be seen that with both measures the null hypothesis can be rejected for all subjects and ranges. The conclusion is that both measures correspond to perceptual relative sharpness.

7 Conclusions and Discussion

We found that we can measure the sharpness of simple line and edge images. We first located these lines and edges in the image. Then we determined the sharpness of these lines and edges by fitting a Gaussian line or edge profile to the Gaussian derivative signature.

We defined two measures: the 5th percentile of the sigma and the fraction of pixels with a sigma smaller than one. We found that the 5th percentile correlates to perceptual sharpness. The fraction of pixels with a sigma smaller than one can be used as a relative sharpness measure.

In the future, we will study the distribution of the sigmas and amplitudes to see if we can define other measures that correlate to the sharpness of images.

Acknowledgments

This research is partly supported by Senter, Agency of the Ministry of Economic Affairs of the Netherlands.

References

1. F. Catté, P.-L. Lions, J.-M. Morel, and T. Coll. Image selective smoothing and edge detection by nonlinear diffusion. *SIAM Journal on Numerical Analysis*, 29(1):182–193, 1992.
2. S. Daly. The visible differences predictor: An algorithm for the assessment of image fidelity. In A. B. Watson, editor, *Digital images and human vision*, chapter 14, pages 179–206. M.I.T. Press, London, England, 1993.
3. J. Dijk, D. de Ridder, P. W. Verbeek, J. Walraven, I. T. Young, and L. J. van Vliet. A new measure for the effect of sharpening and smoothing filters on images. In *Proc. 11th Scandinavian Conference on Image Analysis*, pages 213–220. SCIA '99, 1999.
4. W. T. Freeman and E. H. Adelson. The design and use of steerable filters. *IEEE transactions on Pattern Analysis and Machine Intelligence*, 13(9):891–906, September 1991.
5. M. van Ginkel. *Image Analysis using Orientation Space based on Steerable Filters.* PhD thesis, Delft University of Technology, Delft, The Netherlands, 2002.
6. V. Kayargadde. *Feature extraction for image quality prediction.* PhD thesis, Technische universiteit Eindhoven, 1995.
7. H. Knutsson and G.H. Granlund. Texture analysis using two-dimensional quadrature filters. In *IEEE Computer Society Workshop on Computer Architecture for Pattern Analysis and Image Database Management*, Pasadena, October 1983.
8. T. Lindeberg. On scale selection for differential operators. In *Proc. 8th Scandinavian Conference on Image Analysis*, 1993.
9. S. Mallat and W. L. Hwang. Singularity detection and processing with wavelets. *IEEE transactions on information theory*, 38(2):617–643, March 1992.
10. H. Marmolin. Subjective MSE measures. *IEEE Transactions on Systems, Man and Cybernetics*, 16(3):486–489, 1986.
11. P. Perona, T. Shiota, and J. Malik. Anisotropic diffusion. In B.M. ter Haar Romeny, editor, *Geometry-driven diffusion in computer vision*, pages 73–92, Dordrecht, 1994. Kluwer Academic Publishers.
12. S. Siegel and N. J. Castellan. *Non parametric statistics for the behavioral sciences.* McGraw-Hill, New York, NY, 1988.
13. R. J. van Asselt. Line and edge characterization using mallat wavelets. Master's thesis, Delft University of Technology, December 1997.
14. I. T. Young, J. J. Gerbrands, and L. J. Van Vliet. Image processing fundamentals. In V.K. Madisetti and D.B. Williams, editors, *The Digital Signal Processing handbook*, chapter 51, pages 1 – 81. IEEE Press and CRC Press, 1998.

A New Tracking Technique: Object Tracking and Identification from Motion

Terrence Chen[1,*], Mei Han[2], Wei Hua[2], Yihong Gong[2], and Thomas S. Huang[1]

[1] Beckman Institute, University of Illinois at Urbana Champaign
{tchen5,huang}@ifp.uiuc.edu
[2] NEC Laboratories America
{meihan,wei,ygong}@sv.nec-labs.com

Abstract. Pattern recognition and object tracking play very important roles in various applications, such as motion capture, object detection/recognition, video surveillance, and human computer interface. One very useful method that is rarely mentioned in literature is performing recognition from the motion cue. In many situations, the motion of an object is very representative and informative; therefore, it is possible to identify the object and its behavior from its motion. In this paper, we propose an original method to both identify and track an object in dynamic scenes. The method works on the situations with occlusions, appearance changes and global camera motions. It does not require prior segmentation or initialization. We test this method on a video database containing 18 World Cup soccer videos recorded from TV to detect and track the soccer ball. The results are satisfying. The results are also integrated into a video indexing system and the improvement on video retrieval is described.

1 Introduction

Traditionally, tracking is regarded as an abstract probabilistic inference problem that has three components: prediction, data association and correction. Prediction estimates the object location on current frame based on previous frames; data association connects the object representation with image measurements; correction generates the new object representation based on the current state and relevant measurements. However, in many cases, it is difficult to have reliable and efficient solutions for prediction, data association and correction. Some methods are based on the following two assumptions to simplify the tracking problem [3]: firstly, only the immediate past matters,

$$P(X_i|X_1,\ldots,X_{i-1})-P(X_i|X_{i-1})$$

* This work was conducted while the first author was a summer intern at NEC

N. Petkov and M.A. Westenberg (Eds.): CAIP 2003, LNCS 2756, pp. 157–164, 2003.

where X_i represents the state of the object at the i'th frame; secondly, measurements are only dependent on the current state,

$$P(Y_i, Y_j|X_i) = P(Y_i|X_i)P(Y_j|X_i)$$

where Y_i means the image measurements obtained in the i'th frame. There have been many research activities in this area. Kalman filter [2], condensation algorithm [6] and some more recent methods like co-inferencing [15] give good estimation of tracking under certain constraints or in certain situations. However, in many other cases, the two pre-assumptions are not satisfied and the algorithms mentioned above cannot deal with these situations well. For instance, sometimes the previous state is not known at all, which means the system has to identify at least one state automatically. Sometimes the number of features extracted in any given image is too small to identify the object. This becomes a problem involving both object tracking and recognition.

In this paper, we propose a method to deal with objects with occlusions, appearance changes and global camera motions. The method takes advantage of the temporal context information and accomplishes object identification and tracking at the same time. It works on dynamic scenes where multiple moving objects are included without requirement of pre-segmentation or initialization. The core technique lies on motion trajectory fitting in image volumes. Shi and Malik [12] applied their clustering technique of normalized cut to object tracking and motion segmentation on image volumes. They required good estimations of optical flows which are sensitive to object appearance changes. Peleg and Herman [9] built panoramic images from slices of images. Ngo et al. [8] also worked on volumes of image slices to estimate camera motions from which video shot clustering is achieved. Our method extracts motion trajectory information from image volumes, which is the key characteristic to identify object and its motion.

We test this method on a real world example to identify and track the soccer ball in a broadcasting soccer game. We have no idea of the ball's location in any given image frame. Suppose the small white blobs are detected in the images, we then end up with too many candidates which could possibly be the ball. Furthermore, the ball could be blocked by the players, mix with the lines and goalposts on the field, or even appear as a blurred short line when it is moving fast. Therefore, there is not enough information within individual images. We have to make use of the information across temporal domain. The soccer ball, at most of the time, moves quickly and linearly in the field. There exists a clear motion trajectory of the ball in image volumes. Similar tracking examples can be found in surveillance videos of cluttered environment and data collection tools for traffic or retail monitoring.

Our discussion will proceed as follows. In section 2, we describe the method and explain the details of the algorithm. In section 3, we show our experiments on a video database and its application to video indexing system. In section 4, we conclude.

2 Methodology

In this section, we present object identification and tracking method based on motion information in image volumes. Many tracking algorithms depend on the current image frame to predict the next image frame. This sequential method is incremental and efficient, but it may cause problems in certain cases. First, the object cannot be identified or detected by the system automatically but needs to be identified by a human in the beginning. Second, if the low-level features of the object are not quite consistent, it is very hard to track the object or define the measurements. In order to solve these difficulties, we propose our method to identify and track the object across multiple images at the same time.

Real-time tracking is not always necessary in many applications. If we can tolerate a very short delay like a half second, we can accumulate much more information from the time dimension. In fact, the main difference between a video and an image is that video has the time dimension, so we could utilize features related to this dimension. If the delay is short enough (i.e. less than 1 second), then it should be tolerable by users in most cases, such as analyzing a surveillance video to find out the abnormal patterns or suspicious activities, extracting sports highlights from a broadcasting TV program or summarization documentary videos. With the information gained from videos of the short delay interval, we fit pre-defined motion trajectories in image volumes. In that way, we can detect the moving object and identify its trajectory in one step.

1: $n \leftarrow$ number of frames
2: Split the video V into several segments $S_1, S_2, \ldots, S_m$, each segment S_i contains n frames.
3: Within each frame I_i, clean the noise within a single frame by time-irrelevant features.
4: Within each video segment $S_1,..,S_m$, clean the noise due to correlations between frames.
5: Define constraints C_j ($j = 1$ to p) describing the object behavior over the video segment.
6: $T \leftarrow$ the threshold of number of images where the object appears ($0 \leq T \leq n$).
7: Calculate the rate R_k of each candidate by: $R_k = w_1 C_1^R + w_2 C_2^R + \ldots\ldots + w_p C_p^R$
(*w* is the weighting of each constraint, *p* is number of total constraints, C^R denotes the numerical rating of *C*), $|C_i| \geq T$ ($|C_i|$ means the number of constraint C_i satisfied within the segment, hence, $|C_i| \leq n$)
8: Output the candidate k with the highest rating R_k.

Fig. 1. The proposed algorithm.

Figure 1 shows our algorithm. In step 1, we set *n* as the number of frames we want to analyze together. To reduce the computation overhead and minimize the delay, *n* should not be too large. In step 2, we split the video into several segments and let each segment contains exactly *n* frames. The segments can be overlapped, if needed, to alternatively correct the errors. Step 3 cleans the noise within one single frame, e.g., if we want to find a red flower, we can filter those colors which are far from red. Or if we want to find a wheel, then we can eliminate objects with shapes which are not circular. We try to clean the noise as much as possible using multiple frames in step 4. For example, we can compensate the camera motion using several frames. We can also eliminate some noisy line segments which cannot be identified as noise in a single frame. In Step 5, we define the constraints or characteristics that describe the object's behavior over this period of time, e.g., the trajectory of the object should be a circle, and the velocity of the object should be greater than 5 pixels per frame, etc. Step 6 sets the threshold T which is the number of frames that satisfies the constraints set in step 5, therefore, $0 \leq T \leq n$. This step makes the object need not appear in all the n frames but only T is enough. Step 7 calculates the rating of each candidate by given weights if needed. Step 8 outputs the candidate with the highest rating as the result.

3 Experimental Evaluation

The video database we used to demonstrate our method is a database containing 13 TV broadcasting games in World Cup 2002 and 5 games in World Cup 1998. The problem of soccer ball detection is very difficult. Some apparent difficulties lie in: firstly, the ball is usually only a little white blob. This is annoying since there are many other little white blobs like the shirts, shorts or socks of the players, some vague line segments on the field, and the white patterns on the advertisement boards. Besides, the shape of the ball changes rapidly, especially when the ball moves very fast. Thirdly, the color of the ball is changing during the game due to the lighting, camera motion and its location. Fourthly, the broadcasting cameras are moving almost all of the time. The scene shots change frequently and within each scene shot, the camera may tilt, pan and/or zoom. Finally, the ball is sometimes even not visible in certain frames, maybe blocked by the players or hidden in the auditorium. Even human eyes may not tell where the ball is in some frames. However, the information of the ball is essential in a soccer video.

Much work has been done on understanding or summarizing the sports video content by low level features [4, 5, 7, 16, 18], including American football, soccer, tennis and baseball games. However, lack of identification or tracking of some important objects due to technique limitations makes the result not as good as expected. For example, Yow et al. [17], Retz-Schmidt [11] and Utsumi et al. [14] tried to analyze the soccer game but the results are limited without knowing the position of the soccer ball. Xu et al. [16] only focused on classifying the scene shot by color-based grass detector. Tovinkere and Qian [13] detected the semantic events in soccer games well but it required the position and location information of the players and the ball as inputs. In other words, the ball has to be equipped with a sensor as well as the players. Pingali [10] tracked the ball in tennis broadcasts, however, there are still some pre-assumptions and tracking a tennis ball is much simpler than a soccer ball. This is because the tennis court is much simpler. There are only two players, one at the left hand side and the other at the right hand side. Besides, the ball moves mostly back and forth regularly. We try to overcome the difficulties of tracking the ball in the soccer broadcast video. We also prove that by knowing the position and trajectory of the ball, the learning system can detect the semantic events or highlights of the games more accurately. Our experiments are two folds: First, we tried to recognize and then track the ball in the soccer video database. Later, we added the information to a system used to extract and classify the highlights of the games and see the improvement.

In the first experiment, we ran the proposed algorithm shown in figure 1 by setting n as 16 in step 1. In step 3, we used shape and color filter to select the white blobs as the candidates of the ball in each frame. The filter should be flexible enough to let the real ball be in one of the white blobs. We compensated the global camera motions (pan, tilt, and zoom) and did global noise reduction (removes the lines on the field) in step 4 to get the absolute movements of the objects in the frames. Step 5 defined two constraints, C_1 and C_2, where C_1 means the trajectory of the ball should be nearly a straight line and C_2 gives a range for the ball's velocity. The velocity should be reasonable for a ball moving in a half second. In step 6, we set $T = 10$. This means the candidates satisfying the constraints has to appear in at least 10 frames out of the 16 frames. In step 7, the rating R_k of each candidate k were calculated by:

$$R_k = w_1 C_1^R + w_2 C_2^R$$

where C_j^R means the rating for C_j, $w_1 = 1$, and

$$w_2 = \begin{cases} 1, \ if\ V_{\min} < C_2^R < V_{\max} \\ 0, \ otherwise \end{cases}$$

where V_{min} and V_{max} are given constraints of the velocity.

At last, we simply outputted the candidate k with highest R_k.

Figure 2 shows one of the running examples of our algorithm with the total images (I_0 to I_{15}). The first 16 images represent the original image frames within a selected segment. The 17th image (I_A) in each figure shows the encoding image where the white points indicate the compensated candidate location and their intensities show the time code. The brightest point means the latest point and the darkest point means the earliest point. The 18th image (I_R) shows the selected candidate with its location and direction after running the entire algorithm.

In figure 2, the ball moved towards the player's head by a pass from some other player and then the player shot the ball towards the goal by his head. Although the direction is changed during this segment, we can get the final and the most important direction of the ball. Because half second is short enough, one can believe that the ball does not change direction in most of the segments. Even it does change the direction and we do need to identify the ball in each frame, we can use a cross-validation method to identify and track the ball by overlapping the segments. For example, we can let each segment overlaps each other by 5 frames and validates the correctness of the identified ball. The trade-off is doing cross-validation by overlapping needs more computation, which means the delay may be longer.

As shown, our method can identify the ball and therefore recover its locations and direction, especially when the ball moves very fast (by our given constraint), which is more meaningful in a soccer game. We test our algorithm on 151 highlights (78 shot-on-goals, 4 goals, 54 corner kicks, and 19 free kicks) from the video database containing 18 games to see whether the ball is correctly reported. The precision of our experiment is around 76.8%. Although 76.8% seems not a very good result, using other tracking techniques or different methods can hardly detect the ball, nor track it at all. Besides, if cross-validation is integrated, it is also expected to improve the overall precision of the system. We focus on the highlights, which are more meaningful scene shots.

Fig. 2. A running example of the game Argentina V.S. England in World Cup 2002.

Maximum entropy method (*ME*) [1] has been successfully applied in many applications as well as the sports video summarization by Hua et al. [8]. In Hua's work, they use *ME* to automatically select features with more distinguishing power and then extract the highlights of baseball games based on the selected features. In our second experiment, to demonstrate our work is useful in real applications, we built a similar system to extract the highlights of a soccer video game. However, the most distinguishing but also the most difficult detecting features of a soccer game video might be the motion information of the ball. If we can generate many features of the ball, such as location, direction, velocity, and so on, it is possible to detect the highlights of the soccer games video database as well. Hence, we used *ME* as a test platform to verify the ball tracking results. Our video highlight indexing system automatically selected 100 features (this number is determined by cross validation) while 15 out of them were generated by our ball tracking algorithm, including ball starting location, ending location, velocity, direction. The system not only tried to extract the highlights of the soccer games but also classified the highlights to goal, shot-on-goal, corner kick, or free kick. It is much easier if only highlights need to be extracted without classification. These four highlights were classified by using both low-level features, such as color, edge, camera motion and more elaborated features like goalpost location, corner detection, etc. Table 1 shows the results of extracting and classifying the highlights of a soccer video game with and without identifying and tracking the ball in the sports game. (Based on 18 games in World Cup Series)

Table 1. System performance with and without tracking the ball.

	Precision w/o the ball's features	**Recall w/o the ball's features**	**Precision with the ball's features**	**Recall with the ball's features**
Shot-on-goal (78 total)	55.1%(43 correct)	64.2%(67 detected)	74.4% (58 correct)	89.3%(65 detected)
Goal (4)	50.0% (2)	33.3% (6)	75.0%(3)	60.0%(5)
Corner kick (54)	48.2%(26)	55.3%(47)	68.5%(37)	77.1%(48)
Free kick (19)	10.5% (2)	25.0% (8)	36.8%(7)	43.8%(16)

In table 1, we can see that both the precision and the recall are dramatically improved around 25% with the information of the soccer ball. This demonstrates how important and useful our technique is.

4 Conclusion

In this paper, we propose a novel technique based on the pattern of the object's motion characteristics. It is a batch method using the motion cue, which is a quite reliable feature for many objects. We demonstrated the applicability of the method by doing experiments on a real soccer game video database to identify and track the trajectory of the soccer ball.

Some future works are integrating machine-learning techniques with the method to let the system learn the best weights of each given constraint automatically and make the system easily fit to work on different video databases with various kinds of content. Besides, formalizing a more efficient method to locate the candidate that best matches the given constraints is also important.

In applications to track an object with apparent features, like a human body, or a vehicle, methods like Kalman filter or condensation have been proven to be good estimators. The best merit of our technique is a good alternative method to track object in the situations that other existing methods cannot handle well.

As a result, we propose a novel idea to overcome the difficulties of identifying and tracking an object in videos. The object does not have to be fixed-shape, and it can entirely disappear in several frames. Other work could be done or integrated to refine this idea and it is a very useful alternative technique in many important applications.

References

1. Berger, A. L., Della Pietra, S. A., and Della Pietra, V. J., *A maximum entropy approach to natural language processing*, Computational Linguistics, vol. 22, 1996.
2. Dean, G.C, *An introduction to Kalman filters measurement and control*, V. 19, pp. 69 - 73.
3. Forsyth, D. A., Ponce, J, *Computer Vision: A Modern Approach*, 2002
4. Gong, Y., Sin, L. T., Chuan, C. H., and Sakauchi, M., *Automatic parsing of TV soccer programs*, in IEEE International Conference on Multimedia Computing and Systems, 1995, pp. 167-174.
5. Wei Hua, Mei Han, Yihong Gong, *Baseball Scene classification using multimedia features*, in Proc. IEEE Int'l Conf. on Multimedia and Expo, 2002.
6. Michael Isard, Andrew Blake, *CONDENSATION -- conditional density propagation for visual tracking*, Int. J. Computer Vision, 29, 1, 5-28.
7. Jaimes, A., and Chang, S. F., *Automatic selection of visual features and classifiers*, in SPIE Conference on Storage and Retrieval for Media Databases, 2000.
8. Ngo, C.H., Pong, T.C., and Zhang, H.J., *On clustering and retrieval of video shots*, ACM MM 2001.
9. Peleg, S., and Herman, J., *Panoramic mosaics by manifold projection*, Computer Vision and Pattern Recognition (CVPR), 1997, pp. 338-343.
10. Pingali, G., Opalach, A., and Jean, Y., *Ball tracking and virtual replays for innovative tennis broadcasts*, Proceedings of the International Conference on Pattern Recognition.
11. Retz-Schmidt, G., *A replai of soccer: Recognizing intentions in the domain of soccer games*, Proc. European Conference on Artificial Intelligence, pp.455-457.
12. Shi, J., Malik, J., *Motion Segmentation and Tracking Using Normalized Cuts,* International Conference on Computer Vision (ICCV), 1998.
13. Tovinkere, V., Qian, R. J., *Detecting semantic events in soccer games: Towards a complete solution*, IEEE International Conference on Multimedia and Expo, 2001.
14. Utsumi, O., Miura, K., Ide, I., Sakai, S., Tanaka, H., *An object detection method for describing soccer games from video*, in Proc. IEEE ICME 2002.
15. Wu, Y., and Huang, T. S., *A Co-inference approach to robust visual tracking*, in Proc. IEEE Int'l Conf. on Computer Vision, Vol.II, pp.26-33, Vancouver, Canada.
16. Xu, P., Xie, L., Chang, S.-F., Divakaran, A., Vetro, A., and Sun, H., *Algorithms and systems for segmentation and structure analysis in soccer video*, ICME 2001.
17. Yow, D., Yeo, B.-L., Yeung, M.,and Liu, B., *Analysis and presentation of soccer highlights from digital video*, Proc. Asian Conference on Computer Vision.
18. Zhong, D., and Chang S. F., *Structure analysis of sports video using domain models*, in IEEE Conference on Multimedia and Expo, 2001, pp. 920-923.

Evaluation of an Adaptive Composite Gaussian Model in Video Surveillance

Qi Zang and Reinhard Klette

CITR, Computer Science Department, The University of Auckland
Tamaki Campus, Auckland, New Zealand

Abstract. Video surveillance systems seek to automatically identify events of interest in a variety of situations. Extracting a moving object from a background is the most important step of the whole system. There are many approaches to track moving objects in a video surveillance system. These can be classified into three main groups: feature-based tracking, background subtraction, and optical flow techniques. Background subtraction is a region-based approach where the objective is to identify parts of the image plane that are significantly different to the background. In order to avoid the most common problems introduced by gradual illumination changes, waving trees, shadows, etc., the background scene requires a composite model. A mixture of Gaussian distributions is most popular. In this paper, we classify and discuss several recently proposed composite models. We have chosen one of these for implementation and evaluate its performance. We also analyzed its benefits and drawbacks, and designed an improved version of this model based on our experimental evaluation. One stationary camera has been used.

1 Introduction

Video surveillance is a well-studied subject area with both existing application systems and new approaches still being developed. Research subjects are background modelling, moving object detection and tracking. Normally, video surveillance systems have three separate processing phases:

1. *low-level processes* are based on pixel models, they detect signal changes and update the background model,
2. *middle-level processes* are based on region models, they allow region splitting or merging,
3. *high-level processes* deal with final tasks such as object recognition or tracking.

Obviously, the low-level phase is most fundamental for the whole system: the correct extraction of all pixels defining a moving object and a background is the key step for the next two phases. A variety of methods has been developed and used in video surveillance applications, like *W4* [1] which analyzes pixel changes between frames, records pixel minimum and maximum values that are used in subtracting moving objects from the background; *wallflower* [2] which models and maintains the background in three levels: a pixel level, a region level and a frame level; *P-finder* [3] which models the background using a single Gaussian distribution and uses a multi-class statistical model for the

N. Petkov and M.A. Westenberg (Eds.): CAIP 2003, LNCS 2756, pp. 165–172, 2003.

tracked object; *Stauffer* [4] which uses a mixture of Gaussians to model the background and is considered to be robust against changes in outdoor scenes.

The primary goal of this paper is to critically discuss the use of mixtures of Gaussians to model a background. A second goal is to inform about an implementation of a previously already published method suggesting a mixture of Gaussians, by reporting about its performance and proposing an improvement.

The paper is structured as follows: in Section 2, we discuss recent approaches for modeling a background using Gauss distributions, following [16]. Section 3 presents performance results of the chosen model for implementation. Section 4 introduces and discusses our improvements. Section 5 finally informs about the obtained analysis and gives our conclusion.

2 Previous Work

An important property of Gaussian distributions is that they still remain to be Gaussian distributions after any linear transformation. They are widely used in adaptive systems. Especially in video surveillance applications, normally a Gaussian distribution is assumed in order to make the system adaptive to uncontrolled changes like in illumination, outdoor weather, etc. The Gaussian is defined as

$$p(x) = N(x; \mu, \sigma^2)$$

also expressed by notation

$$x \sim N(\mu, \sigma^2)$$

which states that x is normally distributed with the corresponding mean μ and variance σ^2 [13]. Approaches using the Gaussian can be classified into there categories:

1. *Single Gaussian*: the background distribution is modelled using a single Gaussian in HSV space, see [5];
2. *Combined Gaussians*: use of one Gaussian distribution to model a person's face and another Gaussian to model the body (shirt); this is actually a color-based tracking approach, see [6];
3. *Gaussian Mixture*: model the background by using a mixture model in order to capture changes in illumination, waving trees, etc., see [4].

The Gaussian mixture model belongs to a class of density models which have several functions as additive components. It can be stated as

$$P(\mathbf{X}_t) = \sum_{i=1}^{K} \omega_{i,t} \eta(\mathbf{X}_t; \mu_{i,t}, \Sigma_{i,t}) \ . \tag{1}$$

Here $\mathbf{X}_t$ is the variable which represents the pixel, K is the number of distributions, and t represents time. These functions are combined together to provide a multimodal density function, which can be employed to model colors of a dynamic scene or object. Conditional probabilities can be computed for each color pixel while a model is constructed.

The papers [7–9] are all based on using the Gaussian mixture model. In [9], a number of Gaussian functions are taken as an approximation of a multimodal distribution in color space and conditional probabilities are computed for all color pixels, probability densities are estimated from the background colors and peoples' clothing, heads, hands etc. Two assumptions are made, one is that a person of interest in an image will form a spatially contiguous region in the image plane. Another is that the set of colors for either the person or the background are relatively distinct, the pixels belonging to the person may be treated as a statistical distribution in the image plane.

An adaptive technique based on the Gaussian mixture model is discussed in [4] for the tracker module of a video surveillance system. This technique is to model each background pixel as a mixture of Gaussians. The Gaussians are evaluated using a simple heuristic to hypothesize which are most likely to be part of the "background process". Each pixel is modeled by a mixture of K Gaussians as stated in formula (1): where K is the number of distributions: normally K is between 3 to 5 in practice. $\omega_{i,t}$ is an estimate of the weight of the ith Gaussian in the mixture at time t, $\mu_{i,t}$ is the mean value of the ith Gaussian in the mixture at time t. $\Sigma_{i,t}$ is the covariance matrix of the ith Gaussian in the mixture at time t. Every new pixel value $\mathbf{X}_t$ is checked against the existing K Gaussian distributions until a match is found. Based on the matching results, the background is updated as follows:

$\mathbf{X}_t$ matches component i, that is $\mathbf{X}_t$ decreases by 2.5 standard deviations of the distribution, then the parameters of the ith component are updated as follows:

$$\omega_{i,t} = (1-\alpha)\omega_{i,t-1} + \alpha \tag{2}$$
$$\mu_{i,t} = (1-\rho)\mu_{i,t-1} + \rho\mathbf{I}_t \tag{3}$$
$$\sigma^2_{i,t} = (1-\rho)\sigma^2_{i,t-1} + \rho(\mathbf{I}_t - \mu_{i,t})^{\mathsf{T}}(\mathbf{I}_t - \mu_{i,t}) \tag{4}$$

where $\rho = \alpha \Pr(\mathbf{I}_t|\mu_{i,t-1}, \Sigma_{i,t-1})$. α is the predefined learning parameter, μ_t is the mean value of the pixel at time t, $\mathbf{I}_t$ is the recent pixel at time t.

The parameters for unmatched distributions remain unchanged, i.e., to be precise:

$$\mu_{i,t} = \mu_{i,t-1} \quad \text{and} \tag{5}$$
$$\sigma^2_{i,t} = \sigma^2_{i,t-1}\,. \tag{6}$$

But $\omega_{i,t}$ will be adjusted using formula:

$$\omega_{i,t} = (1-\alpha)\omega_{i,t-1}. \tag{7}$$

If $\mathbf{X}_t$ matches none of the K distributions, then the least probable distribution is replaced by a distribution where the current value acts as its mean value, the variance is chose to be high and the a-priori weight is low [4].

The background estimation problem is solved by specifying the Gaussian distributions, which have the most supporting evidence and the least variance. Because the moving object has larger variance than a background pixel, so in order to represents background processes, first the Gaussians are ordered by the value of $\omega_{i,t}/\|\Sigma_{i,t}\|$ in decreasing order. The background distribution stays on top with the lowest variance by applying a threshold T, where

$$B = \text{argmin}_b \left(\frac{\sum_{i=1}^{b} \omega_{i,t}}{\sum_{i=1}^{K} \omega_{i,t}} > T \right) . \tag{8}$$

All pixels $\mathbf{X}_t$ which do not match any of these components will be marked as foreground.

Paper [10] suggested an improvement of this technique by using depth estimates: a similar Gaussian mixture model as in [4] is used, except that it is formulated in YUV color space, and it also utilizes depth values instead of disparities. This makes the algorithm applicable in systems that compute depth not only by window-matching techniques, but also by methods based on active illumination, lidar, or other means. The progress reported in [10] is about controlling of shadows, color camouflages and high-traffic areas.

Paper [11] also reports improvements on shadow detection based on [4]. Actually this paper combines methods proposed in [4] and [12]. Shadows remained to be the main problem in [4], and [12] uses a chromatic color space model to detect and eliminate moving object shadows. It separates chromatic and brightness components by making use of the [4] mixture model, comparing a non-background pixel against the current background components. If the difference in both chromatic and brightness components are within some thresholds, then the pixel is considered to be shadow.

3 Implementation and Evaluation

We implemented the method reported in [4], 'a statistical adaptive Gaussian mixture model for background subtraction' (Our implementation is on Linux in order to achieve fast processing.) We tested the program both on indoor and outdoor image sequences. In this section we report about our evaluation results.

PLUS: The system can start at any stage, it does not restrict on the background contains any moving objects or not. There are only two parameters that need to be defined in advance, and they do not need to be changed during sequence processing. (These two parameters need to be estimated/fixed during an initialization period.) The method is able to cope with many of the common problems that may happen in video surveillance applications, such as gradual illumination changes, waving trees, etc. It is stable and robust. It suits different types of cameras. It works especially very well for fast moving objects in complex environments.

MINUS: Shadows could not properly be detected/removed in [4]. This is the main problem of the method. Another problem is, while an object is moving very slowly, it will be treated as part of the background, or just detected based on differences between the current frame and previous frames, and the overlapping regions of the moving object cannot be detected as foreground. Similar outcomes happened while testing a large moving object, leaving 'holes' at the overlapping regions. This is because a slowly moving object has a small variance, which will match the background model, and, as a result, the slowly moving object was absorbed by the background. A second learning parameter ρ is not necessary to be recalculated here, because the computed value is not only too small, but also increases the computation time of the system. If the value is too small, the background model will be refined too slowly. Another issue to be considered

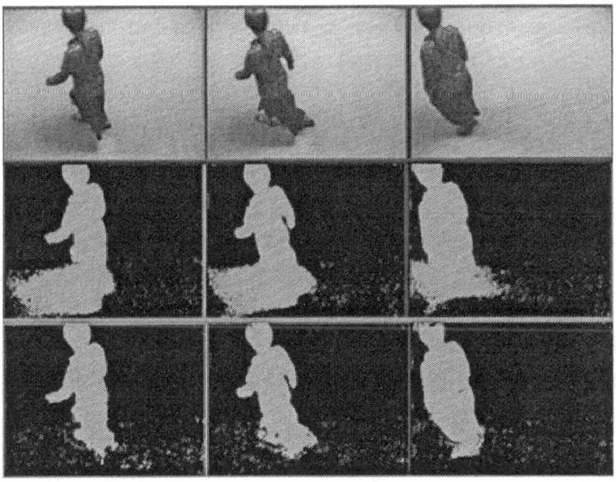

Fig. 1. The top row shows an original indoor image sequence. The middle row shows results after background subtraction, still affected by shadows. The bottom row are the results after eliminating shadows.

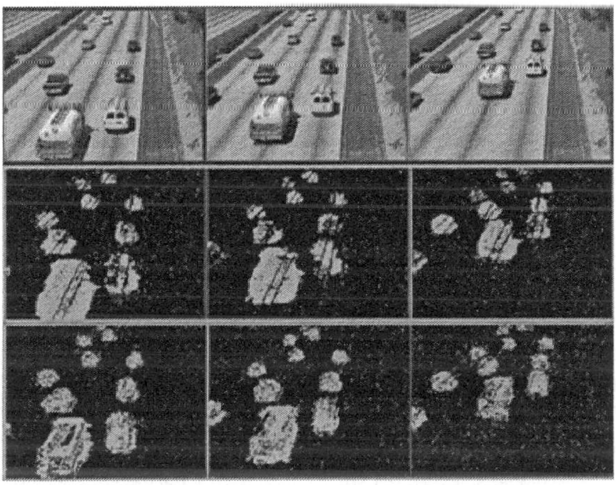

Fig. 2. The top row shows an original image sequence of outdoor traffic on a highway. The middle row are results after background subtraction without shadow elimination, and the bottom row are the results after eliminating shadows.

for simple indoor scenes: there are no problems such as waving trees, the background is not affected by bad weather, etc., so there is actually no need to use a Gaussian mixture model. A single Gaussian is sufficient. In another words, the mixture model is not suitable for simple indoor environments.

4 Improvement

Based on the above analysis of the Gaussian mixture model, we concluded to improve as follows:

(i) Drop the second learning parameter ρ: This value is normally very small. If it is too small, the model will be refined very slowly, and this causes that the system adapts to background changes very slowly. Instead we use a reasonable value: we set this value according to specific situations in the captured scenes to control the speed of adaptation. Originally parameter ρ is still defined in an initialization phase.

(ii) Detect shadows: As we discussed before, [11] proposes to detect shadows by combining a Gaussian mixture model and [12] to detect shadows directly, however from the analysis results reported in [14] we can see that the shadow detection method of [12] works better for indoor scenes compared to outdoor scenes, and the Gaussian mixture model works better for outdoor scenes compared to indoor scenes. We derived another method which works well for outdoor scenes, and combined with a Gaussian mixture model it represents a robust approach for outdoor image sequences processing.

Our system works in RGB space. First we model the background by using a Gaussian mixture model. The number of contributing components will be set according to different environments. The minimum value is $K = 3$. The system can start at any stage, it does not matter whether the background is static at this moment or or not. The initial mean value was set to a very small value, and standard deviation was set to a high value. As in [4], for computational reasons, we also assume that the red, green and blue values are independent and have the same scalar variances. This simplifies the calculation of a covariance matrix: instead we approximate the value by calculating the Mahalanobis distance between the pixel of a current frame and the background model. Values which are within an interval of 2.5 times standard deviation are matching one of the mixture components. After resorting the background model using weight/variance values, the best match is detected: if the matching is within the background component, the pixel will be marked as background, otherwise, the pixel will be marked as foreground and grouped together for further processing. If none of these components match, a new component will be initialized using the current pixel value as its mean value, and using a high variance and a low weight. The parameters of matched components will be updated.

The next step is to remove shadows. Here we use a method similar to [11]. The detection of brightness and chromaticity changes in the HSV space are more accurate than in RGB space, especially in outdoor scenes, and the HSV color space corresponds closely to human perception of color [15]. At this stage, only foreground pixels need to be converted to hue, saturation and intensity triples. Shadow regions can be detected/eliminated as followings: let $\mathbf{E}$ represent the current pixel at time t, and $\mathbf{B}$ represents the background pixel at time t. For each foreground pixel, if it satisfies the constraints

$$\begin{aligned} |\mathbf{E}_h - \hat{\mathbf{B}}_h| &< \mathbf{T}_h \ , \\ |\mathbf{E}_s - \hat{\mathbf{B}}_s| &< \mathbf{T}_s \ , \text{ and} \\ \mathbf{T}_{v1} < \mathbf{E}_v / \hat{\mathbf{B}}_v &< \mathbf{T}_{v2} \end{aligned}$$

then this pixel will be removed from the foreground mask. Parameters of shadow pixels will not be updated.

Now we got the binary mask of moving objects. Normally it contains Salt and Pepper noises and holes. We applied Morphological operations on it: dilation and erosion to remove the noises, and then filling holes. Very small areas were dropped. After that, connected components analysis is used, which is to label each moving objects regions and get the number of elements, at the same time, features like size, centroid and velocity of each moving object were obtained as well. At this stage we finished all necessary works required for moving object extraction and is ready to pass all these information to the next stage of moving object tracking.

The three thresholds used for HSV are obtained from testing data, they are $\mathbf{T}_h$=0.5, $\mathbf{T}_s$=0.1, $\mathbf{T}_{v1}$=0.1,$\mathbf{T}_{v1}$=0.7, respectively. The frame size used was 320 x 240, the real-time processing rate we achieved was 5 to 7 frames per second. The indoor testing data are captured in the CITR vision lab, the background was modelled by using a single multi-dimensional Gaussian distribution. Shadows were eliminated by detecting changes in lighting and chromaticity in RGB space. The outdoor traffic testing data have been downloaded from a website, showing scenes for different weather situations, such as sunny or snowing.

5 Conclusion

The Gaussian mixture models are a type of density models which are composed of a number of components (functions). These functions can be used to model the colors of objects or backgrounds in a scene. This allows to achieve color-based object tracking and background segmentation. When a model is generated, conditional probabilities can be estimated for all color pixels. Adaptive Gaussian distributions are applicable for modelling changes, especially also related to fast moving objects such as cars on a highway. How to use Gaussian distributions has to be based on the application context. It can provide analysis results for long duration scenes. It is also quite suitable for complex scenes or multiply-colored objects. For simple indoor scenes or objects appearing monocolored, a Gaussian mixture model is not necessary if care has to be taken about computation time and system efficiency.

How to assign suitable values to parameters during initialization period will depend on specific applications. The more number of mixture models, the better the results, but the computation time increases. Assign a very small value to the learning rate will avoid slow moving large object melt to background, but will affect the system adaptation. One needs to balance all these according to different applications and environments.

Modelling the pixel of background using Mixture Gaussian distribution will result in a pixel processing, so pixel relationship and its region level analysis is suggested during or after background estimation to achieve better result.

Shadow is a main drawback for all video surveillance applications and affects the accuracy of the system performance. We combined Gaussian mixture models and shadow elimination methods, which resulted into a more robust and efficient system, which may be used in traffic analysis and control systems. Future work will also include IR image data.

References

1. I. Haritaoglu, D. Harwood, L. S. Davis: W4: Who? When? Where? What? A real-time system for detecting and tracking people. In Proc. *3rd Face and Gesture Recognition Conf.*, pages 222 227, 1998.
2. K. Toyama, J. Krumm, B. Brumitt, B. Meyers: Wallflower: principles and practice of background maintenance. In Proc. *Int. Conf. Computer Vision*, pages 255-261, 1999.

3. C. Wren, A. Azabayejani, T. Darrell, A. Pentland: Pfinder: Real-time tracking of the human body. *IEEE Trans. Pattern Analysis Machine Intelligence*, **19**:780-785, 1997.
4. C. Stauffer, W. E. L. Grimson: Adaptive background mixture models for real-time tracking. *Computer Vision and Pattern Recognition*, **2**: 246-252, 1999.
5. A. R. J. François, G. G. Medioni: Adaptive color background modeling for real-time segmentation of video streams. In Proc. *Int. Conf. Imaging Science, Systems, and Technology*, pages 227-232, 1999.
6. S. Waldherr, S. Thrun, R. Romero: A neural-network based recognition of pose and motion gestures on a mobile robot. In Proc. *5th Brazilian Symposium on Neural Networks*, pages 79-84, 1998.
7. S. J. Mckenna, Y. Raja, S. Gong: Object tracking using adaptive colour mixture models. In Proc. *ACCV'98*, pages 615-622, 1998.
8. Y. Raja, S. J. Mckenna, S. Gong: Tracking colour objects using adaptive mixture models. *Image and Vision Computing*, **17**: 225-231, 1999.
9. Y. Raja, S. J. Mckenna, S. Gong: Tracking and segmenting people in varying lighting conditions using colour. In Proc. 3rd IEEE Int. Conf. *Automatic Face and Gesture Recognition*, pages 228-233, 1998.
10. M. Harville, G. Gordon, J. Woodfill: Foreground segmentation using adaptive mixture models in color and depth. In Proc. IEEE Workshop *Detection and Recognition of Events in Video*, pages 3-11, 2001.
11. P. Kaew Tra Kul Pong, R. Bowden: An improved adaptive background mixture model for real-time tracking with shadow detection. In Proc. 2nd European Workshop *Advanced Video Based Surveillance System*, Sept 2001, http://www.ee.surrey.ac.uk/Personal/R.Bowden/publications/avbs01/avbs01.pdf.
12. T. Horparasert, D. Harwood, L. A. Davis: A statistical approach for real-time robust background subtraction and shadow detection. In Proc. *Frame Rate Workshop at ICCV'99*, pages 1-19, 1999.
13. Y. Bar-Shalom, X. R. Li: *Estimation and Tracking: Principles, Techniques, and Software*. Artech House, Boston, 1993.
14. A. Prati, I. Mikic, M. Trivedi, R. Cucchiara: Detecting moving shadows: formulation, algorithms and evaluation. in Proc. *Computer Vision and Pattern Recognition*, Vol. 2, pages 571-576, 2001.
15. N. Herodotou, K. N. Plataniotis, A. N. Venetsanopoulos: A color segmentation scheme for object-based video coding. In Proc. IEEE Symp. *Advances in Digital Filtering and Signal Proc.*, pages 25-29, 1998.
16. A. McIvor, Q. Zang, R. Klette: The background subtraction problem for video surveillance systems. In Proc. Int. Workshop *Robot Vision 2001*, Springer, LNCS 1998, pages 176-183, 2001.

Low Complexity Motion Estimation Based on Spatio-Temporal Correlations and Direction of Motion Vectors

Hyo Sun Yoon and Guee Sang Lee

Department of Computer Science, Chonnam National University
300 Youngbong-dong, Buk-gu, Kwangju 500-757, Korea
estheryoon@hotmail.com, gslee@chonnam.chonnam.ac.kr

Abstract. Motion Estimation (ME) has been developed to remove redundant data contained in a sequence of image. And ME is an important part of video encoding systems, since it can significantly affect the output quality of an encoded sequences. However, ME requires a significant part of the encoding time, when using the Full Search (FS). For this reason, low complexity motion estimation algorithms are viable solutions. In this paper, we present an efficient algorithm based on spatio-temporal correlations and the direction of motion vectors that define the search pattern and the location of search center adaptively. Experiments show that the speedup improvement of the proposed algorithm over Diamond Search algorithm (DS) and Motion Vector Field Adaptive Search Technique (MVFAST) can be up to $0.5 \sim 3$ times faster and the image quality improvement can be better up to $0.1 \sim 1$(dB).

1 Introduction

Recently, great interest has been devoted to the study of different approaches in video compressions. The high correlation between successive frames of a video sequence makes it possible to achieve high coding efficiency by reducing the temporal redundancy. Motion estimation (ME) and motion compensation techniques are an important part of most video encoding, since it could significantly affect the compression ratio and the output quality.

The most popular motion estimation and motion compensation method has been the block-based motion estimation, which uses a block matching algorithm (BMA) to find the best matched block from a reference frame. ME based on the block matching are adopted in many existing video coding standards such as H.261/H.263 and MPEG-1/2/4. If the performance in terms of prediction error is the only criterion for BMA, full search block matching algorithm (FS) is the simplest BMA, guaranteeing an exact result. FS can achieve optimal performance by examining all possible points in search area of the reference frame. However, FS is very computationally intensive and it can hardly be applied to any real time applications. Hence, it is inevitable to develop fast motion estimation algorithms for real time video coding applications. Many low complexity

N. Petkov and M.A. Westenberg (Eds.): CAIP 2003, LNCS 2756, pp. 173–181, 2003.

motion estimation algorithms such as Diamond Search (DS) [1, 2], Three Step Search (TSS)[3], New Three Step Search (NTSS)[4], Four Step Search (FSS)[5], Two Step Search (2SS)[6], Two-dimensional logarithmic search algorithm [7], HEXagon-Based Serch (HEXBS) [8] and the algorithms [9–12] based on temporal or spatial correlations of motion vectors have been proposed. Regardless of the characteristic of the motion of a block, all these most fast block matching algorithms (FBMAs) use a fixed search pattern and the origin of the search area as a search center.

A fixed search pattern and a fixed search center results in the use of many checking points to find a good motion vector (MV). To improve the "speed-quality", the motion estimation method we proposed in this paper uses spatio-temporal correlations and the direction of motion vectors to predict a search center that reflects the current block's motion trend and to choose a search pattern adaptively. Because a properly predicted search center makes the global optimum motion vector closer to the predicted starting center, it increases the chance of finding the optimum or near-optimum motion vector with less search points.

In this paper, we proposed an adaptive block matching algorithm based on spatial and temporal correlations and direction of motion vectors. In this algorithm, the motion vector mv_t of the block with the same coordinate in the reference frame and the median motion vector mv_s of motion vectors of neighboring blocks in the current frame are used as predictors to decide a search center and a search pattern adaptively for the current block. Specifically, the weighted sum of mv_t and median(mv_s) and the direction of mv_t and median(mv_s) are computed to get the search center and to decide the type of the search pattern.

This paper is organized as follows. Section 2 describes the existing motion estimation algorithms. The proposed algorithm is described in Section 3. Section 4 reports the simulation results and conclusions are given in Section 5.

2 Motion Estimation Algorithms

There are many search algorithms for motion estimation. The full search (FS), the simplest algorithm, examines every point in the search area in the reference frame to find the best match. Clearly, it is optimal in terms of finding the best motion vector, but it is computationally very expense. Hence, several sub-optimal search algorithms such as DS [1,2], TSS [3], NTSS [4], FSS [5], 2SS [6], Two-dimensional logarithmic search algorithm [7], HEXagon-Based Serch (HEXBS) [8] and Motion Vector Field Adaptive Search Technique (MVFAST) [11] have been developed. The TSS is a coarse-to-fine search algorithm. The starting step size for search is large and the center of the search is moved in the direction of the best match at the stage, and the step size is reduced by half. In contrast, FSS starts with a fine step size (usually 2) and the center of the search is moved in the direction of the best match without changing the step size, until the best match at that stage is the center itself. The step size is then halved to 1 to find the best match. In other words, in FSS the search process is performed mostly around the original search point (0,0), or it is more center-biased. Based

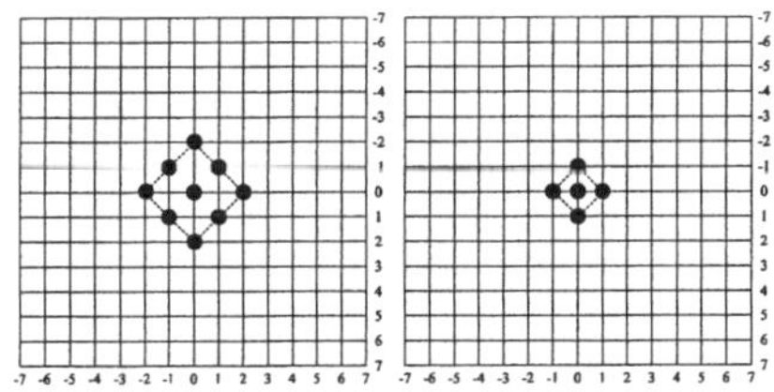

(a) (b)

Fig. 1. Diamond Search Algorithm(DS). (a) Large Diamond Search Pattern (LDSP). (b) Small Diamond Search Pattern (SDSP)

on the characteristics of a center-biased motion vector distribution, NTSS enhanced TSS by using additional search points, which are around the search origin (0,0) of the first step of TSS. The DS is also a center-biased algorithm by exploiting the shape of the motion vector distribution. DS shows the best performance compared to these methods in terms of both average number of search points per motion vector and the PSNR (peak signal to noise ratio) of the predicted image. The DS method uses two diamond search patterns, depicted in Fig. 1. the large diamond search pattern (LDSP) is used for the coarse search. When the centered search position of LDSP show the minimum block distortion, the small diamond search pattern (SDSP) is chosen for the fine search. MVFAST [11] use spatial correlations of MV to get the search center and to decide the search pattern between LDSP and SDSP.

3 The Proposed Algorithm

Since the time interval between successive frames is very short, there are high temporal correlations between successive frames of a video sequence. In other words, the motion of current block is very similar to that of the same coordinate block in the reference frame. And also there are high spatial correlations among the blocks in the same frame. That is to say, the motion of current block is very similar to those of the neighboring blocks in the current frame. If the information of spatially and temporally correlated motion vectors is used to decide the search center and the search pattern for the motion estimation, the motion vector will be found with much less number of search points.

In this paper, the motion vector of the same coordinate block in the reference frame and the motion vectors of the neighboring blocks in the current frame are used as predictors to decide a better search center and a search pattern adaptively for the current block. The proposed method exploiting spatially and temporally correlated motion vectors depicted in Fig. 2, selects one of two search patterns as illustrated in Fig. 3(a) and Fig. 4(a) adaptively.

$$Px = \lfloor dx0 \times \alpha + median(dx1, dx2, dx3) \times \beta \rfloor \quad (1)$$

$$Py = \lfloor dy0 \times \alpha + median(dy1, dy2, dy3) \times \beta \rfloor \quad (2)$$

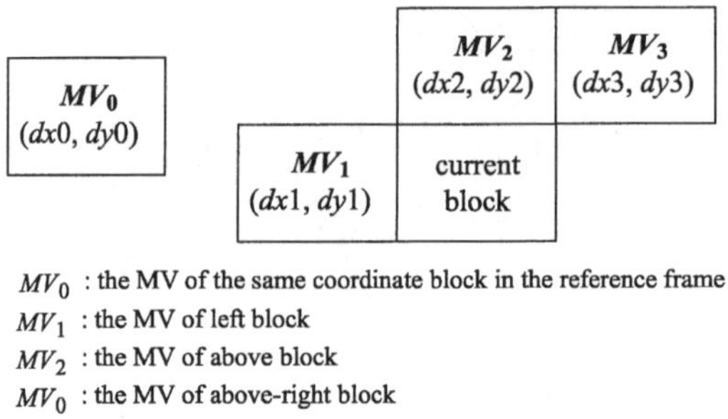

Fig. 2. Blocks for Spatio-Temporal Correlation Information

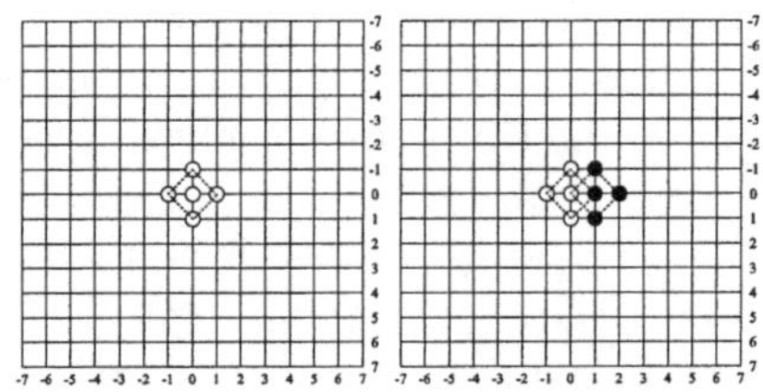

(a) first step (b) second step

Fig. 3. Small Diamond Search Algorithm(SDSP)

At first, (Px, Py) obtained from Eq. (1–2) is used as a search center. (Px, Py) is the weighted sum of the temporal information and the spatial information. In this paper, we experimented with $\alpha = 0.5$ and $\beta = 0.5$. If the Mean Square Error (MSE) of (Px, Py) is less than threshold, (Px, Py) is the final MV and the search procedure terminates. Otherwise, the following search procedure is implemented. If $|Px| < 3$ and $|Py| < 3$, small diamond search pattern (SDSP)[13] as shown in Fig. 3 is selected. In Fig. 3(a), white circles are the initial search points and in Fig. 3(b), black circles are search points added in the second step. Note that the center of black circles is the position which showed the minimum block distortion in the first step.

Otherwise, the next procedure is implemented. The Direction1, that is the direction of the MV mv_t of the same coordinate block in the reference frame, is decided by using [14]. And the Direction2, that is the direction of the median MV mv_s of motion vectors of the neighboring blocks in the current frame, is decided. If the Direction1 is equal to the Direction2, (Px, Py) is a search center and modified diamond search pattern (MDSP) [12], illustrated in Fig. 4 is selected for motion estimation. Otherwise, the distance between mv_t and mv_s is calculated. If the distance is less than threshold, (Px, Py) is a search center and MDSP is selected. Otherwise, the MSE0, that is the MSE of the search origin (0,0), the MSE1, that is the MSE of mv_t and the MSE2, that is the MSE of mv_s, are calculated. And the best candidate predictor $(P'x, P'y)$, that is the MV with the lowest MSE among MSE0, MSE1 and MSE2, is decided

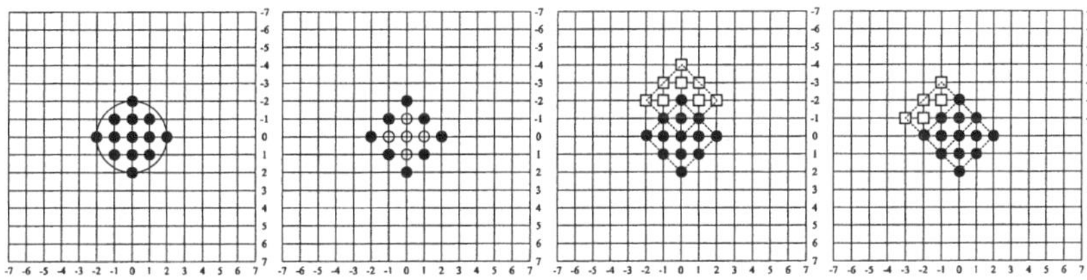

(a) first step (b) last step (c) corner point (d) edge point

Fig. 4. Modify Diamond Search Algorithm(MDSP)

as a search center. And then MDSP [12], illustrated in Fig. 4 is selected for motion estimation. Based on the fact that about 50%(in large motion case) ~ 98%(in small motion case) of motion vectors are enclosed in a circular support, as shown in Fig. 4(a), with a radius of 2 pixels around the search origin (0,0)[1,2], the circular support around the search origin becomes the initial search points in MDSP as shown in Fig. 4(a). If one of $\oplus$ points in Fig. 4(b) shows the minimum block distortion among the search points in the first step of Fig. 4(a), the search procedure terminates. Otherwise, the new search points are set as shown in Fig. 4(c) or Fig. 4(d).

The block diagram of the proposed algorithm appears in Fig. 5. According to the spatio-temporal correlations and direction of motion vectors, the proposed algorithm selects a search center and a search pattern between SDSP and MDSP adaptively. If $|Px| < 3$ and $|Py| < 3$, SDSP is selected as a search pattern. Otherwise, MDSP is chosen. The proposed method is summarized as follows

Step 1 The MSE of (Px, Py) is calculated. If MSE is less than threshold, the (Px, Py) is the final MV of the current block. Otherwise, go to Step 2.

Step 2 If $|Px| < 3$ and $|Py| < 3$, go to Step 3; otherwise, go to Step 4.

Step 3 I. The search origin in search area is moved to the displacement of (Px, Py). Let's call the moved search origin the search center.

II. SDSP is disposed at (Px, Py), and the 5 checking points of SDSP as seen in Fig. 3(a) are tested. If the minimum block distortion (MBD) point calculated is located at the center position of SDSP, then it is the final solution of the motion vector. otherwise go to III.

III. If the MBD point calculated is not located at the center position of SDSP, three additional checking points as shown in Fig. 3(b) are used. The MBD point founded in the previous search step is repositioned as the center point to form a new SDSP. If the new MSD point obtained is located at the center position, then it is the final solution of the motion vector. Otherwise, recursively repeated this step

Step 4 The Direction1, that is the MV mv_t of the same coordinate block in the reference frame, and The Direction2, that is the median MV mv_s of motion vectors of the neighboring blocks in the current frame, are calculated. If Direction1 is not equal to Direction2, go to Step 5; otherwise, go to Step 6.

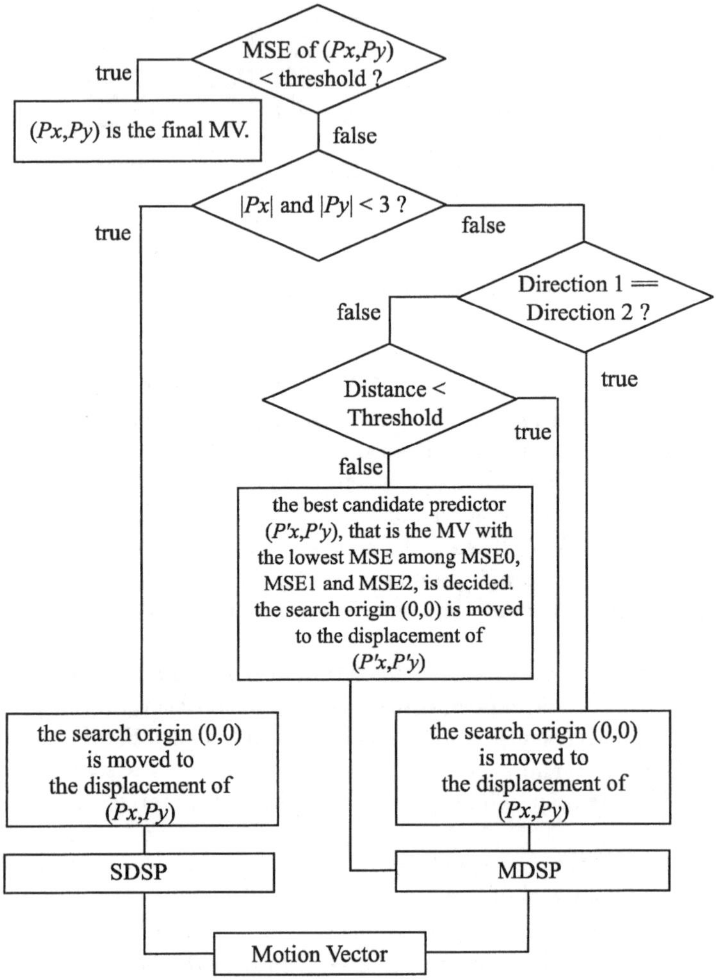

Direction1: the Direction of the MV (mv_t) of the same coordinate block in the reference frame
Direction2: the Direction of the median MV (mv_s) of motion vectors of the neighboring blocks in the current frame
Distance : the Distance between mv_t and mv_s
MSE0 : the MSE of the search origin (0,0)
MSE1 : the MSE of the mv_t
MSE2 : the MSE of the mv_s

Fig. 5. The block diagram of the proposed algorithm

Step 5 The Distance, that is the distance between *mv_t* and *mv_s*, is calculated. If Distance is less than threshold, go to Step 6. Otherwise, the MSE0, that is the MSE of the search origin (0,0), the MSE1, that is MSE of *mv_t* and the MSE2, that is MSE of *mv_s*, are calculated. And the best candidate predictor

$(P'x, P'y)$, that is the MV with the lowest MSE among MSE0, MSE1 and MSE2, is decided as a search center. And then go to Step 7.

Step 6 The search origin is moved to the displacement of (Px, Py). And go to Step 7.

Step 7 I. MDSP is disposed at (Px, Py), and the 13 checking points of MDSP as seen in Fig. 4(a) are tested. If the MBD point calculated is located at the center position of MDSP or one of $\oplus$ points in Fig. 4 (b), then it is the final solution of the motion vector. otherwise go to III.

II. If the MBD point is located at the corner of MDSP, eight additional checking points as shown in Fig. 4(c) are used. If the MBD point is located at the edge of MDSP, five additional checking points as shown in Fig. 4(d) are used. And then the MBD point found in the previous search step is repositioned as the center to from a new MDSP. If the MBD point calculated is located at the center position of MDSP or one of $\oplus$ points in Fig. 4(b), then it is the final solution of the motion vector. Otherwise, recursively repeated this step.

4 Simulation Result

In this section, we show the experiment results for the proposed algorithm. We compared FS, NTSS, FSS, 2SS, DS ,HEXBS and MVFAST to the proposed method in both of image quality and search speed. Eight QCIF test sequences are used for the experiment: Akiyo, Claire, Carphone, Foreman, Mother and Daughter, Salesman, Stefan and Table. The mean square error (MSE) distortion function is used as the block distortion measure (BDM). The quality of the predicted image is measured by the peak signal to noise ratio (PSNR), which is defined by

$$MSE = \left(\frac{1}{MN}\right)\sum_{m=1}^{M}\sum_{n=1}^{N}[x(m,n) - \hat{x}(m,n)]^2 \tag{3}$$

$$PSNR = 10\ log_{10}\frac{255^2}{MSE} \tag{4}$$

In Eq. (3), $x(m,n)$ denotes the original image and $\hat{x}(m,n)$ denotes the motion compensated prediction image. From Table 1 and 2, we can see that proposed method is better than DS and MVFAST in terms of both the computational complexity (as measured by the average number of search points per motion vector) and PSNR of the predicted image. In terms of PSNR, the proposed method is about 0.1(dB) better than MVFAST as well as DS in stationary sequences such as Akiyo, Claire, Carphone, Mother and Daughter, Salesman and about 0.5 $\sim$ 1(dB) in motioned sequences such as Stefan, Table and Foreman in Table 1. The speedup improvement of the proposed method over MVFAST and DS can be up to 0.5 $\sim$ 3 times faster. The 2SS shows the performance in PSNR very close to the proposed method, but the proposed method requires less computation by up to more than 30 times on average as shown in Table 2.

Table 1. Average PSNR of the test image sequence

	FS	2SS	NTSS	FSS	DS	HEXBS	MVFAST	Proposed
Stefan	23.88	23.85	22.24	22.62	22.77	22.59	23.36	23.6
Foreman	29.54	29.24	28.19	28.22	28.66	28.01	29.00	29.02
Akiyo	34.50	34.48	34.48	34.33	34.39	34.30	34.39	34.50
Table	26.50	26.27	26.5	24.81	25.67	24.90	25.49	25.52
Carphone	30.88	30.77	30.14	30.15	30.48	30.07	30.68	30.72
Salesman	32.70	32.70	32.69	32.53	32.62	32.51	32.67	32.69
Claire	35.05	35.01	34.91	34.74	34.85	34.70	34.92	34.93
M&D	31.52	31.51	31.37	31.34	31.42	31.37	31.47	31.48

Table 2. Average number of search points per motion vector estimation

	FS	2SS	NTSS	FSS	DS	HEXBS	MVFAST	Proposed
Stefan	961	255	20.0	18.9	16.2	12.9	10.8	6.54
Foreman	961	255	19.3	18.6	15.4	11.9	8.9	5.21
Akiyo	961	255	17.0	17.0	13.0	11.0	5.05	2.44
Table	961	255	19.7	18.7	15.5	12.5	10.4	7.24
Carphone	961	255	18.6	17.8	14.4	11.7	8.4	5.65
Salesman	961	25	17.1	17.0	13	11.0	5.3	3.52
Claire	961	255	17.2	17.08	13.1	11.0	5.3	3.3
M&D	961	255	17.3	17.1	13.2	11.1	5.6	3.66

5 Conclusion

Based on the spatio-temporal correlations and direction of motion vectors in the reference and the current frame, an adaptive block motion estimation method is proposed in this paper. The proposed method decides a search pattern and a search center based on the spatial-temporal correlations and direction of motion vectors. Experiments show that the speedup improvement of the proposed algorithm over DS and MVFAST can be up to $0.5 \sim 3$ times faster. And the image quality improvement can be better up to $0.1 \sim 1$(dB). The proposed algorithm reduces the computational complexity compared with previously developed fast BMAs, while maintaining better quality.

Acknowledgement

This work was supported by grant No. R05-2003-000-11345-0 from the Korea Science & Engineering Foundation.

References

1. Tham, J.Y., Ranganath, S., Kassim, A.A.: A Novel Unrestricted Center-Biased Diamond Search Algorithm for Block Motion Estimation. IEEE Transactions on Circuits and Systems for Video Technology. **8(4)** (1998) 369–375

2. Shan, Z., Kai-kuang, M.: A New Diamond Search Algorithm for Fast block Matching Motion Estimation. IEEE Transactions on Image Processing. **9(2)** (2000) 287–290
3. Koga, T., Iinuma, K., Hirano, Y., Iijim, Y., Ishiguro, T.: Motion compensated interframe coding for video conference. In Proc. NTC81. (1981) C9.6.1–9.6.5
4. Renxiang, L., Bing, Z., Liou, M.L.: A New Three Step Search Algorithm for Block Motion Estimation. IEEE Transactions on Circuits and Systems for Video Technology. **4(4)** (1994) 438–442
5. Lai-Man, P., Wing-Chung, M.: A Novel Four-Step Search Algorithm for Fast Block Motion Estimation. IEEE Transactions on Circuits and Systems for Video Technology. **6(3)** (1996) 313–317
6. Yuk-Ying, C., Neil, W.B.: Fast search block-matching motion estimation algorithm using FPGA. Visual Communication and Image Processing 2000. Proc. SPIE. **4067** (2000) 913–922
7. Jain, J., Jain, A.: Dispalcement measurement and its application in interframe image coding. IEEE Transactions on Communications. **COM-29** (1981) 1799–1808
8. Zhu, C., Lin, X., Chau, L.P.: Hexagon based Search Pattern for Fast Block Motion Estimation. IEEE Transactions on Circuits and Systems for Video Technology. **12(5)** (2002) 349–355
9. Deepak, S.T., Tsuhan, C.: Estimation and Mode Decision for Spatialy Correlated Motion Sequences. IEEE Transactions on Circuits and Systems for Video Technology. **11(10)** (2002) 1098–1107
10. Xu, J.B., Po, L.M., Cheung, C.K.: Adaptive Motion Tracking Block Matching for Video Coding. IEEE Transactions on Circuits and Systems for Video Technology. **9(7)** (1999) 1025–1029
11. Ma, K.K., Hosur, P.I.: Report on Performance of Fast Motion using Motion Vector Field Adaptive Search Technique. ISO/IEC/JTC1/SC29/WG11.**M5453** (1999)
12. Yoon, H.S., Lee. G.S.: Motion Estimation based on Temporal Correlations. EurAisa-ICT. LNCS.**2510** (2002) 75–83
13. Guy. C. , Michael. G. , Faouzi. K.: Efficient Motion Vector Estimation and Coding for H.263-based very low bit rate video compression. ITU-T SG 16, Q15-A-45. (1997) 18
14. Nam, J.Y., Lee, M.H.: New Block Matching Algorithm for motion estimation based on predicted direction information. Visual Communication and Image Processing 2000. Proc. SPIE. **4067** (2000) 1212–1220

Stereo System for Tracking Moving Object Using Log-Polar Transformation and Zero Disparity Filtering

Il Choi[1], Jong-Gun Yoon[2], Young-Beum Lee[3], and Sung-Il Chien[1]

[1] Department of Electronics, Kyungpook National University
1370 Sankyuk-Dong, Pook-Gu, Taegu 702-701, Korea
{sichien,ichoi}@ee.knu.ac.kr
http://hci.knu.ac.kr/main/main.htm

[2] Digital Information Display Division, LG Electronic Inc.
642 JinPyoung-Dong, Gumi 703-727, Korea
yoonjk@lge.com

[3] Marketing Management, HuHu Inc.
923-14 Mok1-Dong, JingCheun-Gu, Seoul 158-178, Korea
yblee@huhu3.com

Abstract. An active stereo-vision system enables a target object to be localized based on passing small disparities without heavy computation to identify the target. However, this simple method is not applicable to situations where a distracting background is included or the target and other objects are simultaneously located in the zero disparity area. Accordingly, to alleviate these problems, the current study combined filtering and foveation, which employs high resolution in the center of the visual field, while suppressing the periphery. An image pyramid and log-polar transformation are compared for the foveated image representation. The stereo disparity of the target is also extracted using projection to maintain a small stereo disparity during tracking. Experiments demonstrated that a log-polar transformation was superior to both the image pyramid and the traditional method for separating a target from a distracting background, and comparatively enhanced the tracking performance.

1 Introduction

It has been claimed that visually guided behavior can be facilitated by utilizing visual cues commonly found in the biological visual system [1], [2]. For example, when human eyes (stereo camera) converge on a common fixation, the fixation target lies near the horopter and the neighboring points tend to have a small disparity. The horopter is the set of world points with a zero disparity passing through the two nodal points of the stereo camera and the fixation point, as shown in Fig. 1. Objects that stay within the horopter can be easily extracted by suppressing features with large disparities. This is the principle of zero disparity filtering (ZDF) and can be implemented via a logical AND of stereo vertical-edge images [3]. As such, the location of

N. Petkov and M.A. Westenberg (Eds.): CAIP 2003, LNCS 2756, pp. 182–189, 2003.

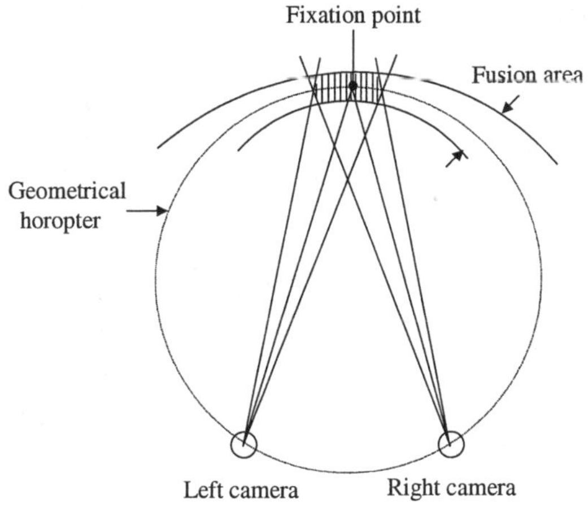

Fig. 1. Horopter where fixation target is located with zero disparity.

a target can be estimated by computing the center of the gravity mass of the ZDF output image. However, ZDF can produce false outputs in a complex scene due to AND results for two different objects. Tanaka et al. [4] proposed a disparity-based segmentation method to track a moving object in a complicated scene. However, they assume that only one object is located in the common space of both cameras' field of view and the horopter. Target windowing is another solution [5]. However, a fixed-size window deteriorates the tracking performance when the size of the target varies, thus the target window needs to be resized adaptively.

Normally, the central area is the major area of concern. Therefore, if the high-resolution portion is located in the center of the visual field, the target object will be dominant over the background. As such, the target can be effectively separated from a distracting background without considering target windowing. Oshiro et al. [6] used log-polar mapping in ZDF to spread the zero disparity area from the gaze point towards the periphery so that a target in the periphery could be found. However, in the current study, instead of a large detectable range of disparities for the target object, each pixel is exclusively mapped in a log polar transformation [7], [8], [9] particularly intended for target enhancement over a background, thereby avoiding target windowing. In addition to a log-polar transformation, a multiresolution image pyramid [10], [11] was also considered for foveation and the ZDF outputs of each method compared. Both methods have important differences, however, they share high central resolution features, which is the main reason for their adoption in the current study.

Since the centroid of a ZDF output only provides a rough measurement of a target location, the stereo disparity also needs to be extracted and then cancelled to fixate on the target object when using a stereo camera. Various disparity extraction methods have already been introduced in binocular tracking, including correlation [4], a virtual horopter [5], a cepstrum operator [12], a phase-based approach [13], and a *lomap* based approach [15]. Whereas most of the above-mentioned methods require heavy computation or arbitrary shifting, the projection of reference edge images proposed in

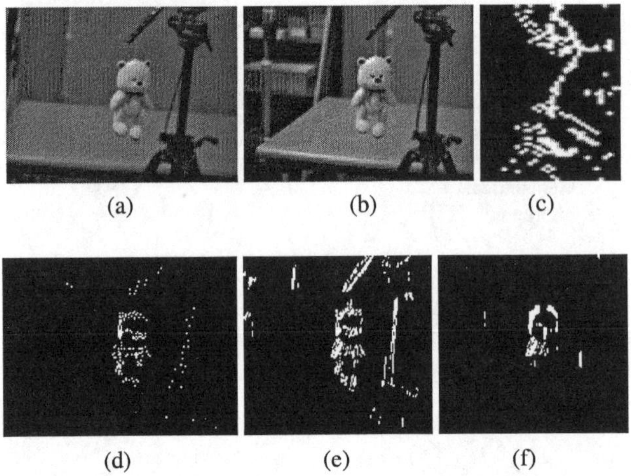

Fig. 2. ZDF outputs. (a) Left image. (b) Right image. (c) Log-polar ZDF. (d) Inverse log-polar ZDF. (e) Traditional ZDF output. (f) Image pyramid ZDF.

the current study can assure a correct steering direction and stereo disparity of the target with less computation cost. The proposed stereo tracking algorithm is implemented in an active vision system and its performance is demonstrated by actual tracking experiments.

2 Target Extraction From Background

The following describes log-polar transformation and foveal image generation using an image pyramid, and shows that ZDF including a log-polar transformation is more efficient in target extraction when compared to either traditional ZDF or ZDF with an image pyramid. Log-polar transformation described in [8] is a well-known space-variant sampling method that decreases the sampling density from the center to the periphery. The generation of a foveal image using an image pyramid has already been explained in [11] where equal-sized central image patches are extracted from each level of the image pyramid, followed by expanding, smoothing, and inserting the finer level of the patch into the center of the present level. Figure 2 shows the ZDF outputs from a log-polar transformation, image pyramid, and the traditional method. In the case of a log-polar transformation, a vertical edge operation is performed for the left and right stereo images and these edge images are then transformed into log-polar coordinates. Next, both log-polar images are binarized based on an appropriate threshold value, then the log-polar ZDF output shown in Fig. 2c is obtained by performing a logical AND of both thresholded log-polar images. Figure 2d shows the inverse log-polar ZDF output, which is obtained by reconverting Fig. 2c into the Cartesian coordinates. Meanwhile, the ZDF output from an image pyramid is obtained by applying the traditional ZDF operation to the foveal image, as shown in Fig. 2f. It can be seen that a log-polar transformation is quite effective, whereas the traditional ZDF shown in Fig. 2e produces background outputs and the image pyramid

ZDF shown in Fig. 2f shows strong vertical edges due to blurring. Although foveation using an image pyramid can suppress the background, part of the target object can also be missing, as shown in Fig. 2f. This implies that the image pyramid struc ture is not as suitable for an exact representation of the central region of gaze when compared to a space-variant resolution structure.

The location of the target is calculated by reconverting the log-polar ZDF output into the Cartesian image and computing its centroid. Due to the subsampling involved in the log-polar processing, the centroid tends to be squeezed toward the image center. However, when the active camera is controlled in a closed loop, the controller will attempt to minimize the error in every frame, as such, this problem does not usually cause much problem.

3 Stereo Disparity Extraction

Let the left and right projections be $p_l(i)$ and $p_r(i)$, respectively, and the centroid of the ZDF output be (x_f, y_f). The sum of the squared difference (SSD) of the intensity values, which is the simplest and most effective criterion in measuring similarity between images [14], is used for the disparity extraction. The SSD of each searching point k in a search area s is defined as

$$e(k) = \sum_{i=-r/2}^{i=r/2} [P_l(x_f + i) - P_r(x_f + i + k)]^2 \tag{1}$$

where $k = -s/2, \cdots, s/2$. Here, r is the size of the window for computing the SSD. The stereo disparity d of a target can be determined by identifying the point with the lowest SSD value.

$$d = \arg\min_k [e(k)] \tag{2}$$

After the stereo disparity is calculated, the desired values for controlling the active stereo system are determined so that the target is located in the image center with a small stereo disparity.

4 Active Stereo Tracking System

The head/eye platform used in the current study, as shown in Fig. 3a, has 5 degrees of freedom (DOF) and is equipped with DC motors and a harmonic driver minimizing the backlash. The maximal pan/tilt angle of each axis is 360°. The focal length of the camera is 25mm and the baseline length is 170mm. The stereo images from the two CCD cameras are digitized into the frame memory using a PCI Matrox Meteor image board. Fig. 3b shows the data flow used to control the active stereo system. The servo loop is controlled by classic proportional control and communication between the host and the active stereo system for camera control is implemented via a GPIB interface. A symmetric pan control is implemented to place the stereo disparity at zero as the positioning mechanism uses an additional pan control system to locate the target in the image center. The entire tracking algorithm is described in Fig. 4.

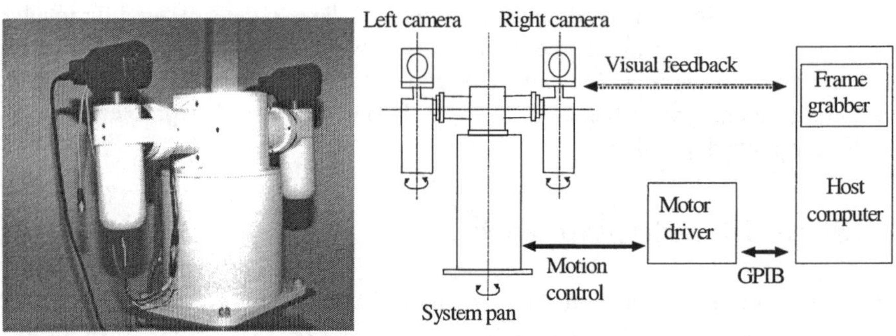

(a) (b)

Fig. 3. (a) Active stereo tracking system. (b) Configuration of tracking system.

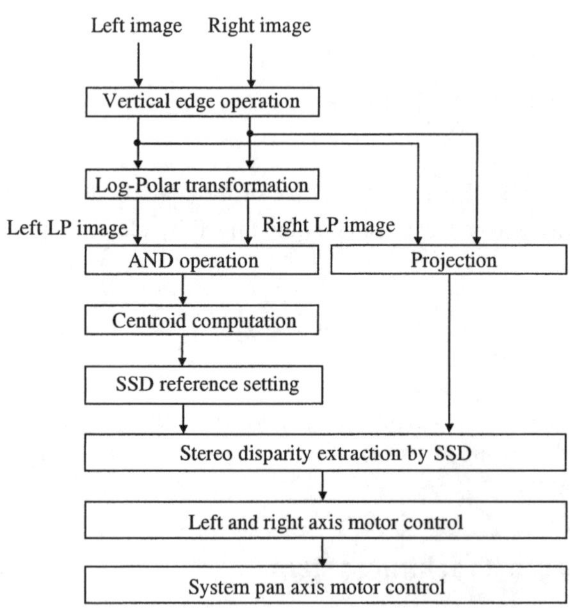

Fig. 4. Data flow of proposed stereo tracking algorithm.

5 Experimental Results

The size of the input image was 160 x 120 pixels, which was transformed into 32 x 64 log-polar images. A stuffed bear rotating round the tripod was used for the experiment. A step motor was attached to the top of the tripod and the stuffed bear rotated at 1.2 cm/sec. The stereo cameras were initially pointed at a target 1.5m away from the stuffed bear. The tracking environment is shown in Fig. 5 and the tracking performance was evaluated based on the difference between the actual camera position and the target location.

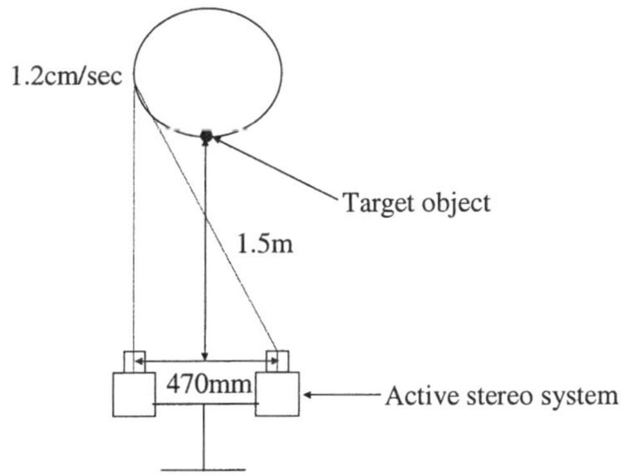

Fig. 5. Experimental setup for tracking.

Figures 6a and 6b show the tracking responses of the three methods: log polar ZDF, image pyramid ZDF, and traditional ZDF. The sinusoidal response shown in Fig. 6a was the rotation angle of the left camera and corresponds to the camera trajectory following the moving target. The rotation angle of the right camera was the same except for a different sign due to symmetric rotation. In the case of the image pyramid ZDF and traditional ZDF, the tracking system began to deviate from the desired trajectory in the 75th frame. The reason for this was directly traced to the situation that the doll and tripod were both located within the same horopter. However, the log-polar transformation was able to track successfully and kept the stuffed bear dominant over the distracting background. Although a partial occlusion occurred at around the 90th frame as shown in Fig. 6c, which led to a system fixation on a random position, the effects were only slight and the tripod lying in the zero disparity area was identified as the main cause of the deviations. The response of the system pan axis is shown in Fig. 6b and the performance was found to be similar to that in Fig. 6a as the rotation angle was linked with the stereo camera movement. Accordingly, the experimental results demonstrated that a log-polar transformation was able to enhance the tracking performance.

6 Conclusions

Foveation coupled to traditional ZDF was proposed for effective target extraction from a distracting background. A log-polar transformation and image pyramid were used for target enhancement and their performances compared based on actual tracking experiments. The results showed that foveation using a log-polar transformation

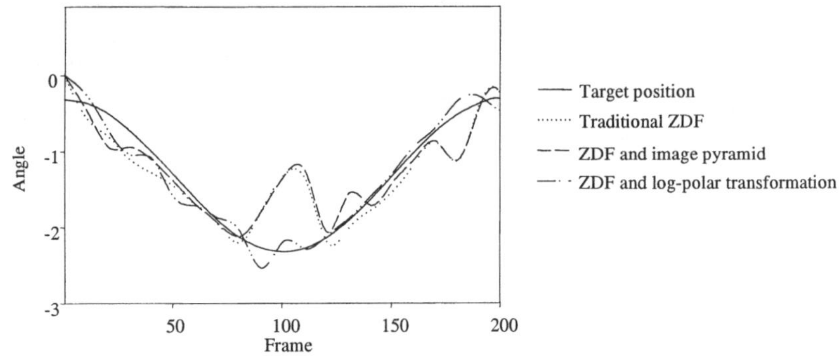

(a)

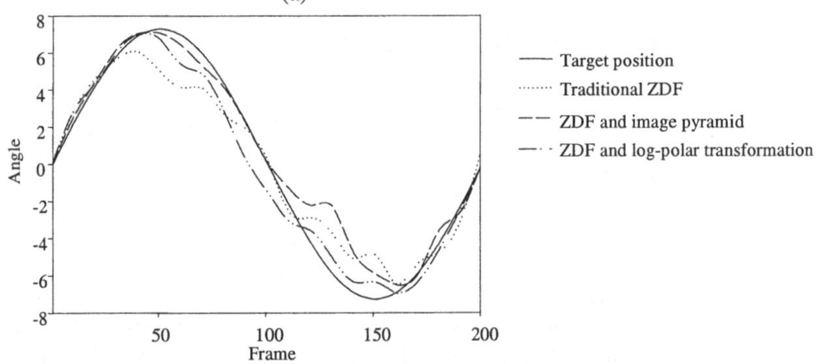

(b)

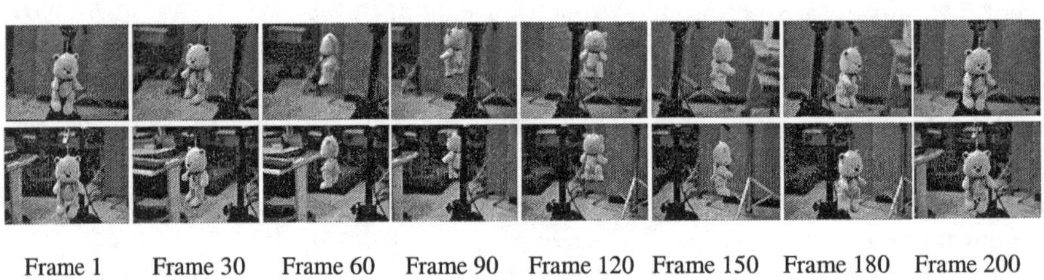

(c)

Fig. 6. Tracking results for rotating stuffed bear. (a) Rotation angle of left camera. (b) Rotation angle of system pan motor. (c) Stuffed bear image frames.

was more helpful in tracking mainly due to effective background suppression without windowing the target. In addition, the stereo disparity was extracted using projection data to fixate on the surface of a moving target and its accuracy was demonstrated based on the experiments. Although the closed-loop controller used in the current study was somewhat coarse, the active stereo system was still capable of tracking a moving target. In further studies, a more reliable PID controller will be designed and incorporated to provide a smoother behavior by the active stereo system.

References

1. Coombs D. J.: Tracking Objects with Eye Movements. Proc. of the Topical Meeting on Image Understanding and Machine Vision, Optical Society of America (1989).
2. Ballard D. H. and Brown C. M.: Principles of Animate Vision. CVGIP: Image Understanding, Vol. 56, No. 1. (1992) 3-21.
3. Coombs D. J. and Brown C. M.: Real-Time Binocular Smooth Pursuit. International Journal of Computer Vision, Vol. 11, No. 2. (1993) 147-164.
4. Tanaka M., Maru N., and Miyazaki F.: Binocular Gaze Holding of a Moving Object with the Active Stereo Vision System. Proc. the 2nd IEEE Workshop on Applications of Computer Vision, Sarasota, Florida, USA. (1994) 250-255.
5. Rougeaux S., Kita N., Kuniyoshi Y., Sakane S., and Chavand F.: Binocular Tracking Based on Virtual Horopters. IROS'94, Vol. 3. (1994) 2052-2057.
6. Oshiro N., Maru N., Nishikawa A., and Miyazaki F.: Binocular Tracking using Log Polar Mapping. IROS'96, Vol. 2. (1996) 791-798.
7. Tistarelli M. and Sandini G.: Dynamic Aspects in Active Vision. CVGIP: Image Undestanding, Vol. 56, No. 1. (1992) 108-129.
8. Messener R. A. and Szu H. H.: An Image Processing Architecture for Real Time Generation of Scale and Rotation. Computer Vision, Graphics, and Image Processing. Vol. 31. (1985) 50-66.
9. Bernardino A. and Santos-Victor J.: Visual Behaviours for Binocular Tracking. 2nd Euro Micro Workshop on Advanced Mobile Robotics - Eurobot97, Brescia, Italy (1997).
10. Olson T. J. and Lockwood R. J.: Fixation-based Filtering. Proc. of the SPIE Intelligent Robots and Computer Vision XI Conference (1992) 685-696.
11. Taylor J. R. and Olson T. J.: Precise Vergence Control in Complex Scenes. SPIE Vol. 2056, Intelligent Robots and Computer Vision XII (1993) 20-30.
12. Olson T. J. and Coombs D. J.: Real-Time Vergence Control for Binocular Robots. International Journal of Computer Vision, Vol. 7, No. 1. (1991) 67-89.
13. Maki A. and Uhlin T.: Disparity Selection in Binocular Pursuit. Technical report, KTH (Royal Institute of Technology) (1995).
14. Okutomi M. and Kanade T.: A Multiple-Baseline Stereo. IEEE Transactions on Pattern Analysis and Machine Intelligence, Vol. 15, No. 4. (1993) 353-363.
15. Bernardino A. and Santos-Victor J.: A Binocular Stereo Algorithm for Log-polar Foveated Systems, 2nd Workshop on BMCV, Tuebingen, Germany, (2002) 127-136.

Monte Carlo Visual Tracking Using Color Histograms and a Spatially Weighted Oriented Hausdorff Measure

Tao Xiong and Christian Debrunner

Center for Robotics, Automation, and Distributed Intelligence
Colorado School of Mines, Engineering Division
1610 Illinois Street, Golden, CO, USA
{txiong,cdebrunn}@mines.edu

Abstract. Color-based and edge-based trackers based on sequential Monte Carlo filters have been shown to be robust and versatile for a modest computational cost. However, background features with characteristics similar to the tracked object can distract them. Robustness can be further improved through the integration of multiple features such that a failure in one feature will not cause the tracker to fail. We present a new method of integrating a shape and a color feature such that even if only a single feature provides correct results, the feature tracker can track correctly. We also introduce a new Hausdorff-based shape similarity metric that we call the spatially weighted oriented Hausdorff similarity measure (SWOHSM). The approach is shown to be robust on both face tracking and automobile tracking applications.

1 Introduction

Visual tracking has been studied extensively by the computer vision community for many applications ranging from face tracking, hand tracking, and human body tracking, to automobile tracking. Several design factors influence the robustness of tracking algorithms. Shape-based trackers and histogram-based color-based trackers (e.g., [1-3]) can be distracted by other regions with similar shape or color characteristics, so some researchers have investigated the integration of measurements from several types of features to increase robustness [1, 3-6]. The reasoning behind this approach is that the various features will fail in different situations, and that at least one feature detector will succeed at most situations. These approaches have shown improvement in tracking results when using multiple cues, but it is not clear how to combine cues such that tracking continues if one or more cues fail.

Other research has explored several methods of integrating multiple cues, including combining measurements as the product of probabilities [7], additively combining edge and color measures [1], *democratic integration* [8, 9] which forms a linear combination of cues and adapts the weights of the linear combination, and sequential Monte Carlo filters using a weighted sum of the cues [8]. Another multiple cue integration method, which we adopt in this work, is *importance sampling,* used in [6]. This method injects new state samples into the standard prediction and diffusion process of a Monte Carlo filter. Wu and Huang [5] use a similar approach that they

N. Petkov and M.A. Westenberg (Eds.): CAIP 2003, LNCS 2756, pp. 190–197, 2003.

refer to as co-inference, in which they maintain three weights for each state sample, one based on each of two cues and one based on the combination of the cues. We also maintain a set of weights based on each feature as well as the combined feature, and draw from the state distributions based on individual features for importance sampling. These earlier works clearly demonstrate the increase in robustness resulting from the integration of multiple cues, and suggest that importance sampling is a powerful method of cue integration. In addition, the methods using Monte Carlo filters appear to be more robust, apparently due to their ability to track multi-modal state distributions.

One of the critical issues in designing a tracking system is the appropriate choice of features. A good choice of features will be independent in that the features fail in different situations and provide statistically independent information when conditioned on a state estimate. Color histogram features appear to be very robust (e.g., [2]) and require little computation to extract or compare. Recently the Hausdorff measure has also been applied to tracking problems and has been shown to be robust [10-12]. Here we define a new variant, the spatially weighted oriented Hausdorff similarity measure (SWOHSM). This method combines the approach of Sim and Park [13] who modify the Hausdorff by weighting edge point matches based on the similarity in edge orientation, and the approach of Lin *et al.* [14] who weight the contributions of edges based on a saliency mask defined on the model edges. We present a tracking method that integrates the SWOHSM and the color histogram similarity measure of [2] in a sequential Monte Carlo filter with importance sampling. This design increases the robustness over earlier approaches in several ways: 1) the SWOHSM increases the reliability of the shape similarity measure, 2) importance sampling from both individual feature distributions allows propagation of the correct hypotheses supported by a single feature, and 3) importance sampling improves the efficiency with which the state space is sampled allowing a reduction in the number of samples required to adequately sample the state space. We demonstrate the tracker on head and vehicle tracking problems using real image sequences.

2 Algorithm Description

To maintain a description of the state of the tracker, we use a sequential Monte Carlo filter. The state of this filter represents the image location of the tracked object, and the state is updated in two steps: a prediction step that predicts the next state in terms of the current state, and a measurement update step that updates the state based on measurements from the image. Denoting by X_t and Z_t respectively the state and the measurement at time t, the sequential Monte Carlo tracking algorithm maintains an estimate of the posterior distribution $p(X_t|Z_t)$ as a set of M weighted samples $\{x_t^m\}_{m=1,\dots,M}$. In the prediction step the samples are propagated to new states at the next time step, and in the measurement update step the weights associated with the samples are updated based on the measurements. The following subsection describes the integration of the shape and color measures in the sequential Monte Carlo filter, and subsequent sections define the color and shape similarity measures.

2.1 Sequential Monte Carlo Filter

The sequential Monte Carlo filter we use in our tracking method is defined in terms of its state, its dynamic model, and its measurement update. The steps of filter algorithm are shown in Fig. 1, where steps 1 and 2 implement the dynamic model and step 3 implements the measurement update. As in [2], the state in our approach consists of the image position and the scale of the target at times t and $t-1$. We maintain for each state sample x_t^m at time t three weights denoted by $\omega_t^{s(m)}$, $\omega_t^{c(m)}$ and $\omega_t^{(m)}$, which are based on the shape measurement, the color measurement, and a linear combination of both measurements, respectively. The combined weight is computed as

$$\omega_t^{(n)} = p_t^s \omega_t^{s(n)} + (1 - p_t^s)\omega_t^{c(n)} , \tag{1}$$

where $p_t^s \in (0,1)$ represents our confidence of the shape cue relative to the color cue at time t.

Importance sampling is a technique developed to improve the efficiency of factored sampling. It applies when auxiliary knowledge is available in the form of an importance function $g(X_t)$ describing which areas of state-space contain most information about the posterior [6]. Importance sampling concentrates samples in those

Generate $\{(x_t^m, \omega_t^{(m)}, \omega_t^{s(m)}, \omega_t^{c(m)})\}$ from $\{(x_{t-1}^m, \omega_{t-1}^{(m)}, \omega_{t-1}^{s(m)}, \omega_{t-1}^{c(m)})\}$, $m = 1,\dots,M$.

Construct the mth of M new samples as follows:

1. Choose the sampling method by generating a uniformly distributed random number $\alpha \in [0,1)$.
2. Sample from the prediction density as follows:
   (a) If $\alpha < q$, choose x_t^m by sampling from $g_{s(t-1)}$ and set
   $\lambda_t^m = f_t(x_t^m) / g_{s(t-1)}(x_t^m)$ where
   $f_t(x_t^m) = \sum_{k=1}^{M} \omega_{t-1}^{(j)} p(X_t = x_t^m \mid X_{t-1} = x_{t-1}^k)$.
   (b) If $q \le \alpha < q + r$, choose x_t^m by sampling from $g_{c(t-1)}$ and set
   $\lambda_t^m = f_t(x_t^m) / g_{c(t-1)}(x_t^m)$, $f_t(x_t^m)$ is the same as above.
   (c) If $\alpha \ge q + r$, choose a base sample x_{t-1}^i with probability $\omega_{t-1}^{(i)}$, then choose x_t^m by sampling from $p(X_t \mid X_{t-1} = x_{t-1}^i)$ and set $\lambda_t^m = 1$
3. Measurement update process
   $\omega_t^{s(m)} = \lambda_t^m * p(Z_{s,t} | X_t = x_t^m)$
   $\omega_t^{c(m)} = \lambda_t^m * p(Z_{c,t} | X_t = x_t^m)$
   Normalize $\omega_t^{c(m)}$ and $\omega_t^{s(m)}$ such that $\sum_{m=1}^{M} \omega_t^{c(m)} = \sum_{m=1}^{M} \omega_t^{s(m)} = 1$
   $\omega_t^{(m)} = p_t^s \omega_t^{s(m)} + (1 - p_t^s)\omega_t^{c(m)}$

Fig. 1. Tracking algorithm with importance sampling

areas of state-space by generating sample positions x_t^m from $g(X_t)$ rather than sampling from the prior $p(X_t|Z_{t-1})$.

To approximate a posterior $p(X_t \mid Z_t)$, instead of sampling directly from the prior $p(X_t \mid Z_{t-1})$, the samples x_t^m can be drawn from the distribution $g_t(X_t)$, and the weight of each sample can be chosen as

$$\omega_t^{(m)} = \frac{f_t(x_t^m)}{g_t(x_t^m)} p(Z_t \mid X_t = x_t^m) \ , \tag{2}$$

where $f_t(x_t^m) = p(X_t = x_t^m \mid Z_{t-1})$.

In step 2 of Fig. 1 we use two importance sampling functions, one from shape $g_{s,t}(X_t) \propto (x_t^m, \omega_t^{s,(m)})$ in step 2(a) and one from color $g_{c,t}(X_t) \propto (x_t^m, \omega_t^{c,(m)})$ in step 2(b). Since we maintain a state distribution for each measurement independently, we track hypotheses that are supported by only a single feature. Step 3 of the figure then implements the weighting of Equation (2). Step 2(c) of the figure implements sampling from the dynamic model as in the standard sequential Monte Carlo filter.

The weighting in the linear combination is selected based on the specific tracking environment. This approach allows us to incorporate our prior knowledge of the reliability of each module. The method used for the initial detection of regions to be tracked will vary with the application. In this paper our focus is on the tracking component of the problem, and we therefore initialize our state samples and our color histogram based on hand-selected regions in the first frame of the sequence.

2.2 Color Similarity

Our color similarity measure is based on the similarity between the color histogram of a reference region in the first image and that of the image region in frame t represented by a sample x_t^m. In order to estimate the proper weight for this sample during the measurement update step (step 3 in Fig. 1), we need the conditional distribution $p(Z_{c,t}|X_t = x_t^m)$ of the color measure $Z_{c,t}$ at time t. This distribution could be estimated from training data, but for simplicity we follow Pérez [2] and define

$$p(Z_{c,t}|X_t = x_t^m) \propto \exp\left\{-\gamma_c D^2\left[q^*, q_t(x_t^m)\right]\right\}, \tag{3}$$

where q^* and $q_t(x_t^m)$ are the N-element color histograms of the reference region and the region defined by x_t^m, respectively. The distance measure D is derived from the Bhattacharyya similarity coefficient and is defined as

$$D\left[q^*, q_t(x_t^m)\right] = \left[1 - \sum_{n=1}^{N} \sqrt{q^*(n) q_t(n; x_t^m)}\right]^{1/2} . \tag{4}$$

2.3 Shape Similarity

Our shape similarity measure captures the similarity between a reference shape and the image edges in a region hypothesized by x_t^m. The measure is based on our Spatially Weighted Oriented Hausdorff Similarity Measure. The SWOHSM computes the similarity of image shapes $\mathbf{A} = \{A_E, A_G(\,), A_W(\,)\}$ and $\mathbf{B} = \{B_E, B_G(\,)\}$, where A_E and B_E are sets of edge points defining the shape, $A_G(\,)$ and $B_G(\,)$ are functions defining the intensity gradient in the two images, and $A_W(\,)$ is a weighting function defining the relative importance of various edge points. Note that the gradient functions and the weighting function need only be defined on the edge points. We define directed SWOHSM of two images as

$$h(\mathbf{A},\mathbf{B}) = \frac{1}{N_A} \sum_{a \in A_E} A_w(a) \left| O_{A_G(a)} \cdot O_{B_G(n_B(a))} \right| \rho_T(d_B(a)) . \tag{5}$$

Here $O_{A_G(x)}$ is the unit vector along the gradient direction at location x in image $\mathbf{A}$ ($O_{B_G(x)}$ is defined similarly), $n_B(a) \in B_E$ such that $\|n_B(a) - a\| \le \|b - a\| \forall b \in B_E$, $d_B(a) = \|n_B(a) - a\|$, $\rho_T(a)$ is a robust distance weighting function which goes to zero for distances greater than T, and N_A is the number points in A_E. Note that this measure differs from that of Sim and Park [13] in several ways: 1) the gradient orientation in image B is taken at location $n_B(a)$ rather than at location a, 2) the absolute value of $O_{A_G(a)} \cdot O_{B_G(n_B(a))}$ is used to allow matching of either sign of gradient, and 3) a spatial weighting function $A_w(a)$ is included.

As in the case of our color similarity metric, we need the conditional probability of the observed shape similarity metric $p(Z_{s,t} | X_t = x_t^m)$ for the measurement update step (step 3 of Fig. 1). We define this distribution as

$$p(Z_{s,t} | X_t = x_t^m) \propto \exp\{-\gamma_s [1 - h(\mathbf{R}(x_t^m), \mathbf{I}_t)]\} . \tag{6}$$

where $h(\mathbf{R}(x_t^m), \mathbf{I}_t)$ is the SWOHSM from the transformed reference shape $\mathbf{R}(x_t^m)$ (transformed based on the state x_t^m) to the current image shape $\mathbf{I}_t$.

3 Experimental Results

We tested our algorithm in an automobile tracking application and a face tracking application. We tested on the former using traffic data collected from a camera on a moving vehicle, and the latter on face data available from [15]. The reference shape models we used are shown in Fig. 2. Equal weights are used for all the points on the automobile reference shape (i.e. $A_w(a) = 1$ in Equation (5)). The face reference shape is modeled as a vertical ellipse with a fixed aspect ratio of 1.2 as in [1] and as illustrated in Fig. 2(b). We set $A_w(a)$ of Equation (5) to 1.2 for the upper part of the head, and to 0.6 for the lower part. In both the automobile and face tracking applications, we set γ_c of Equation (3) to 10, we set γ_s of Equation (6) to 30, and we define $\rho_T(\,)$ of Equation (5) as a triangular pulse function with a width of 12 pixels.

In the automobile tracking experiments, we set p_t^s of Equation (1) to 0.5, which means we trust the shape and color measurement equally well. Some tracking results are shown in Fig. 3. It can be see that the vehicle marked with the white box was tracked robustly even with partial occlusions in a relatively congested traffic scene.

We tested the performance of our algorithm in the face tracking application using the same image sequence used in [1, 5]. This allows a preliminary performance comparison between our method and these earlier methods, and also tests our approach on a relatively difficult sequence that includes a full rotation of the head, tilting of the head, and a large amount of occlusion. In Equation (1), p_t^s is set to 0.6, which means we trust the shape measure more than the color measure. Selected tracking results are shown in Fig. 4. In the first 8 images, the subject moves around in an office environment and makes a full rotation. Algorithms based on just a color cue will fail on the portion of the rotation where only the back of the head (the hair) is visible because of dramatic change in the color histogram and because the wooden door behind the subject is a similar color to the face. Our algorithm is able to track the head very accurately in this sequence. For example, in the third frame shown in Fig. 4, the shape cue is dominating so the tracker can still capture the head without any difficulty. Last 7 images in Fig. 4 show the capability of our algorithm to deal with a large amount of occlusion. In the images, another face moves in front of the subject and largely occludes her face. The combination of shape and color cues helps the tracker to lock on the subject accurately throughout all these difficulties.

Fig. 2. The reference shapes used for (a) automobile tracking and (b) face tracking. The thickness of the boundary line indicates the weighting function $A_w(\,)$ and the arrows indicate the gradient $A_G(\,)$.

Fig. 3. Results of one of the automobile tracking experiments

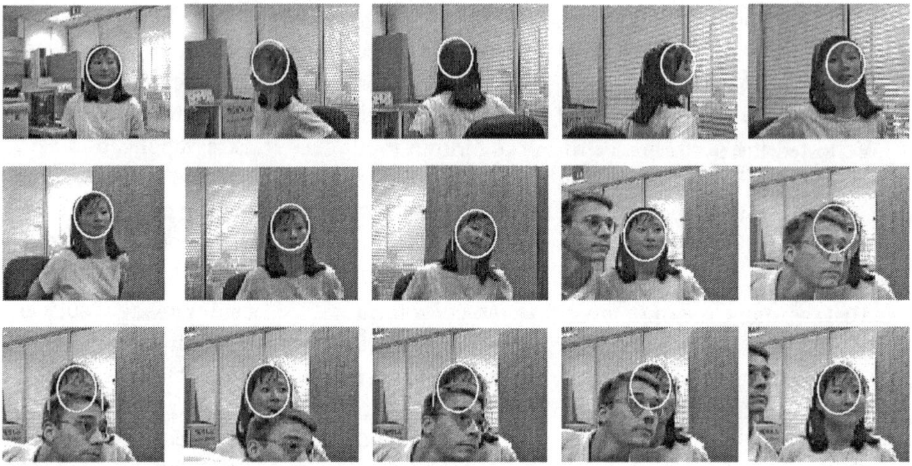

Fig. 4. Results of one of the face tracking experiments

In our experiments, very simple shape models were used. The generic shape models used appear to be adequate for reliable tracking, although it might be useful to also include strong internal edges taken from a reference image. In real-time applications the increase in robustness from using additional edge features must be traded off against additional processing delays.

4 Conclusions

We have demonstrated a sequential Monte Carlo filter-based method for tracking objects in video sequences. The method uses a color histogram similarity feature and a new Hausdorff-based SWOHSM shape feature to locate the object in each new frame. It maintains three estimates of the state distribution based on the color measure, the shape measure, and a linear combination of both measures. New samples are drawn from the shape and color distributions in an importance sampling approach, and from the combined feature using a dynamic model of the tracking process. This method insures that some samples of the state space always capture the information from each of the measures, which captures the state distribution more efficiently and integrates the results of the measures. The approach insures that hypotheses supported by only one feature are considered using importance sampling.

The SWOHSM augments earlier Hausdorff measures by incorporating edge orientation, edge position, and a weighting capturing edge importance into the similarity metric. This increases reliability and robustness of the metric, and improves the performance of the overall tracking approach.

The method was tested on an automobile tracking application and on a face tracking application. In both cases the approach can reliably track the objects in difficult sequences with dramatic color changes, large amounts of occlusion, and many background clutter edges.

References

1. Birchfield, S.: Elliptical Head Tracking Using Intensity Gradients and Color Histograms. In: Proceedings of Computer Vision and Pattern Recognition. (1998)
2. Pérez, P., Hue, C., Vermaak, J. and Gangnet, M.: Color-Based Probabilistic Tracking. In: Proceedings of European Conference on Computer Vision. (2002) 661–675
3. Comaniciu, D., Ramesh, V. and Meer, P.: Real-Time Tracking of Non-Rigid Objects Using Mean Shift. In: Proceedings of Computer Vision and Pattern Recognition. (2000) 142-151
4. Wren, C.R., Azarbayejani, A., Darrell, T. and Pentland, A.P.: Pfinder: Real-Time Tracking of the Human Body. IEEE Transactions on Pattern Analysis and Machine Intelligence, 7 (1997) 780-785
5. Wu, Y. and Huang, T.S.: A Co-Inference Approach to Robust Visual Tracking. In: Proceedings of International Conference on Computer Vision. (2001)
6. Isard, M. and Blake, A.: Icondensation: Unifying Low–Level and High–Level Tracking in a Stochastic Framework. In: Proceedings of European Conference on Computer Vision. (1998)
7. Isard, M. and MacCormick, J.: Bramble: A Bayesian Multiple-Blob Tracker. In: Proceedings of International Conference on Computer Vision. (2001) 34-41
8. Spengler, M. and Schiele, B.: Towards Robust Multi-Cue Integration for Visual Tracking. In: Proceedings of ICVS. (2001)
9. Triesch, J. and Malsburg, C.v.d.: Democratic Integration: Self-Organized Integration of Adaptive Cues. Neural Computation, (2001) 2049–2074
10. Meier, T. and Ngan, K.N.: Automatic Segmentation of Moving Objects for Video Object Plane Generation. IEEE Transactions on Circuits and Systems for Video Technology, 5 (1998) 525-538
11. Hunttenlocher, D.P., Noh, J.J. and Ruckelidge, W.J.: Tracking Non-Rigid Objects in Complex Scenes. In: Proceedings of International Conference on Computer Vision. (1993) 93-101
12. Ayala-Ramirez, V., Parra, C. and Devy, M.: Active Tracking Based on Hausdorff Matching. In: Proceedings of International Conference on Pattern Recognition. (2000)
13. Sim, D.-G. and Park, R.-H.: Two-Dimensional Object Alignment Based on the Robust Oriented Hausdorff Similarity Measure. IEEE Transactions on Image Processing, 3 (2001) 475-483
14. Lin, K.-H., Guo, B., Lam, K.-M. and Siu, W.-C.: Human Face Recognition Using a Spatially Weighted Modified Hausdorff Distance. In: Proceedings of International Symposium on Intelligent Multimedia, Video and Speech Processing. (2001) 477-480
15. Birchfield, S.: Elliptical Head Tracking Using Intensity Gradients and Color Histograms. web page at: http://robotics.stanford.edu/~birch/headtracker

Object Classification and Tracking in Video Surveillance

Qi Zang and Reinhard Klette

CITR, Computer Science Department, The University of Auckland
Tamaki Campus, Auckland, New Zealand

Abstract. The design of a video surveillance system is directed on automatic identification of events of interest, especially on tracking and classification of moving vehicles or pedestrians. In case of any abnormal activities, an alert should be issued. Normally a video surveillance system combines three phases of data processing: moving object extraction, moving object recognition and tracking, and decisions about actions. The extraction of moving objects, followed by object tracking and recognition, can often be defined in very general terms. The final component is largely depended upon the application context, such as pedestrian counting or traffic monitoring. In this paper, we review previous research on moving object tracking techniques, analyze some experimental results, and finally provide our conclusions for improved performances of traffic surveillance systems. One stationary camera has been used.

1 Introduction

Recent research in video surveillance systems is focused on background modelling, moving object classification and tracking. A near-correct extraction of all pixels defining a moving object or the background is crucial for moving object tracking and classification. Major occurrences of moving objects in our data are pedestrians and vehicles. The camera(s) position will affect the selection of an appropriate technique for object tracking. Considering the angle between viewing direction and a horizontal ground plane, this angle is often about 0° which is horizontal, or 90° which is vertical. In situations of about horizontal or vertical viewing, researchers typically prefer the use of region based tracking, or of contour or snake tracking techniques, because the shape of the extracted moving object is not expected to change much. This assumption simplifies feature calculations for tracking, and the main problem is that moving object may be occluded by each other, or by stationary objects such as buildings. But in non-vertical and non-horizontal situations which are typical for traffic monitoring systems, the angle between the viewing direction and the ground plane can take any value. If vehicles move fast, then the shape of the vehicle will change rapidly. In this case feature based tracking is required which extends simple shape matching approaches.

The primary goal of this paper is to critically discuss the use of tracking methods in different situations. A second goal is to present a hybrid method in using feature based object tracking in traffic surveillance, and report about its performance. The paper is structured as follows: in Section 2, we discuss existing approaches for tracking moving objects using different techniques in different situations. Section 3 presents our ideas for moving object tracking. Section 4 discusses our performance experiments, and Section 5 finally informs about the obtained analysis results and gives conclusion.

N. Petkov and M.A. Westenberg (Eds.): CAIP 2003, LNCS 2756, pp. 198–205, 2003.

2 Review of Previous Work

Many applications have been developed for monitoring public areas such as offices, shopping malls or traffic highways. In order to control normal activities in these areas, tracking of pedestrians and vehicles play the key role in video surveillance systems. We classify these tracking techniques into four categories:

Tracking based on a moving object region. This method identifies and tracks a *blob token* or a *bounding box*, which are calculated for connected components of moving objects in 2D space. The method relies on properties of these blobs such as size, color, shape, velocity, or centroid. A benefit of this method is that it time efficient, and it works well for small numbers of moving objects. Its shortcoming is that problems of occlusion cannot be solved properly in "dense" situations. Grouped regions will form a combined blob and cause tracking errors. For example, [11] presents a method for blob tracking. Kalman filters are used to estimate pedestrian parameters. Region splitting and merging are allowed. Partial overlapping and occlusion is corrected by defining a pedestrian model.

Tracking based on an active contour of a moving object. The contour of a moving object is represented by a *snake*, which is updated dynamically. It relies on the boundary curves of the moving object. For example, it is efficient to track pedestrians by selecting the contour of a human's head. This method can improve the time complexity of a system, but its drawback is that it cannot solve the problem of partial occlusion, and if two moving objects are partially overlapping or occluded during the initialization period, this will cause tracking errors. For example, [5] proposes a stochastic algorithm for tracking of objects. This method uses factored sampling, which was previously applied to interpretations of static images, in which the distribution of possible interpretations is represented by a randomly generated set of representatives. It combines factored sampling with learning of dynamical models to propagate an entire probability distribution for object position and shape over time. This improves the mentioned drawback of contour tracking in case of partial occlusions, but increases the computational complexity.

Tracking based on a moving object model. Normally model based tracking refers to a 3D model of a moving object. This method defines a parametric 3D geometry of a moving object. It can solve partially the occlusion problem, but it is (very) time consuming, if it relies on detailed geometric object models. It can only ensure high accuracy for a small number of moving objects. For example, [6] solved the partial occlusion problem by considering 3D models. The definition of parameterized vehicle models make it possible to exploit the a-priori knowledge about the shape of typical objects in traffic scenes. [2].

Tracking based on selected features of moving objects. Feature based tracking is to select common features of moving objects and tracking these features continuously. For example, corners can be selected as features for vehicle tracking. Even if partial occlusion occurs, a fraction of these features is still visible, so it may overcome the partial occlusion problem. The difficult part is how to identify those features which belong to the same object during a tracking procedure (feature clustering). Several papers have been published on this aspect. For example, [10] extracts corners as selected features using the Harris corner detector. These corners then initialize new tracks in each of the corner trackers. Each tracker tracks any current corner to the next image and passes its position to each of the classifiers at the next level. The classifiers use each corner position and several other attributes to determine if the tracker has tracked correctly.

Besides these four main categories, there are also some other approaches on object tracking. [7] presents a tracking method based on wavelet analysis. A wavelet-based neural network (NN) is used for recognizing a vehicle in extracted moving regions. The wavelet transform is adopted to decompose an image and a particular frequency band is selected for input into the NN for vehicle recognition. Vehicles are tracked by using position coordinates and wavelet feature differences for identifying correspondences between vehicle regions [7]. Paper [3] employs a second order motion model for each object to estimate its location in subsequent frames, and a "cardboard model" is used for a person's head and hands. Kalman models and Kalman filters are very important tools and often used for tracking moving objects. Kalman filters are typically used to make predictions for the following frame and to locate the position or to identify related parameters of the moving object. For example, [13] implemented an online method for initializing and maintaining sets of Kalman filters. At each frame, they have an available pool of Kalman models and a new available pool of connected components that they could explain. Paper [12] uses an extended Kalman filter for trajectory prediction. It provides an estimate of each object's position and velocity. But, as pointed out in [5], Kalman filters are only of limited use, because they are based on unimodal Gaussian densities and hence cannot support simultaneous alternative motion hypotheses. So several methods have also been developed to avoid using Kalman filtering. [5] presents a new stochastic algorithm for robust tracking which is superior to previous Kalman filter based approaches. Bregler [1] presents a probabilistic decomposition of human dynamics to learn and recognize human beings in video sequences. [9] presents a much simpler method based on a combination of temporal differencing and image template matching which achieves highly satisfactory tracking performance in the presence of partial occlusions and enables good classification. This avoids probabilistic calculations.

3 A New Approach

Our approach specifies two subprocesses, the extraction of a (new) moving object from the background and tracking of a moving object.

3.1 Object Extraction from Background

Evidently, before we start with tracking of moving objects, we need to extract moving objects from the background. We use background subtraction to segment the moving objects. Each background pixel is modelled using a mixture of Gaussian distributions. The Gaussians are evaluated using a simple heuristic to hypothesize which are most likely to be part of the "background process". Each pixel is modeled by a mixture of K Gaussians as stated in formula (1):

$$P(\mathbf{X}_t) = \sum_{i=1}^{K} \omega_{i,t} \eta(\mathbf{X}_t; \mu_{i,t}, \Sigma_{i,t}) \ . \tag{1}$$

where $\mathbf{X}_t$ is the variable, which represents the pixel, and t represents time. Here K is the number of distributions: normally we choose K between 3 to 5. $\omega_{i,t}$ is an estimate of the weight of the ith Gaussian in the mixture at time t, $\mu_{i,t}$ is the mean value of the ith Gaussian in the mixture at time t. $\Sigma_{i,t}$ is the covariance matrix of the ith Gaussian in the mixture at time t. Every new pixel value $\mathbf{X}_t$ is checked against the existing K Gaussian distributions until a match is found. Based on the matching results, the background is updated as follows: $\mathbf{X}_t$ matches component i, that is $\mathbf{X}_t$ decreases by 2.5 standard deviations of the distribution, then the parameters of the ith component are updated as follows:

$$\omega_{i,t} = (1-\alpha)\omega_{i,t-1} + \alpha \tag{2}$$

$$\mu_{i,t} = (1-\rho)\mu_{i,t-1} + \rho\mathbf{I}_t \tag{3}$$

$$\sigma_{i,t}^2 = (1-\rho)\sigma_{i,t-1}^2 + \rho(\mathbf{I}_t - \mu_{i,t})^\mathsf{T}(\mathbf{I}_t - \mu_{i,t}) \tag{4}$$

where $\rho = \alpha \Pr(\mathbf{I}_t | \mu_{i,t-1}, \Sigma_{i,t-1})$. α is the predefined learning parameter, μ_t is the mean value of the pixel at time t, and $\mathbf{I}_t$ is the recent pixel at time t. The parameters for unmatched distributions remain unchanged, i.e., to be precise:

$$\mu_{i,t} = \mu_{i,t-1} \quad \text{and } \sigma_{i,t}^2 = \sigma_{i,t-1}^2 \, . \tag{5}$$

But $\omega_{i,t}$ will be adjusted using formula: $\omega_{i,t} = (1-\alpha)\omega_{i,t-1}$.

If $\mathbf{X}_t$ matches none of the K distributions, then the least probable distribution is replaced by a distribution where the current value acts as its mean value. The variance is chosen to be high and the a-priori weight is low [13]. The background estimation problem is solved by specifying the Gaussian distributions, which have the most supporting evidence and the least variance. Because the moving object has larger variance than a background pixel, so in order to represents background processes, first the Gaussians are ordered by the value of $\omega_{i,t}/\|\Sigma_{i,t}\|$ in decreasing order. The background distribution stays on top with the lowest variance by applying a threshold T, where

$$B = \operatorname{argmin}_b \left(\frac{\sum_{i=1}^{b} \omega_{i,t}}{\sum_{i=1}^{K} \omega_{i,t}} > T \right) \, . \tag{6}$$

All pixels $\mathbf{X}_t$ which do not match any of these components will be marked as foreground. The next step is to remove shadows. Here we use a method similar to [8]. The detection of brightness and chromaticity changes in the HSV space are more accurate than in RGB space, especially in outdoor scenes, and the HSV color space corresponds closely to human perception of color [4]. At this stage, only foreground pixels need to be converted to hue, saturation and intensity triples. Shadow regions can be detected/eliminated as followings: let $\mathbf{E}$ represent the current pixel at time t, and $\mathbf{B}$ represents the background pixel at time t. For each foreground pixel, if it satisfies the constraints

$$|\mathbf{E}_h - \hat{\mathbf{B}}_h| < \mathbf{T}_h, |\mathbf{E}_s - \hat{\mathbf{B}}_s| < \mathbf{T}_s \text{ and } \mathbf{T}_{v1} < \mathbf{E}_v/\hat{\mathbf{B}}_v < \mathbf{T}_{v2}$$

then this pixel will be removed from the foreground mask. Parameters of shadow pixels will not be updated. Finally, we obtain the moving objects mask, which is applicable for object tracking.

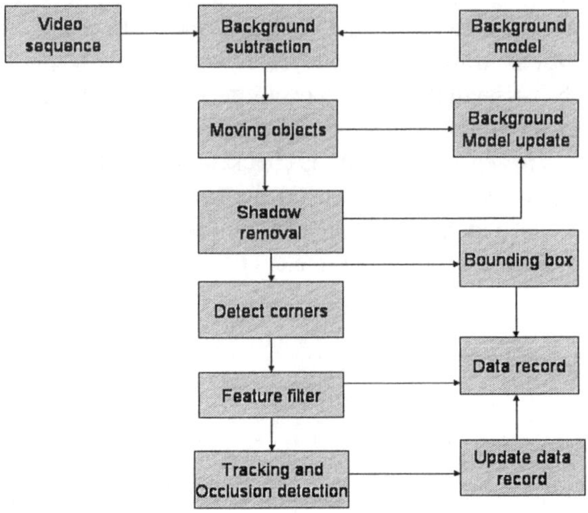

Fig. 1. Flow chart sketch of the proposed approach.

3.2 Object Tracking and Classification

After obtaining an initial mask for a moving object, we have to preprocess the mask. Normally the mask is affected by "salt-and-pepper" noises. We apply morphological filters based on combinations of dilation and erosion to reduce the influence of noise, followed by a connected component analysis for labeling each moving object region. Very small regions are discarded. At this stage we calculate the following features for each moving object region: *bounding rectangle:* the smallest isothetic rectangle that contains the object region. We keep record of the coordinate of the upper left position and the lower right position, what also provides size information (width and height of each rectangle). *color:* the mean R G B values of the moving object. *center:* we use the center of the bounding box as a simple approximation of the centroid of a moving object region. *velocity:* defined as movement of number of pixels/second in both horizontal and vertical direction. In order to track moving objects accurately, especially when objects are partially occluded, and the position of the camera is not restricted to any predefined viewing angle, these features are actually insufficient. We have to add further features that are robust and which can also be extracted even if partial occlusion occurs. From our experiments with traffic video sequences, corners were selected as additional features for tracking. We use the popular SUSAN corner detector to extract corners of vehicles. For each frame, after obtaining a bounding box of the moving object, we then detect corners within the bounding box by applying Susan Quick masks on each pixel. Although sometimes it produces false positives on strong edges, it is faster and can report more stable corners. The corner's position and intensity value is added to a *corner list* of this object. Altogether, the features of a moving object are represented in a five-components vector [bounding box, color, center position, velocity, corner list]. A symbolic flow chart of the proposed method is shown in Figure 1.

Classification of Moving Object Regions. In our captured traffic scenes, moving objects are typically vehicles or pedestrians. We use the ratio of height/width of each bounding box to separate pedestrians and vehicles. For a vehicle, this value should be less than 1.0, for a pedestrian this value should be greater than 1.5. But we also have to provide flexibility for special situations such as a running person, a long or taller vehicle. If the ratio is between 1.0-1.5, then we use the information from the corner list of this object to classify it as a vehicle or a pedestrian (a vehicle produces more corners). This is a simple way to classify moving objects into these two categories.

Tracking of Moving Objects. For moving object tracking we use a hybrid method based on bounding box and feature tracking. During the initialization period a data record is generated for each object: a label for indexing and the five elements of its vector. New positions are predicted using a Kalman filter. For each new frame, the predicted position is searched to see whether it can find any match with the previous data record. If a matching object region is found, it is marked as 'successfully tracked' and belongs to a normal move; if we cannot find any match, then the object may have changed lanes, or stopped, or exceeded the expected speed. So an unmatched object will be checked against already existing objects in the data record. If matched, then it is also marked as 'successfully tracked'; if still not yet matched, it will be marked as a new object and added to the data record. If an existing object is not being tracking for 5 frames, it will be marked as 'stopped'. According to the video capturing speed, we also define a threshold, which is used for marking 'tracking finished'. Matching is performed within certain thresholds for the different feature vector elements. The three main elements used for matching are: same color, a linear change in size, and a constant angle between the line 'corner point-upper left point' versus the line 'corner point-lower bottom point'. Occlusions are reported if bounding boxes are overlapping. In case of partial occlusions, calculated corners and further feature vector elements are tested for making a decision. Finally the data record will be updated using the results of the matching process.

4 Experimental Results

Our approach is implemented on a PC under Linux. Different image sequences have been used: highway with heavy traffic, and a road intersection with vehicles and pedestrians. All sequences are captured in daytime. Figure 2 Left shows moving objects together with bounding boxes and centers marked by white crosses. Figure 2 Right shows examples of detected corners marked by white dots. We set the threshold of the corner detector to a higher value, in order to detect and keep only obvious corners, because "unclear corners" are easily lost, which will affect the tracking accuracy. Corners are only detected within bounding boxes, which not only saves computation time, but also simplifies a common feature tracking problem: how to group features belong to the same objects. After corner detection, we use the identified positions and their intensity values. The average number of corners per vehicle is 26. Our hybrid approach has another advantage, which is to allow the calculation of an important attribute: the angle between the line 'detected corner-upper left position of bounding box' and line 'detected corner-lower right position of bounding box'. This angle is very useful for tracking, because the bounding box shrinks

Fig. 2. Left: An enlarged picture showing detected corners of vehicles marked by white dots. Right: Bounding boxes of moving vehicles and their centers marked by white crosses.

Table 1. Average processing times in seconds.

Step	*Average time*
Object extraction	0.105
Feature extraction	0.025
Object tracking	0.07
Total	0.2

or expands while the object moves, but this angle will still remain unchanged. Of course, this reflects our assumption that the viewing area on a road or highway is basically planar and does not change orientation. The image size is 320 x 240, average processing rate is 4-6 frames/second, on average of 0.2 second per frame. The processing times are given in Table 1.

5 Conclusions

Moving object tracking is a key task in video monitoring applications. The common problem is occlusion detection. In this case the selection of appropriate features is critical for moving object tracking and classification. We propose a hybrid method of both bounding box and feature tracking to achieve a more accurate but simple object tracking system, which can be used in traffic analysis and control applications. Corners are detected only within the bounding rectangle. In this way we reduced computation time and avoided the common feature grouping problem. Corner attribute is very helpful in feature tracking, in our approach we use the stable angle between the line 'detected corner point-upper left point' versus the line 'detected corner point-lower bottom point'. We use the ratio of height/width plus corner information to classify vehicles and pedestrians. This method proved to be easy and efficient, but it only works well on separated regions. So removing shadows is an important preprocessing task [14] for the subsequent extraction of moving objects masks, because shadows merge otherwise separated regions. Future work will also apply 3D analysis (a binocular stereo camera system and an infrared camera), which allows a more detailed classification of cars. The intention is to identify the type of a vehicle. The height value of the car is, for example, easily to extract from the infrared picture.

References

1. C. Bregler: Learning and recognizing human dynamics in video sequences. In Proc. *IEEE Int. Conf. CVPR'97*, pages 568-574, 1997.
2. A. Cavallaro, F. Ziliani, R. Castagno, and T. Ebrahimi: Vehicle extraction based on focus of attention, multi feature segmentation and tracking. In Proc. *European signal processing conference EUSIPCO-2000*, Tampere, Finland, pages 2161-2164, 2000.
3. I. Haritaoglu, D. Harwood, and L. S. Davis: W4: Who? When? Where? What? A real-time system for detecting and tracking people.In Proc. *3rd Face and Gesture Recognition Conf.*, pages 222-227, 1998.
4. N. Herodotou, K. N. Plataniotis, and A. N. Venetsanopoulos: A color segmentation scheme for object-based video coding. In Proc. *IEEE Symp. Advances in Digital Filtering and Signal Proc.*, pages 25-29, 1998.
5. M. Isard, and A. Blake: Contour tracking by stochastic propagation of conditional density. In Proc. *European Conf. Computer Vision, Cambridge, UK*, pages 343-356, 1996.
6. D. Koller, K. Daniilidis, and H. H. Nagel: Model-based object tracking in monocular image sequences of road traffic scenes. *Int. Journal Computer Vision*, **10**:257–281, 1993.
7. J. B. Kim, C. W. Lee, K. M. Lee, T. S. Yun, and H. H. Kim: Wavelet-based vehicle tracking for automatic traffic surveillance. In proc. *IEEE int. Conf. TENCON'01*, Aug, Singapore, Vol. 1, pages 313-316, 2001.
8. P. Kaew Tra Kul Pong, and R. Bowden: An improved adaptive background mixture model for real-time tracking with shadow detection. In Proc. *2nd European Workshop Advanced Video Based Surveillance System*, Sept 2001.
9. A. J. Lipton, H. Fujiyoshi, and R. S. Patil: Moving target classification and tracking from real-time video. In Proc.*IEEE Workshop Application of Computer Vision*, pages 8-14, 1998.
10. B. McCane, B. Galvin, and K. Novins: Algorithmic fusion for more robust feature tracking. *Int. Journal Computer Vision*, **49**: 79–89, 2002.
11. O. Masoud, and N. P. Papanikolopoulos: A novel method for tracking and counting pedestrians in real-time using a single camera. *IEEE Trans. Vehicular Technology*, **50**:1267-1278, 2001.
12. R. Rosales, and S. Sclaroff: Improved tracking of multiple humans with trajectory prediction and occlusion modeling. In Proc. *Workshop on the Interpretation of Visual Motion at CVPR'98*, Santa Barbara, CA, pages 228-233, 1998.
13. C. Stauffer, and W. E. L. Grimson: Adaptive background mixture models for real-time tracking. *Computer Vision and Pattern Recognition*, **2**: 246-252, 1999.
14. Q. Zang, and R. Klette: Evaluation of an adaptive compositeGaussian model in video surveillance. In Proc.*Image and Vision Computing New Zealand 2002*, pages 243-248, 2002.

Video Retrieval by Context-Based Interpretation of Time-to-Collision Descriptors

Ankush Mittal[1] and Wing-Kin Sung[2]

[1] Birla Institute of Technology and Science, Pilani, India 91- 333031
ankush@bits-pilani.ac.in
[2] National University of Singapore, Singapore 117543
ksung@comp.nus.edu.sg

Abstract. Video retrieval using high-level indices is more meaningful than querying using low-level features. In this paper, we show how perceptual features such as time-to-collision (TTC) can lead to several high-level categories. Experiments have been conducted to validate our proposed TTC detection algorithm to compute TTC from the divergence of the image velocity field. A simple and novel method named as the *pilot cue* is used to further refine our algorithm. Our initial system works with a rule-based approach where the extracted TTC shots (low-level feature) are mapped to their corresponding high-level indices. The information conveyed by their neighboring frames or shots (i.e. contextual information) is used to facilitate the mapping process. Several psychological effects (high-level indices) such as intimacy, suspense and terror are recovered as a result.

1 Introduction

Time-To-Collision (TTC) is the time needed for the observer to reach the object, if the instantaneous relative velocity along the optical axis is kept unchanged [12]. According to Marr [13], there exists a specific mechanism in the human visual system, designed to cause one to blink or to avoid a looming object approaching too quickly. Video shot with a small TTC evokes fear because it indicates a scene of impending collision. Thus, TTC can serve as a potent cue for the characterization of an accident or violence.

In this paper, we propose that contextual information of TTC can be used to aid our multimedia indexing system in recovering the semantic contents (high-level indices) of a video sequence. This will be realized in several steps. In Section II, we will examine the conventional use of TTC shots in cinematography to affect the psychological state of the audience. This step is needed because the observations derived from this study can facilitate the formation of several TTC-based high-level indices from low-level features. In Section III, we will attempt to extract a class of contextual information cues – *time-to-collision* (TTC) from the video sequence. The motivation behind this step stem from psychological studies which have shown that human beings are responsive to impending colliding objects [1], and from cinemato-

N. Petkov and M.A. Westenberg (Eds.): CAIP 2003, LNCS 2756, pp. 206–213, 2003.

graphic studies which have shown that filmmakers often gradually shorten the camera-to-subject distance to intensify the audience's emotional involvement with the subject [2], to clarify detail [3], to identify objects of importance [4] or to amplify emotion [5]. Thirdly, in Section IV, we propose to refine our TTC detection algorithm using a simple and novel method, named as the *pilot cue*. Finally, in Section V, we will design a rule-based system that integrates the various contextual information to recover a set of TTC-based high-level indices.

2 Time-to-Collision (TTC) in Cinematography

Depending on how the cinematographer designed and juxtaposed the TTC shots in a scene, it can generate many psychological effects.

1. *Suspense:* Suspense is generated when the audience is led to anticipate an exciting development or payoff. When creating a suspense scene, most directors tend to follow this cue-delay-fulfillment (payoff) pattern [6]. In general, camera movement may be used to create this delay effects. For instance, if the director slowly dolly the camera forward on a detail, gradually enlarging it but delaying the fulfillment of our expectations, the camera movement has contributed to suspense

2. *Intimacy:* By portraying the face in close up, the cinematographer makes it possible for the audience to know intimately the face of the character portrayed and hence by implication to read his/her thoughts and feelings. As a result of that, the audience can get psychologically intimate with the character [7]. Hence, by zooming in or dollying towards (TTC) the subject's face or body, the cinematographer can call the audience's attention.

3. *Terror:* For a lack of a better all-inclusive name, terror in our context can range from fear, panic or shock portrayed by the characters in the scene. Resolution into each of these psychological states depends on what is being portrayed by the cinematographer. For instance, in a chase scene, the director can use a variety of camera movements to dynamically bring out the panicky state that the prey or victim is experiencing as the pursuer is chasing after him/her. Such camera movements include dolly shots that offer the audience views of the characters from the front as they run towards the camera.

2.1 Context-Based Interpretation

In cinematography, besides the incredible psychological effects that can be created through well-choreographed TTC shots in a scene, the cinematographer can also make use of contextual relations to affect TTC shots interpretation. Continuity in the events or the interpretations of the preceding or succeeding shots can affect the ways in which the audience perceives a TTC shot. For instance, a zoom in (TTC) shot can be used within the context of an establishing shot to lead the audience into the environment that the scene will occur. Moreover, the cinematographer can incorporate zoom in (TTC) into the context of other camera movements to direct the audience's attention to a significant object which is a key piece of story information.

3 Time-to-Collision (TTC) Detection

TTC is estimated by computing affine parameters from optical flows. Our optical flow estimation algorithm is similar to the method proposed by Horn and Schunck [8], and Proesmans et al. [9]. The advantage of adopting these two algorithms is that a dense optical flow can be obtained, i.e. for every pixel in the image, an optical flow vector (u, v) can be obtained. The *time-to-collision* (TTC), which is the time that will elapse before the object and the camera collide, is computed as:

$$TTC = \frac{2}{div(\vec{v})} = \frac{2}{u_x + v_y} \quad (1)$$

Here, we have made an assumption that there is no deformation present in the image flow field. The TTC is actually bounded by the deformation term (see [10]). After computing the TTC for each frame in the video sequence, the final step in our TTC detection algorithm is to recover the TTC shots from the video sequence. After experimenting with some training video sequences, we set the threshold for the TTC value in each frame to be 1000, i.e. for TTC value greater than 1000 or less than 0, a default high value of 10000 is set. Finally, the log of the average TTC value for each shot is then computed and evaluated.

3.1 Experimental Results

In this section, a video sequence taken from the action movie – *Tomorrow Never Dies* is used to evaluate the performance of our TTC detection algorithm. The video sequence is about 11 minutes long (total of 16,246 frames).

3.1.1 Performance Evaluation

The performance of the TTC detection algorithm will be expressed in terms of recall and precision.

$$\begin{aligned} recall &= \frac{N_c}{N_c + N_m} \times 100\% = \frac{43}{43+14} \times 100\% = 75.4\% \\ precision &= \frac{N_c}{N_c + N_f} \times 100\% = \frac{43}{43+16} \times 100\% = 72.9\% \end{aligned} \quad (2)$$

where N_c, N_m and N_f correspond to the number of correct detections, number of missed detections and number of false detections respectively.

3.1.2 Shot 1 – Correct Detection

Shot 1 is an image sequence whereby the object is moving closer to the camera. Fig. 2 depicts an example of this type of shot that is correctly detected by our algorithm. In that shot, a jeep is moving closer towards the stationary camera and it will potentially collide with the camera if the cinematographer does not terminate the shot.

Fig. 1. 4th, 12th and 20th frame of a shot showing a jeep moving closer to the camera

3.1.3 Lateral Movement – False Detection

Fig. 4 illustrates a lateral movement shot in which the camera is trying to track the movement of the man as he runs to the left. During the leftward tracking process of the camera, the background is actually moving to the right while the man is running in the direction of the camera movement and is running faster than the camera. Hence, there is an accelerated lateral flow in the horizontal direction (i.e. in the x direction) as depicted in the optical flow diagram in Figure 4. This will cause our algorithm to misclassify this shot as TTC shot even though the man in Fig. 4 is not going to collide with the camera.

Fig. 2. 4th, 13th and 22nd frame of a lateral movement shot and its optical flow – the shot is showing a camera trying to follow a man who is running to the left

4 Improvement To TTC Detection – Pilot Cue

In airline pilots and other fliers' training school, pilots are taught that if another aircraft stays in the same location through their windscreen and grows large, they should immediately take evasive action as the aircraft that they see on their windscreen is on a direct collision course with their aircraft [11]. This method to detect potential collision can also be used in our TTC detection algorithm to extract TTC shots.

4.1 Method

The approach that we take is to first divide the 352x288 image into 99 smaller square regions of size 30x30. The TTC for each square region will be computed and a square will be labeled as TTC square if its TTC falls below a threshold of 100 (determined by some training sequences). Finally, the centroid of the TTC squares, as well as the total number of TTC squares, will be computed for each image frame. The centroids for the entire image sequence are said to stay in the same region of the image frame if the computed centroids fall within a circular boundary with center given by the center of the centroids and the radius given by 90 percent of the average flow strength for each pixel (percentage determined by some training sequences). The average flow strength is considered because it gives a rough indication of the amount of spatial movement present in the image. As for the number of TTC squares, we plot these numbers along the time axis and use least square fit to find the best fitting straight line through these points. A positive line gradient will indicate that the number of TTC squares is increasing. If the image sequence satisfies all the above-mentioned conditions, it will be labeled as a TTC shot.

4.2 Experimental Result – Sequence 1

Sequence 1 is a 38 frames video sequence whereby a man is running towards the camera. Fig. 5 illustrates the 4th, 19th and 35th frame of the video sequence and its corresponding optical flow diagram. The centroid of the TTC squares for each frame in the video sequence is computed and plotted as shown in Fig. 6.

The number of TTC squares for each frame in the video sequence was also plotted as shown in Fig. 7. Using least square fit, the gradient of the straight line that best fit the curve was found to be 0.39 squares/frame. Hence, the second condition is also satisfied.

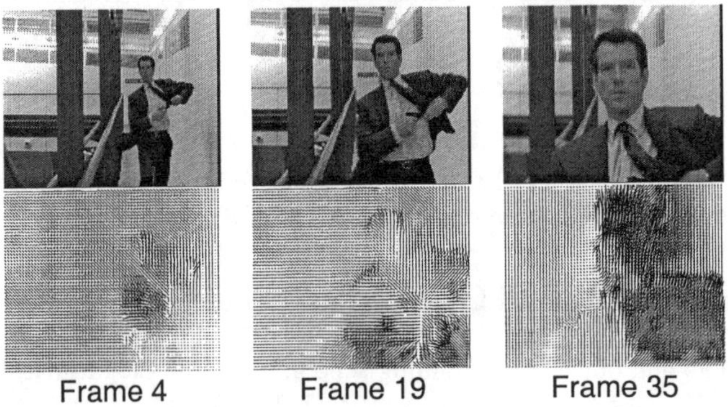

Fig. 3. 4th, 19th and 35th frame of a video sequence and its corresponding optical flow – the video sequence is showing a man running towards the camera

Clearly from the analysis conducted, the *pilot cue*, which requires the object to stay in the same region of the image frame and grows large, has been satisfied. Hence, we have shown that it is feasible to use *pilot cue* to detect TTC shot where the object is moving towards the camera and there is impending collision.

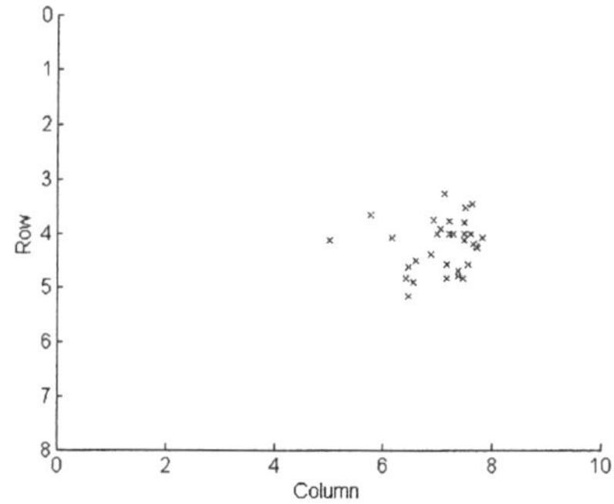

(a)

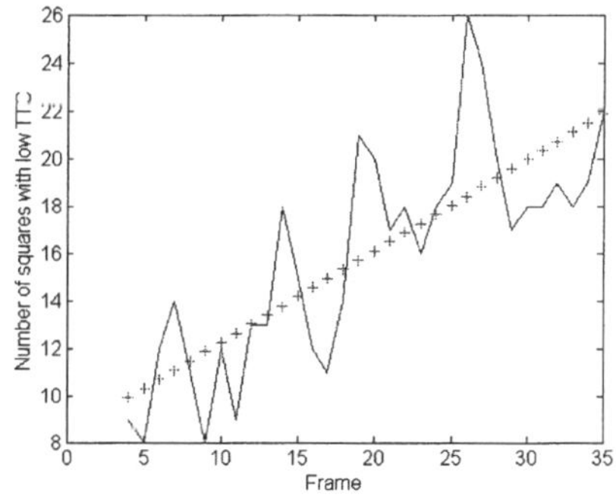

(b)

Fig. 4. (a) A scatter plot for the centroid of the TTC squares in each frame of video sequence (b) A graph of the number of squares with low TTC against the frame number for video sequence 1

Table 1. General Observations

#1	The shot cutting rate during the delay element of the suspense scene is slower (i.e. slow tempo) as compared to the payoff element of the same scene.
#2	High cutting rate (i.e. fast tempo) during a chase scene where the panicky state of the prey or victim is portrayed.
#3	Intimacy shot is likely to end with a scene change. Fade-out or dissolve may be used to denote the end of the scene.
#4	A new scene is likely to start in an establishing shot. Fade-in or dissolve may be used to denote the start of the scene.
#5	In an attention shift shot, fast and short camera pan or tilt normally precedes the TTC frames.
#6	Slow and long camera pan or crane normally precedes the TTC frames in an establishing shot.
#7	Strong camera movements are often used to bring out the sense of panic experienced by the victim or prey.
#8	Frequency of occurrence of TTC shots is very high in the delay element of the suspense scene.
#9	High frequency of occurrence of TTC shots in a chase scene where the panicky state of the victim or prey is portrayed.
#10	Suspense shot, intimacy shot, establishing shot and attention shift shot tend to have longer duration of TTC frames as compared to the terror shot.

5 A Rule Based System

Rule 1 A sequence of shots is marked as ***suspense*** if both of the conditions below are satisfied (from observation #1 and #8):

Condition 1: high frequency of occurrence of TTC shots within a fixed sequence of shots and that sequence has a slow tempo.

Condition 2 the succeeding sequence has a fast tempo.

Rule 2 A shot is marked as ***intimacy*** if both of the conditions below are satisfied (from observation #3 and #10):

Condition 1 the shot is the end of a scene and that scene may transit to the other scene with a fade-out or dissolve.

Condition 2 long duration of TTC frames.

Rule 3 Sections of the sequence are marked as ***terror*** if both of the conditions below are satisfied (from observation #2, #7 and #9):

Condition 1 high frequency of occurrence of TTC shots within a fixed sequence of shots and that sequence has a fast tempo.

Condition 2 there is strong camera movement in that sequence.

Rule 4 A shot is marked as ***attention shift*** if both of the conditions below are satisfied (from observation #5 and #10):

Condition 1 fast pan or tilt at the beginning of the shot.

Condition 2 long duration of TTC frames.

Rule 5 A shot is marked as ***establishing shot*** if both of the conditions below are satisfied (from observation #4, #6 and #10):

Condition 1 the shot is the start of a new scene and that scene may transit from the preceding scene with a fade-in or dissolve.

Condition 2 slow camera pan or crane at the beginning of the shot.

Condition 3 long duration of TTC frames.

Discussion

The five rules that we have formed so far can only manage to recover five high-level indices from the video database. As illustrated in Fig. 8, these five high-level indices are grouped according to how the audience perceives these semantic effects, i.e. TTC shots that affect the psychological state of the audience are classified as psychological effects while TTC shots that depend on the interpretation of the preceding or succeeding shots are classified as context-based interpretation. For instance, if a long duration of TTC frames is found after a sudden pan (attention shift shot), then most likely the cinematographer is trying to direct the audience's attention to a significant object in the scene and as a result, the audience will be able to intuitively interpret that the cinematographer is trying to underline a key piece of story information.

6 Conclusion

In this paper, we have clearly established that it is possible to derive TTC-based high-level indices from low-level features with the help of contextual cues. It is also worthwhile to note that this rule-based system that we have designed has contributed tremendously to a complete framework by which the semantic contents of a video can be fully recovered. To achieve this complete framework, future work may be done to extend our rule-based system to include other categories of high-level indices such as camera or subject movement-related high-level indices.

Acknowledgement

A. Mittal is deeply indebted to his anonymous friend who gave the inspiration for the work. Thanks are also due to our undergraduate students for their help.

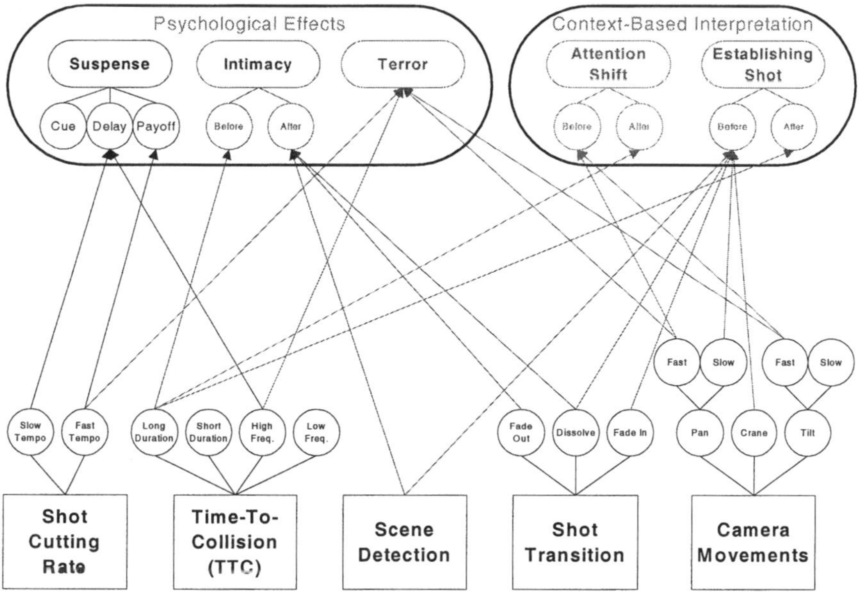

Fig. 5. Mapping from low-level features to their corresponding high-level indices

References

1. W. Ball and E. Tronick, "Infant Responses to Impending Collision: Optical and Real", *Science*, New Series, Vol. 171, Issue 3973, pp. 818 – 820, Feb 1971
2. Stephen Prince, "Movies and Meaning: An Introduction to Film", Allyn & Bacon, 1997
3. J. M. Boggs, "The Art of Watching Films", Fourth Edition, Mayfield Publishing Co., 1996
4. J. Mitry, "The Aesthetics and Psychology of the Cinema translated by Christopher King", Indiana University Press, 1998
5. B. Mamer, "Film Production Technique: Creating the Accomplished Image", Second Edition, Wadsworth – a division of Thomson Learning, 1999
6. W. Miller, "Screenwriting for Film and Television", Allyn and Bacon, 1998
7. R. B. Peacock, "The Art of Movie Making: Script to Screen", Prentice Hall, 2001
8. B. K. P. Horn and B. G. Schunck, "Determining Optical Flow", *A.I. Memo No. 572*, April 1980
9. M. Proesmans, L. Van Gool, E. Pauwels and A. Oosterlinck, "Determining of Optical Flow and its Discontinuities using Non-Linear Diffusion", *3rd European Conference on Computer Vision*, Vol. 2, pp. 295 – 304, 1994
10. M. Subbarao, "Interpretation of Visual Motion: A Computational Study", Pitman Publishing Limited, 1988
11. J. E. Cutting, P. M. Vishton and P. A. Braren, "How We Avoid Collisions With Stationary and Moving Obstacles", *Psychological Review*, Vol. 102, No. 4, pp. 627 – 651, 1995
12. F. G. Meyer, "Time-to-collision from First-order models of the motion fields", *IEEE Transactions of robotics and automation*, pp. 792-798, 1994
13. D. Marr, "Vision: A computational investigation into the human representation and processing of visual information", Freeman. 1982

Trajectory Estimation Based on Globally Consistent Homography

Siwook Nam, Hanjoo Kim, and Jaihie Kim

Dept. of Electrical and Electronic Eng., Yonsei University
Biometrics Engineering Research Center, Seoul, Korea
acesniper@yonsei.ac.kr

Abstract. We propose a method for estimating trajectories of objects moving on a world plane. Motivation of this work is to estimate the field trajectories of players and the ball from uncalibrated monocular soccer image sequences. In order to find mappings between images and the plane, four feature points, no three of them are collinear, should exist in each image. However, many soccer images do not satisfy that condition. In that case, the object positions in the given image are mapped to those in the reference image of the sequence, and then mapped again to those in the soccer field. Conventional mapping between given image and the reference image is given by concatenation of homographies between consecutive image pairs. However, small correspondence error is accumulated in the concatenation of homographies over long image sequence. To overcome this problem, we compute globally consistent homographies for all the feature-sufficient images by solving a sparse linear system of equations which consists of consecutive and non-consecutive homographies of feature-sufficient image pairs. Experimental results with real and synthetic soccer data show that the proposed method is more accurate than existing method.

1 Introduction

In soccer image sequences, objects are moving and the camera is continuously panning and zooming. In addition, objects are nonrigid and frequently occlude each other, and motion blur and change of object size continuously occur.

Many works on the analysis of soccer image sequences are reported, such as trajectory estimation of players and the ball on the ground[1][2][7], estimation of 3D trajectory of the ball[5][9], object tracking[8], soccer image mosaicing[6][10], and so on. Among them, estimating trajectories of players and the ball on the ground from soccer image sequences is especially important since we can obtain a lot of information about the game from that. To estimate field trajectories of objects, we should find point-to-point correspondences between each soccer image and the soccer field, and this correspondence can be given by homography. Homography, a 3×3 mapping matrix, can be determined from four corresponding point features provided that no three of them are collinear. In this paper, an image which satisfy this condition of four-point correspondences for computing homography is referred to as a feature-sufficient image.

N. Petkov and M.A. Westenberg (Eds.): CAIP 2003, LNCS 2756, pp. 214–221, 2003.

Previous works on trajectory estimation fall into two broad categories: works that estimate trajectories of the objects only around the goal area[1][7]; and the work that estimates trajectories of players and the ball over the whole soccer field[2]. Most works deal with just goal area images, since most regions of soccer field except the goal area have few sailent features such as field lines and are low-textured.

Unlike the other works, Choi *et al.*[2] computed trajectories of players and the ball over the whole soccer field from monocular soccer image sequence. They estimated trajectories of objects as follows. First, they tracked object positions in the image sequence using adaptive template matching. Second, they found homographies for all consecutive image pairs and concatenated the homographies to find the mappings between feature-insufficient images and the feature-sufficient reference image. Third, they also found the homography between the reference image and the soccer field using four point correspondences. By applying these two kinds of homographies to the tracking results, they estimated the trajectories of all objects over whole soccer field. But the estimated trajectories is prone to the accumulated errors of concatenated homographies over long image sequence[3].

In this paper, to overcome the accumulated errors of concatenated homographies, we use globally consistent homographies. We compute globally consistent homographies for all the feature-sufficient images by solving a sparse linear system of equations which consists of consecutive and non-consecutive homographies of feature-sufficient image pairs. Experimental results with real soccer image sequences and synthetic soccer data show that the proposed method can provide more accurate trajectories than existing method.

2 Background

Homography is a linear transformation on homogeneous 3-vectors $\mathbf{x}_i$ and $\mathbf{x}'_i$ represented by a nonsingular 3×3 matrix $\mathbf{H}$ as shown in Eq.(1). Given a set of $n(\geq 4)$ points $\mathbf{x}_i = (x_i, y_i, 1)^T$ in the projective plane $\mathbb{P}^2$ and a corresponding set of points $\mathbf{x}'_i = (x'_i, y'_i, 1)^T$ likewise in $\mathbb{P}^2$, we can compute the homography $\mathbf{H}$ that maps each $\mathbf{x}_i$ to $\mathbf{x}'_i$. Here,'$\simeq$' means equality up to a nonzero scale factor.

Homography can exist between a world plane and its image as follows. An image point is represented by a homogeneous 3-vector $\mathbf{x} = (x, y, 1)^T$, and world point by homogeneous 4-vector $\mathbf{X} = (X, Y, Z, 1)^T$. A scene point $\mathbf{X}$ is mapped to an image point $\mathbf{x}$ by perspective projection. This map is represented by a 3×4 camera matrix $\mathbf{P}$, as $\mathbf{x} \simeq \mathbf{PX}$. If we choose the world coordinate system so that the first two axis define the plane $\boldsymbol{\pi}$, that is $Z = 0$, then $\mathbf{P}$ is reduced to a 3×3 homography between two projective planes $\mathbb{P}^2$[4].

$$\begin{bmatrix} x'_i \\ y'_i \\ 1 \end{bmatrix} \simeq \begin{bmatrix} h_{11} & h_{12} & h_{13} \\ h_{21} & h_{22} & h_{23} \\ h_{31} & h_{32} & h_{33} \end{bmatrix} \begin{bmatrix} x_i \\ y_i \\ 1 \end{bmatrix} \quad , \; i.e., \; \mathbf{x}'_i \simeq \mathbf{H}\mathbf{x}_i \; , \; i = 1, 2, \cdots, n(\geq 4) \qquad (1)$$

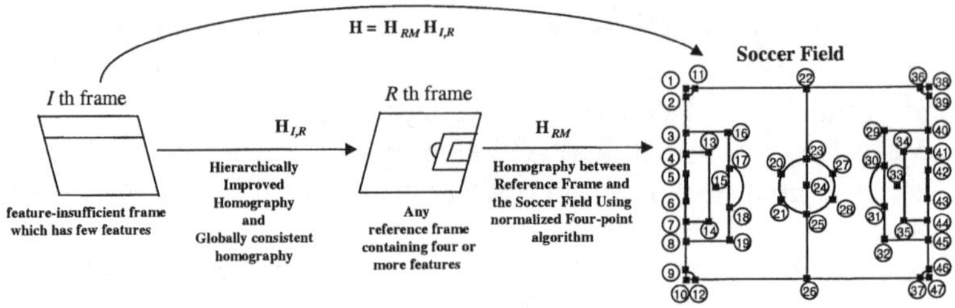

Fig. 1. Proposed homography estimation (Black rectangle indicate feature point)

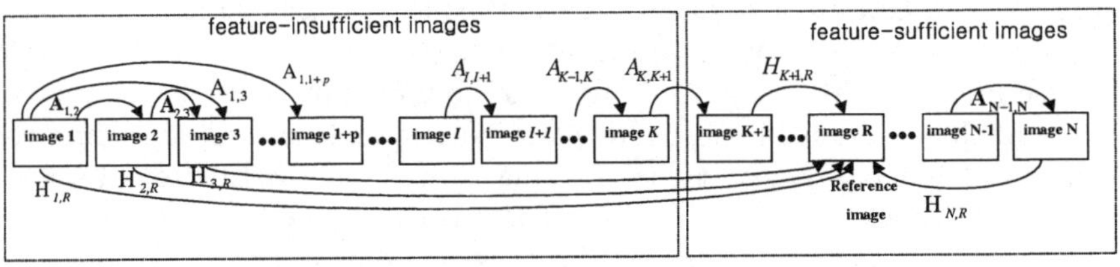

Fig. 2. Homographies between consecutive and non-consecutive image pairs

3 Proposed Method

In situations there are many images of a scene, it is often required to compute the homography relating any given pair of images. A common method is to compute homographies only between temporally consecutive images in the sequence, and then use the concatenation of homographies to obtain the correspondence between temporally non-consecutive images as shown in Eq.(2) and Eq.(3). However, this method is prone to errors which accumulate when concatenating homographies over long image sequence[3].

$$\begin{bmatrix} x_{n+1} \\ y_{n+1} \\ 1 \end{bmatrix} = \mathbf{A}_{n,n+1} \begin{bmatrix} x_n \\ y_n \\ 1 \end{bmatrix} \quad , \; i.e. \; , \; \mathbf{x}_{n+1} = \mathbf{A}_{n,n+1}\mathbf{x}_n \tag{2}$$

$$\mathbf{x}_R = \mathbf{A}_{1,R}\mathbf{x}_1,$$
$$\text{where } \mathbf{A}_{1,R} = \mathbf{A}_{R-1,R}\mathbf{A}_{R-2,R-1}\cdots\mathbf{A}_{2,3}\mathbf{A}_{1,2} = \prod_{i=R-1}^{1} \mathbf{A}_{i,i+1} \tag{3}$$

In order to avoid these accumulated errors, we find globally consistent homography[3] as shown in Fig.1. Suppose consecutive homography $\mathbf{A}_{i,i+1}$ and non-consecutive homographies $\mathbf{A}_{i,i+2}, \cdots, \mathbf{A}_{i,i+p}$ are known as shown in Fig.2. Then, we have unknowns $\mathbf{H}_{k,R}(k = 1, 2, \cdots, N,$ and $k \neq R)$ to be found, and can derive the relation as shown in Eq.(4). By considering for each image, we can build a sparse linear system of equation as shown in Eq.(5) when *Rth* image is the reference image, i.e., $\mathbf{H}_{R,R}$ is 3×3 indentity matrix. Then, we can rewrite Eq.(5) as Eq.(6) where $\mathcal{A}$ and $\mathcal{B}$ are composed of known homographies $\mathbf{A}_{i,j}$, and $\mathcal{H}$ is composed of unknown homographies $\mathbf{H}_{i,R}$ ($k = 1, 2, \cdots, N$, and $k \neq R$) to be found. If we have more constraint equation than the total number of images in the sequence, the system of equations will be overdetermined. Solving this linear system of equations in a least squares sense will produce a set of globally consistent homographies $\mathbf{H}_{i,R}$ that minimally deviate from the set of concatenated homographies $\mathbf{A}_{i,R}$ shown in Eq.(3).

$$\mathbf{H}_{i,R} = \mathbf{A}_{i,j}\mathbf{H}_{j,R} \tag{4}$$

$$\begin{bmatrix} -\mathbf{I} & \mathbf{A}_{1,2} & \mathbf{O} & \mathbf{O} & \mathbf{O} & \mathbf{O} & \mathbf{O} & \mathbf{O} & \mathbf{O} \\ -\mathbf{I} & \mathbf{O} & \mathbf{A}_{1,3} & \mathbf{O} & \mathbf{O} & \mathbf{O} & \mathbf{O} & \mathbf{O} & \mathbf{O} \\ -\mathbf{I} & \mathbf{O} & \mathbf{O} & \mathbf{A}_{1,4} & \mathbf{O} & \mathbf{O} & \mathbf{O} & \mathbf{O} & \mathbf{O} \\ \vdots & \vdots & \vdots & \vdots & \vdots & \vdots & \vdots & \vdots & \vdots \\ \vdots & \vdots & \vdots & \vdots & \vdots & \vdots & \vdots & \vdots & \vdots \\ \vdots & \vdots & \vdots & \vdots & \vdots & \vdots & \vdots & \vdots & \vdots \\ \vdots & \vdots & \vdots & \vdots & \vdots & \vdots & \vdots & \vdots & \vdots \\ \vdots & \vdots & \vdots & \vdots & \vdots & \vdots & \vdots & \vdots & \vdots \\ \mathbf{O} & \mathbf{O} & \mathbf{O} & \mathbf{O} & \mathbf{O} & \mathbf{O} & -\mathbf{I} & \mathbf{A}_{N-2,N-1} & \mathbf{O} \\ \mathbf{O} & \mathbf{O} & \mathbf{O} & \mathbf{O} & \mathbf{O} & \mathbf{O} & -\mathbf{I} & \mathbf{O} & \mathbf{A}_{N-2,N} \\ \mathbf{O} & \mathbf{O} & \mathbf{O} & \mathbf{O} & \mathbf{O} & \mathbf{O} & \mathbf{O} & -\mathbf{I} & \mathbf{A}_{N-1,N} \end{bmatrix} \begin{bmatrix} \mathbf{H}_{1,R} \\ \mathbf{H}_{2,R} \\ \mathbf{H}_{3,R} \\ \vdots \\ \mathbf{H}_{R-1,R} \\ \mathbf{H}_{R+1,R} \\ \vdots \\ \mathbf{H}_{N,R} \end{bmatrix} = \begin{bmatrix} \mathbf{O} \\ \vdots \\ \mathbf{A}_{R-3,R} \\ \mathbf{O} \\ \mathbf{A}_{R-2,R} \\ \mathbf{O} \\ \mathbf{A}_{R-1,R} \\ \vdots \\ \mathbf{I} \\ \vdots \\ \mathbf{O} \end{bmatrix} \tag{5}$$

$$\mathcal{A}\mathcal{H} = \mathcal{B} \tag{6}$$

As explained above, to obtain globally consistent homographies, we first need to find not only consecutive homographies but also non-consecutive homographies. We obtain non-consecutive homographies for feature-sufficient image pairs, which are even temporally distant, using intersetions of lines. Although intersections are not visible in the image, they can be computed(see Fig.3(f)). We extract the lines in the first image of the feature-sufficient images, and track them in the subsequent feature-sufficient images. However, between feture-insufficient image pairs, it is difficult to guarantee the accuracy of non-consecutive homographies (when typically $p > 8$ for $\mathbf{A}_{i,i+p}$) due to low photometric coherency between them. Hence, we find globally consistent homography only for feature-sufficient images. Then, we use hierarchically improved homography[6] to reduce accumulated errors of homographies between feature-insufficient images using non-consecutive, but temporally not so distant, homographies. Homographies between feature-insufficient image pairs are computed using algorithm based on block matching.

Finally, homography between reference image of the sequence and the soccer field, $\mathbf{H}_{RM}$, is obtained using four-point correspondences. Since linear estimation method using features is sensitive to the measurement noise, we normalize the coordinates of the feature points and then estimate the homography[4].

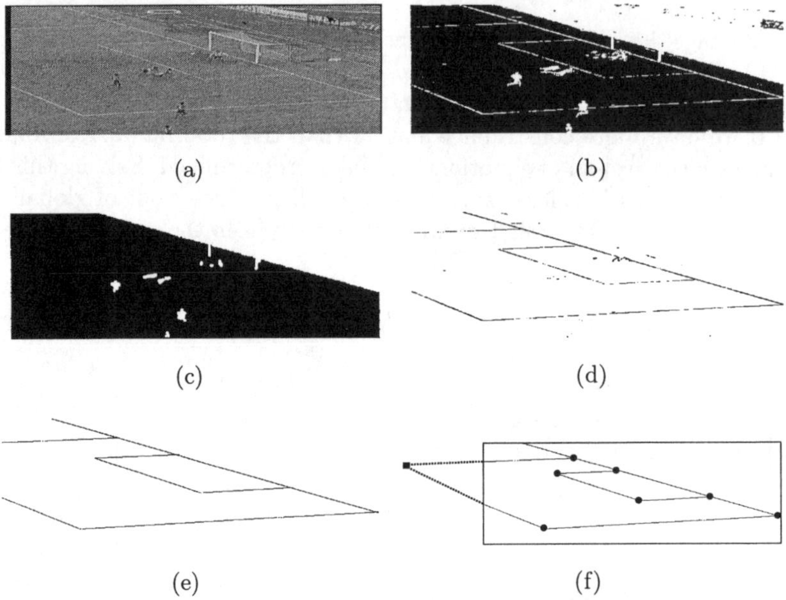

Fig. 3. Preprocessing results: (a) input image, (b) Stage 1: Binarize field region, (c) Stage 2: Morphological filtering and noise filtering, (d) Stage 3: Edge detection for input image(a) over extracted field region in (c), (e) Stage 4: Thinning the line, Hough transform for line extraction, (f) Stage 5: Feature detected in the image (indicated by black circle) and feature outside the image computed by line intersection (indicated by black rectangle)

After three kinds of homogrphies previously explained are obtained, we compute the $\mathbf{H}$ as shown in Eq.(7).

$$\mathbf{H} = \mathbf{H}_{RM}\mathbf{H}_{IR} \tag{7}$$

where

$$\begin{aligned}\mathbf{H}_{IR} = &\quad \mathbf{H}_{K+1,R}\ \mathbf{A}_{K,K+1}\ \cdots\ \mathbf{A}_{I,I+1} \\ &= \mathbf{H}_{K+1,R} \prod_{i=K}^{I} \mathbf{A}_{i,i+1}\ , if\ 1 \leq I \leq K\end{aligned}$$

Suppose $\mathbf{x}_i^k = (x_i^k, y_i^k)$, $\mathbf{x}_R^k = (x_R^k, y_R^k)$ and $\mathbf{X}_p^k = (X_p^k, Y_p^k)$ are the position of kth object in the ith image, in the Rth image(i.e., reference image of the sequence) and the soccer field, respectively. By applying Eq.(8) for all objects and images in the sequence, we can estimate the trajectories of all objects in the sequence.

$$\mathbf{x}_R^k = \mathbf{H}_{IR}\mathbf{x}_i^k\ ,\ \mathbf{X}_P^k = \mathbf{H}_{RM}\mathbf{x}_R^k\ ,\ \mathbf{X}_P^k = \mathbf{H}\mathbf{x}_i^k = \mathbf{H}_{RM}\mathbf{H}_{IR}\mathbf{x}_i^k \tag{8}$$

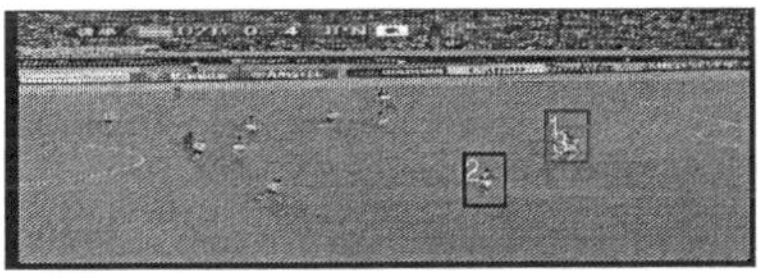

(a)

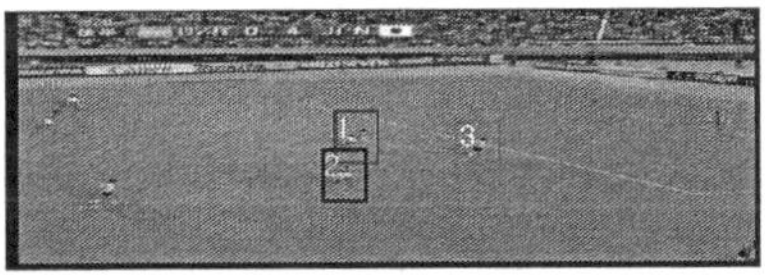

(b)

(c)

(d)

Fig. 4. Test soccer image sequence 1:(a) image 0, (b) image 50, (c) image 80, (d) image 130

4 Experimental Results

We conduct two sets of experiments with real soccer images and synthetic soccer data. In the first set of experiments, proposed method is applied to real image data, i.e., 10 broadcast soccer image sequences. We use RGB color soccer image sequences which consist of about 150 color images on average and have 720×243 pixels. One of the test sequences is shown in Fig.4. Typical soccer image sequences of our interest consist of feature-insufficient images followed by feature-sufficient images. Camera motion is typically panning and tilting followed by zooming. We assume that the boundary of feature-insufficient images and feature-sufficient images is given, and select the middle image of the feature-sufficient images as the reference image (see Fig.2, $R = \frac{N+K+1}{2}$). In the existing method and the proposed method, same reference image is used.

Object tracking, to locate objects in the consecutive images, is performed using adaptive template matching. Adaptive template matching technique updates the template with the segmented object in the current window position in every image of the sequence. The image position of object, foot point, is computed using center of gravity for object region. In Fig.3, preprocessing to extract lines and their intersection is shown. Estimated trajectories using both method is shown in Fig.5. Trajectories of the proposed method is closer to human estimate than those of existing method.

In the second set of experiments, proposed method is applied to synthetic soccer data. Our procedure of experiments is as follows. In the first place, we generate the positions of objects in the soccer field. Then, we obtain the image positions of objects in each image by applying camera matrix which simulate the panning, tilting, and zooming camera to the field positions of objects and add Gaussian noise to the image positions. Homography between two feature-insufficient images can be computed by camera matrices of the two images. Homography between two feature-sufficient images is computed using image positions of feature points. For synthetic data, we compare the proposed method and the existing method. As illustrated in Fig.6, the result of proposed method is

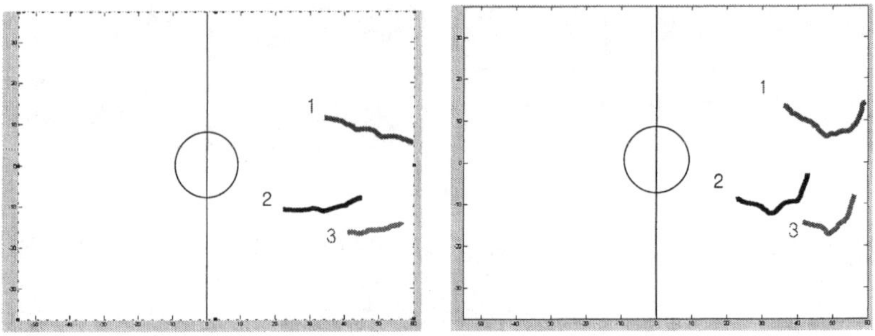

(a) (b)

Fig. 5. Estimated trajectories for Fig.4: (a) proposed method (b) existing method

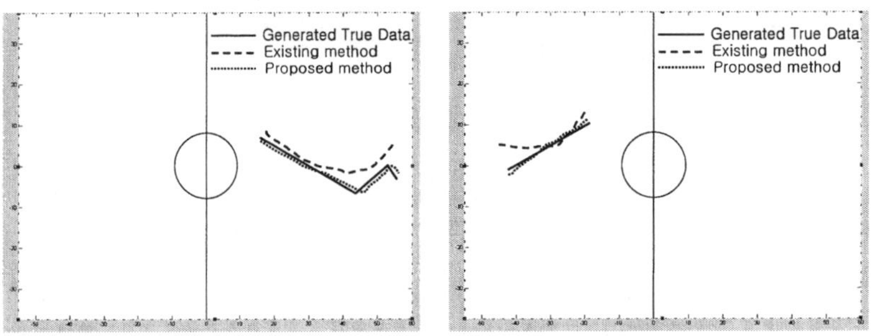

(a) (b)

Fig. 6. Graphical comparison of estimated trajectories for synthetic data: We simulate the camera movement of the real soccer sequence, and generate the synthetic trajectories

more accurate than the existing method. The trajectories estimated by existing method is globally distorted due to the accumulated errors compared to those of proposed method. On the other hand, trajectories estimated by proposed method is similar to the true data than those of existing method. RMS(root-mean-square) error of the proposed method is quite small compared to that of the existing method.

5 Conclusions

In this paper, we propose a method for estimating field trajectories of players and the ball moving on the soccer field from uncalibrated monocular soccer image sequences. Previous work used concatenation of homographies between consecutive images to compute the homography between a feature-insufficient image and the reference image. However, it is prone to the accumulated correspondence errors in the concatenation of homographies over long image sequence.

To overcome this problem, we compute globally consistent homographies for all the feature-sufficient images by solving a sparse linear system of equations which consists of consecutive and non-consecutive homographies of feature-sufficient image pairs. In addition, we find hierarchically improved homography for feature-insufficient images.

We apply the proposed method to the problem of computing the field trajectories of players and the ball from soccer image sequences. Experiments were conducted using real broadcast soccer image sequences and synthetic soccer data. The trajectories estimated by existing method is globally distorted due to the accumulated errors compared to those of proposed method. On the other hand, trajectories estimated by proposed method is similar to the true data than those of existing method.

Proposed method can be applied to 3D animation of soccer game, analysis of soccer tactics of each team, and so on.

Acknowledgements

This work was supported (in part) by Biometrics Engineering Research Center, (KOSEF).

References

1. T.Bebie and H.Bieri, "A Video-Based 3D-Reconstruction of Soccer Games", EUROGRAPHICS 2000, Vol.19, No.3.
2. S. Choi, Y. Seo, H. Kim and K. S. Hong, "Where are the ball and players ? Soccer game analysis with color-based tracking and image mosaik", International Conference on Image Analysis and Processing, Florence, Italy, 1997.
3. J.Davis, "Mosaics of scenes with moving objects", International Conference on Computer Vision and Pattern Recognition, pp.354 -360, 1998.
4. R.Hartley and A.Zisserman, Multiple View Geometry in computer vision, Cambridge University Press, 2000.
5. T. Kim, Y. Seo, and K.-S. Hong, "Physics-based 3D position analysis of a soccer ball from monocular image sequences", International Conference on Computer Vision, pp. 721-726, Jan. 1998.
6. Jae Cheol Lee and Jaihie Kim, "Hierarchical Enhancement of Motion Parameters Using Error Division", IEE Electronic Letters, Vol.36, No.14, pp.1193-1194, July 2000.
7. K. Matsui, M. Iwase, M. Agata, T. Tanaka, and N. Ohnishi, "Soccer Image Sequence Computed by a Virtual Camera", IEEE Computer Society Conference on Computer Vision and Pattern Recognition 23 - 25 June, 1998.
8. Y.Ohno, J.Miura and Y.Shirai, "Tracking Players and a Ball in Soccer Games", International Conference on Multisensor Fusion and Integration for Intelligent Systems", pp. 147-152, 1999.
9. Ian Reid and Andrew Zisserman, "Goal-directed Video Metrology", In Proc. European Conference on Computer Vision, 1996.
10. Heung-Yeung Shum and Richard Szeliski, "Systems and Experiment Paper:Construction of Panoramic Image Mosaics with Global and Local Alignment", International Journal of Computer Vision, Vol.36, No.2, pp.101-130, 2000.

Real-Time Optic Flow Computation with Variational Methods*

Andrés Bruhn[1], Joachim Weickert[1], Christian Feddern[1], Timo Kohlberger[2], and Christoph Schnörr[2]

[1] Mathematical Image Analysis Group
Faculty of Mathematics and Computer Science, Bldg. 27
Saarland University, 66041 Saarbrücken, Germany
{bruhn,weickert,feddern}@mia.uni-saarland.de
http://www.mia.uni-saarland.de

[2] Computer Vision, Graphics, and Pattern Recognition Group
Faculty of Mathematics and Computer Science
University of Mannheim, 68131 Mannheim, Germany
{tkohlber,schnoerr}@uni-mannheim.de
http://www.cvgpr.uni-mannheim.de

Abstract. Variational methods for optic flow computation have the reputation of producing good results at the expense of being too slow for real-time applications. We show that real-time variational computation of optic flow fields is possible when appropriate methods are combined with modern numerical techniques. We consider the CLG method, a recent variational technique that combines the quality of the dense flow fields of the Horn and Schunck approach with the noise robustness of the Lucas–Kanade method. For the linear system of equations resulting from the discretised Euler–Lagrange equations, we present a fast full multigrid scheme in detail. We show that under realistic accuracy requirements this method is 175 times more efficient than the widely used Gauß-Seidel algorithm. On a 3.06 GHz PC, we have computed 27 dense flow fields of size 200×200 pixels within a single second.

1 Introduction

Variational methods belong to the well-established techniques for estimating the displacement field *(optic flow)* in an image sequence. They perform well in terms of different error measures [1, 6], they make all model assumptions explicit in a transparent way, they yield dense flow fields, and it is straightforward to derive continuous models that are rotationally invariant. These properties make continuous variational models appealing for a number of applications. For a survey of these techniques we refer to [12].

Variational methods, however, require the minimisation of a suitable energy functional. Often this is achieved by discretising the associated Euler–Langrange

* Our research is partly funded by the DFG project SCHN 457/4-1. Andrés Bruhn thanks Ulrich Rüde and Mostafa El Kalmoun for interesting multigrid discussions.

N. Petkov and M.A. Westenberg (Eds.): CAIP 2003, LNCS 2756, pp. 222–229, 2003.

equations and solving the resulting systems of equations in an iterative way. Classical iterative methods such as Jacobi or Gauß–Seidel iterations are frequently applied [13]. In this case one observes that the convergence is reasonably fast in the beginning, but after a while it deteriorates significantly such that often several thousands of iterations are needed in order to obtain the required accuracy. As a consequence, variational optic flow methods are usually considered to be too slow when real-time performance is needed.

The goal of the present paper is to show that it is possible to make variational optic flow methods suitable for real-time applications by combining them with state-of-the-art numerical techniques. We use the recently introduced CLG method [4], a variational technique that combines the advantages of two classical optic flow algorithms: the variational Horn and Schunck approach [8], and the local least-square technique of Lucas and Kanade [9]. For the CLG method we derive a fast numerical scheme based on a so-called full multigrid strategy [3]. Such techniques belong to the fastest numerical methods for solving linear systems of equations. We present our algorithm in detail and show that it leads to a speed-up of more than two orders of magnitude compared to widely used iterative methods. As a consequence, it becomes possible to compute 27 optic flow frames per second on a standard PC, when image sequences of size 200×200 pixels are used.

Our paper is organised as follows. In Section 2 we review the CLG model as a representative for variational optic flow methods. Section 3 shows how this problem can be discretised. A fast multigrid strategy for the CLG approach is derived in Section 4. In Section 5 we compare this algorithm with the widely used Gauß–Seidel and SOR schemes and show that it allows real-time computation of optic flow. The paper is concluded with a summary in Section 6.

Related Work. It is quite common to use pyramid strategies for speeding up variational optic flow methods. They use the solution at a coarse grid as initialisation on the next finer grid. Such techniques may be regarded as the simplest multigrid strategy, namely cascading multigrid. Their performance is usually somewhat limited. More advanced multigrid techniques are used not very frequently. First proposals go back to Terzopoulos [11] and Enkelmann [5]. More recently, Ghosal and Vaněk [7] developed an algebraic multigrid method for an anisotropic variational approach that can be related to Nagel's method [10]. Zini et al. [14] proposed a conjugate gradient-based multigrid technique for an extension of the Horn and Schunck functional. To the best of our knowledge, our paper is the first work that reports real-time performance for variational optic flow techniques on standard hardware.

2 Optic Flow Computation with the CLG Approach

In [4] we have introduced the so called *combined local-global (CLG) method* for optic flow computation. It combines the advantages of the global Horn and Schunck approach [8] and the local Lucas–Kanade method [9]. Let $f(x, y, t)$ be an image sequence, where (x, y) denotes the location within a rectangular image domain Ω, and t is the time. The CLG method computes the optic flow field $(u(x,y),v(x,y))^\top$ at some time t as the minimiser of the energy functional

$$E(u,v) = \int_\Omega \left(w^\top J_\rho(\nabla_3 f)\, w + \alpha(|\nabla u|^2 + |\nabla v|^2) \right) dx\, dy, \tag{1}$$

where the vector field $w(x,y) = (u(x,y),v(x,y),1)^\top$ describes the displacement, ∇u is the spatial gradient $(u_x,u_y)^\top$, and $\nabla_3 f$ denotes the spatiotemporal gradient $(f_x,f_y,f_t)^\top$. The matrix $J_\rho(\nabla_3 f)$ is the structure tensor given by $K_\rho * (\nabla_3 f\, \nabla_3 f^\top)$, where $*$ denotes convolution, and K_ρ is a Gaussian with standard deviation ρ. The weight $\alpha > 0$ serves as regularisation parameter.

For $\rho \to 0$ the CLG approach comes down to the Horn and Schunck method, and for $\alpha \to 0$ it becomes the Lucas–Kanade algorithm. It combines the dense flow fields of Horn–Schunck with the high noise robustness of Lucas–Kanade. For a detailed performance evaluation we refer to [4].

In order to recover the optic flow field, the energy functional $E(u,v)$ has to be minimised. This is done by solving its Euler–Lagrange equations

$$\Delta u - \tfrac{1}{\alpha}\left(K_\rho * (f_x^2)\, u + K_\rho * (f_x f_y)\, v + K_\rho * (f_x f_t)\right) = 0, \tag{2}$$

$$\Delta v - \tfrac{1}{\alpha}\left(K_\rho * (f_x f_y)\, u + K_\rho * (f_y^2)\, v + K_\rho * (f_y f_t)\right) = 0, \tag{3}$$

where Δ denotes the Laplacean.

3 Discretisation

Let us now investigate a suitable discretisation for the CLG method (2)–(3). To this end we consider the unknown functions $u(x,y,t)$ and $v(x,y,t)$ on a rectangular pixel grid of size h, and we denote by u_i the approximation to u at some pixel i with $i = 1,\ldots,N$. Gaussian convolution is realised by discrete convolution with a truncated and renormalised Gaussian, where the truncation took place at 3 times the standard deviation. Symmetry and separability have been exploited in order to speed up these discrete convolutions. Spatial derivatives of the image data f have been approximated using a fourth-order approximation with the convolution mask $(-1,8,0,-8,1)/(12h)$, while temporal derivatives are approximated with a simple two-point stencil. Let us denote by J_{nmi} the component (n,m) of the structure tensor $J_\rho(\nabla f)$ in some pixel i. Furthermore, let $\mathcal{N}(i)$ denote the set of neighbours of pixel i. Then a finite difference approximation to the Euler–Lagrange equations (2)–(3) is given by

$$0 = \sum_{j \in \mathcal{N}(i)} \frac{u_i - u_j}{h^2} - \frac{1}{\alpha}\left(J_{11i}\, u_i + J_{12i}\, v_i + J_{13i}\right), \tag{4}$$

$$0 = \sum_{j \in \mathcal{N}(i)} \frac{v_i - v_j}{h^2} - \frac{1}{\alpha}\left(J_{21i}\, u_i + J_{22i}\, v_i + J_{23i}\right) \tag{5}$$

for $i = 1,\ldots,N$. This sparse linear system of equations for the $2N$ unknowns (u_i) and (v_i) may be solved iteratively, e.g. by applying the Gauß–Seidel method [13].

Because of its simplicity it is frequently used in literature. If the upper index denotes the iteration step, the Gauß-Seidel method can be written as

$$u_i^{k+1} = \frac{\sum\limits_{j \in \mathcal{N}^-(i)} u_j^{k+1} + \sum\limits_{j \in \mathcal{N}^+(i)} u_j^k - \frac{h^2}{\alpha}\left(J_{12i}\, v_i^k + J_{13i}\right)}{|\mathcal{N}(i)| + \frac{h^2}{\alpha} J_{11i}}, \tag{6}$$

$$v_i^{k+1} = \frac{\sum\limits_{j \in \mathcal{N}^-(i)} v_j^{k+1} + \sum\limits_{j \in \mathcal{N}^+(i)} v_j^k - \frac{h^2}{\alpha}\left(J_{21i}\, u_i^{k+1} + J_{23i}\right)}{|\mathcal{N}(i)| + \frac{h^2}{\alpha} J_{22i}} \tag{7}$$

where $\mathcal{N}^-(i) := \{j \in \mathcal{N}(i) \mid j < i\}$ and $\mathcal{N}^+(i) := \{j \in \mathcal{N}(i) \mid j > i\}$. By $|\mathcal{N}(i)|$ we denote the number of neighbours of pixel i that belong to the image domain.

Common iterative solvers like the Gauß–Seidel method usually perform very well in removing the higher frequency parts of the error within the first iterations. This behaviour is reflected in a good initial convergence rate. Because of their smoothing properties regarding the error, these solvers are referred to as *smoothers*. After some iterations only low frequency components of the error remain and the convergence slows down significantly. At this point smoothers suffer from their local design and cannot attenuate efficiently low frequencies that have a sufficiently large wavelength in the spatial domain.

4 An Efficient Multigrid Algorithm

Multigrid methods [2, 3] overcome the before mentioned problem by creating a sophisticated fine-to-coarse hierarchy of equation systems with excellent error reduction properties. Low frequencies on the finest grid reappear as higher frequencies on coarser grids, where they can be removed successfully. This strategy allows multigrid methods to compute accurate results much faster than non–hierarchical iterative solvers. Since we focus on the real-time computation of optic flow, we developed such a multigrid algorithm for the CLG approach.

Let us now explain our strategy in detail. We reformulate the linear system of equations given by (4)–(5) as

$$A^h x^h = f^h \tag{8}$$

where h is the grid spacing, x^h is the concatenated vector $(u^h, v^h)^\top$, f^h is the right hand side given by $\frac{1}{\alpha}(J_{13}, J_{23})^\top$ and A^h is the matrix with the corresponding entries. Let $\tilde{x}^h$ be the result computed by the chosen Gauß–Seidel smoother after n_1 iterations. Then the error of the solution is given by

$$e^h = x^h - \tilde{x}^h. \tag{9}$$

Evidently, one is interested in finding e^h in order to correct the approximative solution $\tilde{x}^h$. Since the error cannot be computed directly, we determine the residual error given by

$$r^h = f^h - A^h \tilde{x}^h \tag{10}$$

instead. Since A is a linear operator, we have

$$A^h e^h = r^h. \tag{11}$$

Solving this system of equations would give us the desired correction e^h. Since high frequencies of the error have already been removed by our smoother, we can solve this system at a coarser level. For the sake of clarity the notation for the coarser grid is chosen correspondingly to the original equation on the fine grid (8). Thus, the linear equation system (11) becomes

$$A^{\bar{h}} x^{\bar{h}} = f^{\bar{h}} \tag{12}$$

at the coarser level, where $\bar{h}$ is the new grid spacing with $\bar{h} > h$, and $f^{\bar{h}}$ is a downsampled version of r^h.

At this point we have to make four decisions:

(I) The new grid spacing $\bar{h}$ has to be chosen. In our implementation h is doubled at each level, so $\bar{h} := 2h$.

(II) A *restriction operator* $R^{h\to 2h}$ has to be defined that allows the transfer of vectors from the fine to the coarse grid. By its application to the residual r^h we obtain the right hand side of the equation system on the coarser grid

$$f^{2h} = R^{h\to 2h} r^h. \tag{13}$$

For simplicity, averaging over 2×2 pixels is used for $R^{h\to 2h}$.

(III) A coarser version of the matrix A^h has to be created. All entries of A^h belonging to the discretised Laplacean depend on the grid spacing of the solution x^h. Therefore these entries have to be adapted to the coarser grid scaling. Having their origin in the structure tensor J^h, all other entries of A^h are independent of x^h and are therefore obtained by a componentwise restriction of J^h:

$$J^{2h}_{nm} = R^{h\to 2h} J^h_{nm}. \tag{14}$$

This allows the formulation of the coarse grid equation system

$$0 = \sum_{j\in\mathcal{N}(i)} \frac{u_i^{2h} - u_j^{2h}}{(2h)^2} - \frac{1}{\alpha}\left(J^{2h}_{11i}\, u_i^{2h} + J^{2h}_{12i}\, v_i^{2h} + f^{2h}_{1i}\right), \tag{15}$$

$$0 = \sum_{j\in\mathcal{N}(i)} \frac{v_i^{2h} - v_j^{2h}}{(2h)^2} - \frac{1}{\alpha}\left(J^{2h}_{21i}\, u_i^{2h} + J^{2h}_{22i}\, v_i^{2h} + f^{2h}_{2i}\right) \tag{16}$$

for $i = 1,\ldots,\frac{N}{4}$, where again $(u^{2h}, v^{2h})^\top = x^{2h}$ and $(f_1^{2h}, f_2^{2h})^\top = f^{2h}$. The corresponding Gauß-Seidel iteration step is given by

$$u_i^{2h,k+1} = \frac{\sum\limits_{j\in\mathcal{N}^-(i)} u_j^{2h,k+1} + \sum\limits_{j\in\mathcal{N}^+(i)} u_j^{2h,k} - \frac{(2h)^2}{\alpha}\left(J^{2h}_{12i}\, v_i^{2h,k} + f_i^{2h}\right)}{|\mathcal{N}(i)| + \frac{(2h)^2}{\alpha} J^{2h}_{11i}}, \tag{17}$$

$$v_i^{2h,k+1} = \frac{\sum\limits_{j\in\mathcal{N}^-(i)} v_j^{2h,k+1} + \sum\limits_{j\in\mathcal{N}^+(i)} v_j^{2h,k} - \frac{(2h)^2}{\alpha}\left(J^{2h}_{21i}\, u_i^{2h,k+1} + f_i^{2h}\right)}{|\mathcal{N}(i)| + \frac{(2h)^2}{\alpha} J^{2h}_{22i}}. \tag{18}$$

(IV) After solving $A^{2h}x^{2h} = f^{2h}$ on the coarse grid, a *prolongation operator* $P^{2h \to h}$ has to be defined in order to transfer the solution x^{2h} back to the fine grid:

$$e^h = P^{2h \to h} x^{2h}. \tag{19}$$

We choose constant interpolation as prolongation operator $P^{2h \to h}$.

The obtained correction e^h can be used now for updating the approximated solution of the original equation on the fine grid:

$$\tilde{x}^h_{new} = \tilde{x}^h + e^h. \tag{20}$$

Finally n_2 iterations of the smoother are performed in order to remove high error frequencies introduced by the prolongation of x^{2h}.

The hierarchical application of the explained 2-grid cycle is called *V–cycle*. Repeating two 2-grid cycles at *each* level yields the so called *W–cycle*, that has better convergence properties at the expense of slightly increased computational costs (regarding 2D). Instead of transferring the residual equations between the levels one may think of starting with a coarse version of the *original* equation system. In this case coarse solutions serve as initial guesses for finer levels. This strategy is referred to as *cascading multigrid*. In combination with V or W–cycles the multigrid strategy with the best performance is obtained: *full multigrid*. Our implementation is based on such a full multigrid approach with two W–cycles per level (Fig. 1). At each W-cycle two presmoothing and two postsmoothing iterations are performed ($n_1 = n_2 = 2$).

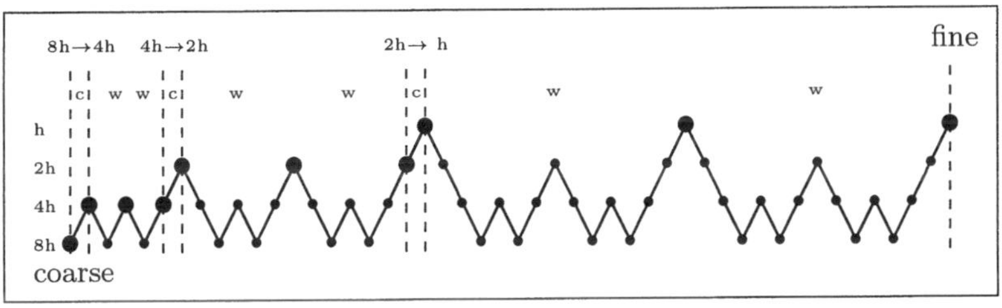

Fig. 1. Example of our full multigrid implementation for 4 levels. Dashed lines separate alternating blocks of the two basic strategies. Blocks belonging to the cascading multigrid strategy are marked with *c*. Starting from a coarse scale the original problem is refined step by step. This is visualised by the → symbol. Thereby the coarser solution serves as an initial approximation for the refined problem. At each refinement level two W–cycles (blocks marked with two *w*) are used as solvers. Performing iterations on the original equation is marked with large black dots, while iterations on residual equations are marked with smaller ones.

5 Results

Our computations are performed with a C implementation on a standard PC with a 3.06 GHz Intel Pentium 4 CPU, and the 200 × 200 pixels office sequence

Table 1. Comparison of the Gauß-Seidel and the SOR method to our full multigrid implementation. Run times refer to the computation of all 19 flow fields for the *office* sequence.

	iterations per frame	run time $[s]$	frames per second $[s^{-1}]$
Gauß–Seidel	6839	120.808	0.157
SOR	252	5.760	3.299
full multigrid	1	0.692	27.440

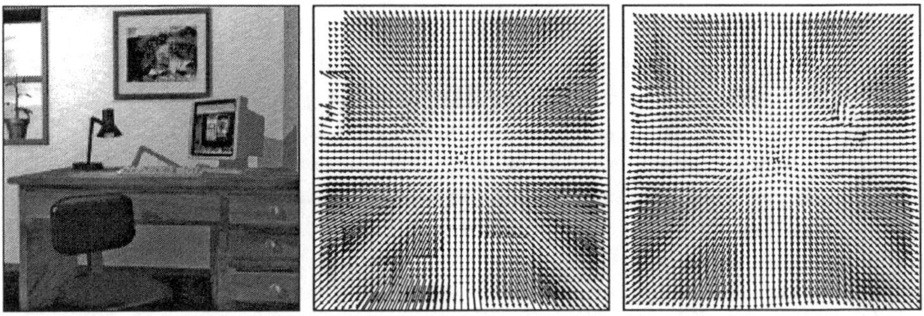

Fig. 2. *(a) Left:* Frame 10 of the *office* sequence. *(b) Center:* Ground truth flow field between frame 10 and 11. *(c) Right:* Computed flow field by our full multigrid CLG method ($\sigma = 0.72$, $\rho = 1.8$, and $\alpha = 2700$).

by Galvin et al. [6] is used. We compared the performance of our full multigrid implementation on four levels with the widely used Gauß–Seidel method and its popular *Successive Overrelaxation* (SOR) variant [13]. Accelerating the Gauß–Seidel method by a weighted extrapolation of its results, the SOR method represents the class of advanced non-hierarchical solvers in this comparison. The iterations are stopped when the relative error $e_{rel} := |x_c - x_e|/|x_c|$ was below 10^{-3}, where the subscripts c and e denote the correct resp. estimated solution.

Table 1 shows the performance of our algorithm. With more than 27 frames per second we are able to compute the optic flow of sequences with 200×200 pixels in real-time. We see that full multigrid is 175 times faster than the Gauß–Seidel method and still one order of magnitude more efficient than SOR. In terms of iterations, the difference is even more drastical: While 6839 Gauß–Seidel iterations were required to reach the desired accuracy, a single full multigrid cycle was sufficient. Qualitative results for this test run are presented in Figure 2 where one of the computed flow fields is shown. We observe that the CLG method matches the ground truth very well. Thereby one should keep in mind that the full multigrid computation of such a single flow field took only 36 milliseconds.

6 Summary and Conclusions

Using the CLG method as a prototype for a noise robust variational technique, we have shown that it is possible to achieve real-time computation of dense optic flow fields of size 200 × 200 on a standard PC. This has been accomplished by using a full multigrid method for solving the linear systems of equations that result from a discretisation of the Euler–Lagrange equations. We have shown that this gives us a speed-up by more than two orders of magnitude compared to commonly used algorithms for variational optic flow computation. In our future work we plan to investigate further acceleration possibilities by means of suitable parallelisations. Moreover, we will investigate the use of multigrid strategies for nonlinear variational optic flow methods.

References

1. J. L. Barron, D. J. Fleet, and S. S. Beauchemin. Performance of optical flow techniques. *International Journal of Computer Vision*, 12(1):43–77, Feb. 1994.
2. A. Brandt. Multi-level adaptive solutions to boundary-value problems. *Mathematics of Computation*, 31(138):333–390, Apr. 1977.
3. W. L. Briggs, V. E. Henson, and S. F. McCormick. *A Multigrid Tutorial.* SIAM, Philadelphia, second edition, 2000.
4. A. Bruhn, J. Weickert, and C. Schnörr. Combining the advantages of local and global optic flow methods. In L. Van Gool, editor, *Pattern Recognition*, volume 2449 of *Lecture Notes in Computer Science*, pages 454–462. Springer, Berlin, 2002.
5. W. Enkelmann. Investigation of multigrid algorithms for the estimation of optical flow fields in image sequences. *Computer Vision, Graphics and Image Processing*, 43:150–177, 1987.
6. B. Galvin, B. McCane, K. Novins, D. Mason, and S. Mills. Recovering motion fields: an analysis of eight optical flow algorithms. In *Proc. 1998 British Machine Vision Conference*, Southampton, England, Sept. 1998.
7. S. Ghosal and P. Č. Vaněk. Scalable algorithm for discontinuous optical flow estimation. *IEEE Transactions on Pattern Analysis and Machine Intelligence*, 18(2):181–194, Feb. 1996.
8. B. Horn and B. Schunck. Determining optical flow. *Artificial Intelligence*, 17:185–203, 1981.
9. B. Lucas and T. Kanade. An iterative image registration technique with an application to stereo vision. In *Proc. Seventh International Joint Conference on Artificial Intelligence*, pages 674–679, Vancouver, Canada, Aug. 1981.
10. H.-H. Nagel. Constraints for the estimation of displacement vector fields from image sequences. In *Proc. Eighth International Joint Conference on Artificial Intelligence*, volume 2, pages 945–951, Karlsruhe, West Germany, August 1983.
11. D. Terzopoulos. Image analysis using multigrid relaxation. *IEEE Transactions on Pattern Analysis and Machine Intelligence*, 8(2):129–139, Mar. 1986.
12. J. Weickert and C. Schnörr. A theoretical framework for convex regularizers in PDE-based computation of image motion. *International Journal of Computer Vision*, 45(3):245–264, Dec. 2001.
13. D. M. Young. *Iterative Solution of Large Linear Systems.* Academic Press, New York, 1971.
14. G. Zini, A. Sarti, and C. Lamberti. Application of continuum theory and multigrid methods to motion evaluation from 3D echocardiography. *IEEE Transactions on Ultrasonics, Ferroelectrics, and Frequency Control*, 44(2):297–308, Mar. 1997.

Adaptive Stabilization of Vibration on Archive Films*

Attila Licsár, László Czúni, and Tamás Szirányi

University of Veszprém, Department of Image Processing and Neurocomputing
H-8200 Veszprém, Egyetem u. 10. Hungary
{licsara,czuni}@almos.vein.hu, sziranyi@sztaki.hu

Abstract. Image vibration is a typical type of degradation that is difficult to restore in an automatic film restoration system. It is usually caused by improper film transportation during the copying or the digitization process. We have developed a method for automatic image stabilization consisting of two main steps: estimating vibration then correction by drifting the whole frame. Earlier stabilization algorithms are unsuccessful in cases of multiple motions and human interaction is necessary to achieve satisfactory results. The proposed technique is automatic and avoids false results for most difficult situations as shown in examples. The paper describes the technique used for motion estimation of regions; the selection of image regions for adequate vibration estimation; and the method of stabilization.

1 Introduction

Archive films suffer from several degradations such as blotches, scratches, flickering, image vibration, fading, etc. [1]. Frame vibration can be defined as a rapid random spatial drift and/or rotation between consecutive frames. It is usually caused by unsteady film transportation in film cameras, telecine and copying machines or other instruments. The observed vibration of films can be very complex since camera egomotion can also cause vibration having serious effects on the 2D projection of 3D sceneries. It is important to note that our vibration model does not deal with the egomotion of the recording camera itself (neither rotation), however our solution has side effects on camera vibration as will be explained and demonstrated later.

The paper is organized as follows: in Section 2 we briefly overview earlier stabilization methods emphasizing differences found in comparison to our model. In Section 3 the model of the new stabilization algorithm is described. We explain motion estimation, vibration estimation and filtering. Then we present some results of automatic stabilization in Section 4. Conclusion and Future Work comes finally in Section 5.

2 Overview of Stabilization Methods

Basically, there are three main sources of image vibration: camera motion (egomotion: translation, rotation, zoom), film vibration (in our article the global drift due

* This paper is based on the research supported by the project NKFP-2/049/2001 and OTKA-T32307 of the Ministry of Education, Hungary.

N. Petkov and M.A. Westenberg (Eds.): CAIP 2003, LNCS 2756, pp. 230–237, 2003.

to unsteady film transfer in a copy or in a telecine machine is called film vibration), object vibration (shaking objects such as a moving car on a rough road).

The removal of the random vibration from motion can be related to a wide area of image processing applications. Taking a closer look, stabilization algorithms can be grouped into three main classes:

1. Methods to remove vibration originating from camera ego-motion (for example [2][3]);
2. Methods to remove film vibration by global motion estimation and filtering (for example [4][5][6]);
3. Methods to remove object vibration (this problem often arises as object tracking).

Methods of the second-class implement stabilization process based on the global motion of a frame, while in the third case local object motion gives a support for stabilization. In some papers local feature points are used to estimate motion vectors to remove film vibration [7].

In contrast, our proposed model combines classes 2 and 3 by automatic **ROF** (**Region Of Fixation**) selection where stabilization will be done based on this specific image region. The ROF can be the whole frame (initial assumption) or a specific fixed region (i.e. an object) of the image; everything depends on the local structure of the motion on the film. In case of manual restoration an operator should mark some areas as ROFs on the image. The purpose of our method is the stabilization of film sequences by automatic ROF selection.

Please, notice here that camera ego-motion filtering is not the target of our method, but our model will not differentiate camera vibration from film vibration at the selected ROF. As found in our experiments, and shown in some examples, this side effect is not disturbing, while differentiating between these two kinds of motion would require 2D/3D parametric models. It results in a considerable increasing of computational costs. Talking about any of the above classes, almost all algorithms contain the following three main steps:

1. estimating motion (of camera, object, or feature points);
2. filtering motion trajectory to estimate the ideal noise-free motion;
3. modify image motion (i.e. warp the image) to get smooth trajectories.

As for the estimation of motion, several techniques can be applied. One can set up 2D or 3D parametric models for ego-motion estimation [3]; can make block matching [8][13][14], feature point tracking [7], image derivatives for measuring local motion; can use phase correlation [6][11] to estimate global motion. Once motion has been measured it is smoothed by different techniques. Simple methods include low-pass filtering, median filtering [5][12] while more complicated solutions apply motion statistics or error propagation control [2], polygonal approximation [3], Kalman filtering, etc. Finally, the input sequence is processed to remove vibration by applying a drift or other warping techniques. Methods adequate for the stabilization of archive films suffer from the following problems:

- 2D/3D parametric models are too time consuming,
- global motion estimation fails in case of complex scenes,
- models based on local features are sensitive to noise (e.g. flickering, blotches),
- in most cases robust and fast tracking algorithms require human interaction.

3 Unsupervised Image Stabilization

The main task of film restoration is to differentiate between the three sources of vibration (in an implicit or explicit way) and to eliminate film vibration effects only. The restoration method should be:

- computationally feasible for high-resolution image sequences,
- robust for flickering and blotches,
- automatic in most cases.

In our model, image vibration affects all image pixels the same way (i.e. we excluded non homogenous shrinking and film rotation from our model at this stage): the same unwanted random motion (separable in x and y directions) is considered to be added to the motion of all image pixels. Image stabilization is the process of removing this noise from the motion of all image points by repositioning the whole frame with a global drift. This can lead to image loss on the borders of a frame but this can be eliminated by applying zooming, with a magnitude proportional to the amplitude of the vibration, or by impainting from a previous/successive frame that has adequate border information.

The main point of estimating and compensating vibration is to find the global drift and reposition the whole frame in the opposite direction. We can estimate global vibration with the help of the vibration of local regions. This process is as follows:

1. Find suitable velocity functions (i.e. find characteristic local motion e.g. the global motion of the selected ROF).
2. Smooth these functions to estimate a stabilized image.
3. Measure temporal deviations of these functions from the smoothed version.
4. Estimate global vibration with the help of these local deviations.

Local deviations will contain the superposition of film vibration and camera vibration. The effect of camera vibration can differ from region to region depending on the 3D structure of the scene, while film vibration is constant over the whole frame. Since it would be very time-consuming to separate camera vibration from film vibration the proposed technique compensates the superposition instead. As shown in the examples in most cases this is not a limitation of our algorithm and even sequences with camera vibration are reconstructed adequately.

3.1 Motion Estimation with Phase Correlation

We have chosen the phase correlation technique for estimating motion of an image region [11]. This method is relatively insensitive to fluctuations in image intensity (flicker and blotches are very typical for archive films) due to two reasons: it uses normalized Fourier coefficients and input images are high-pass filtered first, since edges and textures are less affected by intensity variation (flicker). The phase correlation technique evaluates the phase of the Cross Power Spectrum (CPS) of consecutive images. If one image (f_1) is a shifted version of the other (f_2) then the CPS is as follows:

$$\frac{F_1(\zeta,\eta) * F_2^*(\zeta,\eta)}{\left|F_1(\zeta,\eta) * F_2^*(\zeta,\eta)\right|} = e^{j2\pi(\zeta\, x_0, \eta\, y_0)} \tag{1}$$

where F_1 and F_2 are the Fourier transforms of the images and F_2^* is the complex conjugate of F_2. The inverse Fourier transform of the CPS has an impulse with coordinates located at the required shift (x_0, y_0).

In case of real video sequences successive frames are never perfectly shifted of each other and instead of an impulse a so-called correlation surface can be obtained, containing peaks indicating the motion components in the block. (See later examples.) The phase correlation technique offers a high degree of accuracy and robustness [10][11].

3.2 Automatic ROF Selection

Most stabilization algorithms require the user to select an object (or say an image region) that has a suitable motion trajectory. In our algorithm an image region can describe vibration adequately when the following conditions are met:

- The image area can be characterized with one typical (global) motion.
- The image area should have relatively smooth motion.

The first question is how to find those image areas that represent image vibration suitably: in our algorithm we apply a top-bottom search for adequate ROFs. The motion estimation is often affected by film defects (e.g. blotches, scratches) and non-rigid object motion. For the better estimation accuracy we need the largest regions on the image with unambiguous motion. Accordingly, we use a quad-tree based image splitting method (see Figure 1.). Automatic ROF selection starts with processing the first frame of an image sequence and the selected ROFs are valid for a predefined length of app. 0.5-1.0 seconds (depending on the constancy of the film). The main steps of automatic stabilization follow:

1. The whole image is selected as one ROF to be used for vibration estimation.
2. The motion of the ROF is estimated by the phase correlation technique.
3. Peaks of the inverse Fourier transform of the CPS are analyzed: if a unique peak is found then we suppose that a global motion vector can characterize the ROF. Uniqueness satisfies two constraints: 1. the height of the peak is over a predefined threshold (here 0.023); 2. no other local maximum can reach 30% of the height of the peak. Otherwise the ROF is divided into sub-regions, in a quad-tree manner, until an adequate peak is found (see Figure 1) or the ROF size (maximum depth of the quad-tree) reaches a lower limit (here 3 levels). Calculating all quad-trees in the given sequence we have to compare motion vectors of image regions (ROFs) in time. The motion of a given region is equal to the calculated motion in the leaf that contains it due to the feature of our splitting method.
4. The speed, in both directions of x and y, of ROFs at the leaves of the tree are calculated. Velocity functions are plot for each ROF as a function of time and straight lines are fitted with linear regression. We choose the function with the smallest square error. This function determines the ROF used for further vibration estimation for the whole frame within the short sequence.

If the tree has maximum depth (here 3) and the motion is ambiguous (but the tree cannot be divided into sub-regions) then the motion function can be estimated from different blocks of similar motions. Then we calculated the median of the motion vectors of several ROFs with the smallest square error.

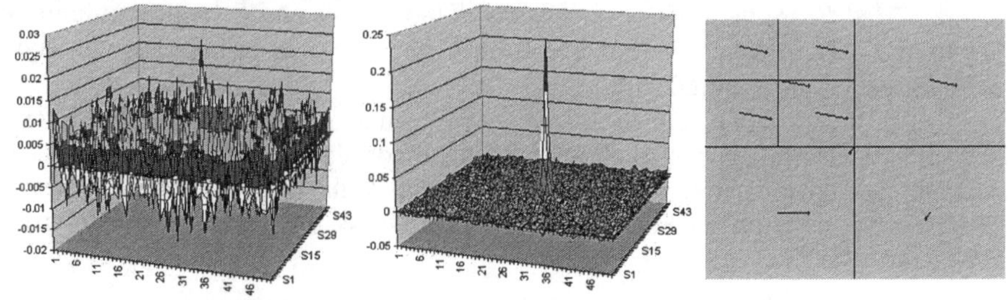

Fig. 1. Ambiguous and unambiguous peaks of the inverse Fourier transform of the CPS and an example of quad-tree with motion vectors.

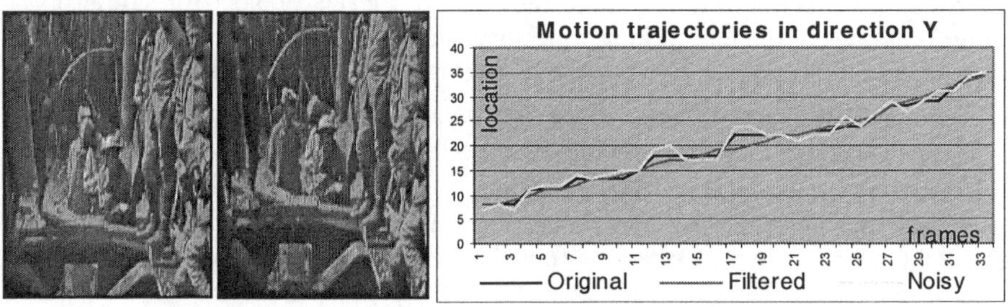

Fig. 2. Left: two frames (#1 and #20) from Soldiers (with camera tilt and central local motion) Right: the corresponding motion trajectories: original, noise added and filtered motion data.

If automatic ROF selection is not satisfactory for some reason, user interaction is still allowed to choose the appropriate region for manual vibration compensation. In this case the system indexes the frame and its features, then at the next occurrence of a similar scene chooses the user selected ROF [9]. In our experiments no such case with necessary manual interaction occurred.

4 Examples

In this Section we illustrate the performance of the proposed stabilization algorithm through several examples.

4.1 Sequence "Soldiers"

The original sequence contains only little local motion in the central region and definite camera tilt. Figure 2 shows two frames from the sequence and illustrates original, noise added and filtered trajectories estimated with the proposed method. As for a test, we added drift of uniform distribution with a deviance of 2 pixels in both directions.

It can be seen that this artificially added vibration is filtered as well as some vibration originating from camera shaking. In this example our top-bottom technique found the whole frame adequate for global motion estimation, there was no need for quad-tree blocks for motion analysis.

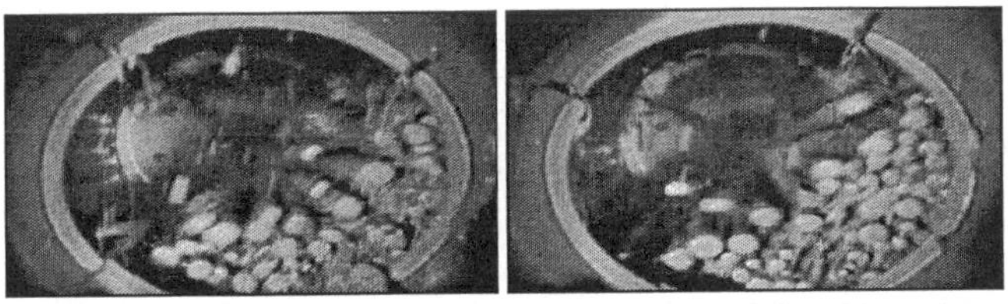

Fig. 3. Frames #10 and #20 from "Rotating Drum" with complex motion.

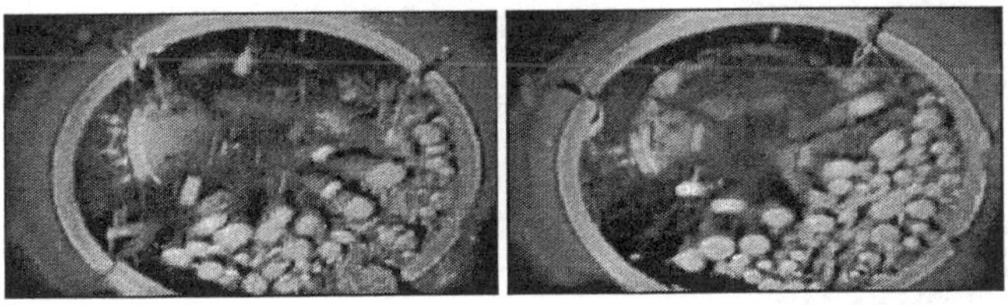

Fig. 4. Filtered "Rotating Drum" frame #10 and #20 with [15]. Automatic filtering fails.

4.2 Sequence "Rotating Drum"

In the second example the input sequence contains complex motion: while the drum rotates, particles inside have turbulent motion (see Figure 3). For the human viewer no vibration is observable.

In this example conventional techniques fail to estimate global motion. Our top-bottom motion analysis, after rejecting the top level of the quad-tree due to the ambiguous nature of the inverse Fourier transform of the CPS, divides the image into non-overlapping ROFs and finds that there is one region with almost no motion at all (top-left corner due to aperture problem; if there was vibration there would be no aperture problem). That is, there is no need for stabilization in this case. We made experiments with two other stabilization algorithms available on the Internet [15][16]. Both of these techniques failed and introduced serious drift instead of stabilization as shown in the example above (Figure 4). Both frames (#10 and #20) are, as can be seen, positioned approximately by 5 pixels to the right.

4.3 Sequence "Night Dancer"

In this example there are two main regions of the sequence with different motion behavior (Figure 5). The dancer in the front has very fast motion while the man in the back is almost unmoving except for some visible vibration.

The adaptive algorithm divides images into four blocks (level of quad-tree is 2) and chooses the bottom-right region of the image for the stabilization. Figure 5 shows estimated motions in the Y direction. Estimation based on the whole frame fails at several points (e.g. at the 19th position). ROF chosen automatically to be the right part of the image gives satisfactory results.

4.4 Sequence "Chevy"

In the last example called "Chevy" we measured the horizontal motion of the car manually. The input sequence contains camera motion, strong local motion and has definite vibration either. The global stabilization technique fails while adaptive ROF selection stabilizes the sequence (see right of Figure 6.) In the left of Figure 6 two frames (upper line frame: #13, bottom line: frame #24) can be compared visually. The horizontal position of the right lamp of the car is rapidly altering when the non-adaptive technique is applied. Automatic ROF selection works well.

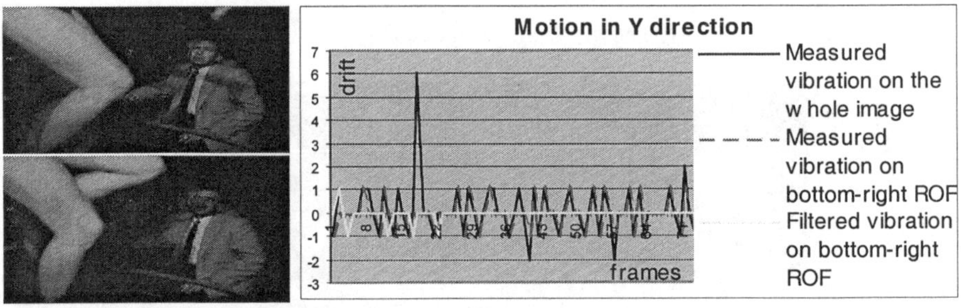

Fig. 5. Left: Examples from sequence "Night Dancer" (Frame #30 and #40). Right: original and filtered global motion of the bottom-right ROF of "Night Dancer".

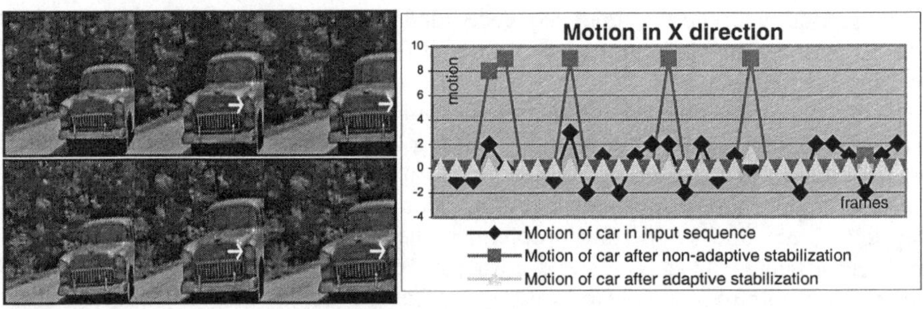

Fig. 6. Left: in columns are input, adaptive and non-adaptive filtered frames #13 and #24 (in rows) of sequence "Chevy". Right: the motion of the car measured manually in direction X.

5 Conclusions and Future Work

We introduced a new adaptive model for film stabilization. It enables automatic operation with minimal human interaction reducing costs in film restoration. The proposed technique is robust for noise and can handle complex scenes. The application of the proposed model is illustrated with several examples. There are two main areas where improvements could be achieved: 1. to introduce rotation and zoom into the vibration model. 2. to increase computation speed by multi-scale processing in case of very high-resolution sequences (2-6K). This means that the first few levels of the tree could be processed at lower resolution with satisfactory results.

For better visual presentation of results please go to:
http://www.knt.vein.hu/~dimorf/demo

References

1. Read, P., Meyer, M.P.: Restoration of Motion Picture Film. Butterworth-Heinemann (2000)
2. Chen, T.: Video Stabilization Algorithm Using a Block-Based Parametric Motion Model. Information System Laboratory, Department of Electrical Engineering, Stanford University (2000)
3. Duric, Z., Rosenfeld, A.: Shooting a Smooth Video with a Shaky Camera. Machine Vision and Applications 13 (2003) 5-6, 303-313
4. Saito, T., Komatsu, T., Hoshi T., Ohuchi, T.: Image Processing for Restoration of Old Film Sequences. 10th International Conference on Image Analysis and Processing (ICIAP), (1999)
5. Schallauer, P., Pinz, A., Haas, W.: Automatic Restoration Algorithms for 35mm Film. VIDERE, MIT press, 1(3), (1999) 60-85
6. Wu, Y., Suter, D.: Noisy Image Sequence Registration and Segmentation. In Proceedings of Second Asian Conference on Computer Vision, ACCV'95, Singapore (1995) 1533-1537
7. Censi, A., Fusiello, A., Roberto, V.: Image Stabilization by Features Tracking. In 10th International Conference on Image Analysis and Processing, Venice, Italy (1999)
8. Irani, M., Rousso, B., Peleg, S.: Recovery of Ego-Motion Using Region Alignment. IEEE Trans. on PAMI, (1997) 268-272
9. Hanis, A., Szirányi, T.: Measuring the Motion Similarity in Video Indexing. 4th EURASIP, Zagreb (2003)
10. Hill, L., Vlachos, T.: On the Estimation of Global Motion Using Phase Correlation for Broadcast Applications. In Proceedings of the IEEE International Conference on Image Processing and it's Applications (IPA), Manchester (1999) 721-725
11. Kuglin, C.D., Hines, D.C.: The Phase Correlation Image Aligment Method. In Proceedings of International Conference on Cybernetics and Society, IEEE (1975) 163-165
12. Tenze, L., Ramponi, G., Carrato, S.: A Complete System for Old Motion Picture Restoration. In Proceedings of EVA, Florence, Italy (2002) 110-114
13. Vlachos, T.: Simple Method for Estimation of Global Motion Parameters Using Sparse Translational Motion Vector Fields. Electronics Letters (1998) 60-62
14. Wang, D., Wang, L.: Global Motion Parameters Estimation Using a Fast and Robust Algorithm. IEEE Trans. Cets. And Sys. For Video Technology (1997) 823-826
15. http://www.dv99.com
16. http://steadyhand.dynapel.com/

A Genetic Algorithm with Automatic Parameter Adaptation for Video Segmentation

Eun Yi Kim[1] and Se Hyun Park[2,*]

[1] College of Internet and Media, Konkuk Univ.
1 Hwayang-dong, Gwangjin-gu, Seoul, Korea
eykim@kkucc.konkuk.ac.kr

[2] Devision of Computer Engineering, College of Electronic and Information, Chosun Univ.
375 Susuk-dong, Dong-gu, Gwangju, Korea
sehyun@chosun.ac.kr

Abstract. We present a novel genetic algorithm (GA) for video sequence segmentation. The novelty of the approach is that the mating rates such as crossover rate and mutation rate are not constant, but spatio-temporally varying. The variation of mating rates depends on the degree of activity of each chromosome in between the successive frames. The effectiveness of the proposed method will be extensively tested in the synthetic and natural video sequences and compared to several other GA-based segmentation method. The results show that the proposed approach is able to enhance the computational efficiency and the quality of the segmentation results than other methods.

1 Introduction

It is widely acknowledged that the segmentation is the first processing steps in the computer vision and is very important processing in the video coding and multimedia systems [1,2]. The segmentation problem is to divide an image into regions based on homogeneity criterion and optimization scheme. That is, segmentation is to estimate the label field from the observed field, based on optimality scheme.

However, it is a very complex combinatorial optimization problem to choose a specific label field from the astronomical size of the solution space [1-4]. This renders deterministic optimization techniques ineffective since they are prone to stalling in a local optimum. Stochastic optimization techniques, on the other hand, are more suitable since they are capable of forgoing the local optima in the solution space in favor of a global optimum. By using simulated annealing (SA), good results are obtained but it is computationally intensive.

Recently, genetic algorithms (GAs) have appeared as a good solution in the field of segmentation problems [3-5]. A GA is a stochastic optimization algorithm based on mechanisms of natural selection and genetics [6]. In a GA, a search is performed based on a population of solutions instead of a single solution. GAs find an optimal or near-optimal solution through iterative modification of a population initiated from

* The corresponding author: Tel.: +82-62-230-7021; Fax: +82-62-230-7021

N. Petkov and M.A. Westenberg (Eds.): CAIP 2003, LNCS 2756, pp. 238–245, 2003.

random values. Their main attractive is their ability to efficiently deal with hard complex combinatorial problem. They are also attractive because they can achieve an efficient parallel exploration of search space without getting stuck in local optima. Therefore, over the last few years, GAs have attracted increasing attention for use in segmenting variety of images. These studies show that GAs are successfully used for image or video segmentation problems, yet relatively low search efficiency is still prevalent problem in GAs.

The search efficiency in GAs is affected by crossover and mutation. Crossover controls the size of the solution space that can be explored, while mutation creates new chromosomes that may be useful. A high mutation rate allows the fast exploration of the whole solution space and reduces the chance of entrapment in local minima. However, it can cause significant disruption to the exploitation of local regions. Meanwhile, a high crossover allows for further exploration of the solution space and reduces the chance of settling for a false optimum; yet, if it is too high, it can waste a lot of computation time in exploring unpromising regions. Consequently, search efficiency has been a problem with traditional genetic algorithms because it is difficult to choose suitable mating rates for those methods.

Accordingly, we present a novel technique for the automatic adaptation of GA parameters within GAs for video sequence segmentation. In our approach, the mating rates are not constant, but spatio-temporally varying. The variation of mating rates depends on the degree of activity of each chromosome in between the successive frames. In the proposed method, the segmentation of the current frame in the video is successively obtained by chromosomes that evolve using DGAs. Unlike the standard DGA, chromosomes are initiated using the segmentation results of the previous frame instead of the random values and then the unstable chromosomes corresponding to the moving objects parts have the larger mating rates than stable chromosomes, to adapt the changes in between the successive frames.

The proposed method with automatic adaptation of GA parameter can provide effective exploitation and exploration of the solution space, thus improving the performance relative to speed and segmentation quality.

2 Problem Definitions

The input image G was considered as degraded by i.i.d (independent identically distributed) zero-mean Gaussian white noise $N=\{n_{ij}\}$. Let $S=\{(i,j):1\leq i\leq M_1, 1\leq j\leq M_2\}$ denote the $M_1 \times M_2$ lattice, such that an element in S indexes an image pixel. Let $\Lambda=\{\lambda_1, \ldots, \lambda_R\}$ denote the label set and $X=\{X_{ij} | X_{ij}\in \Lambda\}$ be the family of random variables defined on S. The neighborhood of S can be defined as $\Gamma=\{\eta_{ij}\}$, where η_{ij} is a set of sites neighboring (i, j). Then, X is an MRF on S with respect to Γ because the two conditions of [2,3] are satisfied. Let ω be a realization of X. The goal is to identify ω which maximizes the posterior distribution for a fixed input image g. That is, to determine

$$\arg\max_{\omega} P(X=\omega \mid G=g) \propto \arg\max_{\omega} P(g \mid \omega) P(\omega) \quad (1)$$

Eq. (1) is divided into likelihood function and prior probability, which are defined in [3]. Using these components, Eq. (1) can be represented by the following equation, which is defined as a *posterior energy function*.

$$\arg\min_{\omega}\{\sum_{c\in C}[S_c(\omega)+T_c(\omega)]+\frac{[g-M(\omega)]^2}{2\sigma^2}+\frac{1}{2}\log(2\pi\sigma^2)\} \tag{2}$$

In Eq. (2), σ is the noise variance and $M(\cdot)$ is the mapping function that the label of a pixel corresponds to the estimated color vector. And C is a possible set of cliques. Then spatial potentials $S_c(\omega)$ and imposes the spatial continuity of the labels and temporal potentials $T_c(\omega)$ is to achieve the temporal continuity of the labels. These potentials are defined in detail in [3]. Let ρ_{ij} denote a set of cliques containg pixel (i,j). Since C is equal to the sum of ρ_{ij} for all pixels, the function in Eq. (2) can be rewritten as the sum of the local energy U_{ij} for all pixels.

$$\arg\min_{\omega}\sum_{(i,j)\in S}U_{ij},\ \text{where}\ U_{ij}=\sum_{c\in\rho_{ij}}\left(S_c(\omega_{ij})+T_c(\omega_{ij})\right)+\frac{\left(g_{ij}-M(\omega_{ij})\right)^2}{2\sigma^2}+\frac{1}{2}\log(2\pi\sigma^2) \tag{3}$$

As a result, instead of maximizing the posterior distribution, the posterior energy function is minimized to identify the optimal label.

3 Proposed Method

Segmentation problem is formulated as minimizing the energy function. This minimization process is performed by chromosomes that evolve using DGAs. A chromosome consists of a label and a feature vector allocated to one. The population of chromosomes is given initial values then evolved by iteratively performing selection, crossover, and mutation, until the stopping criterion is satisfied. These operators eventually lead to a stable label configuration, which is taken as the resulting segmentation.

In this work, new mechanisms are introduced into conventional DGAs, to improve the performance. The first initializes the chromosomes using the segmentation results from the previous frame to segment subsequent frames. The second provides some chromosomes corresponding to moving object parts the larger mating rates. The role of the mating operators in DGAs is to generate an improved new population from the existing population. When considered from the viewpoint of video segmentation, these operators enable the chromosomes initialized by the segmentation results of the previous frame to track the information that changed between the successive frames. Therefore, it is reasonable that the operators are first applied to the chromosomes allocated to actually moving object parts. Consequently, the new mechanisms introduced in the current work facilitate the effective exploitation and exploration of the search space, thereby improving the performance of the proposed method in terms of speed and segmentation quality.

3.1 Chromosome

A chromosome $C_{ij}=(l_{ij}, f_{ij})$ is allocated at site (i,j), wherein l_{ij} is the label and f_{ij} is the estimated RGB-color vector. A chromosome is real-coded. As such, the chromosome is composed of four integer fields, each of which represents a label and each color in the feature vector.

Each chromosome has a fitness value, and then $-U_{ij}$ is a measure of this fitness. Moreover, each chromosome has an *evolution probability* that represents its likelihood of being evolved by crossover and mutation. The probability of a chromosome C_{ij} is denoted as PE_{ij}, and defined as follows:

$$PE_{ij} = \frac{\Delta U(i,j,t)}{\max\{\ \Delta U(0,0,t),\ \ldots\ ,\ \Delta U(i,j,t),\ \ldots\ ,\ \Delta U(M_1-1,M_2-1,t)\ \}},$$

where $\Delta U(i,j,t) = |\ U(i,j,t) - U(i,j,,t-1)\ |$ is the local energy variance of chromosome C_{ij} at time t. Accordingly, the evolution probability of a chromosomes is directly proportional to the variance of its local energy.

Based on their evolution probabilities, the chromosomes are classified as either stable or unstable chromosomes. A chromosome is categorized as unstable if the following condition is satisfied:

$$PE_{ij} \geq \frac{1}{2}(\ 1 - C_r(\text{or } M_r)\ ),$$

where C_r and M_r are crossover rate and mutation rate, respectively. Given the rates of mating operators, certain chromosomes with evolution probabilities above the threshold are selected as unstable.

3.2 Parameter Adaptation

Mating rates of chromosomes are automatically determined based on their evolutional probabilities. The larger the number of unstable chromosomes, the larger the mating rates. Once given the initial values of mating rates, the values are changed in a dynamic way for each generation. In the proposed method, initial mating rates were fixed regardless of the input video sequence: mutation rate as 0.005 and crossover rate as 0.05. Then, the mating rates are automatically adapted according to the type of input video sequences.

Figs. 1 and 2 show the respective variations of mating rates when segmenting a frame in *Claire* and *Table Tennis*, respectively.

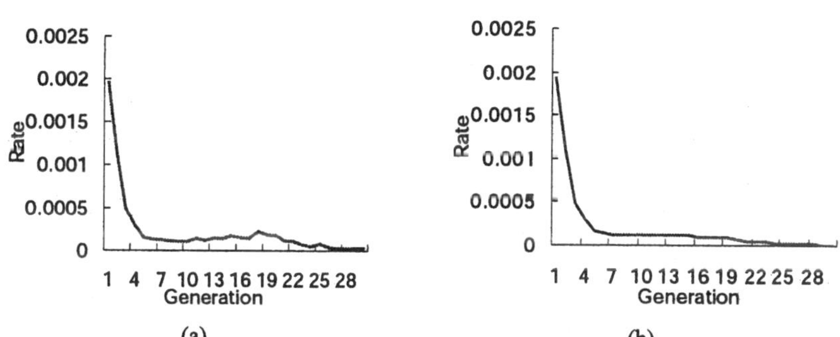

Fig. 1. Variation of mating rates according to the generation, when segmenting *Claire*: (a) crossover rates; (b) mutation rates

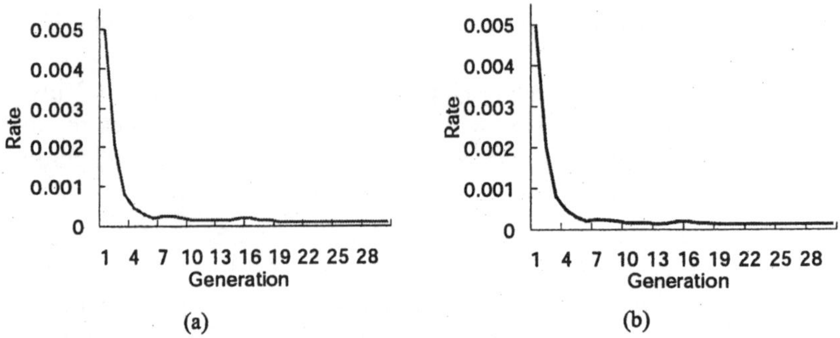

Fig. 2. Variation of mating rates according to the generation, when segmenting *Table Tennis*: (a) crossover rates; (b) mutation rates

When comparing the graphs at Figs. 1 and 2, average mating-rates in the *Table Tennis* are larger than those in *Claire*. These differences are due to the characteristics of the segmented sequences. The *Claire* sequence has the small motion, whereas the *Table Tennis* sequence has relatively large motions during the entire sequence. Accordingly, the more representative solutions are required to enable the chromosomes initialized with the segmentation results of the previous frame to track the changes between successive frames. As a result, the larger mating rates are needed.

3.3 Algorithm

The chromosomes mapped to the first frame are evolved using conventional DGAs [5]. That is, the chromosomes are initialized with totally random values, and all of them have the same evolution probabilities. On the other hand, the chromosomes of the subsequent frames are initiated from the segmentation results of the previous frame, and then classified into stable and unstable ones according to their evolution probabilities. The difference between stable and unstable chromosomes is that the operators applied to stable chromosomes differ from those applied to unstable chromosomes. Stable chromosomes undergo neither crossover nor mutation, whereas unstable chromosomes are evolved using all GA operators for each generation. GA operators and stopping criterion used in the respective evolution mechanisms are described in detail in [3].

4 Experimental Results

This section focuses on evaluating the proposed method. Section 4.1 shows the segmentation results performed by the proposed method and comparisons with other GA-based segmentation methods. Then, the validity of the proposed method is discussed in the following section.

4.1 Segmentation Results

To assess the validity of the proposed method, it was tested on several well-known video sequences. The stopping criterion was described in [3]. The label size at 64. DGA parameters were fixed as follows: the window size at 5×5, mutation rate as 0.005 and crossover rate as 0.05.

Figs. 3–4 show some segmentation results for well-known videos, which are referred to as *Claire* and *Table Tennis*. In respective experiments, the segmentation results of our method were compared with those of other GA-based segmentation methods. Here, Andrey *et al.*'s method was adapted [5].

Fig. 3 shows some segmentation results for the sequence *Claire* when segmented using Andrey *et al's* method and the proposed method. Fig. 3(a) shows the original frames at time 1, 65, 96, and 165. Then, the respective segmentation results are shown in Figs. 3(b) and (c). As shown in Fig. 3(c), the proposed method was able to perfectly determine the boundaries of *Claire* and tracked her motion even though only unstable chromosomes were evolved. There was no significant difference between the respective segmentation results when they were visually inspected.

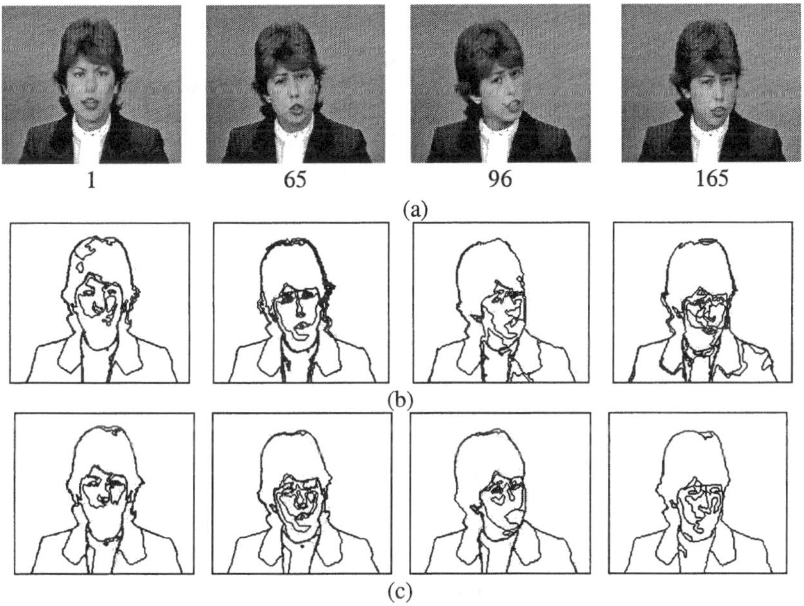

Fig. 3. Segmentation results of sequence *Claire*: (a) Original frames at time 1, 65, 96, and 165; (b) Segmentations using Andrey *et al.*'s method; (c) Segmentations using the proposed method

To fully demonstrate the validity of the proposed methods, they were applied to a video sequence with more than two objects. Fig. 4 shows some segmentation results for the sequence *Table Tennis* when segmented using the respective methods. The scene was decomposed into five objects: the background, ball, left hand, right arm with a racquet, and background. In this sequence, the objects are not absolutely rigid, and different areas have different kinds of motion. In particular, the left hand was not explicitly shown in the simulation results as indeed it disappears as the sequence unravels. The original frames at time 1, 4, 10, and 14 are shown in Fig. 4(a), then the respective segmentation results are shown in Figs. 4(b) and (c). With the proposed method, to improve the computational efficiency, only unstable chromosomes are evolved by crossover and mutation. Nonetheless, the objects boundaries were correctly tracked.

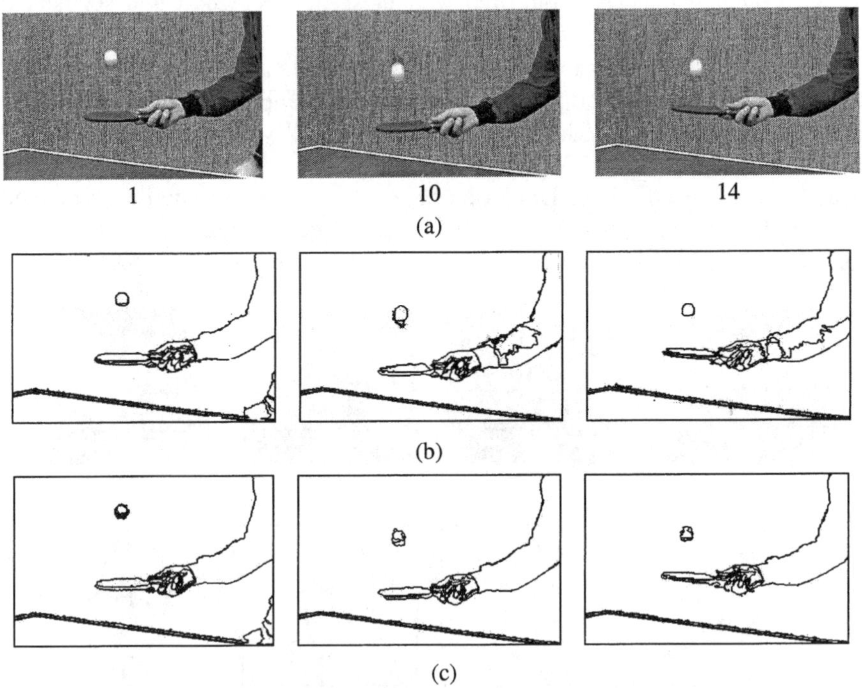

Fig. 4. Segmentation results of sequence *Table Tennis* when segmenting using several methods: (a) Original frames at time 1, 10 and 14; (b) Segmentation results using Andrey *et al.*'s method; (c) Segmentation results using the proposed method

4.2 Performance Comparisons

The proposed GA-based segmentation method was effective in reducing the computational time involved in segmenting the video sequences, while improving the quality of the segmentation results. To prove its effectiveness, the proposed method was compared with Andrey *et al.*'s method as regards the speed and quality of the segmentation results. Then, to quantitatively measure the quality of the segmentation results, the standard uniform function F was applied, as proposed by Liu *et al* and used in [3,7]. The smaller the value of F, the better the segmentation results.

Table 1 shows the performance comparison of the two methods when segmenting the sequences *Claire* and *Table Tennis*. These comparisons show that the proposed method could improve both the quality of the segmentation results and the convergence speed. Consequently, the proposed method demonstrated a superior performance when compared with standard DGA-based algorithms.

Table 1. Summary of Performance Comparisons

Methods	Video sequences	Average number of generations to segment a frame	Average time taken to segment a frame	Average value of $F(\omega)$
Andrey *et al.*'s method	*Claire*	287.92	16.41	155.94
	Table Tennis	89.97	25.82	88.24
Proposed method	*Claire*	26.38	1.42	42.43
	Table Tennis	24.7	4.78	39.38

5 Conclusion

This paper presented a new unsupervised method for segmenting a video sequence. Each frame in a sequence was modeled using an MRF, which is robust to degradation. Since this is computationally intensive, a new segmentation algorithm based on GA that can improve computationally efficiency was developed. Experimental results demonstrated the effectiveness of the proposed method.

Acknowledgement

This work was supported by research funds from Chosun university, 2002.

References

1. Nikhil R. Pal and Sankar K. Pal: A review on image segmentation techniques. Pattern Recognition. 26- 9 (1993) 1277-1294.
2. Gene K. Wu and T. R. Reed: Image sequence processing using spatiotemporal segmentation. IEEE Trans. Circuits Syst. Video Technol., 9-5 (1999) 798-807.
3. Kim, E. Y., S. W. Hwang, S. H. Park and H. J. Kim: Spatiotemporal Segmentation using Genetic Algorithms. Pattern Recognition. 34-10 (2001) 2063-2066.
4. S. M. Bhandarkar and H. Zhang: Image segmentation using evolutionary computation. IEEE Trans. Evolutionary Computation. 3-1 (1999) 1-21.
5. Andrey, P. and P. Tarroux: Unsupervised segmentation of Markov random field modeled textured images using selectionist relaxation. IEEE Trans. Pattern Anal. Machine Intell. 20-3(1998) 659-673.
6. D. E. Goldberg: Genetic Algorithms in Search, Optimization and Machine Learning. Addison Wesley. (1989)
7. J. Liu and Y. H. Yang: Multiresoultion color image segmentation. IEEE Trans. PAMI. 16-7 (1994) 689-700.

Two-Step Unassisted Video Segmentation Using Fast Marching Method

Piotr Steć[1] and Marek Domański[2]

[1] University of Zielona Góra, Institute of Control and Computation Engineering
ul. Podgórna 50, Zielona Góra, Poland
P.Stec@issi.uz.zgora.pl
[2] Poznań University of Technology, Institute of Electronics and Telecommunications
Piotrowo 3A, 60-965, Poznań, Poland
domanski@et.put.poznan.pl

Abstract. The paper presents a fully automatic method of video segmentation that exploits both colour and motion information. A variation of the active contour technique is applied. The method is developed for real-time applications and therefore its low complexity is of high importance. The major part of contour migration is driven by very efficient algorithm known as *Fast Marching*. The result is then locally enhanced using more computationally exhaustive still image segmentation.

1 Introduction

In many forthcoming applications, visual objects should be extracted from video sequences. For example, the multimedia object coding standard MPEG-4 [1] defines encoding of individual visual objects, e.g. foreground objects that differ by motion from the background. Examples are teachers in e-learning sequences, sport players in digital television broadcasts, intruders in video surveillance sequences and so on.

Object-oriented processing provides also tools for efficient video object manipulation, edition and description as defined by MPEG-4 and MPEG-7 [2]. For all these tasks, the first step is video segmentation that results in extraction of visual objects with some semantic meaning like human beings, vehicles, animals etc. In multimedia applications, segmentation must be fully automatic, i.e. unassisted by a human operator. Moreover the computing schemes must be fast enough to ensure real-time implementations.

Semantic object segmentation of video sequences is currently an important research area, and many different approaches have been proposed in the references [3]. Among the great variety of segmentation techniques, those based on active contour or snakes [4 – 7] are of high interest for extraction of single objects. Recently, some variants of the technique [17,18] have been used mostly for semiautomatic segmentation. The technique of classic active contour exploits markers placed along contour. These markers are driven by force that depends on segmented image properties as well as on terms based on contour itself. Such an approach is related to some problems caused by moving markers. When the markers move too far or too close to each other, there is a problem with inserting and removing markers from contour, and the accuracy is determined by the distance between markers. There are also problems

N. Petkov and M.A. Westenberg (Eds.): CAIP 2003, LNCS 2756, pp. 246–253, 2003.

related to topology changes, namely splitting and merging contours. Very complex description of the force that drives markers results in high computational complexity. Solution to some of these problems is *geodesic active contour* [8] which does not relay on markers, thus gives segmentation of higher quality. However this technique still cannot handle changes in topology.

The *Level Set Method* has been proposed by Osher and Sethian [9] in order to overcome the problems related to topology changes. This method converts the two-dimensional problem into a three-dimensional one, i.e. a two-dimensional contour γ at the time instant t is considered as a zero-level set of a three-dimensional surface ϕ that evolves in time

$$\phi(x,t) = 0\,. \tag{1}$$

Propagation of the contour is featured by the speed F, which can be defined in way that is appropriate to a given problem. The surface ϕ evolves in time according to following differential equation

$$\phi_t - F|\nabla\phi| = 0. \tag{2}$$

More detailed description of this method can be found in [9 - 11]

2 Fast Marching Methods

In this paper, *Fast Marching Method* [12,13] is used as a tool for image segmentation. This method is applied to segment frames of video using both color and motion information.

Fast Marching Method is a very fast computational technique related to Level Set Methods which is designed to approximate the solution of the equation

$$|\nabla T|F = 1\,. \tag{3}$$

The gradient in (3) may be calculated at each point using discrete approximations. This can be effectively applied to the curve evolution problem. The limitation of this method consists in one-way contour propagation. The speed F can be positive (propagation outwards) or negative (propagation inwards) but the speed sign have to be fixed before propagation starts. In a two dimensional case, a curve (contour) propagates with speed $F(x,y)$ and arrives at the point (x,y) at the time $T(x,y)$. The surface formed by arrival times is the solution to the problem stated.

All the points in the narrow band of one-grid-step ahead from evolving curve are included into list sorted by the time value computed using Equation (4). The point with the smallest time value is marked as visited and all its neighbours that were not visited are included into a list of the points within the narrow band. The list is sorted with *heapsort* algorithm which makes updates to the narrow band fast and computationally efficient.

3 Calculations of Speed

The key element in the Fast Marching method, that allows its adaptation to many problems, is the contour propagation speed F. In this paper, the speed function F is defined as a product of two terms, an image-related term F_1 and a curvature-related term F_2:

$$F = F_1 F_2 . \tag{4}$$

Here, the curvature-related term is introduced into the speed definition in order to make it more robust. The idea of such a smoothing term was borrowed from the original Level Set method but with an essential modification. In Level Set method, the smoothing term is summed with the main term. Such an approach is appropriate for techniques where the speed can change sign. Smoothing term with the same sign as main term increases speed whereas with the opposite sign reduces speed. In the fast marching method, the speed must be of constant sign, let us say positive. When trying to use the same additive term, it would be possible to obtain negative speed in some cases, which is invalid for Fast Marching. Moreover, if the term F_2 was limited to the non-negative values it would have been able to increase contour speed only.

It was necessary to include smoothing term in another way. Multiplication of F_1 by F_2 allows to keep essential features of the smoothing term that can be found in Level Set method. F_2 is neutral when it has value one, it slows down the propagation for values less then one and increases speed for values greater then one.

The algorithm for calculation of F is described below.

3.1 Image-Related Term

The image-related term F_1 has its values in the range <0,1>. This term is defined as follows

$$F_1 = \frac{1}{\min(dI, \alpha \cdot dM) + 1} \tag{5}$$

where *dIm* and *dM* are scalar measures of local changes of colour and motion, respectively. α is a normalizing coefficient that is described later in this paragraph. Maximum value of colour change depends on pixel representation, and is fixed. This is mapped on the range <0,1>. Maximum value of difference in motion can vary from sequence to sequence. In order to keep sense of the maximum function in Equation (5), the coefficient α is needed to remap the values of *dM* onto the range <0,1>. The value of the parameter α is estimated from the minimum and maximum values of horizontal and vertical motion vector components.

The term *dI* is computed using a contour-adapted difference operator. At the first step, differences are computed along normal direction between both sides of the curve as well as in direction perpendicular to normal vector. Figure 1 shows an exemplary position on a contour. The differences calculated between points in the two areas marked with *a* are summed into the component *dA,* and the differences calculated between points in the two areas marked with *b* are summed into the component *dB* in Equation (6). Multi-point differences are less sensitive to noise as compared to single differences. The measure *dI* of local changes of color are calculated as

$$dI = \max(dA, dB) \tag{6}$$

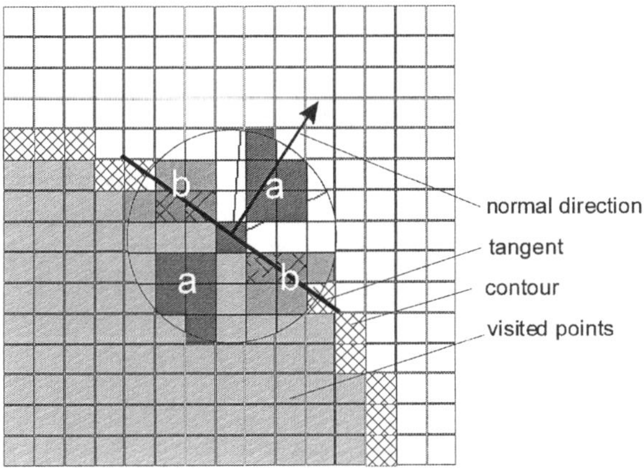

Fig. 1. Illustration of the curve-oriented difference operator.

The motion-related term dM should be robust and insensitive to noise present in the respective motion field. Therefore it is computed by comparison of mean motion vectors at the opposite sides of the curve and as a sum of absolute differences between horizontal and vertical motion vector components:

$$dM = \left| \frac{\sum_{\mathbf{x} \subset W} V_x(\mathbf{x})}{W} - \frac{\sum_{\mathbf{x} \subset B} V_x(\mathbf{x})}{B} \right| + \left| \frac{\sum_{\mathbf{x} \in W} V_y(\mathbf{x})}{W} - \frac{\sum_{\mathbf{x} \in B} V_y(\mathbf{x})}{B} \right|, \quad (7)$$

where W is the area of that part of the window S that is currently located inside the curve, B is the area of the part of S outside the curve, V_x and V_y are the horizontal and vertical motion components, respectively (Fig. 2).

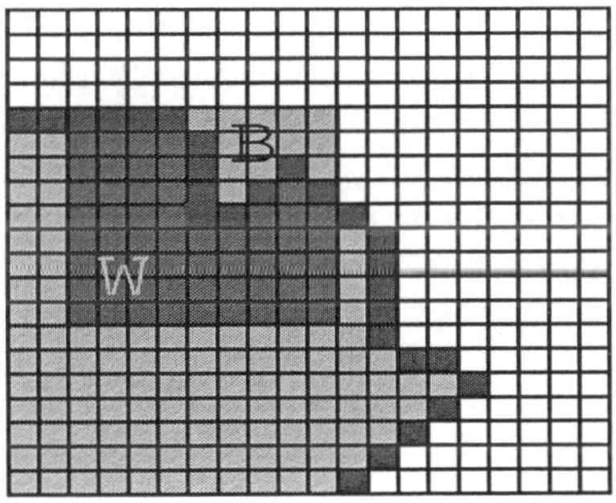

Fig. 2. Areas on which the difference dM is computed.

3.2 Curvature-Based Term

At a point of the contour, where component F_2 has to be estimated, a circle of small radius is placed (Fig. 3). The angle γ defined by the circle centre and curve intersection points defines local curvature (Eq. 8).

$$F_2 = \begin{cases} 0.1, \text{if } \gamma < 90^\circ \\ 10, \text{if } \gamma > 270^\circ \\ 1, \text{in other cases.} \end{cases} \tag{8}$$

The curvature-based term F_2 should have values below one for cusps and values grater then one for corners. The simplified local curvature estimation is proposed to keep performance of the algorithm at the high level. This term also helps to keep contour as short as possible. The shortest contour the smaller number of elements that have to be sorted.

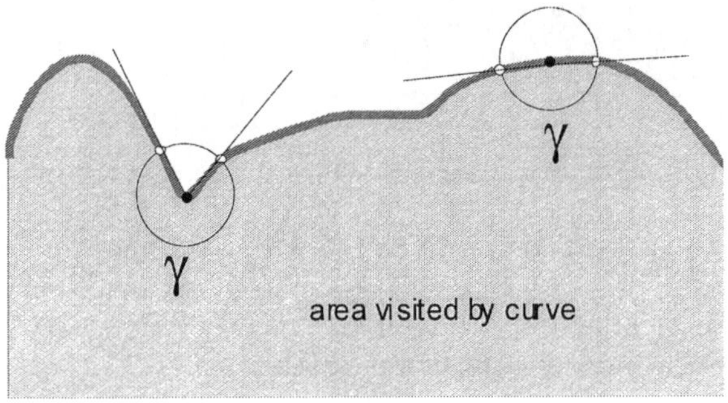

Fig. 3. Local curvature definition. Angle (γ) is measured at the side already visited by curve.

3.3 Stop Condition

In typical applications of active contour, a stop condition is defined in dependence on energy value calculated along the whole contour. Moreover, in classic geodesic active contour and level set methods, calculations are performed along whole contour even when some parts of the contour reached the solution. Here, in our implementation of Fast Marching method, the stop condition is defined locally. This means that parts of the contour which reached solution are no longer considered in calculation. When the speed of the contour at certain point drops below threshold value this point is considered to be at the solution. Points that reached solution does not propagate (narrow band is not updated for them) and are removed from narrow band. This approach lets reduce length of the narrow band list and improve performance of the algorithm. Algorithm stops when the narrow band list is empty.

4 Enhancement Step

The first step of the presented algorithm stops contour before object boundary. This is necessary because Fast Marching Method cannot move contour back. If the object boundary was passed by propagating curve at any point, the curve would leak into the object merging it with the background.

In the second step of the algorithm, segment borders are moved towards nearest edge detected in picture by static image segmentation. Segmentation of the whole image is not necessary. Only the part that is contained in ae band around curve developed in the first stage is considered.

Fig. 4. Exemplary segmentation of the sequence "Stefan". From top and left to bottom and right: the original, the result of the first step, the final result.

Let sr_i be a *i*-th region from static segmentation from static segmentation and *fmr* is a region from Fast Marching segmentation.

```
for i=0 to n
if sr_i ∩ fmr ≠ ∅ add sr_i to fmr
```

where *n* is a total number of segments obtained from static segmentation. Above procedure merges segments from static segmentation to the segment obtained in the first step. The segments with the common parts are merged.

5 Experimental Results

The algorithm was tested using natural sequences with non-rigid objects moving over textured background in presence of camera motion. Algorithm is able to pass highly textured areas that form the same object. Each frame was computed in the time below 2 seconds on 1.5GHz PC. All the sequences were in CIF format.

Even for very dynamic sequences with highly textured background and fast camera motion, the results were quite good (Figs. 4 and 5).

6 Conclusions

The two-step segmentation technique has been proposed in the paper. The two steps include:

Fig. 5. Exemplary segmentation of the sequence "Football". From top and left to bottom and right: the original, the result of the first step, the final result.

- Fast Marching used for fast and rough segmentation,
- local and exact pixel-based segmentation applied only on small area around the previous solution.

To a certain level of motion estimation errors, the algorithm performs quite exactly. However rapid motion in the scene may cause the algorithm to fail, when motion errors become too big. The algorithm is robust to even extremely high motion estimation errors in the areas of low gradient of image. Motion estimation errors near strong edges in image cause a serious problem. Nevertheless, motion estimation is the separate problem that is not considered in this paper.

Low numerical complexity of the Fast Marching Method makes it good candidate for real-time performance. However, real-time performance was not achieved, but the execution times were promising under consideration that test version was not optimized for runtime.

In the nearest future, the method will be compared to other state-of-art techniques.

Acknowledgement

The work has been partially supported by Polish National Committee for Scientific Research in years 2002-2003.

References

1. ISO/IEC IS 14496-2: Generic Coding of Audio-Visual Objects. Part 2: Visual.
2. ISO/IEC DIS 15938-3: Information Technology – Multimedia Content Description Interface. Parts 3: Visual.

3. Guo J., Kuo C.-C. J.: Semantic Video Object Segmentation for Content-Based Multimedia Applications. Kluwer Academic Publishers (2001).
4. Kaas M., Witkin A., Terauzopoulos D.: Snakes: Active Contour Models. International Journal of Computer Vision, 1 (1988) 321-332.
5. Jehan-Besson S., Barlaud M., Aubert G.: Region-Based Active Contours for Video Object Segmentation With Camera Compensation. IEEE Int. Conf. Image Processing, Thessaloniki, Greece (2001) 61-64 .
6. Szczypiński P.: Deformable Models for Quantitative Analysis and Recognition of Objects in Digital Images. Ph.D. thesis, Łódź University of Technology, Łódź, Poland (2000), in Polish.
7. Kühne G., Weickert J., Schuster O., Richter S.: A Tensor-Driven Active Contour Model for Moving Object Segmentation. IEEE Int. Conf. Image Processing, Thessaloniki, Greece (2001) 73-76.
8. Casells V., Kimmel R., Sapiro G.: Geodesic Active Contours. IEEE Int. Conf. on Computer Vision, Boston, USA (1995).
9. Osher S. and Sethian J.A.: Fronts Propagating with Curvature Dependent Speed: Algorithms Based on Hamilton-Jacobi Formulation. Journal of Comp. Physics, 79 (1995) 12-49.
10. Sethian J.A.: Level Set Methods. Cambridge University Press (1996).
11. Adalsteinsson D., Sethian J.A.: A Fast Level Set Method for Propagating Interfaces. Journal of Comp. Physics, (1995) 118-126.
12. Sethian J.A.: Fast marching methods. SIAM Review, vol. 41 (1999) no. 2, 199–235.
13. Sethian J.A., Popovici M.: Three dimensional traveltimes computation using the fast marching method. Geophysics 64 (1999), no. 2.
14. Stec P., Domański M.: Video Segmentation Using Fast Marching Methods. Int. Conf. Computer Vision and Graphics, Zakopane, Poland (2002) 710-715.
15. Mansouri A.-R.: Region Tracking via level Set PDEs without Motion Compensation. IEEE Trans. Pattern Analysis Machine Intelligence, vol. 24 (2002) 947-961.
16. Mansouri A.-R., Konrad J.: Motion Segmentation with Level Sets. IEEE International Conference on Image Processing (1999).
17. Sun S., haynor D., Kim Y.: Semiautomatic Video Object Segmentation Using VSnakes, IEEE Trans. Circuits Systems Video Technol., 13 (2003) 75-82.
18. Wang J., Li X.: Guiding Ziplock Snakes With *a priori* Information, IEEE Trans. Image Proc. 12 (2003) 176-185.

Video Mosaicking for Arbitrary Scene Imaged under Arbitrary Camera Motion

Man-Tai Cheung and Ronald Chung

Department of Automation & Computer-Aided Engineering
The Chinese University of Hong Kong, Shatin, Hong Kong
{mtcheung,rchung}@acae.cuhk.edu.hk

Abstract. Existing mosaic construction algorithms have the following restrictions: (1) the scene is planar or very distant, or (2) the scene is generic but the camera motion is a pure rotation. In either case the registration of images could be captured by a global mapping named planar homography. In this work we address the general case: a generic scene pictured under an arbitrary camera motion. The image data so captured contains parallax that makes the registration of images a difficult problem. We introduce a framework that is capable of constructing mosaic from an image stream of even such a nature. The framework is devised on the basis of an algorithm we refer to as the three-image algorithm that, by the use of a third image, overcomes the parallax problem in registering images. We answer two questions: (1) how an image stream is divided into various 3-image sets for the three-image algorithm to iterate upon; and (2) how intermediate mosaic results over the various 3-image sets are accumulated to compose the overall mosaic at the end. The framework allows uneven sampling, in terms of space or time, of the video stream. Experimental results on real image data are presented to illustrate the performance of the proposed solution.

1 Introduction

Image mosaic construction is about stitching together adjacent images of a scene into an image that displays a wider field of view. Image mosaicking can be used in a wide variety of applications including remote sensing, visual surveillance, virtual reality, and video compression.

There have been a few pieces of work about mosaic construction in recent years [5,6,7,8]. A single global parametric transformation between two images is typically used to register the images and thereby construct the mosaic. Global transformations used include image-plane similarity transformation, affine transformation, bilinear transformation, and planar-projective (homography) transformation. The work [5] uses Gaussian Pyramid to form mosaic and is able to do inverse mosaic for tracking the current image frame, but the work is limited to panoramic scene. The work [6] allows zooming and forward motion in the camera, but it relies on the use of some nonlinear method. The work [10] focuses on constructing panorama from image sequence. It uses planar-projective transformation to register adjacent image frames and refines the mosaic result using global and local alignments. In [7], a nonlinear M-estimator is used to handle parallax in the images, but the nonlinear estimator requires to deal with a large number of unknowns in order to obtain a good result.

N. Petkov and M.A. Westenberg (Eds.): CAIP 2003, LNCS 2756, pp. 254–261, 2003.

In summary, previous work is effective only in constrained situations where the camera motion is a pure rotation or the viewed scene is planar or very distant. The general case, i.e., the case of having a generic scene viewed under a general camera motion, has not been addressed much. What makes the general case difficult is the parallax present in the images. Mosaicking images with parallax is challenging because there is no single global parametric transformation between the images, as is present in the above-mentioned restricted cases [5,6,7,8], that allows the images to be registered and warped to the same image frame for the stitching process.

In an earlier work [1], we proposed a framework that allows a mosaic to be constructed from images with parallax. We argued that in such a case two images could not possibly allow mosaic to be constructed, and we proposed the use of an additional image, termed the intermediate image, that allows intensity region visible only in one of the first two images be warped from one to the other. However, the framework applies only to a discrete set of three images. As the framework involves not two adjacent images but three images, it is not obvious how the framework could be extended to process an image stream. In this paper, we address this issue and propose a mechanism of constructing mosaic from an image stream. The mechanism allows image mosaicking to be no longer limited to planar scene or distant scene or imaging under a pure rotation of the camera. Mosaic can be constructed even from images captured under arbitrary motion of a hand-held camcorder.

2 The Three-Image Algorithm

Here we review how we, with the help of a third image, register two images that contain parallax. Details of the algorithm are available at [1].

Given two images (that are taken from different viewpoints) of a generic scene, we aim at constructing a mosaic that displays all that is visible in the two images. In this paper all image points are represented by their homogeneous coordinates. Let $\mathbf{R}$ and $\mathbf{t}$ be the rotation and translation components of the spatial transformation between the two camera coordinate frames. Let $\mathbf{K}$ denote the intrinsic parameters of the camera (a 3×3 upper-triangular matrix). For any pair of matched pixels or features, $\mathbf{p}_1$ and $\mathbf{p}_2$ in the two images, we have the following equations [2,9]($\cong$ stands for the equality up to a scale factor):

$$\mathbf{p}_2 \cong \mathbf{KRK}^{-1}\mathbf{p}_1 + \frac{1}{z}\mathbf{Kt} \tag{1}$$

where z if the depth of the corresponding 3D feature. Since $\mathbf{KRK}^{-1}$ is the homography at infinity, and $\mathbf{Kt}$ represents the epipole $\mathbf{e}_2$ on the second image, Eq.(1) can be written as:

$$\mathbf{p}_2 \cong \mathbf{H}_\infty \mathbf{p}_1 + \frac{1}{z}\mathbf{e}_2$$

Thus the 2D motion of the feature or pixel can be decomposed into two components (Eq.(1)): (i) a planar component (the first term in the above equation), and (ii) a parallax component (the second term in the above equation). Note that this decomposition can be done with respect to any arbitary plane Π (real or virtual) in the environment [4]. The parallax is the image projection of the deviation of the associated 3D feature from the chosen plane.

The above can be written as

$$\mathbf{p}_2 \cong \mathbf{H}_\infty \mathbf{p}_1 + k\mathbf{e}_2 \tag{2}$$

where k can be considered as the projective depth of the point $\mathbf{p}_1$. In this case, the parallax is defined with respect to this plane.

While the planar transformation can be computed by choosing a physical or virtual plane in the scene, the second component depends on both the camera translation and the individual depth of the considered pixel.

From Eq.(2), one would notice that the knowledge of the correspondence ($\mathbf{p}_1$, $\mathbf{p}_2$) and the knowledge of the scalar k are equivalent in the sense that the knowledge of one yields that of the other. However, due to the intrinsic property of images that their texturedness might not permit a pixel-to-pixel correspondence for the whole image, the parallax component is not known for the majority of pixels even though it is known for some of them (the correspondences over some distinct features). As a consequence, one cannot simply use Eq.(2) to register the two images.

Since in the general case (an arbitrary scene imaged under an arbitrary camera motion) it is impossible to construct a 2D parametric transformation between two images, we make use of a third image.

We are thus left with three images. We call them as follows. The *reference image* R is the image whose viewpoint is where all image data are warped to, and where the final mosaic is constructed. The *target image* T is the image to be warped to the viewpoint of the reference image for constructing a mosaic there. The *intermediate image* I is a third image that is to assist the warping of the target image to the reference image; it should show something in common with the target image as well as with the reference image. It should be noticed that we have two parallax fields: (i) the one associated with the target-reference image pair, and (ii) the one associated with the target-intermediate image pair.

It is well known that uncalibrated images could be related to one another in the appropriate projective space. Suppose we use the projective space of the target image for reference. Each image will have a 3×4 projective mapping that maps that 3D projective space into the image plane. Let **M**, **M'**, and **M"** be the projective mappings associated with the target image, the intermediate image, and the reference image respectively. These three matrices can be easily inferred from a few point matches. We use the following.

Let **F** be the fundamental matrix between the target image and the intermediate image, and **e'** be the corresponding epipole in the intermediate image. It is well known that a solution for the mappings **M** and **M'** is given by [11]:

$$\mathbf{M} \cong \begin{bmatrix} & & 0 \\ \mathbf{I} & & 0 \\ & & 0 \end{bmatrix}, \quad \mathbf{M}' \cong \left[\mathbf{S}(\mathbf{e}')\mathbf{F} + \mathbf{e}'\mathbf{w}^{T} \quad \omega\mathbf{e}'\right]$$

for some 3-vector **w**, and a non-zero scale ω. Matrix **I** represents the 3×3 identity matrix, **S(e')** is the skew-symmetric matrix associated with the 3-vector **e'**.

Once **M** and **M'** are determined, the 3D projective coordinates of all feature matches present in the target image and the intermediate image can be recovered by a simple triangulation. The third mapping **M"** is then obtained by imposing that some reconstructed 3D points are re-projected to their matches in the reference image frame. This can be carried out using linear equations with at least 6 features matches across the three images. Therefore, computing the three projective mappings requires that (i) we have at least 8 matches between the target image and the intermediate image (**F**, **M**, **M'**), and (ii) we have at least 6 matches among the three images (**M''**). To get such matches we used the method developed by Zhang et al. [12] in our implementation.

Our method relies on the following fact. In general, for any pixel of the image to be registered (i.e., target image), if we know the 2D location of its correspondence in the intermediate image we are able to transfer this pixel to the reference image using a projective reconstruction followed by a projection, i.e., using the three projection matrices **M**, **M'**, and **M''**.

3 The n-Image Algorithm

Here we describe how we extend the 3-image algorithm for the case of an image stream.

It could be expected that if the 3-image algorithm is to be extended for an image stream, it would involve (1) iterations of processing over the various 3-image sets of the image stream, and (2) propagation of the intermediate mosaic results across the 3-image sets and at the end to the final mosaic frame. The issues are, how should the image stream be split into various 3-image sets, how the 3 images in each iteration be designated as the image frames *{T,R,I}* in the 3-image algorithm, and most importantly how the mosaic results can be accumulated across the iterations and be propagated to the mosaic frame. In this work we propose a solution to all these questions. The solution contains an orderly splitting of the image stream into 3-image sets as well as a systematic designation of the three images in each set as the *T,R,I* frames. Most importantly, it requires no explicit propagation of intermediate mosaic results across the iterations; all intermediate mosaickings happen at the final mosaic frame.

We first sample the image stream with an equal sampling. We refer to the most current image frame of all these sampled images as *S(t)*, where *t* represent the current time frame, and the second most current image frame as *S(t-1)*, and the third most current image frame as *S(t-2)*, and so on. We assume that the desired mosaic frame is the most current image frame *S(t)*. In other words, we are to warp all the previous images to the most current image frame and construct a mosaic there.

We begin the iterations from the most current end of the image stream. In the first iteration, we pick the images *S(t),S(t-2),S(t-3)* to apply the 3-image algorithm. *S(t)* is designated as the reference image frame *R*, *S(t-2)* as the target image frame *T*, and *S(t-3)* as the intermediate image frame *I*. *S(t-1)* is not used as the target image as very often it resembles the reference image *S(t)* too much and its information content does not justify the mosaicking effort. Using the 3 image algorithm, whatever visible in both *S(t-2)* and *S(t-3)* but not *S(t)* will be warped to *S(t)* to create an intermediate mosaic there. Notice that this mosaic of iteration 1 is constructed at the final mosaic frame *S(t)*. Notice also that in this iteration we have compute a mapping that allows any feature point in *S(t-2)* to be mapped to *S(t)*, the final mosaic frame.

In the second iteration, we pick the images *S(t-2),S(t-4),S(t-5)* to apply the 3-image algorithm, this time with *S(t-2)* as the reference image frame *R*, *S(t-4)* as the target image frame *T*, and *S(t-5)* as the intermediate image frame *I*. However, instead of constructing the intermediate mosaic for these 3 images at the *S(t-2)* frame, we first make use of the mapping from *S(t-2)* to *S(t)* we have calculated in the previous iteration, to transfer the initial set of feature points over the frames *S(t-2),S(t-4),S(t-5)* to a set over the frames *S(t),S(t-4),S(t-5)*. With this transfer, we have initial matches over not *S(t-2),S(t-4),S(t-5),* but *S(t),S(t-4),S(t-5)* instead. Treating *S(t)* as the new reference frame *R'* in the 3-image algorithm, we can construct the intermediate mosaic of this iteration not at the frame *S(t-2)* but the final mosaic frame *S(t)* directly.

The third and the other iterations over even earlier image frames are processed in the same fashion. The iterations are illustrated in Fig. 1. This way, propagation of intermediate mosaic results is no longer necessary, and all the intermediate mosaic results are constructed at the final mosaic frame. Through the iterations over the images up to the very first one a mosaic could be constructed.

4 The Uneven-Sampling n-Image Algorithm

The above n-image algorithm employs an even sampling strategy in picking the reference, target, and intermediate frames over the image stream. Even sampling (with respect to time) is not always desirable, as how dense we should have the video stream sampled at a particular section of it should depend upon how close the scene is toward the camera over that particular section. The closer the scene is toward the camera, the faster the visuals move in the image plane, and the denser the sampling should be so that the images to register are still not too different. On the other hand, the sampling should not be so dense that the reference, target, and intermediate images are actually all displaying the same data. Experimental results echo the argument, as we found that different sampling distance for the reference, target, and intermediate images in each iteration could result in mosaic of different quality. In this section we propose a way to allow the above n-image algorithm to have uneven sampling.

The key is whether we could have a measure of whether the picked images (for the reference, target, and intermediate frames) in any particular iteration are too close or too far apart. The main idea of the 3-image algorithm is first to perform an approximate projective reconstruction from the target image and the intermediate image, and then to project the projective coordinates so estimated to the reference image. We found that the error in projecting the projective coordinates (acquired from the target and intermediate image frames) to the reference image is a good measure.

Before performing the n-image algorithm on a sampled image sequence we have to choose, for each iteration, which image frames will be the target image, the intermediate image, and the reference image.

In the first iteration we still using the frames S(t),S(t-2) as the reference image and target image. But for the intermediate image, we choose a frame which shares the most suitable separation with the target image (frame S(t-2)). We decide which frame will be the best intermediate image by examining the distance between (a) the feature positions projected from the target image to the reference image, and (b) the original feature positions in the reference image. The image frame that contributes the least error will be chosen as the intermediate image of the iteration.

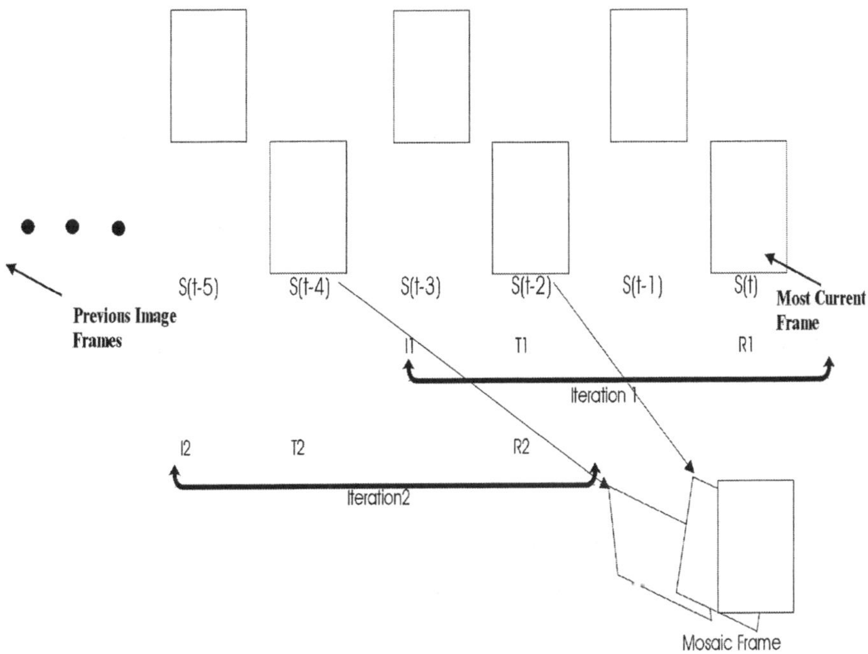

Fig. 1. Illustration of the *n*-image algorithm.

In the second iteration, we pick the frame S(t-2) as the reference image frame, and S(t-4) as the target image. Again we will examine the distance between (a) the feature positions projected from frame S(t-4) to frame S(t-2), and (b) the original feature positions in frame S(t-2), in deciding which frame will be the best intermediate image.

The third and the other iterations over even earlier image frames are processed in the same fashion. With decisions about which image frames are to be the target, intermediate, and reference images in each iteration, we could proceed with the n-image algorithm as detailed in the previous section.

5 Experiments

Here we provide some experimental results on real image data to illustrate the performance of the proposed methods. We have used the software "image-matching" of INRIA to obtain matches between any pair of images.

Fig. 2 shows the result of the uneven-sampling n-image algorithm over an image sequence of 15 images. The result is compared to the mosaic constructed from the software *Photo Vista* (by *livepicture*) [13]. It could be seen from the line alignment quality over the walls (on the right of the mosaic) that our proposed algorithm performs more accurate registration.

(a) Input Image Stream

(b) Mosaic result from Photo Vista, a method that employs global transformation

(c) Final mosaic using the uneven-sampling n-image algorithm

Fig. 2. Comparison between mosaic results of the uneven-sampling n-image algorithm, and of a method Photo Vista that employs global 2D transformation.

6 Conclusion and Future Work

We have presented two algorithms, one employing a fixed-sampling rate of the input video stream, the other an uneven sampling rate, for constructing mosaic from video stream that contains parallax. The work represents a first solution to the problem of constructing mosaic from image data with parallax, i.e., for arbitrary scene pictured under arbitrary camera motion.

Acknowledgment

The work described in this paper was partially supported by a grant from the Research Grants Council of the Hong Kong Special Administrative Region, China (Project No. CUHK4177/01E).

Reference

1. F. Dornaika and R. Chung. *Image Mosaicing under Arbitrary Camera Motion.* In Proc. of the 4th Asian Conference on Computer Vision, January 2000, pages 484-489.
2. O.Faugeras. *Three-Dimensional Computer Vision: a Geometric Viewpoint.* The MIT press, 1993.
3. R. I. Hartley. *Projective Reconstruction and Invariants from Multiple Images.* In IEEE Transactions on Pattern Analysis and Machine Intelligence, pages 1036- 1041, Vol 16, No. 10, October 1994.
4. R.Kumar, P.Ananadon, and K.Hanna. *Direct recovery of shape from multiple views: a parallax based approach.* In IEEE International Conference on Pattern Recognition, 1994.
5. C. Morimoto and R. Chellappa. *Fast 3D Stabilization and Mosaic Construction.* In Proc. of IEEE International Conference on Computer Vision and Pattern Recognition, pages 660-665, June 1997.
6. B. Rousso, S. Peleg, I. Finci and A. Rav-Acha. *Universal Mosaicing using Pipe Projection.* In Proc. of IEEE International Conference on Computer Vision, pages 945-952, January 1998.
7. H. S. Sawhney, S. Ayer and M.Gorkani. *Model-based 2D&3D Dominant Motion Estimation for Mosaicing and Video Representation.* In Proc. of IEEE International Conference on Computer Vision, pages 583-590, 1995.
8. H.S. Sawhney, S. Hsu and R. Kumar. *Robust Video Mosaicing through Topology Inference and Local and Global Alignment.* In Proc. of Fifth European Conference on Computer Vision, pages 103-119, June 1998.
9. A. Shashua. *Algebraic functions for recognition.* IEEE Trans. On Pattern Analysis and Machine Intelligence, pages 779-789, Volume 17, No.10, 1995.
10. H. Shum and R. Szeliski. *Systems and Experiment Paper: Construction of Panoramic Image Mosaics with Global and Local Alignment.* In International Journal of Computer Vision, pages 101-130, Vol 36, No. 2, February 2000
11. Z. Zhang. *Determining the epipolar geometry and its uncertainly: A review.* International Journal of Computer Vision, pages 43-76, Volume 27, No 2, 1998.
12. Z. Zhang, R. Deriche, O. Faugeras, and Q. –T. Luong. *A robust technique for matching two uncalibrated images through the recovery of the unknown epipolar geometry.* Artificial Intelligence Journal, pages 87-119, Volume 78, October 1995
13. www.livepicture.com

Multi-loop Scalable MPEG-2 Video Coders

Sławomir Maćkowiak

Poznań University of Technology
Institute of Electronics and Telecommunication
Piotrowo 3A, 60-965 Poznań, Poland
smack@et.put.poznan.pl
Phone: +48 61 66 52 171 Fax: +48 61 66 52 572

Abstract. In this paper, a structure of a hybrid highly scalable video encoder with fine granularity scalability in a scheme based on a modified version of the classic MPEG-2 scalable encoder is proposed. The assumption is that high level of compatibility with the MPEG video coding standards would be ensured. In particular, it is assumed that the low-resolution base layer bitstream is fully compatible with the MPEG-2 standard. The proposed scalable coder exhibits good satisfactory coding performance. These results are much better than those usually obtained for standard scalable profiles of MPEG-2.

Keywords: MPEG-2, scalable video coding, spatio-temporal scalability, fine granularity scalability

1 Introduction

Video and multimedia communication services have been developing rapidly in the last years. Their availability depends strongly on communication network infrastructure. High bitrates needed for video transmission impose severe requirements on communication networks. The existing networks are very inhomogeneous. Links are characterized by different bitrates, by different error rates, by different levels of Quality of Service (QoS). Different levels of Quality of Service are often related to different available transmission bitrates.

On the other hand, service providers demand the data to be broadcasted only once to a group of users accessed via heterogeneous links. Different networks are indeed different groups of users who have varying expectations. The same content may reach different group of users. For this purpose, the transmitted bitstream should be partitioned into some layers.

Scalability of video means the ability to achieve a video of more than one resolution or quality simultaneously. Scalable video coding involves generating a coded representation (bitstream) in a manner that facilitates the derivation of video of more than one resolution or quality from this bitstream.

For a given overall decoded video quality, scalable coding is not acceptable in common applications, if the bitrate is significantly greater than the bitrate achieved in single-layer coding.

The existing video compression standard MPEG-2 [1,2] defines scalable profiles, which exploit classic Discrete Cosine Transform-(DCT)-based schemes with motion

N. Petkov and M.A. Westenberg (Eds.): CAIP 2003, LNCS 2756, pp. 262–269, 2003.

compensation. Unfortunately, spatial scalability as proposed by the MPEG-2 coding standard is inefficient because the bitrate overhead is too large. Additionally, the solutions defined in MPEG-2 do not allow flexible allocation of the bitrate. There exists a great demand for flexible bit allocation to individual layers, i.e. for fine granularity scalability (FGS) [3], which is also already proposed for MPEG-4, where the fine granular enhancement layers are intraframe encoded.

The scalability is expected to find many applications. The goal of scalable coding is to provide interoperability between different services and to flexibly support receivers characterized by different display capabilities. For example, flexible support of multiple resolutions is of particular importance in interworking between High Definition Television (HDTV) and Standard Definition Television (SDTV), in which case it is important for a HDTV receiver to be compatible with a SDTV application. Compatibility of the receivers can be achieved by means of scalable coding of the HDTV source. Moreover, the transmission of two independent bitstreams to the HDTV and SDTV receivers can be avoided.

The importance of scalability is being more and more recognized as more attention is paid to video transmission in error-prone environments, such as wireless video transmission systems [4]. A video bitstream is error-sensitive due to extensive employment of variable-length coding. A single transmission error may result in a long, undecodable string of bits. It has been shown that an efficient method of improving transmission error resilience is to split the coded video bitstream into a number of separate bitstreams (layers) transmitted via channels with different degrees of error protection. The base layer is better protected, while the enhancement layers exhibit a lower level of protection. A receiver is able to reproduce at least low-resolution pictures if Quality of Service decreases.

In this paper, a structure of a hybrid highly scalable video encoder with fine granularity scalability in a scheme based on a modified version of the classic MPEG-2 scalable encoder coder is proposed. The goal is to achieve total bitrate of all layers of scalable coding possibly close to the bitrate of single-layer coding. The assumption is that high level of compatibility with the MPEG video coding standards would be ensured. In particular, it is assumed that the low-resolution base layer bitstream is fully compatible with the MPEG-2 standard.

2 Spatio-Temporal Scalability

Most scalability proposals are based on one type of scalability. The universal scalable coding has to include different types of scalability [5]. A single scalable video technique cannot serve a broad range of bitrates in networks (e.g. from a few kbps to several Mbps) or a wide selection of terminals with different characteristics.

Among various possibilities, the combination of spatial and temporal scalability called spatio-temporal scalability seems very promising [13]. Spatio-temporal decomposition allows to encode the base layer with a smaller number of bits because the base layer corresponds to reduced information. Here, the term of spatio-temporal scalability describes a functionality of video compression systems where the base layer (low resolution layer) corresponds to frames with reduced spatial and temporal resolution. An enhancement layer (high resolution layer) is used to transmit the information needed for restoration of full spatial and temporal resolution. Fig. 1 shows an example of a video sequence structure obtained after spatio-temporal decomposition, for three layers. For the sake of simplicity, spatio-temporal scalability will be reviewed for the simplest case of a two-layer encoder, i.e. a system that produces one low resolution bitstream and one high resolution bitstream.

Spatio-temporal scalability has been proposed in several versions, in particular:

- with 3-D spatio-temporal subband decomposition [6-8],
- with 2-D spatial subband decomposition and partitioning of B-frames data [8,9],
- exploiting as reference frames the interpolated low resolution images from the base layer [10,11].

The following basic video sequences are processed in the presented encoder:

- The low resolution sequence with reduced picture frequency and reduced horizontal and vertical resolution.
- The high resolution sequence with original resolutions in time and space.

The advantage of this solution is that the low resolution layer is an independently coded layer and does not use any information from the other layer.

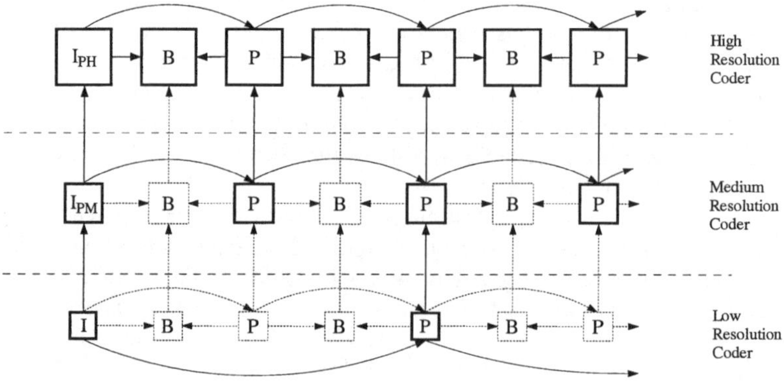

Fig. 1. Exemplary structure of the video sequence.

Temporal scalability is achieved using bi-directionally predicted frames, or B-frames. B-frames are disposable, since they are not used as reference frames for the prediction of any other frames. This property allows B-frames to be discarded without destroying the ability of the decoder to decode the sequence and without adversely affecting the quality of any subsequent frames, thus providing temporal scalability.

In this paper, temporal resolution reduction is achieved by partitioning the stream of B-frames: every second frame is skipped in the low resolution layer.

The choice of the spatial decimator and interpolator has substantial impact on the overall coding efficiency. In the experiments, for decimation, an FIR lowpass zero-phase 7-tap filter has been applied. Of course, these are only exemplary filter parameters that have been applied for the experiments described in this document. One can use other filters providing some trade-off between aliasing attenuation and spatial response length.

3 Coder Structure

The proposed encoder consists of a low resolution encoder and a high resolution encoder (Fig. 1). The low resolution encoder is implemented as a motion-compensated hybrid MPEG-2 encoder of the Main Profile@Main Level (MPEG-2 MP@ML).

The high resolution encoder is a modification of the MPEG-2 encoder. The motion-compensated predictor employed in the high resolution layer uses a modified prediction proposed by Łuczak for B-frames [10,11]. As an extension to the MPEG-2 compression technique, in the modified prediction those B-frames which correspond to B-frames from the base layer can be used as reference frames for predicting other B-frames in the enhancement layer.

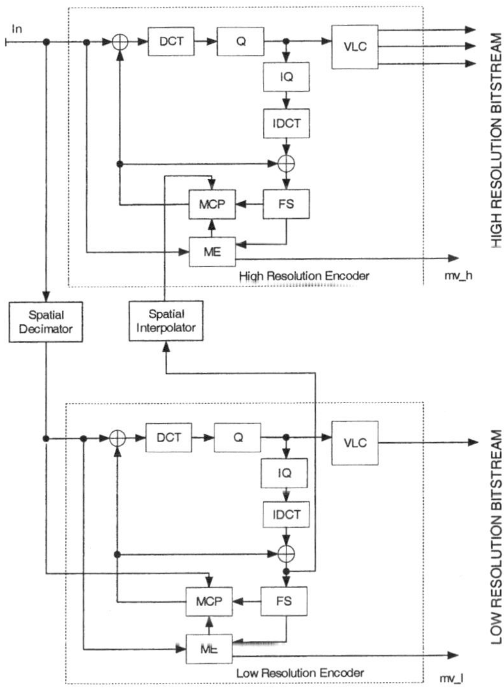

DCT Discret cosine transform
Q Quantization
IQ Dequantization
IDCT Inverse discret cosine transform
FS Frame memory
MCP Motion-compensated predictor
ME Motion estimator
VLC Variable length encoder

Fig. 2. General coder structure.

High efficiency of scalable encoding requires using some information from the base layer in the high resolution encoder. The high resolution layer encoder uses the interpolated decoded frame from the base layer in the prediction of the full resolution frame. It is assumed that the base layer represents a video signal with half the spatial resolution. Therefore one macroblock in the base layer corresponds to four macroblocks in the enhancement layer.

The proposed encoder applies independent motion compensation loops in all layers [13]. The motion vectors mv_b for the low resolution frames are estimated independently from the mv_e, which are estimated for the high resolution images.

Since every second frame is skipped in the low resolution encoder, motion estimation and compensation processes in the low and high resolution layers are performed for the frames from different time moments.

Two independent motion estimation and compensation processes yield the best results because due to the estimation and compensation in the low resolution layer, there is coarse motion compensation for slowly moving objects in the high resolution layer. The second motion estimation and compensation give more precise prediction.

4 Fine Granularity Scalability with Motion Compensation

Fine granularity is obtained by partitioning transform coefficients between layers. Except from headers and motion vectors, the bitstreams can be arbitrarily split into layers and multi-layer fine granularity can be achieved [13]. All header data and the enhancement motion vectors mv_h may be treated as basic granules [11]. The next granules are constituted by DCT coefficients that are encoded as (run, level) pairs, as described in the MPEG-2 standard. The lower layer contains N_m first (run, level) pairs for individual blocks. The control parameter N_m influences bit allocation to layers. The bitrates in subsequent layers can be controlled individually. To some extent, nevertheless, each additional layer increases the bitrate overhead because at least slice headers should be transmitted in all layers in order to guarantee resynchronization after an uncorrected transmission error. The total bitstream increases by about 3% per each layer obtained using data partitioning.

The drawback of this strategy is accumulation of drift. Drift is generated by partitioning the high resolution bitstream. Moreover, when the enhancement layer bitstream is corrupted by errors during transmission, the enhancement layer DCT coefficients cannot be properly reconstructed due to the loss of DCT information. This causes drift between the local decoder and remote decoder. It means that the decoding process exploits only the base layer bitstream.

In some applications, drift is not a significant problem. In particular, the MPEG-2-related encoders mostly use relatively short independently coded Groups of Pictures (GOPs), thus preventing drift from significant accumulation. In the author's solution, drift accumulation is also reduced because the total bitstream is divided into two drift-free parts, i.e. the low and the high resolution bitstream. Drift propagates within one part only when fine granularity is applied to a given bitstream. Furthermore, drift in the high resolution part may be reduced by more extensive use of the low resolution images as reference.

5 Experimental Results

In order to evaluate compression efficiency, a verification model has been written in the C++ language and is currently available for progressive 4CIF (704 x 576), 50 Hz, 4:2:0 video test sequences. This software also provides an implementation of the MPEG-2 encoder, which has been cross-checked with the MPEG-2 verification model [12].

Simulations have been carried out for constant quality coding, for three bitrates, i.e. 3 Mbps, 4 Mbps and 5 Mbps, for non–scalable MPEG–2 coding of SDTV signals. In simulcast coding, each bitstream of video is associated with a certain resolution or quality and is encoded independently. Thus, any bitstream can be decoded by a single-layer decoder. The total bitrate required for transmission of encoded streams is the sum of bitrates of these streams.

The results from Figs 3,4 and 5 prove high efficiency of the two-layer encoder. With the same bitrate as in the MPEG-2 non-scalable profile, the proposed scalable encoder ensures almost the same quality. Bitrate overhead due to scalability is about 0% - 18%.

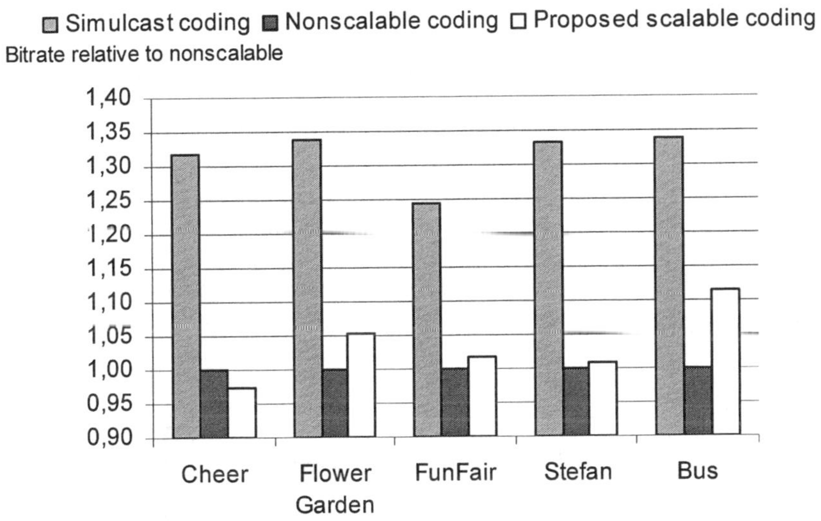

Fig. 3. Approximate bitrate comparison for scalable, nonscalable (single-layer) and simulcast coding at 3 Mbps for non–scalable MPEG–2 coding of SDTV signal.

6 Conclusion

Described is a modified MPEG-2 scalable codec with fine granularity scalability. The basic features of the two-loop coder structure are:

- mixed spatio-temporal scalability with fine granularity scalability,
- independent motion estimation for each motion-compensation loop, i.e. for each spatio-temporal resolution layer,
- BR/BE-frame structure.

The scalable coder exhibits good satisfactory coding performance. These results are much better than those usually obtained for standard scalable profiles of MPEG-2. Scalable coder complexity is similar to that of the simulcast structure.

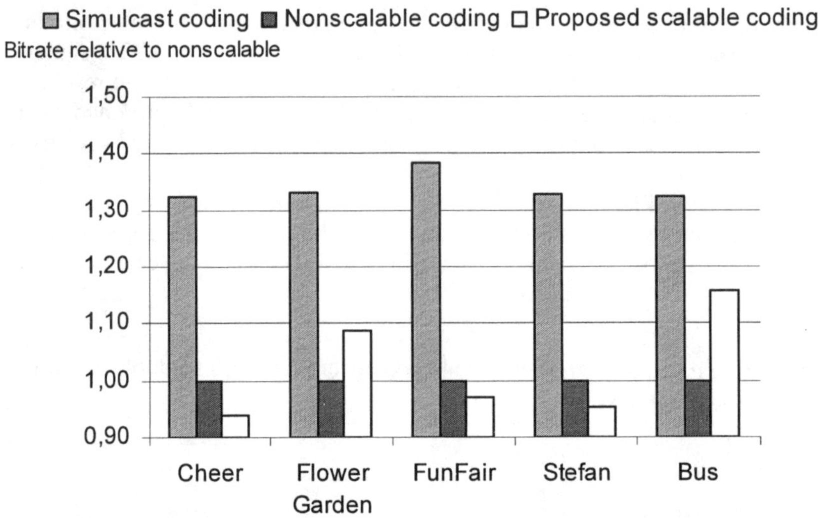

Fig. 4. Approximate bitrate comparison for scalable, nonscalable (single-layer) and simulcast coding at 4 Mbps for non–scalable MPEG–2 coding of SDTV signal.

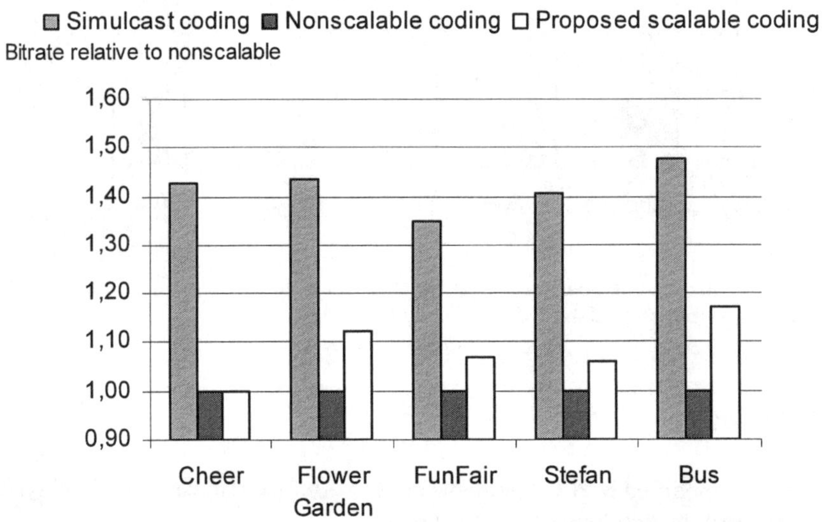

Fig. 5. Approximate bitrate comparison for scalable, nonscalable (single-layer) and simulcast coding at 5 Mbps for non–scalable MPEG–2 coding of SDTV signal.

References

1. ISO/IEC IS 13818-2 / ITU-T Rec. H.262, "Generic coding of moving pictures and associated audio, part 2: video", November 1994.
2. Haskell B.G., Puri A., Netravali A.N., Digital video: an introduction to MPEG-2, New York, Chapman & Hall, September 1996.

3. Li W. "Overview of Fine Granularity Scalability in MPEG-4 Video Standard", IEEE Transactions on Circuits and Systems for Video Technology, Vol. 11 Issue: 3, pp. 301 - 317, March 2001.
4. Girod B., Färber N., "Wireless Video", in Reibman A., Sun M.-T. (eds.), Compressed Video over Networks, Marcel Dekker, 2000.
5. Ohm J.-R., Li W., Ling F., Chun K.-W., Li S., Wu F., Zhang Y.-Q., van der Schaar M., Jiang H., Chen X., Vetro A., Sun H., Wollborn M., "Summary of Discussions on Advanced Scalable Video Coding", ISO/IEC JTC1/SC29/WG11 M7016, Singapore, March 2001.
6. Taubman D. and Zakhor A., "Multirate 3-D subband coding of video", IEEE Trans. Circ. Syst. Video Techn., vol. 3, pp. 572-588, September 1994.
7. Kim B.-J., Xiong Z., Pearlman W.A., "Low Bit-Rate Scalable Video Coding with 3-D Set Partitioning in Hierarchical Trees (3-D SPIHT)", IEEE Transactions on Circuits and Systems for Video Technology, Volume: 10, No. 8, December 2000.
8. Domański M., Łuczak A., Maćkowiak S., Świerczyński R., "Hybrid coding of video with spatio-temporal scalability using subband decomposition", Signal Processing IX: Theories and Applications, pp. 53-56, Typorama, 1998.
9. Domański M., Łuczak A., Maćkowiak S., "Spatio-Temporal Scalability for MPEG", IEEE Transactions on Circuits and Systems for Video Technology, Vol. 10, No. 7, pp. 1088-1093, October 2000.
10. Domański M., Łuczak A., Maćkowiak S., "On improving MPEG Spatial Scalability", Proceedings of the IEEE International Conference on Image Processing ICIP'2000, Vancouver, pp. II-848 - II-851, 2000.
11. Domański M., Maćkowiak S., "Modified MPEG-2 Video Coders with Efficient Multi-Layer Scalability", Proceedings of the IEEE International Conference on Image Processing ICIP'2001, vol. II, pp. 1033-1036, Thessaloniki, 2001.
12. MPEG Software Simulation Group, MPEG-2 Encoder Decoder version 1.2, July 19, 1996, ftp://ftp.mpeg.org/pub/mpeg/mssg.
13. Maćkowiak S., "Scalable Coding of Digital Video", Doctoral dissertation, Poznań University of Technology, Poznań 2002.

Multimedia Simulation of Colour Blindness and Colour Enhancement Assisted Colour Blindness

Chanjira Sinthanayothin and Suthee Phoojaruenchanachai

National Electronics and Computer TEchnology Center (NECTEC)
112 Science Park, Tumbon.Klong 1, Amphur Klong Luang, Pathumthanee 12120, Thailand
{pooh,Suthee}@notes.nectec.or.th

Abstract. This paper presents the development of a multimedia simulation of colour blindness and proposes a colour enhancement technique on streaming data such as a video source or multimedia files. With the red-green colour perception difficulties, the ISH model has been used to develop the algorithms. The simulator and colour enhancement have been tested by colour-blind people and compared to existing simulators for colour-blindness. Multimedia applications based on these techniques will be able to develop the creation of advanced digital multimedia services and distribute activities in the areas of telecommunications and TV broadcasting.

1 Introduction

This paper proposes a multimedia simulation of how sufferers from colour-blindness perceive colours on a Visual Display Unit (VDU). Approximately 5% to 8% of the population have some sort of colour-blindness [1]. The world looks differently to these people because they often find it difficult to separate red and green or unable to see the same colours as people who do not suffer from colour blindness. It is sometimes difficult for colour-blinded people to live in the world with safety such as the problem of the traffic light. The environment and temperature can also effect the perception of colours. In order to solve the problem, people with colour blindness have to use their experiences to predict and decide for the coming events. Therefore, the assistance of multimedia colour enhancement can help a colour blinded person to gain more experiences in order to separate the red and green colour in a video or multimedia file where the clip mimics real events. With the algorithm described in this paper, you will discover how the world appears as a colour-blinded person based on video technology. With this knowledge, this paper also intends to present a colour enhancement technique to assist colour-blinded people to watch a movie or video. Indeed the researchers from Stanford University have developed the techniques called *Vischeck* and *Daltonized*, which simulates colour-blind vision and corrects an image for a colour-blind viewer [2], respectively, but both techniques have been applied on still images while the technique described in this paper is applied on multimedia data. Both Vischeck and Daltonized cannot be found in any publication yet, hence nobody

N. Petkov and M.A. Westenberg (Eds.): CAIP 2003, LNCS 2756, pp. 270–277, 2003.

Fig. 1. Computerized simulation of colour blindness and Colour enhancement assisted colour blindness for multimedia

knows exactly how to apply those techniques. Sinthanayothin [3] has also developed simulations of colour-blind vision and colour enhancement techniques on still images. The ideas implemented in these techniques are innovative because there has been no publication related to this work.

2 Methods

For this research, four windows are designed in a program shown in Figure 1. The first window shows an online multimedia data stream; the second window shows the colour enhancement of the first window; the third window shows the colour blind simulation of the first window; and the last window shows the colour-blind simulation of the second window. In order to manipulate the multimedia source, the copy-rect feature is used to allow an existing rectangle of video stream data (the first window) to be copied and manipulated into new locations (the second through to the fourth window). In order to apply the video processing on the video stream, the process of colour manipulation must be fast. From the previous study [3], the method to calculate and manipulate the colour for colour-blind vision is to perform one-to-one colour matching. The size of arrays must be large enough to carry out this method for colour enhancement (the second window), colour-blind simulation (the third window) and colour-blind simulation on the enhanced windows (the fourth window). However, the dimensioning of an array for 16 million colours (256 x 256 x 256 colours) is greater than its maximum allowable value causing some other memory related error message. Therefore the one-to-one matching method used for images cannot be applied to video data. In order to solve the problem, the data set was reduced to Equation 1-3.

$$R' = F_{CB}(R,G) \quad ; B = 192 \tag{1}$$

$$G' = F_{CB}(R,G) \quad ; B = 192 \tag{2}$$

$$B' = (F_{CB}(R,B) + F_{CB}(G,B))/2 \quad ; B = 64 \tag{3}$$

Where (R,G,B) represents the colour value of the original data, (R', G', B') represents the colour value after manipulation. F_{CB} is a manipulation function, which is a colour enhancement function for the second window, and a colour blind simulation function of the first and second for the third and fourth window respectively. Equations 1 and 2 can be explained as follows. First the image of size 256x256 pixels is created, the blue value is constant at 192 while the red value is increased from 0 to 255, which follows the position from left to right, and the green value is increased from 0 to 255, which follows the position from top to bottom, respectively. Then the manipulation techniques are applied to this image as explain later in this paper. The image after transformation gives a value of R' and G', which depends on R and G. For the Equation 3, the same technique is applied but results in a different image. For F_{CB}(R,B) on an image size of 256x256 pixels, the green value is constant at 64 while the red value is increased from 0 to 255, which follows the position from left to right, and the blue value is increased from 0 to 255, which follows the position from top to bottom, respectively. F_{CB}(G,B) on an image size of 256x256 pixels, the red value is constant at 64 value while the green value is increased from 0 to 255, which follows the position from left to right, and the blue value is increased from 0 to 255, which follows the position from top to bottom, respectively. Therefore, for each manipulation technique, the new value of (R', G', B') can be mapped from the original value (R, G, B). In this paper, three manipulation techniques (F_{CB}) are presented as follows:

1. Colour enhancement assisted colour blindness (presented in the second window).
2. Computerised simulation of colour blindness on the original data (presented in the third window).
3. Computerised simulation of colour blindness on enhanced data (presented in the fourth window).

Both techniques, computerised simulations of colour blindness and colour enhancement assisted colour blindness, can be explained in the following two sections.

2.1 Computerized Simulation of Colour Blindness (F_{CB}: RGB -> R'G'B')

Normally, the RGB (Red-green-Blue) colour cube is used to represent image colours. However, in this paper, the ISH (Intensity-Saturation-Hue) model has been used instead to understand colour appearance due to saturation and hue, where both are closely related to the way we describe colour perception. For the colour-blind simulation method, firstly, the RGB colour model has been transform into ISH model [4].

In order to simulate colour blindness, the saturation value is multiplied to the function curve (R(H)) which runs from 0 to 1 and can be calculated with Equation 4. The R(H) curve is shown in Figure 2(A), where the horizontal axis of the curve is the original hue (h) value ranging from 0° to 359°. The vertical value is the ratio function which is necessary for the multiplication with the original saturation (S) value to form a new set of saturation values (S').

$$R(h) = 1 - Ae^{-\left(\frac{h-x_1}{\sigma}\right)^2} - Be^{-\left(\frac{h-x_2}{\sigma}\right)^2} - Be^{-\left(\frac{360+(h-x_2)}{\sigma}\right)^2} \quad (4)$$

With the assumption that the cyan and red-magenta colours are unsaturated similar to the grey colour, the following parameters can be set to Equation 4: A = 1.0, B = 0.8, $x_1 = 180$, $x_2 = 330$ and $\sigma^2 = 800$.

The hue parameter is shifted and reallocated to the new range because this parameter represents the red appearance. In order to shift and reallocate the new range of the hue value, the transformation curve shown in Figure 2(B) is used. The defect function curve comes from the assumption that all pixels have the hue value in the range 45 to 240 (yellow to blue). With this assumption, the defect function curve proposed in this paper can be calculated by using the function described by Equation 5 and has been shown in Figure 2(B).

Equation (5):

$$h = x_1 + (x_2 - x_1)e^{-\left(\frac{h-x_2}{\sigma}\right)^2} + (x_2 - x_1)e^{-\left(\frac{h-x_3}{\sigma}\right)^2} \quad (5A)$$

Where $x_1 = 45$, $x_2 = 180$, $x_3 = 325$ and $\sigma^2 = 20$.

The equation above applies when the hue value is less than 180 or greater or equal than 330, otherwise the hue value will be:

$$h = x_0 + \sqrt{(R^2 - (h - y_0)^2)} \quad (5B)$$

Where the parameters were calculated by fitting the three points ((180, 180), (240, 240), (360,180)) as part of a circle, which has a radius R and centre at the co-ordinate (x_0, y_0), respectively.

Finally, the new range of hue and saturation are applied and combined with the original intensity, then converted back to R'G'B' for display. Using the technique described above, the red and green colour will be difficult to separate simulating how a colour-blinded person would see.

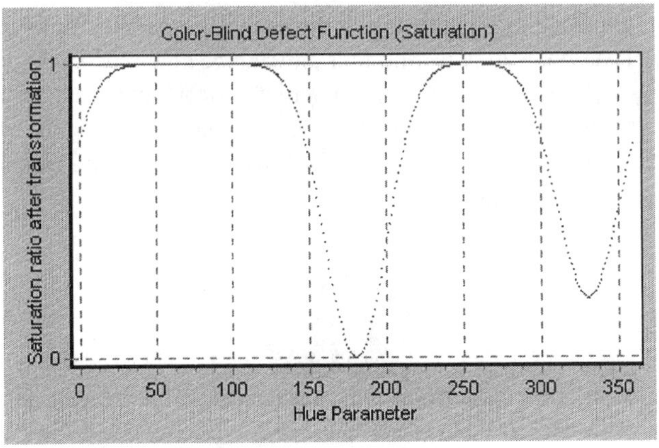

Fig. 2(A). Saturation ratio for Colour-blind simulation

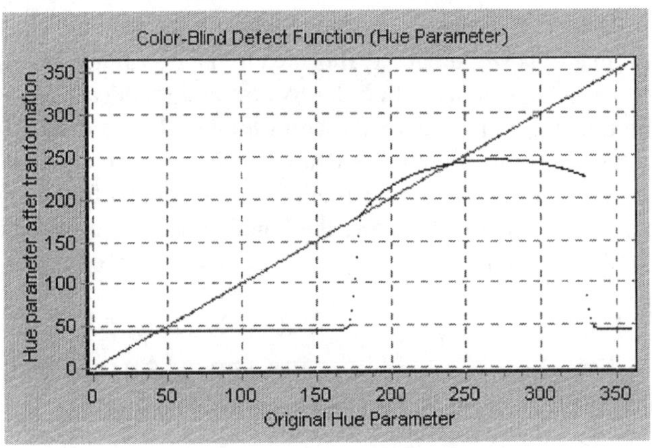

Fig. 2(B). Hue transformation function

Fig. 2. Simulation function of colour blindness on Saturation and Hue parameters

2.2 Colour Enhancement Assisted Colour Blindness (F_{CB}: RGB -> R'G'B')

With the assistance of colour enhancement, colour-blinded people can use the same technique but applied to a different curve as shown in Figure 3. Saturation has been increased as illustrated by the curve in Figure 3(A). The horizontal axis of the curve is the original saturation value ranging from 0 to 255. The vertical axis is the saturation value after the transformation with the saturation function curve (green curve). By fitting the three points ((0, 0), (M_x, M_y), (255,255)) as part of circle, the saturation function can be calculated similar to Equation 2(B). With this technique, saturation is enhanced to give a higher colour.

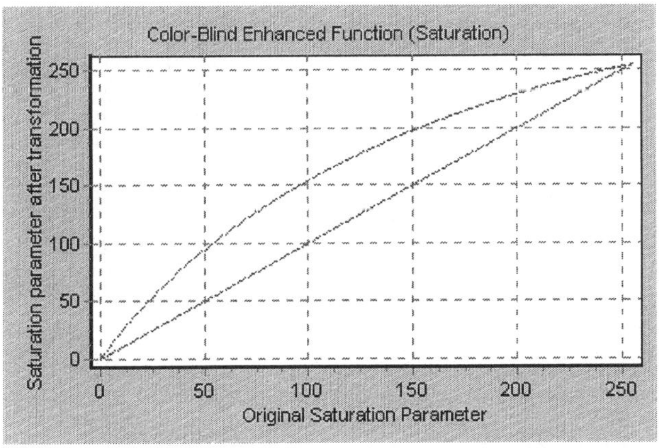

Fig. 3(A). Saturation Transformation function

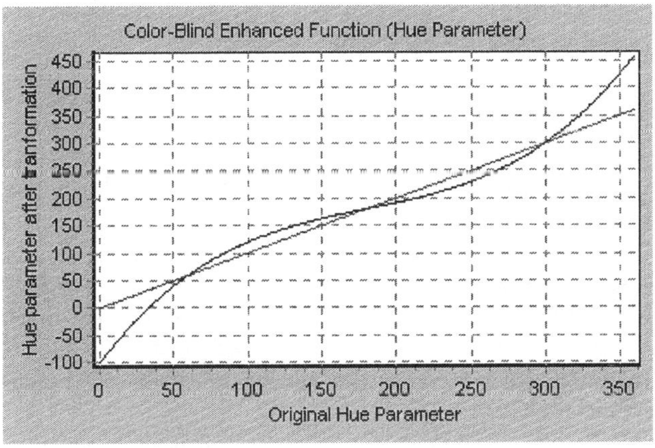

Fig. 3(B). Hue transformation function

Fig. 3. Contrast functions assisted Colour blindness on Saturation and Hue parameters

For the hue parameter, the range of hue is expanded by the transformation curve shown in Figure 3(B). The horizontal axis of the curve is the original hue value ranging from 0° to 359°. The vertical axis is the hue value after the transformation with the enhanced function curve (blue curve). The curve proposed in this paper can be calculated by using the third degree polynomial function, described by Equation 6, fitting on the four co-ordinates ((0, -100), (180, 180), (300, 300), (360, 400)) as shown in Figure 3(B). For hue values higher than 360 and less than 0 are rounded to zero and rounded up to 360, respectively.

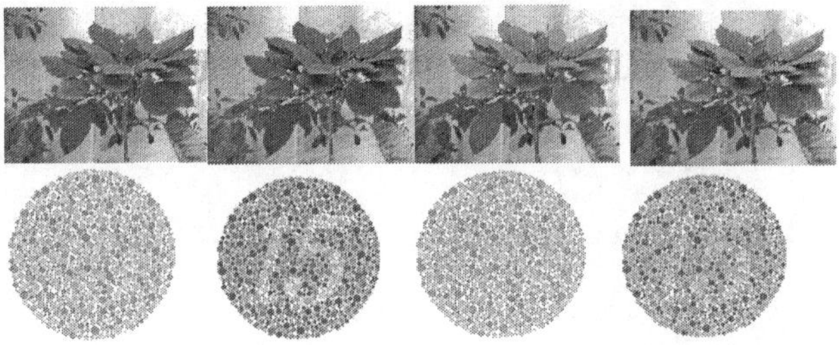

Fig. 4(A). The result of computerized simulation of colour blindness and colour enhancement with the technique in this paper

Fig. 4(B). The result of Vischeck (colour blindness simulation) and Daltonized (colour correction) techniques

Fig. 4. Comparison of colour blindness simulation and colour enhancement results to the Vischeck and Daltonized on a normal picture and Ishihara pattern. The first column shows the original image, the second column shows the enhanced images, the third column shows the simulation of colour blindness of first column and the last column shows the enhanced images of the second column respectively.

$$y = a_0x^3 + a_1x^2 + a_2x + a_3 \tag{6}$$

The result from the algorithm has been tested by a normal person and colour-blinded person and compared to the Vischeck colour blindness simulator.

3 Results

The colour-blind simulation was compared against the Ishihara test for colour blindness. The simulation has shown that the numbers on the test patterns disappear in accordance to the colour blinded person observation. The result was also confirmed by a colour-blinded person who did not pass the Ishihara colour-blind test. With the colour enhancement technique, the person succeeded in reading the number on each pattern. The image after enhancement was also applied to the Vischeck simulator and the simulation algorithm in this paper, both simulators have shown that the number can still be recognised.

The results from the comparison of the Vischeck and Daltonized techniques with the techniques discussed in this paper are shown in Figure 4. The Computerised simulation of colour blindness of both techniques appear to be the same while the colour enhancement or correction technique using in Daltonized lost some detail in the green value area while the technique in this paper can show this detail. With the technique applied on multimedia data, people with colour-blind vision can obtain more information by watching the enhanced window.

The speed of the program at this time is restricted as follows: the first windows shows the data stream with speeds greater than 15 f/s, and the rest of the windows show the result of manipulation with the rate of approximately 3 f/s on an AMD 650 MHz, 256 MB RAM computer. Each window shows a video data size of 400x300 pixels. The program also presents a new function: it displays the (R,G,B) value of the real data during a mouse-over action on the second window which is useful for a normal vision person to understand the colour before enhancement.

4 Conclusion

This paper has proposed a video manipulation system that simulates the colour-blind vision and enhances the colour assisted colour blindness in a video frame. The result has been tested with colour-blinded people who have evaluated that they can see more information from watching the enhanced multimedia. The multimedia manipulation of colour could be processed to achieve higher frame rates – this is currently work in progress.

Acknowledgement

We acknowledge the organization in Thailand, the National Electronics and Computer Technology Center (NECTEC) for the financial support.

References

1. Waggoner TL. "What Is Colour-blindness and the Different Types?" http://members.aol.com/ nocolorvsn/color2.htm
2. Dougherty R, Wade A. "Vischeck simulates colour-blind vision." http://www.vischeck.com/
3. Sinthanayothin C, Computerised Simulation of Colour-Blind and Colour Enhancement Assisted Colour-Blind. ITC-CSCC2002 Proceeding Volume 2 (International Technical Conference on Circuits/Systems, Computers and Communications) page 1149-1152.
4. Gonzalez RC, Woods RE. *Digital Image Processing*. Addison-Wesley Publishing Company, Reading 1993;229-237,583-586.
5. Press WH, Flannery BP, Teukolsky SA, Vetterling WT. *Numerical Recipes in C* Cambridge University Press. 1991;p. 528-534

Coefficient Partitioning Scanning Order Wavelet Packet Algorithm for Satellite Images

Seong-Yun Cho[1] and Su-Young Han[2]

[1] Dept. of Digital Media, Anyang University
Anyang 5-dong, Manan-gu Anyang, Kyonggi-do, Korea, 708-113
scho@aycc.anyang.ac.kr

[2] Dept. of Electronic Engineeriing, Hanyang University
17 Haengdang-dong, Seongdong-Gu Seoul, Korea, 133-791
yejiwon@ihanyang.ac.kr

Abstract. A new embedded wavelet packet image coder algorithm is proposed for an effective image coder using correlation between partitioned coefficients. The new algorithm presents parent-child relationship for reducing image reconstruction error using a coefficient partitioning scanning order (CPSO). It is shown that the new algorithm achieves low bit rates and rate-distortion. It also demonstrates higher PSNR under the same bit rate. These results show that the encoding and decoding processes of the proposed coder are more accurate than SPIHT for texture images that include many high-frequency elements such as satellite photograph images. The experimental results imply the possibility that the proposed method can be applied to on-line image processing which require smaller file size and better resolution.

1 Introduction

In high altitude photograph images such as satellite photograph images, buildings and landscapes are usually represented as recursive textures. After FFT for these images as a preprocessing, it is notified that high frequency components are dominated. The wavelet packet transform usually shows better performance than the conventional wavelet transform in the processing of information which has high frequency component [1][2][3]. Contrary to the dyadic wavelet transform which recursively decomposes low frequency components, the wavelet packet transform is suitable for analyzing or presenting nonstationary signals such as texture images by its adaptability to each frequency band [4].

Many wavelet-based embedded image coders such as EZW (Embedded Wavelet Transform) [2], SPIHT (Set Partitioning In Hierarchical Tree) [5] have provided progressive coding properties. In spite of it simplicity, EZW algorithm has good bit rate distortion performance and the embedding characteristic that the large and major coefficients retransferred earlier than other ones. This characteristic is very helpful to progressive transmission. SPIHT has well known as an improved model of EZW. In opposition to EZW which decides transfer order

N. Petkov and M.A. Westenberg (Eds.): CAIP 2003, LNCS 2756, pp. 278–284, 2003.

using the dominant and subordinate pass, SPIHT decides transfer order more effectively using the LIP (List of Insignificant Pixel) and LIS (List of Insignificant Sets).

These two algorithms construct a tree with zero quantized coefficients using the relationship between bilateral bandwidths. In conclusion, it introduces efficient reduction of the amount of data which are sent to decoder. Because the hierarchical structure with multi-level resolutions is not clear in the wavelet packet, it is not easy to use the relationship between bilateral bandwidths. That is, in the wavelet packet, the parent-child relationship, which is used in the EZW or SPIHT, is not easy to maintain. Because the wavelet packet transformation should lose the multi-resolution structure of wavelet basis function, the zerotree method could not be directly introduced in the wavelet packet transform. That is, it is impossible to construct the tree that has its coefficients located in the same spatial relationship.

In this paper, a coefficient partitioning scanning order (CPSO) is newly defined using decomposition information, which is derived from wavelet packet decomposition. From this definition, a new wavelet packet image coder algorithm, which applies the zerotree by partitioning its coefficient, is developed. Parent-child relationships are defined in the packet-transformed coefficients depending upon its sub-band decomposition information and the essentiality of coefficients. From this relationship, CPSO is constructed. After partitioning the coefficients, each coefficient is quantized hierarchically and decoded.

2 Wavelet Packet Image Coder Algorithm

In this section, the newly defined CPSO (Coefficient Partition Scanning Order) is defined using the parent-child relationship (the relationship of identical space) based on the zerotree method.

2.1 Wavelet Packet Transform

Input images are transformed into wavelet packets using proper wavelet filters over full bandwidth and optimal basis functions are selected on the basis of entropy. Then, parent-child relationships are defined from the transformed coefficients depending upon its sub-band decomposition information and the essentiality of coefficients. From these relationships, the CPSO is constructed. After partitioning the coefficients, each coefficient is hierarchically quantized. Finally, we get the bit stream using entropy coder such as Huffman or Arithmetic coder.

2.2 CPSO (Coefficient Partition Scanning Order)

In the proposed algorithm, CPSO is defined as the next three conditions.

Condition 1. If child sub-band S is more decomposed than band P, which is related with the parent node, it does not have a child node. This bandwidth finds out the significant coefficients through the raster scan after finishing the P band threshold scanning as shown in the Figs. 1-a and 1-b. We call it CPSO0.

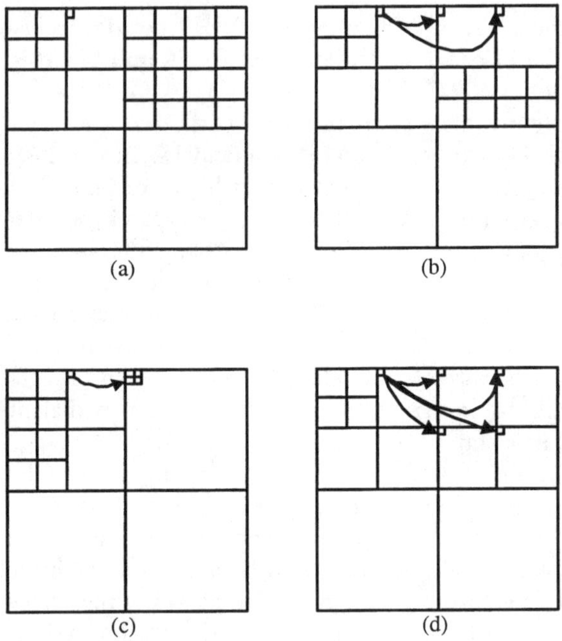

Fig. 1. Examples of CPSO in the wavelet packet transform; (a) example of CPSO0, (b) other example of CPSO0, (c) example of CPSO4, (d) example of CPSO1

Condition 2. If child sub-band S is not decomposed, it has 4 children nodes. It is described in Fig. 1-c. Equation (1) describes condition 2. We call it CPSO4.

$$\{D(x,y) \mid S(x+i,y+j),\ \text{where } i=0,1 \text{ and } j=0,1\}\,. \tag{1}$$

where $D(x,y)$ is the set of children nodes and $S(x,y)$ is a child node in sub-band.

Condition 3. If child sub-band S is decomposed into 4 sub-bands, each coefficient located in the same space of the sub-band becomes a child node. It is described in Equation (2) and Fig. 1-d. We call it CPSO1.

$$\{D(x,y) \mid S_k(x,y),\ \text{where } k=0,1,2,3\}\,. \tag{2}$$

where $D(x,y)$ is the set of children nodes and $S_k(x,y)$ is a child node in sub-band.

2.3 Packet Coder Algorithm Using CPSO

In most of wavelet packet transforms except top-down algorithm, the information, which indicates each band's decomposition, has to be transferred with transformed coefficients in a header format.

In this paper, during the coding process, the child node scheme of each coefficient is verified using this information and CPSO is extracted depending on these results. In this list of decomposition information *SM* (Split Mark), 1 is assigned for the decomposed band and 0 for the un-decomposed band.

Following is a pseudo code for the coding algorithm except the wavelet packet decomposition and the entropy coding. *DC* (The list of the detected coefficients) saves the coordinate of coefficient which has bigger absolute value than the specific threshold in *WC* (the list of waiting coefficients) and in *WCR* (the list of waiting coefficients root) used with the *SM*. The first threshold value T_0 for identifying a significant value is $T_0 = max\{c_{x,y}\}/2$. $c_{x,y}$ is a wavelet packet-transformed coefficient for the coordinate of spatial dimension $\{x, y\}$.

```
while (up to target compression ratio)
    while (each coefficient saved in WC)
        if |c_{x,y}| ≥ T_0
          then
                Output 1, output 1 or 0 for +/- bit,
                add coordinate to the list DC and delete from the WC
          else
                Output 0
        fi
    end
    while (each coefficient saved in WCR)
        if |c_{x,y}| ≥ T_0
          then
                Output 1 and determine scanning order in children
                nodes according to SM.
                if (CPSO0)
                   Add coordinate to the list WCR.
                fi
                if (CPSO1)
                   D(x, y) = { each coefficient located in same with x, y
                             { at S_k(x, y)
                fi
                if (CPSO4)
                   D(x, y) = { (2*x, 2*y), (2*x, 2*y+1)
                             { (2*x+1, 2*y),(2*x+1, 2*y+1)
                fi
                while (in D(x, y))
                      if |c_{x,y}| ≥ T_0
                        then
                              Output 1 and 1 or 0 for +/- bit,
                              add it to the DC.
                        else
                              Output 0, and it to the WC
                      fi
```

```
                        Determine scanning order in descendent nodes
                        according to SM.
                        According to CPSO, determine D(x, y)
                        and move the tree to the WCR
                    end
                else
                    Output 0
            fi
    end
end
```

3 Experiment and Results

The experiment process and the results are presented in this chapter. Two satellite images are chosen for experimental samples as shown in Fig. 2 (sample #1) and Fig. 3 (sample #2). These kinds of images are usually composed by simplified and recursive geometrical structures such as rectangular, circles, and lines due to high altitude view point. Applying the FFT to these images, it is found that satellite images contain a larger quantity of high frequency component than those of portrait images as shown Fig. 4. The wavelet packet decomposition has shown better performance at the image analysis which composed high frequency components [6].

Fig. 2. sample #1

Fig. 3. sample #2

For the wavelet packet decomposition in the experiment, 2D separable length-9-7 biorthogornal wavelet filters are used. The result of the proposed wavelet packet corder using CPSO algorithm is compared with those of conventional SPIHT algorithm. These results of experimental are summarized in Table 1 and Fig. 5 and Fig. 6.

The performances are compared between the proposed and SPIHT algorithm using bit rate and PSNR. The bit rates of the results are referred to the size of

(a) a satellite sample image

(b) lenna image

Fig. 4. FFT Comparision

Table 1. Results of the performance comparison between CPSO and SPIHT

Bit rate	Sample #1 (PSNR)		Sample #2 (PSNR)	
(bpp)	SPIHT	CPSO	SPIHT	CPSO
0.125	23.35	24.52	21.87	23.35
0.25	24.81	26.12	22.83	24.28
0.5	26.80	29.02	24.37	28.23
1.0	29.95	32.44	27.61	30.92

files, which obtained from cording procedure. As same as SPIHT, all of output data of coder indicate only 1 or 0. Therefore, the proposed algorithm can do bit operation for all of the output data and it can be reduced the file size more than the SPIHT. The bit per pixel unit against file size, including header information, is used for the performance of bit rate. The proposed algorithm shows 1 or 2 dB higher performance than SPIHT in the higher compression rates.

Because the parent-child relationship of wavelet packet cannot utilize multi-resolution structure that the wavelet transform does, the CPSO is applied to wavelet packet transform to overcome this problem in this research. The result in Table 1 shows that the image adaptability of wavelet packet transform using CPSO can sufficiently compensate the parent-child relations for the images which has high frequency components such as satellite photograph images.

4 Conclusions

Using the relationships between sub-bands, the new wavelet packet transform image coder algorithm using CPSO is proposed. The proposed algorithm demonstrates improving the image compression algorithm that uses the conventional wavelet transform. In the CPSO algorithm, the new parent-child relationship is

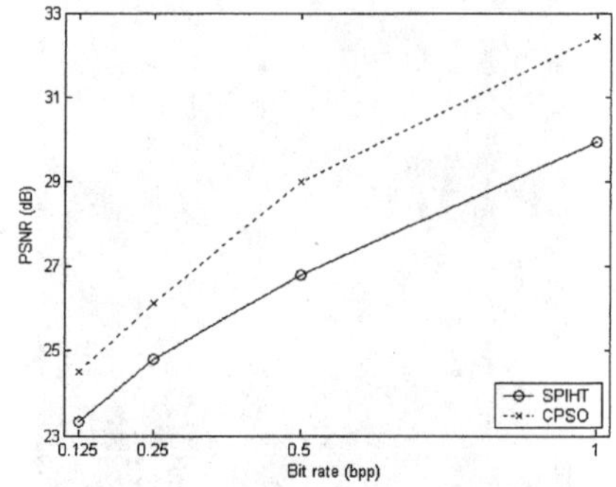

Fig. 5. PSNR of sample #1

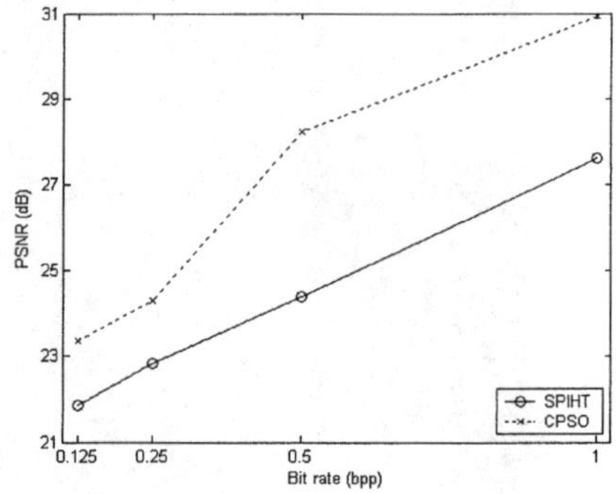

Fig. 6. PSNR of sample #2

extracted using the relationships between individual frequencies sub-bands at the wavelet packet transform, decide the coding order of coefficient to reduce image reconstruction error.

There are improvements in bit rate and distortion performance by decoding wavelet packet transform coefficient with the zerotree method. The experimental results demonstrate higher PSNR at the bit rate.

From these results, it is shown that the encoding and decoding processes of the proposed coder are simpler and more accurate than the conventional method for texture images, which include many high-frequency elements such as satellite photograph images.

It shows that the proposed algorithm has a great possibility to improve on-line image processing.

References

1. Ramchandran K., M. Vetterli: Best wavelet packet bases in a rate-distortion sense. IEEE Trans. on Image Processing, 2(2) (1993) 1760-1785
2. Shapiro J.: Embedded image coding using zerotree wavelet coefficients. IEEE Trans. on Signal Processing, 41 (1993) 3445–3462
3. Meyer J., A. Averbuch, J. Stromberg: Fast adaptive wavelet packet image compression. IEEE Trans. on Image Processing. (1998)
4. Pei-Yuan Huang, Long-Wen Chang: Digital Image Coding with Hybrid Wavelet Packet Transform. PCM 2001, LNCS 2195. (2001) 301–307
5. Said A., W. Pearlman: A new fast and efficient image codec based on set partitioning in hierarchical trees. IEEE Trans. on Circuits and Systems for Video Tech., 6 (1996) 243–250
6. Han S., C. Lim: Embedded wavelet packet image coder using set partitioning. Proc. of IEEE TENCON' 97, Brisbane, Australia. (1997)

Support Vector Machines for Road Extraction from Remotely Sensed Images

Neil Yager and Arcot Sowmya

School of Computer Science and Engineering
University of New South Wales, Sydney, NSW 2052, Australia
{nyager,sowmya}@cse.unsw.edu.au

Abstract. Support Vector Machines (SVMs) have received considerable attention from the pattern recognition community in recent years. They have been successfully applied to many classic recognition problems with results comparable or even superior to traditional classifiers such as decision trees, neural networks, maximum likelihood classifiers, etc. This paper presents encouraging experimental results from applying SVMs to the problem of road recognition and extraction from remotely sensed images using edge-based features.

1 Introduction

Road recognition from remotely sensed images is an important process in the acquisition and updating of Geographical Information Systems, and the automatic extraction of roads is an active area of research. RAIL is a road recognition system that has been under development by our group for a number of years. It serves as a framework to research new directions in machine learning, image understanding, and road recognition [1, 2].

A support vector machine (SVM) is a relatively new classification technique that has grown from the field of statistical learning theory. Despite its recent arrival, it has already proven itself to be a very powerful classifier.

There are two main motivations for incorporating SVMs into RAIL. First of all, SVM classifiers have yielded some excellent results in other application domains. However, at the time of writing there have been no results published on applying SVMs specifically to the problem of road extraction. Therefore, the results of these experiments will be of interest to the remote sensing and pattern recognition communities. Secondly, RAIL is not only a tool for investigating future directions in road extraction. RAIL uses a *meta-learning* framework to learn the strengths and weaknesses of different classification algorithms. Incorporating SVMs into the RAIL framework provides a broader range of base-level algorithms and promotes the development of the meta-learning research.

Section 2 of this paper provides a brief introduction to the field of statistical learning theory and support vector machines. Section 3 discusses some work that has already been done with SVMs in the remote sensing domain. Section 4 describes the RAIL system and the experimental setup, while Section 5 presents the results of the experiments.

N. Petkov and M.A. Westenberg (Eds.): CAIP 2003, LNCS 2756, pp. 285–292, 2003.

2 Support Vector Machines

The field of statistical learning theory was originally proposed by V. Vapnik [3]. The theory provides a robust framework for comparing different classifiers to determine which will give superior performance for a given problem and dataset. The basic idea is that a balance needs to be found between the complexity of a classifier and its performance on a particular training set.

Support Vector Machines (SVMs) are a classifier based on the principles of statistical learning theory. An excellent introduction to SVMs can be found in [4]. SVMs work by finding a hyperplane in the feature space that separates the positive and negative training samples. The *margin* of a hyperplane is the distance between the hyperplane and the closest vectors of each class (known as the *support vectors*). In Figure 1, Hyperplane A has a large margin and Hyperplane B has a small margin. It is known that a hyperplane with a large margin has a greater ability to generalize to unseen data than one with a small margin [3]. Therefore, an SVM finds the separating hyperplane with the largest margin.

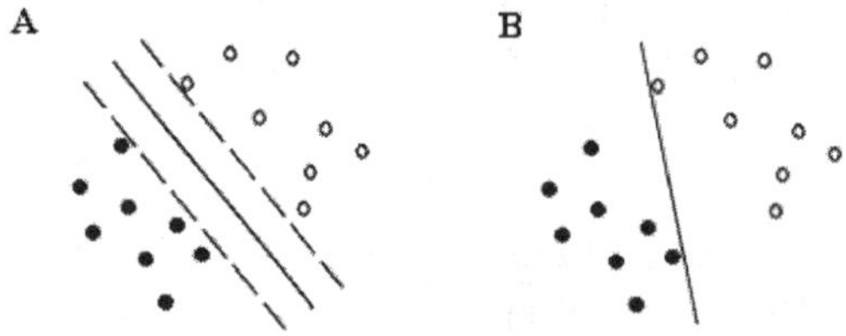

Fig. 1. Maximizing the Hyperplane Margin

When the training samples are not linearly separable in the feature space, *kernel functions* are used to map the training data to a feature space F with a much higher dimension via a nonlinear mapping $\Phi : \mathrm{I\!R}^N \mapsto F$. The optimal separating hyperplane is found in F and is mapped back to a nonlinear surface in the original feature space.

3 SVMs and Remotely Sensed Images

Not only are SVMs interesting from a theoretical viewpoint, they have also proved to be a very powerful classifiers in practice. However, due to the relatively recent arrival of SVMs, there has not yet been much experimentation in the remote sensing domain.

Land cover classification is one of the most important applications of remote sensing technology. It consists of segmenting an image into regions and categorizing the regions based on their land cover. This is one area in remote sensing where some SVM experiments have been conducted. Fukuda and Hirosawa have applied SVMs to land cover classification using polarimetric SAR data [5]. A more extensive assessment of SVMs for land cover classification is presented by

Huang et al [6]. These applications use multi-channel images and use low-level pixel values as the basis for feature extraction. Li et al. have used SVMs in an effort to detect bridges in remotely sensed images [7]. They also use pixel-based feature values. Perkins et al. present a system that uses genetic programming to select features for SVM classification of land cover [8].

4 SVMs and RAIL

The papers mentioned above use low-level features (such as pixel intensities or local textural features) for classification. This approach could very easily be adapted to the road extraction problem. However, using low-level pixel values as features is very similar to the existing approaches for land cover applications and would most likely produce similar results. Our experiments mark a significant departure from this approach, as our experiments use edge-based features extracted from the images.

Most knowledge-based road recognition systems systems use *a priori* heuristic rules to enable road recognition. These rules place explicit constraints on the road properties and scene content that can be successfully classified by the system. For example, a system that is designed to extract roads from rural scenes will perform poorly for city scenes since very different rules are required to distinguish the roads.

RAIL is an adaptive and trainable road recognition system. Starting with low-level objects, RAIL incrementally builds higher-level objects. The output from one level of classification is used as input to the next level. The levels of classification are:

1. Road Edges - Single edges that bound a road on one side.
2. Road Edge Pairs - Pairs of edges that enclose a segment of a road.
3. Linked Road Edge Pairs - Adjacent road edge pairs that form single, continuous roads.
4. Intersections - Road edge pairs that meet to form intersections.
5. Road Networks - Linked roads and intersections.

At each level in RAIL, several algorithms are available as potential classifiers. It is known that different classification algorithms have correspoding strengths and weaknesses. In other words, there is no known classifier that consistently outperforms all others. RAIL uses *meta-learning* to learn which algorithms work well in different situations. For example, it may be the case that the kNN clustering algorithm works very well for recognizing road edges in complicated city scenes, while SVMs are particularly well suited to classifying road edges in rural scenes. It is information like this that RAIL hopes to gain through meta-learning. The various algorithms are executed using images from a wide variety of different environments. The meta-learner uses inductive learning (the C4.5 learning algorithm) to derive rules about when the classification algorithms work well. When unlabeled images are input to the system, the rules are used to automatically select algorithms which will likely be successful at the different levels of classification.

C4.5 decision trees, kNN clustering and kMeans clustering have previously been incorporated into the RAIL framework. Adding SVMs to this suite of algorithms provides more data for learning at the meta-level. Therefore, adding SVMs to RAIL has significant benefits beyond determining their usefulness for road extraction.

4.1 Experiment Dataset

For the SVM experiments, a series of 6 images were used. Images 1 and 2 are of rural areas in France and consist of a single channel (grey scale intensities). The ground resolution is 0.45 m/pixel. Images 3-6 are extracted from a single image of Morpeth in rural Australia and have a similar resolution.

Information about the images is presented in Table 1. The 'Number of Edges' column shows the number of edges detected in the image by a Canny edge operator.

Table 1. Image Properties

	Image Dimensions	Number of Edges
Image 1	776 x 289	6087
Image 2	757 x 821	18660
Image 3	1500 x 848	33125
Image 4	1700 x 1300	50272
Image 5	1400 x 1200	46414
Image 6	1600 x 1100	51243

4.2 Experiment Design

The SVM experiments have been conducted for Level 1 and Level 2 classification in RAIL. The SVM implementation that was used for the experiments is SVM^{light} [1].

Level 1 – Road Edges. The edges in the images are found using a Canny edge detector. Edges that are adjacent are linked together, and are then segmented into smaller edges that are very close to being straight and have a maximum length of 50 pixels. The following features are used to classify edges as road edges or non-road edges:

Edge Length Road edges tend to be long since roads are straight and span large distances in the image. Edges from other artifacts in the image are often much shorter.

Edge Gradient The edge gradient is a measure of the change in image intensity at the edge. At an edge where a road meets its surrounding environment the gradient is usually high.

[1] The SVM^{light} software can be downloaded at http://svmlight.joachims.org/

For each image, sample road edges and non-road edges are selected. This data is used to train an SVM, and the SVM is used to classify all the edges. The edges retained by the SVM are then used as input to Level 2.

Level 2 – Road Edge Pairs. In Level 2 of RAIL, opposite road edges are paired to create road segments. The following features are used:

Pair Width This is the distance between the edge segments. Road pairs for a single road will have a consistent width along the length of the road. Conversely, arbitrary edge pairs will have widely varying widths.

Enclosed Intensity The enclosed intensity of two edges is the average intensity of the pixels between them. All pixels belonging to a road will tend to take on values from a small range.

Positive and negative edge pair samples from the image are selected and are used to train an SVM. This SVM is used to classify all possible edge pairs (from the Level 1 road edges).

For both Level 1 and Level 2, several other features were extracted from the image edge set. For example, for Level 2 bearing difference and length of center line were also computed for the edge pairs. However, the ones listed above were the only ones with a strong ability to discriminate between positive and negative samples, so were the only features used for classification.

5 Experiment Results

The metrics used to evaluate the results are *completeness* and *correctness*. Completeness is the percentage of actual road edges (or road pairs) that are detected by the SVM. Correctness is the percentage of road edges (or road pairs) labeled as positive by the SVM that are true positives. Alternate evaluation measures such as ROC curves display how a system's performance varies as a parameter or threshold is adjusted. There are multiple parameters in our system, but they are implicit in the SVM implementation and cannot be manually adjusted. A completeness and correctness value pair corresponds a single point on an unknown ROC curve.

RAIL road networks are built in stages, with the output from one stage used as the input to the next. This means that data discarded at one level will be lost forever. Therefore, it is very important that high completeness values are achieved at the lower levels. On the other hand, high correctness values are not as important because additional edges will be discarded at the higher levels.

In order to configure the SVMs, experiments with two kernel functions (polynomial and Gaussian) and various kernel parameters (eg. polynomial degree) were conducted. A polynomial kernel of degree 3 consistently gave the best results, therefore it was used for our Level 1 and Level 2 SVMs.

As shown in Table 2, on average about 95% of the edges are discarded by the Level 1 SVM. This is a significant decrease in the number of edges. However,

Table 2. Results of Level 1 Edge Classification

	Number of Edges	Classified Road Edges	Completeness	Correctness
Image 1	6,087	382	90.74	25.65
Image 2	18,660	762	83.20	26.64
Image 3	33,125	2516	80.86	10.41
Image 4	50,272	1314	87.35	33.64
Image 5	46,414	1724	86.13	11.89
Image 6	51,243	1206	89.01	6.72

Table 3. Results of Level 2 Edge Pair Classification

	Number of Pairs	Classified Road Pairs	Completeness	Correctness
Image 1	72,771	1579	90.74	34.88
Image 2	289,941	3405	81.15	34.86
Image 3	3,163,870	19,524	75.31	13.17
Image 4	862,641	17,712	87.13	43.65
Image 5	1,485,226	9,883	86.13	17.94
Image 6	726,615	3254	89.01	16.46

the completeness values remain fairly high, which is exactly the result one would hope for at this level of classification. Table 3 shows that on average about 2% of the possible edge pairs are classified as road pairs. It should be noted that a large portion of the non-road pairs have been rejected due to the presence of a distance threshold. The introduction of a threshold in this case is reasonable since we generate all possible edge pairs, and there is no point in attempting to classify edges that are very far apart. Once again, these results are encouraging because high completeness values are obtained.

Figure 2 shows the SVM results for Image 4. The upper left quadrant shows the original edge set and the upper right quadrant shows the edges in the reference model. The lower left and right quadrants show the output of Level 1 and Level 2 classification respectively.

In order to evaluate the performance on unseen data, the SVMs trained on Image 2 were applied to Image 1. Image 1 and Image 2 contain similar road types, so it is valid to expect the Image 1 SVMs to recognize Image 2 roads. For Level 1, the results of this experiment were 91.67% completeness and 19.68% correctness. For Level 2, completeness and correctness values of 91.67% and 22.00% were obtained. These results are displayed in Figure 3, where the upper left quadrant shows the original Image 2 edge set, the upper right quadrant shows the reference edge set, and the Level 1 and Level 2 results are shown in the lower left and right quadrants respectively. These results suggest that SVMs will perform well on unseen images that contains similar road types.

The results obtained from the SVM experiments are very competitive with previous RAIL experiments using decision trees and clustering techniques. Although a direct empirical comparison is difficult (due to differences in training

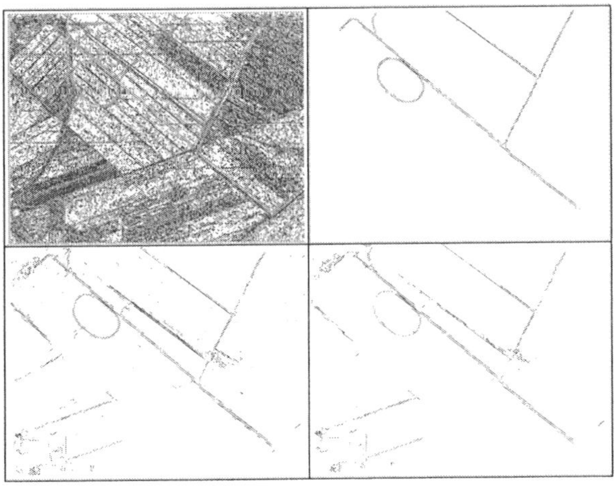

Fig. 2. Image 4 Results

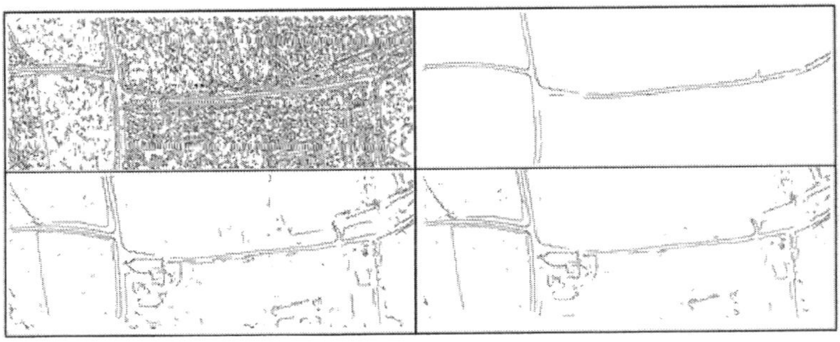

Fig. 3. Results of Applying Image 1's SVMs to Image 2

data, reference models, etc.), a visual comparison of the results shows that the SVM results are similar to those using the C4.5 learning algorithm, and usually superior to those obtained using the kNN and kMeans clustering algorithms.

6 Conclusion

In this paper we have presented the preliminary results from incorporating SVMs into the RAIL framework. This is an interesting experiment since it is significantly different from other work that has been done with SVMs in the remote sensing domain. Furthermore, the data from these experiments will soon be incorporated into RAIL's meta-learning framework, making a significant contribution to the future research and development of RAIL.

The results we have obtained are very encouraging. The correctness values are rather low, but this should be improved with the continued development of higher RAIL levels.

References

1. Chen, A., Donovan, G., Sowmya, A., Trinder, J.: Inductive Clustering: Automating Low-level Segmentation in High Resolution Images. Proc. ISPRS Commission III Symp. Photogrammetric Computer Vision. **34** (2002) 73-78
2. Singh, S., Sowmya, A.: RAIL: Road Recognition from Aerial Images Using Inductive Learning. Proceedings of ISPRS Commission III Symposium Object Recognition and Scene Classification from multispectral and multisensor pixels. (367-378)
3. Vapnik, V.: The Nature of Statistical Learning Theory. Spring-Verlag, New York (1995)
4. Burges, C.: A Tutorial on Support Vector Machines for Pattern Recognition. Data Mining and Knowledge Discovery. **2** (1998) 121-167
5. Fukuda, S., Hirosawa, H.: Support Vector Machine Classification of Land Cover: Application to Polarimetric SAR Data. 2001 Asia-Pacific Radio Science Conference. Tokyo, Japan. (2001) F5-04
6. Huang, C., Davis, L., Townsend, J.: An Assessment of Support Vector Machines for Land Cover Classification. International Journal of Remote Sensing. **4** (2002) 725-749
7. Li, Z., Weida, Z., Licheng, J.: SAR Image Recognition Based on Support Vector Machines. Proceedings of the 2001 CIR International Conference on Radar. (2001) 1044-1046
8. Perkins, S., Harvey, N., Brumby, S., Lacker, K.: Support Vector Machines for Broad Area Feature Classification in Remotely Sensed Images. Proc. SPIE 4381. (2001)

Fingerprint Matching Based on Directional Image Feature in Polar Coordinate System

Chul-Hyun Park[1], Joon-Jae Lee[2], and Kil-Houm Park[1]

[1] School of Electrical Engineering and Computer Science
Kyungpook National University, Daegu, Korea
nagne@palgong.knu.ac.kr, khpark@ee.knu.ac.kr
[2] Division of Internet Engineering, Dongseo University, Busan, Korea
jjlee@dongseo.ac.kr

Abstract. This paper presents a new fingerprint feature extraction and alignment method based on a directional image representation in polar coordinate system. First, the proposed method establishes a region of interest (ROI) for feature extraction using the reference point information. The ROI is then converted from a Cartesian coordinate system to a polar coordinate system to facilitate the following feature extraction and rotational alignment processes. In the proposed method, standard deviation value of each directional subband block is exploited as the fingerprint feature, and the directional subbands are obtained using a directional filter bank (DFB). Input feature vectors, in which various rotations are considered, are extracted by cyclically shifting the decomposed subband outputs and recalculating the directional feature value of each block, and these input feature vectors are matched with the enrolled single template feature vector. Rotational alignment is achieved by finding the minimum Euclidean distance. Experimental results demonstrated the effectiveness of the proposed method in feature extraction and alignment, along with a comparable verification accuracy to that of other leading techniques.

1 Introduction

In an effort to establish more secure and convenient personal authentication, many studies have recently been performed in the field of biometrics, which aims to identify individuals based on their physiological or behavioral characteristics. Among all the biometrics, finger scanning is already widely used for personal identification or verification, since fingerprints essentially satisfy the basic requirements, i.e. universality, uniqueness, and immutability, for a biometric feature and provide highly reliable biometric information [1].

A fingerprint verification system extracts the features of a fingerprint image, which consists of ridges and valleys, and then generates a feature vector used for subsequent matching. According to the matching score, the input fingerprint is then accepted or rejected. Existing fingerprint feature extraction methods can be largely classified into two categories. The first is minutiae-based approaches that extract minutia points where the ridges end or branch, and then utilize

N. Petkov and M.A. Westenberg (Eds.): CAIP 2003, LNCS 2756, pp. 293–300, 2003.

this minutiae information for verification or identification [1], while the second is image-based approaches that directly extract features from a fingerprint image using filtering or a transform without detecting the minutia points [2], [3]. Minutiae-based approaches generally conduct intensive preprocessing, like image enhancement, binarization, thinning etc., and then detect the minutia points. Thereafter, matching is performed using such information as the relative positions of the minutia points to a reference point and directions of the ridges in the minutia points. However, these approaches have the disadvantage that it is not easy to automatically extract sufficient minutia points for reliable verification. In addition, there are also difficulties related to aligning the minutiae patterns from the input and template fingerprints, because the number of minutia points from an input fingerprint generally differs from that of the template fingerprint. To overcome or complement the minutiae-based approaches, many image-based techniques have been introduced. These approaches have advantages that they do not need to extract minutia points and usually generate a small fixed size feature vector. However, most of the techniques do not consider rotations of the input fingerprint, and even in the considered case [2], the compensation procedure is not efficient in that it requires the enrollment of variously rotated version of template feature vectors.

Accordingly, this paper presents a new image-based fingerprint matching method whose rotational alignment procedure is efficient. The proposed method extracts a region of interest (ROI) for feature extraction, then converts the ROI from Cartesian coordinates into polar coordinates to facilitate the rotational alignment procedure. Thereafter, directional feature value of each block is calculated using a directional filter bank (DFB) to form a feature vector. When generating the input feature vector, the proposed method constructs a set of feature vectors where various rotations of the input fingerprint are considered, and then attempts to match these feature vectors with the enrolled template feature vector. A rotational alignment between the input and template feature vectors is achieved by simply identifying the minimum distance. Besides, the proposed method has the additional advantage that its processing speed is very fast due to the efficient DFB structure. Section 2 explains the DFB used in the proposed method, while Sections 3 and 4 describe the feature extraction and subsequent matching procedures. Section 5 presents the experimental results and some final conclusions are given in Section 6.

2 Directional Filter Bank (DFB)

The DFB divides the two-dimensional spectrum of an image into wedge-like directional subbands, as shown in Fig. 1(a) [4], [5]. Eight directional subband outputs can be obtained using the 8-band DFB, as shown in Fig. 1(b). Figure 1(d) shows an example of the directional subband images decomposed by the 8-band DFB, where each directional component is captured in its subband image.

The DFB efficiently and accurately divides an image into directional subband outputs in the spatial domain using quincunx matrices, which rotate and downsample the image, and a low pass filter, which has a diamond-shape filtering

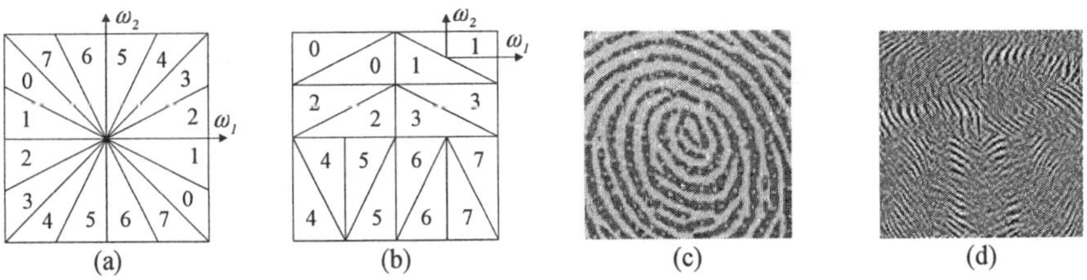

Fig. 1. Frequency partition map of (a) input and (b) 8 subband outputs, (c) example of fingerprint image, and (d) decomposed subband outputs of (c) when using 8-band DFB

characteristic. Each direction subband output has a rectangular shape where the width and height differ due to the back sampling matrices used to remove frequency scrambling [5]. For an $N \times N$ image, the first half of the 2^n subband outputs is $N/2^{n-1} \times N/2$ in size, while the other half is $N/2 \times N/2^{n-1}$.

3 Feature Extraction

The proposed feature extraction scheme basically consists of three steps: ROI extraction, normalization, and feature vector generation.

3.1 ROI Extraction and Normalization

The proposed method first establishes a reference point for the same portion of a fingerprint to be used for extracting features, then the area within a certain range of the reference point is used as the ROI for feature extraction. The reference point is detected using the technique based on a Poincaré index analysis [6].

The area within a certain range from the detected reference point is then used for feature extraction, as illustrated in Fig. 2(a). An innermost band with a radius of less than 20 pixels is not used for feature extraction, because the number of pixels per sector is too small to give a reliable feature value. The detected ROI is then converted from Cartesian coordinates into polar coordinates, as shown in Fig. 2(b), to facilitate the subsequent processes of feature extraction and rotational alignment. The polar coordinates for the ROI are then transformed again into a square form, as the DFB is optimized to filter only square images where the width and height are equal. In the proposed method, the ROI is transformed into a square form by repositioning the right half of the region below the left half, as shown in Fig. 2(c). We can see the discontinuity between the upper and lower parts, however, there is no information loss due to this reformation. The proposed method normalizes the ROI in each block separately to a constant mean and variance in order to remove the effect of gray level deformation due to finger pressure differences [2].

3.2 Feature Vector Generation

Since fingerprint patterns have strong directionality, directional information can be used as a good fingerprint feature. Therefore, the proposed method decom-

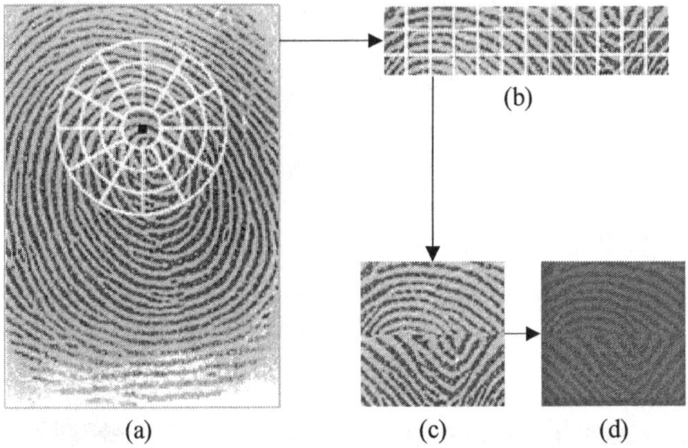

Fig. 2. ROI detection and normalization. (a) Extracted ROI, (b) ROI converted to polar coordinate system, (c) ROI shape converted to square form by changing position of right half to below that of left half, and (d) normalized ROI

poses the normalized ROI into the 8 directional subband outputs using the DFB, then calculates the standard deviation value from each decomposed directional subband block. Let $\sigma_{\theta k}$ denote the standard deviation of the kth block in the θ direction subband image (which we call $S_{\theta k}$), and $c_{\theta k}(x, y)$ is the coefficient value at pixel (x, y) in subband block $S_{\theta k}$, then the feature value of the block, $v_{\theta k}$, is given as

$$v_{\theta k} = \text{nint}\left(\frac{255 \times (\sigma_{\theta k} - \sigma_{min})}{\sigma_{max} - \sigma_{min}}\right) \tag{1}$$

where

$$\sigma_{\theta k} = \sqrt{\frac{1}{N} \sum_{x,y \in S_{\theta k}} \left(c_{\theta k}(x, y) - \bar{c}_{\theta k}\right)^2}\ , \tag{2}$$

nint(x) is the function that returns the nearest integer to x; σ_{max} and σ_{min} are the maximum and minimum values of $\sigma_{\theta k}$, respectively, for all $\theta \in \{0, 1, 2, \ldots, 7\}$ and $k \in \{0, 1, 2, \ldots, 35\}$; N is the number of pixels in $S_{\theta k}$; and $\bar{c}_{\theta k}$ is the mean of pixel values of $c_{\theta k}(x, y)$ in subband block $S_{\theta k}$. Thus, Eq. 1 implies that a feature vector is generated by normalizing and quantizing each feature value to an integer between 0 and 255.

The main difference between the proposed method and the Gabor filter bank-based method in [2] is the use of different subband ranges for feature extraction. With a Gabor filter bank, there are always some overlapping or missing subband regions, whereas a DFB has a directionally accurate subband separation characteristic. Accordingly, a DFB can represent linear patterns, as found in fingerprint patterns, more effectively than a Gabor filter bank. The positive effect of extracting features using a specific directional and frequency subband that emphasizes the dominant frequency information and suppresses noise components is much offset by the suppression of useful information existing outside the specified frequency range. Plus, since each finger has a different dominant inter-ridge frequency, limiting the frequency subband to a small range centered on the average inter-ridge frequency can create a negative effect on the matching result.

4 Matching

Fingerprint matching is carried out by calculating the Euclidean distance between the input feature vector and the template feature vector enrolled in the database. Since the proposed feature extraction process is performed based on blocks and the directions of the ridges change smoothly, the proposed method is robust to a small amount of rotation, even without the rotational alignment procedure. However, if the input image is significantly rotated, the performance is severely deteriorated. In [2], rotational alignment is partially achieved by cyclically rotating the feature values in the feature vector and finding the minimum distance between the input and template feature vector, yet this only provides robustness for a small perturbation within $\pm 11.25°$, that is, half the angle of a sector. However, for this method to be invariant to smaller perturbations, many feature vectors for a variously rotated image must be enrolled in the database.

Instead of using a single feature vector as the input, the proposed method performs matching using several feature vectors, in which various rotations are considered, to effectively compensate for rotation. After an input fingerprint image is decomposed into 8 directional subband images, several feature vectors are obtained by cyclically shifting the subband images and recalculating a standard deviation for each subband block. The minimum unit of horizontal shift in the subband images is a one-pixel shift in 4 to 7 direction subband images, and this one-pixel shift means a four-pixel shift in the image domain. For an $N \times N$ image, a four-pixel shift in the ROI is equivalent to a rotation of $180 \times (4/N)$ degrees in the original image. For a 144×144 image, the minimum unit of rotation that can be effectively compensated for is $5°$, as such, the feature vector generated by the proposed method is invariant to small perturbations within $\pm 2.5°$.

Let $v_{\theta k}^{R}$ denote the feature value for the kth block in the θ direction subband image for an input fingerprint image rotated by $R \times 180 \times (4/N)$ degrees and let $t_{\theta k}$ denote the feature value corresponding to the kth block in the θ direction subband of the template fingerprint, then the distance between the input and template feature vectors, d, is given by

$$d = \min_{R} \sqrt{\sum_{\theta} \sum_{k} (v_{\theta k}^{R} - t_{\theta k})^2} \tag{3}$$

where $R \in \{-10, -9, -8, \ldots, -2, -1, 0, 1, 2, \ldots, 8, 9, 10\}$, and $\theta \in \{0, 1, 2, \ldots, 7\}$. Rotational alignment is achieved by finding the minimum distance between the corresponding feature vectors. According to matching score or distance, the input is accepted or rejected. The proposed alignment procedure is efficient in that it requires only single input and template fingerprint, without needing to enroll the variously rotated version of template feature vectors. The procedures for generating the input feature vectors from the normalized ROI and matching are illustrated in Fig. 3.

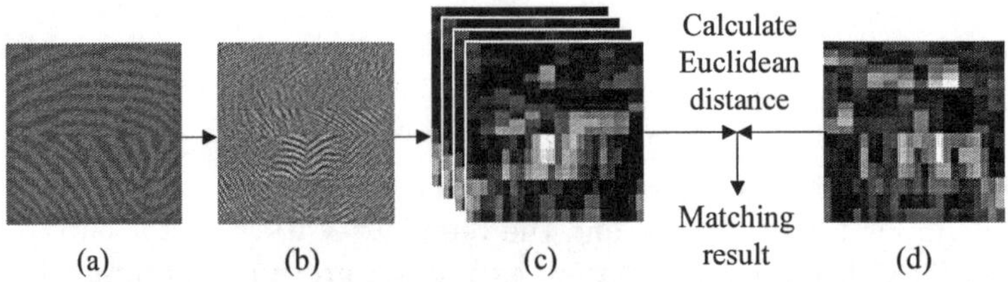

Fig. 3. Feature extraction and matching. (a) Normalized ROI, (b) Decomposed subband outputs, (c) generated input feature vector set, and (d) enrolled template feature vector

5 Experimental Results

A total of 2060 fingerprint images from 105 persons were acquired using a capacitive fingerprint sensor. Each subject was asked to provide about 20 fingerprint images for their right and left thumb. The subjects were guided to place their thumb in the center of the sensor, yet rotation within about $\pm 45°$ was allowed. The acquired fingerprint images were 256 gray scale images and 364×256 in size and the experiments were conducted on a personal computer using a 1 GHz Pentium III processor.

To evaluate the proposed method, its performance was compared with that of the Gabor filter bank-based method in [2], a leading image-based fingerprint feature extraction and matching technique. The fingerprint features were only extracted from 3 band regions due to the small size of the fingerprint images and the width of each band was set at 20 pixels for about a ridge and valley pair for inclusion in a band. In our experiment, each band was divided into 12 sectors, thus a total of $288 (3 \times 12 \times 8)$ feature values were extracted. Since each feature value was an integer between 0 and 255, the entire feature vector only required 288 bytes of storage.

The performance of each method was evaluated in a verification mode. First, genuine and imposter distributions were obtained for each method, then the respective performances were assessed based on the characteristics of the distributions. A genuine distribution indicates the distribution of the Euclidean distances between all possible intra-class image pairs in the database, while an imposter distribution represents the distribution of the Euclidean distances between all possible inter-class image pairs in the database. The more the genuine and imposter distributions are separated and the smaller the standard deviation for each distribution, the more advantageous for a personal verification method.

A decidability index is a good measure of how well the two distributions are separated [1]. Let μ_1 and μ_2 be the means and σ_1 and σ_2 the standard deviations of the two distributions, respectively, then the decidability index d' can be defined as $d' = |\mu_1 - \mu_2| \times ((\sigma_1^2 + \sigma_2^2)/2)^{-1/2}$. In terms of the decidability index, the proposed method with a value of 2.8472 exhibited better characteristics than the Gabor filter bank-based method with a value of 2.6721, implying that the distributions for the proposed method were better separated than those for the Gabor filter bank-based method. When evaluated based on the ROC curve, the proposed method had a similar verification accuracy to the Gabor filter bank-based method (see Fig. 4).

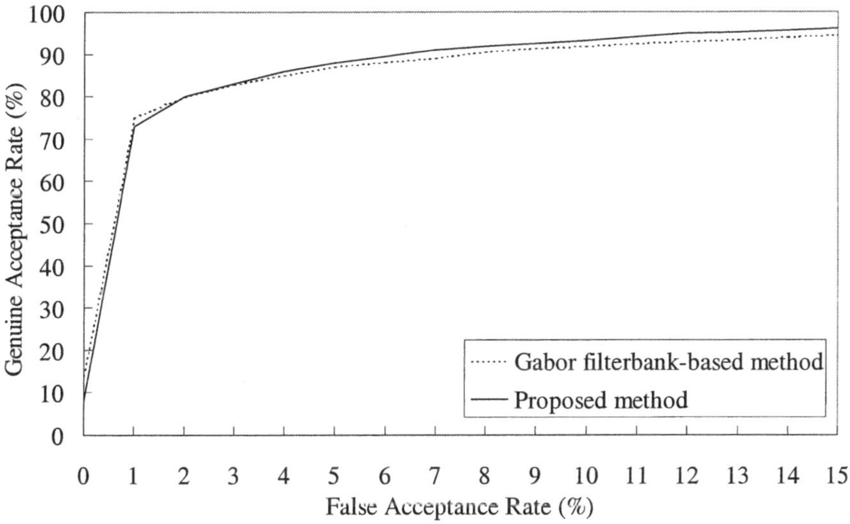

Fig. 4. ROC Curves for proposed method and Gabor filter bank-based method

To estimate how effectively the proposed method achieves a rotational alignment, we investigated the Euclidean distances between the feature vector of the original ROI and those of the shifted ROIs with and without the rotational alignment procedure. Without the rotational alignment procedure, the Euclidean distance between the two feature vectors increased monotonically as the extent of the shift increased. Whereas, with the rotational alignment process, the distances remained almost constant, and when the extent of the shift was a multiple of 4, the distance became the local minimum. This result shows that the rotational alignment procedure of the proposed method is effective.

For the Gabor filter bank-based method, when the Gabor filtering was performed with a mask size of 33 × 33, feature extraction took 4.848 seconds. However, when only pixels with absolute values greater than 0.05 in the filter mask were convolved [2], the Gabor filter bank-based method generated a feature vector in 0.561 seconds. Nonetheless, the processing speed of the proposed method was approximately 2 times faster than that of the Gabor filter bank-based method. The proposed method only took around 0.21 seconds to extract features from the normalized ROI. Half the processing time was taken to filter the ROI and the other half taken to shift the subband images and generate 21 feature vectors based on computing the standard deviation for each subband block. As such, the proposed method was able to perform the entire process from reference point location to matching within about 0.3 seconds.

6 Conclusion

We have proposed a new image-based fingerprint feature extraction method using a DFB. The proposed method can effectively extract both global and local features by utilizing the directional information of each block in the ROI. Furthermore, the proposed verification system is robust to various rotations, as it does not use a single feature vector input, but rather a feature vector set generated by cyclically shifting the directional subband outputs. The feature vector constructed by the proposed method is compact and only requires a fixed storage size. Experimental results using 2060 fingerprint images acquired by a capacitive sensor demonstrated that the proposed method had the comparable verification accuracy to the Gabor filter bank-based method, yet more efficient rotational alignment procedure and faster processing time.

References

1. Jain, A. K., Hong, L., Pankanti, S., Bolle, R.: An identity-authentication system using fingerprints. Proceedings of the IEEE **85** (1997) 1417–1420
2. Jain, A. K., Prabhakar, S., Hong, L., Pankanti, S.: Filterbank-based fingerprint matching. IEEE Trans. Image Processing **9** (2000) 846–859
3. Tico, M, Kuosmanen, P., Saarinen, J.: Wavelet domain features for fingerprint recognition. Electronics Letters **40** (2001) 288–290
4. Bamberger, R. H., Smith, M. J. T.: A filter bank for the directional decomposition of images: Theory and design. IEEE Trans. Signal Processing **40** (1992) 882–893
5. Park, S., Smith, M. J. T., Mersereau, R. M.: A new directional filter bank for image analysis and classification. Proc. IEEE Intl. Conf. on Acoustics, Speech, and Signal Processing **3** (1999) 1417–1420
6. Karu, K., Jain, A. K.: Fingerprint classification. Pattern Recognition **29** (1996) 389–404

Efficient Algorithm of Eye Image Check for Robust Iris Recognition System

Jain Jang[1], Kwiju Kim[2] and Yillbyung Lee[1]

[1] Biometrics Engineering Research Center, Yonsei University, Seoul, Korea
{jijang,yblee}@csai.yonsei.ac.kr
[2] Department of Computer Science, Yonsei University, Seoul, Korea
kamang98@csai.yonsei.ac.kr

Abstract. For the improvement of iris recognition system performance, the filtering algorithm that picks out counterfeit and noisy data is very important. In this paper, as a part of preprocessing step, we propose the efficient algorithm of eye image check, composed of two stages for detecting the fake and noisy eye data. The first stage is to detect the fake iris data evaluating the coefficient of variation of pupil radius and eyelid movement, and analyzing of 2D Fast Fourier Transform (2D-FFT) spectrum. The second stage is to find out the noisy image such as blink, eyelash interference and the truncation of iris region on the eye image. Using this algorithm, the improvement of about 2% at the accuracy rate of the system is achieved. For the experiment, we integrate the algorithm with iris recognition system, made use of Daubechies' Wavelet and Support Vector Machines (SVM) for feature extraction and pattern matching. Experiment results involve 1694 eye images of 111 different people and the accuracy rate of 99.1%.

1 Introduction

The biometric identification and verification system is the method of recognizing individual based on physical and behavioral characteristic. Many biometrics including face, voice, fingerprints, palms, hand geometry, retina, handwriting, gait and eye, have been used for the security applications instead of the traditional security system such as identification tokens, password, personal identification numbers (PINs), etc. Among them, the iris recognition is the most promising method because the iris pattern is unchanged as long as one lives and every one has the unique iris pattern.

The iris recognition system is composed of four steps, image acquisition, preprocessing, feature extraction and pattern matching. By means of excluding the noisy and counterfeit data through the preprocessing step, the system performance can be improved.

We propose an efficient algorithm of eye image checking to detect the fake data and to evaluate the quality of eye image in the real time. It is composed of two stages. At the first stage, the system evaluates the coefficient of variation of pupil radius with 2D bisection-based Hough transform and eyelid movement with a region-based tem-

N. Petkov and M.A. Westenberg (Eds.): CAIP 2003, LNCS 2756, pp. 301–308, 2003.

plate deformation and masking method [1]. If the eye images pass these two tests, 2D-FFT spectrum of eye image is analyzed to detect the fake iris data. At the second stage, the algorithm which checks eye image quality finds out inappropriate images such as blink, eyelash interference and the truncation of iris region. After finishing the algorithm of eye image check, we can get the qualified images for the registration and the identification/verification of the iris recognition system. For the test of algorithm performance, we integrate the algorithm with iris recognition system [2], which uses Daubechies' Wavelet for feature extraction and Support Vector Machine (SVM) for pattern matching.

2 Test of Fake Eye Data

In the image acquisition step, several eye images of each user are rapidly captured by the CCD camera, and stored by 240×320 size. After image acquisition, as a first step of preprocessing, the algorithm evaluates a coefficient of variation of pupil radius. We can find fake eye data with evaluating the pupil radius variation because the size of pupil is continuously changed even under steady illumination. To find the boundary of pupil, we use Canny Edge operator [3] and 2D bisection-based Hough transform. Using these methods, we can compute the average radius of current user's pupil on several images. If data passes the first test, the algorithm performs the second test, which evaluates the coefficient of eyelid movement. To extract the eyelid region from the eye image, we use a region-based template deformation and masking method [1] and Canny edge operator [3]. After extracting eyelid part from the Canny edge image, the algorithm evaluates coefficient of the variation of distance between the center of the pupil and the specific part of the upper eyelid region. Finally, 2D-FFT is used to find the lens image with fake iris pattern printed. It is easily detected in the Fourier plane because the printing process generates a characteristic signature and it appears to four points of symmetric energy in the Fourier spectrum. If eye image proves real eye data in the first stage, it is tested at the second stage by the evaluation algorithm of eye image quality.

2.1 Evaluating the Coefficient of Variation of Pupil Radius

Using 2D bisection-based Hough Transform, we can efficiently find out the pupil radius more than 2D gradient-based Hough transform. To detect the center of pupil, we use 2D bisection-based Hough Transform and Canny edge operator to extract the pupil edge component. The basic idea of the bisection method is that any line connecting two points on the circle is bisected by the perpendicular line which passes through the center of the circle. To get candidate points of center, we compute the intersection point of each perpendicular line made by the specific distance between the two points on connected edge components. Using a maximal frequency determination method, the center and radius of pupil are decided among the many candidate center points. As a result of these processes, we can find out the pupil boundary [2]. Fig. 1 shows a result of the detection of pupil boundary.

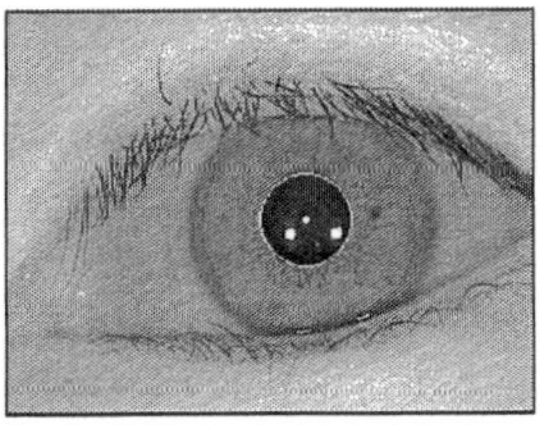

Fig. 1. Result of the detection of pupil boundary

To test the fake eye in the sequentially given images, we have to evaluate the coefficient of radius variation by equation (1). If the coefficient values are given in the range between minimum and maximum coefficient of total eye data, they are treated as a data of living iris. C_t is the coefficient of total iris image and C_n is coefficient of the current user's data. m_n is the mean of the radius of current user's data and r_i is the radius of pupil in each data of current user.

$$C_n = \frac{\sqrt{\sum_i r_i^2 - m_n^2}}{\sum_i r_i} \tag{1}$$

$$Min\,C_t \leq C_n \leq Max\,C_t$$

2.2 Tracking the Eyelid Movement

If data passes the first test, the detecting function of eyelid movement is performed. To extract the eyelid region from the iris image, we use Deng's approach [1] called by region-based template deformation and masking method. It is the improved method of Yuille's energy-minimization algorithm [3] and uses deformable eye template to search and fit the eye region in the face.

To extract the eyelid edge from eye image data, we make the eye image edge data by means of Canny edge operator, first and use the deformable eye template as the eyelid mask. To evaluate the variation of eyelid movement, we compute the average of distance between the center point of pupil and the part of eyelid edge pixels, range of 15° of both side of the axis passed through center of pupil. To evaluate the eyelid movement, we compute the difference of the average between the current user's previous frame and current frame. The eye template and the eyelid mask to extract eyelid edge from the Canny edge component are given in Fig. 2(a) and Fig. 2(b), respectively. Fig. 2(c) shows the eyelid edge extracted by eyelid mask. The variation of eyelid movement is evaluated by equation (2). D_{Avr} is the average of distance between the center point of pupil, (x_c,y_c) and specific region of edge pixel, (x_i,y_i) and n is the number of pixels in the specific region. C means the coefficient of eyelid movement variation and m is the mean of difference between previous and current frame. D_p and D_c mean the average distance of previous and current frame.

$$D_{Avr} = \frac{\sum_i \sqrt{(x_c - x_i)^2 + (y_c - y_i)^2}}{n} \quad (2)$$

$$C = \frac{\sqrt{\sum_{i-1} (D_p - D_c)^2 - m^2}}{\sum_{i-1} | D_p - D_c |}$$

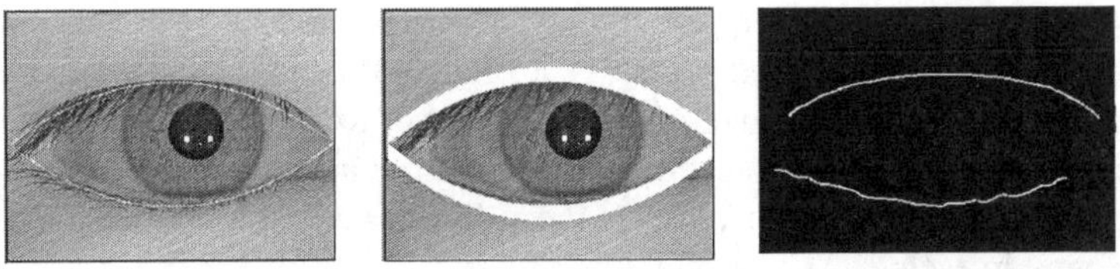

(a) (b) (c)

Fig. 2. (a) Eye template, (b) Eyelid mask, (c) Extraction result of eyelid edge

2.3 Detecting the Data of Fake Contact Lenses

Contact lenses with fake iris pattern printed are also available as a counterfeit data. It is not easy to detect the fake contact lenses in the spatial domain, but can be found in the frequency domain by means of detecting the characteristic signal of printing process. We use contact lenses used to change one's iris color. Using 2D-FFT, we can get the Fourier spectrum shown in Fig. 3(c), which has four points of spurious energy in the Fourier plane. In the natural iris, they do not appear on the Fourier spectrum [5].

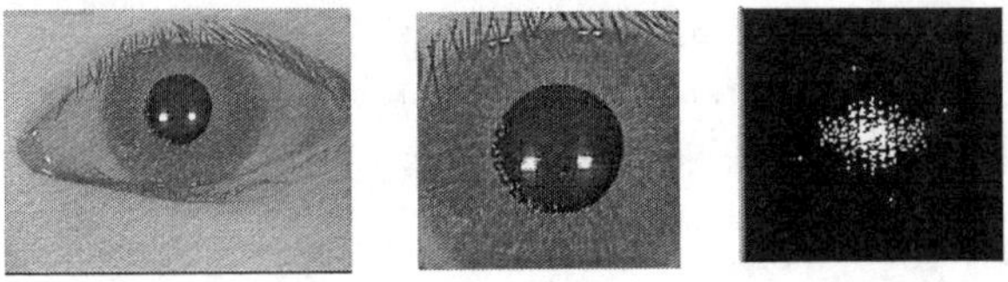

(a) (b) (c)

Fig. 3. (a) Eye data of contact lenses with fake iris pattern printed, (b) Extracting data of iris region, (c) 2D-FFT spectrum

3 Evaluation Algorithm of Eye Image Quality

To extract consistent iris features, we have to exclude noisy images, the obstruction of eyelid or eyelash and iris image that is truncated some part of iris area. Fig. 4 shows an example of good qualified images for the registration and the identification/ verification of the iris recognition system.

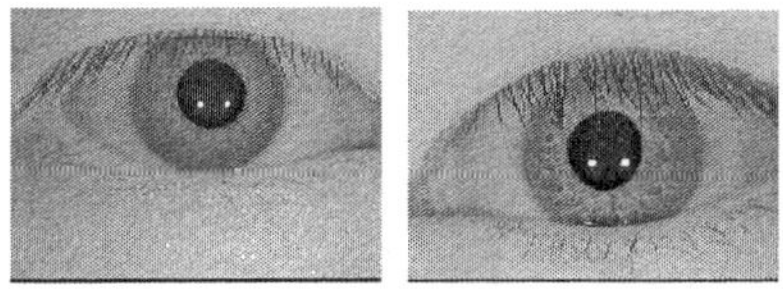

Fig. 4. Qualified eye images for the iris recognition system

Evaluation algorithm of iris image quality involves three steps in order to select appropriate images. The first step detects the image of eye blink shown in Fig. 5(a), and the second step detects the image of iris area interfered by eyelashes shown in Fig. 5(b). Finally, the algorithm finds out the eye data which is truncated some part of iris area. It is shown in Fig. 5(c).

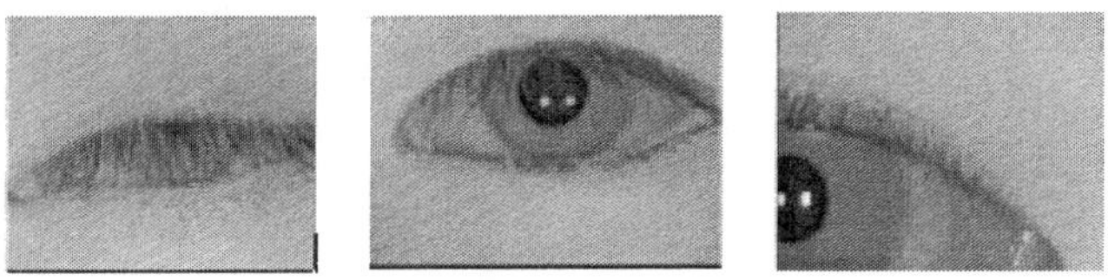

(a) (b) (c)

Fig. 5. Examples of inappropriate eye images (a) eye blink (b) eyelash interference (c) eye data is truncated some part of iris area

In both the first and third cases, we cannot extract iris area because only part of iris area appears in the data. In the second case, the eyelash interference in the iris area is worked as a noise of feature extraction step. For better performance, filtering of eye images through evaluation algorithm is needed. Especially, oriental people's problem occurred by eyelash interference is more frequent than occidental people's.

3.1 Detecting the Eye Image with Blink

Eye data with blink is detected by two kinds of evaluation method. The first method is to decide the threshold value by the gray level of eyelid area. Generally, gray level of pixel in the eyelid area is brighter than other area of eye image. If the average value of intensity of eyelid area is over threshold, we can estimate that eye data have blinking noise. The average value of intensity is computed by equation (3). T is the pre-defined threshold in eyelid area, $f(i, j)$ is intensity function, M is the size of width and N is the size of height.

$$MeanOfLid = \frac{\sum_{i=0}^{M}\sum_{j=0}^{N} f(i, j)}{M \times N} > T \tag{3}$$

The other method is to check the ratio of pupil radius. The shape of pupil is nearly circle and so the ratio of horizontal to vertical radius is almost 1. Based on the characteristics of the shape of pupil, we can decide which one is appropriate eye data or not.

The algorithm reject eye image when the ratio of horizontal to vertical pupil radius is under the ratio of 2 to 3.

3.2 Detecting Interference of Eyelash

Eyelash interference in iris area is serious problem at feature extraction step. As a tool to solve the eyelash problem, we use the line detector to find out line component between inner boundary and iris area. If the endpoint of line component is under the pupil center, the algorithm decides that iris area is interfered by eyelash. Fig. 6 shows the mask for line detection.

Vertical			+45°			Horizontal			-45°		
-1	2	-1	-1	-1	2	-1	-1	-1	2	-1	-1
-1	2	-1	-1	2	-1	2	2	2	-1	2	-1
-1	2	-1	2	-1	-1	-1	-1	-1	-1	-1	2

Fig. 6. Mask for line detection

3.3 Truncation of Iris Area

If the data is accepted in the previous processes, the truncation of iris area is detected by evaluating iris area within a certain boundary. If the center of pupil is not located in the restricted area obtained by the experimental method, the eye image is rejected. Fig. 7 shows the rejected eye image due to truncate the iris area.

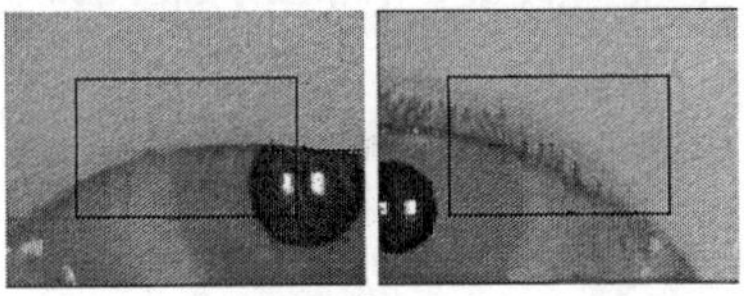

Fig. 7. Eye image with truncated iris area

4 Experimental Results

The experiments have been comparable according to the system performances of two cases. In the first case, we evaluated the performance that algorithm of eye image check was used as a part of the preprocessing step, and in the second one, algorithm was not used. To extract the feature, each iris image was decomposed to three levels by Daubechies' Wavelet (tap-4). Pattern matching algorithm is SVM [2]. Two databases were used during the experiments. One is eye image database from University of Yonsei and the other is eye image database from Senex Technologies. Eye images were captured by the fixed focus CCD camera and the system performance was evaluated with involving 1694 eye images of 111 people.

Analysis

In the algorithm of eye image check, the first method is to detect the fake iris data and the second one is to evaluate the quality of image. If the data pass algorithm of eye image check, iris data are localized for the feature extraction. Iris features were extracted by Wavelet packet and SVM is used as a patterns matching algorithm for data training [2]. We evaluate the success rate of the iris recognition system according to algorithm of eye image check. Data sets are given in Table 1. In case of fake data, the forty data of naked eye were printed on the paper and twenty data of contact lenses with fake eye pattern printed were used.

Table 1. Data Set

	Naked eye	Glasses	Contact lenses	Total
Real data	1,363	160	111	1634
Fake data	40	·	20	60
Total	1,403	160	131	1694

If we do not use the algorithm of eye image check, FAR is 0.7% and FRR is 2.3%. But after using the algorithm in the preprocessing step, both FAR and FRR are reduced as shown in Table 2. D-system means that system is not to use the algorithm of eye image check and U-system means that system is to use the algorithm. Total accuracy rate was improved from 97.4% to 99.1%.

Table 2. Comparison of accuracy rate

	D-System	U-system
FAR	0.7%	0.6%
FRR	2.3%	1.6%
Accuracy Rate	97.4%	99.1%

The failure of 0.9% is due to unfocused image and dim eyelash resulted from the intensity of the eyelash ineffective on determining the threshold value. Another reason of the failure is the glasses data that the lens in glasses has noises like reflection of light and scratch of the lens surface. The other reason comes from the interference of iris area by camera illumination.

5 Conclusion

In this paper, we discussed efficient algorithm of eye image check to detect the fake data and evaluate the quality of eye image. First, we checked the fake eye data by means of evaluating coefficient of variation of pupil radius and eyelid movement. 2D-FFT spectrum was analyzed to check the fake iris pattern printed on the contact lenses. When the data passed the algorithm of fake data checking, we used evaluation algorithm of eye image quality to find out the noisy data such as blink, eyelash interference and truncation of iris area. For the feature extraction and pattern

ference and truncation of iris area. For the feature extraction and pattern matching, we used the iris recognition system of [2]. The experiments performed two cases, in the first case, we evaluated the performance that algorithm of eye image check was used as a part of the preprocessing step, and in the second one, eye image checking algorithm was not used. As a result, the improvement at the accuracy rate of the system was about 2%.

Although eye image checking algorithm improved the system performance, time consuming problem of the 2D-FFT spectrum analysis remains and extension of the eyelash detection method is also needed. In the further work, we will try to solve the time consuming problem and extend the checking algorithm of image quality to be applied with various environments.

Acknowledgements

This work was supported by Biometrics Engineering Research Center, Korea Science and Engineering Foundation (KOSEF).

References

1. J. Deng and F. Lai., Region-Based Template Deformation and Masking for Eye-Feature Extraction and Description. *Pattern Recognition*, 30(3): 403-419, Mar. 1997
2. G. Kee., Iris Recognition System Using Wavelet Packet and Support Vector Machines. *Ph. D thesis, Yoinsei University*, 2003
3. A. Yuille and P. Hallinan., Deformable Templates.: *Active Vision*, A. Blake and A. Yuille, eds., pp.21-38. MIT Press, Cambridge, MA, 1992
4. J. Canny., A Computational Approach to Edge Detection, IEEE Trans. *Pattern Analysis Mach. Intell.* 8(6), 679-698, 1986
5. J. Daugman., Recognizing Persons by Theirs Iris Patterns, *Biometrics Personal Identification in Networked Society*, A. Jain, R. Bolle and S. Pankanti, eds., Kluwer Academy Publishers, 1999

Recognition of Car License Plate by Using Dynamical Thresholding Method and Enhanced Neural Networks

Kwang-Baek Kim[1], Si-Woong Jang[2], and Cheol-Ki Kim[3]

[1] Dept. of Computer Engineering, Silla University, Korea
[2] Research Center for Electronic Ceramics(RCEC) of Dongeui University, Korea
[3] Dept. of Computer Engineering, Miryang National University, Korea

Abstract. In this paper, for the implementation of the recognition system of car license plates, the region extraction algorithm based on the contour tracking and the new enhanced neural networks learning algorithm are proposed, which extracts the areas of car license plate and the character areas from the car images and recognizes the car license numbers from the extracted areas. And a candidate area was selected, whose density rate was corresponding to the properties of the car license plate obtained in the condition of the car license plate. The contour tracking algorithm extracted the feature areas covering the areas of characters from the car license plate. As well, the enhanced neural networks learning algorithm, combining the modified ART1 and supervised learning algorithm, recognized the car license numbers from the feature areas.

1 Introduction

As the number of cars is increasing, it is getting difficult to control all the issues related to traffic. Unfortunately, violations related to vehicles are also gradually increasing. A lot of researches have been done to solve issues related to vehicles. One of them is to identify vehicles by recognizing license plates from entire vehicle images [1,2]. The recognition of a license plate from a vehicle (front) image is basically divided into three parts; Isolation of a license plate region from a vehicle image, Extraction of character strings from an extracted license plate region, and Recognition of extracted character strings. In this paper, we introduce the thresholding method to extract a plate region from an entire vehicle image. For an extracted plate region, we apply the contour-tracking algorithm to extract character strings. Finally we propose the Enhanced Neural Network (ENN) algorithm to recognize character strings. Moreover we see that the ENN algorithm, which creates dynamically nodes in a hidden layer, is designed to make up for the disadvantages in the back propagation algorithm and enhance the recognition ratio of a license plate.

2 Related Works

The conventional methods used single color models such as gray illumination variation, RGB(Red, Green, Blue) color model, and HSI(Hue, Saturation, Intensity) color

N. Petkov and M.A. Westenberg (Eds.): CAIP 2003, LNCS 2756, pp. 309–319, 2003.

model to extract license plate regions from vehicle images. There is the advantage that extraction method using gray illumination variation is scarcely affected by the loss of information due to light. However, it also has the problem of extracting wrong non-license plate region as the corresponding region in case that there exist non-license plate region satisfying the given threshold value, and the same features as license plate[2]. In general, when we are readjusting the threshold of illumination variation, total extracting time is delayed because of additional time of (total image processing time × the number of readjusting threshold value) [2]. Extraction method using RGB color model is affected by the change of brightness[3]. Extraction method using HSI color model can solve the problem arising from RGB color model. However, it takes much time to compute HSI color values[4]. Artificial neural networks(ANNs) are mathematical materialization of biological neural networks, based on parallel distributed processing. Moreover, ANNs can be applicable to new circumstances, because they have the self-adjustment learning function on experiences [5]. In many ANNs, the error BP and the ART algorithm are considered as suitable models for character recognition. In most case of character recognition, the BP algorithm is selected to handle the unformatted data from real life. However, it has basically three disadvantages; local minima, learning time, and stagnation phenomenon [6]. In order to recognize character strings in a license plate, the error BP algorithm should set the number of nodes in a hidden layer empirically. On the other hand, the ART algorithm has complicated structures and requires large volume of memory according as the number of patterns increases [7]. Moreover, the ART algorithm takes vigilance parameters to cluster patterns and determine disagreement tolerance between arbitrary patterns and stored patterns. Thus, when we use the ART algorithm to recognize character strings on a license plate, we may confront a problem that vigilance parameter should be set heuristically.

3 Extraction of Car License Plate Region and Character String by Contour Tracking Algorithm

In this study, we extract the plate region by using thresholding method and the density ratio. We use the following four features to extract a plate region from a vehicle image. First, the ratio of vertical line to horizontal line for the plate region is 2:1. Second, the color of characters is clearly distinguished from that of background in the plate region. Third, the density of the license plate region is higher than that of other regions because characters are in the plate region. Fourth, characters in the plate region have their position information. For extracting a license plate region from the vehicle image by thresholding method, we first convert the vehicle image into a binary formatted form by using threshold value, and compute the density of each line. We note that threshold value plays an important role in the whole process of the license plate recognition, because it is used to distinguish character string of a license plate region from background. In the thresholding method, the average of the brightest value and the darkest value is assigned as threshold value. We define threshold value $V_{threshold}$ by the average intensity of an entire vehicle image and update it dynamically.

$$V_{threshold} := \frac{\sum_{y=0}^{M}\left\{\sum_{x=0}^{N}\{I(x,y)\}\right\}}{M * N} \tag{1}$$

where M and N denote the width and length of an image respectively, and $I(x,y)$ is the brightness value at position (x,y). Because the pixel values of an image are affected by intensity of illumination on the neighborhood as well as color, it is difficult to get an accurate threshold value. Hence we define initial threshold value by average brightness value. If we will fail in extracting a license plate from a vehicle image, we update dynamically threshold value as an approximate value to average brightness value. After thresholding, if we compute the density and extract the plate region from a vehicle image, there is possibility to be extracted one or more license plate regions. Therefore, it is required a filtering process that eliminates a shadow within invariable size of mask. After executing thresholding process and noisy filtering process, we calculate the density and then select high density regions as candidates for the license plate regions. If there are two or more candidate regions, we extract license plate region by using above conditions. If no regions satisfy characteristics of the license plate region, we assume that thresholding has some problems. And we update threshold value and execute thresholding again.

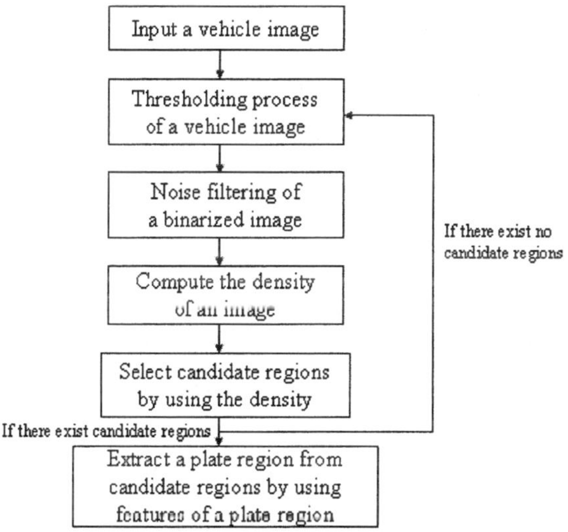

Fig. 1. Extraction process of a license plate region by the proposed method

Fig 1 presents the proposed extraction process of the license plate region. There are some methods based on image processing techniques, which are designed for extracting the characters from an extracted plate region. The method which uses the structure ratio information of characters, a method which uses the boundary information of characters, a method which computes threshold value from gray level histogram, and a method which computes threshold value from an arbitrary threshold value[8,9,10]. In this paper, we use the contour tracking algorithm, a method which uses the boundary information of characters. As methods of extracting contour line, there are methods of extracting contour line into eight directions by using 3×3 mask and into four directions by using 2×2 mask. In extraction method applied in this paper, for license plate region, compute the density indicating histogram for y-axis direction, divide license plate region into higher part and lower part, and extract contour line of each character and digit by using 2×2 mask for each of the divided regions. Fig 2 shows 2×2 mask for extracting contour line. 2×2 mask algorithm locates mask x_k into starting point as Fig 2 by selecting one of boundary pixels in the corresponding region as starting point, and determines the next progressing direction of mask by considering two pixels which correspond to a and b. Contour tracking circulates basically counterclockwise. If a and b are boundary pixel and background pixel respectively, the contour tracking circulates as current status. If a and b are boundary pixels, or a and b are background pixel and boundary respectively, it circulates as Fig 3(a). If a and b are background pixels, it circulates to left and progress direction is converted, as Fig 3(b). Table 1 shows the progressing direction of 2×2 mask.

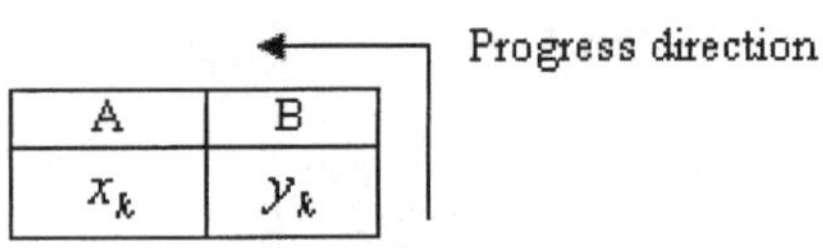

Fig. 2. 2×2 mask for extracting contour line

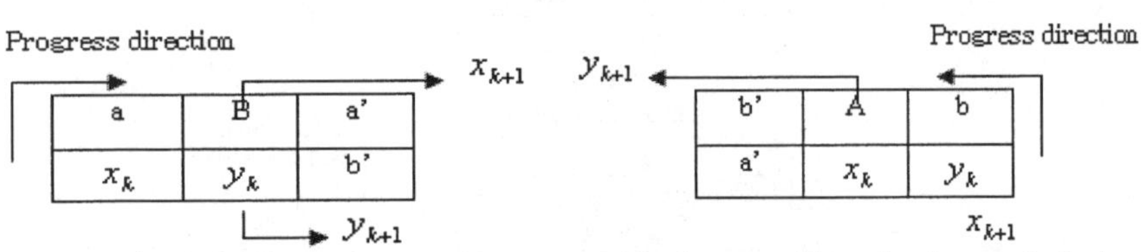

(a) when a and b are boundary pixels (b) when a and b are background pixels

Fig. 3. The progressing direction of a mask according to a and b

Table 1. The progressing direction of a 2×2 mask according to a and b

	a	b	x_{k+1}	y_{k+1}
Forward	1	0	a	b
Right side	0	1	b	y_k
Right side	1	1	a	x_k
Left side	0	0	x_k	a

4 Enhanced Neural Network for License Plate Recognition

We propose the enhanced algorithm combined with the modified ART network, which dynamically changes the number of nodes in a hidden layer. Biological neuron structure to support the enhanced structure is based on the feedback inhibition structures, which reacts on cells activating themselves. The proposed architecture, which creates nodes in a hidden layer by itself, is shown in Figure 4. The connection structure between an input layer and a hidden layer is the same structure as the modified ART1. And an output layer of the modified ART1 is a hidden layer of the proposed structure. Each node of a hidden layer indicates each class. So the structure is fully-connected structure. But, when back-propagating by comparing between target value and real output value, we choose winner-take-all which back-propagates weight value of representative class and connected synapse. Let the learning data of value 0(every input value is 0) affect every hidden layer without taking winner.

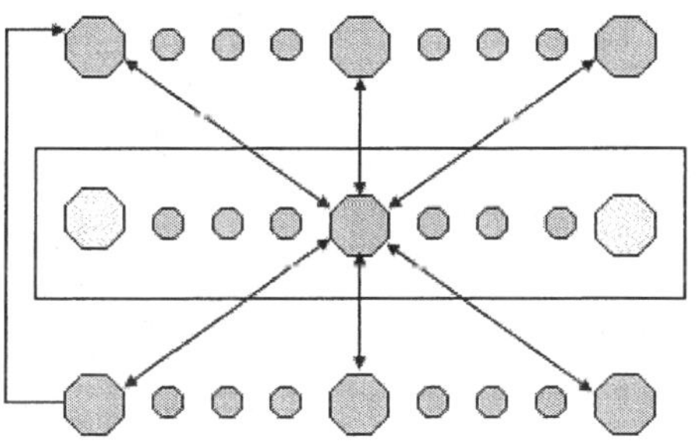

Fig. 4. The enhanced neural network model

Similarity is defined by the ratio of two values as follows in the ART1 learning algorithm;

$$\text{Similarity} := \frac{\|T \cdot X\|}{\|X\|}, \text{(where } T \text{ is the stored pattern, } X \text{ is the input pattern)} \quad (2)$$

In the ART1 learning algorithm, because the similarity is equal to the ratio of the number of 1's in case of binary input, the only pattern 1's value affects the similarity and the pattern 0's value does not affect the similarity. Thus, in the proposed architecture, the similarity is not distinguished by the ratio of the number of 1's but by the number of nodes with the same value. This means that when we consider logical operation, the similarity is defined by the ratio of two values as follows.

$$\text{Similarity} := \frac{\| T * X \|}{\| X \|}, \quad (3)$$

where T is the stored pattern, X is the input pattern and $T * X$ is equivalence(Exclusive NOR) between T and X. The proposed architecture adjusts the weight by taking winner-take-all method in the error back propagation learning algorithm. If we consider the connection between input layer and hidden layer, and the connection between hidden layer and output layer separately, the winner node selected from hidden layer become representative class for the presented patterns. Thus, we adjust weight of the synapse connected to winner node between hidden layer and input layer for reflecting the presented pattern to the stored pattern of representative class (figure 5(a)). Also, in order to reflect the target value of the presented pattern on actual output value by the representative class, we only adjust connection weight value associated with soma in output layer and its representative class (figure 5(b)). The proposed architecture let zero pattern pass through during forward activation process, and adjust weight value to affect every node in a hidden layer during backward activation process. This procedure is designed to solve the fail cases in taking winner because net value of hidden layer always becomes 0 when applying the enhanced ART1 architecture to error back propagation learning architecture. We introduce the ENN learning algorithm for license plate recognition as follows.

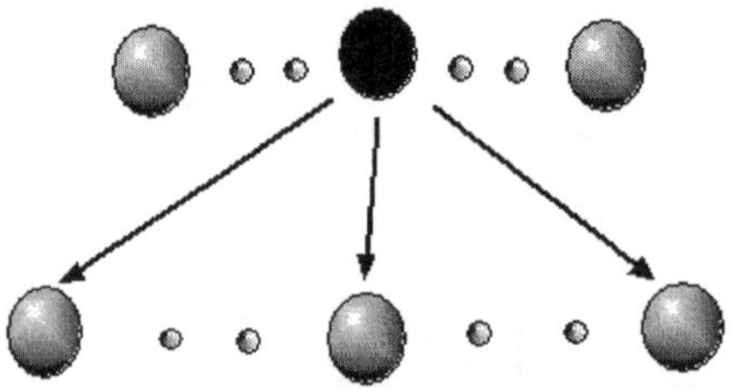

(a) From hidden layer to input layer

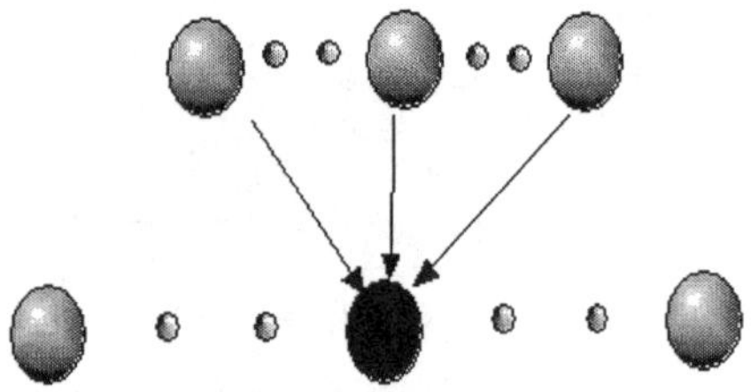

(b) From output layer to hidden layer

Fig. 5. Adjustment of connection weight

[Step 1] Initialize bottom-up weight b_{ij} and top-down weight t_{ij} between input layer and ouput layer, and take a random value between –1 and 1 for the initial weight w_{jk} between a hidden layer and an output layer, where i , j and k denote input layer node, hidden layer node, and output layer node, respectively. That is,

$$t_{ik}(0)=1 \text{ and } b_{ij}(0)=\frac{1}{1+N} \tag{4}$$

where $0 \le i \le N-1$, $0 \le j \le M-1$, and $N-1$ is the number of input patterns and $M-1$ is the number of nodes in a hidden layer.

[Step 2] Input new pattern x_i^p and initialize vigilance parameter ρ and target value t_{kl} , where p is the number of kind of patterns and l is the number of target values for patterns.

[Step 3] Calculate output value of hidden layer by comparing the input with each class of nodes in a hidden layer.

$$O_j=\sum_{i=0}^{N-1} B_{ij}(t)X_i^P \tag{5}$$

[Step 4] Select winner class μ_{j*} from nodes in a hidden layer.

$$\mu_{j*} = Max_j[O_j] \tag{6}$$

[Step 5] Calculate similarity between top-down weight $t_{ij*}(t)$ and input pattern for winner node. If they are similar each other, update the corresponding winner class. If not so, create the class of new node.

$$\|X\| = \sum_{i=0}^{N-1} x_i^p \,, \quad \|T * X\| = \sum_{i=0}^{N-1} t_{ij*}(t) x_i^p \tag{7}$$

$$\text{If } \frac{\|T * X\|}{\|X\|} > \rho \text{ and } \rho \in [0,1], \qquad \text{then goto Step 7} \tag{8}$$

Else, goto Step 6. (where $*$ is Exclusive NOR)

[Step 6] Set the value of current winner class μ_{j*} to 0, and go to Step 3 to calculate class of next winner node.

[Step 7] If the similarity between input pattern and winner node is grater than vigilance parameter, then the similarity are satisfied. Thus we update bottom-up weight and top-down weight of corresponding winner node.

$$t_{ij*}(t+1) = t_{ij*}(t) x_i^p \,, \quad b_{ij*}(t+1) = \frac{t_{ij*}(t) x_i^p}{0.5 + \sum_{i=0}^{N-1} t_{ij*}(t) x_i^p} \tag{9}$$

[Step 8] Calculate output value O_k of node in output layer by using class of node in hidden layer μ_{j*}, connection weight w_{j*k} between hidden layer and output layer, and offset θ_k of node in output layer.

$$Net_k = \sum_{j=0}^{M-1} w_{j*k} \mu_{j*} + \theta_k \,, \quad O_k = \frac{1}{1 + e^{-Net_k}} \tag{10}$$

[Step 9] Calculate error δ_k between connection weight w_{j*k} and the offset θ_k by using difference between target value t_k^l of learning pattern and actual output value O_k.

$$\delta_k = (t_k^l - O_k) O_k (1 - O_k) \tag{11}$$

[Step 10] Adjust w_{j*k} and θ_k by using the error.

$$w_{j*k}(t+1) = w_{j*k}(t) + \alpha \delta_k O_k \,, \quad \theta_k = (t+1) = \theta(t+1) + \alpha \delta_k \,, \tag{12}$$

where α is learning rate and $0 \le \alpha \le 1$.

[Step 11] Go to step 2 to be learned for every pattern.

[Step 12] If the sum of squares of total errors is less than or equal to error criteria, the learning ends. If not so, go to Step 3

5 Experimental Results

For the performance test, we take 114 vehicle front images of 640×480 pixels with 256 colors captured by DC265 Zoom digital camera. For performance evaluation on extracting license plate regions, we restrict our attention to two methods; (1) two known method-using grey illumination variations and RGB color information, and (2) the proposed extraction method. For performance evaluation on character extraction, we considered two methods; (1) the existing extraction method which uses position information and (2) the proposed contour tracking algorithm. For recognition ratio of the extracted characters, we compared the proposed ENN algorithm with the existing error BP algorithm. Table 2 gives the test results of RGB-method, gray-method, and the proposed method on 114 vehicle images. Consequently, when a license plate region is distinguished from other area in vehicle images, RGB-method works properly. Fig 6(a) gives an image for which RGB-method cannot be applied because the green color does not almost appear. However, the proposed method works successfully even in case fig 6(a).

On the other hand, gray-method may extract a non-plate region as a license plate region, when a non-plate region satisfies current threshold value and features of license. However, the proposed method works successfully as shown in Fig 7(b).

Table 2. Comparison for results of extracting license plate regions

	Extraction success	Extraction Fail
Gray-level	107	7
RGB method	104	10
The proposed method	112	2

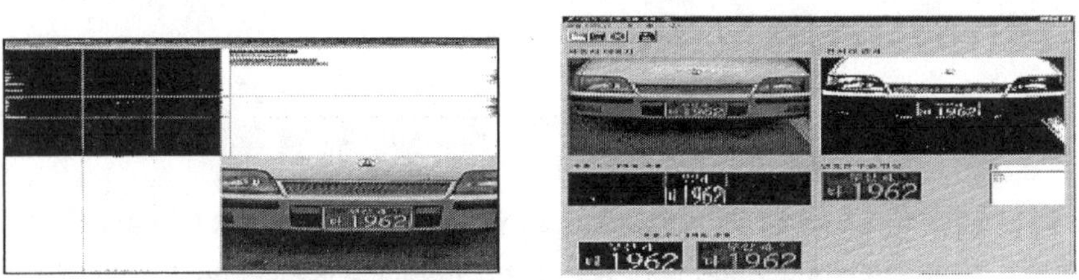

(a) RGB-method : a fail case (b) The proposed method : a success case

Fig. 6. Comparison of RGB-method and the proposed method

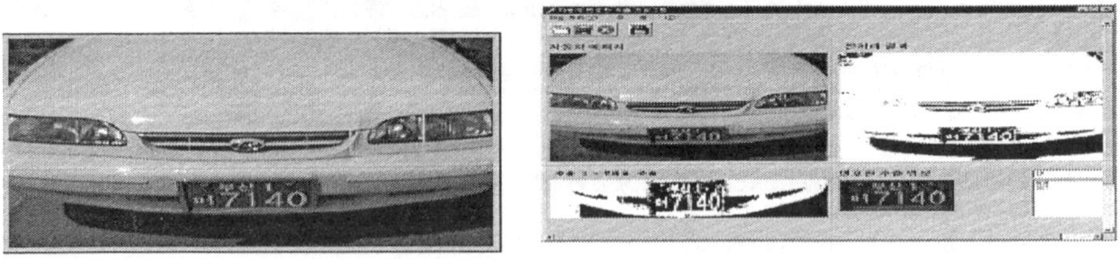

(a) Gray-method : a fail case (b) The proposed method : a success case

Fig. 7. Comparison of Gray-method and the proposed method

We assume that the license plate is composed of 4 codes; area code, vehicle code, purpose code and plate code as shown in Fig 8. Moreover region of the license plate consists of thc white-colored characters on the top of the green-colored back ground. The character extraction results by the existing position information method and the proposed contour tracking algorithm are shown in table 3.

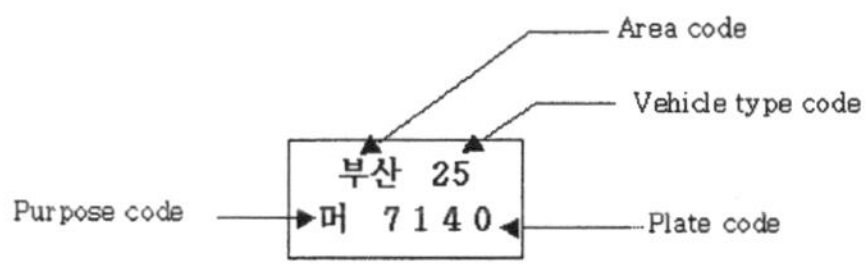

Fig. 8. Organization of license plate

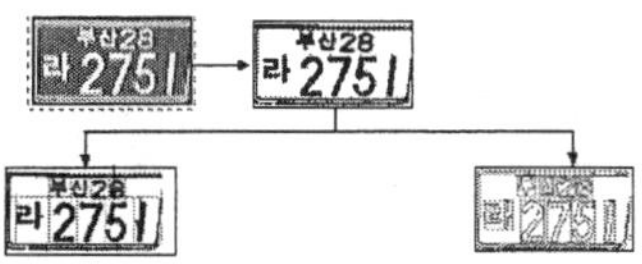

Fig. 9. Character extraction result

Table 3. Experimental results of character extraction

	Number of plates regions	Position information method	Contour tracking algorithm
Area code	200	182	192
Vehicle type code	100	90	95
Purpose code	183	177	180
Plate code	400	385	396
Total	883	834	863

For recognition of characters extracted by contour tracking algorithm, we considered two algorithms; (1) the conventional BP algorithm and (2) the proposed ENN algorithm. Table 4 gives information on the number of nodes in a hidden layer, and recognition results. We set learning rate and momentum for two algorithms by 0.75. Experimental results of the error BP algorithm give the number of nodes in a hidden layer for the minimum learning time in table 4. However there were a few oscillations in learning area code. Hence the recognition ratio for area code is lower than one for other code in the license plate region. As for the ENN, table 4 gives the number of nodes in a hidden layer, which was created dynamically with one initial node. The vigilance parameters for creating or updating nodes in a hidden layer are optimized when area code, vehicle type code, purpose code and plate number are 0.88, 0.93, 0.93 and 0.95, respectively. Consequently on recognition of characters, the ENN works better than the error BP algorithm. Fig 9 shows extraction results by two methods.

Table 4. Comparison of recognition result

		Number of hidden nodes	Recognition results
Error back-propagation	Area code	50	167/192
	Vehicle type code	45	84/93
	Purpose code	30	165/173
	Plate code	80	382/392
Enhanced Neural Network	Area code	99	189/192
	Vehicle type code	61	91/93
	Purpose code	54	171/173
	Plate code	101	390/392

6 Conclusions

In this paper, we presented new method to recognize a license plate from a vehicle image. In the proposed method, extraction of the license plate region is achieved through thresholding method based on dynamic threshold by using characteristics of a license plate. When we were extracting a license plate region, we took average brightness of the entire image as a threshold value, filter noisy and compute the density of each line. When we experimented using 114 vehicle images, 112 license plate regions are successfully extracted. The extraction ratio was better than those of two existing methods using the illumination variation and the RGB information. Furthermore, for extraction of characters, we proposed the contour tracking algorithm. Experimental results showed that the proposed method was more efficient than the existing location information method. For recognition of the extracted characters, we proposed the ENN, which complements disadvantages of error BP algorithm. The experimental results showed that the recognition rate in the proposed ENN is higher than that in conventional error BP algorithm. When learning data of a license plate in error BP algorithm, it was difficult to determine the number of nodes in a hidden layer, and also the convergence was low. However the ENN dynamically creates the number of nodes in a hidden layer and guarantees the convergence to learning. We note that the ENN algorithm creates more nodes in a hidden layer than that in error BP algorithm. In addition, the license plate region was not well presented at night, because the images are represented by only a light from camera.

Acknowledgement

This work was supported by Silla University. And this work was also supported by ECC(Electronic Ceramics Center) at Dong-eui University as RRC·TIC program which is financially supported by KOSEF(Korea Science and Engineering Foundation) under MOST(Ministry of Science and Technology), and ITEP(Korea Institute of Industrial Technology Evaluation and Planning) under MOCIE(Ministry of Commerce, Industry and Energy), and Busan Metropolitan City.

References

1. H. J. Choi, Y. H. Oh, T. Agui and M. Nakajima, "An Extraction Method of Car Number-Plates using Pyramid-Structured Hough Transform," Transaction of Korea Information Science Society (KISS), Vol.14, No.1, pp.312-315, 1987.
2. R. Taktak, m. Dufaut and R. Husson, "Road Modeling and Vehicle Detection by using Image Processing," Proceedings of IEEE SMC, pp.2153-2158, Oct. 1994.
3. E. R. Lee and H. J. Kim, "Automatic Recognition of a car License Plate using Color Image Processing," Proceedings of IEEE Image Processing, Vol.2, pp.301-305.
4. M. Y. Nam, J. H. Lee and K. B. Kim, "Extraction System of a Car License Plate using The Enhanced HIS Color Information," Proceedings of Korea Multimedia Society, Vol.2, No.1, pp.345-349, 1999.

5. Abhijit S. Pandya and Robert B. Macy, "Pattern Recognition with Neural Networks in C++," CRC Press, 1996.
6. Y. Hirose, K. Yammashita and S. Hijiya, "Backpropagation Algorithm which Varies the Number of Hidden Units," Neural Networks, Vol.4, pp.61-66, 1991.
7. K. B. Kim and K. C. Kim," A Study on Face Recognition using New Fuzzy ART," Proceedings of ITC-CSCC, Vol.2, pp.1057-1060, 1998.
8. J. B. Lee, A Study on The Recognition of The Low Contrasted and Titled Car License Plate, MS Thesis, Soong Sil University, Jun, 1995.
9. J. R. Cowell, "Syntactic Pattern Recognizer for Vehicle Identification Numbers," Journal of Image and Vision Computing, Vol.13, No.1, pp.13-19, 1995.
10. E. k. Lim, H. K. Yang and K. B. Kim, "Recognition of Car License Plate using Kohonen Algorithm, Proceedings of ITC-CSCC, Vol.2, pp.785-788, 2000.

Generalizing the Active Shape Model by Integrating Structural Knowledge to Recognize Hand Drawn Sketches

Stephan Al-Zubi and Klaus Tönnies

Otto-von-Guericke University Magdeburg, Department of Simulation and Graphics
P.O.Box 4120, D-39106 Magdeburg, Germany
{stephan,klaus}@isg.cs.uni-magdeburg.de

Abstract. We propose a new deformable shape model Active Shape Structural Model (ASSM) for recognition and reconstruction. The main features of ASSM are: (1) It describes variations of shape not only statistically as Active shape/Appearance model but also by structural variations. (2) Statistical and structural prior knowledge is integrated resulting in a multi-resolution shape description such that the statistical variation becomes more constrained as structural information is added. Experiments on hand drawn sketches of mechanical systems using electronic ink demonstrate the ability of the deformable model to recognize objects structurally and reconstruct them statistically.

1 Introduction

Shape representation, recognition and classification is used for analyzing 2-d and 3-d data as well as to analyze 3-d data from 2-d projections. This work is interested in the former. Various deformable shape models have been developed in recent years and used for segmentation, motion tracking, reconstruction and comparison between shapes. These models can be broadly classified into three paradigms:

1. Statistical models use prior knowledge about shape variation for reconstruction.
2. Dynamic models fit shape data using built-in smoothness constraints.
3. Structural models extract structural features to compare and classify shapes.

One of the important statistical models is the Active Shape and Appearance Model developed by Cootes et. al [1] that utilizes principal component analysis in order to describe variations of landmarks and textures. The Active Appearance Motion Model by Mitchell et. al [2] extends the active appearance model to fit a time varying shape like the heart. Another important example is probabilistic registration by Chen [3] that uses the per-voxel gray level and shift vector distributions to guide a better fit between the brain atlas and brain data.

The restriction in statistical models is that they describe the statistical variations of a fixed-structure shape and not structural differences between different shapes.

An example of dynamic models is the front propagation method by Malladi et. al [4] that simulates an expanding closed curve that eventually fits the shape boundaries. A similar concept is found in dynamic particles by Szeliski et. al [5] that simulate a system of dynamically oriented particles that expand into the object surface guided by

N. Petkov and M.A. Westenberg (Eds.): CAIP 2003, LNCS 2756, pp. 320–328, 2003.

internal forces that maintain an even and smooth distribution between them. Another approach are T-snakes / surfaces by McInerny et. al [6] that use the ACID grid (a decomposition of space) that enable traditional snakes to adapt to complex topologies.

The dynamic models are able to segment and sample shapes of complex topology such as blood vessels. Their restriction is that they cannot characterize the shapes they segment either statistically or structurally.

A good example of structural models is segmentation of shapes into geons as in Wu et. al [11]. This model uses the finite element method to estimate the charge density of a shape surface. This identifies boundaries of high curvature where the shape is divided into subparts. Seven parametric geons such as cylinder or ellipsoid are fitted to the subparts resulting in a simplified structural description of the shape.

A similar concept to geons is shape blending by DeCarlo et. al [8]. It begins by fitting an ellipsoid to the shape. The fitting process tears the surface into two blended surface patches at points where the object has protrusions or holes. The importance of blended surfaces is that we can construct a shape graph of protrusions and holes.

Shape structure can also be extracted using the shock grammar by Siddiqi et. al [7]. This model defines four types of shocks, which are evolving medial axes formed from colliding propagating fronts that originate at shape boundaries. The model defines a shock grammar that restricts how the shock types can combine to form a shape. The grammar is used to eliminate invalid shock combinations. Resulting shock graphs facilitate comparison between shapes.

The structural models are data driven in that they have no prior knowledge about shape structure. They also can not describe the shapes they fit statistically.

The model we propose defines multi-resolution a-priori knowledge about the shape both at the structural and the statistical level. It is called Active Shape Structural Model (ASSM). It extends the ability of statistical models to handle structural variability and structural models to include a-priori shape information.

2 Method

Hand drawn sketches were chosen to demonstrate the ASSM because they have the following properties:

1. Sketches are more suitable for shape oriented models as opposed to feature oriented models such as cursive hand writing recognition.
2. Training and testing data are easy to generate and no preprocessing or postprocessing steps are required.
3. If we impose the constraint that no structure is smaller than a stroke, we can easily separate shape sub-structures from each other.
4. Strokes are suitable for statistical analysis because they vary shape in relationship to each other or when drawn by the same user or different users.

Sketches are gaining increased importance with the shift to pen based interface used for palm and tablet computers. Currently sketching systems are employed in the field of design such as: Design of user interfaces [13], recognition of mechanical designs [14] and content based image retrieval [12, 15].

Many sketching systems restrict sketch recognition to simple shape primitives such as a square, circle, polygons or other specific shapes [14,16]. We propose a new system that studies sketches statistically allowing a richer, more complex and uniform characterization of shapes.

The sketch is represented at three levels: Stroke, object and relation (See Fig. 1). The stroke is the atomic unit of shape. An ordered list of strokes representing a single entity is an object. Groups of objects, that are statistically correlated together, are combined by relations. A relation may also include other relations. The components of a relation are not drawn in any predefined order.

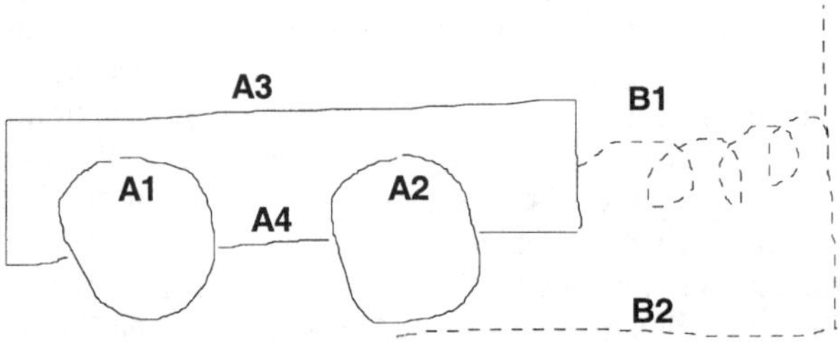

Fig. 1. Levels of a sketch: (1) Strokes {A1... A4, B1, B2} (2) Objects: Cart, spring (3) Relations: Correlation between the length of the spring and the distance between the cart and the wall.

The ASSM consists of a training module and a recognition module. The training module provides prior knowledge to the ASSM. The recognition module uses the prior knowledge of the ASSM to recognize and reconstruct structures from sketches.

2.1 The Training Module

A shape table is constructed from shape samples in four steps:

1. Strokes and multi-strokes are sampled into statistical vectors.
2. Sampled vectors are aligned for statistical analysis.
3. Principal component analysis is applied on the aligned samples.
4. Shape regression parameters are computed for relations.

During sampling, a stroke is defined as a parametric B-spline curve interpolating a sequence of device sampled points: $\mathbf{p}(t)=(\mathrm{x}(t), \mathrm{y}(t))$ where $0 \leq t \leq t_{max}$ is the time in milliseconds. Time is used as the interpolating variable because it samples more of the curve at points of high curvature and high detail. An n-sampling of the stroke $\mathbf{p}$ is a vector $\mathbf{x}_n=(x_1, x_2 \ldots x_n, y_1, y_2 \ldots y_n)^T$ where $(x_i, y_i)=\mathbf{p}((i-1)t_{max} / (n-1))$, $1 \leq i \leq n$. Objects and relations consist of multiple strokes $\mathbf{q}=(\mathbf{p}_1, \mathbf{p}_2 \ldots \mathbf{p}_m)$. $\mathbf{q}$ is statistically sampled by concatenating the corresponding sample vectors $\mathbf{x}=(\mathbf{x}_1^T, \mathbf{x}_2^T \ldots \mathbf{x}_m^T)^T$.

A population of stroke / multiple-stroke samples $S=\{\mathbf{x}_1, \mathbf{x}_2 \ldots \mathbf{x}_p\}$ is then iteratively aligned to an average shape $\bar{\mathbf{x}}$ by finding the transform parameters $\boldsymbol{\theta}_i$ that minimizes the average Euclidian distance between the corresponding n points of $\mathbf{x}_i$ and $\bar{\mathbf{x}}$. $\bar{\mathbf{x}}$ is initialized as $\mathbf{x}_1$ and recalculated after every realignment of S. The transformation parameters $\boldsymbol{\theta}$ are translation and optionally rotation, scale or all three.

After aligning S, we apply principal component analysis to yield a matrix of t principal components $\boldsymbol{\Phi}=[\phi_1, \phi_2 \ldots \phi_t]$. The shape parameters are described by a vector $\mathbf{b}$ such that $\mathbf{x}=\bar{\mathbf{x}}+\boldsymbol{\Phi}\mathbf{b}$. Fig. 2 shows the first three variation modes of a com-

such that $\mathbf{x} = \bar{\mathbf{x}} + \mathbf{\Phi b}$. Fig. 2 shows the first three variation modes of a complex two-stroke shape analyzed from 20 samples. The variation of an object becomes more specific as it becomes a part of a relation. Fig. 3 shows how the variation of a rectangle becomes more constrained as it becomes part of a shape group. The significance of this is that a sub-shape changes its variation modes according to its *context*.

Fig. 2. The effect of varying the first three shape parameters of a two-stroke shape by ±3 standard deviations.

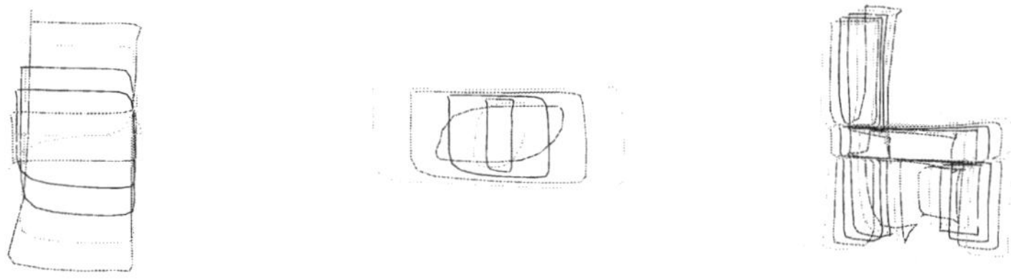

Fig. 3. Left, middle: the first two variation modes of a rectangle object. Right: The first variation mode of a chair relation between four rectangles. The variation of each rectangle becomes more constrained and correlated to other rectangles.

Relations can be used to *predict* new shapes when only some are given using a regression technique. This speeds up searching for relations and also completes missing structures in the image. Principal component regression (PCR) uses the shape parameter space **b** as regression and observation variables. Shape coordinates **x** are not used because they have a high linear correlation. Given a relation $R = \{r_1, r_2, ... r_n\}$ between n objects/relations of which $A \subset R$ are regression objects and $B \subset R, B \cap A = \phi$ are observation objects and given a population of p samples, we compute a regression matrix **B** as follows:

1. We align the p samples and compute $(\bar{\mathbf{x}}, \mathbf{\Phi}_A, \mathbf{\Phi}_B, \boldsymbol{\lambda}_A, \boldsymbol{\lambda}_B)$ where $(\mathbf{\Phi}_A, \boldsymbol{\lambda}_A)$ are the latent vectors and roots of the regressors and similarly $(\mathbf{\Phi}_B, \boldsymbol{\lambda}_B)$ are the latent vectors and roots of the observation objects.
2. For every sample x_i, $1<i<p$ compute the shape coordinates of regressors and observation objects $\mathbf{b}_{i,A} = \mathbf{\Phi}^t(\mathbf{x}_{i,A} - \bar{\mathbf{x}}_A)$, $\mathbf{b}_{i,B} = \mathbf{\Phi}^t(\mathbf{x}_{i,B} - \bar{\mathbf{x}}_B)$.
3. We form a regression matrix from shape parameters $\mathbf{R} = \left[\mathbf{b}_{1,A}^T \dots \mathbf{b}_{p.A}^T\right]^T$ and an observation matrix of shape parameters $\mathbf{S} = \left[\mathbf{b}_{1,B}^T \dots \mathbf{b}_{p,B}^T\right]^T$. Then we compute the regression matrix $\mathbf{B} = (\mathbf{R}^t\mathbf{R})^{-1}\mathbf{R}^t\mathbf{S}$. Let $\boldsymbol{\theta}_{A/B} = (\bar{\mathbf{x}}, \mathbf{\Phi}_\mathbf{x}, \mathbf{\Phi}_\mathbf{y}, \boldsymbol{\lambda}_\mathbf{x}, \boldsymbol{\lambda}_\mathbf{x}, \mathbf{B})$ be the regression parameters of A to B.

4. For a relation R that consists of n objects/relations $\{r_1 \ldots r_n\}$ we compute the regression parameters $\boldsymbol{\theta}_{\{r_1,r_2 \ldots r_{i-1}\}/\{r_i\}}$, $i = 2 \ldots n$.

Fig. 4 shows how PCR is used to predict parts of a chair. We see the match between actual and predicted shapes increases as more shapes are used for regression. The statistical and regression parameters of strokes, objects and relations are then stored in a shape table. For a relation consisting of n objects, regression matrices are stored as $\{\mathbf{B}_2 \ldots \mathbf{B}_{n-1}\}$ where $\mathbf{B}_i$ means that we use the first 1 ... (i-1) objects as regression shapes and the ith object as the observation object (as depicted in Fig. 4).

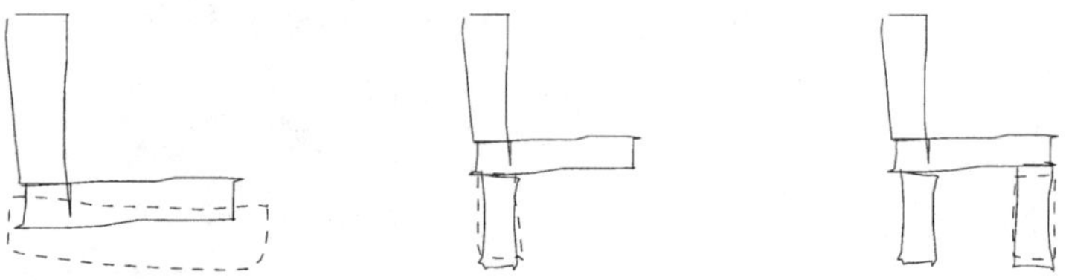

Fig. 4. A chair modeled as a relation between rectangular single-stroke objects. PCR constructs the expected shape given 1, 2 and three regressor objects from left to right respectively. As we can see regression improves its fit to the original data as more regression objects are used.

2.2 The Recognition Module

After constructing the shape table, we can use it to recognize and reconstruct new sketches. The sketch interpretation consists of the following: Sequences of strokes are classified as candidate objects. Then, relations are recognized in the sketch by using the structural prior knowledge to generate new objects given an existing object set. The sketch is then searched for evidence that supports the generated assumption. When there is sufficient data to support the relation then it gets accepted. Finally, conflicting interpretations between candidate objects are resolved using the object's largest context principle. This means that candidate objects that belong to bigger relations are favored to single objects or objects that belong to smaller relations. Once a candidate object is selected for removal , all the relations it belongs to are removed.

The best fitting shape $\mathbf{x}'$ for a shape class with parameters $(\overline{\mathbf{x}}, \boldsymbol{\Phi}, \boldsymbol{\lambda})$ and n-sampled stroke/object/relation $\mathbf{x}$ is computed as follows:

1. Initialize the best fitting model $\mathbf{x}'$ to $\overline{\mathbf{x}}$.
2. Transform $\mathbf{x}$ with rigid body transform $\boldsymbol{\theta}$ into $\mathbf{x}_\theta$ to minimize $\|\mathbf{x}' - \mathbf{x}_\theta\|$.
3. Compute the nearest fitting shape parameters $\mathbf{b} = \boldsymbol{\Phi}^T(\mathbf{x}_\theta - \overline{\mathbf{x}})$.
4. Compute the best fitting shape as $\mathbf{x}' = \overline{\mathbf{x}} + \boldsymbol{\Phi}\mathbf{b}$.
5. Goto (2) and repeat until $\mathbf{x}'$ converges.

The shape similarity measure computed from the best fitting shape $\mathbf{x}'$ as the weighted sum of the deviation of $\mathbf{x}'$ from its mean and the maximum distance between the corresponding points of $\mathbf{x}_\theta$ and $\mathbf{x}'$ as follows

$$dissimilarity(\mathbf{x},\bar{\mathbf{x}},\mathbf{\Phi},\boldsymbol{\lambda}) = deformation(\mathbf{x},\bar{\mathbf{x}},\mathbf{\Phi},\boldsymbol{\lambda}) + \alpha \cdot distance(\mathbf{x},\bar{\mathbf{x}},\mathbf{\Phi},\boldsymbol{\lambda}), \tag{1}$$

$$deformation(\mathbf{x},\bar{\mathbf{x}},\mathbf{\Phi},\boldsymbol{\lambda}) = \sqrt{\sum_{i=1}^{t}\left(\frac{b_i}{\lambda_i}\right)^2} \quad \text{where } \mathbf{b} = \mathbf{\Phi}^t(\mathbf{x}'-\bar{\mathbf{x}}) = (b_1, b_2 ... b_t),$$

$$distance(\mathbf{x},\bar{\mathbf{x}},\mathbf{\Phi},\boldsymbol{\lambda}) = \max_{i=1}^{t}\left|x_i' - x_{\theta,i}\right| \text{ where}$$

$$\mathbf{x}' = (x_1, x_2 \dots x_n), \mathbf{x}_\theta = (x_{\theta,1}, x_{\theta,2} \dots x_{\theta,n})$$

Objects and relations are accepted or rejected by applying a threshold τ to eq. 1.

Ordered sequences of strokes are classified into candidate objects. Given a sequence of strokes $(\mathbf{s}_1, \mathbf{s}_2 \dots \mathbf{s}_k)$ we find candidate objects as follows:

1. For every i=1...k, we classify the first $\{\mathbf{s}_i, \mathbf{s}_{i+1} \dots \mathbf{s}_{i+k}\}$ strokes for some k using the shape table ST. We designate $C(\mathbf{s}_j)$ as all single stroke classes of which the dissimilarity is below the threshold τ in eq. 1.
2. Every object that starts with a stroke sequence in $C(\mathbf{s}_i)\times C(\mathbf{s}_{i+1})\dots C(\mathbf{s}_{i+k})$ is tested by similarity measure in eq. 1 to find the set of acceptable candidate objects $CO = \{o_1, o_2 \dots o_m\}$

A relation $R = \{r_1, r_2 \dots r_n\}$ with PCR parameters $\{\boldsymbol{\theta}_1, \boldsymbol{\theta}_2 \cdots \boldsymbol{\theta}_{n-1}\}$ is recognized by comparing the generated expected object or relation with the actual objects or relations (as depicted in Fig. 4) in the sketch as follows:

1. Find all objects of type r_1 in the sketch. Set i=2.
2. Generate the expected shape of type r_{i+1}, call it $\mathbf{x}'_{i+1}$, using regression parameters $\boldsymbol{\theta}_i$ and previously found shapes $P = \{\mathbf{x}_1, \mathbf{x}_2, \dots \mathbf{x}_i\}$.
3. Find objects or relations of type $r_{i+1} : S = \{\mathbf{x}_1, \mathbf{x}_2 \dots \mathbf{x}_k\}$. Find $\min_{\mathbf{x}_j \in S}\left\|\mathbf{x}_j - \mathbf{x}'_{i+1}\right\|$
4. If $\left\|\mathbf{x}_j - \mathbf{x}'_{i+1}\right\| < \varepsilon$, then add $\mathbf{x}_j$ to P, Increment (i) and goto (2). Otherwise R is not recognized.

The final stage of interpretation is to delete conflicting interpretations. A conflict occurs when two objects o_1, o_2 share one or more strokes (as depicted in fig. 7). Let's denote by $context(o_i)$ as the set of all relations $C = \{r_1, r_2 \dots r_k\}$ of which o_i is a part of such that no relation in C is contains another relation in C. If o_i is not a part of a relation then set $context(o_i) = \{o_i\}$ .We assign a cost function which measures the cost of removing o_i and all its relations as follows

$$cost(o_i) = \sum_{r_i \in context(o_i)} size(r_i) / similarity(r_i), \tag{2}$$

where $size(r_i)$ is a measure of complexity and importance of shape r_i .

3 Experimental Results

The goal of the experiments is to demonstrate the abilities of ASSM on sketches of complex mechanical systems. They demonstrate the ASSM model because objects correspond to machine parts and relations represent scale and connectivity constraints.

The ASSM model was trained with 10-30 samples per object or relation drawn by a single person. The number of principal components ranged between 3 for simple shapes up to 12 for the most complex shape. The number of principal components was set to explain 95% of the variation in samples. The algorithm is well conditioned because the thresholds τ, ε could be set high without compromising the result. This is because most conflicting interpretations were eliminated using the shape's largest context as depicted in Fig. 7.

Fig. 5. Objects: Spring, weight, wheel, joint, force, pivot, Bar and Rope.

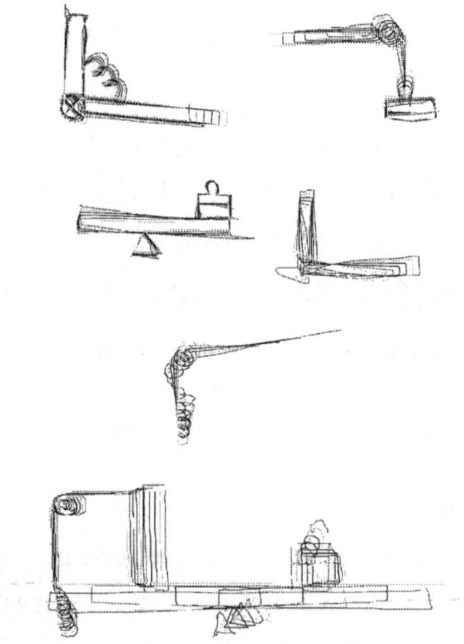

Fig. 6. Relations: Arm, crane, lever, corner, pulley and "ShockAbsorber" consisting of a pulley, lever and corner.

Fig. 5 shows objects used in constructing the sketches. Binary and higher order relations analyze spatial and scale covariance between machine parts as seen in Fig. 6. Fig. 8 shows the results for interpreting a sketch. The left image shows the individual objects with the best fitting shape overlaid and the latent coordinates of each object. The right image shows relations binding these objects. The shock absorber is the largest relation binding three smaller relations.

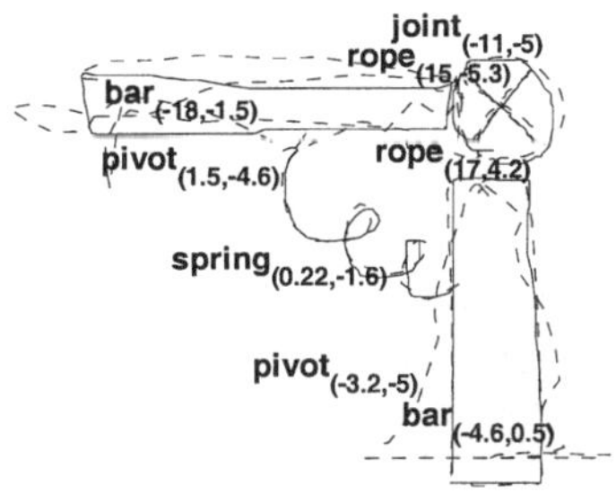

Fig. 7. Conflicting interpretations like the pivot and rope objects above are resolved using the fact that the bars and the joint are part of an arm relation which represents a larger shape context with higher confidence.

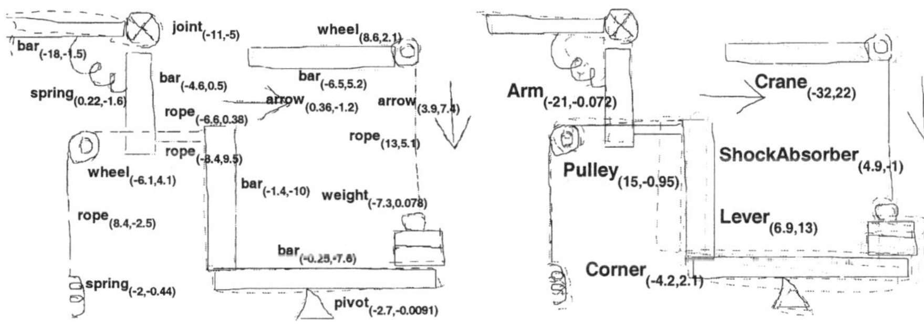

Fig. 8. Example sketch with the overlaid fitted model. Left: Objects, Right: Relations. Each object or relation is characterized by its shape parameters where the first two are shown.

4 Conclusions and Future Work

ASSM demonstrates a way to extend statistical models to handle structural variability. Robustness of statistical models comes from their prior knowledge of shape variation. Extending prior knowledge to structural variations enables us to robustly handle incomplete or false interpretation of structure.

Training of statistical variation was based on sketches by a single person. Future work will include the analysis of sketches from various persons including biometric analysis for the discrimination of individual drawing behavior based on ASSM.

The main problem with ASSM is that a large training set is required where all the structural information is defined beforehand. Automatic learning of shape using support vector machines will be investigated to define a deformable shape model that cyclically acquires and applies prior knowledge about shape.

Future applications of ASSM will be for content based image retrieval (CBIR) of image databases [10]. This is because very few CBIR systems today use shape and most rely on color distribution and low level features like histograms [12].

References

1. Cootes, T., Taylor, C.: Statistical Models of Appearance for Medical Image Analysis and Computer Vision. SPIE Proc. Medical Imaging:Image Processing, Vol.4322 (2001) 236-248
2. Mitchell, S., Lelieveldt, B., van der Geest, et. al.: Time Continuous Segmentation of Cardiac MR Image Sequences using Active Appearance Motion Models. SPIE Proc. Medical Imaging: Image Processing, Vol. 4322 (2001) 249-256
3. Chen M.: 3-D Deformable Registration Using a Statistical Atlas with Applications in Medicine. MICCAI (1999) 621-630
4. Malladi, R., Sethian, J., Vemuri, B.: Shape Modeling with Front Propagation: A Level Set Approach. IEEE PAMI, Vol. 17(2) (1995) 158-175
5. Szeliski, R., Tonnesen, D., Terzopoulos, D.: Modeling Surfaces of Arbitrary Topology with Dynamic particles. Proc. Computer Vision and Vision Recognition (CVPR) (1993) 82-87
6. McInerney, T., Terzopoulos, D.: Topology Adaptive Deformable Surfaces for Medical Image Volume Segmentation. IEEE Trans. on Medical Imaging, Vol. 18(9) (1999) 100-111
7. Siddiqi, K., Kimia, B.: Toward a Shock Grammar for Recognition. IEEE Conf. on Computer Vision and Pattern Recognition (1996)
8. DeCarlo, D., Metaxas, D.: Shape Evolution with Structural and Topological Changes using Blending. IEEE PAMI, Vol. 20(11) (1998) 1186-1205
9. Al-Zubi, S., Tönnies, K.: Extending Active Shape Models to Incorporate a-priori Knowledge about Structural Variability. DAGM Pattern Recognition, Vol. 2449 LNCS. Springer Verlag (2002) 338-344
10. Mokhtarian, F., S. Abbasi, J. Kittler.: Robust and Efficient Shape Indexing through Curvature Scale Space, Proc. British Machine Vision Conference (1996) 53-62
11. Wu, K., Levine, M.: Segmenting 3D Objects into Geons. ICIAP(1995) 321-334
12. Veltcamp, R., Tanase, M.: Content-Based Image retrieval Systems: A Survey. Technical report UU-CS-2000-34, Department of Computing Science, Utrecht University (2000)
13. Lin, J., Newman, M., et al.:DENIM: Finding a Tighter Fit Between Tools and Practice for Web Site Design. CHI Letters: Human Factors in Computing Systems(2000)510-517
14. C. Alvarado, C., R. Davis: Resolving ambiguities to create a natural computer-based sketching environment. IJCAI-2001
15. Chans, Y., Lei, Z., Lopresti, D., S. Kung: A Feature-Based Approach for Image Retrieval by Sketch. SPIE Proc. Multimedia Storage and Archiving Systems (1997)
16. Fonseca, M., J. Jorge: Using Fuzzy Logic to Recognize Geometric Shapes Interactively. FUZZIEEE (2000)

Automatic Segmentation of Diatom Images

Andrei C. Jalba and Jos B.T.M. Roerdink

Institute of Mathematics and Computing Science
University of Groningen, P.O. Box 800
9700 AV, Groningen, The Netherlands
{andrei,roe}@cs.rug.nl
http://www.cs.rug.nl

Abstract. In this paper we present a segmentation technique based on tools from mathematical morphology which can be successfully used for automatic segmentation of diatom images. The proposed method belongs to the class of hybrid segmentation techniques, and is based on the morphological watershed from markers. The novelty of this method is the computation and selection of markers. A new connected operator is used to simplify the input image and to produce candidate marker regions. A further step which selects among these regions is carried out in order to produce the final markers as a label image, and a watershed process initiated from this image is applied on the gradient of the input image. In a post-processing step, the contours of the diatoms present in the resulting image (given as watershed lines) are extracted.

1 Introduction

Segmentation is one of the critical aspects in many image analysis and computer vision tasks, because effective segmentation usually dictates successful analysis. Image segmentation is the process in which an image is divided in its constituent parts, and ideally it should be computationally efficient and correspond well with the physical objects represented in the image. This implies that segmentation should produce a complete partitioning of the image such that object contours are closed and precisely localized.

There are four main approaches [1,9] for the segmentation of grey-scale images: threshold techniques, boundary-based methods, region-based methods, and hybrid techniques which combine both boundary and region criteria. In this paper, we mention only hybrid techniques, while for a complete review on image segmentation we refer to [9].

Two important representatives in the class of hybrid techniques are morphological watershed segmentation [7,10] and seeded region growing [1]. The watershed method regards an image as a landscape where intensity values correspond to elevations, and is generally applied to the gradient of the image. Advantages of watershed segmentation are that it (generally) leads to closed boundaries of the image regions and it can describe edge junctions [8]. As pointed out in [6], the seeds in the seeded region growing method play the same role as the markers

N. Petkov and M.A. Westenberg (Eds.): CAIP 2003, LNCS 2756, pp. 329–336, 2003.

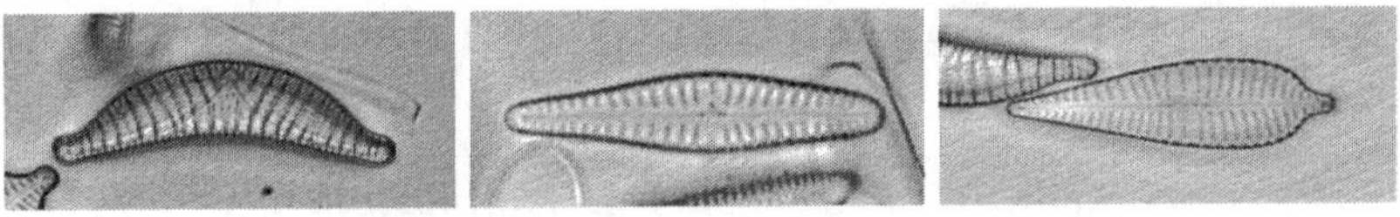

Fig. 1. Some examples of diatom shells.

used in watershed segmentation. Although both methods have the advantages that they are fast and parameter free, the most critical part is the selection of seeds.

Our overall goal in this work is to develop a framework for automatic segmentation of high-magnification, grey-scale diatom images. Diatoms are microscopic, single-celled algae, whose sensitivity to environmental parameters means that they can be used to monitor changes in the environment, or have forensic applications. All these applications require counting and identification of different species present in the sample of interest. However, prior to automatic identification, reliable segmentation should be performed. Therefore, in this paper we propose a hybrid segmentation method which can be successfully used for automatic segmentation of diatom images. The goal is to extract the outline (encoded as chain-codes) of each diatom shell present in the input image (see Fig. 1 for some examples). The typical size of these images is between 600 ... 900 pixels for the horizontal dimension and 200 ... 400 pixels for the vertical dimension. Ideally, each image contains a single diatom shell, but as can be seen in the figure, diatoms may lay on top of each other, may not be in proper focus, or can be very close to each other. Moreover, dust specks and background texture may be visible in some images.

2 A Hybrid Segmentation Technique

The main steps of the proposed method are shown in Fig. 2. The processing flow of the input image branches in two paths according to the desired output. One of the paths ends with the selection of markers which produces the label image, while the other ends with the computation of the gradient-magnitude image. Both resulting images are then used in the watershed-segmentation step.

The novelty of the technique is the computation and selection of markers. A new connected operator is used to simplify the input image and to produce candidate marker regions. The final marker regions are selected based on the area of each candidate region, after some morphological processing is performed.

All main steps of the method are described in the next sections, beginning with the steps which yield the label image.

2.1 Preprocessing

In the pre-processing step, a non-linear method for contrast enhancement [3] is applied to the input image. The basic idea of this algorithm is to perform a sliding

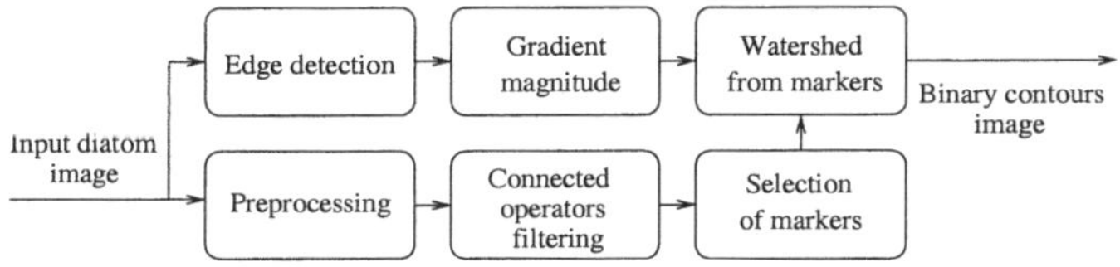

Fig. 2. Hybrid segmentation method diagram.

downhill on the gradient-squared surface until a local minimum is reached. Then all pixels along this path are given the image intensity of this local minimum. The squared image gradient is computed using a Sobel operator [4].

The reasoning for using this method for contrast enhancement is that it performs a (re)quantization of the grey levels in the input image, controlled by the gradient-squared function. Since spurious pixels are linked to homogeneous regions, areas of these regions increase, and in turn, this provides an increased robustness of the operator in Eq. (1). However, the technique is not used on the path which leads to the gradient-magnitude image, since it may introduce false edges which hampers the evolution of the watershed. Nevertheless the method shows desirable results especially for low contrast images, and can be used for marker extraction, even though it may introduce false edges. The regions associated with the false edges can be eliminated either by the subsequent filtering step, or during the selection of marker regions. If some regions still survive, they can be neglected when the contours are extracted (see Sect. 3), due the property of the watershed to allow for T-junctions.

2.2 Connected Operator Filtering

It is common to represent a grey-scale image by its level components (connected components, in the binary case). Let R be the domain of a grey-scale image f. A *flat zone* L_h at level h of grey-scale image f is a connected component of the level set $X_h(f) = \{p \in R | f(p) = h\}$. A *regional maximum* M_h at level h is a flat zone which has only strictly lower neighbours, and a *peak component* P_h at level h is a connected component of the threshold set $T_h(f) = \{p \in R | f(p) \geq h\}$. At each level h there may exist several such components, indexed as L_h^i, P_h^j, M_h^k, with i, j, k from three index sets.

Max-trees were introduced by Salembier *et al.* [11] as a versatile data structure for anti-extensive connected set operators. A max-tree is a rooted tree, in which each of the nodes C_h^k at grey-level h corresponds to a peak component P_h^k. However, C_h^k contains only those pixels in P_h^k which have grey level h. In other words, it is the union of all flat zones $L_h^j \subseteq P_h^k$. An example of a 1-D signal, its peak components and its max-tree representation is shown in Fig. 3.

Once the max-tree has been built, it can be used for processing of the input image, since the tree is its representation. For tasks of filtering, this is a three-step process: construction of the max-tree, criterion assessment and decision, and image restitution. The filtering step analyzes each node C_h^k by evaluating a specific criterion $T(C_h^k)$ and takes a decision on the elimination or preservation of

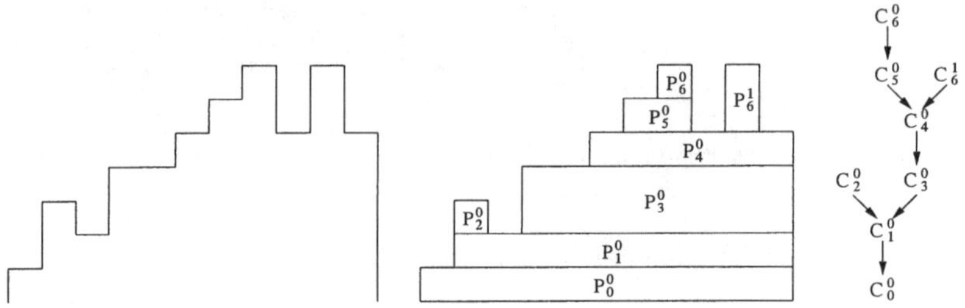

Fig. 3. The max-tree structure. *Left*: a 1-D signal; *center*: peak components P_h^k of the signal; *right*: its corresponding max-tree.

the node. The last step, called here restitution, transforms the filtered max-tree into an output image.

Let us assume that components with large areas compared with the area of their parent component are important and are to be preserved by the filtering process. Let $A_{C_m^n}$ be the area of the component associated with the node C_m^n. We propose to use the *relative percentage difference* as a measure of closeness between the area of the component and the sum of areas of its child components (corresponding to child nodes $C_{h_i}^k$), *i.e.*

$$d_A = 100 \times \frac{|\sum_i A_{C_{h_i}^k} - A_{C_m^n}|}{A_{C_m^n}} \quad (\%), \tag{1}$$

with $h_i > m$, and k, n from two index sets. Starting with the root node, d_A is recursively computed according to Eq. (1). If for a given node C_h^k this value is larger than a threshold λ then *all* its child nodes are marked as deleted. In a subsequent step, all marked nodes are merged with their nearest preserved ancestors; in our implementation $\lambda = 1\%$.

2.3 Selection of Markers

In this subsection a simple method is presented which selects the final markers from candidate marker regions. The selection of markers is the most critical part of the segmentation based on watershed from markers. As the number of markers does not change during the watershed evolution, a marker region lost during marker selection cannot be recovered later. Therefore, special care must be taken during the marker selection process, for which we propose the following procedure.

- Compute the morphological gradient (the difference between dilated and eroded images), and label with zero all pixel positions where its value is greater than zero.
- Do a connected component labeling (with labels greater than zero) of all regions which are not assigned a value of zero;
- Regions with small areas are not considered marker regions, *i.e.* they are marked with a zero label.

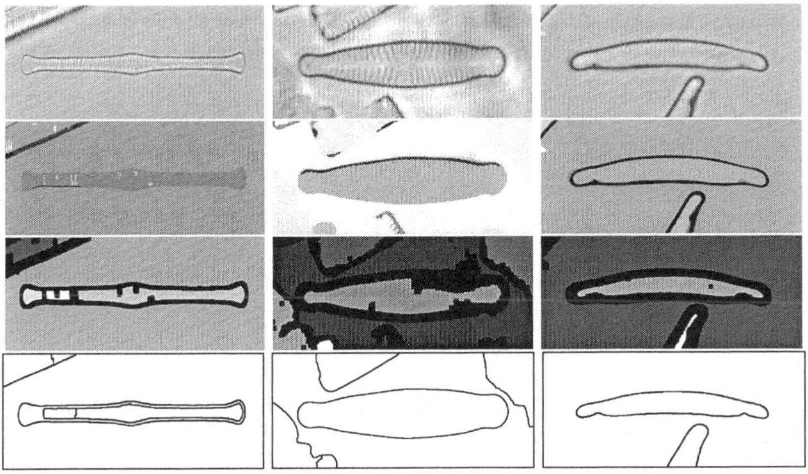

Fig. 4. Hybrid segmentation technique. Examples. *First row*: diatom images; *second row*: filtered images; *third row*: label images; *fourth row*: resulting binary images.

At the end of this procedure, all marker regions are given a unique label greater than zero, and all other regions, with uncertain region membership, are marked with zero. The decision about their region membership is made by the watershed transform by growing basins from marker regions under the control of the magnitudes of edges.

Notice that an initially connected region may be split into more than one during this process, and assigned different labels. Fortunately this problem can be corrected during the post-processing step (see Sect. 3), due to the property of the watershed to allow for T-junctions.

The size of the structuring element for both dilation and erosion was set to 13×13, and the threshold on area, for small region removal, was set to 100 pixels.

2.4 Gradient Magnitude Computation

The gradient of the image along with a certain degree of smoothing is obtained by convolving the initial image with a derivative Gaussian filter. In our implementation the width of the kernel σ was set to 4.0.

2.5 Watershed from Markers

Our implementation of the watershed from markers is based on the Image Foresting Transform (IFT) [5]. An advantage of the IFT compared to the classical watershed is that it guarantees the optimality of the solution, as long as the cost path is a non-decreasing function of the arc weights. Also, similarly to the watershed from markers using an ordered queue, the IFT does not need a change of homotopy (a minima imposition operator which changes the homotopy of the image in such a way that the desired markers are the only regional minima of the image [7]).

All regions in the label image whose pixel values are greater than zero provide the marker regions from which the watershed segmentation is initiated; the watershed propagation is done on the gradient-magnitude image (see Sect. 2.4). As a final step, the watershed lines are drawn in black on a white background, in order to provide a binary image.

2.6 Examples

Some example results produced using the proposed hybrid segmentation technique are shown in Fig. 4. The input diatom images are shown in the first row of the image. The resulting images, after connected operators filtering (see Sect. 2.2), are shown in the second row. The label images (see Sect. 2.3) and the resulting binary images are shown in the third and fourth rows, respectively. Although the large region corresponding to the central diatom, present in the first image, is split by the marker selection procedure, this is not a problem since all extracted contours are flood-filled in the post-processing step (see Sect. 3). The T-junctions produced by the watershed lines can be observed in the first two cases.

3 Post-processing and Contour Extraction

First, *all* contours present in the binary image, produced by the segmentation method, are traced using a standard contour following algorithm [4]. Then, all extracted contours, which are necessarily closed, are filled at grey-level zero by a flood-fill algorithm, and all obtained regions are drawn in the same image. In a further post-processing step, an opening with a structuring element of size 3×3 is performed, in order to prune thin structures, which may still be connected to diatom regions, due to debris or fragments of other diatoms. In this way, the union of all diatom and inner-diatom regions is performed and *all* diatom contours can be found by tracing only *one* contour per region. Finally, contours which enclose regions of areas smaller than 4900 pixels are not considered as diatom regions, and are rejected.

The whole tracing process is illustrated in Fig. 5. The initial diatom image and the binary contour image are shown in Fig. 5(a) and (b), respectively. The above procedure for contour extraction yields three contours depicted in Fig. 5(c). The regions obtained after flood-filling the traced contours are shown in Fig. 5(d). Notice that, surviving inner-diatom regions, which were not removed by filtering or by the marker selection procedure (see Sect. 2.2 and 2.3, respectively), are now merged in one large diatom region. After opening (Fig. 5(e)), and removal of small regions, the final contour(s) can be traced (Fig. 5(f)).

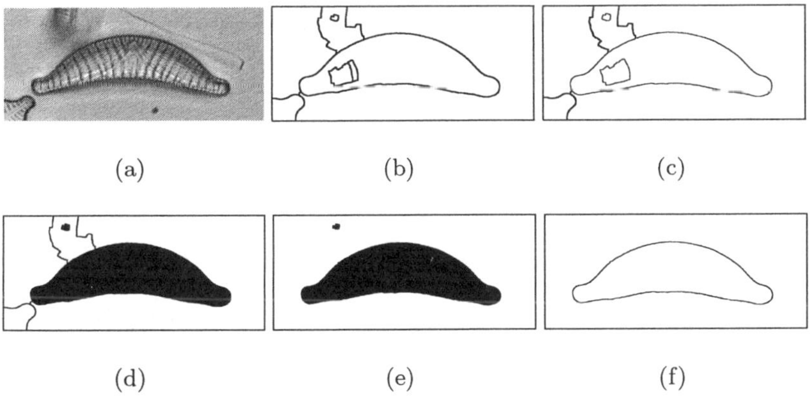

Fig. 5. Contour extraction. Example. (a) initial image; (b) binary image with watershed lines; (c) extracted contours; (d) regions obtained after flood-filling the contours; (e) opened image; (f) the final contour.

4 Experimental Results

The proposed segmentation method was used to extract binary contours from a large set of diatom images [2] comprising 808 files. The quality of the extracted contours was evaluated visually.

Unfortunately, because there is no established theory which defines the quality of a segmentation, we had to rely on some heuristic. Therefore, visual estimation of the quality of the contours was guided by the following criteria: (i) the contours should be smooth, (ii) they should correspond well with the perceived diatom outlines, and (iii) they should not enclose debris or diatom fragments. All contours that did not fulfill the above requirements and all images for which no appropriate contours could be extracted were considered errors. The hybrid technique showed very good segmentation results, with only 16 errors, leading to 98% correctly extracted contours.

5 Conclusions

In this paper we developed a framework for automatic segmentation of microscopic diatom images based on watershed segmentation from markers. The novelty of the proposed segmentation technique is the computation and the selection of markers. As the number of markers does not change during the watershed evolution, a marker region lost during marker selection cannot be recovered later. Therefore, we have proposed procedures which (i) compute candidate marker regions based on connected operators filtering, and (ii) select final markers based on the area of each candidate region, after some morphological post-processing is performed.

The proposed segmentation method was applied on a large set of diatom images and the extracted contours were evaluated qualitatively, by visually estimating the quality of the contours.

The technique yielded good results, obtaining 98% correctly extracted contours, with a very good quality of the contours. Therefore, our conclusion is that the segmentation of diatom images can be performed automatically, and with very good results.

References

1. Adams, R., Bischof, Leanne: Seeded Region Growing. IEEE Trans. on PAMI. **16(6)** (1994) 641–647
2. du Buf, H., Bayer, M.M. (ed.): Automatic Diatom Identification. World Scientific Publishing, Singapore (2002)
3. Fairfield, J.: Toboggan contrast enhancement for contrast segmentation. In: Proc. 10th ICPR. (1990) 712–716
4. Haralick, R.M., Shapiro, L.G.: Computer and Robot Vision. Addison-Wesley, New York (1992)
5. Lotufo, R., Falcao, A.: The ordered queue and the optimality of the watershed approaches. In: Goutsias, J., Vincent, L., Bloomberg, D. (eds.): Math. Morph. and its Application to Image and Sign. Process. Kluwer Academic Publishers, Dordrecht (2000) 341–350
6. Mehnert, A.,Jackway, P.: An improved seeded region growing algorithm. Pattern Rec. Lett. **18** (1997) 1065–1071
7. Meyer, F., Beucher, S.: Morphological segmentation. J. Vis. Comm. Image Repr. **1** (1990) 21–46
8. Najman, L., Schmitt, M.: Watershed of a continuous function. Sign. Proc. **38** (1994) 99–112
9. Pal, N., Pal, S.: A Review of Image Segmentation Techniques. Pattern Rec. **26(9)** (1993) 1277–1294
10. Roerdink, J.B.T.M., Meijster, A.: The watershed transform: Definitions, algorithms and parallelization strategies. Fundamenta Informaticae **41(1-2)** (2000)187–228
11. Salembier, P., Oliveras, A., Garrido, L.: Anti-extensive connected operators for image and sequence processing. IEEE Trans. Im. Proc. **7** (1998) 555–570

Topological Active Volumes

N. Barreira, M.G. Penedo, C. Mariño, and F.M. Ansia

LFCIA Lab, VARPA Group
Fac. de Informática, Universidade de A Coruña
Campus de Elviña s/n, C.P. 15781, A Coruña
castormp@fi.udc.es
http://varpa.lfcia.org

Abstract. In the last years, deformable models raised much interest and found various applications in the field of 2D and 3D computer vision. Active surfaces are usually employed for segmentation and object reconstruction. In this paper, a new model for 3D image segmentation is proposed, the Topological Active Volumes (TAV). This model is based on deformable models, it is able to integrate the most representative characteristics of the region-based and boundary-based segmentation models and it also provides information about the topological properties of the inside of detected objects. This model has the ability to perform topological local changes in its structure during the adjustment phase in order to: obtain a specific adjustment to object's local singularities, find several objects in the scene and identify and delimit holes in detected structures.

Keywords: segmentation, 3D reconstruction, active nets, active volumes.

1 Introduction

Deformable models were introduced by Kass et al. [1] in 2D as explicit deformable contours and generalized to the 3D case by Terzopoulos et al. [2]. In the last years, much models have been developed for the treatment of three-dimensional scenes. Most of those models are deformable surfaces mainly used in segmentation [3, 4] and modelization [5, 6] tasks. The level set approach has proved to be an efficient framework which integrates region and boundary information [7]. Other techniques like geodesic active regions [8] have also been employed in this area.

In this paper a new three-dimensional deformable model is proposed, the *Topological Active Volumes*, as an extension of the *Topological Active Nets* [9], focused on performing segmentation tasks by means of a volumetric distribution of nodes. It tries to solve some intrinsic problems to deformable models. First of all, it solves the initialization problem: in this model the initialization is always the same and includes the whole image. Second, it integrates information of edges and regions in the adjustment process in order to take advantage of both methods. The model allows the obtention of topological information inside the objects found. The model also has a dynamic behavior allowing topological local changes in order to perform accurate adjustments and to find all the objects of interest in the scene.

N. Petkov and M.A. Westenberg (Eds.): CAIP 2003, LNCS 2756, pp. 337–344, 2003.

2 Topological Active Volumes (TAV)

The model presented in this paper is an extension of Topological Active Nets [9] to three-dimensional world. Its operation is focused on extraction, modelization and reconstruction of volumetric objects present in the scene.

A TAV is a 3D structure composed by interrelated nodes where the basic repeated structure is a cube (figure 1). Parametrically, a TAV is defined as $v(r,s,t) = (x(r,s,t), y(r,s,t), z(r,s,t))$, where $(r,s,t) \in ([0,1] \times [0,1] \times [0,1])$. The state of the model is governed by an energy function defined as follows:

$$E(v) = \int_0^1 \int_0^1 \int_0^1 E_{int}(v(r,s,t)) + E_{ext}(v(r,s,t)) dr ds dt \quad (1)$$

where E_{int} and E_{ext} are the internal and the external energy of the TAV, respectively. The former controls the shape and the structure of the net. Its calculus depends on first and second order derivatives which control contraction and bending, respectively. The internal energy term is defined by:

$$\begin{aligned} E_{int}(v(r,s,t)) = &\alpha(|v_r(r,s,t))|^2 + |v_s(r,s,t))|^2 + |v_t(r,s,t))|^2) \\ &+ \beta(|v_{rr}(r,s,t)|^2 + |v_{ss}(r,s,t)|^2 + |v_{tt}(r,s,t)|^2) \\ &+ 2\gamma(|v_{rs}(r,s,t)|^2 + |v_{rt}(r,s,t)|^2 + |v_{st}(r,s,t)|^2) \end{aligned} \quad (2)$$

where subscripts represents partial derivatives and α, β and γ are coefficients controlling the first and second order smoothness of the net. In order to calculate the energy, the parameter domain $[0,1] \times [0,1] \times [0,1]$ is discretized as a regular grid defined by the internode spacing (k,l,m) and the first and second derivatives are estimated using the finite differences technique in 3D.

On the other hand, E_{ext} represents the characteristics of the scene that guide the adjustment process. As can be seen in figure 1, the model has two types of nodes: internal and external. A node is initially internal if it is located inside the grid, and external if it is located on the border of the grid, although as the process of adjustment is performed, the state of an internal node could change to external when a division of the grid takes place. Each type of node is used to represent different characteristics of the object: the external nodes fit the surface of the object and the internal nodes model the internal topology of the object. So the external energy would have to be different for both types of nodes. This fact allows the integration of information based on discontinuities and information based on regions. The former is associated to external nodes and the latter, to internal nodes. In the model presented, this energy term is defined as:

$$\begin{aligned} E_{ext}(v(r,s,t)) = &\omega f[I(v(r,s,t))] \\ &+ \frac{\rho}{\aleph(r,s,t)} \sum_{p \in \aleph(r,s,t)} \frac{1}{\|v(r,s,t) - v(p)\|} f[I(v(p))] \end{aligned} \quad (3)$$

where ω and ρ are weights, $I(v(r,s,t))$ is the intensity value of the original image in the position $v(r,s,t)$, $\aleph(r,s,t)$ is the neighborhood of the node (r,s,t) and f is a function associated to the image intensity and defined differently for both types of nodes.

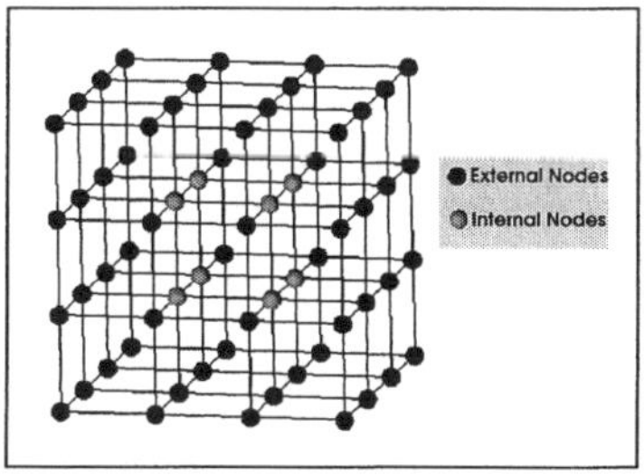

Fig. 1. TAV grid initial state.

On one hand, if the objects to detect are dark and the background is bright, the energy of an internal node would be minimum when it is on a point with a low grey level. On the other hand, the energy of an external node would be minimum when it is on a discontinuity and on a light point outside the object. In that situation, function f is defined as:

$$f[I(v(r,s,t))] = \begin{cases} h[\overline{I(v(r,s,t))_n}] & \text{for internal nodes} \\ h[I_{max} - \overline{I_n(v(r,s,t))_n} + \\ \xi(G_{max} - G(v(r,s,t)))] & \text{for external nodes} \end{cases} \tag{4}$$

where ξ is a weighting term, I_{max} and G_{max} are the maximum intensity values of image I and the image of gradients G, respectively, $I(v(r,s,t))$ and $G(v(r,s,t))$ are the intensity values of the original image and the image of gradients in the position $v(r,s,t)$ of the node, $\overline{I_n(v(r,s,t)}$ is the mean intensity in a $n \times n \times n$ cube and h is an appropriate scaling function.

2.1 Topological Changes

The TAVs have the ability to make topological local changes that give more flexibility to the structure and avoid the limitations of a fixed topology. Those changes consist on removing connections between nodes. This changes allow: (a) enhance the fitting efficacy on those areas where a greater definition is required, (b) detect two or more objects in the image by means of the generation of 2 or more subTAVs, (c) model the found objects and adjust to the existing holes.

The process of removing a connection takes place only between external nodes which are badly located once the minimization process has finished. Removing that connection will affect the elementary structures, that is, the cubes the nodes belong to. Once the connection between two external nodes has disappeared they have a greater freedom of movements. Besides, breaking a link implies labelling some nodes again since some internal nodes will become external (figure 2 (a) and (b)). Those new external nodes will allow a greater definition and adjustment in the area where the breaking takes place.

Only one restriction exists when breaking connections: the cubic structure of the model must be maintained. If it is not possible, the connection will not be broken, unless there were other connections that could be broken simultaneously and, after it, the structure was maintained. Nevertheless, all those connections will only be broken if the implied nodes are badly located. Figures 2 (c) and (d) depict two cases of this particular situation. In (c), to break the connection a, it is necessary to break before b. In (d) the connections a, b, c and d can only be broken simultaneously.

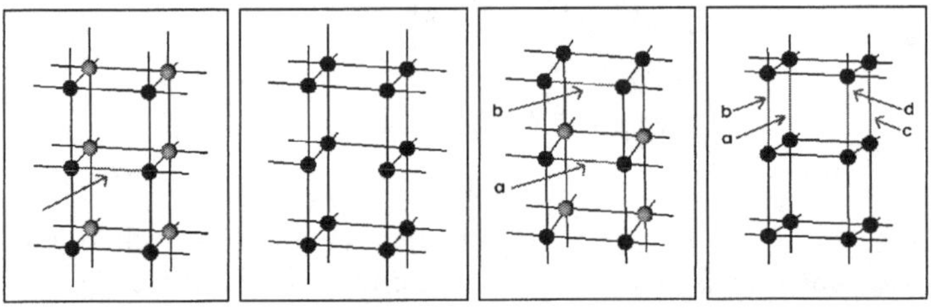

(a) (b) (c) (d)

Fig. 2. (a) and (b) show the conversion of internal nodes in external after breaking a connection. (c) and (d) show cases of multiple breaks. Light nodes represent internal nodes and dark ones, external nodes.

Once the minimization process has finished, the external nodes badly located are chosen by their distance to gradient. That distance will be calculated through an extension of Midpoint algorithm [10] in 3D. A node will be badly located if its distance to the gradient is greater than a certain threshold. In order to obtain the value of this threshold the Tchebycheff's theorem [11] was employed. This theorem identifies the outliers within a population. Thus, an external node $v_{ext}(r,s,t)$ will be badly located if its distance to gradient, $DG_{v_{ext}}(r,s,t)$, verifies that:

$$DG_{v_{ext}}(r,s,t) > \mu DG_{v_{ext}} + c\sigma DG_{v_{ext}} \tag{5}$$

where $\mu DG_{v_{ext}}$ and $\sigma DG_{v_{ext}}$ respectively represent the average and the standard deviation of the distance to gradient of the TAV external nodes. c is a constant so that $1/c^2$ is the percentage of correctly placed nodes. The distance to the gradient is calculated as follows:

$$DG_{v_{ext}}(r,s,t) = minDG^k_{v_{ext}}(r,s,t), \forall k \in \kappa \tag{6}$$

where κ is the set of possible directions defined by a 26-neighborhood.

Once the external nodes badly placed are delimited, it is necessary to select the connection to break. It is the connection formed by the worst located node and its worst neighbor. After breaking a connection and performing the topological changes, the TAV is minimized. The process is repeated until there is no nodes which fulfills the expression 5. To guide the breaking process and to avoid anarchical breakings, a greater cut priority is assigned to the nodes located in the cube in which the cut takes place. Figure 3 (a) and (b) show the following connection to break. The values associated to the external nodes in each image indicate the cut preferences with and without priority respectively. Figure 3 (c)

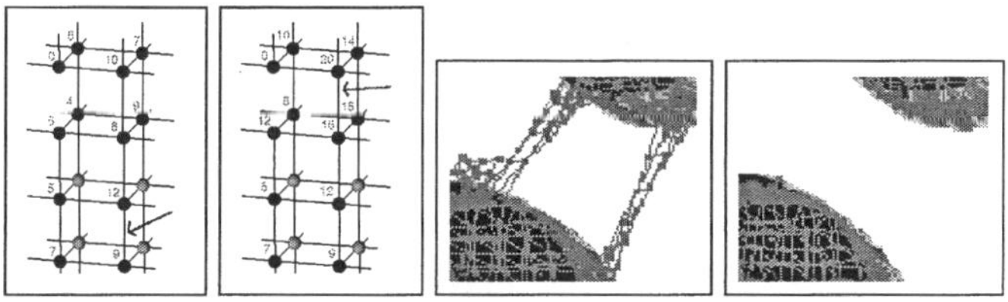

(a) (b) (c) (d)

Fig. 3. (a) Next connection to break without cut priority and (b) with cut priority. (c) Breaks without cut priority and (d) with cut priority.

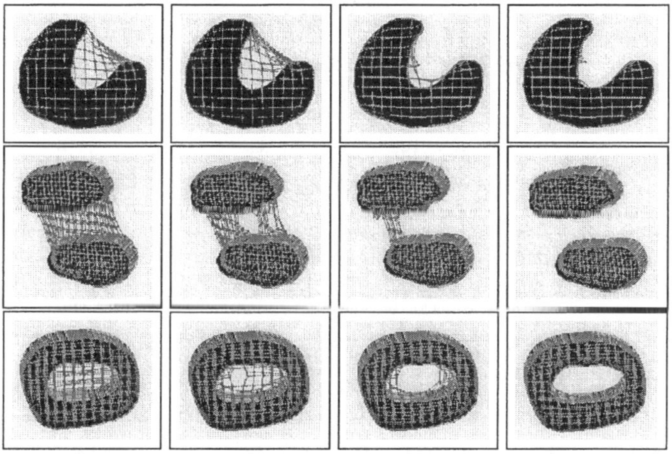

Fig. 4. Topological adaptive changes in TAVs. Upper row: the mesh adapts to an object with a pronounced entrant; second row: the mesh is divided to locate the objects in the image; third row: a hole in the mesh is generated to obtain a good fit to the object.

and (d) depict the consequences of making breakings with or without cut priority. If the cut priority is not considered, the breakings will be chaotic and there could be groups of linked cubes badly placed and whose connections cannot be broken, also called threads. When the cut priority is used, the probability of thread formation diminishes.

Advantages of the topological changes are shown in figure 4. First row shows a perfect adjustment that is achieved by adaptive topological changes in the complex zones. The middle row of the figure shows the detection of several objects in the image by means of a subdivision process, generating as many TAVs as interest objects exist. The last row shows how the model can detect and adjust correctly to holes, obtaining a correct representation of the internal structure of the hole.

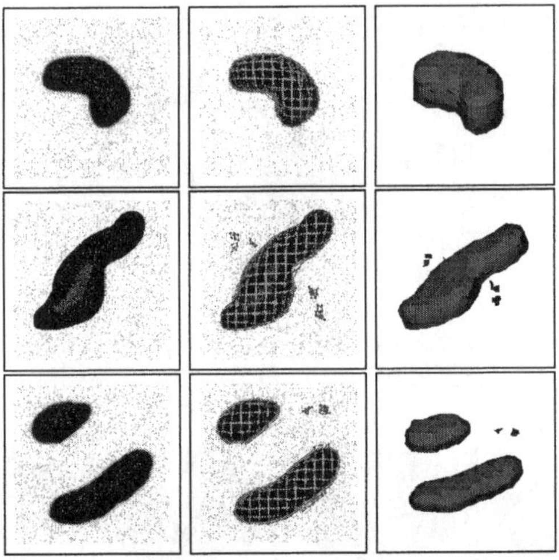

Fig. 5. Results obtained on artificial noisy images. First column shows the original image; second, the result after segmentation and last one, the 3D reconstruction of the detected object from the external nodes.

3 Results

This section shows the results obtained on artificial noisy images. The model presents several aspects to be considered. Firstly, the three-dimensional structure covers the whole image in the initialization. The own model has to detect the number of interest objects in the image based on their properties and, after that, it has to make the adjustment and description of these objects. Energy minimization is performed locally: the best position for each node is chosen in each step from the 26 candidate new positions, corresponding to the 26 neighbor pixels of the 3D image. Once the mesh reaches a stable situation, the dimensions of the mesh are recalculated. This readjustment is based on the size of the object. After that, the TAV is centered over the object. Then, the minimization process is repeated. When it finishes, a search process takes place in order to locate the external nodes badly located, a connection is broken if it is possible and the TAV is minimized. Those three steps are repeated until no external node is badly located or until any connection cannot be broken. In both cases the segmentation process finishes.

Figure 5 shows some examples of segmentation on artificial images with 255 levels of gray. The objects are dark and the background, light. The images are composed by a set of *slices* (256×256) with Gaussian noise (mean 0, variance between 5 and 25). The first image has 80 *slices*, the second, 50 and the third, 40. The initial TAV had $8 \times 8 \times 8$ nodes in all the examples. Table 1 shows the size of the TAV after the readjustment process and the parameters used in the energy formulae. In those examples the image is used as an external energy for both internal and external nodes and the Canny filter [12] itself has been employed to obtain the gradients images.

Table 1. Number of nodes and parameters of TAVs used in figure 5.

	Number of nodes			Parameters					
Image	x	y	z	α	β	γ	ω	ρ	ξ
Top	11	9	6	3.1	0.00001	0.00001	2.0	5.0	3.5
Middle	13	13	4	3.1	0.00001	0.00001	2.0	5.0	3.3
Bottom	15	15	3	4.0	0.00001	0.00001	5.0	5.0	3.0

The middle row of figure 5 depicts the final adjustment of the model and its right behavior in order to detect the different objects present in the scene and the singularities in the border of those objects. Some images present isolated cubes, originated during the breaking process and that are located in areas where the ratio S/N is low. Those cubes are formed only by external nodes and contain no useful information, so they can be removed easily at the end of the process.

The last column in figure 5 represents the 3D reconstruction of the object from the TAV obtained after the segmentation process. The reconstruction is performed from the cubes using the external nodes.

4 Conclusions

This work presents a new deformable model focused on segmentation and reconstruction tasks. The model consists of a volumetric structure and has the ability to integrate information based on discontinuities and regions. The model also allows the detection of two or more objects in the image and a good adjustment to the surfaces and holes in each object. This is due to the distinction of two classes of nodes: internal and external. That distinction allows the assignment of complementary terms of energy to each kind of node which makes possible that internal and external nodes act differently in the same situations.

The model is fully automatic ant it does not need an initialization process like other deformable models. Once the TAV fits the object, the connections between the external nodes allow the definition of the surface of the object and its representation using any reconstruction. On the other hand, the internal nodes show the spatial distribution inside the object. Results shown in figures 4 and 5 were obtained in an AMD Athlon XP 1800MHz, and time taken by the process was about 20 minutes for each image, which were composed by a set of 80 slices each one, with a resolution of 256×256 pixels each slice.

Future work includes the use of new basic structures in the mesh like triangular pyramids, and the introduction of graphical principles in nodes' behavior to obtain a better representation of the surfaces of the objects. Other improvements will include analyzing advanced mininization algorithms for the energy functional, in order to lower the computational time.

Acknowledgements

This paper has been partly funded by the Xunta de Galicia through the grant contract PGIDT01PXI10502PR.

References

1. M. Kass, A. Witkin, and D. Terzopoulos. Active contour models. *International Journal of Computer Vision*, 1(2):321–323, 1988.
2. D. Terzopoulos, A. Witkin, and M. Kass. Constraints on deformable models: Recovering 3D shape and nonrigid motion. *Artificial Intelligence*, 36(1):91–123, 1988.
3. M. Ferrant et al. Surface based atlas matching of the brain using deformable surfaces and volumetric finite elements. In *MICCAI 2001*, 2001.
4. L.Zhukov, I. Guskov J.Bao, J. Wood, and D. Breen. Dynamic deformable models for mri heart segmentation. In *SPIE Medical Imaging 2002*, 2002.
5. J. Montagnat and H. Delingette. Globally constrained deformable models for 3d object reconstruction. *Signal Processing*, 71(2):173–186, 1998.
6. J. Starck, A.Hilton, and J. Illingworth. Reconstruction of animated models from images using constrained deformable surfaces. *Lecture Notes in Computer Science*, 2301:382–391, 2002.
7. D.Magee, A.Bulpitt, and E.Berry. Combining 3d deformable models and level set methods for the segmentation of abdominal aortic aneurysms. In *Proc. of the British Machine Vision Conference*, 2001.
8. Nikos Paragios and Rachid Deriche. Geodesic active contours and level sets for the detection and tracking of moving objects. *IEEE Transactions on Pattern Analysis and Machine Intelligence*, 22(3):266–280, 2000.
9. F. M. Ansia, M. G. Penedo, C. Mariño, and A. Mosquera. A new approach to active nets. *Pattern Recognition and Image Analysis*, 2:76–77, 1999.
10. J. D. Foley, A. van Dam, S. K. Feiner, and J. F. Hughes. *Computer Graphics: Principles and Practice in C, 2/E*, pages 74–81. Addison Wesley Professional, 1996.
11. S. Ehrenfeld and S.B. Littauer. *Introduction to Statistical Method*, page 132. McGraw-Hill, 1964.
12. J. Canny. A computational approach to edge-detection. *IEEE Trans. on Pattern Analysis and Machine Intelligence*, 8(6):679–698, 1986.

Genetic Algorithm to Set Active Contour

Jean-Jacques Rousselle, Nicole Vincent, and Nicolas Verbeke

Laboratoire d'Informatique (LI)
Université François Rabelais de Tours
64, av. Jean Portalis, 37200 Tours, France
(rousselle,vincent)@univ-tours.fr

Abstract. Active contours, very popular in image segmentation, suffer from delicate adjustments of many parameters. We propose to carry out these adjustments using genetic algorithm. Here an active contour is implemented using a greedy algorithm. Within this framework, two approaches are presented. A supervised approach which delivers a global set of parameters. In this case the greedy algorithm is involved in the evaluation function of the genetic algorithm. The second approach is unsupervised. It determines a local set of parameters. The genetic algorithm computes a set of parameters which minimizes the energy at each point in the neighborhood of the current point in the greedy algorithm try to move.

1 Introduction

In image processing, segmentation is an essential phase. The traditional models detect some points of contour which are needed to be chained. This chaining is no more needed when using an active contour "snake". The snake is a curve, deformable under the influence of various forces. These forces must be balanced by the user according to the object of interest and to the images to be analyzed. Generally, the adjustment of these parameters is carried out by trial and error. It is recognized that these adjustments are difficult, but few authors were interested in that problem. We already proposed an approach by experimental design [6] and a method using random parameters search [7]. Here we will use a genetic optimization method. It is based on the natural selection theory.

After having presented active contours then the genetic algorithm technique, we will explain the results of two approaches: one supervised and the other unsupervised.

2 Active Contour

The concept of active contour, or snake, comes first from Kass *et al.*'s works [4]. It is a question of evolving a set of ordered points (describing a closed contour) so that it is nearest as possible to the contour sought for in the image. Such a set of points is called "snake" and the points which make it up are "snaxels".

Let V be a snake that is composed of n points and defined as follows:

$$V = \{v_i, \ldots, v_n\}, \; v_i = (x_i, y_i) \; i \subset \{1, \ldots, n\} \tag{1}$$

In the continuous field, it can be represented parametrically:

N. Petkov and M.A. Westenberg (Eds.): CAIP 2003, LNCS 2756, pp. 345–352, 2003.

$$v(s) = (x(s), y(s)),\ s \in [0,1] \tag{2}$$

The movements of the snake are produced by the minimization of an energy function:

$$E_{\text{snake}} = \int_0^1 E_{\text{internal}}[v(s)]\,ds + \int_0^1 E_{\text{external}}[v(s)]\,ds \tag{3}$$

where E_{internal} is the snake internal energy, and E_{external} is the external energy, i.e. depends on the image. Internal energy manages the coherence of the curve. It is made up of two parts:

$$E_{\text{internal}}(v) = \int_0^1 \left(\frac{\alpha}{2}(s)\left\|v'(s)\right\|^2 + \frac{\beta}{2}(s)\left\|v''(s)\right\|^2 \right) ds \tag{4}$$

$$E_{\text{internal}}(v) = \alpha E_{\text{continuity}}(v) + \beta E_{\text{curvature}}(v) \tag{5}$$

The continuity (α) energy maintains the cohesion of the points. It tends to make the distance between the points of the snake uniform. The curvature (β) energy manages the smoothness of the curve.

External energy is often made up of two terms. One is related to the gradient of the image, the other one is sensitive to the intensity of the image. The gradient can be calculated using a Sobel pseudo gradient.

$$E_{\text{external}}(v) = E_{\text{gradient}}(v) + E_{\text{intensity}}(v) \tag{6}$$

The energy calculation is carried out in the neighborhood of each snaxel. Thus the initialization of the Kass's snake has to be done close to the sought contour so that the gradient influences the calculation.

To avoid this disadvantage, Cohen introduced the concept of balloon energy which will tend, according to the sign, to inflate or retract the contour [2]. The final equation, to be minimized, is thus the following one:

$$E(v) = \alpha E_{\text{continuity}}(v) + \beta E_{\text{curvature}}(v) + \gamma E_{\text{gradient}}(v) + \delta E_{\text{intensity}}(v) \tag{7}$$

We will use an implementation using a greedy algorithm

[8], i.e. that the points are calculated, then moved the one after the other unlike is the variational approach [4]. The greedy algorithm is well-known to have faster processing time [3].

3 Genetic Algorithms

The genetic algorithms like the ant algorithms or the neural networks belong to the biomimetic approaches. They constitute an evolutionnary method of optimization based on natural selection.

3.1 Algorithm Genetic Principles

They are based on a coding of potential solutions using "chromosomes". The whole of the chromosomes, "individuals" forms the "population". A "generation" is the state of the population at one moment *t*.

The population evolves during generations while following some laws. In computing processing, these laws are called "genetic operators". In the basic genetic algorithm there are three: selection, crossing, mutation.

To each individual, is associated, an "adaptation level to its environment". It is the fitness. The following generation is generally built in such way that the individuals of the preceding population having the best fitness are preserved; this allows convergence towards an optimal solution.

3.2 Operators

In the traditional genetic algorithm, its chromosome represents the potential solution. This chromosome is represented by a chain of "genes" (of bits) called "genome". For a given individual, one distinguishes his "genotype", i.e. its internal representation (ex: 1001), of its "phenotype", i.e. its physical reality - what it represents - (here 9 is the physical meaning of the previous genotype, if the genome codes an integer).

3.2.1 Selection

The selection operator copies the chromosome in the new population according to its fitness; i.e. one gives more chance for the "good" individuals to take part in the following generation. It is a question of associating to each individual, i.e. to each chromosome x_i^t : $i^{\text{ème}}$ chromosome of the generation t, a probability of selection $p_s(x_i^t)$.

We will choose a method that is less elitist than the roulette wheel and simpler than the ranks, the K-tournament. It is a question of choosing n times k individuals in the population (randomly and uniformly) and of copying best k individuals in the new population.

3.2.2 Crossing

The aim of the crossing is to combine chromosomes in order to obtain new potentially best ones. It mixes the genomes of two individuals (parents) to generate two other ones (children). The size of the population remains constant.

In the simplest crossing, the genome of the parents is cut in one or more places randomly chosen. The fragments are combined to build the children.

3.2.3 Mutation

The mutation is carried out by a modification of the genes of the new generation chromosomes. This modification is realized with a very low probability (typical 0.1 %). Mutation makes it possible to increase the exploratory efficiency of the algorithm.

The mutation ratio μ strongly influences the effectiveness of the algorithm. There are many methods to optimize it. We will use $\mu = 1/l$ [1], l the chromosome length.

4 Optimization

We recalled in section 2, the existence of several weighted coefficients for the calculation of the snake energy. They are generally regulated in an empirical way by trial -

error experiments. In section 3, we have presented an evolutionary method of optimization. Parametric optimization being one of the fields where the genetic algorithms have good results, we used this method in order to optimize the $\alpha, \beta, \gamma, \delta, \lambda$ parameters of the model.

The general idea is as follows. The main program makes a genetic algorithm evolve, where the chromosome codes the $\alpha, \beta, \gamma, \delta, \lambda$ quadruplet. The fitness function computation comprises two parts. It starts an algorithm of an active contour with the parameters coded by the chromosome. Then it remains to define the evaluation criterion of the quality of the result obtained. It will be used to judge the quality of the set of parameters.

4.1 Chromosomes Coding

Coding is the way in which the physical reality of the snake (phenotype) is transformed into a bit string (genotype). We have five reals to be coded. We use the Michalewicz's method [5]. In this method, it is necessary to know the definition field of each parameter. We take: $[\alpha_{min}, \alpha_{max}], [\beta_{min}, \beta_{max}], [\gamma_{min}, \gamma_{max}], [\delta_{min}, \delta_{max}], [\lambda_{min}, \lambda_{max}]$

To know the length of the chromosome it is necessary to define the maximal precision of each parameter which we note $\Delta\alpha, \Delta\beta, \Delta\gamma, \Delta\delta, \Delta\lambda$. The length l of a chromosome is thus:

$$l = \left\lceil \log_2 \frac{\alpha_{min} - \alpha_{max}}{\Delta\alpha} \right\rceil + \left\lceil \log_2 \frac{\alpha_{min} - \alpha_{max}}{\Delta\alpha} \right\rceil + \left\lceil \log_2 \frac{\alpha_{min} - \alpha_{max}}{\Delta\alpha} \right\rceil + \left\lceil \log_2 \frac{\alpha_{min} - \alpha_{max}}{\Delta\alpha} \right\rceil + \left\lceil \log_2 \frac{\alpha_{min} - \alpha_{max}}{\Delta\alpha} \right\rceil \tag{8}$$

For the tests we used:

$$\begin{aligned} &\alpha_{min} = 0, \alpha_{max} = 1, \Delta\alpha = 0.001; \beta_{min} = 0, \beta_{max} = 1, \Delta\beta = 0.001; \\ &\gamma_{min} = 0, \gamma_{max} = 1, \Delta\gamma = 0.001; \delta_{min} = 0, \delta_{max} = 1, \Delta\delta = 0.001; \\ &\lambda_{min} = 0, \lambda_{max} = 1, \Delta\lambda = 0.001 \end{aligned} \tag{9}$$

These values give a chromosome of 35 bits.

In our case, the genome is rather short. So it encouraged us to take few cut points for the crossing. We took a crossing with two cut points.

In the same way, for the mutation, a rate of change of 0.001 (the most running) was likely to be not adapted because it ensures, on average, only one gene modified for 34 chromosomes at each generation. By applying the second mode of calculation we presented $\mu = 1/l$, we obtain a rate of change of 0.03 which ensures that at least one gene by chromosome will be affected.

In addition, as each evaluation implies the search for the optimal snake for each set of parameters, these operations are very time consuming. We thus took a population of reduced size which evolves on few generations. We used a selection by K-tournaments with a low value of K in order to make the algorithm less elitist.

4.2 Choice of the Evaluation Function

To measure the quality of a set of parameters, it is necessary to determine the fitness of a chromosome. The quality of active contour can be given by the position of a point on the contour or by a minimum of the global energy. As to minimize the equation (7) with $\alpha \in \mathbb{R}^+$, $\beta \in \mathbb{R}^+$, $\gamma \in \mathbb{R}^-$, $\delta \in \mathbb{R}$ and $\lambda \in \mathbb{R}^+$ or $\mathbb{R}^-$ (if retraction or expansion) an obvious solution would be obtained fixing α and β to zero and making γ and δ tend towards $-\infty$. Such parameters cannot provide an energy representative of the quality of the snake.

5 Results

We have tested two approaches, a supervised global solution and an unsupervised local approach.

5.1 Supervised Approach

Within the framework of a work on a series of images a same type, it can be interesting to regulate the set of parameters in a supervised way on one training image then to use this set on the remainder of the series. We thus placed the points of contour manually on an image and thus we defined an optimal contour. We sought to minimize the surface ranging between this optimal contour and the contour obtained by the algorithm. The evaluation function of the genetic algorithm uses the greedy algorithm to determine the fitness of a set of parameters.

The algorithm launched on 100 generations with 100 chromosomes gives the results presented in Fig. 1. The coefficients converge along the generations. All the parameters tend to converge towards a value with more or less precision. It appears for example that the coefficients controlling the continuity, the curvature and the gradient are more sensitive than those which control the intensity or the balloon force.

5.2 Unsupervised Approach

In the supervised approach we determined a set of global parameters. The same set of parameters is used throughout the algorithm, i.e. in any point and at each iteration. On some image, one can notice that the magnitude of the gradient varies. For example in the zone where the magnitude is low, the strategy should be to increase the influence of the internal energy. We would like to adjust the value of the coefficient related to the gradient with a very low value. Indeed, when the same coefficient is kept, the points concerned will tend to move towards the local minima of the gradient whereas it would be preferred that the snake preserves its cohesion.

An active contour evolves in a predefined neighborhood. In the implementation using a greedy algorithm, each term of energy is standardized [8], which already introduces, a local adjustment. We thus propose to make the set of parameters at each snaxel vary. This set is used for the neighborhood of this snaxel. In this approach, it is

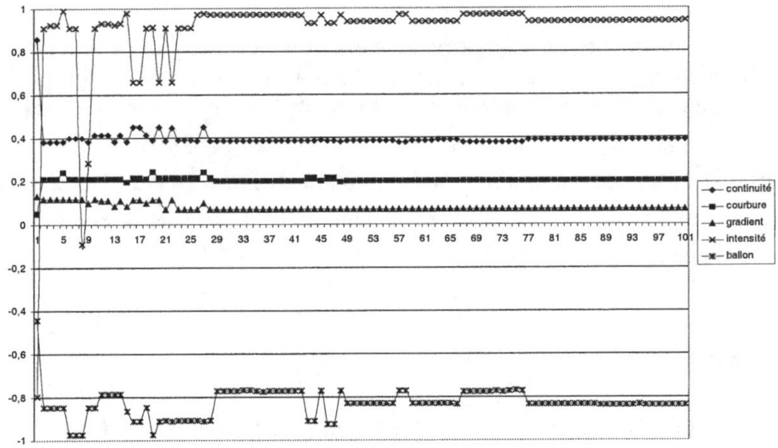

Fig. 1. Evolution of the global set of parameters

Fig. 2. Local adjustment of the parameters on a simple image: 1, 10, 20 iterations

no more a genetic algorithm using a greedy algorithm as evaluation function but a greedy algorithm which uses a genetic algorithm as local search procedure for a set of parameters.

A chromosome codes a set of parameters. We minimize the total energy of the snake and for the fitness we take the minimum of energy in the neighborhood. To prevent that the parameters tend towards zero, we force their sum to be equal to one (see §.4.1)

The execution on a simple image of a black oval on a white zone gives the results that can be seen in Fig. 2.

We can observe, in Fig. 3, the evolution of the parameters during the execution of the genetic algorithm, for a point, during an iteration of the greedy algorithm.

On Fig. 4, we can see how the parameters used evolve during calculation of the global energy at each iteration of the greedy algorithm. In other words they are the final results obtained for each call of the genetic algorithm.

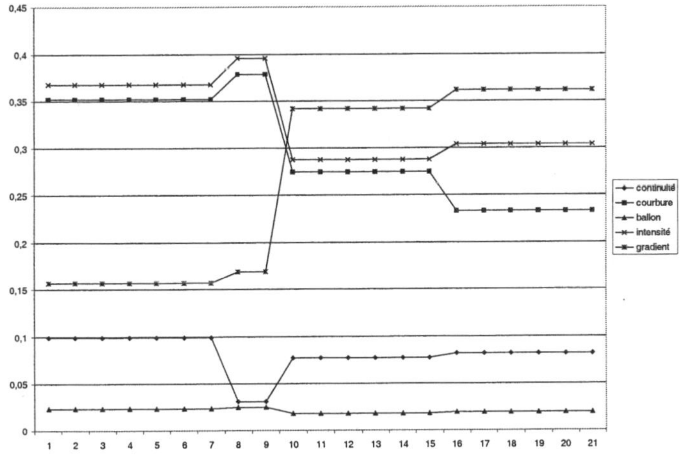

Fig. 3. Evolution of the parameters of a point during a local optimization

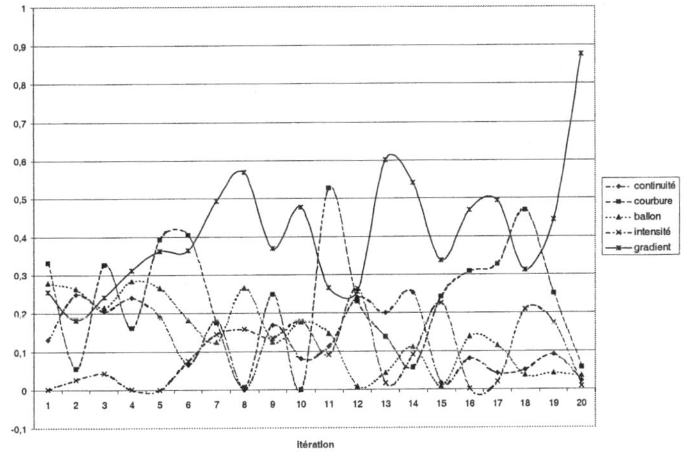

Fig. 4. Evolution of the parameters for each iteration of the greedy algorithm

These curves make it possible to detect certain tendencies of the coefficients. For example, the coefficient of the gradient tends to increase. This is normal since, in an initial state, the snake is in a zone of low gradient magnitude, whereas at the end of the algorithm, the points are on the required contour. The balloon energy coefficient tends to decrease since this energy becomes useless at the end of the move.

In active contours, parameters have to be tuned depending on each image. A new image implies to find a new set of parameters. In genetic algorithms there are also some parameters which have to be tuned but they depend on the problem. Here the problem is to find a set of parameters and that is independent of the image. The results given by genetic algorithm are more robust to a change of parameters value; nevertheless the convergence process would be sensitive to a small modification.

6 Conclusion

We showed in this article that it was possible to put the exploratory power of the genetic algorithms to the service of active contours. They were used first in a supervised approach where the genetic algorithm determines a set of global parameters which is evaluated using a greedy algorithm. In a second approach, unsupervised, the genetic algorithm locally seeks a set of parameters for each point which the greedy algorithm moves. In both cases, the results obtained with these automatically determined parameters using the method are satisfactory.

References

1. Bäck, T. - *Optimal Mutation Rates in Genetic Search.* Fifth International Conference in Genetic algorithm (ICGA'93), San mateo, CA., USA. 1993, p. 2-8.
2. Cohen, L.D. - On Active Contour Models and Balloons, *Computer Vision, Graphics, and Image Processing: Image Understanding,* vol. 53, n° 2, March 1991, p. 211-218.
3. Denzler, J. and Niemann, H. - *Evaluating the Performance of Active Contour Models for Real-time Object Tracking*, Second Asian Conference on Computer Vision, Singapore, 1995, p. II/341-II/345.
4. Kass, M. Witkin, A. Terzopoulos, D. - *Snakes: Active Contour Models*, In Proceedings of the first International Conference on Computer Vision, June 1987, p. 259-268.
5. Michalewicz, Z. - *Genetic Algorithms + Data Structures = Evolution Programs* – Ed. Springer-Verlag – Berlin-Heidelberg 1992, 252 p., ISBN 3-540-55387-8.
6. Rousselle, J-J. Vincent, N. - *Design of Experiments To Set Active Contour*, 6th International Conference on Quality Control by Artificial Vision, 2003, Gattlinburg, Tenessee, USA.
7. Vincent, N. Rousselle, J-J. - *Determination of Optimal Coefficients in active contour method for contour extraction.* Eleven International Colloquium on Numerical Analysis and Computer Sciences with Applications, 12-17 august 2002, Plodiv, Bulgaria, p. 79.
8. Williams, D.J. and Shah, M. - A Fast Algorithm for Active Contours and Curvature Estimation, *CVIGP Computer Vision Graphics Image Process: Image Understanding*, vol. 55, n° 1, January 1992, p. 14-26.

Unsupervised Segmentation Incorporating Colour, Texture, and Motion*

Thomas Brox[1], Mikaël Rousson[2], Rachid Deriche[2], and Joachim Weickert[1]

[1] Mathematical Image Analysis Group, Faculty of Mathematics and Computer Science
Saarland University, Building 27, 66041 Saarbrücken, Germany
{brox,weickert}@mia.uni-saarland.de
www.mia.uni-saarland.de

[2] Projet Odyssée, INRIA Sophia-Antipolis, 2004, route des Lucioles
BP 93, 06902 Sophia-Antipolis, France
{Mikael.Rousson,Rachid.Deriche}@sophia.inria.fr
www-sop.inria.fr/odyssee/presentation/index.en.html

Abstract. In this paper we integrate colour, texture, and motion into a segmentation process. The segmentation consists of two steps, which both combine the given information: a pre-segmentation step based on nonlinear diffusion for improving the quality of the features, and a variational framework for vector-valued data using a level set approach and a statistical model to describe the interior and the complement of a region. For the nonlinear diffusion we apply a novel diffusivity closely related to the total variation diffusivity, but being strictly edge enhancing. A multi-scale implementation is used in order to obtain more robust results. In several experiments we demonstrate the usefulness of integrating many kinds of information. Good results are obtained for both object segmentation and tracking of multiple objects.

1 Introduction

Image segmentation is one of the principal problems in computer vision and has been studied for decades. From recent approaches those using a variational framework are very popular, because in such a framework it is possible to integrate many different cues and models. One can integrate, for instance, boundary information, shape priors as well as region information. Level set theory [12] provides an efficient possibility to find a minimizer of such an energy.

In our paper an unsupervised approach will be proposed that does not depend on previously acquired information. The objective of such an unsupervised approach is to find good segmentations in less difficult image scenes, in order to serve as a knowledge acquisition method for a segmentation based on prior knowledge.

In order to succeed in this task it is necessary to use as much information of an image as possible. This importance to combine different cues in a segmentation algorithm has

* Our research is partly funded by the projects IMAVIS HPMT-CT-2000-00040 within the framework of the *Marie Curie Fellowship Training Sites Programme* as well as the European project *Cogvisys* numbered 3E010361, and the projects WE 2602/1-1 and SO 363/9-1 of the *Deutsche Forschungsgemeinschaft (DFG)*. This is gratefully acknowledged.

N. Petkov and M.A. Westenberg (Eds.): CAIP 2003, LNCS 2756, pp. 353–360, 2003.

also been stressed in the work of Malik et al. [10]. Consequently, we propose to use not only the grey value of an image but also colour, texture, as well as motion information, if they are available. The proposed framework based on the work in [19] allows to integrate all this information.

However, the possibility to integrate different kinds of information is only one step. Another question is how to acquire the information from the image. There is no such problem when using only primary features like grey value or colour, but as soon as secondary features like texture or motion are included, it is not obvious how to extract them the best way. Recently a nonlinear version of the linear structure tensor from [6] has been proposed [22]. Its suitability for texture discrimination is demonstrated in [18]. Considering motion, the optic flow is the principal method to integrate this information. Due to the fact that structure tensor techniques are also useful for optic flow analysis [2, 11], the nonlinear structure tensor can be applied here as well [4].

Since the features are often perturbed by noise or details that are useless for segmentation, a pre-processing step is very useful to obtain better results. Such a pre-processing should meet the following requirements: It must remove the perturbations while not loosing any important information. Moreover, like the segmentation, it should combine all the given information. Finally, it should yield results that are already close to a segmentation. Nonlinear diffusion is a well-suited technique to meet these requirements [15]. In this context, we propose to use a new diffusivity that can especially meet the last item.

As soon as motion information is used, it becomes obvious to perform not only segmentation but also tracking. For our segmentation technique it is rather easy to track an object once it has been detected. It becomes even possible to drop the assumption of having only one object, and to perform simultaneous tracking of multiple objects.

The remainder of this paper is organized as follows. In the next section the acquisition of the texture and motion features is briefly specified. Section 3 then describes how the information is employed in the two parts of our technique. In Section 4 the method is extended to tracking of multiple objects. In the succeeding section we show results of our experiments. The paper is concluded by a summary as well as an outlook on future work. A more detailed description and more experiments can be found in a research report [3] available from the internet.

2 Information Extraction

Information extraction is only interesting for texture and motion, since the grey level or colour information is already given by the image itself. For the acquisition of good texture features the nonlinear structure tensor has been shown to be very powerful [18]. It will also be used here.

For optic flow estimation, we use a modification of the method from [4]. This technique has two advantages: first, it induces only one smoothness parameter, and second it also applies the nonlinear structure tensor, so it is in best accordance with the texture feature acquisition. Thus, instead of the nonlinear structure tensor from [4], the slightly modified scheme described in [18] will be applied.

Provided all information is used, a feature vector with 8 components is considered, 3 colour channels (R, G, B), the optic flow components u and v computed with the above-mentioned method, and 3 texture channels ($\sum_i (I_i)_x^2, \sum_i (I_i)_y^2, \sum_i (I_i)_x (I_i)_y$), where i denotes the colour channel and the other subscripts denote partial derivatives.

3 Integration of Cues

3.1 Integrating Cues for Joint Smoothing

For the joint smoothing of the extracted features we apply nonlinear vector-valued diffusion. Nonlinear diffusion was introduced by Perona and Malik [15]. It was extended to vector-valued data in [7] using

$$\partial_t u_i = \operatorname{div}\left(g\left(\sum_{k=1}^{N} |\nabla u_k|^2\right)\nabla u_i\right) \qquad i = 1, ..., N \tag{1}$$

where u is the evolving feature vector initialized by the previously extracted data, and N is the number of feature channels. The decreasing *diffusivity function* g steers the reduction of smoothing in the presence of discontinuities. Note that g is the same for all channels, so there is a joint smoothing taking the edge information of all channels into account.

The choice of the diffusivity function is a critical point and mainly defines the behaviour of the diffusion process. Since there are first derivatives in the feature vector, the frequently used diffusivities with additional contrast parameters cause problems: Often it is impossible to choose a good global contrast parameter, since the derivatives may have responses of very different magnitude. A diffusivity without a contrast parameter is used in the total variational (TV) flow [1], the diffusion filter corresponding to TV regularization [20]. It leads to piecewise constant results removing oscillations and closing structures. However, TV flow is only one special representative of an entire family of diffusivities having these properties:

$$g(|\nabla u|^2) = \frac{1}{|\nabla u|^p + \epsilon} \tag{2}$$

where ϵ is a small positive constant avoiding the diffusivity to become unbounded. These diffusivities include TV flow for $p = 1$ and so-called *balanced forward backward diffusion* [8] for $p = 2$. While TV flow is exactly the limit between forward and backward diffusion, the diffusivities are strictly edge enhancing for $p > 1$. In the continuous case, well-posedness questions for forward–backward diffusion are still unsolved, but discretization has been shown to resolve this problem [21]. The results for $p > 1$ appear not only to be piecewise constant, they also have steep edges due to the edge enhancement. This is very useful for our application. The exact choice of p is uncritical. It specifies the ratio between edge enhancement and smoothing. As edge enhancement has basically a positive effect for our application, it would be best to use large p. However, this will considerably increase diffusion time necessary to obtain also an appropriate smoothing effect. In our experiments $p = 1.6$ turned out to be a good compromise.

3.2 Integrating Cues for Partitioning

Two-Region Partitioning. Assume the image to consist of only two regions: the object region and the background region. Then a segmentation splits the image domain Ω into two disjoint regions Ω_1 and Ω_2, where the elements of Ω_1 and Ω_2 respectively are not necessarily connected. Let $u : \Omega \to \mathbb{R}^N$ be the computed features of the image and $p_{ij}(x)$ the conditional probability density function of a value $u_j(x)$ to be in region Ω_i. Assuming all partitions to be equally probable and the pixels within each region to be independent, the segmentation problem can be formulated as an energy minimization problem following the idea of *geodesic active regions* [14, 19]:

$$E(\Omega_i, p_{ij}) = -\sum_{j=1}^{N} \left(\int_{\Omega_1} \log p_{1j}(u_j(x))dx + \int_{\Omega_2} \log p_{2j}(u_j(x))dx \right) \quad i = 1, 2. \quad (3)$$

For minimizing this energy a *level set function* is introduced. Let $\Phi : \Omega \to \mathbb{R}$ be the level set function with $\Phi(x) > 0$ if $x \in \Omega_1$, and $\Phi(x) < 0$ if $x \in \Omega_2$. The zero-level line of Φ is the searched boundary between the two regions. We also introduce the regularized heaviside function $H(s)$ with $\lim_{s\to-\infty} H(s) = 0$, $\lim_{s\to\infty} H(s) = 1$, and $H(0) = 0.5$. Furthermore, let $\chi_1(s) = H(s)$ and $\chi_2(s) = 1 - H(s)$. Moreover, we add a regularization term on the length of the interface $\partial\Omega$ between the two regions Ω_1 and Ω_2. Such a regularization can be expressed using the level set representation; see [23] for details. This allows to formulate a continuous form of the above-mentioned energy functional:

$$E(\Phi, p_{ij}) = -\sum_{i=1}^{2} \sum_{j=1}^{N} \left(\int_{\Omega} \log p_{ij}(u_j)\chi_i(\Phi)dx \right) + \alpha \int_{\Omega} |\nabla H(\Phi)|dx \quad (4)$$

The minimization of this energy can be performed using the following gradient descent:

$$\partial_t \Phi = H'(\Phi) \Big(\sum_{j=1}^{N} \log \frac{p_{1j}(u_j)}{p_{2j}(u_j)} + \alpha \operatorname{div} \frac{\nabla\Phi}{|\nabla\Phi|} \Big) \quad (5)$$

where $H'(s)$ is the derivative of $H(s)$ with respect to its argument.

PDF Approximations. The variational framework still lacks the definition of the probability density function (PDF). A reasonable choice is a Gaussian function. Assumed there is no useful correlation between the feature channels, this yields two parameters for the PDF of each region i and channel j: the mean μ_{ij} and the standard deviation σ_{ij}. Although reasonable, choosing a Gaussian function as PDF is not the only possible solution. Kim et al. [9] proposed nonparametric Parzen density estimates instead. Using discrete histograms this approach comes down to smoothing the histograms computed for each region i and channel j by a Gaussian kernel.

Given the probability densities, the energy can be minimized with respect to Φ using the gradient descent in Eq. 5. Thus the segmentation process works according to the *expectation-maximation* principle [5] with some initial partitioning (Ω_1, Ω_2). The nonparametric PDF estimate is much more powerful in describing the statistics within the regions than the Gaussian approximation. Although this yields best usage of the given information, it results in more local minima in the objective function and makes it more dependent on the initialization. This problem can be addressed by applying the basic idea of deterministic annealing [16, 17] using a Gaussian function in the first run to get close to the global minimum of the objective function. Then a second run of the minimization process will finally result in this global minimum or a local minimum that is very close to this global minimum. Although there exist counter-examples where this approach will fail, the heuristic works very well in most cases.

In order to further increase the robustness of our approach, we used a multi-scale implementation: the data from a finer scale is downsampled and serves as input for a segmentation at a coarser scale. This segmentation is then used to initialize the segmentation of the finer scale. This eases the problem of local minima. Two levels were used for our experiments.

In the variational formulation, we did not mention which information each channel contained. This general framework permits to combine any kind of information as we will see in the experiments.

4 Extension to Tracking

One of several applications for the segmentation approach described in the preceding sections is the tracking of moving objects. Since it becomes possible to employ not only the optic flow to follow the objects but also other information, the tracking is expected to be more reliable than with techniques based only on optic flow. In [13] and [19] it has already been demonstrated that it is possible to apply segmentation to tracking. In this section that approach will be combined with the classic idea of tracking using optic flow. Both vector components of the optic flow are used as features.

To allow the tracking of multiple objects, the variational formulation must be slightly modified. First, we suppose the positions of each of the moving objects to be known in the first frame. To each of these moving objects a level set function Φ_k is assigned, with $k = 1, ..., M$ and M being the total number of detected objects. We denote by B the static part of the image (which corresponds to the background of the scene) and by p_B the corresponding probability density function. This region is defined as the region where all the level set functions are negative. The global energy is defined as follows:

$$E = \int_\Omega \sum_{k=1}^{M} \Bigg(\underbrace{-\sum_{j=1}^{N} \log p_{kj}}_{e_k} H(\Phi_k) + \alpha |\nabla H(\Phi_k)| \Bigg) \underbrace{-\sum_{j=1}^{N} \log p_{Bj}}_{e_B} \chi_B \qquad (6)$$

Note that the χ function for the background $\chi_B = \prod_{l=1}^{M}(1 - H(\Phi_l))$ also affects the estimation of the PDFs. The minimization of the new energy leads to the revised gradient descent

$$\partial_t \Phi_k = -H'(\Phi_k)\Big(e_k - e_B \prod_{l \neq k}(1 - H(\Phi_l)) - \alpha \operatorname{div} \frac{\nabla \Phi_k}{|\nabla \Phi_k|}\Big). \qquad (7)$$

5 Results

The performance of our approach was tested with a number of real-world images. For more examples we refer to [3].

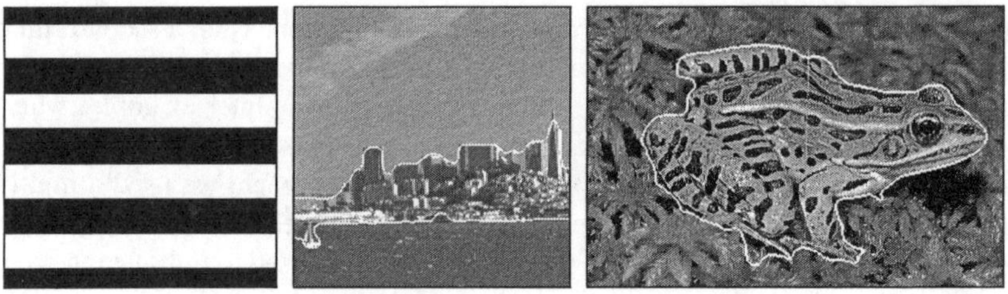

Fig. 1. LEFT: (a) Level set initialization. CENTER: (b) Using colour and texture. RIGHT: (c) Using colour and texture.

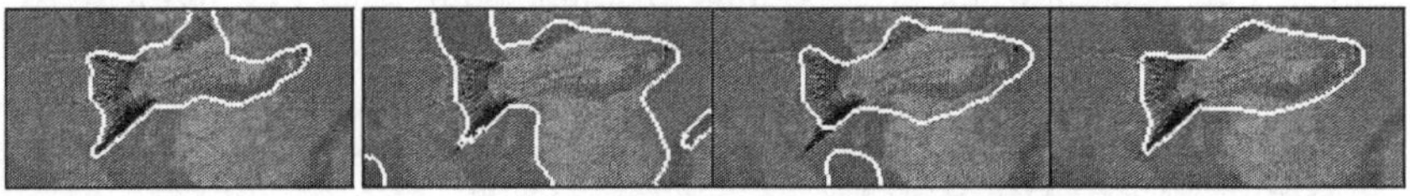

Fig. 2. Segmentation results using different kinds of information. FROM LEFT TO RIGHT: (a) Grey value and texture. (b) Colour (RGB). (c) Colour (CIELAB). (d) Colour and texture.

Fig. 3. Tracking result for 3 out of 30 images of the hand sequence.

First we used static images without motion information to combine texture and colour. Two results are shown in Fig. 1. In Fig. 1a the level set initialization used for all our experiments is depicted. Fig. 2 demonstrates the importance to use all available information for some images. The correct result can only be obtained by using both texture and colour information.

Colour information and optic flow magnitude were integrated on a sequence where a hand is moving in front of a complicated background (Fig. 3). Despite camera noise we obtain a good detection of the hand. Only a small region corresponding to the shadow is merged with the moving object in some frames.

To illustrate the capacities of the tracking method in Section 4, we applied it on the tracking of three players in a soccer sequence with moving camera (Fig. 4). Note that the players are relatively small and close to each other. The tracking initialization is done by clicking on the players we want to track. The results look very promising.

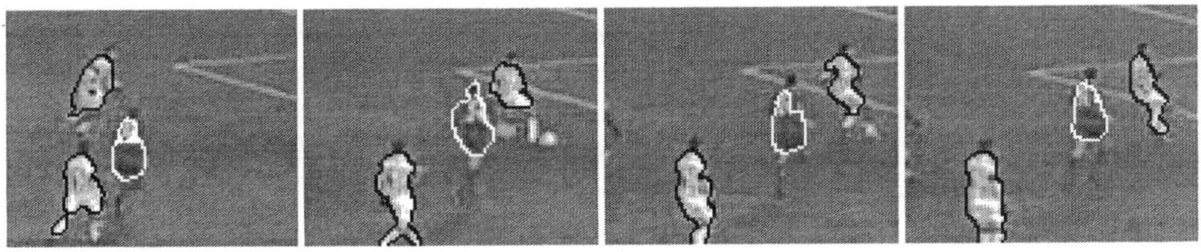

Fig. 4. Tracking result for 4 out of 27 images of the soccer sequence.

6 Conclusions

We have presented an unsupervised segmentation framework that can incorporate many different kinds of information. It has been possible to integrate colour, texture, and motion. The way to compute the features, the coupled nonlinear diffusion with a novel diffusivity, as well as the statistical region model and a multiscale implementation are responsible for the good results. Our approach uses jointly different cues in both parts of the method. Like humans do when analysing a scene, we tried to extract many kinds of information and integrated them in a general framework.

In several experiments it has been shown that our method works very well with all images that are in accordance with our model assumptions. In natural images such assumptions can sometimes be violated. In order to be able to deal also with such images, the assumption of having only two regions has to be dropped. A good solution for this problem will be a very challenging topic for future research. We also think that it could be advantageous to combine our unsupervised technique with learning techniques known from supervised approaches.

References

1. F. Andreu, C. Ballester, V. Caselles, and J. M. Mazón. Minimizing total variation flow. *Differential and Integral Equations*, 14(3):321–360, Mar. 2001.
2. J. Bigün, G. H. Granlund, and J. Wiklund. Multidimensional orientation estimation with applications to texture analysis and optical flow. *IEEE Transactions on Pattern Analysis and Machine Intelligence*, 13(8):775–790, Aug. 1991.
3. T. Brox, M. Rousson, R. Deriche, and J. Weickert. Unsupervised segmentation incorporating colour, texture, and motion. Technical Report 4760, INRIA Sophia-Antipolis, France, 2003.
4. T. Brox and J. Weickert. Nonlinear matrix diffusion for optic flow estimation. In L. Van Gool, editor, *Pattern Recognition*, volume 2449 of *Lecture Notes in Computer Science*, pages 446–453. Springer, Berlin, 2002.
5. A. Dempster, N. Laird, and D. Rubin. Maximum likelihood from incomplete data via the EM algorithm. *Journal of the Royal Statistical Society Series B*, 39:1–38, 1977.
6. W. Förstner and E. Gülch. A fast operator for detection and precise location of distinct points, corners and centres of circular features. In *Proc. ISPRS Intercommission Conference on Fast Processing of Photogrammetric Data*, pages 281–305, Interlaken, Switzerland, June 1987.
7. G. Gerig, O. Kübler, R. Kikinis, and F. A. Jolesz. Nonlinear anisotropic filtering of MRI data. *IEEE Transactions on Medical Imaging*, 11:221–232, 1992.
8. S. Keeling and R. Stollberger. Nonlinear anisotropic diffusion filters for wide range edge sharpening. *Inverse Problems*, 18:175–190, Jan. 2002.

9. J. Kim, J. Fisher, A. Yezzi, M. Cetin, and A. Willsky. Nonparametric methods for image segmentation using information theory and curve evolution. In *IEEE International Conference on Image Processing*, Rochester, NY, Sept. 2002.
10. J. Malik, S. Belongie, T. Leung, and J. Shi. Contour and texture analysis for image segmentation. *International Journal of Computer Vision*, 43(1):7–27, 2001.
11. H.-H. Nagel and A. Gehrke. Spatiotemporally adaptive estimation and segmentation of OF-fields. In H. Burkhardt and B. Neumann, editors, *Computer Vision – ECCV '98*, volume 1407 of *Lecture Notes in Computer Science*, pages 86–102. Springer, Berlin, 1998.
12. S. Osher and J. A. Sethian. Fronts propagating with curvature-dependent speed: Algorithms based on Hamilton–Jacobi formulations. *Journal of Computational Physics*, 79:12–49, 1988.
13. N. Paragios and R. Deriche. Geodesic active contours and level sets for the detection and tracking of moving objects. *IEEE Transactions on Pattern Analysis and Machine Intelligence*, 22(3), Mar. 2000.
14. N. Paragios and R. Deriche. Geodesic active regions: A new paradigm to deal with frame partition problems in computer vision. *Journal of Visual Communication and Image Representation*, pages 249–268, March/June 2002.
15. P. Perona and J. Malik. Scale space and edge detection using anisotropic diffusion. *IEEE Transactions on Pattern Analysis and Machine Intelligence*, 12:629–639, 1990.
16. C. Peterson and B. Söderberg. A new method for mapping optimization problems onto neural networks. *International Journal of Neural Systems*, 1(1):3–22, 1989.
17. J. Puzicha, T. Hofmann, and J. Buhmann. Deterministic annealing: fast physical heuristics for real-time optimization of large systems. In *Proc. 15th IMACS World Conference on Scientific Computation, Modelling and Applied Mathematics*, Berlin, 1997.
18. M. Rousson, T. Brox, and R. Deriche. Active unsupervised texture segmentation on a diffusion based feature space. In *Proc. 2003 IEEE Computer Society Conf. on Computer Vision and Pattern Recognition*, Madison, WI, June 2003. IEEE Computer Society Press. To appear.
19. M. Rousson and R. Deriche. A variational framework for active and adaptive segmentation of vector valued images. In *Proc. IEEE Workshop on Motion and Video Computing*, Orlando, Florida, Dec. 2002.
20. L. I. Rudin, S. Osher, and E. Fatemi. Nonlinear total variation based noise removal algorithms. *Physica D*, 60:259–268, 1992.
21. J. Weickert and B. Benhamouda. A semidiscrete nonlinear scale-space theory and its relation to the Perona–Malik paradox. In F. Solina, W. G. Kropatsch, R. Klette, and R. Bajcsy, editors, *Advances in Computer Vision*, pages 1–10. Springer, Wien, 1997.
22. J. Weickert and T. Brox. Diffusion and regularization of vector- and matrix-valued images. In M. Z. Nashed and O. Scherzer, editors, *Inverse Problems, Image Analysis, and Medical Imaging*, volume 313 of *Contemporary Mathematics*. AMS, Providence, 2002.
23. H. Zhao, T. Chan, B. Merriman, and S. Osher. A variational level set approach to multiphase motion. *Journal of Computational Physics*, 127:179–195, 1996.

Image Segmentation Based on Transformations with Reconstruction Criteria

Iván R. Terol-Villalobos[1] and Jorge D. Mendiola-Santibañez[2]

[1] CIDETEQ,S.C., Parque Tecnológico Querétaro S/N, SanFandila-Pedro Escobedo 76700, Querétaro Mexico
famter@ciateq.net.mx.
[2] Doctorado en Ingeniería, Universidad Autónoma de Querétaro, 76000, México.

Abstract. In this paper, a class of transformations with reconstruction criteria is investigated. This class of transformations was initially proposed for obtaining intermediate results between the morphological opening and the opening by reconstruction. Here, the transformations are presented in the general case, as in the reconstruction transformations case, by imposing some conditions on the marker. The form of selecting the markers to build these transformations is particularly described for binary images. Since the transformations studied in this work use a reconstruction criterion, we illustrate how it can be modified in order to have a better control of the output image. Finally, the interest of these transformations in image segmentation is also shown.

Keywords: filters by reconstruction, image segmentation, transformations with reconstruction criteria, markers

1 Introduction

The main goal in image segmentation consists in extracting the regions of interest of the image. The method must allow the introduction of criteria in order to obtain the desired regions. In mathematical morphology, the watershed-plus-markers approach is the traditional image segmentation method [1]. The watershed is one of the most interesting methods because of its capability to adapt itself to different image problems. However, many applications in image segmentation can be resolved by using only a filtering process. In particular, filters by reconstruction are frequently used ([2],[3], [4]). Nevertheless, the main drawback of the filters by reconstruction is that they reconstruct *too much* and sometimes it is not possible to extract the regions of interest. A solution to this inconvenience is to introduce a criterion which allows the reconstruction to be stopped, as proposed in [5],[6]. The transformations with reconstruction criteria proposed in [5],[6] have a similar behavior than a class of transformations introduced by Serra in [4]. In his work, Serra characterizes the viscous propagations by means of the notion of viscous lattices. In the present work, the transformations with reconstruction criteria are studied. Specifically, this study is focused to the marker notion and its applications to image segmentation. After introducing the morphological filtering tools in Section 2, the transformations with reconstruction

N. Petkov and M.A. Westenberg (Eds.): CAIP 2003, LNCS 2756, pp. 361–368, 2003.

criteria are presented in Section 3. In particular in this section, a study of the marker notion and the reconstruction criteria is made. Finally, in Section 4, the interest of these transformations in image segmentation is shown.

2 Some Basic Concepts of Morphological Filtering

2.1 Basic Notions of Morphological Filtering

The basic morphological filters are the morphological opening $\gamma_{\mu B}$ and the morphological closing $\varphi_{\mu B}$ with a given structuring element. In this work, B is an elementary structuring element (3x3 pixels) containing its origin, $\check{B}$ is the transposed set ($\check{B} = \{-x : x \in B\}$) and μ is an homothetic parameter. The morphological opening and closing are given, respectively, by:

$$\gamma_{\mu B}(f)(x) = \delta_{\mu \check{B}}(\varepsilon_{\mu B}(f))(x) \quad \text{and} \quad \varphi_{\mu B}(f)(x) = \varepsilon_{\mu \check{B}}(\delta_{\mu B}(f))(x) \tag{1}$$

where the morphological erosion $\varepsilon_{\mu B}$ and dilation $\delta_{\mu B}$ are expressed by: $\varepsilon_{\mu B}(f)(x) = \wedge\{f(y) : y \in \mu\check{B}_x\}$ and $\delta_{\mu B}(f)(x) = \vee\{f(y) : y \in \mu\check{B}_x\}$. $\wedge$ is the inf operator and $\vee$ is the sup operator. In the following, we will suppress the set B. The expressions γ_μ,$\gamma_{\mu B}$ are equivalent (i.e. $\gamma_\mu = \gamma_{\mu B}$). When the parameter μ is equal to one, all parameters are suppressed (i.e. $\delta_B = \delta$).

2.2 Opening (Closing) by Reconstruction

Geodesic transformations are used to build the reconstruction transformations [7]. In the binary case, the geodesic dilation of size 1 of a set Y inside the set X is defined as $\delta^1_X(Y) = \delta(Y) \cap X$. To build a geodesic dilation of size m, the geodesic dilation of size 1 is iterated m times. Similarly, a geodesic erosion $\varepsilon^m_X(Y)$ is computed by iterating m times the geodesic erosion of size 1: $\varepsilon^1_X(Y) = \varepsilon(Y) \cup X$. When filters by reconstruction are built, the geodesic transformations are iterated until idempotence is reached. The reconstruction transformation in the gray-level case is a direct extension of the binary one. In this case, the geodesic dilation $\delta^1_f(g)$ (resp. the geodesic erosion $\varepsilon^1_f(g)$) with $g \leq f$ (resp. $g \geq f$) of size 1 given by: $\delta^1_f(g) = f \wedge \delta_B(g)$ (resp. $\varepsilon^1_f(g) = f \vee \varepsilon_B(g)$) is iterated until idempotence. When the function g is equal to the erosion or the dilation of the original function, we obtain the opening and the closing by reconstruction:

$$\widetilde{\gamma}_\mu(f) = \lim_{n\to\infty} \delta^n_f(\varepsilon_\mu(f)) \quad \widetilde{\varphi}_\mu(f) = \lim_{n\to\infty} \varepsilon^n_f(\delta_\mu(f)) \tag{2}$$

3 Transformations with Reconstruction Criteria: Markers and Size Criteria

3.1 Openings (Closings) with Reconstruction Criteria

It is well-known that the use of the opening by reconstruction does not enable the elimination of some structures of the image (this transformation reconstructs all connected regions during the reconstruction process). To attenuate this inconvenience, the openings and closings with reconstruction criteria were introduced in [5]. In [6], a modification in the criterion for building the transformations proposed in [5] permitted a better control of the reconstruction, and also to generate connected transformations according to the notion of connectivity class [8]. This last class of openings and closings ([6]) are introduced in this section. These openings (closings) enable us to obtain intermediate results between the morphological opening (closing) and the opening (closing) by reconstruction. Let us comment the case of the opening with reconstruction criteria obtained by iterating the expression $\omega^1_{\lambda,f}(g) = f \wedge \delta\gamma_\lambda(g)$ using the marker image $g = \gamma_\mu(f)$. Observe that the only difference between this operator and the one $(f \wedge \delta(g))$ for building the opening by reconstruction is the morphological opening of size γ_λ. Under the condition $g = \gamma_\mu(f)$, the output images obtained by iterating the term $\delta\gamma_\lambda(g)$ of the operator $\omega^1_{\lambda,f}$ are the same as those obtained by iterating the basic morphological dilation $\delta(g)$ with the condition $\lambda \leq \mu$. However, when the expressions $f \wedge \delta\gamma_\lambda(g)$ and $f \wedge \delta(g)$ are iterated, different images are obtained. The morphological opening γ_λ in the operator $\omega^1_{\lambda,f}$ plays the role of a reconstruction criterion, by stopping the reconstruction of the regions where the criterion is not verified. Let γ_μ and φ_μ be the morphological opening and closing of size μ, respectively. The transformations given by the following expressions:

$$\widehat{\gamma}_{\lambda,\mu}(f) = \lim_{n\to\infty} \omega^n_{\lambda,f}(\gamma_\mu(f)) \qquad \widehat{\varphi}_{\lambda,\mu}(f) = \lim_{n\to\infty} \alpha^n_{\lambda,f}(\varphi_\mu(f)) \tag{3}$$

are an opening and a closing of size μ with $\lambda \leq \mu$, respectively, where $\omega^1_{\lambda,f} = f \wedge \delta\gamma_\lambda$ and $\alpha^1_{\lambda,f} = f \vee \varepsilon\varphi_\lambda$.

3.2 Marker Selection

Openings and closings with reconstruction criteria require markers given by the morphological opening and closing, respectively. In this section, the general condition that a marker g must verify is analyzed. Consider the operator $\omega^1_{\lambda,f}$ used to build an opening. The following property is satisfied by the morphological opening and the dilation:

Property 1. *For all pairs of parameters λ_1, λ_2 with $\lambda_1 \leq \lambda_2$, $\delta_{\lambda_2}(g) = \gamma_{\lambda_1}(\delta_{\lambda_2}(g))$.*

This means, that the dilation permits the generation of invariants for the morphological opening; the dilation of a function g', $g = \delta_{\lambda_2}(g')$, is an invariant of γ_{λ_1} $(\gamma_{\lambda_1}(g) = g)$. Using this type of marker, the expression $\lim_{n\to\infty} \omega^n_{\lambda,f}(g)$ can be described in terms of geodesic dilations. Observe that at the first iteration of the operator $\omega^1_{\lambda,f}$, we have $\omega^1_{\lambda,f}(g) = f \wedge \delta\gamma_\lambda(g) = f \wedge \delta(g) = \delta^1_f(g)$ which is the geodesic dilation of size 1. At the second iteration, $\omega^2_{\lambda,f}(g) = f \wedge \delta\gamma_\lambda(\omega^1_{\lambda,f}(g)) = f \wedge \delta\gamma_\lambda(\delta^1_f(g)) = \delta^1_f\gamma_\lambda\delta^1_f(g)$ Thus, when stability is reached,

$$\lim_{n\to\infty} \omega^n_{\lambda,f}(g) = \underbrace{\delta^1_f\gamma_\lambda\delta^1_f\gamma_\lambda \cdots \delta^1_f\gamma_\lambda\delta^1_f(g)}_{Until\ stability} \tag{4}$$

When the marker is given by $g = \gamma_\mu(f)$, the opening with reconstruction criterion given by equation (3) is computed. Let us apply to this last equation an opening size λ,

$$R_{\lambda,f}(g) = \gamma_\lambda \lim_{n\to\infty} \omega^n_{\lambda,f}(g) = \underbrace{\gamma_\lambda\delta^1_f\gamma_\lambda\delta^1_f\cdots\gamma_\lambda\delta^1_f(g)}_{Until\ stability} \quad (5)$$

This equation illustrates that, after each elementary geodesic dilation, the output image is tested by the morphological opening. This transformation with reconstruction criteria is used in this work. In fact, the output image computed by eqn. (5) is an invariant for the morphological opening size λ. This is not true when the transformation given by eqn. (4) is used. In the binary case, the algorithm to compute the marker is based on the notion of regional maxima of the distance function. The distance function of a set X is defined by the distance of each point $x \in X$ to the complement set X^c and it is expressed by $\rho_X(x) = d_H(x, X^c)$ (where H refers to the type of distance, which can be square, hexagonal....). The set of points for which $\rho_X(x) > n$ is the erosion of X by a structuring element of size n. The dilation of size λ of the set composed by the points belonging to the maxima of the distance function for which $\rho_X(x) > \lambda$ satisfies the conditions to be a marker. However, if a size criterion is introduced in the transformation, as in the case of the opening $\widehat{\gamma}_{\lambda,\mu}$ with $\lambda \leq \mu$, the points of the maxima for which $\rho_X(x) > \mu$ are selected. The dilation of size λ of this set of points is an invariant set of the morphological opening of size λ.

3.3 Reconstruction Criterion Using a Rank-Max Connected Opening

In equation (5), the morphological opening is used as the reconstruction criterion. However, the morphological opening presents some problems when images have thin regions. Since equation (5) is general, a solution of this inconvenience consists in changing the morphological opening by another opening. We know that a class of non-linear filters, called rank filters, exhibit excellent robustness properties and provide solutions in many cases where other transformations are inappropiate. Moreover, rank filters are used to build an interesting class of transformations called rank-max openings. Ronse introduced the rank-max openings on sets and gray-level functions as a generalization of the morphological opening by a structuring element λB (see [8]). Let $\mathbf{B}_k$ be the set of all subsets $B_i \subseteq \lambda B$ containing k points. The rank-max opening is given by,

$$\gamma_{\lambda B,k}(f) = \vee_i\{\gamma_{B_i}(f); B_i \in \mathbf{B}_k\}$$

The rank-max opening is more flexible than the morphological opening because it preserves the regions which contain at least k points. This opening transforms a binary image X into the supremum of all portions of it, consisting of "sufficiently large" subset of a translate of λB. However, the main drawback of the rank-max opening lies in the interactions between the connected components. In other words, every connected component of an invariant of $\gamma_{\lambda B,k}$ is not itself an invariant of $\gamma_{\lambda B,k}$. This problem leads to a degradation of the filtered image. A solution to this problem is achieved by introducing the connectivity notion. Consider a subset $\mathbf{B}_{C_k}$ of $\mathbf{B}_k$ containing all connected subsets of $\mathbf{B}_k$ which include the origin of λB. Thus, the rank max connected opening is defined by

$$\widetilde{\gamma}_{\lambda B,k}(f) = \vee_i\{\gamma_{B_i}(f); B_i \in \mathbf{B}_{c_k}\}$$

This opening independently processes each connected component. This means, every connected component of an invariant of $\widetilde{\gamma}_{B,k}$ is itself an invariant of $\widetilde{\gamma}_{B,k}$. Figure 1 illustrates the reconstruction process based on a rank max connected opening. Figure 1(a) illustrates the original binary image X, while Fig. 1(b) shows the marker image Y obtained by $\widetilde{\gamma}_{\mu B,k}$, with $\mu = 12, k = 400$ ($Y = \widetilde{\gamma}_{\mu B,k}(X)$). Figures 1(c) and (d) show the output images obtained by $R_{\lambda,X}(Y)$ using the rank-max connected opening as the reconstruction criterion.

Fig. 1. a) Original image, b) Marker image obtained by $\widetilde{\gamma}_{\mu B,k}$, with $\mu = 12, k = 400$, c) Output image with $\lambda = 8, k = 40$, d) Output image with $\lambda = 8, k = 20$

4 Automatic Selection of λ and Its Applications

The idea for automatically selecting the parameter λ comes from the work of Serra [4]. Here, a fast procedure based on a reconstruction function image is proposed. The procedure for the selection of λ consists in choosing the minimum value of λ such that it only permits the reconstruction of the region of interest. First, the maximum parameter λ must be selected. For example, for the opening with reconstruction criteria $\widehat{\gamma}_{\lambda,\mu}$, with μ the critical element of the opening, $\gamma_\mu(X) \neq \emptyset$ and $\gamma_{\mu+1}(X) = \emptyset$, the greatest value of λ is μ. Thus, the reconstruction process begins with the operator $\omega^1_{\mu,X}(Y)$ with $Y = \gamma_\mu(X)$. When stability is reached, $\omega^n_{\mu,X}(Y)$, the parameter λ is decreased by one. The reconstruction process continues using $\omega^n_{\mu,X}(Y)$ as the input image, i.e. $\omega^n_{\mu-1,X}\omega^n_{\mu,X}(Y)$. A similar procedure is made $\omega^n_{\lambda',X}\omega^n_{\lambda'+1,X}\cdots\omega^n_{\mu-1,X}\omega^n_{\mu,X}(Y)$ until a parameter λ, allowing the reconstruction of undesirable regions, is found. In order to know when undesirable regions are reconstructed, a marker signaling these regions must be introduced.

Example 1. *Consider the problem of detecting a contour on the skull of the image shown in figure 2(a).*

Since the highest gray-levels of the image are on the skull, thresholding the image between 221 and 255 will give a set composed only by points on the skull

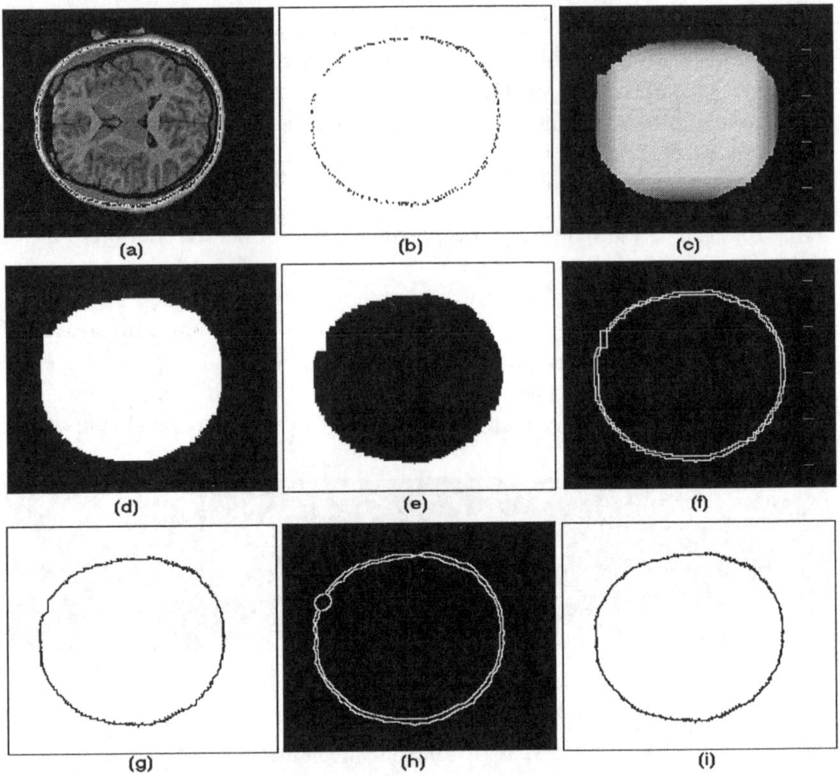

Fig. 2. a) and b) Original image and its threshold, c) Reconstruction function, d) and e) Reconstructed binary image, f) Contours of (d) and (e), g) Interpolation of images (d) and (e), h) Contour detection using disks, i) Interpolation of (h)

(Fig. 2(b)). Observe that the contour is not closed. Below gray-level 221 regions of the brain will appear. Now, the distance function is computed on this set. Due to the form of the brain, it is clear that the distance function will have the global maximum placed in this region. The set formed by the points of this maximum is used as the marker for the reconstruction process. When the parameter λ is small, the reconstruction process goes between the contour points and touches the field borders; when λ increases, the contour points stop the reconstruction. Let μ be the gray-level of the distance function in the global maximum. Then, the greatest value of the reconstruction criterion will be $\lambda = \mu - 1$. Now, in order to have all images for each reconstruction criterion, we use a gray level image Im. The image Im is called in this work reconstruction function image. Initially, this image is set equal to zero. The reconstruction begins with the parameter value $\lambda = \mu - 1$ on a binary image Is. All pixels x achieved by the reconstruction ($Is(x) = 1$) are increased by one in the output image Im. When the reconstruction process of parameter λ stops, a second reconstruction process begins with parameter $\lambda - 1$, by increasing the gray levels in the output image Im

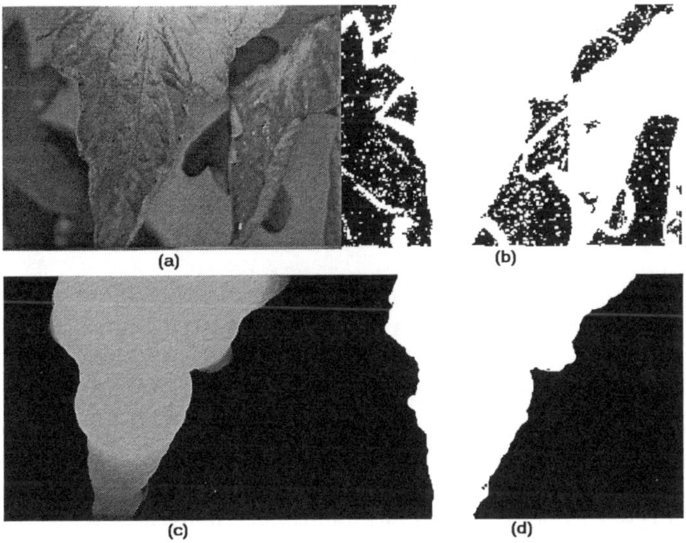

Fig. 3. (a) and (b) Original image and its binary image, (c) Reconstruction function using disks as structuring elements, (d) Segmented image

at each pixel x such that $Is(x) = 1$. The procedure to build the reconstruction function image stops when we find a value λ', such that the reconstruction in Is touches the field borders. Then, the reconstruction criterion has the value $\lambda' + 1$ and its associated reconstruction image is computed by thresholding the gray-level image Im between 2 and 255. Figures 2(c) and 2(d) illustrate the reconstruction function and the binary image obtained with an automatically detected parameter. It is possible to obtain a better contour by carrying out a second reconstruction. In Fig. 2(e) we illustrate the reconstructed binary image obtained from the image in Fig. 2(b), using the field borders as markers to reconstruct the image and the same value for the reconstruction criterion λ. In Fig. 2(f) the contours of both reconstructed images (Figs. 2(d) and 2(e)) are shown. An interpolation between both enables the computation of a better segmentation as illustrated in Fig. 2(g). This result may be improved by using disks as it is shown in Fig. 2(h) and 2(i).

Example 2. *Image segmentation in the tomato plant leaf.*

The same procedure illustrated in example (1) can be under taken in other images. It is only necessary to choose a good marker that will play the role of stop criterion. The goal in this problem consists in extracting the leaf illustrated in Fig. 3(a) of the tomato plant, in order to study the evolution of the *Phytophthora infestans* illness inside the leaf. In the leaf extraction problem, the reconstruction process also begins from the global maximum of the distance function, but the field borders are not used as a stop criterion. In this case, the set playing the role of stop criterion is given by the first maximum touched by the reconstruction process. Also, instead of using squares structuring elements, disks are used to build the reconstruction function. Images in Figs. 3(b)-3(d) show the binary image, the reconstruction function and the output binary image obtained by the reconstruction criterion automatically computed. The contour of the reconstructed binary image gives the segmented image.

5 Conclusion

In this paper, a class of transformations with reconstruction criteria was investigated. In particular, the conditions required for selecting a marker for this type of transformations were studied. It enabled us to have a general expression for these transformations that permitted the use of other reconstruction criteria, in order to have a better control of the output image. The interest of this class of transformations in image segmentation was also shown. Future works on the transformations with reconstructon criteria will be in the direction to study the selection of the λ value by means of a multiscale analysis.

Acknowledgements

We wish to thank the anonymous reviewer whose comments will help us for future works. The author I. Terol would like to thank Diego Rodrigo and Darío T.G. for their great encouragement. This work was funded by the government agency CONACyT (41170), Mexico.

References

1. Meyer, F., Beucher, S.: Morphological segmentation. J. Vis. Comm. Image Represent., **1**, (1990) 21-46.
2. Salembier, Ph., Serra, J.: Morphological Multiscale Image Segmentation. SPIE-Visual Communications and Image Processing, **1818**, (1992) 620–631.
3. Crespo, J., Schafer, R., Serra, J, Gratin, C., Meyer, F.: A flat zone approach: a general low-level region merging segmentation method. Signal Process., **62(1)** (1997) 37-60.
4. Serra, J.: Viscous lattices. In Mathematical Morphology, H. Talbot and R. Beare (Eds.), CSIRO, (2002) 79–89 (Australia).
5. Terol-Villalobos, I.R., Vargas-Vázquez, D.: Openings and closings by reconstruction using propagation criteria, Computer Analysis of Image and Patterns, W. Skarbek Ed., LNCS **2124**, Springer (2001) 502–509.
6. Terol-Villalobos, I.R., Vargas-Vázquez, D.: A study of openings and closing using reconstruction criteria, In Mathematical Morphology, H. Talbot and R. Beare (Eds.), CSIRO, (2002) 413–423 (Australia).
7. Vincent, L.: Morphological grayscale reconstruction: applications and efficient algorithms, IEEE Trans. on Image Processing, **2(2)**, (1993) 176–201.
8. Serra, J.: Image Analysis and Mathematical Morphology, Vol. II, Theoretical advances, Academic Press, 1988.

Gaussian-Weighted Moving-Window Robust Automatic Threshold Selection

Michael H.F. Wilkinson

Institute for Mathematics and Computing Science, University of Groningen
P.O. Box 800, 9700 AV Groningen, The Netherlands
michael@cs.rug.nl
http://www.cs.rug.nl/~michael/

Abstract. A multi-scale, moving-window method for local thresholding based on Robust Automatic Threshold Selection (RATS) is developed. Using a model for the noise response of the optimal edge detector in this context, the reliability of thresholds computed at different scales is determined. The threshold computed at the smallest scale at which the reliability is sufficient is used. The performance on 2-D images is evaluated on synthetic an natural images in the presence of varying background and noise. Results show the method deals better with these problems than earlier versions of RATS at most noise levels.

1 Introduction

In all applications of thresholding, correct selection of the threshold is the key issue, and many methods for automatic selection of optimal thresholds have been published[1–4, 8]. Ideally, thresholds should be computed locally, adapting to the local image statistics, to deal properly with a locally varying background, or variations in the grey level of objects, both of which may occur in a single image [8]. An example is shown in Fig. 1, in which a local variations in object intensity are compensated through local threshold selection.

In this paper I will extend a local thresholding method, called Robust Automatic Threshold Selection (RATS) [1]. A new, moving-window version of the algorithm using Gaussian convolution will be developed. This versions will be extended to a multi-scale method, in which the smallest scale at which reliable thresholds can be computed is finally used. To do this, the effect of Gaussian noise on the computed threshold is derived. Finally, the method is evaluated first on synthetic images with varying noise levels, and later on natural ones.

The applications for the method include 2-D microscopic images of microorganisms, and 3-D angiograms.

2 Robust Automatic Threshold Selection

RATS [1] is a method for bilevel thresholding of grey scale images, which has been applied to images of bacteria [5, 6]. It is based on a simple image statistic,

N. Petkov and M.A. Westenberg (Eds.): CAIP 2003, LNCS 2756, pp. 369–376, 2003.

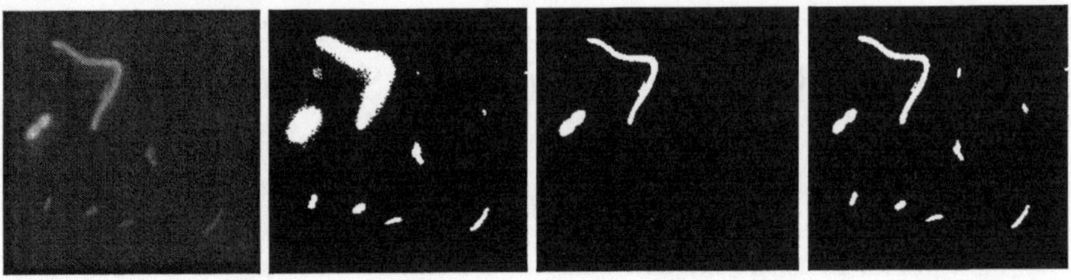

(a) (b) (c) (d)

Fig. 1. Local thresholding: (a) fluorescence image of bacteria; (b) global thresholding using original RATS algorithm without noise correction; (c) global thresholding using RATS algorithm with square Sobel gradient filter and noise correction; (d) locally thresholded result using RATS with the quad-tree approach from [5].

which is the average of grey levels weighted by the edge strength at each point. Kittler et al. [1] show that the optimal threshold in a noise-free image T is

$$T = \frac{\sum e(x,y)p(x,y)}{\sum e(x,y)}, \tag{1}$$

in which $p(x,y)$ is the grey level at (x,y) and the edge strength e is given by

$$e(x,y) = \max(|g_x(x,y)|, |g_y(x,y))|, \tag{2}$$

with

$$g_x(x,y) = p(x-1,y) - p(x+1,y) \quad \text{and} \quad g_y(x,y) = p(x,y-1) - p(x,y+1). \tag{3}$$

Initially the optimality of T was proved only for gradient operator in (2), and for straight edges. It has since been shown that any edge detector with an even response to a step edge at the origin will yield the same optimal result [7]. In particular, the gradient detector

$$g^2(x,y) = g_x^2(x,y) + g_y^2(x,y) \tag{4}$$

shows no curvature bias, is rotation invariant, and has reduced noise bias. However, the reduced noise bias comes at the expense of increased variance, which can be countered by using Sobel filter kernels to compute x and y derivatives [7]. The method readily extends to 3-D images, by replacing the edge detectors to their 3-D counterparts.

In the presence of noise T is biased towards the most common category in the image (usually background) [1]. This noise bias is counteracted by using a threshold on the edge strength below which the pixels receive zero weight. The statistic now becomes

$$T_\lambda = \frac{\sum w_\lambda(x,y)p(x,y)}{\sum w(x,y)}, \tag{5}$$

with

$$w_\lambda(x,y) = \begin{cases} g^2(x,y) & \text{if } g^2(x,y) > \lambda^2\eta^2 \\ 0 & \text{otherwise,} \end{cases} \tag{6}$$

in which η is the standard deviation of the image noise, and λ is an adjustable parameter, which depends on the actual edge strength used. For the edge strength defined in (2) it was shown empirically that $\lambda = 5$ is a good choice for Gaussian noise [7].

2.1 Local Application of RATS

RATS lends itself well to local application [1] for two reasons: (i) the statistic in (5) is robust against noise, and (ii) it is easy to check whether a region contains an edge by checking whether the denominator in (5) is above some threshold [1, 7]. Ideally, we want to compute the threshold in an isotropic surroundings of each pixel. This can be done using a moving-window version of RATS, which can be written as the ratio of two convolutions

$$T_h(x,y) = \frac{(\Pi_h * (w \cdot p))(x,y)}{(\Pi_h * w)(x,y)}, \tag{7}$$

in which $*$ denotes convolution and $\Pi_h(x,y)$ is given by

$$\Pi_h(x) = \begin{cases} 1 & \text{if } |x| \leq h \text{ and } |y| \leq h, \\ 0 & \text{otherwise.} \end{cases} \tag{8}$$

One problem with (7) is that T_h is undefined for all pixels where $(\Pi_h * w)(x,y) = 0$. Thus wherever the distance between edges is greater than the width of the window, no threshold is computed. Besides, the square convolution kernels are not isotropic. However, the convolution formalism allows generalization of the algorithm to other convolution kernels, e.g. Gaussian. Gaussian kernels are separable, and have infinite impulse response (IIR), and so will contribute over the entire image. Besides, can be computed quickly using a recursive implementation which has an IIR [9]. We arrive at

$$T_\sigma(x,y) = \frac{(G_\sigma * (w \cdot p))(x,y)}{(G_\sigma * w)(x,y)}, \tag{9}$$

with G_σ a Gaussian with zero mean and standard deviation of σ. A further advantage (9) over (7) is that edges close to the current pixel are given higher weights than distant edge. However, despite their infinite impulse response, G_σ falls off so rapidly that at large distances from edges thresholds may become unreliable, because a few remaining nearby noise edges may outweigh distant true edges. To counter this, multi-scale approach can be used, by computing T_σ with $\sigma = \sigma_0, 2\sigma_0, 4\sigma_0, \ldots, \sigma_{\max}$, and using the lowest σ for which T_σ can be computed reliably.

2.2 Selecting the Correct Scale

To select the correct scale we need to understand how the noise influences the statistic T_σ. Let us assume that the noise in an image is Gaussian with zero mean and standard deviation η. Its distribution is simply

$$p(x)dx = \frac{1}{\eta\sqrt{2\pi}}e^{-x^2/2\eta^2} \tag{10}$$

This means that the probability distribution p_{g_x} of g_x (or g_y or g_z) is

$$p_{g_x}(x)dx = \frac{1}{2\eta\sqrt{\pi}}e^{-x^2/4\eta^2}. \tag{11}$$

The probability distribution p_1 of g_x^2 is

$$p_1(x)dx = p_{g_x}(\sqrt{x})d\sqrt{x} = \frac{1}{2\eta\sqrt{2\pi x}}e^{-x/4\eta^2}. \tag{12}$$

In 2-D, the probability distribution p_2 of g^2 in (4) is

$$p_2(x)dx = (p_1 * p_1)(x)dx = \frac{1}{4\eta^2}e^{-x/4\eta^2}, \tag{13}$$

The 3-D counterpart of g^2 has a probability distribution p_3 given by

$$p_3(x)dx = (p_2 * p_1)(x)dx = \frac{\sqrt{x}}{4\eta^3\sqrt{2\pi}}e^{-x/4\eta^2}. \tag{14}$$

To select the lowest scale at which the denominator in (9) becomes significantly different from the value expected from noise, we need both the mean value $\langle w_\lambda\rangle$ and the variance σ_w^2 of w_λ. Using (6) and (13) the distribution p_w of w_λ is

$$p_w(x) = \begin{cases} \delta(x)\int_0^{\lambda^2\eta^2} p_2(x')dx' & \text{if } x < \lambda^2\eta^2, \\ p_2(x) & \text{otherwise.} \end{cases} \tag{15}$$

It can be seen from (13) that the probability p_λ that $x > \lambda^2\eta^2$ is $e^{-\lambda^2/4}$. Therefore, the expected value $\langle w_\lambda\rangle$ is

$$\langle w_\lambda\rangle = \int_{\lambda^2\eta^2}^{\infty}\frac{x}{4\eta^2}e^{-x/4\eta^2}dx = e^{-\frac{\lambda^2}{4}}\left(1+\frac{\lambda^2}{4}\right)4\eta^2 \tag{16}$$

and the variance σ_w^2 is

$$\sigma_w^2 = e^{-\frac{\lambda^2}{4}}\left((1-e^{-\frac{\lambda^2}{4}})\left(1+\frac{\lambda^2}{4}\right)^2+1\right)16\eta^4 \approx e^{-\frac{\lambda^2}{4}}\left(1+\frac{\lambda^2}{4}\right)^2 16\eta^4 \tag{17}$$

in the 2-D case. Thus, the standard deviation σ_w is approximately

$$\sigma_w \approx e^{-\frac{\lambda^2}{8}}\left(1+\frac{\lambda^2}{4}\right)4\eta^2. \tag{18}$$

For $\lambda \geq 5$ the approximation is accurate to within 6%. The mean noise response in the Gaussian-convolved edge image is just $\langle w_\lambda \rangle$, whereas the variance of the noise response σ_{Gw}^2 is

$$\sigma_{Gw}^2 = \sigma_w^2 \int_{-\infty}^{\infty} \int_{-\infty}^{\infty} G_{\sigma_i}^2(x, y) dx dy = \frac{1}{4\pi\sigma_i^2} \sigma_w^2. \tag{19}$$

We can select the lowest scale σ_i for which the denominator of (9) is larger than a threshold $T_{Gw} = \langle w_\lambda \rangle + 3\sigma_{Gw}$, or

$$(G_{\sigma_i} * w)(x, y) \geq T_{Gw} = e^{-\frac{\lambda^2}{8}} \left(1 + \frac{\lambda^2}{4}\right) \left(e^{-\frac{\lambda^2}{8}} + \frac{3}{2\sigma_i\sqrt{\pi}}\right) 4\eta^2 \tag{20}$$

Note that as $\sigma_i \to \infty$, the variance $\sigma_{Gw}^2 \to 0$, and so $T_{Gw} \to \langle w_\lambda \rangle$. When using the Sobel kernels in our initial edge detector, the only thing that needs to be changed in this calculation is to replace η with $\sqrt{5}\eta/4$ [7].

3 Algorithm

Let array p contain the original image, array w store the weights, array wp the product $w_\lambda p$, array T the threshold, and a boolean array q the binary output image. All arrays are of the same size as the original image. Let the value Inv denote an invalid threshold (e.g., some value $> \max_{x,y}(p(x, y))$). Finally, we have T_λ to store the global threshold according to (5).

The multi-scale, Gaussian-weighted, moving-window RATS algorithm is summarized in Fig. 2. The only input the algorithm needs is the original image, the desired value of λ, and the image noise η. After computing of w_λ and storing in in w, we compute the product image $w_\lambda p$, and the global threshold T_λ. We initialize all elements of T to Inv, and convolve both w and wp with G_{σ_0} at the lowest scale. After this initial phase, we loop through all scales but the last. During each loop we first compute T_{Gw} at that scale, and then compute T_{σ_i} for all pixels (x, y) which have not yet been assigned a valid threshold (i.e., $T(x, y) = Inv$), *and* for which $w(x, y) \geq T_{Gw}$. We then compute $G_{\sigma_{i+1}} * w$ from $G_{\sigma_i} * w$ by convolving $G_{\sigma_i} * w$ with $G_{\sqrt{3}\sigma_i}$, and likewise for $G_{\sigma_{i+1}} * wp$. At the largest scale, a similar operation is performed, but here $T(x, y)$ is set to the global threshold T_λ if no threshold can be computed at that scale. Finally, for each pixel $q(x, y)$ is set to *true* if $p(x, y) > T(x, y)$ and to false otherwise.

4 Results

The algorithm was implemented, using the Sobel gradient, $\lambda = 7$, and four scales ranging from $\sigma = 2$ to $\sigma = 16$, and tested on synthetic 2-D images of 256×256 pixels containing objects of different sizes and different or constant contrast with respect to the local background. The constant object-intensity images (see Fig. 3(b)) served as reference segmentation for themselves and the

```
For all pixels (x, y) compute w_λ(x, y) from input image p and store in w.
Compute product image w_λ p and store in wp.
Compute T_λ from wp and w.
Set all values in T to Inv.
Convolve w and wp with G_σ0 and store in w and wp respectively.
For all scales i = 0, 1, ..., max −1 do
    Compute T_Gw for this scale
    For all pixels (x, y) with T(x, y) ≠ Inv
        if w(x, y) ≥ T_Gw then
            T(x, y) ← wp(x, y)/w(x, y).
    Convolve w and wp with G_√3σi and store in w and wp respectively.
Compute T_Gw for σ_max
For all pixels (x, y) with T(x, y) ≠ Inv
    if w(x, y) ≥ T_Gw then
        T(x, y) ← wp(x, y)/w(x, y).
    else
        T(x, y) ← T_λ
For all pixels (x, y)
    q(x, y) ← p(x, y) > T(x, y)
```

Fig. 2. The multi-scale, Gaussian-weighted, moving-window RATS algorithm. Note that $\leftarrow$ denotes assignment.

corresponding variable object-intensity images as in Fig. 3(a). A background slope running from 0 at the left and height h_s at the right, and Gaussian noise with standard deviation η were added. The fraction of misclassified pixels was computed as a function of η and h_s. The results are shown in Fig. 3(c)-(h). Using all four scales the performance is generally good up to an η of about 8 (corresponding to an S/N-ratio of about 8 for the faintest objects) for objects of varying intensity (Fig. 3(c), (d) and (f)). Fig. 3(d) shows how omission of the lowest scale results in segmentation errors where faint objects lie close to bright. Fig. 3(f) shows a comparison of the new method with global thresholding by Otsu's method [2]. The latter performs badly at all noise levels, because it classifies fainter foreground objects as background. For the former method the error fraction rises sharply beyond $\eta = 8$ to about 7% at $\eta = 32$. An example is shown in Fig. 3(e). The slope h_s has no impact on segmentation quality (not shown). Segmentation of Fig. 3(b) is easier, the errors never exceeding 0.5 % (not shown). Using just a single scale σ results in rather poor segmentation, unless the smallest scales are used Fig. 3(g). Apparently, the lowest values of σ have a high impact on the quality of segmentation. Finally, Fig 3(h) shows a comparison between the earlier quad-tree method and the new algorithm for $h_s = 16$. Only at $\eta = 16$ does the old method perform better, suggesting that the way noise is dealt with using (20) could be improved, perhaps by giving less weight to the lowest scale. The results in Fig. 3(g) also suggest that using $\sigma = 4$ at $\eta = 16$ is better than the multi-scale approach.

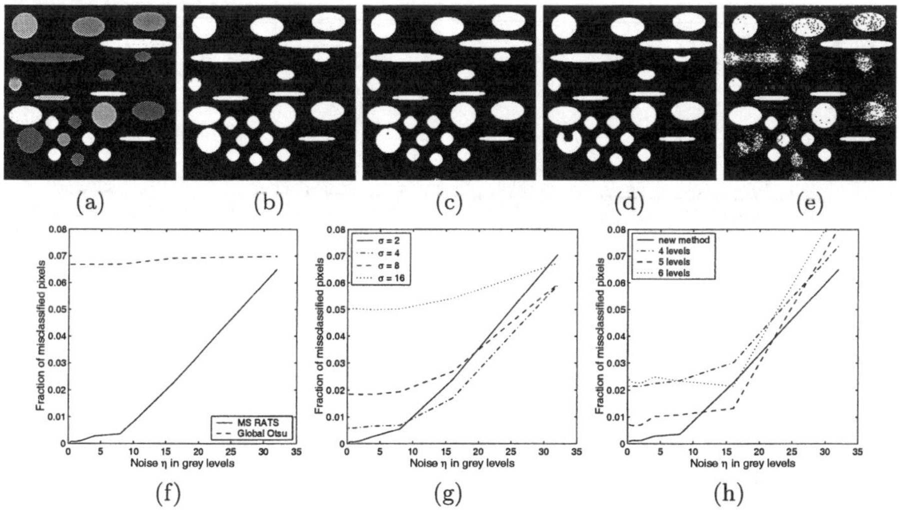

Fig. 3. Segmentation of synthetic images of ellipses: (a) synthetic image of ellipses of differing intensities; (b) same as (a) but with constant intensities; (c) segmentation result of (a) with noise $\eta = 1$ and slope $h_s = 0$ added; (d) as (c) but without using scale $\sigma = 2$; (e) as (c) but $\eta = 32$ and $h_s = 32$; (f) fraction of correctly classified pixels of (a) as a function of η, for multi-scale RATS with $h_s = 0$, using 4 scales plus global threshold T_λ, compared to global thresholding according to Otsu [2]; (g) same as (f) but using just a single scale σ and T_λ; (h) same as (f) but comparing the new method to the quad-tree method [5] for different numbers of levels in the quad-tree.

The method was also tested on images of bacteria, with σ_0 ranging from 2 to 8. As can be seen in Fig. 4, when three scales are used, the method detects a faint object skipped by the quad-tree approach shown in Fig. 1. If $\sigma_0 = 2$, the method detects parts of the diffraction halos around the brighter objects.

5 Discussion

A new, multi-scale version of RATS has been developed which can adapt well to variations in both background and object intensity. A framework to select the appropriate scale has been developed. The experiments show that the method works with a modest number of scales, and with therefore a modest computational cost. A 512×512 image takes just 0.16 s if four scales are used, whereas a 2483×3508 image takes 6.03 s on a Pentium 4 at 1.9 GHz. At a single scale the timings are 0.06 s and 1.83 s, respectively. Extensions to 3-D should be straightforward, provided a 3-D equivalent of (20) is derived. The selection of the lowest scale may need more work. The experiment with synthetic images yielded the best results with $\sigma_0 = 2$, whereas the experiment using images of bacteria yielded the best results with $\sigma_0 = 4$. It might well be that the Gaussian assumptions used in (20) do not hold for small σ. Solving this problem requires analytical solutions or numerical approximations of the distribution of the denominator of (9). This will be studied in future work.

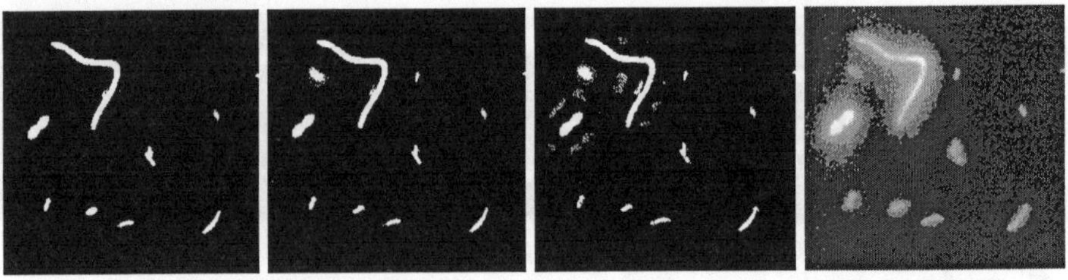
(a) (b) (c) (d)

Fig. 4. Segmentation of image of bacteria from Fig. 1(a) with $\sigma_{max} = 16$, $\lambda = 5$ and $\eta = 2.3$: (a) $\sigma_0 = 8$; (b) $\sigma_0 = 4$; (c) $\sigma_0 = 2$; (d) contrast stretched original showing faint object and diffraction halo around brighter objects.

One drawback of this and many other implementations of RATS is that we need an estimate of the image noise. Ideally, we would like to be able to determine the noise from the image itself, rather than rely on external calibration data, which might be absent. If we assume that the lowest gradient pixels (or voxels) are attributable to noise only, we could estimate η by fitting the histogram of the edge filtered image at these values to the distribution in (13) in 2-D or (14) in 3-D. Work is in progress for just such an extension.

References

1. J. Kittler, J. Illingworth, and J. Föglein. Threshold selection based on a simple image statistic. *Comp. Vision Graph. Image Proc.*, 30:125–147, 1985.
2. N. Otsu. A threshold selection method from gray-level histogram. *IEEE Trans. Syst. Man Cybern.*, 9:62–66, 1979.
3. P. K. Sahoo, S. Soltani, A. K. C. Wong, and Y. C. Chen. A survey of thresholding techniques. *Comp. Vision Graph. Image Proc.*, 41:233–260, 1988.
4. . D. Trier and A. K. Jain. Goal-directed evalution of binarization methods. *IEEE Trans. Image Proc.*, 17(12):1191–1201, 1995.
5. M. H. F. Wilkinson. Rapid automatic segmentation of fluorescent and phase-contrast images of bacteria. In J. Slavik, editor, *Fluorescence Microscopy and Fluorescent Probes*, pages 261–266. Plenum Press, New York, 1996.
6. M. H. F. Wilkinson. Automated and manual segmentation techniques in image analysis of microbes. In M. H. F. Wilkinson and F. Schut, editors, *Digital Image Analysis of Microbes*, pages 135–171. John Wiley and Sons, Ltd, Chichester, UK, 1998.
7. M. H. F. Wilkinson. Optimizing edge detectors for robust automatic threshold selection: coping with edge curvature and noise. *Graph. Mod. Image Proc.*, 60:385–401, 1998.
8. Y. Yang and H. Yan. An adaptive logical method for binarization of degraded document images. *Pattern Recognition*, 33:787–807, 2000.
9. I. T. Young and L. J. van Vliet. Recursive implementation of the Gaussian filter. *Signal Processing*, 44:139–151, 1995.

Shape from Photometric Stereo and Contours

Chia-Yen Chen[1], Reinhard Klette[1], and Chi-Fa Chen[2]

[1] Center for Image Technology and Robotics
The University of Auckland, New Zealand
[2] Department of Electrical Engineering, I-Shou University, Taiwan

Abstract. In this work, we propose an alternative approach to 3D shape recovery by combining photometric stereo and shape from contours methods. Surfaces recovered by photometric stereo are aligned, adjusted and merged according to a preliminary 3D model obtained by shape from contours. Comparisons are conducted to evaluate the performances of different methods. It has been found that the proposed approach provides more accurate shape recovery than the photometric stereo and shape from contours methods.

Keywords: 3D shape recovery, photometric stereo, shape from contours

1 Introduction

The photometric stereo method is able to rapidly obtain dense local surface orientations from intensity images of the object illuminated by calibrated light sources [2–4, 8, 9]. The surface orientation vectors are integrated, either globally or locally, to provide the depth values of the surface. However, independent of integration approaches, the surface depth values recovered by integration of the orientation vectors are scaled with respect to the true surface.

The shape from contours method combines contour images of the object from various known viewing directions to recover a 3D model of the object [4–7]. However, the method is unable to recover some concave regions on the surface and the accuracy of the recovered 3D model depends on the resolution of the viewing directions. Nevertheless, the shape from contours method has less restrictions on the illumination conditions, making it a more robust approach to obtain a preliminary 3D model of an object.

In this work, we propose a 3D shape recovery method to combine the depth information obtained by photometric stereo and shape from contours methods. Our motivation is to design an alternative 3D shape recovery method that combines the advantages of photometric stereo and shape from contours to provide rapid, detailed and reliable 3D surface recovery.

The proposed shape from photometric stereo and contours method uses the 3D model obtained by shape from contours to align and adjust surfaces recovered by photometric stereo in different viewing directions. Neighbouring surface are then merged according to a weighting function associated with the reliability of the photometric stereo method to produce the final 3D model. Comparisons of experimental results have shown that the proposed approach has better performance than the photometric stereo or shape from contours method alone.

N. Petkov and M.A. Westenberg (Eds.): CAIP 2003, LNCS 2756, pp. 377–384, 2003.

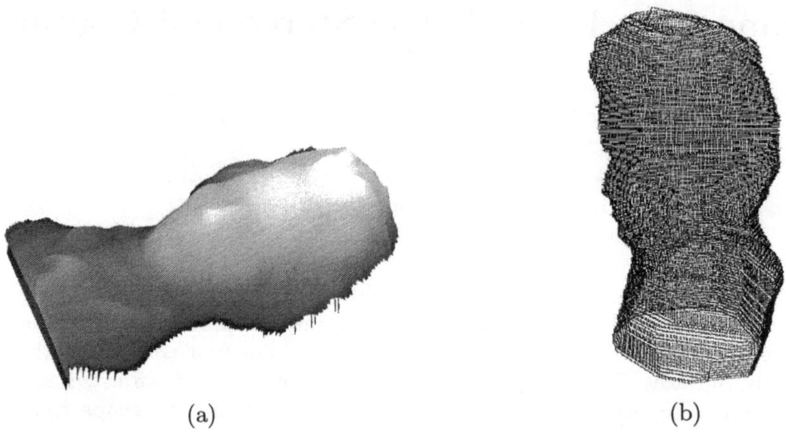

Fig. 1. Examples of input data: (a) partial surface recovered by photometric stereo and (b) preliminary 3D model (*photo hull*) recovered by shape from contours.

2 Shape from Photometric Stereo and Contours

2.1 Input Data

In this section we briefly describe how to apply photometric stereo and shape from contours methods (see [4] for details) for our purposes. The object is rotated in θ degree increments to provide views from different directions. At each viewing direction θ_{psm}, three light sources are used to provide input irradiance images for the albedo-independent photometric stereo method. Local surface orientation vectors are recovered by the photometric stereo method and globally integrated using the Frankot-Chellapa algorithm to obtain surface depth values. Altogether, there are $360/\theta_{psm}$ partial surface reconstructions of the object. A 3D model of the object is constructed by acquiring the contour images of the object at θ_{sfc} degrees increment and applying the shape from contours method. Examples of input partial surfaces and 3D model are shown in Fig. 1. Experiments have been conducted using different combinations of θ_{psm} and θ_{sfc} to investigate the influence of the recovered partial surfaces and the preliminary 3D model on the final 3D model.

Once the input partial surfaces and 3D model have been obtained, they are aligned according to the viewing directions in preparation for the following steps, where the input data will be adjusted and merged according to the proposed method.

2.2 Surface Adjustment

The partial surfaces obtained by photometric stereo are adjusted with respect to corresponding regions on the 3D model obtained by shape from contours [1]. This process is necessary to account for the fact that surface values are obtained by the photometric stereo method through integration, which makes

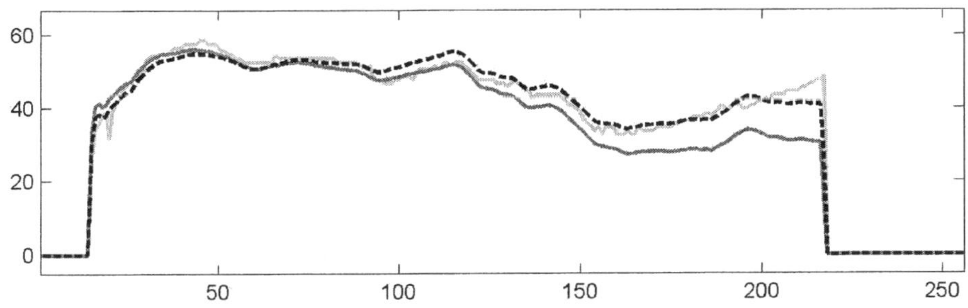

Fig. 2. A vertical cross-section showing profiles extracted from the 3D model, the corresponding partial surface and the adjusted partial surface.

them somewhat scaled with respect to the true surface. On the other hand, the 3D model obtains its shape directly from the contours of the object, hence it can serve as a reference for correcting the scaled surfaces.

A vertical profile extracted from each partial surface is compared with the profile extracted from the 3D model in the same viewing direction and the difference between two profiles is approximated by a linear function. The linear function is then weighed and applied to the partial surface to adjust surface depth values towards those on the 3D model. Figure 2 shows an example of the vertical profiles. In Fig. 2, the solid light gray line represents the profile extracted from the preliminary 3D model, the solid black line represents the profile extracted from the corresponding partial surface obtained by photometric stereo, and the dashed black line is the profile extracted from the adjusted surface.

The adjustment process is performed for each given partial surface. In Fig. 3, a horizontal cross-section from the shape from contours 3D model, profiles from the original partial surfaces and adjusted surfaces, are respectively represented by the solid light gray line, solid black lines, and dashed black lines.

When all partial surfaces have been aligned and adjusted, the next step is to merge these surface with respect to the reliability of depth values on each surface.

2.3 Merging of Surfaces

In the merging step, depth values on overlapping partial surfaces are merged according to weighting functions to produce a 3D model of the object. The weighting functions are based on the characteristics of the photometric stereo method when recovering a given surface. Generally, surface orientations recovered by photometric stereo becomes less accurate as they approach 90 degrees with the viewing direction, since those are regions where shadows begin to occur. Hence depth values towards the edges of a given partial surface are less reliable then values towards the center of the surface.

Suppose $S_{\theta,j}$ represents the jth horizontal cross-section of partial surface obtained from viewing direction θ. Given two overlapping profiles $S_{\theta 1,j}$ and $S_{\theta 2,j}$,

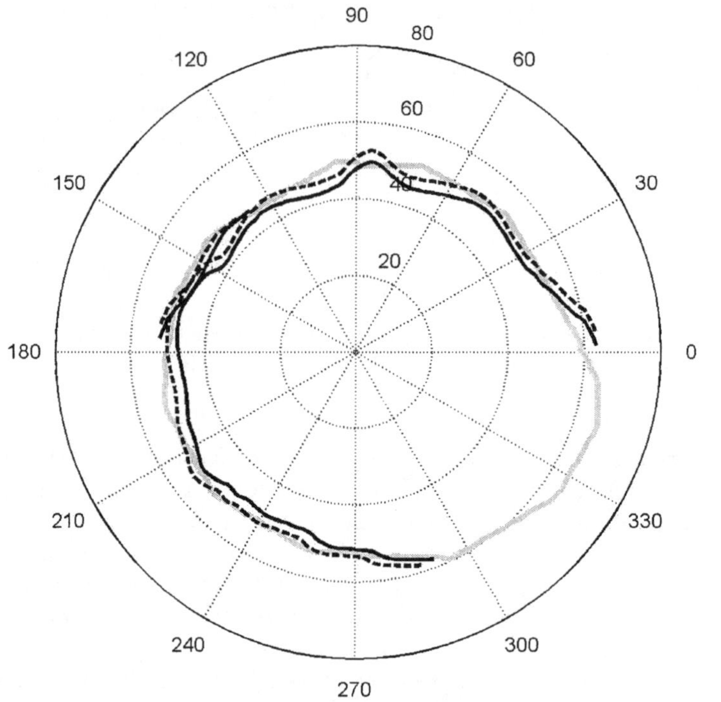

Fig. 3. Horizontal cross-sections from 3D model, the original and adjusted photometric stereo profiles.

let $\phi_{\theta 1,j}$ denote the angle of the overlapping region. The weighting function for each point i within the overlapping region is

$$w_{\theta 1,j}(i) = 1 - i/\phi_{\theta 1,j} \ , \tag{1}$$

and the merged profile is

$$S_j(i) = w_{\theta 1,j}(i) * S_{\theta 1,j}(i) + (1 - w_{\theta 1,j}(i)) * S_{\theta 2,j}(i) \ . \tag{2}$$

Figure 4 shows two overlapping profiles and the resultant merged profile. It can be seen that the merged profile has a smooth transition from one profile into the next, and it retains the details provided by both profiles.

The merging process is repeated for all horizontal profiles for all viewing directions to obtain a 3D model from the partial surfaces.

3 Results

We show the results obtained by fusion of partial surfaces and the preliminary 3D model, and evaluate the reconstruction accuracy of each method. Figure 5(a)

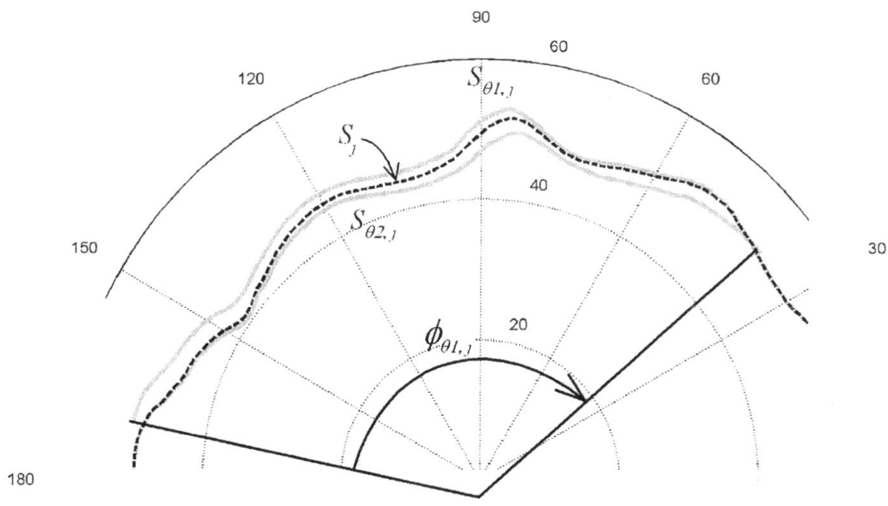

Fig. 4. Overlapping profiles and the resultant merged profile.

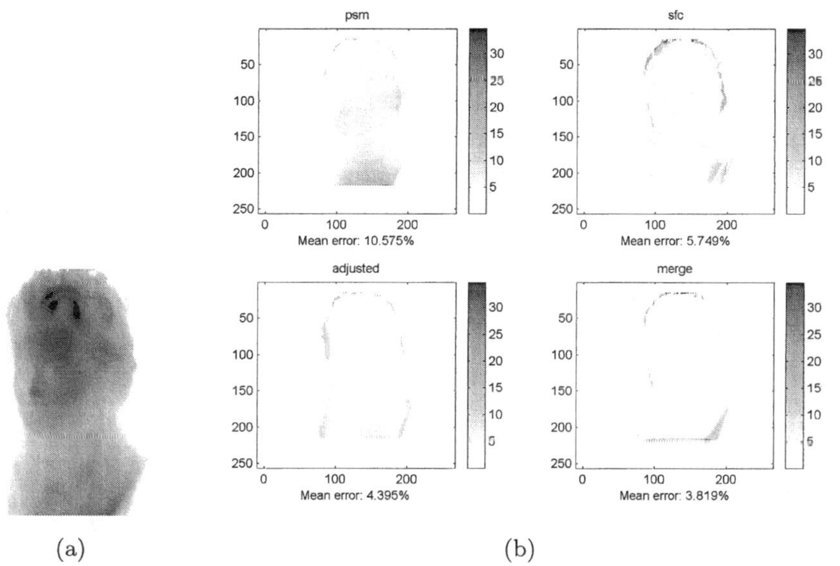

Fig. 5. Comparison of results for *Beethoven* (a) original surface and (b) errors in surfaces reconstructed by different methods.

shows a partial surface of the original 3D model *Beethoven*, Fig. 5(b) shows the errors calculated for corresponding surfaces reconstructed using photometric stereo(top left), shape from contours(top right), photometric stereo surface adjusted using the preliminary 3D model (bottom left), and the surface reconstructed by merging the adjusted surface according to the weighting function.

Table 1. Error for reconstructed models.

(%)	Photometric stereo	Shape from contours	Adjusted photometric stereo	Merge (combined reconstruction)
Beethoven	12.49	4.88	4.92	3.93
Monk	16.21	4.96	5.54	3.83
Mozart	13.17	5.68	5.34	4.06
Penguin	13.35	6.48	5.95	4.39

The intensity of the error images represent the error magnitude, and the mean percentage error is given at the bottom of each image.

It can be seen from Figs. 5 that the surfaces reconstructed by the fusion of photometric stereo and shape from contours are more accurate than surface obtained by the other methods. Reconstructions and comparisons for other models also been performed with similar results as shown in Figs. 5. Figures 6 (a) and 6 (b) show the error plots for two of the models used in this work and Table. 1 shows the overall errors for all four reconstructed 3D models. For the examples, we used $\theta_{psm} = 30$ and $\theta_{sfc} = 30$.

Figures 6 (a) and 6 (b) show that the merged 3D models have generally lower errors than either the surfaces obtained by photometric stereo, shape from contours, or the photometric stereo partial surfaces adjust by the preliminary 3D models obtained by shape from contours. It can be seen from the graphs that the error plots of the merged models approximately follows the error plots of the preliminary 3D model. We also experimented with other combinations of θ_{psm} and θ_{sfc}, and it has been found that if the preliminary 3D model is accurate (e.g., mean error is less than 10%), then the merged model will have improved accuracy. On the other hand, if the preliminary 3D model is not so accurate, then it degrades the effects of the surface adjustment process, resulting in a less accurate 3D model.

The effectiveness of the adjustment and merging functions can be seen from the comparisons. Errors in the partial surfaces are dramatically reduced once the surfaces are adjusted. The merging process also reduced the errors further by discarding the less reliable regions on the partial surface and placing higher weight on the more reliable and detailed regions.

Table 1 summarises the errors for models recovered by each of the three shape recovery methods used in this work, it can be seen that the 3D models recovered by the proposed method have lower overall error than models obtained using other approaches.

4 Conclusion

We proposed an alternative method for 3D shape recovery by combining data provided by photometric stereo and shape from contours. Partial surfaces obtained by photometric stereo in multiple viewing directions are aligned and adjusted with respect to a preliminary 3D model recovered by shape from contours.

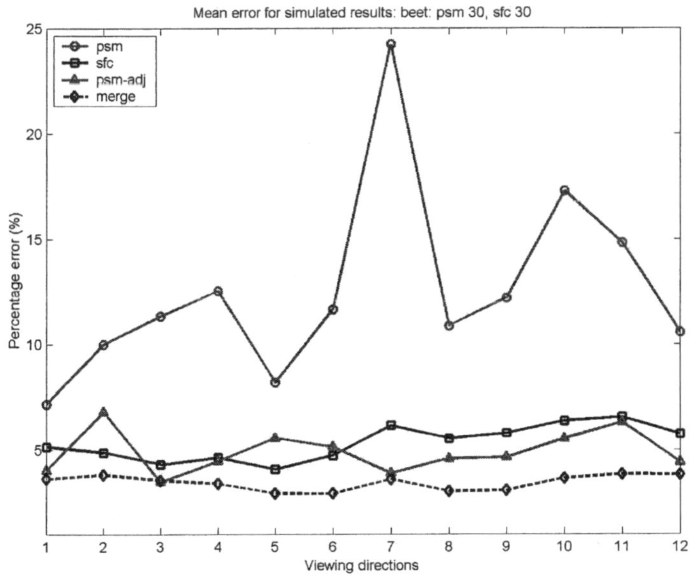

(a)

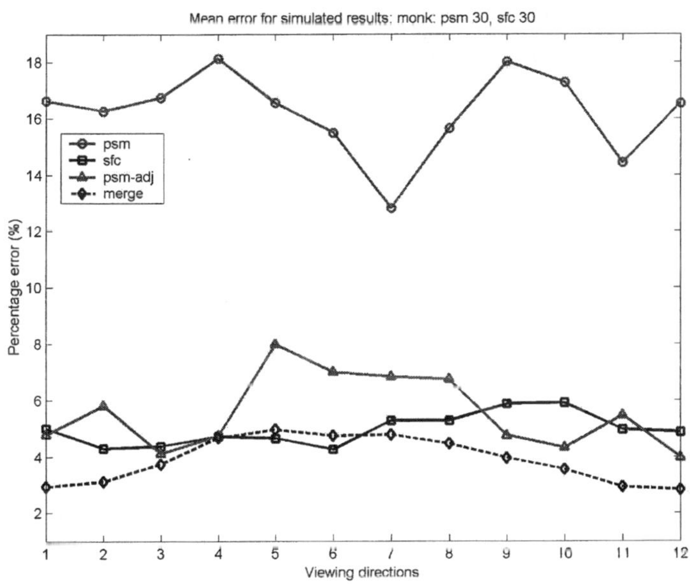

(b)

Fig. 6. Error plots for reconstructed (a) *Beethoven* and (b) *Monk*.

The surfaces are then merged with respect to a weight function to produce a 3D model. The 3D model recovered by the proposed has the advantages from both the photometric stereo and shape from contours methods. The adjusting function adjusts the partial surfaces towards the shape of the preliminary 3D model, and the weighting function merges the partial surfaces together. Both functions have been selected such that while conforming to the shape of the object, it also retains the details on the surface of the object. Experiments and comparisons have been performed using different objects. Overall, the proposed 3D shape recovery approach by combining photometric stereo and shape from contourscan effectively obtain 3D models with higher accuracy than either method alone. Future work may include experiments by merging with surface patches rather than the horizontal profiles, and reconstructing models with different reflectance and geometric properties.

References

1. C. Chen, R. Klette and C. Chen: Improved fusion of photometric stereo and shape from contours. in Proc. *Image Vision Computing New Zealand* (2001) 103–108.
2. R. Frankot, R. Chellappa: A method for enforcing integrability in shape from shading algorithms. *IEEE Trans. Pattern Analysis Machine Intelligence*, **10** (1988) 439–451.
3. R. Klette, K.Schlüns: Height data from gradient fields. in Proc. *SPIE* **2908** (1996) 204–215.
4. R. Klette, K. Schlüns, A. Koschan: *Computer Vision: Three-dimensional Data from Images.* Springer, Singapore (1998).
5. J. J. Koenderink: *Solid Shape.* Cambridge, MA, MIT Press (1990).
6. K. N. Kutulakos and S. M. Seitz: A theory of shape by space carving. Proc. 7th*Int. Conf. Computer Vision* (1999) 307–314.
7. S. Tokai, T. Wada, T. Matsuyama: Real time 3D shape reconstruction using PC cluster system. Proc. 3rd Int. Workshop *Cooperative Distributed Vision* (1999) 171–187.
8. R.J. Woodham: Photometric method for determining surface orientation from multiple images. *Optical Engineering*, **19** (1980) 139–144.
9. R. Zhang, P. S. Tsai, J. E. Cryer and M. Shah: Shape-from-shading: a survey. *IEEE Trans. Pattern Analysis and Machine Intelligence*, **21** (1999) 690–706.

A Fast Algorithm for Constructing Parameterizations of Three-Dimensional Simply Connected Digital Objects

Ola Weistrand

Uppsala University, Department of Mathematics
and Centre for Image Analysis
Lägerhyddsvägen 17, SE-752 37 Uppsala, Sweden
weistrand@math.uu.se

Abstract. In this paper we present a fast algorithm that constructs a parameterization of certain classes of simply connected three-dimensional digital objects. A local search strategy is used to increase the convexity of the object without destroying neighborhood relations of the surface. The resulting object is easily parameterized and by a pull-back of this parameterization, we can approximate the original object in terms of spherical harmonic functions. Finally, limitations of the method as well as different directions for future research are discussed.

1 Introduction

The development of new image acquisition techniques has made volume images a commonly used tool in, for example, the medical community. It is therefore an important challenge to develop methods that can be used for analysis of these, often rather large, data sets. Some concepts from two-dimensional image analysis are easily generalized to handle these new images, some are not. In this paper global shape approximation of simply connected binary objects is discussed. We would like to capture information of the shape in a small set of parameters that can be used for shape analysis, comparison between different objects and matching against predefined templates. Although many methods for global shape description exist, they are often not applicable to three-dimensional objects or they only provide a very rough description. Successful families of methods that avoids these problems are *implicit polynomial* descriptors and *spherical harmonic* descriptors. Two of the most prominent representatives of these approaches are the work of Blane, Lei, Civi and Cooper [1] and the work of Brechbühler, Gerig and Kubler [5]. The method in this paper is related to the latter of these. Although the algorithm in [5] is successful on many objects, it is computationally too expensive for large objects. We see a need for methods that can describe shape of large objects (100,000-200,000 surface voxels) up to an adaptable degree. This paper describes an attempt to do this.

When trying to generalize two-dimensional Fourier descriptors to three dimensions, the difficulty of representing the shape of objects in terms of functions

N. Petkov and M.A. Westenberg (Eds.): CAIP 2003, LNCS 2756, pp. 385–392, 2003.

is soon identified as the main problem. Construction methods of such functions are well-known in two dimensions, but very hard and computationally expensive in three dimensions. Brechbühler [5] solves this problem by a two step method: Initial mapping of surface vertices to a sphere, followed by a non-linear, constrained optimization method that aims at equalizing the distribution of the vertices over the sphere. The initial parameterization is constructed by solving a sparse symmetric system of linear equations and is therefore very fast. This nice feature is not shared by the optimization step. It is very time consuming. The speed of convergence depends on the size of the object as well as the degree of clustering in the initial parameterization.

The method in this paper was originally developed as an alternative method for the initial parameterization step in [5]. The main idea is to construct less clustered initial parameterizations without a significant increase in computational time. For many objects it turns out that the quality is good enough to allow shape approximation without the non-linear optimization. The price to be paid for this is that not all simply connected objects can be handled by the method. Limitations as well as future directions of research are discussed in Section 5.

2 Preliminaries

In this section we discuss the objects and their associated surfaces that will be considered in the remaining part of this article.

2.1 Objects and Surfaces

Let I be a volume image, that is a cubic subset of $\mathbf{Z}^3$ together with a function that assigns a value to each element (voxel) in the subset. For simplicity we will identify I with the function $I\colon \mathbf{Z}^3 \to \mathbf{Z}$. Distances between elements will be measured by the l^1-metric defined by $d_1(x,y) = |x_1 - y_1| + |x_2 - y_2| + |x_3 - y_3|$ or by the l^∞-metric defined by $d_\infty(x,y) = \max(|x_1 - y_1|, |x_2 - y_2|, |x_3 - y_3|)$ for elements x and y in $\mathbf{Z}^3$.

We want to describe the shape of, in general non-convex, subsets of I. Let A be such a set, $I(x) = 1$ for all $x \in A$ and $I(x) = 0$ for all $x \in A^c$. The following assumptions are made about A:

- A is 6-connected.
- A is simply connected (no holes or tunnels).
- A is "thick enough" to admit a meaningful surface representation in terms of voxels.

As we are interested in large objects, we usually have no problems fulfilling the last condition.

Definition 1. *Let A be a set as described above and let $x \in A$. Then x is an* inner point *if the set $\{y; d_\infty(x,y) \leq 1\}$ is included in A.*

We can now define the *surface* of A

Definition 2. *The surface of A, denoted ∂A, consists of all $x \in A$ such that*

- *x is not an inner point of A.*
- *The set $\{y; d_\infty(x, y) \leq 1\}$ contains at least one inner point of A.*

Note that ∂A is a 6-connected subset of A. A drawback of this rather primitive surface definition is that one or two voxel thick parts of the object is not included in ∂A. Also, keeping track of the orientation of the surface is difficult. A surface definition that avoids these problems (although more expensive in terms of storage) is found in [8]. However, for large objects, our surface definition serves well and leads to a good representation.

2.2 The Surface Data Structure

In Section 3 we will present a constrained optimization problem which improves the convexity of A without "tearing" the surface too much. To do this we must specify local adjacency relations between surface elements. It is important not to be too generous when setting up these relations, in the sense that a given surface element cannot be adjacent to many other elements. This would impose hard restrictions on which local moves are possible. For example, a straightforward 18-connected adjacency relation can be shown to be a bad choice. The choice in this article will be 6-connectedness, that is two elements $x, y \in \partial A$ are adjacent if $d_1(x, y) \leq 1$.

Representing the surface of A as a set is not enough for our purposes. In Section 3 we will gradually move the surface elements. It is important to know the identity of each element during this process, see Section 4. The following data structures handles this by assigning ID-numbers to surface elements

```
struct 3d_point { int x1, x2, x3; };

struct surface_element
{
    int id;
    3d_point x;
    int n[1..nr_of_neighbors];
};.
```

Let S_A be an array of *surface_element* as defined above. Given a *surface_element*, $s \in S_A$, we will refer to its associated coordinate, ID-number and array of ID-numbers of neighbors as $s.x$, $s.id$ and $s.n$, respectively.

3 Optimization

We want to approximate the shape of a non-convex, simply 6-connected set, $A \subset I$ using an optimization step that aims at maximizing the object's convexity, without destroying neighborhood relations between surface elements. To do this starting from A, we construct a new set that will guide the process.

First an approximation to the digital convex hull of A is calculated [7]. Algorithms for computing approximate convex hulls are available. Using the (3×3×3) neighborhood algorithm presented in [3], with the set A as input, a new set $\text{CVX}(A) \subset I$ is obtained that is "convex". Using larger neighborhoods, for example (5×5×5), we can construct better approximations to a higher computational cost.

We want to move the surface of A towards the surface of the convex hull. By labeling each element in the concavities, $\text{CVX}(A) \setminus A$, with the shortest distance to the background, $I \setminus \text{CVX}(A)$, this new image will provide guidance for this process. Shortest paths are constrained not to leave the concavities. Many different metrics can be used for approximating distances in digital images. Our interest is not distance measurements. Instead our motivation comes from the fact that at each iteration in the optimization process, we must provide an indication of which local moves are considered favorable. The d_∞-metric has proved to be a good choice. Using algorithms found in [2] the new distance labeled image can be efficiently calculated.

We will consider the optimization problem

$$\min \sum_{s \in S_A} I(s.x)$$

such that

$$\begin{aligned} &d_\infty(s.x, q.x) \leq d_{\max} && \text{for all } q \in s.n \\ &s.x \in \text{CVX}(A) \setminus A && \text{for all } s \in S_A. \end{aligned}$$

An obvious solution to this problem is obtained if the whole surface is placed in a single voxel on the boundary of the convex hull. This solution is not interesting for our purposes. By using the surface of A as input to Algorithm 1, we avoid this. The algorithm is a fast randomized local search method inspired by simulated annealing [6]. If we would iterate over the surface and locally move elements if and only if the degree of convexity increases, we would get stuck in local minima. B y sometimes choosing to move, even if this does not decrease the value of the function or even increases it, we are more likely to reach a better final result.

of the object to which we apply Algorithm 1, it may happen that different surface elements are occupying the same position in $\mathbf{Z}^3$. During the process this does not cause any problems—digital surfaces are not physical objects—but in the final result it is not a desirable situation. If this situation occurs, the surface needs to be moved further out from the object. Making a small adjustment of Algorithm 1 we can accomplish this: Replace the distance transformed concavities by a "thin" layer in each iteration by dilating the surface with a structuring element $\{x; d_\infty(x, 0) \leq 1\}$. In each iteration the image value in the positions of the new layer is labeled with a value that is one unit higher than the value in the previous iteration. This is to make sure that the surface does not start moving backwards.

4 Approximation

By applying Algorithm 1 combined with the expansion step if needed, a new object has been constructed that is convex or at least *starshaped* around the

Algorithm 1: Convexity Optimization

```
Data    : p_eq, p_inc      Probability to make equal and increasing moves
          S_A^ini          Initial surface structure
          I                Volume image to guide optimization
          T                Constant that decreases p_eq and p_inc
          d_max            Maximal distance from neighbors
          non_dec_max      Maximal number of nondecreasing iterations
Result  : S_A^opt          Optimized surface structure
begin
    iteration ⟵ 0
    bettermove ⟵ true
    ctr ⟵ 0
    while bettermove = true or ctr < non_dec_max do
        bettermove ⟵ false
        iteration ⟵ iteration + 1
        for all s ∈ S_A^ini do
            N = (3×3×3)-neighborhood of s in I
            sort N, best moves first
            p = random number between 0 and 1
            for all x ⊂ N do
                if I(x) > I(s.x) and d_∞(x, s.n) ≤ d_max then
                    s.x ⟵ x
                    bettermove ⟵ true
                if I(x) = I(s.x) and d_∞(x, s.n) ≤ d_max and p < p_eq then
                    s.x ⟵ x
                if I(x) < I(s.x) and d_∞(x, s.n) ≤ d_max and p < p_inc then
                    s.x ⟵ x
        if bettermove = false then
            ctr ⟵ ctr + 1
        else
            p_eq ⟵ T × p_eq
            p_inc ⟵ T × p_inc
    S_A^opt ⟵ S_A^ini
    return S_A^opt
end
```

center of mass, x_c, see left column of Figure 1. Projecting the surface voxels down on the sphere centered at x_c and using the bijectivity between the initial surface and the optimized surface, we obtain coordinate functions

$$(\phi, \theta) \mapsto x_i \qquad \text{for } i \in \{1, 2, 3\}$$

that can be approximated by

$$\sum_{l=0}^{N} \sum_{m=-l}^{+l} a_{lm} Y_{lm}(\phi, \theta), \tag{1}$$

Table 1. Summary of experiments. *Size*: The number of surface voxels. $dmax_{\mathrm{cvx}}$: Max distance between surface elements during convexity optimization. $dmax_{\mathrm{exp}}$: Max distance between surface elements during expansion. p_{eq}: Probability to make moves that does not decrease the objective function. p_{inc}: Probability to make moves that increase the objective function. T: Constant that determines how fast the algorithm becomes "greedy", that is only moves that decrease the objective function are accepted. *non_dec_max*: Maximal allowed number of iterations without decreasing the objective function. *Time*: Running time in minutes.

Name	Size	$\mathbf{dmax_{cvx}}$	$\mathbf{dmax_{exp}}$	$\mathbf{p_{eq}}$	$\mathbf{p_{inc}}$	T	non_dec_max	Time
Cube	15,456	3	3	0.8	0.2	0.95	5	3.3
Candle	14,280	5	-	0.8	0.2	0.95	5	1.2

where $Y_{lm}(\phi, \theta)$ are the *spherical harmonics* [4] and N is the *degree* of the approximation. The spherical harmonics form a complete orthonormal set of functions with respect to the inner product

$$\int_{\mathbf{S}^2} Y^*_{l'm'}(\phi, \theta) Y_{lm}(\phi, \theta) dS \tag{2}$$

and therefore (1) will converge as $N \to \infty$. The coefficients in the expansion can be calculated as

$$a_{lm} = \int_{\mathbf{S}^2} x_i(\phi, \theta) Y^*_{lm} dS.$$

Working with discrete data we could discretize these integrals in different ways and calculate the coefficients. A simpler approach, that also gives a better result, is obtained by calculating the coefficients as the solutions to a linear least squares problem. This is a standard method and we do not go into details here.

5 Experimental Results

The algorithm has been implemented in the C++ programming language and tested on real world objects as well as synthetic objects. Due to limited space, only two experiments are presented in this section. Times are measured on a Compaq Alphastation DS10 running TRU64 UNIX. The results are summarized in Table 1 and Figure 1.

The method cannot at this stage be expected to work for all simply connected objects. One reason for this is that there are requirements on the concavities of the objects. There is no guarantee that the distance transform will move the surface in the way we want. One example where the algorithm fails is "L-shaped" objects. The distance transform will try to move surface voxels deep in the concavity along the tangent plane instead of along the surface normals. A solution to this problem is currently being developed.

We are also investigating the possibilities to include an automatic, individual selection of the maximal allowed distance between neighbor voxels based on local thickness of the object.

Fig. 1. *Top-Left*: A cube with a deep concavity. Landmarks have been added. *Top-Right*: A candlestick and candle. *Middle row*: Objects after optimization. Observe the increased convexity. The cube is starshaped around the center of mass. *Bottom row*: Approximation in terms of spherical harmonic functions of degree 8 and 15, respectively.

References

1. M. M. Blane, Z. Lei, H. Civi, D. B. Cooper, The 3L Algorithm for Fitting Implicit Polynomial Curves and Surfaces to Data, *Pattern Analysis and Machine Intelligence*, Vol. **22**, No. 3, 2001, pp. 298-313
2. G. Borgefors, On Digital Distance Transforms in Three Dimensions, *Computer Vision and Image Understanding*, Vol. **64**, No. 3, November 1996, pp. 368-376.

3. G. Borgefors and G. Sanniti di Baja, Analyzing non-convex 2D and 3D patterns, *Computer Vision and Image Understanding*, Vol. **63**, No. 1, January 1996, pp. 145-157.
4. B. H. Bransden and C. J. Joachain, *Introduction to Quantum Mechanics*, Addison Wesley Longman Limited, 1989.
5. C. Brechbühler, G. Gerig and O. Kübler, Parametrization of Closed Surfaces for 3-D Shape Description, *Computer Vision and Image Understanding*, Vol. **61**, No. 2, 1995, pp. 154 – 170.
6. S. Kirkpatrick, C. D. Gelatt and M. P. Vecchi, Optimization by simulated annealing, *Science*, Vol. **220**, No. 4598, 1983, pp. 671-680.
7. V. Kovalevsky, *Interlaced Spheres and Multidimensional Tunnels*, Report University of Rostock, Germany, 2000.
8. J. K. Udupa and V. G. Ajjangadde, Boundary and object labelling in three-dimensional images, *Computer Vision Graphics and Image Processing*, Vol. **51**, No. 3, 1990, pp. 355–369.

A Visual Comparison of Shape Descriptors Using Multi-Dimensional Scaling

J.D. Edwards, K.J. Riley, and J.P. Eakins

Department of Informatics, University of Northumbria
{jonathan.edwards,jon.riley,john.eakins}@unn.ac.uk

Abstract. In this paper, we investigate the descriptive capabilities of a series of well known shape descriptors, using classical Multi-Dimensional Scaling (MDS). Sammon Mapping is applied to a data-set of six hundred shapes from a real-world multi-component trademark data-set, that have been described using traditional perceptual descriptors, Fourier descriptors and Rosin's descriptors. The maps generated offer considerable insight into how the descriptors encode shape, there is evidence to suggest that traditional perceptual descriptors offer better discriminating performance than Fourier and Rosin's, and also strong indications that an intelligently chosen combination of descriptors could offer increased discriminating capacity over any single descriptor.
The mapping techniques discussed in this paper use an arbitrary distance measure, and hence can be easily adapted to map many other forms of image descriptors. This makes them extremely useful for evaluating descriptor performance and also for visual browsing of image databases.

1 Introduction

One of the cornerstone technologies for Content Based Image Retrieval (CBIR) is shape description. These techniques utilise a segmented view of an image to perform further feature extraction, generating a representation that can be utilised for comparison. Applications of this technology are numerous (see [18] for review), from objective matching tasks such as hieroglyphic matching [19] to subjective shape assessment for trademark matching [5]. It is perhaps in the latter area where deficiencies in current technologies start to show, whilst it may be quite possible to find duplicate or near duplicate shapes, when one tries to simulate more subjective comparisons on databases with large variation, it is hard to judge how the shape descriptors will perform. This is further compounded by difficulties in performing comparative studies, which require a concrete set of ground truths, and are also heavily biased by segmentation accuracy.

The aim of our current study is to take a step back from objective assessment of shape descriptors and to explore a more subjective view, using visual mapping. This has a nice synergy, since we are presenting visual information, the shapes, in a visual manner. To perform this task we utilise Multi-Dimensional Scaling (MDS), placing an iconic view of the shape at the projected position in

N. Petkov and M.A. Westenberg (Eds.): CAIP 2003, LNCS 2756, pp. 393–401, 2003.

the mapping. This paper reports the initial application on traditional perceptual descriptors, Fourier descriptors and Rosin's descriptors. Maps are generated using a diverse database of shapes from real-world multi-component trademarks.

2 Multi-Dimensional Scaling

Multi-Dimensional Scaling (MDS) (variously referred to as Non-metric Dimensional Scaling [10] or Sammon Mapping [16]) addresses the problem of *dimensional reduction*. It tackles the problem of embedding multivariate data in a reduced dimension *directly*, by iteratively minimising the distortion of the distance (either metric or measure) between individual features within a data-set. For visualisation applications, this approach offers significant advantages over more commonly used projection methods (such Principal Components Analysis (PCA) [14] [17]) as it can utilise arbitrary distance measures, and hence map non-Euclidean spaces. This added flexibility is particularly vital for shape descriptors, as the distance measure used often encapsulates much of the descriptive complexity.

MDS proceeds as follows. A Distortion measure (In MDS parlance referred to as *Stress*) is used to compare the original distance in the multivariate data-set ($F(x)$) with an equal number of randomly distributed, two-dimensional points ($M(x)$). The Stress measure S is then represented by

$$Stress(S) = f(d_{ij}, \hat{d}_{ij}) \tag{1}$$

with *distance measures*

$$\begin{aligned} d_{ij} &= d(F(i), F(j)) \;\; F(x) \in \mathbb{R}^n \text{ for } x = 1, \ldots, N \\ \hat{d}_{ij} &= d(M(i), M(j)) \; M(x) \in \mathbb{R}^2 \text{ for } x = 1, \ldots, N \end{aligned}$$

typically, $d \equiv \hat{d}$ where $d(x, y) = \sqrt{(x-y)^2}$. Many forms of S (see [1]) have been explored, the most popular function, proposed by Sammon [16], is

$$S = \frac{1}{\sum_{i<j} d_{ij}^2} \sum_{i<j} \frac{(d_{ij} - \hat{d}_{ij})^2}{d_{ij}} \tag{2}$$

S is then minimised using an appropriate iterative error minimisation scheme. Sammon proposes a pseudo-Newtonian method. The vector update function is

$$M_{t+1}(i) = M_t(i) - \alpha \frac{\frac{\partial S_t}{\partial M(i)_t}}{\left|\frac{\partial^2 S_t}{\partial M(i)_t^2}\right|} \tag{3}$$

Note, that the gradient is independent of multivariate domain's distance measure, and hence no manipulation of the gradient descent methods are required when changing d_{ij}. The *magic factor*, α is normally set to 0.3.

It is worth noting that many other implementation and optimisation strategies have been explored [1], including implementation via Neural models [3] [12]. These strategies are aimed at solving the two general deficiencies, that is the speed of optimisation and the addition of new data without re-minimisation.

3 Shape Descriptors

Shape description has been actively researched since the inception of the "computer vision problem" in the early nineteen sixties. Many competing techniques exist [11], with many contradictory performance indications. A first broad classification of these techniques can be performed by considering from what initial shape representation the descriptor is derived, as descriptors are generated from either the **region** or the **boundary** representations.

3.1 Region Descriptors

Techniques that use a region of intensity representation $I(x,y)$ where $I(x,y) \mapsto [0,1]$ utilise the entire region of the shape. Initially, simple perceptually grounded descriptors were implemented [7]. These are still relevant, since they can be used to explain a shape in a comprehendible fashion. The major descriptors in the category are

$$AspectRatio = \frac{w_{mbr}}{l_{mbr}} \tag{4}$$

$$Circularity = \frac{4\pi A_{shape}}{p^2} \tag{5}$$

$$Convexity = \frac{A_{shape}}{A_{convexhull}} \tag{6}$$

$$Rectangularity = \frac{A_{shape}}{A_{mbr}} \tag{7}$$

where w_{mbr} and l_{mbr} are the width and length of the minimum bounding rectangle, A_{shape} is the area of the actual shape, p is the length of the perimeter, $A_{convexhull}$ is the area within the convex hull, and A_{mbr} is the area with the minimum bounding rectangle.

Latterly, moment based methods have gained prominence, due to their robustness to noise and similitude[1] invariance . Moments μ are high-order statistics generated by the combination of shape data $I(x,y)$ with a moment function φ_{pq}, where

$$\mu_{pq} = \sum_x \sum_y \varphi_{pq}(x,y) I(x,y) \tag{8}$$

Many forms of φ have been explored (see [13] for an extensive review), the most popular *standard form* is $(x-\bar{x})^p(y-\bar{y})^q$ which is made invariant by taking

[1] Scale, translation and rotation.

appropriate moment combinations [8]. The major disadvantage of this approach is the descriptors became difficult to comprehend, Rosin describes a set of *natural* descriptors [15] that are generated from the first affine invariant moment [6] I_1 (Equation 9), but are understandable by humans.

Three measures are generated based on a region's deviation from the moment form of the three most recognisable shapes: the triangle (Equation 10), the rectangle (Equation 11,where $A_{moment,shape}$ is the area difference between the moment fitted rectangle and the shape, *and vice-versa*) and the ellipse (equation 12).

$$I_1 = \frac{\mu_{20}\mu_{02} - \mu_{11}^2}{\mu_{00}^4} \tag{9}$$

$$Triangularity = \begin{cases} 108I_1 & \text{if } I_1 \leq 1/108 \\ 1/108I_1 & \text{otherwise} \end{cases} \tag{10}$$

$$RosinRectangularity = 1 - \frac{A_{moment,shape}}{A_{shape}} \tag{11}$$

$$Ellipticity = \begin{cases} 16\pi^2 I_1 & \text{if } I_1 \leq 16\pi^2 I_1 \\ 1/16\pi^2 I_1 & \text{otherwise} \end{cases} \tag{12}$$

It has been shown in [4] that the above measures significantly increase the retrieval performance over both normal, and affine moment invariants.

3.2 Boundary Descriptors

Boundary based shape descriptors transform the boundary chain-code $s(t) \in \mathbb{I}^2$ into an appropriate measure. Chain codes are used extensively in this type of processing as they offer the most compact initial shape description, and are translation invariant. The most popular approach for further processing is to treat the chain code as a periodic function in $\mathbb{C}$, and apply a discrete Fourier transform (Equation 13) [20]. A series of similitude invariant descriptors can then be generated by discarding phase information (for rotation) and the amplitudes normalised by the first harmonic (for scale) (Equation 14).

$$f_n = \frac{1}{N} \sum_{t=0}^{N-1} s(t) \exp \frac{-j2\pi nt}{N} \tag{13}$$

where N and $s(t) \in \mathbb{C}$

$$FourierDescriptors = \frac{\alpha_1}{\alpha_0}, \frac{\alpha_2}{\alpha_0}, \ldots, \frac{\alpha_{\frac{N-1}{2}}}{\alpha_0} \tag{14}$$

Predictably, Fourier descriptors are good at radially symmetric shapes, and not so good at shapes where a large part of the meaning is held in sharp corners (a rectangle is very similar to a circle for instance). These descriptors have been shown to give improved retrieval performance when compared to region based descriptors [4].

Table 1. Table of mapping performance. c=city block metric($|x - y|$), e=Euclidean metric

Data-set(size)	R^n/R^2 measure	Max Iterations	Final Stress	Map
Traditional Measures (4)	c/e	42	0.046	Figure 1
Rosin's Measures (3)	c/e	43	0.045	Figure 2
Fourier Descriptors (8)	c/e	34	0.042	Figure 3
All above descriptors (15)	c/e	31	0.043	Figure 4

Fig. 1. Sammon Map of the traditional descriptors

4 Experimentation and Results

The above techniques were applied to a set of six hundred shape descriptors generated (using segmentation techniques described in [4]) from approximately seventy real world trademarks. Each descriptor was mapped independently, and a further map produced to assess the efficacy of a combined approach. The mappings were performed using standard implementation of Sammon Map (using the excellent free statistical programming environment **R** [9]) initialised with the following values, ($\alpha = 0.3$, max iterations =100, stop at $S < 0.05$) *for all* mappings. Database generation time was approximately 30 minutes. Typical run times for generating the maps were of the order of minutes on a standard Windows based PC (1GHz with 256M RAM). To verify how well the descriptors mapped to $\mathbb{R}^2$, mapping stresses and minimisation iterations were recorded (Table 1). For all maps the stress measurements were below acceptable tolerance (< 0.1), with a relatively small number of iterations (< 100), and hence the maps can be relied on as accurate representations of the multivariate spaces.

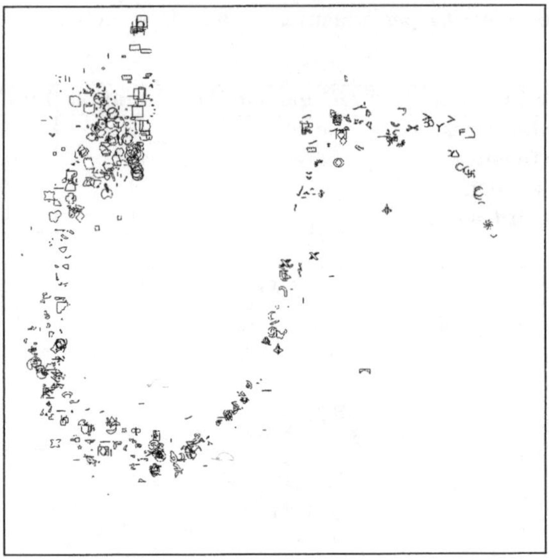

Fig. 2. Sammon Map of the Rosin's descriptors

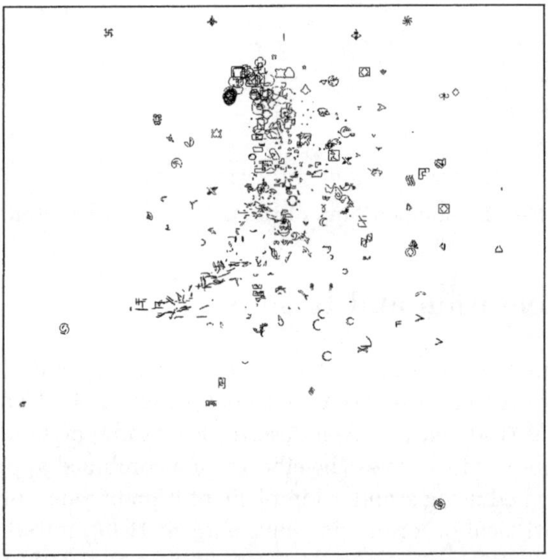

Fig. 3. Sammon Map of the Fourier descriptors

5 Conclusions and Further Work

The mapping results are extremely interesting, and provide a considerable amount of insight into the characteristics of the shape descriptors explored in this experiment. The traditional and Fourier descriptor maps follow a similar

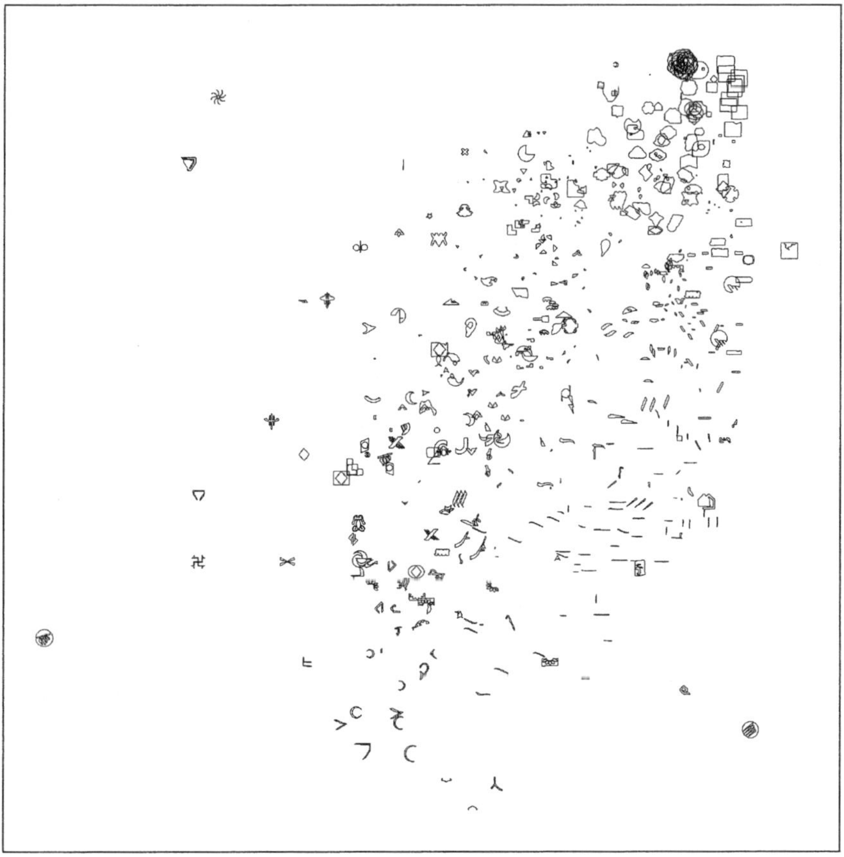

Fig. 4. Sammon Map of the ALL above descriptors

pattern, with shapes arranged primarily along an axis representing aspect ratio. Of the two maps, traditional descriptors appear the most coherent, with less spurious outliers, significantly more coherent clustering of similar shapes, and a greater discrimination between circles and squares.

Rosin's descriptors have discriminated between circles and squares well, but have not performed well on shapes with smaller aspect ratio. The *horseshoe* like nature of the map gives *some* indication that this may be an artifact of the mapping process [2], however this is not supported by the stress and iteration measurements. Clearly, this map is strong evidence to suggest that these descriptors are less suited to subjective comparison on a wide ranging data-set than traditional or Fourier descriptors.

The combined maps give an indication of what can be achieved by taking appropriate combinations. The shapes appear more spread with better discrimination between broad, narrow and irregular shapes. This result is broadly corroborated by the retrieval performance results in [4], where there was strong indications that combining descriptors produced more accurate retrieval. Clearly, by using this approach more intelligently, one could select a combination of descriptors that appeared most effective.

This experiment represents an initial foray into mapping image descriptors, the flexibility of arbitrary distance measures in the mapping process means that many other types of descriptor can be easily explored, both in a scientific context and perhaps more importantly as a user interface for browsing. There are two clear weaknesses that need addressing, firstly MDS does not scale well to large data-sets, a piecewise approach to map generation (perhaps based on a quick clustering partition) may be appropriate in reducing the algorithmic complexity. Interestingly, this may also be beneficial for the second weakness, the overlapping of icons in dense region of the map. A clustering strategy could be used to replace the denser areas, with a representative single icon.

References

1. I. Borg and P. Groenen, *Modern multidimensional scaling*, Springer-Verlag, New York, 1997.
2. M. Carreira-Perpinan, *A review of dimension reduction techniques*, Tech. Report CS–96–09, Dept. of Computer Science, University of Sheffield, January 1997.
3. D. de Ridder and R. Duin, *Sammon's mapping using neural networks: A comparison*, Pattern Recognition Letters **18** (1997), 1307–1316.
4. J.P. Eakins, J. Edwards, J. Riley, and P.L. Rosin, *A comparison of the effectiveness of alternative feature sets in shape retrieval of multi-component images.*, SPIE 2001 San Jose, 2001, pp. 196–207.
5. J.P. Eakins, M.E. Graham, and J.M. Boardman, *Trademark image retrieval by shape similarity*, IEEE Multimedia **5** (1998), no. 2, 53–63.
6. J. Flusser and T. Suk., *Pattern recognition by affine moment invariants*, Pattern Recognition (1993), no. 26, 167–174.
7. R. C. Gonzalez and P. Wintz, *Digital image processing*, Prentice-Hall, 2002.
8. M.K. Hu., *Visual pattern recognition by moment invariants*, IRE Trans. on Information Theory **IT-8** (1962), 179–187.
9. R. Ihaka and R. Gentleman, *R: A language for data analysis and graphics*, Journal of Computational and Graphical Statistics **5** (1996), no. 3, 299–314.
10. J.B. Kruskal, *Multidimensional scaling by optimizing goodness of fit to a nonmetric hypothesis*, Psychometrika **1-27** (1964), no. 29, 115–129.
11. S. Loncaric, *A survey of shape analysis techniques*, Pattern Recognition **31** (1998), no. 8, 983–1001.
12. J. Mao and A.K. Jain, *Artificial neural networks for feature extraction and multivariate data projection.*, IEEE Transactions on Neural Networks **6** (1995), 296–317.
13. R. Mukundan and K. R. Ramakrishnan, *Moment functions in image analysis - theory and applications*, World Scientific, 1998.
14. K. Pearson, *Principal components analysis*, London Edinburgh and Dublin Philosophical Magazine and Journal **6** (1901), no. 2, 559.
15. P.L. Rosin, *Measuring shape: ellipticity, rectangularity and triangularity*, the 15th International Conference on Pattern Recognition, Barcelona, Spain, vol. 1, 2000, pp. 952–955.
16. J. Sammon jnr, *A nonlinear mapping for data structure analysis*, IEEE Transactions on Computers **C-18** (1969), 401–409.

17. Q. Tian, T. Moghaddam, and T.S. Huang, *Visualization, estimation and user-modeling for interactive browsing of image libraries*, International Conference on Image and Video Retrieval (CIVR'02), 2002, pp. 7–16.
18. R.C. Veltkamp and M. Tanase, *Content-based image retrieval systems: A survey.*, UU-CS 2000-34, Utrecht University: Information and Computing Sciences, Utrecht, The Netherlands, 2000.
19. J.M. Vleugels and R.C. Veltkamp, *Efficient image retrieval through vantage objects*, Visual Information and Information Systems: Proceedings of the Third International Conference VISUAL'99, 1999, pp. 575–584.
20. C. Zahn and R. Roskies, *Fourier descriptors for plane closed curves*, IEEE Computer **3** (1972), no. C-21, 269–281.

Part-Based Shape Recognition Using Gradient Vector Field Histograms

Wooi-Boon Goh and Kai-Yun Chan

School of Computer Engineering, Nanyang Technological University,
Nanyang Avenue, Singapore 639798
{aswbgoh,askychan}@ntu.edu.sg

Abstract. The gradient vector field generated from the boundary of a shape describes the regional interaction between the shape boundaries and can therefore be exploited to provide rich and robust shape description. We present a novel part-based shape representation that describes a shape using a set of gradient vector field histograms derived at salient points within the shape. Peaks and ridges derived from the local disparity in the vector field provides a means of locating these salient points called shape axes, from where polar sampling of the vector field is then used to build scale and rotational invariant histograms of the vectors' orientation. A multi-resolution pyramidal framework is proposed for generating the gradient vector field and extracting the shape axes. Results from shape recognition experiments show that the proposed shape descriptor is invariant to similarity transform, robust under boundary distortion and occlusion. This part-based descriptor also supports partial matching and articulation.

1 Introduction

Several researchers in the past have proposed the use of vector fields in the analysis of gray-scale images and shapes [1], [4], [7]. More recently, Shroff and Ben-Arie [7] modeled the gradient of a shape as magnetic dipoles and extracted smooth shape axes at point where the magnetic field interaction resulted in a local minima. Cross and Hancock [4] proposed a multi-scale framework where a vector field is obtained by computing the curl of vector potential found through volume averaging of the tangential edge gradient vectors. Both these works are limited to the task of extracting symmetry axes of shapes, and in the case of the later, the detection of edges as well. Ben-Arie and Wang [1] proposed extracting hierarchical shape descriptors at location of high vectorial disparity (based on a measure they termed Cancellation Energy) when the image gradients at shape boundaries are radially propagated. Their proposed normalized shape feature tokens were shown to be invariant to scaling and rotation. However, the characteristics of the gradient vector field itself were not incorporated into their shape descriptor.

This paper will demonstrate the rich and robust shape descriptive quality of the gradient vector field, especially when the descriptor takes the form of a 1-D histo-

N. Petkov and M.A. Westenberg (Eds.): CAIP 2003, LNCS 2756, pp. 402–409, 2003.

gram of the vectors' orientation. The shape descriptor proposed in this paper does incorporate some form of medial axis representation but unlike [5], [6], [9], we do not represent shapes by graphs or trees. In our approach, the shape axes provide a means to partition the shape into parts. Each part is then described by histograms that contain information about the shape form of the part and its geometric relationship to other parts in its vicinity. Similarity of shape parts is computed by comparing these histograms. Section 2 describes a multi-resolution technique for generating the gradient vector field of a shape and extracting consistent shape axes for shapes at different scales. Section 3 describes the construction of the proposed part-based shape descriptor's and its application to shape recognition. Section 4 presents a series of experiments that will demonstrate various properties of this shape descriptor.

2 The Multi-resolution Pyramidal Framework

In our work, multi-resolution pyramids are used to generate the gradient vector field and vector field disparity map. We first review several useful pyramid operations. The process which generates a lower resolution image from its predecessor will be called a *REDUCE* operation [3]. If G_0 is the original image $I(x,y)$ and G_N is the top level of the pyramid, then for $0 < l \leq N$, $G_l = REDUCE\ [G_{l-1}]$ is defined as

$$G_l(x,y) = \sum_{m,n=-k}^{k}\sum w(m,n)G_{l-1}(2x+m,2y+n) \tag{1}$$

where the generating kernel w of size $(2k+1)$ performs smoothing before the sub-sampling process. In our case, a separable, normalized and symmetric Gaussian kernel of $k = 2$ was used throughout [3]. Another pyramid operation, *EXPAND* is used to expand an image of size $M+1$ to $2M+1$ by interpolating sample values from a low resolution image. If G_l is derive by expanding it low resolution image G_{l+1}, then for $0 \leq l < N$, $G_l = EXPAND\ [G_{l+1}]$ is defined as

$$G_l(x,y) = 4\sum_{m,n=-k}^{k}\sum w(m,n)G_{l+1}\left(\frac{x+m}{2},\frac{y+n}{2}\right) \tag{2}$$

where summation is only carried out when $x+m$ and $y+n$ are even numbers.

2.1 Generating the Gradient Vector Field

It is assumed that the input image is a binary silhouette image $I(x,y)$. Firstly, a Gaussian pyramid $G(l,x,y)$ of $N+1$ levels is created by iteratively applying the *REDUCE* operation N times on each consecutive output image, starting with $I(x,y)$. From the scalar Gaussian pyramid, we then derived the vectorial Gradient pyramid $\boldsymbol{H}(l,x,y)$, which consist of two pyramids $H^x(l,x,y)$ and $H^y(l,x,y)$ given by

$$H_l^x(x,y) = g_{\sigma_H}^x(x,y) * G_l(x,y) \text{ and } H_l^y(x,y) = g_{\sigma_H}^y(x,y) * G_l(x,y) \text{ for } 0 \le l \le N \quad (3)$$

The convolution kernels $g_{\sigma_H}^x$ and $g_{\sigma_H}^y$ are 1st order Gaussian derivatives in the x and y directions, respectively and are given by

$$g_{\sigma_H}^x(x,y) = -\frac{x}{\sigma_H^2}\exp(-\frac{x^2+y^2}{2\sigma_H^2}) \quad \text{and} \quad g_{\sigma_H}^y(x,y) = -\frac{y}{\sigma_H^2}\exp(-\frac{x^2+y^2}{2\sigma_H^2}) \quad (4)$$

Finally, starting at $l=N$-1, each level $\boldsymbol{H}_l$ of the Gradient pyramid is expanded and then combined to derived the Gradient Vector Field pyramid $\boldsymbol{V}(l,x,y)$, where each level $\boldsymbol{V}_l$ is defined as

$$\boldsymbol{V}_l = \alpha\,\boldsymbol{H}_l + (1\text{-}\alpha)\ EXPAND\ [\boldsymbol{V}_{l+1}] \qquad \text{for } 0 \le l < N \quad (5)$$

At the top, where $l = N$, we have $\boldsymbol{V}_N = \boldsymbol{H}_N$ and the parameter $\alpha \in [0,1]$ determines the smoothness of the gradient vector field within the object. Smaller α values result in a smoother vector field.

2.2 The Vector Field Disparity Map

In order to describe a complex shape by decomposing it into suitable parts, the shape axes must first be extracted from the gradient vector field. These shape axes can be located by detecting locations in the vector field where the local gradient vectors exhibit high directional disparity. Given such a disparity map, the shape axes are extracted by locating the local maxima in the disparity measure. Extending the idea in [1], the normalized Vector Field Disparity pyramid $D(l,x,y)$ is derived from $\boldsymbol{V}(l,x,y)$ where each level D_l is define as

$$D_l(x,y) = \frac{g_{\sigma_D}(x,y) * \left\|V_l(x,y)\right\| - \left\|g_{\sigma_D}(x,y) * V_l(x,y)\right\|}{g_{\sigma_D}(x,y) * \left\|V_l(x,y)\right\|} \qquad \text{for } 0 \le l \le N \quad (6)$$

The local disparity measure is computed within a weighted neighbourhood defined by the Gaussian convolution kernel $g_{\sigma_D}(x,y)$ given by

$\exp[-(x^2+y^2)/2\sigma_D^2]/\sqrt{2\pi}\sigma_D$.

The normalized disparity measure $D_l(x,y) \in [0,1]$ gives a value close to 1 in localities of high disparity such as at the center of a circle. To detect consistent shape axes over different scales of a shape, a full resolution vector field disparity map $M(x,y) \in [0,1]$ shown in Fig. 1 is obtained by

$$M(x,y) = \frac{1}{N+1}\sum_{l=0}^{N} d_l(x,y) \quad (7)$$

where $d_l(x,y) = D_l(x,y)$ for $l = N$

$$d_l(x,y) = D_l(x,y) + EXPAND\left[d_{l+1}(x,y)\right] \qquad \text{for } 0 \le l < N \quad (8)$$

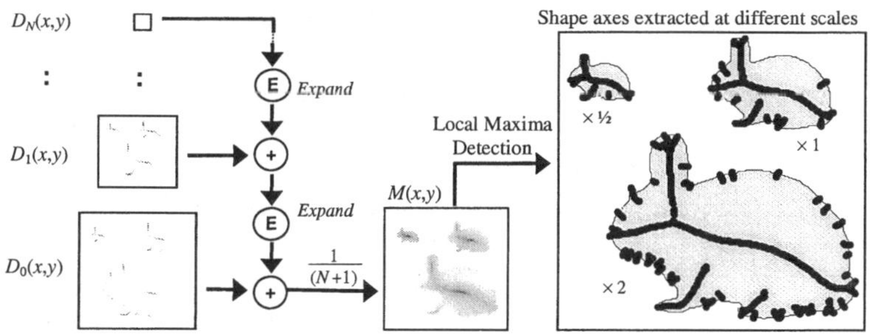

Fig. 1. A multi-level integration technique for generating a vector field disparity map. The extracted shape axes are relatively consistent over scales of two octaves.

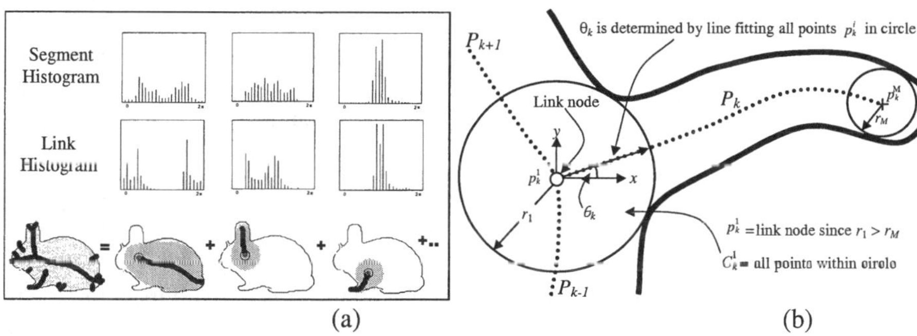

Fig. 2. (a) Decomposition of a rabbit-like shape into parts based of its extracted shape axes. The gray-shaded area in each part shows the locality U_k, in which the segment and link histograms are computed. The small circle marking one end of each of the part axis is a link node. (b) Part axis P_k and relevant parameters for link node determination, histogram normalization and angular compensation for rotation invariance (see text for details).

3 A Part-Based Shape Descriptor

There is much evidence that human perception of shapes involves some form of part-based representation [8]. A more local form of shape description allows for recognition that is more robust to occlusion, articulation of limbs and spatial rearrangement of parts. In our work, a shape is decomposed into parts along segmented sections (part axes) of the extracted shape axes and each part is described by two histograms derived from the local gradient vector field (see Fig. 2a). Although the shape axes extracted by the multi-resolution techniques described in section 2 share many similar characteristics, they are not identical to the shocks of [9] or Blum's MAT-based skeletons [2]. It is characterized by the fact that minor boundary distortions results in a shape axes that remains mainly at the shape's boundary (see Fig. 1). This makes our shape descriptor relatively robust to boundary distortion.

3.1 Part Axes and Its Gradient Vector Field Histograms

Using appropriate ridge extraction and skeleton analysis algorithms, the shape axes are thinned and segmented at every intersections and junctions into Q continuous segments called *part axes*. With reference to Fig. 2b, let the kth part axis $P_k=\{p_k^i\}_{i=1}^M$ be an ordered set of M discrete points starting at one end of a continuous segment and ending at the other. Let r_1 and r_M be the respective radial distances of points p_k^1 and p_k^M to their nearest edge points on the shape boundary. If the ordering of the points $\{p_k^i\}_{i=1}^M$ on P_k is such that $r_1 > r_M$, then the starting point p_k^1 is termed the *link node* of the part axis P_k.

Each part axis is associated with two normalized gradient vector field histograms, the *segment histogram* and the *link histogram*. The segment histogram S_k describes the general shape of the part, such as its length-to-width ratio, its convexity, its taper, etc. The link histogram L_k^1 contains information pertaining to the common space that the part axis k shares with other part axes within its vicinity. This relational information helps differentiate similar looking protrusions, which may be linked to the main shape body at different places and in varying configurations. Link histogram L_k^1 is first constructed by determining the vector orientation associated with all C_k^1 discrete image pixels within the circle of radius r_1, centered about the start point p_k^1 The histogram L_k^1 with n bins representing the value range $[0,2\pi)$ cumulates the quantised orientation of all C_k^1 gradient vectors. The histogram is made rotationally invariant by adding a value θ_k^1 to all orientation values before cumulation. The angle θ_k^1 is derived from the orientation of a straight line fitted along all part axis points $\{p_k^i\}_{i=1}^M \cap C_k^1$ that lie within the circle of radius r_1. By using the link node as an orientation reference for the part, the start point of the straight line is the end closest to p_k^1. The link histogram L_k^1 is normalized with the value C_k^1. The segment histogram S_k is obtained by repeating the procedure described for extracting histogram L_k^1 but this time summing all the computed histograms L_k^i for $1 \le i \le M$ over the entire length of the part axis P_k. More formally, for a part axis P_k, whose locality is define by a region U_k, its segment histogram S_k and its associated normalisation value W_k are given by

$$S_k = \sum_{i=1}^{M} L_k^i \quad \text{and} \quad W_k = \sum_{i=1}^{M} C_k^i \quad \text{and} \quad U_k = \bigcup_{i=1}^{M} C_k^i \tag{9}$$

3.2 Matching Parts of a Shape in a Cluttered Scene

Given a cluttered scene A with Q_A extracted parts, we want to compute the best match for each part in A to a template shape B that contains Q_B parts. The best part match for a part axis $P_{A,k}$ in scene A to all part axes in template shape B is given by

$$cost(P_{A,k}) = \arg \min_{1 \le j \le Q_B} d_p(P_{A,k}, P_{B,j}) \tag{10}$$

where the part distance $d_p(P_{A,k}, P_{B,j}) \in [0,1]$ between two part axes $P_{A,k}$ and $P_{B,j}$ extracted from scene A and shape B is given by the combined χ^2 distance between their respective n-bin link and segment histograms and is given by

$$d_p(P_{A,k}, P_{B,j}) = \frac{\beta}{2}\sum_{i=1}^{n}\frac{[L^1_{A,k}(i) - L^1_{B,j}(i)]^2}{L^1_{A,k}(i) + L^1_{B,j}(i)} + \frac{(1-\beta)}{2}\sum_{i=1}^{n}\frac{[S_{A,k}(i) - S_{B,j}(i)]^2}{S_{A,k}(i) + S_{B,j}(i)} \quad (11)$$

where the parameter $\beta \in [0,1]$, determines the relative importance attached to the matching of the link and segment histograms. A value of $\beta = 0.5$ will give equal emphasis to both when computing the matching cost.

Matching mirrored version of the shape B in scene A can be done by repeating the computation in (11) with $L^1_{Bj}(n-i+1)$ and $S_{Bj}(n-i+1)$ and instead of $L^1_{Bj}(i)$ and S_{Bj} (i), where n is the number of bins in the link and segment histograms. Choosing the lower of the two part distances will ensure invariance to mirror transform.

4 Experimental Results

4.1 Geometric Invariance

A series of shape recognition taks are presented to illustrate the various properties of the proposed part-based shape descriptor. Parameter settings for all experiments are $\sigma_H = 1.0$, $\sigma_D = 1.5$, $\alpha = 0.9$, $\beta = 0.5$, $n = 24$; template and scene image sizes are 129×129 and 257×257 pixels, respectively. The first experiment in Fig. 3 demonstrates its invariance to translation, scaling, rotation and mirror reflection.

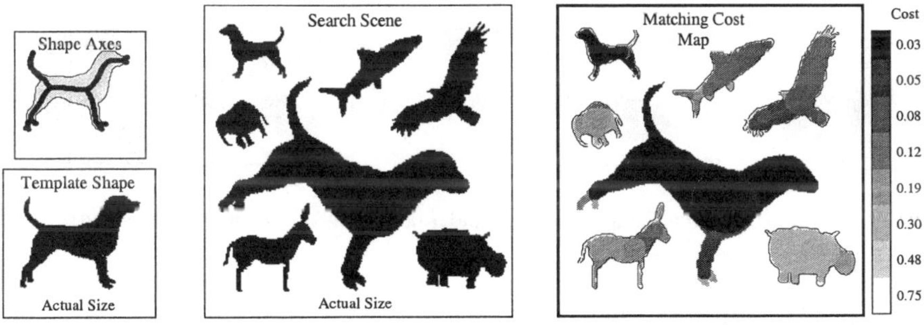

Fig. 3. The search scene contains various animal silhouettes [6] and two dog shapes. The smaller is laterally inverted and × 0.5 times the template size, the larger is rotated by 30° and × 1.6 template size. Both dogs show good part matches to the template shape, demonstrating invariance to translation, scaling, rotation and mirror transform. The extracted shape axes for the template are also shown.

The matching cost maps shown are obtained by assigning $cost(P_{A,k})$ in (10) to all pixels in the locality $U_{A,k}$ of part axis $P_{A,k}$. Darker regions highlights search scene parts that have good shape similarity with subparts in the template. In regions where a set

$\{k_i\}_{i=1}^{J}$ of J part axes localities overlap, the combined cost is weighted based on the saliency (measured by the size of its locality) of each part axis and is given by

$$\sum_{i=1}^{J}\left(cost(P_{A,k_i})U_{A,k_i} \Big/ \sum_{i=1}^{J} U_{A,k_i} \right) \tag{12}$$

4.2 Occlusion and Boundary Distortions

Most boundary-based shape descriptors are sensitive to boundary distortions. Fig. 4 shows that the proposed shape descriptor is robust to substantial boundary noise, as seen in the good matching of the wavy and hairy arctic hares. This is because the shape descriptor integrates both region and boundary information via the gradient vector field histogram. Part axes resulting from boundary noise remain close to the boundary, resulting in small U_k locality values and therefore have minimal impact on the overall matching cost of other more salient part axes. Robustness to occlusion is demonstrated by the relatively good matching of the hare that is occluded by a cage and tree trunk. As the shape changes slightly (see rabbit on the right), the matching cost degrades accordingly. This suggests that the shape descriptor could be useful for shape classification applications where similar shapes are categorized together.

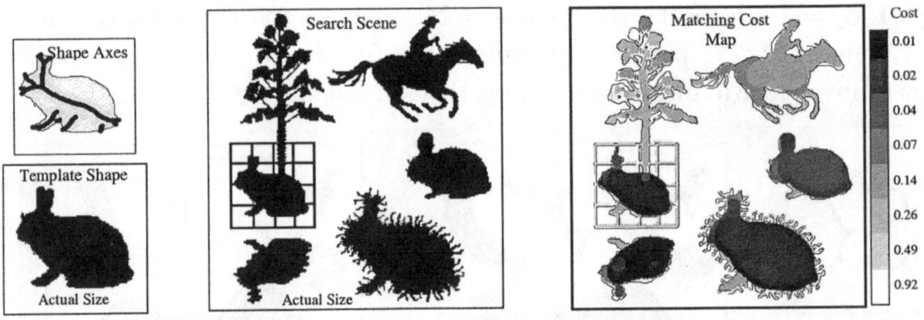

Fig. 4. Robust shape matching under occlusion and boundary distortions.

4.3 Partial Matching and Limb Articulation

The advantage of part-based shape descriptors is their ability to handle partial matches. The rocking horse in template #1 of Fig. 5 found a good match in the horse despite the presence of a rider. Similarly, the cyclist on the bicycle in template #2 found a good partial match in the rider of the horse. This shape descriptor is also able to handle limb articulation, as the gradient vector field histograms are locally re-orientated along the part axes. This is demonstrated by the good matching score of the horse's head and legs to template shape #1 despite their varying postures.

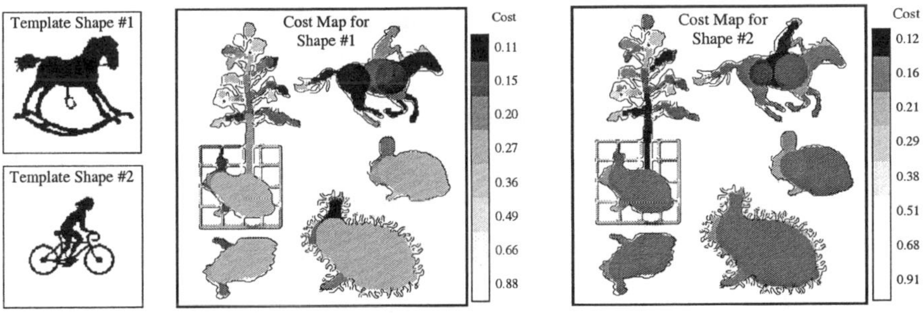

Fig. 5. Results of matching template shapes #1 and #2 to the scene in Fig. 4.

5 Conclusions

We have proposed novel part-based shape descriptor that encapsulates both the form of the part and its relationship with other parts in its vicinity through the use of link and segment gradient vector field histograms. Experimental results show that this shape descriptor is invariant to the similarity transform, robust to occlusion, tolerates significant boundary distortion, handles limb articulation and supports partial matching. We have also described a multi-resolution pyramidal technique for generating the gradient vector field and extracting consistent shape axes over varying scales.

References

1. Ben-Arie, J., Wang, W.: Shape Description and Invariant Recognition Employing Connectionist Approach. Intl. Journal of Pattern Recognition and AI, Vol. 16, No.1 (2002) 69-83
2. Blum, H.: A Transformation for Extracting New Descriptors of Shape. In Proc. Symp. Models for the Perception of Speech and Visual Form, Cambridge, MA: MIT Press (1964)
3. Burt, P.J.: The Pyramid as a Structure for Efficient Computation. In: Rosenfeld, A. (ed.): Multiresolution Image Processing and Analysis. Springer-Verlag, Berlin Heidelberg New York (1984) 6-35
4. Cross, A.D.J., Hancock, E.R.: Scale Space Vector Fields for Symmetry Detection. Image and Vision Computing, Vol. 17 (1999) 337-345
5. Liu, T., Geiger, D.: Approximate Tree Matching and Shape Similarity. In Proc. International Conference on Computer Vision (1999) 456-462
6. Sharvit, D., Chan, J., Tak, H., Kimia, B.: Symmetry-based Indexing of Image Databases. J. Visual Communication and Image Representation (1998) 366-380
7. Shroff, H., Ben-Arie, J.: Finding Shape Axes using Magnetic Field. IEEE Trans. on Image Processing. Vol. 8, No. 10 (1995) 1388-1394
8. Siddiqi, K., Kimia, B.B.: Parts of Visual Form: Computational Aspects. IEEE Trans. On Pattern Analysis and Machine Intelligence, Vol. 17, No. 3 (1995) 239-251
9. Siddiqi, K., Shokoufandeh, A., Dickinson, S., Zucker, S.: Shock Graphs and Shape Matching. International Journal of Computer Vision, Vol. 35, No. 1 (1999) 13-32

Measuring Sigmoidality

Paul L. Rosin

Computer Science, Cardiff University
Queen's Buildings, Newport Road, PO Box 916
Cardiff CF24 3XF, Wales, UK
Paul.Rosin@cs.cf.ac.uk

Abstract. Several new shape measures are proposed for measuring the *sigmoidality* of a region (or more precisely, the region's axis). The correctness of the measures are verified on synthetic data, and then tested quantitatively on a *diatom* classification task.

1 Introduction

The analysis of form is required in many areas. However, notions of shape tend to be vague, and difficult to pin down. Scientific disciplines often provide specialised definitions of shape terms relevant to their subjects of interest. Thus, in botany there are standard descriptors for gross leaf shape, leaf base, leaf margin (i.e. boundary pattern), and so on. In computer vision a more general set of shape descriptors have been developed. Well known examples are symmetry, eccentricity, Euler number, compactness, convexity, and rectangularity [10], while more recent developments have been chirality [5], triangularity [9] and rectilinearity [13].

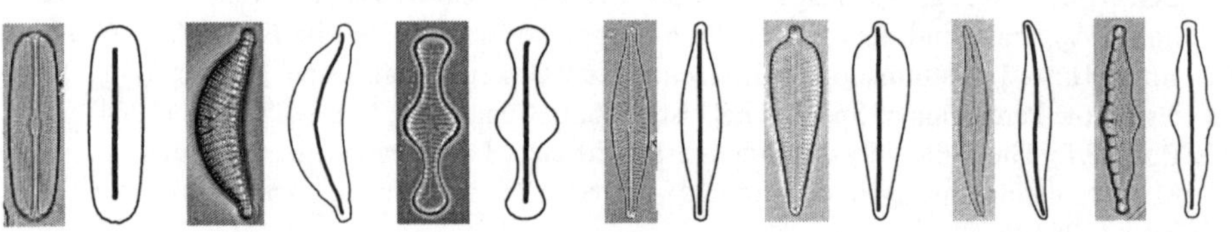

Fig. 1. Examples of diatoms shown next to their extracted contours and axes.

This paper describes a new shape descriptor for *sigmoidality*, motivated[1] by the classification of *diatoms* (see figure 1), which are unicellular algae found in water [2], and have many applications in forensics, geology, etc. There is a limited range of diatom shapes that occur, and so variations in shape between taxa can be quite subtle. While techniques such as Legendre polynomial coefficients [11] and Fourier descriptors [7] have been traditionally used for diatom shape analysis, Fischer and Bunke [4] found that incorporating additional shape descriptors like those listed above improved classification

[1] Other applications of sigmoidal shape are e.g. classification of solar active regions as eruptive/non-eruptive [1], and as a descriptor of the anatomy of bones [12].

N. Petkov and M.A. Westenberg (Eds.): CAIP 2003, LNCS 2756, pp. 410–417, 2003.

rates. Moreover, such intuitive, symbolic descriptors are closer to those currently used by biologists[2].

2 Sigmoidality Measures

The sigmoidal shape is generally described as S shaped, but there is no single precise definition. The measures described in this paper start with a tightly specified function and progress to more general sigmoidal shapes.

While shapes such diatoms are outlines of two dimensional regions, in this paper we only consider the central axis. This is extracted by applying a standard thinning algorithm [14] to the region. If the resulting axis contains vertices then the boundary is iteratively blurred until a simple axis curve is obtained. While this scheme will not work well for substantially branched shapes they are not sigmoidal in any case, and will not be considered further. Also, this paper does not consider details of the shape such as variations in the cross section along the axis, the thickness (width) of the shape, the shape of endings, etc.

Fig. 2. Differents types of variation of a sigmoidal curve.

As shown in figure 2 stretching the shape to increase its curvature has a greater perceptual effect than stretching along its principal axis. Nevertheless, is the right hand shape really more sigmoidal then the others? The measures in this paper do not take the "fullness" of the shape into account.

2.1 Cubic Fit

For diatom classification Fischer and Bunke [4] fit a cubic polynomial and classify the shape based on the coefficient values. We also fit a cubic, but since we are focussing attention on the sigmoid shape we use $y = ax^3 + bx + c$ and miss out the x^2 term to ensure a symmetric curve is fitted. Before the least squares fitting the data is first rotated so that its principal axis lies along the X axis. The correlation coefficient ρ is used to measure the quality of fit. Since we are not expecting inverse correlation the value is truncated at zero, and so the sigmoidality measure is $S_1 = \max(\rho, 0)$. The range of all the measures described in this paper is $0 - 1$.

2.2 Generalized Gaussian Fit

Rather than fit directly to the coordinates the next approach uses the tangent angle instead. This has the advantage that apart from a simple offset of the values the angle is orientation invariant. If we plot the following sigmoid function

[2] Some examples of descriptors (with explanations) commonly used for diatom outlines are: acicular (needle), arcuate (strongly curved), clavate (club), cruciform (cross), cuneate (wedge), elliptical, lenticular (lens), linear, lunate (crescent), panduriform ('8'), sigmoid, stellate (star).

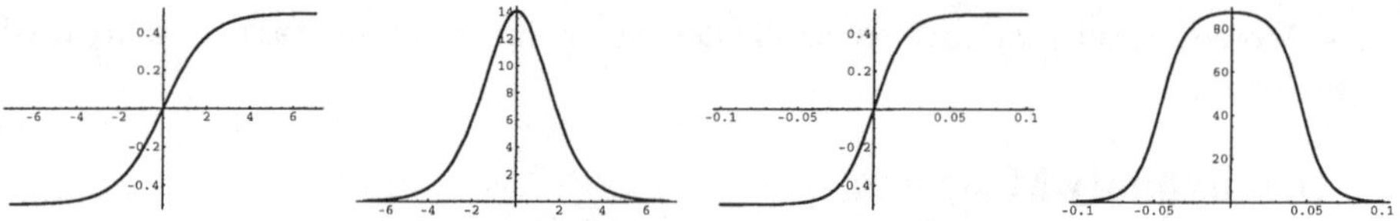

(a) $a = 1$ (b) $a = 1$ (c) $a = 100$ (d) $a = 100$

Fig. 3. Sigmoid function (a & c) and tangent angle (b & d).

$$0.5 - \frac{1}{1 + e^{ax}}$$

we see (figure 3a&c) that increasing the value of a sharpens the transition between the middle section and the outer arms. The corresponding tangent angle looks somewhat Gaussian, but is flattened as the sigmoid function becomes sharper. The shape of the tangent angle plot can be modelled well by the Generalized Gaussian distribution. The probability density function is given by

$$p(x) = \frac{vn(v,s)}{2\Gamma(1/v)} e^{-[n(v,s)|x|]^v} \qquad \text{with} \qquad n(v,s) = \sqrt{\frac{\Gamma(3/v)}{\Gamma(1/v)}}/s$$

where v is a shape parameter controlling the peakiness of the distribution. Since the maximum likelihood estimate requires solving a highly nonlinear equation we use Mallat's method [6] for approximating the solution which is computationally simpler. First the mean absolute value and variance of the data x_i are matched to the Generalized Gaussian. If $m_1 = \frac{1}{n}\sum_{i=1}^{n}|x_i|$ and $m_2 = \frac{1}{n}\sum_{i=1}^{n} x_i^2$ then

$$v = F^{-1}\left(\frac{m_1}{\sqrt{m_2}}\right) \qquad \text{where} \qquad F(\alpha) = \frac{\Gamma(2/\alpha)}{\sqrt{\Gamma(1/\alpha)\Gamma(3/\alpha)}}.$$

In practise, values of $F(\alpha)$ are precomputed, and the inverse function determined by a look-up table with linear interpolation. Finally, the tangent angle is scaled so that the area under the curve sums to one. Again the error of fit was determined using the correlation coefficient, $S_2 = \max(\rho, 0)$.

2.3 Curvature Analysis

A characteristic of the sigmoid is its single, central point of inflection. For perfect, clean data its presence would be easy to test, but in practise, with real data the sensitivity of curvature estimation to noise makes this hopeless. Although the data could be smoothed to eliminate false inflections the parameter for the degree of smoothing would be crucial. Instead of identifying zero crossings of curvature we check the overall distribution of curvature values along the curve. The curvature at each point is estimated as κ_i using kernels of the Gaussian function and its first two derivatives. Since the curvature will be integrated along the curve and the number of zero crossings is not critical then the value for the spread of the Gaussian is not critical either. Separating the positive and negative curvature values as

$$\kappa_i^+ = \begin{cases} 0 & \text{if } \kappa_i < 0 \\ \kappa_i & \text{otherwise} \end{cases} \qquad \kappa_i^- = \begin{cases} 0 & \text{if } \kappa_i > 0 \\ -\kappa_i & \text{otherwise} \end{cases}$$

then the positive and negative curvature values are summed over the curve to the left and right respectively of the midpoint m. In addition the total curvature is computed for normalisation purposes:

$$A^+ = \sum_{i=1}^{m} \kappa_i^+ \qquad A^- = \sum_{i=m}^{n} \kappa_i^- \qquad S = \sum_{i=1}^{n} |\kappa_i| .$$

The sections of positive and negative curvature should be restricted to either side of the inflection point and so the quantity $A^+ + A^-$ should be large. Also, the amount of positive curvature on the left should equal the (absolute) value of the negative curvature on the right, and the discrepancy is measured by $|A^+ - A^-|$. These values are scaled to lie in the range $0 - 1$ and combined using a product to obtain the following measure

$$S_3 = \left[1 - \frac{2\,(A^+ + A^-)}{S}\right]\left[1 - \frac{|A^+ - A^-|}{S}\right].$$

To cope with the curve bending in either direction it is analysed both for κ_i and $-\kappa_i$, and the larger of the two values returned.

Figure 4 shows several examples of curvature plots in which the quantities A^+ and A^- are shaded dark and light gray respectively. Only the first example gets a score of one and the remainder are assigned zero either due to the first (b and c) or the second term (d).

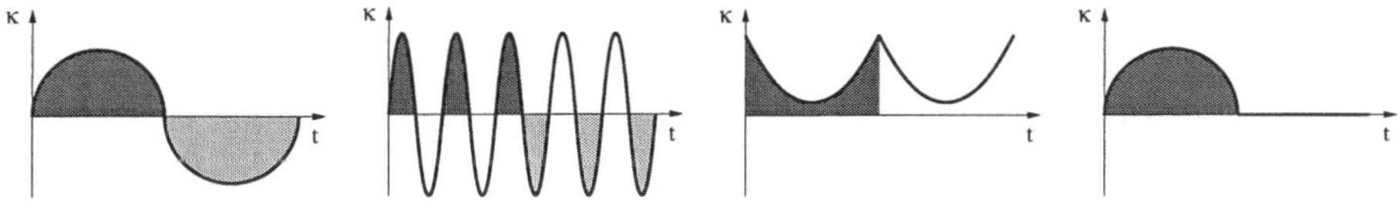

(a) $S_3 = 1 \times 1$ (b) $S_3 = 0 \times 1$ (c) $S_3 = 0 \times 0.5$ (d) $S_3 = 1 \times 0$

Fig. 4. Curvature plots with the shaded regions corresponding to A^+ and A^-.

2.4 Convex Hull Method

The final method splits the curve in two at its midpoint, and the convex hull of each section is determined. Next, each section is traversed from the midpoint to the other end of the curve, and the areas to the left and right sides of the curve are calculated. If these are L_1 and R_1 for section 1, and likewise for section 2, then ideally $L_1 = L_2$ and $R_1 = R_2 = 0$ (or the equivalent with L and R switched). This corresponds to the two sections being convex on opposite sides, and partially enclosing areas of similar sizes. Like S_3, the precise shape of the curve is immaterial. An appropriate normalised measure is

$$S_4 = \left(1 - \frac{|L_1 - L_2|}{L_1 + L_2}\right)\left(1 - \frac{R_1 + R_2}{L_1 + L_2 + R_1 + R_2}\right).$$

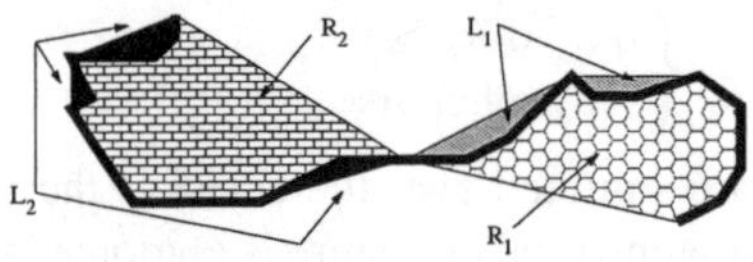

Fig. 5. For the given axis (in bold) the convex hull is determined for each half. The areas to the left/right of each axis section (when traversing from the axis midpoint) are hatched/shaded.

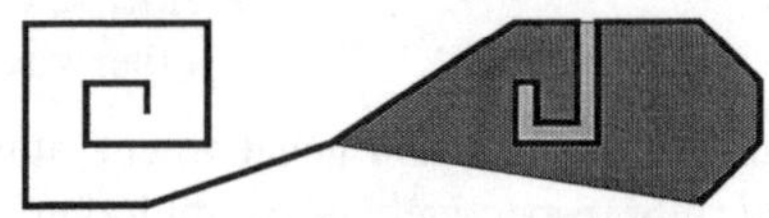

Fig. 6. The areas for the left hand spiral section cannot be calculated, although the other section is not problematic.

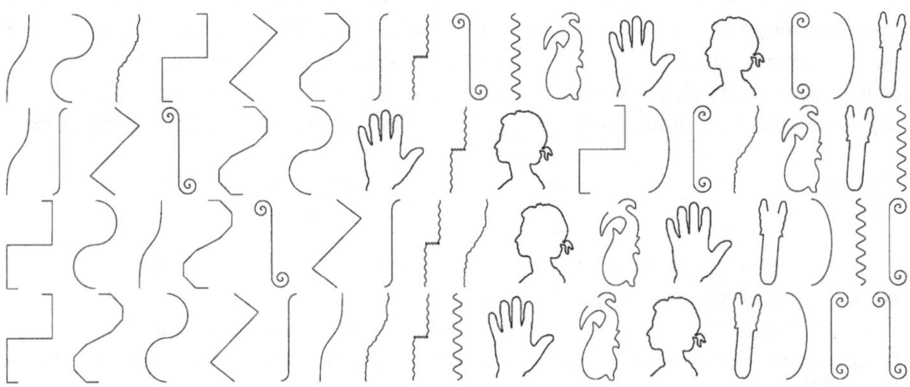

Fig. 7. In each row the curves are ranking in decreasing order according to S_1, S_2, S_3, S_4 respectively.

To be able to determine the areas this method assumes that the endpoints are vertices in the convex hull. Otherwise, problems arise such as shown in the left hand section in figure 6.

3 Experimental Results

3.1 Contour Example

The four measures are first tested on some synthetic curves and a miscellaneous selection of other curves. The curves are shown in figure 7, ranked in descending order of sigmoidality. All measures do reasonable well, generally assigning high scores to sigmoidal curves. Also, as already noted, S_4 cannot cope with the spiral sinusoid.

Examining the distribution of the sigmoidal measures (figure 8) it can be seen that S_2, S_3 and S_4 all correctly give close to peak responses for the first six noise free sinusoids. Due to its more restrictive model S_1 shows a drop-off.

3.2 Diatom Example

The second experiment applies the shape measures to classify diatoms. The mixed genera set from the ADIAC project was used, consisting of 808 contours covering 38 taxa. Out

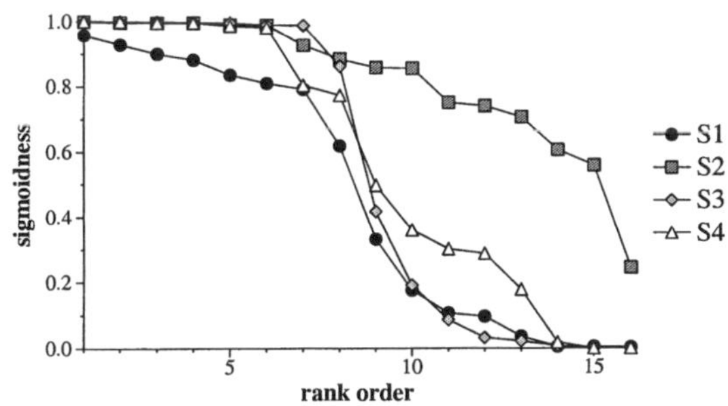

Fig. 8. Distribution of values calculated by sigmoidality measures for data shown in figure 7.

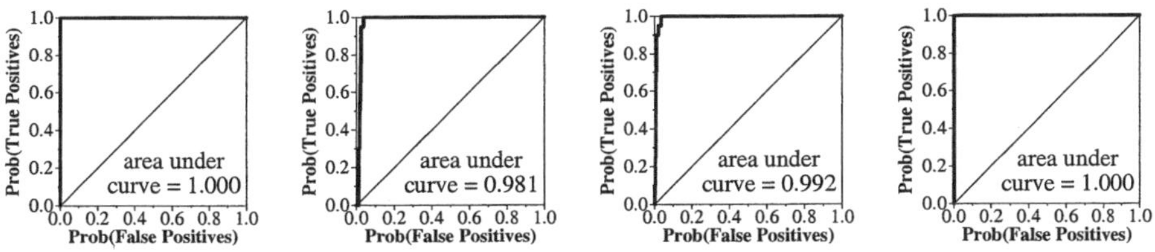

(a) S_1 (b) S_2 (c) S_3 (d) S_4

Fig. 9. ROC curves for identification of *Gyrosigma acuminatum* diatoms.

of the 38 taxa (classes) there is only one with a sigmoidal shape: *Gyrosigma acuminatum*. Between 20 and 29 examples of each taxa were present.

For each sigmoidal shape measure, as well as some standard shape descriptors, their discriminating power was calculated for identifying *Gyrosigma acuminatum* diatoms against all other diatoms (i.e. a two class problem). Receiver operating characteristic (ROC) curves were generated, showing the trade-offs between the amount of true and false positives for all the different threshold values – see figure 9. The area under the ROC curve corresponds to the probability of a correct decision in a two-interval, forced choice task [3], and is listed in table 1. As expected, the sigmoidal shape measures do a good job of discriminating the sigmoidal diatoms, and are clearly better at the task than the other shape descriptors.

Next, classification of the full set of 38 class labels was performed using Murthy *et al.*'s oblique decision trees [8], the set of 15 non-sigmoidal shape descriptors given in table 1, plus one sigmoidal shape measure at a time. Leave-one-out cross validation produced the classification accuracies in table 2 [3]. S_1 was found to perform best, (perhaps since *Gyrosigma acuminatum* have a consistent, regular sigmoidal shape) improving classification accuracy by 3%, while S_2 performs worst. Overall, there seems to be a small but consistent improvement in classification accuracy when one or other of the

[3] Fischer and Bunke [4] reported better accuracies than ours (in excess of 90%). However, they used diatom specific features (e.g. 10 descriptors for valve endings) as well as internal textural details ("ornamentation"). Moreover, by applying bagging they further increased the performance of the decision tree classifiers.

Table 1. Areas under ROC curves for identification of *Gyrosigma* diatoms.

Sigmoidality measures				
method	S_1	S_2	S_3	S_4
area	1.000	0.981	0.992	1.000
Geometric primitives				
method	circularity	ellipticity	rectangularity	triangularity
area	0.142	0.180	0.386	0.060
Classical measures				
method	aspect ratio	compactness	convexity	eccentricity
area	0.203	0.881	0.112	0.818
RTS Moment invariants				
method	ϕ_1	ϕ_2	ϕ_3	ϕ_4
area	0.826	0.825	0.374	0.437
Affine Moment invariants				
method	I_1	I_2	I_3	
area	0.820	0.689	0.708	

Table 2. Diatom classification success rate for all 38 taxa. The columns show which sigmoidality measure was used in addition to the set of general shape descriptors.

S_1	S_2	S_3	S_4	none
78.47	75.62	76.36	77.72	75.25

sigmoidal measures (apart from S_2) are combined with the other descriptors, confirming that sigmoidality does provide some useful discriminating power in this application.

4 Conclusions

Four measures for computing the sigmoidality of a shape have been described. All have linear computational complexity and are straightforward to implement. From the experiments reported in this paper it is not possible to choose any one method as the best. All performed reasonably; S_2 fared worst, but the others produced similar levels of performance considering both the two-way and 38-way diatom classification tasks. The latter three also showed that an improvement in classification could be achieved over using just standard shape descriptors. Future work will investigate testing and comparing the measures over a wider range of applications.

Acknowledgements

The diatom data was kindly provided by the ADIAC project; CEC contract MAS3-CT97-0122.

References

1. R.C. Canfield, H.S. Hudson, and D.E. McKenzie. Sigmoidal morphology and eruptive solar activity. *Geophysical Research Letters*, 26(6):627–630, 1999.
2. J.M.H. du Buf and M.M. Bayer, editors. *Automatic Diatom Identification*. World Scientific, 2002.
3. J.P. Egan. *Signal Detection Theory and ROC Analysis*. Academic Press, 1975.
4. S. Fischer and H. Bunke. Identification using classical and new features in combination with decision tree ensembles. In J.M.H. du Buf and M.M. Bayer, editors, *Automatic Diatom Identification*, pages 109–140. World Scientific, 2002.
5. Y. Hel-Or, S. Peleg, and D. Avnir. Characterization of right handed and left handed shapes. *Computer Vision, Graphics and Image Processing*, 53(2):297–302, 1991.
6. S.G. Mallat. A theory for multiresolution signal decomposition: the wavelet representation. *IEEE Transactions on Pattern Analysis and Machine Intelligence*, 11(7):674–693, 1989.
7. D. Mou and E.F. Stoermer. Separating Tabellaria (Bacillariophyceae) shape groups: A large sample approach based on Fourier descriptor analysis. *J. Phycology*, 28:386–395, 1992.
8. S.K. Murthy, S. Kasif, and S. Salzberg. System for induction of oblique decision trees. *Journal of Artificial Intelligence Research*, 2:1–33, 1994.
9. P.L. Rosin. Measuring shape: Ellipticity, rectangularity, and triangularity. *Machine Vision and Applications*, forthcoming.
10. M. Sonka, V. Hlavac, and R. Boyle. *Image Processing, Analysis, and Machine Vision*. Chapman and Hall, 1993.
11. E.F. Stoermer and T.B. Ladewski. Quantitative analysis of shape variation in type and modern populations of Gomphoneis herculeana. *Nova Hedwigia*, 73:347–386, 1982.
12. A.R. Tolat, J.K. Stanley, and I.A. Trail. A cadaveric study of the anatomy and stability of the distal radioulnar joint in the coronal and transverse planes. *J. Hand Surg. [Br]*, 21:587–594, 1996.
13. J. Žunić and P.L. Rosin. A rectilinearity measurement for polygons. *IEEE Transactions on Pattern Analysis and Machine Intelligence*, forthcoming.
14. T.Y. Zhang and C.Y. Suen. A fast parallel algorithm for thinning digital patterns. *Comm. ACM*, 27(3):236–240, 1984.

Optimization and Tracking of Polygon Vertices for Shape Coding

Janez Zaletelj and Jurij F. Tasic

University of Ljubljana, Faculty of Electrical Engineering
Trzaska 25, SI-1000 Ljubljana, Slovenia
{janez.zaletelj,jurij.tasic}@fe.uni-lj.si
http://ldos.fe.uni-lj.si

Abstract. The efficiency of shape coding is an important problem in low-bitrate object-based video compression. Lossy contour coding methods typically include contour approximation by polygons or splines, spatial and/or temporal prediction of vertices, and entropy coding the of prediction error. In conventional contour coding schemes, however, the coding gain in the interframe mode is typically small. This indicates that the temporal redundancy is not successfully removed. The paper addresses the issue of temporal shape decorrelation by proposing the Kalman filtering-based approach to vertex tracking and prediction. A temporal vertex association procedure is proposed effectively minimizing bit rate in each frame. The prediction error is coded using adaptive arithmetic encoding. Vertex optimization is employed to reduce the shape reconstruction error.

1 Introduction

In the context of object-based video coding, shape information is crucial for content-based access and manipulation of video streams. Because it represents a substantial part of the total bit rate, efficient coding methods are needed. MPEG-4 uses Context Arithmetic Encoding [9], which is a bitmap-based coding method. However, lossy contour-based coding methods can achieve a higher coding efficiency by encoding control points / vertices of spline or polygon approximation. Most contour-based shape coding methods [1,2,3,5,10,11] concentrate on finding a set of polygon vertices / spline control points to minimize the bit rate while satisfying the maximum allowable distortion criterion. Intra-frame relative addressing of vertices is employed and predefined variable length codes are used for entropy coding, which limits the rate-distortion efficiency. Temporal decorrelation of shape is generally not addressed adequately, with the exception of [7] which uses Lagrangian optimization of control point positions to obtain a rate-distortion optimal solution.

The computational complexity of the optimal methods [5], [7] is quadratic in the number of admissible control points. Their optimality can only be claimed within the limitations imposed by the chosen code structure, motion compensation scheme, approximation scheme, width of the admissible control-point band,

N. Petkov and M.A. Westenberg (Eds.): CAIP 2003, LNCS 2756, pp. 418–425, 2003.

and code words. By using different coding schemes or different prediction / motion compensation methods it is thus possible to derive a suboptimal, computationally less intensive method which would yield a similar rate-distortion efficiency.

The proposed method capitalizes on the temporal shape correlation by finding correspondences between polygon vertices in successive frames. In each frame, the video object's shape is approximated by a polygon using a method based on iterative polygon refinement [11]. In Section 2, a vertex optimization procedure is defined which minimizes the distortion of the reconstructed shape. A method of finding a rate-distortion optimal polygon approximation is given in Section 3. Temporal correspondence of vertices in successive frames is determined on the basis of vertex tracking using the Kalman filtering. Using a predicted set of vertices, we find correspondences which minimize the coding rate (see Eqn. 7). This allows using an interframe relative addressing which reduces the dynamic range and consequently the bit rate. A high coding efficiency is achieved by employing adaptive arithmetic encoding of vertices. The encoder uses different probability distributions for each coding mode which are continually adapted to the input signal (Figure 2). Results of the experiments, given in Section 4, indicate that the proposed combination of temporal tracking, adaptive arithmetic encoding and vertex optimization outperforms standard shape coding methods based on the polygon approximation.

2 State of the Art in Vertex-Based Shape Coding

It is clear that the boundaries of the video object in successive frames are highly correlated (see Fig. 1). However, the coding gain achieved by exploiting this redundancy is relatively small compared to the intermode gain for grayscale coders. Algorithms which exploit the interframe redundancy are mostly based on the intraframe techniques adapted to the use of prediction based on a combined spatio-temporal context [9], [7].

The efficiency of such pixel-based approaches is deteriorated by boundary misalignment and boundary noise which are present even if no motion has occurred. A simple translational object motion model used to align boundaries performs poorly under nonrigid object deformations. To compensate for local boundary deformations, two-stage global-local motion compensation was proposed in [8]. Instead of predicting boundary pixels, a spatio-temporal prediction of the angle and size of vectors connecting B-spline control points was proposed in [7]. However, relative encoding of control points is essentially the same as in intramode, so the magnitude of the coded vectors was not reduced.

3 Optimal Encoding Using Distortion Minimization and Vertex Prediction

The computational complexity of the rate-distortion optimal vertex selection methods [7], [5] is high due to exhaustive global search for the optimal vertex positions. By using separate distortion and rate minimizations, it is possible to find a suboptimal, but computationally less intensive solution. We propose an iterative rate-distortion optimization scheme which is based on the polygon refinement method. Polygon vertices are added or removed on the basis of the target bit rate $R^{\max}$. In each iteration, a rate-optimal spatial or temporal correspondence and consequently the coding mode is defined for each vertex. Temporal prediction of the vertex positions based on the Kalman filtering is used to increase the coding gain by reducing the magnitude of the prediction error.

3.1 Distortion-Optimized Polygon Approximation

A number of shape coding methods relies on polygon approximation of the object's contour. In a lossy contour coding scheme, the reconstruction error of the polygon approximation needs to be evaluated. Different distance metrics are defined on the basis of the Euclidean distance between the contour pixel and the closest point on the polygon segment [5]. The peak absolute distance D_p is defined as the maximum of the pixel distances to the polygon and is useful for finding a polygon which satisfies the maximum peak distance criterion $D_p^{\max}$.

However, within MPEG-4 evaluation of shape coders the distortion metric D_n was used, because it is more sensitive to the shape reconstruction error. It is defined on the basis of a comparison of the original and reconstructed binary object masks. Let $B^t = \left(b_j^t : j = 0, \ldots, N_B^t - 1\right)$ denote an ordered set of boundary elements of the object in frame t, and let $S^t = (s_k^t : k = 0, \ldots, N^t - 1)$ denote an ordered set of polygon vertices. Let $\mathcal{O}(B^t)$ denote a set of pixels which belong to the video object in frame t, and let $\mathcal{R}(S^t)$ denote a set of pixels which belong to the reconstruction of the video object. D_n is defined as the relative number of erroneously represented pixels of the reconstructed binary shape mask

$$D_n(S^t, B^t) = \frac{|(\mathcal{O}(B^t)\backslash\mathcal{R}(S^t)) \cup (\mathcal{R}(S^t)\backslash\mathcal{O}(B^t))|}{|\mathcal{O}(B^t)|} . \tag{1}$$

An iterated refinement method [11] is widely used as a polygon approximation technique because of its hierarchical nature. In each iteration it refines a polygon segment with a maximum distance from the boundary by inserting a new vertex. The method finds a polygon satisfying the maximum peak distance $D_p^{\max}$ criterion using a minimal number of vertices. However, because vertex positions are restricted to the contour points, the resulting polygon is suboptimal in terms of the distortion D_n. In [3] a vertex adjustment was proposed which minimizes either average absolute distance D_a or peak absolute distance D_p, however neither of these guarantees the minimization of the distortion D_n. We thus propose to integrate the vertex adjustment using D_n as a criterion into the iterated polygon refinement method.

The iterative optimization procedure seeks for a set of optimal vertices S^{t*}, where each vertex s_k^t is adjusted from its original position $s_k^{t,0}$ within the search range given by $\left\| s_k^t - s_k^{t,0} \right\| \leq D_p^{\max}$

$$\left(s_0^{t*}, \ldots, s_{N^t-1}^{t}{}^{*}\right) = \underset{s_0^t, \ldots, s_{N^t-1}^t}{\arg\min}\; D_n(s_0^t, \ldots, s_{N^t-1}^t, B^t) \,. \tag{2}$$

The obtained polygon yields a minimum shape reconstruction error for the given number of segments N^t.

3.2 Temporal Prediction of Polygon Vertices by Kalman Filtering

The proposed encoding scheme uses a local motion prediction and compensation scheme, based on the Kalman prediction of vertex positions. Fig. 1 shows the polygon approximation of the video object boundary in two successive frames of the Children test sequence. Temporal prediction of the polygon is shown in both frames by a dotted line. Temporally matched polygon vertices are represented by circles, and unmatched vertices are represented by squares. The proposed temporal matching and prediction effectively reduces the magnitude of the coded prediction error vectors (shown by solid lines in Fig. 1, right).

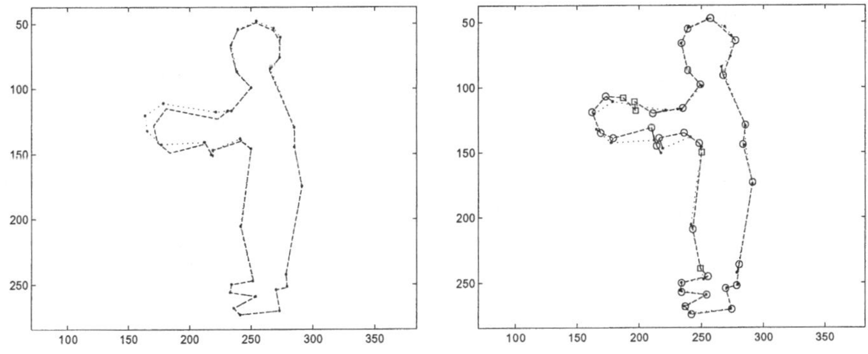

Fig. 1. Polygon approximation (*dashed line*) of two frames from the Children test sequence. Temporally predicted polygon is shown by a dotted line. Temporally matched vertices are represented by circles, and unmatched vertices are represented by squares (*right*). Solid lines (*right*) represent temporal prediction error vectors

Let vector $\mathbf{X}_k^t = (p_k^t, v_k^t)^T$ denote the Kalman state variable which describes the position and velocity of one polygon vertex. The Kalman filtering relates states at different time instants through the equation

$$\mathbf{X}_k^{t+1} = \mathbf{F}\mathbf{X}_k^t + \mathbf{w}_k \,, \tag{3}$$

where $\mathbf{F}$ is a transition matrix, and $\mathbf{w}_k = (w_k^p, w_k^v)^T$ represents the acceleration of the vertex modelled as a white noise process.

The Kalman filter provides a prediction of the vertex position and velocity in each frame $\mathbf{X}_k^{t-} = \mathbf{F}\mathbf{X}_k^{t-1}$, and updates the state variables and error covariance matrices when a new measurement of the vertex position is available. Let $P^{t-} = (p_k^{t-} : k = 0, \ldots, N^{t-1} - 1)$ denote an ordered set of predicted polygon vertices serving as a basis for finding an optimal correspondence between polygon vertices in the current frame S^t and vertices in the previous frame S^{t-1}.

3.3 Problem Formulation

We seek an approximating polygon which effectively minimizes the distortion of the approximation, given the maximum target bit rate $R^{\max}$. We wish to select an optimal number of polygon vertices N^t and an optimal coding mode $\psi(k,t)$ (Eq. 5) for each vertex s_k^t, such that the total distortion is minimized

$$\begin{aligned} &\min_{s_0^t,\cdots,s_{N^t-1}^t} \quad D_n\left(s_0^t,\cdots,s_{N^t-1}^t\right), \\ &\text{subject to } R\left(s_0^t,\cdots,s_{N^t-1}^t\right) \le R^{\max} . \end{aligned} \tag{4}$$

Adding a new polygon vertex, which is a result of polygon refinement and distortion optimization (see Sect. 3.1), generally decreases distortion D_n and increases the bit rate R. In each iteration, the minimum coding rate is found by optimal intra/inter vertex matching, which selects an appropriate coding mode for each vertex.

Given a set of polygon vertices S^t and a set of predicted vertices P^{t-}, the goal of the vertex matching is to find a rate optimal encoding. For each vertex s_k^t two coding modes are available: intraframe, where the prediction error with respect to the spatially predicted position $s_k^{t-} = f(s_{k-1}^t, s_{k-2}^t, \ldots)$ is encoded, and the interframe mode, where the prediction error with respect to the temporal prediction p_l^{t-} is encoded. Because of the temporal redundancy, the interframe compensated coding generally requires less bits. In the context of the Kalman filtering and prediction, the vertex matching is a data association step, necessary to associate a new measurement to each Kalman filter. The problem is to associate a set of N^t optimized polygon vertices to the N^{t-1} predicted vertices. The most likely assignment is the one that minimizes the coding cost function.

Let the binary functions $\psi(k,t)$ and $\chi(k,l,t)$ define the coding mode and the temporal correspondence of the vertex s_k^t, respectively:

$$\psi(k,t) = \begin{cases} 1 \text{ if } s_k^t \text{ is coded in intramode with respect to } s_k^{t-}, \\ 0 \text{ if } s_k^t \text{ is coded in intermode,} \end{cases} \tag{5}$$

$$\chi(k,l,t) = \begin{cases} 1 \text{ if } s_k^t \text{ is coded in intermode with respect to } p_l^{t-} \\ 0 \text{ otherwise.} \end{cases} \tag{6}$$

where $l = 0, \ldots, N^{t-1} - 1$ indexes over the list of the Kalman filters and $k = 0, \ldots, N^t - 1$ indexes over the measurement list. If the vertex s_k^t is coded in intramode, then its intermode correspondence function is zero for all l, $\chi(k,l,t) = 0$. The vertex assignment problem is now formulated as a minimization of a coding rate given by

$$R(\chi,\psi) = \sum_{l=0}^{N^{t-1}-1} \sum_{k=0}^{N^t-1} \left(\psi(k,t) \cdot R^S(s_k^t - s_k^{t-}) + \chi(k,l,t) \cdot R^T(s_k^t - p_l^{t-})\right), \tag{7}$$

where $R^S(s_k^t - s_k^{t-})$ is a coding cost for the intramode encoding (Eq. 9), and $R^T(s_k^t - p_l^{t-})$ is a coding cost for intermode vertex encoding (Eq. 8). The minimization is performed by Dijkstra's algorithm [12] which finds the shortest path in the weighted directed graph, where vertices correspond to the pairs (s_k^t, p_l^{t-}) and edge weights correspond to the coding costs of the prediction error.

3.4 Adaptive Arithmetic Encoding of the Prediction Error

Prediction error vectors $s_k^t - s_k^{t-}$ and $s_k^t - p_l^{t-}$ are losslessly encoded using three components: octant difference index $d_k = o_k - o_{k-1}$, max M_k and min m_k components [3]. This allows that the dynamic range and probability distribution of each component is adjusted independently thus increasing the coding efficiency. Probability distributions are adaptively adjusted with each incoming symbol (see Fig. 2) and they can be initialized to the predefined function, for example Laplacian distribution for M and m components. Typical probability distributions of the M component in the intra and intermode are plotted in Fig. 2. The intermode distribution $p^{M,T}(M_k)$ is highly non-uniform, which explains the higher coding efficiency of the intermode coding.

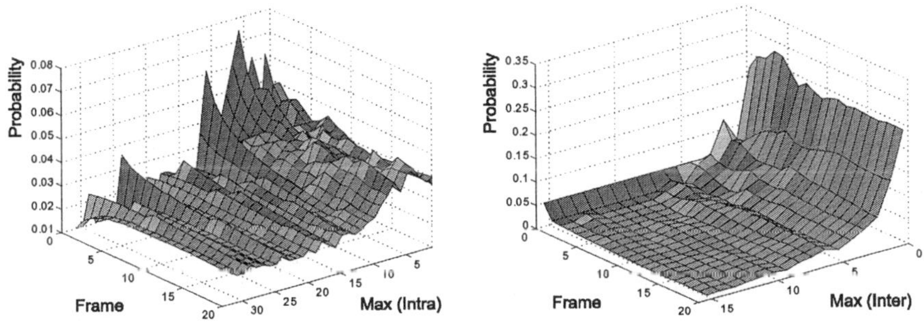

Fig. 2. Probability distributions of the Max component of the prediction error for intramode coding $p^{M,S}(M_k)$ (*left*) and for intermode coding $p^{M,T}(M_k)$ (*right*)

The default coding mode is the interframe mode. An octant difference index 4 is used as an escape symbol, indicating that the next symbol is a control symbol. Control symbols are employed to change the coding mode, indicate a new frame, an overflow of the Min or Max component of a vector, etc. Coding costs for intra and inter encoding can be estimated from the entropies of coding symbols:

$$R^T\left(s_k^t - p_l^{t-}\right) = -\log_2\left(p^d(d_k)\right) - \log_2\left(p^{M,T}(M_k)\right) - \log_2\left(p^{m,T}(m_k)\right) \quad (8)$$

$$R^S\left(s_k^t - s_k^{t-}\right) = -\log_2\left(p^d(\text{esc})\right) - \log_2\left(p^{\text{esc}}(\text{intra})\right) - \log_2\left(p^d(d_k)\right) - \log_2\left(p^{M,S}(M_k)\right) - \log_2\left(p^{m,S}(m_k)\right) \quad (9)$$

4 Experimental Results

Fig. 3 shows the rate-distortion curve of the proposed algorithm for the MPEG-4 test sequence 'Children'. The efficiency of the proposed method is compared to the baseline method [2], object-adaptive vertex encoding method [1] and B-spline-based method [7] (*left*). The proposed method outperforms the baseline and object-adaptive encoding, but the rate-distortion optimized B-spline encoding performs better at all bit rates. This is because of the smaller reconstruction

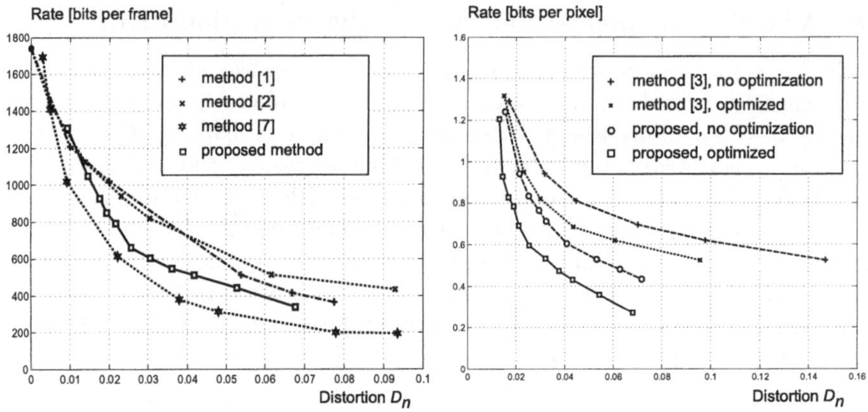

Fig. 3. Rate-distortion efficiency of the proposed method compared to methods [1,2,7] (*left*). Rate-distortion curves of the proposed method with and without vertex optimization compared to method [3] (*right*)

error of B-splines, and also because of global vertex and VLC code word optimization.

Fig. 3 (*right*) demonstrates the effect of vertex optimization. Compared to the vertex coding method [3], which also uses vertex adjustment, the proposed method is more effective, and the bit rate reduction due to optimization ranges up to 40 percent. The coding gain due to the temporal prediction of vertices varies from sequence to sequence and depends on the amount of the contour motion.

5 Conclusion

In this work, we propose a novel approach to the rate-distortion controlled encoding of video object shape information which is based on polygon approximation and vertex encoding. It is a combination of distortion-optimized polygon approximation, Kalman-based tracking and prediction of polygon vertices, and adaptive arithmetic encoding of the prediction error. Its efficiency comes from using a constant-velocity motion model for each vertex separately. The model predicts the position of the vertex in the next frame and allows the tracking of boundary segments moving in different directions. It employs adaptive arithmetic encoding of the prediction error. The coding efficiency outperforms conventional polygon-based shape coding methods, and is close to the rate-distortion optimized B-spline shape coding.

It is expected that further coding gains can be achieved by using a better approximation technique, for example B-splines, by adapting the motion model parameters to the actual sequence and by employing a hybrid intra/inter prediction modes.

References

1. O'Connell, K.J.: Object-adaptive vertex-based shape coding method. IEEE Trans. Circuits Syst. Video Technol., Vol. 7, (1997) 251–255
2. Lee, S., Cho, D., Cho, Y., Son, S., Jang, E., Shin, J.: Binary shape coding using 1-D distance values from baseline. In: Proc. ICIP (1997) I-508–511
3. Chung, J., Lee, J., Moon, J., Kim, J.: A new vertex-based binary shape coder for high coding efficiency. Signal Processing: Image Comm., Vol. 15 (2000) 665–684
4. Freeman, H.: On the encoding of arbitrary geometric configurations. IRE Trans. Electron. Comput., Vol. 10 (1961) 260–268
5. Katsaggelos, A.K., Kondi, L.P., Meier, F.W., Ostermann, J., Schuster, G.M.: MPEG-4 and rate-distortion-based shape-coding techniques. Proc. IEEE, Vol. 86, (1998) 1126–1154.
6. Witten, H., Neal, R.M., Cleary, J.G.: Arithmetic coding for data compression. Commun. ACM, Vol. 30 **6** (1987) 520–540
7. Melnikov, G., Schuster, G.M., Katsaggelos, A.K.: Shape Coding Using Temporal Correlation and Joint VLC Optimization. IEEE Trans. Circ. Syst. Video Techn., Vol. 10 **5** (2000) 744–754
8. Cho, S.H., Kim, R.C., Oh, S.S., Lee, S.U.: A Coding Technique for the Contours in Smoothly Perfect Eight-Connectivity Based on Two-Stage Motion Compensation. IEEE Trans. CSVT, Vol.9 (1999) 59–69
9. Brady, N., Bossen, F.: Shape compression of moving objects using context-based arithmetic encoding. Signal Processing: Image Communication, Vol. 15 (2000) 601–617
10. Kim, J.I., Bovik, A.C., Evans, B.L.: Generalized predictive binary shape coding using polygon approximation. Signal Processing: Image Communication, Vol. 15 (2000) 643–663
11. Gerken, P.: Object-based analysis-synthesis coding of image sequences at very low bit rates. IEEE Trans. CSVT, vol. 4, (1994) 228–235
12. Dijkstra, E.W.: A Note on Two Problems in Connexion with Graphs. Numerische Mathematik, vol. 1, pp. 269-271, 1959.

Greedy Algorithm for a Training Set Reduction in the Kernel Methods*

Vojtěch Franc and Václav Hlaváč

Czech Technical University, Faculty of Electrical Engineering
Department of Cybernetics, Center for Machine Perception
121 35 Prague 2, Karlovo náměstí 13, Czech Republic
{xfrancv,hlavac}@cmp.felk.cvut.cz

Abstract. We propose a technique for a training set approximation and its usage in kernel methods. The approach aims to represent data in a low dimensional space with possibly minimal representation error which is similar to the Principal Component Analysis (PCA). In contrast to the PCA, the basis vectors of the low dimensional space used for data representation are properly selected vectors from the training set and not as their linear combinations. The basis vectors can be selected by a simple algorithm which has low computational requirements and allows on-line processing of huge data sets. The proposed method was used to approximate training sets of the Support Vector Machines and Kernel Fisher Linear Discriminant which are known method for learning classifiers. The experiments show that the proposed approximation can significantly reduce the complexity of the found classifiers (the number of the support vectors) while retaining their accuracy.

1 Introduction

The kernel methods have become a fast developing branch of machine learning and pattern recognition in several past years. The kernel methods use kernel functions to perform the feature space straightening effectively. This technique allows to exploit established theory behind the linear algorithms to design their non-linear counterparts. The representatives of these methods are for instance the Support Vector Machines (SVM) [11] and the Kernel Fisher Linear Discriminant (KFLD) [5] which serve as classifier design or Kernel Principal Component Analysis (KPCA) [10] useful for non-linear feature extraction. The kernel learning methods are generally characterized by the following properties:

- The training data $\mathbf{X} = [\boldsymbol{x}_1, \ldots, \boldsymbol{x}_n]$, $\boldsymbol{x}_i \in \mathcal{X}$ are transformed by a function $\phi: \mathcal{X} \to \mathcal{F}$ to a new high dimensional feature space $\mathcal{F}$. We denote the set of training data transformed to the high dimensional space $\mathcal{F}$ as $\mathbf{F} = [\phi(\boldsymbol{x}_1), \ldots, \phi(\boldsymbol{x}_n)]$.

* The authors were supported by the European Union projects ICA 1-CT-2000- 70002, IST-2001-32184 ActIpret, by the Czech Ministry of Education under project MSM 212300013, by the Grant Agency of the Czech Republic project 102/03/0440. The authors would like to thank to the anonymous reviewers for their useful comments.

N. Petkov and M.A. Westenberg (Eds.): CAIP 2003, LNCS 2756, pp. 426–433, 2003.

- The kernel functions $k: \mathcal{X} \times \mathcal{X} \rightarrow \Re$ are used to avoid problems of high dimensionality of the space $\mathcal{F}$. The value of kernel function corresponds to the dot product of the non-linearly mapped data, i.e., $k(\boldsymbol{x_i}, \boldsymbol{x_j}) = \phi(\boldsymbol{x_i})^T \cdot \phi(\boldsymbol{x_j})$. This implies that the algorithm must use the dot products of training data only. The matrix of all the dot products in the space $\mathcal{F}$ is denoted as the kernel matrix $\mathbf{K}(i,j) = k(\boldsymbol{x_i}, \boldsymbol{x_j})$ and it is of size $[n \times n]$.
- The solution found is linear in the feature space $\mathcal{F}$, i.e. the function $f(\boldsymbol{x}) = \boldsymbol{w}^T \cdot \phi(\boldsymbol{x}) + b$ we search for is characterized by a vector $\boldsymbol{w} \in \mathcal{F}$ and a scalar $b \in \Re$. The function $f(\boldsymbol{x})$ is expressed in terms of kernel expansion $f(\boldsymbol{x}) = \sum_{i=1}^{n} \alpha_i k(\boldsymbol{x}, \boldsymbol{x_i}) + b$, where α_i, $i = 1, ..., n$ are real coefficients. The vector $\boldsymbol{w} \in \mathcal{F}$ is determined as a linear combination of transformed training data, i.e., $\boldsymbol{w} = \sum_{i=1}^{n} \alpha_i \phi(\boldsymbol{x_i})$.

When using the kernel method the following problems can be encountered:

- The storage of the training data in terms of the dot products is too expensive since the size of kernel matrix $\mathbf{K}$ increases quadratically with the number of training data.
- The solution $f(\boldsymbol{x}) = \sum_{i=1}^{n} \alpha_i k(\boldsymbol{x_i}, \boldsymbol{x}) + b$ is not sparse, i.e., many coefficients α_i are nonzero. It can occur for instance in the SVM when the number of support vectors is huge or in the KFLD and the KPCA, since there is the solution expressed using all training data. The non-sparse solution implies an expensive evaluation of the function $f(\boldsymbol{x})$ (e.g., slow classification).

Several approaches to the problem of non-sparse kernel expansion were proposed. These methods are based on approximating the found solution, e.g., the reduced set method [2, 9] or the method by Osuna et. al [7].

We propose a new solution to the problems mentioned above which is based on approximating the training set in the non-linear kernel space $\mathcal{F}$.

The novel approach is described in Section 2. The application of the proposed approach to the SVM and KLFD is described in Section 4. The experiments performed are mentioned in Section 5 and Section 6 concludes the paper.

2 Training Set Approximation

The transformed training data $\mathbf{F} = [\phi(\boldsymbol{x_1}), \ldots, \phi(\boldsymbol{x_n})]$ live in a subspace span($\mathbf{F}$) $\subseteq \mathcal{F}$. Let us suppose that we have a finite set $\mathbf{X_r} = [\boldsymbol{r_1}, \ldots, \boldsymbol{r_m}]$, $\boldsymbol{r_i} \in \mathcal{X}$, $m < n$, and its image in the feature space $\mathcal{F}$, i.e, the set $\mathbf{F_r} = [\phi(\boldsymbol{r_1}), \ldots, \phi(\boldsymbol{r_m})]$. Let us also suppose that the vectors $\phi(\boldsymbol{r_i})$ are linearly independent and so that they form a basis of linear subspace span($\mathbf{F_r}$) $\subseteq \mathcal{F}$. We aim to express the transformed training data $\mathbf{F}$ in a linear basis defined by the set $\mathbf{F_r}$. A method how to properly select the set $\mathbf{X_r}$ is described in the sequel. The $\mathbf{F}' = [\phi(\boldsymbol{x_1})', \ldots, \phi(\boldsymbol{x_n})']$ will denote a set of approximations of vectors $\mathbf{F} = [\phi(\boldsymbol{x_1}), \ldots, \phi(\boldsymbol{x_n})]$ which will be computed as minimal square error projections on the subspace span($\mathbf{F_r}$). It means that the approximation $\phi(\boldsymbol{x})' \in \mathbf{F}'$ of a vector $\phi(\boldsymbol{x}) \in \mathbf{F}$ is expressed as a linear combination of vectors of $\mathbf{F_r}$, i.e., $\phi(\boldsymbol{x})' = \mathbf{F_r} \cdot \boldsymbol{\beta}$ (we used matrix notation). The vector $\boldsymbol{\beta}$ contains real coefficients of linear combination and it is computed as

$$\boldsymbol{\beta} = \underset{\boldsymbol{\beta}'}{\operatorname{argmin}} \left(\phi(\boldsymbol{x}) - \mathbf{F_r} \cdot \boldsymbol{\beta}'\right)^T \cdot \left(\phi(\boldsymbol{x}) - \mathbf{F_r} \cdot \boldsymbol{\beta}'\right) .$$

The well known analytical solution of this problem is

$$\boldsymbol{\beta} = (\mathbf{F_r}^T \cdot \mathbf{F_r})^{-1} \cdot \mathbf{F_r}^T \cdot \phi(\boldsymbol{x}). \tag{1}$$

The solution for $\boldsymbol{\beta}$ in the terms of dot product has form

$$\boldsymbol{\beta} = \mathbf{K_r}^{-1} \cdot \mathbf{k_r}(\boldsymbol{x}) , \tag{2}$$

where $\boldsymbol{x} \in \mathbf{X}$ is a vector to be approximated, $\mathbf{K_r} = \mathbf{F_r}^T \cdot \mathbf{F_r}$ is a kernel matrix $[m \times m]$ of vectors from the set $\mathbf{X_r}$ and $\boldsymbol{k_r}(\boldsymbol{x})$ is a vector $[m \times 1]$ containing values of kernel functions of $\boldsymbol{x}$ and $\boldsymbol{r} \in \mathbf{X_r}$, i.e., $\boldsymbol{k_r}(\boldsymbol{x}) = [k(\boldsymbol{x}, \boldsymbol{r_1}), \ldots, k(\boldsymbol{x}, \boldsymbol{r_m})]$. We denote $\boldsymbol{\beta_i}$ the vector which contains coefficients computed for a vector $\boldsymbol{x_i} \in \mathbf{X}$. Thus the approximated value of kernel function of training vectors $\boldsymbol{x_i}$, $\boldsymbol{x_j} \in \mathbf{X}$ is computed as

$$k'(\boldsymbol{x_i}, \boldsymbol{x_j}) = (\phi(\boldsymbol{x_i})')^T \cdot \phi(\boldsymbol{x_j})' = (\mathbf{F_r} \cdot \boldsymbol{\beta_i})^T \cdot (\mathbf{F_r} \cdot \boldsymbol{\beta_j}) = \boldsymbol{\beta_i}^T \cdot \mathbf{K_r} \cdot \boldsymbol{\beta_j} .$$

As the kernel matrix $\mathbf{K_r}$ is positive definite it can be decomposed by the Choleski factorization as $\mathbf{K_r} = \mathbf{R}^T \cdot \mathbf{R}$, where matrix $\mathbf{R}$ is an upper triangular matrix. We can simplify the computation of the approximated kernel function as

$$k'(\boldsymbol{x_i}, \boldsymbol{x_j}) = \boldsymbol{\beta_i}^T \cdot \mathbf{R}^T \cdot \mathbf{R} \cdot \boldsymbol{\beta_j} = \boldsymbol{\gamma_i}^T \cdot \boldsymbol{\gamma_j} , \tag{3}$$

i.e., a dot product of vectors $\boldsymbol{\gamma_i}$ and $\boldsymbol{\gamma_j}$. Now, we can represent the training set $\mathbf{X}$ mapped to the non-linear space $\mathcal{F}$ by a matrix $\boldsymbol{\Gamma} = [\boldsymbol{\gamma_1}, \ldots, \boldsymbol{\gamma_n}]$ of size $[m \times n]$ instead of the kernel matrix $\mathbf{K}$ $[n \times n]$, where m is the number of vectors $\mathbf{F_r}$ used to approximate subspace $\operatorname{span}(\mathbf{F})$ and n is the number of training vectors. When we put $\mathbf{F_r} = \mathbf{F}$ then $m = n$ and we always obtain the perfect approximation without error, i.e., $k(\boldsymbol{x_i}, \boldsymbol{x_j}) = k'(\boldsymbol{x_i}, \boldsymbol{x_j})$. The perfect approximation is obtained if $\operatorname{span}(\mathbf{F_r}) = \operatorname{span}(\mathbf{F})$, which can occur even if $m < n$, for instance when the number of training data is high and the data are linearly dependent in the space $\mathcal{F}$. However, even if $\operatorname{span}(\mathbf{F_r}) \neq \operatorname{span}(\mathbf{F})$ (actually we always select $\mathbf{F_r}$ such that $\operatorname{span}(\mathbf{F_r}) \subseteq \operatorname{span}(\mathbf{F})$ as will be explained in the sequel) we can obtain a good approximation as experiments show (see below). Let us mention that $\boldsymbol{\gamma}$ is just expression of the vector $\phi(\boldsymbol{x})' = \mathbf{F_r} \cdot \boldsymbol{\beta}$ in the orthonormal basis (columns of matrix $\mathbf{R}$ are basis vectors) of the subspace $\operatorname{span}(\mathbf{F_r})$. The next section describes an approach how to select vectors of the set $\mathbf{X_r}$ used for approximation.

3 Algorithm

Let $\operatorname{se}(\boldsymbol{x})$ denote an approximation error of non-linearly mapped the training vector $\phi(\boldsymbol{x})$ which is defined as

$$\begin{aligned}
\operatorname{se}(\boldsymbol{x}) &= (\phi(\boldsymbol{x}) - \phi(\boldsymbol{x})')^T \cdot (\phi(\boldsymbol{x}) - \phi(\boldsymbol{x})') \\
&= (\phi(\boldsymbol{x}) - \mathbf{F_r} \cdot \boldsymbol{\beta})^T \cdot (\phi(\boldsymbol{x}) - \mathbf{F_r} \cdot \boldsymbol{\beta}) \\
&= k(\boldsymbol{x}, \boldsymbol{x}) - 2\boldsymbol{k_r}(\boldsymbol{x})^T \cdot \boldsymbol{\beta} + \boldsymbol{\beta}^T \cdot \mathbf{K_r} \cdot \boldsymbol{\beta}
\end{aligned}$$

We propose to use a simple greedy algorithm which iteratively adds the vectors with the highest se(x) to the set $\mathbf{X_r}$ and iterates until the prescribed limit on the approximation error is achieved, i.e., se($\boldsymbol{x}$) $< \varepsilon$, $\forall \boldsymbol{x} \in \mathbf{X}$, or until allowed size m (our limitations on memory) of the set $\mathbf{X_r}$ is achieved. Such algorithm can look as follows:

Algorithm 1: **Training set approximation**

1. Initialize the $\mathbf{X_r} = [\boldsymbol{r}]$, where $\boldsymbol{r} = \operatorname{argmax}_{\boldsymbol{x}\in\mathbf{X}} k(x,x)$.
2. Iterate while the size of $\mathbf{X_r}$ is less than m:
   (a) Compute $\mathrm{se}(\boldsymbol{x}) = k(\boldsymbol{x},\boldsymbol{x}) - 2\boldsymbol{k_r}(\boldsymbol{x})^T \cdot \boldsymbol{\beta} + \boldsymbol{\beta}^T \cdot \mathbf{K_r} \cdot \boldsymbol{\beta}$ for all training vectors which are not yet included in $\mathbf{X_r}$, i.e., $\boldsymbol{x} \in \mathbf{X} \setminus \mathbf{X_r}$. It requires to compute $\boldsymbol{\beta} = \mathbf{K_r}^{-1} \cdot \boldsymbol{k_r}(\boldsymbol{x})$ where $\mathbf{K_r}$ is a kernel matrix of the current set $\mathbf{X_r}$.
   (b) If $\max_{\boldsymbol{x}\in\mathbf{X}\setminus\mathbf{X_r}} \mathrm{se}(\boldsymbol{x}) < \varepsilon$ then exit the algorithm else insert the $\boldsymbol{x} = \operatorname{argmax}_{\boldsymbol{x}\in\mathbf{X}\setminus\mathbf{X_r}} \mathrm{se}(\boldsymbol{x})$ to the set $\mathbf{X_r}$ and continue iterations.

The result of the Algorithm 1 is a subset $\mathbf{X_r} \subseteq \mathbf{X}$ which contains the basis vectors as well as the matrix $\mathbf{K_r}^{-1}$ useful to compute the new representation of data using (2).

When using Sherman-Woodbury formula [3] for matrix inverse $\mathbf{K_r}^{-1}$ then the computationally complexity of the algorithm is $O(nm^3)$. The Algorithm 1 does not only minimize the approximation error se($\boldsymbol{x}$) but it also minimizes the mean square error since

$$\mathrm{mse} = \sum_{i=1}^{n} (\phi(\boldsymbol{x}_i) - \phi(\boldsymbol{x}_i)')^T \cdot (\phi(\boldsymbol{x}_i) - \phi(\boldsymbol{x}_i)') = \sum_{i=1}^{n} \mathrm{se}(\boldsymbol{x}_i) \leq (n-m) \max_{\boldsymbol{x}\in\mathbf{X}\setminus\mathbf{X_r}} \mathrm{se}(\boldsymbol{x}).$$

Step 1 can be seen as a selection of the training vector with worst approximation error when the subset $\mathbf{X_r}$ is empty, i.e., all vectors are projected onto the origin. Note, that all vectors $\phi(\boldsymbol{r})$, $\boldsymbol{r} \in X_r$ selected by the Algorithm 1 are vertices of the convex hull of the non-linearly mapped training data[1].

Let us mention the connection to the classical Principal Component Analysis (PCA) or Kernel Principal Component Analysis (KPCA) [10], which exactly minimizes the mean square error mse. However, the basis vectors are linear combinations of all the training data which means that the KPCA requires all training data to represent solution. The basis vectors found by the proposed method are selected vectors from the training set which is more convenient for kernel methods. Moreover, the proposed Algorithm 1 allows on-line processing of data. On the other hand, the Algorithm 1 finds only approximate solution.

Let us note that the found basis vectors can be orthogonalized on-line using well known Gram-Schmidt procedure or using the Choleski factorization which we used as described above (3).

[1] Thanks to J. Matas who pointed out this fact.

4 Applications of Training Set Approximation

In this section we will describe the use of the proposed approximation approach with connection to the Support Vector Machines (SVM) and Kernel Fisher Linear Discriminant (KFLD). The SVM and the KFLD are important representatives of the methods learning the kernel classifiers.

4.1 Approximation of Support Vector Machines

The SVM aim to learn the classifier $f(\boldsymbol{x})\colon \mathcal{X} \rightarrow \{-1,+1\}$ from training data $\mathbf{X} = [\boldsymbol{x}_1, ..., \boldsymbol{x}_n]$ and their hidden states $\boldsymbol{y} = [y_1, ..., y_n]^T, y_i \in \{-1,+1\}$. Learning of the linear SVM classifier $f(\boldsymbol{x}) = \boldsymbol{w}^T \cdot \boldsymbol{x} + b$ is equivalent of solving the following quadratic programming task

$$\boldsymbol{w}, b = \operatorname*{argmin}_{\boldsymbol{w},b} \frac{1}{2}||\boldsymbol{w}||^2 + C\boldsymbol{\xi} \cdot \boldsymbol{e}\,, \quad \text{s.t.} \quad \mathbf{Y} \cdot (\mathbf{X}^T \cdot \boldsymbol{w} + b\boldsymbol{e}) \geq \boldsymbol{e} - \boldsymbol{\xi}\,, \tag{4}$$

where $\mathbf{Y}$ is a diagonal matrix made from the vector of hidden states $\boldsymbol{y}$, $\boldsymbol{e} = [1, 1, ..., 1]^T$ and $\boldsymbol{\xi} = [\xi_1, \xi_2, ..., \xi_n]$ is a vector of slack variables. The non-linear SVM corresponds to the linear SVM learned on the non-linearly transformed training data $\mathbf{F} = [\boldsymbol{\phi}(\boldsymbol{x}_1), ..., \boldsymbol{\phi}(\boldsymbol{x}_n)]$. The non-linear SVM classifier has the form $f(\boldsymbol{x}) = w^T \cdot \phi(\boldsymbol{x}) + b = (\mathbf{F}\boldsymbol{\alpha})^T \cdot \phi(\boldsymbol{x}) + b$. Using the kernel functions we can write $||\boldsymbol{w}||^2 = \boldsymbol{\alpha}^T \cdot \mathbf{K} \cdot \boldsymbol{\alpha}$ and $\mathbf{F}^T \cdot \boldsymbol{w} = \mathbf{K} \cdot \boldsymbol{\alpha}$ which can be substituted to the (4). It results to the quadratic programming task for the non-linear SVM of the form

$$\boldsymbol{\alpha}, b = \operatorname*{argmin}_{\boldsymbol{\alpha},b} \frac{1}{2}\boldsymbol{\alpha}^T \cdot \mathbf{K} \cdot \boldsymbol{\alpha} + C\boldsymbol{\xi} \cdot \boldsymbol{e}\,, \quad \text{s.t.} \quad \mathbf{Y} \cdot (\mathbf{K} \cdot \boldsymbol{\alpha} + b\boldsymbol{e}) \geq \boldsymbol{e} - \boldsymbol{\xi}\,. \tag{5}$$

The proposed method allows to find approximation of the full kernel matrix in the form $\mathbf{K}' = \mathbf{\Gamma}^T \cdot \mathbf{\Gamma}$, where $\mathbf{\Gamma} = [\gamma_1, ..., \gamma]$ is a new representation of the training data (see (3)). It can be easily shown (substituting $\mathbf{K}'$ for $\mathbf{K}$ in (5)) that solving the linear SVM (4) for the data $\mathbf{\Gamma}$ is equivalent to solving the non-linear SVM (5) with the approximated kernel $\mathbf{K}'$. Let $\boldsymbol{w}, b$ be the solution of (4) computed for the data $\mathbf{\Gamma}$. The approximated non-linear SVM classifier can be expressed as

$$f(\boldsymbol{x}) = \sum_{i=1}^{m} \alpha_i k(\boldsymbol{x}, \boldsymbol{r}_i) + b \quad \text{and} \quad \boldsymbol{\alpha} = \mathbf{R}^{-1} \cdot \boldsymbol{w}\,.$$

In other words, we are able to find the approximated non-linear SVM classifier by the use of any solver for the linear SVM. Moreover, we can control the complexity of the resulting classifier since the number of the vectors defining the classifier (virtual support vectors) can be prescribed beforehand by the parameter m of the Algorithm 1.

4.2 Approximation of Kernel Fisher Linear Discriminant

The KFLD [4–6] is a non-linear extension of the classical Fisher Linear Discriminant (FLD) using the kernel trick. The aim here is to learn the binary non-linear classifier $f(\boldsymbol{x}) = \sum_{i=1}^{n} \alpha_i k(\boldsymbol{x}, \boldsymbol{x}_i) + b$ from the given training data. It can be shown [4] that the learning of the KFLD can be expressed as the quadratic programming task

$$\boldsymbol{\alpha} = \operatorname*{argmin}_{\boldsymbol{\alpha}} \boldsymbol{\alpha}^T \cdot \mathbf{N} \cdot \boldsymbol{\alpha} + C\boldsymbol{\alpha}^T \cdot \boldsymbol{\alpha} \quad \text{s.t.} \quad \boldsymbol{\alpha}^T \cdot \mathbf{K} \cdot \boldsymbol{e} = 2\,. \tag{6}$$

The matrix $\mathbf{N}$ is of size $[n \times n]$ is computed from the kernel matrix $\mathbf{K}$. The vector $\boldsymbol{e}$ is of size $[n \times 1]$. Solving the quadratic programming problem (6) is infeasible for large training sets. Moreover, the solution of the problem (6) is not sparse so that all the training data must be stored which results to a slow classification.

The use of the approximated kernel matrix $\mathbf{K}' = \mathbf{\Gamma}^T \cdot \mathbf{\Gamma}$ leads to the essential simplification of the problem (6). Following the derivation of the KFLD from [4], but with approximated kernel matrix $\mathbf{K}'$, yields a new quadratic programming task of the approximated KFLD. This new task has the same form as the original (6) but the matrix $\mathbf{N}$ is now of size $[m \times m]$ and the vector $\boldsymbol{e}$ is of size $[m \times 1]$. Consequently the classifier is determined by m training data. Thus we can control the complexity of the learning as well as the complexity of the resulting classifier by the parameter m of the Algorithm 1.

5 Experiments

We tested the proposed approach described in Section 4 to find the approximated SVM and KFLD classifier on selected problems from the IDA benchmark repository [1]. We used the Sequential Minimal Optimizer [8] to solve the linear SVM and the Matlab Optimization Toolbox to solve the quadratic programming task of the KFLD.

The IDA repository contains both synthetic and real word binary problems. Each problem consists of 100 realizations of training and testing sets. The assessment is done on the all 100 realizations and all the measured values are computed as the mean values.

The Algorithm 1 used for approximation has two parameters: (i) the maximal allowed approximation error ε and (ii) the maximal number of basis vectors m. We set the parameter $\varepsilon = 0.001$ and $m = 0.1n$ (training set reduced to 10% of its original size) for the SVM approximation and $m = 0.25n$ (training set reduced to 25% of its original size) for the KFLD approximation.

Free parameters of both the SVM and KFLD algorithm are the argument of the used RBF kernel function $k(\boldsymbol{x_i}, \boldsymbol{x_j}) = exp(-\sigma||\boldsymbol{x_i} - \boldsymbol{x_j}||^2)$ and regularization constant C. We used first 5 realization of data to select the best combination of parameters $\sigma = [2^{-8}, 2^{-7}, \ldots, 2^3]$ and $C = [2^0, 2^1, \ldots, 2^{12}]$. The pairs of arguments (σ, C) which yielded the smallest testing error were selected.

During the experiments we measured (i) percentage of training errors TrnErr, (ii) percentage of testing errors TestErr, (iii) number of kernel evaluations used in the training stage ker_eval, and (iv) number of the support vectors n_{SV}. In fact, the n_{SV} is a measure of classification speed and ker_eval is a measure of speed of the learning stage. In the case when the approximation was used ker_eval means the number of kernel evaluations used to compute the training set approximation by the Algorithm 1 and the number of kernel evaluations used by the training algorithm (SMO or KFLD) is enlisted in the brackets. The number in the brackets actually means the number of computations of dot products ${\gamma_i}^T \cdot \gamma_j$ which approximate the true kernel evaluations.

Table 1. Comparison of the SVM and the KFLD classifiers trained on full and the approximated training sets.

Data set	Method	TrnErr	TestErr	ker_eval	nsv
BREAST	SVM	20.69	25.36	2.7×10^6	116
dim = 9	SVM+Approx	20.93	26.51	$7.8 \times 10^3 (264 \times 10^6)$	20
$n_{trn} = 200$	KFLD	28.04	29.52	40×10^3	200
$n_{tst} = 77$	KFLD+Approx	20.82	29.82	$18.8 \times 10^3 (10 \times 10^3)$	50
FLARE	SVM	32.48	32.33	8.7×10^6	570
dim = 9	SVM+Approx	32.48	32.33	$49 \times 10^3 (7.5 \times 10^6)$	37
$n_{trn} = 666$	KFLD	33.19	33.09	443.6×10^6	666
$n_{tst} = 400$	KFLD+Approx	33.34	33.97	$49 \times 10^3 (24.6 \times 10^3)$	37
HEART	SVM	13.82	15.31	291.3×10^3	100
dim = 13	SVM+Approx	13.95	15.44	$5.6 \times 10^3 (242.8 \times 10^3)$	17
$n_{trn} = 170$	KFLD	14.43	16.31	28.9×10^3	170
$n_{tst} = 100$	KFLD+Approx	14.06	16.53	$13.4 \times 10^3 (7.3 \times 10^3)$	42
RINGNORM	SVM	0.07	1.60	1.7×10^6	218
dim = 20	SVM+Approx	1.11	1.91	$31.2 \times 10^3 (1.7 \times 10^6)$	40
$n_{trn} = 400$	KFLD	1.43	1.49	160×10^3	400
$n_{tst} = 7000$	KFLD+Approx	1.7	2.01	$75.1 \times 10^3 (40 \times 10^3)$	100
TITANIC	SVM	19.57	22.28	4.3×10^6	85
dim = 3	SVM+Approx	19.56	22.94	$3.4 \times 10^3 (350 \times 10^3)$	11
$n_{trn} = 150$	KFLD	21.99	23.81	22.5×10^3	150
$n_{tst} = 2051$	KFLD+Approx	22.47	24.26	$2.8 \times 10^3 (1.4 \times 10^3)$	9
WAVEFORM	SVM	2.68	9.92	1.0×10^6	175
dim = 21	SVM+Approx	7.14	10.47	$31.2 \times 10^3 (4.4 \times 10^6)$	40
$n_{trn} = 400$	KLFD	6.34	10.39	160×10^3	400
$n_{tst} = 4600$	KFLD+Approx	7.26	10.80	$115 \times 10^3 (75 \times 10^3)$	100

The overall results of the experiments can be seen in Table 1. The experiments show that the testing error TestErr of the classifiers found on the approximated training sets equals or is slightly worse than that of the full training set. The number of kernel evaluations ker_eval used for training set approximation is significantly smaller than that used by the learning algorithm. This can speed up the learning time when the kernel evaluation is significantly more expensive than the evaluation of the dot products ${\gamma_i}^T \cdot \gamma_j$. The number of the support vectors yielded by the approximation method is significantly smaller than that without approximation. This is especially apparent in the case of the KFLD where all the training data are used to represent decision rule.

6 Conclusions

We have proposed a simple method for data set approximation and its use for approximating the kernel methods. The proposed method allows to reduce complexity of the found solution as well as computational and memory demands of the learning algorithms.

The idea of this method is to represent data in a lower dimensional space with possibly minimal representation error which is similar to the Principal Component Analysis (PCA). In contrast to the PCA, the basis vectors used for data representation are selected from the training set and not as their linear combinations. These basis vectors can be selected by a simple greedy algorithm which does not require eigenvalue decomposition (as the PCA does) and its complexity is $O(nm^3)$ where n is size of training set and m the number of the basis vectors. The algorithm is on-line in nature and allows to process huge data.

We tested the proposed training set approximation in connection to the Support Vector Machines and Kernel Fisher Linear Discriminant. The results obtained show that the proposed approximation can significantly reduce the number of the support vectors while retaining the accuracy of the found classifiers.

References

1. Intelligent Data Analysis (IDA) repository. `http://ida.first.gmd.de/~raetsch`.
2. C.J.C Burges. Simplified Support Vector Decision Rule. In *13th Intl. Conf. on Machine Learning*, pages 71–77, San Mateo, 1996. Morgan Kaufmann.
3. G.H. Golub and C.F. van Loan. *Matrix Computations*. John Hopkins University Press, Baltimore, London, 3nd edition edition, 1996.
4. S. Mika, G. Rätsch, and K.R. Müller. A Mathematical Programming Approach to the Kernel Fisher Algorithm. In *NIPS*, pages 591 597, 2000.
5. S. Mika, G. Rätsch, J. Weston, B. Schölkopf, and K.R Müller. Fisher Discriminant Analysis with Kernels. In Y.-H. Hu, J. Larsen, E. Wilson, and S. Douglas, editors, *Neural Networks for Signal Processing IX*, pages 41–48. IEEE, 1999.
6. S. Mika, A. Smola, and B. Scholkopf. An Improved Training Algorithm for Kernel Fisher Discriminants. In *AISTATS 2001*. Morgan Kaufmann, 2001.
7. E. Osuna and F. Girosi. *Advances in Kernel Methods*, chapter Reducing the Runtime Complexity in Support Vector Machines, pages 271–284. MIT Press, 1998.
8. J.C. Platt. Sequential Minimal Optimizer: A Fast Algorithm for Training Support Vector Machines. Technical Report MSR-TR-98-14, Microsoft Research, 1998.
9. B. Schölkopf, P. Knirsch, and C. Smola, A. Burges. Fast Approximation of Support Vector Kernel Expansions, and an Interpretation of Clustering as Approximation in Feature Spaces. In R.-J.Ahler, P.Levi, M.Schanz, and F.May, editors, *Mustererkennung 1998-20. DAGM-Symp.*, pages 124–132, Berlin, Germany, 1998. Springer-Verlag.
10. B. Schölkopf, A. Smola, and K.R. Müller. Nonlinear Component Analysis as a Kernel Eigenvalue Problem. Technical report, Max-Planck-Institute fur biologische Kybernetik, 1996.
11. V. Vapnik. *Statistical Learning Theory*. John Wiley & Sons, Inc., 1998.

Learning Statistical Structure for Object Detection

Henry Schneiderman

Robotics Institute, Carnegie Mellon University
Pittsburgh, PA 15213, USA
hws@cs.cmu.edu
http://www.cs.cmu.edu/~hws/index.html

Abstract. Many classes of images exhibit sparse structuring of statistical dependency. Each variable has strong statistical dependency with a small number of other variables and negligible dependency with the remaining ones. Such structuring makes it possible to construct a powerful classifier by only representing the stronger dependencies among the variables. In particular, a semi-naïve Bayes classifier compactly represents sparseness. A semi-naïve Bayes classifier decomposes the input variables into subsets and represents statistical dependency within each subset, while treating the subsets as statistically independent. However, learning the structure of a semi-naïve Bayes classifier is known to be NP complete. The high dimensionality of images makes statistical structure learning especially challenging. This paper describes an algorithm that searches for the structure of a semi-naïve Bayes classifier in this large space of possible structures. The algorithm seeks to optimize two cost functions: a localized error in the log-likelihood ratio function to restrict the structure and a global classification error to choose the final structure. We use this approach to train detectors for several objects including faces, eyes, ears, telephones, push-carts, and door-handles. These detectors perform robustly with a high detection rate and low false alarm rate in unconstrained settings over a wide range of variation in background scenery and lighting.

1 Introduction

Many classes of images have sparse structuring of statistical dependency. Each variable has strong statistical dependency with a small number of other variables and negligible dependency with the remaining ones. For example, geometrically aligned images of faces, cars, push-carts, and telephones exhibit this property. Figure 1 shows empirical mutual information among wavelet variables representing frontal human face images. (Mutual information measures the strength of the statistical dependence between two variables.) Each "image" is a visualization of the mutual information values between one chosen wavelet variable, indicated by an arrow, and all the other variables in the wavelet transform. The brightness at each location indicates the mutual information between the variable at this location and the chosen variable. These examples illustrate common behavior where a given variable is statistically related with a small number of other variables.

N. Petkov and M.A. Westenberg (Eds.): CAIP 2003, LNCS 2756, pp. 434–441, 2003.

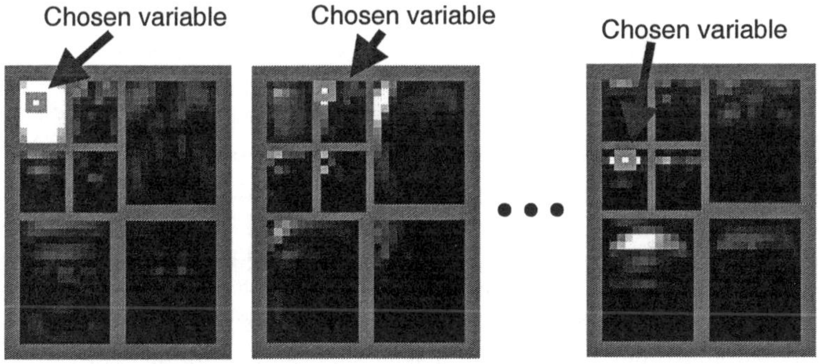

Fig. 1. Empirical mutual information among wavelet variables sampled from frontal faces images.

Sparse structuring of statistical dependency explains the empirical success of "parts-based" methods for face detection and face recognition [1][2][3][4][5]. Such parts-based methods concentrate modeling power on localized regions, in which dependencies tend to be strong and use weaker models over larger areas in which dependencies tend to be less significant.

In general, though, the problem of actually learning the statistical dependency structure for image classification has not received much attention in the computer vision community. Previous "parts-based" methods use hand-picked "parts". In this paper, we propose a method to learn the dependency structure from data and use the dependency structure to build a semi-naïve Bayes classifier.

A semi-naïve Bayes classifier [6] decomposes the input variables into subsets, representing statistical dependency within each subset, while treating the subsets as statistically independent. This classifier, $f(X_1, \ldots, X_n)$, takes the following form when written as a log-likelihood ratio test:

$$f(X_1,\ldots,X_n) = \log\frac{P(S_1|\omega_1)}{P(S_1|\omega_2)} + \log\frac{P(S_2|\omega_1)}{P(S_2|\omega_2)} + \ldots + \log\frac{P(S_r|\omega_1)}{P(S_r|\omega_2)} > \lambda$$
$$S_1,\ldots,S_r \subset \{X_1,\ldots,X_n\} \tag{1}$$

where $X_1 \ldots X_n$ are the input variables, $S_1 \ldots S_r$ are subsets of these variables, and ω_1 and ω_2 indicate the two classes. For the problem of object detection, the classes are "object" and "non-object" where the non-object class represents all possible visual scenery that does not contain the object. For example, ω_1 may correspond to face and ω_2 may correspond to "non-face." In this form, the classifier chooses class ω_1 if $f(X_1, \ldots, X_n) > \lambda$. Otherwise, it chooses class ω_2.

Learning the structure of a semi-naïve Bayes classifier is challenging. The search space is enormous. It is super-exponential in n input variables, where n typically is $\sim 10^3$ for image classification. Moreover, the solution is NP complete; that is, we must compare every possible structure in order to find the optimal solution. The Bayesian score [9][14][15] is an ideal metric for comparing these model structures. It naturally penalizes for overfitting. However, computing the score for one model involves summing the probabilities of the training data over all possible instantiations of the model's parameters. The computational cost of doing so can be quite large.

Solution using heuristic search and approximate metrics is unavoidable. On lower dimensional domains (e.g., under a hundred variables) proposed methods have focused on joining one variable at a time using estimates of pair-wise distributions [6] or accuracy using cross-validation [7]. Another method [8] induces products of decision tree like structures. Our strategy selects a structure by sequentially optimizing two cost functions using greedy search techniques. The first function models local error in the log likelihood ratio function over pairs of variables. This function assumes every pair of variables is independent from the remaining variables. We organize the variables into subsets such that this measure is minimized. In particular, we generate a large semi-redundant pool of candidate subsets. The second optimization chooses the final solution as a subset of these candidate subsets by minimizing a global measure of classification error.

We use this method in the context of object detection. Object detection is the task of finding instances of the given object anywhere in an image and at any size. To perform detection we use a classifier that discriminates between the object and scenery that does not contain the object. This classifier operates on fixed size input "window", e.g., 32x24 for frontal faces, and allows for a limited amount of variation in size and alignment of the object within this window. Therefore, to perform detection, we exhaustively scan the classifier over the input image (e.g., with a step size of 4 pixels) and resized versions of the input image (e.g. with a scale factor step size of 1.189).

We use this approach to construct classifiers for detecting several types of objects: faces, eyes, ears, telephones, push-carts, and door-handles. These detectors perform robustly with a high detection rate and low false alarm rate in unconstrained scenery over a wide range of variation in background scenery and lighting.

2 Construction of the Classifier

There are two aspects to constructing the classifier: learning the structure of the classifier (assignment of the variables to subsets in equation (1)) and estimating probability distributions over each such subset. In our approach, these two steps are coupled. Section 2.1 describes the initial selection of a pool of candidate subsets. Section 2.2 describes the estimation of probability distributions over these candidate subsets. Section 2.3 describes the selection of a subset of the candidate subsets to form the final classifier.

The training data consists of images of the object for class ω_1 and various non-object images for class ω_2. The input to the classifier, $X_1 \ldots X_n$, is a wavelet transform of input window. However, there is nothing about this method that is specific to the wavelet transform. Conceiavably, the raw pixel variables or any transform of the image could be used. For more details about our image pre-processing, training data, and overall system for detection, refer to [12].

2.1 Minimizing Local Error in the Log-Likelihood Ratio

This step creates a large collection of subsets of variables. Such a selection of subsets reduces representational power. Only dependencies within each subset are represented. We therefore must decide which variables we will not represent and which dependencies we will not represent. We evaluate the cost of a proposed reduction by its error in modeling the log-likelihood ratio function. Our error metric is the difference between the true log-likelihood ratio function and the log-likelihood ratio under the given reduction. However, we compute this error only over pairs of variables. In particular, we consider three possible cases given by the following costs:

$$C_1(X_i,X_j)=\sum_{x_i\in X_i}\sum_{x_j\in X_j}P(x_i,x_j)abs[\log\frac{P(x_i,x_j\,|\,\omega_1)}{P(x_i,x_j\,|\,\omega_2)}-\log\frac{P(x_i\,|\,\omega_1)P(x_j\,|\,\omega_1)}{P(x_i\,|\,\omega_2)P(x_j\,|\,\omega_2)}] \quad (2)$$

$$C_2(X_i,X_j)=\sum_{x_i\in X_i}\sum_{x_j\in X_j}P(x_i,x_j)abs[\log\frac{P(x_i,x_j\,|\,\omega_1)}{P(x_i,x_j\,|\,\omega_2)}-\log\frac{P(x_i\,|\,\omega_1)}{P(x_i\,|\,\omega_2)}] \quad (3)$$

$$C_3(X_i,X_j)=\sum_{x_i\in X_i}\sum_{x_j\in X_j}P(x_i,x_j)abs[\log\frac{P(x_i,x_j\,|\,\omega_1)}{P(x_i,x_j\,|\,\omega_2)}] \quad (4)$$

(Note, each of the random variables is assumed to be discrete-valued. We use upper case notation to denote the random variable and lower case notation to denote a particular instantiation of the variable; that is, each sum is over all possible values of the given random variable.) C_1 is the error in modeling the two variables, X_i and X_j, as independent; that is the cost of removing the dependency between the two variables. C_2 is the error of removing one variable, X_j, from the pair. C_3 is the error of removing both variables from the pair. Each of these assumes that the pair, (X_i, X_j), is independent from the remaining input variables. We obtain these measures by empirically estimating the probability distributions, $P(X_i, X_j\,|\omega_1)$ and $P(X, X_j\,|\omega_2)$, for every pairings of variables, X_i, X_j.

Under these approximations, the error associated with a given choice of subsets, $F = \{S_1, \ldots, S_r\}$, can be computed as:

$$E(F)=\sum_{\substack{(X_i,X_j),\forall i,j,i\neq j\\ X_i\cap X_j\notin S_k,\forall S_k\\ X_i\in S_k,\exists S_k\\ X_j\in S_k,\exists S_k}}C_1(X_i,X_j)+\sum_{\substack{(X_i,X_j),\forall i,j,i\neq j\\ X_j\notin S_k,\forall S_k\\ X_i\in S_k,\exists S_k}}C_2(X_i,X_j)+\sum_{\substack{(X_i,X_j),\forall i,j,i\neq j\\ X_i\notin S_k,\forall S_k\\ X_i\notin S_k,\forall S_k}}C_3(X_i,X_j) \quad (5)$$

We seek a set of candidate subsets, F, to minimize this localized error function. We search for such a solution using two steps. The first step assigns the variables to n subsets using n greedy searches, where each input variable is a seed for one search. This guarantees that every variable is represented in at least one subset and, therefore, there are no errors of the form C_2 or C_3 for this step. (This is a fairly reasonable way to optimize $E(F)$ since the errors due to removing a variable tend to be greater than those of removing a dependency.) Each of the greedy searches adds new variables by choosing the one that has the largest sum of C_1 values formed by its pairing with all current members of the subset. Such a selection process will guarantee that the variables within any subset will have strong statistical dependency with each other.

A second search may be desirable to reduce the number of subsets to smaller collection. We propose sequentially removing subsets until some desirable number, q, are remaining. At each step we remove the subset that will lead to the smallest increase in modeling error. In particular, it follows from equation (5) that the error in removing a given subset, S_k, is:

$$\sum_{\substack{X_i \in S_k, X_j \in S_k \\ X_i \cap X_j \notin S_i, \forall S_i, S_i \neq S_k}} C_1(X_i, X_j) + \sum_{\substack{X_i \in S_k, X_j \in S_k \\ X_j \notin Si, \forall S_i, S_i \neq S_k \\ X_i \in S_i, \forall S_i, S_i \neq S_k}} C_2(X_i, X_j) + \sum_{\substack{X_i \in S_k, X_j \in S_k \\ X_j \notin Si, \forall S_i, S_i \neq S_k \\ X_i \notin S_i, \forall S_i, S_i \neq S_k}} C_3(X_i, X_j)$$

In the experiments we describe later, the number of selected candidate subsets, q, ranged from 200 to 1,000. However, computational cost is linear in the number of candidate subsets and is not prohibitive for large numbers.

The sizes of the subsets are somewhat of an open question. Larger subsets have the potential to capture greater dependency. Subset size, however, increases the dimension of the probability distributions in equation (1) and, therefore, size must be balanced against practical limits in representational power and limited training data. One possible way of addressing this issue is terms of VC dimension as described by [4] or by Bayesian scoring techniques [9][14][15] For simplicity we describe the algorithm assuming the subsets will all have the same number of members, however, in our experiments we consider multiple sizes (leading to initially *mn* subsets above, where *m* is the number of sizes) to allow for greater variety in the representation.

2.2 Estimating the Probability Distributions

This step estimates log-likelihood ratio functions, log $(P(S_k|\omega_1) / P(S_k|\omega_2))$, for each candidate subset, S_k. Any functional form (e.g. Gaussian, mixture model, Bayes net, non-parametric, etc.) is admissible as a choice for $P(S_k|\omega_1)$ and $P(S_k|\omega_2)$. In general, classification functions such as linear and quadratic discriminants, neural networks, or decision trees may also be admissible for log $(P(S_k|\omega_1) / P(S_k|\omega_2))$ by proper normalization. In our current experiments, we represent each probability distribution by a table. This representation discretizes each subset of wavelet variables to a discrete feature value by vector quantization. (See [12] for more details on this representation.) The probability tables are then estimated by counting the frequency of occurrence of each feature value in the training data.

2.3 Minimizing Global Classification Error

We now form the overall structure of the semi-naïve Bayes classifier by choosing a group of the candidate subsets to form the final classifier. We choose the combination that minimizes an empirical classification error score. We measure performance by the area under the receiver operating characteristic (ROC) [13]. This measure of classification error accounts for the classifier's full operating range over values for the threshold, λ, in equation (1).

The difficulty in making this selection is that combinatorial space of candidate subsets is enormous. We use greedy search to incrementally combine subsets. In this search, the cost of evaluating each candidate combination on an example is small. In particular, the evaluation over any combination of subsets takes the form of equation (1) and is therefore simply the sum of the evaluations over the individual candidate subsets. Therefore, the individual candidate log-likelihood ratio functions only have to be evaluated once on each example. We then evaluate any combination as a sum of the appropriate pre-computed values.

In practice, it may be desirable to repeat this process several times where each time we prohibit identical choices to the previous searches. In particular, in our experiments we use a two part strategy that first finds l candidate combinations by comparing performance on training data (same images used to estimate probability distributions) then chooses the best of these by comparing performance on cross-validation data (images that are separate from other aspects of training).

3 Object Detection Experiments

We used this method to train detectors for frontal faces, eyes, ears, telephones, push-carts, and door-handles.

In frontal face detection, this method achieves relatively accurate detection rates at a fairly low computational cost. The table below show results on the MIT-CMU test set [10][2].

Recognition rate	86.5%	90.9%	94.0%	96.1%
False detections	3	7	22	65

These results are at least equal, and perhaps superior, to those of other state of the art detectors on this testing set including [1][2][4][5][10][11].

A human eye detector trained by this method has been tested extensively. The eyes were successfully located within a radius of 15 pixels with an accuracy of 98.2% on over 29,000 images of faces in an experiment independently conducted at the National Institute of Standards and Technology (NIST) by NIST employees[1] and reported back to the author. This dataset is sequestered and is not available to the public. The dataset consists of mugshot still images where there is only one face per person in the image and the face is that most prominent object in the image. The algorithm assumed that one face was present per image for this experiment.

The telephone detector was tested on one model of telephone over a set of 43 images with 107 telephones. The telephones had small variations in design, coloring,

[1] The author would like to acknowledge Jonathon Phillips, Patrick Grother, and Sam Trahan for their assistance in running these experiments.

and age, etc. Some examples are shown in Figure 5. The table below gives the performance over different values of the classification threshold in each column:

Recognition rate	61.7%	78.5%	85.5%	91.6%
False Detections	0	9	35	90

Accurate and efficient detectors were also trained for human ears, push-carts, and door-handles and are illustrated in Figures 2–5 where graphic overlays indicate the detected positions of these objects.

Fig. 2. Face, eye, and ear detection

Fig. 3. Door-handle detection

Fig. 4. Telephone detection

Fig. 5. Push-Cart detection

4 Conclusion

Sparse structuring of statistical dependency makes it possible to construct a powerful classifier by only representing the stronger dependencies among a group of variables. We have illustrated how such structure can be exploited by a semi-naïve Bayes classifier model. In particular, we have shown that the structure of the classifier can be learned by a search that optimizes a local error criterion given by equation (5) followed by another search that optimizes a global error criterion described in Section 2.3. We have shown that such a classifier can be effective for difficult object detection tasks. We believe these techniques of learning statistical structure will carry over to more complex models. In particular, a semi-naïve Bayes model is the most basic form of the larger graphical probability family of models including Bayes nets, Markov random fields, factor graphs, chain graphs, and mixtures of trees. Such models make it possible to represent more complex structural relationships such as conditional independence and hold further promise for improved image classification and object recognition.

References

1. Schneiderman, H., Kanade, T. "Object Detection using the Statistics of Parts." To appear in *International Journal of Computer Vision.* (2003)
2. Rowley, H.A., Baluja, S. and Kanade, T. Neural Network-Based Face Detection. *IEEE Transactions on Pattern Analysis and Machine Intelligence*, 20(1):23-38. (1998)
3. Moghaddam, B.; Pentland, A. "Probabilistic visual learning for object representation." *IEEE Transactions on Pattern Analysis and Machine Intelligence*, 19:7, 696 -710 (1997)
4. Heisele, B., T. Serre, M. Pontil and T. Poggio. "Component Based Face Detection." CVPR, 2001. (2001)
5. Viola P. and Jones M. Rapid Object Detection Using a Boosted Cascade of Simple Features. CVPR, 2001. (2001)
6. Kononenko, I. "Semi-Naïve Bayesian Classifier." Sixth European Working Session on Learning. pp. 206-219. (1991)
7. Domingos, P., Pazzani, M.. On the Optimality of the Simple Bayesian Classifier under Zero-One Loss. *Machine Learning*. 29:103-130 (1997)
8. Rokach, L. and Maimon, O. "Theory and Applications of Attribute Decomposition." *IEEE International Conference on Data Mining*. pp. 473-480. (2001)
9. Cooper, G. and Herskovits, E. "A Bayesian Method for the Induction of Probabilistic Networks from Data." *Machine Learning*. 9:303-347. (1992)
10. Sung, K-K., Poggio, T.. Example Based Learning for View-Based Human Face Detection. *IEEE Transactions on Pattern Analysis and Machine Intelligence*, 20(1):39-51. (1998)
11. Roth, D., Yang, M-H., Ahuja, N. A SNoW-Based Face Detector. *NPPS-12*. (1999)
12. Schneiderman, H. CMU Robotics Institute Tech Report. In Preparation.
13. Duda, R. O., Hart, P. E., Stork, D. G. *Pattern Classification*. John Wiley & Sons. (2001)
14. Heckerman, D., Geiger, D., Chickering, D. H. (1995) "Learning Bayesian Networks: The Combination of Knowledge and Statistical Data." *Machine Learning* 20(3): 197-243
15. Friedman, N. and Koller, D. (2002) "Being Bayesian about Network Structure: A Bayesian Approach to Structure Discovery in Bayesian Networks." *Machine Learning Journal*.

Blind Source Separation Using Variational Expectation-Maximization Algorithm

Nikolaos Nasios and Adrian G. Bors

Dept. of Computer Science, University of York, York YO10 5DD, UK
{nn,adrian.bors}@cs.york.ac.uk

Abstract. In this paper we suggest a new variational Bayesian approach. Variational Expectation-Maximization (VEM) algorithm is proposed in order to estimate a set of hyperparameters modelling distributions of parameters characterizing mixtures of Gaussians. We consider maximum log-likelihood (ML) estimation for the initialization of the hyperparameters. The ML estimation is employed on distributions of parameters obtained from successive runs of the EM algorithm on the same data set. The proposed algorithm is used for unsupervised detection of quadrature amplitude and phase-shift-key modulated signals.

1 Introduction

A large variety of algorithms have been employed for data modelling. Expectation-maximization (EM) algorithm has been used successfully in many applications requiring the maximization of the log-likelihood of data [1]. More recently, Bayes- ian approaches consider the integration over distributions of parameters in order to achieve a better data modelling and generalization capability [2]. Various algorithms including stochastic approaches such as Monte Carlo Markov Chains (MCMC) and variational approximations have been used for Bayesian learning of graphical models [3, 4]. Variational Bayes (VB) algorithm is an EM like algorithm which is used in order to estimate hyperparameters characterizing distributions of parameters [5–7]. The performance of both EM and VB algorithms depends on a suitable initialization. In this paper we employ a maximum log-likelihood estimation for the initialization of the hyperparameters. We use distributions of parameters resulted from successive runs of the EM algorithm for the maximum log-likelihood estimation. We consider the graphical model of a mixture of Gaussians and we apply the proposed algorithm for unsupervised detection of modulated signals.

In Section 2 we introduce the variational Bayesian methodology for mixtures of Gaussians, Section 3 provides the maximum log-likelihood estimation for initializing the VEM algorithm while Section 4 describes the variational Bayes algorithm. Section 5 presents experimental results when applying the proposed algorithm in blind source separation of modulated signals and Section 6 provides the conclusions of the present study.

N. Petkov and M.A. Westenberg (Eds.): CAIP 2003, LNCS 2756, pp. 442–450, 2003.

2 Bayesian Methodology for Mixtures of Gaussians

Due to their good approximation properties, mixtures of Gaussians have been used in various applications [5, 8]. A mixture of Gaussians can model any continuous probability function:

$$p(\mathbf{x}) = \sum_{i=1}^{N} \frac{\alpha_i}{\sqrt{(2\pi)^d |\mathbf{\Sigma}_i|}} \exp\left[-\frac{1}{2}(\mathbf{x}-\mu_i)^T \mathbf{\Sigma}_i^{-1}(\mathbf{x}-\mu_i)\right] \tag{1}$$

where d is the dimension, $\{\alpha, \mathbf{\Sigma}, \mu\}$ represent parameters and N is the number of components. Furthermore, we consider that the sum of mixture probabilities is $\sum_{i=1}^{N} \alpha_i = 1$. In the classical estimation we estimate the parameters of the model. In Bayesian approaches we take into account the uncertainty in parameter estimation. Instead of parameters we estimate the hyperparameters modelling distributions of parameters. The *a posteriori* probability is calculated as the integration over the space of parameters replacing the posterior with an approximation. The aim of variational Bayesian learning is to maximize the lower bound of the data log-likelihood probability approximation and therefore make the approximate posterior as close as possible to the true posterior distribution.

The parameters modelling a probability density function have their probabilities modelled as the conjugate priors [5, 6]. In the case of the parameters used for a mixture of Gaussians we have the mean, covariance matrix and mixing probability for each component. The conjugate prior distribution for the means is Gaussian, $\mathcal{N}(\mu|\mathbf{m}, \beta\mathbf{S})$ where β is a scaling factor:

$$\mathcal{N}(\mu|\mathbf{m}, \beta\mathbf{S}) \sim \frac{1}{\sqrt{(2\pi)^d |\beta\mathbf{S}|}} \exp\left[-\frac{1}{2}(\mu-\mathbf{m})^T (\beta\mathbf{S})^{-1}(\mu-\mathbf{m})\right] \tag{2}$$

A Wishart distribution $\mathcal{W}(\Sigma|\nu, \mathbf{S})$ is the conjugate prior for the inverse covariance matrix:

$$\mathcal{W}(\mathbf{\Sigma}|\nu, \mathbf{S}) \sim \frac{|\mathbf{S}|^{-\nu/2} |\mathbf{\Sigma}|^{(\nu-d-1)/2}}{2^{\nu d/2} \pi^{d(d-1)/4} \prod_{k=1}^{d} \Gamma(\frac{\nu+1-k}{2})} \exp\left[-\frac{Tr(\mathbf{S}^{-1}\mathbf{\Sigma})}{2}\right] \tag{3}$$

where ν are the degrees of freedom, Tr denotes the trace of the resulting matrix (the sum of the diagonal elements) and $\Gamma(x)$ represents the Gamma function:

$$\Gamma(x) = \int_0^{\infty} \tau^{x-1} \exp(-\tau) d\tau \tag{4}$$

For the mixture probabilities we consider a Dirichlet distribution $\mathcal{D}(\alpha|\lambda_1, \ldots, \lambda_N)$:

$$\mathcal{D}(\alpha|\lambda_1, \ldots, \lambda_N) = \frac{\Gamma(\sum_{j=1}^{N} \lambda_j)}{\prod_{j=1}^{N} \Gamma(\lambda_j)} \prod_{i=1}^{N} \alpha_i^{\lambda_i - 1} \tag{5}$$

The variational learning is expected to provide better data modelling by taking into account the uncertainty in the parameter estimation. On the other hand it provides better generalization while maintaining the good localization and modelling capabilities.

3 Maximum Log-Likelihood Hyperparameter Initialization

For certain datasets EM algorithm may not converge due to an unsuitable initialization. If we increase the number of parameters used in the modelling we are facing an even more challenging problem in choosing their initial values. Usually, random initialization is employed for EM or Variational Bayes algorithms. In this paper we adopt a hierarchical approach to the hyperparameter estimation. In the first stage we employ the EM algorithm using a set of random initializations. After several runs of the EM algorithm on the same data set, we form distributions of the parameters provided by the EM algorithm. Afterwards, maximum log-likelihood estimation is employed onto these distributions of parameters in order to initialize the hyperparameters for the Variational Expectation-Maximization algorithm.

The EM algorithm for Mixture of Gaussians model is applied on the given data in the first stage. In the E-step the *a posteriori* probabilities are estimated:

$$\hat{P}_{EM}(i|\mathbf{x}_j) = \frac{\hat{\alpha}_i(|\hat{\mathbf{\Sigma}}_i|)^{-1/2}\exp\left[-\frac{1}{2}(\mathbf{x}_j-\hat{\mu}_i)^T\hat{\mathbf{\Sigma}}_i^{-1}(\mathbf{x}_j-\hat{\mu}_i)\right]}{\sum_{k=1}^{N}\hat{\alpha}_k(|\hat{\mathbf{\Sigma}}_k|)^{-1/2}\exp\left[-\frac{1}{2}(\mathbf{x}_j-\hat{\mu}_k)^T\hat{\mathbf{\Sigma}}_k^{-1}(\mathbf{x}_j-\hat{\mu}_k)\right]} \quad (6)$$

In the M-step we update the parameters of the Gaussian mixture model:

$$\hat{\alpha}_i = \frac{\sum_{j=1}^{M}\hat{P}_{EM}(i|\mathbf{x}_j)}{M} \quad (7)$$

$$\hat{\mu}_{i,EM} = \frac{\sum_{j=1}^{M}\mathbf{x}_j\hat{P}_{EM}(i|\mathbf{x}_j)}{\sum_{j=1}^{M}\hat{P}_{EM}(i|\mathbf{x}_j)} \quad (8)$$

$$\hat{\mathbf{\Sigma}}_i = \frac{\sum_{j=1}^{M}\hat{P}_{EM}(i|\mathbf{x}_j)(\mathbf{x}_j-\hat{\mu}_{j,EM})(\mathbf{x}_j-\hat{\mu}_{j,EM})^T}{\sum_{j=1}^{M}\hat{P}_{EM}(i|\mathbf{x}_j)} \quad (9)$$

We run the EM algorithm L times considering random initializations. All the parameters estimated in each of the runs are stored individually, forming parameter distributions. We assume that these distributions can be characterized parametrically by a set of hyperparameters. The parametric description of these probabilities is given by (2) for means μ, by (3) for covariance matrices $\mathbf{\Sigma}$, and by (5) for mixing probabilities α.

The next step consists in estimating the hyperparameters characterizing the distributions formed in the previous step. This estimation would correspond to a second level of embedding, characterizing the initial estimation of the hyperparameters. The distributions of the means resulting from the EM algorithm (the outputs from (8)) can be modelled as a mixture of Gaussians. We apply a second EM algorithm onto the distributions of parameters. The updating equations of the second EM are similar with (6), (7), (8) and (9). In the second EM we consider the given data samples $\mathbf{x}_j$, $j = 1,\ldots,M$ as the initial starting points for the centers of the mean distributions. The hypermeans $\hat{\mathbf{m}}(0)$ are calculated as the average of the means resulting from several runs of the second EM. The corresponding covariance matrices for the Gaussian distribution of means $\mathbf{S}$, are stored as well. The parameter β represents a scaling factor of the covariance matrices corresponding to distribution $\hat{\mathbf{\Sigma}}$, resulting from the given data set according to (9), and that of the mean distribution, $\mathbf{S}$, respectively. This parameter is initialized as the average of the eigenvalues of the matrix $\mathbf{\Sigma}\mathbf{S}^{-1}$, which can be calculated using the trace:

$$\beta_i(0) = \frac{\sum_{k=1}^{L} Tr(\hat{\mathbf{\Sigma}}_{ik}\mathbf{S}_{ik}^{-1})}{Ld} \tag{10}$$

where L is the number of runs for the EM algorithm.

The Wishart distribution $\mathcal{W}(\mathbf{\Sigma}|\nu, \mathbf{S})$ characterizes the covariance matrix. We initialize the degrees of freedom $\nu_i(0) = d$, while for the initialization of $\mathbf{S}$ we consider the distribution of $\hat{\mathbf{\Sigma}}$ resulting from (9). We apply a Cholesky factorization onto the matrices $\hat{\mathbf{\Sigma}}_k$, $k = 1, \ldots, L$ resulted from successive runs of the EM algorithm. The Cholesky factorization results into an upper triangular matrix $\mathbf{R}_k$ and a lower triangular matrix $\mathbf{R}_k^T$ such that:

$$\hat{\mathbf{\Sigma}}_{ik}^{-1} = \mathbf{R}_{ik}\mathbf{R}_{ik}^T \tag{11}$$

We generate d independent samples from a normal distribution of variance 1 $\mathcal{N}(0, 1)$, and form a vector denoted as $\mathbf{N}$. The matrix $\mathbf{S}$ will be initialized as [2]:

$$\mathbf{S}_i(0) = \frac{\sum_{k=1}^{L} \mathbf{R}_{ik}\mathbf{N}_k(\mathbf{N}_k\mathbf{R}_{ik})^T}{L} \tag{12}$$

For the Dirichlet parameters we use the maximum log-likelihood estimation for (5). After applying the logarithm on (5) and differentiating the resulting expression with respect to the parameters λ_i, $i = 1, \ldots, N$ we obtain the following equation which is applied iteratively:

$$\psi(\lambda_{i,t}) = \psi(\sum_{k=1}^{N} \lambda_{i,t}) + \log E[\hat{\alpha}_i] \tag{13}$$

where t is the iteration number, $\log E[\hat{\alpha}_i]$ is the expectation of the mixing probability $\hat{\alpha}_i$, which is derived from the distributions obtained from successive runs of equation (7), and $\psi(x)$ is the digamma function (the logarithmic derivative of the Gamma function):

$$\psi(\lambda_i) = \frac{\Gamma'(\lambda_i)}{\Gamma(\lambda_i)} \tag{14}$$

where $\Gamma(x)$ function is provided in (4) The mean of the mixing probability distribution is considered as an appropriate estimate for $E[\hat{\alpha}_i]$. The parameter λ_i is initialized by inverting the digamma function, $\lambda_{i,0} = \psi^{-1}(\log E[\hat{\alpha}_i])$. The iterative algorithm uses Newton's method for updating λ_i follows:

$$\lambda_{i,t} = \lambda_{i,t-1} - \frac{\psi(\lambda_{i,t}) - \psi(\lambda_{i,t-1})}{\psi'(\lambda_{i,t})} \tag{15}$$

Just a few iterations of (13) and (15) are necessary, and the result achieved at convergence provides the Dirichlet parameters $\lambda_i(0)$, $i = 1, \ldots, N$.

4 Variational Bayes Algorithm

Integrating over the entire parameter space would amount to a very heavy computational task, involving multidimensional integrals. Variational Bayes algorithm has been derived in order to estimate the hyperparameters of a mixture model [5, 6]. In our approach we use the initialization provided by the maximum log-likelihood for the initialization of the Bayesian estimation algorithm. The variational Bayes is an iterative algorithm which consists of two steps at each iteration: variational expectation (VB-E) and variational maximization (VB-M). In the first step we compute the *a posteriori* probabilities, given the hidden variable distributions and their hyperparameters. In the VB-M step we find the hyperparameters that maximize the log-likelihood, given the observed data and their *a posteriori* probabilities.

In the VB-E step for a mixture of Gaussians model we calculate the *a posteriori* probabilities for each data sample x_j, depending on the hyperparameters:

$$\hat{P}(i|\mathbf{x}_j) = \exp\left[-\frac{1}{2}\log|\mathbf{S}_j| + \frac{1}{2}d\log 2 + \frac{1}{2}\sum_{k=1}^{d}\psi\left(\frac{\nu_j+1-k}{2}\right) + \right.$$
$$\left. +\psi(a_i) - \psi(\sum_{k=1}^{N} a_k) - \frac{\nu_j}{2}(\mathbf{x}_j - \mathbf{m}_i)^T \beta_i \mathbf{S}_i^{-1}(\mathbf{x}_j - \mathbf{m}_i) - \frac{d}{2\beta_i}\right] \quad (16)$$

where $i = 1, \ldots, N$ is the mixture component, d is number of dimensions, $j = 1, \ldots, M$ denotes the data index, and $\psi(x)$ is the digamma function from (14).

In the VB-M step we perform an intermediary calculation of the mean parameter as in the EM algorithm, but considering the *a posteriori* probabilities from (16):

$$\hat{\mu}_{i,VEM} = \frac{\sum_{j=1}^{M} \mathbf{x}_j \hat{P}(i|\mathbf{x}_j)}{\sum_{j=1}^{M} \hat{P}(i|\mathbf{x}_j)} \quad (17)$$

The hyperparameters of the distribution of means are updated as follows:

$$\mathbf{m}_i = \frac{\beta_i(0)\mathbf{m}_i(0) + \sum_{j=1}^{M} \hat{P}(i|\mathbf{x}_j)\mathbf{x}_j}{\beta_i(0) + \sum_{j=1}^{M} \hat{P}(i|\mathbf{x}_j)} \quad (18)$$

$$\mathbf{S}_i = \mathbf{S}_i(0) + \sum_{j=1}^{M} \hat{P}(i|\mathbf{x}_j)(\mathbf{x}_j - \hat{\mu}_{i,VEM})(\mathbf{x}_j - \hat{\mu}_{i,VEM})^T +$$
$$+\frac{\beta_i(0)(\hat{\mu}_{i,VEM} - \mathbf{m}_i(0))(\hat{\mu}_{i,VEM} - \mathbf{m}_i(0))^T \sum_{j=1}^{M} \hat{P}(i|\mathbf{x}_j)}{\beta_i(0) + \sum_{j=1}^{M} \hat{P}(i|\mathbf{x}_j)} \quad (19)$$

while the additional hyperparameters for Wishart and Dirichlet distributions are updated as:

$$\beta_i = \beta_i(0) + \sum_{j=1}^{M} \hat{P}(i|\mathbf{x}_j); \quad \nu_i = \nu_i(0) + \sum_{j=1}^{M} \hat{P}(i|\mathbf{x}_j);$$
$$\lambda_i = \lambda_i(0) + \sum_{j=1}^{M} \hat{P}(i|\mathbf{x}_j) \quad (20)$$

The effectiveness of the modelling is shown by the increase in the log-likelihood with each iteration. The convergence, is achieved when we obtain a small variation in the log-likelihood for the given set of *a posteriori* probabilities:

$$|\sum_{j=1}^{M} \log \hat{p}(\mathbf{x}_j|\Phi(t)) - \sum_{j=1}^{M} \log \hat{p}(\mathbf{x}_j|\Phi(t-1))| < \varepsilon \qquad (21)$$

where $\hat{p}(\mathbf{x}_j|\Phi(t))$ is the probability function for the given set of hyperparameters Φ at iteration t, and ε is a small quantity. The number of mixture components is found using minimum description length (MDL) criterion.

5 Experimental Results

We have applied the proposed algorithm in blind signal detection problems. We consider two cases of modulated signals: quadrature amplitude modulated signals (QAM) and phase-shifting-key (PSK) modulated signals. The perturbation channel equations considered in the case of 8-PSK signals are provided by [8]:

$$x_I(t) = I(t) + 0.2I(t-1) - 0.2Q(t) - 0.04Q(t-1) + \mathcal{N}(0, 0.11) \qquad (22)$$

$$x_Q(t) = Q(t) + 0.2Q(t-1) + 0.2I(t) + 0.04I(t-1) + \mathcal{N}(0, 0.11) \qquad (23)$$

where $(x_I(t), x_Q(t))$ makes up the in-phase and in-quadrature signal components at time t on the communication line, and $I(t)$ and $Q(t)$ correspond to the signal symbols (there are eight signal symbols in 8-PSK, equi-distantly located on a circle). The noise considered in this case is Gaussian and corresponds to SNR = 22 dB. We consider all possible symbol combinations for (I, Q) and we generate a total of 64 signals which can be grouped in 8 signal constellations corresponding to the distorted signals [8]. We have generated 960 signals, by assuming equal probabilities for all intersymbol combinations. The signal constellations are represented in Figure 1. For 4-QAM signals we assume only additive noise, with SNR of 8 dB.

The blind detection problem is treated as an unsupervised classification task in which we want to model the superclusters (each formed from 8 clusters). The VEM algorithm properly initialized with the maximum likelihood estimation from distributions of parameters is applied on the given data. The covariance matrices characterizing the Wishart distribution $\mathbf{S}$, and the distribution of the means $\beta\mathbf{S}$, as well as the initial location and the ideal location for the hypermeans are marked in Figure 1. In Figure 2 the convergence of the mean distributions measured by the Kullback-Leibler (KL) divergence [2] is shown, while the global convergence for the proposed algorithm and for the variational Bayes (VB) algorithm considering various random initializations [5, 6] is displayed in Figure 3. The favourable initialization for the VEM algorithm, achieved by applying maximum log-likelihood techniques can be easily identified on the curve marked with circles from Figure 3. The MDL criterion found four components for 4-QAM and eight components for 8-PSK. Table 1 shows comparative results when applying VEM, VB and EM algorithms on 4-QAM and 8-PSK modulated signals. The

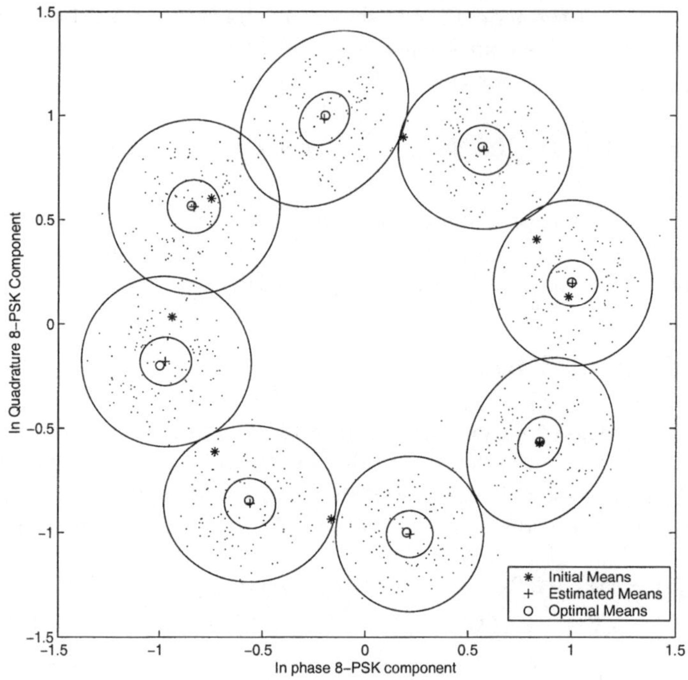

Fig. 1. Blind detection of 8-PSK modulated signals using VEM algorithm.

Table 1. Comparisons among VEM, VB and EM algorithms in blind source separation.

Algorithm	Data Set	Kullback-Leibler of posterior		Misclassification Error (%)		Bias $\|m - \hat{m}\|$	Bias $\|\alpha - \hat{\alpha}\|$	Average No. Iterat.
		Train. Set	Test Set	Train. Set	Test Set			
VEM	4-QAM	0.0255	0.0258	0.63	0.73	0.0319	0.0017	7
VB		0.1273	0.1330	6.08	6.63	0.2654	0.0294	8
EM		0.1448	0.1673	11.94	12.18	0.3134	0.0413	24
VEM	8-PSK	0.0257	0.0383	0.73	0.73	0.0147	0.0029	9
VB		0.0563	0.0735	6.66	6.68	0.1800	0.0169	14
EM		0.1102	0.1458	13.05	13.28	0.4047	0.0332	34

errors are measured in terms of global estimation by using KL divergence for the posterior distributions and misclassification errors on both training and testing set, and locally for the estimation of the individual parameters, respectively for the hypermean bias and for mixing probability bias. We have considered eight different random initializations for the VB and EM algorithms. We can observe from all these results that VEM algorithm provides a better estimation of the model parameters and achieves better source separation while the number of its necessary iterations is lower than in the other algorithms.

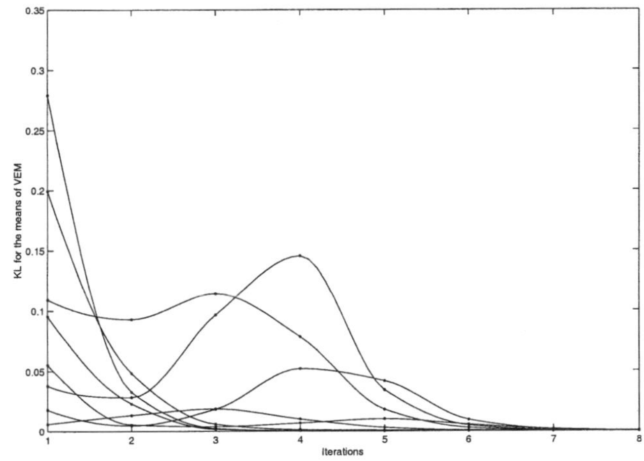

Fig. 2. Kullback-Leibler of mean distributions

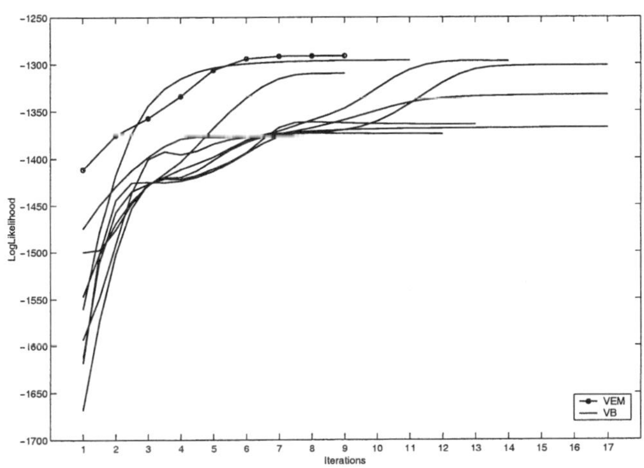

Fig. 3. Convergence of variational algorithms

6 Conclusions

We propose a new Bayesian estimation algorithm applied to mixtures of Gaussians models. The proposed algorithm has two stages. In the first stage we model distributions of parameters resulting from repetitive runs of the EM algorithm on the same data set. In the second stage we apply maximum log-likelihood estimation in order to obtain initial estimators for the proposed variational expectation-maximization algorithm. We have considered appropriate hyperparameter initial estimates for the parameter distributions under consideration: normal for the means, Wishart for the covariance matrix, and Dirichlet for the mixing probabilities. The proposed algorithm is compared with variational Bayes, which considers a similar updating algorithm, but random initialization, and with EM algorithm using random initialization. The algorithms have been tested on data sets representing 8-PSK and 4-QAM modulated signals, under inter-symbol and co-channel interference, when additive Gaussian noise is assumed. The experimental results show that the proposed VEM algorithm eliminates the dependence on the initialization which characterizes EM and VB algorithms and provides better estimation for the individual model parameters.

References

1. A. P. Dempster, N. M. Laird and D. B. Rubin. Maximum Likelihood from Incomplete Data via EM Algorithm, *J. of the Royal Stat. Soc., Series B*, Vol. 39, Issue 1, pp. 1-38, 1977.
2. A. Gelman, J. B. Carlin, H. S. Stern, D. B. Rubin, *Bayesian Data Analysis.* Chapman & Hall, 1995.
3. M. I. Jordan, Z. Ghahramani, T. S. Jaakkola, L. K. Saul, *An introduction to variational methods for graphical models,* pp. 105-161, in *Learning in Graphical Models,* ed. M.I. Jordan, MIT Press, 1999.
4. T. S. Jaakkola, M. I. Jordan, "Bayesian parameter estimation via variational methods," *Statistics and Computing,* vol. 10, pp. 25-37, Sep. 2000.
5. H. Attias, "A Variational Bayesian Framework for Graphical Models," *Advances in Neural Information Processing Systems (NIPS) 12*, 2000, pp. 209-215.
6. Z. Ghahramani, M. Beal, "Propagation Algorithms for Variational Bayesian learning," *Advances in Neural Information Processing Systems (NIPS) 13*, 2001, pp. 294-300.
7. S. J. Roberts, W. D. Penny, "Variational Bayes for Generalized autoregressive models," *IEEE Trans. on Signal Processing,* vol. 50, no. 9, pp. 2245-2257, 2002.
8. A. G. Bors, M. Gabbouj, "Quadrature Modulated Signal Detection Based on Gaussian Neural Networks," *Proc. of IEEE Workshop Visual Signal Processing and Communications,* Melbourne, Australia, Sep. 1993, pp. 113-116.
9. H. Attias, "Inferring parameters and structure of latent variable models by variational Bayes," in *Proc. of 15th Conf. on Uncertainty in Artif. Intel.,* Stockholm, Sweden, 1999, pp. 21-30.

Graph Clustering with Tree-Unions

Andrea Torsello and Edwin R. Hancock

Dept. of Computer Science, University of York, York, YO10 5DD, UK

Abstract. This paper focuses on how to perform unsupervised learning of tree structures in an information theoretic setting. The approach is a purely structural one and is designed to work with representations where the correspondences between nodes are not given, but must be inferred from the structure. This is in contrast with other structural learning algorithms where the node-correspondences are assumed to be known. The learning process fits a mixture of structural models to a set of samples using a minimum descriptor length formulation. The method extracts both a structural archetype that describes the observed structural variation, and the node-correspondences that map nodes from trees in the sample set to nodes in the structural model. We use the algorithm to classify a set of shapes based on their shock graphs

1 Introduction

Graph-based representations have been used with considerable success in computer vision in the abstraction and recognition of object shape and scene structure. Concrete examples include the use of shock graphs to represent shape-skeletons [11], the use of trees to represent articulated objects and the use of aspect graphs for 3D object representation. The attractive feature of structural representations is that they concisely capture the relational arrangement of object primitives, in a manner which can be invariant to changes in object viewpoint. However, despite the many advantages and attractive features of graph representations, the methodology available for learning structural representations from sets of training examples is relatively limited. As a result, the process of constructing shape-spaces which capture the modes of structural variation for sets of graphs has proved to be elusive. Hence, geometric representations of shape such as point distribution models [10, 4], have proved to be more amenable when variable sets of shapes must be analyzed.

Recently there has been considerable interest in learning structural representations from samples of training data, in particular in the context of Bayesian networks [3, 1], mixtures of tree-classifiers [8], or general relational models [2]. The idea is to associate random variables with the nodes of the structure and to use a structural learning process to infer the stochastic dependency between these variables. Although these approaches provide a powerful way to infer the relations between the observable quantities of the model under examination, they rely on the availability of correspondence information for the nodes of the different structures used in learning. However, in many cases the identity of the nodes and their correspondences across samples of training data are not to hand, Instead, the correspondences must be recovered using a graph matching technique during the learning process. Hence, there is a chicken and egg problem in structural

N. Petkov and M.A. Westenberg (Eds.): CAIP 2003, LNCS 2756, pp. 451–459, 2003.

learning. Before the structural model can be learned, the correspondences with it must be available, and yet the model itself must be to hand to locate correspondences.

The aim in this paper is to develop a framework for the unsupervised learning of generative models of tree-structures from sets of examples. We pose the problem as that of learning a union structure from the set of examples with hidden or unknown correspondences. The structure is constructed through a set of edit operations. Associated with each node of the structure is a random variable which represents the probability of the node. There are hence three quantities that must be estimated. The first of these are the correspondences between the nodes in the training examples and the estimated union structure. Secondly, there is the union structure itself. Finally, there are the node probabilities.

We cast the estimation of these three quantities in an information theoretic setting. The problem is that of learning a mixture of trees to represent the classes of tree present in the training data. We use as our information criterion the description length for the union structure and its associated node probabilities given correspondences with the set of training examples [9]. An important contribution is to demonstrate that the description length is related to the edit distance between the union structure and the training examples. >From our analysis it follows that the edit costs are directly related to the entropy associated with the node probabilities. We perform three sets of updates. First, correspondences are located so as to minimize the edit distance. Secondly, the union structure is edited to minimize the description length. Thirdly, we make maximum likelihood estimates of the node probabilities. It is important to note that the union model underpinning our method assumes node independence on the training samples. Using a mixture of unions we condition this independence on the class. This conditional independence assumption, while often unrealistic, is at the basis of the naive Bayes model [6] which has proven to be robust and effective for a wide range of classification problems. We apply the resulting framework to the problem of learning a generative model for sets of shock trees.

2 Tree Edit-Distance

This section introduces the tree edit-distance framework, explains how it can be used to estimate node-correspondences, and gives an overview of the algorithm we use to approximate it.

The idea behind edit distance is that it is possible to identify a set of basic edit operations on nodes and edges of a structure, and to associate with these operations a cost. The edit-distance is found by searching for the sequence of edit operations that will make the two graphs isomorphic with one-another and which have minimum cost. The optimal sequence can be found using only structure reducing operations. This can be explained by the fact that we can transform node insertions in one tree into node removals in the other. This means that the edit distance between two trees is completely determined by the subset of residual nodes left after the optimal removal sequence, or, equivalently, by the nodes that are in correspondence. In particular the distance between two trees t and t' is:

$$D(t,t') = \sum_{i \notin \mathrm{Dom}(\mathcal{M})} r_i + \sum_{j \notin \mathrm{Im}(\mathcal{M})} r_j + \sum_{<i,j> \in \mathcal{M}} m_{ij}. \quad (1)$$

Here r_i and r_j are the costs of removing i and j respectively, $\mathcal{M}$ is the set of pairs of nodes from t and t' that match, $m_{i,j}$ is the cost of matching i to j, and $\text{Dom}(\mathcal{M})$ and $\text{Im}(\mathcal{M})$ are the domain and image of the relation $\mathcal{M}$. Letting $\mathcal{N}^t$ be the set of nodes of tree t, the distance can be rewritten as:

$$D(t,t') = \sum_{i \in \mathcal{N}^t} r_i + \sum_{j \in \mathcal{N}^{t'}} r_j + \sum_{<i,j> \in \mathcal{M}} (m_{ij} - r_i - r_j).$$

Hence the distance is minimized by the set of correspondences that maximizes the utility

$$\mathcal{U}(\mathcal{M}) = \sum_{<i,j> \in \mathcal{M}} (r_i + r_j - m_{ij}). \tag{2}$$

Let O be the set of matches that satisfy the constraints residing on the tree, then the node correspondence that minimize the edit distance is

$$M^* = \underset{M \in O}{\text{argmax}} \, \mathcal{U}(M). \tag{3}$$

Let us assume that we know the utility of the best match rooted at every descendent of nodes i and j of t and t' respectively. We aim to find the set of siblings with greatest total utility. To do this we make use of a derived structure: the association graph. The nodes of this structure are pairs drawn from the Cartesian product of the descendents of i and j and each pair correspond to a particular association between a node in one tree to a node in the other. That is, for each pair of nodes a and b, children of i and j, we have an association node (a, b). We connect two such associations if and only if there is no inconsistency between the two associations, that is the corresponding subtree is obtainable. Furthermore we assign to the association (a, b) a weight equal to the utility of the best match rooted at a and b. The maximum weight clique of this graph is the set of consistent siblings with maximum total utility, hence the set of children of i and j that guarantee the optimal isomorphism. Given a method to obtain a maximum weight clique, we can use it to obtain the solution to our isomorphism problem. We refer to [13] for heuristics for the weighted clique problem.

3 Edit-Intersection and Edit-Union

As shown in the previous section, the edit distance between two trees is completely determined by the set of nodes that do not get removed by edit operations, that is, in a sense, the *intersection* of the sets of nodes. We would like to extend the approach to more than two trees so that we can represent the structural variations present in a set of examples trees T. To this end we assume that there is an underlying "structure model",which determines a distribution of tree structures, and that each tree is a sample drawn from that distribution. In this way edit operations are linked to sampling error, and their cost to the error probability. We, then, need a way to estimate the underlying structural model. Our model has three components: a set of nodes, a partial order relation between these nodes and a sampling probability for each node. Sampling from this distribution means sampling nodes according to their probability and extracting the minimal descriptions of the order relation restricted to the sampled nodes.

Restricting the analysis to the structural part of the model, our interpretation is equivalent to having a generating hierarchical structure, namely the tree-union, and obtaining the various tree samples by applying structure-reducing edit operations to it. The sampling process applies to this structure the edit operation E_i with probability $1-\theta^i$, where θ^i is the sampling probability of node i. Hence, given the structure of the tree-union, the set of correspondences $\mathcal{C} : (\bigcup_t \mathcal{N}^t) \to \mathcal{N}$ from the nodes of the tree samples to the nodes of the union, and the sampling probability of each node $\Theta : \mathcal{N} \to [0, 1]$, we can express the probabilty of sampling a tree t as:

$$\Phi(t|\mathcal{C}, \Theta) = \prod_{i \in \mathcal{N}} E_i(t|\mathcal{C}, \theta^i), \tag{4}$$

where $E_i(t|\theta^i)$ is the sampling probability of node i and is defined as:

$$E_i(t|\theta^i) = \begin{cases} \theta^i & \text{if } \exists j \in \mathcal{N}^t, \mathcal{C}(j) = i \\ 1 - \theta^i & \text{otherwise.} \end{cases} \tag{5}$$

That is $E_i(t|\theta^i)$ is θ^i if tree t samples node i, $1 - \theta^i$ otherwise. The probability of a sample set $\mathcal{D}$ is, hence, $P(\mathcal{D}|\mathcal{C}, \Theta) = \prod_{t \in \mathcal{D}} \Phi(t|\mathcal{C}, \Theta)$.

4 Estimating the Structural Model

To estimate the structural part of the model we need to obtain the set of nodes of the model and correspondences from the nodes in the samples to the nodes of the model. With this correspondences, the nodes of the model span every node in the samples, and hence, the node set can be considered the "union" of the set of nodes of the samples. We refer to [14] for an analysis of the properties of the structure behind this "tree-union".

Formally, we would like to find the set of nodes $\mathcal{N}$, the sampling probability of each node $\Theta : \mathcal{N} \to [0, 1]$, and the set of correspondences $\mathcal{C} : (\bigcup_t \mathcal{N}^t) \to \mathcal{N}$ from the nodes of the tree samples to the nodes of the union. To this purpose, given a sample set $\mathcal{D}$, we could use a maximum likelihood estimator

$$\mathcal{C}^* = \operatorname*{argmax}_{\mathcal{C}} \left[P(\mathcal{D}|\mathcal{C}, \Theta) \right].$$

In many real-world problems the underlying structural model might not be single: when dealing with shock graphs, for example, samples drawn from a single shape-class might be related to a single structural model, but it is reasonable to assume that the structures of the skeletons of shapes that are perceptually very different are not generated by a single model. For this reason, when fitting a generative model of tree distribution, we want to allow for the samples to be drawn from multiple tree-union models . Namely we would like to fit a mixture of tree-unions.

The mixture model is parametrized by the number of mixtures k, their sampling probability α_i, and the various union models U_i. The Union models are defined by their correspondences $\mathcal{C}_i$ and sampling probabilities Θ_i. That is the probabbility of a tree t is

$$P(t|\alpha, \mathcal{C}, \mathbf{\Theta}) = \sum_{m=1}^{k} \alpha_m \Phi(t|\mathcal{C}_m, \Theta_m) \tag{6}$$

Here we use the Minimum Description Length (MDL) principle to describe the cost of the mixture model and the model representing it. Here the model is captured by the mixing proportions α_i, the union structures and the sampling probabilities θ_i^n for each union i and node n. To describe the data, we need, for each tree sample, to describe from which union model the sample was drawn. additionally, for each node in the union, we need to describe whether the node was present in the sample. Asymptotically the cost of describing the mixing components α_i and the component each one of n samples is drawn from is bo unded by $nI(\bar{\alpha})$, where $I(\bar{\alpha}) = -\sum_{m=1}^{k} \alpha_m \log(\alpha_m)$ is the entropy of the mixture distibution α. The cost of describing a the structure of a union mode can be considered proportional to the number of nodes, while the cost of describing the sampling probability θ_i^n of node n of union i and the existence of such node in each samples of $n\alpha_i$ samples generated by union i is asymptotically $n\alpha_i I(\theta_i^n)$. Here $I(\theta_i^n) = -theta_i^n \log(\theta_i^n) - (1-\theta_i^n)\log(1-\theta_i^n)$ is the entropy of the node sampling probability. Hence, given a model $\mathcal{H}$ with k unions, each with d_i nodes and probability α_i of being sampled, and node correspondences $\mathcal{C}$, the descriptor length is:

$$\mathrm{LL}(\mathcal{H}) = nI(\boldsymbol{\alpha}) + \sum_{m=1}^{k} \sum_{j=1}^{dm} \left[n\alpha_m I(\theta_m^j) + c \right]. \tag{7}$$

In this equation, c is the length per node of the description of the structure of the edit union, in our experiments set to 1, while the sample probability θ_m^j is estimated from the correspondences as the fraction of trees generated by union m that sample node j.

5 Minimizing the Descriptor Length

Finding the global minimum of the descriptor length is an intractable combinatorial problem, so we have to resort to some local search technique. A common approach to minimizing the descriptor length of a mixture model is to use the Expectation-Maximization algorithm. Unfortunately, the complexity of the maximization step on our union-tree model grows dramatically with the number of trees in the union. This means that, when we relax the membership variables for the EM algorithm, each union will effectively include every sample-tree.

We have chosen a different approach that would allow us to limit the complexity of the maximization. The approach we have used is as follows.

- Start with an overly-specific model: a structural model per sample-tree, where each model is equiprobable and structurally identical to the respective sample-tree, and each node has sample probability 1.
- Iteratively generalize the model merging two tree-unions. The mixture components to be merged are chosen in such a way that their merger maximally decreases the descriptor length.
- The algorithm stops when there are no merges left that would decrease the descriptor length.

Both the EM algorithm and our approach are descent methods in the sense that each iteration strictly decreases the objective function. The main difference is in the direction of descent. The update direction of the EM algorithm is closer to the gradient, while our approach is, basically, a coordinate descent method: at each iteration we move only along one of the coordinates in the parameter space. The greatest advantage of coordinate descent methods is the extremely low space and time complexity of each it eration step. Furthermore, in our particular case, we are guaranteed convergence to a local minimum with at most a linear number of merges.

5.1 Merging Two Unions

The main requirement of our minimization algorithm is that we can optimally merge two union models. That is that we can find the optimal structure that generates every tree-sample previously assigned to the two models.

From equation 7 we see that the descriptor length is linear with respect to $\mathrm{LL}_i(\mathcal{H}_i)$, the descriptor length of union i. That is $\mathrm{LL}(\mathcal{H}) = nI(\alpha) + \sum_{m=1}^{k} \mathrm{LL}_m(\mathcal{H}_m)$, where $\mathrm{LL}_m(\mathcal{H}_m) = \sum_{j=1}^{dm} \left[na_m I(\theta_m^j) + c\right]$. Here na_m is simply the number of samples assigned to component m and the remaining part of the equation is linear in the nodes.

Given two tree unions U_1 and U_2, we need to construct a union $\hat{U}$ whose structure respects the the hierarchical constraints present in U_1 and U_2 and that minimizes $\mathrm{LL}_m(\mathcal{H}_m)$. Since U_1 and U_2 already assign node correspondences from the samples to the model, we can simply find the correspondences from the nodes in U_1 and U_2 to $\hat{U}$ and transitively extending the correspondences from the samples to the final model $\hat{U}$.

Reduced to two structures, the correspondence problem is reduced to finding the set of nodes in U_1 and U_2 that are in common. Starting with the two structures, we merge the set of nodes that would reduce the descriptor length by the largest amount while still satisfying the hierarchical constraint. That is we merge nodes v and w of U_1 with node v' and w' of U_2 respectively if and only if $v \rightsquigarrow w \Leftrightarrow v' \rightsquigarrow w'$, where $a \rightsquigarrow b$ indicates that a is an ancestor of b. Assuming that the structures of U_1 and U_2 are trees, finding the set of nodes to be merged is equivalent to solving a tree-edit distance problem where the utility of a match is equivalent to the advantage in descriptor length we obtain through the merger. Let n_1 and n_2 be the number of samples in U_1 and U_2 respectively, and p_v and $p_{v'}$ the number of times nodes v and v' are sampled in U_1 and U_2 respectively, the sampling probability of the two nodes if they are not matched is $\theta v = \frac{p_v}{n_1+n_2}$ and $\theta v' = \frac{p'_v}{n_1+n_2}$ respectively, while the sampling probability of the node if the two are merged is $\theta vv' = \frac{p_v+p_{v'}}{n_1+n_2}$. Hence, the advantage in descriptor length we obtain through the merger is:

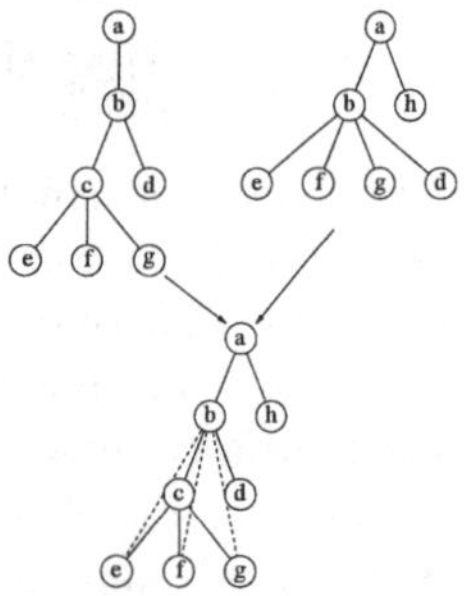

Fig. 1. The Union is defined by the common nodes.

$$\mathcal{U}(v, v') = (n_1 + n_2)\left[I(\theta v) + I(\theta v') - I(\theta vv')\right] + c. \quad (8)$$

From an edit distance point of view this is equivalent to saying that the cost of removing node v is $r_v = (n_1 + n_2)I(\theta v) + c$, while the cost of matching v to v' is $m_{vv'} = (n_1 + n_2)I(\theta vv') + c$.

At the end of the node merging operation we are left with a set of nodes that respects the original partial order defined by the various hierarchies in the sample-trees. The links of our model will be obtained from the partial order by constructing the minimal representation. When this representation is a tree, every sample tree can be obtained from this structure with a sequence of node removal operations.

6 Experimental Results

We evaluate the approach on the problem of shock tree matching. The idea behind the shock formulation of shape is to evolve the boundary of an object to a canonical skeletal form using the eikonal equation. The skeleton represents the singularities (shocks) in the curve evolution, where inward moving boundaries collide. Once the skeleton is to hand, the next step is to devise ways of using it to characterize the shape of the original boundary. Here we follow Zucker, Siddiqi, and others, by labeling points on the skeleton using so-called shock-classes [11]. According to this taxonomy of local differential structure, there are different classes associated with behavior of the radius of the maximal circle bitangent to the boundary. The so-called shocks distinguish between the cases where the local osculating circle has maximum radius, minimum radius, constant radius or a radius which is strictly increasing or decreasing. We abstract the skeletons as trees in which the level in the tree is determined by their time of formation [11]. The later the time of formation, and hence their proximity to the center of the shape, the higher the shock in the hierarchy.

In order to asses the quality of the method we compare clusters defined by the components of the mixture with those obtained with those obtained using the graph clustering method described in [13, 7]. In our experiments we use only structural information to characterize the shapes, while [7] enhance the representation with geometrical information and [13] presents results both with purely structural and enhanced representations.

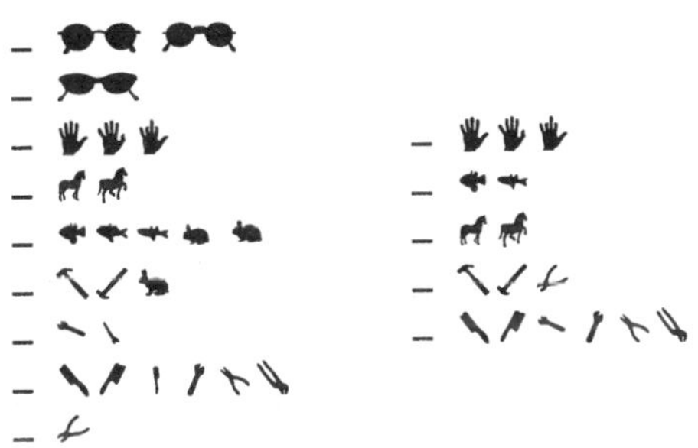

Fig. 2. Clusters extracted by the mixture of trees.

Figure 2 shows the clusters extracted on a database of 25 shapes and on a reduced database of 16 shapes. While there is some merger and leakage, the results outperform those obtained through pairwise clustering of the purely structural skeletal representations. Furthermore, it compares favorably with the pairwise clustering algorithm even where the latter is enhanced with geometrical information linked to the nodes of the trees.

6.1 Synthetic Data

To augment these real world experiments, we have fitted the model on synthetic data. The aim of the experiments is to characterize the sensitivity of the classification approach to class merger. To meet this goal we have randomly generated some prototype trees and, from each tree, we generated structurally perturbed copies. The trees are perturbed by randomly adding the required amount of nodes.

In our experiments we fit samples generated from an increasing number of prototypes and subject to an increasing amount of structural perturbation. We tested the classification performance on samples dawn from 2, 3, and 4 prototypes of 10 nodes each. The amount of noise is increased from an initial 10% of the total number of nodes to a maximum of 50%. Figure 3 plots the fraction of pairs of trees that are correctly classified as belonging to the same or different clusters as the noise is inc reased. From these experiment we can see that the approach works well with compact and well separated classes. The algorithm presents a sudden drop in performance when the structural variability of the class reaches 40% of the total number of nodes of the prototypes. Furthermore, when more prototypes are used, the distance between the clusters is smaller and, consequently the classes are harder to separate.

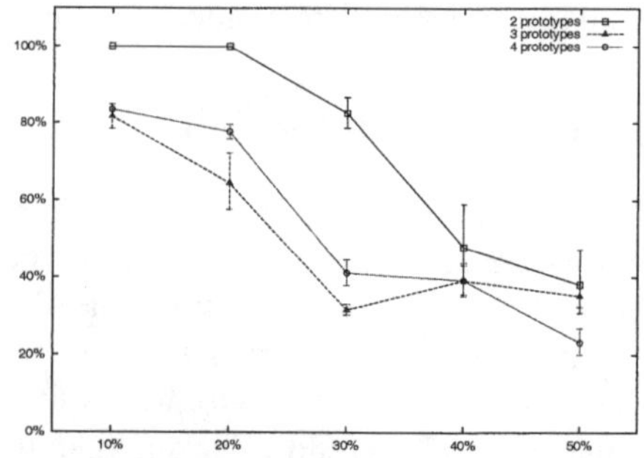

Fig. 3. Percentage of correct classifications under increasing structural noise.

7 Conclusions

This paper presented a novel algorithm to learn a generative model of tree structures. The approach uses the the Tree-Union as the structural archetype for every tree in the distribution and fits a mixture of these structural models using a minimal descriptor length formulation. In a set of experiments we apply the algorithm to the problem of unsupervised classification of shape using the shock-graphs. The results of these experiments are very encouraging, showing that the algorithm,although purely structural, compares favorably with pairwise classification approaches on attributed shock-graph. We are convinced that the results can be further improved by extending the model to take into account node-attributes.

References

1. N. Friedman and D. Koller, Being Bayesian about Network Structure, *Machine Learning*, to appear, 2002
2. L. Getoor et al., Learning Probabilistic models of relational structure, in *8th Int. Conf. on Machine Learning*, 2001.
3. D. Heckerman, D. Geiger, and D. M. Chickering, Learning Bayesian networks: the combination of knowledge and statistical data, *Machine Learning*, Vol. 20(3), pp. 197-243, 1995.
4. T. Heap and D. Hogg, Wormholes in shape space: tracking through discontinuous changes in shape, in *ICCV*, pp. 344-349, 1998.

5. X. Jiang, A. Muenger, and H. Bunke, Computing the generalized mean of a set of graphs, in *Workshop on Graph-based Representations, GbR'99*, pp 115-124, 2000.
6. P. Langley, W. Iba, and K. Thompson, An analysis of Bayesian classifiers, in *AAAI*, pp. 223-228, 1992
7. B. Luo, et al., Clustering shock trees, in *CVPR*, pp. 912-919, 2001.
8. M. Meilă. *Learning with Mixtures of Trees*. PhD thesis, MIT, 1999.
9. J. Riassen, Stochastic complexity and modeling, *Annals of Statistics*, Vol. 14, pp. 1080-1100, 1986.
10. S. Sclaroff and A. P. Pentland, Modal matching for correspondence and recognition, *PAMI*, Vol. 17, pp. 545-661, 1995.
11. K. Siddiqi et al., Shock graphs and shape matching, *Int. J. of Comp. Vision*, Vol. 35, 1999.
12. T. Sebastian, P. Klein, and B. Kimia, Recognition of shapes by editing shock graphs, in *ICCV*, Vol. I, pp. 755-762, 2001.
13. A. Torsello and E. R. Hancock, Efficiently computing weighted tree edit distance using relaxation labeling, in *EMMCVPR*, LNCS 2134, pp. 438-453, 2001.
14. A. Torsello and E. R. Hancock, Matching and embedding through edit-union of trees, in *ECCV*, LNCS 2352, pp. 822-836, 2002.

Writer Style from Oriented Edge Fragments

Marius Bulacu and Lambert Schomaker

AI Institute, Groningen University, The Netherlands
{bulacu,schomaker}@ai.rug.nl

Abstract. In this paper we evaluate the performance of edge-based directional probability distributions extracted from handwriting images as features in forensic writer identification in comparison to a number of non-angular features. We compare the performances of the features on lowercase and uppercase handwriting. In an effort to gain location-specific information, new versions of the features are computed separately on the top and bottom halves of text lines and then fused. The new features deliver significant improvements in performance. We report also on the results obtained by combining features using a voting scheme.

1 Introduction

This paper deals with the problem of writer identification from scanned images of handwriting. Image-based (off-line) writer identification has its principal application mainly confined to the forensic area. It is in the same class with other behavioral biometrics (on-line signature dynamics, voice) which, in contrast, enjoy much wider applicability together with the more powerful, but also more intrusive, physiological biometrics (face, hand geometry, fingerprint, iris pattern, retinal blood vessels).

An essential requirement for the forensic application area is that the writer identification system should have, not only verification capability (authentication in a one-to-one comparison), but also the vastly more demanding identification capability (one-to-many search in a large database with handwriting samples of known authorship and return of a likely list of candidates). As a rule of thumb, in forensic writer identification one strives for close to 100% recall of the correct writer in a hit list of 100 writers, computed on a database of more than 10^4 samples. This amount is based on the pragmatic consideration that a number of one hundred suspects is just about manageable in criminal investigation. Current systems are not powerful enough to attain this goal.

Writer identification is rooted in the older and broader automatic handwriting recognition domain. For automatic handwriting recognition, invariant representations are sought which are capable of eliminating variations between different handwritings in order to classify the shapes of characters and words robustly. The problem of writer identification, on the contrary, requires a specific enhancement of these variations, which are characteristic to a writer's hand. At the same time, such features should, ideally, be independent of the amount and semantic content of the written material. In the extreme case, a single word or

N. Petkov and M.A. Westenberg (Eds.): CAIP 2003, LNCS 2756, pp. 460–469, 2003.

the signature should suffice to identify the writer from his individual handwriting style.

Three categories of image-based features are usually integrated in operational forensic writer identification systems: 1) features extracted automatically on regions of interest from the script image, 2) features measured manually by forensic experts, and 3) character-based features capturing allograph-shape information. The complete process of forensic writer identification is never fully automatic, due to a wide range of scan-quality, scale and foreground/background separation problems.

We analyze in this paper only category 1: features automatically extractable from the handwriting image without any human intervention. It is implicitly assumed that a crisp foreground/background separation has already been realized in a pre-processing phase, yielding a white background with (near-) black ink.

In this paper we summarize the extraction methods for five features: three edge-based directional features, one run-length feature and one ink-distribution feature. In order to gain location-specific information, new versions of the features are computed separately on the top and bottom halves of text lines and then fused. We make a cross comparison of the performance of all features when computed on lowercase and uppercase handwritten text. We report also on results obtained using a voting scheme to combine the different features into a single final ranked hit list.

2 Data

We conducted our study using the *Firemaker* dataset [1]. A number of 250 Dutch subjects, predominantly students, were required to write 4 different A4 pages. On page 1 they were asked to copy a text of 5 paragraphs using normal handwriting style (i.e. predominantly lowercase with some capital letters at the beginning of sentences and names). On page 2 they were asked to copy another text of 2 paragraphs using only uppercase letters. Pages 3 and 4 contain forged- and normal-style handwriting and are not used here. For practical reasons, lineation guidelines were used on the response sheets using a special color "invisible" to the scanner. The added drawback is that vertical line distance can not be used as a discriminatory writer characteristic. However, we gain two important advantages that we will effectively use: automatic line segmentation can be performed reliably and handwriting is never severely skewed. In addition, the subjects were asked to leave an extra blank line between paragraphs making possible automatic paragraph extraction. Recording conditions were standardized: the same kind of paper, ballpoint pen and support were used for all subjects. As a consequence, this also implies that the variations in ink-trace thickness and blackness will be more due to writer differences than due to the recording conditions. The response sheets were scanned with an industrial quality scanner at 300 dpi, 8 bit/pixel, gray-scale.

Being recorded in optimal conditions, the *Firemaker* dataset contains very clean data. This is obviously an idealized situation compared to the conditions in practice. However, the dataset serves well our purpose of evaluating the usefulness for writer identification of different features encoding the ink-trace shape.

Table 1. Features used for writer identification and the used distance function $\Delta(\boldsymbol{u},\boldsymbol{v})$ between a query sample $\boldsymbol{u}$ and a database sample $\boldsymbol{v}$. All features are computed in two scenarios "entire-lines" and "split-lines" (see text for details)

	Feature	Explanation	Dimensions		$\Delta(\boldsymbol{u},\boldsymbol{v})$
			entire	split	
f1	$p(\phi)$	Edge-direction PDF	16	32	χ^2
f2	$p(\phi_1,\phi_2)$	Edge-hinge PDF	464	928	χ^2
f3	$p(rl)$	Horiz. run-length on background PDF	100	200	EUCLID
f4	$p(\phi_1,\phi_3)$	Horiz. edge-angle co-occurrence PDF	256	512	χ^2
f5	$p(brush)$	Ink-density PDF	225	450	χ^2

3 Feature Extraction

All the features used in the present analysis are probability density functions (PDFs) extracted empirically from the handwriting image. Our previous experiments confirmed that the use of PDFs is a sensitive and effective way of representing a writer's uniqueness [2]. Another important advantage of using PDFs is that they allows for homogeneous feature vectors for which excellent distance measures exist. Experiments have been performed with different distance measures: Hamming, Euclidean, Minkowski up to 5th order, Hausdorff, χ^2 and Bhattacharyya. Table 1 shows the features and the corresponding best-performing distance measures used in nearest-neighbor matching.

In the present study, all the features will be computed in two scenarios: either on the entire text lines or separately on the top-halves and the bottom halves of all the text lines. In the first scenario, features are computed on the image without any special provisions. For the second scenario, all text lines are first segmented using the minima of the smoothed horizontal projection. Afterwards, the maxima are used to split horizontally every individual text line into two halves (fig. 1b). All features are then computed separately for the top-halves and the bottom-halves and the resulting two vectors are concatenated into a single final feature vector. Clearly the "split-line" features have double dimensionality compared to their "entire-line" counterparts.

While feature histograms are accumulated over the whole image providing for a very robust probability distribution estimation, they suffer the drawback that all position information is lost. Line splitting is therefore performed in an effort to localize more our features and gain back some position information together also with some writer specificity. What we must pay is the sizeable increase in feature dimensionality.

We describe further the extraction methods for the five considered features.

3.1 Edge-Direction Distribution (f1)

It has long been known from on-line handwriting research [3] that the distribution of directions in handwritten traces, as a polar plot, yields useful information for writer identification or coarse writing-style classification [4].

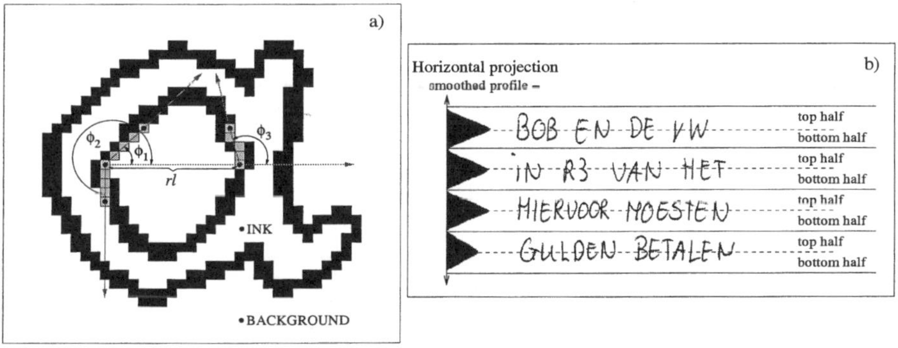

Fig. 1. a) Feature extraction on letter "a", b) Line segmentation and splitting

We recently developed an off-line and edge-based version of the directional distribution. Computation of this feature starts with conventional edge detection: convolution with two orthogonal differential kernels (Sobel), followed by thresholding. This procedure generates a binary image in which only the edge pixels are "on". We then consider each edge pixel in the middle of a square neighborhood and we check, using the logical AND operator, in all directions emerging from the central pixel and ending on the periphery of the neighborhood for the presence of an entire edge fragment (fig. 1a). All the verified instances are counted into a histogram that is normalized to a probability distribution $p(\phi)$ which gives the probability of finding in the image an edge fragment oriented at the angle ϕ measured from the horizontal. In order to avoid redundancy, the algorithm only checks the upper two quadrants in the neighborhood. The orientation is quantized in n directions, n being the number of bins in the histogram and the dimensionality of the feature vector (see [2] for a more detailed description of the method). A number $n = 16$ directions performed best and will be used in the sequel.

As can be seen in fig. 2, the predominant direction in $p(\phi)$ corresponds, as expected, to the slant of writing. It is interesting to note that there is an asymmetry between the directional diagrams for the top halves and the bottom halves of the text lines. This observation is precisely the underpinning of our approach to split the lines in an attempt to recover this writer specific positional information. There is a correlation also with the known fact from on-line handwriting research that upward strokes are slightly more slanted than the downward strokes because they contain also the horizontal progression motion [3]. Even if idealized, the example shown can provide an idea about the "within-writer" variability and "between-writer" variability in the feature space.

3.2 Edge-Hinge Distribution (f2)

In order to capture the curvature of the ink trace, which is very discriminatory between different writers, we designed a novel feature using local angles

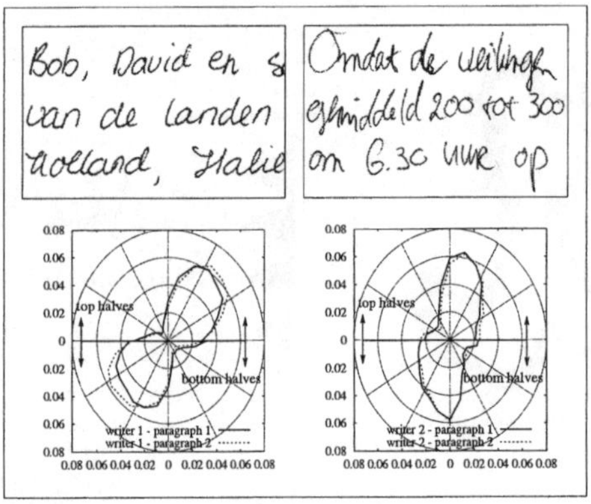

Fig. 2. Examples of lowercase handwriting from two different subjects. We superposed the polar diagrams of the "split-line" direction distribution $p(\phi)$ extracted from the two lowercase handwriting samples for each of the two subjects

along the edges. Computation of this feature is similar to the one previously described, but it has added complexity. The central idea is to consider in the neighborhood, not one, but two edge fragments emerging from the central pixel and, subsequently, compute the joint probability distribution of the orientations of the two edge fragments. All instances found in the image are counted and the final normalized histogram gives the joint probability distribution $p(\phi_1, \phi_2)$ quantifying the chance of finding in the image two "hinged" edge fragments oriented at angles ϕ_1 and ϕ_2 respectively. Orientation is quantized in $2n$ directions for every leg of the "edge-hinge". From the total number of combinations of two angles $(4n^2)$ we will consider only non-redundant ones $(\phi_2 > \phi_1)$ and we will also eliminate the cases when the ending pixels have a common side (see [2] for a more detailed description of the method). The final number of combinations is $C_{2n}^2 - n = n(2n-3)$. For $n = 16$, the edge-hinge feature vector will have 464 dimensions.

3.3 Run-Length Distributions (f3)

Run-lengths have long been used for writer identification. They are determined on the binarized image taking into consideration either the black pixels (the ink) or, more beneficially, the white pixels (the background). There are two basic scanning methods: horizontal along the rows of the image and vertical along the columns of the image. Similar to the edge-based directional features presented above, the histogram of run-lengths is normalized and interpreted as a probability distribution. The run-lengths on white are obviously more informative about the characteristics of handwriting as they capture the regions enclosed inside the letters and also the empty spaces between letters and words. Vertical run-lengths on black are more informative than the horizontal run-lengths on black [2] as the vertical component of handwriting strokes carries more information than the

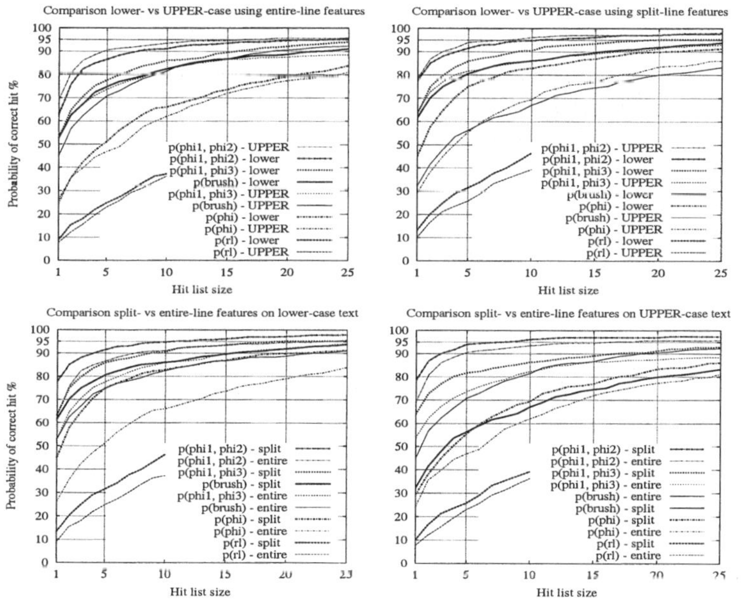

Fig. 3. Performance curves (features are ordered with the most effective at the top)

horizontal one [3]. Our particular implementation considers only run-lengths of up to 100 pixels (comparable to the height of a written line). This feature is not size invariant, however, size normalization could be performed by hand prior to feature extraction. We will consider here only the horizontal run-lengths on white to be able to directly compute this feature both in the "entire-line" and "split-line" scenarios.

3.4 Horizontal Co-occurrence of Edge Angles (f4)

This new feature that we recently developed derives naturally from the previous two. It is a variant of the edge-hinge feature, in that the combination of edge-angles is computed at the ends of run-lengths on white. The joint probability distribution $p(\phi_1, \phi_3)$ of the two edge-angles occurring at both ends of a run-length on white captures longer range correlations between edge-angles and gives a measure of the roundness of the written characters. This feature has n^2 dimensions, namely 256 in our implementation.

3.5 Brush Function: Ink Density PDF (f5)

It is known that axial pen force ('pressure') is a highly informative signal in on-line writer identification [5]. Force variations will be reflected in saturation and width of the ink trace. Additionally, in ink traces of ballpoint pens, there exist lift-off and landing shapes in the form of blobs or tapering [6], which are due to ink-depositing processes. In order to capture the statistics of this process, we designed another new feature. A convolution window of 15x15 pixels was used, only accumulating the local image if the current region obeys the following constraints: a supraliminal ink intensity in the center of the window, co-occurring with a long run of white pixels along minimally 50% of window perimeter and an ink run of at least 5% of window perimeter. After scanning all the image, the accumulator window is normalized, yielding a PDF describing ink distribution. This feature is clearly not size invariant (the window of 15^2 pixels was chosen for capturing the 6-7 pixel-wide ink traces usual in our images), but we use it because the recording conditions have been standardized for all subjects in our dataset.

The edge-based features (f1, f2, f4) that we propose here for writer identification are general texture descriptors and, as such, they have wider applicability (e.g., we use then for the analysis of machine-print as well). However, a more detailed discussion can not be encompassed in the framework of the present paper.

4 Results

We compare the performance of our new "split-line" versions of the features with their former "entire-line" versions. We are also interested to compare the performance of all the features when computed on lowercase as opposed to uppercase handwriting. In order to perform all these comparisons, handwriting samples have been extracted from the database. Two paragraphs have been extracted from page 1 obtaining in this way two separate samples in lowercase for every subject. Similarly, from page 2 we extracted separately the two paragraphs in uppercase handwriting. Special care has been taken to have roughly the same amount of text in lowercase and uppercase (approx. 100 characters in the first paragraphs and approx. 150 characters in the second ones). Using nearest-neighbor matching in a leave-one-out strategy, the writer identification performance has been evaluated for lowercase and uppercase handwriting using both the "entire-line" and the "split-line" versions of our PDF features. The numerical results for the four possible combinations are given in Table 2.

4.1 Comparison Lower- vs Upper-Case and Entire- vs Split-Line

The performance curves have been drawn in fig. 3 to allow a quick visual cross-comparison. There are important differences in performance for the different features. The edge-hinge feature (f2) surpasses all the other features and, quite remarkably, it performs better on uppercase than on lowercase, opposite to the situation for all the other features. This may result from the fact that the "hinge" can capture the sharp angularities present in uppercase letters. Another important observation is that the differences in feature performance between lowercase and uppercase are not as large as one might intuitively expect thinking that it is always easier to identify the author of lowercase rather than uppercase handwriting. In mixed searches (e.g. lowercase query sample / uppercase dataset) writer

Table 2. Writer identification accuracy (in percentages) on the Firemaker data set (250 writers). One selected sample is matched against the remaining 499 samples that contain only one target sample (the pair) and 498 distractors. In the cells, performance figures for lowercase are in the upper-left corner and for uppercase in the lower-right (with boldface characters). 95% confidence limits: ±4%

Hit list size	f1: $p(\phi)$		f2: $p(\phi_1, \phi_2)$		f3: $p(rl)$		f4: $p(\phi_1, \phi_3)$		f5: $p(brush)$	
	entire	split	entire	split	entire	split	entire	split	entire	split
1	26 **24**	45 **29**	63 **69**	78 **79**	9 **8**	13 **10**	53 **54**	64 **64**	53 **45**	62 **32**
2	35 **36**	58 **38**	76 **81**	85 **87**	15 **12**	20 **17**	65 **62**	75 **73**	63 **57**	70 **42**
3	42 **40**	65 **45**	83 **86**	88 **90**	18 **16**	25 **21**	71 **67**	80 **77**	67 **62**	75 **48**
4	47 **44**	71 **50**	85 **89**	90 **92**	22 **19**	29 **24**	75 **71**	84 **80**	72 **67**	78 **54**
5	51 **47**	75 **55**	87 **91**	92 **94**	25 **23**	32 **26**	78 **74**	86 **82**	75 **71**	81 **56**
10	66 **62**	83 **69**	91 **94**	95 **96**	37 **36**	46 **39**	86 **82**	91 **86**	83 **82**	86 **67**

identification is very low. The features used encode the shape of handwriting and, naturally, they are sensitive to major style variations.

The split-line features perform significantly better than their entire-line counterparts, fully justifying the extra cost in terms of dimensionality and computation. The exception is the brush feature (f5) on uppercase and this is due to the fact that there are not sufficient image sampling points on the bottom half of uppercase that comply with the imposed constraints and the PDF estimate is not sufficiently reliable. We emphasize that regaining location specific information, especially for the edge-based orientation PDF features, is a promising way of improving writer identification accuracy.

4.2 Voting Feature Combination

It is important to note that no single feature will be powerful enough for the performance target defined by the forensic application, necessitating the use of classifier-combination schemes. In the present study we explored the Borda count method that considers every feature as a voter and then computes an average rank for each candidate over all voters. Different ranked voting schemes have been tested: min, plurality, majority, median, average, max (e.g. using the median instead of the average). The only voting method that brought some improvement in performance over the top performing feature (f2) was the "min" method (results in Table 3). In this method, the decision of the voter (feature) giving the lowest rank is considered as the final decision.

In the current context, because the individual features have widely different performance, all the other voting schemes lead to some average performance higher than that of the weakest feature, but certainly lower than that of the strongest feature. An additional drawback is that the considered features are not totally orthogonal. Results reported elsewhere [7] confirm that another effective method of combining heterogeneous features is to consider a sequential scheme

Table 3. Writer identification accuracy (in percentages) after feature combination using the Borda "min" voting method. Please refer to Table 2 for more details

Hit list size	1	2	3	4	5	10
entire	67 **72**	77 **82**	83 **87**	86 **89**	87 **91**	91 **94**
split	80 **79**	86 **87**	89 **91**	90 **92**	92 **94**	95 **96**

in which the stronger features vote at later stages against the accumulated votes from the weaker features.

The improvement in performance obtained with Borda "min" voting method is marginal: 0-4% for top 1 and vanishing for longer list sizes. It is however worthwhile mentioning that eliminating some of the weaker features from voting results nevertheless in slight performance drops.

5 Conclusions

We must emphasize that the method for writer identification presented here is automatic and sparse-parametric (no learning takes place) and this approach possesses major advantages in forensic applications given the appreciable size and time-variant content of the sample databases. Nevertheless, our future research interest will include also parameter-greedy methods (e.g. multi-layer perceptron or support vector machine) as more data necessary to train the system becomes available. Although results are far from the requirements in the forensic application domain, it quite evident that global features extracted from the handwriting image will never suffice in writer identification. Detailed character shape knowledge is needed as well. In this respect, it is important to note also the recent advances [8] that have been made at the detailed allographic level, when character segmentation is performed by hand. Only a combination of features at trace-level, allograph-level and text-line-level [9] will yield adequate results.

References

1. Schomaker, L., Vuurpijl, L.: Forensic writer identification [internal report for the Netherlands Forensic Institute]. Technical report, Nijmegen: NICI (2000)
2. Bulacu, M., Schomaker, L., Vuurpijl, L.: Writer identification using edge-based directional features. In: Proc. of ICDAR 2003 [accepted]. (2003)
3. Maarse, F., Thomassen, A.: Produced and perceived writing slant: differences between up and down strokes. Acta Psychologica **54** (1983) 131–147
4. Crettez, J.P.: A set of handwriting families: style recognition. In: Proc. of ICDAR 1995, Montreal, IEEE Computer Society (1995) 489–494
5. Schomaker, L.R.B., Plamondon, R.: The Relation between Pen Force and Pen-Point Kinematics in Handwriting. Biological Cybernetics **63** (1990) 277–289

6. Doermann, D., Rosenfeld, A.: Recovery of temporal information from static images of handwriting. In: Proc. of CVPR92. (1992) 162–168
7. Schomaker, L., Bulacu, M., van Erp, M.: Sparse-parametric writer identification using heterogeneous feature groups. In: Proc. of ICIP 2003 [accepted]. (2003)
8. Srihari, S., Cha, S., Arora, H., Lee, S.: Individuality of handwriting. Journal of Forensic Sciences **47** (2002) 1–17
9. Marti, U.V., Messerli, R., Bunke, H.: Writer identification using text line based features. In: Proc. of ICDAR'01, Seattle, IEEE Computer Society (2001) 101–105

Font Classification Using NMF

Chang Woo Lee[1], Hyun Kang[1], Keechul Jung[2], and Hang Joon Kim[1]

[1] Dept. of Computer Engineering, Kyungpook National Univ., Daegu, Korea
{cwlee,hkang,hjkim}@ailab.knu.ac.kr
[2] School of Media, College of Information Science, Soongsil University, Seoul, Korea
kcjung@ssu.ac.kr

Abstract. In this paper, we propose a font classification method in scanned documents using non-negative matrix factorization (NMF). Using NMF, we automatically extract spatially local features enough to classify each font. The appropriateness of the features to classify a specific font is shown in the experimental results. The proposed method is expected to increase the performance of optical character recognition (OCR), document indexing and retrieval systems if such systems use a font classifier as a preprocessor.

1 Introduction

In many published OCR techniques, there is much room to improve their performance in recognition accuracy and processing time if font classification is preceded or taken into account. Although font classification in document image analysis and recognition area is fundamental, only a few adapt font classification techniques. Font classification, for example, can reduce the burden that various fonts should be considered to recognize characters so that it leads to essentially single-font character recognition [1].

Recently, many research achievements for font classification have been reported [2-5]. Among them, to identify the predominant font and the frequent function words, Khoubyari and Hull [2] proposed an algorithm in which clusters of word images are generated from an input document and matched to a database of function words derived from fonts and document images. In the method used by Shi and Pavlidis [3], they combined font recognition results and contextual information to enhance the accuracy of text recognition. For font information in the paper, two sources, namely the global page properties such as histogram of word length and stroke slopes, and the graph matching result of recognized short words are extracted. To increase the accuracy of text recognition, Shi and Pavlidis focused not on the font types such as Arial, Courier, Gothic, etc., but on font families such as *seriffed* versus *sans-serif* fonts and *upright* versus *slanted* fonts. In the method used by Zramdini and Ingold [4], a statistical approach based on global typographical features is used to identify the typeface, weight, slope, and size of the text from an image block without any knowledge of the content of that text. Zramdini and Ingold define the fonts by using many characteristics that are manually defined. Zhu *et al.* [5] presented a texture-analysis-based approach toward font recognition that is adapted without involving detailed local feature analysis. This method is dissimilar to the existing methods based on local typographi-

N. Petkov and M.A. Westenberg (Eds.): CAIP 2003, LNCS 2756, pp. 470–477, 2003.

cal features that often require connected components analysis. Zhu *et al.* performed their experiments not on optically scanned documents, but on noise-free font images.

In this paper, we propose a font classification method using an NMF technique that decomposes a given matrix into the basis set and their encodings while satisfying its non-negativity constraints, thus representing the original data set as the low-dimensional feature set in a projection space. In Fig. 1, the flow diagram of the proposed font classifier is shown, in which the trained encodings $H_{r\times m}$ are compared with a newly projected encoding $H_{r\times 1}$ using the factorized basis W to classify various fonts. In other word, a newly projected vector is classified using Euclidian distance as one that is nearest from the trained encodings. We refer it as the nearest neighbor classifier (NNC). In this manner, we notice that NMF is able to extract the local features from a set of font images automatically and use the features indicating characteristics to classify fonts.

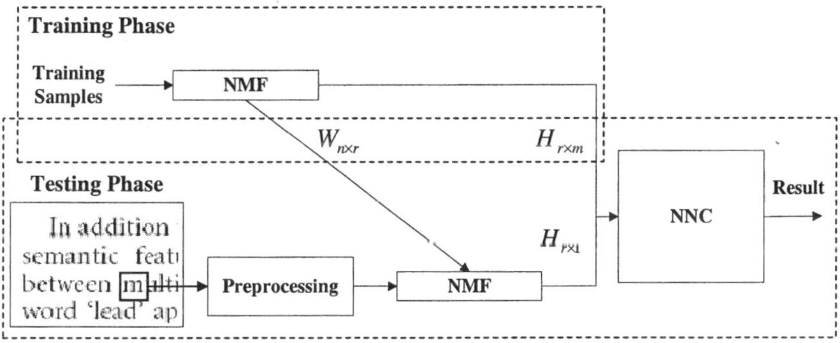

Fig. 1. The flow diagram of the proposed font classifier.

2 Non-negative Matrix Factorization

The NMF algorithm was devised by Lee and Seung [6], and is a method to find a set of basis and their encodings to represent a specific class of objects using non-negativity constraints. Given an original training set, $V_{n\times m}$, in which a column is an n-dimensional non-negative vector of the m vectors, NMF decomposes V into the factorized basis $W_{n\times r}$ and encodings $H_{r\times m}$ in order to approximate the original matrix. Then the NMF algorithm constructs approximate factorizations of the form, Eq. (1).

$$V_{i\mu} \approx (WH)_{i\mu} = \sum_{a=1}^{r} W_{ia} H_{a\mu}, \qquad (1)$$

where the r columns of W are called the basis set, each column of H is called an encoding, and the rank r of the factorization is generally chosen by $(n+m)r < nm$.

To find an approximate factorization as Eq. (1), cost function that quantifies the quality of the approximation should be defined. This cost function is then related to the likelihood of generating the images in V from the basis W and encodings H. The NMF starts by assuming that V is drawn from a Poisson distribution with mean WH -

it is true in real [7]. The distribution therefore takes the form as Eq. (3).. Taking the logarithm of both sides of Eq. (3) is resulted in Eq. (4), in which the term log(V!) can be dropped, because it is a function of V only, and makes no difference when optimizing with respect to W and H. Thus taking the logarithm turns the product into the sum as Eq. (4).

$$F=\sum_{i=1}^{n}\sum_{\mu=1}^{m}V_{i\mu}\log(WH)_{i\mu}-(WH)_{i\mu}\,. \tag{2}$$

$$P(V\mid WH)=\exp(-WH)\frac{(WH)^{V}}{V!}\,. \tag{3}$$

$$\log P(V\mid WH)=V\log(WH)-WH-\log V!\,. \tag{4}$$

It is an iterative algorithm with multiplicative update rules that can be regarded as a special variant of gradient-descent algorithms [8]. The algorithm iteratively updates W and H by multiplicative rules:

$$H_{a\mu}\leftarrow H_{a\mu}\frac{(W^{T}V)_{a\mu}}{(W^{T}WH)_{a\mu}},\ \text{and}\ W_{ia}\leftarrow W_{ia}\frac{(VH^{T})_{ia}}{(WHH^{T})_{ia}},$$
$$W_{ia}\leftarrow W_{ia}\frac{W_{ia}}{\sum_{j}W_{ja}}\,. \tag{5}$$

These update rules maximize the objective function in Eq. (2) updating the basis W and its encodings H using Eq. (5). Now, we have to encode test vector $\boldsymbol{v}$ using the previously trained basis $W_{n\times r}$. By updating only the H matrix that is randomly initialized, we project a new image vector $\boldsymbol{v}$ into the NMF projected space. Therefore an input image is reconstructed using Eq. (6) as shown in Fig. 2. In this way we calculate a new encoding $\boldsymbol{h}_{r\times 1}$ corresponding to an input image, while the trained basis set W is used as a constant reference.

$$v_{n\times 1}\approx(W_{n\times r})h_{r\times 1}=\sum_{a=1}^{r}\sum_{i=1}^{n}W_{ia}h_{a1} \tag{6}$$

3 Font Classifier

The characteristics of each font come from the parts of each font character rather than from the holistic textures. Since NMF technique allows only additive or multiplicative updates using non-negativity constraints, each basis represents more local characteristics of each font. Thus, the basis images provide a more sparse representation instead of the global one provided by Principal Component Analysis (PCA) or Vector Quantization (VQ). Moreover, a sparsely distributed font image encoding is produced in the projected space as shown in Fig. 2.

New image encodings of unknown test fonts obtained from scanned documents are compared with those of a set of the template font encodings. The basis images factorized from training samples are used for projecting a test sample to the NMF projected space, while the encodings compose the template encodings for classifying each font. NNC classifies a test font image as one of the font classes, K, if the following Eq. (4) is satisfied.

$$K = \arg\min_{k} dist(H_k, h), \qquad (7)$$

where $dist(\bullet)$, H_k, and $\boldsymbol{h}$ represent the Euclidean distance measure, the template encodings, and an encoding of a test font image, respectively.

In Fig. 2, 4992 character images of different fonts are applied for establishing the basis and encodings. Each font image consists of $n = 28 \times 28$ pixels, and constitutes an 784×4992 matrix V in which the intensities of every pixels are normalized to the range [0, 1]. An original image is approximately represented by a linear combination of basis images. The coefficients of the linear combination are shown as the one of encodings shown with a bold boundary.

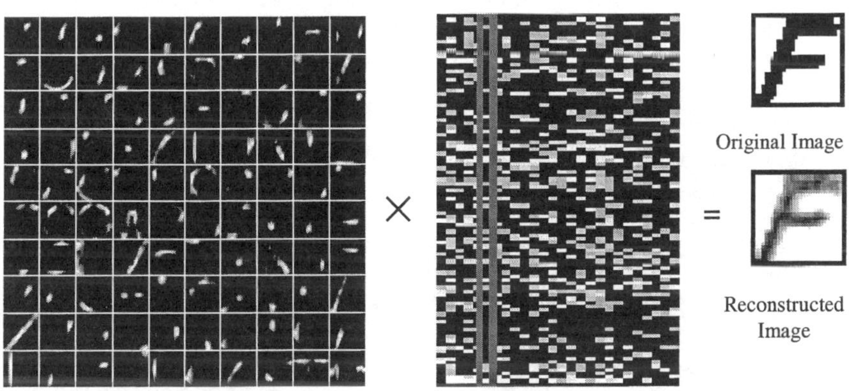

Fig. 2. Font image reconstruction using NMF with the trained basis and encodings.

4 Experimental Results

Six frequently used English fonts (Courier New (CN), Comic Sans MS (CS), Impact (IM), MS Gothic (MG), Microsoft Sans Serif (MS), and Times New Roman (TR)) combined with four styles (regular, bold, italic, and bold italic) and two kinds of letters (small and capital) are trained and tested. This means that we classify an input font image as one of a total of 48 classes (6 fonts × 4 styles × 2 kinds of letters).

The training samples are obtained from both noise-free font images and the document images scanned as a binary image at the resolution 100, 200, and 300 dpi, respectively, in which the number of font images is 4992 and the font size is 14. All of the training samples are normalized as 28 × 28 pixels and then factorized into the basis and encodings. The encodings are used as the template encodings in the testing phase.

The test data are obtained from 144 (48 classes × 3 different resolution levels) document images. The total number of test images is 190830 character images included in the document images, in other words, CN 10368 × 3 characters, CS 8544 × 3 characters, IM 11586 × 3 characters, MG 10416 × 3 characters, MS 11464 × 3 characters, TR 11232 × 3 characters are included. This means a document per class exists. The sizes of the document images range from 651 × 888 to 655 × 920 at the resolution 100 dpi, from 1311 × 1737 to 1287 × 1904 at the resolution 200 dpi, from 1960 × 2642 to 1960 × 2809 at the resolution 300 dpi. To obtain test samples from the documents containing machine-printed characters, we first detect the valleys between text lines using horizontal projection profiles, thus segment text lines from a document image. Second, for each text line vertical projection profiles are used to separate each character. Third, boundaries of all components are adjusted, and the size of each component should be larger than a predefined box size. Finally, the size of each component is normalized to the size 28 × 28 as the same size of the training samples. During the experiments, we assume that overall characters are well separated from each other. This assumption is easily solved because of the merits of the previous works such as [9-12]. But we do not deal with this problem in this paper. Fig. 3 (a) shows training samples and (b) does test samples which are generated by scanning the document images at the resolutions of 100, 200, and 300 dpi.

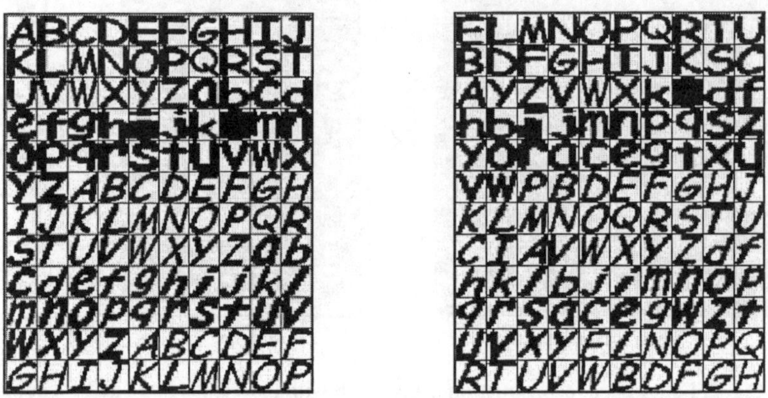

(a) (b)

Fig. 3. Examples of training and test samples; (a) a part of training samples (b) a part of test samples.

To verify that the encodings are proper features for font classification, we illustrate the averages of encodings for each font in Fig. 4. This figure reveals that the basis used to represent each font and its coefficients are sufficiently different to distinguish each font. In Fig. 4, Y axis represents the average encoding of encodings for six fonts and X axis represents the rank used to factorize training samples. As shown in Fig. 4, for example, CN and TR fonts hardly use the 23rd base while Impact font uses all bases with relatively high-valued coefficients.

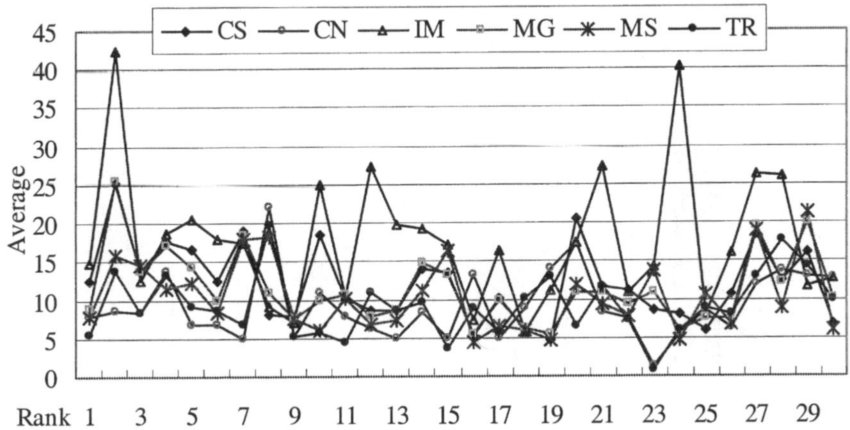

Fig. 4. Average encodings of encodings for six fonts.

Fig. 5 visualizes the difference between the encoding of an input font image and one of the template encodings that has minimum distance. Once an input font image is projected to the NMF projected space, a newly projected vector is compared with the template encodings. In Fig. 5, '•' stands for the one of templates that has the minimum distance from the encoding of a test sample represented by '•'. In this illustration, 100 ranks ($r = 100$) are used to factorize training samples.

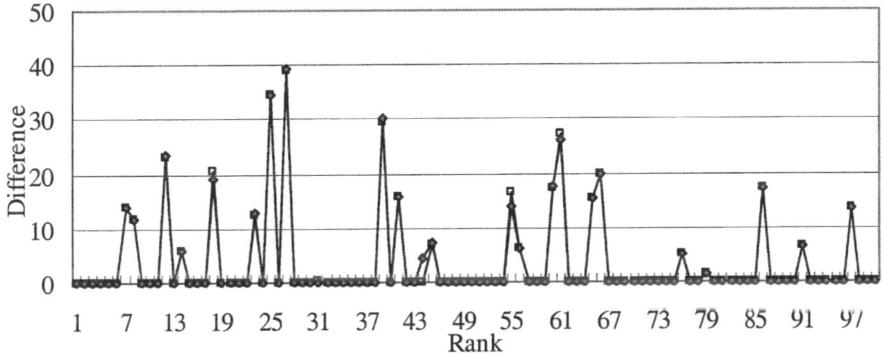

Fig. 5. Example of classification result using the Euclidean distance for Courier capital 'A'.

Fig. 6 shows the classification rates for the scanned documents at different resolution levels in which 30, 50, 70, and 100 ranks are used to factorize the training pattern matrix, respectively. As shown in Fig. 6, the 75 ranks are suitable to factorize a given font matrix of English alphabets. The overall classification rate was 99.65%.

5 Conclusions

In this paper, we presented a new approach for the multi-font classification using NMF technique that is capable of learning a part-based representation of images. The

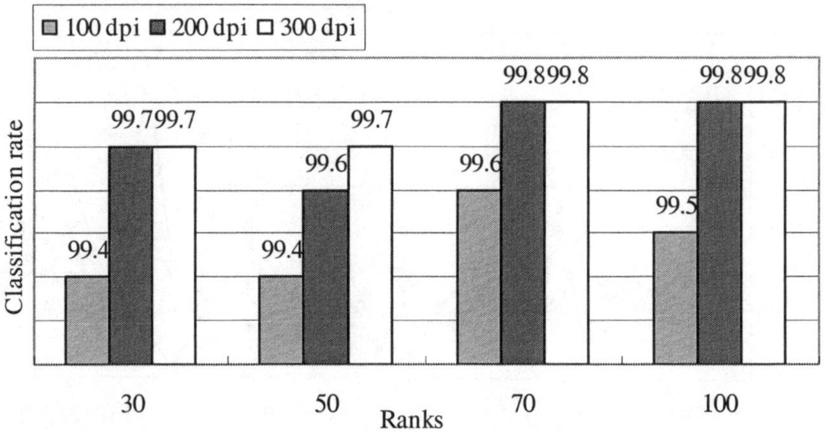

Fig. 6. Font classification rates (percent) according to the different resolutions and different ranks.

proposed font classification method is based on the understanding that the characteristics of fonts are determined by spatially local parts of each font. The appropriateness for the features to classify a specific font was shown in the experimental results. The experimental results were obtained from the character level tests. But if word- or block-level test is performed, the better result might be accomplished. The proposed method is expected to increase the performance of OCR systems, document indexing and retrieval system if such systems use a font classifier as a preprocessor. If the number of template encodings is increased, alternatives for the recognition include neural networks, statistical methods, or clustering algorithms.

Acknowledgement

This work was supported by the Soongsil University Research Fund.

References

1. G. Nagy, 2000, "Twenty Years of Document Image Analysis in PAMI," IEEE Trans. Pattern Analysis and Machine Intelligence,Vol. 22, no. 1, pp. 38-62.
2. S. Khoubyari and J. J.Hull, 1996. Font and function word identification in document recognition, Computer Vision and Image Understanding, Vol. 63, no. 1, pp. 66-74.
3. H. Shi and T. Pavlidis, 1997. Font Recognition and Contextual Processing for More Accurate Text Recognition, ICDAR'97, pp. 39-44, Ulm, Germany, Aug.
4. A. Zramdini and R. Ingold, 1998. Optical Font Recognition Using Typographical Features, IEEE Trans. Pattern Anal. Machine Intell., Vol. 20, no. 8, pp.877-882.
5. Y. Zhu, T. Tan, and Y. Wang, 2001, Font Recognition Based on Global Texture Analysis, Trans. On Pattern Analysis and Machine Intelligence, Vol. 23, no. 10, pp. 1192-1200.
6. D.D Lee, H.S.Seung, 1999. Learning the Parts of Objects by Non-Negative Matrix Factorization. Nature 401, 788-791.
7. H.S.Seung, 1999. Derivation of the objective function (Eq.2), http://jounalclub.mit.edu.

8. D.D.Lee, H.S.Seung, 2001. Algorithms for non-negative matrix factorization. In Advances in Neural Information Processing Systems, volume 13, pages 556–562.
9. J. H. Bae, K. Jung, J. W. Kim, and H. J. Kim, 1998, Segmentation of Touching Characters Using an MLP, Pattern Recognition Letters, Vol.19, no. 8, pp.701-709.
10. K. Jung, 2001. Neural network-based Text Location in Color Images, Pattern Recognition Letters, Vol. 22, No. 14, pp 1503-1515.
11. Veena Bansal and R. M. K. Sinha, 2002, Segmentation of touching and fused Devanagari characters, Pattern Recognition, Vol. 35, no. 4, pp. 875-893.
12. Yi Lu, 1995, Machine printed character segmentation--an overview, Pattern Recognition, Vol. 28, no. 1, pp. 67-80.

Arabic Character Recognition Using Structural Shape Decomposition

Abdullah Al Shaher and Edwin R. Hancock

Department of Computer Science
University of York,York YO1 5DD, UK
{abdullah,erh}@minster.cs.york.ac.uk

Abstract. This paper presents a statistical framework for recognising 2D shapes which are represented as an arrangement of curves or strokes. The approach is a hierarchical one which mixes geometric and symbolic information in a three-layer architecture. Each curve primitive is represented using a point-distribution model which describes how its shape varies over a set of training data. We assign stroke labels to the primitives and these indicate to which class they belong. Shapes are decomposed into an arrangement of primitives and the global shape representation has two components. The first of these is a second point distribution model that is used to represent the geometric arrangement of the curve centre-points. The second component is a string of stroke labels that represents the symbolic arrangement of strokes. Hence each shape can be represented by a set of centre-point deformation parameters and a dictionary of permissible stroke label configurations. The hierarchy is a two-level architecture in which the curve models reside at the nonterminal lower level of the tree. The top level represents the curve arrangements allowed by the dictionary of permissible stroke combinations. The aim in recognition is to minimise the cross entropy between the probability distributions for geometric alignment errors and curve label errors. We show how the stroke parameters, shape-alignment parameters and stroke labels may be recovered by applying the expectation maximization EM algorithm to the utility measure. We apply the resulting shape-recognition method to Arabic character recognition.

Keywords: point distribution models, expectation maximization algorithm, discrete relaxation, hierarchical mixture of experts, Arabic scripts

1 Introduction

The analysis and recognition of curved shapes has attracted considerable attention in the computer vision literature. Current work is nicely exemplified by point distribution models [1] and shape-contexts [2]. However, both of these methods are based on global shape-descriptors. This is potentially a limitation since a new model must be acquired for each class of shape and this is an inefficient process. An alternative and potentially more flexible route is to use a structural approach to the problem, in which shapes are decomposed into arrangements of

N. Petkov and M.A. Westenberg (Eds.): CAIP 2003, LNCS 2756, pp. 478–486, 2003.

primitives. This idea was central to the work of Marr [3]. Shape learning may then be decomposed into a two-stage process. The first stage is to acquire a models of the variability is the distinct primitives. The second stage is to learn the arrangements of the primitives corresponding to different shape classes.

Although this structural approach has found widespread use in the character recognition community, it has not proved popular in the computer vision domain. The reason for this is that the segmentation of shapes into stable primitives has proved to be an elusive problem. Hence, there is a considerable literature on curve polygonalisation, segmentation and grouping. However, one of the reasons that the structural approach has proved fragile is that it has been approached using geometric rather than statistical methods. Hence, the models learned and the recognition results obtained are highly sensitive to segmentation error. In order to overcome these problems, in this paper we explore the use of probabilistic framework for recognition.

We focus on the problem of developing hierarchical shape models for handwritten Arabic characters. These characters are decomposed into concave or convex strokes. Our statistical learning architecture is reminiscent of the hierarchical mixture of experts algorithm. This is a variant of the expectation maximisation algorithm, which can deal with hierarchically structured models. The method was first introduced in 1994 by Jordan and Jacobs [4]. In its simplest form the method models data using a doubly nested mixture model. At the top layer the mixture is over a set of distinct object classes. This is sometimes referred to as the gating layer. At the lower level, the objects are represented as a mixture over object subclasses. These sub-classes feed into the gating later with predetermined weights. The parameters of the architecture reside in the sublayer, which is frequently represented using a Gaussian mixture model. The hierarchical mixture of experts algorithm provides a means of learning both the gating weights and the parameters of the Gaussian mixture model.

Here our structural decomposition of 2D shapes is a hierarchical one which mixes geometric and symbolic information. The hierarchy has a two-layer architecture. At the bottom layer we have strokes or curve primitives. These fall into different classes. For each class the curve primitive is represented using a point-distribution model [5] which describes how its shape varies over a set of training data. We assign stroke labels to the primitives to distinguish their class identity. At the top level of the hierarchy, shapes are represented as an arrangement of primitives. The representation of the arrangement of primitives has two components. The first of these is a second point distribution model that is used to represent how the arrangement of the primitive centre-points varies over the training data. The second component is a dictionary of configurations of stroke labels that represents the arrangements of strokes at a symbolic level. Recognition hence involves assigning stroke symbols to curves primitives, and recovering both stroke and shape deformation parameters. We present a probabilistic framework which can be for the purposes of shape-recognition in the hierarchy. We apply the resulting shape-recognition method to Arabic character recognition.

2 Shape Representation

We are concerned with recognising a shape $W = \{\boldsymbol{w}_1, ..., \boldsymbol{w}_p\}$ which consists of a set of p ordered but unlabelled landmark points with 2D co-ordinate vectors $\boldsymbol{w}_1$, ..., $\boldsymbol{w}_p$. The shape is assumed to be segmented into a set of K non-overlapping strokes. Each stroke consists of a set of consecutive landmark points. The set of points belonging to the stroke indexed k is S_k. For each stroke, we compute the mean position

$$\boldsymbol{c}_k = \frac{1}{|S_k|} \sum_{i \in S_k} \boldsymbol{w}_i$$

The geometry of stroke arrangement is captured by the set of mean position vectors $C = \{\boldsymbol{c}_1, ...\boldsymbol{c}_K\}$.

Our hierarchical model of the characters uses both geometric and symbolic representations of the shapes. The models are constructed from training data. Each training pattern consists of a set of landmark points that are segmented into strokes. We commence by specifying the symbolic components of the representation. Each training pattern is assigned to shape class and each component stroke is assigned to stroke class. The set of shape-labels is Ω_c and the set of stroke labels is Ω_s. The symbolic structure of each shape is represented a permissible arrangement of stroke-labels. For shapes of class $\omega \in \Omega_c$ the permissible arrangement of strokes is denoted by

$$\Lambda_\omega =< \lambda_1^\omega, \lambda_2^\omega, ... >$$

We model the geometry of the strokes and stroke-centre arrangements using point distribution models. To capture the shape variations, we use training data. The data consists of a set of shapes which have been segmented into strokes. Let the tth training pattern consist of the set of p landmark co-ordinate vectors $X^t = \{\boldsymbol{x}_1, ..., \boldsymbol{x}_p\}$. Each training pattern is segmented into strokes. For the training pattern indexed t there are K_t strokes and the index set of the points belonging to the kth stroke is S_k^t. To construct the point distribution model for the strokes and stroke-centre arrangements, we convert the point co-ordinates into long-vectors. For the training pattern indexed t, the long-vector of stroke centres is $X_t = ((\boldsymbol{c}_1^t)^T, (\boldsymbol{c}_2^t)^T, ..., (\boldsymbol{c}_L^t)^T)^T$. Similarly for the stroke indexed k in the training pattern indexed t, the long-vector of co-ordinates is denoted by $z_{t,k}$. For examples shapes belonging to the class ω, to construct the stroke-centre point distribution model we need to first compute the mean long vector

$$Y_\omega = \frac{1}{|T_\omega|} \sum_{t \in T_\omega} X_t \tag{1}$$

where T_ω is the set of index patterns and the associated covariance matrix

$$\Sigma_\omega = \frac{1}{|T_\omega|} \sum_{t \in T_\omega} (X_t - Y_\omega)(X_t - Y_\omega)^T \tag{2}$$

The eigenmodes of the stroke-centre covariance matrix are used to construct the point-distribution model. First, the eigenvalues e of the stroke covariance matrix are found by solving the eigenvalue equation $|\Sigma_\omega - e^\omega I| = 0$ where I is the $2L \times 2L$ identity matrix. The eigen-vector ϕ_i corresponding to the eigenvalue e_i^ω is found by solving the eigenvector equation $\Sigma\phi_i^\omega = e_i^\omega \phi_i^\omega$. According to Cootes and Taylor [6], the landmark points are allowed to undergo displacements relative to the mean-shape in directions defined by the eigenvectors of the covariance matrix Σ_ω. To compute the set of possible displacement directions, the M most significant eigenvectors are ordered according to the magnitudes of their corresponding eigenvalues to form the matrix of column-vectors $\Phi_\omega = (\phi_1^\omega|\phi_2^\omega|...|\phi_M^\omega)$, where $e_1^\omega, e_2^\omega, ..., e_M^\omega$ is the order of the magnitudes of the eigenvectors. The landmark points are allowed to move in a direction which is a linear combination of the eigenvectors. The updated landmark positions are given by $\hat{X} = Y_\omega + \Phi_\omega \gamma_\omega$, where γ_ω is a vector of modal co-efficients. This vector represents the free-parameters of the global shape-model.

This procedure may be repeated to construct a point distribution model for each stroke class. The set of long vectors for strokes of class λ is $T_\lambda = \{Z_{t,k}|\lambda_k^t = \lambda\}$. The mean and covariance matrix for this set of long-vectors are denoted by Y_λ and Σ_λ and the associated modal matrix is Φ_λ. The point distribution model for the stroke landmark points is $\hat{Z} = Y_\lambda + \Phi_\lambda \gamma_\lambda$.

We have recently described how a mixture of point-distribution models may be fitted to samples of shapes. The method is based on the EM algorithm and can be used to learn point distribution models for both the stroke and shape classes in an unsupervised manner. We have used this method to learn the mean shapes and the modal matrices for the strokes. More details of the method are found in [7].

3 Hierarchical Architecture

With the stroke and shape point distribution models to hand, our recognition method proceeds in a hierarchical manner. To commence, we make maximum likelihood estimates of the best-fit parameters of each stroke-model to each set of stroke-points. The best-fit parameters γ_λ^k of the stroke-model with class-label λ to the set of points constituting the stroke indexed k is

$$\gamma_\lambda^k = \arg\max_\gamma p(z_k|\Phi_\lambda, \gamma) \tag{3}$$

We use the best-fit parameters to assign a label to each stroke. The label is that which has maximum a posteriori probability given the stroke parameters. The label assigned to the stroke indexed k is

$$l_k = \arg\max_{\lambda \in \Omega_s} P(l|z_k, \gamma_\lambda, \Phi_\lambda) \tag{4}$$

In practice, we assume that the fit error residuals follow a Gaussian distribution. As a result, the class label is that associated with the minimum squared error.

This process is repeated for each stroke in turn. The class identity of the set of strokes is summarised the string of assigned stroke-labels

$$L =< l_1, l_2, ... > \tag{5}$$

Hence, the input layer is initialised using maximum likelihood stroke parameters and maximum a posteriori probability stroke labels.

The shape-layer takes this information as input. The goal of computation in this second layer is to refine the configuration of stroke labels using global constraints on the arrangement of strokes to form consistent shapes. The constraints come from both geometric and symbolic sources. The geometric constraints are provided by the fit of a stroke-centre point distribution model. The symbolic constraints are provide by a dictionary of permissible stroke-label strings for different shapes.

The parameters of the stroke-centre point distribution model are found using the EM algorithm [8]. Here we borrow ideas from the hierarchical mixture of experts algorithm, and pose the recovery of parameters as that of maximising a gated expected log-likelihood function for the distribution of stroke-centre alignment errors $p(X|\Phi_\omega, \Gamma_\omega)$. The likelihood function is gated by two sets of probabilities. The first of these are the a posteriori probabilities $P(\lambda_k^\omega|z_k, \gamma_{\lambda_k^\omega}, \Phi_{\lambda_k^\omega})$ of the individual strokes. The second are the conditional probabilities $P(L|\Lambda_\omega)$ of the assigned stroke-label string given the dictionary of permissible configurations for shapes of class ω. The expected log-likelihood function is given by

$$\mathcal{L} = \sum_{\omega \in \Omega_c} P(L|\Lambda_\omega) \Big\{ \prod_k P(\lambda_k^\omega|z_k, \gamma_{\lambda_k^\omega}, \Phi_{\lambda_k^\omega}) \Big\} \ln p(X|\Phi_\omega, \Gamma_\omega) \tag{6}$$

The optimal set of stroke-centre alignment parameters satisfies the condition

$$\Gamma_\omega^* = \arg\max_\Gamma P(L|\Lambda_\omega) \Big\{ \prod_k P(\lambda_k^\omega|z_k, \gamma_{\lambda_k^\omega}, \Phi_{\lambda_k^\omega}) \Big\} \ln p(X|\Phi_\omega, \Gamma_\omega) \tag{7}$$

From the maximum likelihood alignment parameters we identify the shape-class of maximum *a posteriori* probability. The class is the one for which

$$\omega^* = \arg\max_{\omega \in \Omega_c} P(\omega|X, \Phi_\omega, \Gamma_\omega^*) \tag{8}$$

The class identity of the maximum *a posteriori* probability shape is passed back to the stroke-layer of the architecture. The stroke labels can then be refined in the light of the consistent assignments for the stroke-label configuration associated with the shape-class ω.

$$l_k = \arg\max_{\lambda \in \Omega_s} P(\lambda|z_k, \gamma_l^k, \Phi_\lambda) P(L(\lambda, k)|\Lambda_\omega) \tag{9}$$

Finally, the maximum likelihood parameters for the strokes are refined

$$\gamma_k = \arg\max_\gamma p(\boldsymbol{z}_k|\Phi_{l_k}, \gamma, \Gamma_\omega^*)) \tag{10}$$

These labels are passed to the shape-layer and the process is iterated to convergence.

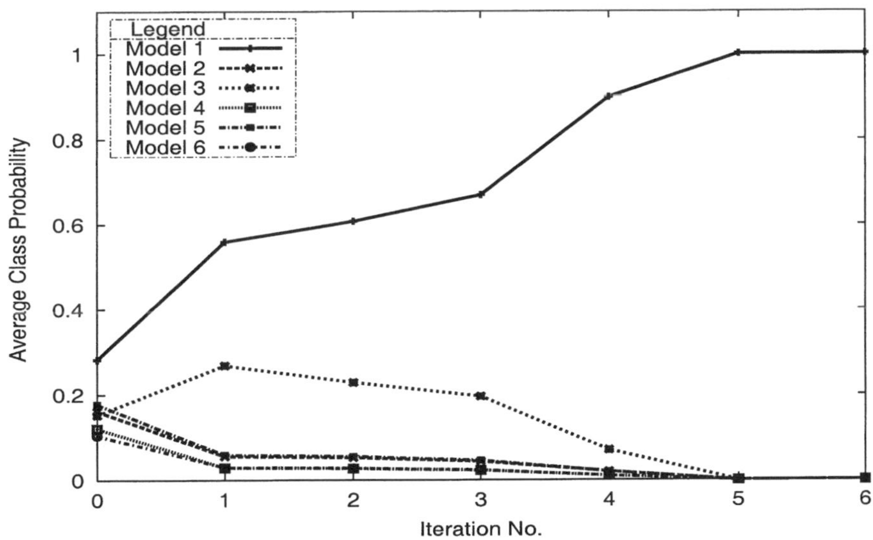

Fig. 2. (a) Alignment convergence rate as a function per iteration no

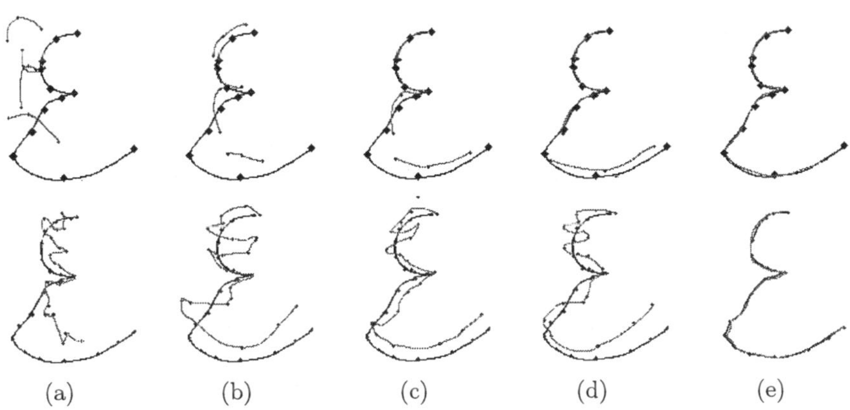

Fig. 3. Alignment. First raw shows hierarchical strokes:(a)iteration 1, (b)iteration 2, (c)iteration 3, (d)iteration 4, (e)iteration 5. Second raw represents character models:(a)iteration 1, (b)iteration 2, (c)iteration 3, (d)iteration 4, (d)iteration 8

Figure 3 compares the fitting of the stroke model (top row) and a global PDM (bottom row) with iteration number. It is clear that the results obtained with the stroke model are better than those obtained with the global PDM, which develops erratic local deformations. Finally, we demonstrate in Figure 4 comparison of stroke decomposition and character with respect to recognition rate as a function of point position error. Stroke decomposition methods shows a better performance when points are moved randomly away of their original location.

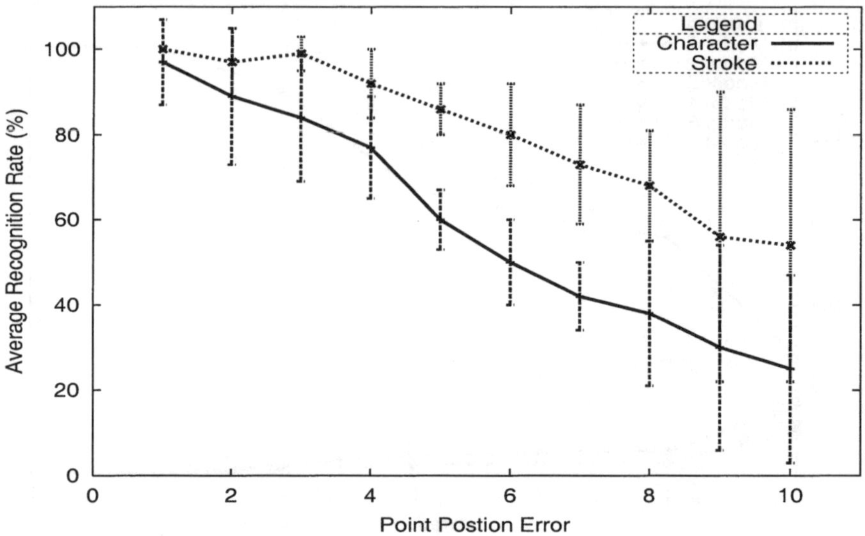

Fig. 4. (a) Recognition rate with respect to random point position

6 Conclusion

In this Paper, we have described a hierarchical probabilistic framework for shape recognition via stroke decomposition. The structural component of the method is represented using symbolic dictionaries, while geometric component is represented using Point Distribution Models. Experiments on Arabic character recognition reveal that the method offers advantages over a global PDM.

References

1. Cootes T.; Taylor C.; Cooper D.; Graham J. Active shape models-their training and application. *Computer Vision and Image Understanding*, 61(1):38–59, 1995.
2. Serge Belongie; Jitendra Malik; and Jan Puzicha. Shape matching and object recognition using shape contexts. *IEEE Transactions on PAMI*, 24(24):509–522, 2002.
3. David Courtenay Marr. *Vision: a computational investigation into the human representation and processing of visual information.* San Francisco, Freeman, 1982.
4. Jordan M.; Jacobs R. Hierarchical mixtures of experts and the em algorithm. *Neural Computation*, 6:181–214, 1994.
5. Cootes T.; Taylor C. A mixture models for representing shape variation. *Image and Vision Computing*, 17:403–409, 1999.
6. Cootes T.; Taylor C. Combining point distribution models with shape models based on finite element analysis. *Image and Vision Computing*, 13(5):403–409, 1995.
7. Abdullah A. Al-Shaher; Edwin R. Hancock. Linear shape recognition with mixtures of point distribution models. In *SSPR2002, Windsor, Canada*, pages 205–215, 2002.
8. Dempster A.; Laird N.; Rubin D. Maximum likelihood from incomplete data via the em algorithm. *Journal of Royal Statistical Soc. Ser.*, 39:1–38, 1977.
9. Edwin R. Hancock; Josef Kittler. Discrete relaxation. *Pattern Recognition*, 23(7):711–733, 1990.

Classifier Combination through Clustering in the Output Spaces

Hakan Altınçay and Buket Çizili

Computer Engineering Department, Eastern Mediterranean University
Gazi Mağusa, KKTC Mersin 10, Turkey
{hakan.altincay,buket.cizili}@emu.edu.tr

Abstract. This paper proposes the use of information about the distribution of the classifier outputs in their output spaces during combination. Two different methods based on the clustering in the output spaces are developed. In the first approach, taking into account the distribution of the output vectors in these clusters, the local reliability of each individual classifier is quantified and used for weighting the classifier outputs during combination. In the second method, the classifier outputs are replaced by the centroids of the nearest clusters during combination. Experimental results have shown that both of the proposed approaches provide more than 3% improvement in the correct classification rate.

1 Introduction

In a pattern classification problem involving N pattern classes, a classifier can be interpreted as a mapping from the input pattern space into the N-dimensional output space. The distribution of the classifier outputs obtained during training is used to select the correct class. The distribution provided by such a mapping is not random. In other words, the output vectors provided for each class have some common properties. For instance, consider the case of two pattern classes, w_1 and w_2 and an arbitrary output vector provided by the classifier e_k as $\mathcal{O}_k = [o_1, o_2]$. If the classifier at hand is a reasonable one and the tested pattern belongs to class w_1, it is expected that $o_1 > o_2$. In the general case where N classes are involved, the decision is selected by considering the relative values of the entries in the output vectors where the pattern class that obtains the maximum output value is selected as the correct class. In other words, if $o_i > o_j$, $\forall j \neq i$, then the correct class is selected as w_i. This is reasonable since the main aim in classifier training is either to maximize the output value of the correct class or the difference in the output values of the correct class and the other classes. Hence, it can be argued that different regions in the output space should be dominated by the outputs of different classes.

If the combination scheme under concern takes only the raw output vectors from each classifier as input, this means that the distribution of the output vectors in the individual classifier's output space is ignored. Typical examples for such combination rules are linear and logarithmic combination schemes, max rule, median rule etc. [1,2]. In order to avoid this drawback, learning based

N. Petkov and M.A. Westenberg (Eds.): CAIP 2003, LNCS 2756, pp. 487–493, 2003.

combiners can be used such as the decision templates proposed by Kuncheva *et al.* which takes into account the mean of the classifier output vectors during the combination operation [3].

In some studies, the distribution of the classifier outputs are estimated using non-parametric techniques like Parzen windows and k-nearest neighbors or, they are assumed to be multi-dimensional Gaussian [4–6]. These distributions are later used to convert the measurement level outputs into a posteriori probabilities. Consequently, instead of the measurement level outputs, frequencies approximately derived from the classifier outputs are used during combination.

This paper proposes two novel classifier combination approaches based on the use of information about the distribution of the measurement level classifier outputs in their output spaces. For this purpose, the output space of each classifier is partitioned into clusters. In the first approach, the output vectors of the classifiers are weighted using the percentage of correctly classified pattern samples in the nearest clusters. In the second approach, the centroids of the clusters are used during the combination instead of the original measurement level classifier outputs. Experimental results have shown that the proposed multiple classifier systems surpassed some well known fixed combination techniques.

2 Output Clustering Based Classifier Combination

The proposed combination schemes depend on the analysis of clustering behavior of the output vectors. Assume that we have N pattern classes, $\Omega = \{w_1, w_2, \ldots, w_N\}$ and K classifiers, $\mathcal{E} = \{e_1, e_2, \ldots, e_K\}$. Let $\mathcal{O}_k = \{o_1, \ldots, o_N\}$ denote an output vector from classifier e_k. Each classifier can be considered as a mapping $e_k : t \mapsto \mathcal{R}^N$ where t denotes an arbitrary pattern sample. Using a clustering algorithm that can be denoted by $\mathcal{F} : \mathcal{R}^N \mapsto \mathcal{M}$, the output vectors are grouped into clusters $\{\mathcal{V}_1, \mathcal{V}_2, \ldots, \mathcal{V}_M\}$. In this mapping, $\mathcal{M} = \{m_1, m_2, \ldots, m_M\}$, $m_i \in \mathcal{R}^N$ denotes the centroids of these clusters [7].

2.1 Cluster Based Weighting (CBW) Approach

The resulting clustering can be considered as an indicator for the classification behavior of each classifier in different regions of the output space. For instance, consider e_k and let n_{ij} denote the number of output vectors from w_i that lie in cluster $\mathcal{V}_j$ and let m_{ij} be the number of output vectors in that cluster that belong to pattern class w_i and the most likely class is also w_i. Assume that the event $\{\mathcal{O}_k \in \mathcal{V}_j\}$ occurs during testing and the most likely class is w_i. Then, the probability that the most likely class is correct can be approximately calculated as $p_{ij} = m_{ij}/n_{ij}$. More specifically, p_{ij} is the approximate probability of correct classification given that the most likely class is w_i and the output vector is in cluster $\mathcal{V}_j$. Taking into account the approximate correct classification probabilities for all classes in a cluster, the reliability of the cluster $\mathcal{V}_j$ is defined as,

$$rel_j = \sum_{i=1}^{N} p_{ij} P(w_i|\mathcal{V}_j) \quad (1)$$

where $P(w_i|\mathcal{V}_j)$ denotes the percentage of the output vectors of class w_i in $\mathcal{V}_j$.

The output space of each individual classifier, e_k is partitioned into clusters using the binary-split LBG algorithm [8]. During testing, the nearest cluster of the output vector provided by a classifier is determined using the Euclidean distance between the output vector and the cluster centroids. Let rel_{kj} denote the rel_j value of the nearest cluster for the output provided by classifier e_k. Then, the weights used during the linear combination of the classifier outputs are defined as $weig_k = (1+rel_{kj})$. These weights carry *local* information about the classifier reliability in the sense that the percentage of successfully classified samples in the neighborhood of the given output is used as a measure of reliability. From this point on, this weighting will be referred as $CBW - L$.

The correct classification performance of each classifier on the whole validation data denoted by q_k can also be used for weighting. q_k is generally considered as a measure of the *global* classifier reliability. In order to use both local and global reliability measures during combination, the classifier weights are modified as,

$$weig_k = (1 + rel_{kj}) \times q_k. \tag{2}$$

From this point on, this weighting will be referred as $CBW - G$. Having computed the classifier weights, the linearly combined output vector is computed as $\mathcal{O}_{comb} = \sum_{k=1}^{K}(weig_k \times \mathcal{O}_k)$ [9].

In the ideal case, it is expected that the number of clusters is equal to the number of pattern classes and each cluster includes output vectors from a single class. However, the output vectors corresponding to misclassifications violate this expectation since the output vector of a misclassified pattern sample may either be similar to the output vectors of other pattern samples or they may form different clusters. Because of this, $\mathcal{M}$ should be selected as larger than N.

If a cluster consists of the output vectors from various classes, it means that the separability of the correct classification and misclassification behaviors is poor in that region of the output space. As a matter of fact, it is desirable that the outputs corresponding to misclassification lie in different clusters than those that are correctly classified. The clusters including the misclassified outputs represent the weaknesses whereas the clusters including the correctly classified outputs represent the strengths of the individual classifiers.

2.2 Cluster Centroids Based (CCB) Approach

Using the output vectors corresponding to the training data, the output space of each classifier is initially partitioned into $2 \times N$ clusters according to the *most likely class* in the output vector. The first set of N clusters contain the output vectors that correspond to correct classification where the correct class receives the maximum output score. The second set of N clusters contains the output vectors for which the most likely class is not the same as the correct class. For instance, cluster 1 contains the output vectors with most likely class equal to 1 where the correct class is also 1. Similarly, cluster $N+1$ contains the output vectors with most likely class equal to 1 but the correct class is *not* 1.

After this clustering, the centroid of each cluster is computed as the mean of all vectors in these clusters. During testing, the nearest cluster for the output

Table 1. Classifiers used in the simulation experiments

Classifier	*Modeling meth.*	*Feature set*	*CMS*	*Accuracy*
e_1	VQ	LPCC		89.4
e_2	VQ	LPCC	√	84.4
e_3	VQ	MFCC		86.3
e_4	VQ	MFCC	√	79.9

vector is determined using the Euclidean distance. Assume that the output vector provided by e_k is nearest to the cluster $\mathcal{V}_j$ which has the centroid $\bar{u}_{k,j}$. Then, during the linear combination, the combined output vector is computed as,

$$\mathcal{O}_{comb} = \sum_{k=1}^{K} \bar{u}_{k,j}. \tag{3}$$

The major advantage of using the cluster centroids is the smoothing of outliers in the output spaces. In other words, the outliers are represented using an average value in that neighborhood.

3 The Classification Problem and Database

The proposed approaches are applied to the closed-set text-independent speaker identification problem. In the simulation experiments, four different classifiers are used. The classifiers are given in Table 1. They are based on Vector Quantization (VQ) modeling where the models are trained with the LBG algorithm and each speaker is represented by 32 code vectors. 12 linear prediction derived cepstral coefficients ($LPCC$) and 12 Mel-frequency cepstral coefficients ($MFCC$) type features are extracted and used in the classifiers [10, 11]. Delta features are also appended to obtain a 24 element feature vector for each speech frame. Cepstral Mean Subtraction (CMS) is also used for some classifiers. The experiments are conducted on 25 speakers from the POLYCOST database. There are approximately 10 sessions for each speaker. The records are done on telephone lines, sampled at 8kHz and a-law coded. First three sessions are used for training and cross validation. There are totally 6675 training and 17709 test tokens. 200 consecutive frames, each 20ms long, are used to form speech tokens where each speech token is treated as a separate training or test sample. Let x_i denote the ith frame. Then, the set of frames $\{x_1, x_2, \ldots, x_{200}\}$ belongs to the first token, $\{x_{11}, \ldots, x_{211}\}$ belongs to the second token etc.

4 Simulation Results and Discussions

In multiple classifier systems, due to the fact that the incomparability of the classifier outputs is a major problem, normalization is generally applied to transform the classifier outputs onto a comparable scale. The success of the proposed approaches heavily depends on obtaining clusters that are dominated by the

Table 2. The accuracies of $CBW-L$ and $CBW-G$ combination methods (in %) for two different normalization techniques

$\mathcal{M}$	*CBW-L with MON*	*CBW-G with MON*	*CBW-L with OSN*	*CBW-G with OSN*
28	92.77	92.85	90.99	91.14
30	**92.81**	92.91	**91.02**	**91.15**
32	92.78	**92.92**	91.00	91.10
34	92.79	92.91	91.00	91.07
36	92.79	92.92	90.91	91.03
38	92.77	92.89	90.85	90.95
40	92.73	92.85	90.87	90.96

outputs of either correctly classified or misclassified samples. Although normalization modifies the distribution of the output vectors, the experimental results have shown that they provide more useful clusters in that sense. Because of this, in all the experiments described below, the output vectors are normalized before clustering where two different output normalization techniques are considered. The first method is minimum output normalization (MON) where the normalized output values are computed as,

$$o_i' = \frac{o_i - o_{min}}{\sum_{j=1}^{N}(o_j - o_{min})} \tag{4}$$

where o_{min} denotes the minimum element in the output vector. In the output sum normalization (OSN) case, $o_i' = \frac{o_i}{\sum_{j=1}^{N} o_j}$.

The experimental results for the Cluster Based Weighting (CBW) approaches, i.e. $CBW-L$ and $CBW-G$ are given in Table 2 for various values of $\mathcal{M}$.

As seen in the table, the combined identification accuracy does not vary too much with the number of clusters where the 30 clusters case provides the best results in general. In the 30 clusters case, the clusters obtained for e_1 involved at most 10 different classes where the average over all clusters is obtained to be less than 4 classes for both MON and OSN. As seen in the table, the use of global classifier reliability (i.e. classification accuracy on the validation data) during combination together with the local, increases the combined accuracy. When only the global classifier reliability is used as classifier weights, i.e. $weig_k = q_k$, the combined accuracy is obtained as 92.19% in the case of MON and 90.82% in the case of OSN. These results show the importance of the information provided by the clustering based local reliability estimation.

The combination experiments are also performed using the Cluster Centroids Based (CCB) approach. Taking into account the fact that the best results were obtained with MON method in the experiments described above, the combination experiments are conducted only for this normalization technique in the CCB approach. Using the proposed class dependent clustering technique and the resulting centroids during combination, the classifiers are linearly combined. The resulting combined identification rate is obtained as 92.52% which is better than

Table 3. The overall results obtained from the combination experiments

Combination methods	*Accuracy (in %)*
CBW-L with MON	92.81
CBW-G with MON	92.91
CCB with MON	92.50
Max with MON	91.74
Median with MON	91.36
Linear Comb. with MON	92.04
CBW-L with OSN	91.02
CBW-G with OSN	91.15
Max with OSN	89.69
Median with OSN	91.48
Linear Comb. with OSN	90.73

the rate provided by the linear combination of the original normalized output vectors, i.e. 92.04%.

The proposed combination schemes are also compared with two other fixed combination rules namely, *max* and *median* which are applied on the original normalized outputs [1]. The whole set of experimental results are presented in Table 3 for comparison. The accuracies of the proposed approaches are given for $\mathcal{M} = 30$. As see in the table, the proposed approaches provided better accuracies for both MON and OSN. The only exception is median rule with OSN.

5 Conclusions

In this paper, two different combination schemes are proposed to take into account the distribution of the output vectors in the output space of each individual classifier. In these approaches, the clusters in the output space of each classifier are initially determined. In the first approach, the reliability of each cluster is defined in terms of correct classification percentage in the corresponding cluster and this quantity is used to assign weights to the individual classifiers during linear combination. In the second approach, the cluster centroids of the nearest clusters are used to replace the measurement level output vectors. In the simulation experiments, the speaker identification problem is considered and the proposed techniques are used to the combine the outputs of four different classifiers. Experimental results have shown that both of the techniques provided more than 3% improvement when compared to the best individual classifier. The proposed approach is also compared with some other fixed combination rules which also make use of the normalized forms of the original outputs. The proposed approaches are observed to provide better accuracies in most of the cases.

References

1. J. Kittler et al. On combining classifiers. *IEEE Transactions on Pattern Analysis and Machine Intelligence*, 20(3):226–239, March 1998.

2. H. Altınçay and M. Demirekler. An information theoretic framework for weight estimation in the combination of probabilistic classifiers for speaker identification. *Speech Communication*, 30(4):255–272, April 2000.
3. L. I. Kuncheva, J. C. Bezdek, and R. P. W. Duin. Decision templates for multiple classifier fusion. *Pattern Recognition*, 34(2):299–314, 2001.
4. J. S. Denker and Y. leCun. Transforming neural-net output levels to probability distributions. Technical report, AT&T Bell Laboratories, 1991.
5. R. P. W. Duin and M. J. Tax. Classifier conditional posteriori probabilities. *SSPR/SPR*, pages 611–619, 1998.
6. G. Giacinto and F. Roli. Methods for dynamic classifier selection. *ICIAP'99, 10th international conference on image analysis and processing, Italy*, pages 659–664, September 1999.
7. R. O. Duda, P. E. Hart, and D. G. Stork. *Pattern Classification.* John Wiley and Sons, 2000.
8. Y. Linde, A. Buzo, and R. M. Gray. An algorithm for vector quantizer design. *IEEE Transactions on Communications*, 28:84–95, 1980.
9. J. A. Benediktsson and P.H. Swain. Consensus theoretic classification methods. *IEEE Transactions on Systems Man and Cybernetics*, 22(4):688–704, July 1992.
10. H. Gish and M. Schmidt. Text-independent speaker identification. *IEEE Signal Processing Magazine*, pages 18–32, October 1994.
11. J. P. Campbell. Speaker recognition: A tutorial. *Proceedings of the IEEE*, 85(9):1437–1462, September 1997.

An Image-Based System for Spoken-Letter Recognition

Khalid Saeed[1] and Marcin Kozłowski[2]

[1] Bialystok University of Technology, Faculty of Computer Science
Wiejska 45a, 15-351 Bialystok, Poland
aidabt@ii.pb.bialystok.pl
http://aragorn.pb.bialystok.pl/~zspinfo/
[2] Department of Informatics, Statistical Office in Bialystok
Krakowska 13, 15-959 Bialystok, Poland
mkoz@interia.pl
http://www.stat.gov.pl/urzedy/bialystok/index-en.htm

Abstract. A new trial on speech recognition from graphical point of view is introduced. Isolated spoken-letters and color-names words are considered. After recording, the speech signal is processed as an image by Power Spectrum Estimation. For feature extraction, classification and hence recognition, the algorithm of minimal eigenvalues of Toeplitz matrices together with other methods of speech processing and recognition are used. A number of examples on applications and comparisons are presented in the work. The efficiency of the method is very high in the case of the six Polish vowels and English color-names, and the results are encouraging to extend the algorithm to cover more word classes.

Keywords: Speech, Image Processing and Recognition, Burg's and Toeplitz Models

1 Introduction

Most of speech classification algorithms are based on neural network theory, among them is that of Burr's [1]. In his paper, Burr used neural networks to classify and recognize written and spoken letters. Another and often used method of recognition is Hidden Markov Models, described for example in [2].

This paper, however, is based on algorithmic approaches and looks at the spoken letter as an image, that is, the speech signal is treated graphically. It is the aim of this paper that the approaches, achieved by the first author [3], which were successfully used in description and classification of written scripts and texts, are applied on speech recognition. Particular attention is paid to the application of Toeplitz forms and the minimal eigenvalues of their determinants for shape description. However, this approach cannot be applied directly because of the speech complicated nature. That is why the authors are using some other methods of speech pre-processing for better feature extract of voice image before entering Toeplitz-based algorithms. The processing methods that gave good results in most cases are LPC – Linear Predictive Coding coefficients [4], Spectral Moments [5] and Zero-Crossing method [6]. All of them have their advantages and also drawbacks. Seeking a simple and also a more stationary way for the graphical speech description, we applied the frequency spectral

N. Petkov and M.A. Westenberg (Eds.): CAIP 2003, LNCS 2756, pp. 494–502, 2003.

estimation method based on linear prediction model introduced in [7] and will thereafter be referred to as Burg's model. This method seems to be very useful for image-spectral pre-processing. The obtained signal spectrum forms the basis to further analysis for spoken-letter classification and recognition.

2 Spoken-Letter Waveform Pre-processing

The input to the system is a recorded speech waveform (Fig. 1). This sound contains silence region before and after the under-analysis signal. The sound also consists of excessive number of samples, which must be reduced without losing the most important feature.

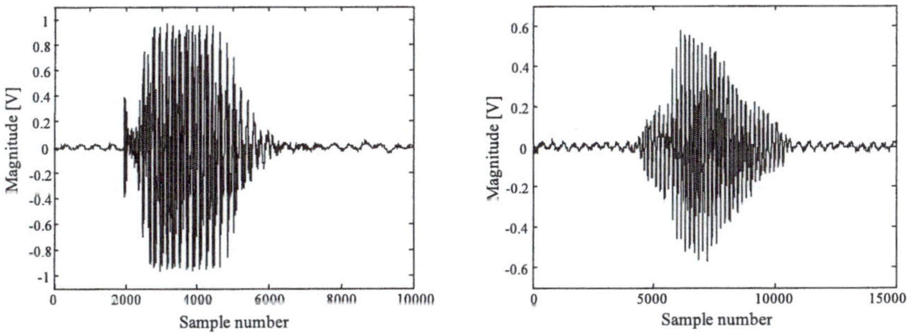

(a) **(b)**

Fig. 1. The waveforms of two recorded speech signals: (a) The Polish vowel *a* - pronounced like '*a*' in 'car', (b) The English word 'blue'.

The process of the speech preparation for feature extraction is given in Fig. 2.

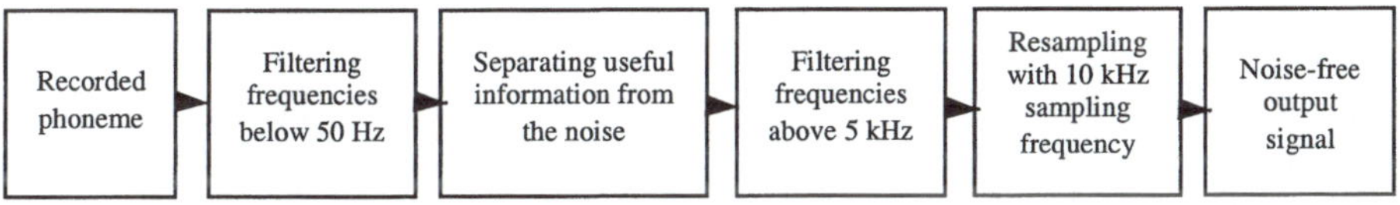

Fig. 2. The flow chart of speech signal preparation for recognition process.

A digital filter is applied to cut frequencies below 50 Hz. Almost all of the recorded speech signals contain this 50-Hz component. After filtering this frequency, the signal is free of such noise. The next step is to extract the valuable information from the rest of the signal. This is very important part of the signal pre-processing. The noise-free signal forms the input data to the algorithm of description and classification.

2.1 Algorithm

Now we can proceed with our algorithm whose input is the amplified signal with frequencies above 3 kHz [8]. This is applied because consonants generally consist of two parts. The first one, with the lower magnitude, consists of the most important features, while the second one sounds like a vowel (the letter *b*, for example, is pronounced *'be'* in Polish, and is analyzed as a consonant plus a vowel - *b+e*). Therefore, when amplifying higher frequencies we separate the first most important part of consonant signal. After this process we still have the signal sampled with 22 kHz frequency so that it consists of frequencies from 0 to 11 kHz, because sampling frequency, according to Nyquist theory, is at least twice higher than the highest frequency in the bandwidth.

Resampling. As we are trying to decrease the time of processing, and hence to speed the algorithm up, it is of great benefit then to reduce the number of samples and also number of computing operations. To realize that, in addition to the low-pass filtering of frequencies below 5 kHz, we resample the signal into one of less number of samples, without losing its essential-for-recognition characteristics.

In our case, after reducing the maximal frequency to 5 kHz, the sampling frequency must be at least 10 kHz in order to meet the requirements of Nyquist theory of sampling. As a result of this resampling process, the number of samples is reduced to less than half its original value (from 22000 to 10000 per second), and the further steps of the analysis will be run on minimal data. This causes the system speed to increase twice. Comparison of the signal with and without resampling is given in Fig. 3.

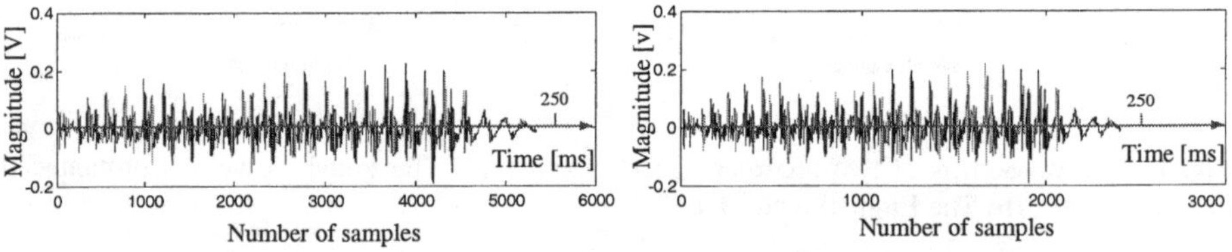

(a) The waveform before resampling (b) The waveform after resampling

Fig. 3. Waveform resampling.

After resampling, the new signal is now prepared to be applied as an input to the next block, namely, Speech Signal Processing. This step is the most important one in the whole process of classification where the features of the acoustic images are extracted.

2.2 Speech Signal Processing

Among many methods of Speech Signal Processing, the authors have chosen the method based on spectrum analysis. This method allows speech image-feature extract from spectral analysis in a simple way. However, the processing is a difficult task because of the very complicated model of speech creation and perception. The advantage of spectral analysis processing is the possibility of analyzing the particular frequencies contained in the speech signal, which are articulation dependent and hence in some manner to allow identifying such components like phonemes. Following this, the authors are working on finding a method for smoothing irregular spectral shape resulting from applying FFT (Fast Fourier Transform). Experiments showed that power spectrum estimation of Burg's model is the best for this purpose. It is based on the Linear Predictive Coding approach (Fig. 4). The theory of linear predictive coding is given in [9], where the sample $u(n)$ can be approximated as the linear combination of the P previous samples, with $n > 0$.

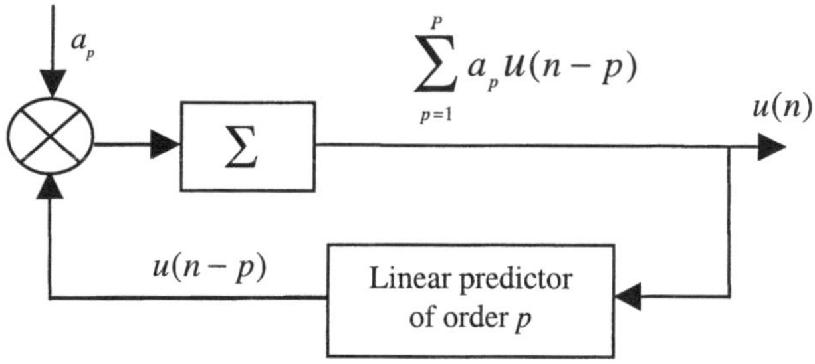

Fig. 4. The main idea of the prediction.

The nth sample estimator $\tilde{u}(n)$ is defined to be:

$$\tilde{u}(n) = -\sum_{p=1}^{P} a_p u(n-p) \tag{1}$$

where a_p – prediction coefficients, p = 1, 2, ..., P, and P – prediction order. The difference between $u(n)$ and $\tilde{u}(n)$ is called the prediction error $e(n)$. Hence,

$$e(n) = u(n) - \tilde{u}(n) = u(n) + \sum_{p=1}^{P} a_p u(n-p) \tag{2}$$

Burg's model together with the whole software implementation is included in [10]. This step is the starting point for further analysis. The analysis is based on minimizing forward and backward prediction errors according to Levinson – Durbin recursion [11,12]. For most of the phonemes, the spectral estimation furnishes a smooth envelope, while local extremes can be seen clearly (Fig. 5).

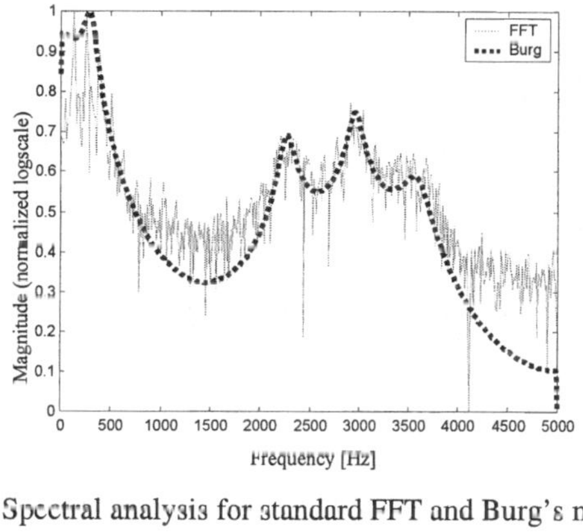

Fig. 5. Spectral analysis for standard FFT and Burg's method.

The obtained power spectrum acoustic images are then analyzed using the known methods of classification and recognition. In this work we use both classical point-to-point algorithms as well as the one based on minimal eigenvalues of Toeplitz matrices [3]. This algorithm has proved to be efficient in image feature extraction of scripts, texts [13,14] and a number of other various image-recognition processes [3,15]. Therefore, Toeplitz algorithm is applied to recognize spoken waveforms looked at as acoustic images. Of course, there are some factors which directly affect the accuracy of the pre-processing algorithms. For example, when applying the method of estimation, one needs to specify the prediction order and the FFT length. The FFT length must give the smoothest shape of the spectrum (the more samples we have, the smoother shape we get), and it cannot be a case when too many samples are considered. This, as very well known, would definitely lower the efficiency of the algorithm. Prediction order is also an important parameter. When it is too low, the envelope doesn't match with FFT shape, and when it's too high, it causes the speed of the algorithm to fall. So it's very important, although very difficult, to choose the best prediction order.

Again, when considering Toeplitz matrices and their minimal eigenvalues, it is essential to know how to select the characteristic points from the spectral estimation curve in order to apply as the feature data for the input to the classifying system. Figure 6 shows this procedure. In Fig. 6a out of 250 points only 25 are selected, that is every tenth point is considered. However, Fig. 6b shows larger number of samples as they are taken every fifth sample. This decreases the number of samples to only 50.

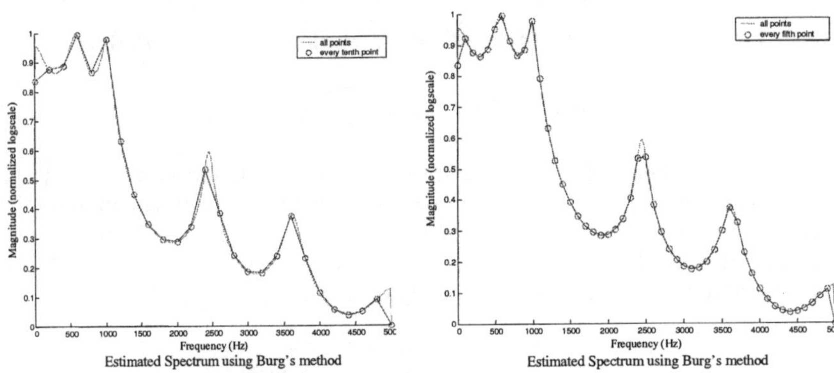

(a) Every tenth point selection **(b)** Every fifth point selection

Fig. 6. Characteristic and feature point selection

As can be seen from this figure, the choice of every-tenth-point selection (Fig. 6a) leads to a distorted curve, while that of Fig. 6b does not cause any mentioned changes or distortion. This means that the last choice (Fig. 6b) is sufficient to assign and deliver the necessary minimized number of characteristic points as the input data to image classifying system based on Toeplitz approach of description. This would certainly decrease the computation size taking place in evaluating the necessary Toeplitz form determinants by at least 5 times.

The next step is to determine the Toeplitz matrices and calculate their corresponding determinants.

3 Classification

For the purpose of classification, the required comparison between the reference pattern Ψ and the resulting one from the input data Φ, is led by the Absolute Deviation classifier [3], defined by the summation of the absolute-values of the differences between Ψ_i and Φ_i elements for $i = 1, 2, \ldots, P$, that is,

$$D = \sum_{i=1}^{P} \left| \Psi_i - \Phi_i \right| \tag{3}$$

The input data Φ_i to this equation is taken from the feature vector of the minimal eigenvalues extracted by the following criterion. To explain how the algorithm of minimal eigenvalues works, we first introduce the way of calculating Toeplitz-matrix determinants.

According to the method given in [3,15], the under-test object-features are described by the following rational function:

$$H(s) = \frac{P(s)}{Q(s)} \tag{4}$$

where $P(s)$ and $Q(s)$ are n-degree polynomials in the complex variable s whose coefficients are the coordinates of the feature points of Fig. 6. They are treated as pairs of complex numbers $s_i = x_i + jy_i$ with $i = 1,2,3\ldots,n$, n being the number of points considered. Therefore,

$$H(s) = \frac{x_0 + x_1 s + x_2 s^2 + \ldots + x_n s^n}{y_0 + y_1 s + y_2 s^2 + \ldots + y_n s^n} \tag{5}$$

Apply the bilinear transformation $s = \frac{1-z}{1+z}$ to have H in another simpler form $H(z)$.

To create Toeplitz matrices and their determinants, evaluate Taylor series for $H(z)$:

$$T(z) = c_0 + c_1 z + c_2 z^2 + \ldots + c_n z^n + \ldots \tag{6}$$

where,

$$c_i = \frac{1}{x_0^{i+1}} \begin{vmatrix} y_i & x_1 & x_2 & \cdots & x_i \\ y_{i-1} & x_0 & x_1 & \cdots & x_{i-1} \\ y_{i-2} & 0 & x_0 & \cdots & x_{i-2} \\ y_{i-3} & 0 & 0 & \cdots & \cdots \\ \cdots & \cdots & \cdots & \cdots & x_1 \\ y_0 & 0 & 0 & \cdots & x_0 \end{vmatrix} \quad \text{for } i = 1,2,\ldots,n \tag{7}$$

These coefficients form the elements of Toeplitz forms:

$$D_i = \begin{vmatrix} c_0 & c_1 & c_2 & \cdots & c_i \\ c_1 & c_0 & c_1 & \cdots & c_{i-1} \\ c_2 & c_1 & c_0 & \cdots & c_{i-2} \\ \cdots & \cdots & \cdots & \cdots & \cdots \\ c_i & c_{i-1} & c_{i-2} & \cdots & c_0 \end{vmatrix}, \quad i = 0, 1, 2, \ldots, n \tag{8}$$

Determine the minimal eigenvalues of the forms in *Eq*. (8):
$\lambda_{\min}\{D_i\} = \lambda_{\min_i} = \lambda_i$ for $i = 1, 2, ..., n$. Hence, the following feature vector is found:

$$\Phi_i = (\lambda_0, \lambda_1, \lambda_2, ..., \lambda_n) \tag{9}$$

Eq.(9), acts as the input data to the classification algorithms when applying the known methods of similarity and comparison for the sake of recognition. The characteristic behavior of this equation lies in the fact, that it forms a monotonically non-increasing series whose limit has something common with the minimal value of the rational function in *Eq*.(5) at $s = jy$. The behavior of this function and its derivatives is beyond the topics of this work. Again, the feature vector of *Eq*.(9) presents a very useful tool in describing an image within a class of similar objects. Simply, each has its own series of minimal eigenvalues Ψ_i descending to a definite limit of specific value differing from the series and their limits of other ones. The obtained results from the theory of both Burg's and Toeplitz according to the authors' approach, are given in the following section.

4 Recognition – Experiments and Result

A number of experiments and calculations have been performed for varieties of parameters and different possibilities of data introducing to *Eq*. (4) through the choice of the feature points and their data-defining variables $s_i = x_i + jy_i$, $i = 1, 2, 3, \ldots n$.

Experiment 1. Here, a direct application to the results obtained from Burg's estimation spectrum is used for classification of characteristic points extracted from the under-test spoken-letter image. The recognition rate is high, and the number of samples is high, too. Table 1 shows the results of this experiment.

Table 1. Recognition results of Experiment 1.

Burg's model prediction order: *P*=12; FFT length: 500; number of input samples: 1000																							Overall Recognition	Recognition Rate
Pattern set	**a**	**b**	**c**	**d**	**e**	**f**	**g**	**h**	**i**	**k**	**l**	**m**	**n**	**o**	**p**	**r**	**s**	**t**	**u**	**w**	**y**	**z**		**93%**
Number of recognized samples out of **5 iterations**	5	3	4	5	5	5	5	4	5	5	5	5	5	5	5	3	5	5	5	4	5	4	**102/110**	

Experiment 2. This time and before applying the classification methods, apply the minimal eigenvalues algorithm of Toeplitz considering only the characteristic points extracted from the transfer function of *Eq*.(4). The first results showed a high efficiency level (88%) for the 14 pronounced-in-Polish letters a, c, d, e, l, m, n, o, p, r, s, t, u, z, but a lower rate for the others, which reduced the overall recognition rate to 65% (see Table 2).

The recent work has shown higher recognition rate especially when the input data to *Eq*.(5) was modified leading to other more distinguishable series of minimal eigenvalues. The results were encouraging to extend the algorithm and test word groups by the Toeplitz-based algorithm. The first tested groups were the color names in two languages Polish and English. Our research group has been working on other spoken-word classes like days of the week, months of the year, and so forth.

Table 2. Recognition results of Experiment 2.

Burg's model prediction order: *P*=12, FFT length: 50; number of input samples: 1000																							Overall Recognition	Recognition Rate
Pattern set	**a**	**b**	**c**	**d**	**e**	**f**	**g**	**h**	**i**	**k**	**l**	**m**	**n**	**o**	**p**	**r**	**s**	**t**	**u**	**w**	**y**	**z**		**65%**
Number of recognized samples out of **5 iterations**	4	2	4	5	5	1	0	0	5	2	2	5	5	5	5	3	5	3	5	0	2	3	**71/110**	

Experiment 3. This experiment shows the results of recognition seven color-names in Polish and another seven-color group in English. The recognition rates are very high; they are **96%** for Polish group and **94%** for the English group (see Table 3 for the English group).

Table 3. Recognition results of English seven-color names group of Experiment 3.

Burg's model prediction order: *P*=12; FFT length: 50; number of input samples: 1000								Overall Recognition	Recognition Rate
Pattern set	**Green**	**Yellow**	**Pink**	**Red**	**Orange**	**Blue**	**White**		**94%**
Number of recognized samples out of **10 iterations**	10	6	10	10	10	10	10	**66/70**	

5 Conclusions

The image-based approach in speech classification and processing has proved to be as good as other known methods in their recognition efficiency. In the case of using 22 letter-pattern classes, a recognition accuracy of above 93% was achieved. Experiments have shown that spectrum estimation parameters are very important for the recognition quality. Moreover, results improvement lies in choosing the suitable sampling window, for example Blackman's window [10,16] is adequate to our needs. Other methods are based on various modifications of the minimal eigenvalues algorithm based on Toeplitz matrices [3,13]. This algorithm has given very good results in case of scripts, texts and two-dimensional object images [3,13,15]. In the case of speech signals and their spectral images, this kind of image is more complicated. Speech images, no matter what form they are described in, they always represent a complex of a lot of various elements and they need special and specific ways of processing.

Researches, focused on developing methods based on the minimal eigenvalues algorithm are still being working on. The accuracy of these methods is mainly affected by the minimization of the number of characteristic points. Another important factor that may lower the recognition accuracy, is the fact, that power spectrum is too similar for different phonemes. This is why more efforts are employed to apply Toeplitz approach directly on recorded voice just after filtering and noise removing so that the recognition is processed in the real time. The successful application of the Toeplitz-based algorithm to color-names classes in two languages, Polish (96% recognition rate) and English (94%), has proved that the presented work is promising. Experiments are being done on Arabic classes, as well. Some recent results [17] seem to be helpful in the pre-processing steps, which will certainly improve the level of accuracy and give much better results. Moreover, the results achieved in [18] are being used for better feature extract and improved voice-signal image processing. The near future publications will show more interesting results, hopefully of higher recognition rate and wider applications.

Acknowledgement

This work was supported by the Rector of Bialystok University of Technology (grant number W/II/3/01).

References

1. D. J. Burr, "Experiments on Neural Net Recognition of Spoken and Written Text," IEEE Transactions on Acoustic, Speech, and Signal Processing, vol. 36, July 1988.
2. J. L. MacDonald, W. Zucchini, W. Zucchi, "Hidden Markov and Other Models for Discrete-Valued Time Series," CRC Press, Jan. 1, 1997.
3. K. Saeed, "Computer Graphics Analysis: A Criterion for Image Feature Extraction and Recognition," Vol. 10, Issue 2, 2001, pp. 185-194, MGV - International Journal on Machine Graphics and Vision, Institute of Computer Science, Polish Academy of Sciences, Warsaw.
4. R. W. Schafer, L. R. Rabiner, "System for Automatic Formant Analysis of Voiced Speech," J. Acoust. Soc. Amer. Vol.47, Feb. 1970.
5. L. Grad, "Obrazowa reprezentacja sygnału mowy," Biuletyn IAiR WAT, nr 11, Warsaw 2000.
6. Cz. Basztura, "Modele analizy i procedury w komputerowym rozpoznawaniu głosów," Prace naukowe ITiA Politechniki Wrocławskiej, nr 30, Wrocław 1989.
7. L. S. Marple, "Digital Spectral Analysis," Englewood Cliffs, NJ: Prentice Hall, 1987.
8. K. Saeed, M. Kozłowski, A. Kaczanowski, "Metoda do rozpoznawania obrazów akustycznych izolowanych liter mowy," Zeszyty Politechniki Białostockiej (in Polish), I-1/2002, pp.181-207, Białystok 2002.
9. R. Tadeusiewicz, "Sygnałmowy," WKiŁ (in Polish), Warsaw 1988.
10. V. K. Ingle, J. G. Proakis, "Digital Signal Processing Using MATLAB," Brooks Cole, July 1999.
11. N. Levinson, "The Wiener RMS (Root Mean Square) Error Criterion in Filter Design and Prediction," Journal Math. Phys. Vol. 25, 1947.
12. J. Durbin, "Efficient Estimation of Parameters in Moving Average Models," Biometrics, Vol. 46, part 1, 2, 1969.
13. Khalid Saeed, "Experimental Algorithm for Testing The Realization of Transfer Functions," Proceedings of the Fourteenth IASTED International Conference, Austria 1995.
14. R. Niedzielski, "Kryterium do rozpoznawania znaków maszynowych alfabetu łukowego," MSc Thesis, Ins. Informatyki PB, Białystok 1999.
15. K. Saeed, A. Dardzinska, "Language Processing: Word Recognition without Segmentation," *JASIST - Journal of the American Society for Information Science and Technology*, Volume 52, Issue 14, 2001, pp. 1275-1279, John Wiley and Sons.
16. R. G. Lyons, "Wprowadzenie do cyfrowego przetwarzania sygnałów," WKiŁ (in Polish), Warsaw 1999.
17. Sadaoki Furui, "Digital Speech Processing, Synthesis, and Recognition," Marcel Dekker, Inc. 2001.
18. K. Saeed, M. Rybnik, M. Tabędzki, "More Results and Applications about the Algorithm of Thinning Images to One-Pixel-width," 9th CAIP Int. Conference on Computer Analysis of Images and Patterns, Sept. 5-7, 2001, pp. 601-609, Springer-Verlag, Warsaw 2001.

A Comparative Study of Morphological and Other Texture Features for the Characterization of Atherosclerotic Carotid Plaques

C.I. Christodoulou[1], E. Kyriacou[2], M.S. Pattichis[3], C.S. Pattichis[2], and A. Nicolaides

[1] Cyprus Institute of Neurology and Genetics, P.O.Box 3462, 1683 Nicosia, Cyprus
cschr2@ucy.ac.cy

[2] Dept. of Computer Science, University of Cyprus, P.O.Box 20578, 1678 Nicosia, Cyprus
{ekyriac,pattichi}@ucy.ac.cy

[3] Dep. of Electrical and Computer Engineering, University of New Mexico, NM, USA
pattichis@eece.unm.edu

Abstract. The extraction of features characterizing the structure of atherosclerotic carotid plaques, obtained by high-resolution ultrasound imaging is important for the correct plaque classification and the estimation of the risk of stroke. In this study morphological features were extracted and compared with the well-known texture features spatial gray level dependence matrices (SGLDM), gray level difference statistics (GLDS) and the first order statistics (FOS) for the classification of 330 carotid plaques. For the classification the neural self-organizing map (SOM) classifier and the statistical k-nearest neighbor (KNN) classifier were used. The results showed that morphological and other texture features are comparable, with the morphological and the GLDS feature sets to perform slightly better than the SGLDM and the FOS features. The highest diagnostic yield was achieved with the GLDS feature set and it was about 70%.

1 Introduction

There are indications that the morphology of atherosclerotic carotid plaques, obtained by high-resolution ultrasound imaging, has prognostic implications [1-5]. Smooth surface, echogenicity and a homogenous texture are characteristics of stable plaques, whereas irregular surface, echolucency and a heterogeneous texture are characteristics of potentially unstable plaques. The extraction of features characterizing efficiently the structure of ultrasound carotid plaques is important for the correct plaque classification. The objective of this work was to investigate the usefulness of morphological features for the characterization of carotid plaques for the identification of individuals with asymptomatic carotid stenosis at risk of stroke. The developed system should be able, based on extracted morphological and other texture features to classify plaques into one of the following types: 1) symptomatic because of ipsilateral hemispheric symptoms, and 2) asymptomatic because they were not connected with ipsilateral hemispheric events. The aim is to identify subjects at risk of stroke.

N. Petkov and M.A. Westenberg (Eds.): CAIP 2003, LNCS 2756, pp. 503–511, 2003.

2 Material

A total of 330 carotid plaque ultrasound images (194 asymptomatic and 136 symptomatic) were analyzed. The carotid plaques were labeled as symptomatic after one of the following symptoms was identified: 1) Stroke, 2) Transient Ischemic Attack (TIA) or 3) Amaurosis Fugax (AF). Two sets of data were selected: 1) for training the system, and 2) for evaluating its performance. For training the system 90 asymptomatic and 90 symptomatic plaques were used, whereas for evaluation of the system the remaining 104 asymptomatic and 46 symptomatic plaques were used. The ultrasound images were collected at the Irvine Laboratory for Cardiovascular Investigation and Research, Saint Mary's Hospital, UK, by two ultrasonographers using an ATL duplex scanner with a 7-4 MHz multifrequency probe. Longitudinal scans were performed using duplex scanning and color flow imaging [6].

Before processing, the images were standardized manually by linearly adjusting the image so that the median gray level value of the blood was 0, and the median gray level value of the adventitia (artery wall) was 190. The scale of the gray level of the images ranged from 0 to 255. This standardization using blood and adventitia as reference points was necessary in order to extract comparable measurements in case of processing images obtained by different operators or different equipment [6]. Following the image standardization, the expert physician using as guide their corresponding color blood flow images segmented the plaques manually. Figure 1 shows ultrasound images with the plaque region outlined.

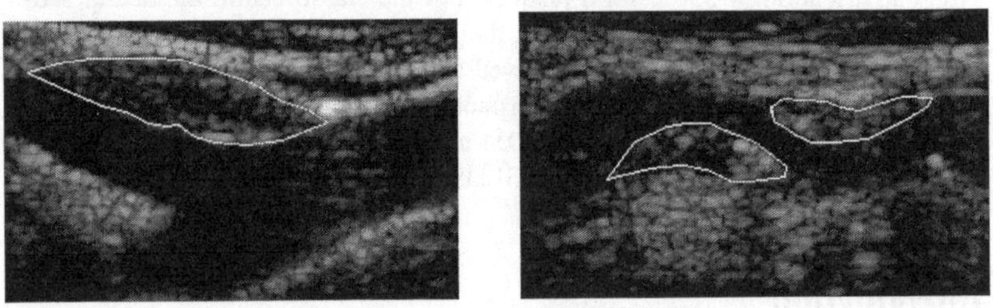

Fig. 1. Ultrasound images of the carotid artery with the atherosclerotic carotid plaques outlined

3 Feature Extraction and Selection

In order for the pattern recognition process to be tractable it is necessary to convert patterns into features, which are condensed representations of the patterns, containing only salient information. Features contain the characteristics of a pattern in a comparable form making the pattern classification possible. The extraction from the signal patterns of good features and the selection from them of the ones with the most discriminatory power can be very crucial for the success of the classification process. In this work morphological and other texture features were extracted from the segmented plaque images in order to be used for the classification of the carotid plaques.

3.1 Morphological Features

Morphological image processing allows us to detect the presence of specified patterns at different scales. We consider the detection of isotropic features that show no preference to particular directions. The simplest structural element for near-isotropic detection is the cross '+' consisting of 5 image pixels.

Thus, we considered pattern spectra based on a flat '+' structural element B. Formally, the Pattern Spectrum is defined in terms of the Discrete Size Transform (DST). We define the DST using [7, 8, 9]:

$$f \rightarrow (\ldots, d_{-k}(f;B), \ldots d_{-1}(f;B), d_0(f;B), \ldots, d_1(f;B), \ldots, d_k(f;B), \ldots) \tag{1}$$

where

$$d_k(f;B) = \begin{cases} fokB - fo(k+1)B, k \geq 0 \\ f \bullet |k|B - f \bullet (|k|-1)B, k \leq 0 \end{cases} \tag{2}$$

o denotes an open operation, and $\bullet$ denotes the close operation. The grayscale DST is a multi-resolution image decomposition scheme, which decomposes an image f into residual images $f \circ kB - f \circ (k+1)B$, for $k > 0$, and $f \bullet |k|B - f \bullet (|k|+1)B$ for $k < 0$. The pattern spectrum of a grayscale image f, in terms of a structuring element B, is given by:

$$P_{f;B}(k) = \|d_k(f;B)\| = \begin{cases} \|fokB - fo(k+1)B\|, k \geq 0 \\ \|f \bullet |k|B - f \bullet (|k|-1)B\|, k \leq 0 \end{cases} \tag{3}$$

where

$$\|f\| = \sum_{x,y} f(x,y), \quad f(x,y) \geq 0. \tag{4}$$

We note that in the limit, as $k \rightarrow \infty$, we have that the resulting image $f \circ kB - f \circ (k+1)B$ converges to the zero image. Also, we note that with increasing values of k, $f \circ kB$ is a subset of the original image. For $k \geq 0$, we may thus normalize the Pattern Spectrum by dividing by the norm of the original image $\|f\|$. Similarly, as $k \rightarrow \infty$, $\|f \bullet kB\|$ converges to $NM \max f(x,y)$, where it is assumed that the image is of size N by M. Hence, for $k < 0$, we can normalize the pattern spectrum by dividing by $NM \max f(x,y) - \|f\|$. Thus, to eliminate undesired variations, all the pattern spectra were normalized.

3.2 Texture Features

Texture refers to the spatial interrelationships and arrangement of the basic elements of an image. Visually, these spatial interrelationships and arrangements of the image pixels are seen as variations in the intensity patterns or gray tones. Therefore texture features have to be derived from the gray tones of the image.

The following feature sets were computed:

(a) First Order Statistics (FOS):

1) Mean value, 2) Variance, 3) Median value, 4) Skewness, 5) Kurtosis, 6) Energy, 7) Entropy.

(b) Spatial Gray Level Dependence Matrices (SGLDM). The spatial gray level dependence (co-occurrence) matrices as proposed by Haralick et al. [10] are based on the estimation of the second-order joint conditional probability density functions that two pixels (k,l) and (m,n) with distance d in direction specified by the angle θ, have intensities of gray level i and gray level j. Based on the probability density functions the following texture measures [7] were computed:

1) Angular second moment, 2) Contrast, 3) Correlation, 4) Sum of squares: variance, 5) Inverse difference moment, 6) Sum average, 7) Sum variance, 8) Sum entropy, 9) Entropy, 10) Difference variance, 11) Difference entropy, and 12), 13) Information measures of correlation.

For a chosen distance d (in this work d=10 was used) and for angles $\theta = 0°, 45°, 90°$ and $135°$ we computed four values for each of the above 13 texture measures. In this work, the mean of these four values were computed for each feature and it was used for classification.

(c) Gray Level Difference Statistics (GLDS). The GLDS algorithm [11] uses first order statistics of local property values based on absolute differences between pairs of gray levels or of average gray levels in order to extract the following texture measures:

1) Homogeneity, 2) Contrast, 3) Energy, 4) Entropy, and 5) Mean.

The above features were calculated for displacements $\delta = (0, 1), (1, 1), (1,0), (1,-1)$, where $\delta \equiv (\Delta x,\Delta y)$, and their mean values were taken.

3.3 Feature Selection

A simple way for calculating the discriminatory power of each individual feature can be defined by computing the distance between the two classes for each feature as:

$$dis = \frac{|m_1 - m_2|}{\sqrt{\sigma_1^2 + \sigma_2^2}} \tag{5}$$

where m_1 and m_2 are the mean values and σ_1 and σ_2 are the standard deviations of the two classes for each feature. The features with the highest discriminatory power are considered to be the ones with the greatest distance.

4 Plaque Classification

For the classification of the carotid plaques into symptomatic or asymptomatic two different classifiers were used: (i) the neural network self-organizing map (SOM) classifier [12] and (ii) the statistical K-Nearest Neighbor (KNN) classifier. All features were normalized before use by subtracting their mean value and dividing with their standard deviation:

$$n(x_i)=(x_i-m_i)/\sigma_i \qquad (6)$$

where m_i is the mean value and σ_i is the standard deviation of the feature i.

4.1 The SOM Classifier

The SOM was chosen because it is an unsupervised learning algorithm where the input patterns are freely distributed over the output node matrix [12]. The weights are adapted without supervision in such a way, so that the density distribution of the input data is preserved and represented on the output nodes. This mapping of similar input patterns to output nodes, which are close to each other, represents a discretisation of the input space, allowing a visualization of the distribution of the input data. The output nodes are usually ordered in a two dimensional grid and at the end of the training phase, the output nodes are labeled with the class of the majority of the input patterns of the training set, assigned to each node.

In the evaluation phase, a new input pattern was assigned to the winning output node with the weight vector closest to the new input vector. In order to classify the new input pattern, the majority of the labels of the output nodes in a *RxR* neighborhood window centered at the winning node, were considered. The number of the input patterns in the neighborhood window for the two classes $m=\{1, 2\}$, (1=symptomatic, 2=asymptomatic), was computed as:

$$SN_m = \sum_{i=1}^{L} W_i N_{mi} \qquad (7)$$

where L is the number of the output nodes in the *R*x*R* neighborhood window with $L=R^2$ (e.g. $L=9$ using a 3x3 window), and N_{mi} is the number of the training patterns of the class m assigned to the output node i. $W_i=1/(2\ d_i)$, is a weighting factor based on the distance d_i of the output node i to the winning output node. W_i gives the output nodes near to the winning output node a greater weight than the ones farther away (e.g. in a 3x3 window, for the winning node $W_i=1$, for the four nodes perpendicular to the winning node $W_i=0.5$ and for the four nodes diagonally located $W_i=0.3536$, etc). The evaluation input pattern was classified to the class m of the SN_m with the greatest value, as symptomatic or asymptomatic. In this work five different window sizes were tested: 1x1, 3x3, 5x5, 7x7, 9x9.

Figure 2 illustrates the distribution of the 180 plaques of the training set on a 10x10 SOM using as input the 5 best morphological features. The figure illustrates the degree of overlap between the two classes.

4.2 The KNN Classifier

The statistical k-nearest neighbor (KNN) classifier was also used for the classification of the carotid plaques. In the KNN algorithm, in order to classify a new input pattern,

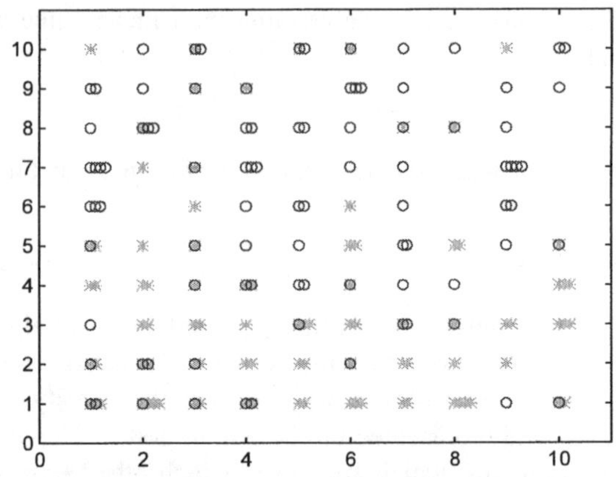

Fig. 2. Distribution of 180 carotid plaques of the training set (90 asymptomatic and 90 symptomatic) on a 10x10 SOM using as input the 5 best morphological features (* = asymptomatic, o = symptomatic). Similar plaques are assigned to neighboring output matrix nodes. A new plaque will be assigned to one winning output node and will be classified based on the labels of the neighboring nodes in a *RxR* neighborhood window. The output nodes near to the winning node are given a greater weight than the ones farther away.

its k nearest neighbors from the training set are identified. The new pattern is classified to the most frequent class among its neighbors based on a similarity measure that is usually the Euclidean distance. In this work the KNN carotid plaque classification system was implemented for different values of k = 1, 3, 5, 7, 9, 11, 19 and it was tested using for input the different feature sets.

5 Results

A total of 330 ultrasound images of carotid atherosclerotic plaques were analyzed and four different feature sets (morphological, FOS, SGLDM and GLDS) were extracted from the manually segmented plaque images as described in section 3. The morphological algorithm extracted 98 features from the plaque images. Using the entire pattern spectra for classification yielded poor results. Using Eq. 5 the number of features used was reduced to only five, which proved to yield satisfactory classification results. The selected features represent the most significant normalized pattern spectra components. We determined that small features due to: $P_{1,'+'}$, $P_{2,'+'}$, $P_{3,'+'}$, $P_{-4,'+'}$ and $P_{-5,'+'}$ (see Eq. 3) yield the best results. It is noted the good performance of $P_{1,'+'}$, which may be susceptible to noise but it is also the feature that is most sensitive to turbulent flow effects around the carotid plaques. Table 1 tabulates the statistics for the five selected morphological features, for the two classes and their interclass distance as computed with Eq. 5.

Table 1. Statistical analysis of the five best morphological features computed from the 330 (194 asymptomatic and 136 symptomatic) ultrasound images of carotid plaques. For each feature the mean and standard deviation were computed for the asymptomatic group and for the symptomatic group. The distance between the symptomatic and the asymptomatic groups was computed as described in Eq. 5

	Asymptomatic		*Symptomatic*		*Distance*
Feature	***Mean*** M_1	***Std*** σ_1	***Mean*** M_2	***Std*** σ_2	$dis = \frac{\lvert m_1 - m_2 \rvert}{\sqrt{\sigma_1^2 + \sigma_2^2}}$
$P_{1,'+'}$	0.0249	0.0229	0.0433	0.0407	0.3934
$P_{3,'+'}$	0.1355	0.0870	0.1922	0.1218	0.3787
$P_{2,'+'}$	0.0713	0.0520	0.1102	0.0888	0.3782
$P_{-4,'+'}$	0.0119	0.0084	0.0080	0.0061	0.3701
$P_{-5,'+'}$	0.0158	0.0109	0.0108	0.0079	0.3675

For the classification task, the neural SOM classifier and the statistical KNN classifier were implemented. For training the classifier, 90 symptomatic and 90 asymptomatic plaques were used, whereas for evaluation of the system the remaining 104 asymptomatic and 46 symptomatic plaques were used. Table 2 tabulates the diagnostic yield for the SOM classifier for the different feature sets and for different neighborhood window sizes on the self-organizing map. Table 3 tabulates the diagnostic yield of the KNN classifier for the different feature sets, for different values of *k*. The diagnostic yield is defined as the percentage of the correctly classified plaques to the total number of the tested plaques. The estimated success rate for the two classes was about similar.

The unsupervised neural SOM classifier was implemented with a 10x10 output node architecture and it was trained for 5000 learning epochs. In order to obtain a more reliable estimate of the diagnostic yield, the SOM was trained and evaluated three times and the average of the three runs was used. Different neighborhood window sizes were tested, where larger window sizes tend to yield higher success rate. The significantly lower success rate for the 1x1 window size is attributed to the many 'undefined' cases where the evaluation input pattern was assigned to a node on the SOM (s. Fig. 2), where no training patterns were assigned during the training phase. The highest diagnostic yield was 69.6% and it was obtained with a 9x9 window size, using as input the GLDS feature set. On average, the results with the highest diagnostic yield were obtained by the GLDS feature set, which was 64.6%, followed by the morphological feature set with a diagnostic yield of 62.9%, the SGLDM with 62.2% and the FOS with 59.9%.

For comparison reasons the statistical KNN classifier was also implemented for different values of *k*, which also performed well. The best diagnostic yield was 68.7% and it was obtained with a *k*=3, using as input the morphological feature set. In average, the best results were obtained by the morphological feature set which was 66.3%, followed closely by the GLDS feature set with a diagnostic yield of 65.6%, the FOS with 63.9% and the SGLDM with 63.8%. Overall the classification results

Table 2. Diagnostic yield (%) of the SOM classifier for the different feature sets and different neighborhood window sizes on the self-organizing map

Window Size	Morphological	FOS	SGLDM	GLDS
1x1	52.4	40.5	44.2	50.0
3x3	66.7	61.6	66.0	66.0
5x5	64.7	65.8	64.4	68.0
7x7	64.7	66.2	67.8	69.3
9x9	65.8	65.5	68.7	69.6
Average	*62.9*	*59.9*	*62.2*	*64.6*

Table 3. Diagnostic yield (%) of the KNN classifier for the different feature sets, for different values of *k*

K	Morphological	FOS	SGLDM	GLDS
1	62.7	60.0	62.7	65.3
3	68.7	63.3	58.7	64.0
5	66.7	63.3	67.3	62.7
7	68.0	65.3	62.7	68.0
9	64.0	62.0	64.7	67.3
11	66.7	67.3	66.0	66.7
19	67.3	66.0	64.7	65.3
Average	*66.3*	*63.9*	*63.8*	*65.6*

for the two classifiers are comparable, with the morphological and the GLDS feature sets to perform slightly better than the SGLDM and the FOS features.

6 Discussion

In this study the usefulness of morphological features is investigated for the characterization of carotid plaques for the identification of individuals with asymptomatic carotid stenosis at risk of stroke. Previous work [4, 5] has shown that texture features can successfully be used for carotid plaque classification. In this work it is shown that morphological features are compare well with the most successful texture feature sets and provide an additional tool for the identification of individuals at risk of stroke. In future work the extracted morphological features will be extended to investigate the classification performance of larger components, and linear, directional structural elements. Also other feature selection methods such as principal component analysis and/or moments of pattern spectra can be considered in future studies, for the selection of the features with the highest discriminatory power. It is hoped that these enhancements will lead to a higher classification performance.

In conclusion, the results in this work show that it is possible to identify a group of patients at risk of stroke based on morphological and other texture features extracted from high resolution ultrasound images of carotid plaques. This group of patients may benefit from a carotid endarterectomy whereas other patients may be spared from an unnecessary operation. Because of the difficulty of the problem and the high degree of overlap of the symptomatic and asymptomatic classes, the above results should be verified with more images from more patients. Furthermore other source of information may be used for classification, for example information obtained by a 3-dimensional reconstruction of the carotid plaque, which may lead to a better diagnostic yield.

Acknowledgements

This work was partly funded through the project *Integrated System for the Support of the Diagnosis for the Risk of Stroke (IASIS),* of the 5th Annual Program for the Financing of Research, of the Research Promotion Foundation of Cyprus.

References

1. Elatrozy T., Nicolaides A., Tegos T., Griffin M., "The Objective Characterisation of Ultrasonic Carotid Plaque Features", *Eur J Vasc Endovasc Surg 16*, pp. 223-230, 1998.
2. Wilhjelm J.E., Gronholdt L.M., Wiebe B., Jespersen S.K., Hansen L.K., Sillesen H., "Quantitative Analysis of Ultrasound B-Mode Images of Carotid Atherosclerotic Plaque: Correlation with Visual Classification and Histological Examination", *IEEE Trans. on Medical Imaging,* Vol. 17, No. 6, pp.910-922, December 1998.
3. Polak J., Shemanski L., O'Leary D., Lefkowitz D., Price T., Savage P., Brand W., Reld C., "Hypoechoic Plaque at US of the Carotid Artery: An Independent Risk Factor for Incident Stroke in Adults Aged 65 Years or Older", *Radiology*, Vol. 208, No 3, pp. 649-654, Sept. 1998.
4. Christodoulou C.I., Pattichis C.S., Pantziaris M., Tegos T., Nicolaides A., Elatrozy T., Sabetai M., Dhanjil S., "Multi-feature texture analysis for the classification of carotid plaques", *Int. Joint Conf. on Neural Networks IJCNN '99*, Washington DC, July, 1999.
5. Christodoulou C.I., Pattichis C.S., Pantziaris M., Nicolaides A., "Texture Based Classification of Atherosclerotic Carotid Plaques", to be published in *IEEE Trans. on Medical Imaging,* 2003.
6. Elatrozy T., Nicolaides A., Tegos T., Zarka A., Griffin M., Sabetai M., "The effect of B-mode ultrasonic image standardisation on the echogenicity of symptomatic and asymptomatic carotid bifurcation plaques", *International Angiology*, Vol. 17, No 3, pp. 179-186, Sept. 1998.
7. Dougherty E.R., *An Introduction to Morphological Image Processing*, Belingham, Washington, SPIE Optical Engineering Press, 1992.
8. Dougherty E. R., Astola J., *An Introduction to Nonlinear Image Processing*, Belingham, Washington, SPIE Optical Engineering Press, 1994.
9. Maragos P., "Pattern spectrum and multiscale shape representation", *IEEE Trans. on Pattern Analysis and Machine Intelligence*, 11:701 715, 1989.
10. Haralick R.M., Shanmugam K., Dinstein I., "Texture Features for Image Classification", *IEEE Trans. on Systems, Man., and Cybernetics,* Vol. SMC-3, pp. 610-621, Nov. 1973.
11. Weszka J.S., Dyer C.R., Rosenfield A., "A Comparative Study of Texture Measures for Terrain Classification", *IEEE Trans. on Systems, Man. & Cybern.,* Vol. SMC-6, April 1976.
12. Kohonen T., "The Self-Organizing Map", *Proceedings of the IEEE*, Vol. 78, No. 9, pp. 1464-1480, Sept. 1990.

A Computation of Fingerprint Similarity Measures Based on Bayesian Probability Modeling

Sungwook Joun, Eungbong Yi, Choonwoo Ryu, and Hakil Kim

Graduate School of Information Technology & Telecommunication, INHA University
253 Yonghyun-dong, Nam-ku, Incheon, Korea
Biometrics Engineering Research Center
{mistral,atropiny,ryusrain}@dreamwiz.com, hikim@inha.ac.kr

Abstract. One of the primary functions of minutia-based fingerprint recognition algorithms is to compute a similarity measure between two fingerprints. The similarity measure is generally based on the type, angle-difference, and position-difference of corresponding minutiae. This paper proposes a Bayesian probability modeling method for computing the fingerprint similarity measure. The proposed method models the distributions of the angle-differences and the position-differences according to the type-difference between the corresponding minutia pairs. Also, the similarity measure is represented by a posteriori probability assuming that their distributions are statistically independent. This method has been applied to two different cases of fingerprint verification and demonstrated its effectiveness by reducing the equal error rates with the average of 40%.

1 Introduction

A fingerprint matching method can be divided into one of two methods according to the information which the method utilizes. The first is a template matching method where the correlation between two fingerprints is computed, either in the spatial domain or in the frequency domain [1,2,3,4]. The second is a minutia matching method, in which a numerical similarity is calculated from a set of corresponding minutiae [5]. The minutia matching method can be further developed to a ridge counting method through the process of updating the similarity based on the coincidence of ridge lines between a corresponding pair of minutiae [6]. Recently, the minutia matching method has been studied vigorously because of its efficiency and flexibility. Fig. 1 shows the two prominent minutia types, *ending* and *bifurcation*. The ending is defined where a ridge ends abruptly, and the bifurcation is where a ridge is divided [5].

A minutia-based fingerprint matching algorithm is generally decomposed into three stages [7];

- *alignment* stage: the parameters of a transformation between the two fingerprint images are estimated, and the input minutiae are aligned with the enrolled minutiae according to the estimated parameters,
- *matching* stage: the corresponding minutiae are decided and the differences in angle and in position of each pair of corresponding minutiae are computed,

N. Petkov and M.A. Westenberg (Eds.): CAIP 2003, LNCS 2756, pp. 512–520, 2003.

- *scoring* stage: a similarity measure between the two fingerprints is calculated using a decision strategy.

In a current scoring stage, a similarity measure has been computed by separately considering the position-difference, the angle-difference, and the type-difference between the matched pairs of corresponding minutiae [7]. This method, however, has overlooked the tendency of the feature vectors in the genuine matching and in the impostor matching, respectively, and ignored the probabilistic distributions of the components of the feature vector. In order to refine the current scoring strategy and to compute more reliable fingerprint similarity measures. This paper proposes a Bayesian probability modeling in which the probabilistic distributions and the tendency of the feature vectors are dealt with.

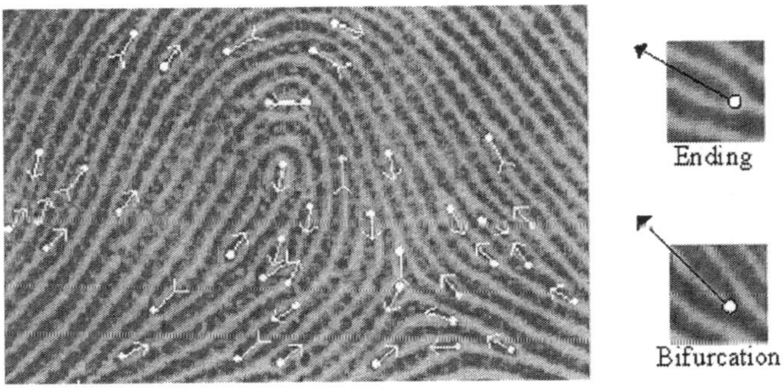

Fig. 1. Definition of fingerprint minutia types.

2 Bayesian Decision Theory

The Bayesian decision theory is a fundamental statistical approach to the problem of pattern classification. This approach is based on quantifying the tradeoffs between various classification decision which uses the probability and the costs that accompany such decision under the assumption that the decision problem is posed in probabilistic term and all of the relevant probability values are known [8].

In the framework of fingerprint verification, ω_j denotes the state of nature, with j=1 for genuine matching and j=2 for impostor matching. Then, $P(\omega_j)$ are their prior probabilities. Given two sets of minutiae obtained from two different fingerprints, where one is enrolled and the other is tested, the feature vector, $\boldsymbol{x}$ consists of three quantities, position-difference, angle-difference, and type-difference between the pairs of minutiae from the two fingerprints. The conditional probability, $p(\boldsymbol{x}|\omega_j)$ is the probability density function for $\boldsymbol{x}$ given that the state of nature is ω_j.

Suppose that the prior probabilities $P(\omega_j)$ and the conditional probabilities $p(\boldsymbol{x}|\omega_j)$ are known for j=1, 2, and that a feature vector $\boldsymbol{x}$ is observed. Then, the feature vector influences the decision concerning the state of nature by calculating the posterior probability $P(\omega_j|\,\boldsymbol{x})$ based on the *Bayesian formula* :

$$P(\omega_j \mid x) = \frac{p(x \mid \omega_j)P(\omega_j)}{\sum_{j=1}^{2} p(x \mid \omega_j)P(\omega_j)} \qquad (j = 1,2) \tag{1}$$

Fig. 2 shows the overall procedure of computing the similarity measure based on the Bayesian decision theory. The following two modules are the primary components of the proposed computational method of the fingerprint similarity.

1. Training module: The prior probabilities and the conditional probabilities are obtained from a set of training samples. Then, the obtained stochastic information is generalized using a modeling process.
2. Evaluation module: The posterior probabilities are calculated by the Bayesian formula that inputs the prior probabilities and the modeled conditional probabilities.

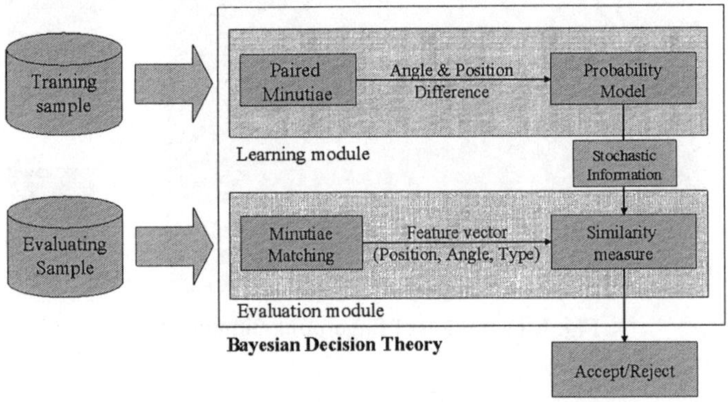

Fig. 2. Overall block diagram of the proposed method.

3 The Proposed Method

3.1 Search for Corresponding Minutiae

The attribute of each minutia is composed of position (***x***-, ***y***-coordinates of minutia), angle (counter-clockwise direction from the ***x***-axis), and type (type of minutia). For each minutia in the enrolled fingerprint, the corresponding minutia in the tested fingerprint is found by comparing their attributes. As shown in Fig. 3, a tolerance region is defined as a circle centered at the given minutia. Among the candidate minutiae residing in the tolerance region, the most likely corresponding minutia is the one which has the smallest value of multiplying the normalized position-difference with the normalized angle-difference. We have empirically determined a radius of the tolerance region as 15 pixels, the position-difference and the angle-difference as 30 pixels and 30 degrees, respectively. Once the corresponding minutia is determined, the feature vector representing the likelihood of the pair of minutiae is defined as following [7]:

$$\boldsymbol{x} = \{\textit{Position-difference, Angle-difference, Type-difference}\} = \{D, A, T\} \quad (2)$$

where D is the Euclidean distance in pixel, A is the angle in degree, and $T = 0$ for different type.,$T = 1$ for same type.

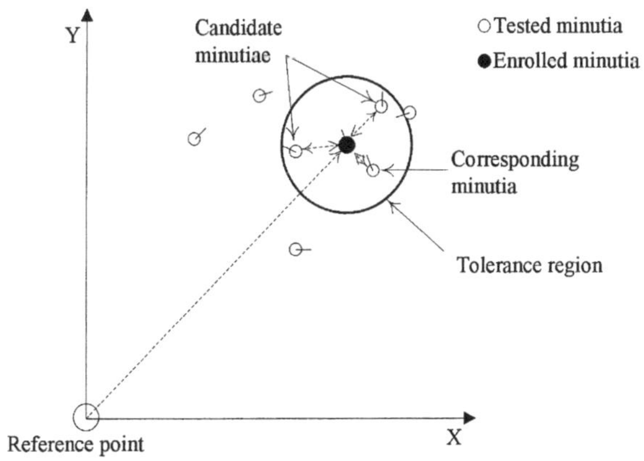

Fig. 3. Search for a corresponding minutia.

3.2 Bayesian Probability Modeling

In this study, the problem of matching two fingerprints is modeled as the classification of a set of feature vectors $\boldsymbol{X} = \{\boldsymbol{x}_i, i=1, ..., N\}$ defined in equation (2) into one of the two classes, $\{\omega_1$=Genuine, ω_2=Impostor$\}$, where N is the number of matched minutiae pairs between the two fingerprints. Without the loss of generality, the two classes are assumed to be equally likely, and their prior probabilities are given as $P(\omega_1) = P(\omega_2) = 0.5$. Meanwhile, the conditional probabilities of each feature components given a known class are computed from a set of training samples. Basically, this process is a supervised learning, where the distributions of the feature components are modeled by parametric probability density functions (PDF) for genuine matching and impostor matching, respectively

Furthermore, it has been observed that the genuine matching and the impostor matching produce distinctive distributions in the minutia-type difference. For a certain set of training samples, our feature extraction algorithm gives the conditional probabilities of the type-difference as follows :

$$P(\boldsymbol{T}|\omega_1) = \begin{cases} 0.3, & \boldsymbol{T}=0 \\ 0.7, & \boldsymbol{T}=1 \end{cases}, \quad P(\boldsymbol{T}|\omega_2) = \begin{cases} 0.5, & \boldsymbol{T}=0 \\ 0.5, & \boldsymbol{T}=1 \end{cases} \quad (3)$$

These conditional probabilities are in accordance with our observation that the minutia type is more highly preserved in the genuine matching than the impostor matching where it is preserved or exchanged with the equal rate.

Especially in the genuine matching, if the types of the truly corresponding minu tiae are different, then it affects the tested minutia to move to a neighboring ridge causing a position-difference offset of a half of the ridge interval. This is depicted in Fig. 4. While Fig. 5(a) shows that the angle-difference is distributed similarly regardless of the type changes, Fig. 5(b) describes that the position-difference with the type change occurrence is shifted to 7 pixels which is equal to the half of the average ridge interval. These distributions are modeled parametrically by the discrete Gamma function as shown in equation (4) and displayed as curves in Fig. 5 [9].

$$P(A \mid \omega_1, T) = C_a \cdot A^{\alpha-1} e^{-A/\beta} \quad \begin{cases} \text{for } T = 0, \alpha = 2.2 \text{ and } \beta = 2.1 \\ \text{for } T = 1, \alpha = 1.7 \text{ and } \beta = 3.9 \end{cases} \quad \text{and} \quad P(D \mid \omega_1, T) = C_d \cdot D^{\alpha-1} e^{-D/\beta} \quad \begin{cases} \text{for } T = 0, \alpha = 2.4 \text{ and } \beta = 1.9 \\ \text{for } T = 1, \alpha = 5.8 \text{ and } \beta = 1.3 \end{cases} \tag{4}$$

where $\boldsymbol{C_a}$ and $\boldsymbol{C_d}$ are normalizing constants and $\boldsymbol{A}$ and $\boldsymbol{D}$ are integers from 0 to 30.

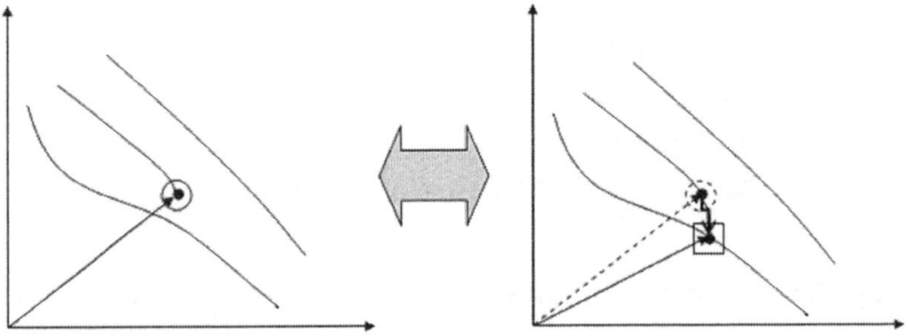

Fig. 4. Example of minutia-type change.

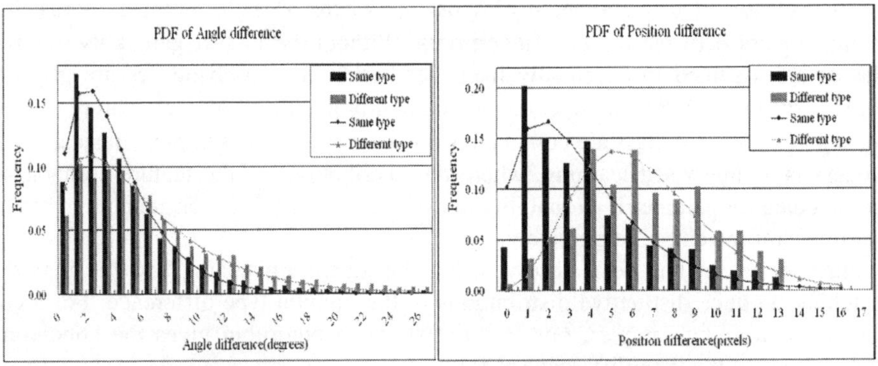

(a) angle-difference (b) position-difference

Fig. 5. Distribution of features in the genuine matching.

In contrast, the impostor matching has almost uniform distributions for both feature components, and they are estimated by using polynomial regression. The distribution models are expressed in equation (5) and displayed as curves in Fig. 6 over the sample distributions. It must be noted that the distributions are the same regardless of the changes in type.

$$P(A \mid \omega_2, T) = -0.0012A + 0.0552$$
$$P(D \mid \omega_2, T) = -0.017D^2 + 0.0238D + 0.0175 \tag{5}$$

In order to resolve the correlation between the angle-difference and the position-difference, their scatter plot for the training samples is obtained as shown in Fig. 7. Regardless of the fact that the types of the corresponding minutiae pairs are either same or different, the plots of 1,000 pairs are widely scattered enough to conclude that the angle-difference and the position-difference are statistically independent. Hence, for each pair of corresponding minutiae, the combined conditional probability is computed as:

$$\begin{aligned} P(x \mid \omega_j) &= P(D,A,T \mid \omega_j) = P(D,T \mid \omega_j) \cdot P(A,T \mid \omega_j) \\ &= \left\{ \frac{P(D \cap T \cap \omega_j)}{P(\omega_j)} \right\} \cdot \left\{ \frac{P(A \cap T \cap \omega_j)}{P(\omega_j)} \right\} \\ &= \{P(T \mid \omega_j) P(D \mid \omega_j, T)\} \cdot \{P(T \mid \omega_j) P(A \mid \omega_j, T)\} \quad \text{for } j = 1,2 \\ &= P(T \mid \omega_j)^2 P(D \mid \omega_j, T) P(A \mid \omega_j, T)\} \end{aligned} \tag{6}$$

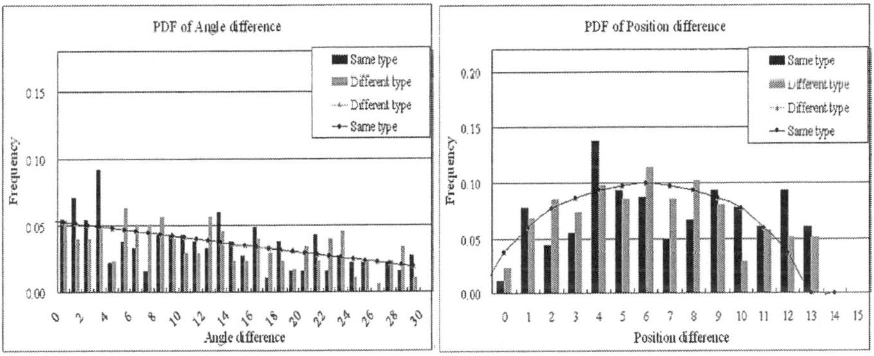

(a) Angle-difference (b) Position-difference.

Fig. 6. Distribution of features in the impostor matching.

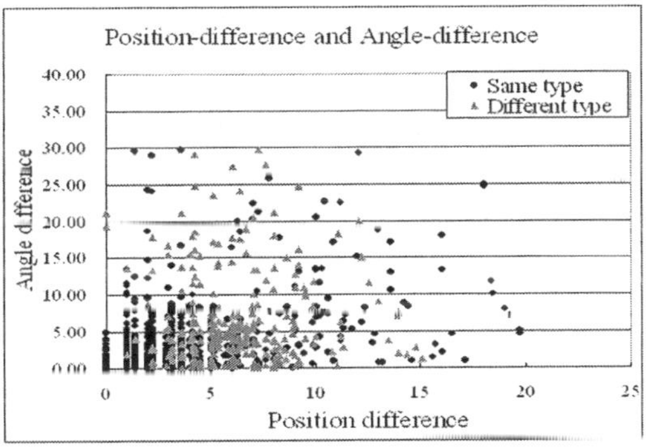

Fig. 7. Scatter plot of angle-difference and position-difference of corresponding minutia pairs.

3.3 Similarity Measure

Once a fingerprint has been enrolled and a tested fingerprint is input for the verification, there exists a set of corresponding minutiae pairs between the two fingerprints. Denoting $\boldsymbol{X} = \{\boldsymbol{x}_i, i=1, ..., N\}$ the set of feature vectors between corresponding minutiae pairs, the posterior probability $P(\omega_j|\boldsymbol{x}_i)$ of each $\boldsymbol{x}_i$, is computed from the prior probability and the combined conditional probability using equation (1). Then, the similarity measure between the two fingerprints based on $\boldsymbol{X}$ is defined as following :

$$\text{Similarity Measure} = \frac{1}{C}\sum_{i=1}^{N}\{P(\omega_1 \mid x_i) - P(\omega_2 \mid x_i)\} \tag{7}$$

where $\boldsymbol{C}$ is a normalizing constant.

4 Experimental Results

The first fingerprint database(I) tested in the experiment is the DB2 provided by FVC2002 (Fingerprint Verification Competition 2002) [10]. 880 images (110 fingers × 8 impressions) are captured by an optical sensor for the database(I). The fingerprint image is of the size 296×560 and the resolution 569 dpi. The second database(II) consists of 800 fingerprints (80 fingers × 10 impressions) captured by an optical sensor. The size and the resolution of images are 248×292 and 500dpi, respectively. Each database is divided as following: For the learning stage, Set-B consists of 90% images of each database. Then, Set-A is for the verification, which consists of 10% images.

The proposed method has been implemented and tested over the above data sets, and the results are summarized in Table 1 and Fig. 8. Table 1 compares EER (Equal Error Rates) of our lab-made fingerprint matching algorithm without and with the proposed method, respectively method A and B. The matching algorithm is more optimized for images of database(I). Fig. 8 depicts more thorough comparison by DET (Detection Error Trade-off) curves. For both databases, the EER is reduced by a considerable amount, with the average 40%.

Table 1. Performance of the proposed method in the equal error rate.

DB	EER(%)	
	Method A	Method B
Database(I)	0.82	0.46
Database(II)	3.80	2.44

5 Conclusion

The problem of matching two fingerprints is considered as the classification of a set of feature vectors into either the genuine class or the impostor class. The decision

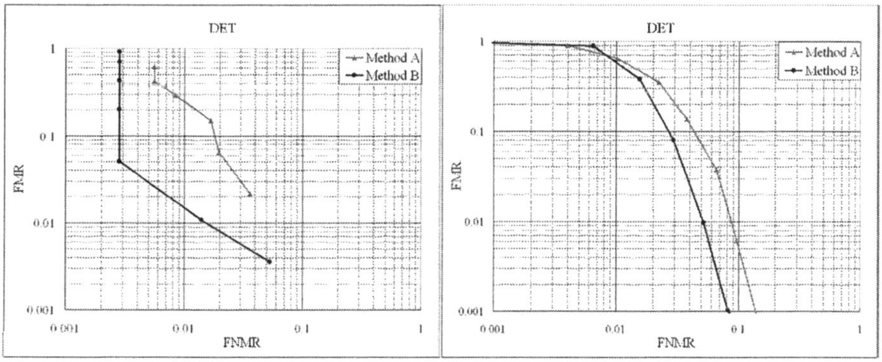

(a) Database(I) (b) Database(II)

Fig. 8. Performance comparison of the proposed method in DET curves.

boundary function is represented by a similarity measure between the pair of fingerprints. In computing the similarity measure, a Bayesian probability modeling is utilized, where the distributions of the angle-difference and the position-difference between the corresponding minutiae pairs are modeled by conditional probability density functions. It has been observed that the angle-difference and the position-difference are uncorrelated enough to be assumed being statistically independent. Letting the prior probabilities be equally likely, the similarity measure is given as the posterior probability using the Bayesian updating formula. The proposed method has been implemented and demonstrated how the equal error rate in fingerprint verification can be lowered.

Acknowledgement

This work was supported in part by Biometrics Engineering Research Center, KOSEF.

References

[1] K.H.Fielding et al. "Optical fingerprint identification by binary joint transform correlation", *Optical Engineering,* Vol. 30, No. 12, pp.1958-1961, Dec. 1991.

[2] R. Bahuguna, "Fingerprint verification using hologram matched filterings," in *Proc. Biometric Consortium Eighth Meeting*, San Jose, CA, June, 1996.

[3] E. C. Driscoll, C. O. Martin, K. Ruby, J. J. Russel, and J. G. Watson, "Method and apparatus for verifying identity using image correlation," *U.S. Patent* 5067162, 1991.

[4] A. Sibbald, "Method and apparatus for fingerprint characterization and recognition using auto-correlation pattern," *U.S. Patent* 5633947, 1994.

[5] N.K. Ratha, K. Karu, S. Chen, and A.K. Jain, "A real-time matching system for large fingerprint databases," *IEEE Trans. On PAMI,* Vol. 18, No. 8, pp. 799-813, August, 1996.

[6] R.M. Bolle et al, "System and method for detecting ridge counts in fingerprint image processing," U.S.Patent No.6266433, Jul.24, 2001.
[7] A.K. Jain, et al, "On-line fingerprint verification," *IEEE Trans. On PAMI*, Vol. 19, No. 4, pp. 302-314, 1997.
[8] R.O. Duda, P.E. Hart, D.G. Stork, *Pattern Classification*, 2nd ed. Wiley Publication, pp. 20-64, 2000.
[9] A. L.Garcia, *Probability and Random Processing for Electrical Engineering*, 2nd ed Addison-Wesly Publication, pp116-119, May 2000.
[10] D.Maio, D.Maltoni, R. Cappelli, J.wayman and A.K Jain, "FVC2002: Fingerprint verification competition," *Pattern Recognition, Proceedings, 16th International Conference on*, Vol. 3, pp.811-814, 2002..

Classifying Sketches of Animals Using an Agent-Based System

Graham Mackenzie and Natasha Alechina

Nottingham University, Nottingham, NG8 1BB, UK
gjm@cs.nott.ac.uk
http://www.cs.nott.ac.uk/~gjm

Abstract. A technique for the classification and understanding of child-like sketches of animals, using a live pen-based input device is demonstrated. A method of segmenting the sketch using curve differentials in addition to pen speed is shown. Once this stage is completed, an agent-based search of the resultant data begins in an attempt to isolate recognisable high-level features within the sketch. The context between probable matches for these features is used by the agents in assessing their success in identifying features correctly.

1 Introduction

This paper describes work in progress on classifying objects in free-hand drawings or sketches. We have concentrated on recognising drawings of animals: classifying a free-hand sketch as a cat, or a dog, or a fish, etc.

The drawings we use are discretised pen drawings (not optical images) although the general methodology proposed in the paper could be easily adapted for optical images. At the moment the sketches are represented as sets of components which in turn are arrays of coordinate points. We plan to move to the UNIPEN format[5] in the near future.

This work is intended to explore possibilities of using agent techniques in conjunction with context resolution more generally in computer vision. The decision to use sketch based input was taken simply to reduce the problem in scope - leaving the agent-based context resolution system independent of less relevant low-level computer vision problems.

Our method of classification uses a hierarchical database of animal body parts (heads, tails, paws,...) which is described in section 4. Classification proceeds by parsing the sketch into a set of meaningful components on the basis of their geometry, matching those components to generalised animal body parts contained in a database and then using those match results to match the overall sketch to a particular animal.

Parsing of the sketch into components is done using two different techniques. This is described in section 2. Classifying components of a sketch as heads, tails or other animal parts is a hard combinatorial problem. To avoid brute force matching of every component to every entry in the database we use a technique involving 'agents', able to communicate via a blackboard-like architecture [6, 10]. Each component in the database has an associated agent. Agents move around the sketch getting 'more confident' if they seem to be successfully matching their component and also if they encounter other

N. Petkov and M.A. Westenberg (Eds.): CAIP 2003, LNCS 2756, pp. 521–529, 2003.

agents in the neighbourhood which they are more comfortable with, (e.g. eyes and ears) and don't encounter agents they are 'repulsed' by (e.g. an ear and a tail). Having reached a certain level of confidence the agents 'settle' on their component. Completely unsuccessful agents are removed from the sketch and replaced by agents corresponding to other components. Another agent then recognises the arrangement of other agents as an animal and gives us a final result.

Unlike most visual classifiers this one attempts to achieve recognition by 'understanding' the image presented to it, at least to a degree. Once a successful match is achieved, we can expect that most of the component parts of the sketch will also have been identified correctly.

More details on the agents control is given in section 5. The algorithm for comparing a stroke in the database and a stroke in the sketch is described in section 3. Some simple experimental results are described in section 6.

2 Parsing a Sketch

The input to our system is via a 'pen-based' interface, rather than a scan of a previously drawn sketch. Data arrives as a series of Cartesian points grouped into strokes, which together comprise a complete sketch. What we need to do, in essence, is search through the strokes finding and separating out probable high-level features from the collection of strokes. We make the fairly strong assumption that there must be some change of direction or other interference within a pen-stroke to denote a transition from one high-level feature to another, or else a completely new pen-stroke. By separating every combination of change of directions we have a collection of stroke fragments, of which some tiny portion will be complete, identifiable high-level features.

Each sketched 'stroke' is first of all processed to locate probable corners or changes from one subsection of the sketch to another. This is achieved using a combination of measuring pen-speed (the sketcher's pen speed drops significantly at corners) and by measuring the perpendicular distance from a chord across a small section of the stroke to the stroke itself at sample points along the sketch.

Each potential corner is flagged. It is preferable to be over-sensitive in corner-detection, rather than under-sensitive at this stage, since spurious corners can be ignored during the matching stage. We then examine each drawn stroke's relationships with others - attempting to establish points in the sketch that were intended by the sketcher to connect, and ignoring those when sections of line were supposed merely to come close together. Points of probable intersection are flagged along with the corners. Clusters of close flagged points are 'joined' to form a single point to reference that particular event.

What results is a network of edges drawn by the sketcher, and nodes that represent a either a possible change from one primitive component of the sketch to another, or an event of potential significance within one such component.

Once we have this 'graph-like' structure describing a sketch we can consider plausible paths through it as possible components representing high-level features.

We introduce a simple grammar used to describe these components in a concise manner. Each component extracted from the sketch consists of sections of line and the joins between sections. Our grammar, therefore contains these two basic symbols. Each

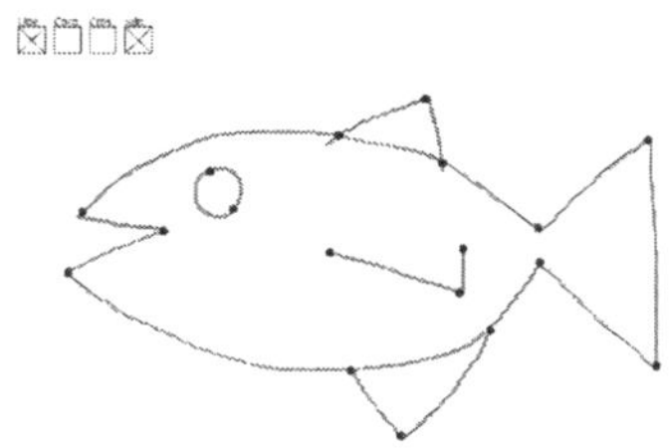

Fig. 1. Parsing a sketch to identify points of interest

line is expanded to provide information regarding its length (relative to the sketch size) and its curvature (direction and magnitude). Each 'join' provides the angle between the two adjoining line sections.

Given a list of coordinate points $C[1..n]$ between two 'join' points A and B we

- assess the curvature: measure the perpendicular distance between each point in C and the straight-line AB and find the maximum value.
  Curvature direction is determined by assessing whether any point $C[i]$ between A and B is to the 'right' or 'left' of AB from the perspective of travelling along AB.
- find the length: the distance along C from A to B (not just the length of AB).

For each corner, we must record the change in direction at corners: examine a corner Y by inspecting straight lines XY and YZ (where X, Y, and Z are corners on C). The angle at Y is ordained to be the change in direction required to change from bearing XY to bearing YZ.

3 Matching

It is easy enough to define a matching algorithm that will return a positive match between two components if, and only if, they are exactly the same (after scaling). Assuming the starting points of both components are fixed, we could match their grammatical representations section by section and return a positive match if they are identical.

In reality we want to match successfully two components that the artist/sketcher intended to represent the same concept. This means that the matching process should be relaxed: lengths of the sections, angles between them, and curvature of the lines may vary within some limits, which depend on how precise a match we need for a particular feature.

We mentioned earlier that when parsing we aim to be over-sensitive in our detection of corners and other 'points of interest'. When matching two components with non-equal sizes we can remove corners from the more numerous in an attempt to facilitate a match, imposing a penalty on the match likelihood for each corner removed.

The outcome of matching is determined by three results from the matching algorithm: similarity of corresponding angles, lengths and curvatures.

4 Database of Components

A database of matchable components is needed to compare the components found in a sketch with. Since the larger part of the aim is to classify the overall sketch, our database must do more than identify individual components - we must concern ourselves with the relations between those components that lead us to build up the 'big picture'.

As section 5 describes, 'agents' are responsible for applying the above matching test on the components in the sketch, so each database entry must contain all the information that a agent might require for its search to be successful.

Often, a given component we want to match as a general case will have many different incarnations, which are completely incompatible with the matching algorithm. The database must therefore be hierarchical in nature - with sub-classes of features for recognising using low-level matches and parent classes that simplify relationships between agents.

Certain database entries (those at the very top level, for example) are designed such that an agent constructed from it can be satisfied by diverse range of possible sketches. For these agents no components-based models are required whatsoever, since the range would be too great. Only the layout of other agents within the system affects the judged success of these agents.

Each database entry includes some of the following:

- a model, for the purposes of matching components at the low-level;
- a parent, from which it can inherit rules from the more general case that still apply;
- neighbour relationships: rules to define what features are to expected in the vicinity of, and what constitutes a 'correct' layout relationship between features;
- alternatives, for the purposes of introducing different agents.

5 Agent Control

We use agents to reduce the search space of features that could be part of a sketch by using relationships between parts already identified or partially identified. Examining conflicts and complementary features as we continue the recognition process allows us to reject certain branches of the space of features and order our search more appropriately. By using agents' contextual comparisons to minimise unnecessary calls to the curve matching routine we hope to avoid the combinatorial explosion which is inherent in the 'brute force' approach of matching each component with each feature in the database.

Knowledge-based solutions to image understanding problems are relatively scarce [3] but have been explored [9, 4]. Utilising a similar approach to SIGMA [9], we attempt to improve over time our interpretation of an 'image' by allowing collaborative agents brought into play by the identification of certain components to search the available data for additional components that are expected to be present.

We define an 'arena' for our agent system to exist in. The potential features extracted from the graph are added to the arena 'floor', where all agents have access to them.

Roaming the arena are several agents, each tasked individually with finding a specific high-level feature. An agent, in this context, is an independent but communicative 'sub-program' endowed with its own objective and set of skills. By striving to reach its own goals it aids the whole process of identifying sketches. The agents 'wander' the floor exerting an influence on, and being influenced by the other agents in the image, searching for features that their grammar compliant word matches.

Agents are aided in their task by their own sense of achievement and restlessness - a measure of their confidence in having found their individual goal. The mobile agents gradually become more and more restless over time if they are unsuccessful in their task - leading them to become less careful about steering clear of other agents that it might otherwise consider inappropriate to consort with, and take more risks regarding unusual positioning within the image. The more restless an agent is, the less influence it has over other agents, whereas if an agent is satisfied with where it is other agents will consider its input more reputable.

An *agent's confidence* at its current location is a combination of three factors; a measure of how near it is to the feature it is trying to find (c_{target}), and a measure of how compatible its current position is with other agents with respect to the local (c_{local}) and global (c_{global}) rules. These values are computed using the two 'sensors': the target sensor and agent sensor.

The *target sensor* searches the vicinity of the agent (the part of the arena floor around the agent's location) for patterns that match its target specifications. This means running matching tests provided by this agent against fragments found around the agent. Output from the matching sensor directly effects the confidence level that agent advertises, and therefore its subsequent motion.

The *agent sensor* is responsible for interacting with the other agents that are active within the system. This allows an implicit co-operation between agents - one agent knows it should (typically) be 'above' a second agent within the image, so it is 'pushed' that way, and its confidence level increases to reflect that it believes it is in the correct area of the image - at least with respect to the former agent. Two agents can also be repulsed or attracted, depending upon issues regarding their respective targets (insisting on their closeness, for example) and the agent with the least confidence will be most affected.

An agent contains 'rules' regarding its relations with other agents in the image. These rules are split into two sets: local and global. A local rule applies to agents which are in the vicinity of the given agent. A global rule applies to the entire system of agents. Such rules could be that one feature must remain below another, or that one feature must remain horizontally between two others etc.

To compute the exact value of the agent confidence, the system is currently using the following formula. Let $\mathcal{F}$ be the set of potential features, $\mathcal{A}$ the set of all agents, $A \in \mathcal{A}$, R the range within which agents and features are noticed by the agent A, $DIST(x_1, x_2)$ a function that gives the distance between two features x_1 and x_2 in the arena, $CLOSE(x_1, x_2)$ gives a normalised (relative to the size of the sketch) measure of the distance between x_1 and x_2 in the sketch, where higher is closer, $A.MODEL$ the feature the agent is looking for, $MATCH(x_1, x_2)$ is the probability that a potential feature x_1 is an example of an abstract feature x_2, $A.RULES$ the set of local rules belonging to A, $RULE(a_1, a_2)$ the result of an application of a rule to agents a_1 and a_2 (higher is a better compliance with the rule).

$$c_{target}(A) = \frac{\Sigma_{x \in X}(CLOSE(x, A) \times MATCH(x, A.MODEL))}{|X|}$$

where $X = \{x \in \mathcal{F} \text{ and } DIST(x, A) < R\}$ (the set of features visible to A).

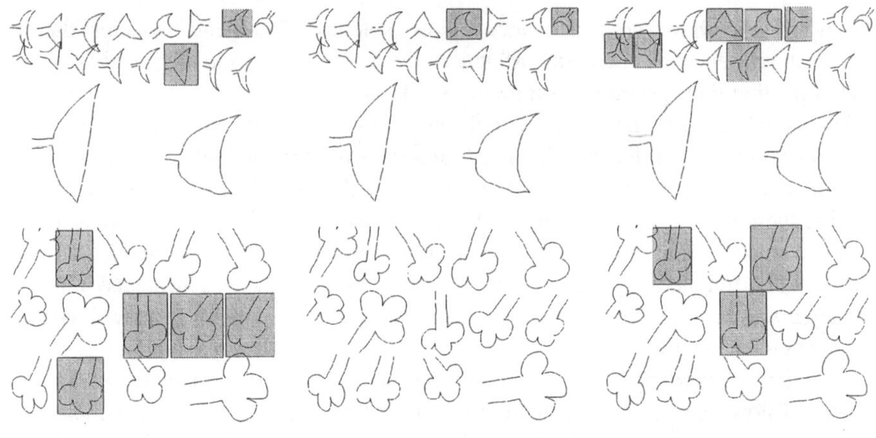

Fig. 2. Highlighted components were matched to the wrong model using the length *(left)*, Perpendicular distance *(centre)* and bearing *(right)* match tests respectively for the 'fish-tails' test *(top)*, and the 'dog-paw' test *(bottom)*

$c_{local}(A) = \frac{\Sigma_{a \in X}(\Sigma_{RULE \in A.RULES}(CLOSE(a,A) \times RULE(a,A))/|A.RULES|)}{|X|}$
where $X = \{a \in \mathcal{A} \text{ and } DIST(a, A) < R\}$ (the set of agents visible to A).

$c_{global}(A)$ is computed similarly to $h_{local}(A)$ but with respect to the set of global rules associated with A.

The agent will move in the direction that causes an increase in the value of c_{target}, c_{local} and c_{global} if possible. If one value increases radically whilst the others do not, it is an indication that perhaps it has found a false success.

Only a certain amount of agents are allowed into the image at any one time. Their introduction into the system of active agents follows a period of queueing, waiting to be 'voted' on by the agents that are already active within the image. A voting cycle is set up, and on each iteration of it, an active agent requests an agent that would help satisfy it, that is currently not active. The queue of inactive agents is ordered by the number of votes each agent has received and when a space in the image becomes available, the highest voted agent is released from the queue. Such a 'space' would be made after an agent is rejected from the image. This occurs if an agent's satisfaction drops too low. The dissatisfied agent is removed from the image and added to the back of the queue of waiting agents.

6 Experimental Results

We demonstrate some of the results from testing of the low-level, component matching technique below. For this purpose, a user was asked to draw several primitive 'fish-tails' and 'dog-paws' (figure 2), which were matched against a small library of alternative components using the technique described in section 3.

As is apparent each of the matching tests produces different results. The three tests complement each other, as each is more or less applicable in differing circumstances. For

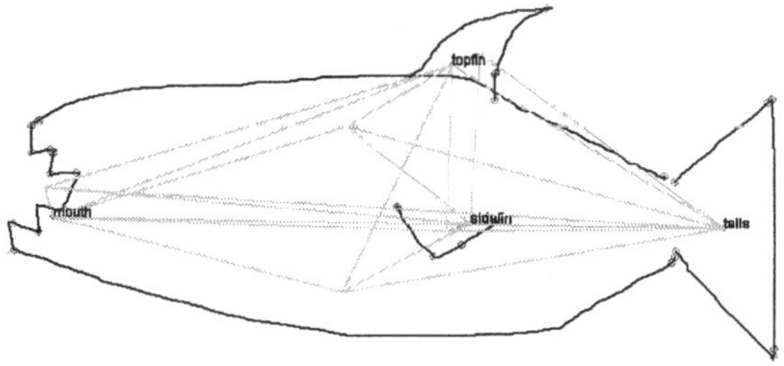

Fig. 3. Appropriate agents working on an example sketch

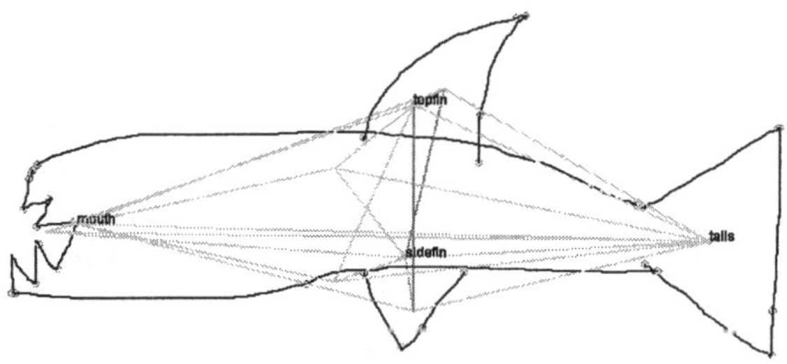

Fig. 4. A feature is in an unexpected location

example, using the length-based test several 'dog-paws' are mis-identified as 'fish-tails' simply because the ratio of lengths of each section of the component are likely to be the similar in this case.

The 'dog-paw' test demonstrates that the perpendicular distance test (curvature) is advantageous for models with obvious curves, as their are no incorrect matches. Models with no curves will not benefit from this test.

Preliminary tests using the agents resulted in some promising results, an example is shown in figure 3 - a hastily drawn sharp-toothed fish. The appropriate agents, given a small match database and simple ruleset are introduced and they quickly find their valid component match, aided by their own interaction, as described above. Sketches do not have to be oriented specifically - the agents should arrange themselves regardless of the orientation of the overall sketch.

In the image, the black lines comprise the sketch, the dark grey lines represent strong potential matches that have been ignored and the faint grey lines show weak or where there is no match between agent and feature in the image. The agent's location is denoted by the word that describes its target. The image shows the agents after they have settled. Although the 'side-fin' and 'top-fin' agents have correctly found their targets, it is evident from the strongly coloured lines leading from each agent to their other possible feature matches that they each might have settled on the other's target, if based on sketch data only.

Figure 4 shows an example where a feature has appeared in an unexpected location. This demonstrates the interplay between agents - although the 'side-fin' agent has identified the fin on the bottom of the fish it is kept from settling there by rules regarding the

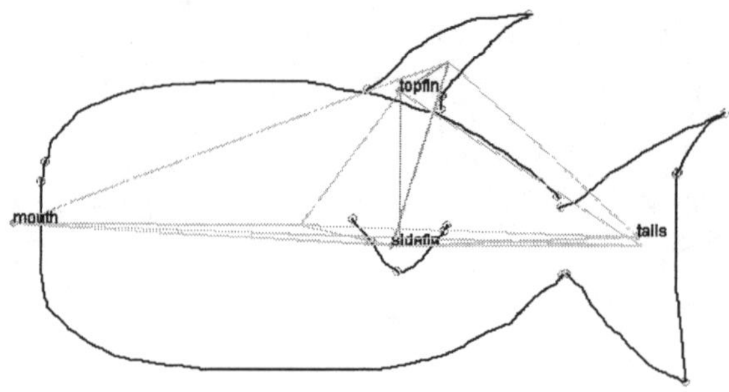

Fig. 5. A feature's location is inferred by an agent

location of *side-fins*. The relevant rule states that *side-fins* 'prefer' to be in a line with tails and mouths - both of which have matched comfortably. A decision now needs to be taken as to whether to reject this agent and replace it with one from the queue, or whether to relax the problematic rule and allow the agent to settle.

Figure 5 shows how the location of a missing feature can be inferred using the agent interaction - the mouth agent has moved to the approximate location of the undrawn mouth of the fish using only rules regarding the locations of the other agents - specifically that it must preferably be in line with tail and sidefin, and be far away from the tail.

7 Related Work

We utilise a similar approach to SIGMA [9], by allowing collaborative agents brought into play by the identification of certain components to search the available data for additional components that are expected to be present.

An interesting comparison could be drawn between our system and the *SketchIT* [12] system. However, that system relies on having a limited model database of individually drawn schematic representations (mechanical engineering components, electrical components, UML components, etc) and uses knowledge of the *function* of the system to aid in the recognition process.

Some research has been done on interpreting freehand sketches [12, 8, 7, 2, 1] all of which requires a small restricted 'visual grammar' to operate or recognise simple, one-stroke geometric shapes. Our system segments completely before attempting recognition, not requiring the sketcher to draw strokes in a particular order and the recognition solution discussed should scale-up easily.

8 Conclusions and Future Work

We have described an approach to classifying hand drawings of animals using agents which move around a sketch trying to find 'their' feature (an eye, or a tail) and attracting and repulsing other agents. A prototype version of the system (parsing a sketch into components, matching components to features in a database, small hierarchical database, agent control mechanism) has been implemented and tested on small samples of data. The experiments testing the matching implementations demonstrate the need for a mechanism to combine the three simple match tests in a manner appropriate to the model being matched against. Early results of using agents are encouraging.

The subject of our future work is to find out whether the system scales when applied to a large collection of data. Much work is also needed in experimentally adjusting optimal matching parameters for various features as the database of features is being extended.

References

1. J. Arvo and K. Novins. Fluid sketches: Continuous recognition and morphing of simple hand-drawn shapes.
2. C. Calhoun, T. Stahovich, T. Kurtoglu, and L. B. Kara. Recognizing multi-stroke symbols. Technical report, 2002.
3. D. Crevier and R. Lepage. Knowledge-based image understanding systems: A survey. *Computer Vision and Image Understanding*, 67(2):161–185, 1997.
4. B.A. Draper, R. Collins, A. Brolio, A. Hansen, and E. Riseman. The schema system. *The International Journal of Computer Vision*, 2:209–250, 1989.
5. I. Guyon, L. Schomaker, Plamondonm R., M. Liberman, and S. Janet. Unipen project of on-line data exchange and recognizer benchmarks. 1994.
6. B. Hayes-Roth. A blackboard architecture for control. *Artificial Intelligence*, 26:251–321, 1985.
7. J. A. Landay and B. A. Myers. Interactive sketching for the early stages of user interface design. In *Human Factors in Computing Systems*, 1995.
8. J. A. Landay and B. A Myers. Sketching interfaces: Toward more human interface design. *IEEE Computer*, 34(3):56–64, 2001.
9. T. Matsuyama and V. Hwang. Sigma: A knowledge-based aerial image understanding system. *Plenum*, 1990.
10. H. P. Nii. Blackboard systems: The blackboard model of problem solving and the evolution of blackboard architectures. *AI Magazine*, 7(2):38–53, 1986.
11. S. Russel and P. Norvig. *Artificial Intelligence: A Modern Approach.* Prentice-Hall, 1995.
12. T. F. Stahovich. *SketchIT: A Sketch Interpretation Tool for Conceptual Mechanical Design.* PhD thesis, Massachusetts Institute of Technology, Cambridge, Massachusetts, USA, 1995.

Iris Recognition for Iris Tilted in Depth

Chun-Nam Chun and Ronald Chung

Department of Automation and Computer-Aided Engineering
The Chinese University of Hong Kong, Shatin, Hong Kong
{cnchun,rchung}@acae.cuhk.edu.hk

Abstract. The capability of conducting unconscious recognition, in the sense of identifying people without them knowing it, is increasingly important in security and surveillance applications. Iris recognition is one of the few biometric recognition technologies that could serve the purpose. Yet, previous work on iris recognition have all assumed that iris appears as a radially symmetric print in the image data, which might not the case if people do not consciously position their eyes properly to the camera. In unconscious recognition applications iris could be imaged at oblique angle and could appear with substantial eccentricity in the image. This work investigates the improvement of the recognition performance as the image model of iris is allowed to carry substantial eccentricity. Experimental results on real image data show that the improvement could be significant.

1 Introduction

Ophthalmologists noted from clinical experience that every iris had a highly detailed and unique texture [2]. Moreover, the texture is relatively stable across one's life and is rarely subject to the sort of damage one's fingers could be. Owing to all these uniqueness and stability properties of iris, there have been extensive investigations ([1],[2],[3],[5] to name a few) in the last ten years on how iris image could be used for automatic identification of people.

Compared with other biometric recognition cues, iris recognition has the advantage of requiring no physical contact with the subject or even the awareness of the subject that he/she is being screened. On this, there is facial recognition that has the same advantage, but then facial features are far less distinct than iris texture in terms of capturing a person's identity. Clinical evidence has shown that even twins have different iris patterns.

The above advantage is essential in applications where it is desired that people could be screened without them aware of it. Such a recognition mode, which we refer to as unconscious recognition, is increasingly important in security and surveillance applications.

However, previous works on iris recognition all assume that iris appears as a radially symmetric print in the image. Typically, they use the polar coordinate system to unfold the Cartesian-coordinated iris image before they match the image against reference data. The assumption requires people to position their eyes head-on to the camera, and is clearly not enforceable in unconscious recognition applications. In unconscious recognition, iris could be pictured from oblique angle and could appear

N. Petkov and M.A. Westenberg (Eds.): CAIP 2003, LNCS 2756, pp. 530–539, 2003.

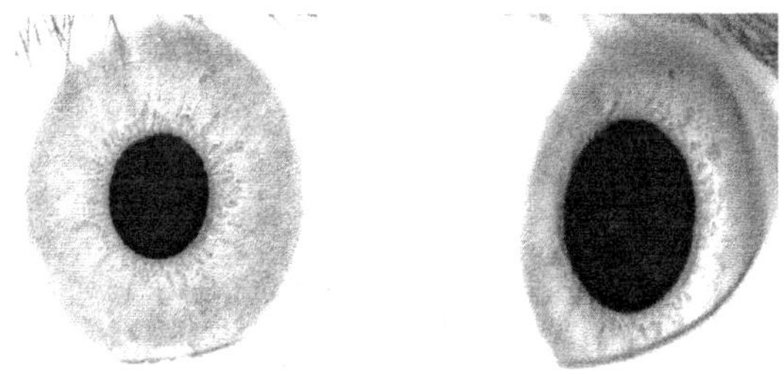

(a) (b)

Fig. 1. Eccentric deformation of iris in an image upon lateral viewing. (a) Iris viewed from a near-orthogonal angle. (b) Iris viewed from an oblique angle. Substantial eccentricity of the iris pattern is observed.

with substantial eccentricity in the image. Fig. 1 illustrates the degree of eccentric deformation an iris could have in an image.

This work investigates how, and by how much, the recognition performance could be boosted by including the possible eccentricity of iris print into consideration, thereby allowing iris recognition be used for unconscious applications.

Our idea is to extend the image model of iris from being circular to being elliptical, thereby allowing it to carry arbitrary eccentricity. The eccentricity will be taken into account in the coding of the iris before matching takes place.

We first describe a simple elliptical edge detector that could be applied to image to detect ellipse that has strong edgel support. Given an image, we use the detector to extract two ellipses, one for the inside boundary and the other for the outside boundary of the eye's iris portion. We then use a coordinate system modified from the polar coordinate system, which we refer to as the eccentric-polar coordinate system, to represent the iris data. The coordinate system allows the same iris to be coded the same way regardless of the eccentricity it displays under the particular viewing angle.

Experimental results with real image data show, by taking eccentricity into consideration, the recognition performance could be significantly improved.

2 Previous Work

Previous works on iris recognition include [1],[2],[3],[5], and others. Iris recognition could be described as the composition of four modules: iris image acquisition, iris localization, image encoding, and database matching.

The general mechanism of image acquisition has been well addressed in [2],[5], although image acquisition for Asians could be tricky as Asian irises tend to have dark background which makes iris texture not as visible. Our experience shows the use of near-IR cameras is effective in making the iris texture stand out in the image.

On image localization, previous works all rely upon the use of circle detector to detect the outside and inside boundaries of iris which typically appears as a ring in the image of an eye. The two boundaries (the pupil and sclera boundaries) encapsulate and define the ring that contains the iris texture. Once the iris ring is extracted, polar coordinate system is typically used to unfold the ring.

Image encoding and matching are often related., as matching depends upon how the input image and the reference data are encoded. A number of coding schemes have been proposed, ranging from as direct as raw intensity data [5], to as abstract as the coefficients of wavelet transformation, in particular the coefficients of 2D Gabor wavelet filter [2]. For direct codings like the raw intensity data, direct comparison schemes like cross-correlation are typically used for matching. For codings like the coefficients of Gabor transformation, Hamming distances between codes in the coefficient space are typically used to describe how similar two codes are.

This work addresses mainly the iris localization module. For the rest, we adopt the modules of Daugman's system [2] in our experimentation.

3 Isolating the Region of Interest

Iris appears in image as a ring between the pupil and sclera of the eye. The region of interest in iris image is thus the part between the pupil boundary and the sclera boundary, which needs be extracted. Previous works assume the two boundaries to be circular, and use circle detector to extract them. Here we allow the two boundaries to display certain degree of eccentricities, and for that we need to generalize the detector to an ellipse detector.

A number of elliptical edge detectors have been proposed in the literature, such as [4] which makes use of Hough transform. Our elliptical edge detector is one that is generalized from the circular edge detector described in [2].

As illustrated by Fig. 2, a general ellipse consists of five parameters: x_0, y_0, φ, a, and b, which represent the coordinates of the ellipse center, the orientation of the major-axis, the length of the major-axis, and the length of the minor axis respectively.

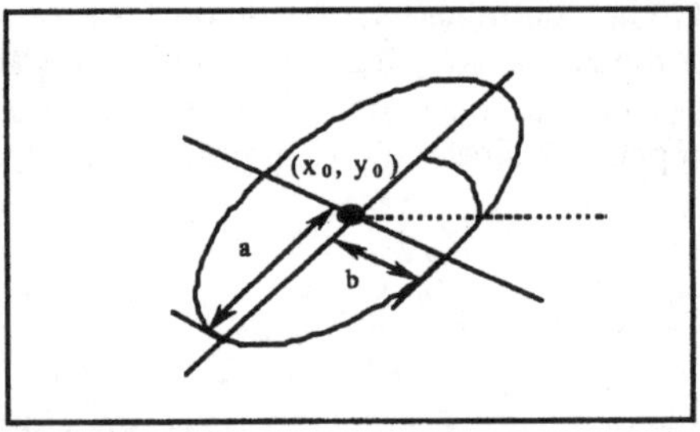

Fig. 2. The five parameters of a general ellipse.

To extract an ellipse that is of strong edgel support, we find the values of the five parameters using the following integro-differential operator:

$$\underset{(x_0,y_0,\varphi,a,b)}{\text{Max}} \left| \frac{\partial}{\partial r} \oint_{x_0,y_0,\varphi,a,b} \frac{I(x,y)}{2\pi r} ds \right| \tag{1}$$

where s is the arc length parameter that traverses the ellipse, $I(x, y)$ is the image intensity value on the ellipse at arc position s that has (x, y) as its image position, and r is the distance of the arc position s from the center (x_0, y_0) of the ellipse. The differential

$\partial / \partial r$ is there to maximize the intensity gradient in the direction that is orthogonal to the ellipse contour, the integration is to sum all the intensity gradients over the entire ellipse, and the denominator $2\pi r$ is to normalize the sum by the length of the ellipse so as to avoid bias toward bigger ellipse.

The operator searches over the parameter space of x_0, y_0, φ, a, b for an ellipse (of the image space $\{(x,y)\}$) that maximizes the value of Expression (1). The operator demands iterative processing. For the initialization of the five parameters, we use the end-result of the circular edge detector described in [2]: (x_0, y_0) are initialized as the center of that circle, a and b as its radius, and φ as $\pi/2$.

We use the above elliptical edge detector to extract the pupil and sclera boundaries. Figure 3 shows a typical result. The pupil boundary and sclera boundary are displayed as white and black contours respectively.

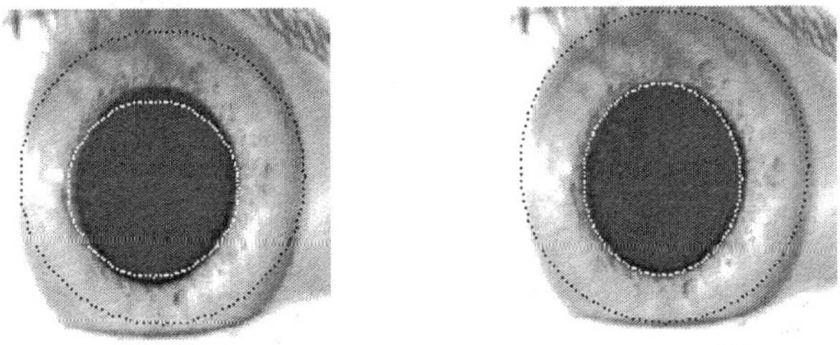

(a) (b)

Fig. 3. Result of our elliptical iris-ring boundary detection. (a) Result of circular edge detector. (b) Result of elliptical edge detector.

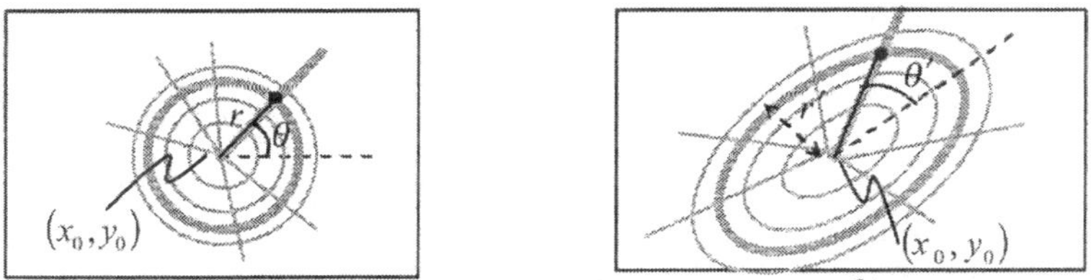

(a) (b)

Fig. 4. (a) The polar coordinate system with respect to (x_0, y_0) (b) The eccentric-polar coordinate system with respect to a certain reference center (x_0, y_0), a certain orientation φ, and a certain eccentricity s.

4 Eccentric-Polar Coordinate System

As illustrated by Fig. 4 (a), a circle in a 2D space, say $(x - x_0)^2 + (y - y_0)^2 = R^2$, defines for that space two sets of coordinate lines: the r-lines and the θ-lines, with respect to the reference center (x_0, y_0). While positions on the same r-line have the same radial distance r from the reference center, positions on the same θ-line have the same inclination θ from the x-axis. Using the two sets of coordinate lines to index positions of the 2D space, we have the polar coordinates (r, θ) with respect to the reference center (x_0, y_0).

In the same vein, as illustrated by Fig. 4 (b), an ellipse of center (x_0, y_0), orientation φ, major-axis length a, and minor-axis length b could be used to define two sets of coordinate lines: the r'-lines and the θ'–lines, with respect to the reference center (x_0, y_0), orientation φ, and eccentricity (ratio of the major-axis length to the minor-axis length) $s = a / b$. r'-lines are the different ellipses of the same ellipse center (x_0, y_0), the same orientation φ, and the same ratio s of the major-axis and minor-axis lengths. All positions on the same ellipse have the same r', whose value could be assigned as the minor-axis length of the corresponding ellipse. θ'–lines are still loci of positions having the same inclination with the x-axis. However, for convenience, we use $\tan^{-1}(sy'/x')$ as the value of θ', where x' and y' are respectively the parallel- and perpendicular displacements of the position with respect to the major axis. We thus in a way measure θ' against the direction of the major axis (which is common among all the ellipses) not that of the x-axis, and have the eccentricity s of the ellipses scaled away in θ'.

The two sets of coordinate lines could also be used to index positions of the 2D space, and in that case we have the coordinates (r', θ') which we call the eccentric-polar coordinates.

5 Iris-Ring Unfolding and Normalization

The next step to iris-ring extraction is to unfold the ring and normalize the data. The purpose is to maintain reference to the same region of iris tissue regardless of both the papillary dilation or contraction (due to illumination change), the zoom factor (due to change in the imaging distance), and the 2D displacement (due to viewpoint change) of the iris image. In this work we would go as far as to make the data independent of the viewing angle.

To achieve the above, previous works use polar coordinate system to unfold the iris-ring. However, polar coordinate system falls short of freeing the data from the effect of oblique viewpoint. In this work, we use the eccentric-polar coordinate system instead to unfold the iris ring.

Once the iris-ring is extracted, we have access to its inside and outside boundaries in the form of two ellipses. We then use the ellipses to define an eccentric-polar coordinate system to represent the iris data. Ideally, the two ellipses have the same center, eccentricity, and orientation, and they define the same eccentric-polar coordinate system for the image space. In case they do not, we use the average of their centers, eccentricities, and orientations to define the eccentric-polar coordinate system. Our experience shows the two boundaries generally do not differ by much in the above parameters.

Suppose we have reference center (x_0,y_0), orientation φ, and eccentricity s to define the eccentric-polar coordinates.

Let (x, y) be the Cartesian coordinates of a position in image I. (x, y) are first transformed into (x', y') by first a rotation specified by φ, and second a translation specified by (x_0, y_0):

$$\begin{bmatrix} x' \\ y' \end{bmatrix} = \begin{bmatrix} \cos(-\varphi) & -\sin(-\varphi) \\ \sin(-\varphi) & \cos(-\varphi) \end{bmatrix} \begin{bmatrix} x - x_0 \\ y - y_0 \end{bmatrix} \tag{2}$$

Under the coordinates (x', y'), positions which should have the same r' value are those lying on

$$\frac{x'^2}{a^2} + \frac{y'^2}{b^2} = 1 \tag{3}$$

for some a and b, where $a / b = s$.

We then transform (x', y') to (r'', θ') using the following transformation:

$$r'' = \sqrt{\frac{x'^2}{s^2} + y'^2} \tag{4}$$

$$\theta' = \tan^{-1} \frac{sy'}{x'} \tag{5}$$

Suppose the iris-ring in image $I(x,y)$ has b_1 and b_2 as the minor-axis lengths of the inside and outside boundaries. Then in the (r'', θ') coordinate space, the iris ring will be a rectangular strip with r'' as the vertical axis ranging from b_1 to b_2.

To normalize the range of r'', we further convert r'' to r' by making $r' = \frac{r'' - b_1}{b_2 - b_1}$.

In the coordinate space of (r', θ'), the iris ring is a rectangular strip with θ' as the horizontal axis ranging from 0 to 2π, and r' as the vertical axis ranging from 0 to 1. The coordinate system (r', θ') is thus dimensionless, and the iris-ring in $I(r', \theta')$ is invariant with the papillary dilation or contraction, imaging distance, the iris offset and rotation in the image, and even the imaging angle.

Fig. 5 shows the transformation result of one iris image.

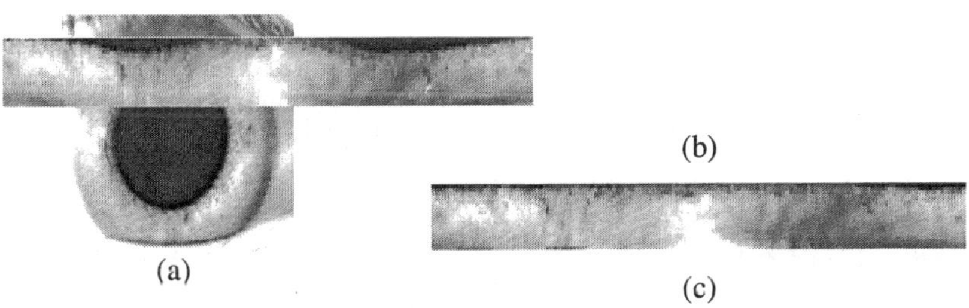

Fig. 5. Image transformation from Cartesian coordinates to Eccentric-polar coordinates. (a) Image in the Cartesian coordinates. (b) Image in the polar coordinates defined by the iris-boundary. Some portion of the pupil is included undesirably. (c) Image in the Eccentric-polar coordinates defined by the iris-boundary. Undesirable inclusion of the pupil portion is reduced.

6 Performance Measure of Recognition

We use the following measure for comparing recognition performances. Suppose we have K classes $\{\{I_{k,n} : n = 1,\cdots,N\} : k = 1,\cdots,K\}$ of iris images, each class being the different images of the same iris, with N images in each class. Suppose for every class of images, say the kth class $\{I_{k,n} : n = 1,\cdots,N\}$, there is a reference image $\bar{I}_k$ as the norm or reference of the class for recognition. Iris recognition is thus about classifying any given image into the class to which it belongs.

Suppose by whatever coding and matching schemes we could compute the matching distance between any two iris images I_i and I_j as $\left\| I_i - I_j \right\|$. To correctly classify the images as their own class, we desire that the matching distance within the same class be as small as possible, and the matching distance between classes be as large as possible.

We measure the inter-class matching distance between any k^{th} class with the rest of the classes as

$$A_k = \sum_{j\in\{1,\cdots,K\}-\{k\}} \left\| \bar{I}_k - \bar{I}_j \right\| \Big/ K-1 \tag{6}$$

The average inter-class matching distance of all classes is then $A = \sum_{k=1}^{K} A_k \Big/ K$.

We measure the intra-class matching distance for any k^{th} class as

$$B_k = \sum_{n\in\{1,\ldots,N\}} \left\| \bar{I}_k - I_{k,n} \right\| \Big/ N \tag{7}$$

The average intra-class matching distance of all classes is then $B = \sum_{k=1}^{K} B_k \Big/ K$.

With the above, the overall performance of a recognition scheme could be measured in terms of the following:

$$C = \sum_{k=1}^{K} \frac{A_k}{B_k} \Big/ K \tag{8}$$

We refer to measure C as the *classification power*. C represents how large is the average inter-class matching distance (over all classes) compared with the average intra-class distance. A recognition scheme is more favorable should it have a larger C.

7 Experimental Result

We have implemented the proposed idea and compared its recognition performance, on real image data, with that of using polar coordinates to unfold the iris data. Below we present some of the results.

On the image encoding and matching parts, those of the system described in [2] are what the comparison experiment borrowed, but those of other systems will serve the purpose just as well, for image localization and normalization – the focus of this work – are necessary pre-processing steps to any image encoding and matching mechanisms. Under the image matching mechanism described in [2], the matching distance $\|I_i - I_j\|$ between any two iris images I_i and I_j, is the Hamming distance expressed in terms of the fraction of disagreeing bits between the Gabor-wavelet transformed codes of the two images. We used the Pulnix TM-300 NIR camera to capture iris images. Figure 1 shows samples of the images.

Our experiment was conducted in the following way. A total of 32 images over 8 irises were involved. In other words, there were 8 distinct classes of images, with four images available in each class. Among the four images of each class, two were captured under the conscious situation, i.e., with each iris positioned head-on to the camera, and the other two were captured from oblique angles. Our first experiment consisted of using only the consciously-taken iris data for recognition. It was expected that the classification power would not differ much with the use of eccentric-polar coordinate system. The second experiment consisted of using the unconsciously-taken iris data for recognition.

Fig. 6 (a) and (b) show results of the first experiment. The inter-class matching distance A_i and the intra-class matching distance B_i of the respective iris-classes, when only the consciously-taken iris data were used, are displayed. It could be observed that the polar-coordinates based system and the eccentric-polar coordinates based system are about the same in A_i's, but the eccentric polar coordinates are still slightly better in B_i's even though the subjects have consciously made the effort to position their irises directly to the camera. Table 1 shows the classification powers C of the two systems. The eccentric polar coordinates based system has an improvement of about 8% over the polar-coordinates based system.

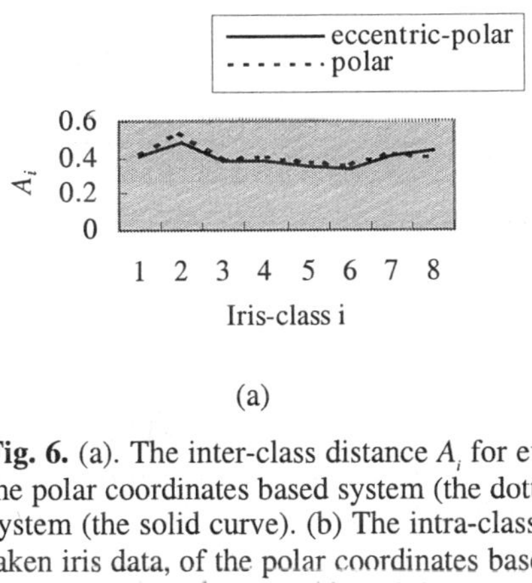

(a)

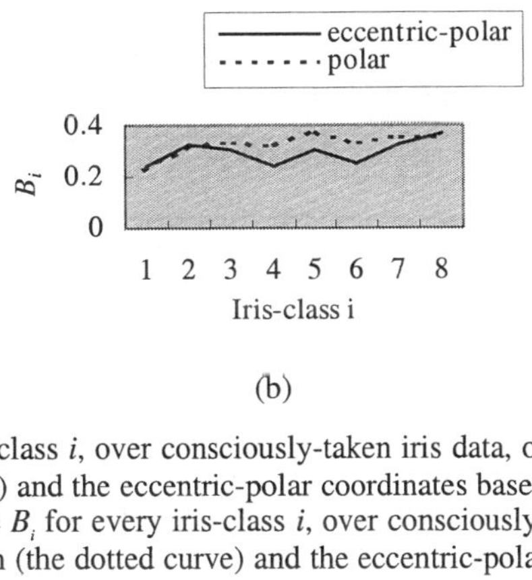

(b)

Fig. 6. (a). The inter-class distance A_i for every iris-class i, over consciously-taken iris data, of the polar coordinates based system (the dotted curve) and the eccentric-polar coordinates based system (the solid curve). (b) The intra-class distance B_i for every iris-class i, over consciously-taken iris data, of the polar coordinates based system (the dotted curve) and the eccentric-polar coordinates based system (the solid curve).

Table 1. The classification power C, over consciously-taken iris data, of the polar coordinates based system and the eccentric-polar coordinates based system

	Polar Coordinate System	Eccentric-polar Coordinate System
C	1.7396	1.8848

Fig. 7 (a) and (b) show results of the second experiment in which only iris data taken from oblique angles were used. It could be observed that the polar-coordinates-based system and the eccentric-polar-coordinates-based system are still not too different in A_i's, but the eccentric-polar coordinates are generally much better in B_i's. Table 2 shows the classification powers C of the two systems. The eccentric-polar-coordinates-based system has an improvement of more than 16% over the polar-coordinates-based system. We attribute the substantial improvement to the more accurate modeling of iris image by the eccentric-polar coordinates, especially when the irises are pictured from oblique angles.

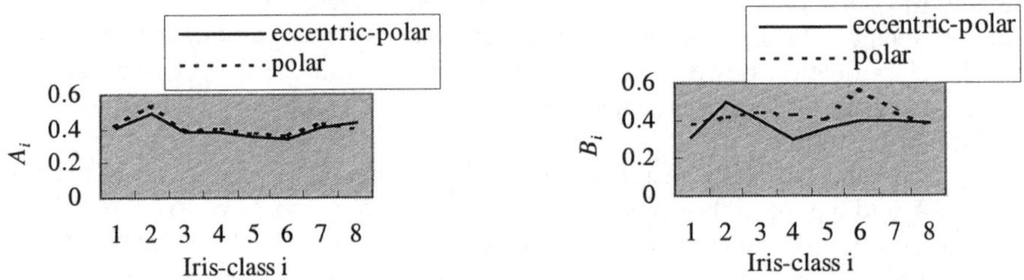

(a) (b)

Fig. 7. (a) The inter-class distance A_i for every iris-class i, over iris data taken from oblique angles, of the polar coordinates based system (the dotted curve) and the eccentric-polar coordinates based system (the solid curve). (b) The intra-class distance B_i for every iris-class i, over iris data taken from oblique angles, of the polar coordinates based system (the dotted curve) and the eccentric-polar coordinates based system (the solid curve).

Table 2. The classification power C, over iris data taken from oblique angles, of the polar coordinates based system and the eccentric-polar coordinates based system.

	Polar Coordinate System	Eccentric-polar Coordinate System
C	0.9706	1.1281

8 Conclusion and Future Work

Security and surveillance applications are increasingly important in recent years. Not only could the capability of achieving unconscious recognition add versatility to the applications and avoid bad feelings from the examined people, it could even prevent raising alarm to the solicited subjects, thereby increasing the effectiveness of the security system.

Iris recognition is one of the few biometric cues that could serve the purpose. In this work, we generalized the iris model to give it the additional freedom of carrying eccentricity, so that iris image data could be captured from oblique viewpoints which are likely the case in unconscious recognition. More precisely, we proposed to use the eccentric-polar coordinates in place of the polar coordinates in unfolding the iris-ring of the image data and normalizing it. Empirical results on real image data show, in so doing the recognition performance could be significantly improved.

Future work would include how a system of multiple cameras, some for picturing a wider field of view of a scene and locating where the irises are, and the other with active drives for picturing close-up pictures of the extracted irises, could be devised and compose a complete iris recognition system.

Acknowledgment

The work described in this paper was partially supported by a grant from the Research Grants Council of the Hong Kong Special Administrative Region, China (Project No. CUHK4177/01E).

References

1. W. W. Boles. A Security System Based on Human Iris Identification Using Wavelet Transform. IEEE Proceedings of First International Conference on Knowledge-Based Intelligent Electronic Systems, Vol. 2, pp. 533-541, 1997.
2. John G. Daugman. High Confidence Visual Recognition of Persons by a Test of Statistical Independence. IEEE Transactions on Pattern Analysis and Machine Intelligence, Vol. 15, No. 11, pp.1148-1161, Nov. 1993.
3. P. W. Hallinan. Recognizing human eyes. Geometric Methods Comput. Vision, Vol. 1570, pp. 214-226, 1991.
4. Clark F. Olson. Constrained Hough Transforms for Curve Detection. Computer Vision and Image Understanding, Vol. 73, No. 3, pp. 329-345, March, 1999.
5. Richard P. Wildes. Iris Recognition: An Emerging Biometric Technology. Proceedings of the IEEE, Vol. 85, No. 9, pp. 1348-1363, September, 1997.

Spectral Clustering of Graphs

B. Luo, R.C. Wilson, and E.R. Hancock

Department of Computer Science, Univerisity of York, York Y01 5DD, UK

Abstract. In this paper we explore how to use spectral methods for embedding and clustering unweighted graphs. We use the leading eigenvectors of the graph adjacency matrix to define eigenmodes of the adjacency matrix. For each eigenmode, we compute vectors of spectral properties. These include the eigenmode perimeter, eigenmode volume, Cheeger number, inter-mode adjacency matrices and intermode edge-distance. We embed these vectors in a pattern-space using two contrasting approaches. The first of these involves performing principal or independent components analysis on the covariance matrix for the spectral pattern vectors. The second approach involves performing multidimensional scaling on the L2 norm for pairs of pattern vectors. We illustrate the utility of the embedding methods on neighbourhood graphs representing the arrangement of corner features in 2D images of 3D polyhedral objects.

1 Introduction

Many of the foundations of current work on graph-structures for vision and pattern recognition were laid by the pioneers of structural pattern recognition in the early 1980's [2, 8]. However, despite recent progress in accurately measuring the similarity of graphs and performing robust inexact graph-matching, one of challenges that ramains is how to cluster graphs. Graph-clustering allows the unsupervised learning of the class-structure from sets of graphs. The problem is of practical importance in the organisation of large structural data-bases [9] or the discovery of the view-structure of objects [1].

One of the problems that hinders the graph-clustering that graphs are neither vectorial in nature nor easily transformed into vectors. The reasons for this are twofold. First, there is no canonical ordering of the nodes or edges of a graph. Hence, there is no natural way to map the nodes or edges to the components of a vector. Second, most graph-matching or graph manipulation problems are inexact in nature. That is to say that the graphs are noisy in nature and hence contain different numbers of nodes or edges. Hence, even if an ordering can be established then there needs to be a means of dealing with pattern-vectors of different length. Since they are not easily vectorised, it is not straightforward to characterise the mean and variance of a set of graphs. Hence, standard pattern recognition methods can not be used to analyse or cluster sets of graphs. One way around this problem is to adopt a pairwise clustering approach [3]. This involves measuring the pairwise similarity of the graphs and clustering them by searching for sets of graphs which exhibit a strong mutual affinity to one-another.

N. Petkov and M.A. Westenberg (Eds.): CAIP 2003, LNCS 2756, pp. 540–548, 2003.

We have recently attempted to overcome this problem by adopting a spectral representation of graphs [6] which allows the structure of a graph onto a vector of fixed length. We work with the spectral decomposition (or eigendecomposition) of the adjacency matrix. Each component of the vector is taken to represent a different spectral mode of the original graph adjacency matrix. The order of the components of the vector is the magnitude order of the eigenvalues of the adjacency matrix. For each spectral mode, we use the components of the associated eigenvectors to compute spectral attributes. In this way we solve the problem of finding correspondences between nodes and vector-components. Empirical results showed that the feature-vectors resulted in well structured pattern spaces, where siliar graphs were cloese together. The aim in this paper is to investigate in more detail how the spectral feature-vectors can be used to the purposes of clustering. The aim is to investigate a numnber of different strategies including principal components analysis, independant components analysis and multidimensional scaling.

2 Graph Spectra

In this paper we are concerned with the set of graphs $G_1, G_2, .., G_k, ..., G_N$. The kth graph is denoted by $G_k = (V_k, E_k)$, where V_k is the set of nodes and $E_k \subseteq V_k \times V_k$ is the edge-set. Our approach in this paper is a graph-spectral one. For each graph G_k we compute the adjacency matrix A_k. This is a $|V_k| \times |V_k|$ matrix whose element with row index i and column index j is

$$A_k(i,j) = \begin{cases} 1 & \text{if } (i,j) \in E_k \\ 0 & \text{otherwise} \end{cases} . \tag{1}$$

From the adjacency matrices $A_k, k = 1...N$ at hand, we can calculate the eigenvalues λ_k by solving the equation $|A_k - \lambda_k I| = 0$ and the associated eigenvectors ϕ_k^ω by solving the system of equations $A_k \phi_k^\omega = \lambda_k^\omega \phi_k^\omega$, where ω is the eigenmode index. We order the eigenvectors according to the decreasing magnitude of the eigenvalues, i.e. $|\lambda_k^1| > |\lambda_k^2| > \ldots |\lambda_k^{|V_k|}|$. The eigenvectors are stacked in order to construct the modal matrix $\Phi_k = (\phi_k^1|\phi_k^2|\ldots|\phi_k^{|V_k|})$.

With the eigenvalues and eigenvectors of the adjacency matrix to hand, the spectral decomposition for the adjacency matrix of the graph indexed k is $A_k = \sum_{\omega=1}^{|V_k|} \lambda_k^\omega \phi_k^\omega (\phi_k^\omega)^T$.. If $\Lambda_k = diag(\lambda_k^1, ..., \lambda_k^{|V_k|})$ is the diagonal matrix with the eigenvalues of A_k as diagonal elements, then the spectral decomposition of the adjacency matrix can be written as $A_k = \Phi_k \Lambda_k \Phi_k^T$.. Associated with the eigenmode with index ω is the mode adjacency matrix $S_k^\omega = \phi_k^\omega (\phi_k^\omega)^T$.. The aim in this paper is to explore whether the properties of these matrices can be used to construct feature vectors for the graphs under study. We explore two different approaches. The first of these involves computing features for individual mode adjacency matrices. The second involves the use of relational features which describe the arrangement of mode adjacency matrices.

For each graph, we use only the first n eigenmodes of the adjacency matrix. The truncated modal matrix is $.\Phi_k = (\phi_k^1|\phi_k^2|\ldots|\phi_k^n)$..

3 Spectral Features

Our aim is to use spectral features computed from the eigenmodes of the adjacency matrices for graphs under study to construct feature-vectors. To overcome the correspondence problem, we use the order of the eigenvalues to establish the order of the components of the feature-vectors. We study a number of features suggested by spectral graph theory.

3.1 Unary Features

We commence by considering unary features for the eigenmodes of the adjacency matrix. The features studied are listed below:

Leading Eigenvalues: Our first vector of spectral features is constructed from the ordered eigenvalues of the adjacency matrix. For the graph indexed k, the vector is $B_k = (\lambda_k^1, \lambda_k^2, ..., \lambda_k^n)^T$.. This vector represents the spectrum of the graph G_k.

Eigenmode Volume: The volume $Vol(S)$ of a subgraph S of a graph G_k is defined to be the sum of the degrees of the nodes belonging to the subgraph, i.e $Vol_k(S) = \sum_{i \in S} D_k(i)$, where $D_k(i) = \sum_{j \in V_k} E_{i,j}$. is the degree of node i in the graph G_k. If D_k is the degree vector for the graph G_k, then the vector of volumes for the eigenmodes is found using the projection $Vol_k = \Phi_k^T D_k$. In other words, the volume associated with the eigenmode indexed ω in the graph-indexed k is $Vol_k(\omega) = \sum_{i \in V_k} \Phi_k(i, \omega) D_k(i)$. The eigenmodes volume feature-vector for the graph-indexed k is $B_k = (Vol_k(1), Vol_k(2)), ., Vol_k(n))^T$.

Eigenmode Perimeter: For a subgraph S the set of perimeter nodes is $\Delta(S) = \{(u, v)|(u, v) \in E \wedge u \in S \wedge v \notin S\}$. The perimeter length of the subgraph is defined to be the number of edges in the perimeter set, i.e. $\Gamma(S) = |\Delta(S)|$. Again, by analogy, the perimeter length of the adjacency matrix for the eigenmode indexed ω is $\Gamma_k(\omega) = \sum_{\nu \neq \omega} \sum_{i \in V_k} \sum_{j \in V_k} \Phi_k(i, \omega) \Phi_k(j, \nu) A_k(i, j)$. The perimeter values are ordered according to the modal index to form the graph feature vector $B_k = (\Gamma_k^1, \Gamma_k^2, ..., \Gamma_k^n)^T$.

Cheeger Constant: The Cheeger constant for the subgraph S is defined as $H(S) = \frac{|\Delta(S)|}{min[Vol(S), Vol(\hat{S})]}$.. The analogue of the Cheeger constants for the eigenmodes of the adjacency matrix is $H_k(\omega) = \frac{\Gamma_k(\omega)}{min[Vol_k(\omega), Vol_k(\hat{\omega})]}$, where $Vol_k(\hat{\omega}) = \sum_{\omega=1}^{n} \sum_{i \in V_k} \Phi_k(i, \omega) D_k(i) - Vol_k(\omega)$ is the volume of the complement of the eigenmode indexed ω. Again, the eigenmode Cheeger numbers are ordered to form a spectral feature-vector $B_k = (H_k(1), H_k(2), ..., H_k(n))^T$.

3.2 Binary Features

In addition to the unary features, we have studied pairwise attributes for the eigenmodes.

Mode Association Matrix: Our first pairwise representation is found by projecting the adjacency matrix onto the basis spanned by the eigenvector to compute a matrix of mode associations. The projection or inter-mode adjacency matrix is $U_k = \Phi_k^T A_k \Phi_k$. The element of the matrix with row index u and column index v is $U_k(u,v) = \sum_{i \in V_k} \sum_{j \in V_k} \Phi_k(i,u)\Phi_k(j,v)A_k(i,j)$. This is infact the association between clusters u and v. These matrices are converted into long vectors. This is done by stacking the columns of the matrix U_k in eigenvalue order. The resulting vector is $B_k = (U_k(1,1), U_k(1,2), ..., ...U_k(n,n))^T$. Each entry in the long-vector corresponds to a different pair of spectral eigenmodes.

Inter-mode Distances: The between mode distance is defined as the path length, i.e. the minimum number of edges, between the most significant nodes associated with each eigenmode of the adjacency matrix. The most significant node associated a particular eigenmode of the adjacency matrix is the one having the largest co-efficient in the associated eigenvector. For the eigenmode indexed u in the graph indexed k, the most significant node is $i_u^k = \arg\max_i \Phi_k(i,u)$. To compute the distance, we note that if we multiply the adjacency matrix A_k by itself l times, then the matrix $(A_k)^l$ represents the distribution of paths of length l in the graph G_k. In particular, the element $(A_k)^l(i,j)$ is the number of paths of length l edges between the nodes i and j. Hence the minimum distance between the most significant nodes of the eigenmode indexed u and v is $d_{u,v} = \arg\min_l (A_k)^l(i_u^k, i_v^k)$..

If we only use the first n leading eigenvectors to describe the graphs, the between mode distances for each graph can be written as a n by n matrix which can be converted to a $n \times n$ long-vector $B_k = (d_{1,1}, d_{1,2}, ...d_{1,n}, d_{2,1} .....d_{n,n})^T$.

4 Embedding the Spectral Vectors in a Pattern Space

In this section we describe three methods for embedding graphs in eigenspaces. The first of these involves performing principal components analysis on the covariance matrices for the spectral pattern-vectors. The second involves independent component analysis. The third method involves performing multidimensional scaling on a set of pairwise distance between vectors.

PCA: Our first method makes use principal components analysis and follows the parametric eigenspace idea of Murase and Nayar [7]. The graphs extracted from each image are vectorised in the way outlined in Section 3. The N different image vectors are arranged in view order as the columns of the matrix $T = [B_1|B_2|\ldots|B_k|\ldots|B_N]$.. Next, we compute the covariance matrix for the elements in the different rows of the matrix T. This is found by taking the matrix product $C = TT^T$.. We extract the principal components directions for the relational data by performing an eigendecomposition on the covariance matrix C. The eigenvalues λ_i are found by solving the eigenvalue equation $|C - \lambda I| = 0$, and the corresponding eigenvalues $\mathbf{e}_i$ are found by solving the eigenvector equation $C\mathbf{e}_i = \lambda_i \mathbf{e}_i$..

We use the first 3 leading eigenvectors to represent the graphs extracted from the images. The co-ordinate system of the eigenspace is spanned by the three orthogonal vectors by $\boldsymbol{e} = (\boldsymbol{e}_1, \boldsymbol{e}_2, \boldsymbol{e}_3)$. The individual graphs represented by the long vectors $B_k, k = 1, 2, \ldots, N$ can be projected onto this eigenspace using the formula $\boldsymbol{x}_k = \boldsymbol{e}^T B_k$.. Hence each graph G_k is represented by a 3-component vector $\boldsymbol{x}_k$ in the eigenspace.

ICA: Our second approach uses Independent Components Analysis(ICA) to embed the graphs in a pattern space. We explore how to decompose a set of graphs into significantly different independent components. These can then be used for graph clustering by projecting the original graphs into the pattern space spanned by the independent components.

The ICA algorithm used in this paper is Cardoso and Soulourniac's JADE algorithm[3]. JADE is a statistically based algorithm. The main features of the algorithm are as follows. As with other ICA algorithms, the first step is data whitening or sphering. The aim is to eliminate correlations from the data. This can be achieved by removing the mean of the data and using PCA on the data covariance matrix. As a result, the whitened vector set is $Z = WB$, where W is the estimated whitening matrix. The second step of JADE is estimate the 4th-order cumulants Q_z. In the noiseless case, Q_z can be calculated as follows, $Q_Z(I_n) = E\{|Z|^2 ZZ^T\} - (n+1)I_n$, where I_n is the n-order identity matrix and $E(.)$ is the expectation operator. Next, a joint diagonalisation is performed to find a matrix $\hat{V}$ to minimise the non-diagonal entries of the cumulants matrices, $\hat{V} = \arg\min \Sigma_i Off(V^T Q_Z V)$.. Again we use the first 3 most significant independent components to represent the graphs extracted from the images. The co-ordinate system of the pattern-space is spanned by the three independent components by $\hat{e} = (\hat{V}_l, \hat{V}_2, \hat{V}_3)$. The individual graphs represented by the long vectors $Z_k,\ k = 1, 2, ..., N$ can be projected onto this pattern space using the formula $\boldsymbol{x}_k = \boldsymbol{e}^T Z_k$. Hence each graph G_k is represented by a 3-component vector $\boldsymbol{x}_k$ in the pattern space.

MDS: Multidimensional scaling(MDS) is a procedure which allows data specified in terms of a matrix of pairwise distances to be embedded in a Euclidean space. The classical multidimensional scaling method was proposed by Torgenson[10] and Gower[5]. Shepard and Kruskal developed a different scaling technique called ordinal scaling[4]. Here we intend to use the method to embed the graphs extracted from different viewpoints in a low-dimensional space.

To commence we require pairwise distances between graphs. We do this by computing the L2 norms between the spectral pattern vectors for the graphs. For the graphs indexed $i1$ and $i2$, the distance is $d_{i1,i2} = \sum_{\alpha=1}^{K} [B_{i1}(\alpha) - B_{i2}(\alpha)]^2$..

The pairwise similarities $d_{i1,i2}$ are used as the elements of an $N \times N$ dissimilarity matrix D, whose elements are defined as follows

$$D_{i1,i2} = \begin{cases} d_{i1,i2} & \text{if } i_1 \neq i2 \\ 0 & \text{if } i1 = i2 \end{cases} . \tag{2}$$

In this paper, we use the classical multidimensional scaling method to embed the view-graphs in a Euclidean space using the matrix of pairwise dissimilarities D. The first step of MDS is to calculate a matrix T whose element with row r and column c is given by $T_{rc} = -\frac{1}{2}[d_{rc}^2 - \hat{d}_{r.}^2 - \hat{d}_{.c}^2 + \hat{d}_{..}^2]$, where $\hat{d}_{r.} = \frac{1}{N}\sum_{c=1}^{N} d_{rc}$

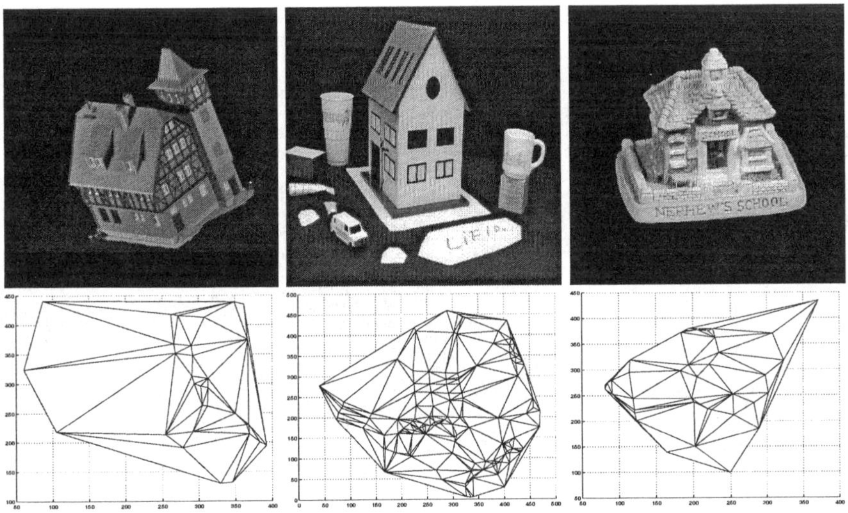

Fig. 1. Example images from the three sequences and their corner-feature Delaunay graphs.

is the average dissimilarity value over the rth row, $\hat{d}_{.c}$ is the similarly defined average value over the cth column and $\hat{d}_{..} = \frac{1}{N^2}\sum_{r=1}^{N}\sum_{c=1}^{N} d_{r,c}$ is the average similarity value over all rows and columns of the similarity matrix T.

We subject the matrix T to an eigenvector analysis to obtain a matrix of embedding co-ordinates X. If the rank of T is $k, k \leq N$, then we will have k non-zero eigenvalues. We arrange these k non-zero eigenvalues in descending order, i.e. $\lambda_1 \geq \lambda_2 \geq \ldots \geq \lambda_k > 0$. The corresponding ordered eigenvectors are denoted by $\boldsymbol{e}_i$ where λ_i is the ith eigenvalue. The embedding co-ordinate system for the graphs obtained from different views is $X = [\boldsymbol{f}_1, \boldsymbol{f}_2, \ldots, \boldsymbol{f}_k]$, where $\boldsymbol{f}_i = \sqrt{\lambda_i}\boldsymbol{e}_i$ are the scaled eigenvectors. For the graph indexed i, the embedded vector of co-ordinates is $\boldsymbol{x}_i = (X_{i,1}, X_{i,2}, X_{i,3})^T$..

5 Experiments

Our experimental vehicle is provided by object recognition from 2D views of 3D objects. We have collected sequences of views for a number of objects. For the different objects the image sequences are obtained under slowly varying changes in viewer angle. From each image in each view sequence, we extract corner features. We use the extracted corner points to construct Delaunay graphs. In our experiments we use three different sequences. Each sequence contains images with equally spaced viewing directions. The sequences contain different numbers of frames, but for each we have selected 10 uniformly spaced images. In Figure 1 we show example images and their associated graphs from the three sequences. From left-to-right the images belong to the CMU, MOVI and chalet sequences. There is considerable variability in the number of feature-points detected in the

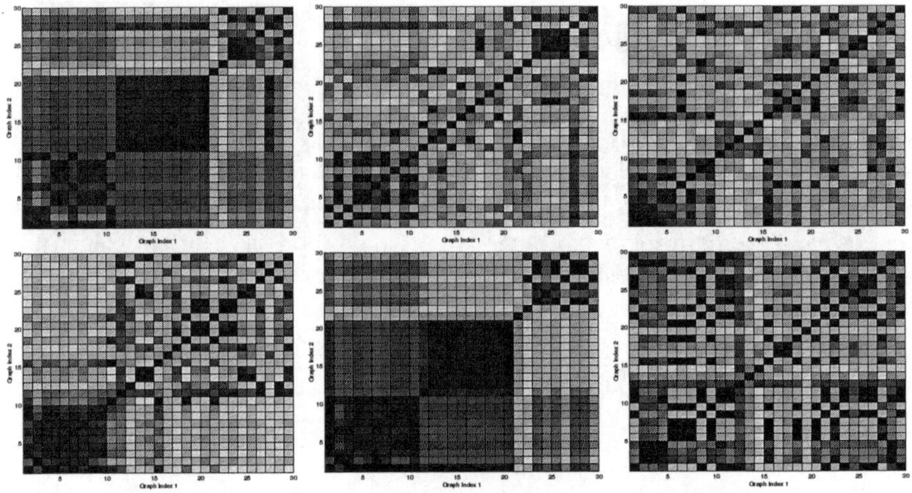

Fig. 2. Distance maps using the spectral features of binary adjacency graph spectra, volumes, perimeters, Cheeger constants, inter-mode adjacency matrix and inter-mode distances.

different sequences. For the CMU sequence the minumum number of points is 30 and the maximum is 35. For the MOVI sequence the minimum is 130 and the maximum is 140, For the chalet sequence the minimum is 40 and the maximum 113; this is the most variable sequence in terms of view structure.

We commence by investigating which combination of spectral feature-vector and embedding strategy gives the best set of graph-clusters. In other words, we aim to explore which method gives the best definition of clusters for the different objects. In Figure 2 we compare the results obtained with the different spectral feature vectors. In the figure we show the matrix of pairwise Euclidean distances between the feature-vectors for the different graphs (this is best viewed in colour). The matrix has 30 rows and columns (i.e. one for each of the images in the three sequences with the three sequences concatenated), and the images are ordered according to the position in the sequence. From left-to-right and top-to-bottom, the different panels show the results obtained when the feature-vectors are constructed using the eigenvalues of the adjacency matrix, the volumes, the perimeters, the Cheeger constants, the inter-mode adjacency matrix and the inter-mode distance. From the pattern of pairwise distances, it is clear that the eigenvalues and the inter-mode adjacency matrix give the best block structure in the matrix. Hence these two attributes may be expected to result in the best clusters.

Next, we show the clustering results for the two well behaved features. i.e. the vector of leading eigenvalues and the inter-mode adjacency matrix. In Figure 3, we show the clustering results obtained with vectors of different spectral attributes. For clarity, the results are displayed by positioning image "thumbnails" at the position associated with the corresponding spectral feature vector in relevant eigenspace. In each case we visualise the thumbnails in the space spanned by the leading two eigenvectors generated by the embedding method (PCA, ICA or MDS). The top row shows the results obtained using the vector of leading eigenvalues of the adjacency matrix. The left-most panel shows the result obtained using PCA, the centre panel that obtained using ICA and the right-most panel that obtained using MDS. There are a number of conclusions that can be drawn from these plots. First, the cluster associated with the Swiss chalet is always the least compact. Second, the best clusters are produces using MDS. That is to say the clusters are most compact and best separated. This is perhaps surprising, since this method uses only the set of pairwise distances between graphs, and overlooks the finer information residing in the vectors of spectral features. Although the clusters delivered by PCA are poorer, the results can be improved by using ICA. However, in none of the three cases is there any overlap between clusters. More importantly, they can be separated by straight-lines, i.e. they are linearly separable.

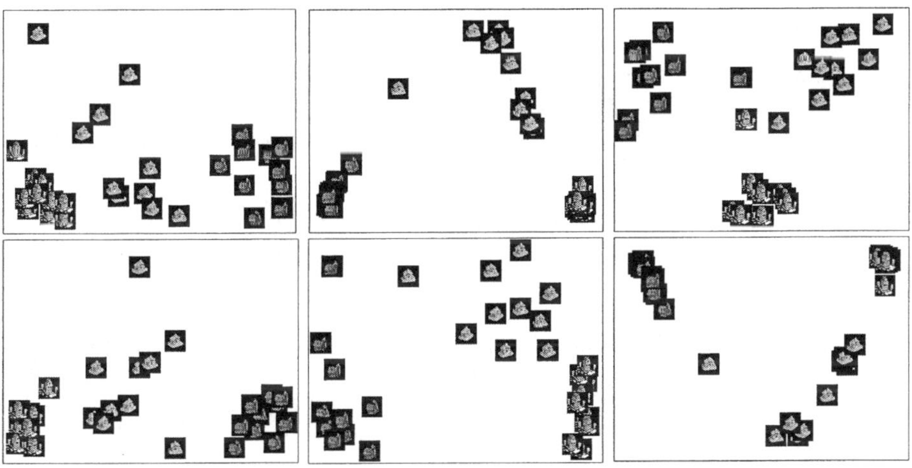

Fig. 3. Clustoring Results.

In the bottom of Figure 3 we repeat this sequence of experiments for the inter-mode adjacency matrix. This is a pairwise relational attribute. In each case the clusters are slightly improved. This is most marked when PCA is used to perform the embedding.

6 Conclusions

In this paper we have investigated how vectors of graph-spectral attributes can be used for the purposes of graph clustering. To do this we must first select attributes from which to construct feature vectors, and then select a means by which to embed the feature-vectors in a pattern space. The attributes studied are the leading eigenvalues, the volumes, perimeters, Cheeger numbers, inter-mode adjacency matrices and inter-mode edge-distance for the eigenmodes of the adjacency matrix. The embedding strategies are PCA, ICA and MDS. Our empirical study is based on corner adjacency graphs extracted from 2D views of 3D objects. We investigate two problems. The first of these is that of clustering the different views of the three objects together. The second problem is that of organising different views of the same object into well structured trajectories, in which subsequent views are adjacent to one another and there are distinct clusters associated with different views. In both cases the best results are obtained when we apply MDS to the vectors of leading eigenvalues.

References

1. C.M. Cyr and B.B. Kimia. 3D Object Recognition Using Shape Similarity-Based Aspect Graph. In *ICCV01*, pages I: 254–261, 2001.
2. M.A. Eshera and K.S. Fu. An image understanding system using attributed symbolic representation and inexact graph-matching. *Journal of the Association for Computing Machinery*, 8(5):604–618, 1986.
3. T. Hofmann and J.M. Buhmann. Pairwise data clustering by deterministic annealing. *PAMI*, 19(2):192–192, February 1997.
4. Kruskal J.B. Nonmetric multidimensional scaling: A numerical method. *Psychometrika*, 29:115–129, 1964.
5. Gower J.C. Some distance properties of latent root and vector methods used in multivariate analysis. *Biometrika*, 53:325–328, 1966.
6. Luo N, Wilson R.C and Hancock E.R. Spectral Feture Vectors for Graph Clustering multivariate analysis.
   Proc. SSPR02, LNCS 2396, pp. 83–93, 2002.
7. H. Murase and S.K. Nayar. Illumination planning for object recognition using parametric eigenspaces. *IEEE Transactions on Pattern Analysis and Machine Intelligence*, 16(12):1219–1227, 1994.
8. A. Sanfeliu and K.S. Fu. A distance measure between attributed relational graphs for pattern recognition. *IEEE Transactions Systems, Man and Cybernetics*, 13(3):353–362, May 1983.
9. K. Sengupta and K.L. Boyer. Organizing large structural modelbases. *PAMI*, 17(4):321–332, April 1995.
10. Torgerson W.S. Multidimensional scaling. i. theory and method. *Psychometrika*, 17:401–419, 1952.

Adaptive Segmentation of Remote-Sensing Images for Aerial Surveillance

Sung W. Baik[1], Sung M. Ahn[2], Jong W. Lee[1], and Khin K. Win[3]

[1] Sejong University, Seoul 143-747, KOREA
{sbaik,jwlee}@sejong.ac.kr
[2] Kookmin University, Seoul 136-702, KOREA
sahn@kookmin.ac.kr
[3] Yangon University, Yangon, Myanmar
physics@mptmail.net.mm

Abstract. The paper focuses on the adaptive segmentation of aerial images for aerial surveillance. The adaptive segmentation is achieved by the cooperation of on-line model modification and model based image segmentation through RBF neural network classifier. The on-line model modification allows the RBF classifier to adapt to the changes of geographical features on the aerial images. In addition, the Gabor filtering method for feature extraction is proposed in this experiment to discriminate between geographical features for better image segmentation.

1 Introduction

Aerial surveillance is now popular in the military for observing enemy force activities and detecting its military facilities, in the industrial world for management of restorable resources, classification and evaluation of earthy resources, land use mapping, plantation and vegetation monitoring. As examples, the state forestry department conducts regular aerial surveillance over its forest areas bordering neighboring countries or states to detect the occurrence of illegal logging, and the aerial surveillance is carried out by the maritime frontier guard to monitor illegal oil discharges from ships within fishing boundaries and maritime zone of interest to prevent oil pollution [1].

As the amount of aerial images collected under surveillance rapidly increased, it became very tedious for human analysts to examine these aerial images in order to derive information of interest. Therefore image analysis such as image segmentation became the norm. Image segmentation for scene understanding is one of very important aerial image analysis techniques for aerial surveillance. Some research [2,3,4] for the segmentation of aerial images has been conducted with extensive efforts in image processing, pattern recognition, intelligent system and computer vision fields. Also, there are some attempts [3,5] to perform image analysis considering spatial changes in aerial images.

This paper presents adaptive and intelligent image segmentation through geographical feature classification required for aerial surveillance of extensive regions, which are divided and registered into many aerial images. In this paper, we regard the shapeless regions of natural resources such as forests, river and sea, or regions with a collection of tiny and complicated structures such as man-made features including

N. Petkov and M.A. Westenberg (Eds.): CAIP 2003, LNCS 2756, pp. 549–554, 2003.

buildings, roads and bridges in the aerial images as texture as in previous research papers [2,3]. Furthermore, this paper considers the aerial image segmentation with the help of on-line model modification [6] for geographical texture features that change over different locations, on the assumption that texture features may substantially but smoothly change over different locations. The developed approach includes texture feature extraction for geographical features (geographical feature representation), and the aerial image segmentation through the close-loop of on-line model modification and Radial Basis Function network (adaptive image segmentation).

2 Geographical Feature Representation

To represent geographical features for aerial image segmentation, we use three texture feature extraction methods 1) Gabor spectral filtering [7], 2) Laws' energy filtering [8,9], and 3) Wavelet Transformation [10-13]; which have been widely used by researchers and perform very well for various classification and image segmentation tasks. To achieve the best segmentation, we need to select the best of these methods.

Gabor filters are useful to deal with the texture characterized by local frequency and orientation information. Gabor filters are obtained through a systematic mathematical approach. A Gabor function consists of a sinusoidal plane of particular frequency and orientation modulated by a two-dimensional Gaussian envelope. A two-dimensional Gabor filter is given by:

$$G(x, y) = \exp[\frac{1}{2}(\frac{x}{\sigma_x^2} + \frac{y}{\sigma_y^2})]\cos(\frac{2\pi x}{n_0} + \alpha) \tag{1}$$

By orienting the sinusoid at an angle α and changing the frequency n_0, many Gabor filtering sets can be obtained. An example of a set of eight Gabor filters is decided with different parameter values (n_0 = 2.82 and 5.66 pixels/cycle and orientations α = 0°, 45°, 90°, and 135°).

Laws' convolution kernels based on five dimensional vectors are used as an energy filter bank. It consists of 25 filters which can be derived from the weights of L5=[1,4,6,4,1], E5=[-1,-2,0,2,1], S5=[-1,0,2,0,-1], R5=[1,-4,6,-4,1], and W5=[-1,2,0,-2,1]. The respective specifications are Level, Edge, Spot, Ripple and Wave detection, in which convolving and transposing each other produce various square masks of 25 filters.

Texture feature extraction algorithm based on wavelet transform provides a non redundant signal representation with accurate reconstruction capability, and forms a precise and uniform framework for the signal analysis at different scales [10]. The pyramidal wavelet transform is used because of its non data redundancy and less complexity. Basically, in pyramidal wavelet transform, original image is decomposed into four sub-images which are one approximation (LL) and three details (LH, HL, HH) frequency components at each level. The HH, LH, HL and LL sub-images represents diagonal details (higher frequencies in both directions, corners), vertical higher frequencies (horizontal edges), horizontal higher frequencies (vertical edges) and lowest frequencies, respectively [11]. The decomposition procedures are performed repeatedly on approximation component at each level, and hence 3n+1 numbers of sub-images are produced for 'n' level decompositions. Thus, many wavelet transform sub-images can be achieved from different level, and the variance of each sub-image is used as a texture feature [12]. However, most significant information appears in middle frequency regions for texture images [13], LH and HL sub-images are selected from each decomposition level to compute the channel variances of feature image. Since there is no criterion to determine the decomposition level that yields the best discriminations, it is necessary to define the desired (optimal) level. In practice, deeper level decompositions could not contain significant information and will give unreliable data. In this work, 24 wavelet filters are generated by using three Daubechies wavelets (db1, db2, db3) and five biorthogonal wavelets (bior1.3, bior2.4, bior3.7, bior4.4, bior5.5) at one, two and three scale decomposition. From experimental observations, it has no drastic change between the wavelet feature images even though 24 wavelet filters are used.

3 Adaptive Image Segmentation

RBF neural network classifier [14-17] has been chosen for remote sensing image analysis by many researchers. And it has been used as an adaptively trained neural network [16-19] since its well-defined mathematical model allows for further modifications with its parameters and structure.

The key idea in this paper is image segmentation mechanism to sensitively adapt to the spatial changes of geographical features on the aerial images. Such mechanism can be achieved by the cooperation of on-line model modification and the model based image segmentation through RBF neural network classifier.

A RBF function Fr consists of a set of basis functions that form localized decision regions. Overlapping local regions formed by simple basis functions can create a complex distribution. For Gaussian distribution, as a basis function, each region is represented by its center and width corresponding to a mean vector and a covariance matrix (μ, Σ). For a multi-modal distribution of a class r, a RBF can be formed through the following linear combination of these basis functions:

$$F_r(X) = w_0 + \sum_i w_i f_{ri}(X) \tag{2}$$

where: w_i is the trainable weight vector (for $i = 0,\ldots, N_r$);r is the class membership number; N_r is the number of nodes (basis functions) in class r; and

$$f(X) = \exp[-\frac{1}{2}(X-\mu)^T \Sigma^{-1} (X-\mu)]. \tag{3}$$

The RBF classifier models complex multi-modal data distribution through its decomposition into multiple independent Gaussians. The RBF classifier models a complex multi-modal data distribution through its decomposition into multiple independent Gaussians. The model can be dynamically adjusted by changing mode parameters over time.

There are four behaviors for the RBF classifier modification that can be selected and executed independently: (1) Accommodation, (2) Translation, (3) Generation, and (4) Extinction. Each behavior is implemented separately using mathematical rules transposing reinforcement parameters onto actions of RBF modification.

Accommodation and Translation behaviors modify the classifier parameters only. This modification is performed over selected nodes of the RBF net. The basis for Accommodation is to combine reinforcement parameters with the existing node parameters. The result of Accommodation is adjusted function spread. The node center does not change/shift through the feature space. The goal for Translation is to shift the node center in the direction of reinforcement without modifying the spread of the function. Combining Accommodation and Translation, the system can fully modify an existing RBF node of the classifier.

Generation and Extinction behaviors modify the classifier structure by expanding or pruning the number of RBF nodes. The basic idea behind Generation is to create a new node. A node is generated when there is (1) a significant progressive shift in function location and/or (2) an increase in complexity of feature space, for example, caused by the increase in the multi-modality of data distribution. The goal of Extinction is to eliminate useless nodes from a classifier. Extinction is activated by the utilization of classifier nodes in the image classification process. Nodes, which constantly do not contribute to the classifier, are disposed. This allows for controlling the complexity of the classifier over time.

4 Experiments

Experimental data have been obtained from UC Berkeley Library Web [20]. They are aerial black/white colored photographs of the San Francisco Bay area, California, where there are natural resource features such as forests, river and sea, and man-made features such as buildings, roads, and bridges. An aerial image (1308 by 1536 pixels) of a certain area is shown in Figure 1-(a), where a gray-colored curved arrow indicates a surveillance path for discriminating the target area from the background. Along this path, a sequence of 30 sub-images (240 by 320 pixels) can be selected for target segmentation. Figure 1-(b) shows three sample sub-images of the sequence. The experiment focuses on the segmentation between densely built-up areas and the other areas on each aerial image in a sequence. For better segmentation, an appropriate feature extraction method should be selected. Gabor filtering method finally is selected according to the evaluation of feature extraction results.

The initial step for the model based image segmentation is to design the RBF neural network by training it from the first image of the sequence. In the next step, the RBF network is applied to segment geographical features of interest on the next image and then the RBF network's parameters are adjusted according to intermediate segmentation results with some or serious errors caused due to the difference between new geographical features on the next image and estimated parameters of the RBF network designed in the initial step. Furthermore, RBF parameter adjustment process is repeatedly performed until the intermediate results are satisfied with the given criteria.

Figure 1-(c) shows the segmentation results of these images. In the segmentation result, the black regions represent non-target areas and the regions with several other gray colors are for target areas. The gray color indicates the confidence of segmentation. In other words, the pixel value of the gray colored regions indicates the measurement of confidence for the classification of its corresponding pixel of the original images.

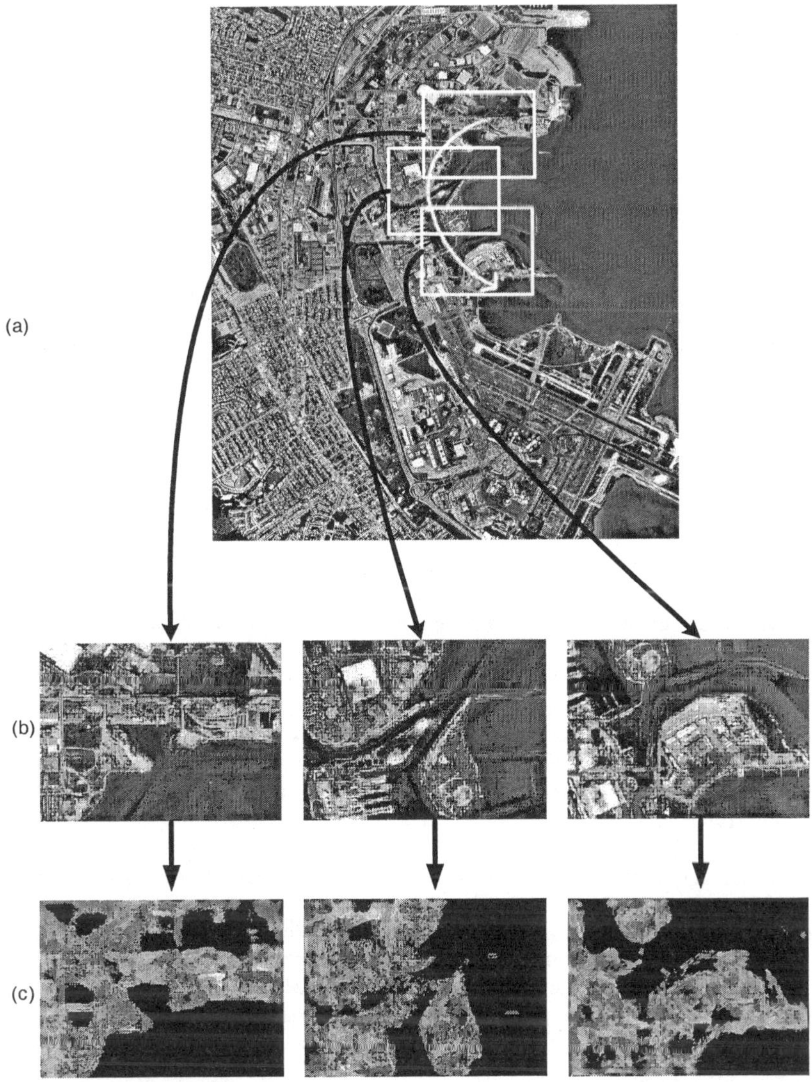

Fig. 1. An aerial image, three sample sub-images and segmentation results of these images

5 Conclusions

On-line model modification approach was applied to the aerial image segmentation for aerial surveillance. The approach has been tested on a variety of geographical feature segmentation problems in image sequences. Considering the difficulties in aerial image analysis, a major problem has been identified. Since a close-loop cooperation of on-line model modification and segmentation process is required, the effectiveness of model modification depends on the quality of image segmentation. As a future work, we need the further investigation of geographical feature extraction to improve the quality of image segmentation.

References

1. F. Volckaert, G. Kayens, R. Schallier and T. Jacques. Aerial surveillance of operational oil pollution in Belgium's maritime zone of interest. *Marine Pollution Bulletin*, 40(11), 1051-1056, 2000.
2. B. Lofy and J. Sklansky. Segmenting multisensor aerial images in class-scale space. *Pattern Recognition.* 34, 1825-1839, 2001.
3. P. Robertson and J. Michael Brady. Adaptive image analysis for aerial surveillance. *IEEE Transaction on Intelligent Systems*, 14(3), 30-36, 1999.
4. D. McCoy and V. Devarajan. Artificial immune systems and aerial image segmentation. *IEEE International Conference on Systems, Man, and Cybernetics*, 1, 12-15, 1997.
5. R. Kumar and H. Sawhney. Aerial video surveillance and exploitation. *Proceedings of the IEEE*, 89(10), 1518-1526, 2001.
6. S. Baik and P. Pachowicz. Online model modification for adaptive texture recognition in image sequences. *IEEE Transactions on Systems, Man, and Cybernetics, Part A*, 32(6), 625-639, 2002.
7. M. Farrokhnia and A. Jain. A multi-channel filtering approach to texture segmentation. *Proceedings of IEEE Computer Vision and Pattern Recognition Conference*, 346-370, 1990.
8. M. Chantler, The effect of variation in illuminant direction on texture classification, *Ph D Thesis,* Dept. Computing and Electrical Engineering, Heriot-Watt University, 1994.
9. K. Laws. Textured image segmentation. *Ph.D. Thesis*. Dept. of Electrical Engineering, University of Southern California, Los Angeles, 1980.
10. M. Unser. Texture classification and segmentation using wavelet frames, *IEEE Transactions on Image Processing*. 4(11), 1549-1560, 1995.
11. S. Mallat. Multifrequency channel decompositions of images and wavelet models, *IEEE Transactions on Acoustics, Speech and Signal Processing*, 37(12), 2091-2110, 1989.
12. C. Chen. Filtering methods for texture discrimination, *Pattern Recognition Letters*, 20, 783-790, 1999.
13. T. Chang and C. Kuo. A wavelet transform approach to texture analysis, *Proceedings of IEEE International Conference on Acoustics, Speech, and Signal Processing,* 4, 661-664, 1992.
14. C. H. Chen and B. Shrestha. Classification of multi-sensor remote sensing images using self-organizing feature maps and radial basis function networks. *Proceedings of IEEE 2000 International Geoscience and Remote Sensing Symposium*, 2, 711 -713, 2000.
15. L. Bastos, R. Bastos and W. Nishida. Radial basis function for classification of remote sensing images. *Proceedings of International Joint Conference on Neural Networks*, 1959-1962, 1999.
16. L. Bruzzone and D. Prieto. A technique for the selection of kernel-function parameters in RBF neural networks for classification of remote-sensing images. *IEEE Transactions on Geoscience and Remote Sensing*, 37(2), 1179-1184, 1999.
17. L. Bruzzone and D. Fernàndez Prieto. An incremental-learning neural network for the classification of remote-sensing images. *Pattern Recognition Letters*, 20(11-13), 1241-1248, 1999.
18. D. Park, M. El-Sharkawi and R. Marks II. An adaptively trained neural network. *IEEE Transactions* on Neural Networks, 2(3), 334-345, 1991.
19. P. Robertson and J. M. Brady. Adaptive image analysis for aerial surveillance. *IEEE Transaction on Intelligent Systems*, 14(3), 30-36, 1999.
20. http://sunsite.berkeley.edu/AerialPhotos/vbzj.html#index

Detecting and Classifying Road Turn Directions from a Sequence of Images

A.P. Leitão[1], S. Tilie[1], S.-S. Ieng[1], and V. Vigneron[2]

[1] LIVIC (INRETS–LCPC)
13, route de la Minière – bat 140, 78150 Versailles, France
{leitao,ieng}@inrets.fr, tilie@lcpc.fr
[2] LSC (Université d'Evry)
40, Rue du Pelvoux – CE 1455, Courcouronnes 91020 Evry Cedex, France
vvigne@iup.univ-evry.fr

Abstract. We propose a detection and classification system for road curvature, which is robust to light changes and different road markings. The road curves in an image are first filtered to detect the road marks and borders. The contrast gradient angle of the detected regions are accumulated in a histogram. The resulting histograms are used to train a Kohonen Neural Network. The final output classification shows the mapping of a sequence of scenes on the network centroids, giving a correlation of the transitions between classes and represented situations. This may be used later to improve road security, indicating dangerous situations to the driver or feeding a driving control system.

1 Introduction

In this work, we analyze a sequence of gray-level images, in order to describe the road shape. On vision-based intelligent driving-systems, different approaches [1], [2], [3] have been proposed to deal with lane detection in complex situations. Using a single camera as sensor, we want to create a simple and fast solution, which is robust for noise, discontinuities in line-marks, contrast variations, and shadows (Fig. 1). The system should be capable of detecting and classifying road singularities, such as shape and relative turn orientation. A dynamic process may then guide the analysis of the following images in the sequence, showing the evolution of the scene transitions within the network centroids.

Fig. 1. Different image configurations on the same road situation.

N. Petkov and M.A. Westenberg (Eds.): CAIP 2003, LNCS 2756, pp. 555–562, 2003.

The next section describes the implemented preprocessing method: the band detecting filter, used to extract the regions that should be used to describe the road shape. Section 3 presents the Self-Organizing Map (SOM), used as classification method for the established histograms. Section 4 gives a quality index for evaluating the training results and its applications on some simulations. The last section presents conclusions and proposals for future work.

2 Preprocessing

In a system that aims to characterize objects which are present in an image, we must first establish a representation that may better describe the information. We use object contours, which has been promoted in the litterature over absolute luminance values (gray levels) [4], [5], [6]. This representation is robust for luminance intensity and to direction changes.

2.1 Feature Extraction

Feature extraction in image data can be seen as a special kind of data reduction for which the goal is to find a subset of informative variables. Since image data is, by nature, very high dimensional, feature extraction is often a necessary step for object recognition to be successful. It is also a means for controlling the so–called curse–of–dimensionality. When used as further inputs, one wants to extract those features that best describe the objects in the image, preserving the class separability.

Band Detection. Ieng and Tarel [7] propose a lane-marking features extractor based only on the geometry of lane-markings, which is robust to lighting variations. Its goal is to obtain the maximum number of features present on the lane-markings while largelly reducing the number of outliers. The remaining outliers should be later taken into account in the processing.

With the frontal camera, the observed lane-marking width decreases linearly and reaches zero at the horizon line, thus a valid width interval $[S_{min}, S_{max}]$ will be adjusted to each line of the image. At first, the horizontal and vertical gradient components are computed using Canny-Deriche filter [8]. Then, at each line, the detector of white bands search for a pair od positive and negative gradients (G_+ and G_-) with a value higher then a threshold G_0 in absolute value and within the defined range distance $[S_{min}, S_{max}]$ adequate to the processed line (Fig. 2). The threshold G_0 is set small to a small value to compensate adverse lighting conditions.

As an adaptation to this method, we included the detection of dark bands (see Fig. 3). This should enhance the road shape detection, increasing the number of extracted features. It should specially concern the scenes where the lane-marking is not continuous or not clear, where the darker borders are the only contour information. To implement this dark band detector we adjusted a new initial gradient G_0^d and a new range distance $[S_{min}^d, S_{max}^d]$. As for the matching pair of

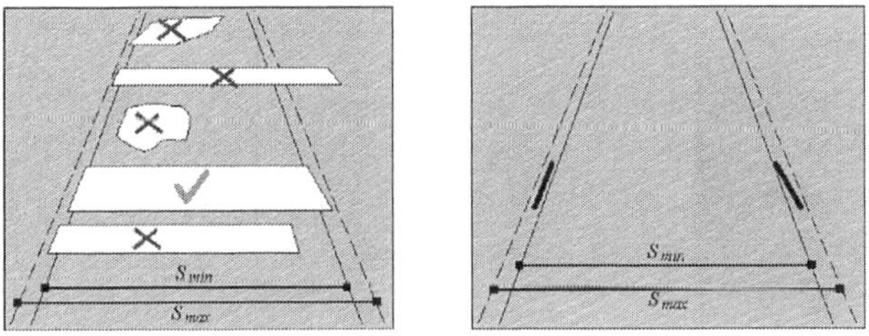

Fig. 2. Using Ieng and Tarel constraints, objects having exactly both borders within the interval $[S_{min}, S_{max}]$ are detected. The right image shows the output of this filter.

(a) (b)

Fig. 3. The extraction of bands on sintesized (a) and real (b) images .

gradients, the search is inverted: first a negative and then a positive values are detected (G^d_- and G^d_+). Fig. 3 shows the detection on both synthesized and real road scenes: (a) only the light (white) bands are detected on the synthesized image; (b) the result shows the extraction of both white and dark bands.

Gradient Angle Histograms. Intuitively, road contours may be simplified as a set of curves. Recent works have tried to describe these curves as polynomial equations, splines, etc. [9], [10], [11].

Suppose that the pixel (P_x, P_y) can be represented by a function of the luminance intensity $I(x, y)$. The output of the geometric filter is a set of pixels that indicates the position where the road marks and contours should be found (regardless the noise). Instead of calculating the precise description of the curve composed by these pixels, we propose to describe the gradient vector angle in each position detected by the above filter and accumulate it in a histogram. In this way, the detection of courves is given by a set of possible curves (which can be summarized) while small inconsistencies (noise) will be dispersed.

Fig. 4 shows the results of the gradient marginal calculation, considering the dark-light and light-dark contrast directions. In Fig. 4-(b), all the pixels under the estimated horizon line are used and the very contrasted shadows create peaks around 105 and -85 degrees on the graph (described by the dashed lines). In the second histogram, presented at Fig. 4-(c), only the points detected by the geometric filter are included. The direction of the road contour (described

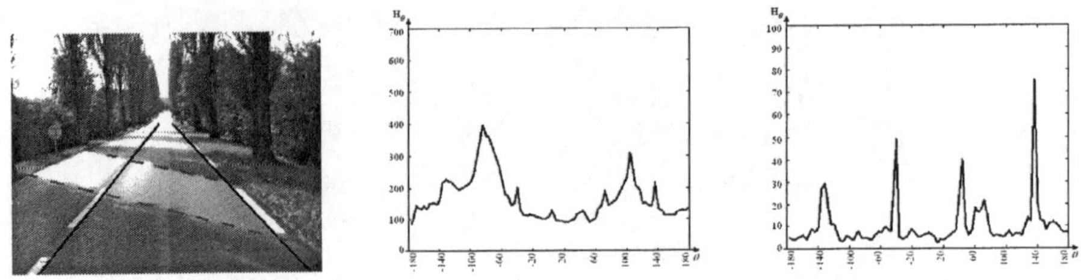

(a) (b) (c)

Fig. 4. Using the same gray scale image (a), we calculated two gradient vector angle θ histograms using: (b) every pixel under an estimated horizon; (c) pixels selected with the geometric filter described above.

by the full lines) becomes a clear information, and the peaks are placed at the contrast-pairs (50,-135) and (135,-40).

3 Classification

A wide class of artificial neural networks can be trained to perform classification. In this paper, we apply a SOM [12] to organize structural road changes in topological manner. The structural information obtained by the previous feature extraction step is collected in a d dimensional vector x (where d is the dimension of the histogram). These vectors are quantized into a finite number of so–called *centroids* using a SOM that offers several advantages such as the ability to quantize adaptively depending on the changes in the ranges of the attributes and the ability to deal with the curse–of–dimensionality.

The network has one layer of n units arranged in a grid. Let w_{ij} represent the jth component of the input x_i. The unit i is defined by the vector:

$$\boldsymbol{w}_i = (w_{i1}, w_{i2}, ..., w_{id}) \tag{1}$$

The set $I = 1, ..., n$ of units is composed in a topological structure. This is provided by a symmetrical and decreasing neighborhood function $\Lambda(i, j)$, defined on $(i, j) \in I \times I$ (Equation 3). The input space X is included in $\mathbb{R}^d$. The units are fully connected to the inputs.

For a given state S of the network, the network response to input x is the winner unit i_o, *i.e.* the closest unit to input x. At the end, the network defines a map $\Phi_S : \boldsymbol{x} \longmapsto i(\boldsymbol{x}, S)$, from $\boldsymbol{w}$ to $I = 1, ..., n$, and the goal of the learning algorithm is to converge to a network state such that the corresponding map will preserve topology. The learning rule is formalized at each interation step as in Equation (2), where $\varepsilon(t)$ is a decreasing learning function.

$$\boldsymbol{w}_i(t+1) = \boldsymbol{w}_i(t) - \varepsilon(t)\Lambda(i_o, i)(\boldsymbol{x}(t) - \boldsymbol{w}_i(t)), \tag{2}$$

Fig. 5. Result of the Ward group clustering applied to the trained 9-classes network.

If N is the number of iterations, we applied the following Gaussian function as a linear decreasing neighborhood function $\Lambda(i_o, i)$

$$\Lambda(i_o, i) = e^{\left(\frac{-\|i_o - i\|^2}{2\sigma(t)^2}\right)} \quad \text{where} \quad \sigma(t) = 1 + (\sigma(0) - 1) * \left(1 - \frac{t}{N}\right) \tag{3}$$

There are no known proof to the SOM training convergence, but some statistical measures can be made to evaluate the quality of the map [13]. To improve the choice of the $\varepsilon(t)$, in [14], we studied the *mean quantization error* during the training phase. The error evolution (the square distance of an input $\boldsymbol{x}(t)$ and its winner centroid) showed that the best performance was achieved with the inversed decreasing function described bellow. Let

$$\varepsilon(t) = \varepsilon(0) * \left(\frac{\left(\frac{N}{\beta}\right)}{\left(\frac{N}{\beta}\right) + t} \right) \tag{4}$$

be such a learning function, and β and initialization parameter (here $\beta = 200$).

4 Simulations

A database of gray scale images, with 384*288 pixels, was collected with a camera installed on the roof of the experiment car. Several lighting conditions were encountered, taking into account the position of the sun and on the shadows provided by trees and various objects.

The described methodology was applied to a training set of 550 images, and their collected histograms were used as vector input to the SOM. These histograms were down-sampled with a scale of 4, creating input vectors of $d = 90$. The work was focused in three situations: *turn to the right*, *turn to the left*, and *straight road*. From the final network map, Ward's hierarchical clustering was used to define three different labels to the centroids (Fig. 5).

In the Ward's method, the criterion for cells fusion is that it should produce the smallest possible increase in the error sum of squares [15]. In Fig. 5, for each centroid, the main directions of the road contour are illustrated by lines representing the highest histogram θ peaks. The neighborhood topology built by the SOM is represented on the clusters distribution. From left to right the neurons show the *turn to the right*, the *straight road* and the *turn to the left*.

Fig. 6 presents the evolution of the gradient vector histogram in a sequence of images (or in time). The vertical axis represents the time and the horizontal axis the gradient vector angles of each image. Thus, the intensity of each image

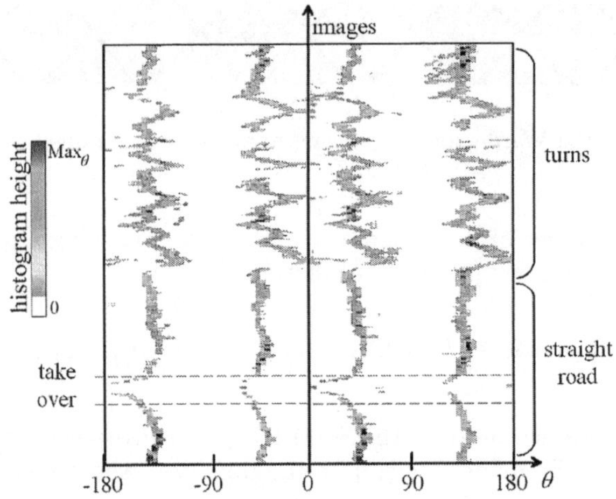

Fig. 6. The evolution of the θ histogram on an image sequence showing all the tree three different situations. First a straight road then curves to the right and to the left in a zigzag. On the histogram we can analyze the changes on the images following the higher peaks that indicate the main directions. MAX_θ is the highest peak on all the sequence of histograms. *Take over* represents the sequence where the car takes over a bicycle.

histogram is represented in a colorful line of the new graph. We clearly notice the simultaneity of the changes in the road situations with the appearance of histogram peaks. Our results show that the same relation can be found while classifying the sequence on a trained Kohonen map.

Tests were run for validation with a sequence of 500 images presenting the three established situations to the network. On these first results, the map is able to follow the transitions that occur in the sequence (Fig. 7). The straight roads images are always on classified on the central cluster. All 5 *turns to the right* were well classified on the correct clusters and only one of the 5 *turns to the left* is not fully recognized. This turn arrives to the closest centroid between the *straight road* and the *turn to the left* clusters.

5 Conclusion and Future Work

In this paper, we describe an original solution for detecting and classifying road turn directions by tracing the analogy between the scenes transitions and the classes transitions on a sequence of images.

The scene geometry is first processed with a band–detecting filter. This result is then represented on a histogram that describes the gradient's contrast vector angles. These parameters are treated by a SOM network. Although the first results indicate that changes on the road can be traced during the classification phase, a quantitative analysis should be implemented to justify the chosen approach.

Fig. 7. The transitions from the different situations are reflected on the Kohonen map. On the top of each image we represent the classification on the same map represented in Fig. 5. We also mark the history of the transitions that occur in the sequence.

To improve the results of the band extract filter we are testing adapting methods to automatically adjust the G_0 and G_0^d initial gradients values, establishing a filter independent to luminance variations within a single image (shadows) and within a sequence (over exposure caused by sun light).

References

1. Batavia, P., Pomerleau, D., and Thorpe C. Applying Advanced Learning Algorithms to ALVINN. Techinical report CMU-RI-TR-96-31, Robotics Institute, Carnegie Mellon University (1996)
2. Crisman, J.D., Thorpe, C.E.: SCARF – A color vision system that tracks roads and intersections. IEEE Transactions on Robotics and Automation. **9** 1 (1993) 49–58
3. Kim, K.I., Kim, S.W., and Oh, S.Y.: Autonomous Land Vehicle: PRV III. Proceedings 6th Korea-Japan Joint Workshop on Computer Vision. Nagoya, Japan (2000) 32–37
4. Brunelli, R., Poggio, T.: Face recognition: Features versus Templates. IEEE Transactions on Pattern Analysis and Machine Intelligence.**15** 10 (1993) 1042–1052
5. Edelman, S., Intrator, N., Poggio, T.: Complex cells and object recognition. submitted (1997)
6. Marr, D.: Vision. Freeman and Company, New York (1982)
7. Ieng, S. S., Tarel, J.-P.: On the design of a single lane-markings detector regardless the on-board camera's position. To appear in Proceedings of IEEE Intelligent Vehicles Symposium, IV'2003. Columbus, OH, USA. (2003)
8. Deriche, R.: Using Canny's criteria to derive a recursively implemented optimal edge detector. International Journal of Computer Vision.**1** 2 (1987) 167–187
9. Tarel J.-P., Guichard, F.: Combined dynamic tracking and recognition of curves with application to road detection. Proceedings of International Conference on Image Processing, IEEE ICIP'2000.**I** Vancouver, Canada. (2000) 216–219

10. Risack, R., Klausmann, P., Kruger, W., Enkelmann, W.: Robust lane recognition embedded in a real time driver assistance system. Proceedings of Intelligent Vehicles Symposium, IV'98.**1** Stuttgart, Germany. (1998) 35–40
11. Wang, Y., Shen, D., Teoh, E.K.: Lane detection using catmull-rom spline. Proceedings of Intelligent Vehicles Symposium, IV'98.**1** Stuttgart, Germany. (1998) 51–57
12. Kohonen, T.: Self-organizing maps. Springer, Berlin (1995)
13. de Bold, E., Cotrell, M., Verleysen, M.: Statistical tools to asses the reliability of self-organizing maps. Neural Networks. **15** (2002) 967–978
14. Leitão, A.P., Tilie, S., Mangeas, M., Tarel, J.-P., Vigneron, V., Lelandais, S.: Road Singularities Detection and Classification. Proceedings of the 11th European Symposium on Artificial Neural Networks, ESANN'2003. Bruges, Belgium. (2003) 301–306
15. Ward, J. H.: Hierarchical Grouping to Optimize an Objective Function Journal of the American Statistical Association.**58** (1963) 236–244

Classification of Connecting Points in Thai Printed Characters by Combining Inductive Logic Programming with Backpropagation Neural Network

Luepol Pipanmaekaporn and Amornthep Sachdev

Department of Computer Science, Thammasart University
99 Klongnuang, Prathumtani, Thailand
luepol@cs.tu.ac.th, thep@sachdev.co.th

Abstract. An important problem that decreases the accuracy in Thai Printed Character Recognition system is the errors in segmentation process. In vertical connected character segmentation, we can easily use the reference lines of Thai language structure. This paper thus proposes a method for detecting the connecting points in horizontal connected characters. First, we extract the features of the connecting points in the character images. Then, we employ Inductive Logic Programming to produce the rules that will be used to classify the unseen examples. Finally, we use Backpropagation Neural Network to make these rules more flexible. The results show that our method achieves 94.94% of accuracy.

1 Introduction

One of the most important problems that decrease the accuracy in Thai Printed Character Recognition systems is connected character in a document image. Major issues that lead to the connecting of characters are that a scanned document is usually contaminated with noise, style, and size of fonts and ink absorbing in the paper. These could cause the errors in recognition process because the incorrectly segmented characters are not likely to be correctly recognized.

There have been many good performance researches on English character segmentation [1]. However, Thai character segmentation much differs from English approaches because Thai characters are categorized into 4 different levels [8], and therefore we must apply horizontal segmentation process together with vertical segmentation. So the English character segmentation techniques cannot be directly used with Thai characters correctly due to the differences in the nature of the language. Various approaches have been proposed for Thai character segmentation such as the method of detection horizontally touching characters by shortest path algorithm [3], In [5], the templates of touching characters are determined by boundary of horizontal and vertical histograms, which is then encoded by modified freeman coding techniques. And the segmentation of horizontal and vertical touching characters using multi-level structure combined with the width and the height of character [8]. However, problems of connected characters such as crossing and overlapping characters have not been solved. In this paper, we present a new method for detection of the

N. Petkov and M.A. Westenberg (Eds.): CAIP 2003, LNCS 2756, pp. 563–570, 2003.

connecting points in Thai printed characters, which combines two learning algorithms, i.e. Inductive logic programming (ILP) and the Backpropagation Neural network (BNN)[10]. First, we extract the features of the connecting points in the character images. Then, we employ ILP to produce the rules that will be used to classify the unseen images. Finally, we use BNN to make these rules more flexible.

2 Connected Characters in Thai Documents

In Thai language structure, all characters are categorized into 4 different level [8]. We can partition the connected characters in a Thai sentence into 2 groups, i.e. vertical and horizontal connecting. Vertical connected characters are those characters connected among different levels. Horizontal connected characters are those characters connected in the same level, as shown in Fig. 1.

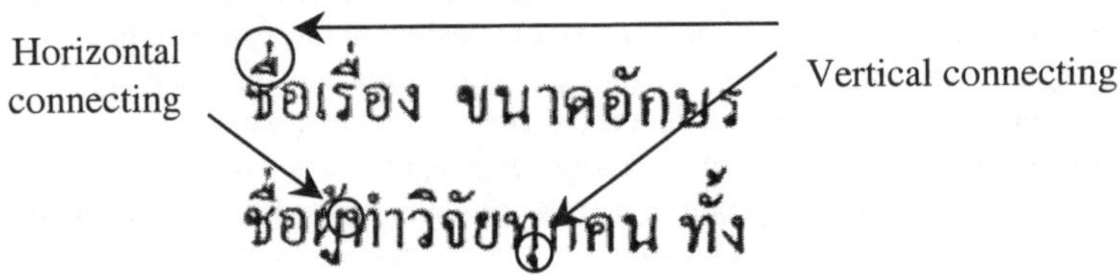

Fig. 1. Examples of connected characters.

3 Connected Characters in Thai Documents

3.1 Detection of Reference Lines, and Boundary Determination of Connected Pixels

In order to determine the level of characters, the reference line must be known. First, we apply the salt and pepper noise-reduction algorithm to a scanned document. Then, we detect the reference line using horizontal projection on the document image. The local minimums of the horizontal projection on the reference line are used as the level separation lines, as shown in Fig. 2.

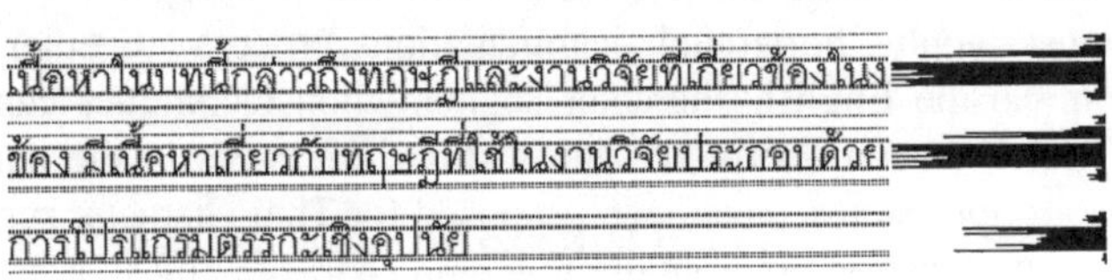

Fig. 2. The result of detection of the reference line level.

Boundary of connected pixels is determined using Breadth-First Search (BFS), in order to separate document image into sub-images, which contain only one group of connected pixels. First, the document image is scanned from left to right, then top to bottom. When a black pixel is encountered, the BFS process starts by adding the black pixel to be the root of the queue; adjacent black pixels are then recruited into the queue. Continue the BFS process until the queue is empty. Black pixels, which have been considered, will be eliminated from the document image. The connected pixels could be an isolated character or connected characters, as shown in Fig. 3.

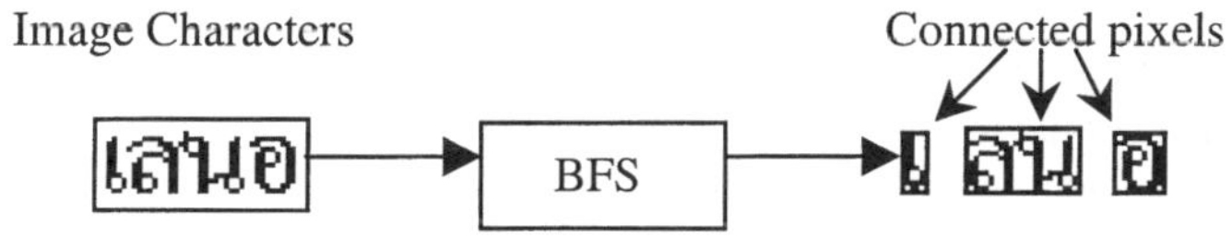

Fig. 3. The result of the Boundary determination of Connected pixels.

3.2 Preprocessing

The medial axes thinning algorithm [2] is applied to each image of connected pixels. Then, each image is resized into 36 x 36 pixels. Zoning is then applied to divide the image into 9 zones, as shown in Fig. 4.

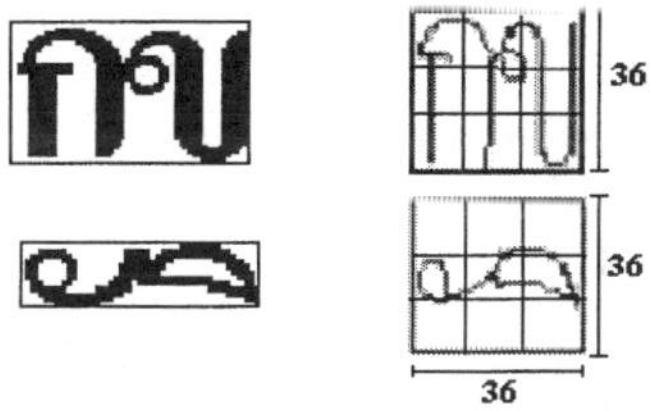

Fig. 4. (a) Image before preprocessing and (b) Image after preprocessing.

3.3 Detection of Connecting Points

The process starts with matching the pattern of the pixels on each black pixel of the connected pixels to define the connecting point. As shown in Fig. 6, the black boxes in the pattern indicate that those pixels must be black. The white boxes in the pattern indicate that those pixels must be white. If there is at least one black pixel found on the gray area, the middle pixel (PC) will be first considered as a connecting point. The pattern is shown in Fig. 5

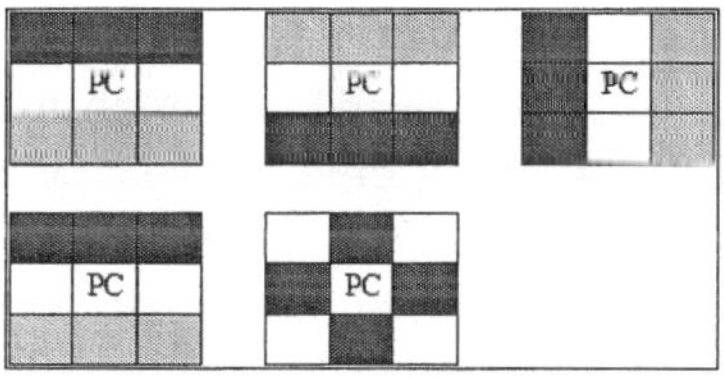

Fig. 5. The patterns for detection of connecting points.

3.4 Feature Extraction

We extract several features from the connecting points. These features will be further fed into the learning algorithm. The following features are shown in Fig. 6.

- *neighbor* is the list of position of black neighbor pixels.
- *sum_neighbor* is the number of neighbor points.
- *zone* is the area zone of the connecting point on the connected pixels.
- *height* is the original height of the connected pixels.
- *width* is the original width of the connected pixels.
- *link_point* is the pair of connecting points found in the same column or within 2-column distance of the connected pixels.
- *sum_link* is the amount of connection between connecting points.

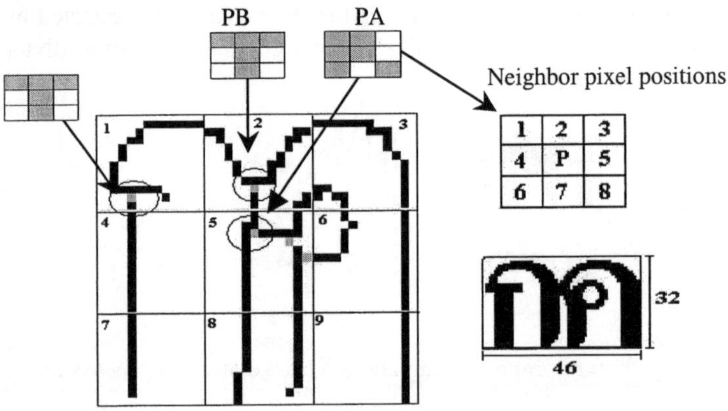

Extracted Features: The height of the connected pixels is 32 points. The width is 46 points. PA has the features; the list of black neighbor pixels of PA are 1,2,4,6 and 8, the area zone is 5 and PA is only connected to PB.

Fig. 6. An example of features extracted from connected pixels.

3.5 Leaning Rules with ILP

The ILP is a fast growing research area, which combines Logic Programming and Machine Learning [6]. The general setting for ILP is, given background knowledge or theory in the form of first-order clauses and sets of positive and negative examples, find a hypothesis which covers all the positive but none of the negative examples.

The ILP system used in our experiment is Progol [7]. Input of Progol composes of positive examples, negative examples and background knowledge. The positive examples are connecting points found between characters, and the negative examples contain all possible connecting points other than those found in positive examples. Each example is represented in the form "active(A)" , where active is the head of rules, A is name of the connecting point e.g., active(p21).

Background knowledge is a set of predicates, which are used to describe hypotheses about connecting points. It is a group of knowledge we know about the domain, and is defined by logic programs. All features extracted from the connecting points in the previous subsection are used as background knowledge. The output of ILP is a set of rules, which are used to classify connecting point. For instance, some of rules are shown in Fig. 7.

```
active(A) :- neighbor (A,6), zone(A,2), inpic_width(A).

active(A) :- neighbor (A,4), zone(A,5), link_point
(A,B), zone(B,8) , inpic_height(A).

active(A) :- neighbor (A,1), neighbor (A,2), neighbor
(A,4), zone(A,2), inpic_width(A).

inpic_width(X) :- width(X,Y) , Y >30 , Y <50.

inpic_height(X) :- height(X,Y) , Y >20,  Y < 25.
```

Fig. 7. Examples of learned rules from Progol.

In Fig. 8, the first rule defines that the examined point is considered to be a connecting point between connected characters if it has black pixel on the 6th neighbor position, locates in the zone 2 and the width of the connected pixels is beyond 30 points, but, less than 50 points. If the rule is false, the other rule will be considered respectively.

3.6 Combining Backpropagation Neural Network for Approximate Partially Match of Rules [4, 11]

Rules obtained from the ILP algorithm are then used to classify the connecting points by comparing the input features with the rule that exactly match with the features. Therefore it is possible that some correct rules are not exactly matched with the input features, especially with features obtained from noisy or unseen images. BNN is designed to choose the best matching rule, which approximately matches with the input features. The structure of BNN is composed of three layers; the input layer having neurons representing the truth values of predicates from each rule, the hidden layer having neurons representing each rule and the output layer with 2 neurons representing the classes of connected characters. The links from the input neurons to the hidden neurons are partially connected, linking predicates and corresponding rule. The hidden neurons fully connect to the output neurons, as shown in Fig. 8.

In the input layer, some predicates cannot appear alone, e.g. zone(B,8) in the second rule in Fig. 8., because the new variable B is introduced in predicate link_point(A,B). So the introducing predicate, link_point(A,B) must be combined with zone(B,8) and we then use both predicates to evaluate the truth value of the example. In case of more than one possible variable binding, we use the binding that gives maximum true predicates [4].

In the training process, the training examples are examined with the rules from ILP; the result of matching predicates of each rule is fed into the input layer of the neural network. We assign 1 for the true predicates and assign –1 for the false predicates. The output neuron that corresponds to the training connecting point is set to 1,

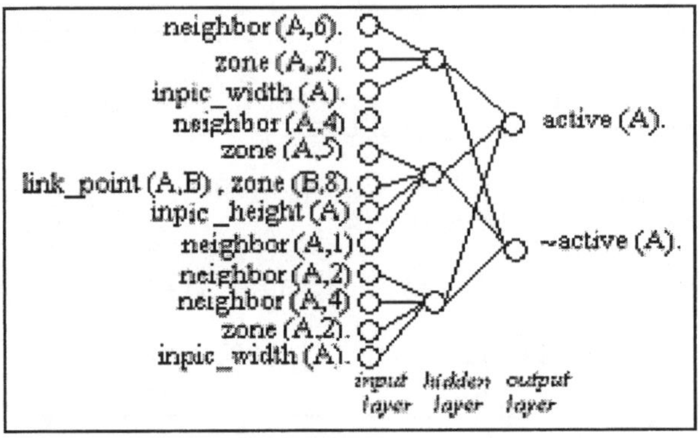

Fig. 8. The Backpropagation Neural Network stracture.

4 Experimental Results

In our experiment, we used 2,208 connecting points from connected characters and isolated characters of image documents of the fonts Angsana and Cordia of sizes 14, 16, 18 and 20. All examples are divided into 2 classes, connecting points found between 2 connected characters and connecting points appearing in isolated characters. In order to estimate the accuracy of the rules obtained by ILP, we carried out a 10 fold cross-validation test.

We compared our method with C4.5 Decision Tree Learning Algorithm (DTL) [9]. To make DTL be comparable with ILP, we used only predicates that represent the propositional attributes of the connecting point. Then we employed BNN to help ILP approximate rules. The experimental results are shown in Table 1.

The results show that the accuracy of ILP&BNN was higher than ILP alone with 95% confidence level and higher than C4.5 with 99% confidence level using a one-tailed paired t-test. And the accuracy of ILP alone was higher than C4.5 with 95% confidence level using the same method. To demonstrate the advantage of the use of first order predicates by ILP, we added a new predicate, link_point (A, B), to the background knowledge. The function of this predicate is to introduce new variable(s) in the rule production process and make the rules more expressive. The results are shown below in Table 2.

The results in Table 2 show that when we added the predicate, link_point (A, B), to the background knowledge, the accuracy of ILP was higher than ILP without link_point and when BNN was combined with ILP, the performance was better and higher than other methods with 99.5% confidence level.

Table 1. The experiment results using only propositional attributes.

Fold	C4.5	ILP	ILP & BNN
1	89.88	90.05	90.14
2	85.14	89.71	92.40
3	88.51	88.69	90.52
4	80.14	88.42	92.60
5	88.51	86.43	90.00
6	85.51	87.78	91.47
7	89.81	89.69	90.00
8	89.81	90.95	91.82
9	87.61	95.26	90.84
10	90.00	88.64	89.92
AVG	**87.52**	**88.56**	**90.97**

Table 2. The experiment results show the recognition rate of all methods.

Fold	C4.5	ILP	ILP &BNN	ILP*	ILP* & BNN
1	89.88	90.05	90.14	92.31	95.55
2	85.14	89.71	92.40	87.87	96.29
3	88.51	88.69	90.52	90.95	96.10
4	80.14	88.42	92.60	89.14	93.92
5	88.51	86.43	90.00	88.69	93.95
6	85.51	87.78	91.47	91.86	95.28
7	89.81	89.69	90.00	90.50	94.24
8	89.81	90.95	91.82	91.86	94.31
9	87.61	95.26	90.84	90.95	95.13
10	90.00	88.64	89.92	88.28	94.67
AVG	**87.52**	**88.56**	**90.97**	**90.24**	**94.94**

* Denotes the methods using predicate *link_point and sum_link.*

5 Conclusion

We have presented a method for detection and classification of the connecting points in Thai printed characters. First, we ran the experiments comparing ILP and DTL using the same set of propositional attributes. The accuracies of both algorithms are very close to each other. And with the help of BNN, the performance of ILP is better and higher than DTL. Our experiments also show the improvement when the first order background knowledge predicates are added to make the produced rules more meaningful.

References

1. G. Casey and E.Lecolinet , "A Survey of Methods and Strategies in Character Segmentation", IEEE on pattern Analysis and machine intelligence, vol. 18, 1996.
2. A. K. Jain, The Fundamental Digital Image Processing, Prentice-Hall International Editions, 1989, pp.382-383.

3. J. Keittisirianan and B. Kurtachoo, "A Segmentation of Thai Printed Characters Using Shortest Path Algorithm", Proceedings of 21st EECON98', 1998, pp.561-564.
4. B. Kijsirikul, S. Sinthupinyo and K. Chongkasemwongse, "Approximate Match of Rules Using Backpropagation Neural Network", Machine Learning, Vol. 44(3), 2001.
5. S. Kongthawornwattana, and S. Jitapunkul, "Segmentation of Thai-Printed Character String by Modified Freeman Coding of Boundary of Histogram", Proceedings of 19th EECON96', 1996, pp. DS-73-DS-77.
6. S. Muggleton, "Inductive Logic Programming", New Generation Computing, 1991, pp. 295-318.
7. S. Muggleton, ,"Inverse entailment and PROGOL", New Generation Computing, 1995, 13:2454-286.
8. N. Premchaiswadi ,W. Premchaiswadi and S. Narita , "Segmentation of Horizontal and Vertical Touching Thai Characters", IEICE TRANS 2000, VOL 83-A, NO 6.
9. J. R. Quinlan , C4.5 Programs for machine learning, Morgan Kaufmann, San Mateo C.A, 1993.
10. D. E. Rumelhart, G. E. Hinton & R. J. Williams, "Learning Internal Representations by Error Propagation", In D. E. Rumelhart, & J. L. McClelland (Eds.), Parallel distributed processing, (Vol 1). Cambridge, MA:MIT Press. 1986.
11. S. Sinthupinyo and B. Kijsirikul, "Approximation of First-Order Rules by the Backpropagation Neural Network", The First National Computer Science and Engineering Conference, 2000.

Design of a Multilayered Feed-Forward Neural Network Using Hypersphere Neurons

Vladimir Banarer, Christian Perwass, and Gerald Sommer

Institut für Informatik und Praktische Mathematik
Christian-Albrechts-Universität zu Kiel
Christian-Albrechts-Platz 4, 24118 Kiel, Germany
{vlb,chp,gs}@ks.informatik.uni-kiel.de

Abstract. In this paper a special higher order neuron, the hypersphere neuron, is introduced. By embedding Euclidean space in a conformal space, hyperspheres can be expressed as vectors. The scalar product of points and spheres in conformal space, gives a measure for how far a point lies inside or outside a hypersphere. It will be shown that a hypersphere neuron may be implemented as a perceptron with two bias inputs. By using hyperspheres instead of hyperplanes as decision surfaces, a reduction in computational complexity can be achieved for certain types of problems. This is shown in two experiments using classical test data for neural computing. Furthermore, in this setup, a reliability measure can be associated with data points in a straight forward way.

1 Introduction

The basic idea behind a single standard perceptron is that it separates its input space into two classes by a hyperplane [12]. For most practical purposes such a linear separation is, of course, not sufficient. In general, data is to be separated into a number of classes, where each class covers a particular region in the input space. The basic idea behind classifying using a multi-layer perceptron (MLP), is to use a number of perceptrons and to combine their linear decision planes, to approximate the surfaces of the different class regions. In principle, a MLP can approximate any type of class configuration, which implies that it is an universal approximator [3, 6].

However, being an universal approximator alone says nothing about the complexity a MLP would need to have in order to approximate a particular surface. In fact, depending on the structure of the data it may be advantageous to not use perceptrons but instead another type of neuron which uses a non-linear 'decision surface' to separate classes. Such neurons are called *higher-order* neurons. There has been a lot of effort to design higher-order neurons for different applications. For example, there are hyperbolic neurons [2], tensor neurons [11] and hyperbolic SOMs [13]. Typically, the more complex the decision surface a neuron has is, the higher its computational complexity. It is hoped that a complex decision surface will allow to solve a task with fewer neurons. However, the computational complexity of each neuron should not offset this advantage.

N. Petkov and M.A. Westenberg (Eds.): CAIP 2003, LNCS 2756, pp. 571–578, 2003.

In this paper we present a simple extension of a perceptron, such that its decision surface is not a hyperplane but a hypersphere. The representation used is taken from a conformal space representation introduced in the context of Clifford algebra [10]. The advantage of this representation is that only a standard scalar product has to be evaluated in order to decide whether an input vector is inside or outside a hypersphere. That is, the computational complexity stays low, while a non-linear decision plane is obtained. This will be explained in some detail later on. The main advantages of such a hypersphere neuron over a standard perceptron are the following:

- A hypersphere with infinite radius becomes a hyperplane. Since the hypersphere representation used is homogeneous, hyperspheres with infinite radius can be represented through finite vectors. Therefore, a standard perceptron is just a special case of a hypersphere neuron.
- The VC-dimension [1] of a hypersphere neuron for a 1-dimensional input space is three and not two, as it is for a standard perceptron. However, for higher input dimensions, the VC-dimensions of a hypersphere neuron and a standard perceptron are the same.

Although the VC-dimensions of a hypersphere neuron and a standard perceptron are the same for input dimensions higher than one, it is advantageous to use a hypersphere neuron, if the classification of the data is orientation invariant about some point in the input space. For example, let $\{\mathbf{x}_i\} \subseteq \mathbb{R}^n$ and $\{\mathbf{y}_i\} \subseteq \mathbb{R}^n$ denote the input vectors of two different classes. If there exists a point $\mathbf{c} \in \mathbb{R}^n$, such that $\max_i |\mathbf{x}_i - \mathbf{c}| < \min_i |\mathbf{y}_i - \mathbf{c}|$ or $\max_i |\mathbf{y}_i - \mathbf{c}| < \min_i |\mathbf{x}_i - \mathbf{c}|$, then the classification of the data is basically a 1-dimensional problem, and the two classes can be separated by a single hypersphere, independent of the input dimension. A multi-layer hypersphere perceptron (MLHP), therefore separates the input space into regions where the classification is orientation invariant.

The remainder of this paper is structured as follows. First the representation of hyperspheres used is described in some more detail. Then some important aspects concerning the actual implementation of a hypersphere neuron in a single- and multi-layer network are discussed. Afterwards some experiments with the Iris data set and the two spirals benchmark are presented. Finally, some conclusions are drawn from this work.

2 The Representation of Hyperspheres

There is not enough space here to give a full treatment of the mathematics involved. Therefore, only the most important aspects will be discussed. For a more detailed introduction see [9, 10].

Consider the Minkowski space $\mathbb{R}^{1,1}$ with basis $\{e_+, e_-\}$, where $e_+^2 = +1$ and $e_-^2 = -1$. The following two null-vectors can be constructed from this basis, $e_\infty := e_- + e_+$ and $e_0 := \frac{1}{2}(e_- - e_+)$, such that $e_\infty^2 = e_0^2 = 0$ and $e_\infty \cdot e_0 = -1$. Given an n-dimensional Euclidean vector space $\mathbb{R}^n$, the conformal space $\mathbb{R}^{n+1,1} = \mathbb{R}^n \oplus \mathbb{R}^{1,1}$ can be constructed. Such a conformal space will also be denoted as $\mathbb{ME}^n \equiv \mathbb{R}^{n+1,1}$. A vector $\mathbf{x} \in \mathbb{R}^n$ may be embedded in conformal space as

$$X = \mathbf{x} + \tfrac{1}{2}\mathbf{x}^2 e_\infty + e_0, \tag{1}$$

such that $X^2 = 0$. It may be shown that this embedding represents the stereographic projection of $\mathbf{x} \in \mathbb{R}^n$ onto an appropriately defined projection sphere in $\mathbb{ME}^n$. Note that the embedding is also homogeneous, i.e. αX, with $\alpha \in \mathbb{R}$, represents the same vector $\mathbf{x}$ as X. In other words, any vector $A \in \mathbb{ME}^n$ that lies in the null space of X, i.e. satisfies $A \cdot X = 0$, represents the same vector $\mathbf{x}$.

The nomenclature e_0 and e_∞ is motivated by the fact that the origin of $\mathbb{R}^n$ maps to e_0 when using equation(1). Furthermore, as $|\mathbf{x}|$ with $\mathbf{x} \in \mathbb{R}^n$ tends to infinity, the dominant term of the mapping of $\mathbf{x}$ into $\mathbb{ME}^n$ is e_∞.

A null-vector in $\mathbb{ME}^n$ whose e_0 component is unity, is called *normalized.* Given the normalized null-vector X from equation (1) and $Y = \mathbf{y} + \frac{1}{2}\mathbf{y}^2 e_\infty + e_0$, it can be shown that $X \cdot Y = -\frac{1}{2}(\mathbf{x} - \mathbf{y})^2$. That is, the scalar product of two null-vectors in conformal space, gives a distance measure of the corresponding Euclidean vectors. This forms the foundation for the representation of hyperspheres. A normalized hypersphere $S \in \mathbb{ME}^n$ with center $Y \in \mathbb{ME}^n$ and radius $r \in \mathbb{R}$ is given by $S = Y - \frac{1}{2} r^2 e_\infty$, since then

$$X \cdot S = X \cdot Y - \tfrac{1}{2} r^2\, X \cdot e_\infty = -\tfrac{1}{2}(\mathbf{x} - \mathbf{y})^2 + \tfrac{1}{2} r^2, \tag{2}$$

and thus $X \cdot S = 0$ iff $|\mathbf{x} - \mathbf{y}| = |r|$. That is, the null space of S consists of all those vectors $X \in \mathbb{ME}^n$ that represent vectors in $\mathbb{R}^n$ that lie on a hypersphere. It can also be seen that the scalar product of a null-vector X with a normalized hypersphere S is negative, zero or positive, if X is outside, on or inside the hypersphere. Scaling the normalized hypersphere vector S with a scalar does not change the hypersphere it represents. However, scaling S with a negative scalar interchanges the signs that indicate inside and outside of the hypersphere.

The change in sign of $X \cdot S$ between X being inside and outside the hypersphere, may be used to classify a data vector $\mathbf{x} \in \mathbb{R}^n$ embedded in $\mathbb{ME}^n$. That is, by interpreting the components of S as the weights of a perceptron, and embedding the data points into $\mathbb{ME}^n$, a perceptron can be constructed whose decision plane is a hypersphere.

From the definition of a hypersphere in $\mathbb{ME}^n$ it follows that a null-vector $X \in \mathbb{ME}^n$ may be interpreted as a sphere with zero radius. Similarly, a vector in $\mathbb{ME}^n$ with no e_0 component represents a hypersphere with infinite radius, i.e. a plane. In fact, given two normalized null-vectors $X, Y \in \mathbb{ME}^n$, $X - Y$ represents a plane. This can be seen quite easily, since it is again the null space of $X - Y$ that gives the geometric entity represented by the algebraic object. That is, all those vectors $A \in \mathbb{ME}^n$ that satisfy $A \cdot (X - Y) = 0$ lie on the geometric entity represented by $X - Y$. Clearly,

$$A \cdot (X - Y) = A \cdot X - A \cdot Y = -\tfrac{1}{2}(\mathbf{a} - \mathbf{x})^2 + \tfrac{1}{2}(\mathbf{a} - \mathbf{y})^2 = 0, \tag{3}$$

which is satisfied for all points $\mathbf{a}$ that are equidistant to $\mathbf{x}$ and $\mathbf{y}$. All these points lie on the plane located half way between $\mathbf{x}$ and $\mathbf{y}$ with normal $\mathbf{x} - \mathbf{y}$.

Such a plane still has a sidedness, that is, the scalar product of a null-vector with a plane is either positive, zero or negative depending on whether the test vector is off to one side, on the plane or off to the other side. Therefore, a hypersphere neuron may also represent a hyperplane.

3 Implementation

The propagation function of a hypersphere neuron may actually be implemented as a standard scalar product, by representing the input data as follows. Let a data vector $\mathbf{x} = (x_1, x_2, \ldots, x_n) \in \mathbb{R}^n$ be embedded in $\mathbb{R}^{n+2}$ (*not* $\mathbb{ME}^n$) as $\boldsymbol{X} = (x_1, \ldots, x_n, -1, -\frac{1}{2}\mathbf{x}^2) \in \mathbb{R}^{n+2}$. Then, representing a hypersphere $S = \mathbf{c} + \frac{1}{2}(\mathbf{c}^2 - r^2)e_\infty + e_0 \in \mathbb{ME}^n$ in $\mathbb{R}^{n+2}$ as $\boldsymbol{S} = (c_1, \ldots, c_n, \frac{1}{2}(\mathbf{c}^2 - r^2), 1)$, one finds that $X \cdot S = \boldsymbol{X} \cdot \boldsymbol{S}$. During the training phase of a hypersphere neuron, the components of $\boldsymbol{S}$ are regarded as independent, such that $\boldsymbol{S}$ may simply be written as $\boldsymbol{S} = (s_1, \ldots, s_{n+2})$. This embedding also allows hyperspheres with imaginary radii. However, since such a hypersphere cannot include any points, it does not produce spurious solutions. It may indeed contribute to a successful learning.

Therefore, a hypersphere neuron may be regarded as a standard perceptron with a second 'bias' component. Of course, the input data must be of a particular form. That is, after embedding the input data in $\mathbb{R}^{n+2}$ appropriately, a decision plane in $\mathbb{R}^{n+2}$ represents a decision hypersphere in $\mathbb{R}^n$. In this respect, it is similar to a kernel method, where the embedding of the data in a different space is implicit in the scalar product.

The computational complexity of a hypersphere neuron is as follows. Apart from the standard bias, which is simply set to unity, the magnitude of the input data vector has to be evaluated. However, for a multi-layer hypersphere network, this magnitude only has to be evaluated once for each layer. In terms of complexity this compares to adding an additional perceptron to each layer in a MLP.

It follows from equation (2), that the value of the scalar product of a data point with a normalized hypersphere is bounded by the radius of the hypersphere for data points lying within (class $\mathcal{I}$), but it is not limited for data points lying outside (class $\mathcal{O}$). Since the result of this scalar product is the input to an activation function, the type of activation function appears to have an influence on how large the radius of a hypersphere will tend to be. However, since the weights of a hypersphere neuron are treated as independent components, they represent an un-normalized hypersphere. The overall scale factor of the hypersphere vector then allows the scalar product of the hypersphere with points lying within it to take on arbitrarily large values.

For example, denote by $X \in \mathbb{ME}^n$ the representation of data point $\mathbf{x} \in \mathbb{R}^n$, and denote by $S \in \mathbb{ME}^n$ the representation of a hypersphere neuron with center $\mathbf{c} \in \mathbb{R}^n$, radius $r \in \mathbb{R}^+$ and scale $\kappa \in \mathbb{R}\backslash\{0\}$. Furthermore, let the activation function of the hypersphere neuron be the sigmoidal function $\sigma(\lambda, z) = (1 + e^{-\lambda z})^{-1}$. Training the hypersphere neuron to classify $\mathbf{x}$ as belonging to $\mathcal{I}$ then means to vary $\mathbf{c}$, r and κ, such that $\sigma(\lambda, X \cdot S) > 1 - \epsilon$, where $\epsilon \in \mathbb{R}^+$ gives the

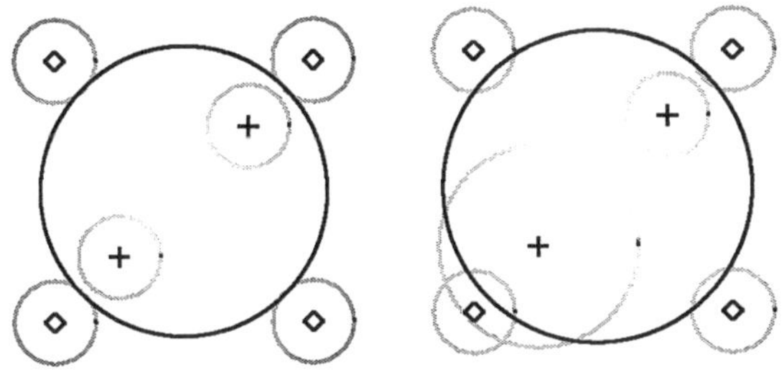

Fig. 1. Position of the decision hypersphere can be influenced by confidence. Left picture shows the position of decision hypersphere (black circle) for uniformly distributed confidences (grey circles). After increasing of confidence for left bottom point, the decision circle is moved in such a way, that the affected point is placed further inside.

decision threshold. If $\mathbf{x}$ is to be classified as belonging to $\mathcal{O}$, then one demands that $\sigma(\lambda, X \cdot S) < \epsilon$. With respect to the radius this means that

$$r^2 > \frac{2}{\lambda\kappa} \ln \frac{1-\epsilon}{\epsilon} + (\mathbf{c} - \mathbf{x})^2 \quad \text{if} \quad \mathbf{x} \in \mathcal{I}, \tag{4}$$

$$r^2 < \frac{2}{\lambda\kappa} \ln \frac{\epsilon}{1-\epsilon} + (\mathbf{c} - \mathbf{x})^2 \quad \text{if} \quad \mathbf{x} \in \mathcal{O}, \tag{5}$$

It can be seen that for fixed ϵ, $\mathbf{c}$ and κ, the radius of the hypersphere depends on the parameter λ of the sigmoid function. The effect of this is that the smaller λ, the larger the radius of the hypersphere tends to be. Note that the above equations are valid for $\kappa > 0$, whence $X \cdot S = \frac{1}{2}|\kappa|\,(r^2 - (\mathbf{x} - \mathbf{y})^2)$. However, for $\kappa < 0$, this becomes $X \cdot S = \frac{1}{2}|\kappa|\,((\mathbf{x} - \mathbf{y})^2 - r^2)$, such that data points inside S belong to class $\mathcal{O}$ and outside S to class $\mathcal{I}$.

We can introduce a measure for the reliability of a particular data point by extending data points in the following way. Given a data point $\mathbf{x}$ with some confidence measure r_{conf}, it is embedded in $\mathbb{ME}^n$ as $X_{\text{conf}} = \mathbf{x} + \frac{1}{2}\,(\mathbf{x}^2 + r^2_{\text{conf}})\, e_\infty + e_0$. This is equivalent to a hypersphere with imaginary radius. It will therefore be called an imaginary hypersphere. The scalar product between a hypersphere S and X then yields,

$$S \cdot X_{\text{conf}} = \tfrac{1}{2}\Big(r^2 - \big((\mathbf{c} - \mathbf{x})^2 + r^2_{\text{conf}}\big)\Big). \tag{6}$$

That is, the vector $\mathbf{x}$ appears to be further away from the center $\mathbf{c}$ than it actually is. Therefore, a training algorithm will try to place a decision hypersphere such that $\mathbf{x}$ lies further to the inside of the hypersphere's surface, than without confidence. This effect is shown in figure 1.

4 Experiments

In an initial experiment, a multi-layer hypersphere perceptron was tested on Fisher's Iris data set [5]. This set consists of 150 four-dimensional data vectors, which are classified into three classes. Visualizing the data [7] shows that one class can be separated linearly from the other two. The two remaining classes, however, are somewhat entangled. The data set was separated into a training data set of 39 randomly chosen data vectors and a test data set of the remaining 111 data vectors. A standard single-layer perceptron (SLP) and a single-layer hypersphere perceptron (SLHP) were then trained on the training data set in two different configurations. In the first configuration (C1) the network consisted of one layer with three neurons, each representing one class. In the second configuration (C2) there was a single layer with only two neurons, whereby the three classes were coded in a binary code. That is, the output of the two neurons had to be $(1, 0)$, $(0, 1)$ and $(1, 1)$, respectively, to indicate the three classes.

The following tables give the number of *incorrectly* classified data vectors after training in configuration C1 and C2, respectively, for the training and the test data set using the SLP and the SLHP.

Net	C1 Train. Data	C1 Test Data	C2 Train. Data	C2 Test Data
SLP	0	2	9	31
SLHP	0	7	0	7

It can be seen that both the SLP and the SLHP in C1, classify the training data perfectly. However, the SLP is somewhat better in the classification of the test data set. For C2, where only two neurons were used, the SLP cannot give an error free classification of the training data set. This is in contrast to the SLHP where an error free classification is still possible. Also for the test data set the SLHP gives much better results than the SLP. In fact, the SLHP does equally well with two and with three neurons.

The results in C2 basically show that the data set cannot be separated into three classes by two hyperplanes. However, such a separation is possible with two hyperspheres.

In the second experiment the two spirals benchmark [4] was used, to compare a MLHP with a classical MLP. The task of this benchmark is, to learn to discriminate between two sets of training points, which lie on two distinct spirals in the 2D plane. These spirals coil three times around the origin and around one another. This can be a very difficult task for back-propagation networks and comparable networks [8, 14].

Figure 2 shows the results of training for two-layer-networks with classical perceptrons (MLP) and hypersphere neurons (MLHP) in dependance of the amount of units in the hidden layer. All network configurations were trained with a backpropagation-algorithm. Two different methods were used to train the MLHP, with complete derivatives and with simplified derivatives under the assumption, that the quadratic component of the input for each neuron is independent (MLHPS). The figure shows, that the MLHP gives much better results in comparison to the MLP. The simplification of derivatives leads to ‘smoother’ minimization surfaces and increased stability of solution, while at the same time accelerating the convergence. Also the comparison in dependence of the number

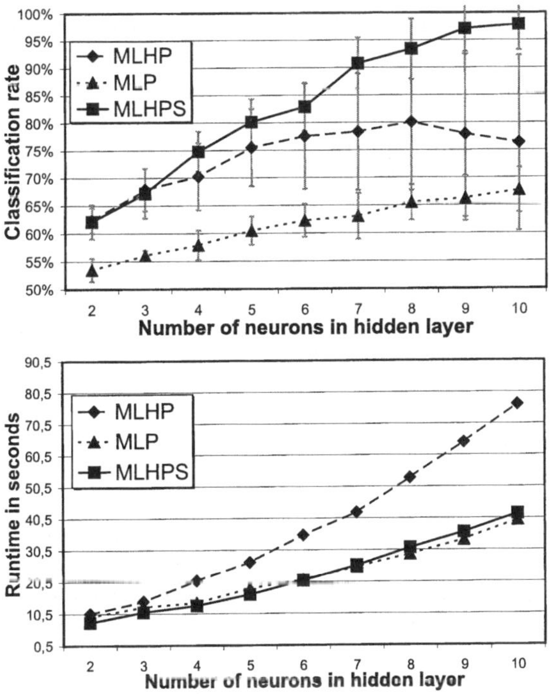

Fig. 2. Top - Comparison of classification rates (y-axis) for MLP, MLHP and MLHPS for different number of neurons used in the hidden layer (x-axis). The results are averaged over 100 trials. Bottom - Time performance of the different network configurations.

of free parameters (weights) of the whole net shows, that the MLHP produces better results than the MLP. For example, the classification with a MLHPS with 5 neurons in the hidden layer (24 weights) is significantly better, than with a MLP with 7 neurons in the hidden layer (also 24 weights).

5 Conclusions

In this paper a higher-order neuron was presented which has the effect of placing a decision hypersphere in the input space, whereas a standard perceptron uses a hyperplane to linearly separate the input data. It was shown that a hypersphere neuron may also represent a hypersphere with infinite radius, i.e. a hyperplane, and thus includes the case of a standard perceptron. Advantages that may be gained by using hypersphere neurons, are the possibility to classify compact regions with a single neuron in n-dimensions, while the computational complexity is kept low. A single-layer hypersphere perceptron was tested and compared to a standard single-layer perceptron on the Iris data of R.A. Fisher. The data could be successfully classified with two hypersphere neurons. At least three standard neurons were necessary to achieve similar results. Furthermore multi-layered network architecture was tested with the two spirals benchmark. Also in this case better results are achieved with hypersphere neurons then with a classical MLP. An the error-free classification can already be achieved by MLHP with eight neurons in the hidden layer. For a MLP larger networks are necessary [14]. This shows that using hypersphere neurons is advantageous for certain types of data.

Acknowledgment

This work has been supported by DFG Graduiertenkolleg No. 357 and by EC Grant IST-2001-3422 (VISATEC).

References

1. Y. S. Abu-Mostafa. The Vapnik-Chervonenkis dimension: Information versus complexity in learning. *Neural Computation*, 1(3):312–317, 1989.
2. S. Buchholz and G. Sommer. A hyperbolic multilayer perceptron. In S.-I. Amari, C.L. Giles, M. Gori, and V. Piuri, editors, *International Joint Conference on Neural Networks, IJCNN 2000, Como, Italy*, volume 2, pages 129–133. IEEE Computer Society Press, 2000.
3. G. Cybenko. Approximation by superposition of a sigmoidal function. *Mathematics of Control, Signals and Systems*, 2:303–314, 1989.
4. S. E. Fahlman and C. Lebiere. The cascade-correlation learning architecture. In D. S. Touretzky, editor, *Advances in Neural Information Processing Systems*, volume 2, pages 524–532, Denver 1989, 1990. Morgan Kaufmann, San Mateo.
5. R. A. Fisher. The use of multiple measurements in axonomic problems. *Annals of Eugenics 7*, pages 179–188, 1936.
6. K. Hornik. Approximation capabilities of multilayer feedforward neural networks. *Neural Networks*, 4:251–257, 1990.
7. Larry Hoyle. http://www.ku.edu/cwis/units/IPPBR/java/iris/irisglyph.html.
8. K.J. Lang and M.J. Witbrock. Learning to tell two spirals apart. In D.S. Touretzky, G.E. Hinton, and T. Sejnowski, editors, *Connectionist Models Summer School*. Morgan Kaufmann, 1988.
9. H. Li, D. Hestenes, and A. Rockwood. Generalized homogeneous coordinates for computational geometry. In G. Sommer, editor, *Geometric Computing with Clifford Algebra*, pages 27–52. Springer-Verlag, 2001.
10. H. Li, D. Hestenes, and A. Rockwood. A universal model for conformal geometries. In G. Sommer, editor, *Geometric Computing with Clifford Algebra*, pages 77–118. Springer-Verlag, 2001.
11. H. Lipson and H.T. Siegelmann. Clustering irregular shapes using high-order neurons. *Neural Computation*, 12(10):2331–2353, 2000.
12. M. Minsky and S. Papert. *Perceptrons*. Cambridge: MIT Press, 1969.
13. H. Ritter. Self-organising maps in non-Euclidean spaces. In E. Oja and S. Kaski, editors, *Kohonen Maps*, pages 97–108. Amer Elsevier, 1999.
14. Alexis Wieland and Scott E. Fahlman. http://www.ibiblio.org/pub/academic/computer-science/neural-networks/programs/bench/two-spirals, 1993.

Analytical Decision Boundary Feature Extraction for Neural Networks with Multiple Hidden Layers*

Jinwook Go and Chulhee Lee

Department of Electrical and Electronic Engineering, BERC, Yonsei University
134 Shinchon-Dong, Seodaemoon-Gu, Seoul, KOREA
chulhee@yonsei.ac.kr
Tel: (82-2) 2123-2779 Fax: (82-2) 312-4584

Abstract. A feature extraction method based on decision boundaries has been proposed for neural networks. The method is based on the fact that normal vectors to the decision boundary provide the information necessary for discriminating between classes. However, it is observed that the previous implementation of numerical approximation of the gradient has resulted in some performance loss and a long processing time. In this paper, we propose a new method to calculate normal vectors analytically for neural networks with multiple hidden layers. Experiments showed noticeable improvements in performance and speed.

1 Introduction

Neural networks have been successfully applied in various fields such as pattern recognition, remote sensing, and dynamic modeling. However, relatively few feature extraction algorithms are available for neural networks. Although one may use the conventional feature extraction methods such as principal component analysis and discriminant analysis [1], such methods do not take full advantage of neural networks that can define complex decision boundaries.

A feature extraction algorithm based on decision boundaries has been proposed [2] and the method has been successfully applied to neural networks [3]. By extracting features directly from decision boundaries, it is possible to take a full advantage of neural networks that can construct arbitrary decision boundaries without assuming any underlying probability density function. The performance of the decision boundary feature extraction (DBFE) algorithm doesn't deteriorate even if there is no mean difference while the discriminant analysis fails in such a circumstance [2]. The decision boundary feature extraction algorithm can be used for a parametric classifier [2] and non-parametric classifiers such as the kNN classifier and neural networks [3, 4]. In the previous implementation of the decision boundary feature extraction for neural networks, normal vectors to decision boundaries were computed numerically, resulting in performance loss and a long processing time. However, normal vectors to the

* This work was supported in part by Biometrics Engineering Research Center (KOSEF).

N. Petkov and M.A. Westenberg (Eds.): CAIP 2003, LNCS 2756, pp. 579–587, 2003.

decision boundary can be computed analytically once the decision boundary is found. In this paper, we derive all the necessary equations to analytically compute normal vectors to decision boundaries of neural networks.

2 Decision Boundary Feature Extraction [2]

For a two-pattern classification problem, the Bayes' decision rule is given by

$$\text{Decide class } \omega_1 \text{ if } h(\mathbf{X}) < t \text{. Otherwise, decide class } \omega_2$$

where $\mathbf{X}$ is an observation, $h(\mathbf{X}) = -\ln \frac{p(\mathbf{X} \mid \omega_1)}{p(\mathbf{X} \mid \omega_2)}$, $t = P(\omega_1)/P(\omega_2)$, $p(\mathbf{X} \mid \omega_i)$ and $P(\omega_i)$ are a conditional density function and a prior probability of class ω_i, respectively. Then, feature extraction can be viewed as finding a subspace, $\mathbf{W}$, with the minimum dimension M and the spanning vectors $\{ \vec{\beta}_k \}$ of the subspace where the same classification accuracy can be obtained as in the original space. In other words, for any observation $\mathbf{X}$

$$(h(\mathbf{X}) - t)(h(\hat{\mathbf{X}}) - t) > 0$$

where $\hat{\mathbf{X}}$ is an approximation of $\mathbf{X}$ in the subspace $\mathbf{W}$. It was shown that discriminantly informative features, which provide useful information for discriminating among classes, and discriminantly redundant features, which provide no useful information for discriminating among classes, are related to decision boundaries. Fig. 1a shows an example of a discriminantly redundant feature. In this case, even though $\hat{\mathbf{X}}$ is moved along the direction of vector $\vec{\beta}_k$, the classification result will remain unchanged. In other words, vector $\vec{\beta}_k$ makes no contribution in discriminating classes. Thus, vector $\vec{\beta}_k$ is redundant for the purpose of classification. Fig. 1b shows an example of a discriminantly informative feature. In this case, as $\hat{\mathbf{Y}}$ is moved along the direction of vector $\vec{\beta}_k$, the classification result will be changed. It is noted that the discriminantly informative feature vector has a component that is normal to the decision boundary and the discriminantly redundant feature vector is orthogonal to the vector normal to decision boundary at every point on decision boundary. In order to extract discriminantly informative features, the decision boundary feature matrix was defined as follows:

Definition 1. The decision boundary feature matrix ($\mathbf{\Sigma}_{\mathbf{DBFM}}$): Let $\mathbf{N}(\mathbf{X})$ be the unit vector normal to the decision boundary at a point $\mathbf{X}$ on the decision boundary for a given pattern classification problem. Then the decision boundary feature matrix is defined as

$$\mathbf{\Sigma}_{\mathbf{DBFM}} = \frac{1}{\mathrm{K}} \int_S \mathbf{N}(\mathbf{X}) \mathbf{N}^{\mathrm{T}}(\mathbf{X}) p(\mathbf{X}) d\mathbf{X} \quad (\mathrm{K} = \int_S p(\mathbf{X}) d\mathbf{X})$$

where $p(\mathbf{X})$ is a probability density function, S is the decision boundary, and the integral is performed over the decision boundary. The decision boundary feature matrix can be used to extract discriminantly informative features and the following two theorems were derived [2]:

Theorem 1. The rank of the decision boundary feature matrix Σ_{DBFM} of a pattern classification problem will be the smallest dimension where the same classification could be obtained as in the original space.

Theorem 2. The eigenvectors of the decision boundary feature matrix of a pattern recognition problem corresponding to non-zero eigenvalues are the necessary feature vectors to achieve the same classification accuracy as in the original space for the pattern recognition problem.

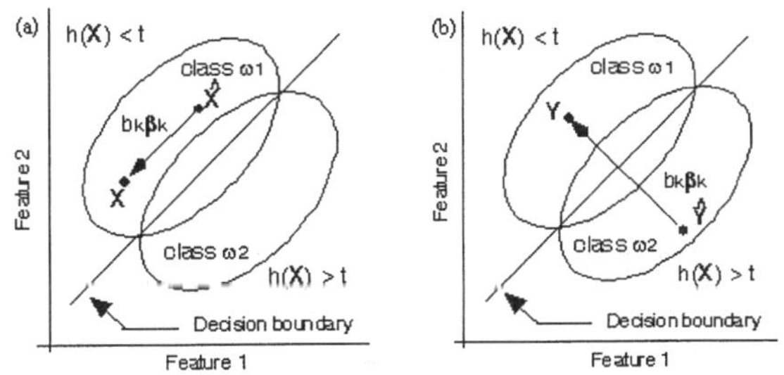

Fig. 1. (a) a discriminantly redundant feature. (b) a discriminantly informative feature

In order to obtain the decision boundary feature matrix for a two-class problem, the following procedure was proposed [2, 3, 4]:

Step 1: Classify training samples using all features.
Step 2: Find pairs of samples which are correctly classified as different classes.
Step 3: Find decision boundary points on the lines that connect the pairs from Step 2 and compute normal vectors at the decision boundary points ($\mathbf{N} = \nabla h(\mathbf{X}) / |\nabla h(\mathbf{X})|$ where $\mathbf{X}$ is a decision boundary point, i.e. $h(\mathbf{X}) = \mathrm{t}$).
Step 4: Estimate Σ_{DBFM} using the normal vectors found in Step 3 as follows:

$$\Sigma_{DBFM} = \frac{1}{L} \sum_i \mathbf{N}_i \mathbf{N}_i^T$$

where L is the number of normal vectors.
Step 5: Select the eigenvectors of the decision boundary feature matrix corresponding to non-zero eigenvalues as a new feature vector set.

In case of neural networks, the neural network is trained twice. First, a neural network is trained using all features in order to determine the decision boundary in the original feature space. Then, the DBFE algorithm is used to produce a reduced feature set and the neural networks is trained again with the reduced feature set. In general, neural networks need a long training time but a relatively short classification time for test data. However, if the dimensionality of the input of neural networks is large as in the case of high dimensional data and multi-source data, the resulting neural network

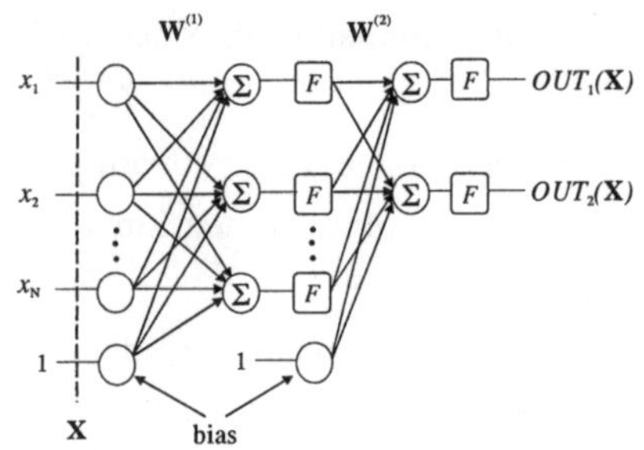

Fig. 2. An example of 2-layer feedforward neural networks

can be very complex, resulting in a long processing. Furthermore, the cost of hardware implementation is high. Thus, the benefit of the reduced input dimensionality without sacrificing the performance is a short processing time or reduced complexity of hardware implementation. With the proposed feature extraction method, the neural network can be made much faster and simpler.

If there are more than two classes, the procedure can be repeated for each pair of classes. If there are M classes, the total decision boundary feature matrix can be calculated as

$$\mathbf{\Sigma}_{\mathbf{DBFM}} = \sum_{i}^{M} \sum_{j,j \neq i}^{M} P(\omega_i) P(\omega_j) \mathbf{\Sigma}_{\mathbf{DBFM}}^{ij}$$

where $\mathbf{\Sigma}_{\mathbf{DBFM}}$ is a decision boundary feature matrix between class ω_i and class ω_j and $P(\omega_i)$ is the prior probability of class ω_i if available. Otherwise let $P(\omega_i) = 1/\mathrm{M}$.

3 Analytical Decision Boundary Feature Extraction for Neural Networks

3.1 Computing Normal Vectors in Neural Networks

Fig. 2 shows an example of 2-layer feedforward neural networks with 2 outputs. The decision rule is to select the class corresponding to the output neuron with the largest output. If we denote the activation of i-th output neuron as $OUT_i(\mathbf{X})$ where $\mathbf{X} = [x_1, x_2, ..., x_N, 1]^T$ is an input vector, the decision boundary of two pattern classes is defined as follows:

$$\{\mathbf{X} \mid h(\mathbf{X}) = OUT_1(\mathbf{X}) - OUT_2(\mathbf{X}) = 0\} \text{ or } \left\{\mathbf{X} \middle| h(\mathbf{X}) = F(\mathbf{w}_1^{(2)^T} F(\mathbf{W}^{(1)}\mathbf{X})) - F(\mathbf{w}_2^{(2)^T} F(\mathbf{W}^{(1)}\mathbf{X})) = 0\right\}$$

where $\mathbf{W}^{(1)}$ is the weight matrix between input layer and hidden layer, $\mathbf{w}_i^{(2)}$ the weight vector between hidden layer and i-th output neuron, and F an activation function. It is noted that $\mathbf{W}^{(2)^T} = [\mathbf{w}_1^{(2)}, \mathbf{w}_2^{(2)}]$ in Fig. 2. In [3], due to the nested sigmoid function in $h(\mathbf{X})$, $\nabla h(\mathbf{X})$ was calculated using a numerical approximation as follows:

$$\nabla h(\mathbf{X}) \approx \frac{\Delta h}{\Delta x_1}\mathbf{x}_1 + \frac{\Delta h}{\Delta x_2}\mathbf{x}_2 + \frac{\Delta h}{\Delta x_3}\mathbf{x}_3 + \ldots + \frac{\Delta h}{\Delta x_N}\mathbf{x}_N$$

where $\{\mathbf{x}_i\}$ is a basis of N-dimensional input space. A problem with this numerical approximation is that it is time-consuming and may not be accurate. In order to solve these problems, we propose an analytical method to compute the gradient of $h(\mathbf{X})$.

In order to simplify the equation for the decision boundary, we first note that, once a neural network is trained, the sigmoid functions in the output neurons are irrelevant for the purpose of pattern classification since the activation functions are monotonically increasing. Therefore, the equivalent decision boundary will be obtained with the following equation:

$$\left\{\mathbf{X} \middle| \mathbf{w}_1^{(2)\mathrm{T}} F(\mathbf{W}^{(1)}\mathbf{X}) - \mathbf{w}_2^{(2)\mathrm{T}} F(\mathbf{W}^{(1)}\mathbf{X}) = 0\right\} \tag{1}$$

3.2 Computing Normal Vectors in Neural Networks with Multiple Hidden Layers

Fig. 3 shows an example of 3-layer feedforward neural networks. In Fig. 3, differentiating $h(\mathbf{X})$ with respect to input x_i can be expressed as follows:

$$\frac{\partial h(\mathbf{X})}{\partial x_i} = \frac{\partial (y_1'(\mathbf{X}) - y_2'(\mathbf{X}))}{\partial x_i} = \frac{\partial y_1'(\mathbf{X})}{\partial x_i} - \frac{\partial y_2'(\mathbf{X})}{\partial x_i} \tag{2}$$

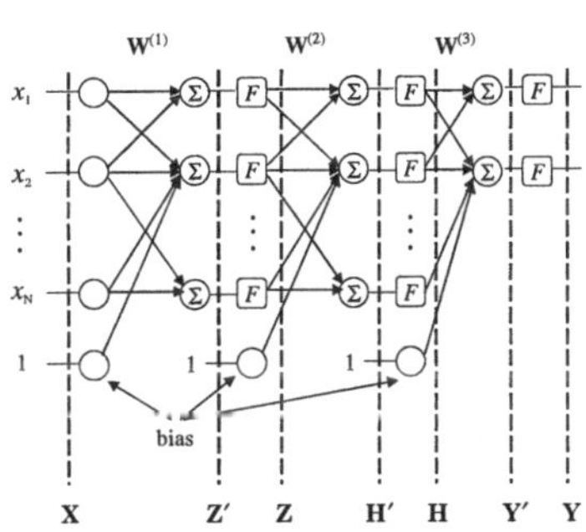

Fig. 3. An example of 3-layer feedforward neural networks (2 pattern classes)

We assume that the network shown in Fig. 3 has N inputs, M neurons in the first hidden layer, K neurons in the second hidden layer, and 2 output neurons. Without a loss of generality, the bias value can be considered as 1. In Fig. 3, $\mathbf{Z}'$ represents a vector that is given by

$$\mathbf{Z}' = \mathbf{W}^{(1)}\mathbf{X} = (z_1', z_2', \ldots, z_M')^{\mathrm{T}}$$

where $\mathbf{W}^{(1)}$ is the weight matrix between input layer and hidden layer, $z'_j = \sum_{s=1}^{N+1} w_{j,s}^{(1)} x_s$, $x_{N+1} = 1$ and $w_{j,s}^{(1)}$ is the weight between s-th input neuron and j-th neuron in the first hidden layer. And $\mathbf{Z}$ is obtained by applying the activation function F to each element of $\mathbf{Z}'$ as follows:

$$\mathbf{Z} = (z_1, z_2, ..., z_M, z_{M+1})^{\mathrm{T}} = (F(z'_1), F(z'_2), ..., F(z'_M), 1)^{\mathrm{T}} \text{ where } z_{M+1} = 1 .$$

Similarly, $\mathbf{H}'$ and $\mathbf{H}$ are defined as follows:

$$\mathbf{H}' = (h'_1, h'_2, ..., h'_K)^{\mathrm{T}} = \mathbf{W}^{(2)}\mathbf{Z} \quad \text{where } h'_k = \sum_{s=1}^{M+1} w_{k,s}^{(2)} z_s \quad (k = 1, ..., K).$$

$$\mathbf{H} = (h_1, h_2, ..., h_K, h_{K+1})^{\mathrm{T}} = (F(h'_1), F(h'_2), ..., F(h'_K), 1)^{\mathrm{T}} \quad \text{where } h_{K+1} = 1.$$

Finally, $\mathbf{Y}'$ and $\mathbf{Y}$ are defined as follows:

$$\mathbf{Y}' = (y'_1, y'_2)^{\mathrm{T}} = \mathbf{W}^{(3)}\mathbf{H} \quad \text{where } y'_l = \sum_{s=1}^{K+1} w_{l,s}^{(3)} h_s \quad (l = 1,2).$$

$$\mathbf{Y} = (y_1, y_2)^{\mathrm{T}} = (F(y'_1), F(y'_2))^{\mathrm{T}}.$$

Now, we will derive the partial derivative of the net input to each layer with respect to the input. Differentiating the net input to the first hidden layer, z'_j, with respect to input x_i yields

$$\frac{\partial z'_j}{\partial x_i} = w_{j,i}^{(1)}$$

where $j = 1, ..., M$. And differentiating the net input to second hidden layer, h'_k, with respect to input x_i yields

$$\begin{aligned} \frac{\partial h'_k}{\partial x_i} &= \sum_{s=1}^{M+1} w_{k,s}^{(2)} \frac{\partial z_s}{\partial x_i} = \sum_{s=1}^{M} w_{k,s}^{(2)} \frac{\partial z_s}{\partial x_i} + w_{k,M+1}^{(2)} \frac{\partial z_{M+1}}{\partial x_i} = \sum_{s=1}^{M} w_{k,s}^{(2)} \frac{\partial z_s}{\partial x_i} \\ &= \sum_{s=1}^{M} w_{k,s}^{(2)} \frac{\partial z_s}{\partial z'_s} \frac{\partial z'_s}{\partial x_i} = \sum_{s=1}^{M} w_{k,s}^{(2)} \frac{\partial F(z'_s)}{\partial z'_s} \frac{\partial z'_s}{\partial x_i} = \sum_{s=1}^{M} w_{k,s}^{(2)} F'(z'_s) w_{s,i}^{(1)} \end{aligned}$$

where $k = 1, ..., K$ and $z_{M+1} = 1$. Finally, differentiating the net input to output layer, y'_l, with respect to input x_i yields

$$\begin{aligned} \frac{\partial y'_l}{\partial x_i} &= \sum_{s=1}^{K+1} w_{l,s}^{(3)} \frac{\partial h_s}{\partial x_i} = \sum_{s=1}^{K} w_{l,s}^{(3)} \frac{\partial h_s}{\partial x_i} + w_{l,K+1}^{(3)} \frac{\partial h_{K+1}}{\partial x_i} = \sum_{s=1}^{K} w_{l,s}^{(3)} \frac{\partial h_s}{\partial x_i} \\ &= \sum_{s=1}^{K} w_{l,s}^{(3)} \frac{\partial h_s}{\partial h'_s} \frac{\partial h'_s}{\partial x_i} = \sum_{s=1}^{K} w_{l,s}^{(3)} \frac{\partial F(h'_s)}{\partial h'_s} \frac{\partial h'_s}{\partial x_i} = \sum_{s=1}^{K} w_{l,s}^{(3)} F'(h'_s) \frac{\partial h'_s}{\partial x_i} \\ &= \sum_{s=1}^{K} w_{l,s}^{(3)} F'(h'_s) \left[\sum_{t=1}^{M} w_{s,t}^{(2)} F'(z'_t) w_{t,i}^{(1)} \right] \end{aligned}$$

where $l = 1,2$ and $h_{K+1} = 1$. Thus, $\partial h(\mathbf{X}) / \partial x_i$ in (2) can be computed as follows:

$$\frac{\partial h(\mathbf{X})}{\partial x_i}=\frac{\partial y_1'(\mathbf{X})}{\partial x_i}-\frac{\partial y_2'(\mathbf{X})}{\partial x_i}=\sum_{s=1}^{K} w_{1,s}^{(3)}F'(h_s')\left[\sum_{t=1}^{M} w_{s,t}^{(2)}F'(z_t')w_{t,i}^{(1)}\right]-\sum_{s=1}^{K} w_{2,s}^{(3)}F'(h_s')\left[\sum_{t=1}^{M} w_{s,t}^{(2)}F'(z_t')w_{t,i}^{(1)}\right]$$

$$=\sum_{s=1}^{K}(w_{1,s}^{(3)}-w_{2,s}^{(3)})F'(h_s')\left[\sum_{t=1}^{M} w_{s,t}^{(2)}F'(z_t')w_{t,i}^{(1)}\right].$$

Using the equations derived above, we can obtain a general expression for normal vector to the decision boundary of feedforward neural networks that have an arbitrary number of hidden layers as follows:

$$\frac{\partial h(\mathbf{X})}{\partial x_i}=\sum_{s=1}^{N_H}(w_{1,s}^{(H+1)}-w_{2,s}^{(H+1)})F'(\tilde{y}_s^{(H)})\frac{\partial \tilde{y}_s^{(H)}}{\partial x_i} \tag{3}$$

where $\frac{\partial \tilde{y}_s^{(l-1)}}{\partial x_i}=\begin{cases}\sum_{t=1}^{N_{l-2}} w_{s,t}^{(l-1)}F'(\tilde{y}_t^{(l-2)})\frac{\partial \tilde{y}_t^{(l-2)}}{\partial x_i} & \text{for } l=H+1,H,\ldots,3\\ w_{s,i}^{(l-1)} & \text{for } l=2\end{cases}$ $(s=1,\ldots,N_{l-1})$.

Here, H is number of hidden layers, N_l number of neurons in layer l $(l=0,1,\ldots,H+1)$, $w_{j,i}^{(l)}$ the weight vector between the i-th neuron in layer $(l-1)$ and the j-th neuron in layer l $(l=1,2,\ldots,H+1)$, and $\tilde{y}_j^{(l)}$ the net input to the j-th neuron in layer l. Using $\partial h(\mathbf{X})/\partial x_i$ in (3), we compute the normal vector to the decision boundary at $\mathbf{X}$ as follows:

$$\nabla h(\mathbf{X})=\frac{\partial h}{\partial x_1}\mathbf{x}_1+\frac{\partial h}{\partial x_2}\mathbf{x}_2+\frac{\partial h}{\partial x_3}\mathbf{x}_3+\ldots+\frac{\partial h}{\partial x_N}\mathbf{x}_N.$$

4 Experiments and Results

In order to evaluate the performance of the proposed method, tests were conducted using real multi-spectral remotely-sensed data from the field spectrometer system (FSS), which were collected as a part of the LACIE remote sensing programs [5]. The data are multi-spectral and multi-temporal in the agricultural area. Three-layer feed-forward neural networks were used and the number of hidden neurons in each hidden layer is two times the number of input neurons. Along with the proposed analytical DBFE method (ADBNN), we tested the principal component analysis (PCA), the discriminant analysis (DA), and the numerically implemented DBFE method (DBNN) [3].

We tested the performances of the various feature extraction algorithms in a multimodal situation, which is more difficult. We selected 8 classes randomly from the FSS data set and combined two classes to form a new class. Consequently, there are four classes and each class has two subclasses. Table 1 gives information on the classes. 800 randomly selected samples from each class were used as training data and the rest were used as test data. Since the number of training samples is not enough for the number of features, we reduced the original 60-dimensional data to 20-dimensional data by combining adjacent bands [2]. The test was repeated 10 times with different initial weights and Fig. 4 shows the average classification accuracy.

Table 1. Class description of the multi-modal 4 classes

Class	Date	Location	Species	No. samples
Class 1st	Mar 8, 1977	Finney Co. KS.	Winter Wheat	691
	May 3, 1977	Finney Co. KS.	Winter Wheat	657
Class 2nd	Oct.18, 1977	Hand Co. SD.	Winter Wheat	660
	Oct 26, 1978	Hand Co. SD.	Winter Wheat	393
Class 3rd	June 2, 1978	Hand Co. SD.	Spring Wheat	515
	May 15, 1978	Hand Co. SD.	Spring Wheat	474
Class 4th	Sep 20, 1977	Hand Co. SD.	Unknown Crops	1316
	Oct 18, 1977	Hand Co. SD.	Unknown Crops	445

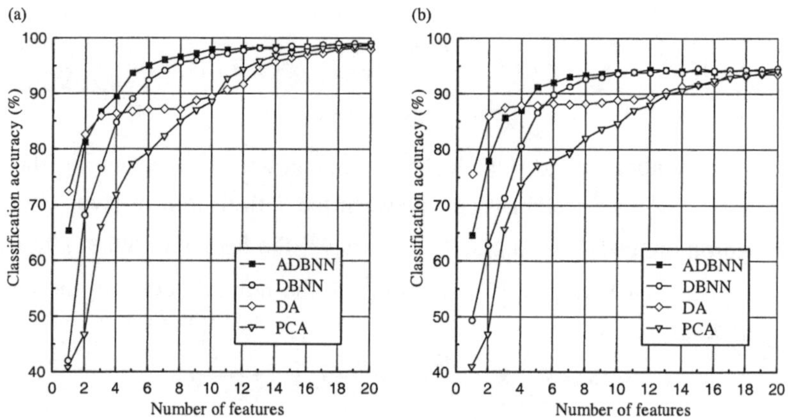

Fig. 4. Performance comparison of ADBNN(analytical decision boundary feature extraction), DBNN(numerical decision boundary feature extraction), DA(discriminant analysis), and PCA(principal component analysis). (a) training data, (b) test data

With 20 features, the classification accuracies of training data and test data are 98% and 94%, respectively. The ADBNN method achieves about 93% classification accuracy with 7 features for test data while the DA and the PCA need more than 17 features to achieve the same classification accuracy. Also, at lower dimensionality (number of features ≤ 5), the classification accuracies of the numerically calculated DBNN method are much lower than those of the ADBNN method. It is observed that the analytical method significantly outperforms the numerically calculated decision boundary feature extraction method. Experiments with other data sets showed that the proposed method consistently outperforms the other methods.

5 Conclusion

In this paper, we derived the gradient equations of the decision boundary of feedforward neural networks with multiple hidden layers. Experiments with various data sets show that the analytical decision boundary feature extraction for neural networks compares favorably with the conventional feature extraction methods (the principal component analysis, the discriminant analysis) and provides noticeable improvements in performance and processing time, compared to the numerical decision boundary feature extraction.

References

1. J. A. Richards, Remote Sensing Digital Image Analysis: Springer-Verlag, 1993
2. C. Lee and D. A. Landgrebe, Feature extraction based on decision boundaries. *IEEE Trans. on Pattern Analysis and Machine Intelligence*, vol. 15, 388-400, 1993.
3. C. Lee and D. A. Landgrebe, Decision boundary feature extraction for neural networks. *IEEE Trans. Neural Networks*, vol. 8, 75-83, 1997.
4. C. Lee and D. A. Landgrebe, Decision Boundary Feature Extraction for Non-Parametric Classification. *IEEE Trans. on Systems, Man, and Cybernetics*, vol. 23, no. 2, 433-444, 1993.
5. L. L. Biehl and et. al., A crops and soils data base for scene radiation research. *Proc. Machine Process. of Remotely Sensed Data Symp., West Lafayette, Indiana*, 169-177, 1982.

Feasible Adaptation Criteria for Hybrid Wavelet – Large Margin Classifiers

Julia Neumann, Christoph Schnörr, and Gabriele Steidl

Dept. of Mathematics and Computer Science
University of Mannheim, D-68131 Mannheim, Germany
{jneumann,schnoerr,steidl}@uni-mannheim.de
http://www.cvgpr.uni-mannheim.de, http://kiwi.math.uni-mannheim.de

Abstract. Hybrid wavelet – large margin classifiers have recently proven to solve difficult signal classification problems in cases where merely using a large margin classifier like, e.g., the Support Vector Machine may fail. The features for our hybrid classifier are selected from the outputs of *all* orthonormal filter banks of fixed length with respect to criteria measuring class separability and generalisation error.

In this paper, we evaluate a range of such adaptation criteria to perform feature selection for hybrid wavelet – large margin classifiers. The two main points we focus on are (i) approximation of the radius – margin error bound as the ultimate criterion for the target classifier, and (ii) computational costs of the approximating criterion for feature selection relative to those for the classifier design.

We show that by virtue of the adaptivity of the filter bank, criteria which are more efficient than computing the radius – margin are sufficient for wavelet adaptation and, hence, feature selection. Our results are relevant for image– and arbitrary–dimensional signal classification by utilising the standard tensor product design of wavelets.

1 Introduction

Motivation. A persistent problem in signal and image classification concerns filter design for feature extraction and selection [6, 7, 11]. In most cases, this problem is addressed *irrespective of* the subsequent classification stage. However, using 'off–the–shelf' filters like Daubechies' wavelets [2] may result in an unacceptably large classification error. Fig. 1 shows a typical example for a difficult signal classification problem.

In this context, our approach is to take the target classifier and data into consideration for filter design and the selection of appropriate features. Given a sample set of labelled patterns, the main idea is to *adapt* the filter bank based on a criterion measuring class separability and generalisation error to obtain the *optimal features* for the particular problem under consideration.

It has recently been shown for a number of difficult applications that *jointly* designing both the filter stage and the classifier in this way may considerably outperform standard approaches based on a *separate* design of both stages [10].

N. Petkov and M.A. Westenberg (Eds.): CAIP 2003, LNCS 2756, pp. 588–595, 2003.

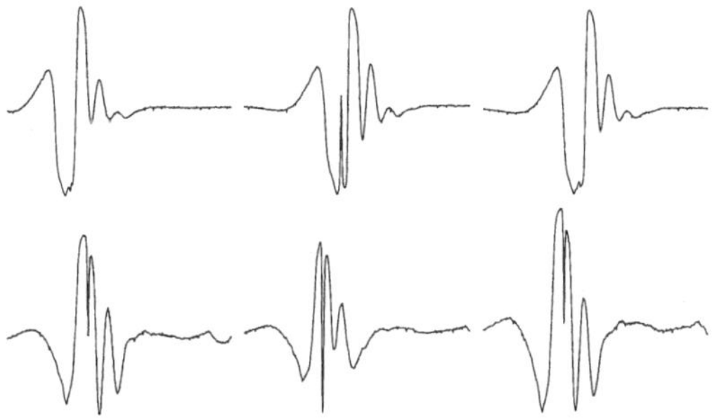

Fig. 1. Two–class problem (heart beats: sinus rhythm (SR) and ventricular tachycardia(VT)): Choosing standard wavelets for feature extraction may result in a classification error up to 31%!

This motivates the investigation of suitable adaptation criteria which is summarised in the present paper.

Problem Statement. The target classifier in our hybrid approach is the Support Vector Machine (SVM) which is well known to belong to the most competitive approaches and has favourable properties from the perspective of optimisation during the learning stage [12]. Accordingly, a suitable criterion for feature selection is the radius – margin bound which captures the generalisation error [12]. The direct application of this criterion to feature selection has been studied in [13].

In the hybrid approach studied here, however, the objective function with respect to the filters is quite complex and can be minimised by exhaustive search only. In contrast to related work [3], this is nevertheless computationally feasible and efficient in our case, due to the lattice factorisation of orthonormal filter banks (see Sec. 2 and [5, Sec. 5.3]).

On the other hand, determining the optimally adapted filter bank requires many evaluations of the objective function. This is no longer computationally feasible if the objective function is based on a criterion the evaluation of which is as time consuming as the design of the classifier itself! Since this holds for the radius – margin bound as criterion of our target classifier – each evaluation requires to solve two quadratic programs! –, approximations of this criterion have to be investigated which are suitable for the overall design of the hybrid approach.

Organisation of the Paper. We summarise the hybrid architecture in Sec. 2. Next, in Sec. 3, we discuss a range of criteria in view of the problems stated above, along with a confirmation and illustrations by numerical evaluations in Sec. 4.

2 Hybrid Wavelet – SVM Architecture

In this section we briefly introduce our hybrid architecture for feature extraction and subsequent classification of the resulting feature vectors.

Feature Extraction. Our feature extraction process consists of two steps, namely filtering by an orthogonal two-channel octave band filter bank, and energy computation of the resulting coefficients in the different frequency bands.

We deal with input signals $\mathbf{s} \in \mathbb{R}^N$, where N is a power of 2. Fundamental for our filter adaptation process is that any orthogonal two-channel filter bank with filters of length $2L+2$ is determined by L angles $\boldsymbol{\theta} = (\theta_0, \ldots, \theta_{L-1}) \in [0,\pi)^L$ by the so–called lattice decomposition of the corresponding polyphase matrix [9, Theorems 4.6 and 4.9]. Filtering by the d-level octave band filter bank given by $\boldsymbol{\theta}$ can then be considered as orthogonal discrete wavelet transform

$$F_{\boldsymbol{\theta}} : \mathbb{R}^N \to \mathbb{R}^N , \; \mathbf{s} \mapsto (\mathbf{c^d}, \mathbf{d^d}, \ldots, \mathbf{d^1}) \;\; ,$$

which maps the input signal $\mathbf{s}$ to its wavelet coefficients $\mathbf{d^j} = (d_1^j, \ldots, d_{N/2^j}^j)$ in the jth frequency band, $j = 1, \ldots, d$. The mapping $F_{\boldsymbol{\theta}}$ is norm preserving with respect to the Euclidean norm $\|\cdot\|_2$, i.e., $\|F_{\boldsymbol{\theta}}\mathbf{s}\|_2 = \|\mathbf{s}\|_2$.

To generate a handy number of features that still make the signals well distinguishable, we introduce the energy operator

$$E_{\|\,\|} : \mathbb{R}^N \to \mathbb{R}^d , \; (\mathbf{c^d}, \mathbf{d^d}, \ldots, \mathbf{d^1}) \mapsto (\|\mathbf{d^d}\|, \ldots, \|\mathbf{d^1}\|) \;\; .$$

As possible norms for $E_{\|\,\|}$ we consider besides the Euclidean norm the weighted Euclidean norm $\sqrt{\frac{1}{n}\sum_{i=1}^n c_i^2}$, which was proposed by Unser [11] to represent the channel variance. Other Hölder norms may be used as well.

In summary our feature extraction process produces the feature vectors $\mathbf{x} := E_{\|\,\|}F_{\boldsymbol{\theta}}\mathbf{s}$. For later considerations it is important that the norm preserving property of the orthogonal wavelet transform implies

$$\|E_{\|\,\|}F_{\boldsymbol{\theta}}\mathbf{s}\|_2 \leq \|\mathbf{s}\|_2 \;\; . \tag{1}$$

In our experiments we deal w.l.o.g. with input signals $\mathbf{s}$ with fixed Euclidean norm and average value zero and apply the full wavelet decomposition, i.e., $N/2^d = 1$. Then it is easy to check that $\mathbf{c}^d = 0$. Now (1) implies that the feature vectors lie within a sphere in $\mathbb{R}^d$ centred at the origin. Moreover, if we use the Euclidean norm in $E_{\|\,\|}$, then we have equality in (1).

Classification. To rate a set of feature vectors according to their classification ability, it is essential to take into account the classifier in use. We intend to apply a SVM as classifier. Let $\mathcal{X}$ be a compact subset of $\mathbb{R}^d$ containing the feature vectors. Given a training set $\mathcal{Z} := \{(\mathbf{x}_i, y_i) \in \mathcal{X} \times \{-1, 1\} : i = 1, \ldots, n\}$ of n associations, we are interested in the construction of a real valued function f defined on $\mathcal{X}$ such that $\mathrm{sgn}(f)$ well predicts the class labels y. Let $\mathbf{y} := (y_1, \ldots, y_n)$ denote the vector of class labels and let $\mathbf{Y} := \mathrm{diag}\,\mathbf{y}$. We introduce a so–called *kernel* function $K : \mathcal{X} \times \mathcal{X} \to \mathbb{R}$ which is square integrable, positive definite and symmetric. In our applications we will use Gaussian kernels $K(\mathbf{x}, \mathbf{y}) := e^{-\frac{\|\mathbf{x}-\mathbf{y}\|_2^2}{2\sigma^2}}$ where $\sigma > 0$. With the kernel K we associate the kernel matrix $\mathbf{K} := (K(\mathbf{x}_i, \mathbf{x}_j))_{i,j=1}^n$. Then the standard SVM finds f as linear combination

$$f(\mathbf{x}) = \sum_{i=1}^n y_i \alpha_i K(\mathbf{x}_i, \mathbf{x}) \;\; , \tag{2}$$

where the coefficients $\boldsymbol{\alpha} = (\alpha_1, \ldots, \alpha_n)$ are given by the solution of the quadratic optimisation problem (QP)

$$\max_{\boldsymbol{\alpha}} -\frac{1}{2}\boldsymbol{\alpha}^T \mathbf{YKY}\boldsymbol{\alpha} + \mathbf{e}^T\boldsymbol{\alpha} \quad \text{subject to} \quad \mathbf{0} \leq \boldsymbol{\alpha} \leq C\mathbf{e} \ . \tag{3}$$

For $C = \infty$ the resulting classifier is called *hard margin SVM*, otherwise *soft margin SVM*. The *support vectors* (SVs) are those training patterns $\mathbf{x}_i$ for which the coefficients α_i in the solution of (3) do not vanish. Then the sum (2) involves only SVs. The *margin* separating the classes is defined by $\rho := (\boldsymbol{\alpha}^T\mathbf{YKY}\boldsymbol{\alpha})^{-\frac{1}{2}}$. Note that (3) originates from the unconstrained optimisation problem

$$\min_{f \in \mathcal{H}_K} C\sum_{i=1}^{n}(1 - y_i f(\mathbf{x}_i))_+ + \frac{1}{2}||f||^2_{\mathcal{H}_K}, \qquad (\tau)_+ := \begin{cases} \tau & \text{if } \tau \geq 0, \\ 0 & \text{otherwise,} \end{cases}$$

where $\mathcal{H}_K$ denotes the reproducing kernel Hilbert space associated with K. For details see [12].

3 Criteria for Feature Adaptation

To steer the parameters $\boldsymbol{\theta}$ in our feature extraction process according to the subsequent SVM classifier we want to find a measure that allows for fast comparison of different sets of feature vectors based on maximising the SVM performance. In this paper, we restrict our attention to hard margin SVMs for simplicity. All results can be formulated for soft margin SVMs as well [4]. Possible criteria for adaptation are obtained by bounds for the *generalisation error*, i.e., the probability that $\text{sgn} f(\mathbf{x}) \neq y$ for a randomly chosen example $(\mathbf{x}, y) \in \mathcal{X} \times \{-1, 1\}$. In our experiments we investigate five criteria:

Radius – Margin. Since the expectation of the quotient

$$\mathcal{C}_1 := \frac{1}{n}\frac{R^2}{\rho^2} \tag{4}$$

forms an upper bound on the SVM generalisation error [12, Theorem 10.6] we consider a minimal value $\mathcal{C}_1$ as the ultimate criterion for the SVM classifier. Here R is the radius of the smallest sphere in $\mathcal{H}_K$ enclosing all $K(\cdot, \mathbf{x}_j)$, i.e., the solution of

$$\min_{a \in \mathcal{H}_K, R \in \mathbb{R}} R^2 \quad \text{subject to} \quad ||K(\cdot, \mathbf{x}_j) - a||^2_{\mathcal{H}_K} \leq R^2 \ , \quad j = 1, \ldots, n \ . \tag{5}$$

In [4] we proved that (5) can be also solved by the QP (3):

Proposition 1. *Let K be a kernel with $K(\mathbf{x}, \mathbf{x}) = \kappa \ \forall \mathbf{x} \in \mathcal{X}$. Then the optimal radius R in (5) can be obtained by solving (3) with $\mathbf{Y} = \mathbf{I}$. If $\boldsymbol{\alpha}$ is the solution of (3) and j an index of a SV, then $R^2 = \kappa + \boldsymbol{\beta}^T\mathbf{K}\boldsymbol{\beta} - 2(\mathbf{K}\boldsymbol{\beta})_j$, where $\boldsymbol{\beta} := \frac{\boldsymbol{\alpha}}{\mathbf{e}^T\boldsymbol{\alpha}}$.*

However, the computation of ρ and R in (4) still requires the solution of two QPs for each parameter vector $\boldsymbol{\theta}$.

Margin. Due to (1), the radius R is bounded. This motivates to consider only the denominator of (4), i.e., to use a maximal $\mathcal{C}_2 = \rho$ as objective criterion. Indeed, our experiments indicate that if training and test data have the same underlying distribution, the margin behaves much like the classification error.

Alignment. As a measure of classification ability for kernel problems, the alignment

$$\mathcal{C}_3 := \frac{\mathbf{y}^T \mathbf{K} \mathbf{y}}{n \|\mathbf{K}\|_F} \tag{6}$$

with Frobenius norm $\|\cdot\|_F$ was proposed in [1]. By [1, Theorem 4], the generalisation accuracy of the expected Parzen window estimator which is related to an SVM is bounded by a function of the alignment.

Class Centre Distance. In all our experiments, the denominator in (6) doesn't influence the alignment much. Furthermore, supposing normed training vectors $\|\mathbf{x}_i\|_2 = c$ and a Gaussian kernel with large deviation σ, the numerator in (6) is approximately proportional to $\mathbf{y}^T(\langle \mathbf{x}_i, \mathbf{x}_j \rangle)_{i,j=1}^n \, \mathbf{y}$. Introducing the class means $\boldsymbol{\mu}_i := \frac{1}{n_i} \sum_{y_j=i} \mathbf{x}_j$ with class cardinalities n_i $(i = \pm 1)$, for $n_1 = n_{-1}$ this can be rewritten as $\|\boldsymbol{\mu}_1 - \boldsymbol{\mu}_{-1}\|_2^2$. The criterion $\mathcal{C}_4 := \|\boldsymbol{\mu}_1 - \boldsymbol{\mu}_{-1}\|_2$ can be simply evaluated and is also easily differentiable. It was successfully applied in [10].

Scatter Measures. While $\mathcal{C}_4$ only takes into account the mean values of the classes we are now looking for classes that are distant from each other and at the same time concentrated around their means. A generalisation of $\mathcal{C}_4$ are measures using scatter matrices. We consider the generalised Fisher criterion

$$\mathcal{C}_5 := \frac{\operatorname{tr}(\mathbf{S}_b)}{\operatorname{tr}(\mathbf{S}_w)} = \frac{\frac{n_1}{n}\|\boldsymbol{\mu}_1 - \boldsymbol{\mu}\|^2 + \frac{n_{-1}}{n}\|\boldsymbol{\mu}_{-1} - \boldsymbol{\mu}\|^2}{\frac{n_1}{n}\sum_{k=1}^d \sigma_{1k}^2 + \frac{n_{-1}}{n}\sum_{k=1}^d \sigma_{-1k}^2}, \quad \boldsymbol{\mu} := \sum_{i \in \{-1,1\}} \frac{n_i}{n} \boldsymbol{\mu}_i$$

where σ_{ik}^2 is the marginal variance of class i along dimension k and

$$\mathbf{S}_w := \frac{1}{n} \sum_{i \in \{-1,1\}} \sum_{y_j = i} (\mathbf{x}_j - \boldsymbol{\mu}_i)(\mathbf{x}_j - \boldsymbol{\mu}_i)^T, \quad \mathbf{S}_b := \sum_{i \in \{-1,1\}} \frac{n_i}{n} (\boldsymbol{\mu}_i - \boldsymbol{\mu})(\boldsymbol{\mu}_i - \boldsymbol{\mu})^T$$

denote the *within-class scatter matrix* and the *between-class scatter matrix*, respectively. For equiprobable classes, $\mathcal{C}_5$ is proportional to $\mathcal{C}_4^2 / \sum_{k=1}^d (\sigma_{1k}^2 + \sigma_{-1k}^2)$.

4 Numerical Evaluation

So far we have proposed several criteria for judging the discrimination ability of a set of feature vectors and have shown some connections between the criteria. We now want to see how these links show up when analysing real data.

We use two structurally different real data sets: The first electro–physiological data set originates from the detection of ventricular tachycardia as in [10]. For

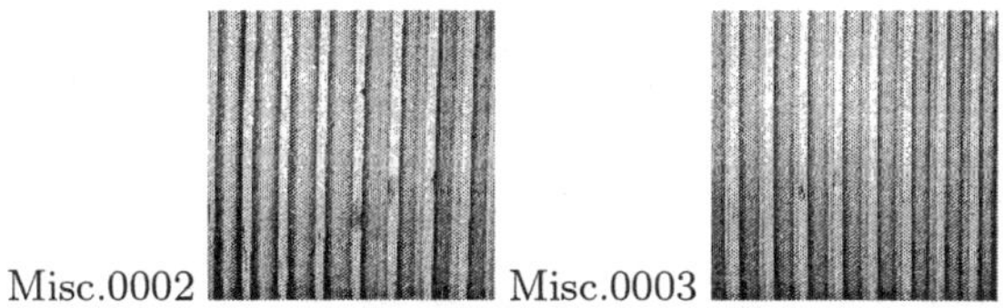

Fig. 2. texture sample: linearly rescaled images

each patient, eight beats from a single episode are used for classifier training. Some exemplary beats for a sample patient are shown in Fig. 1. The second group of data are the texture images from the MeasTex collection [8]. We use single rows of the corrugated iron images 'Misc.0002' and 'Misc.0003' shown in Fig. 2 to have one–dimensional data as in the first data set. Here, the first 32 rows of each texture are used for classifier training. We normalised all samples by $\|\mathbf{s}_i\|_2 = 1000$ and set their average value to zero.

We apply orthogonal filter banks with filters of length ≤ 6 which can be parameterised by two angles $\boldsymbol{\theta} = (\theta_0, \theta_1) \in [0, \pi)^2$. The parameter space was discretised with 128 angles per dimension. For the classification, a hard–margin SVM with Gaussian kernel of width $\sigma = 100$ is used. The highest alignment $\mathcal{C}_3$ is achieved with $\sigma \approx 150$ and $\sigma \approx 80$ for the Euclidean and the weighted Euclidean norm, respectively.

To control the filter design, we generate plots that show the values of the five criteria subject to the two–dimensional parameter space. The values are plotted using a linear grey scale except for the radius – margin bound which is plotted on a logarithmic scale due to its large variation. Additionally, the larger values are clipped to the trivial error bound 1 to enhance the contrast. To assess the effect of the clipping, the distribution of the logarithm of the bound is indicated by a histogram. The resulting images are shown in Fig. 3, where the plots (a) – (e) are ordered from the simplest and computationally most efficient criterion to the most expensive one.

For all three problems, the overall impression is that all shown criteria are alike. Moreover, all criteria show a detailed structure for the parameter space. This indicates that effectively finding the optimal wavelet according to the chosen criterion is not easy even for the simple criteria. The class centre distance and particularly the alignment resemble the margin. That is, the wavelets that generate a high class centre distance or alignment also guarantee a large margin. Although the scatter criterion $\mathcal{C}_5$ also takes into account the variances, it doesn't seem to be superior to the simplest criterion $\mathcal{C}_4$.

The radius – margin bound $\mathcal{C}_1$ covers a large range of values from 10 resp. 3% to 100%. This indicates the significance of the wavelet choice which is also emphasised in Fig. 4. Apart from the different distribution of the values, the radius – margin bound rates the features mostly like the margin.

For specific signals there may be an important difference between using the Euclidean and the weighted Euclidean norm as exhibited by Fig. 3–2 and 3–3.

The plots show that simple adaptation criteria suffice to promisingly design filters for hybrid wavelet – large margin classifiers with Gaussian kernels.

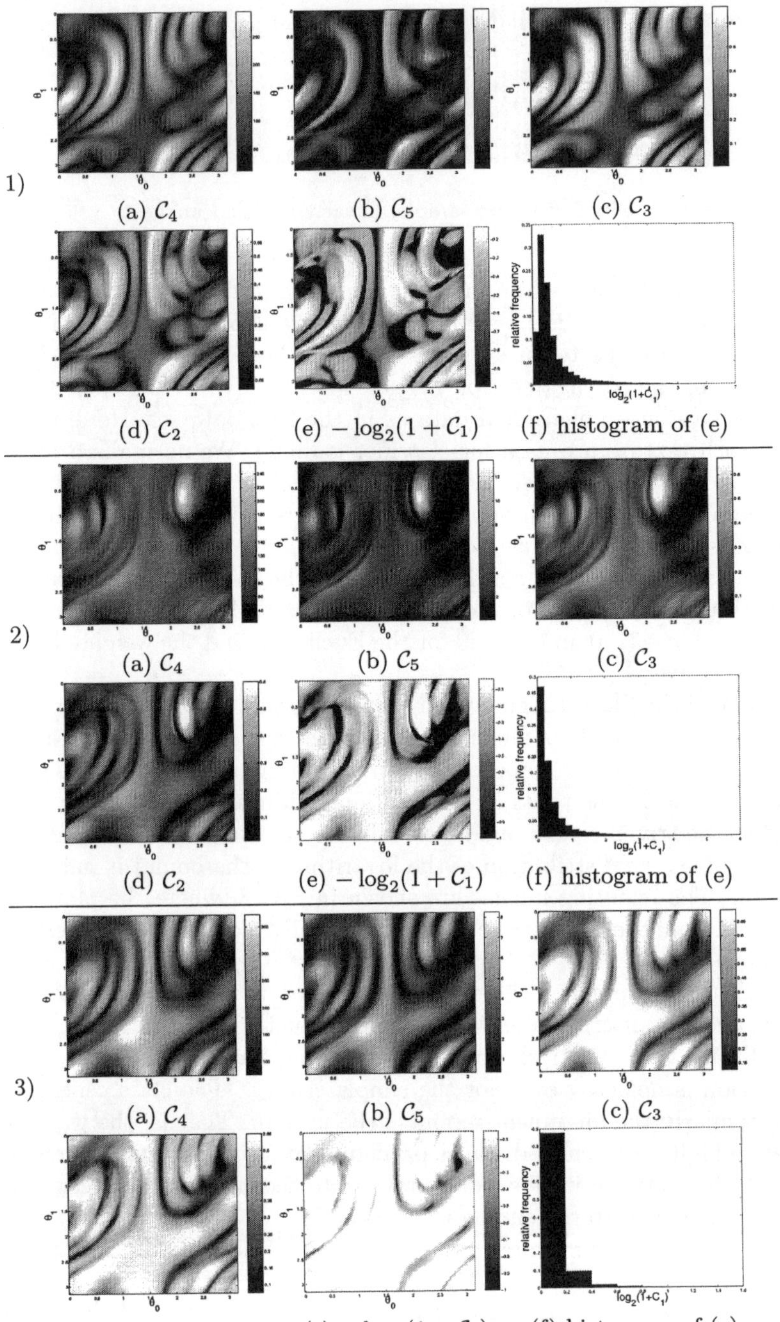

Fig. 3. Criteria values for 1) heartbeat classification with weighted Euclidean norm in $E_{\| \|}$, 2) texture row classification with weighted Euclidean norm in $E_{\| \|}$, 3) texture row classification with Euclidean norm in $E_{\| \|}$; light spots represent favourable criterion values and, hence, beneficial filter banks

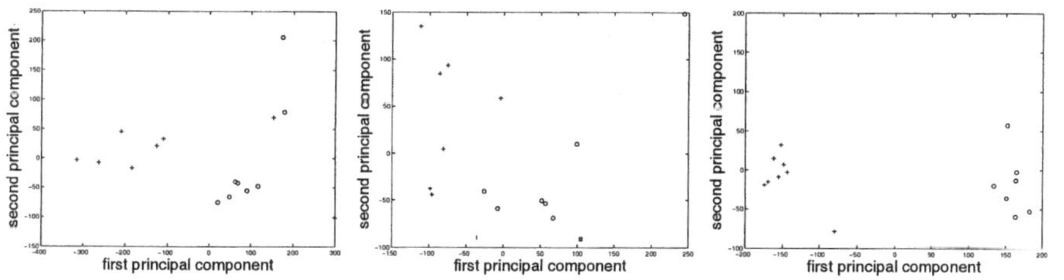

(a) (b) (c)

Fig. 4. Principal components of training vectors for heartbeat classification with Euclidean norm in $E_{\|\ \|}$: (a) for the Haar wavelet, (b) for the Daubechies wavelet with three vanishing moments, (c) for the optimally aligned wavelet ($\mathcal{C}_3$); these results show that wavelet adaptation may considerably improve class separability

Acknowledgements

This work is funded by the DFG, Grant Sch 457/5-1.

References

1. N. Cristianini, J. Shawe-Taylor, A. Elisseeff, and J. Kandola. On kernel-target alignment. In *NIPS*, volume 14, pages 367–373. The MIT Press, 2002.
2. I. Daubechies. Orthonormal bases of compactly supported wavelets. *Communications on Pure and Applied Mathematics*, 41:909–996, 1988.
3. E. Jones, P. Runkle, N. Dasgupta, L. Couchman, and L. Carin. Genetic algorithm wavelet design for signal classification. *IEEE TPAMI*, 23(8):890–895, 2001.
4. J. Neumann, C. Schnörr, and G. Steidl. Feasible adaptation criteria for hybrid wavelet – large margin classifiers. Technical Report TR-02-015, Dept. of Mathematics and Computer Science, University of Mannheim, 2002.
5. J. Neumann, C. Schnörr, and G. Steidl. Effectively finding the optimal wavelet for hybrid wavelet – large margin signal classification. Technical Report TR-03-005, Dept. of Mathematics and Computer Science, University of Mannheim, 2003.
6. T. Randen and J. H. Husøy. Filtering for texture classification: A comparative study. *IEEE TPAMI*, 21(4):291–310, Apr. 1999.
7. P. Scheunders, S. Livens, G. Van de Wouwer, P. Vautrot, and D. Van Dyck. Wavelet-based texture analysis. *International Journal on Computer Science and Information Management*, 1(2):22–34, 1998.
8. G. Smith. MeasTex image texture database and test suite. Available at `http://www.cssip.uq.edu.au/meastex/meastex.html`, May 1997. Version 1.1.
9. G. Strang and T. Nguyen. *Wavelets and Filter Banks*. Wellesley-Cambridge Press, Wellesley, 1996.
10. D. Strauß and G. Steidl. Hybrid wavelet-support vector classification of waveforms. *Journal of Computational and Applied Mathematics*, 148:375–400, 2002.
11. M. Unser. Texture classification and segmentation using wavelet frames. *IEEE Transactions on Image Processing*, 4(11):1549–1560, 1995.
12. V. Vapnik. *Statistical Learning Theory*. Wiley, New York, 1998.
13. J. Weston, S. Mukherjee, O. Chapelle, M. Pontil, T. Poggio, and V. Vapnik. Feature selection for SVMs. In *NIPS*, pages 668–674. The MIT Press, 2000.

A New Fisher-Based Method Applied to Face Recognition

Carlos E. Thomaz and Duncan F. Gillies

Imperial College London, Department of Computing
180 Queen's Gate, London SW7 2BZ, United Kingdom
{cet,dfg}@doc.ic.ac.uk

Abstract. A critical issue of applying Linear (or Fisher) Discriminant Analysis (LDA) is the singularity and instability of the within-class scatter matrix. In practice, particularly in image recognition applications such as face recognition, there are often a large number of pixels or pre-processed features available, but the total number of training patterns is limited and commonly less than the dimension of the feature space. Hence, a considerable amount of effort has been devoted to the design of Fisher-based methods, for targeting limited sample and high dimensional problems. In this paper, a new Fisher-based method is proposed. It is based on a novel regularisation approach for the within-class scatter matrix. In order to evaluate its effectiveness, experiments on face recognition using the well-known ORL and FERET face databases were carried out and compared with similar methods, such as Fisherfaces, Chen et al.'s, Yu and Yang's, and Yang and Yang's LDA-based methods. In both databases, our method improved the LDA classification performance without a PCA intermediate step and using less discriminant features.

1 Introduction

Linear Discriminant Analysis (LDA), also called Fisher Discriminant Analysis, has been used successfully as a feature extraction technique in several classification problems.

A critical issue in using LDA is, however, the singularity and instability of the within-class scatter matrix. In practice, particularly in image recognition applications such as face recognition, there are often a large number of pixels or pre-processed features available, but the total number of training patterns is limited and commonly less than the dimension of the feature space. This implies that the within-class scatter matrix either will be singular if its rank is less than the number of features or might be unstable (or poorly estimated) if the total number of training patterns is not at least five to ten times the dimension of the feature space [6]. Hence, a considerable amount of effort has been devoted to the design of other Fisher-based methods, for targeting limited sample and high dimensional problems [1,2,7,12,15,16,17].

In this paper, a new Fisher-based method is proposed. It is based on a straightforward regularisation approach that overcomes the singularity and instability of the within-class scatter matrix when LDA is applied directly in limited sample and high

N. Petkov and M.A. Westenberg (Eds.): CAIP 2003, LNCS 2756, pp. 596–605, 2003.

dimensional problems. In order to evaluate its effectiveness, experiments on face recognition using the well-known ORL and FERET face databases were carried out and compared with other LDA-based methods, such as the popular Fisherfaces [1,12,17] and the more recent Chen et al.'s [2], Yu and Yang's [16], and Yang and Yang's [15] methods. The results indicate that our method improved the LDA classification performance when the within-class scatter matrix is singular as well as poorly estimated, without a PCA intermediate step and using less discriminant features.

2 Linear Discriminant Analysis (LDA)

Linear Discriminant Analysis (LDA) is a well-known feature extraction technique that maximizes between-class separability and minimizes within-class variability.

Let the between-class scatter matrix S_b and the within-class scatter matrix S_w be defined as

$$S_b = \sum_{i=1}^{g} n_i(\overline{x}_i - \overline{x})(\overline{x}_i - \overline{x})^T \quad \text{and} \quad S_w = \sum_{i=1}^{g}\sum_{j=1}^{n_i}(x_{i,j} - \overline{x}_i)(x_{i,j} - \overline{x}_i)^T , \tag{1}$$

where $x_{i,j}$ is the p-dimensional pattern j from class i, n_i is the number of training patterns from class i, g is the number of classes or groups, and $\overline{x}_i$ and $\overline{x}$ are the class and grand mean vectors, given respectively by

$$\overline{x}_i = \frac{1}{n_i}\sum_{j=1}^{n_i} x_{i,j} \quad \text{and} \quad \overline{x} = \frac{\sum_{i=1}^{g} n_i \overline{x}_i}{N} , \tag{2}$$

where $N = n_1 + n_2 + \cdots + n_g$.

The main objective of LDA is to find a projection matrix P_{lda} that maximizes the ratio of the determinant of the between-class scatter matrix to the determinant of the within-class scatter matrix (Fisher's criterion), that is,

$$P_{lda} = \arg\max_{P} \frac{\left|PS_bP^T\right|}{\left|PS_wP^T\right|} . \tag{3}$$

It has been proved [4] that if S_w is a non-singular matrix then the Fisher's criterion is maximised when the column vectors of the projection matrix P_{lda} are the eigenvectors of $S_w^{-1}S_b$ with at most $g-1$ nonzero corresponding eigenvalues. This is the standard LDA.

In the next sub-sections, recent LDA methods with application to face recognition are briefly described. A new LDA-based approach is detailed in section 3.

2.1 Fisherfaces

The Fisherfaces [1, 17] or Most Discriminant Features (MDF) [12] method is one of the most successful feature extraction approaches for solving limited sample size problems in face recognition.

It is essentially a two-stage dimensionality reduction technique. First the face images from the original vector space are projected to a lower dimensional space (face subspace) using Principal Component Analysis (PCA) [14] and then LDA is applied next to find the best linear discriminant features on that face subspace. Since the number of retained principal components may vary from at least g to at most $N-g$ PCA features [1,12,17], the singularity problem of the within-class scatter matrix S_w is overcome.

2.2 Other LDA Methods

Chen et al. [2] have proposed another LDA-based method, here called CLDA, that overcomes the singularity problems related to the direct use of LDA in small sample size applications, particularly in face recognition. The main idea of their approach is basically to use either the discriminative information of the null space of the within-class scatter matrix to maximise the between-class scatter matrix whenever S_w is singular, or the eigenvectors corresponding to the set of the largest eigenvalues of matrix $(S_b + S_w)^{-1} S_b$ whenever S_w is non-singular. Although experimental results have shown that CLDA improves the performance of a face recognition system compared with Liu et al.'s approach [7] and template matching, Chen et al.'s approach will select the same linear discriminant features as the standard LDA when S_w is non-singular [4] but poorly estimated.

Yu and Yang [16] have developed a direct LDA algorithm (DLDA) for high dimensional data with application to face recognition. The key idea of their method is to discard the null space of S_b rather than discarding the null space of S_w by diagonalizing S_b first and then diagonalizing S_w [16]. This diagonalization ordering process avoids the singularity problems related to the use of the pure LDA in high dimensional data where the within-class scatter matrix S_w is likely to be singular. Using computational techniques to handle large scatter matrices, experimental results have shown that DLDA can be applied on the original vector space of face images without any explicit intermediate dimensionality reduction step.

More recently, Yang and Yang [15] have proposed a feature extraction method that is capable of deriving all discriminatory information of the LDA in singular cases (YLDA). Analogous to the Fisherfaces, it is a two-stage dimensionality reduction technique. That is, PCA is used firstly to reduce the dimensionality of the original space and then LDA (using the OFLD [15] method) is applied next to find the best linear discriminant features on that PCA subspace. They have shown that the number of principal components to retain for a best LDA performance should be equal to the rank of the total scatter matrix S_T, given by $S_T = S_b + S_w$ and calculated on the original space [15]. Although YLDA addresses the PCA+LDA problems when the total scatter matrix is singular, such PCA strategy does not avoid the within-class scatter instability when S_T is non-singular but poorly estimated.

3 A New LDA (NLDA)

In order to avoid the singularity and instability critical issues of the within-class scatter matrix S_w when LDA is applied directly in limited sample and high dimensional problems, we propose a new LDA approach based on a straightforward regularisation method for the S_w matrix.

3.1 Reguralisation Methods

Regularisation methods have been used successfully in solving poorly and ill-posed inverse problems [9]. The idea behind the term "regularisation" is to decrease the variance associated with the limited sample based estimate at the expense of potentially increased bias [3].

Several researchers (see, e.g., [10]) have proposed a regularisation in LDA in which ridge-like estimates of the form $S_p + kI$ are substituted for S_p, where S_p is the corresponding covariance matrix to scatter matrix S_w (that is, $S_w = (N-g)S_p$), I is the p by p identity matrix, and $k \geq 0$. This modification makes the problem mathematically feasible and increases the stability of the resulting LDA when S_p has small eigenvalues.

Rayens [10] has suggested that a reasonable grid of potential parameter values for the optimal k could be $\lambda_{\min} \leq k \leq \lambda_{\max}$. The values $\lambda_{\min}$ and $\lambda_{\max}$ are respectively the non-zero smallest and largest eigenvalues of S_p and a more productive searching process should be based on values near $\lambda_{\min}$ rather than $\lambda_{\max}$ [10]. As pointed out by Rayens, however, this reasoning is context-dependent and a leave-one-out optimisation process must be done in order to determine the optimal k regarding an appropriate loss function [10].

Other researchers have imposed different regularisation methods to overcome the singularity and instability in sample based covariance estimation, especially to improve quadratic classification performance (see, e.g., [3, 5]). Most of these works have used shrinkage parameters other than k and involve a convex combination between a singular or unstable covariance matrix, such as S_p, and a multiple of the identity matrix. In other words, the poorly or ill-posed S_p estimate could be replaced with a symmetric matrix of the form $(1-\gamma)S_p + (\gamma)\bar{\lambda}I$, where the shrinkage parameter γ takes on values $0 \leq \gamma \leq 1$ and the identity matrix multiplier is just the average eigenvalue of S_p. The parameter γ could be selected to maximise the leave-one-out classification accuracy. This regularisation idea would have the effect of decreasing the larger eigenvalues and increasing the smaller ones, thereby counteracting the biasing inherent in sample-based estimation of eigenvalues [3].

3.2 The Proposed Method

The proposed method considers the issue of regularising the S_p estimate with a multiple of the identity matrix by selecting the largest dispersions regarding the S_p average eigenvalue. It is based on the concept of the maximum entropy covariance selection method developed to improve quadratic classification performance on limited sample size problems [13].

Let a combination of S_p and a p by p identity matrix I be given by

$$\hat{S}_p(k) = S_p + kI \,, \tag{4}$$

where k is just an identity matrix multiplier. The eigen-decomposition of equation (4) can be written as

$$\begin{aligned} \hat{S}_p(k) &= \sum_{j=1}^{r} \lambda_j \phi_j (\phi_j)^T + \sum_{j=1}^{p} k \phi_j (\phi_j)^T \\ &= \sum_{j=1}^{r} (\lambda_j + k) \phi_j (\phi_j)^T + \sum_{j=r+1}^{p} k \phi_j (\phi_j)^T \end{aligned} \,, \tag{5}$$

where r is the rank of S_p ($r \leq p$), λ_j is the jth non-zero eigenvalue of S_p, and ϕ_j is the corresponding eigenvector. As can be seen from equation (5), a combination of S_p and a multiple of the identity matrix I as described in equation (4) expands all the S_p eigenvalues, independently whether these eigenvalues are either null, small, or even large.

A possible regularisation method should be the one that decreases the larger eigenvalues and increases the smaller ones, as proposed by [3, 5] to improve quadratic classification performance. According to this approach, briefly described in the previous sub-section, the eigen-decomposition of a convex combination of S_p and a p by p identity matrix I can be written as

$$\hat{S}_p(\gamma) = (1-\gamma) \sum_{j=1}^{r} (\lambda_j + \bar{\lambda}) \phi_j (\phi_j)^T + \gamma \sum_{j=r+1}^{p} \bar{\lambda} \phi_j (\phi_j)^T \,, \tag{6}$$

where the mixing parameter γ takes on values $0 \leq \gamma \leq 1$, and $\bar{\lambda}$ is the average eigenvalue of S_p.

Despite the substantial amount of computation saved by taking advantage of matrix updating formulas [3, 10], the regularisation method described in equation (6) requires the computation of the eigenvalues and eigenvectors of a p by p matrix for each training observation of all the classes and each value of the mixing parameter γ. In recognition applications where a large number of classes and several training observations are considered, such as face recognition, this reguralisation method can be unfeasible.

Thus, as it is well-known that the estimation errors of the non-dominant eigenvalues are much greater than those of the dominant eigenvalues [4], we propose the following selection method in order to expand only the smaller and consequently less reliable eigenvalues of S_p, and keep most of its larger eigenvalues unchanged:

1) Find the Φ eigenvectors and Λ eigenvalues of S_p, where $S_p = S_w/[N-g]$;
2) Calculate the S_p average eigenvalue $\bar{\lambda}$ given by

$$\overline{\lambda} = \left(\sum_{j=1}^{p} \lambda_j \right) / p \, ; \tag{7}$$

3) Form a new matrix of eigenvalues based on the following largest dispersion values

$$\Lambda^* = diag[\max(\lambda_1, \overline{\lambda}), \max(\lambda_2, \overline{\lambda}), ..., \max(\lambda_p, \overline{\lambda})] \, ; \tag{8}$$

4) Form the regularised within-class scatter matrix

$$S_w^* = S_p^* (N - g) = (\Phi \Lambda^* (\Phi)^T)(N - g) \, . \tag{9}$$

The new LDA (NLDA) is constructed by replacing S_w with S_w^* in the Fisher's criterion formula described in equation 3. It is a straightforward method that overcomes both the singularity and instability of the within-class scatter matrix S_w when LDA is applied directly in limited sample and high dimensional problems. NLDA also avoids the computational costs inherent to the aforementioned regularisation processes.

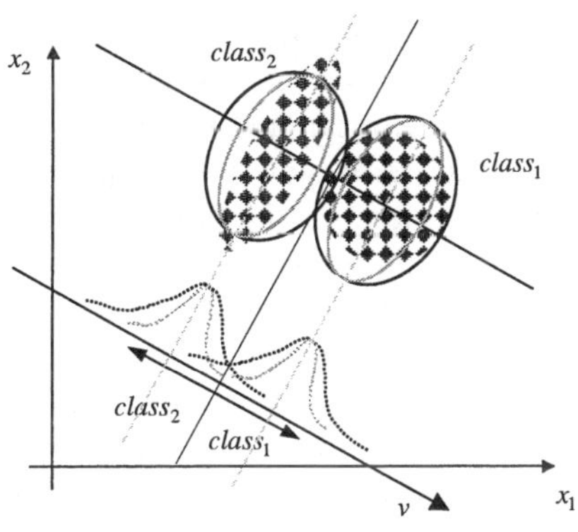

Fig. 1. Geometric idea of the new LDA-based method.

Figure 1 illustrates the geometric idea of the new S_p reguralisation on a two-dimensional feature space. The constant probability density contours of a well-defined S_p and S_p^* for two hypothetical "Gaussian-like" sample classes are represented respectively by the grey and black ellipses. As can be seen, the new regularisation expands S_p and increases slightly the two classes overlap. However, the same optimum linear mapping v would be found by a Fisher's criterion based on the within-class variability given by S_p or S_p^*.

The main idea of the NLDA can be summarised as follows. In limited sample size and high dimensional problems where the within-class scatter matrix is singular or poorly estimated, it is reasonable to expect that the Fisher's linear basis found by minimizing a more difficult "inflated" within-class S_p^* estimate would also minimize a less reliable "shrivelled" within-class S_p estimate.

4 Experiments

In order to evaluate the effectiveness of our new LDA (NLDA) on face recognition, comparisons with LDA (when possible), Fisherfaces, CLDA, DLDA, and YLDA, were performed using the ORL and FERET face databases.

The ORL database contains a set of face images taken between April 1992 and April 1994 at the Olivetti Research Laboratory in Cambridge, U.K., with ten images for each of 40 individuals, a total of 400 images. All images were taken against a dark homogeneous background with the person in an upright frontal position, with tolerance for some tilting and rotation up to about 20 degrees. Scale varies about 10%.

The FERET database is the US Face Recognition Technology facial database that has become the standard data set for benchmark studies. Sets containing 4 "frontal b series" images for each of 200 total subjects were considered. Each image set is composed of a regular facial expression (referred as "ba" images in the FERET database), an alternative expression ("bj" images), and two symmetric images ("be" and "bf" images) taken with the intention of investigating 15 degrees pose angle effects.

A simple Euclidean distance classifier was used to perform classification in the projective feature space, analogously to the other approaches we investigated. Each experiment was repeated 25 times using several features. Distinct training and test sets were randomly drawn, and the mean and standard deviation of the recognition rate were calculated. The ORL classification was computed using for each individual 5 images to train and 5 images to test. In the FERET database, the training and test sets were respectively composed of 3 and 1 images. For implementation convenience, the ORL face images were resized to 32x32 pixels, representing a recognition problem where the within-class scatter matrix is singular. The FERET images were resized to 16x16 pixels in order to pose an alternative pattern recognition problem where the within-class scatter matrix is non-singular but poorly estimated.

To determine the number of principal components to be retained in the intermediate step of Fisherfaces, experimental analyses were carried out based on the best classification accuracy of several PCA features in between the corresponding interval $(g, N-g)$. In order to determine the number of YLDA optimal discriminant vectors derived from the within-scatter matrix eigenvectors space, we used for the ORL experiments the eigenvectors corresponding to the first 10 largest eigenvalues, as suggested by Yang and Yang's work [15]. For the FERET database, the eigenvectors corresponding to the first 20 largest eigenvectors were sufficient to determine the respective YLDA optimal discriminant vectors.

5 Results

Tables 1 and 2 present the maximum test average recognition rates (with standard deviations) of the ORL and FERET databases over the corresponding number of PCA (when applicable) and LDA features.

Table 1. ORL (32x32 pixels) results.

Method	Features PCA	Features LDA	Recognition Rate
Fisherfaces	60	39	94.9% (1.9%)
YLDA	199	45	96.1% (1.4%)
LDA	-	-	-
CLDA		39	95.4% (1.5%)
DLDA		39	94.9% (1.6%)
NLDA		39	95.8% (1.6%)

Table 2. FERET (16x16 pixels) results.

Method	Features PCA	Features LDA	Recognition Rate
Fisherfaces	200	20	91.5% (1.9%)
YLDA	256	92	94.7% (1.4%)
LDA		20	86.2% (1.9%)
CLDA		20	86.2% (1.9%)
DLDA		20	94.5% (1.3%)
NLDA		10	95.4% (1.4%)

Table 1 shows that the new LDA (NLDA) led to higher classification accuracies than the other one-stage approaches. The overall best classification result was reached by Yang and Yang's approach (YLDA) – 96.1% (1.4%) – which was not significantly greater than the NLDA one – 95.8% (1.6%). However, the YLDA used a much larger two-stage linear transformation matrix compared to the one-stage methods. In terms of how sensitive the NLDA results were to the choice of the training and test sets, it is fair to say that the new LDA standard deviations were similar to the other methods.

Table 2 presents the results of the FERET database. In this application, the within-class scatter was non-singular but poorly estimated and the standard LDA (LDA) could be applied directly on the face images. As can be seen, the overall best classification result was achieved by NLDA – 95.4% (1.4%) – using only 10 features. Again, regarding the standard deviations, NLDA showed to be as sensitive to the choice of the training and test sets as the other compared approaches.

6 Conclusion

In this paper, a new LDA-based method (NLDA) was introduced. It is a one-stage straightforward regularisation approach that overcomes the singularity and instability of the within-class scatter matrix when the standard LDA is applied directly in limited sample and high dimensional problems. Although regularisation has been used before, our method is based on selection and therefore avoids the computational costs inherent to the commonly used optimisation processes.

Experiments were carried out to evaluate this approach on face recognition, using the well-known ORL and FERET databases. Comparisons with similar methods, such as Fisherfaces [1,17], Chen et al.'s [2], Yu and Yang's [16], and Yang and Yang's [15] LDA-based methods, were made. In both databases, our method improved the LDA classification performance without a PCA intermediate step and using less discriminant features. Regarding the sensitivity to the choice of the training and test sets, the new LDA gave a similar performance to the compared approaches.

Although in face recognition 32x32 images with at least 4 bits per pixel is sufficient for identification [11], it is possible that memory computation problems would arise when scatter matrices larger than 1024x1024 elements are used. Despite this possibility, we believe that the new LDA regularisation approach might be suitable for solving not only the singularity and instability issues of the linear Fisher methods, but also the non-linear Fisher Discriminant Analysis with Kernels [8].

Acknowledgment

The first author was partially supported by the Brazilian Government Agency CAPES under grant No. 1168/99-1. Also, portions of the research in this paper use the FERET database of facial images collected under the FERET program.

References

1. P. N. Belhumeur, J. P. Hespanha, and D. J. Kriegman, "Eigenfaces vs. Fisherfaces: Recognition Using Class Specific Linear Projection", *IEEE Trans. Pattern Analysis and Machine Intelligence*, vol. 19, no. 7, pp. 711-720, 1997.
2. L. Chen, H. Liao, M. Ko, J. Lin, and G. Yu, "A new LDA-based face recognition system which can solve the small sample size problem", *Pattern Recognition*, 33 (10), pp. 1713-1726, 2000.
3. J. H. Friedman, "Reguralized discriminant analysis", *Journal of the American Statistical Association*, vol. 84, no. 405, pp. 165-175, March 1989.
4. K. Fukunaga, *Introduction to Statistical Pattern Recognition*, Academic Press, New York, 1990.
5. T. Greene and W. S. Rayens, "Covariance pooling and stabilization for classification", *Computational Statistics & Data Analysis*, vol. 11, pp. 17-42, 1991.
6. A. K. Jain and B. Chandrasekaran, "Dimensionality and sample size considerations in pattern recognition practice", *Handbook of Statistics*, P. R. Krishnaiah and L. N. Kanal Eds., North Holland, vol. 2, pp. 835-855, 1982.
7. K. Liu, Y. Cheng, and J. Yang, "Algebraic feature extraction for image recognition based on an optimal discriminant criterion", *Pattern Recognition*, 26 (6), pp. 903-911, 1993.
8. S. Mika, G. Ratsch, J. Weston, B. Scholkopf, and K.–R. Muller, "Fisher discriminant analysis with kernels", *IEEE Neural Networks for Signal Processing IX*, pp. 41-48, 1999.
9. F. O'Sullivan, "A Statistical Perspective on Ill-Posed Inverse Problems", *Statistical Science*, vol. 1, pp. 502-527, 1986.
10. W. S. Rayens, "A Role for Covariance Stabilization in the Construction of the Classical Mixture Surface", *Journal of Chemometrics*, vol. 4, pp. 159-169, 1990.
11. A. Samal and P. Iyengar, "Automatic Recognition and Analysis of Human Faces and Facial Expressions: A Survey", Pattern Recognition, 25 (1), pp. 65-77, 1992.
12. D. L. Swets and J. J. Weng, "Using Discriminant Eigenfeatures for Image Retrieval", *IEEE Trans. Pattern Analysis and Machine Intelligence*, vol. 18, no. 8, pp. 831-836, 1996.

13. C. E. Thomaz, D. F. Gillies, and R. Q. Feitosa, "A New Quadratic Classifier applied to Biometric Recognition", *Proc.of the Post-ECCV Workshop on Biometric Authentication, Springer-Verlag LNCS 2359*, pp. 186-196, Copenhagen, Denmark, June 2002
14. M. Turk and A. Pentland, "Eigenfaces for Recognition", Journal of Cognitive Neuroscience 3, pp. 71-86, 1991.
15. J. Yang and J. Yang, "Why can LDA be performed in PCA transformed space?", *Pattern Recognition*, vol. 36, pp. 563-566, 2003.
16. H. Yu and J. Yang, "A direct LDA algorithm for high dimensional data – with application to face recognition", *Pattern Recognition*, vol. 34, pp. 2067-2070, 2001.
17. W. Zhao, R. Chellappa, and A. Krishnaswamy, "Discriminant Analysis of Principal Components for Face Recognition", *Proc. 2nd Int'l. Conference on Automatic Face and Gesture Recognition*, pp. 336-341, 1998.

Merging Subspace Models for Face Recognition

Władysław Skarbek

Faculty of Electronics and Information Technology
Warsaw University of Technology
W.Skarbek@ire.pw.edu.pl

Abstract. The merging problem for principal subspace (PS) models is considered in the form: given two principal subspace models $\mathcal{M}_i$ for independent training data sequences, assuming that the original data is not available, find the subspace model for the union of the original data sets. The principal subspace merging (PSM) algorithm and its approximated version (APSM) are proposed to solve the problem. The accuracy and the complexity of the approach has been mathematically analyzed and verified on face image models. If data vectors are modeled by projections into a linear subspace of dimension r in N dimensional feature space then the algorithm has $O(r(4N^2 + 13r^2))$ time complexity.

1 Introduction

In multivariate data analysis, the principal component analysis (PCA) is one of the most popular methods (cf. [4]). PCA is a procedure which finds for the data matrix (vector data sequence) $X = [x_1, \ldots, x_L]$, the principal subspace model $\mathcal{M}(X)$. In image analysis projections to relatively low dimensional principal subspace is used as compact representation for modeling images of objects such as human faces. The model can be used for recognition object's identity (e.g. face recognition) or its specific features (e.g. face location, face pose).

Suppose that there are two subspace models $\mathcal{M}(X_i)$ which have been produced for two independent training collections $X_i \in \mathbb{R}^{N \times L_i}$, $i = 1, 2$. We want to establish the new subspace model $\mathcal{M}(X)$ for the join $X = [X_1, X_2]$ of the training data. The question can be raised: can we use both models to build the joined subspace model without accessing to the original data ? This paper shows that the answer is positive.

The above scenario can happen in context of using PCA based face recognition descriptor included in MPEG-7 standard (cf. [1]) when somebody wishes to improve recognition rate on his/her data using facial MPEG-7 descriptor but with extended model by training it on the new data. However, the MPEG-7 facial data base is not available for public use and the subspace model as part of MPEG-7 standard can be only used.

The merging algorithm of two principal subspace models is based on computing singular subspace model for a new data sequence which is generated using only information contained in input models.

The paper is organized as follows. In sections 2 and 3 necessary definitions are reminded and useful properties are presented. The algorithm for merging

N. Petkov and M.A. Westenberg (Eds.): CAIP 2003, LNCS 2756, pp. 606–613, 2003.

principal subspaces is given in section 4 and its approximated version in section 5. Description of experiments, conclusions, and references are the last sections of the paper.

2 Principal Subspace Data Model

The principal subspace model $\mathcal{M}(X)$ of the data matrix $X = [x_1, \ldots, x_L]$, $x_i \in \mathbb{R}^N$ defines parameters describing the ascending family of principal subspaces:

$$S_0(X) \subset S_1(X) \subset S_M(X) \subset \cdots \subset S_{N-1}(X) \subset S_N(X) = \mathbb{R}^N .$$

The principal subspace $S_M(X)$ is the M-dimensional hyperplane which is the best linear approximation of data sequence X, i.e. the mean squared error of orthogonal projection P_M of X onto S_M is minimum for all M dimensional affine subspaces included in $\mathbb{R}^N$. The affine subspace of dimension M can be created by the linear translation of the linear subspace which is spanned by M independent vectors.

The properties 1 explain how the principal subspace model can be built using eigenvalue decomposition of the covariance matrix $R(X) = (X - \overline{X})(X - \overline{X})^t/L$, where the vector $\overline{X} = \sum_{i=1}^{L} x_i/L$ and the matrix $X - \overline{X}$ is built from X by subtracting from each of its column the vector $\overline{X}$.

Properties 1. Principal Subspace Model
Let $R(X) = U\Lambda U^t$ be the reduced eigenvalue decomposition of the covariance matrix $R(X)$, i.e. $r = rank(R(X))$, $U \in \mathbb{R}^{N\times r}$, $\Lambda = diag(\lambda_1, \ldots, \lambda_r) \in \mathbb{R}^{r\times r}$, $\lambda_1 \geq \cdots \geq \lambda_r > 0$. Let also $U = [u_1, \ldots, u_r]$, $U_M = [u_1, \ldots, u_M]$ for $M = 1, \ldots, r$. Then

1. *The zero dimensional subspace consists of the mean vector: $S_0(X) = \{\overline{X}\}$*
2. *For $1 \leq M \leq r$ the M dimensional principal subspace is spanned by columns of U_M and shifted by mean vector: $S_M(X) = \overline{X} + span(U_M)$*
3. *For $r < M \leq N$ the M dimensional principal subspace $S_M(X)$ is any M dimensional linear subspace shifted by $\overline{X}$ which includes $S_r(X)$: $S_M(X) = \overline{X} + span(U_M)$ where $U_M = [U_r, U_{M-r}^{\perp}]$, and $U_{M-r}^{\perp} \in \mathbb{R}^{N\times(M-r)}$ is arbitrary orthonormal matrix orthogonal to U_r.*
4. *The variance of the projected data $P_M X$, $M \leq r$, depends only on first M eigenvalues: $var(P_M X) = \|P_M X - \overline{X}\|_F^2/L = \sum_{i=1}^{M} \lambda_i$*
5. *The variance for the error $X - P_M X$ of projected data, $M \leq r$, depends only on ending $r - M$ eigenvalues: $var(X - P_M X) = \|X - P_M X\|_F^2/L = \sum_{i=M+1}^{r} \lambda_i$*
6. *If we consider the principal subspace $S_{r(\epsilon)}$ with error $\epsilon < 1$, where*
$$r(\epsilon) \doteq \arg \min_{1\leq M\leq r} [\|X - P_M X\|_F^2 \leq L\epsilon] \tag{1}$$
and the covariance matrix $R(X(\epsilon))$ for the projected data $X(\epsilon) \doteq P_{r(\epsilon)}X$ included in $S_{r(\epsilon)}$ then $R(X(\epsilon)) = U_{r(\epsilon)}\Lambda_{r(\epsilon)}U_{r(\epsilon)}^t$ and the covariance matrix change measured by the squared Frobenius norm is bounded by ϵ :
$$\|R(X) - R(X(\epsilon))\|_F^2 \leq \epsilon \tag{2}$$

Hence the principal subspace model for L element data vector sample X can be specified by $\mathcal{M}(X) = (\overline{X}, U, \Lambda, L)$. Though the principal subspace is uniquely defined by its anchor point $\overline{X}$ and local orthonormal base U, we extend the model by information on data variances for each principal axis Λ and the original number of data vectors. Both elements will be useful at merging principal subspaces for different data sequences. Note, that the memory overhead for this elements is a fraction of the basic storage requirement equal to $(r+1)/(N(r+1)) = 1/N$ which is negligible for N encountered in image processing applications.

In applications such as face recognition usually we retain not full model, but its ϵ approximation $\mathcal{M}(X(\epsilon)) = (\overline{X}, U_{r(\epsilon)}, \Lambda_{r(\epsilon)}, L, \epsilon)$.

3 Singular Subspace Data Model

Similarly to the principal subspace model, the singular subspace model $\mathcal{M}'(X)$ of the data matrix $X = [x_1, \ldots, x_L]$, $x_i \in \mathbb{R}^N$ defines parameters describing the ascending family of singular linear subspaces:

$$S'_0(X) = \{0\} \subset S'_1(X) \subset S'_M(X) \subset \cdots \subset S'_r(X) = \text{span}(X) ,$$

where $r = \text{rank}(X)$.

The singular subspace $S'_M(X)$ is the M-dimensional subspace which is the best linear approximation of the data sequence X, i.e. the mean squared error of orthogonal projection P_M of X onto S_M is minimum for all M dimensional linear subspaces included in $\mathbb{R}^N$.

While the principal subspace for X is associated with eigenvalue decomposition of the covariance matrix $R(X)$, the singular subspace associates to the correlation matrix $C(X) = XX^t/L$.

The following properties explain also how the singular subspaces can be found using eigenvalue decomposition of $C(X)$:

Properties 2. Singular Subspace Model
Let $C(X) = U\Lambda U^t$ be the reduced eigenvalue decomposition of the matrix $C(X)$, i.e. $r = \text{rank}(X)$, $U \in \mathbb{R}^{N\times r}$, $\Lambda = \text{diag}(\lambda_1, \ldots, \lambda_r) \in \mathbb{R}^{r\times r}$, $\lambda_1 \geq \cdots \geq \lambda_r > 0$. Let also $U = [u_1, \ldots, u_r]$, $U_M = [u_1, \ldots, u_M]$ for $M = 1, \ldots, r$. Then

1. *For $1 \leq M \leq r$ the M dimensional singular subspace is spanned by columns of U_M : $S'_M(X) = \text{span}(U_M)$*
2. *The mean of squared norms for the projected data $P_M X$, $M \leq r$, depends only on first M eigenvalues: $\|P_M X\|_F^2/L = \sum_{i=1}^M \lambda_i$*
3. *The mean of squared norms for errors $X - P_M X$, $M \leq r$, depends only on ending $r - M$ eigenvalues: $\|X - P_M X\|_F^2/L = \sum_{i=M+1}^r \lambda_i$*
4. *If we consider the singular subspace $S'_{r(\epsilon)}$ with error $\epsilon < 1$, where*

$$r(\epsilon) \doteq \arg \min_{1\leq M\leq r} [\|X - P_M X\|_F^2 \leq L\epsilon] \tag{3}$$

and the correlation matrix $C(X(\epsilon))$ for the projected data onto $S'_{r(\epsilon)}$ then $C(X(\epsilon)) = U_{r(\epsilon)}\Lambda_{r(\epsilon)}U^t_{r(\epsilon)}$ and the correlation matrix change measured by the squared Frobenius norm is bounded by ϵ:

$$\|C(X) - C(X(\epsilon))\|_F^2 \leq \epsilon \tag{4}$$

5. *Let* $Y = [y_1, \ldots, y_L]$, *where* $y_i \doteq x_i - \overline{X}$. *Then* $C(Y) = R(X)$ *and singular subspaces for* Y *are obtained from principal subspaces of the same dimension using translation by the vector* $-\overline{X}$: $S'_M(Y) = S_M(X) - \overline{X}$, $M = 0, 1, \ldots, r$, $r = rank(X)$.

For large data vector dimension N and long data sequence computing $C(X)$ is costly in both time and space resource. More efficient is computing singular subspaces using Singular Value Decomposition (SVD) method directly for the data matrix $X = U\Sigma V^t$, where U is defined in the properties 2 ($C(X) = U\Lambda U^t$), $\Sigma \doteq \sqrt{L}\Lambda^{1/2} = \text{diag}(\sqrt{L\lambda_1}, \ldots, \sqrt{L\lambda_r})$, $V \doteq X^t U \Sigma^{-1}$.

Obviously, the matrix V is orthonormal: $V^t V = \Sigma^{-1} U^t X X^t U \Sigma^{-1} = \Sigma^{-1} U^t (LU\Lambda U^t U)\Sigma^{-1} = \Sigma^{-1} IL\Lambda I \Sigma^{-1} = \Sigma^{-1}\Sigma^2\Sigma^{-1} = I$.

Using the singular subspace of the dimension $r(\epsilon) < r$ we get the data matrix $X(\epsilon) \doteq P_{r(\epsilon)} X$ for which SVD is called the singular value ϵ approximation (SVA) of the original data matrix X. It can be shown that:

$$X(\epsilon) = U_{r(\epsilon)} \Sigma_{r(\epsilon)} V^t_{r(\epsilon)} \tag{5}$$

The mathematical properties of SVA are given below.

Properties 3. Singular Value Approximation

1. *The coefficients of the projected vector* $P_M x_i$ *in the base* U_M *can be obtained by scaling the columns of* V_M : $U_M^t X = \Sigma_M V_M^t$
2. *The column* v_i *of the matrix* V_M *can be obtained by scaling the coefficients of the projected vector* $P_M x_i$ *in the base* $U_M, i = 1, \ldots, M$: $V_M = \Sigma_M^{-1}(U_M^t X)^t$.
3. *The singular value* ϵ *approximation* $X(\epsilon)$ *of data matrix* X *based on singular subspace of dimension* $r(\epsilon)$ *differs in squared Frobenius norm from the original matrix not more than* $L\epsilon$:

$$\|X - X(\epsilon)\|_F^2 = \sum_{i=r(\epsilon)+1}^{r} \sigma_i^2 = L \sum_{i=r(\epsilon)+1}^{r} \lambda_i < L\epsilon \tag{6}$$

4. *The singular value* ϵ *approximation* $X(\epsilon)$ *is the closest to* X *matrix of rank* $r(\epsilon)$ *in matrix space* $\mathbb{R}^{N\times L}$ *with Frobenius norm.*

4 Principal Subspace Merge

The following algorithm describes merging process for principal subspace models.

Algorithm 1. PSM - Principal Subspace Merge
Input: $\mathcal{M}_i = (\overline{X_i}, U^{(i)}, \Lambda^{(i)}, L_i)$, $i = 1, 2$, $r = rank(R(X_1)) + rank(R(X_2)) + 1$.
Output: $\mathcal{M} = \mathcal{M}(X) = (\overline{X}, U, \Lambda, L)$ *for unknown* $X = [X_1, X_2]$.

Method:

1. *Compute total number of training data:* $L = L_1 + L_2$
2. *Compute model merging weights:* $\alpha_1 = L_1/L;\ \alpha_2 = L_2/L$
3. *Compute the joined mean vector:* $\overline{X} = \alpha_1\overline{X_1} + \alpha_2\overline{X_2}$
4. *Generate artificial training data:*

$$Y = \left[\sqrt{\alpha_1}U^{(1)}(\Lambda^{(1)})^{1/2}, \sqrt{\alpha_2}U^{(2)}(\Lambda^{(2)})^{1/2}, \sqrt{\alpha_1\alpha_2}(\overline{X_1} - \overline{X_2})\right] ,$$

5. *Find the singular value decomposition for* $Y : Y = U\Sigma V^t,\ U \in \mathbb{R}^{N\times rank(Y)}$, $\Sigma \in \mathbb{R}^{rank(Y)\times rank(Y)}$
6. *Compute eigenvalues for the merged model:* $\Lambda = \Sigma^2$
7. *Return principal subspace model for* $X : \mathcal{M} = (\overline{X}, U, \Lambda, L)$

The correctness of merged subspace parameters in the above algorithm follows from the following observations collected in the next lemma.

Lemma 1. On Correctness of PSM Algorithm

1. *Covariance by correlation:* $R(X) = C(X) - \overline{X}\,\overline{X}^t$
2. *Recursive relation for mean:* $\overline{X} = (L_1\overline{X_1} + L_2\overline{X_2})/L$.
3. *Recursive relation for correlation matrix:* $C(X) = \alpha_1 C(X_1) + \alpha_2 C(X_2)$.
4. *Recursive relation for outer product of mean vector:*

$$\overline{X}\,\overline{X}^t = \alpha_1^2\overline{X_1}\,\overline{X_1}^t + \alpha_1\alpha_2\overline{X_1}\,\overline{X_2}^t + \alpha_1\alpha_2\overline{X_2}\,\overline{X_1}^t + \alpha_2^2\overline{X_1}\,\overline{X_1}^t$$

5. *Recursive relation for covariance matrix:*

$$R(X) = \alpha_1 R(X_1) + \alpha_2 R(X_2) + \alpha_1\alpha_2(\overline{X_1} - \overline{X_2})(\overline{X_1} - \overline{X_2})^t$$

6. *Equality of second order statistics:* $C(\sqrt{r}Y) = R(X)$
7. *Final corollary: the singular subspace for* Y *shifted by* $\overline{X}$ *is the principal subspace for* X.

The execution time of PSM algorithm is dominated by SVD algorithm used in step (5). Using the modified Goloub-Reinsch algorithm (cf. [3, 5]) which is especially fast when the number of columns r in Y is small relatively to N, we have the time complexity $O(r(4N^2 + 13r^2))$.

5 Approximated Principal Subspace Merge

In image analysis applications ϵ approximation of principal subspaces are used. Usually relatively small dimension $r(\epsilon)$ is useful for recognition tasks. For instance in MPEG-7 version of face recognition descriptor $r(\epsilon) = 48$ for facial images with more than two thousands pixels.

The following algorithm describes approximated merging process for approximated principal subspace models. The approximation is controlled by ϵ_1, ϵ_2, respectively for the input models and ϵ_3 for the output model.

Algorithm 2. APSM - Approximated Principal Subspace Merge
Input: $\mathcal{M}(X_i(\epsilon_i)) = (\overline{X_i}, U^{(i)}_{r_i(\epsilon_i)}, \Lambda^{(i)}_{r_i(\epsilon_i)}, L_i, \epsilon_i)$, $i = 1, 2$, $r = r_1(\epsilon_1) + r_2(\epsilon_2) + 1$, $\epsilon_3 > 0$
Output: $\mathcal{M} = \mathcal{M}(\tilde{X}(\epsilon_3)) = (\overline{X}, U, \Lambda, L, \epsilon 3)$ *for unknown* $\tilde{X} \doteq [X_1(\epsilon_1), X_2(\epsilon_2)]$ *and the bound* ϵ_b *for the approximation error of this model for the data sequence* $X = [X_1, X_2]$.
Method:

1. *Compute total number of training data:* $L = L_1 + L_2$
2. *Compute model merging weights:* $\alpha_1 = L_1/L$; $\alpha_2 = L_2/L$
3. *Compute the joined mean vector:* $\overline{X} = \alpha_1 \overline{X_1} + \alpha_2 \overline{X_2}$
4. *Generate artificial training data* Y :

$$Y_1 = \sqrt{\alpha_1} U^{(1)}_{r_1(\epsilon_1)} (\Lambda^{(1)}_{r_1(\epsilon_1)})^{1/2}, \; Y_2 = \sqrt{\alpha_2} U^{(2)}_{r_2(\epsilon_2)} (\Lambda^{(2)}_{r_2(\epsilon_2)})^{1/2}$$
$$Y = \left[Y_1, Y_2, \sqrt{\alpha_1 \alpha_2}(\overline{X_1} - \overline{X_2})\right]$$

5. *Find the singular value* ϵ_3 *approximation for* Y :
   (a) *Find the singular value decomposition for* Y : $Y = U \Sigma V^t$
   (b) *Establish the number of significant singular values:*

$$r_3(\epsilon_3) \doteq \arg \min_{1 \leq i \leq r} [\sigma^2_{i+1} + \cdots + \sigma^2_r \leq \epsilon]$$

   (c) *Compute the singular* ϵ_3 *approximation* $U_{r_3(\epsilon_3)}, \Sigma_{r_3}$ *by choosing first* r_3 *columns in* U *and* Σ, *respectively*
6. *Compute eigenvalues for the merged model:* $\Lambda_{r_3(\epsilon_3)} = \Sigma^2_{r_3(\epsilon_3)}$
7. *Return the approximated principal subspace model for* X :

$$\mathcal{M} = (\overline{X}, U_{r_3(\epsilon_3)}, \Lambda_{r_3(\epsilon_3)}, L)$$

8. *Compute the error bound:* $\epsilon_b = 2(\alpha_1 \epsilon_1 + \alpha_2 \epsilon_2 + \epsilon_3)$.

The correctness of merged subspace parameters in APSM algorithm follows from the facts demonstrated in the next lemma.

Lemma 2. On Correctness of APSM Algorithm

1. *The mean is invariant to subspace projections:* $\overline{X(\epsilon)} = \overline{X}$
2. *Global projection error bound:* $\|X - X(\epsilon)\|_F \leq \sqrt{L\epsilon}$
3. *Correspondence of second order statistics for unknown and artificially generated data:*

$$R(X_i(\epsilon_i)) = C(\sqrt{r_i} Y_i(\epsilon_i)), \; i = 1, 2, \; R(\tilde{X}(\epsilon_3)) = C(\sqrt{r} Y(\epsilon_3))$$

4. *Let* $[X_1(\epsilon_1)(\epsilon_3), X_2(\epsilon_2)(\epsilon_3)] \doteq \tilde{X}(\epsilon_3)$. *Then*

$$\|X - \tilde{X}(\epsilon_3)\|^2_F = \|X_1 - X_1(\epsilon_1)(\epsilon_3)\|^2_F + \|X_2 - X_2(\epsilon_2)(\epsilon_3)\|^2_F$$

5. *The bound of combined projection error by one step projection errors for* $i = 1, 2:$

$$\|X_i - X_i(\epsilon_i)(\epsilon_3)\|_F^2 \leq 2\left(\|X_i - X_i(\epsilon_i)\|_F^2 + \|X_i(\epsilon_i) - X_i(\epsilon_i)(\epsilon_3)\|_F^2\right)$$

6. *Gathering projection errors:*

$$\|X_1(\epsilon_1) - X_1(\epsilon_1)(\epsilon_3)\|_F^2 + \|X_2(\epsilon_2) - X_2(\epsilon_2)(\epsilon_3)\|_F^2 = \|\tilde{X} - \tilde{X}(\epsilon_3)\|_F^2$$

7. *The average squared error* $\|X - \tilde{X}(\epsilon_3)\|_F^2/L$ *between original merged unknown data and combined projections of unknown data is bounded by* $2(\alpha_1\epsilon_1 + \alpha_2\epsilon_2 + \epsilon_3):$

$$\|X - \tilde{X}(\epsilon_3)\|_F^2/L \leq 2(\alpha_1\epsilon_1 + \alpha_2\epsilon_2 + \epsilon_3)$$

8. *The bound for the mean squared error of the projection of the unknown data* $X = [X_1, X_2]$ *onto the* ϵ_3 *approximation of principal subspace found for data* $\tilde{X} = [X_1(\epsilon_1), X_2(\epsilon_2]:$

$$\|X - P_{r_3(\epsilon_3)}X\|_F^2/L \leq 2(\alpha_1\epsilon_1 + \alpha_2\epsilon_2 + \epsilon_3) \quad (7)$$

9. *If modeling errors are* $\epsilon_1 = \epsilon_2 = \epsilon_3 = \epsilon/4$ *then the average error for the projected data in the merged model is bounded by* ϵ.

The execution time of APSM algorithm is dominated by SVA algorithm used in step (5). Using the Modified Goloub-Reinsch algorithm (cf. [3, 5]) for SVD step we have the time complexity $O(r(4N^2 + 13r^2))$. In case of MPEG-7 model where $r \approx 100$ and $N \approx 2500$, the time complexity formula can be approximated by $O(rN^2)$.

6 Experiments

We considered several subspace models for merging: the principal subspace model built for training data used in MPEG-7 core experiments conducted for version 1 of face descriptor and other principal subspace models built for training part of Altkom database used in VCE for version 2 of the descriptor (cf.[1, 2]).

The table 1 shows the results of experiments for principal subspace dimensions $M_1 = 48$ (fixed in MPEG-7 standard) $M_2 = 30, 48, 60, 100$. The column "Bits" gives the number of bits used in the target descriptor (5 bits per component is used) The column "Time(build-merge)" gives the time in seconds of building the target model when data for input models is known and unknown, respectively. The column "Error(build-merge-bound)" gives the subspace projection mean squared error per one image pixel when the model is obtained on the original merged data (part "build") and by merging models (part "merge") with theoretical error bound (part "bound") computed by the formula (7). The last column gives percent loss of accuracy of the approximated data model.

The experiments with face image retrieval conducted for all computed models show consistently little decrease of performance for merged models but on very low level. Namely for descriptor size less than 250 bits the drop is less than 0.1% while for 500 bits it is less than one percent.

Table 1. The performance of APSM algorithm

M_2	M_3	Bits	Time(b-m)	Error(b-m-b)	δE[%]
30	30	150	450-5.7	582-583-1182	0.2
30	40	200	450-5.7	491-493-1022	0.4
48	48	240	450-7.1	439-441-902	0.4
48	58	290	450-7.1	388-395-849	1.8
70	70	350	450-8.9	342-355-793	3.8
70	80	400	450-8.9	312-330-768	5.8
100	100	500	450-11.4	266-291-719	9.4
100	110	550	450-11.4	248-276-705	11.3

7 Conclusions

The principal subspace merge is important for applications where original data is not available. For full rank subspaces the PSM algorithm builds the model without representation error. For subspaces with approximation error, the APSM algorithm gives very good approximation of the exact model. In face modeling the increase of the representation error is less than two percent. In this application, the PSM and APSM algorithms are very fast. When descriptor size is less than 300 bits, the speed-up of the model computing for merged data is about 50 times. For such compact descriptor size, the recognition performance drop is negligible.

References

1. Information technology - Multimedia content description interface - Part 3: Visual, Part 8: Extraction and Use. ISO/IEC FDIS 15938-[1-8]:2002 (E) (2002)
2. Bober M., Description of MPEG-7 Visual Core Experiments, ISO/IEC JTC1/SC29/WG11, report N4925, July 2002, Klagenfurt.
3. Chan T.F., Improved Algorithm for Computing the Singular Value Decomposition, ACM Transactions on Mathematical Software, **8** (1982) 72-83
4. Jolliffe I.T., Principal Component Analysis. New York: Springer, 2002
5. Golub G., Van Loan C., Matrix Computations. Baltimore: Johns Hopkins University Press, 1996

A Face Processing System Based on Committee Machine: The Approach and Experimental Results

Kim-Fung Jang, Ho-Man Tang, Michael R. Lyu, and Irwin King

Department of Computer Science and Engineering
The Chinese University of Hong Kong
Shatin N.T. Hong Kong
{kfjang,hmtang,lyu,king}@cse.cuhk.edu.hk

Abstract. In this paper, we propose a heterogeneous committee machine for face processing including face detection and recognition. Our proposed system consists of two components, Face Detection Committee Machine (FDCM) and Face Recognition Committee Machine (FRCM), which employs three and five well-known state-of-the-art approaches respectively. We engage different methodologies to solve the face detection and face recognition problems. We provide a rigorous architecture set-up and experimentation protocol to demonstrate the improved performance of FDCM and FRCM over the individual experts.

1 Introduction

In recent years, the committee machine, an ensemble of estimators, has proven to give more accurate results than the use of a single predictor. The basic idea is to train a committee of estimators and combine the individual predictions to achieve improved generalization performance. Different approaches are proposed by researchers within the last ten years such as ensemble averaging, bagging, gating network and hierarchical mixtures of experts [1]. Recently, researchers have applied the committee machine in face processing, Gutta et al. used an ensemble of Radial Basis Function (RBF) network and decision tree in the face processing problem [2]. Huang et al. formulated an ensemble of neural networks for pose invariant face recognition [3].

Previous researchers applied homogeneous experts (neural networks or RBF) trained by different training data sets to arrive at a union decision. However, no one has yet focused on heterogeneous experts on face detection and recognition problems in the current status. We propose the engagement of committee machine with heterogeneous experts in this paper. This is the first effort to employ different state-of-the-art algorithms as heterogeneous experts on committee machines in face detection and recognition. We include neural networks (NN), Sparse Network of Winnows (SNoW) algorithm, and SVM in face detection to validate any possible face images. In face recognition, we investigate Eigenface, Fisherface, EGM, SVM and NN to classify a face image. All the algorithms

N. Petkov and M.A. Westenberg (Eds.): CAIP 2003, LNCS 2756, pp. 614–622, 2003.

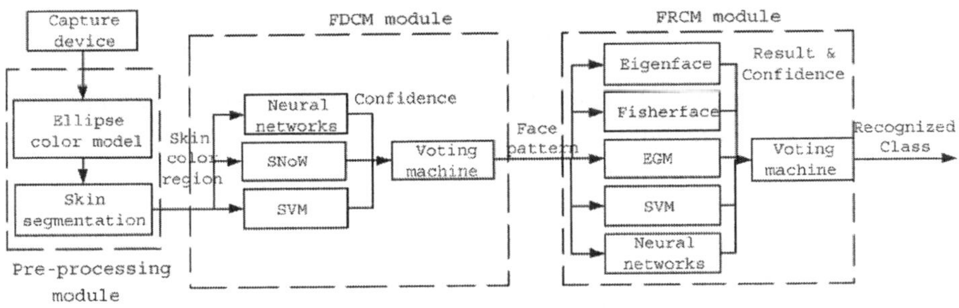

Fig. 1. The system architecture

used are well-known in the field. The results based on the committee machine approach are satisfactory.

2 Background

Within these few years, numerous face detection and recognition methods were proposed by researchers. Turk and Pentland applied Principal Component Analysis (PCA) to face detection [4]. In [5], Rowley et al. used neural networks to learn face and non-face patterns for face detection. Support Vector Machine (SVM) was studied by [6] and demonstrated for the success in detecting frontal faces. Roth et al. proposed Sparse Network of Winnows algorithm [7], which applied the primitive feature space for the learning process. Among the face recognition methods, Eigenface [8] is the most popular one due to its effectiveness. It made use of PCA to find a feature space for projection of face images. A similar approach, Fisherface [9], was proposed later which makes use of Fisher's Linear Discriminant (FLD) instead of PCA. Apart from template matching approaches, Elastic Graph Matching (EGM) [10] was proposed to take into account the human facial features by extracting the features with Gabor wavelet transform. Recently, SVM [11] has gained a wider acceptance in face recognition and were proven with impressive result.

3 A Face Processing System

We propose a face processing system consisting of three main modules: 1) Pre-processing, 2) **Face Detection** and 3) **Face Recognition**. The system architecture is shown in Fig. 1. We employ the color model to reduce the search space for face finding in the Face Detection module. The detected face is then passed to the Face Recognition module for further recognition.

3.1 Pre-processing

Firstly, image data from the capture device or video file are transformed from RGB color model to YCrCb color model. In many studies, human skin color is

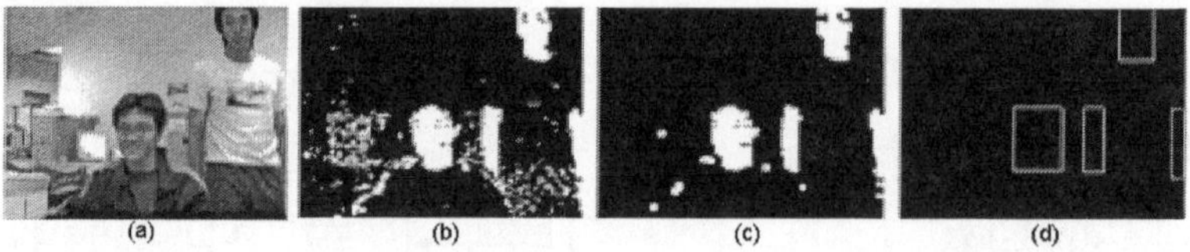

Fig. 2. The image for (*a*) original image, (*b*) binary skin mask, (*c*) binary skin mask after morphological operation and (*d*) face candidates are found

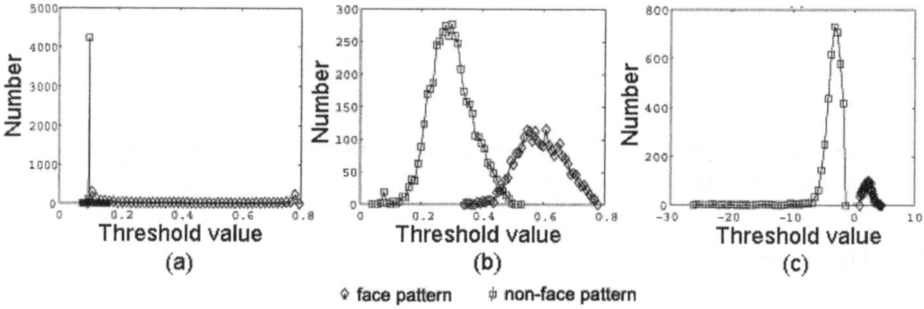

Fig. 3. The distribution of confident value of the training data from *(a)* NN, *(b)* SNoW and *(c)* SVM

not a uniform distribution around the whole color space. Most of human skin tone can be represented by an elliptical equation in the YCrCb color space [12]. We use the ellipse color model to locate all the flesh color to form a binary mask. Morphological operation is then applied to the binary mask to form a new binary mask. This step can reduce noisy components especially when taking image data from the web camera. The skin segmentation is performed to the image by applying the new binary mask to find out face candidates regions from the image. The pre-processing steps are shown in Fig. 2. This module uses the color information to reduce the search space for finding face candidates. New face candidate regions will be passed into the FDCM.

3.2 Face Detection Committee Machine (FDCM)

The FDCM works according to the confidence value T_i of each expert i. However, the confidence value T_i from each of the experts cannot be used directly. Figure 3 shows that the distribution of the confidence value of each expert varies in a large range. Thus, we need to normalize the value T_i by using the statistical information obtained from the training data:

$$\alpha_i = (T_i - \mu_i)/\sigma_i, \tag{1}$$

where T_i is the confidence value from expert i, μ_i is the mean value of training face pattern data from expert i, and σ_i is the standard derivation of training data from expert i.

One of the reasons why we need to normalize the confidence value is that they are not a uniform function. Another reason is that not all the experts have a fixed range of confidence value e.g., [-1,1] or [0,1]. Using statistical approach to model the problem, the information of confidence value from experts can be preserved. The output value of the committee machine can then be calculated using equation:

$$\beta = \sum_i w_i * (\alpha_i + \sigma_i * \delta_i), \tag{2}$$

where δ_i is the criteria factor for expert i and w_i is the weight of the expert i. The data is classified as face when the value of β is larger than 0 and non-face pattern when the value is smaller than or equal to 0.

3.3 Face Recognition Committee Machine (FRCM)

Our proposed FRCM adopts the static structure with five well-known experts. As shown in Fig. 1, input image is sent into the five experts for recognition. Apart from using result of each expert, we introduce the use of confidence as a weighted vote for the voting machine to avoid low confidence result of individual expert from affecting the final result. Due to different nature of the experts, we adopt different approaches to find the results and the associated confidence.

- **Eigenface, Fisherface** and **EGM:** We employ K nearest-neighbor classifiers, where five nearest training set images with the test image are chosen. The final result for expert i is defined as the class j with the highest votes v in J classes among the five results:

$$r_i = \arg\max_j(v(j)), \tag{3}$$

  where its confidence is defined as the number of votes of the result class divided by K, i.e.,

$$c_i = \frac{v(r_i)}{K}. \tag{4}$$

- **SVM:** As SVM was originally developed for two-class classification, multi-class classification can be extended by using "one-against-one" approach. To recognize a test image in J different classes, ${}_JC_2$ (i.e., $\frac{J(J-1)}{2}$) SVMs are constructed. The image is tested against each SVM and the class j with the highest votes in all SVMs is selected as the recognition result $r(i)$. The confidence is defined like Equation 4 with $J-1$ (the maximum number of votes a class) instead of K.
- **NN:** We choose a binary vector of size J for the target representation. The target class is set to one and the others are set to zero. The class j with output value closest to 1 is chosen as the result and the output value is chosen as the confidence.

The weights w in FRCM are evaluated in our testing for different algorithms under ORL and Yale face database (shown in Table 4 and Table 7 respectively). We

Table 1. CBCL face database

	Training Set	**Testing Set**
Face Pattern	2429	472
Non-face Pattern	4548	23573

Table 2. CBCL results

	True Positive	**False Positive**
NN	71.4%	15.2%
SNoW	71.6%	15.1%
SVM	81.2%	13.2%
FDCM	**84.1%**	**11.4%**

take the average accuracy for the algorithms from prior cross validation experiments and normalize them with weights by an exponential mapping function:

$$w_i = \frac{\exp(a_i)}{\sum_{i=1}^{5}\exp(a_i)}, \tag{5}$$

where a_i is the average accuracy of expert i. The use of weights in the voting machine further reduces the chance for an expert who performs poorly on average from affecting the ensemble result even if it has high confidence on the result. The voting machine assembles the results by calculating the score s of each class as follows:

$$s_j = \sum_{i=1}^{5} w_i * c_i, \forall j \in r_i. \tag{6}$$

We define the score in such a way that only experts with high performance on average and high confidence on the result would take the most significant score in the final decision.

4 Experimental Results

4.1 FDCM

We applied the CBCL face database from MIT for training and testing each of the expert systems to control the condition. Table 1 shows some data for the CBCL face database. The outputs from each single approach are determined by a threshold. When the threshold increases, the detection rate and the number of false detection will increase at the same time. For the FDCM, output value is calculated based on the experts' confidence values. When we change the value of criteria factor δ_i, the sensitivity of the committee machine will be affected. Input images classified as face patterns will be increased if we increase the value of criteria factor δ_i. This property is shown in Fig. 4.

The Receiver Operating Characteristics (ROC) curves are employed to show the characteristic of each approach. The area under the ROC curve provides

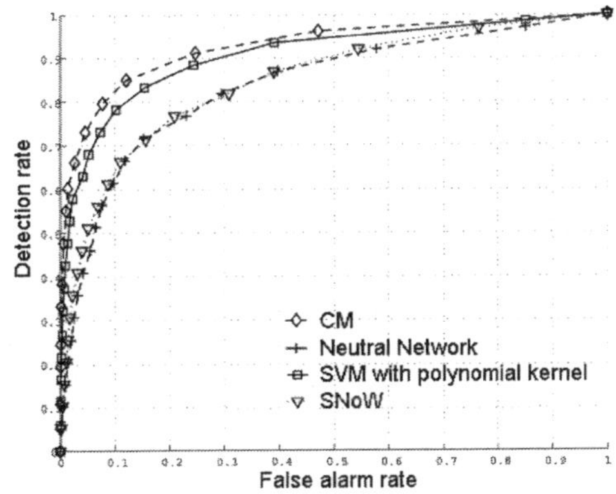

Fig. 4. The ROC curves of three different approaches and committee machine

Table 3. Experimetal results on images from the CBCL testing set

	False Alarm Rate			
Detection Rate	**NN**	**SNoW**	**SVM**	**FDCM**
10%	0.56%	0.41%	0.05%	0.02%
20%	1.37%	1.09%	0.16%	0.07%
30%	2.54%	1.67%	0.44%	0.14%
40%	4.11%	2.92%	0.83%	0.41%
50%	6.32%	4.91%	1.60%	0.77%
60%	9.47%	8.47%	3.07%	1.41%
70%	13.89%	14.67%	5.98%	3.90%
80%	**26.97%**	**27.62%**	**12.32%**	**7.79%**
90%	48.95%	49.26%	28.60%	22.92%

a convenient way to compare classifiers. Table 3 shows the false alarm rate of each approach under the same detection rate. The false alarm rate of FDCM is nearly half of the other approach with 80% detection rate. FDCM archives lower false alarm rate than the other methods with same detection rate. Table 2 lists the best operating point of each classifier. Our approach obtains the highest true positive rate while maintaining the lowest false positive rate. By observation, the statistical model of the committee machine can be engaged in the face detection problem and can improve the accuracy in classifying face and non-face pattern.

4.2 FRCM

Two sets of experiments are presented to evaluate the performance of FRCM and the individual algorithms. We adopt leaving-one-out cross validation method for the experiment to produce a thorough result. Table 6 lists the average running time for the algorithms and FRCM on the face databases.

Table 4. ORL recognition results

Set	Eigenface	Fisherface	EGM	SVM	NN	FRCM
1	92.5%	**100.0%**	90.0%	95.0%	92.5%	**95.0%**
2	85.0%	**100.0%**	72.5%	**100.0%**	95.0%	**100.0%**
3	87.5%	**100.0%**	85.0%	**100.0%**	95.0%	**100.0%**
4	90.0%	97.5%	70.0%	**100.0%**	92.5%	**100.0%**
5	85[.0%	**100.0%**	82.5%	**100.0%**	95.0%	**100.0%**
6	87.5%	**97.5%**	70.0%	**97.5%**	92.5%	**97.5%**
7	82.5%	**95.0%**	75.0%	**95.0%**	**95.0%**	**100.0%**
8	92.5%	95.0%	80.0%	**97.5%**	90.0%	**97.5%**
9	90.0%	**100.0%**	72.5%	97.5%	90.0%	**100.0%**
10	85.0%	**97.5%**	80.0%	95.0%	92.5%	**97.5%**
Average	87.5%	**98.3%**	77.8%	97.8%	93.0%	**98.8%**

Table 5. Result explanation FRCM in Image Set 1 and 7

		Recognized Class(Confidence)					
Set	**Image**	**Eigenface**	**Fisherface**	**EGM**	**SVM**	**NN**	**FRCM**
1	0	15(0.40)	**0**(0.60)	20(0.20)	15(1.00)	23(0.44)	**15**(0.29)
	34	14(0.60)	**34**(0.80)	28(0.40)	14(1.00)	14(0.63)	**14**(0.46)
7	25	27(0.40)	**27**(1.00)	10(0.20)	25(1.00)	25(0.51)	**25**(0.32)
	34	26(0.40)	**18**(0.60)	34(0.40)	34(1.00)	34(0.37)	**34**(0.36)

The ORL Database of Faces. The experiment is performed on the ORL face database (400 images) from AT&T Laboratories in Cambridge. From Table 4, FRCM (98.8%) achieves improvement in accuracy over the individual algorithms in the testing. We notice that Fisherface and SVM obtain higher accuracy (over 97%) than the others. This is due to the fact that both Fisherface and SVM inherit better classification ability in general cases. Table 5 shows the details of the underlying data in Image Set 1 and 7 to demonstrate how the committee machine works. We can see the effect of the committee machine in Set 7 that none of the experts has 100% accuracy but FRCM achieves it.

Yale Face Database. The experiment is performed on Yale face database (165 images) from Yale University. From Table 7, FRCM (86.1%) also outperforms all the individuals on average. The main reason for some non-satisfactory results (i.e., leftlight and rightlight) is due to the fact that Yale database contains variations in strong left and right lighting. The accuracy for both leftlight and rightlight in FRCM is 33.0% only. For algorithms taking the whole image as input like Eigenface, the accuracy would drop significantly because the lighting would greatly affect the pixel values. Without the lighting variations, FRCM achieves 97.8% accuracy, which is comparable to the ORL result (98.8%).

Table 6. Average running time(s)

	Eigenface	Fisherface	EGM	SVM	NN	FRCM
ORL	2.1	1.5	16.3	6	1.4	27.3
Yale	0.9	0.2	6.5	0.6	0.3	8.5

Table 7. Yale recognition results

Set	Eigenface	Fisherface	EGM	SVM	NN	FRCM
centerlight	53.3%	**93.3%**	66.7%	86.7%	73.3%	**93.3%**
glasses	80.0%	**100.0%**	53.3%	86.7%	86.7%	**100.0%**
happy	93.3%	**100.0%**	80.0%	**100.0%**	93.3%	**100.0%**
leftlight	26.7%	26.7%	**33.3%**	26.7%	26.7%	**33.3%**
noglasses	**100.0%**	**100.0%**	80.0%	**100.0%**	**100.0%**	**100.0%**
normal	86.7%	**100.0%**	86.7%	**100.0%**	93.3%	**100.0%**
rightlight	26.7%	**40.0%**	**40.0%**	13.3%	26.7%	**33.3%**
sad	86.7%	93.3%	93.3%	**100.0%**	93.3%	**100.0%**
sleepy	86.7%	**100.0%**	73.3%	**100.0%**	**100.0%**	**100.0%**
surprised	**86.7%**	66.7%	33.3%	73.3%	66.7%	**86.67%**
wink	**100.0%**	**100.0%**	66.7%	93.3%	93.3%	**100.0%**
Average	75.2%	**83.6%**	64.2%	80.0%	77.6%	**86.1%**
No Light	85.9%	**94.8%**	70.4%	93.3%	88.9%	**97.8%**

5 Conclusion

In this paper, we present a heterogeneous committee machine based face processing system which can automatically recognize people from camera. We employ the confidence information on experts' results and weight function on the FDCM and FRCM which can reduce the chance for poor result of certain expert from affecting the ensemble result. The success of the FDCM and FRCM has been demonstrated on the result of CBCL database, and ORL and Yale database, respectively. In our experiment, FDCM achieves 84.1% for true positive rate and 11.4% for false positive rate, which perform better than other three individual approaches. FRCM achieves 98.8% accuracy in ORL test and 97.8% accuracy in Yale test (without lighting variation), which also outperforms other state-of-the-art algorithms. These results show that the use of committee machine works in improving the accuracy of face detection and face recognition.

References

1. Jacobs, R.A., Jordan, M.I., Steven, J.N., Geoffrey, E.H.: Adaptive mixtures of local experts. In: Neural Computation. Volume 3. (1991) 79–87
2. Gutta, S., Huang, J.R.J., Jonathon, P., Wechsler, H.: Mixture of experts for classification of gender, ethnic origin, and pose of human faces. IEEE Trans. on Neural Networks **11** (2000) 948–960

3. Huang, F., Zhang, H., Chen, T., Zhou, Z.: Pose invariant face recognition. In: Proc. IEEE Int'l Conf. on Automatic Face and Gesture Recognition. (2000) 245–250
4. Turk, M., Pentland, A.: Face recognition using eigenfaces. In: Proc. IEEE Conf. on Computer Vision and Pattern Recognition. (1991) 586–591
5. Rowley, H., Baluja, S., Kanade, T.: Neural network-based face detection. IEEE Trans. on Pattern Analysis and Machine Intelligence **20** (1998) 23–38
6. Osuna, E., Freund, R., Girosit, F.: Training support vector machines: an application to face detection. In: Proc. IEEE Computer Society Conf. on Computer Vision and Pattern Recognition. (1997) 130–136
7. Yang, M.H., Roth, D., Ahuja, N.: A snow-based face detector. In: Advances in Neural Information Processing Systems. Volume 12. (1999) 862–868
8. Sirovich, L., Kirby, M.: A low-dimensional procedure for the characterization of human faces. In: J. Opt. Soc. Amer. A. Volume 4. (1987) 519–524
9. Belhumeur, P., Hespanha, J., Kriegman, D.: Eigenfaces vs. fisherfaces: recognition using class specific linear projection. IEEE Trans. on Pattern Analysis and Machine Intelligence **19** (1997) 711–720
10. Lades, M., Vorbruggen, J., von der Malsburg, C., Wurtz, R.P., Konen, W.: Distortion invariant object recognition in the dynamic link architecture. IEEE Trans. on Computers **42** (1993) 300–311
11. Vapnik, V.: Statistical Learning Theory. John Wiley and Sons, Inc. (1998)
12. Hsu, R.L., Abdel-Mottaleb, M., Jain, A.: Face detection in color images. IEEE Trans. on Pattern Analysis and Machine Intelligence **24** (2002) 696–706

Multi-class Support Vector Machines with Case-Based Combination for Face Recognition

Jaepil Ko and Hyeran Byun

Dept. of Computer Science, Yonsei University
134, Shinchon-dong Sudaemoon-ku, Seoul, 120-749, Korea
{nonezero,hrbyun}@csai.yonsei.c.kr

Abstract. The support vector machine is basically to deal with a two-class classification problem. To get *M*-class classifiers for face recognition, it is common to construct a set of binary classifiers $f_1,\ldots,f_M$, each trained to separate one class from the rest. The multi-class classification method has a main shortcoming that the binary classifiers used are obtained by training on different binary classification problems, and thus it is unclear whether their real-valued outputs are on comparable scales. In this paper, we try to use additional information, relative outputs of the machines, for final decision. We propose case-based combination with reject option to use the information. The experiments on the ORL face database shows that the proposed method achieves a slight better performance than the previous multi-class support vector machines.

1 Introduction

Face recognition is one of the active research areas in computer vision and pattern recognition. A various approaches have been proposed in the literature. However, there are still problems to be solved on face image representation and classification. Classical issues in pattern recognition problem are feature extraction for effective representation and classifier for good generalization performance. The commonly used techniques of feature extraction for face image representation are principal components analysis (PCA), linear discriminant analysis (LDA) and independent components analysis (ICA) in image based recognition. The popular system is the ones based on subspace method such as eighenfaces [1] and fisherfaces [2] with nearest neighbor classifier. For better performance, Support Vector Machines (SVM) whih are recently proposed by Vapnik [3] have been adopted as a classifier in face recognition [4,5,6].

SVM is based on the idea of structural risk minimization and shows good generalization performance. However, SVM is basically to deal with a two-class classification problem. To apply SVM to face recognition, we need some methods for multi-class SVM. It is common to construct a set of binary classifiers $f_1,\ldots,f_M$, each trained to separate one class from the rest. The main drawback of the method is that it is unclear whether their real-valued outputs of each two-class SVM are on comparable scales [7]. Some methods have been proposed to deal with this scaling problem [8].

N. Petkov and M.A. Westenberg (Eds.): CAIP 2003, LNCS 2756, pp. 623–629, 2003.

In this paper, we try to use additional information, relative outputs of the machines, for final decision. We propose case-based combination with reject option to use the information. In our approach, we adopt the one-versus-all strategy that is commonly used for multi-class SVM and use PCA technique for face image representation.

The paper organized as follows: In Section 2 we will give a brief overview of SVM and two general methods for multi-class expansion. In Section 3, it is explained about our method. Then we present experimental results in Section 4. The conclusion is given in Section 5.

2 Support Vector Machines for Pattern Classification

We give a brief overview of SVM and then review two methods for dealing with multi-class SVM [3,7].

2.1 Support Vector Machines

Given a set of M training set $\{(\boldsymbol{x}_i, y_i)\}$, where $\boldsymbol{x}_i$ is data and $y_i=1$ or -1 is the associated label, SVM finds the optimal linear hyperplane for good generalization performance by maximizing the margin which is the distance between the hyperplane and the nearest data point of each class in which the nearest data point is called support vector. By SVM learning, we can construct the following decision surface:

$$f(x) = \mathrm{sgn}(g(x))\mathrm{sgn}(< w, x > +b) = \sum_{i=1}^{Ns} \alpha_i y_i K(x, x_i) + b = 0 \quad (1)$$

where N_s is the number of support vectors, α_i is coefficient weight, $\boldsymbol{x}_i$ is support vector, and $\boldsymbol{K}$ is a kernel function to transform input space into feature space. The output of the $g(x)$ gives an algebraic measure of the distance from $\boldsymbol{x}$ to the optimal hyperplane [9]. This measure can be understood as a confidence value of an input $\boldsymbol{x}$ for a given SVM.

2.2 Multi-class SVM

To get multi-class classifiers, it is common to construct a set of binary classifiers. One can construct M-class classifier using the following procedure [3, 7]:

- one-versus-all strategy

A set of binary classifiers, $f_1, \ldots f_M$, are trained to separate one class from the rest. Combined function $F(x)$ is obtained by finding the maximal output among the outputs of those M classifiers. This can be denoted as follows:

$$F(x) = \arg\max_{i=1,\ldots,M} f_i(x), where\ f_i(x) = \sum_{k=1}^{m} y_k \alpha_k^i k(x, x_k) + b^i \quad (2)$$

- pairwise strategy

A set of binary classifiers is constructed for each possible pair of classes. For *M* class, this results in *M(M-1)/2* binary classifiers. In this case, the winner can be decided in *M-1* comparison times by tournament method in tree structure. Though there are some differences in training and testing phase between one-versus-all strategy and pairwise strategy, the experiments on person recognition show similar classification performance [6].

In our approach, we adopt the one-versus-all strategy and explain the next section in details.

3 Case-Based Combination

We try to use relative outputs of the machines for the problem; real-valued outputs of different machines are not on comparable scales. We store a series of real-valued outputs for each machine as an instance for a given input in training phase. We assume that the scale of the outputs of a machine is almost the same if input data come from the same class. Then, a series of real-valued outputs for each machine can form a consistence pattern. We will use this information. However, we do not always use this information. We use this information when output of one-versus-all strategy is unclear.

Fig. 1 shows the system flow. Our system consists of three parts; PCA preprocessor, base classifiers composed of two-class SVM, and aggregation module combining them.

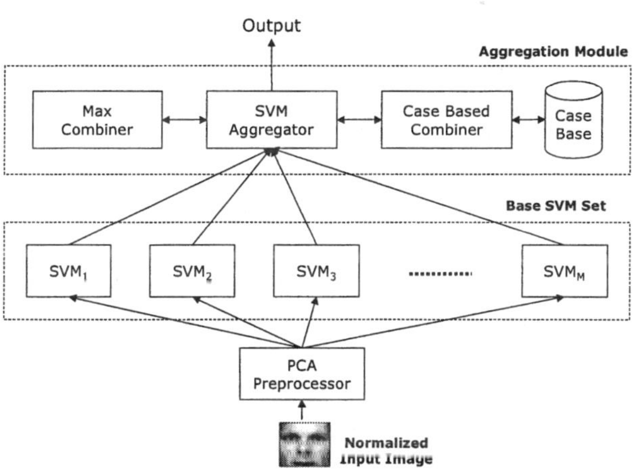

Fig. 1. The proposed face recognition system flow

The PCA preprocessor transforms the original input image to the feature vector. The base classifiers are composed of *M* SVMs for *M* class problem. Each SVM is a binary classifier trained to separate one class from the rest. When an unknown image is given, all members in base SVMs try to identify it. The results from those classifiers are fed to the high-level combination module called SVM aggregator. The SVM aggregator is the second component of our system. To solve multi-class problem with SVM, the most of previous approaches try to finds the winner classifier whose output value is the largest among the outputs from base SVMs. Then, the input is assigned to the class that the winner classifier designates. In our method, high-level combination module, i.e. SVM aggregator, selects a method used for the outputs from base SVMs. The SVM aggregator has two strategies; max combination strategy and case-based combination strategy.

When the outputs are given from base support vector machines, the SVM aggregator checks reject condition first. If reject condition is satisfied, case-based combination strategy is chosen. Otherwise, the common combining method is chosen for dealing with the problem, finding maximum value among those outputs from the base SVMs.

3.1 Rejection Condition

The SVM aggregator chooses the combination method by checking the reject condition. Let us assume that we have *M* support vector machines as base classifiers. The rejection condition used for our system is given by,

$$R(F) = \begin{cases} 1 & \textit{if } f_{\max}(x) < 0 \;\; \textit{or} \;\; \left| f_{\max}(x) - f_{s\max}(x) \right| < \xi \\ 0 & \qquad\qquad \textit{otherwise} \end{cases} \tag{3}$$

where $F=\{f_1(x), f_2(x), \ldots, f_M(x)\}$ is *M*-dimensional vector whose *i*th value $f_i(x)$ is the output from *i*th SVM, $f_{max}(x)$ denotes the largest value among $f_i(x)$, $f_{max}(x)$ means the second largest value, and ξ is the rejection threshold.

If all outputs from base SVMs are negative or the difference between the largest value and the second largest value is not bigger than a threshold, the rejection condition is satisfied and the rejection function *R(F)* returns 1. Otherwise, it returns *0*.

Then, the *Aggr(F)*, final decision of SVMs aggregator, can be described as follows:

$$Aggr(F) = \begin{cases} CB\_Comb(F) & \textit{if } R(F) = 1 \\ Max\_Comb(F) & \textit{otherwise} \end{cases} \tag{4}$$

where *CB_Comb*(*F*) denotes the decision of case-based combination module, and *Max_Comb*(*F*) means the decision of max combination module.

We assume that unclear situation can occur when the range of a classifier having the largest value for a given input is significantly larger than that of a classifier having the second largest value, and yet the difference of outputs values are almost the same. In such a case, it is not desirable to choose the class that has the largest value as winner class. The alternative is to reject the max-win strategy and then use another information. We think that relative outputs of the machines can be useful information.

3.2 Case-Based Combination

When the rejection condition is satisfied, the SVM aggregator calls the case-based combiner shown in Fig. 1. The case-based combiner employs a case base, storing the presented training data. The each instance stored in case base contains the outputs from base SVMs and the target value. It can be relative outputs of the machines.

$$(f_1(\boldsymbol{x}), f_2(\boldsymbol{x}), \ldots, f_M(\boldsymbol{x}), y)$$

where $f_i(\boldsymbol{x})$ is the output from ith SVM in base SVM and y is the target value for the given input $\boldsymbol{x}$.

Our case-based combiner employs a distance-weighted k-nearest neighbor algorithm. Learning in case-based combiner consists of simply storing the pair of outputs from base SVMs and target value on the presented training data. The query instance of case-based combiner is not the image for base SVM but the outputs of base SVMs on the given image. When the outputs from base SVMs on a new image are given, the case-based combiner retrieves a set of similar related cases from the case base and use them to classify the input. The nearest neighbors of an instance are defined in terms of the standard Euclidean distance. The distance between two instances $\boldsymbol{c}_i$, and $\boldsymbol{c}_j$ is defined to be $d(\boldsymbol{c}_i, \boldsymbol{c}_j)$, where

$$d(c_i, c_j) = \sqrt{\sum_{r=1}^{M} (f_r^i(x) - f_r^j(x))^2} \tag{5}$$

The final decision of case-based combiner is given as follows:

$$CB\_Comb(F) = \arg\max_{v \in V} \sum_{i=1}^{k} \delta(v, d(F, c_i), y_{c_i}) \tag{6}$$

where V is the set of class labels, c_i is the i th nearest neighbor in case base, y_{c_i} is the target value of the instance c_i, $\delta(v, d(F, c_i), y_{c_i}) = w(d(F, c_i))$ if $v = y_{c_i}$, $\delta(v, d(F, c_i), y_{c_i})$ =0 otherwise, and $w(\cdot)$ is a function transforming distance measure to weight (similarity) measure as follows:

$$w(d) = 1/(1 + \exp(Ad + B)) \tag{7}$$

A and B are constants of exponential function and they can be usually fixed through experiments.

4 Experimental Results

We demonstrate our method on 400 face images from the ORL dataset of facial images. The 400 images consisted of ten images of 40 individuals. There are variations in lighting, facial expression and pose slightly. The preprocessing for experiments was carried out as follows. First, The preprocessing procedure such as rotation, scaling, and translation were performed that is based on manually localized eye positions. Then we applied histogram equalization to flatten the distribution of image intensity values. Fig. 2 shows examples of the normalized face images whose dimension is 1024.

Fig. 2. Normalized face images for one individuals in the ORL face images

We performed PCA to transform input space into face space. First, we scale facial pixels to have zero mean and unit variance that is required for PCA inputs. To find the best feature dimension, we use all the face images for PCA transformation, and divide it into two parts equally; one is for gallery set, and the other is probe set. We varied the dimension of face space by changing the number of eigenvectors, and obtained the highest recognition rate at 48-dimension with a PCA-based algorithm, which is the base algorithm for the performance test protocol described in FERET [10]. We selected the number of eigenvectors according to the procedure mentioned above because the classification performance of our proposed method was the focus.

In the SVM experiments, the outputs of the PCA were shifted using the mean and scaled by their standard deviation. We used SVM with Radial Basis Function (RBF) kernel for the experiment. We select randomly nine images of each person for training and the remaining one for testing and repeat it ten times. We chose the best average recognition rate among them with the same parameters for ten times and the results are shown in Table 1.

Table 1 compares the performance of the traditional SVM with one-versus-all strategy and that of our proposed method, in accuracy rate. The width σ of RBF kernel was set to 1.0. Several SVMs were trained by varying *C*, the trade-off between margin maximization and training error minimization.

Table 1. Accuracy of SVMs (varying *C*) and the proposed method (varying *k*), $\xi = 0.2$

C	SVM	Case Based Combination									
		k=1	k=2	k=3	k=4	k=5	k=6	k=7	k=8	k=9	k=10
1	90.25	90.75	90.75	90.75	90.25	91.5	91	90	89.5	90	89.25
2	91	91	91	91	91.5	90.5	91	90	90.75	91	89.75
3	91.25	91.5	91.5	91.5	91.75	91	92	91	92	91	92
4	91.25	93.25	93.25	92.75	93	92.5	93	93	92.5	93	93.25
5	91.25	**93.75**	**93.75**	93	92.25	92.5	93	92.75	93	93	92.5
6	91.5	93.5	93.5	92.25	92.5	92	93	93	92.75	93	93.25
7	**92**	93	93	91.75	92.25	92	93	93	92.25	93	92.75
8	**92**	92.75	92.75	92.25	92.5	92.25	93	93	92.5	93	93
9	**92**	92.75	92.75	92.25	92.5	92	93	93	92.5	93	93.25
10	**92**	92.75	92.75	92.25	92.5	92.5	93	93	92.5	93	93.25

From Table 1 the best accuracy of our method is *93.75%* when *k* is *1* and *2* and *C* is *5*, the best accuracy of the previous combination method for SVM is *92%* when *C* is above *7*. We can see that our proposed method achieves the better accuracy than the simple SVM with one-versus-all strategy.

5 Conclusion

Recently, SVM has attracted considerable attention and has been adopted as a classifier in the face recognition system to improve the performance. The support vector machine is basically to deal with a two-class classification problem. Extending the binary classifier to multi-class classifier with SVM still suffers from some problems such as scaling output values from base SVMs. The problems can produce unclear situation with one-against-all strategy.

In this paper, we propose case-based combination with reject option to try to use additional information, relative outputs of the machines, for final decision. The experimental results obtained on the ORL face dataset shows the possibility that the relative outputs of machines can be information to describe each class. However, the proposed method requires additional parameters, threshold value for rejection and the number of nearest neighbors.

Acknowledgements

This work was supported by grant No. (R04-2001-000075-0) from the Basic Research Program (woman's science) of the Korea Science & Engineering Foundation.

References

1. M.A. Turk, A.P. Pentland: Eigenfaces for recognition, Cognitive Neuroscience 3 (1) (1991) 71-86
2. V. Belhumeur, J. Hespanha, and D. Kriegman: Eigenfaces vs. Fisherfaces : Recognition using class specific linear projection, IEEE Trans. On Pattern Analysis and Machine Intellignece 19(7) (1997) 711-720
3. V.N. Vapnik: Statistical learning theory, John Wiley & Sons, New York (1998)
4. P.J. Phillips.: Support vector machines applied to face recognition, Advances in Neural Information Processing Systems II, MIT Press (1998) 803-809
5. G. Guo, S.Z. Li, K.L. Chan: Support vector machines for face recognition, Image and Vision Computing 19 (2001) 631-638
6. B. Heisele, P. Ho, T. Poggio: Face recognition with support vector machines: Global versus Component-based Approach, Proc. of IEEE International Conference on ICCV (2001) 688-694
7. B. Scholkopf, A.J. Smola: Learning with Kernels, MIT Press, Cambridge Massachusetts London (2002)
8. E. Mayoraz, E. Alpaydm: Support Vector Machines for Multi-class Classification, Proc. of International Workshop on Artificial Neural Networks (1999), IDIAP Technical Report 98-06
9. S. Haykin: Neural Networks-A comprehensive foundation, 2nd Edn. Prentice-Hall Inc. New Jersey (1999)
10. P.J. Phillips, H. Moon, S.A. Rizvi and P.J. Rauss : The FERET evaluation methodology for face-recognition algorithms, IEEE Trans. PAMI 22 (2000) pp.1090-1104

Partial Faces for Face Recognition: Left vs Right Half

Srinivas Gutta[1] and Harry Wechsler[2]

[1] Philips Research - USA
345 Scarborough Rd, Briarcliff Manor, NY 10598
Srinivas.Gutta@philips.com
[2] Department of Computer Science
George Mason University, Fairfax, VA 22030
wechsler@cs.gmu.edu

Abstract. Most research on face recognition has focused so far on identification from full frontal/profile facial images. We have reported earlier on a study that assesses the usefulness of partial faces for face recognition. We expand on our earlier results as we now assess if face recognition performance changes if the left half or the right half of the face is chosen for analysis. Our approach employs Ensemble of Radial Basis Functions (ERBF) networks. The motivation for ERBF comes from their ability to cope with the inherent variability in the image formation and data acquisition process. The database used to assess the comparative merit of the left vs. right half of the face consists of face images from 150 different subjects. The subjects pose across $\pm 5^0$ rotation for a total of 3,000 images. The experimental results, using average Cross Validation performance, indicate that there is no significant difference if the left half (96%) or the right half (94%) of the face is used.

1 Introduction

Faces are accessible 'windows' into the mechanisms that govern our emotional and social lives. The face is a unique feature of human beings. Even the faces of "identical twins" differ in some respects. Humans can detect and identify faces in a scene with little or no effort even if only partial views of the faces are available. This skill is quite robust, despite large changes in the visual stimulus due to viewing conditions, expression, aging, and distractions such as glasses or changes in hairstyle.

Automated recognition requires computer systems to look through many stored sets of characteristics ('the gallery') and pick the one that matches best those features of the unknown individual ('the probe'). In most practical scenarios there are two possible recognition tasks to be considered - (i) *Identification*: An image of an unknown individual is collected ('probe" and the identity is found searching a large set of images ('gallery'), and (ii) *Verification*: Rather than identifying a person, the system is now involved with verification and checks if a given probe belongs to a relatively small gallery, sometimes labeled as a set of intruders. In this paper we limit ourselves to the task of identification.

N. Petkov and M.A. Westenberg (Eds.): CAIP 2003, LNCS 2756, pp. 630–637, 2003.

There are two major approaches for automated recognition of human faces. The first approach, the abstractive one, extracts (and measures) discrete *local* features 'indexes' for retrieving and identifying faces, so subsequently standard statistical pattern recognition techniques can be employed for probing amongst faces using these measurements. The other approach, the holistic one, conceptually related to template matching, attempts to recognize faces using *global* representations [1][2]. Common examples of these approaches include (a) Eigen Faces [3], (b) Elastic Bunch Graph Matching [4], (c) Linear Discriminant Analysis [5] and (d) Radial Basis Function Networks [6]. Most research to date has primarily focussed on identification from full frontal/profile facial images. The only other paper that we are aware of that has performed identification from partial images is [7]. They have used partial face images – eye, nose and ear images separately for identification. They report an accuracy of 100 % recognition/rejection on a database of 720 images corresponding to 120 subjects. Recently, we have conducted a study to assess the usefulness of partial faces for face recognition [8]. In our experiments we found that, the performance is the same irrespective of whether partial face or full face is used for recognition.

In this paper we extend our previous work to assess if there is a difference in performance if the right half or the left half of the face is used. Experiments were conducted by using a radial basis function based network ensemble that was developed earlier [6]. In our experiments we limit our attention to recognition of faces from approximately frontal images. Specifically, we attempt to recognize subjects from partial face images. As an example if the face image is of dimension 64x72, our input to the recognition module is of dimension 32x72.

2 Face Recognition

An overall architecture, appropriate for face recognition, is shown in Fig. 1. Face recognition usually starts with the detection of a pattern as a face, proceeds by normalizing the face image to account for geometrical and illumination changes using information from the box surrounding the face and/or eye locations, and finally it identifies the face using appropriate image representation and classification algorithms. The tools needed to detect face patterns and normalize them are discussed elsewhere [9], while this paper describes only the tools developed to realize and implement those stages of face recognition involved in identification tasks.

3 Radial Basis Function Networks

The construction of the RBF network involves three different layers. The input layer is made up of source nodes (sensory units). The second layer is a hidden layer whose goal is to cluster the data and reduce its dimensionality. The output layer supplies the response of the network to the activation patterns applied to the input layer. The transformation from the input space to the hidden-unit space is *non-linear*, whereas the transformation from the hidden-unit space to the output space is *linear*[10].

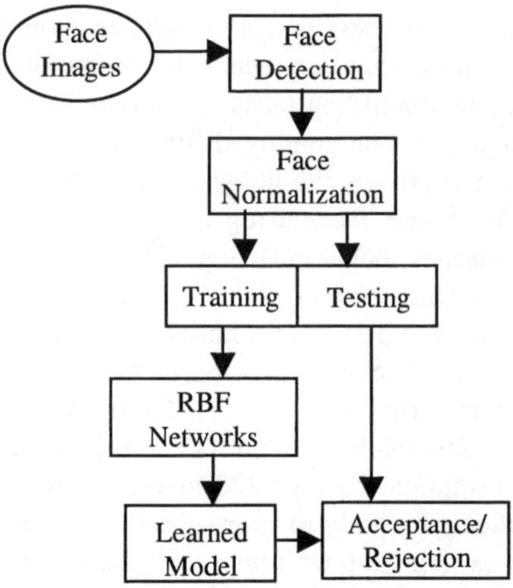

Fig. 1. Automated Face Recognition Architecture

An RBF classifier has an architecture that is very similar to that of a traditional three-layer back-propagation network. Connections between the input and middle layers have unit weights and, as a result, do not have to be trained. Nodes in the middle layer, called BF nodes, produce a localized response to the input using Gaussian kernels. Each hidden unit can be viewed as a localized receptive field (RF). The hidden layer is trained using k-means clustering. The most common basis function (BF) used are Gaussians, where the activation level y_i of the hidden unit i is given by:

$$y_i = \Phi_i(\|X - \mu_i\|) = \exp\left[-\sum_{k=1}^{D} \frac{(x_k - \mu_{ik})^2}{2h\sigma_{ik}^2 o}\right]$$

where h is a proportionality constant for the variance, x_k is the kth component of the input vector $X=[x_1, x_2, \ldots, x_D]$, and μ_{ik} and σ_{ik}^2 are the kth components of the mean and variance vectors, and o is the overlap factor, respectively, of basis function node i. The outputs of the hidden unit lie between 0 and 1, and could be interpreted as fuzzy memberships; the closer the input to the center of the Gaussian, the larger the response of the node. The activation level Z_j of an output unit is given by:

$$Z_j = \sum_i w_{ij} y_i + w_{0j}$$

where Z_j is the output of the jth output node, y_i is the activation of the ith BF node, w_{ij} is the weight connecting the ith BF node to the jth output node, and w_{0j} is the bias or the threshold of the jth output node. The bias comes from the weights associated with a BF node that has a constant unit output regardless of the input. An unknown vector X is classified as belonging to the class associated with the output node j with the largest output Z_j.

The RBF input consists of n normalized face images pixels fed to the network as 1D vectors. The hidden (unsupervised) layer, implements an enhanced k-means clustering procedure, where both the number of Gaussian cluster nodes and their variance are dynamically set. The number of clusters varies, in steps of 5, from 1/5 of the number of training images to n, the total number of training images. The width of the Gaussian for each cluster, is set to the maximum of {*the distance between the center of the cluster and the member of the cluster that is farthest away - within class diameter, the distance between the center of the cluster and closest pattern from all other clusters*} multiplied by an overlap factor o, in our experiment equal to 2. The width is further dynamically refined using different proportionality constants h. The hidden layer yields the equivalent of a functional facial base, where each cluster node encodes some common characteristics across the face space. The output (supervised) layer maps face encodings ('expansions') along such a space to their corresponding class and finds the corresponding expansion ('weight') coefficients using pseudo-inverse techniques. In our case the number of nodes in the output layer correspond to the number of people we wish to identify.

For a connectionist architecture to be successful it has to cope with the variability available in the data acquisition process. One possible solution to the above problem is to implement the equivalent of query by consensus using ensembles of radial basis functions (ERBF). Ensembles are defined in terms of their specific topology (connections and RBF nodes) and the data they are trained on. Specifically, both original data and distortions caused by geometrical changes and blur are used to induce robustness to those very distortions via generalization [7].

The ERBF architecture is shown in Fig. 2. Each RBF component is further defined in terms of three RBF nodes, each of which specified in terms of the number of clusters and the overlap factors. The overlap factors o, defined earlier, for the RBF nodes RBF (11, 21, 31), RBF(12, 22, 32), and RBF(13, 23, 33) are set to 2, 2.5, and 3, respectively. The same RBF nodes were trained on original images, and on the same original images with either some Gaussian noise added or subject to some degree of geometrical ('rotation'), respectively. The intermediate nodes C_1, C_2, and C_3 act as buffers for the transfer of the normalized images to the various RBF components. Training is performed until 100% recognition accuracy is achieved for each RBF node. The nine output vectors generated by the RBF nodes are passed to a *judge* who would make a decision on whether the probe ('input') belongs to that particular class or not. The specific decision used is - if the average of 5 of the 9 network outputs is greater than θ then that probe belongs to that class.

4 Experiments

The number of unique individuals in our database corresponds to 150 subjects. During image acquisition each subject was asked to sit in front of the computer equipped with a Matrox frame grabber and a Philips CCD camera. The distance from the subject and the camera was approximately 3 feet.

Each subject was asked to first look at the camera for approximately 5 seconds and turn his/her head ± 5^0. The subjects were asked to make different kind of facial expressions, which include smiling, surprise, etc. The frame grabber was set to acquire imagery at the rate of 5 fps. The images were acquired at a resolution of 640x480 pixels and encoded in 255 gray scale levels. The images are then passed to the face detection module [9]. Detected faces greater than the set threshold of 0.95 were stored. The faces are then normalized to account for geometrical and illumination changes using information about the eye location. The final face obtained at the end of detection and normalization is of a standard resolution of 64x72 pixels. Since we know the location of the eyes from the detection module, we create the partial-face by cutting the normalized facial image vertically at the point where the distance from one end of the image to the center is 1/2 the eye distance. A sample set of face images and their corresponding partial faces are shown in Figs. 3, 4 and 5 respectively.

In Section 4.1 we report on the experiments conducted for the recognition of subjects from partial faces when left half of the face is used, while in Section 4.2 we report the results when right half of the face is used.

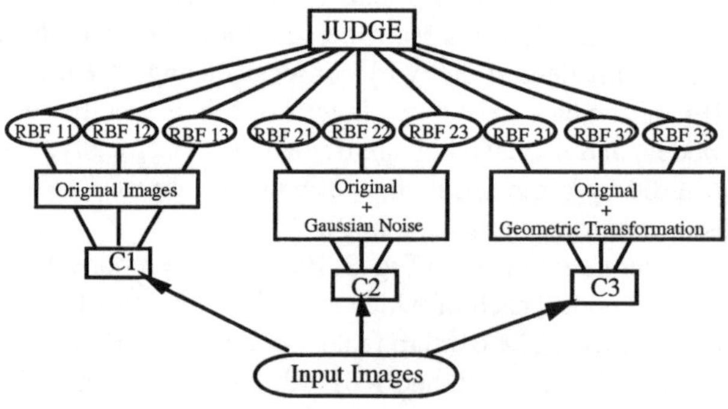

Fig. 2. ERBF Architecture

4.1 Partial Face Recognition Using Left Half of the Face

First we report on experiments when only one instance of the subjects facial image was used for training ('Experiment 1') followed by the case in which multiple instances were used for training. The training and testing strategy used in both cases is similar to that of k - fold cross validation (CV) [11]. In k - fold cross validation, the cases are randomly divided into k mutually exclusive partitions of approximately equal size. The cases not found in one partition are used for training, and the resulting classifier is then tested on the partition left out of training. The average error rates over all k partitions are the CV error rate. Each partition in our case consists of images corresponding to 50 unique subjects. Each CV cycle consists of 20 iterations. As an example, the first CV cycle on its first iteration would randomly pick one image corresponding to each of the 50 subjects ('gallery') in the first partition while testing on the remaining images of the subjects in the gallery plus the images ('probes') corresponding to 100 subjects. For each cycle this process is repeated for a total of 20 times. Table 1 shows the average CV results over all cycles and all iterations when the threshold was set at 0.70 for the case when a single RBF network is used. Similarly Table 1 also shows results when the number of images per individual has been increased to 5 ('Experiment 2') and 9 ('Experiment 3'), respectively. Table 2 below shows the average CV results over all cycles and iterations for cases when 1, 5, 9 images per individual were used when an ensemble is used.

Fig. 3. Examples of detected frontal faces

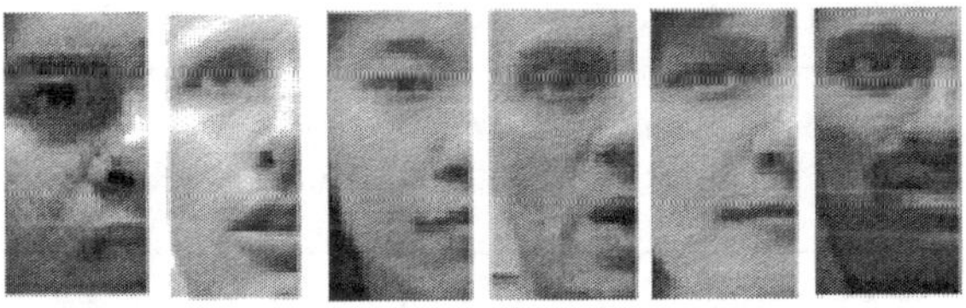

Fig. 4. Examples of partial left half of the face

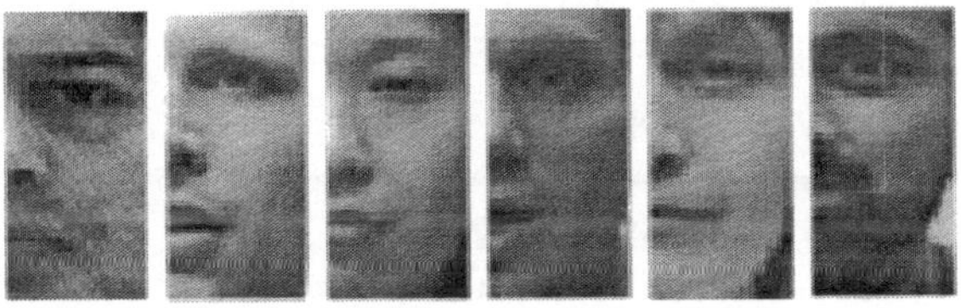

Fig. 5. Examples of partial right half of the face

4.2 Partial Face Recognition Using Right Half of the Face

The specific training and testing procedure remains the same as that was used in section 4.1. The average CV results over all cycles and iterations when the number of images per individual is 1, 5 and 9 for the case when a single RBF network is used are shown below in Table 3. The threshold for acceptance/rejection is the same as that was used earlier – 0.70. Similarly, results for the case when an ensemble is used is shown below in Table 4.

Table 1. Average CV results when a single RBF network is used with left-half of the face

Ave. CV Results	Accepted (Correct) %	False Negative %	Rejected (Correct) %	False Positive %
Exp 1	78	22	80	20
Exp 2	85	15	92	8
Exp 3	91	9	95	5

Table 2. Average CV results when an ensemble is used with left-half of the face

Ave. CV Results	Accepted (Correct) %	False Negative %	Rejected (Correct) %	False Positive %
Exp 1	85	15	87	13
Exp 2	91	9	93	7
Exp 3	96	4	97	3

Table 3. Average CV results when a single RBF network is used with right-half of the face

CV Cycle	Accepted (Correct) %	False Negative %	Rejected (Correct) %	False Positive %
Exp 1	73	27	78	22
Exp 2	80	20	88	12
Exp 3	89	11	95	5

Table 4. Average CV results when an ensemble is used with right-half of the face

CV Cycle	Accepted (Correct) %	False Negative %	Rejected (Correct) %	False Positive %
Exp 1	82	8	85	15
Exp 2	90	10	94	6
Exp 3	94	6	98	2

5 Conclusions

We have proposed in this paper an ensemble of RBF networks for partial-face identification and showed their feasibility on a collection of 3,000 face images corresponding to 150 subjects with $\pm 5^0$ rotation. Cross Validation (CV) results yield an average accuracy rate of (**a**) 96% when left half of the face is used and (**b**) 94% when right half of the face is used. Based on the experimental results, we believe it does not matter whether left half or right half of the face is used for identification.

We are currently adapting the RBF network so that it could be trained on left half of the face image but accepts right half of the face image as the probe during testing and vice versa. This feature is especially useful, as only a left half or a right half of the image is available due to occlusion, local illumination or other factors.

Acknowledgements

Harry Wechsler has been partly supported by TSWG SC-AS-1649.

References

1. Wechsler, H., Phillips, P.J., Bruce, V., Soulie F.F., Huang, T.S.(ed.): Face Recognition: From Theory to Applications, Springer-Verlag, New York (1998)
2. Gong, S., McKenna, S. J., Psarrou, A.: Dynamic Vision: From Images to Face Recognition, 1st edn. Imperial College Press, London (2000)
3. Turk, M., Pentland, A.: Eigenfaces for Recognition. Int. J. Cognitive Neuroscience. 3 (1991) 71-86
4. Wiskott, L., Fellous, J. M., Krüger, N., Malsburg, C.: Face Recognition by Elastic Graph Matching, IEEE PAMI 19(7) (1996) 775-779
5. Etemad, K., Chellappa, R: Discriminant Analysis for Recognition of Human Face Images, J. Optical Society of America 14 (1997) 1724-1733
6. Gutta, S., Wechsler, H.: Face Recognition using Hybrid Classifiers, Int. J. Pattern Recognition. 30(4) (1997) 539-553.
7. Sato, K., Shah, S., Aggarwal, J.K.: Partial Face Recognition using Radial Basis Function networks, in Proc. of the 3rd International Conference on Face and Gesture Recognition. (1998) 288-293, Nara, Japan
8. Gutta, S., Philomin, V., Trajkovic, M.: An Investigation into the use of Partial Faces for Face Recognition, in Proc. of the 5th International Conference on Face and Gesture Recognition. (2002) 33-38, Washington D.C., USA.
9. Colmenarez, A., Frey, B., Huang, T. S.: Detection and Tracking of Faces and Facial Features, in Proc. of International Conference on Image Processing. (1999) 268-272, Kobe, Japan
10. Lippmann, R.P., Ng, K.: A Comparative Study of the Practical Characteristic of Neural Networks and Pattern Classifiers, MIT Lincoln Labs. Tech. Report 894 (1991)
11. Weiss, S.M., Kulikowski, C.A.: Computer Systems That Learn, Morgan Kaufmann, San Francisco (1991).

Face Recognition by Fisher and Scatter Linear Discriminant Analysis

Mirosław Bober[1], Krzysztof Kucharski[2], and Władysław Skarbek[2]

[1] Visual Information Laboratory, Mitsubishi Electric, Guilford, UK
[2] Faculty of Electronics and Information Technology
Warsaw University of Technology, Poland
W.Skarbek@ire.pw.edu.pl

Abstract. Fisher linear discriminant analysis (FLDA) based on variance ratio is compared with scatter linear discriminant (SLDA) analysis based on determinant ratio. It is shown that each optimal FLDA data model is optimal SLDA data model but not opposite. The novel algorithm 2SS4LDA (*two singular subspaces for LDA*) is presented using two singular value decompositions applied directly to normalized multiclass input data matrix and normalized class means data matrix. It is controlled by two singular subspace dimension parameters q and r, respectively. It appears in face recognition experiments on the union of MPEG-7, Altkom, and Feret facial databases that 2SS4LDA reaches about 94% person identification rate and about 0.21 average normalized mean retrieval rank. The best face recognition performance measures are achieved for those combinations of q, r values for which the variance ratio is close to its maximum, too. None such correlation is observed for SLDA separation measure.

1 Introduction

Linear Discriminant Analysis, shortly LDA, deals with the training sequence $X = [x_1, \ldots, x_L]$ of multidimensional data vectors ($x_i \in \mathbb{R}^N,\ i = 1, \ldots, L$).

In general the data vectors are obtained using a measurement process for objects from certain classes $\mathcal{C}_1, \ldots, \mathcal{C}_J$, i.e. i-th element of X belongs to class $\mathcal{C}_{j(i)}$. Let the number of elements x_i which represent class j be L_j, i.e. $L = L_1 + \cdots + L_J$. We can identify elements in X extracted from j-th class by the index set I_j: $I_j \doteq \{i : x_i \text{ represents class } \mathcal{C}_j\}$.

LDA is based on statistical concepts of data variances and covariances. The *unbiased vector within-class variance* $\mathrm{var}_w(X)$ and the *unbiased vector between-class variance* $\mathrm{var}_b(X)$ have the form : $\mathrm{var}_w(X) \doteq \frac{1}{L-J}\sum_{j=1}^{J}\sum_{i\in I_j}\|x_i - \overline{x}^j\|^2$, $\mathrm{var}_b(X) \doteq \frac{1}{J-1}\sum_{j=1}^{J} L_j\|\overline{x}^j - \overline{x}\|^2$, where the class vector mean $\overline{x}^j$ and grand vector mean $\overline{x}$ are: $\overline{x}^j \doteq \sum_{i\in I_j} x_i/L_j$, $\overline{x} \doteq \sum_{i=1}^{L} x_i/L$.

The data covariances within classes are represented by the *within-class scatter matrix* $S_w(X) \doteq \sum_{j=1}^{J}\sum_{i\in I_j}(x_i - \overline{x}^j)(x_i - \overline{x}^j)^t/(L-J)$, while the between class covariances are defined by the matrix $S_b(X) \doteq \sum_{j=1}^{J} L_j(\overline{x}^j - \overline{x})(\overline{x}^j - \overline{x})^t/(J-1)$ called the *between-class scatter matrix.*

N. Petkov and M.A. Westenberg (Eds.): CAIP 2003, LNCS 2756, pp. 638–645, 2003.

For the given dimension r of the feature vector $y = W^t x$, LDA attempts to find a linear transformation matrix $W \in \mathbb{R}^{N\times r}$, $W = [w_1, \ldots, w_r]$, $w_i \in \mathbb{R}^N$ for the training sequence X which gives the best separation for the classes. Then the scatter matrices and data variances are transformed accordingly: $S_w(Y) = W^t S_w(X) W$, $\mathrm{var}_w(Y) = \mathrm{tr}(W^t S_w(X) W)$, $S_b(Y) = W^t S_b(X) W$, $\mathrm{var}_b(Y) = \mathrm{tr}(W^t S_b(X) W)$, where $Y = [W^t x_1, \ldots, W^t x_L]$ is the sequence of feature vectors for X.

In this paper two measures $f(W)$ and $g(W)$ of separation concept are considered. The first one, originally proposed by Fisher ([5]), takes into account the ratio of between-class variance to within-class variance. While the second one, very commonly cited in face recognition applications (e.g. [4, 6, 7]) replaces variances by determinants ($|\cdot|$) of corresponding scatter matrices ([2]) as measures of data scattering. Both measures lead to two modeling techniques with two different families of LDA models $\mathcal{F}_r$ and $\mathcal{S}_r$ defined for $1 \le r \le N$:

1. Fisher linear discriminant analysis (FLDA) with models in $\mathcal{F}_r(X)$:

$$f(W) \doteq \frac{\mathrm{tr}(W^t S_b W)}{\mathrm{tr}(W^t S_w W)}$$

$$\mathcal{F}_r(X) \doteq \{W \in \mathbb{R}^{N\times r} : W = \arg\max f(W),\ W^t S_w W = I,\ W \perp \ker(S_w)\}$$

2. Scatter linear discriminant (SLDA) with models in $\mathcal{S}_r(X)$:

$$g(W) \doteq \frac{|W^t S_b W|}{|W^t S_w W|}$$

$$\mathcal{S}_r(X) \doteq \{W \in \mathbb{R}^{N\times r} : W = \arg\max g(W),\ |W^t S_w W| \neq 0\}$$

The paper is organized as follows. In section 2 algorithmic characterization of FLDA models is given and efficient algorithm 2SS4LDA is described. In section 3 mutual relations between FLDA and SLDA models are presented. Experiments on facial databases are discussed in section 4.

2 Algorithm for FLDA Models

The requirement $W^t S_w W = I$ for FLDA model ensures that class mean shifted, data vector components become decorrelated and of unit variance in LDA coordinates. The column vectors of $W = [w_1, \ldots, w_r]$ of FLDA model are sought within the hyper-ellipsoid $\mathcal{B} \doteq \{x : x^t S_w x = 1, x \perp \ker(S_w)\}$.

Let us consider the reduced eigenvalue decomposition (REVD) for $S_w = U_{q_0} \Lambda_{q_0} U_{q_0}^t$, where the first $q_0 = \mathrm{rank}(S_w)$, columns in U and Λ are chosen, $\Lambda = \mathrm{diag}(\lambda_1, \ldots, \lambda_N)$, $\lambda_1 \ge \cdots \ge \lambda_N$. Then the search space has the form: $\mathcal{B} = \{x : x^t S_w x = 1, x \perp \ker(S_w)\} = \{A\alpha : A \doteq U_{q_0} \Lambda_{q_0}^{-1/2},\ \alpha \in \mathbb{R}^{q_0}, \|\alpha\| = 1\}$. Now, the behavior of the objective function $w^t S_b w$ can be analyzed using REVD for $A^t S_b A \doteq V_{r_0} \Sigma_{r_0} V_{r_0}^t$, where $r_0 = \mathrm{rank}(A^t S_b A) : w^t S_b w = \alpha^t A^t S_b A \alpha = \alpha^t V_{r_0} \Sigma_{r_0} V_{r_0}^t \alpha$. Maximization of $w^t S_b w$ with the constraint $1 - \alpha^t \alpha = 0$ by Lagrangian multipliers leads to the stationary points $\alpha_k = v_k$ with value σ_k,

$k = 1, \ldots, r_0$. Therefore the optimal point for the Fisher goal function $f(W) = f(w_1, \ldots, w_r)$ can be combined from locally optimal points $w_k = Av_k$ of the quadratic form $w^t S_w w$ for $r \le r_0$:

$$f(W) = \mathrm{tr}(W^t S_b W)/r = \sum_{k=1}^{r} w_k^t S_b w_k / r \tag{1}$$

$$rf(W) \le \sum_{k=1}^{r} v_k^t A^t S_b A v_k = \sum_{k=1}^{r} v_k^t V_{r_0} \Sigma_{r_0} V_{r_0}^t v_k = \sum_{k=1}^{r} \sigma_k \tag{2}$$

Hence the optimal $W = AV_r$, $r \le r_0$, and FLDA models can be compactly characterized as follows: $\mathcal{F}_r(X) = \{W \in \mathbb{R}^{N \times r} : W = U_{q_0} \Lambda_{q_0}^{-1/2} V_r\}$, $S_w = U_{q_0} \Lambda_{q_0} U_{q_0}^t$, $A = U_{q_0} \Lambda_{q_0}^{-1/2}$, $A^t S_b A = V_{r_0} \Sigma_{r_0} V_{r_0}^t$, and for $r \le r_0$ $W^t S_b W = V_r^t (A^t S_b A) V_r = V_r^t V_{r_0} \Sigma_{r_0} V_{r_0}^t V_r = \Sigma_r$.

By the above FLDA properties we propose the novel algorithm 2SS4LDA (*two singular subspaces for LDA*). It is based on two singular value approximations applied directly for the normalized multiclass input data matrix and the normalized class means data matrix. It is controlled by subspace dimension parameters q and r. The first singular subspace of dimension q is designed for original data and it used to compute new coordinates for class means. The second singular subspace is built in this new coordinates. In a sense it is nested SVD procedure. The feature vectors are computed using r left singular vectors spanning the second singular subspace.

Algorithm 1. 2SS4LDA - Two Singular Subspaces for LDA

Input. *Data sequence* $X = [x_1, \ldots, x_L], x_i \in \mathbb{R}^N$, *class membership vector* I, *desired LDA feature vector dimension* r, *and desired first singular subspace dimension* q.

Output. *Corrected values of singular subspace dimensions* q, r *and FLDA model* $W \in \mathbb{R}^{N \times r}$.

Method. *Perform the following steps:*

1. *Compute the global centroid* c *and class centroids:* $C \leftarrow [c_1, \ldots, c_J]$
2. *Perform centroid shifting and normalization for data matrices* X, C :

$$\text{if } i \in I_j \text{ then } y_i \leftarrow (x_i - c_j)/\sqrt{L - J}, i = 1, \ldots, L,$$

$$d_j \leftarrow (c_j - c)\sqrt{L_j/(J-1)},\ j = 1, \ldots, J$$

3. *Find the singular subspace of* $Y = [y_1, \ldots, y_L]$ *by performing SVD for* Y *obtaining* $q_0 \doteq rank(Y)$ *left singular vectors* $U_{q_0} \leftarrow [u_1, \ldots, u_{q_0}]$ *corresponding to positive singular values* $\Lambda_{q_0}^{1/2} \leftarrow [\sqrt{\lambda_1}, \ldots, \sqrt{\lambda_{q_0}}]$
4. *If* $q > q_0$ *then* $q \leftarrow q_0$
   If $q < q_0$ *then* $U_q \leftarrow [u_1, \ldots, u_q]$ *and* $\Lambda_q^{1/2} \leftarrow [\sqrt{\lambda_1}, \ldots, \sqrt{\lambda_q}]$
5. *Compute whitening projection matrix:* $A_q \leftarrow U_q \Lambda_q^{-1/2}$

6. *Make whitening projection for normalized class means:*

$$d_j \leftarrow A_w^t d_j,\ j = 1, \ldots, J$$

7. *Find the singular subspace of* $D \doteq [d_1, \ldots, d_J]$ *by performing SVD for* D *obtaining* $r_0 \doteq rank(D)$ *left singular vectors* $V_{r_0} \leftarrow [v_1, \ldots, v_{r_0}]$ *corresponding to positive singular values*
8. *If* $r > r_0$ *then* $r \leftarrow r_0$
   If $r < r_0$ *then* $V_r \leftarrow [v_1, \ldots, v_r]$
9. *Compute FLDA model, i.e. the projection matrix* W: $W \leftarrow A_q V_r$

Note that for $q_0 = \mathrm{rank}(S_w)$ the above algorithm produces the exact FLDA model and for $q < q_0$ its approximation is obtained. In face recognition problem the optimal value of the measure $f(W)$ is obtained for q much less than the rank of normalized data matrix Y. It means that the better mean class separation occurs for Y projected (with whitening) onto its singular subspace of much lower dimension than the dimension of subspace spanned by vectors in Y.

Note that q_0, the rank of Y (equal to the rank of S_w) is bounded by $\min(L-J, N)$, while r_0, the rank of D (equal to the rank of S_b) is bounded by $\min(J-1, q_0)$. Therefore, the constraint for the feature vector size is $r \leq \min(L-J, J-1, N)$.

In FLDA modeling for face recognition, J is the number of persons in the training database and in our experiments it is less than N and $L-J$. Hence if $q = q_0$ then the rank of data matrix D is equal to the number of training persons minus one: $r_0 = J - 1$.

3 On Relation of FLDA and SLDA Models

It is well known (by the analysis of stationary points for $g(W)$) that the optimal SLDA models are sought by solving the generalized eigenvalue problem (cf. [2]) of the following form $S_b W = S_w W \Lambda_r$, where $\Lambda_r = \mathrm{diag}(\lambda_1, \ldots, \lambda_r)$, $\lambda_1 \geq \cdots \geq \lambda_r > 0$.

Let $\mathcal{E}_r(X)$ denotes the set of all solutions of the above generalized eigenvalue problem. It means that $\mathcal{S}_r(X) \subset \mathcal{E}_r(X)$.

It can be easily proved that local maxima for $g(W)$ are always global, i.e. for optimal $W \in \mathcal{S}_r(X)$ the scatter separation measure has always the same value:

$$g(W) = \frac{|W^t S_b W|}{|W^t S_w W|} = \frac{|W^t S_w W \Lambda_r|}{|W^t S_w W|} = \frac{|W^t S_w W||\Lambda_r|}{|W^t S_w W|} = \prod_{k=1}^{r} \lambda_i$$

It also implies that $\mathcal{E}_r(X) \subset \mathcal{S}_r(X)$ and in conclusion $\mathcal{S}_r(X) = \mathcal{E}_r(X)$.

By Lagrangian optimization of $w^t S_b w$ at $w^t S_w w = 1$ we get $S_b w = \mu S_w w$. Hence the optimal FLDA models have to satisfy the generalized eigenvalue equation and therefore $\mathcal{F}_r(X) \subset \mathcal{E}_r(X)$.

The above inclusion is strict. To show it let us observe that by equation (2) and by $\mathrm{tr}(I) = r$ if $W \in \mathcal{F}_r(X)$ we have $f(W) = \sum_{k=1} \sigma_k / r$.

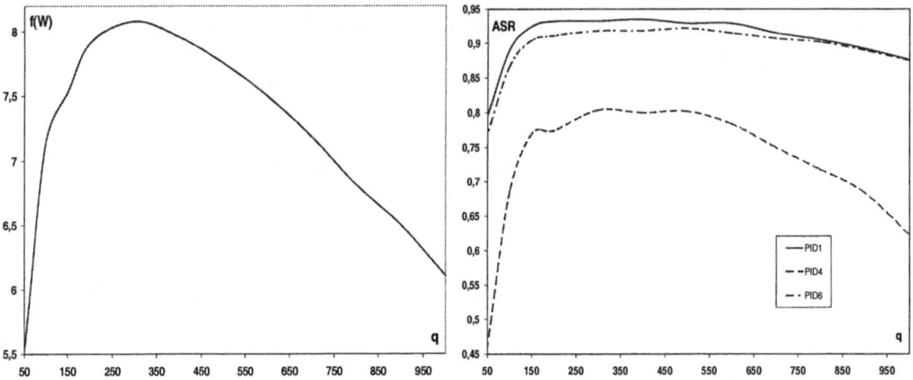

Fig. 1. Left: FLDA separation measure $f(W)$ as function of singular subspace dimension q for class mean shifted original data (model dimension $r = 48$). **Right:** Corresponding average success rate (ASR) using 2SS4LDA algorithm in three person identification experiments (descriptor size: 240 bits).

On the other hand there is simple relation between any two models $W_1, W_2 \in \mathcal{E}_r(X)$: there exists a block diagonal matrix $\Gamma = \text{diag}(B_1, \ldots, B_{r'})$ such that $W_1 = W_2\Gamma$. Suppose that also $W_2 \in \mathcal{F}_r(X)$. If there is no multiple eigenvalues then $\Gamma = \text{diag}(\gamma_1, \ldots, \gamma_r)$ is diagonal what is the case for real life data matrices. Then for any matrix $Z \in \mathbb{R}^{r\times r}$: $\text{tr}(\Gamma^t Z\Gamma) = \sum_{k=1}^{r} \gamma_k^2 Z_{kk}$. Hence if there is no multiple eigenvalues:

$$f(W_1) = f(W_2\Gamma) = \frac{\text{tr}(\Gamma^t W_2^t S_b W_2 \Gamma)}{\text{tr}(\Gamma^t W_2^t S_w W_2 \Gamma)} = \sum_{k=1}^{r} \alpha_k \sigma_k \leq \frac{\sum_{k=1}^{r} \sigma_k}{r}$$

where $\alpha_k \doteq \gamma_k^2/(\gamma_1^2 + \cdots + \gamma_r^2)$. The above inequality becomes equality only if $\gamma_1 = \cdots = \gamma_r$.

In general case when $\Gamma = \text{diag}(B_1, \ldots, B_{r'})$, denoting by $Z_{kk}^{(b)}$ the submatrix of Z corresponding to B_k we have: $\text{tr}(\Gamma^t Z\Gamma) = \sum_{k=1}^{r'} \text{tr}(B_k^t Z_{kk}^{(b)} B_k)$. Hence

$$f(W_1) = f(W_2\Gamma) = \frac{\text{tr}(\Gamma^t W_2^t S_b W_2 \Gamma)}{\text{tr}(\Gamma^t W_2^t S_w W_2 \Gamma)} = \frac{\text{tr}(\Gamma^t \Sigma_r \Gamma)}{\text{tr}(\Gamma^t \Gamma)} = \sum_{k=1}^{r'} \alpha_k \sigma_k \leq \frac{\sum_{k=1}^{r} \sigma_k}{r}$$

where $\alpha_k \doteq \text{tr}(B_k^t B_k)/(\text{tr}(B_1^t B_1) + \cdots + \text{tr}(B_{r'}^t B_{r'}))$. The above inequality becomes equality only if $\text{tr}(B_1^t B_1) = \cdots = \text{tr}(B_{r'}^t B_{r'})$.

Therefore, independently of multiplicity of eigenvalues, there are always optimal models in SLDA which are not optimal in FLDA. In summary:

$$\mathcal{F}_r(X) \subsetneq \mathcal{S}_r(X) = \mathcal{E}_r(X)$$

We have shown that there are optimal SLDA models which are not optimal FLDA models. Can we find optimal SLDA which are not FLDA models, but they achieve maximum value of $f(W)$? The answer is positive. Namely, those

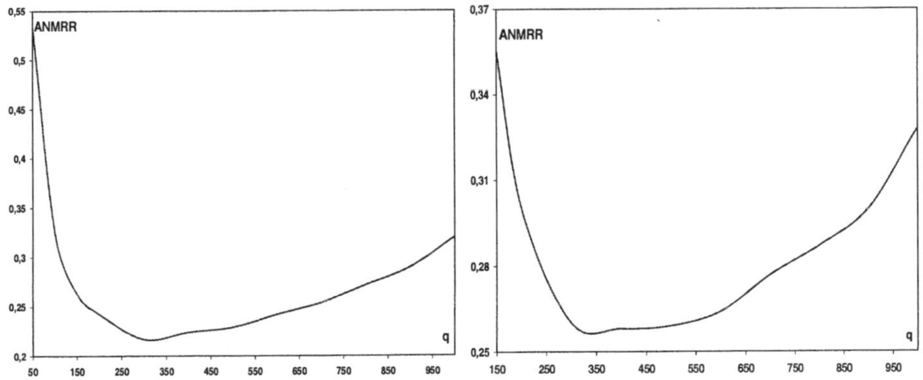

Fig. 2. Average normalized mean retrieval ratio (ANMRR) in function of subspace dimension q in FLDA experiments (**Left:** $r = 48$, 240 bits; **Right:** $r = 128$, 640 bits).

SLDA models $W \in \mathbb{R}^{N \times r}$ for which all diagonal elements of the within-class scatter matrix $W^t S_w W$ are identical, give maximum value of LDA separation measure $f(W)$, i.e. for W satisfying the equation $S_b W = S_w W \Lambda$:

$$f(W) = \frac{\mathrm{tr}(W^t S_b W)}{\mathrm{tr}(W^t S_w W)} = \frac{\mathrm{tr}(W^t S_w W \Lambda)}{\mathrm{tr}(W^t S_w W)} = \frac{\sum_{k=1}^{r} \alpha_k \lambda_k}{\sum_{k=1}^{r} \alpha_k}$$

where $\alpha_k \doteq (W^t S_w W)_{kk} \geq 0$.

Hence, the maximum value of $f(W)$ (equal to $\sum_k \lambda_k / r$) is achieved if and only if $\alpha_1 = \cdots = \alpha_r$. Of course, the class of such matrices W includes $\mathcal{F}_r(X)$. Inclusion is strict as any matrix $W' = \sqrt{\alpha} W$ obtained by uniform scaling by $\sqrt{\alpha} \neq 1$ of FLDA optimal model W gives SLDA optimal model which is not FLDA (since $W'^t S_w W' = \alpha I$). Let us denote the class of such models by $\mathcal{F}_r^{(\alpha)}(X)$. Then $\mathcal{F}_r(X) = \mathcal{F}_r^{(1)}(X)$.

Another observation: if multiplicities of all eigenvalues in Λ_r are equal to one then any SLDA model makes diagonalisation of S_w : $W^t S_w W = \Gamma^t \Gamma$, i.e. LDA projected variables are uncorrelated. This very commonly happens in practice.

If $\Gamma^t \Gamma$ is not a scalable form of unit matrix, i.e. $\Gamma^t \Gamma \neq \alpha I$, then the model W is optimal SLDA model which achieves less value of separation measure $f(W)$ than optimal FLDA models: $W \in \mathcal{S}_r(X) - \bigcup_{\alpha > 0} \mathcal{F}_r^{(\alpha)}(X)$.

Finally, the relation between two concepts of optimal separation of classes can be summarised by the following inclusions:

$$\mathcal{F}_r(X) \subsetneq \bigcup_{\alpha > 0} \mathcal{F}_r^{(\alpha)}(X) \subsetneq \mathcal{S}_r(X) = \mathcal{E}_r(X) \ .$$

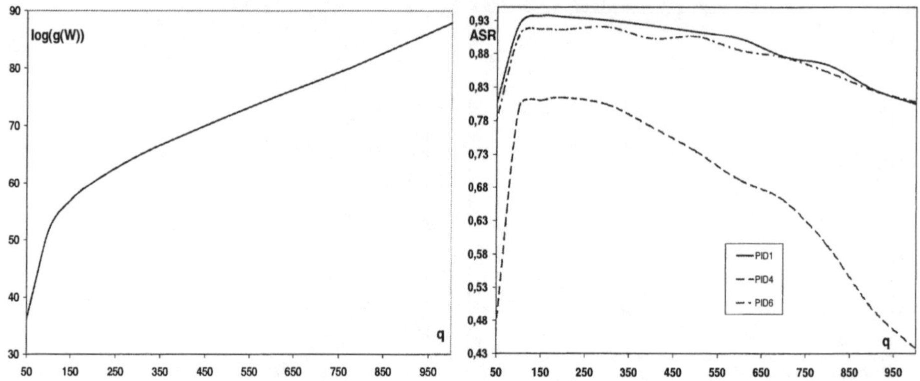

Fig. 3. Left: SLDA separation measure $g(W)$ as function of dimension q for principal subspace which is used for input data matrix singularity conditioning (model dimension $r = 48$). **Right:** Corresponding average success rate (ASR) using GSCHUR algorithm in three person identification experiments (descriptor size: 240 bits).

4 Experiments

In order to perform comparative tests of our method in face recognition task we use images from three databases: Altkom (1200 images, 80 persons), MPEG-7 (3175 images, 635 persons) and FERET subset (4000 images, 875 persons).

Every image has size 46x56 and eyes manually located. Initial preprocessing includes automatic background cutting off.

The half of Altkom and MPEG databases constitutes the training set on which the model matrix W is calculated according to the proposed algorithm 2SS4LDA for FLDA models and generalized Schur algorithm (GSCHUR) for SLDA models (cf. [3]). The other half along with FERET images is used for extracting feature vectors and testing.

The four experiments are considered conforming MPEG-VCE face recognition visual core experiment (cf. [1]): image retrieval(FIR) and three various person identifications(PID). In FIR every single image from testing set becomes a query while in PID the specific disjoint subsets of testing set are chosen for query and test respectively.

5 Conclusions

We have proved that each optimal model of data sequence X in Fisher linear discriminant analysis is also optimal in scatter linear data discriminant analysis. Moreover, there is infinity of models optimal in SLDA which are not optimal in FLDA. There is also infinity of SLDA models which maximize Fisher class separation measure $f(W)$. There exists mathematically closed formulas for those interesting subclasses of SLDA class of data models. They are based on the types of within-class scatter matrix diagonalisation.

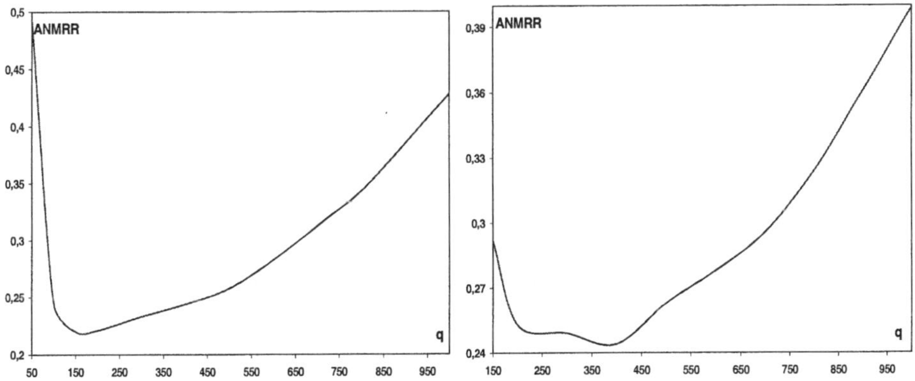

Fig. 4. Average normalized mean retrieval ratio (ANMRR) in function of subspace dimension q in SLDA experiments (**Left:** $r = 48$, 240 bits; **Right:** $r = 128$, 640 bits).

The proposed algorithm 2SS4LDA performs two singular value decompositions applied directly to normalized multiclass input data matrix and normalized class means data matrix. By tuning two singular subspace dimension parameters q and r, we can optimize ratio of between and within-class variance what leads to better performance in face recognition application.

We have observed that using GSCHUR algorithm with regularization by projection of the original data X onto singular subspace of dimension q gives the best results very close to the best results of 2SS4LDA but for quite different settings of q and r.

High correlation of the class separation measure in FLDA with face recognition performance was found in contrary to SLDA case.

On very demanding facial databases of MPEG-7 VCE, the LDA classifier built by proposed algorithm gives 94% for the person identification rate and about 0.21 for the average normalized mean retrieval rank.

References

1. Bober M., Description of MPEG-7 Visual Core Experiments, ISO/IEC JTC1/SC29/WG11, report N4925, July 2002, Klagenfurt.
2. Devijver P.A., Kittler J., Pattern Recognition: A Statistical Approach, Prentice Hall, Englewood Cliffs, N.J., 1982
3. Golub G., Van Loan C., Matrix Computations. Baltimore: Johns Hopkins University Press, 1996
4. Li Y., Kittler J., Matas J., Effective Implementation of Linear Discriminant Analysis for Face Recognition and Verification, CAIP'99, pages 234-242, 1999
5. Ripley B.D., Pattern Recognition and Neural Networks. Cambridge University Press, 1996
6. Swets D.L., Weng J., Using Discriminant Eigenfeatures for Image Retrieval, IEEE Trans. on PAMI, 18(8):831-837, August 1996
7. Zhao W., Krishnaswamy A., Chellappa R., Swets D.L., Weng J., Discriminant Analysis of Principal Components for Face Recognition, In 3rd International Conference on Automatic Face and Gesture Recognition, pages 336-341, 1998

Optimizing Eigenfaces by Face Masks for Facial Expression Recognition

Carmen Frank and Elmar Nöth

Lehrstuhl für Mustererkennung, Universität Erlangen-Nürnberg
Martensstraße 3, 91058 Erlangen, Germany
frank@informatik.uni-erlangen.de,noeth@informatik.uni-erlangen.de
http://www5.informatik.uni-erlangen.de

Abstract. A new direction in improving modern dialogue systems is to make a human-machine dialogue more similar to a human-human dialogue. This can be done by adding more input modalities. One additional modality for automatic dialogue systems is the facial expression of the human user. A common problem in a human-machine dialogue where the angry face may give a clue is the recurrent misunderstanding of the user by the system. Or an helpless face may indicate a naive user who does not know how to utilize the system and should be led through the dialogue step by step.

This paper describes recognizing facial expressions in frontal images using eigenspaces. For the classification of facial expressions, rather than using the face whole image we classify regions which do not differ between subjects and at the same time are meaningful for facial expressions.

Important regions change when projecting the same face to eigenspaces trained with examples of different facial expressions. The average of different faces showing different facial expressions forms a face mask. This face mask fades out unnecessary or mistakable regions and emphasizes regions changing between facial expressions.

Using this face mask for training and classification of *neutral* and *angry* expressions of the face, we achieved an improvement of up to 5% points. The proposed method may improve other classification problems that use eigenspace methods as well.

1 Introduction

Dialogue systems nowadays are constructed to be used by a normal human being, i.e. a naive user. Neither are these users familiar with "drag and drop" nor do they want to read thick manuals about a lot of unnecessary functionality. Rather modern dialogue systems try to behave similar to a human-human dialogue in order to be used by such naive users. But what does a human-human dialogue looks like?

A human being uses much more input information than the spoken words during a conversation with another human being: the ears to hear the words and the tone of the voice, the eyes to recognize movements of the body and facial muscles, the nose to smell where somebody has been, and the skin to recognize

N. Petkov and M.A. Westenberg (Eds.): CAIP 2003, LNCS 2756, pp. 646–654, 2003.

physical contact. In the following we will concentrate on facial expressions. Facial expressions are not only emotional states of a user but also internal states affecting his interaction with a dialogue system, e.g. helplessness or irritation.

At the moment, there are several approaches to enhance modern dialogue systems. The dialogue system *SmartKom* introduced in [Wah01] which is funded by the BMBF[1] is also one of the new powerful dialogue systems. It is a multimodal multimedial system which uses speech, gesture and facial expression as input channels for a human-machine dialogue. The output is a combination of images, animation and speech synthesis.
One idea of facial expression recognition is to get as soon as possible a hint for an angry user in order to modify the dialogue strategies of the system and to give more support. This prevents the users from getting disappointed up to such an extent that they would never ever use the system again.
If a system wants to know about the users internal state by observing the face, it first has to localize the face and then recognize the facial expression.

Face localization aims to determine the image position of a single face. The literature shows various methods. In [Cha98] a combination of skin color and luminance is used to find the face in an head-shoulder image. A combination of facial components (like eyes and nostrils) found by SVMs and their geometric relation is used in [Hei00]. They used this method to detect faces in frontal and near-frontal views of still grey level images. A probabilistic face detection method for faces of different pose, with different expression and under different lighting conditions is the mixture of factor analyzers used by [Yan99]. Only color information is used by [Jon99] to form a statistical model for person detection in web images.
The task of facial expression recognition is to determine the emotional state of a person. A common method is to identify facial action units (AU). These AU were defined by Paul Ekman in [Ekm78]. In [Tia01] a neural-network is used to recognize AU from the coordinates of facial features like lip corners or the curve of eye brows. To determine the muscle movement from the optical flow when showing facial expressions is the task in [Ess95]. It is supplemented by temporal information to form a spatial-temporal motion energy model which can be compared to different models for the facial expressions

In this paper we only deal with the second part, the analysis of an already found face.

2 Algorithm

In the method proposed by us, only pixels that are significant for facial expressions are used to create an eigenspace for facial expression recognition. These significant pixels are selected automatically by a training set of face images showing facial expressions. There is no assumption about the spatial relation of these

[1] This research is being supported by the German Federal Ministry of Education and Research (*BMBF*) in the framework of the SmartKom project under Grant 01 IL 905 K7. The responsibility for the contents of this study lies with the authors.

pixels in contrast to [Kir90] where only an oval region of the face is used to omit background and hair. First we give a short introduction to standard eigenspaces. Then we show their disadvantages and introduce our face mask as improvement.

2.1 Introduction to Eigenspaces

Eigenspace methods are well known in the topic of face recognition ([Tur91], [Yam00], [Mog94]). In a standard face recognition system, one eigenspace for each person is created using different images of this person. Later, when classifying a photo of an unknown person, this image is projected using each of the eigenspaces. The reconstruction error of the principal component representation is an effective indicator of a match.

To create an eigenspace with training images a partial Karhunen-Loéve transformation, also called principal component analysis (PCA) is used. It is a dimensionality reduction scheme that maximizes the scatter of all projected samples, using N sample images of a person $\{\boldsymbol{x}_1, \boldsymbol{x}_2, \ldots, \boldsymbol{x}_N\}$ taking values in an n-dimensional feature space. Let $\boldsymbol{\mu}$ be the mean image of all feature vectors. The total scatter matrix is then defined as

$$S_T = \sum_{k=1}^{N} (\boldsymbol{x}_k - \boldsymbol{\mu})(\boldsymbol{x}_k - \boldsymbol{\mu})^T \tag{1}$$

In PCA, the optimal projection W_{opt} to a lower dimensional subspace is chosen to maximize the determinant of the total scatter matrix of the projected samples,

$$W_{opt} = arg \max_{W} |W^T S_T W| = [w_1, w_2, \ldots, w_m] \tag{2}$$

where $\{w_i | i = 1, 2, \ldots m\}$ is the set of n-dimensional eigenvectors of S_T corresponding to the set of decreasing eigenvalues. These eigenvectors have the same dimension as the input vectors and are referred to as Eigenfaces.

In the following sections we assume that high order eigenvectors correspond to high eigenvalues. Therefore high order eigenvectors hold more relevant information.

2.2 Disadvantages of Standard Eigenspaces

An advantage and as well a disadvantage of eigenspace methods is their capability of finding the significant differences between the input samples. This feature enables eigenspace methods to model a given sample of a n-dimensional feature space in an optimal way using only a m-dimensional space.

But if one has significant differences between training samples not relevant for separating the classes, nevertheless they appear in the high order eigenvalues and maybe fudge the classifying result. An example for such differences of training samples is lighting. Training samples created under different lighting conditions constitute an eigenspace which model the light in high order eigenvectors. In Figure 1 the first three eigenvectors (often called eigenfaces) from an

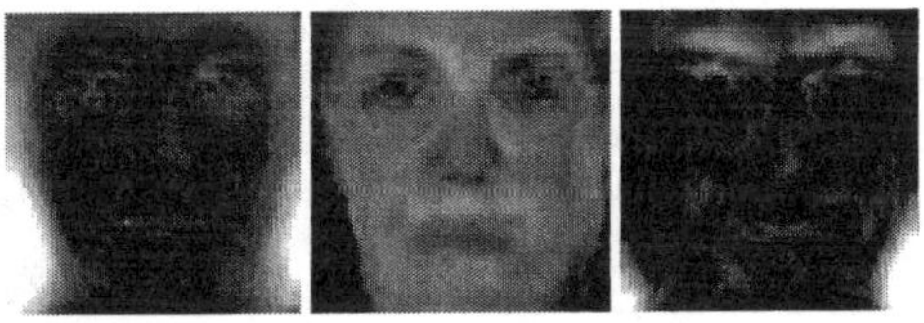

Fig. 1. The first three eigenvectors (eigenfaces) of an *anger*-eigenspace, which model face shape, lighting and eyebrows.

anger eigenspace can be seen modeling light and face contour but not facial expressions. Therefore in face recognition often the first p eigenvectors are deleted as described in [Bel96].

2.3 Eigenfaces for Facial Expression Recognition

When using eigenfaces for facial expression recognition of unknown faces, one possibility is to calculate one eigenspace for each facial expression from a labeled database of different persons.
The classification procedure corresponds to that of face recognition: project a new image to each eigenspace and select the eigenspace which best describes the input image. This is accomplished by calculating the residual description error.

In addition to the disadvantage mentioned above, a problem for facial expression classification is that the person itself, whose facial expression should be classified, is unknown.
Each person uses a different smile. Each person has a different appearance of the neutral face. But each smile of each person should be classified as *smile*. And even facial expressions result from very subtle changes in the face and therefore do not show up in the high order eigenvectors.

2.4 Adapting Eigenfaces for Facial Expression Recognition

In order to deal with this fact we tried to eliminate parts of the face with a high level of changes between different persons which do not contribute to facial expressions. To find out which parts of the face are unnecessary for classifying facial expression, we also use an eigenspace approach.

Imagine we have a training set F_κ of l samples with similar characteristics for each class Ω_κ, $\kappa \in 1, \ldots k$. Thus there is different illumination, different face shape etc. in each set F_κ. Reconstructing one image with each of our eigenspaces results in k different samples. The reconstructed images do not differ in characteristics like illumination, because this is modeled by each eigenspace. But they differ in facial expression specific regions, such as the mouth area.

So we can obtain a mask vector $\boldsymbol{m}$ as the average of difference images using a training set T. For a two class problem this is done in the following way,

$$\boldsymbol{m} = \frac{1}{|T|} \sum_{\boldsymbol{y}_i \in T} V_1^T(\boldsymbol{y}_i - \boldsymbol{\mu}_1) - V_2^T(\boldsymbol{y}_i - \boldsymbol{\mu}_2) \tag{3}$$

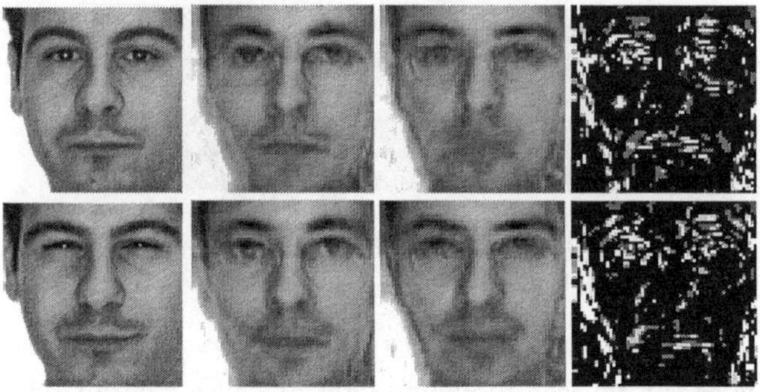

Fig. 2. In the first row the original neutral face, the face reconstructed by a neutral and an anger eigenspace and the difference image of both is shown. In the second row an anger face was used.

where $|T|$ stands for the cardinality of set T and V_κ^T is the eigenspace for class κ. In Figure 2 the neutral and anger face of a man are projected in both eigenspace and the resulting difference images are shown. Before training an eigenspace, we now delete vector components (in this case pixels) from all training samples whose corresponding component of the mask vector $\boldsymbol{m}$ is smaller than a threshold θ. The threshold is selected heuristically at the moment.

The same components must be deleted from an image before classification. A positive side effect is the reduction of feature dimension. The face mask used for our experiments (see. Figure 3) eliminates about 50% of all pixels.

3 Data

All experiments described in this article are performed using the AR-Face Database [Mar98]. From this database we selected one image per person showing a neutral or angry facial expression. The included faces do not show full blown emotion, but natural, weak facial expression. This results in 264 images altogether. The whole set was split into 4 parts (equivalent to the cdroms of the database), 3 parts were used for training and one for testing in a leave one out method. No normalization was done. The tip of the nose, marked by a naive person, served as a reference point to cut the face from the whole image.

4 Experiments

4.1 Facial Expression Mask

The first task is to generate a mask which emphasizes regions of the face important for facial expressions and deletes other regions. We use a set of training images, to create one *anger*- and one *neutral*- eigenspace. The same set of images is used to create a mask using Equation 3.

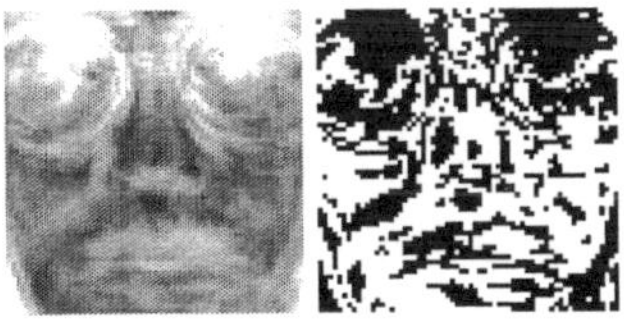

Fig. 3. The left image is an average of faces projected to different eigenspaces. This image binarised with a threshold $\theta = 135$ can be seen on the right side. All *white* pixels are deleted before classification.

This means in detail: project and reproject one image with each eigenspace, subtract the resulting images, calculate an average image over all difference images created from the training set.

Using a threshold θ the mask image is converted to a binary image. Preliminary experiments showed 135 to be a suitable value when using 1 byte of color information for each channel. Such a binarised mask with the corresponding average image can be seen in Figure 3.

4.2 Facial Expression Classification

The images used for the experiments are similar to the faces in Figure 2 and have a size of 64×64 pixels. The classes used were *anger* and *neutral*.

To get an idea of the obtained improvement by the face mask, we show both ROC-curves in one figure. When using *rgb* information of an image the improvement is about 2% points for a medium false alarm rate; this can be seen in Figure 4. False alarm rate means the percentage of *neutral* faces which are classified as *anger*.

The improvement in Figure 5 is much clearer to see. Here we used only the intensity information of a given image. This is more reasonable, because the color of a face does not give a clue about the facial expression, except if the person is ashamed.

The reason why the improvement for the *rgb* case does not have these good values as for the grey value, may be the way the face mask is defined and used. There is only one face mask and not three, for each color channel a separate one. So a constant red value at one position means the green and blue channels are not used either.

5 Application

The knowledge about a users internal state is important to a modern personalized dialogue system. The possible internal user state not only include anger and happiness but also helplessness or confusing. An example application for giving useful information to an automatic dialogue system by analyzing facial expression is a dialogue about current television program. A happy face of a user when getting information about a thriller indicates an affectation for thriller. From

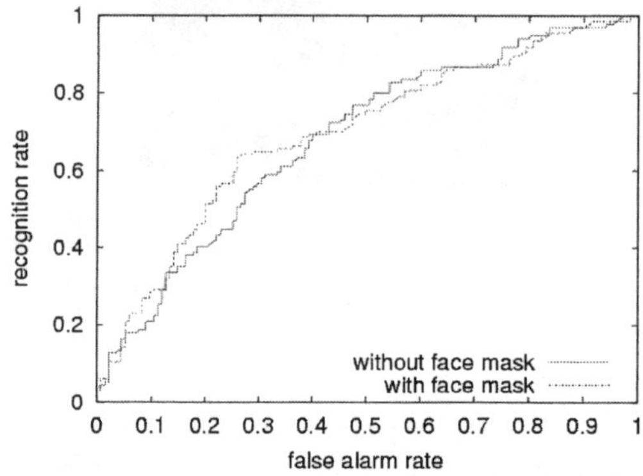

Fig. 4. The percentage of *neutral* faces classified as *anger* is shown on the x-axis (false alarm rate). On the y-axis the percentage of *anger* face classified as *angry* (recognition rate) is shown when using rgb information.

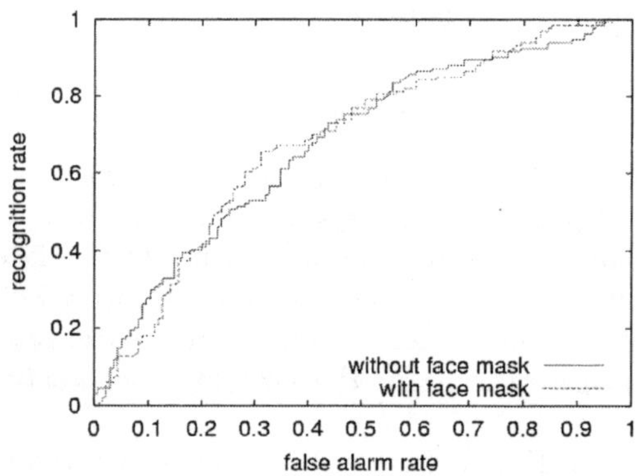

Fig. 5. Recognition rate compared to false alarm rate when using grey level images.

now on this user can be lead to a happy mood when thriller are presented to him first while information about other genres is presented afterwards.

Up to now there are no results from naive persons using a dialogue system which uses information about their emotional state. The reason for this is that on the one hand the users must not know about this functionality of the dialogue system in order to show natural behavior. On the other hand they should be familiar with the system because the dialogue must be as similar as possible to a human-human interaction.

In Wizard-of-Oz experiments the users seemed not to be confused by the facial camera, they forgot being filmed during the dialogue. The questionnaires which are filled out after each dialogue showed the users are not aware of facial expressions influencing the dialogue. They are content with the system and would like to use it an other time.

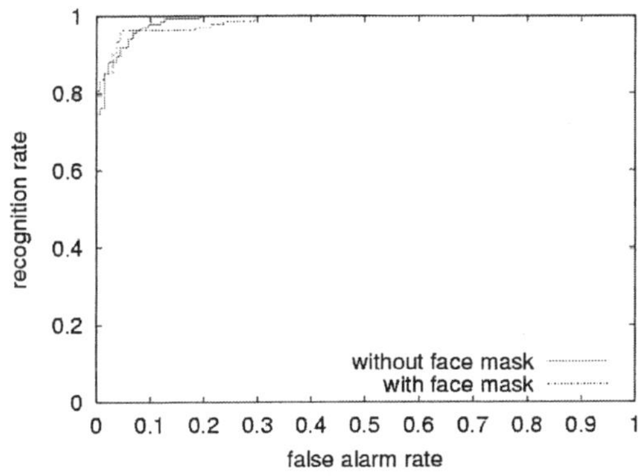

Fig. 6. This is the recognition rate compared to false alarm rate when using rgb-images for classifying *joy* vs. *angry* using a mask with a threshold of $\theta = 135$.

6 Conclusion

Our experiments show that significant information for discriminating facial expressions can not be found in the high order eigenvectors of standard eigenspaces. Moreover fudging information is represented by the high order eigenvectors. This is avoided by using masked faces for the eigenspace training. The used facial mask is automatically trained from a set of faces showing different expressions. It emphasizes discriminating facial regions and fades out unnecessary or mistakable parts.

Using this face mask for training and classification of *neutral* and *angry* expressions of the face, we achieve an improvement of 5% when using grey level images. The described method for data selection to train eigenspaces for facial expression recognition may be used for other classification tasks by changing the training data for the mask.

The next steps for us will be to increase the recognition rates for the rgb case by a more detailed mask and the application of the mask method to the detection of faces using eigenspace methods.

7 Remarks

There are lots of differences between facial expressions. E.g.neither does each smile result from the same positive emotional state of a person nor does each person express a positive emotional state with the same smile. A smile may express love to someone else but a slightly different smile says 'I am sorry'.

The same is true for anger. And especially anger is an emotional state which is expressed in very different manners by different individuals. Some form wrinkles at the forehead, others nearly close their eyes, knit their eyebrows or press the lips together.

But *angry* is besides *helplessness* the most important state for an automatic human-machine dialogue system a user can be in. The anger of a user gives a hint for dialogue problems which should be solved by the dialogue system. Of course it would be nice to know that a user is happy and satisfied with the system but in this case no system reaction is necessary.

The *angry* and *neutral* state of a person are those states which are most difficult to discriminate. A human person produced 50% false alarms and 95% recognition rate when classifying our samples. The reason for this high false alarm rate is that, as mentioned above anger is expressed in very different ways and people often hide anger. The classification of facial expressions of a familiar person is much easier for the human as well as for an automatic system.

The recognition rates for the classification of *angry* and *joyful* user states are much higher than for *angry* and *neutral.* They are shown in Figure 6. A human reaches 97% recognition rate with no false alarms.

References

[Bel96] Belhumeur, P.; Hespanha, J.; Kriegman, D.: *Eigenfaces vs. Fisherfaces: Recognition Using Class Specific Linear Projection*, in *European Conference on Computer Vision '96*, 1996, S. 45–58.

[Cha98] Chai, D.; Ngan, K. N.: *Locating Facial Regions of a Head-and-Shoulders Color Image*, in *Proceedings of the International Conference on Automatic Face and Gesture Recognition*, 1998, S. 124–129.

[Ekm78] Ekman, P.; Friesen, W.: *The Facial Action Coding System: A Technique for the Measurement of Facial Movement*, in *Consulting Psychologists Press, Palo Alto, CA*, 1978.

[Ess95] Essa, I.; Pentland, A.: *Facial Expression Recognition Using a Dynamic Model and Motion Energy*, in *Proceedings of the Fifth International Conference on Computer Vision*, 1995, S. 360–367.

[Hei00] Heisele, B.; Poggio, T.; Pontil, M.: *Face Detection in Still Gray Images*, in *MIT AI Memo, AIM-1687*, 2000.

[Jon99] Jones, M.; Rehg, J.: *Statistical Color Models with Application to Skin Detection*, in *Proceedings of Computer Vision and Pattern Recognition*, 1999, S. I:274–280.

[Kir90] Kirby, M.; Sirovich, L.: *Application of the Karhunen-Loève Procedure for the Characterization of Human Faces*, *TPAMI*, Bd. 12, Nr. 1, 1990, S. 103–108.

[Mar98] Martinez, A.; Benavente., R.: *The AR Face Database*, Purdue University, West Lafayette, IN 47907-1285, 1998.

[Mog94] Moghaddam, B.; Pentland, A.: *Face Recognition Using View-Based and Modular Eigenspaces*, in *Vismod, TR-301*, 1994.

[Tia01] Tian, Y.; Kanade, T.; Cohn, J.: *Recognizing Action Units for Facial Expression Analysis*, *IEEE Transactions on Pattern Analysis and Machine Intelligence (PAMI)*, Bd. 23, Nr. 2, 2001, S. 97–115.

[Tur91] Turk, M.; Pentland, A.: *Face Recognition Using Eigenfaces*, in *Proceedings of Computer Vision and Pattern Recognition*, 1991, S. 586–591.

[Wah01] Wahlster, W.; Reithinger, N.; Blocher, A.: *SmartKom: Multimodal Communication with a Life-Like Character*, in *Eurospeech 2001*, 2001, S. 1547–1550.

[Yam00] Yambor, W. S.; Draper, B. A.; Beveridge, J. R.: *Analyzing PCA-based Face Recognition Algorithms: Eigenvector Selection and Distance Measures*, in *Second Workshop on Empirical Evaluation Methods in Computer Vision*, 2000.

[Yan99] Yang, M.; Ahuja, M.; Kriegman, D.: *Face Detection using a Mixture of Factor Analyzers*, in *Proceedings of the International Conference on Image Processing*, Bd. 3, 1999, S. 612–616.

Polyhedral Scene: Mosaic Construction from 2 Images Taken under the General Case

Yong He and Ronald Chung

Department of Automation & Computer-Aided Engineering
The Chinese University of Hong Kong
Shatin, Hong Kong
{yhe,rchung}@acae.cuhk.edu.hk

Abstract. Image mosaicking is about constructing an image of a large field of view called mosaic from adjacent images, typically two, of the same scene. The problem is particularly difficult if the camera motion is arbitrary and the imaged scene is not planar and is in close range of the camera. In this paper, a novel mosaicking scheme applicable to polyhedral scene in the above scenario is described. The scheme requires only a few initial correspondences over the input images to work. A particular essence of the scheme is that it could handle surfaces that are visible in only one of the input images, and include them into the mosaic. In mosaic construction one has to line up, in the mosaic, surface boundaries that are corresponding but warped from the respective input images. A simple solution to that is also described, which requires only a minimum number of correspondences over the involved surfaces to have the task achieved seamlessly. Experimental results on real images show that the proposed mosaicking scheme is effective.

1 Introduction

In recent years digital cameras of increasingly high image resolution have become available at affordable prices. However, the physical structure of the lenses and camera body still limit the field of view of the images. The field of view could be enlarged with the use of lenses of shorter focal length or even fish-eye lenses, yet it is still bounded by the physical limitation, and with the same number of pixels (picture elements) dedicated to a wider field of view the image quality would also be compromised. Image mosaicking is about putting together a number of images, each with a partially different field of view about the same scene, to form a single image named mosaic that displays a larger field of view. As the mosaic is not something physically captured by any single camera, the accumulated field of view is without physical limit and could be as wide as a 360 degree panorama, and in principle that is achievable without the image resolution sacrificed. The technique could also be used to convert a video to a panoramic or omni- picture of high resolution. It finds uses in a large variety of applications including real image based virtual reality, robotics, and even image compression by reducing redundancy in the image data.

In the simplest form, image mosaic construction is about stitching images two at a time, and about estimating a particular image-to-image mapping named planar homography (or collineation) of every two such images. Planar homography could be ex-

N. Petkov and M.A. Westenberg (Eds.): CAIP 2003, LNCS 2756, pp. 655–663, 2003.

pressed in terms of a nonsingular 3×3 matrix whose overall scale is arbitrary, and it could be estimated from just 4 point correspondences over the images. Once the homography is known, one image (termed the *additive image* here) could be warped to the 2D projective space of the other image (termed the *base image* here), and the two images could be merged under the same image coordinate frame (that of the base image) to form a mosaic. Most of the previous works are based upon this framework (examples: [4] [9]), although there are variations in the local re-alignment of the image-to-image registration they use for achieving better mosaic quality.

However, describing the scene using a single homography is only applicable in the following 3 cases: imaged scene is either planar, or very distant from the cameras, or imaged under a pure rotation of the camera. This paper is about how image mosaic could be constructed for scenes that are pictured under general imaging condition and that could be described as consisting of multiple surface patches, each of which approximately planar. In such a case, no single homography could capture the image-to-image transformation that is needed in the mosaicking process.

An obvious approach to solving the problem is the divide-and-conquer methodology, which is to tackle the planar patches of the imaged scene one by one. Should enough correspondences be established over each of the surface patches, the existing solution framework could be applied to each individual surface patch and at the end constructs a final mosaic. Yet, the above approach requires not only each planar patch to be visible in both input images, enough correspondences must also be available over each of the patches. That also excludes surfaces that are visible in only the additive image not the base image, termed the singly visible surfaces here, from the final mosaic, since with no correspondence physically possible over them the planar homographies that allow them to be warped across the images are simply not available.

In this paper, we describe a novel scheme that could achieve mosaicking with only a few correspondences over the entire scene (not over every surface), and could even include singly visible surfaces into the final mosaic. The trick of the scheme is to take advantage of the connectivity property of the surfaces.

A headache to most if not all mosaicking systems is how to ensure that surface boundaries warped from the additive image and the corresponding surface boundaries in the base image line up perfectly, so as to have the mosaic appear seamless. Previous works focused on ways to estimate the warping-related homographies more accurately, and they include the use of more correspondences over the involved surfaces, the incorporation of robust estimation techniques (that remove outliers of the correspondences), and so on. However, as long as the given correspondences are over-determining for the needed homographies, any estimation method is bound to offer only compromise. We have tried nonlinear estimation methods like Szeliski's [7], yet gaps and undesirable over-writing are inevitable in the mosaic.

In this paper, we provide a very simple solution to the above image registration problem. We go back to the basic form: the just-determined case over some key correspondences that capture the visual quality of the mosaic, and come up with a solution that has a closed-form expression for the required homographies, requiring no iterative computations in the estimation process. Simple the solution is, experiments show it is very effective in coming up with seamless mosaic.

This paper is organized in the following way. In Section 2, we review some preliminaries on planar homography and describe an inference mechanism that allows correspondences to be propagated across surfaces. In Section 3, we describe the line-mapping form of homography and outline how it could be exploited in mosaic construction. In Section 4, we present experimental results on real image data. In Section 5 we give the conclusion.

2 Correspondence Inference Mechanism for Handling the Singly Visible Surfaces

The relationship between two cameras looking at the same plane π in the 3-D space can be represented as homography [3] (also called collineation earlier). It is a linear projective transform in the 2-D image plane, due to some reference plane π in 3-D, denoted by a 3×3 matrix H. That is, all points in one view can be transformed to another view by H, realizing the full correspondence. Four points P_j, j=1,..., 4, in the same 3-D plane π is enough to set up the homography up to a scaling factor.

$$[x', y', 1]^T \cong H[x, y, 1]^T \tag{1}$$

where $\cong$ denotes equality up to a scale, [x, y, 1] and [x', y', 1] is the homogenous co ordinate form of p and p'. Note that the epipoles' existence save us one point in the computation of H, for the line determined by the two camera's centers O and O' always intersects plane π. With three corresponding points p_j and p'_j, j=1,...,3, in the base view and input view, which are the vertex of two corresponding triangle, we can estimate homography H, and then every point (x, y) on the plane defined by the three points in the input view will have the image position (x', y') in the base view according to (1).

For images of a scene that could be approximated as consisting of a number of planar surfaces $\{\Pi_i\}$, there exists a homography associated with every planar partition Π_i. As long as such homographs are known, the corresponding surface patches could be warped across the images to the mosaic frame and construct the mosaic. The problem is, asking for initial correspondences over every surface patch enough for the associated homograph to be determined is too demanding a pre-requisite. In addition, surfaces that are only singly visible do not allow correspondences at all and thus are not mosaicable that way.

As illustrated in Figure 1, suppose we have initial correspondences over two neighboring surfaces *A* and *B*, of the imaged scene, and suppose the correspondences are enough for the homographies associated with *A* and *B* be determined. The homographies could be used to pinpoint all other correspondences over surfaces *A* and *B*. In other words, surfaces *A* and *B* are fully matched across the images (they are shaded in Fig. 1). In particular, the homographies could be used to predict correspondences over their boundaries that are shared with their common neighbor: surface *C*. For example, the homography for *A* could be used to pinpoint correspondence over point *q* (or any other point on the boundary), the homography for *B* could be used to pinpoint correspondence over point *r* (or any other point on the boundary), and either homography could be used to pinpoint correspondence over point *p*. Thus even without any initial correspondence at all over surface *C* at the very beginning, now we have three point correspondences over the surface. These three correspondences, in combination with knowledge about the epipole pair of the image pair, would just be enough to allow the homography associated with surface C to be determined. With the homography all other correspondences over surface C could be predicted, and surface C is fully matched. The same mechanism of propagating correspondences from $\{A,B\}$ to C could be applied to other common neighbors of $\{A,B\}$. Furthermore, the same mechanism could be carried forward to the surfaces that are the common neighbors of $\{B,C\}$, $\{C,A\}$, and so on. The correspondences could even be propagated to singly visible surfaces, like surface D displayed in Fig. 1.

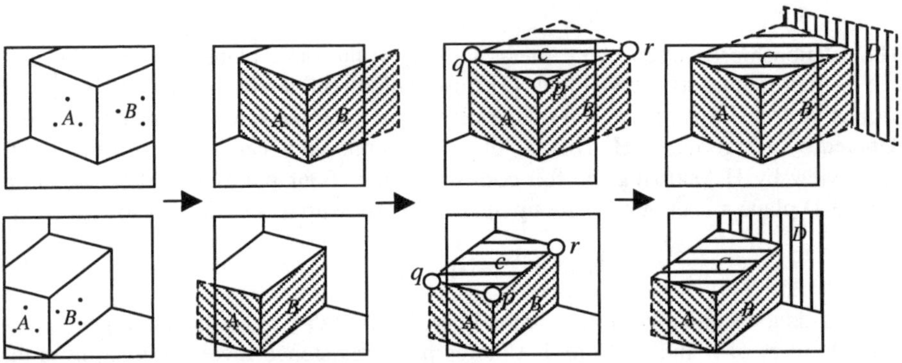

Fig. 1. Operation of the correspondence propagation mechanism. Initial correspondences over surfaces A and B allows the homographies associated with them to be determined. Such homographies then allow points, say p, q, r (or any other points), over the boundary of their common neighbor – surface C – to be inferred, which in turn determine the homography associated with C. The same process could even determine the homography associated with singly visible surfaces like D

The mechanism was first used for object locating in [1] and [2]. It works toward piecewise planar scene like the homography toward planar scene: dense correspondence can be pinpointed from a few initial ones. There are two differences, however. While homography predicts correspondences over a surface, the mechanism propagates correspondences across surfaces. While homography could predict correspondences randomly (over the surface), the mechanism has to predict correspondences over surfaces of an object sequentially: from the initial point correspondences to the first layer of surfaces that contain these point correspondences, to the second layer of surfaces that is the common neighbor of (at least) two of the surfaces in the first layer, and so on.

To implement this algorithm, followings are to be considered firstly:

1. We need to have the input image divided into joint surfaces and get the boundaries of each surface, because each homography only valid for a certain surface area.
2. As a necessary condition for the propagation to be conducted in the current layer, each surface should have two neighboring surfaces, which are predecessor corresponding surface (i.e. the surface that has established full correspondences from previous inference).
3. After that, select a proper start where three planar surfaces intersect to form a 4-tuple and establish the initial correspondences over two of the three surfaces form-

ing this 4-tuple. The propagation path should be one that can go through all the surfaces while fulfill condition 2.

Then, with a few initial correspondences we can realize the correspondence propagation, mapping the exclusive part of the input view to the base view, achieving a mosaicking.

3 Self-duality of Homography and Its Application to Image Mosaicking

First, let us recall some basic law that governs the relation of points and lines in the same projective space and their transformation.
Assume that image plane is a 2-D projective plane and the world in which the camera embedded is a 3-D projective space, things happened conforms to what projective geometry [6] tells us.

Rewrite (1) as

$$\mathbf{p'} = \mathbf{H} \times \mathbf{p} \tag{2}$$

in which p and p' is the homogenous coordinate form of corresponding point (x y) and (x', y') in base view and input view respectively. Here we only consider the non-singular homography, and thus | H | ≠ 0. So

$$\mathbf{p} = \mathbf{H}^{-1} \times \mathbf{p'} \tag{3}$$

Line $\boldsymbol{l}$ can be regarded as the locus of a variable point $\boldsymbol{p}$, then

$$\mathbf{l}^{T}\mathbf{p} = 0 \tag{4}$$

Substitute (3) into (4), we have

$$\mathbf{l}^{T}\mathbf{H}^{-1}\mathbf{p'} = 0 \tag{5}$$

We know that

$$\mathbf{l'}^{T}\,\mathbf{p'} = 0 \tag{6}$$

This imply that

$$\mathbf{l'}^{T} = \mathbf{l}^{T}\mathbf{H}^{-1} \tag{7}$$

i.e.,

$$\mathbf{l'} = \mathbf{H}^{-1T}\mathbf{l} \tag{8}$$

That is to say, the transformation (1) of points into points induces the reciprocal transformation (8) of lines into lines. Also, Points and lines are dual according to projective geometry. It follows, therefore, if

$$\mathbf{l'} = \mathbf{H} \times \mathbf{l} \tag{9}$$

transforms lines to lines, then it induces

$$\mathbf{p'} = \mathbf{H}^{-1T}\mathbf{p} \tag{10}$$

which transforms points to points. In (9) and (10), line l' and l are the locus of point p' and p respectively.

The equation (9) and (10) express a self-dual character of homography. The usage of the above equation can be illustrated through Figure 2, which is redrawn from Fig. 1.

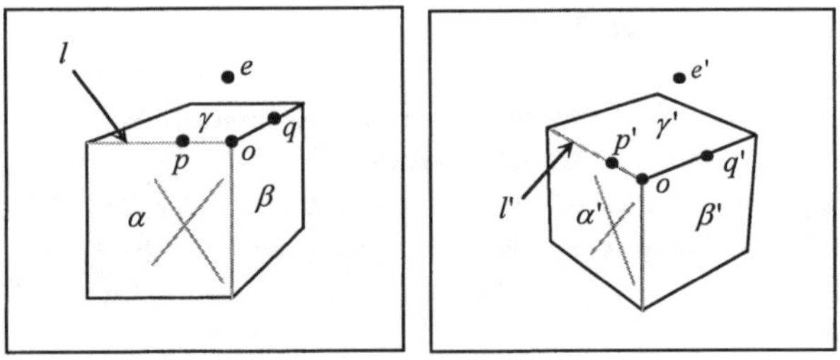

Fig. 2. 4-tuple in different view

The line-mapping form of homography H_A between α and α′, induced by plane A in 3-D, can be estimated by four corresponding lines (drawn with light color) according to equation (5). Note that when system of equations is solved in justdetermined case, the solution exactly fit the input data. In our case, the solution H_A maps l' to l and a randomly selected point $p' \in l'$ to $p \in l$ according to equation (6). Then we get a point correspondence over γ and γ′. The line-mapping form of homography H_B between β and β′, induced by plane B in 3-D, can also be estimated in the same way. Another correspondence q and q', over γ and γ′, is inferred. The third one is the vertex of the 4-tuple o and o'. It can be inferred either from H_A or H_B or a mean of the result from H_A and H_B, for it locate in the common boundary of plane A and B. Epipoles e and e' can be regarded as a universal correspondence over all surfaces, so it can be adopted as the fourth correspondence over γ and γ′.

Having these four correspondences, we link them from p to o, to q, to e, to p in the base view and input view respectively and get four corresponding lines. Using these four line correspondences, the homography H_C between γ and γ′, induced by plane C in 3-D, can be estimated. Therefore the image patch γ′ can be transformed to base view point by point, keeping its boundaries superposition with α and β's boundary.

Though p inferred by H_C may differ from its true position due to some input noise, the difference must be along line l, and is always negligible and bearable as a mosaicking result. It is also worth noting that we don't use any information from γ and γ′, that's where the highlight lies.

4 Experiment and Result

We have coded the proposed system and experimented it with various sets of real image data. Below we present one set of result to illustrate the performance of the system.

As to the estimation of fundamental matrix and epipoles, we used the "Image Matching" system [8] developed by the INRIA group. The accuracy of the epipoles is rather satisfactory.

In all experiments we used a feature detector slightly modified from that proposed by Nevatia and Babu [5], to detect edges and lines in each image.

On line matching there already exist a number of line matchers in the literature (e.g., the one in [2]). We have developed in-house a line matcher that could also serve the purpose. It matches distinct image features hierarchically, from tri-junctions (co-intersections of three lines), to bi-junctions (co-intersections of two lines), and finally to line segments, making full use of the knowledge of the epipolar geometry extracted earlier, and with each level's matching benefiting from the matching results of the previous levels. Feature matching is a nontrivial problem, and indeed our matching system occasionally misses out correct correspondences. Nonetheless, what are required in our system are only a few initial correspondences over two surfaces (three correspondences on each surface), and our experience has been that the line matcher we used is adequate for the purpose.

In all the mosaics presented below, the luminance difference between the additive image and the base image is not adjusted. It is done on purpose so as to make more visible which parts of the final mosaic are original from the base image and which are warped from the additive image, and how good the surface boundaries are lining up in the mosaic.

5 Conclusion and Future Work

We have proposed a system that could construct mosaic for scene that is describable approximately as consisting of multiple planar surfaces. The system does not require the scene to be pictured at far distance. It does not require initial correspondences to be available over each of the surfaces either, nor does it require all the imaged surfaces to be visible in both input images. To our knowledge no existing system is able to achieve the same task.

The system is based upon the use of not one planar homography but multiple homographies to describe the imaged scene, as well as of a correspondence inference mechanism that could propagate correspondences across neighboring surface patches and even to surfaces that are visible in only one of the input images, thereby allowing the homographies associated with those surfaces to be estimatible.

The homographies, even estimatible, could not be estimated very accurately because of the often sparse nature of the correspondences. That leads to compromised quality of the mosaic. We have also proposed a seam elimination mechanism that could ensure seamless mosaicking with even the minimum number (but necessary number for homography determination) of correspondences available.

Experimental results show that the system is effective in achieving the stated task. Future work will address how the system performs for scenes that have substantial curvature.

Fig. 3. (left)Base view of an elevator lobby scene. Again, made of multiple surface patches, the scene is more accurately described by multiple homographies not a single homography. (right) Additive view of the elevator lobby scene. Notice that the surface patch that contains the door entrance and the wall on the right is visible only in this view not in the base view

Fig. 4. Mosaic of the elevator lobby scene resulted from multiple-homography processing plus the seam-elimination mechanism. Even the surface patch on the right that is visible only in the additive view could be warped and form part of the mosaic

Acknowledgment

The work described in this paper was partially supported by a grant from the Research Grants Council of the Hong Kong Special Administrative Region, China (Project No. CUHK4177/01E).

Reference

1. R. Chung, "Object Locating using a single Model View", in *Proc. of IEEE International Symposium on Computer Vision*, Florida, November 1995, pp. 545-550

2. R. Chung and H.S. Wong, "Polyhedral Object Localization by referencing to a Single Model View", to appear in *International Journal of Computer Vision*
3. O. Faugeras, "Stratification of three-dimensional vision: projective, affine, and metric representations", in *Journal of the Optical Society of America: A*, March 1995, Vol. 12, No. 3, pp. 465-484
4. S. Mann and R. Picard, "Virtual bellows: Constructing high quality stills from video", *First IEEE International Conference on Image Processing*, volume I, Austin, Texas, Nov 1994, pp. 363-367
5. R. Nevatia, K. R. Babu, "Linear feature extraction and description", *Computer Graphics and image processing*, 13, 1980, pp.257-269
6. J. G. Semple and G. T. Kneebone, *Algebraic Projective Geometry*, Oxford University Press, London, 1952
7. R. Szeliski, "Video mosaics for virtual environments", in *IEEE Computer Graphics and Applications*, March 1996, Vol. 16, No. 2, pp.22-30
8. Z. Zhang, R. Deriche, O. Faugeras, Q.-T. Luong, "A Robust Technique for Matching Two Uncalibrated Images Through the Recovery of the Unknown Epipolar Geometry", *Artificial Intelligence Journal*, October 1995, Vol.78, pages 87-119
9. I. Zoghlami, O. Faugeras and R. Deriche, "Using Geometry Corners to Build a 2D Mosaic from a set of Images", In *Proc. of IEEE International Conference on Computer Vision and Pattern Recognition*, June 1997, pp. 420-425

Modeling Adaptive Deformations during Free-Form Pose Estimation

Bodo Rosenhahn, Christian Perwass, and Gerald Sommer

Institut für Informatik und Praktische Mathematik
Christian-Albrechts-Universität zu Kiel
Preußerstrasse 1-9, 24105 Kiel, Germany
{bro,chp,gs}@ks.informatik.uni-kiel.de

Abstract. In this article we discuss the 2D-3D pose estimation problem of deformable 3D free-form contours. In our scenario we observe objects of any 3D shape in an image of a calibrated camera. Pose estimation means to estimate the relative position and orientation of the 3D object to the reference camera system. The object itself is modeled as free-form contour. The fusion of modeling free-form contours within the pose estimation problem is achieved by using the conformal geometric algebra: Free-form contours are modeled as unique entities with 3D Fourier descriptors and combined with an ICP (Iterative Closest Point) algorithm they are embedded in the pose problem. The modeling of object deformations within free-form pose estimation is achieved by a combination of adaptive kinematic chain segments within Fourier descriptors.

Keywords: Pose estimation, Fourier descriptors, kinematic chains

1 Introduction

Pose estimation itself is one of the oldest computer vision problems. Algebraic solutions with different camera models have been proposed for several variations of this problem. Pose estimation means to estimate the relative position and orientation of the 3D object to the reference camera system: We assume a 3D object model and extracted corresponding features in an image of a calibrated camera. The aim is to find the rotation $\boldsymbol{R}$ and translation $\boldsymbol{t}$ of the object, which leads to the best fit of the reference model with the actually extracted entities. Pioneering work was done in the 80's and 90's by Lowe [6], Grimson [5] and others. In their work, point correspondences are used. More abstract entities can be found in [15, 2]. In the literature we find circles, cylinders, kinematic chains or other multi-part curved objects as entities. Works concerning free-form curves can be found in [3, 13]. Contour point sets, affine snakes, or active contours are used for visual servoing in these works.

To relate 2D image information to 3D entities we interpret an extracted image entity, resulting from the perspective projection, as a one dimension higher entity, gained through projective reconstruction from the image entity. This idea will be used to formulate the scenario as a pure 3D problem. Our recent work [11]

N. Petkov and M.A. Westenberg (Eds.): CAIP 2003, LNCS 2756, pp. 664–672, 2003.

concentrates on modeling objects by using features of the object (e.g. corners, edges). Instead, we now deal with 3D contours of the object. The problem with feature based pose estimation is that there exist many scenarios (e.g. in natural environments) in which it is not possible to extract point-like features such as corners or edges. In such cases there is need to deal for example with the silhouette of the object as a whole, instead of with sparse local features of the silhouette. In these scenarios free-form contours are applied. The motivation for modeling object deformations within free-form contours is shown in figure 1. In

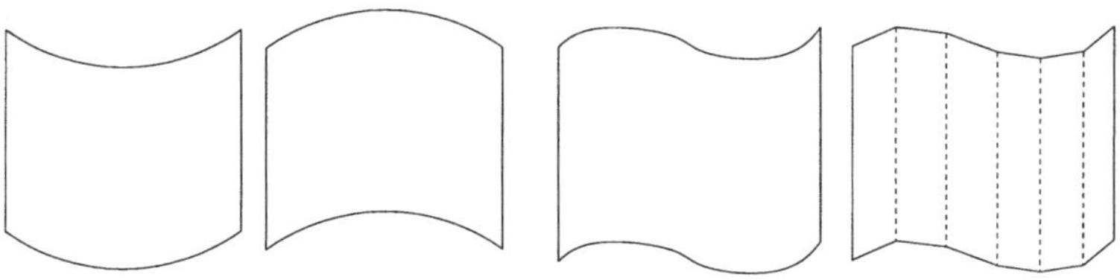

Fig. 1. Possible deformations of a sheet of paper along the y-axis and their representation as kinematic chain.

our experiments we use a planar object, which is printed on a sheet of paper. To model deformations of the sheet of paper we combine kinematic chains within the object contour as shown in the right image of figure 1. Another main point in this contribution is additionally to model object deformations in an adaptive manner: Kinematic chains are used within free-form contours. But the scenario during an image sequence may change, so that it is not useful to take a fixed number of joints along the kinematic chain. Instead, we present a real-time system, which chooses the number of joints adaptively. This leads to more stable and time-optimized algorithms.

2 The Pose Problem in Conformal Geometric Algebra

This section concerns the formalization of the free-form pose estimation problem in conformal geometric algebra. Geometric algebras are the language we use for our pose problem and the main arguments for using this language are its possibility of coupling projective, kinematic and Euclidean geometry by using a conformal model and its dense symbolic representation. A more detailed introduction concerning geometric algebras can be found in [12].

The main idea of geometric algebras $\mathcal{G}$ is to define a product on basis vectors, which extends the linear vector space V of dimension n to a linear space of dimension 2^n. The elements are so-called multivectors as higher order algebraic entities in comparison to vectors of a vector space as first order entities. A geometric algebra is denoted as $\mathcal{G}_{p,q}$ with $n = p + q$. Here p and q indicate the numbers of basis vectors which square to $+1$ and -1, respectively. The product defining a geometric algebra is called *geometric product* and is denoted by juxtaposition, e.g. $\boldsymbol{uv}$ for two multivectors $\boldsymbol{u}$ and $\boldsymbol{v}$. Operations between multivectors

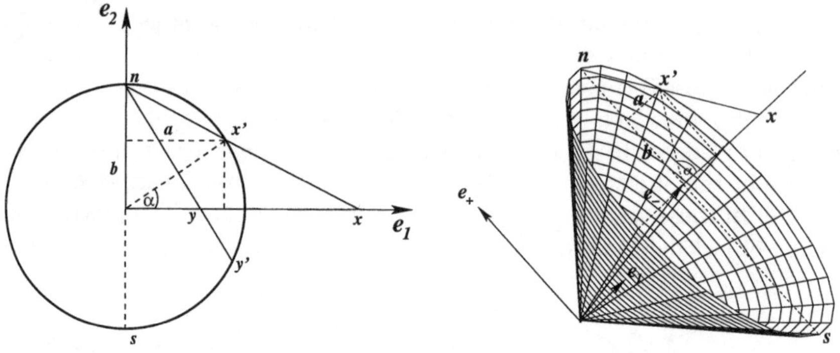

Fig. 2. Left: Visualization of a stereographic projection for the 1D case: Points on the line $\mathbf{e}_1$ are projected on the (unit) circle. Right: Visualization of the homogeneous model for a stereographic projection in the 1D case. All stereographic projected points are on a cone, which is a null-cone in the Minkowski space.

can be expressed by special products, called *inner* $\cdot$, *outer* $\wedge$, *commutator* $\underline{\times}$ and *anticommutator* $\overline{\times}$ product. The idea behind conformal geometry is to interpret points as *stereographically projected* points. This means augmenting the dimension of space by one. The method used in a stereographic projection is visualized for the 1D case in the left image of figure 2: Points $\boldsymbol{x}$ on the line $\mathbf{e}_1$ are mapped to points $\boldsymbol{x}'$ on the unit circle by intersecting the line spanned by the *north pole* $\boldsymbol{n}$ and $\boldsymbol{x}$ with the circle. The basic formulas for projecting points in space on the sphere and vice versa are for example given in [9]. Using a homogeneous model for stereographic projected points means to augment the coordinate system by a further additional coordinate whose unit vector now squares to minus one. In 1D this leads to a cone in space, which is visualized in the right image of figure 2. This cone is spanned by the original coordinate system, the augmented one of the stereographic projection and the homogeneous one. This space introduces a Minkowski metric and will lead to a representation of any Euclidean point on a null-cone (1D case) or a hyper-null-cone (3D case). In [12] it is further shown that the conformal group of $\mathbb{R}^n$ is isomorphic to the Lorentz group of $\mathbb{R}^{n+1,1}$ which has a spinor representation in $\mathcal{G}_{n+1,1}$. We will take advantage of both properties of the constructed embedding which are the representation of points as null-vectors and the spinor representation of the conformal group.

The conformal geometric algebra $\mathcal{G}_{4,1}$ (CGA) [7] is suited to describe conformal geometry. It contains spheres as geometric basis entities and the conformal transformations as geometric manipulations. The point at infinity, $\mathbf{e} \simeq \boldsymbol{n}$, and the origin, $\mathbf{e}_0 \simeq \boldsymbol{s}$, are special elements of the representation which are used as basis vectors instead of $\mathbf{e}_+$ and $\mathbf{e}_-$ because they define a null space in the conformal geometric algebra. A Euclidean point $\boldsymbol{x} \in \mathbb{R}^3$ can be represented as a point $\underline{\boldsymbol{x}}$ on the null-cone by taking $\underline{\boldsymbol{x}} = \boldsymbol{x} + \frac{1}{2}\boldsymbol{x}^2\mathbf{e} + \mathbf{e}_0$. This point representation can be interpreted as a sphere with radius zero. A general sphere, defined by the center $\boldsymbol{p}$ and the radius ρ, is given as $\underline{\boldsymbol{s}} = \boldsymbol{p} + \frac{1}{2}(\boldsymbol{p}^2 - \rho^2)\mathbf{e} + \mathbf{e}_0$, and a point $\underline{\boldsymbol{x}}$ is on a sphere $\underline{\boldsymbol{s}}$ iff $\underline{\boldsymbol{x}} \cdot \underline{\boldsymbol{s}} = 0$. The multivector concepts of geometric algebras then allow to define entities like points, lines, planes or circles as subspaces, generated from spheres.

Rotations are represented by rotors, $\boldsymbol{R} = \exp\left(-\frac{\theta}{2}\boldsymbol{l}\right)$. The parameter of a rotor $\boldsymbol{R}$ is the rotation angle θ applied on a unit bivector $\boldsymbol{l}$ which represents the dual of the rotation axis. The rotation of an entity can be performed by its spinor product $\underline{\boldsymbol{X}}' = \boldsymbol{R}\underline{\boldsymbol{X}}\widetilde{\boldsymbol{R}}$. The multivector $\widetilde{\boldsymbol{R}}$ denotes the reverse of $\boldsymbol{R}$. A translation can be expressed by a translator, $\boldsymbol{T} = (1 + \frac{\mathbf{e}\boldsymbol{t}}{2}) = \exp\left(\frac{\mathbf{e}\boldsymbol{t}}{2}\right)$. A rigid body motion can be expressed by a screw motion [8]. For every screw motion $g \in SE(3)$ exists a $\xi \in se(3)$ and a $\theta \in \mathbb{R}$ such that $g = \exp(\xi\theta)$. The element ξ is also called a *twist*. The motor $\boldsymbol{M}$ describing a screw motion has the general form $\boldsymbol{M} = \exp(-\frac{\theta}{2}(\boldsymbol{n}+\mathbf{e}\boldsymbol{m}))$, with a unit bivector $\boldsymbol{n}$ and an arbitrary 3D vector $\boldsymbol{m}$. The triple $(\theta, \boldsymbol{n}, \boldsymbol{m})$ in the exponential term represent the twist parameters. Whereas in Euclidean geometry, Lie groups and Lie algebras are only applied on point concepts, the motors and twists of the CGA can also be applied on other entities like lines, planes, circles, spheres, etc.

Constraint Equations for Pose Estimation.
Now we start to express the 2D-3D pose estimation problem for pure point correspondences: *a transformed object point has to lie on a projection ray, reconstructed from an image point.* Let $\underline{\boldsymbol{X}}$ be a 3D object point given in CGA. The (unknown) transformation of the point can be described as $\boldsymbol{M}\underline{\boldsymbol{X}}\widetilde{\boldsymbol{M}}$. Let $\boldsymbol{x}$ be an image point on a projective plane. The projective reconstruction of an image point in CGA can be written as $\underline{\boldsymbol{L}}_x = \mathbf{e} \wedge \boldsymbol{O} \wedge \boldsymbol{x}$. The line $\underline{\boldsymbol{L}}_x$ is calculated from the optical center $\boldsymbol{O}$, the image point $\boldsymbol{x}$ and the vector $\mathbf{e}$ as the point at infinity. The line $\underline{\boldsymbol{L}}_x$ is given in a Plücker representation. Collinearity can be described by the commutator product. Thus, the 2D-3D pose estimation from an image point can be formalized as constraint equation in CGA,

$$(\boldsymbol{M}\underline{\boldsymbol{X}}\widetilde{\boldsymbol{M}}) \underline{\times} (\mathbf{e} \wedge \boldsymbol{O} \wedge \boldsymbol{x}) = 0.$$

Constraint equations which relate 2D image lines to 3D object points or 2D image lines to 3D object lines can be expressed in a similar manner. Note: The constraint equations in the unknown motor $\boldsymbol{M}$ express a distance measure which has to be zero.

Fourier Descriptors in CGA.
Fourier descriptors are often used for object recognition [4] and affine pose estimation [1] of closed contours. We are now concerned with the formalization of 3D Fourier descriptors in CGA in order to combine these with our previously introduced pose estimation constraints. Let $\boldsymbol{R}_i^{\phi} := \exp(-\pi u_i \phi/T)\,\boldsymbol{l})$, where $T \in \mathbb{R}$ is the length of the closed curve, $u_i \in \mathbb{Z}$ is a frequency number and $\boldsymbol{l}$ is a unit bivector which defines the rotation plane. Furthermore, $\widetilde{\boldsymbol{R}}_i^{\phi} = \exp(\pi u_i \phi/T\,\boldsymbol{l})$. Because $\boldsymbol{l}^2 = -1$ we can write the exponential function as $\exp(\phi \boldsymbol{l}) = \cos(\phi) + \boldsymbol{l}\sin(\phi)$. We can now formulate any closed curve $C(\phi)$ of the Euclidean plane as a series expansion

$$C(\phi) = \lim_{N\to\infty} \sum_{k=-N}^{N} \boldsymbol{p}_k \exp\left(\frac{2\pi k\phi}{T}\boldsymbol{l}\right) = \lim_{N\to\infty} \sum_{k=-N}^{N} \boldsymbol{R}_k^{\phi} \boldsymbol{p}_k \widetilde{\boldsymbol{R}}_k^{\phi}.$$

This can be interpreted as a Fourier series expansion, where we have replaced the imaginary unit $i = \sqrt{-1}$ with $\boldsymbol{l}$ and the complex Fourier series coefficients with vectors that lie in the plane spanned by $\boldsymbol{l}$. The vectors $\boldsymbol{p}_k$ are the phase vectors. In general it may be shown that for every closed plane curve there is a unique set of phase vectors $\{\boldsymbol{p}_k\}$ that parameterize the curve. To represent a general closed, discretizied 3D curve this can easily be extended to 3D by interpreting the projections along x, y, and z as three infinite 1D-signals and applying a DFT and an IDFT separately, leads to the representation

$$C(\phi) = \sum_{m=1}^{3} \sum_{k=-N}^{N} \boldsymbol{p}_k^m \exp(\frac{2\pi k\phi}{2N+1}\boldsymbol{l}_m).$$

This means we now replace a Fourier series development by the inverse discrete Fourier transform.

Pose Estimation of Free-Form Contours.
We assume a given closed, discretizied 3D curve, that is a 3D contour C with $2N+1$ sampled points in both the spatial and spectral domain with phase vectors $\boldsymbol{p}_k^m$ of the contour. Substituting the representation of the Fourier descriptors in the conformal space within the pose estimation constraint equations leads to

$$\left(\boldsymbol{M}\,(\mathbf{e} \wedge (C(\phi) + \mathbf{e}_-))\,\widetilde{\boldsymbol{M}}\right) \underline{\times}\, (\mathbf{e} \wedge (\boldsymbol{O} \wedge \boldsymbol{x})) = 0.$$

To model any additional deformation, a kinematic chain is added within the pose constraint. This means encapsulating n motors $\boldsymbol{M}_i$ of the deformations within the constraint equation,

$$\left(\boldsymbol{M}\left(\prod_{i=1}^{n} \boldsymbol{M}_i^{\theta_i}\,(\mathbf{e} \wedge (C(\phi) + \mathbf{e}_-))\,\widetilde{\boldsymbol{M}}_i^{\theta_i}\right)\widetilde{\boldsymbol{M}}\right) \underline{\times}\, (\mathbf{e} \wedge (\boldsymbol{O} \wedge \boldsymbol{x})) = 0.$$

This constraint equation is easy to interpret: The inner parenthesis contains the inverse Fourier transformed phase vectors transformed to a representation in the conformal space. The next parenthesis contains the motors $\boldsymbol{M}_i^{\theta_i}$, which are exponentials of twists modeling the joints of the kinematic chain. The last parenthesis contains the motor $\boldsymbol{M}$ with the unknown pose. This is then coupled with the reconstructed projection ray in the conformal space. The unknowns are the pose parameters $\boldsymbol{M}$, the angles θ_i of the kinematic chain and the angle ϕ of the Fourier descriptors.

Solving a set of constraint equations for a free-form contour with respect to the unknown motor $\boldsymbol{M}$ is a non-trivial task, since a motor corresponds to a polynomial of infinite degree. In [10] we presented a method which does not estimate the rigid body motion on the Lie group, $SE(3)$, but the parameters which generate their Lie algebra, $se(3)$, comparable to the ideas, presented in

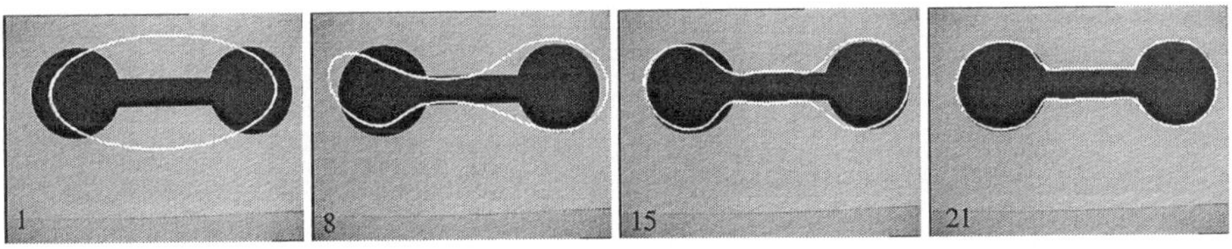

Fig. 3. Pose results of the low-pass filtered contour during the iteration.

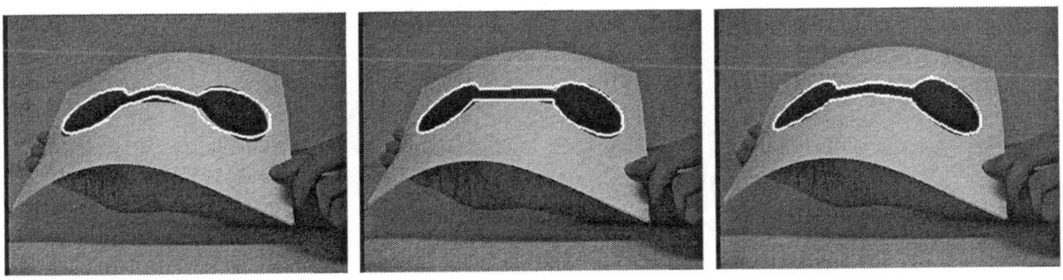

Fig. 4. Pose result of a free-form contour containing one, two or three joints.

[2, 6]. Note, that though the equations are expressed in a linear manner with respect to the group action, the equations in the unknown generators of the group action are non-linear and in our approach they will be linearized and iterated. This corresponds to a gradient descent method in 3D space.

3 Experiments

In this section we present experimental results of free-form pose estimation. The algorithm for deformable free-form pose estimation is basically a modified ICP-algorithm [14]. The convergence behavior of the ICP-algorithm during an image sequence is shown in figure 3. As can be seen, we refine the pose results by using a low-pass approximation for pose estimation and by adding successively higher frequencies during the iteration. This is basically a multi-resolution method and helps to avoid local minima during the iteration.

To model object deformations, the effect of introducing different numbers of joints (as twists) within the pose scenario is visualized in figure 4. It can be seen, that only a few twists are needed to get a good approximation of the deformation. There are two major problems in dealing with a fixed set of twists modeling the object deformation: Firstly, the use of too many twists can lead to local minima and wrong poses. This occurs for example in case of using too many twists for modeling only a slight object deformation. Secondly does the use of many twists increase the computing time of the pose estimation algorithm, since additionally unknowns are modeled which are not always needed. Therefore, a modification of the algorithm is done which chooses the number of twists adaptively, depending on the level of deformation. An example of an image

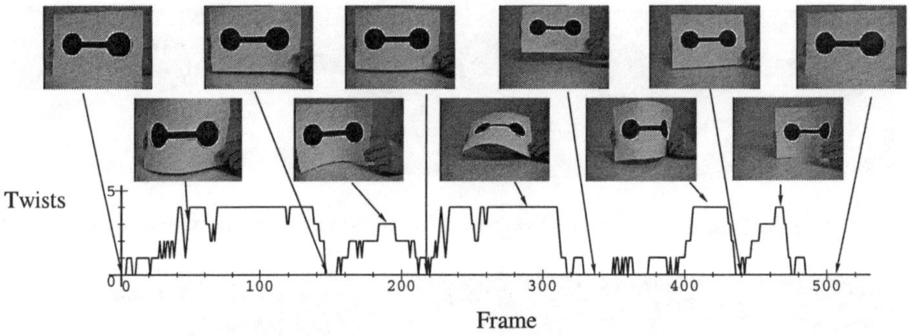

Fig. 5. Adaptive choice of twists for modeling object deformations during an image sequence. For slight deformations less twists are used then for larger ones.

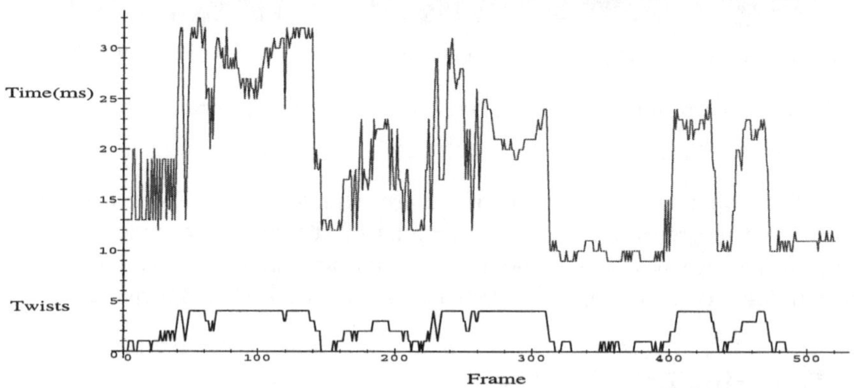

Fig. 6. Time performance for using different numbers of twists in an image sequence.

sequence is shown in figure 5. The diagram shows the frame number during the image sequence on the x-axis and the used number of twists on the y-axis. The example images show that the used number of twists is consistent with the degree of deformation. The increased time performance is shown in figure 6. The y-axis shows on the one hand the used number of twists (consistent with figure 5) and on the other hand the computing time for estimating one pose during the ICP-algorithm. As can be seen, the use of more twists increases the computing time, and the adaptive choice of the number of twists during the image sequence leads to a situation dependent optimized time performance. Note that only the time for estimating one pose is shown. Combined with the ICP-algorithm (which takes between two and eight iteration steps), the overall computing time for one frame varies between $20ms$ and $250ms$. The adaptive behavior is achieved by evaluating the twist angles after each processed image. If the angles are below or above a threshold, twists are eliminated or added and rearranged, respectively. The experiments are performed with a Linux 2 GHz machine.

4 Discussion

This work presents a novel approach to deal with plane dynamic deformations of 3D free-form curves during pose estimation. Free-form contours are modeled by 3D Fourier descriptors which are combined with pose estimation constraints. This coupling of geometry with signal theory is achieved by using the conformal geometric algebra. In this language we are able to fuse concepts, like complex numbers, Plücker lines, twists, Lie algebras and Lie groups in a compact manner. The chosen framework shows, that it is possible to extend scenarios to more complex ones, without loosing the geometric oversight since the equations are given in closed and easily interpretable forms. Our future work will concentrate on dealing with more complex scenarios, e.g. the modeling of free-form surfaces.

Acknowledgements

This work has been supported by DFG Graduiertenkolleg No. 357 and by EC Grant IST-2001-3422 (VISATEC).

References

1. Arbter K. and Burkhardt H. Ein Fourier-Verfahren zur Bestimmung von Merkmalen und Schätzung der Lageparameter ebener Raumkurven *Informationstechnik*, Vol. 33, No. 1, pp.19-26, 1991.
2. Bregler C. and Malik J. Tracking people with twists and exponential maps. *IEEE Computer Society Conference on Computer Vision and Pattern Recognition*, Santa Barbara, California, pp.8-15 1998.
3. Drummond T. and Cipolla R. Real-time tracking of multiple articulated structures in multiple views. In *6th European Conference on Computer Vision, ECCV 2000, Dubline, Ireland*, Part II, pp.20-36, 2000.
4. Granlund G. Fourier preprocessing for hand print character recognition. *IEEE Transactions on Computers*, Vol. 21, pp. 195-201, 1972.
5. Grimson W. E. L. Object Recognition by Computer. *The MIT Press, Cambridge, MA*, 1990.
6. Lowe D.G. Solving for the parameters of object models from image descriptions. in *Proc. ARPA Image Understanding Workshop*, pp. 121-127, 1980.
7. Li H., Hestenes D. and Rockwood A. Generalized homogeneous coordinates for computational geometry. In [12], pp. 27-52, 2001.
8. Murray R.M., Li Z. and Sastry S.S. A Mathematical Introduction to Robotic Manipulation. *CRC Press*, 1994.
9. Needham T. Visual Complex Analysis. *Oxford University Press*, 1997
10. Rosenhahn B., Perwass Ch. and Sommer G. Pose estimation of 3D free-form contours in conformal geometry In *Proceedings of Image and Vision Computing (IVCNZ) D. Kenwright (Ed.)*, New Zealand, pp 29-34, 2002.
11. Rosenhahn B. and Sommer G. Adaptive Pose Estimation for Different Corresponding Entities. In *Pattern Recognition, 24th DAGM Symposium, L. Van Gool (Ed.)*, Springer-Verlag, Berling Heidelberg, LNCS 2449, pp. 265-273, 2002.

12. Sommer G., editor. Geometric Computing with Clifford Algebra. *Springer Verlag*, 2001.
13. Stark K. A method for tracking the pose of known 3D objects based on an active contour model. *Technical Report TUD / FI 96 10*, TU Dresden, 1996.
14. Zang Z. Iterative point matching for registration of free-form curves and surfaces. *IJCV: International Journal of Computer Vision*, Vol. 13, No. 2, pp. 119-152, 1999.
15. Zerroug, M. and Nevatia, R. Pose estimation of multi-part curved objects. *Image Understanding Workshop (IUW)*, pp. 831-835, 1996

Super-resolution Capabilities of the Hough-Green Transform

Vladimir Shapiro

Orbograph Ltd., P.O.Box 215, Yavne 81102, Israel
vladimir.shapiro@orbograph.com

Abstract. A novel approach to the Hough Transform (HT) calculation, based on tracing object contours on bitonal imagery, has recently been proposed. This approach, called the Hough-Green Transform (HGT), is typically much more computationally effective and accurate than the Standard HT (SHT). The additional potential of the HGT lies in its natural ability to compute the complete HT domain with sub-cell resolution. The paper focuses on achieving HT domain super-resolution, i.e., the derivation of a high-resolution HT domain from a downsampled spatial one, which enables significant acceleration of HGT evaluation. The related tradeoffs are also discussed.

1 Introduction

The Hough Transform (HT) has probably been one of the most frequently addressed topics in computer-vision literature over the past 20-30 years; see the canonical survey [1]. The popular (θ, ρ) parameterization is frequently referred to as the Standard HT (SHT). Both the SHT and the Hough-Green Transform (HGT) represent the major HT flavor, known as the *straight-line* HT. The line described by Eq.(1) is frequently referred to as a *line* or *voting support* of an HT domain cell (θ, ρ) [5], which contains a number of object pixels lying along this line, here AB (see Fig. 2a).

$$x \cos\theta_{AB} + y \sin\theta_{AB} = \rho_{AB} \,. \tag{1}$$

The straight-line HT intends to obtain the HT domain, i.e., the projection space.

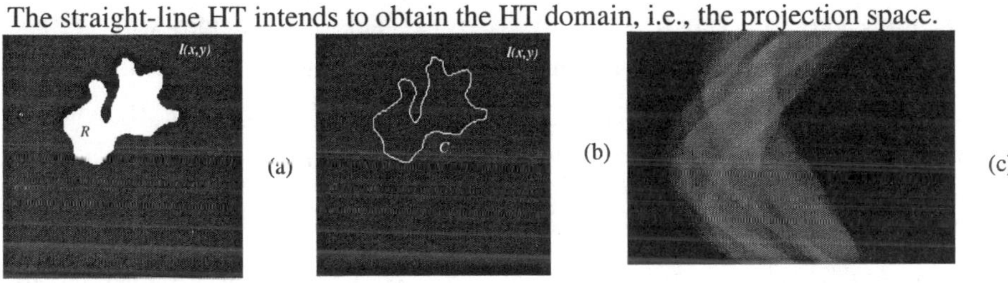

Fig. 1. (a) An object R (binary image size is 256x256 pixels); (b) Its closed boundary C ; (c) The *SHT* (θ, ρ) domain of region R from (a) – the vertical axis represents θ, quantized into 180 samples (degrees); the horizontal axis represents ρ , quantized into 256 samples

N. Petkov and M.A. Westenberg (Eds.): CAIP 2003, LNCS 2756, pp. 673–680, 2003.

There is substantial potential in computing various object features via tracing contours, rather than by tackling the object's interior pixels. The recently proposed HGT [2], which is an approach to HT calculation based on tracing object contours, has been shown to be much more computationally effective than the SHT in most cases. The HGT is a general-purpose HT, which works on objects of any shape, including those with holes and non-closed contours (a non-closed contour can be followed to constitute a closed path by retracing the same pixels whenever required). The HGT provides more accurate and less distorted projection space than the SHT [2]. It will be shown below that the HGT has the potential of achieving either sub-cell resolution or super-resolution with regard to ρ and/or θ.

Issues of SHT accuracy as a function of the projection space quantization, which is due to the voting nature of the SHT, are analyzed in [4]. Parameter quantization does not have the same impact on the accuracy in the HGT where, instead of counting *votes*, distances are measured *directly*.

This paper is structured in the following manner. In Section 2, SHT tradeoffs are considered, and in Section 3, the HGT concept is briefly introduced. Section 4 presents two scenarios for utilizing the HGT's super-resolution capabilities, and in Section 5, simulations and experiments are described. Conclusions are presented at the end of the paper.

2 The Standard HT

The SHT has many useful features: a) It is robust and noise resistant; b) The algorithm is straightforward and simple for implementation; c) It is well understood, and a great deal of positive experience and knowledge has been accumulated by both academics and industry.

However, the SHT has the following main disadvantages: a) High computational costs, as the real-time HT setups require optics or dedicated hardware; b) Uneven accuracy for various θ, expressed in the *aliasing* artifact [3].

3 The Hough-Green Transform

Let us consider the simplest particular HGT case of $\theta = 0°$ (see Fig. 2a). Eq. (1) for $\theta = 0°$ turns into $\rho = x\cos 0° + y\sin 0° \Rightarrow \rho = x$, i.e., ρ coincides with x, and $\theta = 0°$ projection can be obtained simply by integration along the y-axis. Considering the ray AB, determined by ρ_{AB}, which crosses C in points M and N, $HGT(0°, \rho_{AB})$ can be calculated as follows:

$$HGT(0°, \rho_{AB}) = y_M \Delta\rho_M + y_N \Delta\rho_N = y_M - y_N, \tag{2}$$

where $\Delta\rho_M = \rho_M - \rho_{M-1} = 1$ and $\Delta\rho_N = \rho_N - \rho_{N-1} = -1$. Note, that Eq. (2) holds for the continuous case. On digital lattices the boundary width should be accounted for.

For an arbitrary ρ, there might be more than just two points of contour crossing. $\theta = 0°$ projection can be computed from the closed contour C trace as:

$$HGT(0°, \rho_l) = \sum_{l \in C} y_l \Delta\rho_l , \tag{3}$$

where $l = 0,1,\ldots, N_l$. N_l is a number of pixels in contour C .

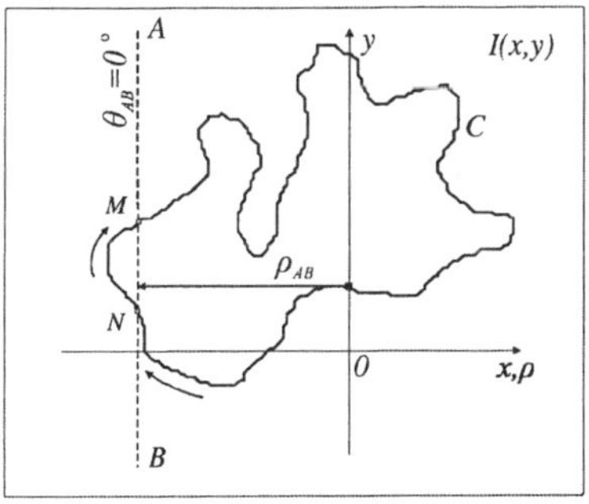

(a)

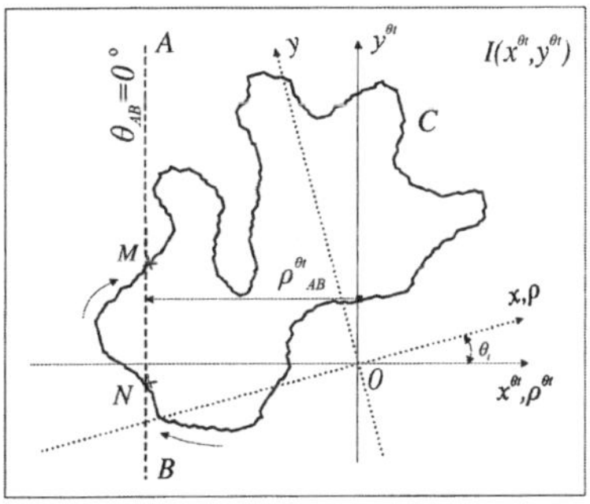

(b)

Fig. 2. (a) Understanding the HGT: $\theta = 0°$ -projection case. Contour C traversing direction is shown by arrows; (b) Coordinate system $(x^{\theta_t}, y^{\theta_t})$ is obtained by θ_t rotation of the source $I(x, y)$ plane from Fig. 2a. The original x, y axes are shown by a dotted line.

Let us turn to an arbitrary projection angle θ_t case (see Fig. 2b). It is equivalent to having the source plane (x, y) rotated by θ_t. After axes variables substitution, the newly rotated plane $I(x^{\theta_t}, y^{\theta_t})$ can be handled similarly to Fig. 2a, and Eqs. (2) and (3) become applicable. New $(x^{\theta_t}, y^{\theta_t})$ coordinates are derived from the original x, y via rotation equations:

$$\begin{cases} x^{\theta_t} = \rho^{\theta_t} = x\cos\theta_t + y\sin\theta_t \\ y^{\theta_t} = -x\sin\theta_t + y\cos\theta_t . \end{cases} \tag{4}$$

Note that ρ^{θ_t} again coincides with x^{θ_t} , thus Eq. (2) for contour points M and N and arbitrary θ angle becomes:

$$HGT(\theta_t, \rho^{\theta_t}) = y_M^{\theta_t} \Delta\rho_M + y_N^{\theta_t} \Delta\rho_N = y_M^{\theta_t} - y_N^{\theta_t} , \tag{5}$$

where the conditions $\Delta\rho_M = \rho_M - \rho_{M-1} = 1$ and $\Delta\rho_N = \rho_N - \rho_{N-1} = -1$ require x^{θ_t} or ρ^{θ_t} resampling to tightly pack the new discrete lattice. This is assumed in the case of $\theta = 0°$, but for an arbitrary θ_t, the new ρ^{θ_t} will be spread unevenly. The full final form of the HGT for an arbitrary crossing point number, and involving original (x_l, y_l) coordinates of all N_l pixels of a contour C in the source image plane prior to the rotation (4) is:

$$\begin{aligned} HGT(\theta, \rho_l) &= \sum_{l \in C} (-x_l \sin\theta + y_l \cos\theta) \Delta\rho_l \\ \Delta\rho_l &= (x_l - x_{l-1})\cos\theta + (y_l - y_{l-1})\sin\theta . \end{aligned} \tag{6}$$

Generalization to more topologically complicated objects than just solids, including those containing holes, is quite straightforward. The algorithm produces a closed path and traverses the external contours counterclockwise, and the internal contours clockwise (see [2]). It must be repeated for each hole and each contour in the image.

3.1 The HGT Algorithm Sketch

The HGT algorithm is derived from (7) (see [2] for details). The external loop, iterating through all image contours, is omitted for the sake of simplicity.

```
    {Trace object's R contour C ; store all x_l, y_l pairs}
    {Decimate x_l, y_l if acceleration requested}
for all θ
  for all l ∈ C
    begin
      rotation by θ
      ρ_l - resampling   //to fractional ρ_l if high resolution requested
      update HGT(θ, ρ_l) //for interpolated θ if acceleration requested
    end
```

3.2 The HGT Complexity

The SHT complexity for an object R is $O(A_R N_\theta N_\rho)$, while HGT's $O(N_l N_\theta N_\rho)$. N_l is a number of pixels constituting contour C_R. Compared to the SHT, the HGT is favorable for shapes with more inner pixels than those lying on the boundary, i.e., N_l must be less than object area A_R.

4 The HGT Super-resolution Capacity

Having a sequence of contour elements, one can easily interpolate them and generate intermediate samples. This is inherent to the HGT property, and is the basis for its super-resolution capabilities. The latter are beneficial in any of two directions, either: acceleration oriented (see Section 4.1) or higher-resolution oriented (see Section 4.2).

4.1 Further HGT Acceleration

Further HGT acceleration may be achieved by reducing the number of contour pixels N_l. There are various options, such as downsampling the source image, e.g., transforming a 256x256 pixel image into 128x128, and so on. Every traced contour will then automatically be of lower resolution. As a traced contour is constituted by a sequence of contour element x, y pairs, a more advantageous way of downsampling would be achievable via *decimation*, i.e., skipping some of the elements prior to the HGT (see Fig. 3b,c and Section 3.1). Let us define a decimation factor df, meaning that only $0, df, 2df, \ldots, ndf$ contour elements remain out of the initial N_l. After decimation, the total number of remaining contour elements will be approximately $M_l = N_l / df$. Note that the starting and ending points must not be eliminated regardless of df.

Contour decimation leads to a significant drop in HGT complexity. It will not, however, reach $O(M_l N_\theta N_\rho)$ due to algorithm stages such as resampling and updating the HT domain, which still have a complexity of $O(N_l)$.

Technically, the interpolation is carried out at the "ρ resampling" stage (see Section 3.1), which is a mandatory stage in the HGT framework even if no super-resolution is required. This stage intends avoiding the *aliasing* artifact inherent to the SHT (see [3]). Without this stage, the contour pixel coordinates, which are generally real numbers, would not necessarily produce at least one sample for each ρ value.

Obviously, a similar approach is applicable to θ, as several implementation schemes are possible. The most computationally effective among them seems to be a scheme of interpolating a given contour C projections $HGT(\theta)_C$ and $HGT(\theta + \Delta\theta)_C$, as shown in Fig. 4b. Applying the technique to both ρ and θ simultaneously would multiply the efficiency gain.

4.2 Sub-Cell Resolution of the Parameter Space

In the SHT framework, the HT parameter space resolution is dictated by the θ, ρ quantization in Eq. (1). As the computation complexity of the SHT is $O(A_R N_\theta N_\rho)$, the price of having higher resolution by, for example, ρ, is proportional to A_R. In the HGT framework, the corresponding price is proportional to N_l, which is typically much smaller than A_R. Implementation-wise, fractional resolution by ρ is again carried out at the "ρ resampling" stage in the HGT algorithm (see Section 3.1).

5 Simulations and Analysis

The HGT with a non-unit decimation factor may be considered as an approximation of the HGT obtained without decimation (i.e., with $df = 1$). Below, we will measure two aspects of the approximation quality for $df = n$: Error uniformity $E_{HGT}(\theta)$ with regard to θ, and mean square HGT error E_{HGT}. These are evaluated with the "Ideal" HT being either, for example, the HGT of the original resolution, or the SHT, as shown in Table 1 and Table 2:

$$E_{HGT}(\theta) = 1/N_\rho \sum\nolimits_{\text{all}\,\rho} \sqrt{\left|\text{Ideal}HT(\theta,\rho)^2 - HGT(\theta,\rho)^2\right|}. \tag{7}$$

$$E_{HGT} = 1/N_\theta \sum\nolimits_{\text{all}\,\theta} E_{HGT}(\theta). \tag{8}$$

For the artificial image in Fig. 1a, the acceleration factor is more than three times greater for $df = 10$ than for $df = 1$ (see Table 1). The $E_{df=n}$ error was not high even for $n = 10$. Error uniformity with regard to θ was remarkable as well (see Fig. 3f).

θ interpolation of the same Fig. 1a image also allowed substantial computation gain to be reached (see Table 2 and Fig. 4). The error was again quite uniformly distributed along the θ axis (see Fig. 4d). As expected, errors rose in the intervals between the non-skipped samples. On an image with many short contours, as in Fig. 5a, the behavior was very different. Computational gain was minor due to the relatively high interpolation cost. E_{HGT}, however, did not grow either, again due to a large quantity of contours (see Fig. 5).

Obviously, actual errors may vary with the image resolution, object shape, area and interpolation scheme. A simple piecewise-linear interpolation has been used in this research. Intuitively, having applied polynomial or spline interpolations, which more precisely represent the contour trace, a lower approximation error, Eq. (8), might be expected. This will however be reflected in a somewhat higher computational cost. The related tradeoffs and consequences are the subject of future research.

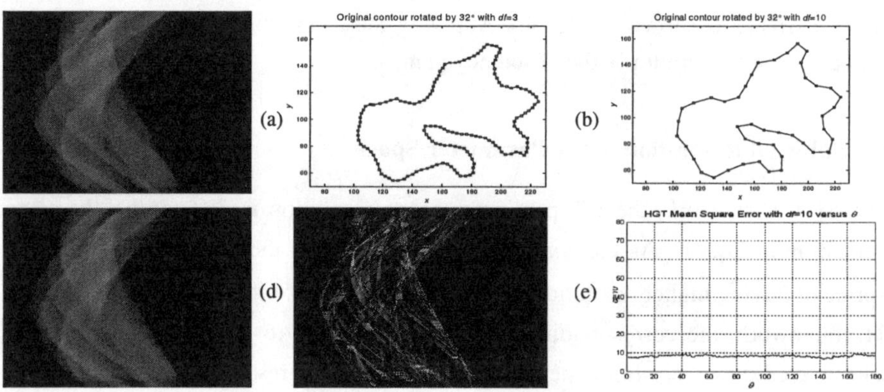

Fig. 3. HGT of the image in Fig. 1. (a) $df = 1$ (no decimation), see the contour in Fig. 1b; (b) Contour with $df = 3$ rotated by arbitrary θ of $32°$; (c) The same with $df = 10$; (d) HGT of $df = 10$; (e) Absolute difference of $df = 1$ vs. $df = 10$ amplified 5 times; (f) See the title.

Contour decimation deforms a shape. For an object of complex shape and size containing holes, the object might lose consistency for a high df.

Let us consider the source of HGT super-resolution capabilities. The SHT framework implies independent voting by each object pixel. If a pixel is skipped due to downsampling, its impact on the HT domain will be irrecoverably lost and the corresponding line support will be reduced. The HGT, however, "remembers" the object shape as it relies on connected contours. If a contour pixel is skipped, its neighbors from both sides close the gap by producing a new interpolated sample instead of the skipped one. Unless the skipped sample was too "spiky", the new sample is a good approximation of the old one. Formally speaking, instead of reducing the line support as a result of downsampling, the HGT only "deforms" it, usually slightly. The same happens in a θ downsampling case. The HGT "remembers" the rotated states adjacent to the skipped θ contour, and restores the missing ones via interpolation.

Table 1. HGT Computation time t for various decimation factors df

		SHT	HGT					
Fig.#	Decimation factor df	NA	1	2	3	4	5	10
Fig. 3	Area/Contour # pixels	6473	441	221	147	111	89	45
	t (ms, PC 1 Ghz)	236	18.7	13.3	10.1	8.6	7.8	6.0
	E_{HGT}	-	4.48	5.42	5.86	6.29	6.71	8.85
Fig. 5	Area/Contour # pixels	52707	19818	9976	6732	5087	4219	3626
	t (ms, PC 1 Ghz)	1485	767	528	408	345	309	275
	E_{HGT}	-	29.3	33.5	35.65	38.1	40.6	53

Table 2. HGT Computation time t for various θ quantizations $(df = 1)$

		SHT	HGT					
Fig.#	θ quantization (degrees)	NA	1°	2°	3°	4°	5°	10°
Fig. 3	t (ms, PC 1 Ghz)	236	18.7	13.7	11.6	10.5	9.9	8.5
	E_{HGT}	-	4.48	4.66	4.88	5.17	5.5	7.17
Fig. 5	t (ms, PC 1 Ghz)	1485	767	757	756	757	759	760
	E_{HGT}	-	29.36	29.41	29.47	29.55	29.67	30.

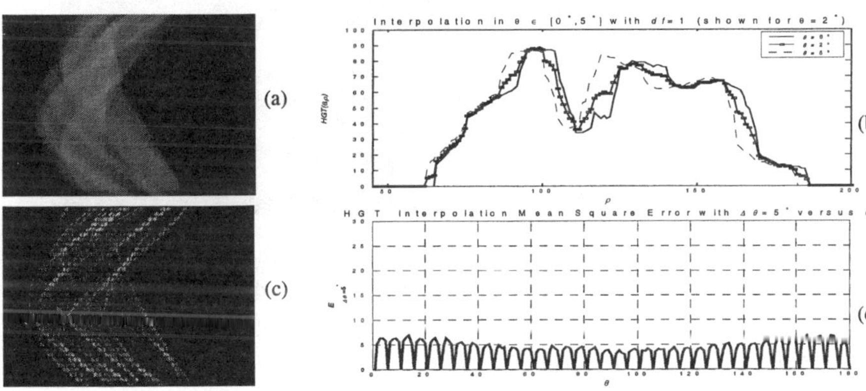

Fig. 4. θ interpolation: (a) HGT of the contour in Fig. 1b with $df = 1$, $\Delta\theta = 5°$; (b),(d) See the title, $\theta = 0°$ and $\theta = 5°$ are original samples, $\theta = 2°$ interpolated; (c) Absolute difference of HGT with $\Delta\theta = 1°$ (Fig. 3a) and $\Delta\theta = 5°$ amplified 10 times.

6 Conclusions

The recently proposed Hough-Green Transform (HGT) is typically a much more effective way of complete Hough Transform (HT) computation than the Standard straight-line HT (SHT). Additional HGT potential lies in achieving a super-resolution of the parameter space. Along with the straightforward resampling of ρ, θ parameters to fractional sub-pixel intervals, this paper proposes a method of further reducing HGT complexity based either on θ downsampling or on contour trace decimating, as the “missing” samples are obtained via interpolation. Significant acceleration gain is traded for affordable accuracy reduction.

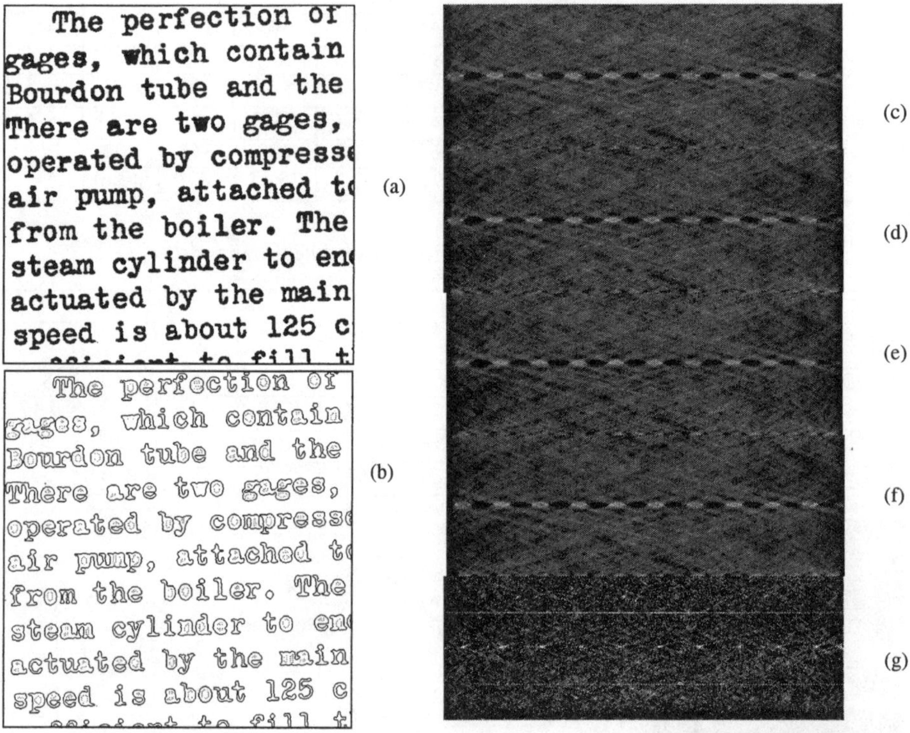

Fig. 5. (a) A 300dpi document image of 512x512 pixels; (b) Its 185 external and 116 internal (lighter) contours; (c) SHT of Fig. 5a; (d) HGT with $df = 1$ (no decimation); (e) HGT with $df = 5$, $\Delta\theta = 1°$;(f) HGT with $df = 1, \Delta\theta = 10°$;(g) Absolute difference of SHT (Fig. 5a) and $df = 5$ (Fig. 5e) amplified 5 times.

References

1. Illingworth, J., Kittler, J.: A Survey of the Hough Transform. CVGIP 44 (1988) 87-116
2. Shapiro, V.: The Hough-Green Transform. ICCV 2003 (submitted), Beijing, China
3. Srihari, S., Govindaraju, V.: Analysis of Textual Images Using the Hough Transform. Machine Vision and Applications 2 (1989) 141-153
4. Van Veen, T.M., Groen, F.C.A.: Discretisation Errors In the Hough Transform. Pattern Recognition 14 (1981) 137-145

Hansen, K., Andersen, J.: Understanding the Hough Transform: Hough Cell Support and Its Utilisation. Image and Vision Computing 15 (1997) 205-218

The Generalised Radon Transform: Sampling and Memory Considerations

C.L. Luengo Hendriks, M. van Ginkel, P.W. Verbeek, and L.J. van Vliet

Pattern Recognition Group, Delft University of Technology
Lorentzweg 1, 2628 CJ Delft, The Netherlands
{cris,michael,piet,lucas}@ph.tn.tudelft.nl

Abstract. The generalised Radon transform is a well-known tool for detecting parameterised shapes in an image. Applying the Radon transform to an image results in a parameter response function (PRF). Curves in the image become peaks in the PRF. The location of a peak corresponds to the parameters of a shape, and the amplitude to the amount of evidence for that shape. In this paper we discuss two important aspects of the Radon transform. The first aspect is discretisation. Using concepts from sampling theory we derive a set of sampling criteria for the Radon transform. The second aspect concerns a projection-based algorithm to reduce memory requirements.

1 The Radon Transform

The (generalised) Radon transform is a technique for detecting parameterised shapes. Given a model of the shape, it defines a mapping from the image space onto a parameter space. The axes of the parameter space correspond to the parameters of the model. When applied to an image, the Radon transform yields a parameter response function (PRF) defined on the parameter space. A shape in the image becomes a peak in the PRF. The location of the peak corresponds to the parameters of the shape. Shape detection is thus reduced to peak detection. We discuss two aspects of the Radon transform: its discretisation and an algorithm to reduce its storage requirements. We focus on the Radon transform for (hyper-)spheres, but the discussion of the discretisation holds for arbitrary shapes. In its most general form, the Radon transform is

$$P(\boldsymbol{p}) = \int_{\boldsymbol{s} \text{ on } \boldsymbol{c}(\boldsymbol{p})} I(\boldsymbol{s}) d\boldsymbol{s}, \tag{1}$$

with $P(\boldsymbol{p})$ the PRF, $I(\boldsymbol{s})$ the image and $\boldsymbol{c}(\boldsymbol{p})$ the shape for parameter vector $\boldsymbol{p}$.

There are two common approaches to the discretisation of the Radon transform. The first is a straight-forward discretisation of the integral using standard numerical algorithms. It chooses a point in parameter space and computes its value by integrating the image over all the points belonging to the curve. In the second algorithm we choose a point in the image and add its contribution to all the appropriate points (or bins) of the PRF, a process known as voting. This

N. Petkov and M.A. Westenberg (Eds.): CAIP 2003, LNCS 2756, pp. 681–688, 2003.

approach is traditionally known as the Hough transform. We stress that the two are identical in the continuous domain [3]. An advantage of the Radon paradigm is that it gives us control over how we visit the points in parameter space. Later we use this property to reduce the memory requirements for storing the PRF.

2 Sampling the Radon Transform

Several authors have addressed discretisation-related effects, in particular binning effects, of the Hough transform [1, 7] and references therein. Here, we pursue a different approach: we apply the principles of sampling theory to the Radon transform, thus trying to avoid discretisation errors altogether. Sampling theory gives us the conditions under which a signal can be sampled without loss of information. The same theory is also applicable to the discretisation of an arbitrary linear *operator*, including the Radon transform. We start by writing the Radon transform in the form of a general linear operator:

$$P(\boldsymbol{p}) = \int_{\mathbb{R}} C(\boldsymbol{p}, \boldsymbol{s}) I(\boldsymbol{s}) d\boldsymbol{s}. \tag{2}$$

This equation becomes a Radon transform by choosing the function $C(\boldsymbol{p}, \boldsymbol{s})$ appropriately. If a subset $\boldsymbol{x}$ of the parameters $\boldsymbol{p}$ represents the spatial position of the shape, then C has a special form:

$$C(\boldsymbol{p}, \boldsymbol{s}) = K(\{\boldsymbol{p} \setminus \boldsymbol{x}\}, \boldsymbol{x} - \boldsymbol{s}), \tag{3}$$

where $\{\boldsymbol{p} \setminus \boldsymbol{x}\}$ denotes all the parameters in $\boldsymbol{p}$ except those in $\boldsymbol{x}$. Along the dimensions $\boldsymbol{x}$ the integral reduces to a convolution [8, 9]. Using the convolution property of the Fourier transform, the operation reduces to a multiplication in the Fourier domain resulting in a huge speed-up.

Following [4], we will now investigate sampling criteria for equation (2). There are two aspects. Keeping $\boldsymbol{p}$ fixed, we will first consider under which conditions we may replace I and C by sampled (along $\boldsymbol{s}$) versions and the integral by a summation. If these conditions are satisfied, we may compute $P(\boldsymbol{p})$ for an arbitrarily chosen $\boldsymbol{p}$. We must then show that it is possible to sample the PRF $P(\boldsymbol{p})$, so that we only need to evaluate $P(\boldsymbol{p})$ on a discrete set of points. For simplicity we restrict ourselves to a one-dimensional example: $\boldsymbol{p} \to p$ and $\boldsymbol{s} \to s$. The Fourier axes corresponding to p and s are denoted by $\tilde{p}$ and $\tilde{s}$ respectively. The sampling distance along s is Δs. The discrete coordinate corresponding to s is n, i.e. the sampled version of I is $I(n\Delta s)$. We first investigate under which conditions the following is true:

$$P(p) = \int_{\mathbb{R}} C(p, s) I(s) ds = \Delta s \sum_{n \in \mathbb{Z}} C(p, n\Delta s) I(n\Delta s). \tag{4}$$

We denote the band-limit (along s) of the product $C(p, s)I(s)$ by $\mathrm{b}_s\{CI\}$. With p fixed, the sampling criterion for the computation of this integral, $\tilde{s}_s > \mathrm{b}_s\{CI\}$, is a relaxed version of the Nyquist criterion [10]. Also the band-limit of CI can be expressed in that of C and I:

$$\mathrm{b}_s\{CI\} \leq \mathrm{b}_s\{C\} + \mathrm{b}_s\{I\}. \tag{5}$$

It follows that both the operator function C and the image I must be band-limited to allow discretisation. Proper sampling of the image I is a prerequisite for any image analysis and poses no specific problem. This is not true for the operator function C, which is not band-limited in general. We must impose a band-limit on C. This clearly leads to a different Radon transform, but this reflects a conscious choice with well-understood consequences. The alternative, sampling C without imposing a band-limit first, leads to aliasing effects.

We can compute $P(p)$ for an arbitrary value of p. If $P(p)$ is band-limited, we may sample $P(p)$ at the correct (Nyquist) rate. We determine whether $P(p)$ is band-limited by computing its Fourier transform:

$$\mathcal{F}\{P\}(\tilde{p}) = \mathcal{F}\left\{\int_{\mathbb{R}} C(p,s)I(s)ds\right\}(\tilde{p}) = \int_{\mathbb{R}} \mathcal{F}_p\{C(p,s)\}(\tilde{p},s)I(s)ds. \tag{6}$$

If C is band-limited along the p axis with band-limit $\mathrm{b}_p\{C\}$, then the integral above evaluates to zero for $\tilde{p} > \mathrm{b}_p\{C\}$, which means that $P(p)$ is band-limited as well.

The discussion above also holds for the complete multi-dimensional operation: our argument holds for each spatial dimension s_i separately and for each parameter dimension p_j as well. The same ideas also extend trivially to other sampling schemes, such as the hexagonal grid.

Kiryati and Bruckstein [6] have proposed band-limitation of the Hough transform. Their approach consists of replacing the sinusoids that are stamped in parameter space by band-limited versions (see also the references in [6]), in essence the same technique used by the Parzen estimator. In our formalism, this corresponds to imposing a band-limit on $C(\boldsymbol{p}, \boldsymbol{s})$ along the $\boldsymbol{p}$ axes. The difference between their and our approach lies mainly in the model for the input data: in their case a set of mathematical points in a continuous space, in our case a sampled image.

2.1 Band-Limiting the Operator Function $\mathbf{C}(\boldsymbol{p}, \boldsymbol{s})$

The Gaussian filter is approximately band-limited with critical sample spacing σ [11] and corresponding band-limit $b = \frac{1}{2}\sigma^{-1}$. Its properties, in particular good simultaneous frequency and spatial localisation, make it a good choice for band-limiting $C(\boldsymbol{p}, \boldsymbol{s})$: We obtain C_b, a band limited version of C, as follows:

$$C_b(\boldsymbol{p}, \boldsymbol{s}) = C(\boldsymbol{p}, \boldsymbol{s}) * G(\boldsymbol{p}, \boldsymbol{s}; \boldsymbol{\Sigma}). \tag{7}$$

The diagonal covariance matrix $\boldsymbol{\Sigma}$ reflects that we impose band-limitation along each dimension separately.

The function $C(\boldsymbol{p}, \boldsymbol{s})$ is in general very sparse. This follows directly from equation (1): for any given $\boldsymbol{p}$, the points $\boldsymbol{s}$ which belong to the shape span some curve or manifold in $C(\boldsymbol{p},\boldsymbol{s})$. The Radon transform for hyper-spheres provides a convenient example to investigate the structure of $C(\boldsymbol{p},\boldsymbol{s})$ and the effects of band-limitation in some detail. The parameter vector $\boldsymbol{p}$ consists of the centre $\boldsymbol{x}$ of the D-dimensional sphere and its radius r: $\boldsymbol{p} = (x_1, \cdots, x_D, r)$. The operator function C becomes

$$C(\boldsymbol{p},\boldsymbol{s}) = K(r, \boldsymbol{x} - \boldsymbol{s}) \quad \text{with} \quad K(r, \boldsymbol{\xi}) = \delta(\frac{1}{2}\sqrt{2}(\|\boldsymbol{\xi}\| - r)) \tag{8}$$

for a sphere. The function K represents a cone. If we consider a sufficiently small surface patch of the cone, we may consider it as a plane. Along the normal to this plane, the function K should behave like a Dirac delta. Hence the factor $\frac{1}{2}\sqrt{2}$ in (8). With this normalisation we have that $\int_0^R \int_{\mathbb{R}^D} K(r,\boldsymbol{\xi}) d\boldsymbol{\xi} dr$ equals the surface area of the truncated cone with a base of radius R.

What is the effect on K of the Gaussian smoothing applied to C? Let us first consider the effect of the smoothing applied along the $\boldsymbol{p}$ axes. All parameters share the same units and it is therefore logical to use the same σ_K along each dimension. The effect on a local surface patch, if it can be considered planar locally ($\sigma_K \ll r$), is that the Dirac profile is substituted by a Gaussian profile

$$K_b(r, \boldsymbol{x} - \boldsymbol{s}; \sigma) = K(r, \boldsymbol{x} - \boldsymbol{s}) *_{\boldsymbol{x},r} G(\boldsymbol{x}, r; \sigma_K) \approx G(\frac{1}{2}\sqrt{2}(\|\boldsymbol{x} - \boldsymbol{s}\| - r); \sigma_K). \tag{9}$$

The next step is to apply a Gaussian along the $\boldsymbol{s}$ axes; but this is, in fact, unnecessary. The structure of K along axes $\boldsymbol{x}$ and $\boldsymbol{s}$ is not independent. The Gaussian smoothing along $\boldsymbol{x}$ implies a Gaussian smoothing along $\boldsymbol{s}$, as is evident from (9). It is unnecessary to apply the Gaussian smoothing along the $\boldsymbol{s}$ axes, unless the required smoothing σ_s along the $\boldsymbol{s}$ axes is larger than that required along the $\boldsymbol{p}$ axes.

The Gaussian smoothing has been chosen to allow a sampling distance of σ_K along the normal to the plane. The actual sampling will be along $\boldsymbol{\xi}$ and r. When using a rectangular sampling grid, the off-axis band-limit is larger than the on-axis band-limit. In the case of our cone, this means that we can reduce the size of the Gaussian by a factor of $\sqrt{2}$:

$$K_b(r, \boldsymbol{\xi}) = \sqrt{2}\, G(\|\boldsymbol{\xi}\| - r; \sigma_K). \tag{10}$$

The consequences of the imposed band-limitation are as follows: as long as the Gaussian is small with respect to the curvature of the manifolds represented by the operator function C, the effects of the Gaussian are negligible. In fact, it is possible to interpolate the PRF and obtain sub-pixel accuracy. High-curvature patches of C correspond either to highly curved shapes or to shapes which vary rapidly as a function of the parameters. In neither case is it reasonable to expect good results.

3 Reducing Memory Requirements

The parameter space for the Radon transform typically has more dimensions than the input image. This implies that the PRF might not fit into the available computer memory. This constraint has traditionally prevented wide-spread use of these transforms for 3D images.

Many authors have tackled this problem in a variety of manners. Most notably, Ballard and Sabbah [2] propose to partition the parameter space into two or more spaces with independent parameters, which can be computed sequentially. Hsu and Huang [5] apply this method to detect 3D ellipsoids (with 6 parameters, the axes are supposed to lie on the grid). They split the 6D parameter space into two 4D parameter spaces, which have to be combined to find the objects.

Another method often employed involves splitting the parameter space into overlapping regions, from which the maxima are extracted. This does not involve a reduction of dimensionality, but incurs a penalty in computational cost because of the overlap. In the case of a sphere, it is natural to split the parameter space along the r-axis, since a slice $P(r_i, \boldsymbol{x})$ is computed by a single convolution. We will call this method the Sliding Window method (SW).

We propose a different approach to reduce the memory requirements. Spheres can be detected very efficiently by storing only the maximum projection along the r-axis of P, together with the location of these values on the r-axis (if one is prepared to ignore concentric spheres). That is, we keep

$$S(\boldsymbol{x}) = \max_r \{P(r, \boldsymbol{x})\} \quad \text{and} \quad R(\boldsymbol{x}) = \arg\max_r \{P(r, \boldsymbol{x})\} . \tag{11}$$

The local maxima in $S(\boldsymbol{x})$ indicate the location of the center of the spheres, and $R(\boldsymbol{x})$ gives the corresponding radii. Both of these can be computed by a small modification of the Radon algorithm. Instead of storing all the $P(r_i, \boldsymbol{x})$ slices, we propose to take the point-wise maximum of each slice with the previously computed intermediate result. This does not add any computational cost to the algorithm, since finding the local maxima needs to be done anyway. This maximum projection even simplifies this task. We call this method the Maximum Projection method (MP), and should be both faster and much less memory-hungry than the SW method.

The resulting PRF $S(\boldsymbol{x})$ is not band-limited. But, if the spheres are clearly identifiable and well separated, it turns out to have nicely-shaped peaks (i.e. the neighbourhoods of the local maxima are band-limited or nearly so). Thus, it is still possible to obtain the center of the sphere with sub-pixel accuracy. However, the r-axis at each location has been discretised to sampling locations. The accuracy to which r can be estimated depends on the number of samples taken, not the band-limitation of $K_b(r, \boldsymbol{x})$ along the r-axis.

It is possible to implement such a Radon transform for other shapes as well, in which the maximum projection can be taken over more than one dimension. That is, only the spatial dimensions need to be kept, all other dimensions can be collapsed into one maximum image and one or more maximum position images, of which there are as many as parameter dimensions are reduced.

4 Results

To demonstrate the claims made in the previous sections, we computed the Radon transform of 25 synthetically generated, 3D test images, 128^3 pixels in size, each containing 20 spheres of different radii (between 6 and 18 pixels) at random, sub-pixel locations. Some of the spheres were touching, but none were overlapping. These spheres had a Gaussian profile (with $\sigma = 1$), thereby approximating band-limitness. We computed the Radon transform with the two methods explained above (setting $\sigma_K = 1$ in equation (10)): SW and MP. The SW method uses a window of 7 slices in the radius direction, from which 2 slices overlap other regions. It required five times as much memory, and took three times as much time to finish, as the MP method. Apparently the local maxima algorithm we used is relatively expensive compared to the convolutions themselves. We evaluated both methods by computing the differences between the true parameters of the spheres and the computed ones. The average error and the standard deviation give a quantitative performance measure for the algorithm. These results are summarized in Table 1.

We found that both methods found the location of the spheres with the same accuracy (actually the parameters found for an individual sphere were very similar). The bias is very small, not significant in relation to the standard deviation. Both methods underestimate the radius in the same way, but the MP method found the rounded values of the radii found by the SW method. The underestimation of the radius depends on r, and it is possible to correct for it by increasing the radius of the functional $K_b(r, \boldsymbol{x})$.

We added Gaussian noise with standard deviation σ_N such that the signal-to-noise ratio $SNR = \frac{\max I(\boldsymbol{s})}{\sigma_N} = 2$ (with $I(\boldsymbol{s})$ the uncorrupted image). The standard deviation in the error of the spatial coordinate increases by about 50% for this noise level, but is still very small. This shows that the projection method is a good approximation with or without noise, and shows that the Radon transform itself is very insensitive to noise.

4.1 Ballotini

As a demonstration application, we used a rather poor quality X-ray micro-CT image of ballotini (small, hollow glass beads, see Fig. 1, the two images on the top left). Some of the glass walls give a very wide response in the imager (probably caused by refraction or reflection). In one such region many small spheres can be fitted. To avoid this, we replaced the kernel K_b by a kernel K_b' that penalizes for high grey-values inside the sphere:

$$K_b'(r, \boldsymbol{x}) = K_b(r, \boldsymbol{x}) - K_b(r - 4, \boldsymbol{x}) , \qquad (12)$$

with K_b the original kernel as given in Eq. (9).

By requiring that the inner part of the sphere be empty, the discriminating abilities of the transform (for these images) are greatly enhanced (see Fig. 1). The computational cost is increased minimally, since only generating the image

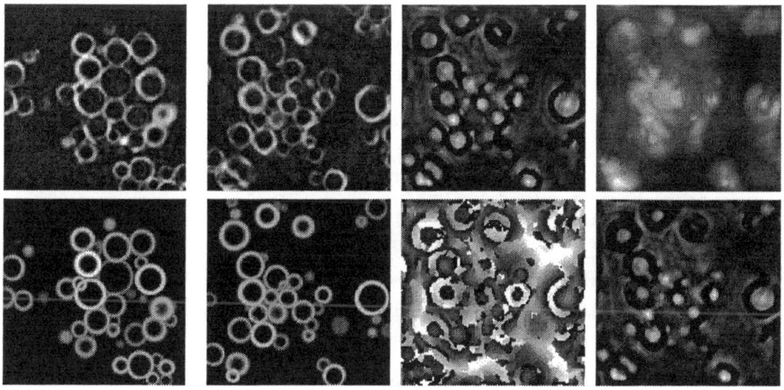

Fig. 1. Two slices of the 3D ballotini image and the results of the Radon transform. Top to bottom, left to right: Slice of the input image; corresponding slice of the image reconstructed with the found parameters. Another slice of the input image; corresponding slice of the output. Corresponding slice of $S(\boldsymbol{x})$; slice of $R(\boldsymbol{x})$. $S(\boldsymbol{x})$ without the inner sphere; $S(\boldsymbol{x})$ when the inner sphere has a diameter 2 pixels smaller than the outer sphere (instead of 4 as actually used).

for the functional $K_b'(r, \boldsymbol{x})$ is more expensive. The "magic number" 4 used in this functional was chosen such that the sphere $K_b(r, \boldsymbol{x})$ was not affected too much ($2 \cdot 2\sigma_K = 4$), since that would cause a heavier underestimation of the radius. In the synthetic test images used in above, this setting leads to an average underestimation of the radius of 0.3 pixels (v.s. 0.2 pixels for the transform with K_b as the kernel). As before, this systematic error can be corrected for.

To find the spheres in the PRF $S(\boldsymbol{x})$, a threshold is used to decide which local maxima are important enough to represent a sphere in the input images. More complex decision rules could be used, but are outside the scope of this paper. Figure 1 shows the results for two different slices from the 3D image.

5 Conclusions

We have given the conditions under which the Radon transform can be computed free of discretisation errors. In general these conditions must be imposed by actively band-limiting the operator function C. This has no consequences for sufficiently smooth shapes. The PRF that results is band-limited, allowing interpolation, and sub-pixel accuracy in the estimated parameters.

The Radon transform reduces to a convolution for position-type parameters, yielding a large speed-up. We propose a memory-efficient implementation computing a single r slice of $P(r, \boldsymbol{x})$ (through convolution) at a time. We keep track of the maximum projection and the argument-maximum projection along the r axis as we compute the slices. We argue that this approach can be used for other shapes as well.

We have applied this modified Radon transform to a 3D image of glass hollow beads. To compute its PRF we have employed a convolution kernel that contains

Table 1. Error made when estimating parameters of spheres in synthetic 3D images. The error in the position ($\delta x = \hat{x} - x$) and the error in the radius ($\delta r = \hat{r} - r$) are shown separately (the units are pixels for both). The error in the position considers the first spatial coordinate only.

	SNR = ∞		SNR = 2	
	MP Method	SW Method	MP Method	SW Method
$E(\delta x)$	−0.00130	−0.00127	−0.00356	−0.00385
$std(\delta x)$	0.02917	0.02938	0.04478	0.04605
$E(\delta r)$	−0.20706	−0.21850	−0.20906	−0.21986
$std(\delta r)$	0.30502	0.07142	0.30683	0.07326

not only a sphere, but also a second, smaller, concentric sphere with negative grey-values. The resulting PRF has a much higher discriminating ability than that which would result from the same computation with a single sphere.

Acknowledgements

The authors wish to thank Scott Singleton and Dave Rowlands at Unilever R&D Colworth (UK), for their hospitality and permission to use the ballotini image in this paper. This work was partially supported by the Dutch Ministry of Economic Affairs through their IOP program and by Unilever R&D Vlaardingen (NL).

References

1. A.S. Aguado, E. Montiel, and M.S. Nixon. Bias error analysis of the generalised Hough transform. *Journal of Mathematical Imaging and Vision*, 12(1):25–42, 2000.
2. D.H. Ballard and D. Sabbah. Viewer independent shape recognition. *IEEE Transactions on Pattern Analysis and Machine Intelligence*, 5(6):653–660, 1983.
3. S.R. Deans. Hough transform from the Radon transform. *IEEE Transactions on Pattern Analysis and Machine Intelligence*, 3(2):185–188, March 1981.
4. M. van Ginkel. *Image Analysis using Orientation Space based on Steerable Filters.* PhD thesis, Delft University of Technology, Delft, The Netherlands, 2002.
5. C.-C. Hsu and J.S. Huang. Partitioned Hough transform for ellipsoid detection. *Pattern Recognition*, 23:275–282, 1990.
6. N. Kiryati and A.M. Bruckstein. Antialiasing the Hough transform. *CVGIP: Graphical Models and Image Processing*, 53(3):213–222, May 1991.
7. J. Princen, J. Illingworth, and J. Kittler. Hypothesis testing: a framework for analyzing and optimizing Hough transform performance. *IEEE Transactions on Pattern Analysis and Machine Intelligence*, 16(4):329–341, April 1994.
8. J. Sklansky. On the Hough technique for curve detection. *IEEE Transactions on Computers*, 27(10):923–926, October 1978.
9. G.C. Stockman and A.K. Agrawala. Equivalence of Hough curve detection to template matching. *Communications of the ACM*, 20(11):820–822, 1977.
10. P.W. Verbeek. A class of sampling-error free measures in oversampled band-limited images. *Pattern Recognition Letters*, 3:287–292, 1985.
11. L.J. van Vliet. *Grey-Scale Measurements in Multi-Dimensional Digitized Images.* PhD thesis, Delft University of Technology, Delft, The Netherlands, October 1993.

Monocentric Optical Space

Jan J. Koenderink

Universiteit Utrecht, Department of Physics & Astronomy
Princetonplein 5, 3584 CC Utrecht, The Netherlands
j.j.koenderink@phys.uu.nl

Abstract. The objective content of the visual world of a monocular, immobile observer is entirely due to "monocular cues". These cues only partially constrain the geometry, the remaining ambiguities define a freedom of the observer to commit "mental changes of viewpoint". Though fully idiosyncratic, such changes cannot possibly violate the optical data. We use this group of "visual congruences" (for that they must be) to deduce the geometry of monocentric visual space. Visual space is a homogeneous, flat non–Euclidean space. Homogeneity implies that the space admits of a group of isometries (the aforementioned cue ambiguities) or "free mobility of rigid configurations". Thus visual space is the same near any one of its points. The theory has many applications, among more in the rendering of scenes at inappropriate sizes as is typical in printing.

1 Introduction

There have been several attempts to construct the geometry of bicentric optical space, perhaps the best known instance being the work by Luneburg[11]. In contradistinction, there does not exist a formal account of monocentric visual space. The reason possibly is that the third dimension of optical space, that is its "depth", seems particularly ill defined. Bishop Berkeley[3] indeed denied the very possibility of a monocular visual space on these grounds. The depth dimension is a mental construction based on a large number of more or less ill defined "cues" (also due to Berkeley[3]). Perhaps unfortunately so, only a few of the cues known to be important are formally understood (largely due to developments in computer vision[6]). Notice that Berkeley's view turns "vision" into something akin to "image interpretation".

I distinguish between monocentric optical space and physical space (or space proper). Monocentric optical space refers to space as experienced from a single vantage point. "Space" proper refers to the case where an observer is free to move, and, even when stationary, entertains multiple virtual copies of herself located at various positions in the space. In space proper opaque objects may occlude, thus hide other things (as apparent from the actual vantage point), *e.g.*, their own backsides. But in monocentric space the very notion of "hiding" is void. Everything that can possibly belong to the space is necessarily in plain sight. There is nothing else but what is seen. The optical facts are fixed. Nevertheless monocentric optical space, like pictorial space, is 3-dimensional though its

N. Petkov and M.A. Westenberg (Eds.): CAIP 2003, LNCS 2756, pp. 689–696, 2003.

third dimension, "depth", is purely virtual. Being "computed" does not render it "real", although it is "actual" to the observer.

2 Construction of the Geometry

My point of departure is not so much a novel analysis of the cues as the exploitation of generally agreed upon invariance properties of monocentric optical space. Two of such invariances have been recognized from the earliest times on. These are the invariance with respect to Euclidean dilations and rotations about the eye (here "eye" means "vantage point" or "perspective center", one may take the first nodal point for the stationary or the geometrical center of the eyeball for the mobile eye).

Consider the case of rotations first. When the world is rotated with respect to the observer the visual field undergoes an isometry, that is to say, all geometrical relations are invariant. Indeed, an eye movement suffices to restore the exact retinal image. Since all cues are untouched one draws the inevitable conclusion that the visual world has to be conserved *in toto*. Next consider the case of dilations. If the physical world is shrunk or expanded with the eye as the single fixed point, the visual field is subjected to the identity transformation. Optically nothing changes, hence the visual world must again be conserved *in toto*. The case of dilations is discussed by Helmholtz[8] and Poincaré[13], however, it was understood well before, even by the general public. Prior to the introduction of Gulliver the worlds of Lilliput or Brobdingnag are (optically) exactly like ours[16].

In this paper I consider the "flatland" case[1]. Consider a visual observer at the origin of the punctured Euclidean plane. There exist curves that are shifted along themselves under central dilation–rotations, they are the logarithmic spirals[5]. Special cases include the equidistance circles and the visual rays. The former can be regarded as spirals of zero and the latter spirals of infinite slope. The logarithmic spirals are special because a dilation can be undone through a Euclidean movement.

From a formal perspective the logarithmic spirals are *linear manifolds* in terms of the logarithmic distance to the origin and the azimuth, that is the (signed) angle of the visual direction with a fiducial "straight ahead" direction. Thus $\log \rho/\rho_0 = \alpha + \sigma\varphi$, ρ the distance, φ the azimuth, ρ_0 and α constants, σ the slope. The pair $\{\log \rho/\rho_0, \varphi\}$ are indeed natural "Cartesian coordinates" of optical space. This is immediately intuitive in case of the azimuth. That the depth coordinate should be logarithmic (in terms of the Euclidean description) is also intuitive when you remember that absolute distance is irrelevant because only distance ratios (differences of logarithmic distances) are optically relevant.

The property of being shift invariant singles out the straight lines in Euclidean geometry, thus it is natural to interpret the logarithmic spirals as the straight lines of visual space. When you do this it becomes evident that Euclidean (central) dilation–rotations must correspond to the *translations* of visual space. You may distinguish two components of such translations, lateral displacements—which correspond to Euclidean central rotations, and depth displacements, which correspond to Euclidean central dilations. The lateral displacements ($\varphi' = \varphi + \lambda$ for some shift λ) conserve equidistance circles and interchange visual rays, whereas the depth displacements ($\log \rho'/\rho_0 = \log \rho/\rho_0 + \mu$ for some shift μ) conserve visual rays and interchange equidistance circles. Thus the visual rays and equidistance circles must be considered two mutually orthogonal families of parallel straight lines of visual space. Although this appears contrived from a Euclidean perspective, it should be a very natural interpretation to the visual observer. The lateral shifts can be undone through eye movements (which are Euclidean rotations) which are experienced as displacements, rather than rotations. Likewise, central dilations are experienced as displacements in the depth dimension. Although the latter are less often experienced than the former, we have some experience with minified scale models (*e.g.*, with architectural models, or doll's houses).

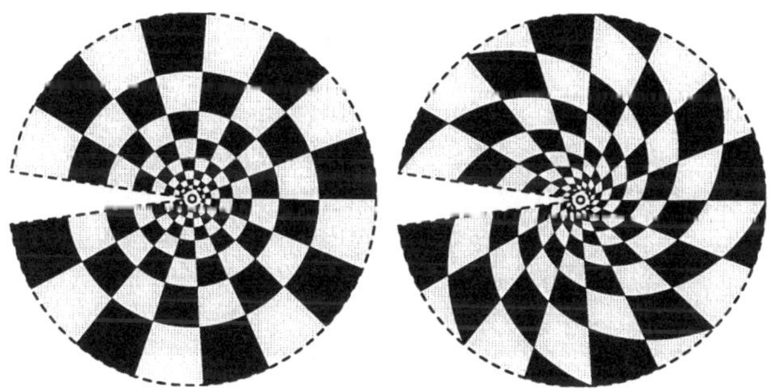

Fig. 1. At the left a pavement of square tiles (in the metric of visual space), neatly lined up with respect to the straight ahead direction. At the right the same pavement rotated in visual space. In these figures "straight ahead" towards the right, on the left the visual field is limited, here to an almost panoramic view.

In the Euclidean plane any rotation changes the slopes of all straight lines by the same amount. You may use this property to identify the analog group of transformations in visual space. The "slope" of a spiral can be understood as the angle subtended with the equidistance circles (the angle subtended with the visual rays is simply the Euclidean complement) for this angle is constant along the length of the spiral (in fact, its defining property). This angle determines the foreshortening and is thus a natural slope parameter. Since we have set out to characterize the spirals as the straight lines of visual space (curves of constant slope) the visual slope has to be a monotonic function of this Euclidean slope. A "rotation" in visual space should change the slopes of straight lines by the same amount and the effect of successive rotations should be additive. This happens when one sets $\log \rho'/\rho_0 = \log \rho/\rho_0 + \xi\,\varphi$ for a "rotation angle ξ". (See figure 1.)

In this interpretation the angle subtended by two spirals is simply the parameter of the rotation that will transform the one into the other. An important constraint in visual space is that visual rays cannot be rotated any further: For all points on a visual ray coincide in the visual field and no transformation can possibly undo that. If the vantage point is fixed there is no way to lift the degeneracy. This was indeed the major point of Berkeley's[3] *New Theory of Vision*, and it is a point that cannot rationally be rejected. Thus the rotations of visual space should conserve the visual rays. In the interpretation attempted here this is an immediate consequence of the geometry though. The visual rays have slopes of $\pm\infty$ (depending upon whether they are understood as pointing away or towards the egocenter), thus any additive angle of rotation must be ineffective (infinity is not changed by the addition of any finite amount). "The" slope in visual space is the tangent of the Euclidean slope and rotations in visual space simply add a constant to all slopes. Because the visual rays have slopes of $\pm\infty$, their slopes are invariant under rotations.

Notice that you can rotate an equidistance circle either way (sloping to the left or the right of the observer), but not further than the visual ray oriented towards or away from the observer. The slopes range from minus to plus infinity, and the angle measure in visual space has to be *parabolic*, that is to say, *non-periodic.*

The shifts and rotations of visual space together constitute its group of proper movements. The group of similarities of visual space is richer than that of the Euclidean plane because of the symmetry between distance and angle. In the Euclidean plane a similarity can scale distances, but not angles. In visual space one has similarities of the first kind, scaling distances, and of the second kind, scaling angles.

Thus the group of proper movements and similarities can be written in homogeneous coordinates as

$$\begin{pmatrix} \varphi' \\ \log \frac{\rho'}{\rho_0} \\ 1 \end{pmatrix} = \mu \begin{pmatrix} \kappa_1 & 0 & \tau_1 \\ \sigma & \kappa & \tau_2 \\ 0 & 0 & 1 \end{pmatrix} \begin{pmatrix} \varphi \\ \log \frac{\rho}{\rho_0} \\ 1 \end{pmatrix},$$

with $\mu \neq 0$. Here τ_1 denotes a lateral, τ_2 a radial shift; σ denotes a rotation, κ_1 and $\kappa_2 = \kappa/\kappa_1$ are the moduli of similarities and are both equal to one for proper movements.

Consider the effect of arbitrary proper movements on the relation between two points in visual space. Because visual rays are conserved as a family and this family is rotated in a rigid fashion (in terms of the geometry of the punctured Euclidean plane), the azimuthal separation is invariant. Call it the "proper distance" of the points. Notice that two points on a single visual ray have zero proper distance but are nevertheless distinct. I call them "parallel points". Here we see the full metric duality of points and lines in visual space. For parallel points the logarithm of their distance ratio is invariant under proper motions. Call it their "special distance". I define the distance of any two points as either their proper or special distance, whichever applies. This is a good definition because the distance is invariant under arbitrary proper movements. Likewise the slope difference of two spirals is invariant under proper movements. Call it the "proper angle". Notice that two spirals may subtend zero angle yet be different (they are related by a lateral shift). I call such spirals "parallel". Parallel spirals possess an invariant separation, which is the logarithm of the distance ratio of their intersection with any visual ray. Call it their "special angle". I define the angle subtended by two spirals as either the proper or the special angle, whichever applies. The angle is invariant under arbitrary proper movements, thus this definition is a good one. Notice the perfect duality between lines (spirals) and points, angles and distances.

The non-Euclidean distance measure of visual space is very different from the Euclidean distance measure of the punctured Euclidean plane. For instance, a point on a logarithmic spiral is at finite distance from the origin, even when measured along the curve (which winds infinitely many times about the origin!) in the Euclidean case, but at infinite distance in the sense of the non-Euclidean metric. Indeed, the origin (location of the eye) is at infinite distance from any real point of the visual space. In this very real sense the eye is outside the visual world!

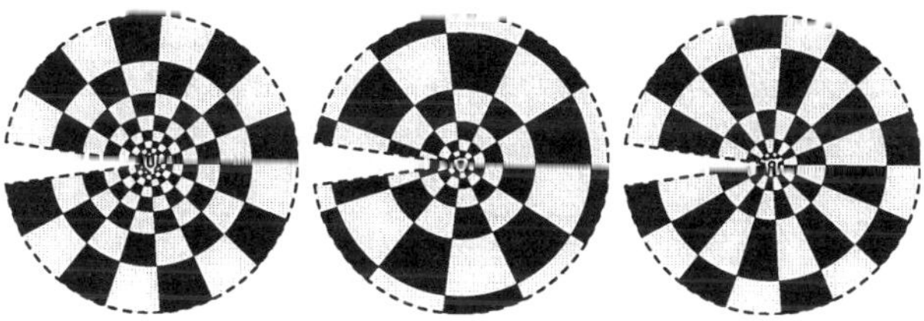

Fig. 2. At the left a square pavement. At the center we show an example of a similarity of the first kind. This transformation affects only the distances. It represents a change of apparent size and is important when a viewer is confronted with minified copies, etc. At the right we show an example of a similarity of the second kind. This transformation affects only the angles. It represents a change of apparent relief, the type of transformation discussed by Adolf Hildebrand[9].

Suppose I raise all radial distances to a certain power κ_2. This transformation multiples the slopes of all logarithmic spirals by the same factor (namely the power κ_2). Thus this transformation scales the angles in visual space, it is a "similarity of the second kind". Notice that the similarity conserves the spirals (straight lines of visual space) as a family and that it conserves parallellity and bisection of distances and angles. Thus it is an "affinity" of visual space. A somewhat stranger transformation (from a Euclidean viewpoint) scales all azimuths by the same factor κ_1. Thus only the straight ahead direction (zero azimuth) remains unaffected. Of course one needs to limit the extent of the visual field suitably in order to avoid "overlaps" or "gaps". Such a transformation scales both distances and angles in visual space. The angles are not affected if you combine the azimuth scaling with a suitable powerscaling of the radial distances. Such a transformation that affects only the azimuths only scales distances in visual space and is a "similarity of the first kind". Such a similarity is again an affinity in visual space since it conserves parallellity and bisection of distances and angles. (See figure 2.)

The geometry I have obtained informally is well known (thus the existence of a formal account is guaranteed). It is one of the 9 Cayley–Klein planes[4, 10], the one with a single isotropic direction. It is a non–Euclidean geometry with parabolic distance and angle measures and a full metric duality between points and lines. It is a homogeneous space that admits of a group of congruences (exactly the linear transformations) or "free mobility of rigid configurations". Thus visual space is the same near any one of its points. The mathematics is all neatly in place[15, 17, 14], one needs only a few minor "patches" to arrive at a formally fully coherent framework.

3 Application: The Minification of Wideangle Scenes

It has been remarked repeatedly that in paintings of wide scenes (over 100° say) that are purportedly in "true linear perspective" it is often the case that local, spherical objects (or roughly globular objects such as human heads) are not depicted as the elongated ellipses they ought to be according to linear perspective. It is generally agreed that although this "is wrong" it nevertheless "looks more real". One "explanation" often encountered is that observers tend to change their station points and look at details or (with fixed station point) often look at minified replicas. This general type of explanation can be formalized in the present framework.

A similarity of the first kind is a conformal transformation (locally a similarity) whereas it changes the angular width of a scene by a factor κ_1. This corresponds to the minified copy viewed in such a way that the angular extent of the depicted scene has shrunk as compared to the "intended" angular extent as evident from an analysis of the linear perspective of the original on the basis of familiarity cues (that is the only analysis possible in the absence of written records or availability of the historical setting). In such a representation local details should appear undeformed because it is a conformal transformation of visual space. Since spheres remain spheres in such a transformation, a depiction of small angular extent should represent spheres with circular outlines, even though they represent spheres at the very periphery of the linear perspective rendering.

One thus obtains a simple, formal account of the matter. The present theory allows for the scaling of the angular extent of a scene, something lacking (to the best of our knowledge) from any existent treatment. This has numerous practical applications. Many book illustrations have standard size (4″ wide say) and are meant to be viewed at some standard distance (about a foot say) whereas they may represent wildly varying angular extents. As is well known such illustrations often "look wrong" (especially with very wide or narrow angle scenes[12, 7]). The present formalism suggests a quantitative method to "predeform them" in order to "look right" at a given size and viewing distance. In the limit for very high minification (e.g., a 180° panorama to a 2″ figure on reading distance (which amounts to about a 20–fold angular minification) one arrives at the perspective renderings of Barre and Flocon[2]. Indeed, these were introduced precisely because of their agreeable representation of the visual field, though these authors use only informal arguments as to why that might be the case.

Fig. 3. The perspectively "correct" viewing distance of the photograph on top is 4cm, thus the regular reading distance (of about 300mm) is far too long. This "explains" the severe wide angle "distorsion". The version at bottom has been transformed to look correct from normal reading distance. Notice the curvature of straight lines in the scene as apparent from the chequered floor.

We supply an example in figure 3. The scene subtends an unusually wide view (a 12mm super wideangle objective on a conventional 35mm camera, about 112° wide). All vases are rotationally symmetric (except for handles, etc.), the dish on the floor is circular, the framed print rectangular. Several of the vases occur as identical pairs (shape–wise, the decorations are different) at different locations, thus the perspectival distortions are readily evident. Notice the "fattening" of the vases near the edges of the photograph, this is the effect often discussed in the literature[12, 7]. The (upper) photograph thus clearly illustrates the well known "distortion of wide angle lenses". Actually the linear perspective rendering is perfect of course. In the bottom image I have corrected the rendering for normal reading distance, using a similarity of monocentric visual space. The fattening effect is gone and the distortions are much less apparent. This is bought at a price: Straight lines become curved, as is apparent from the chequering of the floor. These are exactly the "deformations" often seen in paintings of wide scenes of the middle ages, before linear perspective came into vogue[2].

References

1. Abbot, E. A. Flatland: A Romance of many Dimensions. orig. 1884. Dover, New York (1992)
2. Barre, A., Flocon, A. La perspective curviligne, de l'espace visuel a l'image construite. Flammarion, Paris (1968)
3. Berkeley, B. An Essay towards a New Theory of Vision. Orig. 1709. In: Theory of Vision and Other Writing by Bishop Berkeley, 1925, Dent and Sons, New York (1925)
4. Cayley, A. Sixth memoir upon the quantics. Philosophical Transactions of the Royal Society London **149** (1859) 61-70
5. Coxeter, H. S. M. Introduction to Geometry. Wiley, New York (1989)
6. Forsyth, D., Ponce, J. Computer Vision—A modern Approach, Prentice Hall, Upper Saddle River, NJ (2002)
7. Hauck, G. Die subjektive Perspektive und die horizontalen Curvaturen des Dorischen Styls. Wittwer, Stuttgart (1875)
8. Helmholtz, H. On the Facts underlying Geometry. Orig. 1868. In Cohen and Elkana (1977) 39-71
9. Hildebrand, A. The Problem of Form in painting and sculpture. Translated by M. Meyer and R. M. Ogden. First, German edition, Das Problem der Form, 1893. Stechert, New York (1945)
10. Klein, F. Vergleichende Betrachtungen über neuere geometrische Forschungen. Mathematische Annalen **43** (1893) 63-100
11. Luneburg, R. K. Mathematical analysis of binocular vision. Princeton University Press, Princeton New Jersey (1947)
12. Pirenne, M. H. Optics, Painting and Photography. Cambridge University Press, Cambridge (1970)
13. Poincaré, H. Science et la méthode. Flammarion, Paris (1908)
14. Sachs, H. Ebene isotrope Geometrie. Friedrich Vieweg & Sohn, Braunschweig (1987)
15. Strubecker, K. Differentialgeometrie des isotropen Raumes I. Sitzungsberichte der Akademie der Wissenschaften Wien **150** (1941) 1-43
16. Swift, J. Gulliver's Travels and Other Works. Routledge (orig. 1726) (1906)
17. Yaglom, I. M. A simple non–Euclidean geometry and its physical basis. Springer, New York (1979)

Cumulative Chord Piecewise-Quartics for Length and Curve Estimation

Ryszard Kozera

School of Computer Science and Software Engineering
The University of Western Australia
35 Stirling Highway, Crawley 6009 WA, Perth, Australia
ryszard@csse.uwa.edu.au
http://www.csse.uwa.edu.au/~ryszard/

Abstract. We discuss the problem of estimating an arbitrary regular parameterized curve and its length from an ordered sample of interpolation points in n-dimensional Euclidean space. The corresponding tabular parameters are assumed to be *unknown*. In this paper the convergence rates for estimating both curve and its length with cumulative chord piecewise-quartics are established for different types of unparameterized data including ε-*uniform* samplings. The latter extends previous results on cumulative chord piecewise-quadratics and piecewise-cubics. The numerical experiments carried out for planar and space curves confirm sharpness of the derived asymptotics. A high quality approximation property of piecewise-quartic cumulative chords is also experimentally verified on sporadic data. Our results may be of interest in computer vision (e.g. in edge and range image segmentation or in tracking), digital image processing, computer graphics, approximation and complexity theory or digital and computational geometry.

Keywords: shape, length, curve interpolation, image analysis and features

1 Introduction

The layout of this paper is as follows. The first section is mainly expository and closes with some motivation standing behind this work. The second part extends approximation results established for piecewise-quadratics and piecewise-cubics [24], [25] to piecewise-quartic cumulative chords. Next we verify experimentally the sharpness of herein presented results for planar and space curves tested with different samplings. We close this paper with conclusions.
Let $\gamma : [0,T] \to \mathbb{R}^n$ be a smooth regular curve of class C^k for some $k \geq 1$, where $\dot\gamma(t) \neq \mathbf{0}$ for all $t \in [0,T]$ (with $0 < T < \infty$). Consider the problem of estimating γ and its length $d(\gamma) = \int_0^T \|\dot\gamma(t)\| dt$ from *an ordered* $m+1$-tuple $\mathcal{Q} = (q_0, q_1, \ldots, q_m)$ of points in $\mathbb{R}^n$, where $q_i = \gamma(t_i)$, and $0 = t_0 < t_1 < \ldots < t_m = T$. As γ is regular without loss one can assume that γ is parameterized by arc-length i.e. $\|\dot\gamma(t)\| = 1$ (see [14]; Chapter 1, Prop. 1.1.5). Assume now

$$\delta = max\{t_i - t_{i-1} : i = 1,2,...,m\} \quad \text{and} \quad \delta \to 0 \ . \tag{1}$$

N. Petkov and M.A. Westenberg (Eds.): CAIP 2003, LNCS 2756, pp. 697–705, 2003.

Definition 1. *A family* $\{f_\delta, \delta > 0\}$ *of functions* $f_\delta : [0,T] \to \mathbb{R}$ *is said to be* $O(\delta^p)$ *when there is a constant* $K > 0$ *such that, for some* $\delta_0 > 0$, $|f_\delta(t)| < K\delta^p$, *for all* $\delta \in (0, \delta_0)$ *and all* $t \in [0,T]$. *In such a case write* $f_\delta = O(\delta^p)$. *For a family of vector-valued functions* $F_\delta : [0,T] \to \mathbb{R}^n$, *write* $F_\delta = O(\delta^p)$ *when* $\|F_\delta\| = O(\delta^p)$, *where* $\|\cdot\|$ *denotes the Euclidean norm. An approximation* $\tilde{\gamma} : [0,T] \to \mathbb{R}^n$ *to* γ *determined by* $\mathcal{Q}$ *is said to have* order p *when* $\tilde{\gamma} - \gamma = O(\delta^p)$.

It is well-known that if the t_i's *are given*, then the following holds:

Example 1. Let γ be C^{r+2}, where $r > 0$, and take m to be a multiple of r. Assume $\mathcal{Q}$ consists of $\frac{m}{r}$ consecutive tuples of points $\mathcal{Q}_j = (q_{jr}, q_{jr+1}, \ldots, q_{r(j+1)})$, for $0 \le j \le \frac{m}{r} - 1$. Let $\hat{\gamma}_r^k$ (with $k = jr$) be a piecewise r-degree polynomial interpolating γ over $\mathcal{Q}_j$ and $\hat{\gamma}_r$ be the corresponding track-sum of $\hat{\gamma}_r^k$. If t_i's are known and satisfy (1) then $\hat{\gamma}_r = \gamma + O(\delta^{r+1})$, uniformly for $t \in [0,T]$. Similarly, the error in length can be shown to be $O(\delta^{r+1})$ (see e.g. [16]). For special types of samplings this result can be tightened. Indeed (see also Example 2) if sampling is uniform $t_i = \frac{i}{m}$ the length is approximated with $O(\delta^{r+1})$ or $O(\delta^{r+2})$, accordingly as r is odd or even (see Theorem 1 in [26]). All estimates are experimentally confirmed to be sharp. By *sharpness* we understand the existence of at least one C^{r+2} regular curve which when sampled according to (1) yields rates specified above.

In practice (e.g. in edge or image segmentation) the t_i's might *not be given*. If then t_i's are guessed blindly, the results from Example 1 can be severely crippled (see Example 2). Indeed, γ can then at most be approximated up to reparameterizations. Namely we seek piecewise-r degree polynomial curves $\hat{\gamma}_r : [0,\hat{T}] \to \mathbb{R}^n$ with $\tilde{\gamma} \equiv \hat{\gamma}_r \circ \psi$ uniformly close to $\gamma \in C^{r+2}$, for some piecewise-C^{r+2} $\psi : [0,T] \to [0,\hat{T}]$.

Example 2. Let γ be a C^4 curve in $\mathbb{R}^n$. For $\varepsilon \ge 0$ t_i's are *ε-uniformly sampled* when there is an a C^k reparameterization $\phi : [0,T] \to [0,T]$ such that $\dot{\phi} > 0$ and

$$t_i = \phi(\frac{iT}{m}) + O(\frac{1}{m^{1+\varepsilon}}) \,. \tag{2}$$

Note that ε-uniformity is invariant with respect to arbitrary reparameterization of γ (including arc-length). Clearly, as $t_i - t_{i-1} = \dot{\phi}(\frac{(i-1)T}{m})\frac{T}{m} + O(\frac{1}{m^{1+\varepsilon}}) \to 0$ with $m \to \infty$ (here $1 \le i \le m-1$), formula (2) defines a sub-sampling of (1). Then if γ is sampled according to (2), a piecewise-quadratic *uniform* Lagrange interpolation $\hat{\gamma}_2 : [0,1] \to \mathbb{R}^n$ with times guessed as $\hat{t}_i = \frac{i}{m}$ yields

$$\hat{\gamma}_2 \circ \psi = \gamma + O(\delta^{\min\{3,1+2\varepsilon\}}) \quad \text{and} \quad d(\hat{\gamma}_2) = d(\gamma) + O(\delta^{\min\{4,4\varepsilon\}}) \,,$$

where $\psi : [0,T] \to [0,1]$ defines a piecewise quadratic diffeomorphism (see Theorem 1 in [26]). Visibly, for $\varepsilon \approx 0$ the respective convergence rates are very slow. In particular [27], if $\varepsilon = 0$ (despite $\hat{\gamma}_2 \circ \psi = \gamma + O(\delta)$) length $d(\hat{\gamma}_2) = d(\hat{\gamma}_2 \circ \psi)$ may*not even converge* to $d(\gamma)$. On the other hand, if t_i's satisfying (2) (and thus

(1)) are known then, as expected, the corresponding convergence rates are faster and either match or improve those from Example 1. Namely [16], for a regular $\gamma \in C^{r+2}$ the following holds $\hat{\gamma}_r = \gamma + O(\delta^{r+1})$ and

$$d(\hat{\gamma}_r) = d(\gamma) + O(\delta^{r+1}) \quad \text{or} \quad d(\hat{\gamma}_r) = d(\gamma) + O(\delta^{r+1+\min\{1,\varepsilon\}}) ,$$

according to whether r is odd or even. Tests confirm sharpness of the above estimates. The natural question arises:

Question (i): Can the t_i's be estimated merely from $\mathcal{Q}$ so that the corresponding convergence rates match those established for t_i's known?
A partial solution is to use a piecewise-4-point quadratics interpolating quadruplets of points from $\mathcal{Q}$ [18], [21], [22], [23]. It is, however, limited only to planar strictly convex C^4 curves sampled more-or-less uniformly:

Example 3. The t_i's are sampled *more-or-less uniformly* if there are constants $0 < K_l < K_u$ such that, for any sufficiently large integer m, and all $1 \leq i \leq m$,

$$\frac{K_l}{m} \leq t_i - t_{i-1} \leq \frac{K_u}{m} . \tag{3}$$

From (3) it is clear that increments between successive t_i's are neither large nor small in proportion to $\frac{T}{m}$. Note also that (3) is invariant with respect to any reparameterization of γ. Clearly, as $max_{1 \leq i \leq m}\{t_i - t_{i-1}\} \to 0$ with $m \to \infty$ sampling (3) belongs to (1). Assume now that γ is planar, regular, strictly convex and C^r, where $r \geq 4$. Let $\mathcal{Q}$ be sampled according to (3). Then [22] there is a piecewise-quadratic curve $\hat{\gamma} : [0,1] \to \mathbb{R}^2$, calculable in terms of $\mathcal{Q}$, and a piecewise-cubic reparameterization $\psi : [0,T] \to [0,1]$, with $\hat{\gamma} \circ \psi = \gamma + O(\delta^4)$, and $d(\hat{\gamma}) = d(\gamma) + O(\delta^4)$. Both estimates are sharp [23].

Other approaches referring to Question (i) [5], [21], [29], [31] usually require solutions of systems of nonlinear equations yielding $\hat{t}_i$'s only implicitly. A possible solution to Question (i) is hinted in Chapter 11 of [17] or [8], [19], where *cumulative chord length parameterization* is introduced. Namely, let

$$\hat{t}_0 = 0 , \quad \hat{t}_j = \hat{t}_{j-1} + \|q_j - q_{j-1}\| , \quad \text{and} \quad \hat{T} = \hat{t}_m , \tag{4}$$

with $j = 1, 2, \ldots, m$. For k dividing m and $i = 0, k, 2k, \ldots m-k$, let $\hat{\gamma}_k$ be the curve satisfying $\hat{\gamma}_k(\hat{t}_j) = q_j$ for all $j = 0, 1, 2, \ldots, m$, and whose restriction $\hat{\gamma}_k^i$ to each $[\hat{t}_i, \hat{t}_{i+k}]$ is a polynomial of degree at most k. Call $\hat{\gamma}_k$ the *cumulative chord piecewise degree-k* approximation to γ defined by $\mathcal{Q}$. We have (see [24], [25]):

Theorem 1. *Suppose γ sampled according to (1) is a regular C^r curve in $\mathbb{R}^n$, where $r \geq k+1$ and $k = 2, 3$. Let $\hat{\gamma}_k : [0, \hat{T}] \to \mathbb{R}^n$ be the cumulative chord piecewise degree-k approximation defined by $\mathcal{Q}$. Then there is a piecewise-C^r $\psi_k : [0,T] \to [0,\hat{T}]$, with*

$$\hat{\gamma}_k \circ \psi_k = \gamma + O(\delta^{k+1}) \quad \textit{and} \quad d(\hat{\gamma}_k) = d(\gamma) + O(\delta^{k+1}) .$$

Also, if $r \geq 4$, $k = 2$ and t_i's satisfy (2) then

$$d(\hat{\gamma}_2) = d(\gamma) + O(\delta^{\min\{4,3+\varepsilon\}}) .$$

Theorem 1 together with Examples 1, 2, 3 provide a partial answer to Question (i) at least for $k = 2, 3$. In this paper we address the special case of Question (i):

Question (ii): Can the claim of Theorem 1 be extended to piecewise-quartic cumulative chords ($k = 4$) and if yes, is further speed up on convergence attainable?

The answer to Question (ii), is given here for a special subfamilies of (1) satisfying (2) or (3). In addition, the experiments (conducted only for curves in $\mathbb{R}^2$ or $\mathbb{R}^3$) verifying the sharpness of Theorems 2, 3 (valid for arbitrary regular curves in $\mathbb{R}^n$) are also performed accordingly. Finally, a high quality approximation property of the piecewise-quartic cumulative chord interpolating sporadic data is also experimentally confirmed. Our paper focuses on curve interpolation only. As a special case it provides also upper bounds for optimal rates of convergence when piecewise polynomials are applied to digitized curves [2], [6], [7], [10], [11], [12], [33]. In its current form this work can also be applicable to some computer vision problems such as edge and range image segmentation or tracking some points of a moving rigid body.

This work forms an extension of [25] and refers closely to [16], [26] or [27]. It is also an announcement of [15], where detailed proofs are established. For related work see also [1], [3], [4], [8], [9], [17], [20], [28], [32], [34] or [35].

2 Cumulative Chord Piecewise-Quartics

Recall now that the *first divided difference* [30] for $\phi : I \to \mathbb{R}^n$ at different knot points $t_i, t_{i+1} \in I = [a, b]$ is defined as:

$$\phi[t_i, t_{i+1}] = \frac{\phi(t_{i+1}) - \phi(t_i)}{t_{i+1} - t_i}$$

and, for $k = 2, 3, \ldots, m - i$, the kth *divided difference* at $t_i, t_{i+1}, \ldots, t_{i+k}$ is

$$\phi[t_i, t_{i+1}, \ldots, t_{i+k}] = \frac{\phi[t_{i+1}, t_{i+2}, \ldots, t_{i+k}] - \phi[t_i, t_{i+1}, \ldots, t_{i+k-1}]}{t_{i+k} - t_i} , \quad (5)$$

for $t_{i+k} \neq t_i$. For each $i = 0, 4, 8, \ldots, m - 4$, let $\psi_4^i : [t_i, t_{i+4}] \to [\hat{t}_i, \hat{t}_{i+4}]$ be the quartic polynomial and $\hat{\gamma}_4^i : [\hat{t}_i, \hat{t}_{i+4}] \to \mathbb{R}^n$ be the cumulative chord quartic both satisfying $\psi_4^i(t_{i+j}) = \hat{t}_{i+j}$ and $\hat{\gamma}_4^i(\hat{t}_{i+j}) = q_{i+j}$, for $0 \leq j \leq 4$, respectively. The proof of Theorem 1 [25] exploits boundedness of all kth divided differences of ψ_r^i (and also of ψ_4^i) with $k = 1, 2, 3$ and $r = 2, 3$. Here $\psi_r^i : [t_i, t_{i+r}] \to [\hat{t}_i, \hat{t}_{i+r}]$ is a degree-r polynomial satisfying $\psi_r^i(t_{i+j}) = \hat{t}_{i+j}$, for $0 \leq j \leq r$,. Unfortunately, a closing example in [25] reveals that $\psi_4^i[t_i, t_{i+1}, t_{i+2}, t_{i+3}, t_{i+4}]$ can be unbounded. To extend somehow Theorem 1 to $k = 4$ we resort to three lemmas holding for each ε-uniform samplings (subsumed in (1)) and for any regular $\gamma \in C^4$ in $\mathbb{R}^n$.

Lemma 1. *For t_i's satisfying* (2) *the following holds:*

$$\begin{aligned}
\psi_4^i[t_{i+j}, t_{i+j+1}] &= 1 + O(\delta^2)\,, & j = 0,1,2,3\\
\psi_4^i[t_{i+j}, t_{i+j+1}, t_{i+j+2}] &= O(\delta^{\min\{2,1+\varepsilon\}})\,, & j = 0,1,2\\
\psi_4^i[t_{i+j}, t_{i+j+1}, t_{i+j+2}, t_{i+j+3}] &= -\frac{\kappa^2}{24}\frac{(t_{i+j+3} - 3t_{i+j+2} + 3t_{i+j+1} - t_{i+j})}{t_{i+j+3} - t_{i+j}} & \\
&\quad + O(t_{i+j+3} - t_{i+j}) = O(1)\,, & j = 0,1\\
\psi_4^i[t_i, t_{i+1}, t_{i+2}, t_{i+3}, t_{i+4}] &= O(\delta^{\min\{0,\varepsilon-1\}})\,, & (6)
\end{aligned}$$

where κ is the curvature of γ evaluated at t_i.

The proof is omitted. Note however, that the first three formulas in (6) follow from [25] and the fourth one is fully justified in [15]. Differentiating ψ_4^i expressed in Newton Interpolation formula [30] yields, for each $t \in [t_i, t_{i+4}]$

$$\begin{aligned}
\psi_4^i(t) &= \psi_4^i(t) + (t - t_i)\psi_4^i[t_i, t_{i+1}] + (t - t_i)(t - t_{i+1})\psi_4^i[t_i, t_{i+1}, t_{i+2}]\\
&\quad + (t - t_i)(t - t_{i+1})(t - t_{i+2})\psi_4^i[t_i, t_{i+1}, t_{i+2}, t_{i+3}]\\
&\quad + (t - t_i)(t - t_{i+1})(t - t_{i+2})(t - t_{i+3})\psi_4^i[t_i, t_{i+1}, t_{i+2}, t_{i+3}, t_{i+4}]\,. \quad (7)
\end{aligned}$$

The latter combined with Lemma 1 renders:

Lemma 2. $\dot\psi_4^i = 1 + O(\delta^2)$, $\ddot\psi_4^i = O(\delta)$, $\frac{d^3\psi_4^i}{dt^3} = O(1)$, *and* $\frac{d^4\psi_4^i}{dt^4} = O(\delta^{\min\{0,\varepsilon-1\}})$.

In particular ψ_4^i is a C^∞ diffeomorphism. Furthermore, Lemma 2, (7) and chain rule applied to $\gamma \circ (\psi_4^i)^{-1}$, which interpolates $\hat\gamma_4^i$ (defined for $s \in [\hat t_i, \hat t_{i+4}]$) yield:

Lemma 3. $\frac{d^j\hat\gamma_4^i}{ds^j} = O(1)$, *for $j = 1,2,3$ and* $\frac{d^4\hat\gamma_4^i}{ds^4} = O(\delta^{\min\{0,\varepsilon-1\}})$.

Using Lemma 3 leads to our main result (for proof see [15] extending on [25]):

Theorem 2. *Suppose γ is a regular C^{4+l} curve in $\mathbb{R}^n$, for $l = 1,2$ sampled ε-uniformly with $\varepsilon > 0$. Let $\hat\gamma_4 : [0, \hat T] \to \mathbb{R}^n$ be the cumulative chord piecewise-quartic approximation defined by $\mathcal{Q}$. Then there is a piecewise-C^∞ reparameterization $\psi : [0,T] \to [0, \hat T]$, with*

$$\hat\gamma_4 \circ \psi = \gamma + O(\delta^{\min\{5,4+\varepsilon\}})\,, \quad \textit{and} \quad d(\hat\gamma_4) = d(\gamma) + O(\delta^{\min\{4+l,4+l\varepsilon\}})\,. \quad (8)$$

Though the proof of Lemma 1 fails for $\varepsilon = 0$, Theorem 2 can still be extended to those 0-uniform samplings which also satisfy more-or-less uniformity. Indeed, (3), (5) and $\psi_4^i[t_{i+j}, t_{i+j+1}, t_{i+j+2}, t_{i+j+3}] = O(1)$ (for $j = 0,1$) render $\psi_4^i[t_i, t_{i+1}, t_{i+2}, t_{i+3}, t_{i+4}] = O(\delta^{-1})$. Hence, upon revisiting the proofs of Lemmas 2, 3 and Theorem 2 we arrive at:

Theorem 3. *Let $\gamma \in C^5$ be a regular curve in $\mathbb{R}^n$, sampled as in* (3) *and let $\hat\gamma_4 : [0, \hat T] \to \mathbb{R}^n$ be the cumulative chord piecewise-quartic defined by $\mathcal{Q}$. Then there is a piecewise-C^∞ reparameterization $\psi : [0,T] \to [0, \hat T]$, with*

$$\hat\gamma_4 \circ \psi = \gamma + O(\delta^4) \qquad \textit{and} \qquad d(\hat\gamma_4) = d(\gamma) + O(\delta^4)\,. \quad (9)$$

Note that for uniform sampling $t_i = \frac{Ti}{m}$ (here $\varepsilon = \infty$ and $\phi \equiv id$) formula (6) yields the fourth divided differences of $\psi_4^i = O(1)$. This combined with the proof of Theorem 2 yields $\hat\gamma_4 \circ \psi = \gamma + O(\delta^5)$ and $d(\hat\gamma_4) = d(\gamma) + O(\delta^6)$ which coincides with the uniform piecewise-quartic interpolation with t_i's guessed as $\hat t_i = i/m$.

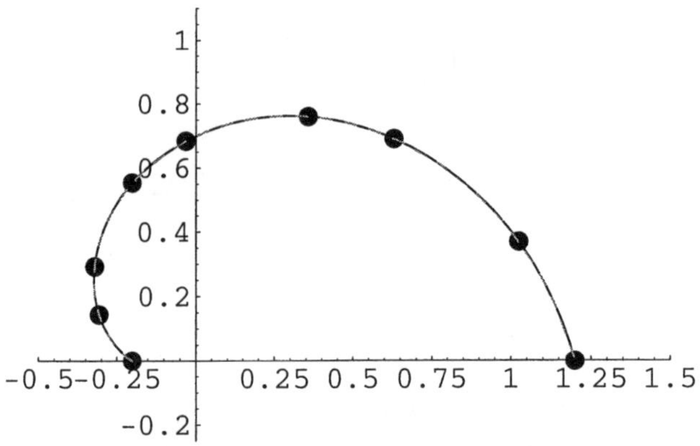

Fig. 1. 9 data points, with 2 successive quintuplets interpolated by piecewise-quartic cumulative chord (black) with length estimate $d(\gamma_s)+0.000237026$ for γ_s (grey dashed).

3 Experimentation

We verify now the sharpness of Theorem 2, 3 tested only for the length estimation, $n = 2, 3$ and for the generic case of regularity of γ i.e. $l = 2$ (in fact here $l = \infty$). The implementation of piecewise-quartic cumulative chord is performed in Mathematica. First, two planar curves $\gamma_c, \gamma_s : [0,1] \to \mathbb{R}^2$ representing *a semi-circle* $\gamma_c(t) = (\cos(\pi(1-t)), \sin(\pi(1-t))$ and *a spiral curve* $\gamma_s(t) = (t+0.2)(\cos(\pi(1-t), \sin(\pi(1-t))$ (see Figure 1; grey dashed) are tested, with true lengths $d(\gamma_c) = \pi$ and $d(\gamma_s) = 2.45171$, respectively. The unknown ε-uniform knot parameters t_i's satisfying $t_0 = 0$, $t_m = 1$ and

$$t_i = \frac{i}{m} + \frac{(-1)^{i+1}}{3m^{1+\varepsilon}} \quad \textit{for} \quad 1 \leq i \leq m-1 \tag{10}$$

are chosen merely to synthetically generate ordered sequences of interpolation points $\mathcal{Q}$. Finally, one space curve $\gamma_h : [0, 2\pi] \to \mathbb{R}^3$ representing *an elliptical helix* $\gamma_h(t) = (1.5\cos(t), \sin(t), t/4)$ (see Figure 2; grey dashed) is tested with true length $d(\gamma_h) = 8.08972$. For the helix γ_h the experiments are carried out with two families of ε-uniform samplings i.e. with (10) and with

$$t_i = \frac{2\pi i}{m} + (Random[\,] - 0.5)\frac{2\pi}{m^{1+\varepsilon}} \quad \textit{for} \quad 1 \leq i \leq m-1; \quad t_0 = 0; \; t_m = 2\pi, \tag{11}$$

where *Random*[ ] takes the pseudo-random values from the interval $[0, 1]$. Different sampling points are generated with $\varepsilon_0 = 0$, $\varepsilon_{1/10} = 0.1$, $\varepsilon_{1/5} = 0.2$, $\varepsilon_{1/4} = 0.25$, $\varepsilon_{1/3} = 0.33$, $\varepsilon_{1/2} = 0.5$, $\varepsilon_{2/3} = 0.66$, $\varepsilon_{3/4} = 0.75$, $\varepsilon_{9/10} = 0.9$, $\varepsilon_1 = 1$, and $\varepsilon_\infty = \infty$ (here $O(\frac{1}{m^\infty})$ vanishes), respectively. Note also that as $T = \sum_{i=1}^{m}(t_i - t_{i-1}) \leq m\delta$ to verify sharpness of (8) and (9) in terms of $O(\delta^\alpha)$ it is sufficient to confirm both of them in terms of $O(\frac{1}{m^\alpha})$. The experiments are carried out for $m = 4k$ with $k_{min} = 3 \leq k \leq k_{max} = 70$. From the set of absolute errors $E_m(\gamma) = |d(\gamma) - d(\hat{\gamma}_4)|$, for $4 * k_{min} \leq m \leq 4 * k_{max}$, the estimate of

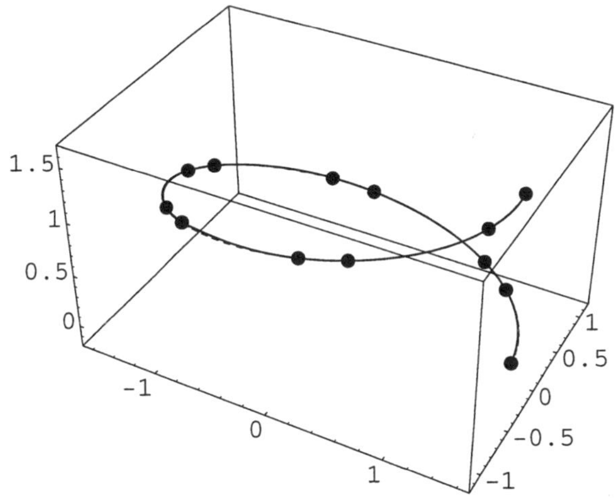

Fig. 2. 13 data points, with 3 successive quintuplets interpolated by piecewise-quartic cumulative chord (black), giving length estimate $d(\gamma_h) - 0.0164562$ for γ_h (grey dashed).

Table 1. Piecewise-quartic cumulative chord estimates of $d(\gamma)$ for γ_c, γ_s, and γ_h.

	ε_0	$\varepsilon_{1/10}$	$\varepsilon_{1/5}$	$\varepsilon_{1/4}$	$\varepsilon_{1/3}$	$\varepsilon_{1/2}$	$\varepsilon_{2/3}$	$\varepsilon_{3/4}$	$\varepsilon_{9/10}$	ε_1	ε_∞
α for γ_c & (10)	3.98	4.19	4.39	4.48	4.65	4.97	5.30	5.42	5.71	6.05	5.99
α for γ_s & (10)	3.95	4.14	4.31	4.38	4.49	4.68	5.27	5.67	6.08	6.02	5.96
α for γ_h & (10)	4.02	4.19	4.39	4.48	4.66	5.02	5.35	7.09	5.84	5.97	6.01
α for γ_h & (11)	4.11	4.30	4.46	4.54	4.85	5.33	5.72	5.75	5.78	5.95	6.01
minimal α	4.00	4.20	4.40	4.50	4.66	5.00	5.33	5.50	5.80	6.00	6.00

convergence rate $O(\frac{1}{m^\alpha})$ is computed by applying *a linear regression* to pairs of points $(\log(m), -\log(E_m(\gamma))$, with $4 * k_{min} \leq m \leq 4 * k_{max}$ - see Table 1.

The results from Table 1 confirm sharpness of (8). Note that the case when $\varepsilon = 0$ is covered by (9) (at least for sampling (10) satisfying (3)). Visibly some α's are slightly smaller as compared with those predicted by Theorems 2, 3. Reaching a high accuracy in performed computation with $m << \infty$, hinders the exact verification of herein presented results proved merely for $m \approx \infty$. As it happens with cumulative chord piecewise-quadratics and piecewise-cubics [24], Figures 1, 2 demonstrate highly accurate curve and length estimation by cumulative chord piecewise-quartics yielded on sporadic data (i.e. when m is small). Here for (10) and curves γ_s and γ_h we set $\varepsilon = 0.5$ and $\varepsilon = 0.1$, respectively. Figures 1, 2 show also that at joint points q_{4j} (where $1 \leq j \leq \frac{m}{4} - 1$) between two consecutive chords the discontinuities in *geomertical smoothness* [5] of $\hat{\gamma}_4$ are indiscernible.

4 Conclusions

We showed and verified that for ε-uniform samplings cumulative chord piecewise-quartics in $\mathbb{R}^n$ improve convergence rates for γ and $d(\gamma)$ estimation over cumulative chord piecewise-cubics and piecewise-quadratics. The asymptotic estimates in question are confirmed to be sharp and the performance of $\hat{\gamma}_4$ on sporadic data is very accurate. Discontinuities in geometrical smoothness at joint points between two consecutive chords seems to be marginal at least for the curves and samplings tested in this paper. Recall that no convexity assumption imposed on $\gamma \in C^{4+l}(\mathbb{R}^n)$ (where $l = 1, 2$) is needed for cumulative chord interpolation.

References

1. Barsky, B.A., DeRose, T.D.: Geometric Continuity of Parametric Curves: Three Equivalent Characterizations. IEEE. Comp. Graph. Appl. **9**:6 (1989) 60–68
2. Bertrand, G., Imiya, A., Klette, R. (eds): Digital and Image Geometry. LNCS Vol. 2243, Springer-Verlag, Berlin Heidelberg New York (2001)
3. Bézier, P.E.: Numerical Control: Mathematics and Applications. John Wiley, New York (1972)
4. Boehm, W., Farin, G., Kahmann, J.: A Survey of Curve and Surface Methods in CAGD. Comput. Aid. Geom. Des. **1** (1988) 1–60
5. de Boor, C., Höllig, K., Sabin, M.: High Accuracy Geometric Hermite Interpolation. Comput. Aided Geom. Design **4** (1987) 269–278.
6. Bülow, T., Klette, R.: Rubber Band Algorithm for Estimating the Length of Digitized Space-Curves. In: Sneliu, A., Villanva, V.V., Vanrell, M., Alquézar, R., Crowley. J., Shirai, Y. (eds): Proceedings of 15th International Conference on Pattern Recognition. Barcelona, Spain. IEEE, Vol. III. (2000) 551-555
7. Dorst, L., Smeulders, A.W.M.: Discrete Straight Line Segments: Parameters, Primitives and Properties. In: Melter, R., Bhattacharya, P., Rosenfeld, A. (eds): Ser. Contemp. Maths, Vol. 119. Amer. Math. Soc. (1991) 45–62
8. Epstein, M.P.: On the Influence of Parametrization in Parametric Interpolation. SIAM. J. Numer. Anal. **13**:2 (1976) 261–268
9. Hoschek, J.: Intrinsic Parametrization for Approximation. Comput. Aid. Geom. Des. **5** (1988) 27–31
10. Klette, R.: Approximation and Representation of 3D Objects. In: Klette, R., Rosenfeld, A., Sloboda, F. (eds): Advances in Digital and Computational Geometry. Springer, Singapore (1998) 161–194
11. Klette, R., Kovalevsky, V., Yip, B.: On the Length Estimation of Digital Curves. In: Latecki, L.J., Melter, R.A., Mount, D.A., Wu, A.Y. (eds): Proceedings of SPIE Conference, Vision Geometry VIII, Vol. 3811. Denver, USA. The International Society for Optical Engineering (1999) 52–63
12. Klette, R., Yip, B.: The Length of Digital Curves. Machine Graphics and Vision **9** (2000) 673–703
13. Klette, R., Rosenfeld, A., Sloboda, F. (eds): Advances in Digital and Computational Geometry. Springer, Singapore (1998) 161–194
14. Klingenberg, W.: A Course in Differential Geometry. Springer-Verlag (1978)
15. Kozera, R.: Cumulative Chord Piecewise-Quartics. Submitted
16. Kozera, R., Noakes, L., Klette, R.: External versus Internal Parameterizations for Lengths of Curves with Nonuniform Samplings. In: Asano, T., Klette, R. Ronse, C., (eds): Theoretical Foundations of Computer Vision, Geometry and Computational Imaging. LNCS Vol. 2616, Springer-Verlag, Berlin Heidelberg New York, 403–418 (2003)

17. Kvasov, B. I.: Method of Shape-Preserving Spline Approximation. World Scientific Pub. Co., Singapore, New Jersey, London, Hong Kong (2000)
18. Lachance, M. A., Schwartz, A. J. : Four Point Parabolic Interpolation. Comput. Aided Geom. Design **8** (1991) 143–149
19. Lee, E.T Y. : Corners, Cusps, and Parameterization: Variations on a Theorem of Epstein. SIAM J. Numer. Anal. **29** (1992) 553–565
20. Moran, P.: Measuring the Length of a Curve. Biometrika **53**:3/4 (1966) 359–364
21. Mørken, K., Scherer, K.: A General Framework for High-accuracy Parametric Interpolation. Maths Comput. **66**:217 (1997) 237–260.
22. Noakes, L., Kozera, R.: More-or-Less Uniform Sampling and Lengths of Curves. Quart. Appl. Maths. In press
23. Noakes, L., Kozera, R.: Interpolating Sporadic Data. In: Heyden, A., Sparr, G., Nielsen, M., and Johansen, P. (eds): Proceedings of 7th International Conference on Computer Vision. Copenhagen, Denmark. LNCS Vol. 2351. Springer-Verlag, Berlin Heidelberg New York, (2002) 613–625
24. Noakes, L., Kozera, R.: Cumulative Chords and Piecewise-Quadratics. Proceedings of International Conference on Computer Vision and Graphics. Zakopane, Poland. Vol. 2, (2002) 589–595
25. Noakes, L., Kozera, R.: Cumulative Chords, Piecewise-Quadratics and Piecewise-Cubics. Submitted
26. Noakes, L., Kozera, R., Klette R.: Length Estimation for Curves with Different Samplings. In: Bertrand, G., Imiya, A., Klette, R. (eds): Digital and Image Geometry. LNCS Vol. 2243, Springer-Verlag, Berlin Heidelberg New York, (2001) 339–351
27. Noakes, L., Kozera, R., Klette R.: Length Estimation for Curves with ε-Uniform Sampling. In: Skarbek, W. (ed.): Proceedings of 9th International Conference on Computer Analysis of Images and Pattterns. Warsaw, Poland. LNCS Vol. 2124. Springer-Verlag, Berlin Heidelberg New York, (2001) 518–526
28. Piegl, L., Tiller, W.: The *NURBS* Book. Springer-Verlag, Berlin Heidelberg (1997)
29. Rababah, A.: High Order Approximation Methods for Curves. Computer Aided Geom. Design **12** (1995) 89–102.
30. Ralston, A.: A First Course in Numerical Analysis. McGraw-Hill (1965)
31. Schaback, R.: Optimal Geometric Hermite Interpolation of Curves. In: Dæhlen, M., Lyche, T., Schumaker, L. (eds), Mathematical Methods for Curves and Surfaces II, Vanderbilt University Press, (1998) 1–12.
32. Sederberg, T.W., Zhao, J., Zundel, A.K.: Approximate Parametrization of Algebraic Curves. In: Strasser, W., Seidel, H.P. (eds): Theory and Practice in Geometric Modelling. Springer-Verlag, Berlin (1989) 33–54
33. Sloboda, F., Zaťko, B., Stör, J.: On Approximation of Planar One-Dimensional Continua. In: Klette, R., Rosenfeld, A., Sloboda, F. (eds): Advances in Digital and Computational Geometry. Springer, Singapore (1998) 113–160
34. Taubin, T. : Estimation of Planar Curves, Surfaces, and Nonplanar Space Curves Defined by Implicit Equations with Applications to Edge and Range Image Segmentation. IEEE Trans. Patt. Mach. Intell. **13**:11 (1991) 1115–1138
35. Traub, J.F., Werschulz, A.G.: Complexity and Information. Cambridge Uni. Press, Cambridge (1998)

PDE Based Method for Superresolution of Gray-Level Images

A. Torii[1], Y. Wakazono[1], H. Murakami[1], and A. Imiya[2,3]

[1] School of Science and Technology, Chiba University, Japan
[2] National Institute of Informatics, Japan
[3] Institute of Media and Information Technology, Chiba University, Japan

Abstract. We propose a superresolution method for gray-level images. The method is based on resolution conversion of discrete terrains in a space by regarding gray-level images as discrete terrains. The deformation process using a discrete diffusion enables us to estimate the smooth boundary surface from a low-resolution data of discrete terrain. Furthermore, the resampling process of the estimated smooth boundary surface produces a high-resolution data of discrete terrain.

1 Introduction

In this paper, we propose a superresolution method for gray-level images based on resolution conversion of discrete terrain in a space. Our resolution-conversion method first considers a gray-level image as a discrete terrain in a space. Second, a boundary surface of the discrete terrain is deformed by a discrete diffusion process. Third, a smooth surface is estimated from the deformed boundary surface using B-spline interpolation. Finally, a high-resolution surface for the profile of gray-level image is generated by resampling the estimated smooth surface.

The resolution conversion of digital surfaces for the recovery of a smooth surface and a series of iso-level counters on it are solved using variational problems. This is a surface reconstruction method which is commonly used in computer vision and aerial data processing communities. The expansion and superresolution of discrete surfaces are mathematically equivalent problems because, for the achievement of these processes, we are required to construct a smooth boundary surface as an estimation of the original boundary, from a digitized surface which is expressed as a collection of voxels.

Spline curves and surfaces are described as the solution of a variational problem for the fitting of smooth functions to a sequence of samples along a curve and an array of sample points on a surface. Splines are, therefore, utilized for the estimation of the smooth boundary from a collection of samples [1–4]. The families of splines are considered by several authors in the computer vision community with respect to curve fitting [5], corner detection [6], shape recovery [7], and detection of discontinuities along the boundary [8]. The spline curves has also been closely examined in meteorology for the description of iso-level curves on weather charts [2, 3]. Furthermore, a family of splines has recently been studied theoretically in the context of wavelets and practically in shape description for

N. Petkov and M.A. Westenberg (Eds.): CAIP 2003, LNCS 2756, pp. 706–713, 2003.

the application of shape expression for data transmission through the internet [9, 10]. These applications partially refer to the application of splines in computer vision for the data compression of boundary information.

Section 2.1 describes the definition of discrete objects, since a discrete terrain is an infinite discrete object in a space. Furthermore, we describe a parallel method for the boundary extraction of discrete objects. Section 2.2 describes the resampling procedure for generating high-resolution images from a given discrete boundary surface which is derived in Section 2.1. The properties of discrete objects which are derived in Sections 2.1 and 2.2 permit us to derive the deformation process in Section 2.3. The deformation process in Section 2.3 enables us to estimate the smooth surfaces from the discrete terrain surfaces. Section 3 shows numerical examples for the resolution conversion of terrains and gray-level images.

2 Resolution Conversion

2.1 Boundary Extraction

We deal with two- and three-dimensional discrete space $\mathbf{Z}^2$ and $\mathbf{Z}^3$, respectively. Here after, we call $\mathbf{R}^2$ and $\mathbf{R}^3$ two- and three-dimensional space. Therefore $\mathbf{Z}^2$ and $\mathbf{Z}^3$ are two- and three-dimensional discrete space, respectively. For $(k,m,n)^\top \in \mathbf{Z}^3$, we set $\mathbf{Z}_1^2(k)$, $\mathbf{Z}_2^2(m)$, and $\mathbf{Z}_3^2(n)$ as two-dimensional planes $x=k$, $y=m$, and $z=n$, respectively. Plane $\mathbf{Z}_i(\alpha)$ is perpendicular to $\boldsymbol{e}_i$ for $i=1,2,3$, for $\boldsymbol{e}_1=(1,0,0)^\top$, $\boldsymbol{e}_2=(0,1,0)^\top$, and $\boldsymbol{e}=(0,0,1)^\top$. For points $(m,n)^\top$ and $(k,m,n)^\top$ in $\mathbf{Z}^2$ and $\mathbf{Z}^3$, respectively, $(m',n')^\top$ and $(k',m',n')^\top$ such that

$$(m'-m)^2+(n'-n)^2 \leq 1,\ (k'-k)^2+(m'-m)^2+(n'-n)^2 \leq 1, \quad (1)$$

are 4-connected and 6-connected points on a plane and in a space, respectively. Furthermore, for points $(m,n)^\top$ and $(k,m,n)^\top$ in $\mathbf{Z}^2$ and $\mathbf{Z}^3$, respectively, $(m',n')^\top$ and $(k',m',n')^\top$ such that

$$(m'-m)^2+(n'-n)^2 \leq 2,\ (k'-k)^2+(m'-m)^2+(n'-n)^2 \leq 3, \quad (2)$$

are 8-connected and 26-connected points on a plane and in a space, respectively. We express them as $\mathbf{N}_4(\boldsymbol{x})$, $\mathbf{N}_8(\boldsymbol{x})$, $\boldsymbol{N}_6(\boldsymbol{x})$, and $\mathbf{N}_{26}(\boldsymbol{x})$.

In $\mathbf{Z}_\alpha(\beta)$, we express 4-connected points as $\mathbf{N}_\alpha^4(\beta)$. For $\boldsymbol{x}=(k,m,n)^\top$, the neighbourhood in a space and on planes satisfies the relation

$$\mathbf{N}_6(\boldsymbol{x}) = \mathbf{N}_1^4(k) \bigcup \mathbf{N}_2^4(m) \bigcup \mathbf{N}_3^4(n). \quad (3)$$

Here after, we affix 0 and 1 to points in $\mathbf{Z}^2$ and $\mathbf{Z}^3$, and our object is the collection of pixels and voxels in two- and three-dimensional space whose centers are points in $\mathbf{Z}^2$ and $\mathbf{Z}^3$. We set $\boldsymbol{x}=(m,n)^\top$

$$\boldsymbol{u}(\boldsymbol{x}) = \begin{cases} 1, & |m-\frac{1}{2}| \leq 1, \text{ and } |n-\frac{1}{2}| \leq 1, \\ 0, & \text{otherwise,} \end{cases} \quad (4)$$

and, $\boldsymbol{x}=(k,m,n)^\top$

$$v(\boldsymbol{x}) = \begin{cases} 1, \text{ if } |k-\frac{1}{2}| \leq 1, \ |m-\frac{1}{2}| \leq 1, \text{ and } |n-\frac{1}{2}| \leq 1, \\ 0, \text{ otherwise,} \end{cases} \tag{5}$$

respectively. $\boldsymbol{u}(\boldsymbol{x})$ and $\boldsymbol{v}(\boldsymbol{x})$ is a pixel and a voxel, respectively, whose center is at $\boldsymbol{x} = (m,n)^\top$ and $\boldsymbol{x} = (k,m,n)^\top$. Therefore setting $\boldsymbol{F}$ to be the set of 1-points, our object is expressed as in two- and three-dimensional space

$$\boldsymbol{D} = \bigcup_{\boldsymbol{x}\in\boldsymbol{F}} \boldsymbol{u}(\boldsymbol{x}),\ \boldsymbol{D} = \bigcup_{\boldsymbol{x}\in\boldsymbol{F}} \boldsymbol{v}(\boldsymbol{x}), \tag{6}$$

We call the boundary of $\boldsymbol{D}$ the edge polygon and the surface polyhedron, for the collection of pixels and voxels, respectively. The edge polygon and surface polyhedron are extracted as

$$\begin{aligned} \Delta\boldsymbol{F} &= \{(\boldsymbol{F} \oplus \mathrm{N}_8) \setminus \boldsymbol{F}\} \bigcup \{\boldsymbol{F} \setminus (\boldsymbol{F} \ominus \mathrm{N}_8)\}, \\ \Delta\boldsymbol{F} &= \{(\boldsymbol{F} \oplus \mathrm{N}_{26}) \setminus \boldsymbol{F}\} \bigcup \{\boldsymbol{F} \setminus (\boldsymbol{F} \ominus \mathrm{N}_{26})\}, \end{aligned} \tag{7}$$

where $\oplus$ and $\ominus$ are the Minkowski addition and subtraction, respectively, of two sets in a vector space.
Next, we define edge polygon and surfel polyhedron in $\mathbf{Z}^2$ and $\mathbf{Z}^3$, respectively, for a set of points $\boldsymbol{F}$, denoting $\lambda\boldsymbol{F} = \{\lambda\boldsymbol{x} \,|\, \boldsymbol{x} \in \boldsymbol{F}, \lambda > 0\}$. The edge polygon is extracted as follows.

- Search for a pair of vertices $\boldsymbol{p}_1$ and $\boldsymbol{p}_2$ on $\boldsymbol{u}(\boldsymbol{x})$ for the boundary of $\Delta\boldsymbol{F}$.
- Follow points which satisfy the relations $|\boldsymbol{p}_{i+1} - \boldsymbol{p}_i| = |\boldsymbol{p}_i - \boldsymbol{p}_{i-1}|$, and $(\boldsymbol{p}_{i+1} - \boldsymbol{p}_i)^\top(\boldsymbol{p}_i - \boldsymbol{p}_{i-1})$ is 0 or 1, for $i \leq 2$.

The surfel polyhedron of three-dimensional discrete object is obtained applying the procedure slice by slice in axes directions $(1,0,0)^\top, (0,1,0)^\top, (0,0,1)^\top$. Since we deal with the 6-connected discrete objects, for a plane $\mathbf{P}_i(k)$ which is a perpendicular vector $\boldsymbol{e}_i$ for $i = 1,2,3$, and passes through point $k\boldsymbol{e}_i$, the vertices of object $\mathbf{O}$ lie on the cross sections of object $\mathbf{O}$ with respect to $\mathbf{P}_i(k)$, and the degree of vertices is three or four. Furthermore, adjacent vertices of a vertex exist in the 6-neighbourhood of the vertex, since we deal with 6-connected discrete objects. The surface polyhedron is extracted by applying this algorithm slice-by-slice in each $\mathbf{P}_i(k)$. For a terrain such that $z = f(x,y)$, we assume that we are dealing with discrete objects which are infinite in the direction of $(0,0,-1)^\top$.

2.2 Generation of High-Resolution Images

We set an object $f(\boldsymbol{x})$, where $\boldsymbol{x} = (x,y)^\top$ and $\boldsymbol{x} = (x,y,z)^\top$ for two- and three-dimensional objects, respectively. We define the set of points $\boldsymbol{A} = \{\boldsymbol{x} \,|\, f(\boldsymbol{x}) > 1, \boldsymbol{x} \in \mathbf{R}^n\}$ in $\mathbf{R}^n$ for $n = 2,3$. Setting f_m, $\boldsymbol{m} \in \mathbf{Z}^n$ for $n = 2,3$ to be the average of volume of $f(\boldsymbol{x})$ in a pixel and a voxel in two- and three-dimensional space. The inverse quantization is to estimate $\boldsymbol{A}$ from $\boldsymbol{F} = \{\boldsymbol{m} \,|\, f_m > \frac{1}{2}\}$ and resolution conversion is described as the computation of $\frac{1}{m}\boldsymbol{F}_m$, where $\boldsymbol{F}_m$ is a binary set computed from the binary object $f(m\boldsymbol{x})$. Furthermore, set $\frac{1}{m}\boldsymbol{F}_m$

enables us to generate an approximation of high-resolution images of $f(\boldsymbol{x})$ for an arbitrary resolution. If $\boldsymbol{A}$ and its boundary $\partial\boldsymbol{A}$ is estimated from $\boldsymbol{F}$, it is easy to generate $\boldsymbol{F}_m$ by computing average in the pixels and the voxels where edge length is $\frac{1}{m}$ unit.

In the previous paper [11, 12], we proposed an algorithm for the estimation of boundary curve $\partial\boldsymbol{A}$ from digital set $\boldsymbol{F}$. Therefore, using the estimation of $\boldsymbol{D}$ we generate set $\frac{1}{m}\boldsymbol{F}_m$ according to the following steps.

1. Compute $\boldsymbol{D}$ from $\boldsymbol{F}$.
2. Compute the B-spline curve from $m\boldsymbol{D}$, and adopt its closure as the estimator of $m\partial\boldsymbol{A}$.
3. Apply the sampling scheme to the closure of the curve using unit pixels and voxels.
4. Reduce the size of pixels and voxels uniformly.

2.3 Deformation of Terrain

It is possible to deal with a terrain as an open polyhedron in $\mathbf{Z}^3$. We can extract the discrete boundary of terrain using eq. (7). Furthermore, for points on the boundary of terrain, we consider slices along x and y axis. Then, we introduce a method for the resolution conversion using the boundary deformation procedure.

For vector $\boldsymbol{p}_{ij} = (i, j, f(i,j))^\top$, $i, j = 1, 2, \cdots, n$, setting

$$D_1^2\boldsymbol{p}_{ij} = \boldsymbol{p}_{i+1\,j} - 2\boldsymbol{p}_{ij} + \boldsymbol{p}_{i-1\,j},\ D_2^2\boldsymbol{p}_{ij} = \boldsymbol{p}_{i\,j+1} - 2\boldsymbol{p}_{ij} + \boldsymbol{p}_{ij-1}, \tag{8}$$

we have the equation

$$D_1^2\boldsymbol{p}_{ij} + D_2^2\boldsymbol{p}_{ij} = (0, 0, \Delta_4 f(i,j))^\top, \tag{9}$$

where Δ_4 is the 4-connected discrete Laplacian operation for two-valued discrete function $f(i,j)$. Assuming that function $f(i,j)$ is a function of time t, we have the relation

$$\boldsymbol{p}_{ij}(t+1) - \boldsymbol{p}_{ij}(t) = (0, 0, f(i,j,t+1) - f(i,j,t))^\top \tag{10}$$

Therefore, the equation

$$\boldsymbol{p}_{ij}(t+1) - \boldsymbol{p}_{ij}(t) = c(D_1^2\boldsymbol{p}_{ij} + D_2^2\boldsymbol{p}_{ij}), \tag{11}$$

where c is a constant, implies the equation $f(i,j,t+1) - f(i,j,t) = \Delta_4 f(i,j,t)$. These mathematical properties of the deformation for discrete terrains lead to the conclusion that our deformation for discrete terrains based on the vertex Laplacian operation for a polyhedron is equivalent to the deformation by the linear diffusion equation, if we consider the height of each point as the gray-level of each point. Furthermore, equation (11) implies that, in the numerical computation, a serial application of the operations D_1^2 and D_2^2 is possible.

For the deformation of the discrete height model of a topographical map, we are required to preserve the height values of a map, since the height values depend on the measurement of heights. Therefore, we generate new control points for the points of the discrete height model according to the following rules.

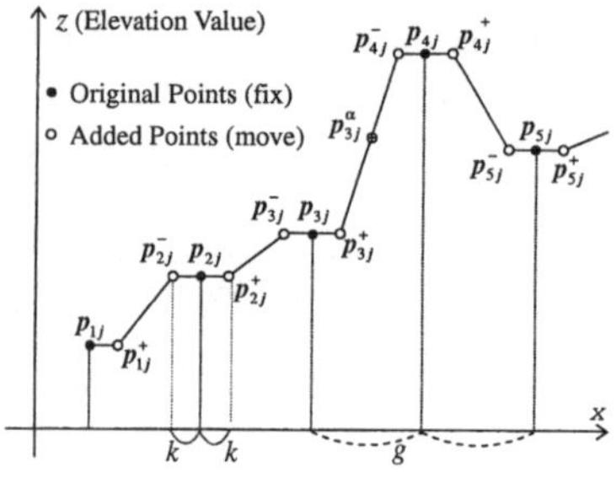

Fig. 1. Control Point Generation.

Table 1. The sum $r_{\alpha\alpha}$ of the ratio $r_{\alpha\alpha}(i,j)$ in figure 2 and the average difference r of gray values in figures 3.

	$r_{\alpha\alpha}$ in Figure 2	r in Figure 3
(a) & (c)	1.229	4.097
(a) & (d)	1.692	5.422

1. For $i,j = 1,2,\cdots,n-1$, $\boldsymbol{p}_{ij}{}^{+} = (i+k, j+k, f(i,j))^\top$, where $0 < k < 1$.
2. For $i,j = 2,3,\cdots,n$, $\boldsymbol{p}_{ij}{}^{-} = (i-k, j-k, f(i,j))^\top$, where $0 < k < 1$.
3. For $i,j = 1,2,\cdots,n-1$, and if $|f(i+1,j) - f(i,j)| \geq 2k$, then $\boldsymbol{p}_{ij}{}^{\alpha} = (i+k, j+k, f(i,j)+\alpha l)^\top$, where $\alpha = 1,2,\cdots,\lceil l \rceil - 1$ and $l = \frac{|f(i+1,j)-f(i,j)|}{k}$.
4. For $i,j = 1,2,\cdots,n-1$, and if $|f(i,j+1) - f(i,j)| \geq 2k$, then $\boldsymbol{p}_{ij}{}^{\beta} = (i+k+\beta m, j+k\beta m, f(i,j)+\beta m)^\top$, where $\beta = 1,2,\cdots,\lceil m \rceil - 1$ and $m = \frac{|f(i,j+1)-f(i,j)|}{k}$.

3 Numerical Examples

Figure 2 shows the results of the resolution conversion of discrete terrain surface by our method. In Figure 2, (a) shows the original topographical map which is a part of 1/5000 digital height map of a country. (b) shows a low-resolution map by reducing the original data points to 1/16. (c) shows a high-resolution map reconstructed from (b) by our super-resolution method. (d) shows a topographical map reconstructed from (b) by the traditional B-spline interpolation.

Since the positions and heights of local minima and maxima are cue-features for the evaluation of roughness of the interpolated functions, we computed the sum ratio $r_{\alpha\alpha}(i,j) = \frac{|\bar{f}_{\alpha\alpha}(i,j) - f_{\alpha\alpha}(i,j)|}{|f_{\alpha\alpha}(i,j)|} \times 100$ such that

$$r_{\alpha\alpha} = \sum\nolimits_{(i,j)^\top \text{in the region of interest}} r_{\alpha\alpha}(i,j) \tag{12}$$

for points $f_{\alpha\alpha}(i,j) = 0$, where $\alpha \in \{x, y\}$. Table 1 shows the sum of $r_{\alpha\alpha}(i,j)$ for all points in the region of interest.

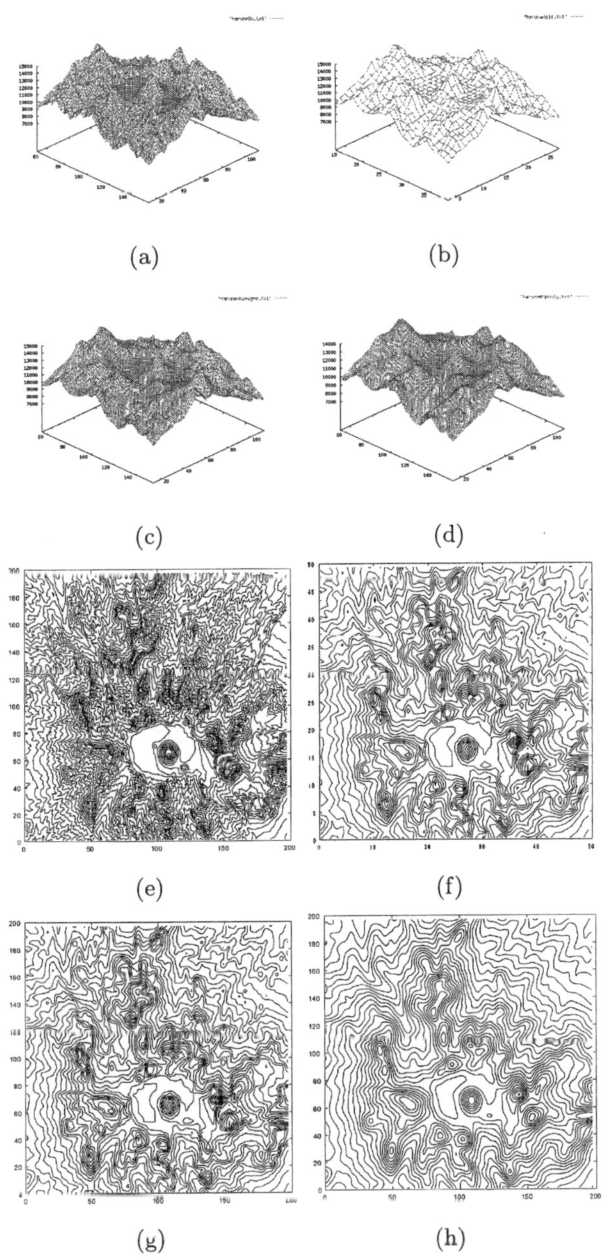

Fig. 2. Super-resolution for a Terrain: Digital Terrain Model raw data [13] visualized by Gnuplot. (a) an original surface: 200 × 200 resolution. (b) the low resolution surface: 50 × 50 resolution. (c) the reconstructed surface by our super-resolution method: 200 × 200 resolution. (d) the reconstructed surface without deformation process: 200 × 200 resolution. (e), (f), (g), and (h) are equi-level contour representation of (a), (b), (c), and (d), respectively.

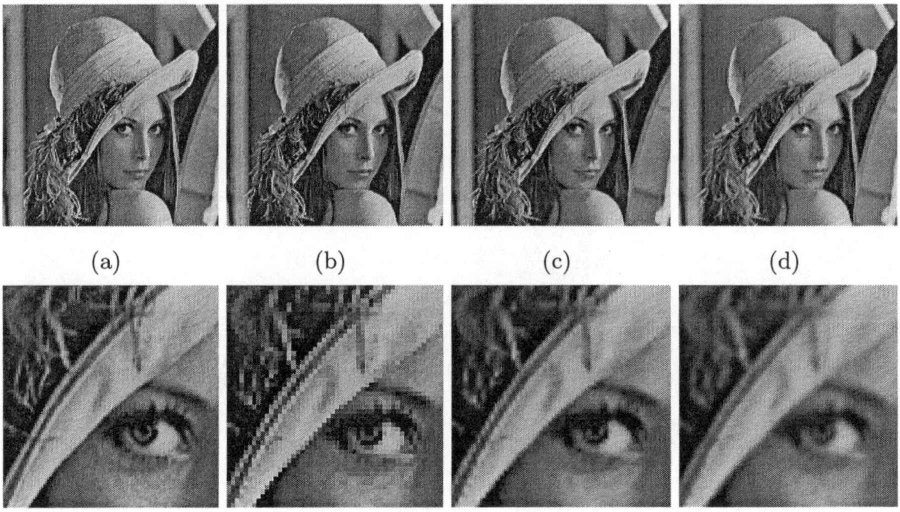

(a) (b) (c) (d)

(e) (f) (g) (h)

Fig. 3. Super-resolution for a 256 Gray-Value Image of Lenna: (a) the original image: 440 × 440 resolution. (b) the low resolution image: 220 × 220 resolution. (c) the reconstructed image by our super-resolution method: 440 × 440 resolution. (d) the reconstructed image without deformation process: 440 × 440 resolution. (e), (f), (g), and (h) are the expanded parts of (a), (b), (c), and (d), respectively.

In Figure 2, (e), (f), (g), and (h) are equi-level-contour representation of (a), (b), (c), and (d), respectively. The contour line is the collection of the same height-values of the terrain surface which is constructed from linear interpolation for discrete terrain surface. Equi-level-contour representation in Figure 2 illustrates the efficiency of our method which is the combination of deformation and interpolation.

We applied the super-resolution to gray-value images considering the gray-values of images as the discrete terrain. Figure 3 shows the results of the super-resolution of gray-value images. In Figure 3, (a), (b), (c), and (d) are the original images, low-resolution images, high resolution images reconstructed by our method, and images reconstructed by B-spline interpolation for the low-resolution images, respectively. (e), (f), (g), and (h) are expanded parts of (a), (b), (c), and (d), respectively.

For the quantitative evaluation of the reconstructed image, we computed the average difference of gray values of images $r = \frac{1}{mn}\sum_{i=1,j=1}^{m,n}|f(i,j) - \bar{f}(i,j)|$, where $f(i,j)$ and $\bar{f}(i,j)$ are the gray values of the original and the reconstructed images, respectively. mn is the size of the images. Table 1 shows the average difference r for all points in the images.

Comparing (e) and (g) in Figure 3, our method for the super-resolution efficiently works for the practical test images. In Figure 3, (e) and (g) show that our method recovers small parts in almost same gray values.

4 Conclusions

In this paper, we constructed an algorithm for estimating a smooth boundary surface of the original image from an isotactic polygon using a morphological operation and a discrete diffusion. The isotactic polygon is the boundary of connected voxels in a space from given discrete surfaces through which the original boundary surface should pass. This estimation of the boundary surface enables us to generate discrete surface at any resolution. The classical PDE based interpolation method [14] has also the property of resolution conversion. That is, the method produces high-resolution images by deforming equi-level surfaces as a profile of gray-level images. Although the classical PDE method [14] deforms a set of curves in a two-dimensional plane, our method deforms terrain surfaces in a three-dimensional space as a profile of gray-level images.

Since we consider the gray levels as the height data of points, a two-dimensional gray-level image is a topographical map in three-dimensional space and, generally, an n-dimensional gray-level image is a topographical map in $(n+1)$-dimensional space. Therefore, our method enable us to generate high-resolution gray-level images of n-dimensional. Numerical examples confirmed the suitable performance of the proposed method for terrains and two-dimensional gray-level images.

References

1. Lu, F., Milios, E.E.: Optimal spline fitting to plane shape, *Signal Processing*, **37** 129-140, 1994.
2. Wahba, G.: Surface fitting with scattered noisy data on Euclidean D-space and on the sphere, *Rocky Mountain Journal of Mathematics*, **14**, 281-299, 1984.
3. Wahba, G., Johnson, D.R.: Partial spline models for the inclusion of tropopause and frontal boundary information in otherwise smooth two- and three-dimensional objective analysis, *J. Atmospheric and Oceanic Technology*, **3**, 714-725, 1986.
4. Chen, M. H., Chin, R.T.: Partial smoothing spline for noisy+boundary with corners, *IEEE Trans. on PAMI*, **15**, 1208-1216, 1993.
5. Paglieroni, D., Jain, A. K.: Control point transformation for shape representation and measurement, *Computer Graphics and Image Processing*, **42**, 87-111, 1988.
6. Medioni, G., Yasumoto, Y.: Corner detection and curve representation using cubic B-spline, *Computer Graphics and Image Processing*, **39**, 267-278, 1987.
7. Terzopoulos, D.: The computation of visible-surface representations, *IEEE Trans. on PAMI*, **10**, 417-438, 1988.
8. Langridge, D.J.: Curve encoding and the detection of discontinuities, *Computer Graphics and Image Processing*, **20**, 58-71, 1982.
9. Daubechies, I., Guskov, I., Sweldens, W.: Regularity of irregular subdivision, *Constructive Approximation*, **15**, 381-426, 1999.
10. Daubechies, I., Guskov, I., Schröder, P., Sweldens, W.: Wavelets on irregular point sets, *Phil. Trans. R. Soc. Lond. A*, to be published.
11. Imiya, A., Ito, A., Kenmochi, Y.: Inverse quantization of digital binary images for resolution conversion, *LNCS* 2106 Springer: Berlin, 426-431.
12. Torii, A., Ichinose, T., Wakazono, Y., Imiya, A.: Inverse quantization for resolution conversion, *LNCS* 2616 Springer: Berlin, 282-300.
13. Geographical Survey Institute, Japan. Digital Map 50 Grid CD-ROM, NIPPON-II.
14. V. Caselles, J. M. Morel, C. Sbert: An axiomatic approch to image interpolation, *IEEE Trans. Image Processing*, **17**, 376-386, 1998.

Interpolating Camera Configurations

Lyle Noakes

Department of Mathematics & Statistics
The University of Western Australia, 35 Stirling Highway
Crawley 6009 WA, Perth, Australia
lyle@maths.uwa.edu.au
http://www.maths.uwa.edu.au/~lyle/

Abstract. A surprisingly rich variety of tools has been developed for interpolating camera orientations, including traditional methods based on charts, corner-cutting schemes from computer graphics, and Riemannian cubic interpolants. Piecewise geodesic and generalized deCastlejau interpolants are described in sufficient detail to permit implementation. Experimental comparisons are made between generalized deCastlejau curves and Riemannian cubics.

Keywords: rotations, cubic interpolation, motion analysis, trajectory planning

1 Camera Trajectories

Let K be a camera, free to rotate about some fixed point O in Euclidean 3-space E^3. Camera orientations, and posibly angular velocities, are prescribed at times $0, T$, where $T > 0$ is given. A camera orientation is specified by an orthonormal frame (x_1, x_2) fixed relative to the focal plane of K, where the vector product $x_1 \times x_3$ points away from the focal plane in the direction of the lens. The frame is then equivalent to the 3×3 matrix $x = \begin{bmatrix} x_1 & x_2 & x_1 \times x_2 \end{bmatrix}$, which is a *rotation* of E^3, namely an orthogonal matrix of determinant $+1$. A curve of camera orientations amounts to a curve $t \mapsto x(t)$ in the space $SO(3)$ of all such rotations. In the simplest nontrivial case $x : [0, T] \to SO(3)$ is required to satisfy

$$x(0) = x_0 \quad \text{and} \quad x(T) = x_T, \tag{1}$$

where $x_0, x_T \in SO(3)$ and $T \in \mathbb{R}$ are given. Of course $SO(3)$ can be locally parameterized by E^3.

Example 1. The rotation matrix $\mathbf{e}(\psi, \theta, \phi)$ with *Euler angles* $(\psi, \theta, \phi) \in [0, 2\pi) \times [0, \pi) \times [0, 2\pi)$ is

$$\begin{bmatrix} \cos\phi\cos\psi - \cos\theta\sin\phi\sin\psi & \cos\psi\cos\theta\sin\phi + \cos\phi\sin\psi & \sin\phi\sin\theta \\ -\cos\psi\sin\phi - \cos\phi\cos\theta\sin\psi & \cos\phi\cos\psi\cos\theta - \sin\phi\sin\psi & \cos\phi\sin\theta \\ \sin\psi\sin\theta & -\cos\psi\sin\theta & \cos\theta \end{bmatrix}$$

Although $\mathbf{e}$ maps onto $SO(3)$, it is not one-to-one: $\mathbf{e}(\psi, 0, 2\pi - \psi)$ is the identity matrix $\mathbf{1}$ for all $\psi \in [0, \pi)$. On the other hand, given $\theta \neq 0$, the last row and

N. Petkov and M.A. Westenberg (Eds.): CAIP 2003, LNCS 2756, pp. 714–721, 2003.

column of $\mathbf{e}(\psi, \theta, \phi)$ uniquely determine ψ, ϕ. The restriction of $\mathbf{e}$ to $(0, 2\pi) \times (0, \pi) \times (0, 2\pi)$ is a diffeomorphism onto an open subset U of $SO(3)$, and the inverse $\Phi : U \to (0, 2\pi) \times (0, \pi) \times (0, 2\pi)$ is a *coordinate chart.* Curves x in U correspond to curves $\Phi \circ x$ in $(0, 2\pi) \times (0, \pi) \times (0, 2\pi) \subset E^3$. So if $x_0, x_T \in U$ we can interpolate in $(0, 2\pi) \times (0, \pi) \times (0, 2\pi)$ and use $\mathbf{e}$ to map back to $SO(3)$:

$$x(sT) = \mathbf{e}((1-s)(\psi_0, \theta_0, \phi_0) + s(\psi_1, \theta_1, \phi_1)),$$

where $s \in [0, 1]$, and $(\psi_i, \theta_i, \phi_i) = \Phi(x_{iT})$ for $i = 0, 1$. If this recipe is followed when one of the x_{iT} is $\mathbf{1}$, ψ_i can be chosen arbitrarily in $[0, 2\pi)$. Unfortunately, when θ_i is nearly 0, small perturbations in x_{iT} can correspond to large changes in ψ_i, ϕ_i. So the interpolant does not depend stably on endpoints. Also, whether the θ_i are small or not, x may not be a natural choice of interpolant. Setting

$$x_{iT} = \begin{bmatrix} 1 & 0 & 0 \\ 0 & \sqrt{3}/2 & (-1)^i/2 \\ 0 & (-1)^{i+1}/2 & \sqrt{3}/2 \end{bmatrix},$$

the curve of unit vectors in the direction of the camera lens is illustrated in Figure 1. It takes the long way round. Such problems can be reduced by switching between several charts, but this complicates implementation and has unpleasant side-effects. For instance, the interpolant from x_T to x_0 need not be the reverse of the interpolant from x_0 to x_T. □

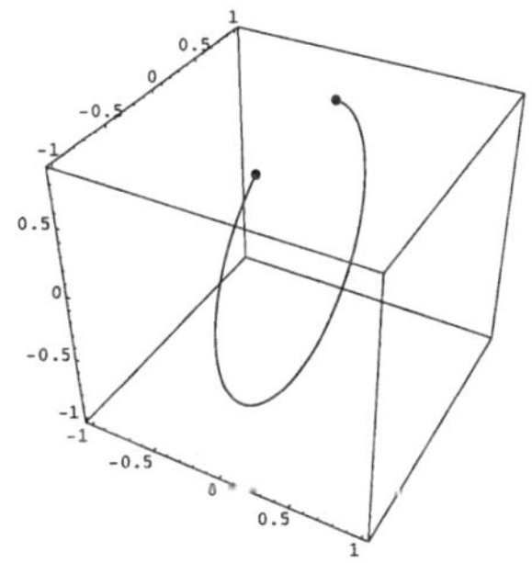

Fig. 1. Lens directions in Example 1.

The most serious defects of chart-based interpolation can be traced to a failure to consider the geometry of $SO(3)$. In the simplest case this has a high degree of symmetry.

Example 2. A geometry of $SO(3)$ is determined by a system for smoothly computing inner products of vectors tangent to $SO(3)$ at the same point, namely by a *Riemannian metric.* Riemannian metrics that are invariant with respect to left and right rotations are said to be *bi-invariant.* They are unique up to positive scalar multiples, and geometrically equivalent.

Given a Riemannian metric, the *length* $\lambda(x)$ and *energy* $\epsilon(x)$ of a smooth curve $x : [0,T] \to SO(3)$ are defined by

$$\lambda(x) = \int_0^T \|\dot{x}(t)\| \, dt, \quad \text{and} \quad \epsilon(x) = \int_0^T \|\dot{x}(t)\|^2 \, dt, \tag{2}$$

where $\| \ \|$ is the Riemannian norm. When the Riemannian metric is bi-invariant and K is spherically symmetric about O, $\epsilon(x)$ is proportional to the average rotational kinetic energy. Bearing in mind Figure 1, a natural condition to impose on x is to be of minimum length and uniform speed among all smooth curves satisfying (1). Such curves, called *minimal geodesics*, also minimise energy [17]. For a bi-invariant Riemannian metric, geodesics have a very simple closed form, using quaternionic multiplication as follows.

Identify the unit 3-sphere S^3 in E^4 with the space of unit quaternions, and E^3 with the space of quaternions whose real parts are 0. Define a homomorphism $\Psi : S^3 \to SO(3)$ by $\Psi(q)r = qrq^{-1}$, where $q \in S^3$, $r \in \mathbb{R}^3$, and on the right hand side multiplication and inversion are quaternionic. Then Ψ is surjective with kernel ± 1, and maps great circle arcs in S^3 to geodesic segments in $SO(3)$. So a unit vector[1] $q = \begin{bmatrix} q_1 & q_2 & q_3 & q_4 \end{bmatrix}^{\mathbf{T}} \in S^3 \subset E^4$ gives a rotation

$$\Psi(\pm q) = \mathbf{1} - 2 \begin{bmatrix} q_3^2 + q_4^2 & -q_2q_3 - q_1q_4 & q_1q_3 - q_2q_4 \\ -q_2q_3 + q_1q_4 & q_2^2 + q_4^2 & -q_1q_2 - q_3q_4 \\ -q_1q_3 - q_2q_4 & q_1q_2 - q_3q_4 & q_2^2 + q_3^2 \end{bmatrix},$$

and conversely any rotation can be written in this form. Choosing $q_{(i)}$ so that $\Psi(q_{(i)}) = x_{iT}$ for $i = 0, 1$, let $y : [0,T] \to S^3$ be the shortest great circle arc from $q_{(0)}$ to $\pm q_{(1)}$. Then $x = \Psi \circ y$ is a minimal geodesic from x_0 to x_T. In the situation of Example 1,

$$q_{(i)} = \frac{1}{2} \begin{bmatrix} \frac{(-1)^i}{\sqrt{2-\sqrt{3}}} & \sqrt{2-\sqrt{3}} & 0 & 0 \end{bmatrix}^{\mathbf{T}},$$

and the curve of lens directions does not behave in the peculiar way shown in Figure 1. □

2 Hermite Interpolation

Piecewise-geodesic interpolants are of little use when data are given at times $0 < T_1 < T_2 < \ldots$, because nondifferentiability at the T_j, corresponds to sudden changes of angular velocities. The simplest way to rule this out is by additional conditions on our elementary interpolant $x : [0,T] \to SO(3)$:

$$x(0) = x_0, \ \dot{x}(0) = v_0, \ x(T) = x_T, \ \dot{x}(T) = v_T, \tag{3}$$

where $x_0, x_T \in SO(3)$ are given, together with v_0, v_T tangent to $SO(3)$ at x_0, x_T respectively. Geodesics seldom satisfy (3) and so some larger family of curves

[1] **T** means "transpose".

is needed, analogous to cubic polynomials in E^3. Of course $SO(3)$ is a subset of the space $M_{3\times 3}$ of 3×3 real matrices, and so we might consider polynomial curves $x : [0,T] \to M_{3\times 3}$, namely matrix-valued functions with all entries x_{ij} polynomial.

Proposition 1. *Let $x : [0,T] \to M_{3\times 3}$ be a polynomial curve of degree $n > 0$. Then the image of x intersects $SO(3)$ in at most $2n$ points.*

Proof: Choose $1 \leq i,j \leq 3$ so that x_{ij} is polynomial of degree n. Then the real-valued polynomial $p(t) = x_{i1}(t)^2 + x_{i2}(t)^2 + x_{i3}(t)^2 - 1$ has degree $2n$. So $p(t) = 0$ for at most $2n$ values of t. But $p(t) = 0$ when $x(t) \in SO(3)$. □

So $SO(3)$ contains no nonconstant polynomial curves in the usual sense; other kinds of curves are needed to satisfy (3). One possibility is to use coordinate charts, as in Example 1, enabling interpolation in $SO(3)$ by reference to cubic polynomials in E^3, but this leads to the difficulties noted in Example 1. A more geometrical approach, analogous to Considering the effectiveness and ease of geodesic Example 2, is to adapt the deCastlejau algorithm [12] which generates polynomial curves in E^3 from line segments.

Example 3. Because geodesic arcs in curved spaces are analogous to line segments in E^3, the deCastlejau algorithm can be adapted to generate curves in $SO(3)$, as done in [26] for the double cover S^3. Small changes are needed for $SO(3)$, as follows. Let $f_{0,1}, f_{2,3} : [0,1] \to SO(3)$ be the minimal geodesics satisfying

$$f_{0,1}(0) = x_0, \quad \dot{f}_{0,1}(0) = v_0/T, \quad f_{2,3}(1) = x_T, \quad \dot{f}_{2,3}(1) = v_T/T,$$

and let $f_{1,2} : [0,1] \to SO(3)$ be the minimal geodesic from $f_{0,1}(1)$ to $f_{2,3}(0)$. For $r \in [0,1]$ and $j = 1,2,3$, let $x_j(r) = f_{j-1,j}(r)$. For $k = 2,3$, let $g_{k-1,k} : [0,1] \to SO(3)$ be the minimal geodesic from x_{k-1} to x_k, and set $y_k = g_{k-1,k}(r)$. Finally, let $h : [0,1] \to SO(3)$ be the minimal geodesic from y_2 to y_3, and set $x(rT) = h(r)$. Then $x : [0,T] \to SO(3)$ is smooth and satisfies (3). This elegant method is also explored in [9]. Imposing (3) instead of (1) in the situation of Example 2, with

$$v_0 = \begin{bmatrix} 0.0000 & 0.9280 & -0.3725 \\ -0.6175 & -0.1225 & 0.2121 \\ 0.7866 & -0.2121 & -0.1225 \end{bmatrix}, \quad v_T = \begin{bmatrix} 0.0000 & -0.2708 & -0.2380 \\ 0.1155 & -0.0224 & -0.0388 \\ 0.3415 & 0.0388 & -0.0224 \end{bmatrix},$$

we obtain an interpolant whose curve of lens directions is shown (thinner) in Figure 2. The deCastlejau algorithm in E^3 also has a recursive form, requiring only computations of midpoints of arcs. In [18], [20] the recursive algorithm is adapted to the Riemannian situation, yielding interpolants with properties related to constructions of von Koch, de Rham, and Dahmen-Micchelli. For related work see [19], [21], [22]. □

3 A Performance Criterion

Just as line segments minimise length among curves joining points in E^3, cubic polynomials minimise an integral of the form $\epsilon_2(x) = \int_0^T \|\ddot{x}(t)\|^2\, dt$ over constrained curves $x : [0,T] \to E^3$. This *variation-diminishing* property of cubic polynomials is important in applications in CAGD. The analogue of ϵ_2 for curves in a Riemannian manifold is the functional

$$\tilde{\epsilon}_2(x) \; = \; \int_0^T \|\nabla_{d/dt}\dot{x}\|^2\, dt, \tag{4}$$

where ∇ is the *Levi-Civita covariant derivative* [17], [13], and $\|\ \|$ the *Riemannian norm.* Interpolants minimizing $\tilde{\epsilon}_2$ may be considered optimal, and compared with the more classical curves of Example 3. Critical points of $\tilde{\epsilon}_2$ are called *Riemannian cubics.* In [11], [23], the Euler-Lagrange equation of $\tilde{\epsilon}_2$ is found to be

$$\nabla^3_{d/dt}\dot{x} + R(\nabla_{d/dt}\dot{x}, \dot{x})\dot{x} \; = \; \mathbf{0}. \tag{5}$$

To see what (5) says about curves in $SO(3)$, define a linear isomorphism from E^3 to the space $so(3) = TSO(3)_1$ of skew-symmetric 3×3 matrices by $b(v)w \; = \; v \times w$ where $v, w \in E^3$. Let $c : S \to SO(3)$ be C^∞. A *vector field along* c is a lifting $X : S \to TSO(3)$ of c. Then the assignment $X \mapsto \bar{X}$, where

$$b(\bar{X}(s)) = c(s)^{-1} X_s,$$

is a one-to-one correspondence from vector fields defined along c to the set of functions $\bar{X} : S \mapsto E^3$. For S an open interval, the *covariant derivative* of X is the vector field $W = \nabla_{d/dt}X$ along c such that

$$\bar{W}(t) = \dot{\bar{X}}(t) + \frac{1}{2}\bar{\dot{c}}(t) \times \bar{X}(t).$$

When c is constant, $\bar{X}$ is a curve in $TSO(3)_c$. Then $\bar{W} = \dot{\bar{X}}$. When $\dot{c}(t) \neq \mathbf{0}$, write X near t in the form $X' \circ c$. Then X' is a vector field defined along the inclusion of part of the image of c, and $(\nabla_{d/dt}X)'$ is denoted $\nabla_{\dot{c}}X'$. The *Riemannian curvature* $R(X,Y)Z$ is the vector field R with

$$\bar{R} = -\frac{1}{4}(\bar{X} \times \bar{Y}) \times \bar{Z}.$$

So (5) stands for a 4th order system of nonlinear ordinary differential equations on E^9 (amounting to 36 nonlinear first order ODEs for 36 real-valued functions) with 24 equality constraints, and 36 scalar boundary conditions corresponding to (3). One way to reduce these numbers is to locally represent curves in $SO(3)$ by curves in E^3, using charts of $SO(3)$, and swapping charts as necessary to avoid numerical instabilities. Because Riemannian cubics are defined independently of charts, this approach is better than using charts to interpolate with cubic polynomials. Each step of classical shooting [14] for the boundary value problem requires solutions of an initial value problem for 84 real valued functions. This is a lot for an elementary CAGD task. Despite substantial progress since [23] on other fronts [5], [6], [7], [8], [9], [16], [15], [24], a practical implementation of shooting to give Riemannian cubics satisfying (3) has been lacking until recently[2]. An effective method known as *Lie shooting* has been implemented, but is more computationally intensive than the non-optimal classical generalized deCastlejau scheme of Example 3. The author's current work in this area aims to improve performance of Lie shooting by exploiting quadratures and closed-form solutions for systems of ODEs associated with (5).

Example 4. It takes around 7 seconds with Mathematica on a 2GHZ PC for Lie shooting to calculate a Riemannian cubic in $SO(3)$ satisfying the conditions in Example 3. The curve of lens directions (shown thick) in Figure 2 is significantly less wavy than the curve of lens directions (shown thin) obtained from the generalized deCastlejau curve of Example 3. So the quality of the cubic interpolant seems relatively high. On the other hand, the generalized deCastlejau interpolant is calculated more or less immediately. □

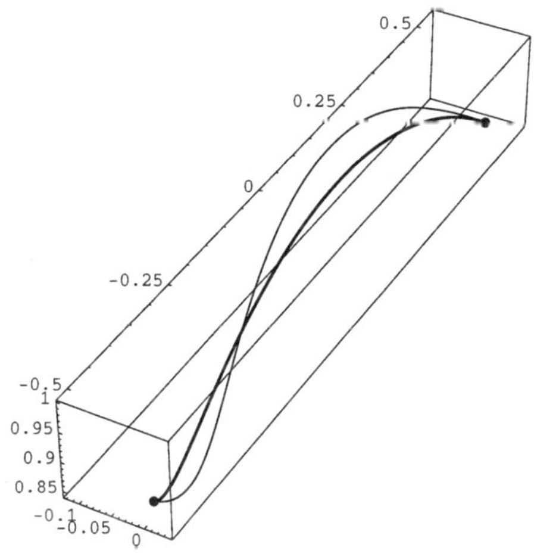

Fig. 2. Lens directions in Examples 3, 4.

4 Experimentation

Experiments were carried out in the situation of Example 4 by varying v_T from the given matrix, and calculating corresponding values of the performance index $\tilde{\epsilon}_2$ for the generalized deCastlejau curve and the Riemannian cubic interpolant. Writing v_T in the form $d\Psi_{q_1}(w_T)$, where $w_T \in E^4$ is tangent to S^3 at q_1, we obtain Table 1 below. In the first row, w_T corresponds to the matrix v_T in Examples 3, 4. In every row $\tilde{\epsilon}_2$ is markedly smaller for the cubic.

[2] For more background see [3], [4], [10], [25], [27], [28].

Table 1. $\tilde{\epsilon}_2$ of Generalized deCastlejau and Riemannian Cubic Interpolants.

w_T^{T}	deCastlejau	Cubic
$[-0.006\ -0.022\ \ 0.150\ -0.100]$	62.06	20.90
$[-0.015\ -0.056\ -0.067\ -0.058]$	55.82	19.25
$[-0.013\ -0.047\ \ 0.057\ -0.022]$	56.79	19.76
$[\ 0.025\ \ 0.095\ \ 0.099\ -0.002]$	74.59	24.27
$[-0.016\ -0.060\ \ 0.097\ -0.082]$	55.57	19.45
$[\ 0.000\ \ 0.000\ \ 0.009\ -0.028]$	57.77	20.73
$[-0.013\ -0.049\ \ 0.003\ -0.079]$	50.98	19.07
$[-0.011\ -0.042\ \ 0.014\ \ 0.067]$	60.73	20.37
$[\ 0.005\ \ 0.017\ -0.004\ -0.060]$	57.14	20.94
$[-0.022\ -0.083\ \ 0.061\ \ 0.053]$	59.32	19.45

5 Conclusions

Whereas interpolation in E^3 is standard [1], typically performed with piecewise polynomial curves, interpolation in $SO(3$ is a more delicate task. The classical generalized deCastlejau curves of Example 3 are readily computed but suboptimal with respect to the performance measure $\tilde{\epsilon}_2$. Riemannian cubics optimizing $\tilde{\epsilon}_2$ can now be calculated, but they are still expensive to compute compared with the classical curves.

References

1. J.H. Ahlberg, E.N. Nilson, J.H. Walsh, *The Theory of Splines and Their Applications*, Mathematics in Science and Engineering 38, Academic Press, 1967.
2. J. Angeles and R. Akras, "Cartesian Trajectory Planning for 3-DOF Spherical Wrists", *IEEE Conference on Robotics and Automation,* Scottsdale, AZ, May (1989) 68-74.
3. A.H. Barr, B. Currin, S. Gabriel and J.F. Hughes, "Smooth Interpolation of Orientations with Angular Velocity Constraints Using Quaternions", *Computer Graphics* 26 (2) (1992), 313-320.
4. J.M. Brady, J.M. Hollerbach, T.L. Johnson, T.Lozano-Perez, and M.T. Masson, *Robot Motion: Planning and Control,* MIT Press, Cambridge MA (1982).
5. M. Camarinha, F. Silva Leite, P. Crouch, "On the Geometry of Riemannian Cubic Polynomials", *Differential Geom. Appl.* 15 (2001) no.2 107-135.
6. M. Camarinha, F. Silva Leite, P. Crouch, "Splines of Class C^k on Non-Euclidean Spaces", *IMA J. Math. Control & Information* 12 (1995) no.4 399-410.
7. P.B. Chapman and Lyle Noakes, "Singular Perturbations and Interpolation - a Problem in Robotics", *Nonlinear Analysis TMA* 16 no.10 (1991), 849-859.
8. P. Crouch and F. Silva Leite, "The Dynamic Interpolation Problem: on Riemannian Manifolds, Lie Groups, and Symmetric Spaces", *J. Dynam. Control Systems* 1 (1995) no.2 177-202.

9. P. Crouch, G. Kun, and F. Silva Leite, "The De Castlejau Algorithm on Lie Groups and Spheres", *J. Dynam. Control Systems* 5 (1999) no. 3 397-429.
10. T. Duff, "Quaternion Splines for Animating Rotations", *Second Summer Graphics Workshop, Monterey, CA*, 12-13 December 1985 (Usenix Association) 54-62.
11. S.A. Gabriel and J.T. Kajiya, "Spline Interpolation in Curved Manifolds", *unpublished manuscript*, 1985.
12. R.N. Goldman, "Recursive Triangles", in *Computations of Curves and Surfaces*", eds W. Dahmen, M. Gasca, & C.A. Micchelli, NATO Adv. Sci. Inst. Ser. C Math. Phys. Sci. 307 (Kluwer, Dordrecht, 1989) 27-72.
13. Jürgen Jost, *Riemannian Geometry and Geometrical Analysis*, Springer-Verlag Universitext 1995.
14. Herbert B. Keller, *Numerical Methods for Two-Point Boundary-Value Problems*, Blaisdell, Waltham Mass. 1968.
15. K. Krakowski, PhD Thesis, *University of Western Australia*, submitted 2002.
16. F. Silva Leite, M. Camarinha, P. Crouch, "Elastic Curves as Solutions of Riemannian and Sub-Riemannian Control Problems", *Math. Control Signals Systems* 13 (2000) no. 2 140-155.
17. J. Milnor, *Morse Theory*, Annals of Math Studies 51, Princeton UP 1963.
18. Lyle Noakes, "Asymptotically Smooth Splines", *World Scientific Series in Approximations and Decompositions* 4 (1994) 131-137.
19. Lyle Noakes, "Riemannian Quadratics", in *Curves and Surfaces with Applications in CAGD*, Alain Le Méhauté, Christopher Rabut, Larry L. Schumaker (eds), Vanderbilt University Press, 1 (1997) 319-328.
20. Lyle Noakes, "Nonlinear Corner-Cutting", *Advances in Computational Math.* 8 (1998) 165-177.
21. Lyle Noakes, "Accelerations of Riemannian Quadratics", *Proc. Amer. Math. Soc.* 127 (1999) 1827-1836.
22. Lyle Noakes, "Quadratic Interpolation on Spheres", *Advances in Computational Math.*, in-press.
23. Lyle Noakes, Greg Heinzinger, and Brad Paden, "Cubic Splines on Curved Spaces", *J. Math. Control & Information* 6 (1989), 465-473.
24. Lyle Noakes, "Null Cubics and Lie Quadratics", *J. Math. Physics* in-press.
25. R.P. Paul, "Manipulator Path Control", *IEEE Trans. Syst. Man. Cybern.* SMC-9 (1979), 702-711.
26. K. Shoemake, "Animating Rotation with Quaternion Curves", *SIGGRAPH* 19 (3) (1985) 245-254.
27. H.H. Tan and R.B. Potts, "A Discrete Path/Trajectory Planner for Robotic Arms", *J. Austral. Math. Soc.* Series B 31 (1989), 1-28.
28. R.H. Taylor, "Planning and Execution of Straight-Line Manipulator Trajectories", *IBM J. Res. Develop.* 23 (1979), 424-436.

Discrete Morphology with Line Structuring Elements

C.L. Luengo Hendriks and L.J. van Vliet

Pattern Recognition Group, Delft University of Technology
Lorentzweg 1, 2628 CJ Delft, The Netherlands
cris@ph.tn.tudelft.nl

Abstract. Discrete morphological operations with line segments are notoriously hard to implement. In this paper we study different possible implementations of the line structuring element, compare them, and examine their rotation and translation invariance in the continuous domain. That is, we are interested in obtaining a morphological operator that is invariant to rotations and translations of the image before sampling.

1 Introduction

Morphological operations use a structuring element (SE), which plays the role of a neighborhood or convolution kernel in other image-processing operations. Often, these SEs are composed of line segments. For example, the square, hexagon and octagon, which are increasingly accurate approximations of the disk, can be decomposed into two, three and four line segments respectively [6]. Thus, it is possible to create an arbitrarily accurate approximation of a disk by increasing the number of line segments used. The advantage of using line segments instead of N-dimensional structuring elements is a reduction in the computational complexity. Furthermore, it is possible to implement a dilation or erosion by a line segment under an arbitrary angle with only 3 comparisons per pixel, irrespective of the length of the line segment [10, 7].

Our reason to study the implementation of the line SE is to improve on the result of morphological operations used to detect and measure linear features in images. Examples are roads in airborne images [2], grid patterns on stamped metal sheets [9], and structure orientation estimation [8]. We also use line SEs in RIA Morphology [5].

The property we are most interested in is similarity to the continuous-domain operation. That is, we are interested in invariance to rotation and translation of the sampling grid. Thus, when we talk about translation-invariance, we actually mean invariance to sub-pixel shifts (unless explicitly stated otherwise).

2 Implementations of the Line SE

2.1 Basic Discrete Lines: Bresenham Lines

Bresenham lines [1] are formed by steps in the eight cardinal directions of the grid, and are the basic discrete lines. The most simple implementation of a

N. Petkov and M.A. Westenberg (Eds.): CAIP 2003, LNCS 2756, pp. 722–729, 2003.

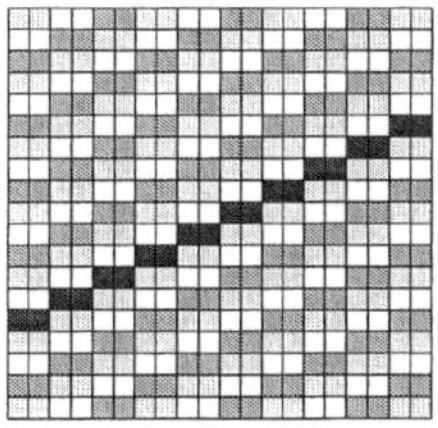

Fig. 1. A Bresenham line across the image can be tiled so that each pixel in the image belongs to a single line. Along these lines it is possible to perform an operation.

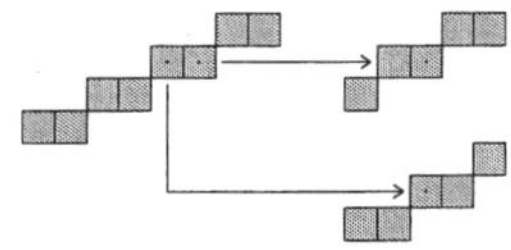

Fig. 2. The problem with a Bresenham line is that each pixel along the line is embedded in a differently shaped neighborhood.

morphological operation with a line SE uses a Bresenham line segment as the SE.

To efficiently implement a dilation with a line segment, the recursive algorithm proposed by van Herk [10] can be applied to a Bresenham line crossing the image [7], as in Figure 1 (lines can be tiled to cover the whole image). This results in, at each point, the maximum over some pixels along the line. The problem is that, for neighboring pixels, the configuration of the SE is different. Take as an example a line that goes up one pixel for each two that it goes right. Such a line is drawn by making one step right and one diagonally up (see Figure 2). There are two ways of starting this line (one of the two steps must be taken first), and each pixel along this line is embedded in one of two different neighborhoods. The dilation along this line will therefore be computed with two different SEs, alternated from pixel to pixel. When the image is translated horizontally by one pixel, and translated back after the operation, a different result is produced than when the operation is computed without translation. This should not pose a significant problem for band-limited images. All shapes used are equally poor approximations of the continuous line segment. The error introduced because of this outweighs the problems caused by the shape-change due to the recursive implementation.

We implemented this method by skewing the image in such a way that all pixels belonging to the Bresenham line are aligned on a row (or column, depending on the orientation of the line) of the image (that is, each column is shifted by an integer number of pixels). On this skewed image the operations can be applied along the rows, and the result must be skewed back.

Another problem with the discrete line segment (whether implemented with a recursive algorithm or not) is that the length, defined by an integer number of pixels, depends on the orientation of the segment. For each orientation, there is a different set of lengths that are possible to construct.

2.2 Periodic Lines

Periodic lines were introduced by Jones and Soille [3] as a remedy to the (discrete) translation-invariance of the morphological operations along Bresenham

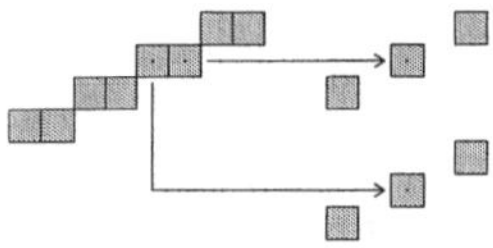

Fig. 3. A periodic line is defined by only those pixels that fall exactly on the continuous line.

Fig. 4. By dilating a periodic line segment with a small SE, it is possible to join up the SE.

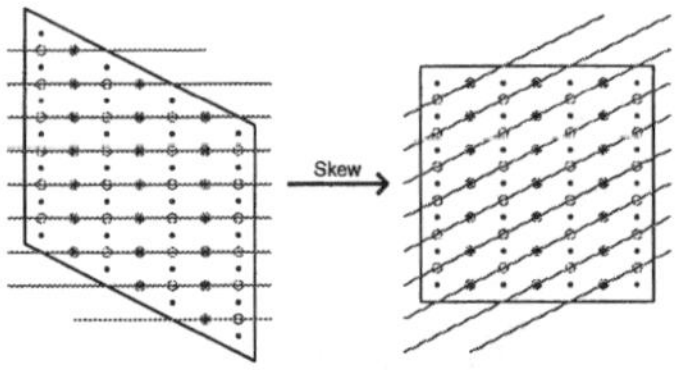

Fig. 5. After skewing the image, horizontal lines correspond to lines under a certain angle with respect to the image data. Some of the original image samples fall exactly on these lines (·), but most samples used (○) lie in between original grid points.

lines. A periodic line is composed of only those points of the continuous line that fall exactly on a grid point, see Figure 3. These lines are thus formed of disconnected pixels, except for lines of one of the three cardinal orientations. When considering only these points, it is possible to use a recursive implementation along the periodic lines that is translation-invariant in the discrete sense. However, because of the sparseness of the points along such a line, they are not useful except in constructing more complex structuring elements. For example, by dilating a periodic line segment with a small connected segment, one creates a connected line segment, as in Figure 4.

The drawbacks of this method are the small number of orientations for which it is useful (there are only few orientations that produce a short periodicity; for longer periodicities the line segment needed to connect the periodic line is longer as well), and the limited number of lengths that can be created (the length is a multiple of the periodicity, which depends on the orientation).

Because the result of this implementation is the same as that obtained by a direct (non-recursive) implementation using a Bresenham line segment as SE, we do not consider it separately in the comparison in Section 3.

2.3 Interpolated Lines by Skewing of the Image

We mentioned above that operations along a Bresenham line can be implemented by skewing the image, applying the operation along a column (or row), and skewing the image back. In this section we consider image skews with interpolation (that is, the rows or columns of the image are not shifted by an integer number of pixels, but by a real value). See Figure 5.

The interpolation method used is an important factor in the correctness of the output. We used cubic convolution [4] to implement the skews. This method is a good compromise between accuracy, computational cost and window size.

The lines obtained in this way are interpolated, but have the same number of samples as the Bresenham line of the same parameters. It is expected that these result in a somewhat better translation-invariance. The mayor drawback is that the result needs to be skewed back. Morphological operations do not produce band-limited images, and therefore the results are not sampled properly. Interpolating the result of a morphological operation is questionable at best.

The reason we need to interpolate in the output image is that the result of the morphological operation is computed at the points along the continuous line laid across the image, and not at the grid points of the output image. There are few columns (as many as there are points in the periodic line representation for the selected orientation) with zero or integer shift. For these columns, no interpolation of the output is required, and the result is at its best.

2.4 True Interpolated Lines

The interpolated lines presented above are at their best on only a few columns (or rows) of the image. It is, of course, also possible to accomplish the same accuracy for all output pixels. In this case, for each output pixel, samples along a line that goes exactly through it are computed by interpolation. On these computed samples the operation is performed. This can be implemented with one skew for each column (or row) of the image.

Again, as for all discrete line segments mentioned up to now, the number of samples used in the computation of the morphological operation depends on both the length of the segment and the orientation. Line segments along the grid are the densest, and diagonal segments have the least number of samples. Thus, for some orientations it is more probable to miss a local maximum (i.e. the maximum falls in between samples) than for others. This makes the continuous-domain translation-invariance better for horizontal and vertical lines than for diagonal lines, and also has repercussions for the rotation-invariance. Ideally, one would like to sample each of these lines equally densely by adding columns to the image when skewing. This also enables the creation of sub-pixel segment lengths. We have not corrected for the number of samples along the line segment in the comparison below.

2.5 Band-Limited Lines

A last option when implementing morphology with discrete line segments is to use grey-value SEs, which allows to construct band-limited lines. Such a segment is rotation and translation invariant, and does not have a limited set of available lengths. The drawback is that the line is thicker, but this should not be a problem for band-limited images, since it should contain only thick lines as well.

A Gaussian function, as well as its integral, are band-limited in good approximation, and can be sampled at a rate of σ with a very small error [11].

An approximately band-limited line segment can be generated using the error-function along the length of the segment, and using the Gaussian function in the other dimensions.

Let us define a two-dimensional image $L_{(\ell,\sigma)}$, to be used as a structuring element, by

$$L_{(\ell,\sigma)}(x,y) = A \cdot \exp\left(\frac{-y^2}{2\sigma^2}\right) \cdot \frac{1}{2}\left\{1 - \operatorname{erf}\left(\frac{\ell - 2|x|}{2\sigma}\right)\right\} \quad , \tag{1}$$

where ℓ is the length of the line segment, x is the coordinate axis in the direction of the segment, and y is the coordinate axis perpendicular to it[1]. Again, setting σ to 1 is enough to obtain a correctly sampled SE.

Note that the grey-value of the segment is 0, and the background has a value of $-A$. A is the scaling of the SE image, and should depend on the grey-value range in the image to be processed. It is not directly clear, however, how to scale this image $L_{(\ell,\sigma)}$. It is obvious that the height A of the line segment must be larger than the range of grey-values in the image. If it is not, the edge of the image used as SE will influence the morphological operation, which is not desirable. We obtained the best results by setting A just a little larger than the image grey-value range. We used the factor 1.0853, which sets the region of the SE that can interact with the image to $|x| \leq \ell/2 + \sigma$.

3 Comparison of Discrete Line Implementations

We have implemented the following versions of the dilation and the opening with a line segment SE:

- Method 1: with a Bresenham line segment as SE.
- Method 2: along Bresenham lines across the image.
- Method 3: with periodic lines.
- Method 4: along interpolated lines across the image.
- Method 5: with true interpolated lines.
- Method 6: with an approximately band-limited line segment as SE.

Figure 6 shows the dilation with each of these methods applied to an image with a discrete delta pulse and a Gaussian blob. This figure gives an idea of the shape used in the operation.

To compare these different methods, an image was generated that contains many line segments of fixed length and orientation, but varying sub-pixel position. They were drawn using (1). Openings were applied to this image, changing both the length and orientation of the SE, and using each of the implemented methods. The result of each operation is integrated (taking the sum of the pixel values), and plotted in a graph (see Figure 7). It is expected that this results in a value of 1 for the openings in which the angle of the SE matches that of the

[1] Of course, generating line segments in higher-dimensional images is trivial: y needs to be substituted by a vector.

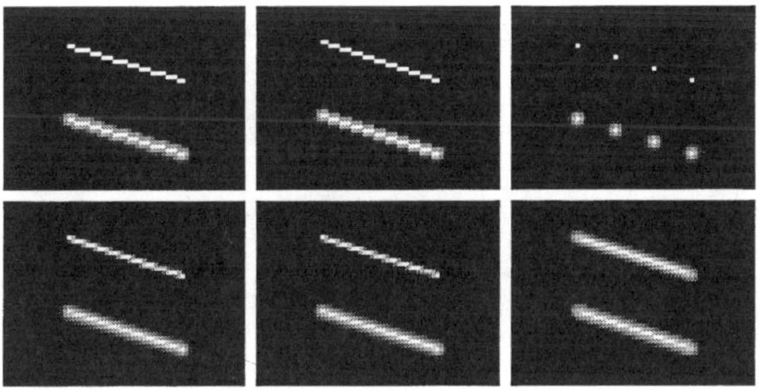

Fig. 6. Sample dilation with different implementations of the line segment structuring element. This gives an of about the shape of the structuring element used. Top row, from left to right: methods 1, 2 and 3. Bottom row: methods 4, 5 and 6.

segments in the input image, and the length ℓ is smaller or equal to the length of these segments. The result should be 0 for any other parameter of the SE, but in practice will decrease slowly when moving away from the correct parameters. This is due to the smoothness of the line segments in the input image.

There are a couple of things that readily come to mind when comparing these graphs:

- All methods produce a similar result, with the exception of the periodic lines (method 3). This is due to the fact that the periodic line segment is disjoint, and therefore can "fit" inside two image features at once. For most of the orientations, the periodic line segment consists of only 2 points.
- The two discrete, non-interpolated implementations (methods 1 and 2), never reach values approximating 1. The interpolated and grey-value methods (methods 4, 5 and 6) reach higher values, closer to the ideal value of 1.
- The three methods that work along lines across the image (methods 2, 4 and 5) show a stair-like dependency on the length. This is because of the discretized lengths of these segments. For method 1, there is also a stair-like dependency on the angle, because it is discrete as well.
- There are very few differences between the two interpolated methods (methods 4 and 5).
- The result of the grey-value method (method 6) is very smooth, but shows some "ringing". This effect is angle-dependent (graphs not shown).

Taking these observations into account, it can be said that the interpolated methods and the grey-value method produce results more consistent with the expectations than the discrete methods. Also, it does not appear to be necessary to use method 5, since it produces a result very similar to method 4. Method 4 is, of course, much simpler and computationally cheaper.

To further examine the interpolated method (method 4), the experiment was repeated changing the length and orientation of the line segments in the image. The results are shown in Figure 8. As seen in these graphs, increasing the length increases the angular selectivity of the filter. Also, for each orientation there is

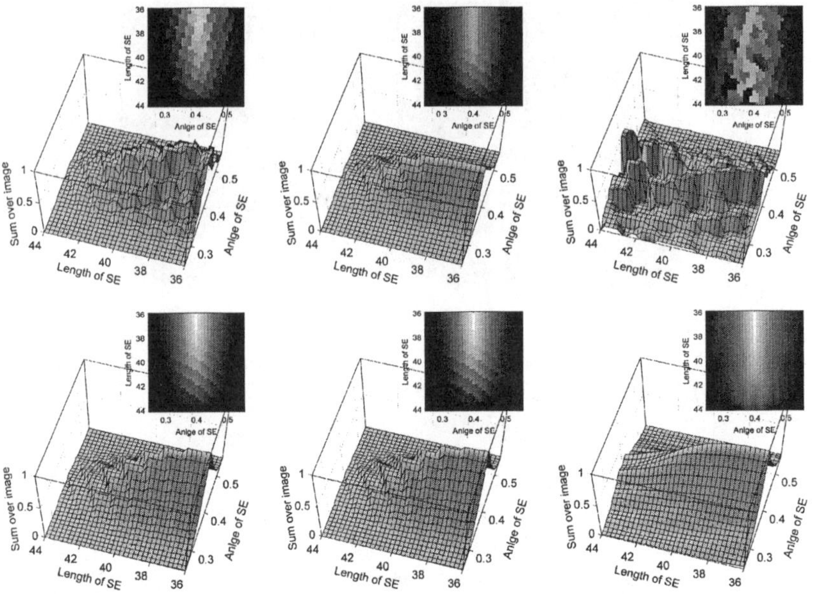

Fig. 7. Comparison of different implementations of the opening with a line segment structuring element. See text for details. The input image has line segments of length 40 pixels, under an angle of 0.4 rad. Top row, from left to right: methods 1, 2 and 3. Bottom row: methods 4, 5 and 6.

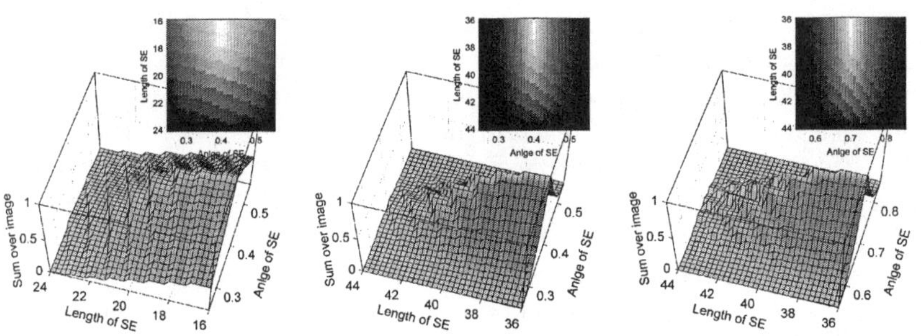

Fig. 8. Evaluation of method 4 (opening along an interpolated line). These graphs were obtained by changing the angle and length of the line segments in the input image. From left to right: 0.4 rad, 20 pixels; 0.4 rad, 40 pixels; and 0.7 rad, 40 pixels.

a different set of possible lengths. This does not happen with the grey-value morphology (graphs not shown).

4 Conclusion

In this paper we reviewed some common methods to implement morphological operations with line structuring elements on digitized images. Besides these methods we also proposed some methods that use interpolation, under the assumption that this will increase the similarity of the operator to its continuous-domain counterpart. We also investigate the use of an approximately band-limited line segment as a grey-value structuring element.

After comparing these methods, we conclude that using interpolation indeed improves the performance of the operator. However, we also note that the available lengths are still discrete and depend on the orientation of the line segment. Using a grey-value structuring element produces satisfactory results as well, and removes the discreteness of the length and angle of the structuring element.

References

1. J. E. Bresenham. Algorithm for computer control of a digital plotter. *IBS Systems Journal*, 4(1):25–30, 1965.
2. J. Chanussot and P. Lambert. An application of mathematical morphology to road network extractions on SAR images. In *Mathematical Morphology and its Applications to Image and Signal Processing*, pages 399–406, Dordrecht, 1998. Kluwer Academic Publishers.
3. R. Jones and P. Soille. Periodic lines: Definition, cascades, and application to granulometries. *Pattern Recognition Letters*, 17(10):1057–1063, 1996.
4. R. G. Keys. Cubic convolution interpolation for digital image processing. *IEEE Transactions on Acoustics, Speech, and Signal Processing*, 29(6):1153–1160, 1981.
5. C. L. Luengo Hendriks and L. J. van Vliet. A rotation-invariant morphology for shape analysis of anisotropic objects and structures. In *Proceedings 4th International Workshop on Visual Form, IWVF4*, LNCS 2059, pages 378–387. Springer, Berlin, 2001.
6. G. Matheron. *Random Sets and Integral Geometry*. Wiley, New York, 1975.
7. P. Soille, E. J. Breen, and R. Jones. Recursive implementation of erosions and dilations along discrete lines at arbitrary angles. *IEEE Transactions on Pattern Analysis and Machine Intelligence*, 18(5):562–567, 1996.
8. P. Soille and H. Talbot. Directional morphological filtering. *IEEE Transactions on Pattern Analysis and Machine Intelligence*, 23(11):1313–1329, 2001.
9. A. Tuzikov, P. Soille, D. Jeulin, H. Bruneel, and M. Vermeulen. Extraction of grid patterns on stamped metal sheets using mathematical morphology. In *Proceedings of the 11th International Conference on Pattern Recognition*, volume 1, pages 425–428, The Hague, 1992.
10. M. van Herk. A fast algorithm for local minimum and maximum filters on rectangular and octagonal kernels. *Pattern Recognition Letters*, 13:517–521, 1992.
11. L. J. van Vliet. *Grey-Scale Measurements in Multi-Dimensional Digitized Images*. PhD thesis, Pattern Recognition Group, Delft University of Technology, Delft, 1993.

Weighted Thin-Plate Spline Image Denoising

Roman Kašpar and Barbara Zitová*

Institute of Information Theory and Automation
Academy of Sciences of the Czech Republic
Pod vodárenskou věží 4, 182 08 Prague 8, Czech Republic
{kaspar,zitova}@utia.cas.cz

Abstract. This paper aims to present new denoising method based on thin-plate splines (*TPS*). The proposed approach is based on the general *TPS* denoising [1], however, its unfavorable smoothing of edges and details is suppressed by introduction of a weighting approach applied locally. The performance of the method is shown and compared to the original *TPS* denoising. The application of the method for denoising of infrared images of old paintings is presented.

1 Introduction

Image denoising problem appeared already in the very beginnings of digital image processing, however, it still attracts research attention and wide range of various approaches has been proposed and studied.

The aim of the noise removal is a construction of the original image estimate given the noisy observation. The additive noise modeled as random variable with zero-mean Gaussian distribution is often expected. Low-pass filters and rank filters belong among the traditional means for image denoising [2]. A lot of attention is paid to wavelet decomposition and proper handling of its coefficients in order to obtain the denoised images [3]. The non-linear diffusions, level sets methods and total variation methods represent the most current direction of the research [4].

Two main issues of denoising methods are efficiency of the noise removal and preservation of edge sharpness and small details. Often a good performance with respect to the denoising is accompanied by a loss of the sharpness and vice versa.

Approximation based thin-plate splines denoising (*TPS*) is one of the classical approaches. The denoised estimate is created as an approximation of the given noisy image by means of locally defined base functions — thin plate splines [5]. The key application of the *TPS* for image denoising was published by Berman [1]. The classical method sets the same merit for approximation to all pixels, independently of the underlying image structures.

The goal of the new method is to achieve an acceptable trade-off between the noise removal and smoothing of the edges and details by introducing a weighting function reflecting the image variance.

* Corresponding author. Tel.: +420 2 6605 2390; Fax: +420 2 8468 0730

N. Petkov and M.A. Westenberg (Eds.): CAIP 2003, LNCS 2756, pp. 730–737, 2003.

2 Description of the Method

The proposed method is based on the general thin-plate spline (*TPS*) approximation of image data, computed sequentially over small overlapping *patches*, centered at each pixel.

In the standard *TPS* method the approximating surface $s(\mathbf{x})$ minimizing

$$\Theta_{approx}(s) = \sum_{i=1}^{N}[s(x_i,y_i) - f(x_i,y_i)]^2 + \lambda \iint (s_{xx}^2 + 2s_{xy}^2 + s_{yy}^2)\mathrm{d}x\mathrm{d}y. \tag{1}$$

can be written as:

$$s(\mathbf{x}) = \sum_{j=1}^{3} b_j h_j(\mathbf{x}) + \sum_{i=1}^{N} a_i g(\mathbf{x},\mathbf{x}_i), \tag{2}$$

where $\mathbf{x}$, $\mathbf{x}_i$ denotes the coordinate vector (x,y), (x_i,y_i) respectively, $h_j(\mathbf{x})$ represents linear functions $h_1(\mathbf{x}) = 1$, $h_2(\mathbf{x}) = x$, $h_3(\mathbf{x}) = y$, N is the number of pixels in the patch, and $g(\mathbf{x},\mathbf{x}_i)$ are radial basis functions, defined as:

$$g(\mathbf{x},\mathbf{x}_i) = \|\mathbf{x}-\mathbf{x}_i\|^2 \ln \|\mathbf{x}-\mathbf{x}_i\|^2. \tag{3}$$

The relative weight between the interpolation and the smoothness in the resulting surface is determined by the regularization parameter $\lambda > 0$ in Eq. 1. If λ is small, a solution with good adaption to the local structure of the deformation is obtained, if the λ is large, a very smooth surface with little adaption to the deformations is acquired.

To compute the coefficients $\mathbf{b} = (b_1,b_2,b_3)^{\mathrm{T}}$ and $\mathbf{a} = (a_1,a_2,\ldots,a_N)^{\mathrm{T}}$, the following system of linear equations has to be solved:

$$(\mathbf{G}+\lambda\mathbf{I})\mathbf{a} + \mathbf{P}\mathbf{b} = \mathbf{v} \tag{4}$$

$$\mathbf{P}^{\mathrm{T}}\mathbf{a} = 0. \tag{5}$$

Matrix $\mathbf{G}$ is defined as $\mathbf{G}_{ij} = g(\mathbf{x}_i,\mathbf{x}_j)$, $\mathbf{I}$ is the identity matrix, λ is a constant that controls the trade-off between noise removal and structure preservation, matrix $\mathbf{P}$ is defined as $\mathbf{P}_{ij} = h_j(\mathbf{x}_i)$, and in $\mathbf{v}$ there are digital image values $f(\mathbf{x}_i)$ written line-wise. Eq. (5) ensures consistent behavior of $s(\mathbf{x})$ in infinity.

As we can see from Eq. (4), each pixel has the same merit (the constant λ) regardless of its position and similarity to surrounding pixels. As the proposed technique should be structure-preserving, the weighting function w, which diversifies the influence of individual pixels, is introduced. The weight of the pixel is a real number within the interval $\langle 0,1\rangle$.

The function w reflects the distance and the similarity of intensity values between any pixel $p(i,j)$ and the central pixel $p(k,l)$ of the patch p. The rule for defining the distance-dependent part of the weight follows the concept, in which the importance of the furthest pixels is set to 25%, and the central pixel itself has 100% weight, i.e. 1.0. For pixels between these two extremes, the weight value is distributed as e^{-r^2}. The intensity-dependent part of the weight uses estimation of noise variance σ^2 in the image. If the difference between intensity values is smaller than 2σ, the pixels are considered to be two noisy pixels of the same homogenous area. If the difference is greater than 3σ, the pixels are probably in different structures of the image. The formula for intensity-dependent part of the weight is then $w(i,j) = e^{\left(\frac{p(k,l)-p(i,j)}{2\sigma}\right)^6}$.

The resulting weighting function w is defined as a product of both parts:

$$w(i,j) = e^{-\left[\frac{(i-k)^2+(j-l)^2}{d}+\left(\frac{p(k,l)-p(i,j)}{2\sigma}\right)^6\right]}, \tag{6}$$

where (i,j), (k,l) are positions of the referred and the central patch pixel respectively, $p(i,j)$, $p(k,l)$ are their intensity values, and the constant $d = \frac{\left(\frac{k-1}{2}\right)^2+\left(\frac{l-1}{2}\right)^2}{\ln(4)}$ performs the normalization with respect to the size of the patch p.

The weight of the central pixel is solved separately. From Eq. (6) it follows that $w(k,l)$ would be 1.0 every time. Therefore, the formula is modified using the count of similar patch pixels close to the central pixel:

$$w(k,l) = \frac{1}{1+c}, \tag{7}$$

where c is the number of patch pixels with computed weight greater than e^{-1}.

Once the weight w is computed, we replace λ in Eq. (4) by line-wise written values of Φ:

$$\Phi_{ij} = \sigma^2 + 2\left(\frac{1}{w(i,j)} - 1\right). \tag{8}$$

When **b** and **a** are resolved using modified Eq. (4) and (5), the approximating surface $s(\mathbf{x})$ for the patch can be calculated as in Eq. (2).

Then, the output image is formed from the patch approximations. It can be assembled using either only central pixels from the computed surfaces (*WTPS(CO)* version — weighted *TPS*: central only), or the combination of all relevant pixels from the computed surfaces (*WTPS(AV)* version — weighted *TPS*: averaged).

In the *WTPS(CO)* version, the output intensity $o(u,v)$ can be expressed as:

$$o(u,v) = p_{uv}(k,l), \tag{9}$$

where p_{uv} is the computed surface centered around (u,v), and (k,l) is the position of the central pixel of p_{uv}.

In the *WTPS(AV)* version, the formula defining the output brightness $o(u,v)$ is as follows:

$$o(u,v) = \frac{\sum_{n=1}^{N} p_n(i_n,j_n) \cdot w_n}{\sum_{n=1}^{N} w_n}. \tag{10}$$

N is the number of computed surfaces that contain the pixel (u,v). $p_n(i_n,j_n)$ is the intensity value computed for the pixel (u,v) in the n-th surface. w_n is the weight defined in Eq. (6) assigned to the pixel (u,v) in the n-th patch.

3 Numerical Experiments

Examples in this section demonstrate the applicability of the proposed method. As it is the modification of standard *TPS* approach, comparison to this technique is also presented. Testing was performed both on synthetic and real scenes. The additive Gaussian noise (zero-mean, $\sigma^2 = 80$) was added to the images. For detailed comparison with state-of-the-art methods, please refer to [6].

The noise variation in homogenous area after denoising σ^2_{out} and the amount of edge blurring in the output images were two major criteria for comparing the methods. The edge blurring was evaluated using δ^2_{edge} criterion — the average of squared differences between vectors computed from the ideal step edge (see Fig. 1 (a)) in the original noise-free and the denoised images. The vectors are obtained as image average along the edge direction in order to minimize the noise influence.

Testing the approaches on synthetic data with added noise was realized by comparing the σ^2_{out}-equivalent and δ^2_{edge}-equivalent results by means of δ^2_{edge} and σ^2_{out} criteria, respectively. Images using the *WTPS(CO)* and *WTPS(AV)* were computed, both with σ^2 input parameter equal to 80 (experiments showing the stability of the method against an inaccurate estimate of σ^2 were performed, see [6]). The σ^2_{out} and δ^2_{edge} were computed for resulting images. To get σ^2_{out}-equivalent *TPS* results, appropriate λ's were found, by means of which *TPS* denoising generates images with the same output noise variation. Thus, the *TPS* denoised images were produced and δ^2_{edge} was computed and compared (see Tab. 1). In the same manner δ^2_{edge}-equivalent *TPS* results were generated and corresponding σ^2_{out} analyzed. Example of collected data forms Table 1. In Fig. 1 the synthetic scene with results of *WTPS* and *TPS* denoising are presented.

Denoising of the *Barbara* image demonstrates the applicability of the method on real scene images. Results using the *WTPS(CO)* and *WTPS(AV)* were computed (the input parameter $\sigma^2 = 80$) and σ^2_{out}-best *TPS* denoising output was generated. Achieved σ^2_{out} for *WTPS(CO)* was 3.4, for *WTPS(AV)* 3.2 and for *TPS* 4.2. Figure 2 shows the results.

For given output noise variation the *WTPS* methods keep blurring smaller near edges than *TPS*. The *TPS* denoising for fixed δ^2_{edge} results in much noisier images than *WTPS*. For general real scenes, the difference between methods *WTPS(CO)* and *WTPS(AV)* is not so important as for synthetic scenes. For artificial data with sharp edges or large homogenous areas, the method *WTPS(AV)* is more effective in denoising and also in edge blurring prevention.

Table 1. Numerical experiments — synthetic data: criteria values (σ^2_{out} and δ^2_{edge}) computed on results of *WTPS* methods, and corresponding *TPS* σ^2_{out}-equivalent results (lines 3, 4) and δ^2_{edge}-equivalent results (lines 5, 6).

Method	λ	σ^2_{out}	δ^2_{edge}
WTPS(CO)		5.74	43.68
WTPS(AV)		3.44	28.80
TPS	22.4	5.74 (fixed)	127.94
TPS	89.8	3.48 (fixed)	211.21
TPS	3.2	18.62	43.13 (fixed)
TPS	2.0	24.67	28.74 (fixed)

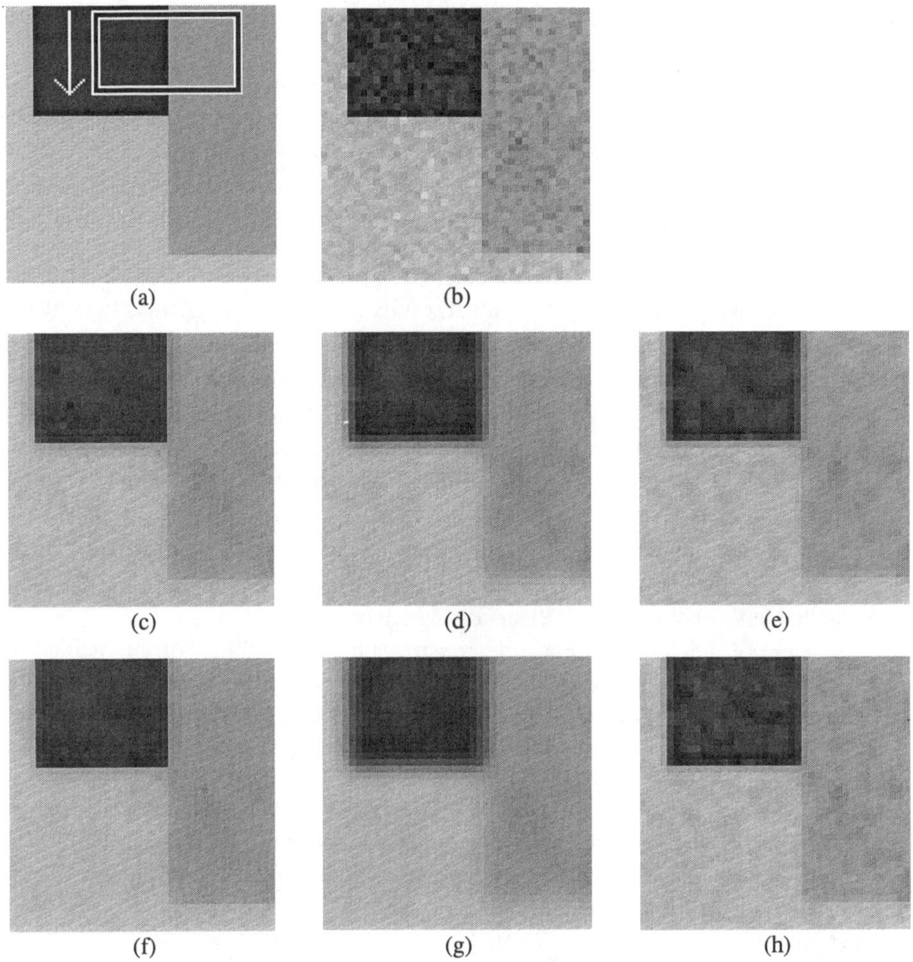

Fig. 1. Synthetic data: (a) noise-free original, the rectangle shows the area for computing the δ^2_{edge} criterion, the arrow implies the direction of averaging, (b) original with added Gaussian noise (zero-mean, $\sigma^2 = 80$), (c) result of *WTPS(CO)* method, (d) *TPS* result σ^2_{out}-equivalent to (c), (e) *TPS* result δ^2_{edge}-equivalent to (c), (f) result of *WTPS(AV)* method, (g) *TPS* result σ^2_{out}-equivalent to (f), (h) *TPS* result δ^2_{edge}-equivalent to (f).

4 Practical Application

In cooperation with the Studio of the Restoration of the Academy of Fine Arts in Prague, Czech Republic, the method was applied for denoising of infrared images. Infrared analysis has long been used in the fields of art history and restoration to determine the authenticity of artwork, to establish the period of an anonymous work, and above all to unmask underdrawings. An underdrawing is a preparatory drawing for a painting, sketched directly on a ground. Underdrawings are typically sketched using charcoal, but

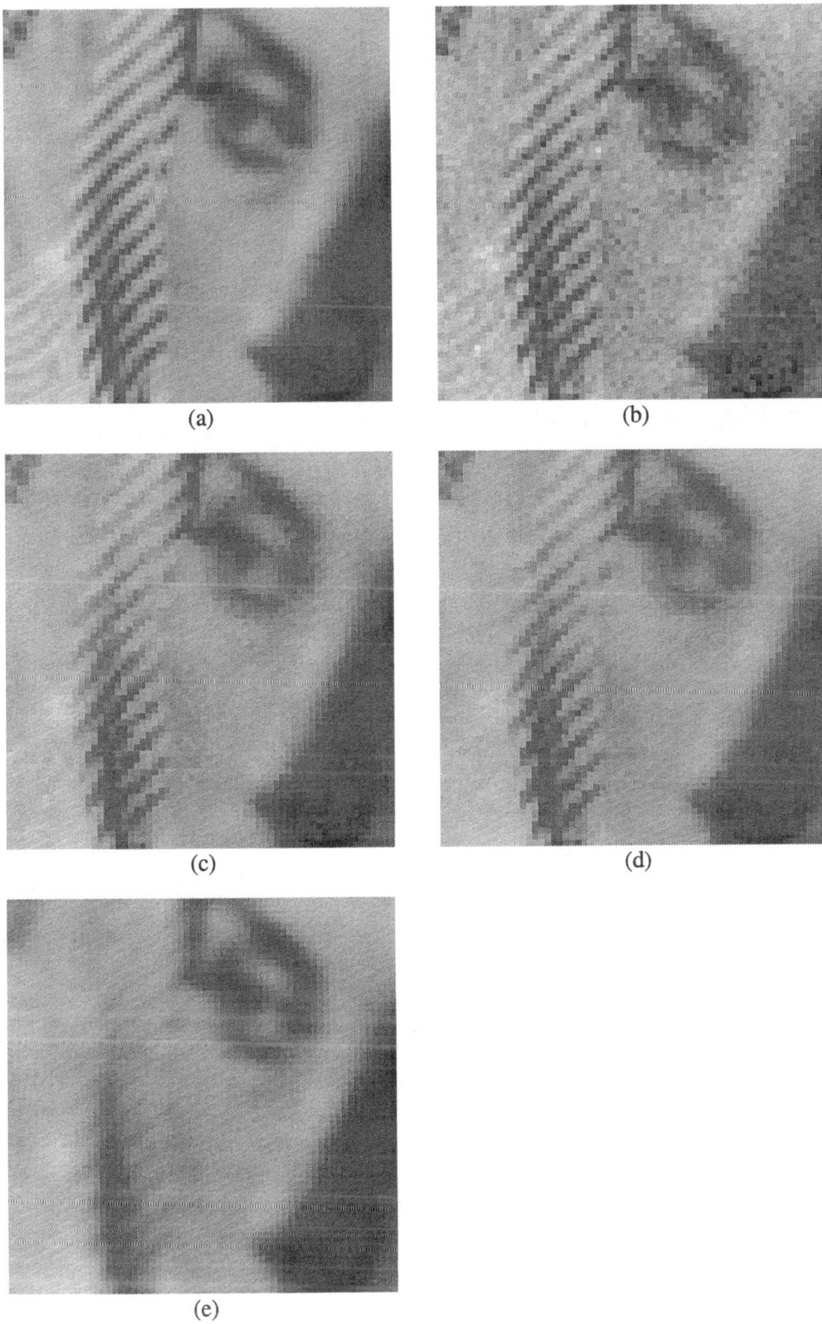

Fig. 2. Barbara image: (a) original, (b) original with added Gaussian noise (zero-mean, $\sigma^2 = 80$), (c) result of *WTPS(CO)* method, (d) result of *WTPS(AV)* method, (e) result of *TPS* method with the best σ^2_{out} value.

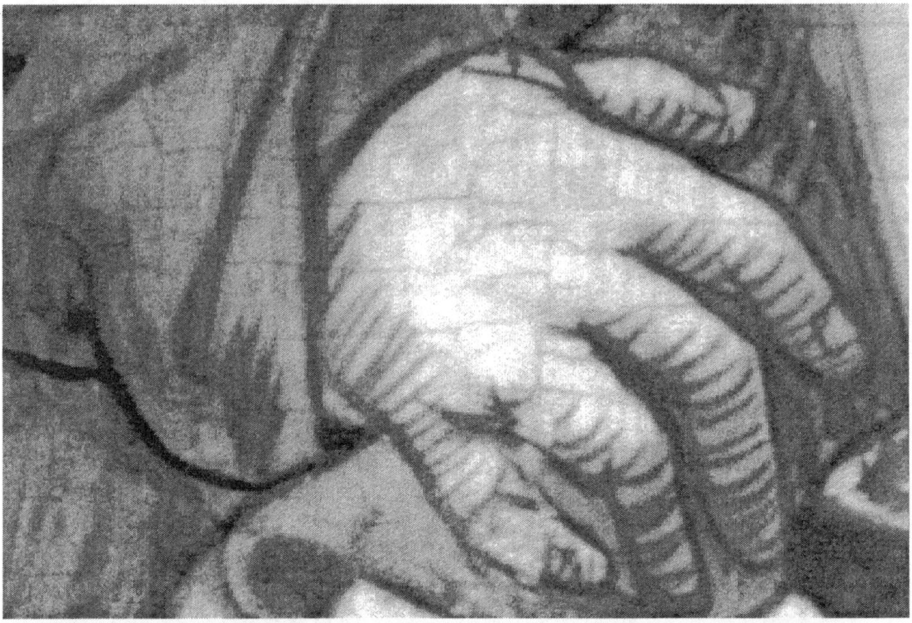

(a)

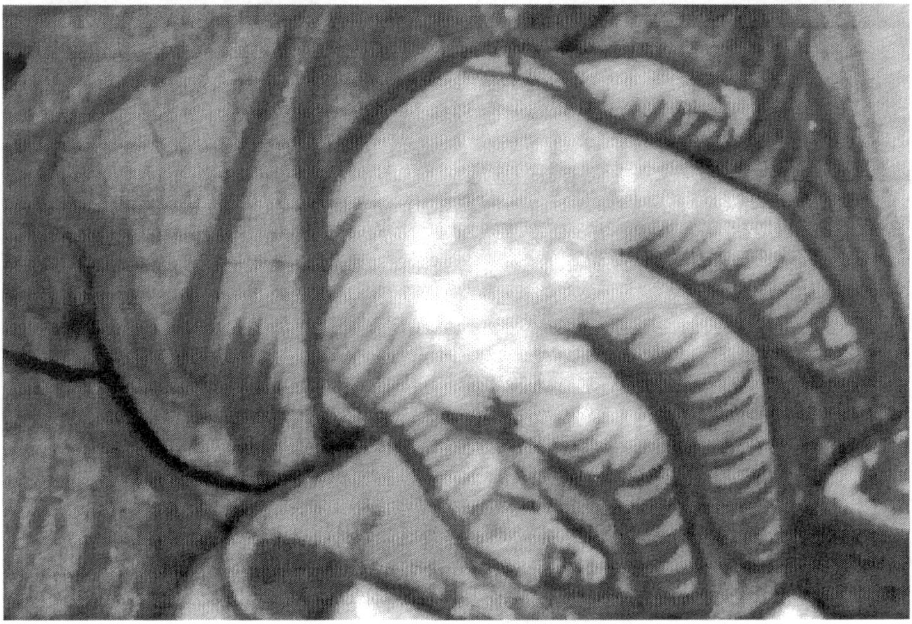

(b)

Fig. 3. Real infrared image: (a) original, (b) result of *WTPS(AV)* method, computed with estimation of noise in image (a) $\sigma^2 = 64.3$.

artists have been known to also use chalk, pencil or paint and brush and other media. The underdrawings are later covered with the artist's medium, and the underdrawings are not visible any more. Infrared analysis provides an easy nondestructive mean of eliminating the overlying paint on the underdrawings of many artworks.

Images acquired with infrared camera appear grayish (and may therefore have poor contrast) and large amount of noise is often present. The following analysis of infrared images of artworks is much easier in case of denoised images.

After testing other methods for image denosing on IR images, we used our proposed *WTPS* method, which gave satisfactory results. The Figure 3 gives an example of original infrared and *WTPS(AV)*-denoised image. More details about the IR denosing project can be found in [6].

5 Conclusion

In this note, the new method for image denoising has been presented. The method is based on the thin-plate spline denoising. The new weighting function has been introduced, which diversifies the influence of individual pixels for computation of approximating surfaces. This approach enables to decrease unwanted smoothing effect of *TPS* denoising on edges and small image details while achieving even bigger noise removal than the original method. Two ways for final image composition have been described. The applicability of the approach has been shown on both synthetic and real scene images with added Gaussian noise. The *WTPS* efficiency has been compared to the standard *TPS* denoising, showing the superiority of the new approach. The applicability of the method for denosing of real data has been demonstrated on infrared images of old paintings.

Acknowledgement

This work has been supported by the grant No. 102/01/P065 of the Grant Agency of the Czech Republic.

References

1. Berman, M.: Automated Smoothing of Image and Other Regularly Spaced Data, IEEE Trans. on Pattern Analysis and Machine Intelligence, Vol. 16 (1994) 460–468
2. Sonka, M., Hlavac, V., Boyle, R.: Image Processing, Understanding, and Machine Vision, 2nd edition, PWS Boston (1999)
3. Donoho, D. L.: De-noising by soft tresholding, IEEE Transactions on Information Theory Vol. 41 (1995, No. 3) 613–627
4. Rudin, L. I., Osher, S., Fatemi, E.: Nonlinear Total Variation Based Noise Removal Algorithms, Phisica D 60, North Holland (1992) 259–268
5. Bookstein, F. L.: Principal Warps: Thin-Plate Splines and the Decomposition of Deformations, IEEE Trans. on Pattern Analysis and Machine Intelligence, Vol. 11 (1989) 567–585
6. Kašpar, R.: Reducing Noise in IR Images, Master's Thesis, Faculty of Mathematics and Physics, Charles University in Prague (2002)

The D-Dimensional Inverse Vector-Gradient Operator and Its Application for Scale-Free Image Enhancement

Piet W. Verbeek and Judith Dijk

Delft University of Technology, Faculty of Applied Sciences
Pattern Recognition Group, Lorentzweg 1
2628CJ Delft The Netherlands
piet@ph.tn.tudelft.nl

Abstract. A class of enhancement techniques is proposed for images in arbitrary dimension *D*. They are free from either space/frequency (scale) or grey references. There are two subclasses. One subclass is the chain: {Negative Laplace operator, Multiplication by Power (γ–1) of modulus-Laplace value, Inverse Negative Laplace operator} together with generalized versions. The generalization of the Negative Laplace operator consists of replacing its isotropic frequency square transfer function by an (equally isotropic) modulus-frequency to-the-power-*p* transfer-function. The inverse is defined accordingly. The second subclass is the chain: {Vector-Gradient operator, Multiplication by Power (γ–1) of modulus-gradient value, Inverse Vector-Gradient operator} together with generalized versions. We believe the Inverse Vector-Gradient operator (and its generalized version) to be a novel operation in image processing. The generalization of the Vector-Gradient operator consists of multiplying its transfer functions by an isotropic modulus-frequency to-the-power-(p–1) transfer-function. The inverse is defined accordingly. Although the generalized (Inverse) Negative Laplace and Vector-Gradient operators are best implemented via the frequency domain, their point spread functions are checked for too large footprints in order to avoid spatial aliasing in practical (periodic image) implementations. The limitations of frequency-power *p* for given dimension *D* are studied.

1 Introduction

Scale-free operators in image processing are operators that contain no reference length, reference frequency or reference grey value. A scale-free operation is based on a function of the form $out = in^{power}$. Examples are spatial differentiation, where the Fourier transform is multiplied by $frequency^{power}$ and grey-value gamma-correction where $out_{grey} = \left(in_{grey}\right)^{\gamma}$. In practice regularization may introduce a reference, but we shall assume it to be far outside the range of interest.

We shall apply scale-free operators to image enhancement in a three step way. First we use a scale-free derivative operator, next we process the derivative i.e. we apply a gamma correction (e.g. to reduce small derivatives probably due to noise) and then we apply the (again scale-free) inverse of the derivative operator. The method can be similarly applied when the second step is replaced by a (noisy) transmission channel. Then the third step is reconstruction or de-emphasis.

N. Petkov and M.A. Westenberg (Eds.): CAIP 2003, LNCS 2756, pp. 738–745, 2003.

A similar approach has been proposed by Fattal et al. [3] for contrast compression of the logarithm of luminance in 2D images. They perform a numerical reconstruction, as they cannot guarantee integrability after the non-linear operation (cf. our gamma correction). We shall show this to be a minor problem in 2D images.

A series of *D*-dimensional derivative operators and corresponding inverse operators is studied, for arbitrary dimension. The simplest are the Negative-Laplace operator (frequency power =2) and the first derivative along a line, which is anisotropic. The direction average of reconstructions from the latter is isotropic. The (vector-)gradient is also isotropic. So far no reconstruction from the vector-gradient was available. We shall prove that the direction average of reconstructions from the first derivative along a line is equivalent to a reconstruction from the vector-gradient. Thus we have found the inverse vector-gradient operator.

Like the Negative-Laplace operator and its inverse also the vector-gradient and its inverse can be generalized to arbitrary frequency power and be used for enhancement or pre-emphasis / de-emphasis. For frequency to the power zero the generalized vector gradient is a multidimensional Vector Hilbert Transform as discussed by Felsberg and Sommer [4].

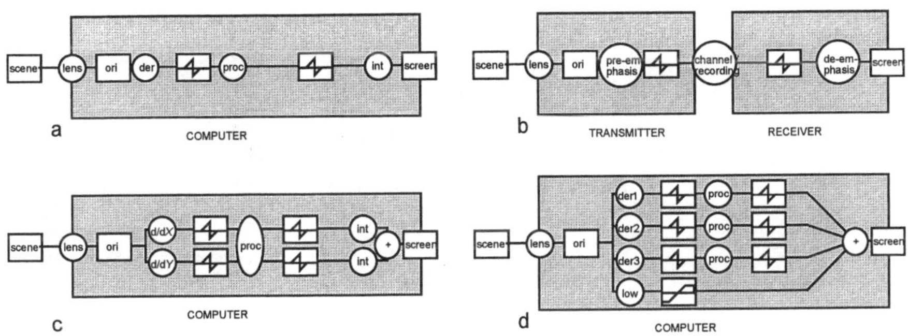

Fig. 1. Related methods (ori=image of the scene, der=derivative, proc=(non-linear) point operation, int=integrating reconstruction). a) Derivative enhancement. b) Pre-emphasized transmission. c) Vector Gradient enhancement. d) Granlund enhancement [1].

2 Related Methods

The derivative methods (fig.1a) are high emphasis methods like the ones used in the (one dimensional) Dolby system for audio recording and in coding systems for signal transmission (fig.1b). Such systems lack the vector approach of the vector-gradient method (fig.1c). Indeed, the vector approach is present in the enhancement methods of the Granlund school [1]. The Transfer Functions of Granlund's directed derivative filters are carefully made to add to an isotropic sum. The essential difference with the vector-gradient method is that no integration step is applied. Instead the low frequencies are removed before processing and reinstalled in the last step (fig.1d).

3 Reconstruction from the Directed Line Derivative

A simple model for derivative and integration is the single line 1D model (fig.2a). The derivative along an X'-direction (direction vector $\vec{n}$) can be integrated along that direction starting from a zero reference rim around the image, which may be extended to infinity. Differentiation followed by integration yields the identity operator, such that the output image equals the input image, $O = I$

$$O_{\vec{n}}(X',,Y') = \int_{X'_{ref}-X'}^{0} dx'[dI(x'+X',,Y')/dx']$$

Expressed in the usual image coordinates $\vec{X} \equiv (X,,Y)$

$$O_{\vec{n}}(\vec{X}) = \int_{-\infty}^{0} dx'\vec{n} \bullet \vec{\nabla} I(x'\vec{n}+\vec{X})$$

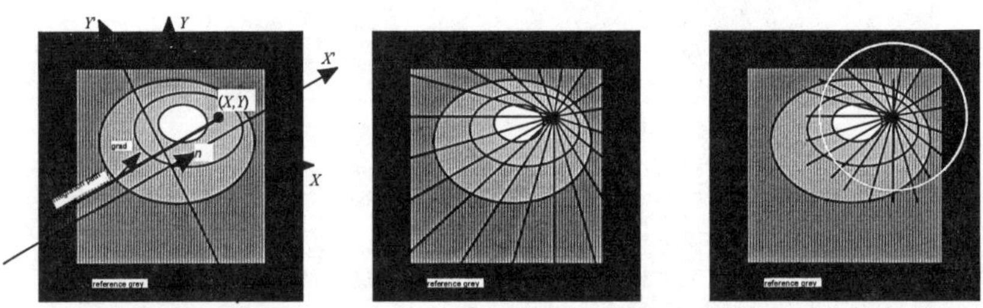

Fig. 2. 1D derivatives and integration. a. Single oriented line. b. Average of many lines in different orientations. c. Average of many lines with limited range integration footprint.

4 Reconstruction from the Vector Gradient

There is no natural preferred X'-direction. Hence an average of directed line reconstructions is a better (more transmission noise robust) method (fig.2b)

$$O(\vec{X}) = \frac{1}{\sum_{\vec{n}} 1} \sum_{\vec{n}} O_{\vec{n}}(\vec{X}) = \frac{1}{S(D)} \int d\Omega \int_0^{\infty} dr \frac{\vec{x}}{-r} \bullet \vec{\nabla} I(\vec{x}+\vec{X})$$

with $\vec{x} = x'\vec{n}, \quad r \equiv |\vec{x}| = -x'$ and full solid angle $S(D) = \int d\Omega$

where $S(D=2m) = D\pi^m / m!, \quad S(D=2m+1) = D\pi^m 2^D m!/D!$

e.g. $S(1) = 2,\ S(2) = 2\pi,\ S(3) = 4\pi$.

Moreover, as

$$\int_{image} d\vec{x}\, f(\vec{x}) \equiv \iint_{image} dx..dy\, f(\vec{x}) = \int d\Omega \int dr\, r^{D-1} f(\vec{x}) \Rightarrow \int d\Omega \int dr\, g(\vec{x}) = \int_{image} d\vec{x}\, \frac{g(\vec{x})}{r^{D-1}}$$

the average of directed line reconstructions can be written as a sum of convolutions

$$O(\vec{X}) = -\frac{1}{S(D)} \int_{image} d\vec{x}\, \left|\vec{x}\right|^{-D} \vec{x} \bullet \vec{\nabla} I(\vec{x}+\vec{X}) = \sum_{k=1}^{D} \left\{ \frac{X_k}{S(D)\left|\vec{X}\right|^{D}} \right\} * \left\{ \frac{\partial I(\vec{X})}{\partial X_k} \right\}$$

In the frequency domain this can only correspond to the identity

$$\tilde{O}(\vec{u}) = \sum_{k=1}^{D} \left\{ \frac{-2\pi i u_k}{(2\pi\left|\vec{u}\right|)^2} \right\} \left\{ 2\pi i u_k\ \tilde{I}(\vec{u}) \right\} \equiv \tilde{I}(\vec{u}) \quad \text{based on} \quad \frac{\vec{u}}{\left|\vec{u}\right|^2} \bullet \vec{u} \equiv 1.$$

Thus we have found that the reconstruction corresponding to the vector gradient operator, the inverse vector-gradient operator, is a sum of axis-wise convolutions with the (Integration) Point Spread Functions (IPSF's)

$$\frac{X_k}{S(D)\, R^D} \quad \text{with} \quad R \equiv \left|\vec{X}\right|.$$

The (Integration) Transfer Functions (ITF's) corresponding to these IPSF's are

$$\frac{-2\pi i u_k}{(2\pi\rho)^2} \quad with \quad \rho \equiv \left|\vec{u}\right|.$$

Note that only D convolutions are needed to get the average over all directions.
The vector gradient model is seen to have a Derivative Transfer Function with characteristic power of frequency p=1.

We generalize the vector gradient to arbitrary p inserting an isotropic factor $(2\pi\rho)^{p-1}$.

5 Derivative Operators and Their Inverse Operators (Integrations)

According to the chain (cf. fig. 1c)

{Derivative operator, Non-linear Point Processing, Inverse Derivative operator}
a variety of enhancement methods can be constructed. Table 1 gives a survey of the derivatives to be chosen. The integrations are up to zero-derivative terms. The derivation of the Fourier transforms is given in [2]. The functions α and β allow non-integer powers of frequency. They are based on the Γ-function and defined in Table 2. Integrations can be of limited range (IPSF truncated by Gaussian, fig. 1c).

In implementations we avoid the infinities of IPSF's or ITF's using Cauchy functions $(R^2+T^2)^{-1}$ instead of R^{-2} and $(\rho^2+\tau^2)^{-1}$ instead of ρ^{-2}. Cauchy functions are related to electronic-integration where τ = resistance × capacity.

Table 1. Derivatives and their inverses: reconstructions by integration. D is the dimension. p is the characteristic (also non-integer) power of frequency in the Derivative Transfer Function. Note that for p=0 the Generalized Vector Gradient and its Inverse are equal to the Vector Hilbert Transform and its Inverse as discussed in [4].

Derivative Type	Derivative DPSF	Derivative DTF	Integration ITF	Integration IPSF
	$R \equiv \lvert\vec{X}\rvert$	$\rho \equiv \lvert\vec{u}\rvert$		$R \equiv \lvert\vec{X}\rvert$
Directed Line Der.	d^n / dX'^n	$(2\pi i u')^n$	$(2\pi i u')^{-n}$	$\left(\int dX'\right)^n$
Negative Laplace	$-\nabla^2$	$(2\pi\rho)^2$	$(2\pi\rho)^{-2}$	$R^{2-D}\alpha(2,D)$ $D-2 \neq 0$
(Negative Laplace)^n	$\left\{-\nabla^2\right\}^n$	$(2\pi\rho)^{2n}$	$(2\pi\rho)^{-2n}$	$R^{2n-D}\alpha(2n,D)$ $D-2n \neq 0,-2,-4,$
General-ized NL	$R^{-p-D}\alpha(-p,D)$ $-p,\ D+p \neq 0,-2,-4,$	$(2\pi\rho)^p$	$(2\pi\rho)^{-p}$	$R^{p-D}\alpha(p,D)$ $p,\ D-p \neq 0,-2,-4$
Vector Gradient	$\vec{\nabla}$	$2\pi i\vec{u}$	$-(2\pi\rho)^{-2}\, 2\pi i\vec{u}$	$R^{-D}\ \beta(1,D)\ \vec{X}$ $\beta(1,D)=1/S(D)$
VG (NL)^n	$\vec{\nabla}\left\{-\nabla^2\right\}^n$	$(2\pi\rho)^{2n}\, 2\pi i\vec{u}$	$-(2\pi\rho)^{-2n-2}\, 2\pi i\vec{u}$	$R^{-D}\ \beta(2n+1,D)\ \vec{X}$ $D-2n \neq 0,-2,-4,$
General-ized VG	$R^{-(D+p)-1}\beta(-p,D)\ \vec{X}$ $-p+1, D+p+1 \neq 0,-2,-4,$	$(2\pi\rho)^{p-1}\, 2\pi i\vec{u}$	$-(2\pi\rho)^{-p-1}\, 2\pi i\vec{u}$	$R^{-(D-p)-1}\ \beta(p,D)\vec{X}$ $p+1, D-p+1 \neq 0,-2,-4,$
Modulus of Grad	$\lvert\vec{\nabla} I\rvert$		Grey-weighted Distance Transform	

Table 2. The functions α and β that allow non-integer powers of frequency.

$\alpha(p,D) \equiv 2^{-p}\pi^{-D/2}\,\Gamma\big((D-p)/2\big)/\Gamma\big(p/2\big),$	$p,\ D-p \neq 0,-2,-4,$
$\beta(p,D) \equiv 2^{-p}\pi^{-D/2}\Gamma((D-(p-1))/2)/\Gamma((p+1)/2),$	$p+1,\ D-(p-1) \neq 0,-2,-4,$
$(D-(p+1))\alpha(p+1,D) = \beta(p,D) = \alpha(p-1,D)\big/(p-1)$	

6 Limited Range Integration

Although the generalized (Inverse) Negative-Laplace and Vector-Gradient operators are best implemented via the frequency domain, their point spread functions are checked for too large footprints in order to avoid spatial aliasing in practical implementations (with periodic images, like in discrete and fast Fourier transforms).

We emulate limited range by truncation of the IPSF by a Gaussian window $W(\vec{X})$, with standard deviation σ_{Gauss}, e.g. for the Vector Gradient model (fig.1c)

$$O(\vec{X}) = \sum_{k=1}^{D}\left\{W(\vec{X})\ X_k\ S^{-1}(D)\ R^{-D}\right\} * \left\{\partial I(\vec{X})/\partial X_k\right\}$$

In the frequency domain this reads as applying a smoothed ITF

$$\tilde{W}(\vec{u}) * [(2\pi\rho)^{-2}\, 2\pi i u_k].$$

Also in the other models truncated integration is tantamount to a smoothed ITF, i.e. $\tilde{W}(\vec{u})*(2\pi\rho)^{-2}$ for the Negative-Laplacemodel, $\tilde{W}(\vec{u})*(2\pi\rho)^{-p}$ for the Generalized NL-model and $\tilde{W}(\vec{u})*(2\pi\rho)^{-p-1}2\pi i u_k$ for the Generalized Vector Gradient model. How do the different derivatives react to truncated integration? In our two-dimensional experiment (D=2) the GVG integration allows IPSF truncation without problems whereas the GNL integration is very sensitive to truncation of its IPSF. The reason might be the following.

In the frequency domain the GNL-ITF $(\rho^2)^{-p/2}$ (or in practice $(\rho^2+\tau^2)^{-p/2}$) has a (very) sharp peak at zero frequency (0,0) which is blunted by the smoothing. The GVG-ITF components $(\rho^2)^{(-p-1)/2}$ (iu_k) have zero crossings at u_1=0 and u_2=0 respectively, the zero value of which is not affected by the smoothing.

7 Derivative Enhancement

The different types of derivatives constitute as many image representations. In each representation one can apply a non-linear operation. In particular a non-linear function can be applied (point operation). Reconstruction by integration then yields a non linearly processed image. By an appropriate choice of the non-linear function the processing can be made an enhancement.

Noise suppression can be achieved by removing or reducing small modulus-derivatives (this encompasses the vector gradient). As a reference for what is small one can take the maximum modulus encountered in the image. This emulates the automatic contrast stretching we are used to in our luminance perception. For the reduction one may think of several functions of relative modulus-derivative: thresholding, smooth thresholding, and symmetric gammacorrection. We shall use the latter in our tests. The non-linear point operation

$$out_{grey} = \operatorname{sign}\left(in_{grey}\right)\left|in_{grey}\right|^{\gamma} = \left|in_{grey}\right|^{\gamma-1} in_{grey}$$

is applied to the derivatives: the (G)NL or the components of the (G)VG.

For $\gamma>1$ this produces noise suppression, as demonstrated in fig. 3, for $\gamma<1$ it compresses contrast as in [3].

8 Integrability of 2D Vector-Gradient Field after Non-linear Point-Operation

Fattal et al. [3] propose the chain {Vector Gradient operator, Multiplication by a function of Modulus Gradient, Numerical Inversion of Vector Gradient} for contrast compression of the logarithm of luminance in two-dimensional images. Following a long tradition of discretized or iterative solution schemes [5, 6, 7] they perform a numerical reconstruction, as they cannot guarantee integrability of the multiplication result (our gamma correction) for other than globally one dimensional images.

We shall show this to be a minor problem as it is sufficient that the image is locally one-dimensional. So the numerical reconstruction can be avoided.

The first step in the chain is to produce the image vector gradient

$$(\partial I/\partial X, \partial I/\partial Y) \equiv (I_X, I_Y) \text{ with modulus } M \equiv \left(I_X^2 + I_Y^2\right)^{\frac{1}{2}}$$

Note that a vector gradient (V_1, V_2) is a special kind of vector field in that it satisfies

$$\partial V_1/\partial Y - \partial V_2/\partial X = 0 \tag{1}$$

The second step, the multiplication of the image vector gradient by a function of modulus gradient yields a product (e.g. for the gamma correction $\Phi(M) = M^{\gamma-1}$)

$$(P_1, P_2) \equiv \Phi(M)\,(I_X, I_Y)$$

In general $\Phi(M) \neq 1$ is a *dis*integrating factor, the product is not a vector gradient

$$\partial P_1/\partial Y - \partial P_2/\partial X \neq 0 \tag{2}$$

and in general it cannot be integrated to a result image.

In [3] this is put forward as a problem unless I is *globally* one-dimensional. Our D-dimensional method always gives a result, the average of 1-D integrations

$$O_\Phi(\vec{X}) = \sum_{k=1}^{D} \left\{X_k\; S^{-1}(D)\; R^{-D}\right\} * P_k$$

What can go wrong is that $\partial O_\Phi/\partial X_j \neq P_j$. The relation with eq. 2 is

$$\partial O_\Phi/\partial X_j = P_j + \sum_{k=1}^{D} \left\{X_k\; S^{-1}(D)\; R^{-D}\right\} * \left\{\partial P_k/\partial X_j - \partial P_j/\partial X_k\right\}$$

For arbitrary two-dimensional I we check eq. 2 and find

$$\begin{aligned}
&\partial P_1/\partial Y - \partial P_2/\partial X = \partial\Phi I_X/\partial Y - \partial\Phi I_Y/\partial X = \\
&= \Phi_Y I_X + \Phi I_{XY} - \Phi_X I_Y - \Phi I_{XY} = \Phi_M M_Y I_X - \Phi_M M_X I_Y = \\
&= \tfrac{1}{2}\Phi_M M^{-1}\left(2I_{XY}(I_X^2 - I_Y^2) - 2I_X I_Y (I_{XX} - I_{YY})\right) = \\
&= \tfrac{1}{2}\Phi_M M\; (\max I_{X'X'} - \min I_{X'X'})\,\sin(2\phi - 2\theta)
\end{aligned}$$

where θ and ϕ are the orientations of largest modulus gradient and largest second derivative of I respectively.

In *locally* one-dimensional images [1] which have local translation or rotation invariance these orientations coincide and eq. 1 is satisfied. In *locally* one-dimensional images the result of the non-linear multiplication of the vector gradient by a function of gradient size is integrable.

9 Conclusions

The Inverse Vector Gradient operator is introduced. It can be applied in image transmission and has been succesfully used for scale-free image enhancement.
A survey of generalizations is given for arbitrary dimension. One of these is the Vector Hilbert Transform.

Gradient manipulation through multiplication by an arbitrary function of modulus gradient is seen to allow reconstruction by the Inverse Vector Gradient operator if the image is two-dimensional and locally one-dimensional as commonly assumed.

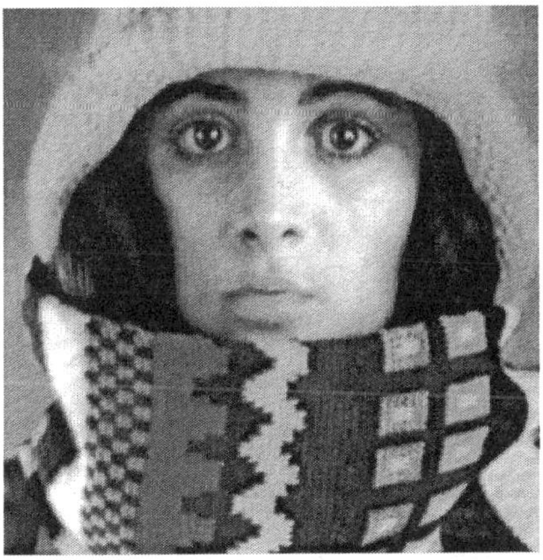

Fig. 3a. Noisefree image 256^2 (0,255)

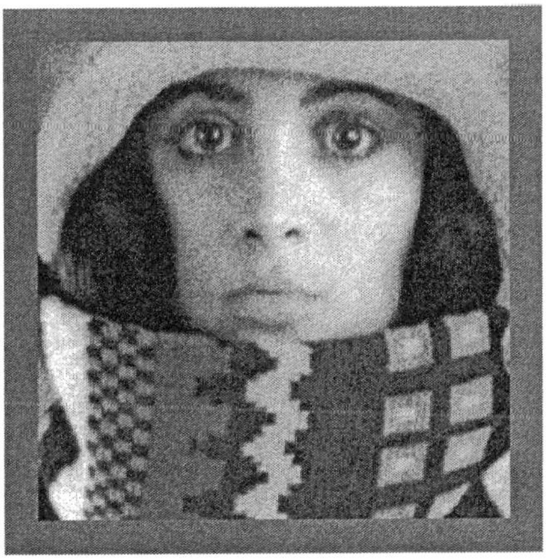

Fig. 3b. Uniform noise added (−12, 12)

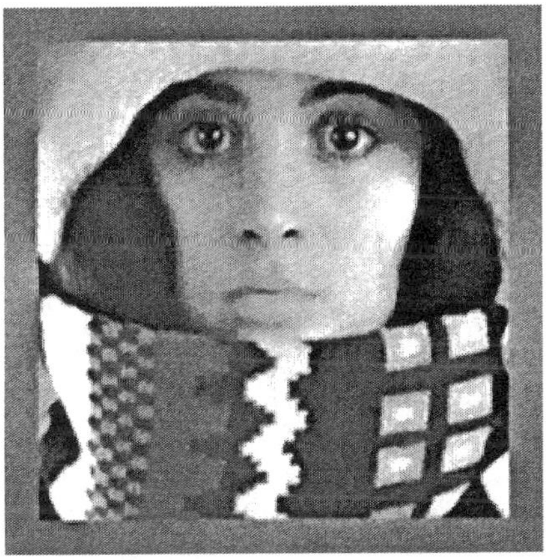

Fig. 3c. Vector Gradient enhanced, σ_{Gauss}=40, T=10^{-6}, γ=1.8

References

1. Granlund, G.H., H. Knutsson: Signal Processing for Computer Vision. Kluwer Academic Publishers (1994)
2. Verbeek, P.W.: Technical report PH 1123. (2001)
3. Fattal, R., D. Lischinski, M. Werman: Gradient domain high dynamic range compression. ACM Transactions on Graphics (Proc. ACM SIGGRAPH 2002) (2002)
4. Felsberg M., G. Sommer: The Monogenic Signal. IEEE Trans. Signal Processing, Vol. 49 **12** (2001) 3136-3144
5. Frankot R.T., R. Chellappa: A method of enforcing integrability in shape from shading algorithms. IEEE PAMI, Vol. 10 **4** (1988) 439-451
6. Simchony T., R. Chellappa, M. Shao: Direct analytical methods for solving Poisson equations in computer vision problems. IEEE PAMI, Vol. 12 **5** (1990) 435-446
7. Noakes L., R. Kozera: 2D Leap-Frog: Integrability Noise and Digitization. LNCS, 2243 (2001) 352-364

A Simple and Efficient Algorithm for Detection of High Curvature Points in Planar Curves*

Dmitry Chetverikov

Computer and Automation Research Institute
1111 Budapest, Kende u.13-17, Hungary
`http://visual.ipan.sztaki.hu`

Abstract. A new algorithm is presented for detection of corners and other high curvature points in planar curves. A corner is defined as a location where a triangle with specified opening angle and size can be inscribed in the curve. The tests compare the new algorithm to four alternative algorithms for corner detection.

Keywords: Planar curves, curvature, corner detection, algorithms

1 Introduction

This paper deals with detection of high curvature points in planar curves. It is well known [1] that these points play a dominant role in shape perception by humans. Locations of significant changes in curve slope are in that respect similar to intensity edges. If these characteristic contour points are identified properly, a shape can be represented in an efficient and compact way with accuracy sufficient in many shape analysis problems.

Corner detection in planar curves is related to corner detection in grayscale images which is not addressed here. Characteristic contour points have traditionally been in the focus of the scale space theory [7] that allows for a 'natural', although sophisticated and computationally demanding, definition of such points at varying scale. However, in many real-time applications, especially in industry, processing time is a crucial issue. Computational load should be minimised without significant loss of robustness.

Various less complicated corner detection algorithms have been developed. A number of frequently cited approaches are discussed in the survey by Liu and Srinath [5], where comparative experimental results are also given. Four of the algorithms considered in [5] are used in our tests as well, namely those by Rosenfeld and Johnston [8], Rosenfeld and Weszka[9], Freeman and Davis [4], and Beus and Tiu [2]. In this paper, these algorithms are referred to as RJ73, RW75, FD77, and BT87, respectively. RW75 is a modification of RJ73, while BT87 is a modification of FD77. A summary of the four algorithms is given in section 2.

Although the notion of corner seems to be intuitively clear, no generally accepted mathematical definition exists, at least for digital curves. In a sense,

* This work was supported by grants OTKA T026592 and M28078.

N. Petkov and M.A. Westenberg (Eds.): CAIP 2003, LNCS 2756, pp. 746–753, 2003.

different approaches give different — but conceptually related — computational definitions to a visual phenomenon. The lack of ground truth makes comparative performance evaluation tests less significant than they could be.

In this paper we present a new, fast and efficient algorithm for detection of high curvature points. (For simplicity, they will be called 'corner points'.) The algorithm is called the IPAN Corner Detector; IPAN stands for Image and Pattern Analysis group. An online Internet demo of the IPAN Corner Detector has been available since early 2000. A remote user can compare our algorithm to four other techniques. This paper is mainly motivated by the popularity of the demo and the frequent requests for description and software.

The parameters of the IPAN Corner Detector are easy to understand and tune to particular sharpness and scale. The algorithm is described in section 3. Experimental results shown in section 4 compare the our method to the alternative methods mentioned above.

2 A Summary of Four Corner Detectors

This section gives a brief summary of the four alternative corner detection algorithms used in our tests. The summary is based on the survey [5] by Liu and Srinath. This study mentions three other techniques, which are not considered in the present paper. Two of them, Medioni-Yasumoto [6] and Cheng-Hsu [3], were found in [5] to be very noise-sensitive. The third one, the weighted-K-curvature corner detector [10], needs selection of a large set of weights; no procedure for this is given. Liu and Srinath conclude that the Beus-Tiu detector [2] seems to best correspond to human perception of corners.

Each corner detector inputs a chain-coded curve, which is converted into a connected sequence of grid points $\mathbf{p}_i = (x_i, y_i)$, $i = 1, 2 \ldots, N$. A measure of corner strength is assigned to each point, then corner points are selected based on this measure. For each approach, we summarise these two main steps and list the parameters of the algorithm and their default ('best') values. The setting of the parameters is discussed in more detail in section 4.

When processing a point $\mathbf{p}_i$, the algorithms consider a number of the previous and subsequent points as candidates for the arms of a potential corner in $\mathbf{p}_i$. For a positive integer k, the forward and the backward *k-vectors* in $\mathbf{p}_i$ are defined as

$$\mathbf{a}_{ik} = (x_i - x_{i+k}, y_i - y_{i+k}) = (X_{ik}^+, Y_{ik}^+) \tag{1}$$

$$\mathbf{b}_{ik} = (x_i - x_{i-k}, y_i - y_{i-k}) = (X_{ik}^-, Y_{ik}^-) \tag{2}$$

where X_{ik}^+, Y_{ik}^+ and X_{ik}^-, Y_{ik}^- are the components of $\mathbf{a}_{ik}$ and $\mathbf{b}_{ik}$, respectively.

2.1 Rosenfeld and Johnston RJ73

Corner Strength. The k-cosine of the angle between the k-vectors is used, which is defined as

$$c_{ik} = \frac{(\mathbf{a}_{ik} \cdot \mathbf{b}_{ik})}{|\mathbf{a}_{ik}||\mathbf{b}_{ik}|} \tag{3}$$

Selection Procedure. Starting from $m = \kappa N$, k is decremented until c_{ik} stops to increase: $c_{im} < c_{i,m-1} < \ldots < c_{in} \not< c_{i,n-1}$. The value $k = n$ is then selected as the best value for the point i. A corner is indicated in i if $c_{in} > c_{jp}$ for all j such that $|i - j| \leq n/2$, where p is the best value of k for the point j.

Parameter. The single parameter κ specifies the maximum considered value of k as a fraction of the total number of curve points N. This limits the length of an arm at κN. The default value is $\kappa = 0.05$.

2.2 Rosenfeld and Weszka RW75

Corner Strength. The average k-cosine of the angle between the k-vectors is used, defined as

$$\bar{c}_{ik} = \begin{cases} \frac{2}{k+2} \sum\limits_{t=k/2}^{k} c_{it} & \text{if } k \text{ is even,} \\ \frac{2}{k+3} \sum\limits_{t=(k-1)/2}^{k} c_{it} & \text{if } k \text{ is odd,} \end{cases} \tag{4}$$

where c_{it} are given by (3).

Selection Procedure. Same as in RJ73, but for $\bar{c}_{ik}$.

Parameter. Same as in RJ73, with the same default $\kappa = 0.05$.

2.3 Freeman and Davis FD77

Corner Strength. In a point i, the angle between the x-axis and the backward k-vector defined in (2) is given by

$$\theta_{ik} = \begin{cases} \tan^{-1}(Y_{ik}^{-}/X_{ik}^{-}) & \text{if } |X_{ik}^{-}| \geq |Y_{ik}^{-}|, \\ \cot^{-1}(X_{ik}^{-}/Y_{ik}^{-}) & \text{otherwise,} \end{cases}$$

The incremental curvature is then defined as

$$\delta_{ik} = \theta_{i+1,k} - \theta_{i-1,k} \tag{5}$$

Finally, the k-strength in i is computed as

$$S_{ik} = \ln t_1 \cdot \ln t_2 \cdot \sum_{j=i}^{i+k} \delta_{jk} \tag{6}$$

where

$$t_1 = \max\{t : \delta_{i-v,k} \in (-\Delta, \Delta), \forall\, 1 \leq v \leq t\} \text{ and}$$
$$t_2 = \max\{t : \delta_{i+k+v,k} \in (-\Delta, \Delta), \forall\, 1 \leq v \leq t\}$$

account for the effect of the forward and backward arms as the maximum spacings (numbers of steps from i) that still keep the incremental curvature δ_{ik} within the limit $\pm\Delta$. The latter is set as

$$\Delta = \arctan\frac{1}{k-1} \tag{7}$$

Selection Procedure. A point i is selected as a corner if S_{ik} exceeds a given threshold S and individual corners are separated by a spacing of at least $k+1$ steps.

Parameters. The two parameters are the spacing k and the corner strength threshold S. The default values are $k = 5$ and $S = 1500$.

2.4 Beus and Tiu BT87

Corner Strength. Similar to FD77, with the following modifications. The arm cutoff parameter τ is introduced to specify the upper limit for t_1 and t_2 as a fraction of N:

$$t_1 = \max\{t : \delta_{i-v,k} \in (-\Delta, \Delta), \forall\ 1 \le v \le t,\ \text{and } t \le \tau N\}$$
$$t_2 = \max\{t : \delta_{i+k+v,k} \in (-\Delta, \Delta), \forall\ 1 \le v \le t,\ \text{and } t \le \tau N\},$$

where δ_{ik} and Δ are given by (5) and (7), respectively. The corner strength is obtained by averaging (6) between two values k_1 and k_2:

$$S_i = \frac{1}{k_2 - k_1 + 1}\sum_{k=k_1}^{k_2} S_{ik} \tag{8}$$

Selection Procedure. Same as in FD77.

Parameters. The four parameters are the averaging limits k_1 and k_2, the arm cutoff parameter τ, and the corner strength threshold S. The default values are $k_1 = 4$, $k_2 = 7$, $\tau = 0.05$, and $S = 1500$.

3 The New Algorithm

The proposed two-pass algorithm defines a corner in a simple and intuitively appealing way, as a location where a triangle of specified size and opening angle can be inscribed in the curve. A curve is represented by a sequence of points $\mathbf{p}_i$ in the plane. The ordered points are densely sampled along the curve, but, contrary to the other four algorithms, no regular spacing between them is assumed. A chain-coded curve can also be handled if converted to a sequence of grid points. In the first pass the algorithm scans the sequence and selects candidate corner points. The second pass is a post-processing step to remove superfluous candidates.

First Pass. In each curve point $\mathbf{p}$ the detector tries to inscribe in the curve a variable triangle $(\mathbf{p}^-, \mathbf{p}, \mathbf{p}^+)$. The triangle is constrained by a set of simple rules:

$$\begin{aligned} d_{min}^2 &\le \|\mathbf{p} - \mathbf{p}^+\|^2 \le d_{max}^2 \\ d_{min}^2 &\le \|\mathbf{p} - \mathbf{p}^-\|^2 \le d_{max}^2 \\ 0 &\le |\alpha| \le \alpha_{max}, \end{aligned} \tag{9}$$

where $\|\mathbf{p} - \mathbf{q}\|$ is the distance between points $\mathbf{p}$ and $\mathbf{q}$ and $\alpha \in [-\pi, \pi]$ is the opening angle of the triangle.

The limits d_{min}, d_{max} and α_{max} are the parameters of the algorithm. Those variations of the triangle that satisfy the conditions (9) are called *admissible*. The search for the admissible variations starts from $\mathbf{p}$ outwards and stops if any of the conditions (9) is violated. That is, a limited number of neighbouring points is only considered.

Among the admissible variations, the least opening angle $|\alpha(\mathbf{p})|$ is selected. The angle $\beta(\mathbf{p}) = \pi - |\alpha(\mathbf{p})|$ is assigned to $\mathbf{p}$ as the *sharpness* of the candidate. If no admissible triangle can be inscribed, $\mathbf{p}$ is rejected and no sharpness is assigned.

Second Pass. A corner detector can respond to the same corner in a few consecutive points. Similarly to edge detection, a post-processing step is needed to select the strongest response by discarding the non-maxima points. A candidate point $\mathbf{p}$ is discarded if it has a *valid neighbour* $\mathbf{p}_v$ which is sharper than $\mathbf{p}$: $\beta(\mathbf{p}_v) > \beta(\mathbf{p})$. In the current implementation, another candidate point $\mathbf{p}_v$ is a valid neighbour of $\mathbf{p}$ if $\|\mathbf{p} - \mathbf{p}_v\|^2 \le d_{max}^2$. Alternatively, one can use d_{min}^2 instead of d_{max}^2. Still another possibility is to simply consider the points adjacent to $\mathbf{p}$.

Parameters. The IPAN Corner Detector has three parameters: d_{min}, d_{max} and α_{max}. d_{min} sets the scale (resolution), with small values responding to fine corners. The upper limit d_{max} is necessary to avoid false sharp triangles formed by distant points in highly varying curves. In practice, we usually set $d_{max} = d_{min} + 2$ and tune the remaining two parameters, d_{min} and α_{max}. This was done in the tests as well. Parameter α_{max} is the angle limit that determines the minimum sharpness accepted as high curvature. The default values are $d_{min} = 7$ and $\alpha_{max} = 150°$.

4 Tests

Five corner detection algorithms were implemented and tested. One of them is the proposed algorithm, while the other four are those listed in section 2. The test shapes were taken from the study [5]. The printed images of [5] were scanned, which introduced some noise into the original noise-free pictures. In addition, some random noise was added to the scanned images to better test the robustness of the algorithms.

To evaluate performance of corner detectors, one needs a large reference database with ground truth. Such databases are available for edge detection.

Fig. 1. Results of RJ73.

Unfortunately, to our best knowledge, no ground-truthed database has been created for corner detection. Partially, this is because the notion of a corner seems to be more task-dependent and subjective than the notion of an intensity edge.

Traditionally, standard collections of shapes have been used to compare corner detectors. The collection we use has also appeared in several studies, including that by Liu and Srinath [5]. However, our version is slightly different because of the scanning and the differently generated noise.

A more important difference lies in the handling of the parameters of an algorithm. Liu and Srinath tune the parameters to each of the shapes separately, so as to obtain the best possible result for each particular shape. In most practical tasks, there is no way to manually set the parameters for each particular input. For this reason, we decided to consider the default 'best' values, as those values that provide the best overall performance for the whole collection of the input shapes. These default values were given in sections 2 and 3. Only when the default parameters gave an obviously poor result, they were modified until the best possible output was obtained. Because of the lack of ground truth, a subjective judgement of detection quality was used.

The main pictorial results are displayed in figures 1–5. Our algorithm distinguishes convex and concave corners, which are marked differently. The algorithm works reasonably well with the default values in all the eight cases. FD77 and BT87 need more frequent modification of their parameters. (For BT87, only S had to be varied.) However, if this is done, they usually yield better results than the other two techniques; this is consistent with the study [5]. Because the parameters were not tuned to each shape, the overall performance of the four alternative algorithms is worse than that reported in [5].

5 Conclusion

We have presented a new corner detection algorithm and compared it to four other techniques. Our experience shows that the proposed algorithm is easy to

Fig. 2. Results of RW75.

Fig. 3. Results of FD77.

Fig. 4. Results of BT87.

use, fast and reliable. It competes with the other techniques in detection performance, while being more stable under changing input data. Another positive feature is that its principle of operation and its results are easy to understand. Consequently, one can find the reason of a failure and figure out if and how the result can be improved.

Fig. 5. Results of IPAN for the default parameter values.

The corner detection algorithms described in this paper are available for online testing over the Internet at the web site of the IPAN research group.

References

1. H. Asada and M. Brady. The curvature primal sketch. *IEEE Trans. Pattern Analysis and Machine Intelligence*, 8:2–14, 1986.
2. H.L. Beus and S.S.H. Tiu. An improved corner detection algorithm based on chain-coded plane curves. *Pattern Recognition*, 20:291–296, 1987.
3. F. Cheng and W. Hsu. Parallel algorithm for corner finding on digital curves. *Pattern Recognition Lett.*, 8:47–53, 1988.
4. H. Freeman and L.S. Davis. A corner finding algorithm for chain-coded curves. *IEEE Trans. Computers*, 26:297–303, 1977.
5. H.-C. Liu and M.D. Srinath. Corner detection from chain-code. *Pattern Recognition*, 23:51–68, 1990.
6. G. Medioni and Y. Yasumoto. Corner detection and curve representation using cubic *B*-splines. *Comput. Vision Graphics Image Process*, 39:267–278, 1987.
7. F. Mokhtarian and A.K. Mackworth. A theory of multiscale, curvature-based shape representation for planar curves. *IEEE Trans. Pattern Analysis and Machine Intelligence*, 14:789–805, 1992.
8. A. Rosenfeld and E. Johnston. Angle detection on digital curves. *IEEE Trans. Computers*, 22:875–878, 1973.
9. A. Rosenfeld and J.S. Weszka. An improved method of angle detection on digital curves. *IEEE Trans. Computers*, 24:940–941, 1975.
10. W.S. Rutkowski and A. Rosenfeld. A comparison of corner-detection techniques for chain-coded curves. Technical Report TR-623, Computer Science Center, University of Maryland, 1978.

Modelling Non-linearities in Images Using an Auto-associative Neural Network

Felix Wehrmann and Ewert Bengtsson

Uppsala University, 75237 Uppsala, Sweden
felix@cb.uu.se
http://www.cb.uu.se/~felix

Abstract. In this paper, we address non-linearities in images to approach flexible templates. Templates reflect objects of a single class and are extended to have the special ability to cover the variations present about the object. An auto-associative neural network learns these variations from examples. We consider images to be related to an artificial retina where the appearance of observed objects is represented. From this point of view, non-linear grey-level changes are the consequences of global and local variations of the object. Image variation is considered in a high-dimensional image space. Thus, varying objects from the same class leave a manifold in the image space, which is modeled by the introduced network.

1 Introduction

Images taken from a natural scene are comparable to the information reaching the retina in the eye. An observed object may vary in position, pose, and shape, and therefore affect different regions on the retina. Still, the object can be a sample from the same class. How is it possible to recognise objects subject to such variations?

When prior knowledge about geometry is available, the shape of the object can be modeled with the necessary degree of freedom, thus allowing to extract object information from images according to its shape.

However, often geometry is not easily extracted and this is when adaptive methods get into place. We desire to build flexible templates that cover the variations that objects may be subject to. Moreover, modelling of templates should be on the level of appearance, i.e. how does the image change when the object undergoes variation. A proper description of the appearance is suitably derived from examples of images about the desired object.

The methods addressed take advantage of all the information found in a set of training images, since it is not obvious which parts about an object characterise its appearance. The central aspect is to provide a compact description of the sub-space or manifold the images reside in, which has been examined in various approaches.

In Cootes et al. [3], active appearance models (AAM) are introduced. In combination with a shape model, AAM provide a low-dimensional representation

N. Petkov and M.A. Westenberg (Eds.): CAIP 2003, LNCS 2756, pp. 754–761, 2003.

of the content of images that belong to the same class. The model uses an orthogonal basis spanning a sub-space that encompasses the image contents. The basis consists of the modes of variation, derived from training data by a principal component analysis (PCA), which cover most of the variation found in the images. Once established, the model is in the position to describe unseen images from the same class by means of the new basis, using a comparably small number of parameters.

However, since the sub-space spanned is linear, the data distribution in the image space is assumed ellipsoid-shaped. It is important to note that this is no restriction considering the dimensional reduction of the data, but it limits the use of these models for recognition purposes.

Non-linear appearance modelling has been addressed where more complex data distributions are allowed. In [8], a one-dimensional trajectory of image samples is interpolated in image space using piece-wise linear functions. Another approach by [2] approximates the training data more closely fitting a spline function to the manifold.

Under this scope, our aim is to provide an alternative model that provides the desired variations in an image. It turns out that a solution would involve non-linear functions to provide higher accuracy compared to the previous cases. In this paper, we apply an auto-associative neural network (AANN) to the problem. This type of network is, as discussed in the next section, well suited for the presented task as it can be considered a non-linear PCA with adjustable kernel functions.

This paper restricts itself to a discussion on modelling and does not consider classification of objects. The initial training data for the first experiment is generated artificially, providing only desired, non-linear, variations. Then, an AANN is composed from two non-linear networks and trained on the data. It will create an implicit representation of the data. Finally, the trained network is separated again, providing one network for encoding and one for reconstruction of images. A more realistic application is given at the end.

2 Methods

2.1 Image Data

The training images should reflect non-linear variations that enable us to understand the modeling quality of the neural network. Therefore, we start the examination using generated data that resembles the desired characteristics.

According to the network, images are regarded as a collection of pixels containing grey-level information, aligned on a lattice. Moreover, an image of size $m \times n$ composes a vector $\boldsymbol{x}$ of $N = mn$ pixels, whose values are addressed x_i. Obviously, this vector can be considered an element in an N-dimensional image space, and is therefore called an image vector. For practical reasons, the grey-levels are normalized to range between zero and one.

We turn our attention to the image space. An individual image is equivalent to a single point in the image space. In this manner, a smooth change of the pixels of an image would move the image vector in the image space to a new location. In particular, imaging an object under variation will necessarily establish a subspace or manifold in the image space.

Although we only consider images taken from objects of one single class, variations can occur from different object transformations. For example, the mere translation or rotation of the imaged object produces non-linear changes in the pixels. Moreover, deformations of the object itself have similar effect, as well as changes in illumination. On the other hand, to brighten or darken the image uniformly is a linear transformation.

The appearance of samples from a class of objects is defined as a continuous and parameterized function f that maps an object to an image according to

$$f : R^M \to R^N,\ \boldsymbol{\theta} \to f(\boldsymbol{\theta}).$$

The parameter $\boldsymbol{\theta}$ reflects the (stochastic) transformations of the object, and represents a feature space of dimensionality M.

Initially, we apply the model to images that are subject to rather simple variations. The set of training images reflect a vertical bar shown at different locations, comparable to time series. The bar is drawn as a Gaussian blurred pixel column with high brightness against dark background, i.e. taking values between one and zero. The images are of size 16×16 to restrict the dimensional load on the network.

2.2 Neural Network Model

The heart of the model is a non-linear AANN, as sketched in Figure 1. This particular type of network has originally been used for data compression of different kinds, and is used here to learn the mapping f. The particular design of the network makes it suitable for modelling the desired variations in the data for two reasons. First, the network is capable of representing highly non-linear functions, a feature which lies partly in the transfer function and partly in the inter-connection scheme of the neurons.

Second, the network establishes an intermediate representation of the data in a so called feature space. This is essential for the proposed problem. Since no information about the initial mapping f is available, we would not have anything to train the network on. In particular, regression approaches would not be applicable. AANNs on the other hand comprise two interrelated functions. In a combined adaption procedure the encoding part learns an approximative mapping $\boldsymbol{x} \to \boldsymbol{\theta}$ such that the reconstruction part is in the position to learn the desired mapping $\boldsymbol{\theta} \to f(\theta)$. When training is completed, the trick is to associate the feature space of the trained network with the parameter space of $\boldsymbol{\theta}$. The feature space is spanned by the neurons of the smallest layer, because here we can assume the most compact representation of the training data.

Auto-associative networks are trained supervised such that the input and output data are pairwise the same. The model is a feed-forward neural network and thus can be trained using common backpropagation strategies. We tested

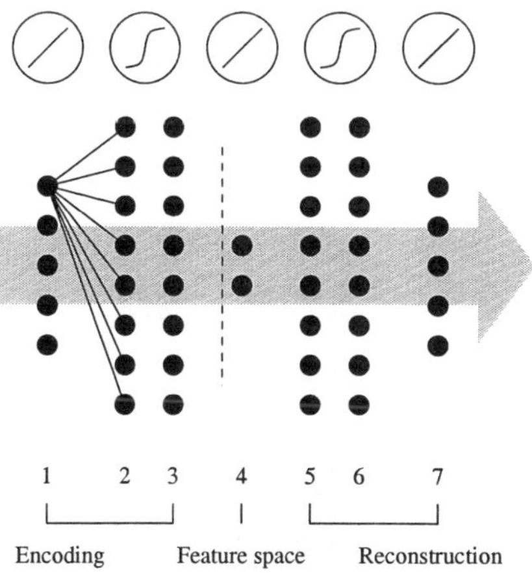

Fig. 1. An auto-associative neural network is composed of two feed-forward networks (glued together at the dotted line). After training, the left network performs a mapping from image space into feature space, while the right one performs the inverse mapping used to reconstruct image vectors. Layers 2, 3, 5, and 6 have sigmoidal transfer functions to model non-linearities, layers 1, 4, and 7 are linear nodes, as common for a function approximator. The network is fully interconnected as sketched in layers 1, 2.

different gradient based methods (gradient decent with/without momentum), as well as resilient backpropagation (RProp). The latter yielded fastest convergence and turned out to be stable.

3 Results

In the experiment, the network is trained on the bar data, shown in Figure 2, left. The network contains $N = 256$ input and output neurons and has 10 neuron in each of the sigmoidal hidden layers. A single linear neuron represents the feature space associated with the translation capability of the bar. The network is trained on the training data for 10000 epochs, while the training set consist of 16 images. Note that this is a very small amount of data compared to a network of this size.

The behaviour of the trained network is shown in Figure 2, middle. The images are obtained by simulating the right part of the network with parameters $\boldsymbol{\theta}$ drawn from the score interval. The scores of the training set are the values that the left part of the network produces as output when simulated on the training set. They can be considered the range of $\boldsymbol{\theta}$ in feature space. The resulting images show that the network adapted to the task rather well. The line structure is reconstructed accurately in all images. Furthermore, the line is subject to $\boldsymbol{\theta}$, which corresponds to a translational transformation of an object observed.

In comparison, the linear model obtained from PCA is depicted in Figure 2, right. Only the largest mode of variation is sampled here. It is shown that

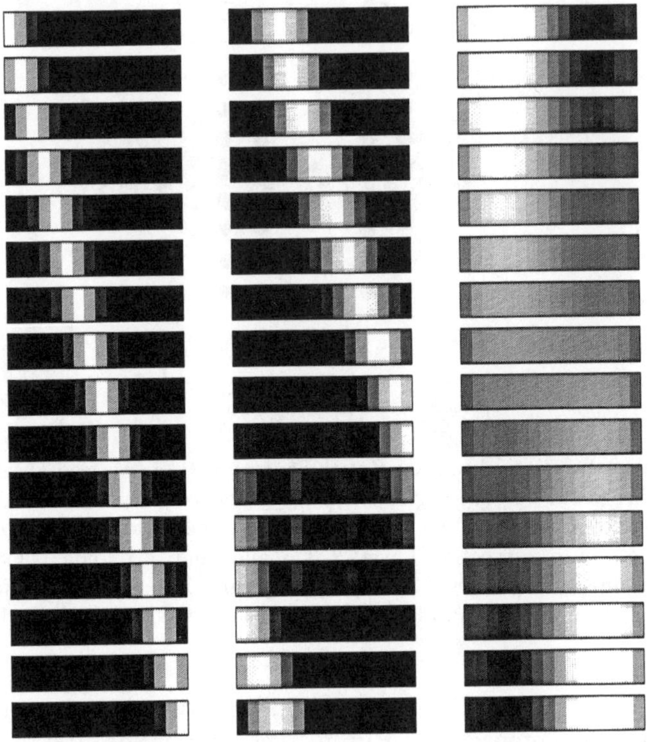

Fig. 2. Gaussian blurred bar translated under an artificial retina used as training images (left). Bar as simulated by the trained network. The right part of the network is reconstructing images corresponding to values of $\boldsymbol{\theta}$ drawn from the feature space, with increasing $\boldsymbol{\theta}$ beginning from the top row (middle). Comparison to principal component analysis of the variation within the training set. We see the effect of varying the largest eigenvector which represents the direction of largest variation in image space. Obviously, a single parameter is not sufficient to model the data completely using PCA (right).

the data is not approximated in all detail, giving reason that a higher number of principle components is required in a linear model. The parameter $\boldsymbol{\theta}$ that is weighting the components is varied within an interval of 2σ. In fact, analyzing the set of principal components, there is only a very small reduction in dimensionality, because the one-dimensional trajectory of the data traverses almost the whole image space.

In Figure 3, we take a look at a small sub-space of the image space. Three pixels (with linear addresses 49, 97, and 129) are observed, spanning a space of three dimensions. A star marks the location where the training data resides when projected onto the three dimensions. In addition, the trajectory as seen from the AANN is shown as a curve. It results from the translation of the object and their corresponding changes in appearance.

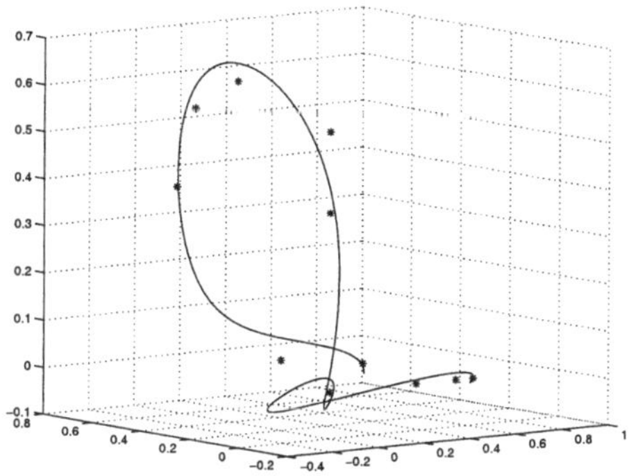

Fig. 3. The trajectory of the training data (marked with stars) in combination with the simulated trajectory of the AANN. The data shown is projected into a three-dimensional sub-space representing three pixels in the image.

Another example shows a more realistic application of the method at hand. A set of 165 pictures of the eye are taken, showing different gaze directions. The AANN establishes a model about the variations that occur when observing the eye in different situations. Figure 4 shows an excerpt of the training set used. The apparent variations address mainly the variation of the iris and the lid, while it was taken care of a rather constant location and illumination of the eye. Each image is of size 64×48 pixels, yielding an image vector of $N = 3072$ pixel values.

To simplify the burden for the network, noise has been reduced by applying a Gaussian filter with $\sigma = 2$ pixels, providing smoother variations. Theoretically, considering initial dimensional reduction as provided by PCA, could reduce the size of the network. However, this experiment is to show the application to the full range of data.

The AANN used in this experiment contained $N = 3072$ neurons in the input and output layers and 70 neurons in each hidden layer, which seems rather large in comparison to the previous experiment. Furthermore, we assume that exactly two parameters are required to model the variations in the eye, which reflect the local translation of the iris and deformation of the lid in a plane. The two parameters can intuitively be considered gaze angles. Training continued for a period of 50000 epochs. The reconstructed images from the score distribution is depicted in Figure 5. Note that resampled images at the border of the modelled distribution still are not as accurate as in the centre.

4 Conclusion

We presented an approach to generate general templates covering image variation in image space and suggested the application of AANN to non-linearly model object appearances. The initial experiments, based on relatively simple

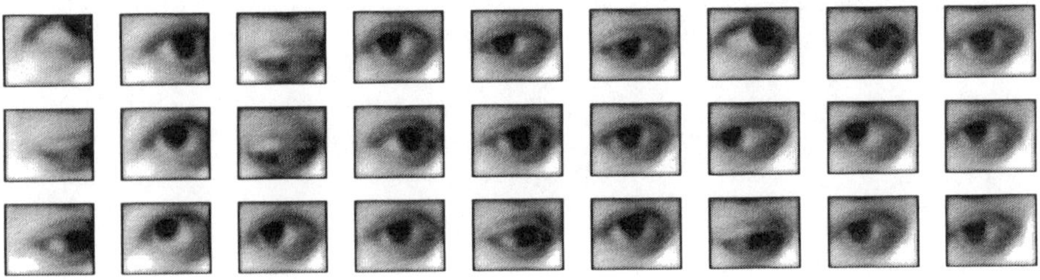

Fig. 4. Excerpt of images of the right eye used as training data.

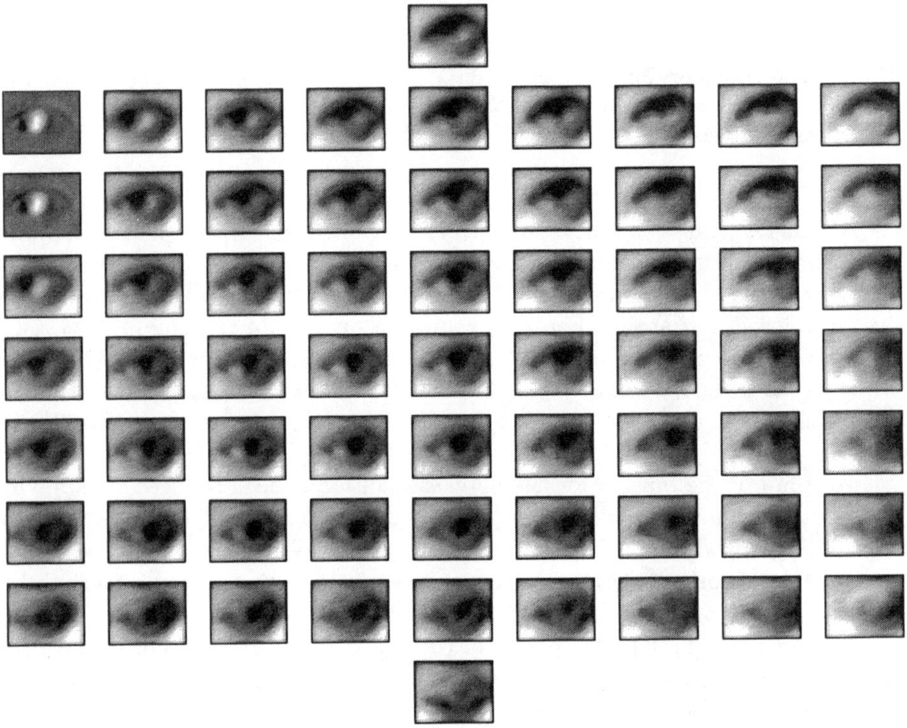

Fig. 5. Stepping through the two-dimensional feature space of the trained network produces the results above. Images are reconstructed due the AANN from samples along two feature variables. Adjusting the value controlling the horizontal variable changes the gaze from left to right. Likewise, changes about the vertical variable changes the appearance of the eye to move upwards and downwards.

variations, reduced the image data to one or two parameters related to both an encoding function and a restoration function, each realised by means of a neural network. However, it is important to note that a larger number of feature neurons can be applied, thus decomposing the images into an increased number of components, if present.

The network has been able to cover variation in the examples shown, and produced results superior to those obtained by linear models. However, the AANN restricts the size of the image. Due to the connectivity scheme, the number of weights that have to be adjusted increases with an increasing number of pixels. Besides training duration, much larger training sets would be required to give the training algorithm the necessary stability to converge.

The complexity of the image function is another aspect related to network size. The more complex the image function is in conjunction with appearance variations, the larger the hidden layers.

The size of the image was clamped to a fixed dimension of $m \times n$, an artificial analogy to the eye's retina. This means that the applied network learns the appearance of objects in correspondence to the fixed lattice, which cannot be changed afterwards. Furthermore, it should be emphasised that the function learned by the AANN in the bar example represents the translation of a *particular* object only. The network is not in the position to realise a general understanding of translation of arbitrary objects. Obviously, the variations in the appearance of objects under translation correspond to the grey-level curvature in an image, which changes with the image.

During the experiments we realised that correlation between the training images must be present for the network to converge to the desired state. In case of the bar images, overlap between the bars was a requirement.

References

1. David P. Casasent and Leonard M. Neiberg. Classifier and shift-invariant automatic target recognition neural networks. *Neural networks*, 8(7–8):1117–1129, 1995.
2. Bernard Chalmond and Stéphane C. Girard. Nonlinear modeling of scattered multivariate data and its application to shape change. *IEEE Transactions on pattern analysis and machine intelligence*, 21(5):422–432, May 1999.
3. T.F. Cootes, G.J. Edwards, and C.J. Taylor. Active appearance models. In H. Burkhardt and B. Neumann, editors, *Proc. European Conference on Computer Vision 1998*, volume 2, pages 484–498. Springer, 1998.
4. Daniel Freedman. Efficient simplicial reconstructions of manifolds from their samples. *IEEE transactions on pattern analysis and machine intelligence*, 24(10):1349–1357, October 2002.
5. Stéphane Girard and Serge Iovleff. Auto-associative models and generalized principal component analysis. Technical Report 4364, INRIA, January 2002.
6. Hermann Haken. *Synergetic computers and cognition: A top-down approach to neural nets*. Springer-Verlag, 1991.
7. Simon Haykin. *Neural networks*. Prentice Hall, 2 edition, 1999.
8. Michael A. Sipe, David P. Casasent, and Leonard M. Neiberg. Feature space trajectory representation for active vision. *SPIE*, 1997.

Conditions of Similarity between Hermite and Gabor Filters as Models of the Human Visual System

Carlos Joel Rivero-Moreno and Stéphane Bres

LIRIS-RFV, FRE 2672 CNRS, Lab. d'InfoRmatique en Images et Systèmes d'information
INSA de Lyon, Bât. Jules Verne, 17 av. Jean Capelle, Villeurbanne Cedex, 69621 France
{rivero,sbres}@rfv.insa-lyon.fr

Abstract. Among the suggested mathematical models for receptive field profiles, the Gabor model is well known and widely used. Another less used model that agrees with the Gaussian derivative model for human vision is the Hermite model which is based on analysis filters of the Hermite transform. It has the advantage of an orthogonal basis and a better fit to cortical data. In this paper we present an analytical comparison based on minimization of the energy error between the two models, and so the optimal parameters letting the two models be close to each other are found. The results show that both models are equivalent and extract about the same frequency information. Actually, we can implement a Hermite filter with an equivalent Gabor filter and vice versa, provided that conditions leading to error minimization are held.

1 Introduction

Image processing has been much inspired by the human vision, in particular with regard to early vision. The latter refers to the earliest stage of visual processing responsible for the measurement of local structures such as points, lines, edges, and textures in order to facilitate subsequent interpretation of these structures in higher stages (known as high level vision) of the human visual system (HVS) [13]. These elementary visual structures are relevant to human visual perception since they often encode a great portion of the information contained in the image. This low level visual computation is carried out by cortical simple cells of the primary visual cortex (area V1). Each cell's receptive field is localized in a small region of the retina. A receptive field profile (RFP) can be interpreted as the impulse response of the cell, which is then considered as a filter. These responses were found experimentally [3] [4] [7] and some assumptions on the nature of filtering carried out by these cells were then deduced [22] [18] [19] [12], thus leading to the mathematical models of RFPs. It makes possible to have a model of the way the HVS extracts information, in particular, its salient tuning properties of spatial localization, orientation selectivity, and spatial-frequency selectivity; which let visual structures be characterized using a small set of parameters that are locally defined such as position, orientation, characteristic size or scale, and phase [17]. The set of these assumptions allows, on the one hand, to establish a general structure of an image [9], and on the other hand, to derive a generic model representing the possible families of RFPs [10] [11] [23].

Among the mathematical models suggested for the RFPs of the HVS and satisfying the properties mentioned, there are two of them which held our attention: the first,

N. Petkov and M.A. Westenberg (Eds.): CAIP 2003, LNCS 2756, pp. 762–769, 2003.

which is more used in image processing (essentially for texture), is that of Gabor [8] [14] [2] [20]; the second, which is more adapted to a local analysis (generally to process edges), is that of the Gaussian derivative [25]. The latter can be given by an equivalent representation based on Hermite polynomials (as we will see later) which is also an interesting model of the HVS [6] [15] [16] [24].

In this paper we present an analytical comparison based on minimization of the energy error between the two models, Gabor and Hermite, in order to obtain the optimal parameters under which the two models are equivalent to each other. In practice, the model of the HVS generally used is that of Gabor and we endeavoured to show that both Hermite and Gabor models are equivalent from the visual perception point of view. Thus, applications using the Gabor model could be extended to that of Hermite.

It is important to point out that a comparison between *cortical data* and RFPs given by these two models was already made by Richard A. Young [25]. Its conclusions show that the two models give a very satisfactory approximation of RFPs. However, a theoretical result showing conditions under which both models are equivalent is now presented for the first time. Furthermore, these optimal conditions minimize the error between the two models and let it be only expressed as function of the derivative order of Hermite filters, i.e. the *order* of the RFP [11].

The paper is organized as follows. In section 2, we give the definitions of both Hermite and real Gabor models. In section 3, we compare the two models by finding the mean square error. In section 4 we show the results. Section 5 is final conclusions.

2 Hermite and Gabor Filters

The analysis done throughout this paper is considering models in one-dimension (1D) since extension to two-dimensions (2D), as the case of images, is straightforward since both models satisfy the property of separability.

The real Gabor model is based on real Gabor functions [5] built by products of a either sine or cosine wave by a Gaussian function. The Fourier transform of a Gabor filter corresponds to a Gaussian function shifted in frequency and centered on the sine or cosine wave's frequency. A complex Gabor function is obtained by multiplying a Gaussian by a complex exponential (real part for cosine and imaginary part for sine). Nevertheless, we are interested in real Gabor functions since signals we are dealing (i.e. images) are real and for the sake of computational efficiency.

Hermite filters were introduced by Martens into the Hermite transform [15] [16]. The latter corresponds to a local transformation of a signal or image, into polynomials multiplied by a Gaussian function. The set of these linear filters gives an orthogonal representation corresponding to derivatives of Gaussians where the maximum derivative order is the order of the expansion. The Fourier transform of a Hermite filter of order n is a Gaussian modulated by a monomial of degree n. It produces a shift in frequency of this Gaussian and introduces a certain asymmetry to it.

Both models have a Gaussian function with a free parameter: the scale of analysis or localization represented by the Gaussian's spread (i.e. its standard deviation). This Gaussian is multiplied by another function with a free parameter. In the Gabor case, it is a cosine and its free parameter is its frequency. In the Hermite case, it is a polynomial (of Hermite), which has the same scale as the Gaussian function, and its free parameter is the polynomial degree which is equivalent to the derivative order.

Hermite filters are linked to Gaussian derivative filters by the definition of *Hermite polynomials* which is given by Rodrigues' formula [1]:

$$H_n(x) = (-1)^n e^{x^2} \frac{d^n}{dx^n} e^{-x^2} \ . \tag{1}$$

These polynomials are orthogonal with respect to the weighting function e^{-x^2} which is given by [1]:

$$\int_{-\infty}^{+\infty} e^{-x^2} H_n(x) H_m(x) dx = 2^n \cdot n! \sqrt{\pi} \delta_{nm} \ . \tag{2}$$

Therefore, the difference between Gaussian derivative filters and Hermite filters is only a scale factor. Hermite filters of parameters σ_h and n are defined in spatial and frequency domains, respectively, by:

$$d_n(x) = \frac{\sigma_h^n}{\sqrt{2^n \cdot n!}} \frac{1}{\sigma_h \sqrt{\pi}} \frac{d^n}{dx^n} \left[e^{-x^2/\sigma_h^2} \right] . \tag{3}$$

$$D_n(\omega) = j^n \frac{\sigma_h^n}{\sqrt{2^n \cdot n!}} \omega^n e^{-\sigma_h^2 \omega^2 / 4} \ . \tag{4}$$

Gabor filters of parameters σ_g and ω_0 are defined in spatial and frequency domains, respectively, by:

$$g(x) = e^{-\frac{x^2}{2\sigma_g^2}} \cdot \cos(\omega_0 x) \ . \tag{5}$$

$$G(\omega) = \frac{\sigma_g \sqrt{2\pi}}{2} \left[e^{-\sigma_g^2 (\omega - \omega_0)^2 / 2} + e^{-\sigma_g^2 (\omega + \omega_0)^2 / 2} \right] . \tag{6}$$

3 Comparison between the Two Models

In order to validate analytically the equivalence between the two models, we first made some insights into their spatial structure and frequency behavior. Fig. 1 shows some spatial filter responses, Hermite on the left-hand, real Gabor at the center as it was defined by equation (5), and Gabor in phase with Hermite on the right-hand. In addition, fig. 2 shows the magnitude spectra: Hermite on the left-hand and real Gabor on the right-hand. Phase of real Gabor filters is always null whereas Hermite filters have a quadrature phase, i.e. $\varphi = k\pi/2$, k=mod(n,4) where mod( ) is the modulus function. Having the same phase, the only important effect in the transfer function behavior is the magnitude spectra. Thus, we will calculate the error between the two models by means of them. In fig. 1 we can see the oscillatory nature in spatial domain of these filters while fig. 2 shows that a similar frequency behavior of the transfer function arises in both models, even though we can see certain differences which lie in the definition of the filters. Thus, the two models correspond to band-pass filters with a *Gaussian* shape. The value of localized frequency of Hermite filters, which we have named ω_m, is not obvious, however it corresponds to the maximum of its spectrum. By setting the derivative of $D_n(\omega)$ with respect to ω equal to zero, we get that $\omega_m = \pm\sqrt{2n}/\sigma_h$. In the case of Gabor filters, the value of central frequency, ω_0, is that of their cosine wave. Two differences in the frequency domain are remarkable:

- Hermite filters have an antisymetry with respect to their central frequency because they are not "pure" Gaussians (they are modulated by a monomial of order n).
- Hermite filters do not have DC components, whereas Gabor filters do. The more the Gabor's central frequency moves away from the origin, the less the DC component is important.

As we have seen, the frequency of oscillatory functions is ω_m and ω_0, for Hermite and Gabor filters, respectively. They correspond to the selective frequency of modeled RFP of the HVS. Intuitively but not obvious, the two models come closer each other when their spectra *are centered* on the same frequency and when they have the same standard deviation.

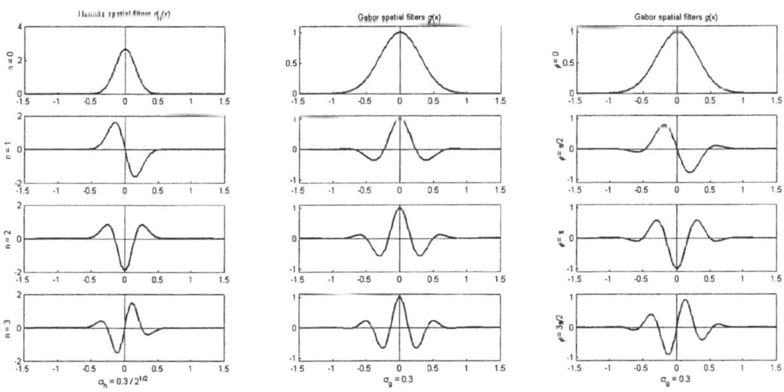

Fig. 1. Receptive field profiles in spatial domain up to order 3 (*from left to right: Hermite, Gabor, and Gabor in phase with Hermite*)

Fig. 3 shows the right-hand of the magnitudes spectra when $\omega_m=\omega_0$, $\sigma_h=\sigma_g$ (n =2). Even if there is a similarity in the magnitude density spectra when provided the latter conditions, it is not sure that they minimize the error between the two models. Nevertheless, they give an idea about their values.

In order to find the *optimal values* of parameters ($\sigma_g,\omega_0,\sigma_h,n$) which minimize the error between the two models, we have to define an error measure as a function of them. We have chosen as *error* measure, ε, the *energy of their difference*, i.e. the mean square error (MSE), which is defined by:

$$\varepsilon = \int_{-\infty}^{+\infty} [D-G]^2 \, d\omega = \int_{-\infty}^{+\infty} D^2 d\omega + \int_{-\infty}^{+\infty} G^2 d\omega - 2\int_{-\infty}^{+\infty} DG d\omega \ . \tag{7}$$

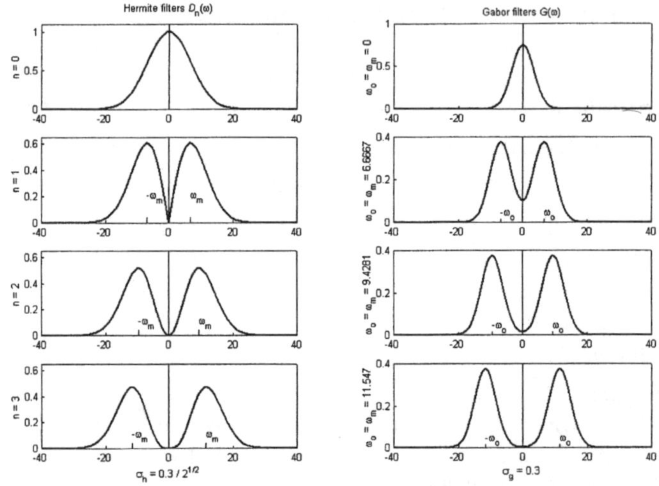

Fig. 2. Receptive field profiles in frequency domain up to order 3 (*left: Hermite, right: Gabor*)

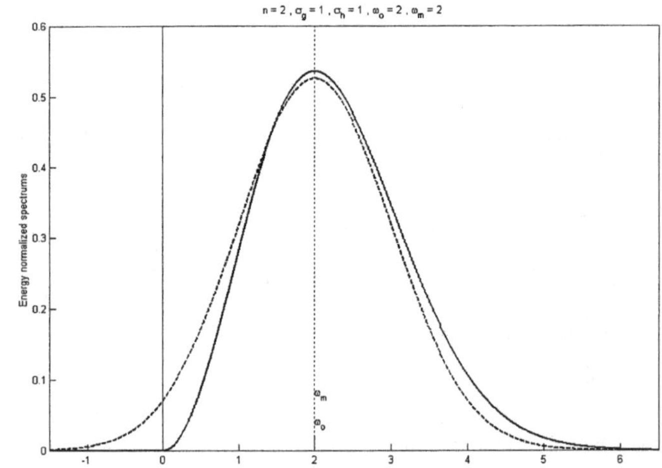

Fig. 3. Matching between the right-hand of Hermite (*solid*) and Gabor (*dashed*) spectra when they are centered on the same frequency

where both filters $D(\omega)$ and $G(\omega)$ are normalized energy versions of filters defined by equations (4) and (6). The norm is obtained as the square root of its energy E_F. Energy normalization is important because it enables to compare the two models. It is achieved by dividing each filter by its norm, which implies $E_D= E_G=1$. In consequence, equation (7) can be rewritten as:

$$\varepsilon = \int_{-\infty}^{+\infty} [D-G]^2 \, d\omega = 2\left(1-\int_{-\infty}^{+\infty} DG d\omega\right) . \tag{8}$$

The latter is equivalent to a measure of cross-correlation (combined energy) between the two filters. If they are highly correlated, which means that they represent the same model, then their cross-correlation will be maximum and consequently the error ε will be minimal. After integrating expression (8), the error is a function of four parameters, i.e. $\varepsilon = E(\sigma_g,\omega_0,\sigma_h,n)$. In order to get the optimal parameter values that minimize the error, we will simplify the expression of ε. For doing this, we consider the parameter n as a constant so that the error function is transformed into a family of *volume* error functions $E_n(\sigma_g,\omega_0,\sigma_h)$ for each order n.

Analysis of expression (8) leads to simplification of the error function [21] with the next results:

$$E(\sigma_g,\omega_0,\sigma_h,n) = E(1,\omega_0',\sigma_h',n) \;. \tag{9}$$

$$\omega_0' = \sigma_g\omega_0 \,,\; \sigma_h' = \sigma_h / \sigma_g \,,\; \omega' = \sigma_g\omega \;. \tag{10}$$

4 Results

We calculated numerically the minimal error for a value set of parameters in order to determine the general conditions which validates equations (9) and (10). Nevertheless, an explicit expression of the error can be obtained by calculating the integral in (8). Such a result and a detailed development are presented in [21]. In this paper we are most interested in the methodology used to find out the optimal parameters. In any case, we will give an explicit expression of the error function. Table 1 shows the numerical solution giving the optimal parameters corresponding to minima of the error $E_{\min} = E_n(1,\omega_0',\sigma_h')$. Using these results and (10) we can find minima of the error function $E_n(\sigma_g,\omega_0,\sigma_h)$ by a simple change of variables given by:

$$\sigma_g^{OPT} = \sigma_g \,,\; \omega_0^{OPT} = \frac{\omega_0'^{OPT}}{\sigma_g} \,,\; \sigma_h^{OPT} = \sigma_g\sigma_h'^{OPT} \;. \tag{11}$$

Thus, an optimal solution minimizing the error between the two models is $\sigma_h=\sigma_g$. In addition, we can deduce (11) that $\omega_0^{OPT}\sigma_h^{OPT}=\omega_0'^{OPT}\sigma_h'^{OPT}= K_n$, where the constant K_n depends on order n. This last expression corresponds to an hyperbole which defines the optimal value locus for all values of σ_g.

Table 1. Optimal solutions (ω_0',σ_h') for σ_g=1 minimizing the error function

n	ω_0'	σ_h'	$\sqrt{2n}$	$\omega_0'\sigma_h'$	$E_{\min}$	δ	E_n
0	0.0000	1.5000	0.0000	0.0000	0.0017	0.0000	–
1	1.8250	1.0000	1.4142	1.8250	0.1154	0.4108	0.2588
2	2.1500	1.0000	2.0000	2.1500	0.0128	0.1500	0.0280
3	2.5750	1.0000	2.4495	2.5750	0.0070	0.1255	0.0145
4	2.9250	1.0000	2.8284	2.9250	0.0036	0.0966	0.0082
5	3.2500	1.0000	3.1623	3.2500	0.0027	0.0877	0.0062
6	3.5500	1.0000	3.4641	3.5500	0.0022	0.0859	0.0050
7	3.8000	1.0000	3.7417	3.8000	0.0018	0.0583	0.0042
8	4.0750	1.0000	4.0000	4.0750	0.0016	0.0750	0.0036
9	4.3000	1.0000	4.2426	4.3000	0.0013	0.0574	0.0032

Since both filters are around about the same central frequency, $K_n^2 \approx 2n = (\omega_0'\sigma_h')^2$. This one is verified by *error of approximation* δ. From these results, we can conclude that the two models are analytically equivalent and the conditions to obtain this similarity are given by:

$$\sigma_g = \sigma_h \quad , \quad \omega_0 = \sqrt{2n}/\sigma_h \ . \tag{12}$$

When conditions of (12) are taken into account, the *minimal error* between the two models expressed by (8) becomes then exclusively function of order n:

$$E_n = 2\left[1 - \frac{2^{3/4}(2/3)^{n+1/2}(2n)^{n/2}e^{-n/3}}{\sqrt{1+e^{-2n}}\sqrt{(2n-1)!!}} \bullet \sum_{k=0}^{n}\binom{n}{2k}(2k-1)!!\left(\frac{3}{4n}\right)^k\right] . \tag{13}$$

The minimal error E_n is a measure of the real error between the two models when they take the similarity conditions expressed by the optimal values of (12).

5 Conclusion

Hermite and Gabor filters are good models of receptive fields profile of the human visual system because they well match to cortical data. However, their definition is not the same one and it can be confusing in deciding which model is more suitable. Even if the Gabor model is more widely used than the Hermite one, the latter has some advantages like being an orthogonal base and having better match to experimental physiological data. In this article, we have found in an analytical fashion the conditions under which the two models are similar in an optimal way. The results show that when these conditions are verified, the two models have a similar behavior in frequency (i.e. band-pass filters around the same frequency and with the same bandwidth). The presence of these similarities enable, in an equivalent manner, to use one model or the other. Thus, applications using Gabor can be implemented by also using Hermite, while keeping the advantages of the latter.

Acknowledgements

This work was supported by the National Council of Science and Technology (CONACyT) of Mexico, grant 111539, and by the SEP of Mexico.

References

1. Abramowitz, M. Stegun, I.A.: Handbook of Mathematical Functions with Formulas, Graphs, and Mathematical Tables. 9th printing. Dover, New York (1972)
2. Daugman, J.G.: Complete 2-D Discrete Gabor Transforms by Neural Networks for Image Analysis and Compression. IEEE Trans. Acoust. Speech Signal Processing. Vol. 36 (1988) 1169-1179

3. De Valois, R.L., Albrecht, D.G., Thorell, L.G.: Spatial Frequency Selectivity of Cells in Macaque Visual Cortex. Vision Research. Vol. 22 (1982) 545-560
4. De Valois, R.L., Yund, E.W., Hepler, N.: The Orientation and Directional Selectivity of Cells in Macaque Visual Cortex. Vision Research. Vol. 22 (1982) 531-544
5. Gabor, D.: Theory of Communication. J. Inst. Electr. Eng. Vol. 93 (1946) 429-457
6. Gertner, I., Geri, G.A.: Image Representation using Hermite Functions. Biological Cybernetics. Vol. 71 (1994) 147-151
7. Jones, J.P., Palmer, L.A.: The Two-Dimensional Spatial Structure of Simple Receptive Fields in Cat Striate Cortex. J. Neurophysiol. Vol. 58 (1987) 1187-1211
8. Jones, J.P., Palmer, L.A.: An Evaluation of the Two-Dimensional Gabor Filter Model of Simple Receptive Fields in Cat Striate Cortex. J. Neurophysiol. Vol. 58 (1987) 1233-1258
9. Koenderink, J.J.: The Structure of Images. Biological Cybernetics. Vol. 50 (1984) 363-370
10. Koenderink, J.J., van Doorn, A.J.: Receptive Field Families. Biological Cybernetics. Vol. 63 (1990) 291-297
11. Koenderink, J.J., van Doorn, A.J.: Generic Neighborhood Operators. IEEE Trans. Pattern Analysis Mach. Intell. Vol. 14 (1992) 597-605
12. Kulikowski, J.J., Marčelja, S., Bishop, P.O.: Theory of Spatial Position and Spatial Frequency Relations in the Receptive Fields of Simple Cells in the Visual Cortex. Biological Cybernetics. Vol. 43 (1982) 187-198
13. Lee, T.S., Mumford, D., Romero, R., Lamme, V.A.F.: The Role of the Primary Visual Cortex in Higher Level Vision. Vision Research. Vol. 38 (1998) 2429-2454
14. Marčelja, S.: Mathematical Description of the Responses of Simple Cortical Cells. J. Opt. Soc. Amer. Vol. 70 (1980) 1297-1300
15. Martens, J.-B.: The Hermite Transform – Theory. IEEE Trans. Acoust. Speech Signal Processing. Vol. 38 **9** (1990) 1595-1606
16. Martens, J.-B.: Local Orientation Analysis in Images by Means of the Hermite Transform. IEEE Trans. Image Processing. Vol. 6 **8** (1997) 1103-1116
17. Perona, P.: Deformable Kernels for Early Vision. IEEE Trans. Pattern Analysis Mach. Intell. Vol. 17 (1995) 488-499
18. Pollen D.A., Ronner, S.F.: Phase Relationships between Adjacent Simple Cells in the Visual Cortex. Science. Vol. 212 (1981) 1409-1411
19. Pollen D.A., Ronner, S.F.: Visual Cortical Neurons as Localized Spatial Frequency Filters. IEEE Trans. Syst. Man Cybern. Vol. 13 (1983) 907-916
20. Porat, M., Zeevi, Y.Y.: The Generalized Gabor Scheme of Image Representation in Biological and Machine Vision. IEEE Trans. Pattern Analysis Mach. Intell. Vol. 10 (1988) 452-468
21. Rivero-Moreno, C.J., Bres, S.: Les Filtres de Hermite et de Gabor Donnent-ils des Modèles Équivalents du Système Visuel Humain?. In: ORASIS'03. Journées Francophones des Jeunes Chercheurs en Vision par Ordinateur. Gérardmer, France. May (2003) 423-432
22. Sakitt, B., Barlow, H.: A Model for the Economical Encoding of the Visual Image in Cerebral Cortex. Biological Cybernetics. Vol. 43 (1982) 97-108
23. Wallis, G.M.: Linear Models of Simple Cells: Correspondence to Real Cell Responses and Space Spanning Properties. Spatial Vision. Vol. 14 (2001) 237-260
24. Yang, J., Reeves, A.J.: Bottom-Up Visual Image Processing Probed with Weighted Hermite Polynomials. Neural Networks. Vol. 8 **5** (1995) 669-691
25. Young, R.A., Lesperance, R.M., Meyer, W.W.: The Gaussian Derivative Model for Spatial-Temporal Vision: I. Cortical Model. Spatial Vision. Vol. 14 **3,4** (2001) 261-319

Offset Smoothing Using the USAN's Principle

Giovanni Gallo and Alessandro Lo Giuoco

Dipartimento di Matematica e Informatica, Università di Catania
V.le A. Doria n. 6A, Catania, Italy
gallo@dmi.unict.it, logiuoco@videobank.it

Abstract. In this paper the problem of reducing the noise in a digital image preserving information about edges and corners is addressed. To this aim a new technique is described, based on the USAN principle [8]. This principle at each image point swaps the pixel value with a new value, which is more representative of the region where the point lies. This technique is a practical alternative for efficiency and quality of the produced image to the offset-filtering technique proposed by Fischl and Schwartz in [4]. A set of experimental results on artificial and natural noisy images highlights that the new technique has a greater noise reduction capability and preserves edges and corners from smoothing better than other published methods.

1 Introduction

Image enhancement through noise reduction is a low-level image-processing step needed to many image processing applications: image restoration, pre-processing step for image segmentation or contours tracing. In particular the authors have been attracted to this processing phase since recognizing its relevance in higher frequency preserving zooming techniques [1]. Many systems have been considered in the literature in order to enhance the contrast in regions that correspond to borders between different objects in the input image. Usually, a filter is applied at each point of an image to swap the value for the pixel in such a way that it is more representative of the region in which the pixel lies. Unfortunately inaccurate smoothing algorithms may produce a value that is not representative neither of the pixels belonging to the object neither of the external pixels. This event is more probable when the kernel of the smoothing filter lies across the border of an object. In such cases, it would be preferable to substitute the border pixel with a pixel inside the object.

Specifically, Nitzberg and Shiota in [2] proposed an offset term that displaces kernel centers away from the presumed edge location, thus enhancing the contrast between adjacent regions without blurring their boundaries. The theory introduced by Nitzberg and Shiota, named "offset filtering", is a practical alternative to non-linear anisotropic diffusion introduced by Perona and Malik in [3]. Starting from this theory, B. Fischl and E. Schwartz introduced in [4] a new offset technique as a fast alternative to anisotropic diffusion. Other similar, more recent approaches the bilateral filtering [5], PDE filtering [6], mean shift filtering [7] have been proposed.

We have developed a new method for the enhancement of noisy images based on the "USAN" principle introduced in [8] by Brady and Smith. The new method compares very well in term of velocity and capabilities of noise reduction with the other techniques.

N. Petkov and M.A. Westenberg (Eds.): CAIP 2003, LNCS 2756, pp. 770–777, 2003.

To have a preliminary qualitative idea of the capabilities of the newly proposed technique, consider figure 1. In the first row is reported the noisy image restored respectively by the median filter, the median filter coupled with the new offset algorithm, the median filter coupled with the Fischl & Schwartz offset. The second row of Fig.1 shows the throughputs of the Canny edge detector. As can be observed the median filter suppresses the noise, but many details are irremediably lost. The median filter coupled with the offset of Fischl & Schwartz suppresses the noise preserving many details, but the new technique preserves better edges and corners and introduces a lesser quantity of artifacts.

Experimental results, presented in Section 3, numerically support the robustness to noise of the proposed technique.

The present paper is organized as follows: Section 1 contains a brief review of SUSAN algorithm, Section 2 introduces the new algorithm, Section 3 reports some experimental results and Section 4 draws some final conclusions.

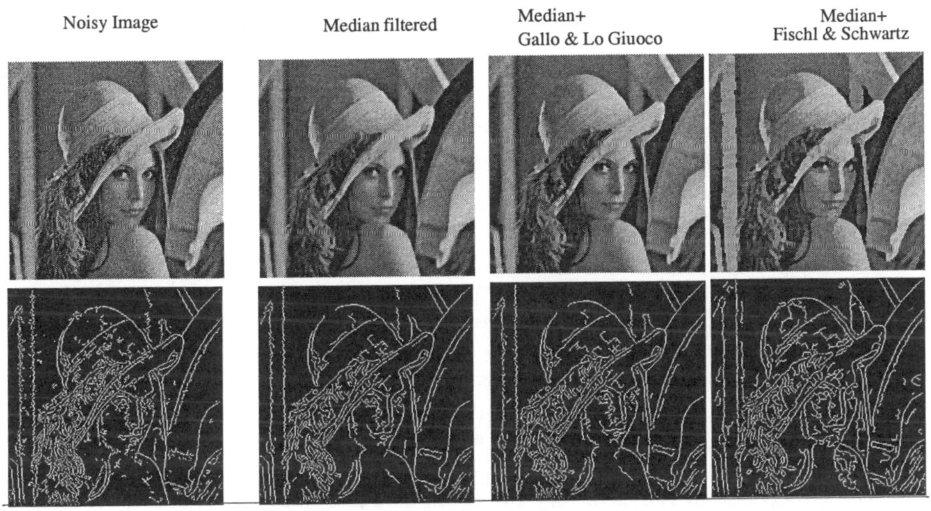

Fig. 1. The original image is corrupted with Gaussian noise of mean=0 and variance=0.02. Successively the images are restored using different techniques. A map of edges, produced by Canny edge finder, is drawn on the second row of the figure to esteem qualitatively the results. As can be seen, the image filtered with the new offset preserves edges and corners better and minimizes the number of artifacts.

1.1 The Susan Algorithm

S.M. Smith and J.M. Brady have introduced the SUSAN algorithm in 1997 in [8] to detect edges and corners and to suppress noise in corrupted images.

The idea behind their edge and corner finder is the computation of a local feature named USAN, which characterizes edges and corners.

Although following this line of thought more recent algorithms are available [5][7], we started from the USAN approach because of its low complexity and simplicity.

To illustrate the USAN strategy, consider the situation in Fig. 2 where a circular mask at five image positions is shown. The central point of this mask is termed as the "nucleus". Comparing the brightness of each pixel inside the mask with the brightness of the nucleus, a region of similarity may be defined. The highlighted area of the mask is called USAN, an acronym standing for "Univalue Segment Assimilating Nucleus".

The USAN span is maximum when the nucleus lies in a flat region of the image, it falls to the half of the mask extension if the nucleus is near to a straight edge and falls even further when the nucleus is inside a corner. Variation in the USAN area provides hence strong evidence for edges and corners.

The USAN area is computed, according to the original proposal of Smith and Brady, as follows:

$$n(\vec{r}_0,t) = \sum_{\vec{r}\in Mask} c(\vec{r},\vec{r}_0,t) = \sum_{\vec{r}\in Mask} e^{-\left(\frac{I(\vec{r})-I(\vec{r}_0)}{t}\right)^6} \tag{1}$$

where c is the weighting function that estimates the similarity between the brightness of the points $\vec{r}_0$ and $\vec{r}$, with $\vec{r}$ within the circular mask.

The parameter t inside the similarity function controls the minimum contrast, which will be detected, and the maximum amount of noise, which will be ignored or discarded. Edges are located, with a single step of non-maxima suppression, at local maxima of the response R thus computed:

$$R(\vec{r}_0,t) = \begin{cases} 3/4 - n(\vec{r}_0,t) & \text{if } n(\vec{r}_0,t) < 3/4 \\ 0 & \text{otherwise} \end{cases} \tag{2}$$

The application of non-maxima suppression requires moreover the evaluation of the edge direction, which is computed in two ways depending on the classification of the nucleus. The nucleus is classified as "intra pixel" if it coincides with the centre of gravity of the USAN area, otherwise it is an "inter pixel".

For an inter-pixel the vector between the centre of gravity and the nucleus is perpendicular to the local edge direction, while for an intra-pixel the edge direction is calculated by finding the longest axis of symmetry of the USAN area.

The USAN corner finder is very similar to the edge finder in its preliminary steps. Corners are localized with a step of non–maxima suppression upon the corner response RC computed as follows:

$$RC(\vec{r}_0,t) = \begin{cases} 1/2 - n(\vec{r}_0,t) & \text{if } n(\vec{r}_0,t) < 1/2 \\ 0 & \text{otherwise} \end{cases} \tag{3}$$

The thresholds used in equations (2) and (3) have been heuristically proven good choices in [8].

2 The New Offset Algorithm

Adaptive filtering uses a term of offset to displace the center of the smoothing mask far from the edge location; the kernel is displaced in the direction perpendicular to the border of the observed region. Unfortunately to know the border location requires gradient information and the approaches based over the derivatives of the original image are known to be quite sensitive to noise.

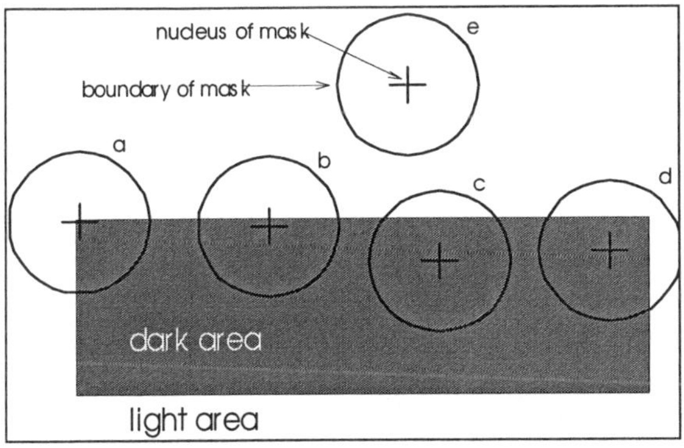

Fig. 2. Susan mask at five distinct image positions is showed, the background is entirely white and the foreground is composed by a dark rectangle. As can be observed, the USAN's area reaches the maximum when the mask lies in a flatten region and falls to less than the half of the mask when the nucleus is positioned on a corner.

We believe that it must be used a more robust mechanism to detect the edge orientation instead of the gradient orientation of the smoothed image, as proposed by Fischl and Schwartz. In the Section 1, we have reported the USAN principle and some of the details about edge and corner finding based on such approach. Starting from these ideas, we have formulated a new method to compute the offset.

In our formulation, the offset field is the vector between the nucleus of a circular mask and the center of gravity of the similarity region of the nucleus. The region of similarity is determined using a brightness comparison. For inter-pixels the vector determined in this way is perpendicular to the edge direction and pushes the nucleus on the side of those pixels having similar brightness, for intra-pixels no offset is done; this avoids, at least when the noise level is not strong enough to "scramble" the dark and light areas, that smoothing is performed across edges.

Let two points $r \equiv (x, y)$ and $r_0 \equiv (x_0, y_0)$ be inside the intensity image *I*, and let *t* be a similarity threshold. The two points are judged similar with a weight *w* computed as follows:

$$w(r, r_0, t) = e^{-\left(\frac{I(r)-I(r_0)}{t}\right)^2} \tag{4}$$

The choice of a Gaussian weight is, of course, quite natural and since it has provided us with better experimental results than results obtained using high polynomial powers, we have adopted it in our implementation.

In our specific implementation, the center of gravity *g* is computed applying a circular mask (composed by 37 pixels) at each image point and calculating the weights of similarity with the nucleus of the digital mask.

$$cg(\vec{r}_0) = \frac{\sum_{\vec{r} \in USAN\_mask \wedge \vec{r} \neq \vec{r}_0} \vec{r} * w(\vec{r}, \vec{r}_0, t)}{\sum_{\vec{r} \in USAN\_mask \wedge \vec{r} \neq \vec{r}_0} w(\vec{r}, \vec{r}_0, t)} \tag{5}$$

The unitary weight $w(\vec{r}_0, \vec{r}_0, t)$ is excluded by the computation, because it may push with an excessive force the center of gravity to be close to the nucleus. This effect should be avoided starting from the following observation: when the image is noisy the nucleus with high probability may be corrupted.

The vector $\vec{v}$ between the nucleus r_0 and the center of gravity $cg(r_0)$ is the offset, which must be applied to displace the nucleus of the smoothing filter.

$$\vec{v} = cg(\vec{r}_0) - \vec{r}_0 \cdot \tag{6}$$

The offset computed with the above algorithm is perpendicular to the edge direction, when the point is an inter-pixel, otherwise it is null. If the point is an intra-pixel the offset vanishes, in this case the pixel is representative of the contour in which lies and for this reason it must not be displaced.

The new offset gives good results for noise suppression and improves the quality of the reconstructed image (optimal peak signal to noise ratio). The final impact of the noise is reduced by two simultaneous actions: the first action is performed by the similarity function and the second one is performed during the computation of the center of gravity by the average.

The throughput is not easily comparable with the offset proposed by Fischl and Schwartz, because even if it behaves like a "diffusion" the variation that it introduces over the image is much less intense. The new exposed method, hence, for its capability of image smoothing preserving the relevant details, can be used in noisy images for edges and corners enhancement. Moreover the proposed technique has been proved very well suited in higher preserving zooming techniques.

3 Experimental Results

The main goal of an offset-filtering technique should be the noise suppression and the enhancement of edges and corners, in order to facilitate applications deputed to the phase of contours tracing. We have performed some experiments aimed to measure the efficiency of the proposed new offset (GL), comparing at the same time its throughputs with the outputs provided by Fischl-Schwartz offset (FS) and the Gaussian and median filters. The testing set, chosen for comparison purpose, is composed by artificial images, which have known edges locations. The noiseless test images are corrupted in a controlled way by Gaussian noise with zero mean and increasing variance. The behavior of the tested filters is verified over: vertical edges in Fig. 3a, horizontal edges in Fig. 3b and radial edges in Fig. 3c, 3d. The standard Canny's edge-detector produces the edge-maps useful to compare qualitatively and quantitatively the different filtering techniques. We report respectively in tables 1a, 1b, 1c, 1d, the percentage of erroneous classifications registered at a given noise variation for the examples in Fig. 3. Edge-maps are reported in figures 3a, 3b, 3c, 3d.

All the experiments confirm the superiority of the offset-filtering techniques over traditional methods, at least when synthetic images and tamed noise model are considered, and also highlight the comparable quality of the proposed method with the Fischl & Schwartz algorithm. It should pointed out that the results obtained on a small set of non synthetic images show the same kind of improvements observed for synthetic images. For example, the error rate for the Lena image corrupted at noise 0.02 when reconstructed with our technique is 45%, when reconstructed with FS is 78%.

Table 1. Percentage of erroneous classifications for the images in Fig. 3

Noise Var	Median	Med-GL	Med-FS	Gaussian	Gauss-GL	Gauss-FS
(a)						
10^{-6}	2.7%	0%	0%	33%	13%	29%
$3x10^{-6}$	51%	3%	7%	75%	30%	77%
10^{-5}	87%	35%	51%	85%	59%	77%
(b)						
Noise Var	Median	Med-GL	Med-FS	Gaussian	Gauss-GL	Gauss-FS
10^{-6}	2%	0%	14%	3%	8%	11%
$3x10^{-6}$	21%	1%	7%	37%	23%	33%
10^{-5}	34%	13%	22%	44%	24%	27%
(c)						
Noise Var	Median	Med-GL	Med-FS	Gaussian	Gauss-GL	Gauss-FS
$3x10^{-6}$	15%	12%	33%	18,86%	13,67%	32%
10^{-5}	15,42%	11.84%	31.21%	18,71%	13,88%	33,55%
$6x10^{-4}$	28,44%	24%	65,64%	26,9%	20,76%	53,36%
(d)						
Noise Var	Median	Med-GL	Med-FS	Gaussian	Gauss-GL	Gauss-FS
$3x10^{-6}$	23,88%	18,73%	41,73%	39,9%	21,38%	49,6%
10^{-5}	25,42%	19,7%	38,94%	39,89%	21,23%	55,4%
$6x10^{-4}$	110%	66,42%	122,77%	109,18%	50,92%	87,50%

4 Conclusions

In this paper, we have introduced a new offset filtering technique based on the USAN principle proposed by Smith and Brady in [8]. The new technique is compared with another good offset-filtering method proposed by Fischl and Schwartz in [4]. A set of experimental results over artificial images demonstrates that this technique is more robust to the digital noise and guarantees a suitable offset to displace smoothing filters. The authors are working on the application of these techniques to the problem of higher frequency preserving zooming of digital images.

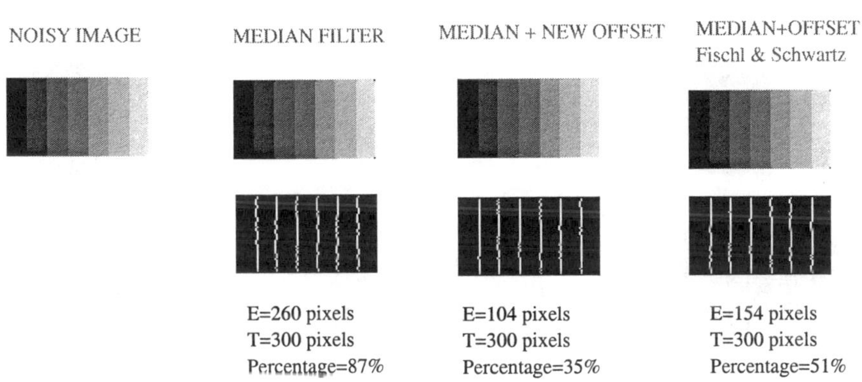

Fig. 3a. Image corrupted with Gaussian noise (m=0, v=10^{-5}).

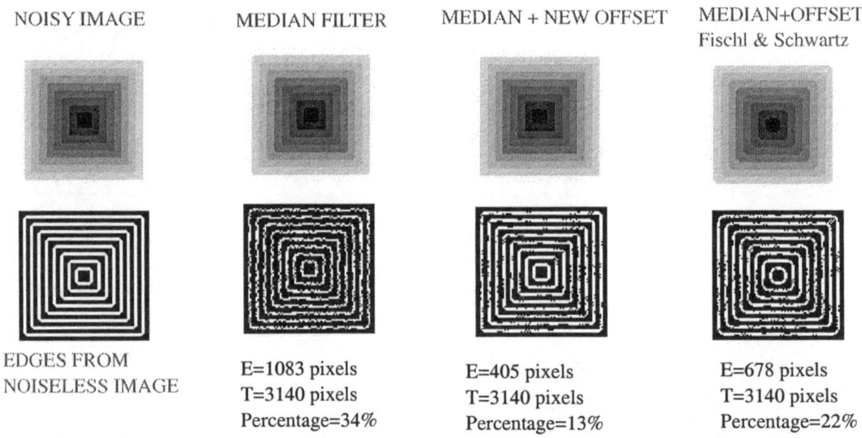

Fig. 3b. Image corrupted with Gaussian noise (m=0, v=10^{-5}).

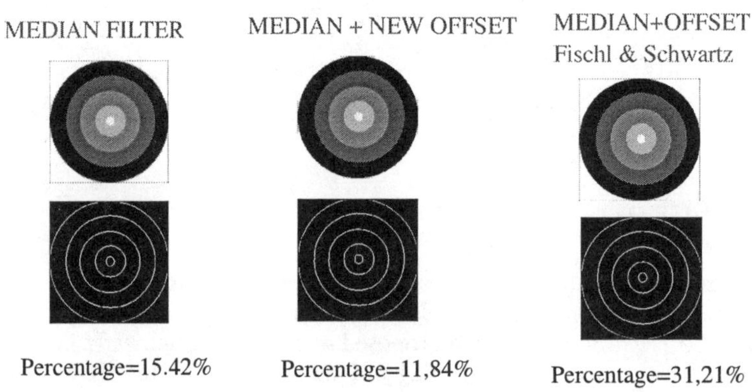

Fig. 3c. Image corrupted with Gaussian noise (m=0, v=10^{-5}).

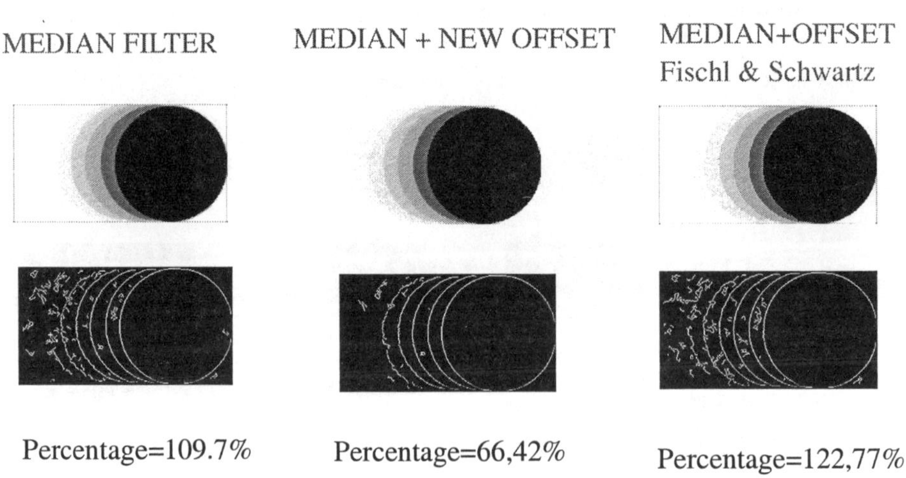

Fig. 3d. Image corrupted with Gaussian noise (m=0, v=$6x10^{-4}$).

References

1. S. Battiato, G. Gallo, F. Stanco, "Smart Interpolation Anisotropic Diffusion", Proceedings of ICIAP 2003, Mantua, Italy.
2. M. Nitzberg and T. Shiota, "Non Linear Filtering with Edge and Corner Enhancement", IEEE Trans. on PAMI, Vol. 6, No 8, pp. 826-833, Aug. 1992.
3. P. Perona and J. Malik, "Scale Space and Edge Detection Using Anisotropic Diffusion", IEEE Trans. on PAMI, Vol.12, No. 7, pp. 629- 639, Jul. 1990.
4. B. Fischl and E. L. Schwartz, "Adaptive Non Local Filtering: A Fast Alternative to Anisotropic Diffusion for Image Enhancement", IEEE Trans. on PAMI, Vol. 21, No 1, Jan.1999.
5. C. Tomasi, R. Mundachi, "Bilateral Filtering for Gray and Color Images", Proceedings of IEEE ICCV 1998, Bombay, India
6. Z. Lin, Q. Shi, "An Anisotropic Diffusion PDE for Noise Reduction and Thin Edge Preservation", Proceedings of Int. Conf. on Image Analysis and Processing,1999, Venice, Italy.
7. D. Comaniciu and P. Meer, "Mean Shift Analysis and Applications", IEEE Int. Conf. Computer Vision, Kerkyra, Greece, pp. 1197-1203, 1999.
8. M. Smith and J. M. Brady, "SUSAN- A New Approach to Low Level Image Processing", Internal Journal of Computer Vision, Vol. 23, No 1, pp. 45-78, May 1997.

Author Index